D1356640

THE CONCISE
OXFORD DICTIONARY OF
ENGLISH
LITERATURE

THE CONCISE
OXFORD DICTIONARY OF
ENGLISH
LITERATURE

SECOND EDITION

OXFORD
AT THE CLARENDON PRESS

Oxford University Press, Walton Street, Oxford OX2 6DP

OXFORD LONDON GLASGOW
NEW YORK TORONTO MELBOURNE WELLINGTON
KUALA LUMPUR SINGAPORE JAKARTA HONG KONG TOKYO
DELHI BOMBAY CALCUTTA MADRAS KARACHI
NAIROBI DAR ES SALAAM CAPE TOWN

ISBN 0 19 866108 8

© *Oxford University Press 1970*

First edition 1939
Second edition 1970
Reprinted with corrections 1979

*Printed in Great Britain
at the University Press, Oxford
by Eric Buckley
Printer to the University*

PREFACE TO THE SECOND EDITION

THIS edition, based on the fourth edition of the *Oxford Companion to English Literature*, contains much new and revised material, especially with reference to the literature of the twentieth century. There are new entries for authors who have become established since the *Companion* and the *Concise Dictionary of English Literature* were first published, and the latest editions of the works and correspondence of earlier writers have been noted. The articles on general literary topics have been revised to take account of developments and research during the last thirty years.

I am grateful to Miss Phoebe Allen for her invaluable help throughout the preparation of this book, and also to the many readers whose suggestions and comments contributed to the work of revision.

DOROTHY EAGLE

January 1970

PREFACE TO THE FIRST EDITION

THIS work is based upon Sir Paul Harvey's *Oxford Companion to English Literature*, which, first published in 1932, several times reprinted, and now in its second edition, has established itself as a standard work. In preparing the abridgment, it has been necessary to eliminate a great deal of the detailed information which is contained in the original work. But all those entries which deal with the central matter of English literature have been retained, though often in a shortened form; authors and works of importance, characters from books and plays, and mythological and historical entries which relate directly to English literature, are included. Certain articles have been added, summarizing in concise form periods of literary history and general literary subjects. A somewhat greater number of entries are also included dealing with contemporary writers, both English and American.

The editor wishes to thank Sir Paul Harvey for his care in reading the proofs of this abridgment. At the same time, it should be made clear that the editor alone is responsible for such differences as there are between the material in this volume and in the *Oxford Companion to English Literature*.

The editor wishes also to thank Mr. J. A. W. Bennett of Merton College, Oxford, Mr. Frederick Page, and Mr. Charles Williams for the contributions of accuracy which they have made to this volume, and Dr. R. W. Chapman particularly for his notes on questions of pronunciation.

JOHN MULGAN

July 1939

NOTE

THE names of AUTHORS at the head of articles and other subjects of articles are printed in ordinary bold type (e.g. **Keats**, JOHN; **Gotham**, WISE MEN OF); the TITLES OF LITERARY WORKS in bold italics (e.g. *Lycidas*).

CHARACTERS IN FICTION and PERSONS IN REAL LIFE are entered under their surnames, e.g. 'Samuel Weller' under 'Weller'; 'John Dryden' under 'Dryden'; unless the two names form in current use an indissoluble whole, or the surname is little known. Thus 'Peter Pan' appears under 'Peter', 'Little Nell (TRENT)' under 'Little Nell'.

Where the TITLE OF A WORK consists of Christian name and a surname it is entered under the Christian name, e.g. *Barnaby Rudge* under *Barnaby*.

Dates of publication are given as a rule in brackets after the title of a work.

General information on matters of literary history will be found summarized under the following heads:

Allegory, Alliteration, Anachronism, Anglo-Saxon Literature, Augustan Age, Autobiography, Ballad, Biography, Blank verse, Burlesque, Carol, Caroline, Cavaliers, Censorship, Classicism, Comedy, Copyright, Criticism, Dialect, Edwardian, Elegiac, Elizabethan Age, English, Epic, Gothic novels, Heroic couplet, Heroic drama, Historians, Interludes, Masques, Metaphysical Poets, Middle English, Miracle Plays, Moralities, Newspaper, Novel, Ode, Opera, Parody, Pastoral, Philosophy, Poetic diction, Proverb, Restoration, Romantic Movement, Saga, Satire, Science Fiction, Senecan tragedy, Sonnet, Standard English, Stream of consciousness, Theatre, Tragedy, Victorian.

ABBREVIATIONS

a.	*ante*, before.
A.-N.	Anglo-Norman.
b.	born.
c.	*circa*, about.
c. or ch.	chapter.
cent.	century.
cf.	*confer*, compare.
C.H.E.L.	*Cambridge History of English Literature.*
d.	died.
D.N.B.	*Dictionary of National Biography.*
E.B.	*Encyclopædia Britannica.*
ed.	edition or edited by.
fl.	flourished.

L.	Latin.
l., ll.	line, lines.
ME.	Middle English.
N.T.	New Testament.
OE.	Old English (Anglo-Saxon).
OED.	*Oxford English Dictionary.*
O.T.	Old Testament.
pron.	pronounced.
q.v.	*quod vide*, which see.
qq.v.	*quae vide*, both which, or all which, see.
s.v.	*sub verbo*, under the word.
tr.	translation or translated by.
vol.	volume.

A

Abana and **Pharpar,** rivers of Damascus, 'better than all the waters of Israel' (2 Kings v. 12).

Abbey Theatre, Dublin, THE, opened in 1904. Miss A. E. Horniman built the theatre for the Fays' National Theatre Company. Yeats and Lady Gregory (qq.v.) were the initial directors. In 1951 the theatre was burnt down; the new Abbey opened in 1966.

Abbot, The, a novel by Sir W. Scott (q.v.) (1820), a sequel to 'The Monastery' (q.v.). The work is concerned with the imprisonment of Mary Queen of Scots.

Abbot of Misrule, see *Misrule.*

Abbotsford, Sir W. Scott's property near Melrose on the Tweed.

Abdera, a city on the coast of Thrace, birthplace of Democritus and Protagoras; in spite of which its inhabitants were proverbial for stupidity.

Abdiel, in 'Paradise Lost' (q.v.), v. 805 and 896, the seraph who resists Satan's proposal to revolt.

Abélard, PIERRE (1079-1142), a brilliant disputant at Ste Geneviève and Notre Dame in Paris, where John of Salisbury (q.v.) was among his pupils. He fell in love with Héloïse, the niece of an old canon of Notre Dame, in whose house he lodged. Their love ended in a tragic separation, and in a famous correspondence.

Cf. Pope's poem 'Eloisa to Abelard' (1717); G. Moore's 'Héloïse and Abélard' (1921). See also 'Peter Abelard' by Helen Waddell (1933).

Abercrombie, LASCELLES (1881-1938), poet and critic, notable for his attempt to revive the poetic drama. His chief published works are: 'Interludes and Poems' (1908), 'Deborah' (1912), poetry; 'Thomas Hardy, a Critical Study' (1912), 'Theory of Art' (1922), critical; 'Collected Poems' (in the 'Oxford Poets', 1930).

Abessa, in Spenser's 'Faerie Queene', I. iii, the personification of superstition.

Abigail (1 Sam. xxv), came to signify a waiting-woman from the name of a character in Beaumont and Fletcher's 'The Scornful Lady'.

Abora, MOUNT, in Coleridge's 'Kubla Khan', is perhaps to be identified with Milton's Mount Amara (q.v.). It occurs as 'Amhara' in an early manuscript version of Coleridge's poem.

Abou Ben Adhem, may his tribe increase, the first line of a poem by Leigh Hunt (q.v.).

Abracadábra, a cabalistic word used as a charm, which first occurs in a poem by Q. Severus Sammonicus, 2nd cent.

Absalom, the son of David, who rebelled against his father. His death occasioned David's lament in 2 Sam. xviii. 33.

Absalom and Achitophel, a satirical poem, in heroic couplets, by Dryden (q.v.) (1681). The poem deals in allegorical form with the attempt by Lord Shaftesbury's party to exclude the Duke of York from the succession and to set the Duke of Monmouth in his place. Chief among the characters are: Monmouth (Absalom); Shaftesbury (the false tempter, Achitophel); the Duke of Buckingham (Zimri), who, as responsible for 'The Rehearsal' (q.v.), was particularly obnoxious to Dryden; Charles II (David); Titus Oates (Corah).

The poem, which was immensely popular, was followed in 1682 by a second part, which was in the main written by Nahum Tate (q.v.), but revised by Dryden, who contributed the famous characters of Doeg (Settle, q.v.) and Og (Shadwell, q.v.).

Absentee, The, a novel by M. Edgeworth (q.v.) (1812).

Absolute, SIR ANTHONY, and his son CAPTAIN ABSOLUTE, characters in Sheridan's 'The Rivals' (q.v.).

Abt Vogler, a poem by R. Browning (q.v.).

Abydos, a city on the shores of the Hellespont, famous for the loves of Hero and Leander. See *Bride of Abydos*.

Academy or ACADEME, from *Academia*, a grove near Athens, sacred to the hero Academus, near which Plato (q.v.) opened his school of philosophy.

Academy, THE BRITISH, a society, incorporated in 1902, for promoting the study of learning and the moral and political sciences. Its first secretary was Sir Israel Gollancz.

Academy, THE DELLA CRUSCA, see *Della Crusca*.

Academy, THE FRENCH (*Académie française*), founded by Cardinal Richelieu in 1635, is essentially a literary academy, and is responsible for a dictionary of the French language (first edition, 1694). See *Immortals*.

Academy of Arts, THE ROYAL, founded in 1768, for the annual exhibition of works of contemporary artists and for the establishment of a school of art. Sir Joshua Reynolds was its first president.

Acadia, the name given to Nova Scotia by the first French settlers there. Their expulsion in the 18th cent. forms the theme of Longfellow's poem, 'Evangeline'.

Acapulco ship, a Spanish ship which sailed annually with treasure from Mexico for Spain.

Acatalectic, 'not *catalectic*' (q.v.), applied to a verse whose syllables are complete, not wanting a syllable in the last foot.

Achates, 'Fidus Achates', a friend of Aeneas (q.v.), whose fidelity has become proverbial.

Acheron, a river of Hades, interpreted as ὁ ἄχεα ῥέων, the river of woe. See *Styx*.

Achilles, son of Peleus and Thetis (qq.v.), the bravest of the Greeks in the Trojan War. During his infancy Thetis plunged him in the Styx, thus making his body invulnerable, except the heel, by which she held him. In the Trojan War he was deprived by Agamemnon of Briseis, who had fallen to his lot. He retired and sulked in his tent until the death of his friend Patroclus recalled him to action. In armour made for him by Hephaestus, he slew Hector and dragged his corpse to the Greek ships. He was wounded in the heel by Paris and died.

The TENDON OF ACHILLES, the tendon by which the muscles of the calf of the leg are attached to the heel, is so called from the above story of the vulnerable heel of Achilles.

The story that Telephus, wounded by Achilles, was cured by rust from his spear is alluded to by Chaucer ('Squire's Tale', 232) and Shakespeare ('2 Henry VI', v. 1).

Achitophel, see *Absalom and Achitophel*.

Acis, the shepherd lover of Galatea (q.v.).

Acrasia, in Spenser's 'Faerie Queene', II. xii, typifies Intemperance. She is captured by Sir Guyon, and her Bower of Bliss destroyed.

Acres, BOB, a character in Sheridan's 'The Rivals' (q.v.).

Actaeon, a famous hunter, who saw Artemis and her attendants bathing. For this he was changed into a stag, and devoured by his own dogs.

Actes and Monuments of these latter perilous times touching matters of the Church, popularly known as the BOOK OF MARTYRS, by Foxe (q.v.), first published at Strasburg in Latin in 1559, and printed in English in 1563. This enormous work is a history of the Christian Church, with special reference to the sufferings of the Christian martyrs, but more particularly of the Protestant martyrs of Mary's reign. It is written in a simple homely style.

Acton, SIR JOHN EMERICH EDWARD DALBERG, *first Baron Acton* (1834–1902), Regius professor of modern history at Cambridge, friend of Gladstone and author of 'Lectures on Modern History' (1906), etc. He planned the 'Cambridge Modern History' (1902–12), for which he wrote the first chapter.

Actors, and **Acting,** see under *Theatre*.

Ada Clare, one of the two wards in Chancery in Dickens's 'Bleak House' (q.v.).

Adam, a 12th-cent. Norman-French dramatic representation of scriptural history, in eight-syllabled verse, probably written in England, important in the evolution of the drama in England.

Adam, in Shakespeare's 'As You Like It' (q.v.), the old servant who accompanies Orlando in exile.

Adam, ROBERT (1728-92), architect, the most famous of four brothers. His best-known building was the Adelphi. He also designed the screen and gate of the Admiralty, Portland Place, and other buildings in London and Edinburgh. He influenced English furniture as well as architecture, and produced beautiful ceilings and mantelpieces.

Adamastor, in the 'Lusiads' (v. li) of Camoëns (q.v.), the spirit of the Cape of Storms. Also the title of a poem by Roy Campbell (q.v.).

Adam Bede, a novel by G. Eliot (q.v.) (1859).

Hetty Sorrel, pretty, vain, and selfish, niece of the genial farmer, Martin Poyser, is loved by Adam Bede, a village carpenter, but is deluded by the prospect of marriage with the young squire, Arthur Donnithorne, and is seduced by him. Arthur leaves her, and Hetty, broken-hearted, consents to marry Adam. But before the marriage, Hetty discovers that she is pregnant, flies from her home to seek Arthur, fails to find him, is arrested, convicted of the murder of her child, and transported. After a time Adam discovers that he has won the heart of Dinah Morris, a young Methodist preacher, whose serene influence pervades the whole story, and whom Adam's brother, Seth, has long loved, and now with a fine unselfishness resigns to him.

Adam Bell, Clym of the Clough (or CLEUGH), and **William of Cloudesley**, three outlaws, as famous for their skill in archery in northern England as Robin Hood and his fellows in the Midlands.

Adam Cupid, in Shakespeare's 'Romeo and Juliet', II. i. 13, perhaps alludes to Adam Bell (q.v.).

Adamnan, ST. (*c.* 625-704), abbot of Iona from 679. The life of St. Columba is generally attributed to him.

Adams, PARSON ABRAHAM, a character in Fielding's 'Joseph Andrews' (q.v.).

Adams, HENRY BROOKS (1838-1918), American man of letters, remembered chiefly by 'Mont-Saint-Michel and Chartres' (1904), and 'The Education of Henry Adams' (1907), an autobiography.

Adam's Ale, a humorous expression for water, as the only drink of our first parents.

Addison, JOSEPH (1672-1719), poet, dramatist, and essayist, educated at the Charterhouse with Steele, and at Queen's College and Magdalen, Oxford. He was distinguished as a classical scholar and attracted the notice of Dryden by his Latin poems. He travelled on the Continent (1699-1703) to qualify for the diplomatic service. In 1704 he published 'The Campaign', a poem in heroic couplets, in celebration of the victory of Blenheim. He was appointed under-secretary of state in 1706, and was M.P. from 1708 till his death. In 1709 he went to Ireland as chief secretary to Lord Wharton, the Lord Lieutenant. He formed a close friendship with Swift, Steele, and other writers, and was a member of the Kit-Cat Club (q.v.). Addison lost office on the fall of the Whigs in 1711. Between 1709 and 1711 he contributed a number of papers to Steele's 'Tatler' (q.v.), and joined with him in the production of 'The Spectator' (q.v.) in 1711-12. His tragedy 'Cato' was produced with great success in 1713, and during the same year he contributed to Steele's periodical, the 'Guardian' (q.v.), and during 1714 to the revived 'Spectator'. On the return of the Whigs to power, Addison was again appointed chief secretary for Ireland, and started his political newspaper, the 'Freeholder' (1715-16). In 1716 he became a lord commissioner of trade, and married the countess of Warwick. In 1718 he retired from office with a pension of £1,500. Addison was buried in Westminster Abbey, and lamented in a noble elegy by Tickell (q.v.).

He was satirized by Pope in the character of 'Atticus' (q.v.).

Addison is remarkable in the history of English literature for his simple and un-ornamented prose style which marked the end of the mannerisms and eccentricities of the 17th cent. His most famous works are the 'Coverley essays', originated by Steele, and contributed to 'The Spectator'. See *Coverley (Sir R. de)*.

Adicia, in Spenser's 'Faerie Queene', v. viii, the wife of the Soldan (Philip of Spain), the symbol of injustice.

Admirable Crichton, THE, see *Crichton.*

Adonais, An Elegy on the Death of John Keats, a poem in Spenserian stanzas by P. B. Shelley (q.v.) (1821).

The death of Keats moved Shelley not only to sorrow but to indignation at the savage criticisms on Keats's work which he believed had hastened his end. In this elegy (founded on Bion's lament for Adonis) the poet pictures the throng of mourners, the Muse Urania, Dreams and Desires, Sorrow and Pleasure, Morning and Spring, and the fellow poets, all bringing their tribute to the bier of Adonais. The lament then changes to a triumphant declaration of the poet's immortality.

Adonis, a beautiful youth beloved by Aphrodite. He received a mortal wound from a wild boar, and the flower anemone was said to have sprung from his blood. Proserpine restored him to life, on condition that he should spend six months with her and the rest of the year with Aphrodite, a symbol of winter and summer. His death and revival were widely celebrated. See also *Venus and Adonis.*

Gardens were a feature of this worship and are referred to in Spenser (F.Q. III. vi. 29), Milton (P.L. ix. 440), etc.

Adramelech, in 'Paradise Lost', vi. 365, one of the rebel angels.

Adrastus, king of Argos, leader of the expedition of 'The Seven against Thebes' (see *Eteocles*).

Adriana, in Shakespeare's 'The Comedy of Errors' (q.v.), wife of Antipholus of Ephesus.

Adullamites, name applied to a group of liberal M.P.s who seceded from the Reform party in 1866. The name was first given by John Bright to Horsman, who, he said, 'had retired into what may be called his political cave of Adullam'. (Cf. 1 Sam. xxii. 1–2.)

Advancement of Learning, The, a philosophical treatise in English by Francis Bacon (q.v.) (1605). The author considers methods of advancing knowledge and the defects in present practice. The divisions of knowledge—history, poetry, and philosophy—are enumerated and analysed. This work was later expanded in Bacon's 'De Augmentis'.

Adventurer, The, a periodical conducted, 1752–4, by John Hawkesworth, to which Samuel Johnson and Joseph Warton (qq.v.) contributed.

Adventures of a Guinea, Chrysal, or the, a satirical narrative (1760–5) by C. Johnstone, in which several chapters are devoted to the 'Hell-fire Club' (q.v.).

Adventures of an Atom, The, see *Atom.*

Adventures of a Younger Son, The, a novel by E. J. Trelawny (q.v.) (1831).

The work, which is partly autobiographical, is the story of the life of a wild Byronic character who deserts from the navy and takes to a life of piracy in the Indian Ocean, encountering many exciting adventures.

Adventures of Philip, The, see *Philip.*

Advice to a Painter, see *Instructions to a Painter.*

Advocates' Library, THE, in Edinburgh, founded by Sir George Mackenzie of Rosehaugh (1636–91), and opened in 1689. It became the National Library of Scotland in 1925.

Advocatus Diaboli, or *Devil's Advocate,* the popular name for the *Promotor Fidei,* who, in a proposal for canonization in the R.C. Church, advances what there is to be said against the candidate's claim.

Æ, AE., or **A.E.,** see *Russell (G. W.).*

Aegeon, in Shakespeare's 'The Comedy of Errors' (q.v.), the father of the Antipholus twins.

Aegeus, father of Theseus (q.v.).

Aegisthus, the son of Thyestes (the son of Pelops) and his daughter Pelopia. As a result of the feud between Thyestes and his brother Atreus (q.v.), Aegisthus murdered Atreus. When the sons of Atreus, Agamemnon (q.v.) and Menelaus went to the Trojan War, Aegisthus was left guardian of Agamemnon's kingdom and of his wife Clytemnestra (q.v.). But he became the paramour of Clytemnestra, and with her murdered Agamemnon on his return from Troy. Orestes (q.v.), the son of Agamemnon, subsequently avenged his father by killing Aegisthus and Clytemnestra.

Aeglogue, an obsolete spelling of 'Eclogue' (q.v.).

Aegyptus, see *Danaïdes*.

Ælfred, see *Alfred*.

Ælfric, called GRAMMATICUS (*d. c.* 1020). His chief works are Catholic Homilies (990-2), largely drawn from the works of St. Augustine, St. Jerome, St. Gregory, and other Latin writers, and 'Lives of Saints' (993-6), a series of sermons in alliterative rhythms. Several other works of his survive, including a Latin grammar and a paraphrase in the vernacular of the first seven books of the Bible (not all of it his own work). Ælfric is a prominent figure in Anglo-Saxon literature, and the greatest prose writer of his time.

Ælla, Songe to, a poem by Chatterton (q.v.).

Aeneas, son of Anchises and Aphrodite, and husband of Creusa, daughter of Priam, king of Troy, by whom he had a son, Ascanius. At the end of the Trojan War, he escaped with his father Anchises and his son, but his wife was separated from him and lost. His adventures are told by Virgil and by other Latin authors, who traced the descent of the Roman emperors to Aeneas. Leaving Troy with twenty ships, he was shipwrecked near Carthage, where Dido the queen fell in love with him. But Aeneas left Carthage by order of the gods, and Dido in despair took her own life. Coming to Cumæ,

Aeneas was conducted by the Sibyl to the nether world, that he might hear from his father's shade the fates of his posterity. After a voyage of seven years he reached the Tiber, where he married Lavinia, the daughter of King Latinus, having slain in single combat his rival Turnus. Aeneas succeeded his father-in-law as king of the Latins and after a short reign was killed in a battle with the Etruscans.

Aeneid, The, a poem in Latin hexameters by Virgil (q.v.), recounting the adventures of Aeneas (q.v.) from the fall of Troy.

Aeolus, the god of the winds.

Aeschylus (525-456 B.C.), the great Athenian tragic poet. Of his tragedies only seven have survived: 'The Persians' (on the triumph of Greece over the Persian invaders), 'The Seven against Thebes' (the story of Eteocles and Polyneices), the 'Prometheus Bound', 'The Suppliants' (i.e. the fifty daughters of Danaus), and the great trilogy on the story of Orestes, the 'Agamemnon', the 'Choephorœ', and the 'Eumenides'. Aeschylus may be regarded as the founder of Greek tragedy, having introduced a second actor and subordinated the chorus to the dialogue.

Aesculapius (ASCLEPIUS), son of Apollo and Coronis, the god of medicine. Among his children was a daughter, Hygieia (q.v.).

Aesir, in Scandinavian mythology, the collective name of the gods.

Aeson, father of Jason (q.v.). He was restored to youth by the arts of Medea (q.v.).

Aesop, the traditional composer of Greek fables about animals, is said by Herodotus to have lived in the 6th cent. B.C., and to have been a slave. But the fables attributed to him are probably compiled from many sources.

Aesthetic Movement, a movement during the eighties of the 19th cent. which adopted the doctrine of 'art for art's sake', sometimes with ostentatious extravagance. It was much ridiculed, e.g. in 'Punch' and in Gilbert and Sullivan's opera 'Patience'.

Æthelred, king of Wessex, 866-71.

Æthelred the Unready, king of England, 979-1016. 'Unready' is properly 'Redeless', the man without counsel.

Æthelstan, king of England, 925-40. In his reign considerable progress was made towards the unification of the English people. He is celebrated in the OE. poem 'Brunanburh' (q.v.).

Æthelwold or ETHELWOLD, ST. (908?-984), re-established a monastic house at Abingdon, introducing the strict Benedictine rule from Fleury; and when Eadgar became king of England, was appointed bishop of Winchester. He co-operated with Dunstan and Oswald (qq.v.) in reforming religion, rebuilt the church of Peterborough, and built a new cathedral at Winchester. He exerted his influence also for the revival of learning. He is commemorated on 1 August.

Aetion, in Spenser's 'Colin Clouts come home againe' (q.v.), possibly represents Shakespeare.

Affectionate Shepherd, The, a poem by Barnfield (q.v.).

Agag, in Dryden's 'Absalom and Achitophel' (q.v.), i. 675 (cf. 1 Sam. xv), is supposed to represent Sir Edmund Godfrey, who took the depositions of Titus Oates and was soon after murdered.

Agamemnon, king of Argos, the son or grandson of Atreus (q.v.). He married Clytemnestra (q.v.) and was elected commander of the Greek host that went to Troy. The Greek fleet was detained at Aulis, where Agamemnon sacrificed his daughter Iphigenia (q.v.) to appease Artemis. After the fall of Troy he was murdered by Clytemnestra and her paramour Aegisthus (q.v.).

Aganippe, a fountain on Mt. Helicon (q.v.), sacred to the Muses.

Age of Reason, The, by Thomas Paine (q.v.) (1795).

This work, which sets forth Paine's 'thoughts on religion', was written in Paris at the height of the Terror.

Agincourt, a village in France where, on St. Crispin's day, 25 Oct. 1415, Henry V of England defeated a superior force of French.

Aglaia, one of the Graces (q.v.).

Agnes, ST., patron saint of virgins, commemorated on 21 Jan. It was a popular belief that by performing certain ceremonies on St. Agnes's Eve, one would dream of the person whom one was destined to marry.

For Keats's poem see *Eve of St. Agnes*. Tennyson wrote a religious poem, 'St. Agnes' Eve'.

Agnes Grey, a novel by Anne Brontë (q.v.) (1847), is the story of a rector's daughter who takes service as a governess, and is ill-treated and lonely. She experiences kindness from no one but the curate, Mr. Weston, whom she finally marries.

Agnes Wickfield, a character in Dickens's 'David Copperfield' (q.v.).

Agravain, SIR, in Malory's 'Morte Darthur' (q.v.), conspires against Launcelot, and discloses to King Arthur Launcelot's love for Guinevere.

Agricola, GNAEUS JULIUS (A.D. 37-93), was Roman governor of Britain and subdued most of the country. Tacitus, his son-in-law, wrote his life.

Agrippa, see *Herod Agrippa I*.

Aguecheek, SIR ANDREW, in Shakespeare's 'Twelfth Night' (q.v.), a ridiculous foppish knight.

Ahab, CAPTAIN, a character in Herman Melville's 'Moby Dick' (q.v.).

Ahasuerus, see *Wandering Jew*.

Aids to Reflection, a philosophical treatise by S. T. Coleridge (q.v.) in the form of aphorisms and comments (1825).

Aiken, CONRAD POTTER (1889-1973), American poet and novelist, resident for many years in England. His publications include: 'Earth Triumphant' (verse, 1914), 'Blue Voyage' (novel, 1927), 'Ushant' (autobiographical novel, 1952), 'Collected Poems' (1953), and 'Reviewer's ABC' (criticism, 1958). His edition (1924) of the poetry of Emily Dickinson (q.v.) did much to make her known.

Ainger, ALFRED (1837-1904), a popular lecturer and preacher, and author of a life of Charles Lamb (1882) and an edition of Lamb's Works (1883-8).

Ainsworth, WILLIAM HARRISON (1805-82), wrote thirty-nine novels, chiefly with some historical basis, of which the best known are 'The Tower of London' (1840), 'Old St. Paul's' (1841), and 'Windsor Castle' (1843).

Ajax, the son of Telamon, king of Salamis, was, after Achilles, the bravest of the Greek host that besieged Troy. After the death of Achilles, Ajax and Odysseus contended for the arms of the dead hero. When they were allotted to Odysseus, Ajax, maddened with rage, slaughtered a flock of sheep, thinking them the sons of Atreus who had given the preference to Odysseus, and stabbed himself.

He was known as *Telamonian Ajax* to distinguish him from *Ajax son of Oïleus*, king of Locris, who went with forty ships to the Trojan War. On his return homewards, his ship was wrecked and he was drowned.

Akbar Khan, the great Mogul emperor, who reigned 1556-1605.

Akenside, MARK (1721-70), author of 'The Pleasures of Imagination' (1744), also of a number of odes and minor poems.

Alabaster, WILLIAM (1567-1640), an Elizabethan divine and Latin poet. Between 1588 and 1592 he produced two notable poems in Latin: an unfinished epic on Queen Elizabeth, admired by Spenser, and the tragedy 'Roxana', which Dr. Johnson thought contained the best Latin verse written in England before Milton. In 1597 Alabaster became a Roman Catholic and was arrested. His sonnets (first published in 1959) were probably written about this time. In his own day Alabaster was known chiefly as a theologian.

Aladdin and the Wonderful Lamp, an oriental tale generally regarded as belonging to the 'Arabian Nights' (q.v.), but not contained in any manuscript of the collected tales. Aladdin acquires wealth by the use of a magic lamp which his former master recovers, though only for a time, by offering to Aladdin's wife 'new lamps for old'.

Alaham, a tragedy by Fulke Greville (q.v.), Lord Brooke, posthumously published in 1633.

Alastor, or The Spirit of Solitude, a poem by P. B. Shelley (q.v.) (1816). 'Alastor' is Greek for 'avenger'.

This, the poet's first important work, is an allegory in which the idealist is depicted happy in contemplation. Presently he seeks in reality the counterpart of his dreams. He meets with frustration, is plunged into despair, and dies. The poem is a condemnation of self-centred idealism, and at the same time a lament for a world in which 'many worms and beasts and men live on', while 'some surpassing spirit' is borne away.

Alban, ST. (*d.* ? 304), the first British martyr. He is commemorated on 22 June.

Albany, ALBAINN, ALBANIA, ALBIN, poetic names of Gaelic origin for the north of Britain.

Albany, DUKE OF, a character in Shakespeare's 'King Lear' (q.v.).

Albany, THE, Piccadilly, originally a single mansion, subsequently divided into bachelor chambers. Lord Byron, Macaulay, George Canning, 'Monk' Lewis, and Bulwer Lytton (qq.v.) lived there.

Albert Memorial, THE, erected in Hyde Park in memory of the Prince Consort (*d.* 1861), was designed by Sir Gilbert Scott.

Albertus Magnus, (1193-1280), a Dominican friar and scholastic philosopher. He was an interpreter of Aristotle, whose doctrine he expounded at Cologne and Paris. Thomas Aquinas was among his pupils. His wide learning earned him the name of *Doctor Universalis.*

Albigenses, a Christian sect living in Provence in the 12th cent. conspicuous for their extravagant asceticism. They were accused of holding Manichaean (q.v.) doctrines. A crusade against them was conducted with great cruelty by Simon de Montfort (1208-13).

Albion, an old poetical name for Britain, perhaps derived from its white (Lat. *albus*) cliffs.

Albion's England, see *Warner*.

Albovine, a tragedy by D'Avenant (q.v.) (1629), the author's first play. The same subject, drawn from the history of the Lombards, is treated in 'The Witch' by Middleton and in Swinburne's 'Rosamund, Queen of the Lombards'.

Alcaeus (*fl. c.* 611–580 B.C.), lyric poet of Mitylene in Lesbos, author of hymns and songs, of which only a few fragments survive; the inventor of the Alcaic (q.v.) metre.

Alcaic, the metre invented by Alcaeus (q.v.), a stanza of four lines, as follows:

$$--\cup--|-\cup\cup-\cup\underset{\smile}{} \text{ (twice)}$$
$$--\cup---\cup--$$
$$-\cup\cup-\cup\cup-\cup-\cup$$

Tennyson experimented in this metre.

Alceste, see *Misanthrope*.

Alcestis, daughter of Pelias (q.v.), and wife of Admetus. Alcestis gave her life to redeem her husband from death, but was rescued by Hercules from the messenger of Hades. She is the subject of one of the plays of Euripides. See *Balaustion's Adventure*.

Alchemist, The, a comedy by Jonson (q.v.) (acted, 1610; printed, 1612), perhaps the greatest of his plays. Love-wit, during an epidemic of the plague, leaves his house in London in charge of his servant, Face. The latter, with Subtle, the Alchemist, and Dol Common, use the house as a place for deluding people, by holding out to them promise of the philosophers' stone. Surly, the gamester, attempts to expose the fraud; and the return of Love-wit puts Subtle and Dol to flight. Face makes peace with his master by marrying him to Dame Pliant.

Alcides, a name of Hercules (q.v.).

Alcinous, king of Phaeacia and father of Nausicaa (q.v.), who entertained Odysseus.

Alciphron, a Greek writer of about A.D. 200, author of letters depicting Athenian life in the 4th cent. B.C.

Alciphron, or The Minute Philosopher, a philosophical treatise in dialogue form by Berkeley (q.v.) (1732).

Alcman (*fl.* 630 B.C.), the principal lyric poet of Sparta, gave artistic form to the choral lyric, by introducing the *strophe* and *antistrophe* (qq.v.).

Alcmena, see *Amphitryon*.

Alcott, LOUISA M. (1832–88), American author of books for girls, including 'Little Women' (q.v., 1868).

Alcuin or ALBINUS (English name EALHWINE) (735–804), theologian and coadjutor of Charlemagne in educational reforms. Educated in the cloister school of York under Archbishop Egbert, he settled on the Continent, becoming abbot of Tours. He wrote liturgical, grammatical, and philosophical works and numerous letters and poems.

Aldhelm, ST. (640?–709), author of a number of Latin works (including treatises in prose and verse on the merits of virginity, with illustrious examples of chaste living), which reveal a wide knowledge of classical and Christian authors. He is commemorated on 25 May.

Aldine Press, see *Aldus Manutius*.

Aldington, RICHARD (1892–1962), poet and novelist. He published several volumes of poetry, as well as critical and biographical work, but was best known for his novels: 'Death of a Hero' (1929), 'The Colonel's Daughter' (1931), and 'All Men are Enemies' (1932). 'Portrait of a Genius, But . . .' (1950) is a biography of D. H. Lawrence; 'Lawrence of Arabia' (1955) is a bitter denigration of T. E. Lawrence and his career.

Aldrich, THOMAS BAILEY (1836–1907), a New England author, who edited the 'Atlantic Monthly' (q.v.) from 1881 to 1890. His best-known work is 'The Story of a Bad Boy' (1870). He also wrote *vers de société*.

Aldus Manutius (ALDO MANUZIO, 1449–1515), the Venetian printer, who founded the Aldine Press, whence he issued the first printed editions of the works of a large number of Greek authors.

Alecto, see *Allecto*.

Alexander, a name borne by Paris (q.v.).

Alexander VI, see *Borgia* (*Rodrigo*).

Alexander, SIR WILLIAM, *Earl of Stirling* (1567?-1640), a courtier, and a friend of Drummond of Hawthornden (q.v.). His chief poetical works are a collection of sonnets called 'Aurora' (1604), and four tragedies.

Alexander and Campaspe, see *Campaspe*.

Alexander of Hales (*d.* 1245), a native of Gloucestershire, studied at Paris and taught theology there. For a short time he held various ecclesiastical appointments in England. Returning to Paris he entered the Franciscan order and continued to teach theology. He was the author of glosses on the 'Sententiae' of Peter Lombard. The 'Summa Theologiae' which goes under his name was put together by other Franciscan theologians, partly drawing on his teachings. In the later Middle Ages he was known as the 'Irrefragable Doctor'.

Alexander's Feast, see *Dryden*.

Alexander the Great (356-323 B.C.), son of Philip II of Macedon and Olympias, educated by Aristotle, became king of Macedon in 336 B.C. He caused the Greek states to nominate him to conduct the war against Persia. He captured the family of Darius and extended his conquests to Egypt, where he founded Alexandria; and after completely defeating the Persians in 331, to India. He married Roxana, and a second wife, Barsine. His horse was named Bucephalus.

Alexander was made the centre of a cluster of medieval legends, comparable to those of the Carlovingian and Arthurian cycles.

Alexandrian Library, THE, was formed at Alexandria during the reign of the Ptolemies (beginning 323 B.C.). It is said to have contained at one time about 400,000 manuscripts, of which a part were accidentally burnt when Julius Caesar was besieged in Alexandria.

Alexandrine, an iambic line of six feet, which is the French heroic verse, and in English is used, e.g., as the last line of the Spenserian stanza, or as a variant in a poem of heroic couplets. Cf. Pope's 'Essay on Criticism':

A needless Alexandrine ends the song,
That like a wounded snake drags its
    slow length along.

Bridges' 'loose Alexandrines' in the 'Testament of Beauty' are noteworthy.

The name is derived from the fact that certain 12th- and 13th-cent. French poems on Alexander the Great were written in this metre.

Alfieri, VITTORIO (1749-1803), Italian dramatist and author of a remarkable autobiography.

Alfred (ÆLFRED) (849-899), king of the West Saxons (871-899), is important in the history of literature for the revival of letters that he effected. He translated into English the 'Cura Pastoralis' of Pope Gregory, and the writings of Orosius (qq.v.). He had a translation made of Bede's 'Historia Ecclesiastica'. He also translated the 'De Consolatione Philosophiae' of Boëthius (q.v.), with some original additions. 'The Anglo-Saxon Chronicle' (q.v.) may represent in part his work or inspiration.

Alfred, a masque, containing 'Rule, Britannia', see *Thomson* (*J.*, 1700-48).

Algarsife, one of the two sons of King Cambuscan, in Chaucer's 'The Squire's Tale' (see *Canterbury Tales*).

Algrind, in Spenser's 'Shepheards Calender' (q.v.), Edmund Grindal, archbishop of Canterbury, 1576-83.

Ali Baba and the Forty Thieves, an oriental tale generally regarded as one of the 'Arabian Nights' (q.v.), but not included in any manuscript of these.

It concerns the adventures of Ali Baba who discovers how to enter the secret cave of a robber band by uttering the magic formula, 'Open, Sesame'.

Alice Brand, a ballad in the 4th canto of Scott's 'The Lady of the Lake' (q.v.).

Alice's Adventures in Wonderland, a

story for children by Lewis Carroll (see *Dodgson*) (1865).

Alice is a little girl who dreams that she pursues a White Rabbit down a rabbit-hole, and there meets with strange adventures and odd characters, the Duchess and the Cheshire Cat, the Mad Hatter and the March Hare, the King and Queen of Hearts, and the Mock Turtle. See also *Through the Looking-Glass.*

Alisaunder, King, the legendary story of Alexander the Great, a verse romance of the early 14th cent., some 8,000 lines in octosyllabic couplets.

Allan-a-Dale, one of the companions of Robin Hood (q.v.); the subject of a song in Scott's 'Rokeby' (q.v.).

Allecto, one of the Furies (q.v.).

Allegory, a figurative narrative or description, conveying a veiled moral meaning; an extended metaphor, or a sustained personification. Famous examples in English literature are Spenser's 'Faerie Queene' and Bunyan's 'The Pilgrim's Progress' (qq.v.), in both of which virtues and vices are personified.

Allegro, *L'*, a poem by Milton (q.v.), written in 1632. The Italian title means 'the cheerful man', and this idyll is an invocation to the goddess Mirth to allow the poet to live with her, first amid the delights of rustic scenes, then amid those of 'towered cities' and the 'busy hum of men'. Cf. *Penseroso (Il).*

Allen, BENJAMIN and ARABELLA, characters in Dickens's 'The Pickwick Papers' (q.v.).

Alleyn, CHIEF DETECTIVE INSPECTOR, the hero of Ngaio Marsh's detective stories.

Alleyn, EDWARD (1566-1626), an actor (Richard Burbage's chief rival) and partner of Philip Henslowe, with whom he built the Fortune Theatre, Cripplegate. There he acted at the head of the Lord Admiral's company, playing among other parts the hero in Marlowe's 'Tamburlaine', 'The Jew of Malta', and 'Doctor Faustus'. He acquired great wealth, bought the Manor of Dulwich, and built and endowed Dulwich College. His first wife was

Henslowe's step-daughter, his second the daughter of Dr. Donne. He was a patron of Dekker, John Taylor, and other writers.

All Fools, a comedy by George Chapman (q.v.) (1605).

All Fools' Day, see *April Fool's Day.*

All for Love, or *A Sinner well saved,* a poem by Southey (q.v.) (1829).

All for Love, or *The World well lost,* a tragedy by Dryden (q.v.) (1678).

In this, his finest play, Dryden abandoned the rhymed couplet for blank verse. The plot deals with the story of Antony and Cleopatra, but, as compared with Shakespeare's treatment of it, Dryden gains concentration by confining his play to the last few days of Antony's career.

All-Hallows' Day, All Saints' Day, 1 November. ALL-HALLOW EVE, or *Hallow-e'en,* 31 October, was in the old Celtic calendar the last night of the old year. Many superstitious and ancient customs attached to it. See Burns's 'Halloween' for Scottish customs.

Alliteration, Alliterative verse, the beginning of two or more syllables close together with the same sound, as, for example, in Coleridge's 'the furrow followed free'.

In OE. verse, alliteration of the stressed syllables in a line was the chief metrical device. As a rule there were three (or four) syllables in a line beginning with the same consonant or a vowel, two in the first half of the line, one (or two) in the second half. The main stresses fell on these syllables. Alliterative verse of this kind survived into the 14th and 15th cent., notably in Langland (q.v.) and later in association with rhyme.

In modern times alliteration has been used for onomatopoeic or emphatic effects. Swinburne's verse is remarkable for its clever but sometimes excessive use of the device. It is an integral part of some of the verse of G. M. Hopkins (q.v.); and certain later poets have used a modified form of the OE. alliterative line.

All Saints' Day, 1 November.

All's Lost by Lust, a tragedy by W. Rowley (q.v.), printed in 1633.

All Souls College, Oxford, founded by Henry VI in 1438, with Archbishop Chichele (q.v.) as co-founder, to pray for the souls of all the faithful and especially of those who fell in the wars against France. It is a unique foundation, consisting of a warden and fellows (originally 40), and no undergraduates.

All Souls' Day, 2 November.

All's Well that Ends Well, a comedy by Shakespeare (q.v.), composed at an uncertain date, placed by some as late as about 1604 (E. K. Chambers, 1602-3), first printed in the folio of 1623.

The plot is drawn from Painter's 'Palace of Pleasure' (q.v.) (No. xxxviii). Bertram, the young count of Rousillon, on the death of his father is summoned to the court of the king of France, leaving his mother and with her Helena, daughter of the famous physician Gerard de Narbon. The king is sick of a disease said to be incurable. Helena, who loves Bertram, conceives the project of going to Paris to attempt the king's cure by means of a prescription left by her father, and Bertram's mother, discovering Helena's love for her son, furthers its accomplishment. Helena effects the cure and as a reward is allowed to choose her husband, and names Bertram, who unwillingly obeys the king's order to wed her. But under the influence of the worthless braggart Parolles, he at once takes service with the duke of Florence, writing to Helena that until she can get the ring from his finger 'which never shall come off', and is with child by him, she may not call him husband. Helena, passing through Florence on a pilgrimage, finds Bertram courting Diana, the daughter of her hostess there. Disclosing herself as his wife to these, she obtains permission to replace Diana at a midnight interview with Bertram, having that day caused him to be informed that Helena is dead. Thereby she obtains from Bertram his ring, and gives him one that the king had given her. Bertram returns to his mother's house, where the king is on a visit. The latter sees on Bertram's finger the ring that he had given Helena, suspects Bertram of having destroyed her, and demands an explanation on pain of death. Helena herself now appears, explains what has passed, and claims that the conditions named in Bertram's letter have been fulfilled. Bertram, filled with remorse, accepts her as his wife.

All the Year Round, see *Dickens*.

Allworthy, Squire and Bridget, characters in Fielding's 'Tom Jones' (q.v.).

Alma (Ital., 'soul', 'spirit'), in Spenser's 'Faerie Queene', II. ix and xi, represents the virgin soul. She is the Lady of the House of Temperance, visited by Prince Arthur and Sir Guyon, and defended against her enemies by the former.

Alma, a poem by Matthew Prior (q.v.).

Almagest, the name applied to the astronomical treatise of Ptolemy (q.v.), and extended in the Middle Ages to other textbooks of astrology and alchemy.

Alma Mater, 'bounteous mother', a title given by the Romans to several goddesses; used in England to refer to one's former school or university.

Almanzor and Almahide, see *Conquest of Granada*.

Almayer's Folly, a novel by Joseph Conrad (q.v.) (1895).

Almeria, the heroine of Congreve's 'The Mourning Bride' (q.v.).

Aloysius, St., see *Eloi*.

Alph, in Coleridge's 'Kubla Khan' (q.v.), the sacred river in Xanadu. For its connection with the river Alpheus and with the Nile see J. L. Lowes, 'The Road to Xanadu' (1927).

Alsatia, a cant name for the precinct of Whitefriars in London which until 1697 was a sanctuary for debtors. See Shadwell, 'The Squire of Alsatia', and Scott's 'The Fortunes of Nigel'.

Altamont, a character in Rowe's 'The Fair Penitent' (q.v.).

Altamont, Frederick, a character in Thackeray's 'Memoirs of Mr. C. J. Yellowplush'.

Altamont, COLONEL JACK, *alias* AMORY, or ARMSTRONG, a character in Thackeray's 'Pendennis' (q.v.).

Althaea, in Greek mythology, see *Meleager*.

Althea, To, a poem by Lovelace (q.v.).

Alton Locke, Tailor and Poet, a novel by C. Kingsley (q.v.) (1850), concerned with Chartism and the social conditions of the time.

Amadis of Gaul (Amadis de Gaula), a Spanish or Portuguese romance, written by Garcia de Montalvo in the second half of the 15th and printed early in the 16th cents. An abridged version of it was published (1803) by R. Southey (q.v.).

Amalthea, the nymph who nursed the infant Zeus (q.v.) in Crete. The horn of Amalthea was the 'horn of plenty' or cornucopia, the symbol of abundance.

Amara, MOUNT, in Abyssinia, where the kings secluded their sons, to protect themselves from sedition (Milton, 'Paradise Lost', iv. 281). It figures as 'Amhara' in Johnson's 'Rasselas' (q.v.). See also *Abora*.

Amaryllis, the name given to a shepherdess by Theocritus, Virgil, and Ovid.

Amaurote, the capital of More's 'Utopia' (q.v.).

Amazing Marriage, The, a novel by G. Meredith (q.v.) (1895).

Amazons, a race of female warriors alleged by Herodotus to exist in Scythia. They figure also in the legends of Hercules, Theseus, etc.

The word is explained by the Greeks from ἀ privative and μαζός a breast (in connection with the fable that they destroyed the right breast so as not to interfere with the use of the bow), but this is probably the popular etymology of an unknown foreign word.

Ambassadors, The, a novel by H. James (q.v.) (1903).

Ambrose, ST. (*c.* 340–97), a celebrated bishop of Milan, one of the Fathers of the Church, and a vigorous opponent of the Arians. He developed the use of music in the church, founding what is known as the Ambrosian chant (as opposed to the Gregorian chant). He composed several hymns, including, according to one tradition, the 'Te Deum' (q.v.).

Ambrosian Library, THE, at Milan, founded in 1609, was named after St. Ambrose.

Ambrosio, the hero of M. G. Lewis's 'The Monk' (q.v.).

Amelia, a novel by H. Fielding (q.v.) (1751). It is the last of Fielding's novels and the story is less successfully told than that of 'Tom Jones'. A good deal of the book is devoted to exposing various social evils of the time, such as the defects in the law of debt, and the scandals of the prisons.

American, The, a novel by H. James (q.v.) (1877).

American Taxation, On, a speech by E. Burke (q.v.), made in 1774 on a motion for the repeal of the American Tea Duty.

Amerigo Vespucci (1451–1512), a Florentine merchant who sailed in 1499 and again in 1501 in an expedition to the West. His name was given to the continent of America.

Amhara, see *Amara*.

Amharic, the principal language of Abyssinia, partly Semitic, partly Hamitic, in origin.

Amiatinus Codex, the best extant MS. of the Vulgate, written in England, early in the 8th cent., at Wearmouth or Jarrow, and now in the Laurentian Library at Florence.

Amintor, the hero of Beaumont and Fletcher's 'The Maid's Tragedy'.

Amis and Amiloun, a metrical romance of the Middle English period, in which the virtue of friendship is exalted. The story is also told by Pater and W. Morris.

Ammon, or AMON, the supreme god of the Egyptians.

Amoret, in Spenser's 'Faerie Queene', III. vi and xii, and IV. vii, 'of grace and beauty noble Paragon', is married to Sir Scudamour, but carried off by the enchanter Busirane and imprisoned by him until released by Britomart.

Amoretti, a series of sonnets by Spenser (q.v.), which probably illustrate his wooing of Elizabeth Boyle, whom he married. These were printed with the 'Epithalamion' (q.v.) in 1595.

Amory, BLANCHE, a character in Thackeray's 'Pendennis' (q.v.).

Amory, THOMAS (1691?-1788), the author of two eccentric works of fiction, 'Memoirs of several Ladies of Great Britain' (1755), and 'The Life of John Buncle, Esq.' (1756-66). 'John Buncle' (q.v.) is virtually a sequel of the 'Memoirs', but is more entertaining.

Amos Barton, one of the tales in *Scenes of Clerical Life* (q.v.).

Amphibology, AMPHIBOLY, ambiguity arising from the uncertain construction of a sentence.

Amphibrach, a metrical foot, ◡–◡.

Amphion, son of Zeus and Antiope. Hermes gave him a lyre on which he played with such skill that the stones of Thebes moved of their own accord and formed a wall.

Amphisbaena, a fabulous serpent with a head at each end and able to move in either direction.

Amphitryon, a Theban prince, who obtained the hand of Alcmena. Zeus borrowed the features of Amphitryon while he was gone to the wars, and introduced himself to her as her victorious husband. The son of Zeus and Alcmena was Hercules. The legend is the subject of plays by Plautus, Molière, Dryden, and Giraudoux (qq.v.).

Amram, the father of Moses (Exod. vi. 20). There is a reference to 'Amram's son' in Milton, 'Paradise Lost', i. 339.

Amurath (MURAD), the name of several Turkish sultans in the 14th-16th cents. 'Not Amurath an Amurath succeeds, But Harry Harry' (Shakespeare, '2 Henry IV', v. ii).

Amyas, in Spenser's 'Faerie Queene', 'the Squire of low degree'.

Amymone, a daughter of Danaus (see *Danaides*). Mentioned by Milton, 'Paradise Regained', ii. 188, as a 'beauty rare'.

Amyntas, see *Colin Clouts come home againe*.

Amyot, JACQUES (1513-93), a French writer, whose version of Plutarch was translated into English by Sir T. North (q.v.).

Amys and Amylion, see *Amis and Amiloun*.

Ana, a Latin termination, used of a collection of sayings or anecdotes of a person, as in *Johnsoniana*.

Anabaptist, one who baptizes over again, as the due performance of a rite ineffectually performed in infancy; the name of a sect that arose in Germany in 1521.

Anabasis, see *Xenophon*.

Anachronism, a reference, occurring commonly in historical plays or novels, to something which could not have existed at the time described, e.g. Shakespeare's mention of clocks striking in 'Julius Caesar'. The concept is in some ways a modern one; the Elizabethans and later ages (e.g. the 18th-cent. stage regularly 'dressed' all plays in the costume of their own time) were not troubled by it. Anachronism can be used for humorous effect, e.g. the opening of Shaw's 'Caesar and Cleopatra', or Mark Twain's 'Yankee at the Court of King Arthur'.

Anacoluthon (Greek, 'wanting sequence'), a sentence in which a fresh construction is adopted before the former is complete.

Anacreon (6th cent. B.C.), lyric poet of Teos in Ionia, author of many melodious verses on love and wine. Of his poems only a few genuine fragments have survived. T. Moore (q.v.) published in 1800 a translation of the 'Odes of Anacreon' into English verse, and Herrick wrote 'Anacreonticks'.

Anacrusis, 'striking up', an additional syllable at the beginning of a verse before the normal rhythm, e.g. the 'and' in the second of the following lines:

Till danger's troubled night depart
And the star of peace return.

Anagram, the rearrangement of letters in a word to make another word. Thus

Caliban ('The Tempest') is an anagram of Cannibal (often spelt *Canibal* in Elizabethan times). Exponents of the Baconian theory (q.v.) find anagrams in support of it, e.g. in 'honorificabilitudinitatibus' ('Love's Labour's Lost', v. 1). George Herbert employed the anagram as a literary device in his poems.

Analogy of Religion, Natural and Revealed, to the Constitution and Course of Nature, The, a treatise in defence of the Christian religion, by J. Butler (q.v.) (1736).

Ananias, (1) the Jewish high-priest before whom Paul was brought and who caused him to be smitten on the mouth (Acts xxiii); (2) the husband of Sapphira who was struck dead because he 'lied unto God' (Acts v); (3) a character in Jonson's 'The Alchemist' (q.v.).

Anapaest (Greek, 'reversed'), a reversed dactyl, a metrical foot ⌣⌣— .

Anaphora, 'carrying back', the repetition of the same word or phrase in several successive clauses; for instance, 'Awake up, my glory; awake, lute and harp; I myself will awake right early.'

Anarchy, The Masque of, a poem by P. B. Shelley (q.v.), 'written on the occasion of the Massacre of Manchester' (the Peterloo (q.v.) affair, August 1819).

Anatomie of Abuses, The, see *Stubbes.*

Anatomy of Melancholy, The, a treatise by Robert Burton (q.v.) (1621).

In purpose the treatise is a medical work. The introduction sets out that melancholy is 'an inbred malady in every one of us'. But the subject is expanded until it covers the whole life of man. The treatment is marked by a sense of humour and pathos, and a tolerant spirit in religion. In the exposition and illustration of his argument, Burton uses quotation (or paraphrase) to an extreme degree, drawing on a very wide field of literature.

Anchises, a Trojan prince, who became by Venus father of Aeneas (q.v.).

Ancien régime, a French phrase signifying the old order before the Revolution.

Ancient Mariner, The Rime of the, a poem by S. T. Coleridge (q.v.), which first appeared in 1798 in Wordsworth's and Coleridge's 'Lyrical Ballads' (q.v.).

An ancient mariner meets three gallants on their way to a marriage feast and detains one to recount his story. He tells how his ship was drawn towards the South Pole by a storm. When the ship is surrounded by ice, an albatross comes through the snow-fog and is received with joy, but is presently shot by the mariner. For this act of cruelty a curse falls on the ship. She is driven north to the Line, and becalmed. The crew die of thirst except the mariner, who beholding God's creatures, blesses them in his heart. The spell breaks and the ship is brought back to England, but the mariner is condemned to travel from land to land and to teach love and reverence to all God's creatures.

Ancients and Moderns, Quarrel of the, see *Battle of the Books.*

Ancrene Riwle, or *Ancrene Wisse, The,* i.e. a rule for anchoresses, a devotional manual in prose written for the rule and guidance of certain English nuns. The author is unknown. The work belongs to the early Middle English period (c. 1200–50).

Andersen, HANS CHRISTIAN (1805–75), Danish poet and author of dramas, novels, and books of travel, is chiefly known in England for his fairy tales, of which the first volume appeared in 1835.

Anderson, SHERWOOD (1876–1941), American writer. He excelled in the short story and published the collections, 'Winesburg, Ohio' (1919), 'The Triumph of the Egg' (1921), 'Horses and Men' (1923), and 'Death in the Woods' (1933), in which he illustrated the frustrations of contemporary life, a theme also explored in his novels. His best novels are 'Poor White' (1920) and 'Dark Laughter' (1925).

Andrea del Sarto, a poem by R. Browning (q.v.), included in 'Men and Women' (1855).

Andrea del Sarto was called 'The Faultless Painter'. The poet presents him as reflecting, in a monologue addressed to Lucrezia, his wife, on his deficiencies.

Andreas, an OE. poem formerly attributed by some to Cynewulf (q.v.), included in the 'Vercelli Book' (q.v.). It is remarkable for its description of a sea voyage.

Andrewes, LANCELOT (1555-1626), bishop successively of Chichester, Ely, and Winchester (1619). He was renowned for his learning, wrote theological works, and was among the divines appointed to make the 'Authorized Version' of the Bible.

Andrew of Wyntoun, see *Wyntoun*.

Androcles, or *Androclus, and the Lion*, a story told by Aulus Gellius (v. 14) of a slave who, running away from his master and hiding in a cave, was confronted by a lion. The animal presented to him a swollen paw, from which he extracted a thorn. Androcles was captured and sentenced to fight with a lion in the arena. It chanced that this lion was the same that he had relieved. The lion recognized him and instead of attacking him, showed every sign of affection. Bernard Shaw wrote a play 'Androcles and the Lion' (1912).

Andromache, wife of Hector (q.v.) and mother of Astyanax. Her parting with Hector before a battle is the most pathetic passage in Homer's 'Iliad' (Book VI).

Andromeda, daughter of Cepheus, king of Ethiopia, and Cassiopea. Cassiopea boasted herself (or her daughter) more beautiful than the Nereids. Whereupon Poseidon sent a sea-monster to ravage the country. To abate his wrath, Andromeda was exposed on a rock to the monster, but was rescued by Perseus (q.v.). Charles Kingsley (q.v.) wrote a poem on this myth, entitled 'Andromeda'.

Aneirin, The Book of, see *Aneurin*.

Anelida and Arcite, an early poem in rhyme-royal by Chaucer (q.v.), the lament of Queen Anelida for the falseness of Arcite her lover.

Aneurin or ANEIRIN (*fl.* 600?), a Welsh bard whose compositions are contained in a MS. 'Book of Aneirin' of the 13th cent.

Angel, from the Greek word ἄγγελος, a messenger. The angels in the Scriptures are prominent chiefly in the apocalyptic books; the apocryphal Book of Enoch enumerates seven archangels: Uriel, Raphael, Raguel, Michael, Sariel, Gabriel, and Jerahmeel. According to a 4th-cent. work, the heavenly beings are divided into three hierarchies, each containing three orders, viz. seraphim, cherubim, thrones; dominions, virtues, powers; principalities, archangels, angels.

Angel, the coin, see *Noble*.

Angelica, a character in 'Orlando Innamorato' (q.v.) and 'Orlando Furioso' (q.v.). Cf. Milton, 'Paradise Regained', iii. 341.

Angelic Doctor, THE, Thomas Aquinas (q.v.).

Angelico, FRA (*c.* 1387-1455), born GUIDO DI PIETRO. He became Fra Giovanni, a Dominican friar of Fiesole. He painted religious subjects.

Angel in the House, The, see *Patmore*.

Angell, SIR NORMAN (1874-1967), writer and lecturer on politics and economics. His most famous work, 'The Great Illusion' (1910), demonstrated the futility of war.

Angelo, a character in Shakespeare's 'Measure for Measure' (q.v.).

Angles, THE, one of the Low German tribes that settled in Britain and finally gave their name to the whole English people.

Anglo-Catholic, see *Catholic Church*.

Anglo-Norman (or ANGLO-FRENCH) designates the French language as spoken and written in the British Isles from the Norman Conquest until roughly the end of the 14th cent. It developed characteristics of its own.

Anglo-Norman literature is rich in didactic and religious or moralizing works, in chronicles and pseudo-historical 'Bruts' (q.v.), and in manuals or treatises of a practical nature, many being based on Latin originals. The first outstanding dramatic production French has to show, the 12th-cent. semi-liturgical play 'Adam' (q.v.), was probably written in England.

An A.-N. type of French was used for official documents and in courts of law long after it had ceased to be a 'living' language.

Anglo-Saxon, originally a collective name for the Saxons of England as distinct from the 'Old Saxons' of the Continent, was extended to the entire Old English people and language before the Conquest. In this book the English language before the Conquest is referred to as 'Old English' (see *English*). See also *Angles* and *Saxon*.

Anglo-Saxon Chronicle, The, compiled by monks working at different centres, notably Winchester, Canterbury, and Peterborough, is a chronological record, in vernacular, of events in England from the beginning of the Christian era to the middle of the 12th cent. It contains some vivid and detailed passages. In the portion of the 'Chronicle' relating to the 10th cent. are inserted some important poems, among others the 'Brunanburh' (q.v.). The earlier part of the 'Chronicle', down to 892, may represent the work or inspiration of King Alfred.

Anglo-Saxon Literature, the literature of the period from the Anglian invasion of the 5th and 6th cents. to about A.D. 1100–50. Comparatively little Anglo-Saxon poetry survives, most of it in four manuscripts: in the Junius MS., the biblical paraphrases attributed to Cædmon (q.v.); in the 'Exeter Book', a medley of religious and half-pagan verse; in the Cottonian MS., 'Beowulf' and 'Judith' (qq.v.); and in the 'Vercelli Book', religious poems and lives of saints.

'Beowulf' and two fragments, 'Widsith' and 'Waldhere' (qq.v.), belong to the genre of heroic poetry (though 'Beowulf' has a Christian tinge) comparable to early German lays. So, too, do poems of lyric power like 'The Wanderer' and 'The Seafarer' and the much later 'Maldon' (qq.v.). The religious poems, formerly attributed to Cædmon, are

mainly biblical paraphrases. The 'Cynewulf [q.v.] poems', 'Elene', 'St. Juliana', etc., probably belong to the late 8th or 9th cent. A.D., and are notable for a clearer narrative style. Two other poems of uncertain date, 'The Phoenix' and 'The Dream of the Rood', have a marked religious inspiration.

Anglo-Saxon verse was based upon a long descended technique, peculiar to the Germanic race, a trochaic metre with four stresses in a line marked by alliteration, and a strong caesura. (See also *Alliteration*.) It had a rich vocabulary of compound phrases and metaphors and was suited to narrative rather than lyric poetry. Though often marred by awkwardness and periphrasis, it could be strong and effective.

The earliest scholars of the period wrote mainly in Latin prose. Alfred (q.v.), as he explains in his preface to the 'Cura Pastoralis', was instrumental in encouraging vernacular prose writing. Besides the many translations which he himself performed or inspired, he probably caused 'The Anglo-Saxon Chronicle' (q.v.) to be written. A great development in prose followed, notably in the writings of Ælfric (q.v.) and of his contemporary Wulfstan (q.v.). Their prose was energetic and often eloquent.

Anglo-Saxon literature ceased for the most part with the Norman Conquest. For the writing which followed, see under *Middle English*.

Animal Farm, a novel by George Orwell (q.v.) (1945). It is a satire in fable form on Revolutionary and post-Revolutionary Russia, and, by extension, on all revolutions. The animals of Mr. Jones's farm revolt against their human masters and drive them out, the pigs becoming the leaders. Eventually the pigs are corrupted by power and a new tyranny replaces the old. The ultimate slogan runs 'All animals are equal but some animals are more equal than others'.

Anima Poetae, a collection of aphorisms, reflections, and other literary material, extracted from the note-books of S. T. Coleridge (q.v.), and published by Ernest Hartley Coleridge in 1895.

Anna Christie, a play by Eugene O'Neill (q.v.) (1921), which was one of the playwright's early successes.

Anna Comnena (*b.* 1083), the daughter of the emperor Alexius Comnenus, and author of the 'Alexiad' (a history in fifteen books, mainly of her father's life). She figures in Scott's 'Count Robert of Paris' (q.v.).

Anna Karenina, a novel by Tolstoy (q.v.) (1875-6).

Annales Cambriae, ancient annals of Wales, of which the earliest extant manuscript dates from the second half of the 10th cent. They have a special literary interest on account of their reference to the Battle of Badon, which is one of the sources of the subsequent Arthurian legend.

Annals of the Parish, a novel by J. Galt (q.v.) (1821) which chronicles the events, great and small, that affected the homely lives of the parishioners of Dalmailing in Ayrshire during the period 1760-1810.

Anne, queen of England, 1702-14.

Anne of Geierstein, or The Maiden of the Mist, a novel by Sir W. Scott (q.v.) (1829). The period of the story is the reign of Edward IV.

Annual Register, The, an annual review of events, founded by Dodsley (q.v.) in 1758.

Annus Mirabilis, a poem by Dryden (q.v.) (1667). It is written in quatrains on the model of 'Gondibert' (q.v.), and deals with the sea-fights against the Dutch and the Fire of London in the year 1666.

Anselm, ST. (1033-1109), Italian by birth, a pupil of Lanfranc at the abbey of Bec in Normandy. William Rufus appointed Anselm archbishop (1093), but in 1097 he withdrew to Rome. He returned to England as archbishop under Henry I. Anselm wrote many theological and philosophical works, including the famous 'Cur Deus Homo'. Commemorated on 21 April.

Anson, GEORGE, *Baron Anson* (1697-1762), made his famous voyage round the world in 1740-4. The account of it, compiled by his chaplain, R. Walter, was published in 1748, and is a stirring narrative of the sea.

Anstey, CHRISTOPHER (1724-1805), author of the 'New Bath Guide' (1766), a series of letters in anapaestic verse, describing the adventures of the 'Blunderhead Family' at Bath.

Anstey, F., the pseudonym of THOMAS ANSTEY GUTHRIE (1856-1934), author of many novels and dialogues, including 'Vice Versa' (q.v., 1882), 'The Tinted Venus' (1885), 'Voces Populi' (1890), 'The Man from Blankley's' (1893), and 'Salted Almonds' (1906).

Antaeus, giant, son of Poseidon and Ge (the Earth). Hercules attacked him, and as Antaeus drew new strength from his mother whenever he touched the earth, Hercules lifted him in the air and squeezed him to death in his arms.

Antenor, a wise counsellor of Priam (q.v.), king of Troy.

Anthology, The Greek, a collection of about 6,000 poems, inscriptions, etc., by more than 300 writers (7th cent. B.C.-10th cent. A.D.), originating in a collection by Meleager of Gadara (*c.* 60 B.C.), which grew by successive additions.

Anthropophagi, in Greek legend, a people of Scythia that fed on human flesh.

Antichrist, the personal opponent of Christ and his Kingdom, expected by the early Church to appear before the end of the world, and much referred to in the Middle Ages.

Anticlimax, see *Bathos*.

Antigone, daughter of Oedipus (q.v.) and Jocasta. When the strife between her brothers Eteocles (q.v.) and Polyneices had led to the latter's death, she buried his body against the order of Creon, and was ordered by him to be buried alive. She took her own life, and Haemon, the king's son, who loved her, killed himself on her grave. This is the subject of a tragedy by Sophocles.

Antigonus, a character in Shakespeare's 'The Winter's Tale' (q.v.).

Anti-Jacobin, The, a journal founded by Canning (q.v.) at the end of the 18th cent., edited by Gifford (q.v.), and including among its contributors Canning, Ellis, and Frere (qq.v.).

Antiope, a daughter of Nycteus, beloved by Zeus, by whom she became mother of Amphion (q.v.) and Zethus.

Antipholus, the name of the twin brothers, sons of Aegeon, in Shakespeare's 'The Comedy of Errors' (q.v.).

Antiquaries, THE SOCIETY OF, was founded about 1572 at the instance of Archbishop Parker, but was suppressed on the accession of James I. The present Society was founded in Jan. 1717–18.

Antiquary, The, a novel by Sir W. Scott (q.v.) (1816).

A young officer, Major Neville, whose birth is supposed to be illegitimate, falls in love with Isabella Wardour, who, in deference to the prejudices of her father, Sir Arthur Wardour, repulses him. Under the assumed name of Lovel, he follows her to Scotland, falling in on the way with Jonathan Oldbuck, laird of Monkbarns, a learned antiquary, and a neighbour of Sir Arthur. Lovel saves the lives of Sir Arthur and his daughter at the peril of his own. He finally turns out to be the son and heir of the earl of Glenallan, and all ends happily. The charm of the book, Scott's 'chief favourite among all his novels', lies in the character of the Antiquary, in which we may recognize a caricature of Scott himself.

Antiquary, The, a comedy by Shackerley Marmion (q.v.).

Antisthenes, the founder of the Cynic school of philosophy. He lived in the 5th cent. B.C., and was a pupil of Socrates. He taught that virtue consists in the avoidance of evil and independence of needs. Diogenes (q.v.) was the most famous of his pupils.

Antistrophe, in a Greek chorus, recited as the chorus proceeded in the opposite direction to that followed in the strophe.

The metre of *strophe* and *antistrophe* was the same.

Antoninus Pius, Roman emperor from 138 to 161. The wall of Antoninus between the Forth and the Clyde was built in his reign.

Antonio, (1) the Merchant of Venice, in Shakespeare's play of that name (q.v.); (2) the brother of Prospero in 'The Tempest' (q.v.); (3) a sea-captain in 'Twelfth Night' (q.v.); (4) the brother of Leonato in 'Much Ado about Nothing' (q.v.); (5) the father of Proteus in 'The Two Gentlemen of Verona' (q.v.).

Antonio and Mellida, History of, a tragedy by J. Marston (q.v.). It provided Ben Jonson with material for his ridicule of Marston in 'The Poetaster' (q.v.).

Antony and Cleopatra, a historical tragedy by Shakespeare (q.v.), probably written about 1606–7, and first printed in the folio of 1623. In it the poet closely follows North's 'Plutarch'.

The play presents Mark Antony at Alexandria, enthralled by the beauty of the Egyptian queen, Cleopatra. Recalled by the death of his wife Fulvia and political developments, he returns to Rome, where the estrangement between him and Octavius Caesar is terminated by his marriage to Octavia, Caesar's sister. But the reconciliation is short-lived, and Antony returns to Egypt. At the battle of Actium, the flight of the Egyptian squadron is followed by the retreat of Antony, pursued to Alexandria by Caesar. There, after a momentary success, Antony is defeated. On the false report of Cleopatra's death, he falls upon his sword. He is borne to Cleopatra and dies in her arms. Cleopatra, fallen into Caesar's power, but determined not to grace his triumph, takes her own life by the bite of an asp.

See also *Cleopatra* and *All for Love.*

Anubis, ancient Egyptian jackal-headed deity, ruler of the dead.

Anville, MISS, the name borne by the heroine of Fanny Burney's 'Evelina' (q.v.), until she is recognized by her father.

Aonia, a part of Boeotia which includes Mt. Helicon and the fountain Aganippe, sacred to the Muses. Hence Milton speaks of 'the Aonian Mount' ('Paradise Lost', i. 15).

Apelles, a celebrated Greek painter, of the time of Alexander the Great. He is a character in Lyly's 'Alexander and Campaspe' (see *Campaspe*).

Apemantus, the 'churlish philosopher' in Shakespeare's 'Timon of Athens' (q.v.).

Aphaeresis, the suppression of a letter or syllable at the beginning of a word.

Aphorism or APOPHTHEGM, a short pithy sentence into which much thought or observation is compressed.

Aphrodite, see *Venus*.

Apis, ancient bull-headed Egyptian deity.

Apocrypha, THE, in its special sense, those books received by the early Church as part of the Greek version of the O.T., but not included in the Hebrew Bible, being excluded by the non-Hellenistic Jews from their Canon. They are Esdras (I and II), Tobit, Judith, the Rest of Esther, the Wisdom of Solomon, Ecclesiasticus, Baruch (with the Epistle of Jeremiah), the Song of the Three Holy Children, the History of Susanna, Bel and the Dragon, the Prayer of Manasses, Maccabees (I and II).

Apodosis, the main or consequent clause of a conditional sentence.

Apollo, called also PHOEBUS, often identified with the sun, was the son of Zeus and Latona. He was the god who brings back sunshine in spring, who sends plagues, and who founds states and colonies. He was the god of music and poetry (cf. Shelley's 'Hymn of Apollo') and had the gift of knowing the future. He was the type of manly youth and beauty, and was represented in the famous Colossus (q.v.) at Rhodes.

Apollonius of Tyre, the subject of a popular medieval romance. See *Pericles* (Shakespeare's drama).

Apollonius Rhodius, a poet and grammarian of Alexandria, 3rd cent. B.C.

Apollyon, 'The Destroyer', the angel of the bottomless pit (Rev. ix. 11). He figures in Bunyan's 'The Pilgrim's Progress' (q.v.).

Apologia pro Vita sua, see *Newman*.

Apologie for Poetrie, The, or *Defence of Poesie,* a prose essay by Sir P. Sidney (q.v.). A treatise by Stephen Gosson (q.v.), the 'Schoole of Abuse', dedicated to Sidney, was probably the occasion. The 'Apologie' was published in 1595, after Sidney's death.

It is a methodical examination of the art of poetry and a critical discussion of the state of English poetry in the author's time, such as had not before appeared in English. The author classifies the various kinds of poetry, and discusses English poetry from Chaucer to his own day. He next deals with the principles that should be observed in tragedy and comedy, laments the poverty of English lyrical poetry and the affectation of the current English style. Lastly, he deals with prosody in its special relation to the English language.

Apologue, a fable conveying a moral lesson.

Apophthegm, see *Aphorism*.

Aposiopesis, a rhetorical artifice, in which the speaker comes to a sudden halt in the middle of a sentence, as if unable or unwilling to proceed.

Appian Way, THE, the first great Roman road, constructed in the censorship of Appius Claudius Caecus (312 B.C.) from Rome to Capua and thence to Brundusium (Brindisi).

Appius, see *Virginia*.

Appius and Virginia, (1) a tragedy attributed to J. Webster (q.v.); (2) a tragedy by John Dennis (q.v.).

April Fool's Day, 1 April, probably the survival of ancient festivities held at the spring equinox.

Apuleius (*b. c.* A.D. 114), author of the 'Metamorphoses seu de Asino Aureo', 'The Golden Ass' (q.v.).

Aquarius, the eleventh sign of the zodiac; also a constellation.

Aquilo, see *Boreas*.

Aquinas, St. Thomas (*c.* 1225–74), Italian philosopher and Christian apologist. His 'Summa Totius Philosophiae' was a vast synthesis of the moral and political sciences, within a theological framework. His followers were called Thomists.

Arabesque, the Arabian or Moorish style of mural decoration, composed in flowing lines of branches, leaves, and scroll-work fancifully intertwined.

Arabia Deserta, Felix, Petraea, the several parts of the desert region between Egypt, Syria, and the Euphrates.

Arabia Deserta, see *Doughty.*

Arabian Nights' Entertainments, or *The Thousand and One Nights,* a collection of Arabic stories made known in Europe in the 18th cent. by the French translation of Antoine Galland. They were translated into English in 1839–41, and again, by Sir Richard Burton, in 1885–8.

The framework of the tales (the story of the king who killed his wives successively on the morning after their marriage, until he married Scheherazade, who saved her life by the tales she told him) is of Persian origin. But the stories are, for the most part, Arabian in character.

Arachne, a weaver who challenged Athene (q.v.) to a contest. She aroused the wrath of Athene, who tore her work in pieces. Arachne in despair hanged herself, but she was changed into a spider.

Aramis, see *Three Musketeers.*

Ara vos prec, a poem by T. S. Eliot (q.v.). The words are Provençal, 'Now I do pray you'.

Arber, Edward (1836–1912), became professor of English at Mason College, Birmingham, in 1881. He produced 'English Reprints' (1868–71), 'Transcripts of the Registers of the Company of Stationers of London, 1554–1640' (1875–94), and 'Term Catalogues, 1668–1709' (1903–6).

Arbiter elegantiae, see *Petronius.*

Arblay, Madame D', see *Burney.*

Arbuthnot, John (1667–1735), physician in ordinary to Queen Anne. He formed a close friendship with Swift and was acquainted with Pope and most of the literary men of his day. His 'History of John Bull', a collection of pamphlets issued in 1712 advocating the termination of the war with France, was included in Pope and Swift's 'Miscellanies' of 1727. This work was the origin of John Bull, the typical Englishman. Dr. Arbuthnot was the principal author of the 'Memoirs of Martinus Scriblerus' (q.v.), which were published with Pope's 'Works' in 1741. He also wrote medical works, which proved him to be in advance of his age in medical science.

Arcades, Part of an Entertainment presented to the Countess-Dowager of Derby, by Milton (q.v.), written about 1633. It was probably composed at the request of Henry Lawes, the musician, while Milton was at Horton.

The piece is short, and consists of a song by nymphs and shepherds as they approach the seat of state of the countess, an address to them by the Genius of the Wood, in decasyllabic couplets, describing his occupations and praising music, and two further songs, one by the Genius, the other by the chorus.

Arcadia, a mountainous district in the Peloponnese, taken as an ideal region of rustic contentment.

Arcades ambo, 'Arcadians both', is applied by Virgil (Ecl. vii. 4) to Corydon and Thyrsis, young shepherds and poets.

The phrase 'Et in Arcadia ego' is first found in a picture by Guercino (1590–1666), as an inscription on a tomb, meaning 'Even in Arcadia am I' (i.e. Death).

Arcadia, The, a prose romance by Sir P. Sidney (q.v.), including at the end of each book a pastoral eclogue, begun in 1580 for the amusement of his sister, the countess of Pembroke, but not published until 1590, after Sidney's death. Sidney had no high opinion of the work and is said to have asked when dying that it should be destroyed. But it has an important place in the history of English literature.

The scene is laid in Arcadia, with its

flowery meads, where 'shepherd boys pipe as tho' they would never be old'.

The story is a maze of diversified incidents of romantic adventure, told in a flowery, repetitive style but with passages of occasional beauty and pathos. A prayer from it acquired celebrity: Charles I on the scaffold handed a copy of the prayer to Bishop Juxon, incurring thereby the censure of Milton.

The miscellaneous poems printed with the 'Arcadia' contain little that is comparable to Sidney's other work, but they include the splendid dirge 'Ring out your bells, let mourning shews be spread', and the song 'My true love hath my heart'.

Archangel, an angel of the highest rank. For the seven archangels enumerated by the Book of Enoch see under *Angel.*

Archer, WILLIAM (1856-1924), dramatic critic, translator of Ibsen, and author of a play, 'The Green Goddess'.

Archilochus of Paros (*fl.* 648 B.C.), celebrated for his satirical iambic verses, and proverbial for his bitterness.

Archimago, in Spenser's 'Faerie Queene', the great enchanter, symbolizing Hypocrisy, who deceives Una by assuming the appearance of the Red Cross Knight (I. i). His deceits are exposed, but in Book II he seeks vengeance on Sir Guyon for what he has suffered at the hands of the Red Cross Knight.

Archimedes (287-212 B.C.), famous mathematician and inventor, of Syracuse, many of whose works are extant. See also *Eureka.*

Arch-poet, the name given to the anonymous German Latin poet whose patron was Rainald of Dessel, arch-chancellor of Frederick Barbarossa and archbishop of Cologne (1161-7). His best-known poem is the 'Confession' in which occur the lines later used as a drinking song:

meum est propositum in taberna mori,
ut sint vina proxima morientis ori.

tunc cantabunt letius angelorum chori:
'sit deus propitius huic potatori.'

This term is also applied in Philemon Holland's translation of Camden's 'Britannia' to 'Henrie of Aurenches, Archpoet to King Henrie the Third', and used by Pope and Fielding as equivalent to poet laureate (q.v.).

Arcite, see *Palamon and Arcite.*

Arden, a forest, centred in Warwickshire, which figures frequently in Elizabethan literature. The scene of the greater part of Shakespeare's 'As You Like It' is laid there.

Ardennes, THE WILD BOAR OF THE, William de la Marck, so called because of his ferocity and acts of rapine. He was beheaded in 1485 by order of the emperor Maximilian. He figures in Scott's 'Quentin Durward'.

Arden of Feversham, The Tragedy of Mr., a play (1592) which has been attributed by some to Shakespeare. It deals with the persistent attempts, finally successful, of Mistress Arden and her paramour, Mosbie, to murder Arden. See under *Tragedy.*

Areopagitica, by Milton (q.v.) (1644). The title is derived from *Areopagus* (q.v.).

In this discourse Milton, addressing the 'Lords and Commons of England', attacks their recent order 'that no book . . . shall be henceforth printed unless the same be first approved and licensed by such . . . as shall be thereto appointed'. He shows, first that licensing has been chiefly the practice of those whom the Presbyterian Government most detest, viz. the Papacy and the Inquisition. Next, that promiscuous reading is necessary to the constituting of human virtue. And thirdly, that licensing will be a grave discouragement to learning; and he quotes the case of the imprisoned Galileo. Milton ends with a magnificent exhortation in which he compares England to an 'eagle mewing its mighty youth', and urges that it should not be shackled and restricted.

Areopagus, the hill of Ares (Mars), at Athens, the place of meeting of the highest judicial tribunal of the city.

Ares, the god of war of the ancient Greeks, identified by the Romans with MARS.

Arethusa, one of the Nereids (q.v.), and nymph of the fountain that bore her name in the island of Ortygia near Syracuse. See Shelley's poem, 'Arethusa'.

Aretino, PIETRO, or the ARETINE (1492-1556), author of five comedies and a tragedy, and also of poems of a scandalous or licentious character. He is frequently mentioned in English works of the Elizabethan and later periods.

Argante, (1) in the Arthurian legend, Morgan le Fay (q.v.), the fairy queen to whom Arthur, after the last battle, is borne to be healed of his wounds; (2) in Spenser's 'Faerie Queene' (III. vii), a mighty and licentious giantess, whom Satyrane puts to flight.

Argonauts, the heroes who accompanied Jason (q.v.) on board the ship 'Argo' to Colchis to recover the Golden Fleece.

Argos or ARGUS, (1) a herdsman with a hundred eyes; (2) the dog of Odysseus (q.v.), who recognized his master on his return from Troy.

Argyle, 'ARCHIBALD CAMPBELL, *eighth earl, first marquess of* (1598-1661), figures in Scott's 'A Legend of Montrose' (q.v.), where his character is contrasted with that of his great rival, the earl of Montrose. Beheaded 1661.

Argyle, JOHN CAMPBELL, *second duke of* (1678-1743), a distinguished military commander and statesman, figures in Scott's 'The Heart of Midlothian' (q.v.).

Ariadne, daughter of Minos (q.v.), of Crete. See under *Theseus*.

Arian heresy. The heresy, formulated by Arius, an Alexandrian priest in the time of Constantine, which denied the deity of Christ. The heresy was repudiated in the Nicene Creed and in the Athanasian Creed.

Ariel, (1) in Shakespeare's 'The Tempest' (q.v.), a spirit whom the witch Sycorax has imprisoned in a cloven pine and whom Prospero releases and employs in his designs; (2) in Milton's 'Paradise Lost' (vi. 371), a rebel angel; (3) in Pope's 'The Rape of the Lock' (ii. 53 et seq.), the chief of the sylphs.

Aries, see *Ram*.

Arimaspians, a Scythian people, of whom Herodotus (iv. 27) relates that they had only one eye.

Arioch, in 'Paradise Lost', vi. 371, one of the rebel angels.

Arion (*fl.* 600 B.C.?), poet and musician of Lesbos, said to have perfected the dithyramb or hymn to Dionysus. Legends relate that dolphins, charmed by his song, wafted him to land, when he had been thrown overboard by the sailors conveying him.

Ariosto, LUDOVICO (1474-1533), author of 'Orlando Furioso' (q.v.) (1532), the greatest of Italian romantic epics.

Aristides, an Athenian general and statesman, surnamed 'The Just', of the 5th cent. B.C. He was the advocate of a conservative policy as opposed to the 'strong navy' policy of Themistocles, and was 'ostracised' or banished.

Aristippus, founder of the Cyrenaic school of philosophy, was born about 428 B.C. He taught that man should devote himself to extracting from life the maximum of pleasure. But he held that the pleasant was identical with the good, and must be obtained by self-control.

Aristophanes (*c.* 448-*c.* 380 B.C.), the Athenian comic poet, whose comedies are of great historical value for their caricatures of the leading personages of the time and their comments on current affairs. The following are his extant comedies: the 'Acharnians', the 'Knights', the 'Clouds' (a criticism of the new spirit of philosophical inquiry), the 'Peace', the 'Wasps', the 'Birds', the 'Frogs' (Euripides and Aeschylus contending for the tragic prize among the dead), the 'Plutus', the 'Lysistrata' and 'Ecclesiazusae', and the 'Thesmophoriazusae' (Euripides tried and convicted at the female festival of the Thesmophoria).

Aristophanes' Apology, a poem by R. Browning (q.v.) (1875), an imaginary defence of comedy against the tragic poet, Euripides.

Aristotle (384–322 B.C.), the great Greek philosopher, studied at Athens under Plato, and stayed there for twenty years, was subsequently appointed by Philip of Macedon to be tutor to his son Alexander. On the accession of the latter to the throne (335), Aristotle returned to Athens, where he lectured to many scholars (see *Peripatetics*) and composed the greater part of his works. His writings, which had an immense influence on thought, cover an extraordinarily wide field: logic, moral philosophy, metaphysics, poetry, physics, zoology, politics, and rhetoric. His most famous works are his 'Ethics', an introduction to moral philosophy, 'Poetics', and 'Politics', though the scope of this last is limited to the city-state of his day.

Ark, The, Sir W. Ralegh's ship in the battle with the Armada.

Armada, THE INVINCIBLE, a fleet of some 130 ships, was dispatched by Philip II of Spain in 1588 to invade England. It was defeated by the English fleet under Lord Howard, Drake, Frobisher, Hawkins, etc.

Armado, DON ADRIANO DE, a character in Shakespeare's 'Love's Labour's Lost' (q.v.).

Armageddon (Rev. xvi. 16), where the Kings of the Earth are to be gathered for battle.

Arminianism, the doctrine of James Arminius (*d.* 1609); opposed to that of Calvin particularly with regard to predestination.

Armstrong, JOHN (1709–79), physician and poet, author of the 'Art of Preserving Health' (1744).

Arnold, SIR EDWIN (1832–1904), author of 'The Light of Asia, or The Great Renunciation' (q.v., 1879), a poem of which Buddha is the subject. He made a number of translations from the Sanskrit.

Arnold, MATTHEW (1822–88), son of T. Arnold (q.v.), the great headmaster of Rugby, became fellow of Oriel College, Oxford, and an inspector of schools, and was professor of poetry at Oxford (1857–67). His first volume of poems (1849) contained 'The Forsaken Merman' and the sonnet on Shakespeare. 'Empedocles on Etna, and other Poems' (1852), contained 'Tristram and Iseult'. In 1853 appeared a volume of 'Poems' containing extracts from the earlier books, 'Sohrab and Rustum' and 'The Scholar-Gipsy' (qq.v.); also the 'Church of Brou', 'Requiescat', the 'Memorial Verses to Wordsworth', and the 'Stanzas in Memory of the Author of Obermann'. 'Poems, Second Series', including 'Balder Dead' (q.v.), appeared in 1855; 'Merope, a Tragedy' in 1858; and 'New Poems', including 'Thyrsis' (q.v.), 'Rugby Chapel', 'Heine's Grave', 'A Southern Night' (a lament for one of his brothers), and other well-known pieces, in 1867.

The bulk of Matthew Arnold's prose works appeared after 1860. The most important of these were the 'Essays in Criticism' (1865 and 1888), in which he gave literary criticism an unusually wide scope, extending it to an attack on the 'philistinism' or 'provinciality' then, in his opinion, prevailing in England. He also published lectures 'On Translating Homer' (1861) and 'The Study of Celtic Literature' (1867). His 'Culture and Anarchy', a criticism of English social and political life, appeared in 1869; and this was followed by various works of religious criticism.

Special reference is due to Arnold's attempts to secure the improvement of education in England. He was sent in 1859, and again in 1865, to study educational systems on the Continent, and his reports drew attention to our deficiencies in this respect. There are further references to his views on education in other writings, e.g. in 'Culture and Anarchy' (1869).

Arnold, THOMAS (1795–1842), is principally remembered as the headmaster (1828–42) who raised Rugby to the rank of a great public school. He was the author of an unfinished 'History of Rome' (1838–42) and of an edition of Thucydides (1830–5), and is celebrated in 'Tom Brown's Schooldays' (q.v.).

Arraignment of Paris, *The*, a pastoral play in verse by G. Peele (q.v.) (1584).

Arsis, the strong or accented syllable in English metre. The precise meaning of the word in Greek is uncertain.

Artegall, SIR, in Spenser's 'Faerie Queene', Bk. V, the champion of justice.

Artemis, see *Diana*.

Artemisia, (1) a queen of Halicarnassus in Caria, who accompanied Xerxes in his invasion of Greece and fought with distinction at the battle of Salamis; (2) the wife of Mausolus, king of Caria, to whose memory she erected the Mausoleum.

Arte of English Poesie, see *Puttenham*.

Artful Dodger, THE, a character in Dickens's 'Oliver Twist' (q.v.).

Arthur, KING. The romantic figure of King Arthur has some historical basis. He was probably a chieftain or general in the 5th or 6th cents.

He first takes form as a romantic hero in the 'Historia Regum Britanniae' of Geoffrey of Monmouth (12th cent.), and this story was developed by the Norman writer Wace (q.v.), who added many details. The 'Round Table' is first mentioned by him, a device to settle the disputes as to precedence among Arthur's knights. Wace's work served as the basis of the 'Brut' of Layamon (q.v.), the first English record, which adds many romantic details, and a fairy element, to the story.

The Arthurian story was then developed in French (see *Chrétien de Troyes*) and Arthur became the centre of a mass of legends in various tongues.

The story of Arthur is the foundation of Malory's 'Morte Darthur' (q.v.), but most of this work is occupied with the exploits of the Knights of the Round Table, the quest of the Holy Grail, the loves of Launcelot and Guinevere and of Tristram and Iseult. For Tennyson's presentation of the story see *Idylls of the King*.

Arthur, PRINCE, in Spenser's 'Faerie Queene', symbolizes 'Magnificence' (? Magnanimity), in the Aristotelian sense of perfection of the virtues. He enters into the adventures of the several knights and brings them to a fortunate conclusion.

Articles of Religion, THE, or THE THIRTY-NINE ARTICLES, the thirty-nine statements to which those who take orders in the Church of England subscribe. These received parliamentary sanction in 1571.

Art of English Poesy, Observations on the, an attack on rhyme in English poetry by Thomas Campion (*d.* 1619), to which S. Daniel (q.v.) replied.

Art of Rhetorique, see *Wilson* (*T.*).

Arundel Marbles, THE, part of a collection of statuary, pictures, gems, and books made by Thomas Howard, second earl of Arundel (1585?-1646), and given by his grandson to the University of Oxford.

Arveragus, in Chaucer's 'Franklin's Tale' (see 'Canterbury Tales'), husband of Dorigen.

Arviragus, in Shakespeare's 'Cymbeline' (q.v.), one of the king's sons.

Aryan, a term applied by some to the great division of languages which includes Sanskrit, Zend, Persian, Greek, Latin, Celtic, Teutonic, and Slavonic, with their modern representatives; also called Indo-European and Indo-Germanic. Also applied to one belonging to or descended from the ancient people who spoke the parent Aryan language, particularly, though often fallaciously, in this sense by the administration of the Third German Reich.

Asaph, in the part of 'Absalom and Achitophel' (q.v.) written by Tate, is Dryden. (Cf. 1 Chron. xvi. 4-7.)

Ascanius, the son of Aeneas (q.v.).

Ascendant, see *House* (*Astrological*).

Ascham, ROGER (1515-68), was educated at Cambridge, where he distinguished himself in classics and became Greek reader in 1538. He published in 1545 'Toxophilus', a treatise in English in dialogue form on archery, urging the importance of physical training in education. In 1553 he became Latin secretary to Queen Mary, and in 1558 private tutor to Queen Elizabeth. In his 'Scholemaster', published after his death, he dealt with the education of boys of position. He contributed notably to the development of a simple English prose style.

Asclepiades, a lyric poet of Samos (3rd cent. B.C.), inventor of the Asclepiadic metre (a spondee, two or three choriambs, and an iambus).

Asclepius, see *Aesculapius.*

Ashley Library, a private library, collected by T. J. Wise, acquired on his death by the British Museum.

Ashmolean Building (the 'Old Ashmolean'), Oxford. Erected 1679-83 by the University, for the reception of the collection of curiosities given by Elias Ashmole (1617-92). The claim that the designer was Wren is debated. The collection was moved to a new building in 1897.

Ashtaroth, see *Astarte.*

Ash Wednesday, the first day of Lent.

Ash Wednesday, the title of a poem by T. S. Eliot (q.v.).

Asmadai ('Asmodæus'), in 'Paradise Lost', vi. 365, one of the rebel angels.

Asmodæus, in Tobit iii. 8, the evil spirit who loved Sarah, and slew the seven husbands given to her in succession. The spirit was driven away by Tobias according to instructions given by the angel; after which he was able to marry Sarah.

Asolando, the title of the collection of the last poems of R. Browning (q.v.) (1889). It contains some of the author's most beautiful short pieces, and ends with the well-known 'Epilogue'—'At the midnight in the silence of the sleep-time'.

Aspasia, the famous Greek courtesan, acquired fame at Athens by her beauty and wit. Pericles (q.v.) made her his life-long companion. See *Pericles and Aspasia.*

Asphodel, a genus of liliaceous plants. The poets make it the flower of the Elysian fields. 'Daffodil' is a corruption of 'asphodel'.

Aspramont, Aspramonte in Calabria, in the Charlemagne legends, the scene of a fictitious war against the Saracens.

Asser (*d.* 909?), a monk of St. David's, who entered the household of King Alfred. He wrote a Latin life of Alfred and a chronicle of English history between 849 and 887. The authenticity of these has been disputed.

Assonance, the correspondence or rhyming of one word with another in the accented and following vowels, but not in the consonants, as, e.g., in Old French versification. Milton, Tennyson, and other poets used it consistently as a literary device for securing melodious and onomatopoeic effects. Wilfrid Owen was remarkable for his development of 'assonance and dissonance' as a substitute for rhyme.

Astarte, ASHTAROTH, ASHTORETH, ISHTAR, the eastern equivalent of the Greek Aphrodite, the goddess of love and fruitful increase.

ASTARTE is the name under which Augusta (Byron's half-sister) figures in his poem 'Manfred' (q.v.). The story of Byron and Augusta is told in 'Astarte', by Ralph Milbanke, earl of Lovelace (issued privately in 1905 and for general sale in 1921).

Astolat, in Malory's 'Morte Darthur', is Guildford in Surrey. For the 'Fair Maid of Astolat' see *Elaine le Blank.*

Astraea Redux, a poem on the Restoration of Charles II, by Dryden (q.v.) (1660). (Astraea, a daughter of Zeus, was said to have lived on earth in the Golden Age and to have been a source of blessing to men.)

Astrophel, a pastoral elegy, by Spenser (q.v.) (1586) on the death of Sir Philip Sidney. Spenser again lamented him in 'The Ruines of Time'.

Astrophel and Stella, the sonnet series in which Sir P. Sidney (q.v.) expressed his love for Penelope Devereux, daughter of the first earl of Essex. In 1580 she married Lord Rich against her will, and Sidney's disappointment and passion are supposed to have found voice in these poems.

As You Like It, a comedy by Shakespeare (q.v.), probably produced about 1599, not printed till the folio of 1623. It is a dramatic adaptation of Lodge's (q.v.) romance 'Rosalynde', with the addition of the characters of Jaques and Touchstone, the humorous scenes, and other minor alterations.

Frederick has usurped the dominions of the Duke his brother, who is living with his faithful followers in the forest of Arden (q.v.). Celia, Frederick's daughter, and Rosalind, the Duke's daughter, living at Frederick's court, witness a wrestling match in which Orlando, son of Sir Rowland de Boys, defeats a powerful adversary, and Rosalind falls in love with Orlando and he with her. Orlando, who at his father's death has been left in the charge of his elder brother Oliver, has been driven from home by Oliver's cruelty. Frederick, learning that Orlando is the son of Sir Rowland, who was a friend of the exiled Duke, has his anger against the latter revived, and banishes Rosalind from his court, and Celia accompanies her. Rosalind assumes a countryman's dress and takes the name Ganymede; Celia passes as Aliena his sister. They live in the forest of Arden, and fall in with Orlando, who has joined the banished Duke. Ganymede encourages Orlando to make love to her as though she were his Rosalind. Oliver comes to the forest to kill Orlando, but is saved by him from a lioness, and is filled with remorse for his cruelty. He falls in love with Aliena, and their wedding is arranged for the morrow. Ganymede undertakes to Orlando that she will by magic produce Rosalind at the same time to be married to him. When all are assembled in the presence of the banished Duke to celebrate the double nuptials, Celia and Rosalind put off their disguise and appear in their own characters. News is brought that Frederick the usurper, setting out to seize and destroy his brother and his followers, has been converted from his intention to 'an old religious man' and has made restitution of the dukedom.

Jaques, a lord attending on the banished Duke, a contemplative character, compounded of humour and melancholy, and Touchstone, a cynical philosopher in the garb of a buffoon, who marries the country wench, Audrey, are among the delightful minor characters of the play.

Atabalipa, in 'Paradise Lost', xi. 409, is Atahualpa, the Inca of Peru.

Atalanta, in Greek mythology, a great huntress, whose beauty gained her many admirers. She required her suitors to run a race with her; those who lost were to die. Many suitors perished in the attempt, till Milanion presented himself. Aphrodite had given him three golden apples. He cunningly threw down the apples, and Atalanta stopped to gather them, so that Milanion arrived first at the goal. For Swinburne's 'Atalanta in Calydon' see *Swinburne*.

Atalantis, *The New*, see *Manley*.

Ate, a daughter of Zeus, who incites men to wickedness and strife.

Atellan or OSCAN FABLES, *Atellanae Fabulae*, a comic but not wanton kind of popular farce, performed not by professional actors, but by amateurs. They were written in the Oscan language of southern Italy.

Athanasian Creed, THE, the creed *Quicunque vult*, called in some manuscripts the creed of St. Athanasius (q.v.). Its origin has been the subject of much controversy.

Athanasius, ST. (*c.* 296-373), bishop of Alexandria in the reign of the Emperor Constantine, and a vigorous opponent of the Arian heresy.

Atheism, On the Necessity of, see *Shelley* (*P. B.*).

Atheist's Tragedie, The, a tragedy by Tourneur (q.v.) (1611).

Athelston, a verse romance of about the year 1350, of some 800 lines. Four messengers meeting by chance in the forest swear brotherhood. One, Athelston, becomes king of England, and makes one of the brothers archbishop of Canterbury, one earl of Dover, and one earl of Stane and husband of Athelston's sister.

Athenae Oxonienses, see *Wood* (*A.*).

Athenaeum, The, a literary and artistic review, founded in 1828. It rose to eminence under Charles Wentworth Dilke (q.v.), and many of the greatest English writers of the nineteenth century were among its contributors. 'The Athenaeum' was incorporated in 'The Nation and Athenaeum' in 1921, and this in turn in 'The New Statesman' in 1931.

Athenaeum Club, THE, in London, was founded in 1824 as an association of persons of literary, scientific, and artistic attainments, patrons of learning, etc.

Athene, the patron goddess of Athens and other Greek cities, and of urban crafts, identified by the Romans with MINERVA. The origin of her other name *Pallas* is unknown. She is represented generally with a countenance marked by masculine firmness and composure rather than by softness and grace. See also *Arachne.*

Atherton, GERTRUDE FRANKLIN (1857–1948), American novelist. Her chief works are: 'The Conqueror' (1902), a fictional biography of Alexander Hamilton, 'Julia France and Her Times' (1912), 'Black Oxen' (1923), and 'Adventures of a Novelist' (1932), her autobiography.

Athos, MOUNT, the 'Holy Mountain' in Greece, the easternmost of the three Chalcidic peninsulas. It has been occupied since the Middle Ages by various communities of monks.

Athos, Porthos, and **Aramis,** the 'Three Musketeers' (q.v.).

Atkins, see *Tommy Atkins.*

Atlantic Monthly, The, an American magazine of literature, the arts, and politics, founded in 1857. J. R. Lowell (q.v.) was its first editor, and W. D. Howells and T. B. Aldrich (qq.v.) were among his successors. Although no longer in the pre-eminent place it held in the 19th cent., it includes many leading American men of letters among its contributors.

Atlantis, a fabulous island in the ocean west of the Pillars of Hercules, a beautiful and prosperous country. But owing to the impiety of its inhabitants, it was swallowed up by the sea. The story is told by Plato in the 'Timaeus'.

Atlantis, New, see *New Atlantis.*

Atlas, one of the Titans (q.v.), punished for rebellion by having to support the sky. Perseus (q.v.), by means of the Medusa's head, turned him into a mountain, which runs across the deserts of North Africa.

Atom, The History and Adventures of an, a satire by Smollett (q.v.) (1769).

Atossa, see *Moral Essays.*

Atreus, a son of Pelops (q.v.) and king of Argos. The post-Homeric poets relate that Atreus, to revenge himself on his brother Thyestes for seducing his wife, invited Thyestes to a banquet and served him the flesh of his children to eat. Thyestes fled in horror, cursing the house of Atreus, which was visited by various calamities. Atreus was the father (or the grandfather) of Agamemnon and Menelaus (qq.v.).

Atropos, see *Parcae.*

Atterbury, FRANCIS (1662–1732), bishop of Rochester, engaged in the Phalaris (q.v.) controversy, and in the political and theological disputes of the day. He was a notable preacher and a trenchant political writer.

Attic, a dialect of ancient Greek spoken at Athens. As an epithet, it is applied to a pure, simple, polished style, as being characteristic of the best Greek writers. See also *Order.*

Attic boy, THE, in Milton's 'Il Penseroso' (q.v.); see *Cephalus.*

Attic salt, refined, delicate, poignant wit.

Atticus, the character under which Pope (q.v.) satirized Addison (q.v.) in lines published in 1723. The lines reappeared in Pope's 'Epistle to Dr. Arbuthnot', 1735. The original Atticus was Cicero's friend and correspondent.

Attila, king of the Huns. He ravaged the Eastern Empire during the years 445–50, and died in 453.

Aubrey, JOHN (1626–97), antiquary, author of a collection of 'Lives' of eminent persons, much used by Anthony à Wood (q.v.).

Auburn, see *Deserted Village.*

Aucassin and Nicolette, a late 13th-cent. legend of Provence, which has been translated or adapted by F. W. Bourdillon, Swinburne, Andrew Lang, and Eugene Mason. With 'Amis and Amile' it forms the subject of one of Pater's 'Studies in the History of the Renaissance'. The original is in prose interspersed with songs telling of the thwarted but faithful love and adventures of a youth and captive maid.

Auchinleck (pron. 'Affleck'), the name of the family estate of James Boswell (q.v.).

Auden, WYSTAN HUGH (1907–73), educated at Christ Church, Oxford, where he was known as a leader of the poets of his generation. He lived for a time in Berlin under the Weimar Republic, when Nazism was already becoming a threat. His early work was verse of social criticism and protest and showed the influence of psycho-analytical as well as of Marxist ideas. He published 'Poems' (1930) and 'The Orators' (1932) and, with Louis MacNeice, 'Letters from Iceland' (1937). He experimented, in collaboration with Christopher Isherwood, in drama, including 'The Dog Beneath the Skin' (1935) and 'The Ascent of F6' (1936). Auden emigrated to the United States in 1939, and later became an American citizen. His later verse, including 'New Year Letter' (1941), 'The Age of Anxiety' (1948), 'The Shield of Achilles' (1959), 'Homage to Clio' (1960), and 'About the House' (1966), to some extent abandons his earlier ideas and is written from a standpoint of Christian commitment.

Audrey, in Shakespeare's 'As You Like It' (q.v.), the country wench wooed and won by Touchstone.

Audrey, ST., St. Etheldreda, patron saint of Ely.

TAWDRY LACE appears in the earliest quotation as *St. Audrey's lace.* It was probably offered for sale at her fair, and this doubtless led to the production of cheap and showy qualities of the article, which at length gave to *tawdry* its later meaning.

Aufidius, a character in Shakespeare's 'Coriolanus' (q.v.).

Augean Stables. Augeas, king of Elis, had an immense herd of oxen, whose stables had never been cleansed. The cleansing in one day was one of the labours of Hercules (q.v.). Hercules accomplished it by changing the course of the river Alpheus so that it should flow into the stables.

Augusta Leigh, Byron's half-sister, see *Leigh.*

Augustan Age, a period of literary eminence in the life of a nation, so named because during the reign of the emperor Augustus (27 B.C.–A.D. 14) Virgil, Horace, Ovid, Tibullus, etc., flourished. The term is usually applied in the history of English literature to the period of Pope and Addison. Among other famous writers of the time were Steele, Swift, Defoe, Gay, Prior, and Congreve. It was notable for the perfection of the heroic couplet (q.v.) and the development of a clear logical prose style. Some of these characteristics are to be found in the time of Dryden, but the Elizabethan qualities of rhetoric and eloquence in prose, conceits and bombast in verse, still remained. The 'Age of Pope' had a classical evenness, a preference for wit and elegance, and for intellectual rather than emotional satisfaction. (See also *Classicism.*) Its traditions survived throughout the greater part of the 18th cent., notably in the writings of Johnson, Goldsmith, and Sheridan. (See Goldsmith's 'Augustan Age in England'; Saintsbury's 'Peace of the Augustans'; and Austin Dobson's 'Eighteenth-Century Vignettes'.) (In French literature the term is applied to the period of Corneille, Racine, and Molière.)

Augustin or AUSTIN FRIARS, an order of mendicant friars, formed in the 13th cent. under the rule of St. Augustine.

Augustine, ST., OF HIPPO (354–430), was for a time a Manichaean, but was converted after hearing the sermons of

Ambrose, bishop of Milan. He became bishop of Hippo, and was engaged in constant theological controversy. The most famous of his numerous works is the 'De Civitate Dei' ('City of God'), a treatise in vindication of the Christian Church. His 'Confessions' contain a striking account of his early life.

Augustine, ST. (*d.* 604), first archbishop of Canterbury, was sent by Pope Gregory with forty monks to preach the Gospel in England. He is commemorated on 26 May.

Augustinian Canons, an order of canons who adopted the Rule of St. Augustine in the 11th cent.

Augustus, GAIUS JULIUS CAESAR OCTAVIANUS (63 B.C.–A.D. 14), the nephew of Julius Caesar, and first Roman emperor, occupying the throne from 27 B.C. till his death.

Auld Lang Syne, a song not entirely of Burns's composition, but taken down by him 'from an old man's singing'. The refrain, at least, had long been in print. The original version has been attributed to Sir Robert Aytoun (1570–1638).

Auld Reekie, a term applied to Edinburgh, in allusion to its smoky atmosphere.

Auld Robin Gray, see under *Lindsay* (*Lady A.*).

Aulus Gellius, see *Gellius.*

Aureng-Zebe, a tragedy by Dryden (q.v.) (1676). It was his last rhymed play.

Aurora, the Greek Eos, a daughter of Hyperion (q.v.) and the goddess of the dawn.

Aurora Leigh, a romance in blank verse by E. B. Browning (q.v.) (1856).

Aurora Leigh tells the story of her life, and the story is made the vehicle for the expression of the author's views on a variety of subjects.

Aurora Raby, a character in Byron's 'Don Juan' (q.v.), a beautiful and innocent young heiress.

Ausonius, DECIMUS MAGNUS (*c.* A.D. 310–90), a Roman poet who sang of the Moselle, its wine and trout.

Austen, JANE (1775–1817), was born at Steventon in Hampshire, of which her father was rector, and lived an uneventful life at her birthplace, at Bath, Southampton, and Chawton. She is buried at Winchester. Of her completed novels (for which see under their titles) 'Sense and Sensibility' appeared in 1811, 'Pride and Prejudice' in 1813, 'Mansfield Park' in 1814, 'Emma' in Dec. 1815, 'Northanger Abbey' and 'Persuasion' posthumously in 1818. The order in which they were written is somewhat different. 'Pride and Prejudice', in its original form and entitled 'First Impressions', was begun in 1796, refused by a publisher in 1797, and revised before ultimate publication. 'Sense and Sensibility' was begun in 1797, but apparently left unfinished for many years. 'Northanger Abbey' was begun in 1798, sold to a publisher in 1803, but not then published. The manuscript was recovered in 1816, and may have been revised, but appears to represent the earliest of her work as we have it in the six published novels. 'Mansfield Park' was begun in 1811, 'Emma' in 1814, and 'Persuasion' in 1815. Besides these Jane Austen was author of two works which she did not publish, 'Lady Susan' (the story, written about 1805, and told in letters, of a designing coquette, the widow Lady Susan Vernon) and a fragment, 'The Watsons'. A further fragment, written in 1817, known to her family as 'Sanditon', was published in 1925. The standard edition of Jane Austen is that of R. W. Chapman, 1923–54; Letters, 1932, 1952.

Auster, see *Notus.*

Austin, ALFRED (1835–1913), between 1871 and 1908 published twenty volumes of verse, of little merit. A prose work, 'The Garden that I love' (1894), proved very popular, and in 1896 Austin was made poet laureate, shortly afterwards publishing in 'The Times' an unfortunate ode celebrating the Jameson Raid. Some of his pleasantest work is to be found in his prose writings. His 'Autobiography' appeared in 1911.

Austin Friars, see *Augustin Friars.*

Authorized Version, see *Bible* (*The English*).

Authors, THE SOCIETY OF, founded in 1884 and devoted to protecting and promoting the rights and interests of its members at home and abroad. Its quarterly publication is 'The Author'.

Autobiography, the story of one's life, written by one's self. (The word does not occur before the 19th cent., though as a form of literature it occurs from the earliest period.) Autobiography has become increasingly popular in modern times. Among famous examples in English literature are Gibbon's 'Memoirs' (1796), Trelawny's 'Adventures of a Younger Son' (1831), Mill's 'Autobiography' (1873), and Gosse's 'Father and Son' (1907). Samuel Butler's 'The Way of All Flesh' (1903) is a good example of an autobiographical novel, in which the events of one's life slightly disguised are presented as fiction.

Auto-da-fé, a Portuguese expression meaning 'act of faith', popularly applied to the burning alive of heretics.

Autocrat of the Breakfast Table, The, see *Holmes* (*O. W.*).

Autolycus, (1) a son of Hermes, celebrated for his craft as a thief; (2) the witty rogue and pedlar in Shakespeare's 'The Winter's Tale' (q.v.).

Automedon, the charioteer of Achilles.

Avalon, in Arthurian legend, a mythical land like the Fortunate Isles (q.v.). It is to Avalon that Arthur is borne after his death. It has been identified with Glastonbury (q.v.).

Avatar, in Hindu mythology, the descent of a deity to earth in incarnate form; hence loosely, a manifestation, display, phase.

Ave atque vale, Latin, 'hail and farewell!', as a farewell to the dead, notably in the poem of Catullus in memory of his brother, to which Tennyson refers in his poem "Frater, ave atque vale'.

Ave Maria, 'Hail Mary!', the angelic salutation to the Virgin (Luke i. 28) combined with that of Elizabeth (v. 42), used as a devotional recitation.

Avenel, MARY, a character in Scott's 'The Monastery' and 'The Abbot' (qq.v.), and JULIAN, her uncle, a character in the former. ROLAND AVENEL is the hero of the latter work.

Avernus, a lake of Campania. The ancients regarded it as the entrance to hell.

Avignon, a city on the Rhône in France. Clement V removed the papal seat to Avignon in 1308, and there it remained until 1377.

Avon, THE SWAN OF, Shakespeare, born at Stratford-on-Avon, so called by Jonson.

Awntyrs (*Adventures*) *of Arthure at the Terne Wathelyne*, an alliterative verse romance of the 14th cent.

Ayala's Angel, a novel by A. Trollope (q.v.) (1881).

Ayenbite of Inwit, 'Remorse of Conscience', a prose translation from the French, made by the monk Michel of Northgate, Canterbury, about 1340, and chiefly of philological interest.

Aylwin, a novel by W. T. Watts-Dunton (q.v.).

Aytoun, WILLIAM EDMONDSTONE (1813-65). He is chiefly remembered for his share in the 'Bon Gaultier Ballads' (q.v., 1845), for his 'Lays of the Scottish Cavaliers' (q.v., 1849), and for his 'Firmilian, or the Student of Badajoz' (1854), a mock-tragedy.

Azazel, see *Scapegoat*. In 'Paradise Lost' (i. 534) Azazel raises the standard of the host of Satan.

Aztecs, a native American people, conquered by the Spaniards under Cortez early in the 16th cent.

B

Baal, name of the chief god of the Phoenician and Canaanitish nations; hence, a false god.

Bab Ballads, a collection of humorous ballads by W. S. Gilbert (q.v.) (1869, and 'More Bab Ballads', 1873).

Babbitt, a novel by S. Lewis (q.v.) (1922). The book depicts life in Zenith, a prosperous American town of the present century, where minds and electrical appliances are equally standardized. Against this background the author draws in minute detail the character and mode of life of George F. Babbitt, a successful real-estate broker.

Babbitt, IRVING (1865-1933), American critic and professor at Harvard; with Paul Elmer More, a leader of the New Humanist movement in the 1920s, and a fierce critic of romanticism.

Babel, Hebrew word in the O.T. for Babylon (q.v.).

For the story of the TOWER OF BABEL see Gen. xi.

Babes in the Wood, see *Children in the Wood.*

Babu, or BABOO, a Hindu title of respect answering to our Mr. or Esquire; hence, a native Hindu gentleman; also (in Anglo-Indian) a native official who writes in English.

Babylon, a magnificent city, once the capital of the Chaldean empire; also the mystical city of the Apocalypse; whence in modern times applied rhetorically to any great and luxurious city.

THE WHORE OF BABYLON is a term applied to the Roman Catholic Church by the early Puritans, with reference to Rev. xvii.

The HANGING GARDENS OF BABYLON, one of the seven wonders of the world, may have been built by Nebuchadnezzar (king of Babylon 605-562 B.C.).

Babylon, an old ballad, of three sisters, to each of whom in turn an outlaw proposes the alternative of becoming a 'rank robber's wife' or death. The first two choose death. The third threatens the vengeance of her brother 'Baby Lon'. This is the outlaw himself, who thus discovers that he has murdered his own sisters, and thereupon takes his own life.

Babylonian Captivity, the period (*c.* 603-536 B.C.) during which the Jews were captive in Babylon; allusively, the period of the Papacy at Avignon (1309-77).

Bacchanalia, the mysteries celebrated in ancient Rome in honour of Bacchus (q.v.).

Bacchantes, priestesses of Bacchus, represented with dishevelled hair and garlands.

Bacchus, a name of the Greek god Dionysus (q.v.).

Bacchylides, the most important Greek lyric poet after Pindar, since the publication (1897) of extensive papyrus fragments. He lived about 470 B.C.

Bach, JOHANN SEBASTIAN (1685-1750), one of the greatest composers of all time. He was for many years musical director of two churches at Leipzig, where he composed most of his music. Much of this is of a sacred character, highly intellectual, and showing a supreme command of counterpoint and fugue.

Back Kitchen, THE, in Thackeray's 'Pendennis' (q.v.), was 'The Cyder Cellars' in Maiden Lane, frequented by Porson, Maginn, Charles Dickens, etc.

Backbite, SIR BENJAMIN, a character in Sheridan's 'The School for Scandal' (q.v.).

Bacon, FRIAR, see *Friar Bacon and Friar Bungay.*

Bacon, FRANCIS, *first Baron Verulam* and *Viscount St. Albans* (1561-1626), younger son of Sir Nicholas Bacon, Lord Keeper in Queen Elizabeth's reign. He went through the various steps of the legal profession, entered Parliament in 1584, and then wrote papers on public affairs, including a 'Letter of Advice to Queen Elizabeth' urging strong measures against the Catholics. He made the acquaintance of the earl of Essex, who treated him with generosity and endeavoured to advance him in his career. Nevertheless, having been appointed to investigate the causes of Essex's revolt in 1601, he was largely responsible for the earl's conviction. He became Solicitor-General in 1607, Attorney-General in 1613, Lord Keeper in 1617, and Lord Chancellor in 1618. In 1621 he was charged before the House of Lords with bribery, and confessed that he had been guilty of 'corruption and neglect' but denied that he had ever perverted justice. He was deprived of the great seal, fined, and condemned to confinement. He remained in the Tower only a few days. The remaining years of his life were spent in literary and philosophical work. Pope described him as 'the wisest, brightest, meanest of mankind'.

Bacon's works may be divided into three classes, the philosophical (which form by far the greatest portion), the literary, and the professional works. The principal and best known of the philosophical works are: (1) 'The Advancement of Learning' (q.v.), published in English in 1605; (2) the 'Novum Organum' (q.v.), published in Latin in 1620; and (3) the 'De Augmentis', published in Latin in 1623. It was Bacon's ambition to create a new system of philosophy, based on a right interpretation of nature, to replace that of Aristotle. Of Bacon's literary works, the most important are the 'Essays' (q.v.), first published in 1597, and issued in final form, 1625; the 'New Atlantis' (q.v.) in 1626; and the 'History of Henry the Seventh', in 1622. The most important of his professional works are the treatises entitled 'Maxims of the Law' and 'Reading on the Statute of Uses'.

Bacon wrote in Latin the works to which he attached importance, with a view, as he supposed, to their greater permanence. Yet he was capable of varied and beautiful styles in English, and there is a magnificence in much of his writing. Many of the sentences in the 'Essays' have assumed almost the character of proverbs.

Bacon, ROGER (1214?-94), student at Oxford and Paris, may be described as the founder of English philosophy; he advocated the substitution of an appeal to experience for the method of argument from premisses based on authority. Bacon had a wide knowledge of the sciences, was an accomplished Greek scholar, and knew Hebrew and Aramaic. As a practical scientist he invented spectacles, and indicated the manner in which a telescope might be constructed.

Bacon and **Bungay,** (1) the rival publishers in Thackeray's 'Pendennis' (q.v.); (2) see *Friar Bacon and Friar Bungay*.

Baconian Theory, the theory that Francis Bacon (q.v.) wrote the plays attributed to Shakespeare, started, apparently, in the middle of the 18th cent.; it is based partly on (supposed) internal evidence in Shakespeare's plays and partly on external circumstances. Some holders of the theory have found in the plays cryptograms in support of it, e.g. in the nonce-word 'honorificabilitudinitatibus' in 'Love's Labour's Lost' (v. i), which has been rendered in Latin as 'These plays, F. Bacon's offspring, are preserved for the World'; the word, however, is found elsewhere as early as 1460. The American cryptologists, W. S. and E. F. Friedman ('The Shakespearean Ciphers Examined', 1957), have convincingly shown that none of the cipher 'evidence' supports the theory.

Badman, The Life and Death of Mr., an allegory by Bunyan (q.v.) (1680).

The allegory takes the form of a dialogue in which Mr. Wiseman relates the life of Mr. Badman, recently deceased, and Mr. Attentive comments on it. The story is entertaining as well as edifying, and has a place in the evolution of the English novel.

Badon, MOUNT, the scene of a battle connected with the legends of Arthur. It is first mentioned by Gildas (q.v.), but without reference to Arthur. The 'Annales Cambriae' (q.v.) give the date of the battle as 518. Badon is identified by some authorities with Bath, by others with Badbury near Wimborne.

Baedeker, KARL (1801–59), editor and publisher, in Coblenz, Germany, of the famous guide-books.

Baffin, WILLIAM (*d.* 1622), navigator and discoverer. He was pilot in the Muscovy Company's expeditions of 1615 and 1616 in search of the North-West Passage. He wrote accounts of most of his voyages.

Bagehot, WALTER (1826–77), a banker and shipowner, joint-editor with R. H. Hutton of the 'National Review' after 1855, and editor of the 'Economist' from 1860 till his death. His remarkable insight into economic and political questions is shown in his 'The English Constitution' (1867) and 'Lombard Street' (1873). His 'Literary Studies' (1879) contain some excellent and individual criticism.

Bagnet, MR. and MRS., characters in Dickens's 'Bleak House' (q.v.).

Bagstock, MAJOR JOE, a character in Dickens's 'Dombey and Son' (q.v.).

Baiae, a town on a small bay near Naples, a favourite resort of the Romans. Its site is now covered by the sea.

Bailey, NATHAN or NATHANIEL (*d.* 1742), author of an English dictionary (1721), forerunner of Dr. Johnson's.

Bailey, PHILIP JAMES (1816–1902), author of a long poem 'Festus' (q.v., 1839). Bailey is often regarded as the father of the 'Spasmodic School' (q.v.).

Bailey, THE OLD, on the site of Newgate gaol, the seat of the Central Criminal Court in London.

Baillie, JOANNA (1762–1851), Scottish dramatist and poetess, was a close friend of Sir Walter Scott, who admired her 'Plays on the Passions' (1798).

Bailly, HENRY, in Chaucer's 'The Canterbury Tales' (q.v.), host of the Tabard Inn.

Baines, CONSTANCE and SOPHIA, characters in Bennett's 'The Old Wives' Tale' (q.v.).

Bajazet or BAJAYET, ruler of the Ottomans (1389–1402), figures in Marlowe's 'Tamburlaine the Great' (q.v.).

Balaam, warned by God not to move against the invading Israelites yet did so on his ass. He would have been killed by an angel had not his ass saved him. When he beat the ass, it opened its mouth and reproved him. (Num. xxii–xxiv.)

Balaam, SIR, the subject of a satire in Pope's 'Moral Essays', Ep. iii, a religious, frugal citizen tempted by the Devil through wealth, who becomes a corrupt courtier.

Balaclava, a small seaport on the coast of the Crimea, near Sebastopol, was the scene in the Crimean War of the famous charge of the Light Brigade (26 Sept. 1854), celebrated in Tennyson's poem.

Balade of Charitie, The, one of the 'Thomas Rowley' poems, see *Chatterton.*

Balaustion's Adventure, a poem by R. Browning (q.v.) (1871), which discusses and translates from Euripides' 'Alcestis'. Balaustion appears again in 'Aristophanes' Apology' (q.v.).

Balboa, VASCO NUÑEZ DE (1475–1517), one of the companions of Cortez, the conqueror of Mexico. It was he who first, in 1513, discovered the Pacific Ocean, not Cortez, as Keats supposed.

Balchristie, JENNY, a character in Scott's 'The Heart of Midlothian'.

Balder, or BALDUR, in Scandinavian mythology, a son of Odin (q.v.), the god of the summer sun, beloved by all, but threatened with death. Frigga, his mother, has persuaded all things to vow not to injure him, but has overlooked the mistletoe. Loki (q.v.) induces the blind god Hödur to throw a branch of mistletoe at Balder, and this kills him.

Balder, a dramatic poem by Dobell (q.v.) (1854), the most notable production of the 'Spasmodic School' (q.v.).

Balder Dead, a poem by M. Arnold (q.v.) (1853).

Balder (q.v.) has been slain by the blind Hödur through the scheming of Loki. The poem tells of the lament of the gods for him, and of Hermod's journey to the shades to persuade Hela to give him up.

Balderstone, CALEB, a character in Scott's 'The Bride of Lammermoor'.

Baldur, see *Balder*.

Baldwin, WILLIAM, see *Mirror for Magistrates*.

Bale, JOHN (1495-1563), notable as having written 'King John', the first English historical play.

Balfour, DAVID, a character in R. L. Stevenson's 'Kidnapped' (q.v.) and 'Catriona'.

Balfour of Burley, JOHN, leader of the Cameronian sect, figures in Scott's 'Old Mortality' (q.v.).

Balin le Savage and **Balan**, two brothers, whose deeds and death at each other's hands are told in Malory's 'Morte Darthur', Bk. II, and in Tennyson's 'Idylls of the King' (q.v.); also in Swinburne's 'Tale of Balen' (1896).

Balkis, or BELKIS, the name given by the Arabs to the queen of Sheba who visited Solomon (1 Kings x).

Ball, JOHN, a leader of the Peasants' Revolt (1381); the subject of W. Morris's 'The Dream of John Ball'.

Ballad, originally a song intended as the accompaniment to a dance; hence a light, simple song of any kind, or a popular song, often one celebrating or attacking persons or institutions. From this last is derived the modern sense in which a ballad is a simple spirited *poem* in short stanzas in which some popular story is graphically narrated.

Most English ballads, in the form in which we know them, date from the 15th cent.; but the 13th-cent. 'Judas' ranks as a ballad and it is certain that from Anglo-Saxon times there existed short alliterative lays from which ballads later developed. The standard ballad verse form is a quatrain, often with only one rhyming pair (a b c b) and iambic lines of eight and six syllables alternately. Its characteristics are: (1) that it tells a story in verse; (2) that the story is a single inci-

dent dramatically treated, not a continuous narrative; (3) that its statements are impersonal and do not express the author's emotions directly. (Oral tradition has played a great part in the composition of genuine ballads. The theory of communal authorship, long held by Grimm (q.v.) and others, is now generally replaced by a belief that an individual may have composed a ballad initially which would be added to or altered by successive reciters.)

With the introduction of printing, the ballad form was used for political and topical purposes (see *Broadside*), and these continued to be popular until the 19th cent. The genuine ancient ballads were collected, often from oral tradition, notably by Pepys, Bagford, and Percy: later by Alan Cunningham, Scott, and others. The standard modern collection is that of Child (q.v.), who printed 305 ballads in their different versions. Many of the stories which they relate can be paralleled in the folklore of other European and even Eastern countries.

Imitations of the ballad, both in form and style, have been made, often with great success. Of these 'literary ballads' Coleridge's 'The Ancient Mariner' and Keats's 'La Belle Dame sans Merci' (qq.v.) are outstanding examples.

Ballade, strictly, a poem of one or more triplets of seven- (or eight-) lined stanzas, each ending with the same line as refrain, e.g. Chaucer's 'Compleynt of Venus'. More generally, a poem divided into stanzas of equal length, usually of seven or eight lines.

Ballantyne, JAMES (1772-1833), at first a solicitor, then a printer in Kelso, printed Sir W. Scott's 'Minstrelsy of the Scottish Border' in 1802, and thenceforth continued to print Scott's works. He was ruined by the bankruptcy of Constable & Co. in 1826.

Ballantyne, JOHN (1774-1821), brother of James Ballantyne (q.v.), became in 1809 manager of the publishing firm started by Sir Walter Scott.

Ballantyne, ROBERT MICHAEL (1825-94), writer of stories for boys, was a nephew of James and John Ballantyne (qq.v.). His popular books include: 'The Young Fur Traders', 'The Coral Island', etc.

Balliol College, Oxford, was founded by John de Baliol in 1263. Among famous masters of this college have been John Wycliffe and Benjamin Jowett (qq.v.), and among its many distinguished members a large proportion of the British statesmen of the last hundred years.

Balthazar ('possessor of treasure'), one of the three Magi (q.v.) or 'wise men of the East'. He is represented as king of Chaldea.

BALTHAZAR, the name assumed by Portia as a lawyer in Shakespeare's 'The Merchant of Venice' (q.v.).

Baltic, The Battle of the, see *Campbell* (*T.*).

Balwhidder, THE REVD. MICAH, in Galt's 'Annals of the Parish' (q.v.), the minister of Dalmailing.

Balzac, HONORÉ DE (1799-1850), French novelist, author of the great collection of romances entitled 'La Comédie humaine' in which he endeavoured to represent, faithfully and minutely, the whole complex system of French society.

Banbury, a town in Oxfordshire, formerly noted for the number and zeal of its Puritan inhabitants. Whence 'Banbury man' is used by Ben Jonson and others for a sanctimonious fellow.

BANBURY CHEESES were thin, and Bardolph in Shakespeare's 'The Merry Wives of Windsor' (I. i) addresses Slender as 'You Banbury cheese!'

BANBURY CROSS, destroyed by the Puritans, has been restored in recent times.

Bandello, MATTEO (1485-1561), the best Italian writer of short stories in the 16th cent. Painter's 'Palace of Pleasure' (q.v.) includes twenty-five of Bandello's tales.

Bandusia, a fountain celebrated by Horace, probably on his Sabine farm.

Bangorian Controversy, a Church controversy of the early years of the reign of George I. Benjamin Hoadly, bishop of Bangor, published a pamphlet and preached a sermon in 1717 reducing Church authority to a minimum and making sincerity the chief test of true religion. These gave rise to the 'Bangorian controversy', in which a great number of pamphlets were issued.

Bankes's Horse, see under *Marocco*.

Bank of England, THE, founded on the basis of a scheme put forward by William Paterson (1658-1719) with a view to raising money for William III's foreign campaigns.

Banks, SIR JOSEPH (1743-1820), explorer and natural historian, who accompanied Cook (q.v.) in his expedition round the world. Banks left a narrative of Cook's voyage.

Bannatyne Club, THE, was founded in 1823, with Sir W. Scott as president, for the publication of old Scottish documents. The club was dissolved in 1861. George Bannatyne (1545-1608), in whose honour it was named, was the compiler (1568) of a large collection of Scottish poems.

Bannockburn, BATTLE OF, 1314, in which the English were defeated by Robert Bruce, is described in Scott's 'Lord of the Isles', vi.

Banquo, a character in Shakespeare's 'Macbeth' (q.v.). Though mentioned by Holinshed, he is not regarded as a historical character.

Banshee, a supernatural being supposed by the peasantry of Ireland and the Highlands to wail under the windows of a house when one of the inmates is about to die.

Bantam, ANGELO CYRUS, in Dickens's 'The Pickwick Papers' (q.v.), Grand Master of the Ceremonies at Bath.

Barabas, the 'Jew of Malta' in Marlowe's play of that name (q.v.).

Barabbas, the robber, released instead of Jesus (Matt. xxvii. 16-26).

Barataria, in 'Don Quixote' (q.v.), the island of which Sancho Panza is governor.

Barbara Allan, a Scottish ballad included in Percy's 'Reliques', on the subject of the death of Sir John Grehme for unrequited love of Barbara Allan, and her subsequent remorse.

Barbarossa, the nickname ('Red-Beard') of the emperor Frederick I of Germany (1152-90). Barbarossa was drowned in a river in the course of the Third Crusade, but legend says that he still sleeps in a cavern in the Kyffhäuser mountain, with his companions about him and his beard grown round a stone table. There is a poem, 'Sleeping Heroes', on the subject by Edward Shanks.

Barbary Corsairs, the cruisers of Barbary (the Saracen countries along the N. coast of Africa), to whose attacks the ships and coasts of the Christian countries were incessantly exposed in the 9th and 10th cents.

Barbason, a demon mentioned by Shakespeare in 'The Merry Wives of Windsor', II. ii, and 'Henry V', II. i.

Barbauld, MRS. ANNA LETITIA (1743-1825), *née* AIKIN, was author of miscellaneous poems and prose essays.

Barbour, JOHN (1316?-95), Scottish poet, was archdeacon of Aberdeen in 1357. He composed his poem 'The Bruce', celebrating the war of independence and deeds of King Robert and James Douglas, about 1375.

Barchester Towers, a novel by A. Trollope (q.v.) (1857).

This is the second in the Barsetshire series, the sequel to 'The Warden', and is mainly occupied with the struggle between Mr. Slope and Mrs. Proudie for the control of the diocese, and in particular for the disposal of the wardenship of Hiram's Hospital.

Barclay, ALEXANDER (1475?-1552), poet, scholar, and divine, translated Brant's 'Narrenschiff' into English verse as 'The Ship of Fools' (q.v.) (1509).

Bard, The, a Pindaric ode by Gray (q.v.) (1757).

The ode is based on a Welsh tradition that Edward I ordered all the bards that fell into his hands to be put to death. It is a lamentation by a Welsh bard, and a curse pronounced by him and the ghosts of his slaughtered companions on Edward's race. Then the bard sings of the glories that will come with the house of Tudor, and of the poets of that age.

Bardell, MRS., in Dickens's 'The Pickwick Papers' (q.v.), Mr. Pickwick's landlady, who sues him for breach of promise.

Bardolph, in Shakespeare's 'Henry IV' and 'Henry V' (qq.v.), one of Falstaff's boon companions. He is hanged for looting in the French war. In 'The Merry Wives of Windsor' (q.v.) he is discarded by Falstaff and employed as tapster at the Garter Inn.

Bareacres, EARL and COUNTESS OF, characters in Thackeray's 'Vanity Fair' (q.v.).

Barebones Parliament, the assembly summoned by Cromwell in 1653, consisting of 133 members, so called from one of its members, Praise-God Barbon, an Anabaptist leather-seller.

Baretti, GIUSEPPE MARC' ANTONIO (1719-89), came to London and opened a school for teaching Italian in 1751. He was a friend of Johnson and Mrs. Thrale (qq.v.).

Barham, RICHARD HARRIS (1788-1845), a clergyman, author of 'The Ingoldsby Legends', first published in 'Bentley's Miscellany' and 'The New Monthly Magazine', and reissued in 1840. He was particularly successful in the comic treatment of medieval legend.

Baring, MAURICE (1874-1945), poet and novelist. His 'Collected Poems' were published in 1925. He wrote novels, short stories, and essays, of which the best known are 'C' (1924), 'Cat's Cradle' (1925), 'Tinker's Leave' (1927), and 'In the End is my Beginning' (1931).

Baring-Gould, SABINE (1834-1924), author of a large number of religious works and novels, including 'John Herring' (1883), 'Richard Cable' (1888).

Barker, GEORGE GRANVILLE (1913-), poet. He published 'Thirty Preliminary Poems' in 1933 and early attracted the admiration of W. B. Yeats. His 'Collected Poems' appeared in 1957. They are marked by a rhetorical style and a preoccupation with human suffering and guilt.

Barker, HARLEY GRANVILLE GRANVILLE-,
see *Granville-Barker*.

Barkis, in Dickens's 'David Copperfield'
(q.v.), the carrier, who sent a message by
David to Clara Peggotty that 'Barkis is
willin''.

Barleycorn, JOHN, the personification of
barley, as the grain from which malt
liquor is made.

Barlow, JOEL (1754-1812), American
poet and diplomat remembered as the
author of 'The Columbiad' (q.v.), and as
one of the 'Hartford Wits' (q.v.).

Barmecide, a family of princes ruling at
Baghdad, concerning one of whom the
story is told in the 'Arabian Nights' that
he put a succession of imaginary dishes
before a beggar. The beggar pretended
to be intoxicated by the imaginary wine,
and fell upon his entertainer. Hence
'Barmecide' is used of one who offers
illusory benefits.

Barnaby Rudge, a novel by Dickens
(q.v.) (1841), the earlier of his two historical novels (see *Tale of Two Cities*), the
period dealt with being that of the Gordon
anti-popery riots of 1780. Reuben Haredale, a country gentleman, has been
murdered, and the murderer has never
been discovered. Geoffrey Haredale, his
brother, a Roman Catholic, and Sir John
Chester are enemies. Chester's son
Edward is in love with Haredale's niece,
Emma; and the elders combine to thwart
the match. The Gordon riots supervene,
fomented secretly by Chester. Haredale's
house is burnt, and Emma carried off.
Edward saves the lives of Haredale and
Emma, and wins Haredale's consent to
his marriage. Haredale discovers the
murderer of his brother, the steward
Rudge, the father of the half-witted Barnaby. Rudge pays the penalty of his crime.
Chester is killed by Haredale in a duel.

The principal interest of the book lies
in the vivid descriptions of the riots, and
in the accessory characters: the pathetic
figure of Barnaby; the sturdy locksmith
Gabriel Varden; Simon Tappertit his
apprentice, small in body but aspiring and

anarchical in soul, and Miss Miggs, his
mean and treacherous servant; Dennis
the Hangman; and lastly Grip, Barnaby's
raven.

Barnacles, THE, in Dickens's 'Little
Dorrit' (q.v.), types of government officials
in the 'Circumlocution Office'.

Barnard, LADY ANNE, see *Lindsay
(Lady A.)*.

Barnardine, a character in Shakespeare's
'Measure for Measure' (q.v.).

Barnavelt, Sir John van Olden, a historical tragedy, probably by J. Fletcher (q.v.),
acted in 1619.

Barnes, BARNABE (1569?-1609), a voluminous writer of verse, issued his 'Parthenophil and Parthenophe' in 1593.

Barnes, WILLIAM (1801-86), rector of
Came, wrote a number of poems in the
Dorset dialect ('Poems of Rural Life',
three series, 1844, 1859, and 1863).

Barney, a character in Dickens's 'Oliver
Twist' (q.v.).

Barnfield, RICHARD (1574-1627), poet;
two of his pieces, in 'The Passionate
Pilgrim' (q.v.) (1599), were long attributed
to Shakespeare, the better known of these
being, 'As it fell upon a day, In the merry
month of May'.

Barnum, PHINEAS TAYLOR (1810-91),
the great American showman.

Barnwell, George, see *George Barnwell*.

Baroque, from the Portuguese *barroco*,
meaning a rough or imperfect pearl;
originally a term of abuse applied to 17th-
cent. Italian art and that of other countries,
especially Germany, influenced by Italy.
It is characterized by the unclassical use
of classical forms, and by the interpenetra-
tion of architecture, sculpture, and painting to produce grandiose and emotional
effects.

Barrès, MAURICE (1862-1923), French
writer and politician known outside France
for the extreme nationalism of his views.
At his death he ranked with Anatole
France as one of the representative literary
figures of his time.

Barrie, SIR JAMES MATTHEW (1860-
1937), in his early days a journalist (cf.

'The Greenwood Hat', 1937). As a dramatist his most original work is to be found in 'Quality Street' (1901), 'The Admirable Crichton' (1902), 'What Every Woman Knows' (in which he pricks the bubble of male self-sufficiency, 1908), and 'The Twelve-Pound Look' (the exposure of a pompous egoist, 1910); while he gained immense popularity with 'Peter Pan' (q.v.) (1904). His other publications include: 'My Lady Nicotine' (1890), 'The Little Minister' (1891), 'Sentimental Tommy' (1896), 'The Little White Bird' (1902), 'Peter Pan in Kensington Gardens' (1906), and 'Peter and Wendy' (1911).

Barry, ELIZABETH (1658-1713), a celebrated actress who owed her entrance to the stage to Rochester (q.v.). Otway was passionately devoted to her, but she did not return his affection.

Barry Cornwall, see *Procter (B. W.)*.

Barry Lyndon, The Luck of, a Romance of the Last Century, by Fitzboodle, a satirical romance by Thackeray (q.v.) ('Fraser's Magazine', 1844), subsequently entitled 'The Memoirs of Barry Lyndon, Esq., by Himself'.

Barsetshire Novels, The, of A. Trollope (q.v.) are the following: 'The Warden', 'Barchester Towers', 'Doctor Thorne', 'Framley Parsonage', 'The Small House at Allington', and 'The Last Chronicle of Barset'.

Bartholomew, MASSACRE OF ST., the massacre of Huguenots throughout France on the morning of the festival, 24 Aug. 1572.

Bartholomew Fair, a famous London fair held at least from Henry II's time within the churchyard of the priory of St. Bartholomew, Smithfield. The fair was continued as a pleasure-fair until 1855. For a description of it in the 17th cent. see Ben Jonson's 'Bartholomew Fayre'.

Bartholomew Fayre, a farcical comedy by Jonson (q.v.), produced in 1614. The play, the plot of which is very slight, presents with much humour the scenes of a London holiday fair, with its ballad-singers, stall-keepers, bullies, bawds, and cut-purses.

Bartholomew's Hospital, ST., built in London by Rahere (*d.* 1144), cleric and formerly king's jester.

Barton, SIR ANDREW, the subject of a ballad in two parts, included in Percy's 'Reliques'. He was a Scottish sea officer who lived in the 16th cent.

Baruch, a book of the Apocrypha, attributed to Baruch the scribe of Jeremiah (Jer. xxxvi). It is a composite work, probably written after A.D. 70.

Bas Bleu, see *Blue Stocking*.

Basil, Pot of, see *Isabella, or the Pot of Basil*.

Basilikon Doron, see *James I* (1603-25).

Basilisk, a fabulous reptile, alleged to be hatched by a serpent from a cock's egg; its breath, even its look, was fatal.

Baskerville, JOHN (1706-75), the famous printer. His first work, a quarto edition of Virgil, appeared in 1757.

Baskett, JOHN (*d.* 1742), king's printer, was printer to the University of Oxford, 1711-42.

Bassanio, a character in Shakespeare's 'The Merchant of Venice' (q.v.).

Bassianus, a character in Shakespeare's 'Titus Andronicus' (q.v.).

Bastard, The, see *Savage (R.)*.

Bastard, PHILIP THE, son of Sir Robert Faulconbridge, in Shakespeare's 'King John' (q.v.).

Bastard, WILLIAM THE, in English history, is William the Conqueror.

Bastille, THE, in Paris, used as a state prison, was destroyed by the populace of Paris on 14 July 1789.

Bates, CHARLEY, in Dickens's 'Oliver Twist' (q.v.), one of the pickpockets in Fagin's gang.

Bates, HENRY WALTER (1825-92), naturalist. His 'The Naturalist on the Amazons' was published in 1863.

Bates, JOHN, in Shakespeare's 'Henry V' (q.v.), one of the English soldiers with whom the king converses before the battle.

Bates, MISS, a character in Jane Austen's 'Emma' (q.v.).

Bath, in Somerset, is the site of a Roman spa, probably built in the 1st and 2nd cents. A.D. Bath's modern reputation dates from the 17th cent., but it rose to the zenith of its fame and prosperity under the rule of Richard ('Beau') Nash, the 'King of Bath' in the 18th cent. It is the subject of very frequent literary allusion, having been visited among many others by Smollett, Fielding, Sheridan, Fanny Burney, Goldsmith, Southey, Landor, Jane Austen, Wordsworth, Cowper, Scott, Moore, and Dickens.

Bath, Wife of, see *Canterbury Tales.*

Bathos, Greek, 'depth'. The current usage for 'descent from the sublime to the ridiculous' is due to Pope's satire, 'Bathos, the art of sinking in Poetry' ('Miscellanies', 1727-8). The title was a travesty of Longinus's essay, 'On the Sublime'.

Batrachomyomachia, or *Battle of the Frogs and the Mice,* a mock-heroic Greek poem, at one time erroneously attributed to Homer.

Thomas Parnell (q.v.) wrote a satirical 'Homer's Battle of the Frogs and the Mice' (1717), against Theobald and Dennis.

Battle, SARAH, the subject of one of Lamb's 'Essays of Elia' (q.v.), a character drawn from Mrs. Burney, the sister-in-law of Fanny Burney (q.v.).

Battledore-book, see *Horn-book.*

Battle of Alcazar, The, a play in verse by G. Peele (q.v.) (1594).

Battle of Britain, the name popularly given to the series of encounters over London and SE. England between the R.A.F. and the German Air Force in 1940 in which British victory ended the threat of German invasion. The prime minister, Winston Churchill, in his survey of the air warfare in the House of Commons on 20 Aug. said: 'Never in the field of human conflict was so much owed by so many to so few.'

Battle of Lake Regillus, The, the title of one of Macaulay's 'Lays of Ancient Rome' (q.v.), which describes the great victory of the Romans over the Latins under Tarquin in *c.* 496 B.C.

Battle of Maldon, see *Maldon.*

Battle of Otterbourne, see *Otterbourne.*

Battle of the Books, The, a prose satire by Swift (q.v.), written in 1697, when Swift was residing with Sir W. Temple, and published in 1704.

Temple had written an essay on the comparative merits of 'Ancient and Modern Learning', in which he had drawn on himself the censure of William Wotton and Bentley. Swift, in his 'Battle of the Books', treats the whole question with satirical humour. The ancients, under the patronage of Pallas, are led by Homer, Pindar, Euclid, Aristotle, and Plato, with Sir W. Temple commanding the allies; the moderns by Milton, Dryden, Descartes, Hobbes, Scotus, and others. The fight is conducted with great spirit. Aristotle aims an arrow at Bacon but hits Descartes. Homer overthrows Gondibert. Virgil encounters his translator Dryden, in a helmet nine times too big. Boyle transfixes Bentley and Wotton.

Battle of the Frogs and the Mice, see *Batrachomyomachia.*

Baucis, see *Philemon.*

Baudelaire, CHARLES (1821-67), French poet, whose chief work is his 'Les Fleurs du Mal' (1857), poems of a melancholy romantic spirit remarkable for their originality and peculiar charm.

Baviad, The, see *Gifford.*

Baxter, RICHARD (1615-91), a presbyterian divine and military chaplain during the Civil War. The author of 'The Saint's Everlasting Rest' (1650) and a lengthy autobiography, 'Reliquiae Baxterianae' (1696).

Bayard, the magic horse given by Charlemagne to Rinaldo (q.v.).

Bayard, PIERRE DU TERRAIL, SEIGNEUR DE (*c.* 1473-1524), a famous captain in the Italian wars of Charles VIII, the 'chevalier sans peur et sans reproche'.

Bayes, the name under which Dryden is ridiculed in Buckingham's 'The Rehearsal' (q.v.).

Bayeux Tapestry, THE, an embroidered strip of linen, about 80 yards long by 19 inches wide, belonging to Bayeux in Normandy. It was probably commissioned by Bishop Odo of Bayeux and made in Kent, c. 1070-80. It depicts the events leading up to and including the Norman Conquest.

Bayham, FRED, a character in Thackeray's 'The Newcomes' (q.v.).

Bayle, PIERRE (1647-1706), French philosopher, author of the 'Dictionnaire historique et critique' (1697-1702), a pioneer work in scientific biography.

Bayona, see *Namancos*.

Bazzard, MR., a character in Dickens's 'Edwin Drood' (q.v.).

Beaconsfield, EARL OF, see *Disraeli*.

Beagle, H.M.S., see *Darwin* (*C. R.*).

Bear, THE, AT THE BRIDGE FOOT, a tavern at the Southwark end of old London Bridge frequently mentioned by Pepys.

Beardsley, AUBREY VINCENT (1872-98), black-and-white illustrator whose fantastic, mannered style was highly individual yet typical of *art nouveau*. He became art editor of 'The Yellow Book' in 1894. He illustrated Oscar Wilde's 'Salome', 'The Rape of the Lock', and other books, achieving a remarkable output before his early death from tuberculosis.

Beatrice, a character in Shakespeare's 'Much Ado about Nothing' (q.v.).

Beatrice, DANTE'S, see *Dante*.

Beattie, JAMES (1735-1803), professor of moral philosophy and poet, the author of 'The Minstrel', a poem in Spenserian stanzas, of which Book I appeared in 1771, Book II in 1774.

Beau Brummell, see *Brummell*.

Beauchamp's Career, a novel by G. Meredith (q.v.), published serially 1875, in volume form 1876.

Beaumains, in Malory's 'Morte Darthur', the nickname given to Gareth.

Beaumanoir, SIR LUCAS, in Scott's 'Ivanhoe' (q.v.), Master of the Knights Templars.

Beaumarchais, PIERRE AUGUSTIN CARON DE (1732-99), author of the famous comedies 'Le Barbier de Séville' (1775) and 'Le Mariage de Figaro' (1784).

Beaumont, FRANCIS (1584-1616), collaborated with John Fletcher in dramatic works from about 1606 to 1616 (for a list of the plays so produced see under *Fletcher, J.*). Dryden states that Beaumont was 'so accurate a judge of plays that Ben Jonson, while he lived, submitted all his writings to his censure'. His superior faculty for the construction of plots is discernible in some of the plays that he wrote in collaboration with Fletcher.

Beau Nash, see *Nash* (*R.*).

Beau Tibbs, a character in Goldsmith's 'The Citizen of the World' (q.v.); an absurd creature, poor and unknown, but affecting the airs of a man of fashion.

Beauvoir, SIMONE DE (1908-), French novelist and essayist, with J.-P. Sartre (q.v.) one of the leading Existentialist writers, author of: 'L'Invitée' (1943), 'Le Sang des Autres' (1944), 'Les Mandarins' (1954), etc., novels; 'Le Deuxième Sexe' (1949) and other essays; also 'Mémoires d'une Jeune Fille rangée' (1958) and subsequent volumes of autobiography.

Beaux' Stratagem, The, a comedy by Farquhar (q.v.) (1707).

Beazeley, OLD TOM and YOUNG TOM, characters in Marryat's 'Jacob Faithful' (q.v.).

Beck, MADAME, a character in Charlotte Brontë's 'Villette' (q.v.).

Becket, a tragedy by Lord Tennyson (q.v.) (1884). The subject of the play is the bitter quarrel that arose between Henry II and Thomas à Becket. T. S. Eliot's verse drama, 'Murder in the Cathedral', deals with the same subject.

Becket, THOMAS À, see *Thomas à Becket*.

Beckett, SAMUEL BARCLAY (1906-), novelist and dramatist, born in Dublin. He went to Paris about 1928 to study and teach and has lived there since 1938. He was a friend of James Joyce (q.v.) and at one time his amanuensis. Many of Beckett's works were written first in French. They include poetry, novels, and a number of short plays, notably 'En attendant Godot' (1952, 'Waiting for Godot', produced in London, 1956). He received the Nobel Prize in 1969.

Beckford, WILLIAM (1759-1844), remembered chiefly as the author of the fantastic oriental tale 'Vathek' (q.v.), but also for his two books of travel, 'Dreams, Waking Thoughts, and Incidents' (1783, revised 1834), and 'Recollections of an Excursion to the Monasteries of Alcobaça and Batalha' (1835).

Beddoes, THOMAS LOVELL (1803-49), went abroad to study medicine and settled at Zürich in 1835. He published in 1821 'The Improvisatore' and in 1822 'The Bride's Tragedy'. His most important work, 'Death's Jest-Book' (q.v.), a play in the Elizabethan spirit, was begun in 1825 and repeatedly altered at various times, not being published until 1850, after his death by suicide. Beddoes showed, besides a taste for the *macabre* and supernatural, a capacity for occasionally fine blank verse, and more especially a poignant lyrical gift.

Bede or BÆDA (673-735), historian and scholar, was when young placed under the charge of Benedict Biscop, abbot of Wearmouth. Thence he went to the monastery of Jarrow, where he spent the greater part of his life. He appears from his writings to have been wise, learned, and humble. His 'Historia Ecclesiastica Gentis Anglorum' (q.v.) was brought to an end in 731, and by that year he had written nearly forty works, chiefly biblical commentaries. The treatise 'De Natura Rerum', one of his earliest works, contains such physical science as was then known.

Bede, CUTHBERT, pseudonym of E. BRADLEY (q.v.).

Bedivere, SIR, in Malory's 'Morte Darthur', one of Arthur's knights. He and his brother Sir Lucan, with Arthur, alone survived the last battle, and he, at Arthur's bidding, threw Excalibur into the water, and bore the king to the barge that carried him away to Avalon.

Bed of Ware, THE GREAT, an oak bed referred to by Shakespeare ('Twelfth Night', III. ii), Jonson, and Farquhar. It is now in the Victoria and Albert Museum.

Bedlam, a corruption of Bethlehem, applied to the Hospital of St. Mary of Bethlehem, in Bishopsgate, London, which became a hospital for lunatics. From Bedlam are derived such expressions as Tom o' Bedlam (q.v.) for wandering lunatics.

Bee, The, see *Goldsmith.*

Beecher, HENRY WARD, see *Stowe.*

Beefeater, a popular appellation of the Yeomen of the Guard.

Beelzebub, one of the fallen angels, next to Satan in power ('Paradise Lost', i. 79).

Beerbohm, SIR MAX (1872-1956), critic, essayist, and caricaturist, published his first book, 'The Works of Max Beerbohm', in 1896. A master of wit, irony, and satire, and of a polished and incisive style, he directed his criticism at literary mannerisms and social pretences. 'Zuleika Dobson' (1911) is an amusing story of the devastating effect on the youth of Oxford of a beautiful adventuress. His other principal works are: 'More', 'Yet Again', 'And Even Now' (essays); 'Seven Men' (stories); also volumes of caricatures.

Bees, Fable of the, see *Mandeville* (*B. de*).

Beethoven, LUDWIG VAN (1770-1827), the famous German musical composer. He studied under Haydn. He became afflicted with deafness in 1802, which increased until it became complete, but did not arrest his creative genius. His musical conceptions have an intellectual and moral quality that was previously unknown. He perfected the symphony. His compositions included one opera ('Fidelio'), two masses, nine symphonies, and a large number of concertos, sonatas, quartets, and trios.

Beeton, MRS. ISABELLA MARY (1836-65), *née* MAYSON, author of a famous book of cookery and domestic economy (1859-61).

Beggars Bush, The, a drama by J. Fletcher (q.v.), and perhaps Massinger, probably produced in 1622.

Beggar's Daughter of Bednall Green, The, a ballad written in the reign of Elizabeth and included in Percy's 'Reliques'.

The story forms the basis of Chettle and Day's 'The Blind Beggar of Bednal Green' (1600, printed 1659). J. S. Knowles (q.v.) wrote a comedy called 'The Beggar's Daughter of Bethnal Green'; and R. Dodsley (q.v.) wrote a musical play, 'The Blind Beggar of Bethnal Green'.

Beggar's Opera, The, a musical play by J. Gay (q.v.), produced in 1728.

The play arose out of a suggestion by Swift to Gay that a Newgate pastoral 'might make an odd pretty sort of thing'. The principal characters are Peachum, a receiver of stolen goods; his wife, and his pretty daughter, Polly; Lockit, warder of Newgate, and his daughter Lucy; and Captain Macheath, highwayman and light-hearted winner of women's hearts. The play was a great success and Gay is said to have made £800 by it.

Behemoth, an animal mentioned in Job xl. 10, probably a hippopotamus. Used in modern literature as a general expression for one of the largest and strongest animals.

Behn, MRS. APHRA (1640–89), playwright and novelist. Between 1671 and 1689 she produced fifteen plays, of which the most popular was 'The Rover' (in two parts, 1677–81). 'The City Heiress', 1682, is one of her typical coarse comedies of contemporary London life. She also wrote poems (including the beautiful 'Love in fantastic triumph sat'), and novels, of which her 'Oroonoko, or the History of the Royal Slave' (q.v.) is the best known.

Bel and the Dragon, one of the apocryphal books of the O.T., detached from the Book of Daniel. Bel was an idol worshipped by the Babylonians, and the story tells how Daniel convinced King Astyages that it was a mere image of brass. The dragon, a living animal, was also worshipped. Daniel disproved its divine character by giving it lumps of pitch, fat, and hair to eat, so that it burst.

Belarius, a character in Shakespeare's 'Cymbeline' (q.v.).

Belch, SIR TOBY, in Shakespeare's 'Twelfth Night' (q.v.), a roistering knight, uncle to Olivia.

Belial, the spirit of evil personified, used by Milton ('Paradise Lost', i. 490) as the name of one of the fallen angels.

Belinda, the heroine of Pope's 'The Rape of the Lock' (q.v.).

Belkis, see *Balkis*.

Bell, ADAM, see *Adam Bell*.

Bell, CURRER, ELLIS, and ACTON, see *Brontë (C., E., and A.)*.

Bell, LAURA, the heroine of Thackeray's 'Pendennis' (q.v.).

Bellafront, in Dekker's 'The Honest Whore' (q.v.), the repentant courtesan.

Bellamira, a comedy by Sir C. Sedley (q.v.), produced in 1687.

Bellamy, EDWARD (1850–98), American author, whose fame rests upon his popular Utopian romance, 'Looking Backward' (1888).

The work had an immense vogue; a Nationalist Party was formed to advocate its principles; and Bellamy's ideas are still of considerable influence in the United States.

Bellario, (1) the name assumed by the heroine of Beaumont and Fletcher's 'Philaster' when disguised as a page; (2) in Shakespeare's 'The Merchant of Venice' (q.v.), Portia's lawyer cousin.

Bellaston, LADY, a character in Fielding's 'Tom Jones' (q.v.).

Bella Wilfer, a character in Dickens's 'Our Mutual Friend' (q.v.).

Belle or ISOPEL **Berners,** in Borrow's 'Lavengro' (q.v.), a wandering lass, acts as second to Lavengro in his fight with the Flaming Tinman.

Belle Dame sans Merci, La, a ballad by Keats (q.v.), written in 1819.

The knight-at-arms, enthralled by an elf, wakes from the dream of his lady, to find not his dream realized, but the cold hill's side, where 'no birds sing'. 'La Belle Dame sans Merci' is also the title of a poem, in rhyme royal and octaves, translated from Alain Chartier, attributed at one time to Chaucer.

Bellenden, LADY MARGARET, EDITH, and MAJOR, characters in Scott's 'Old Mortality' (q.v.).

Bellerophon, son of Glaucus, king of Corinth. He was banished for a murder, and fled to the court of Proetus, king of Argos, where Anteia, the king's wife, fell in love with him. As he slighted her passion, she accused him to her husband of an attempt on her virtue. Proetus dispatched him to his father-in-law, Iobates, bearing a letter signifying that he should be killed (whence the expression *Bellerophontis litterae*). Iobates accordingly sent Bellerophon against the monster Chimaera (q.v.); but Bellerophon, with the aid of the winged horse Pegasus (q.v.), overcame it. Iobates, despairing of killing the hero, gave him his daughter to wife and the succession to his throne. Other legends relate that he attempted to fly to heaven on Pegasus, but that Zeus by means of a gadfly caused the horse to throw its rider.

Bellerus, a fabulous person introduced by Milton in his 'Lycidas' to account for *Bellerium*, the Roman name of Land's End.

Belle's Stratagem, The, a comedy by Mrs. H. Cowley (q.v.), produced in 1780.

Belloc, JOSEPH HILARY PIERRE (1870-1953), who wrote as HILAIRE BELLOC, born in France, educated at Balliol College, Oxford, a writer of essays, novels, verse, travels, history, biography, and criticism. Among his best works is 'The Path to Rome' (1902). His other writings include: 'Hills and the Sea' (1906), 'The Bad Child's Book of Beasts', 'Cautionary Tales' (all light verse); 'Mr. Clutterbuck's Election', 'A Change in the Cabinet' (novels); 'The Four Men' (fantastic travel); 'History of England'; and books of essays on 'Nothing', 'Something', 'Everything'.

Bellona, the Roman goddess of war.

Bells, The, a dramatic adaptation by L. Lewis of 'The Polish Jew' of Erckmann-Chatrian, the story of a burgomaster

haunted by the consciousness of an undiscovered murder that he has committed. It provided Sir H. Irving with one of his most successful parts.

Bells and Pomegranates (the reference is to Exod. xxviii. 34), a series of poems, published by R. Browning (q.v.) between 1841 and 1846, including 'Pippa Passes', 'The Pied Piper', etc.

Bell-the-Cat, nickname of Archibald Douglas, fifth earl of Angus (1449?-1514). He figures in Scott's 'Marmion' (q.v.).

Belmont, Portia's house in Shakespeare's 'The Merchant of Venice' (q.v.).

Belmont, SIR JOHN, the heroine's father in Fanny Burney's 'Evelina' (q.v.).

Belphoebe, in Spenser's 'Faerie Queene', the chaste huntress, twin sister of Amoret.

Belshazzar's Feast, the feast made by Belshazzar, the last king of Babylonia, at which his doom was foretold by a writing on the wall, as interpreted by Daniel (Dan. v). Belshazzar was killed in the sack of Babylon (538 B.C.).

Belton Estate, The, a novel by A. Trollope (q.v.) (1865).

Belvedere Apollo, a statue of Apollo (q.v.) in the Vatican.

Belvidera, the heroine of Otway's 'Venice Preserv'd' (q.v.).

Benavente y Martinez, JACINTO (1866-1954), Spanish playwright and critic, the author of many light and pleasant comedies.

Benedicite, see *Song of the Three Holy Children.*

Benedick, a character in Shakespeare's 'Much Ado about Nothing' (q.v.). The name is used (also erroneously in the form 'Benedict') of an apparently confirmed bachelor who marries.

Benedict Biscop, ST. (628?-690), founded (in 674) the monastery of St. Peter at the mouth of the river Wear. After this he founded the sister monastery of St. Paul at Jarrow. He is regarded as one of the originators of the artistic and literary development of Northumbria in the next century. He is commemorated on 12 Feb.

Benedictines, the order of monks, also known from their dress as 'Black Monks', established by St. Benedict (480-543) about the year 529, when he founded the monastery on Monte Cassino in Campania; the first in time, as in fame, of the great Western Church orders.

Benét, STEPHEN VINCENT (1898-1943), American writer, known chiefly for his narrative poem on the Civil War, 'John Brown's Body' (1928). His collected 'Ballads and Poems' appeared in 1930. He also wrote several novels and the libretto for the folk-opera, 'The Devil and Daniel Webster' (1943).

Benét, WILLIAM ROSE (1886-1950), American poet, and brother of S. V. Benét (q.v.). He published many volumes of romantic verse and two verse novels, the best of which is the autobiographical 'The Dust Which Is God' (1941).

Ben Hur: A Tale of the Christ, a historical novel about the early days of Christianity, by Lewis Wallace (American novelist, 1827-1905), published in 1880.

Bennet, MR., MRS., JANE, ELIZABETH, MARY, KITTY, and LYDIA, characters in Jane Austen's 'Pride and Prejudice' (q.v.).

Bennett, ENOCH ARNOLD (1867-1931), became a solicitor's clerk in London and in 1893 assistant editor and subsequently editor of the periodical 'Woman'. After 1900 he devoted himself exclusively to writing, theatre journalism being among his special interests.

His fame as a novelist rests chiefly on 'The Old Wives' Tale' (q.v., 1908) and the 'Clayhanger' series: 'Clayhanger' (1910), 'Hilda Lessways' (1911), 'These Twain' (1916), reprinted as 'The Clayhanger Family' (1925). The 'Five Towns' which figure prominently in these works are Tunstall, Burslem, Hanley, Stoke-upon-Trent, and Longton, centres of the pottery industry; and the features, often ugly and sordid, of this background are skilfully woven into stories of lives which he presents dispassionately, with an in-

finite delight in significant detail. Among Bennett's other best-known works are: 'Riceyman Steps' (1923), 'The Grand Babylon Hotel' (1902), 'Milestones' (play, with E. Knoblock), and 'The Matador of the Five Towns' (short stories, 1912).

Benoît de Sainte-Maure, a 12th-cent. *trouvère* (q.v.). His best-known work is the 'Roman de Troie', which served as a source on which many subsequent writers drew, including Boccaccio, followed by Chaucer and Shakespeare, in the story of 'Troilus and Cressida'.

Benson, EDWARD FREDERIC (1867-1940), the author of the popular novel 'Dodo' (1893), and many other stories.

Benson, STELLA (1892-1933), novelist, whose chief works are 'Living Alone' (1919), 'The Poor Man' (1922), 'Goodbye, Stranger' (1926), 'Worlds within Worlds' (1928), 'Tobit Transplanted' (1931), and her 'Collected Short Stories' (1936).

Bentham, JEREMY (1748-1832), published anonymously in 1776 his 'Fragment on Government', in which he first sketches his theory of government. In 1789 he published his 'Introduction to Principles of Morals and Legislation'. Besides these he produced a number of works on ethics, jurisprudence, logic, and political economy, his influence proving greatest in the first two of these spheres.

It is the political and ethical theory of 'Utility' by which Bentham is principally remembered. 'It is the greatest happiness of the greatest number that is the measure of right and wrong.' He also propounded a number of reforms in the administration of English justice, which have since his time been applied. In 1824 Bentham, with the assistance of James Mill (q.v.), founded the 'Westminster Review', the organ of the philosophical radicals, which lasted until 1907.

Bentley, EDMUND CLERIHEW (1875-1956), author of 'Trent's Last Case' (1913), a famous detective story. He invented the clerihew (q.v.).

Bentley, RICHARD (1662-1742), was brought into great repute as a scholar by his 'Epistola ad Millium' in 1691, a critical letter in Latin on the Greek dramatists. He became keeper of the king's libraries in 1694. During 1697-9 he was engaged in the famous controversy relating to the 'Epistles of Phalaris' (see *Phalaris*), which he proved to be spurious. In 1699 he was appointed Master of Trinity College, Cambridge. Among his greatest critical works were his bold revisions of the text of Horace and Manilius. His arbitrary revision of Milton's 'Paradise Lost', on the other hand, was a venture in a field unsuited to his genius. Bentley is caricatured by Pope in 'The Dunciad' (Bk. IV, 201 et seq.).

Benvolio, a character in Shakespeare's 'Romeo and Juliet' (q.v.).

Benwick, CAPTAIN, a character in Jane Austen's 'Persuasion' (q.v.).

Beowulf, an Old English poem of some 3,200 lines, perhaps the earliest considerable poem in any modern language. The manuscript, of the late 10th cent., formed part of the collection of Sir Robert Bruce Cotton, whence it passed into the British Museum.

The poem opens with praise of the deeds of the Danes, Scyld their king, and his descendants. One of these, Hrothgar, builds a great hall, Heorot. The monster Grendel enters the hall at night and carries off thirty of Hrothgar's thanes, and haunts the hall for twelve years, accomplishing more murders. Beowulf, the nephew of Higelac, king of the Geats, comes with fourteen companions across the sea to give assistance. Beowulf and his men sleep in the hall; Grendel breaks in and seizes Beowulf, who unarmed wrestles with him and tears out his arm. Grendel, mortally wounded, makes off to his lair. Grendel's mother, a water-hag, enters the hall to revenge her son, and carries off Aeschere, the counsellor of Hrothgar. Beowulf dives into the mere where the witch's lair is, and fights with her. She nearly kills him, but his woven armour, with God's assistance, saves him, and he cuts off her head. Beowulf and his Geats return to their own land.

After the death of Higelac and Heardred his son, Beowulf succeeds to the kingdom of the Geats, where he reigns for fifty years. A dragon devastates the country. Beowulf and eleven companions go out to meet it. All the companions, save Wiglaf, fly to a wood. Beowulf's sword breaks, and the dragon sets its teeth in Beowulf's neck. Wiglaf wounds it, and its strength wanes. Beowulf kills it, but is mortally wounded. Wiglaf rebukes his companions and sends word of Beowulf's death. Beowulf's body is burnt on a pyre, with his armour.

It is possible to fix the date of the historical events in the first part of the 6th cent. The date of the composition of the poem is more uncertain; it has been strongly argued that it is the work of a Christian poet of the 8th cent.

There are good editions of the poem by F. Klaeber (1922) and C. L. Wrenn (1953) and a number of translations, one of them by William Morris in collaboration with A. J. Wyatt (1892).

Beppo: A Venetian Story, a poem by Lord Byron (q.v.) (1818).

Béranger, PIERRE JEAN DE (1780-1857), French poet, the author of popular light verse (*chansons*), usually cheerful satire of contemporary society and events.

Bergamask or BERGOMASK, a dance 'framed in imitation of the people of Bergamo' (a province in the state of Venice) (Nares), referred to in Shakespeare's 'A Midsummer Night's Dream', v. 360.

Bergerac, CYRANO DE (1619-55), a French soldier, and an author of comedies. He is the subject of a highly successful play by the French dramatist, Edmond Rostand (1898).

Bergson, HENRI (1859-1941), French philosopher. His principal works include: 'Matière et mémoire' (1896), 'L'Évolution créatrice' (1907), 'La perception du changement' (Oxford lecture, 1911).

Berkeley, GEORGE (1685-1753), philosopher, educated at Trinity College, Dublin. He came to England in 1713, and became associated with Steele, Addison, Pope, Swift, and others.

His chief works were the 'Essay towards a New Theory of Vision' (1709) and the 'Principles of Human Knowledge' (1710). His dialogues of 'Alciphron' (1732) combated deism.

Berkeley takes up the evolution of English philosophy where Locke left it (see *Essay concerning the Human Understanding*), and his work is primarily a destructive criticism of Locke's external, material, reality. According to him, spirit is the only real cause or power. Berkeley was a master of English prose; he is remarkable for his lucidity, grace, and dignity of expression.

Bermoothes, THE, in Shakespeare's 'The Tempest', I. ii, are the Bermuda islands.

Bermudas, The, a poem by Marvell (q.v.).

Bernard, ST. (1090-1153), a great French ecclesiastic, founder of the abbey of Clairvaux, one of the 'Latin Fathers', the glory of the Cistercian order, and practically dictator of Christendom. He was an adversary of Abélard (q.v.), and left some remarkable letters and treatises.

Bernardines, see *Cistercians.*

Bernard of Morlaix, a Benedictine monk of the monastery of Cluny in Burgundy, lived in the 12th cent., and was author of the beautiful Latin poem, 'De Contemptu Mundi', which inspired the hymn, 'Jerusalem the Golden', by J. M. Neale (q.v.).

Berners, BELLE or ISOPEL, see *Belle Berners.*

Berners, JOHN BOURCHIER, *second Baron* (1467-1533), statesman and author. He translated the 'Chronicles' of Froissart (q.v.) (1523-5); 'Huon of Bordeaux' (q.v., probably printed in 1534); Guevara's 'El Relox de Principes' under the title of the 'Golden Boke of Marcus Aurelius' (1535).

Berners, JULIANA, see *Book of St. Albans.*

Bernhardt, SARAH (ROSINE BERNARD) (1844-1923), a celebrated French actress, partly of Jewish descent. Her successes were largely due to her beautiful voice and magnetic personality. She was frequently seen in London.

Bernstein, BARONESS, see *Virginians (The).*

Berowne or BIRON, in Shakespeare's 'Love's Labour's Lost' (q.v.), one of the lords attending the king of Navarre.

Berserk, BERSERKER (Icelandic), a Norse name for a warrior who fought in the battlefield with a frenzied fury known as the 'berserker rage'.

Bertha, a character (1) in Scott's 'Count Robert of Paris'; (2) in Dickens's 'The Cricket on the Hearth'.

Bertram, COUNT OF ROUSILLON, a character in Shakespeare's 'All's Well that Ends Well' (q.v.).

Bertram, HARRY, a character in Scott's 'Guy Mannering' (q.v.).

Bertram, SIR THOMAS and LADY, and their sons and daughters, characters in Jane Austen's 'Mansfield Park' (q.v.).

Besant, MRS. ANNIE (1847-1933), *née* WOOD, an ardent supporter of Liberal causes, once President of the Theosophical Society, and active in the cause of Indian self-government.

Besant, SIR WALTER (1836-1901), became acquainted in 1869 with James Rice, with whom he collaborated in several novels, including 'The Golden Butterfly' (1876) and 'The Chaplain of the Fleet' (1881). From 1882 he continued to write fiction without collaboration, chiefly based on historical incident. In 'All Sorts and Conditions of Men' (1882) and 'Children of Gibeon' (1886) he called attention to social evils in East London. In 1894 Besant commenced the 'Survey of London', which he unfortunately left unfinished (the work appeared in 1902-12). His 'Autobiography' appeared in 1902.

Bestiaries, medieval treatises derived from the Greek Physiologus, which was a collection of some fifty fabulous anecdotes from natural history, of a moralizing and symbolical character. It was translated into many languages. In the 12th cent. additions began to be made to the Latin version from the popular encyclopaedia of the Middle Ages, the 'Etymologiae' of Isidore of Seville (q.v.). The bestiaries were often richly illustrated with miniatures, especially those written in England in the 12th and 13th cents.

Bethnal Green, see *Beggar's Daughter of Bednall Green*.

Betjeman, SIR JOHN (1906-   ), poet. His books of verse include 'Continual Dew' (1937), 'Old Lights for New Chancels' (1940), and 'A Few Late Chrysanthemums' (1954). His 'Collected Poems' were published in 1958, and 'Summoned by Bells', an autobiography in verse, in 1960. He became Poet Laureate in 1972.

Betrothed, The, a novel by Sir W. Scott (q.v.) (1825).
    The scene is laid in the Welsh Marches, in the reign of Henry II.

Betterton, MRS. (*d.* 1711), the wife of Thomas Betterton (q.v.), the first notable actress on the English stage (until 1660 female parts were taken by men or boys).

Betterton, THOMAS (1635?-1710), actor and dramatist, joined Sir John D'Avenant's company at Lincoln's Inn Fields in 1661, and was associated in the management of the Dorset Garden Theatre from 1671. He was a man of high character, and was much esteemed as an actor by his contemporaries.

Betty, MISS, in Fielding's 'Amelia', the spiteful and rapacious sister of the heroine.

Beulah, LAND OF, see Isa. lxii. 4. In Bunyan's 'The Pilgrim's Progress' it is beyond the valley of the Shadow of Death and where the pilgrims were in sight of the Heavenly City.

Bevis of Hampton, a popular verse romance of 4,000 lines, of the early 14th cent., translated from the French.

Beyle, HENRI, see *Stendhal*.

Bezonian, from Italian *bisogno*, a raw recruit, knave, rascal. 'Under which king, Bezonian? speak, or die' (Shakespeare, '2 Henry IV', v. iii. 116).

Bianca, (1) a character in Shakespeare's 'The Taming of the Shrew' (q.v.); (2) in his 'Othello' (q.v.), Cassio's mistress.

BIAΘANATOΣ [Biathanatos], A Declaration of that Paradoxe or Thesis that Self-Homicide is not so Naturally Sinne, by John Donne (q.v.) (1624).

Bible, THE. (1) THE OLD TESTAMENT. The oldest Hebrew manuscripts of the O.T. date only from the 9th-11th cents. A.D. The Greek translation known as the *Septuagint* (q.v.), of the 3rd cent. B.C., is the most important of the ancient versions. About the end of the 2nd cent. A.D. the Old Latin Version, based on the Septuagint was made. It was superseded by Jerome's Latin text, known as the *Vulgate* (q.v.).

    (2) THE NEW TESTAMENT. Of this we possess manuscripts in Greek, and manuscripts of translations from the Greek into Latin, Syriac, and Coptic. The most important of these are the Greek, of which the chief are the *Codex Vaticanus* and the *Codex Sinaiticus*, uncial manuscripts of the 4th cent.; there is also the *Codex Alexandrinus* (5th cent.).

    See also *Bible (The English)*, *Mazarin Bible*, *Polyglot Bible*, and *Luther*.

Bible, THE ENGLISH. Apart from paraphrases at one time attributed to Cædmon (q.v.) and the translation by Bede (q.v.) of part of the Gospel of St. John, the earliest attempts at translation into English of the Holy Scriptures are the 9th- and 10th-cent. glosses, and Ælfric's translation of the O.T. at the close of the 10th cent. After this little was done until the time of Wycliffe (q.v.), to whom and his followers we owe two 14th-cent. versions, the first complete renderings into English of the Scriptures.

    William Tyndale (q.v.) was the first to translate the N.T. into English from the Greek text; this he probably did in Wittenberg, the translation being printed first at Cologne, and when this was interrupted, at Worms (1525-6). Our 'Authorized Version' (see below) is essentially the text of Tyndale. The complete English

Bible that bears the name of Miles Coverdale (q.v.) was printed in 1535. The Prayer-book text of the Psalms is largely Coverdale's version.

The 'Great Bible', also called 'Cranmer's Bible', was brought out in 1539 under the auspices of Henry VIII; Coverdale was placed by Cromwell in charge of its preparation. The printing of it was begun in Paris and finished in London.

During Mary's reign, the reformers took refuge, some in Frankfort-on-the-Main, some in Geneva, where in 1560 appeared the Genevan or 'Breeches Bible' (q.v.). It had a marginal commentary which proved agreeable to the Puritans.

The 'Authorized Version' arose out of a conference at Hampton Court, convened by James I in 1604 (it was not authorized by any official pronouncement) and appeared in 1611. It is practically the version of Tyndale with some admixture from Wycliffe.

In 1870 the Convocation of Canterbury appointed a committee to consider the question of revision, and two companies were constituted to revise the authorized versions of the O.T. and N.T. respectively. The revised text was published, of the N.T. in 1881, of the O.T. in 1885. That of the N.T. was unfavourably received, owing to many irritating and apparently unnecessary alterations of familiar passages. The 'Revised Version' of the O.T., though not altogether free from these, was in many respects an improvement on the authorized text. In 1922 the Revd. James Moffat produced a 'New Translation of the New Testament', and in 1924 'The Old Testament, a new Translation', both of which caused some controversy. The Rt. Revd. Monsignor Ronald Knox (q.v.) published a new translation of the Bible based on the Vulgate text; the N.T. in 1945 and the O.T. in 1949.

In 1947 a new translation of the Bible into modern English was undertaken by a Joint Committee of all the major churches (except the Roman Catholic) in the British Isles. The work was to be carried out by panels of translators for the O.T., Apocrypha, and N.T., with the help of literary advisers, and published by the University Presses of Oxford and Cambridge. 'The New English Bible' N.T. was published in 1961 and the O.T. and Apocrypha in 1970.

Bible in Spain, The, by George Borrow (q.v.) (1843).

Borrow travelled in Spain as colporteur of bibles from 1835 to 1840, and this book is an account of the adventures that he met with at the time of the Carlist troubles. It is impossible to say how far the incidents recounted actually occurred; but the vivid picture of Spain is unquestionably true, and the work is one of the best of English books of travel.

Bibliographical Society, THE, founded in 1892. It issued in 1926 the invaluable 'Short-Title Catalogue of English Books, 1475-1640'.

Bickerstaff, ISAAC, a fictitious person invented by Swift (q.v.). A cobbler, John Partridge, had published predictions in the form of an almanac. Swift in the beginning of 1708 produced 'Predictions for the ensuing year, by Isaac Bickerstaff', in which he foretold the death of Partridge on 29 March. On 30 March he published a letter giving an account of Partridge's end. Partridge indignantly protested that he was still alive, but Swift retorted in a 'Vindication' proving that he was really dead. Other writers took up the joke, and Steele, when he launched 'The Tatler' in 1709, adopted the name of Bickerstaff for the supposed author.

Bierce, AMBROSE (1842-1914?), American writer. He served in the Civil War and afterwards became a prominent journalist. He published much, and collected his writings together in twelve volumes (1909-12), but is best known for his short stories, realistic, sardonic, and strongly influenced by E. A. Poe (q.v.). In 1913 he went to Mexico and disappeared mysteriously, it is thought in the fighting of the Civil War.

Big Brother, in Orwell's 'Nineteen Eighty-four' (q.v.), is the head of the Party, who never appears in person, but whose portrait in every public place, with the caption *Big Brother is watching you*, is inescapable.

Big-endians and Little-endians, see *Gulliver's Travels*.

Biglow Papers, see *Lowell (J. R.)*.

Billickin, MRS., a character in Dickens's 'Edwin Drood' (q.v.).

Billings, JOSH, see *Shaw (H. W.)*.

Billingsgate, one of the gates of London on the river side, and hence the fish market there. There are frequent references in 17th-cent. literature to the abusive language of the Billingsgate market; hence foul language is called 'billingsgate'.

Billy Budd, Sailor, a short novel by H. Melville (q.v.), published posthumously in 1924. Billy Budd, a handsome and innocent sailor in an English naval ship, is persecuted by a malevolent petty officer, Claggart. Billy unintentionally kills Claggart, and Captain Vere, though recognizing his true character, has no alternative but to have him hanged. Benjamin Britten (q.v.) wrote an opera (1951) to a libretto from the story, written by E. M. Forster (q.v.) and Eric Crozier.

Bingley, CHARLES, a character in Jane Austen's 'Pride and Prejudice' (q.v.).

Binyon, LAURENCE (1869–1943), poet, keeper of prints and drawings in the British Museum, noted as an authority in many branches of art, especially Oriental painting. He was the author of many volumes of poems, of which the first was 'Lyric Poems' (1894), and of some plays. His poem 'For the Fallen' (1914) contains the lines:

They shall grow not old, as we that are
　　left grow old:
Age shall not weary them, nor the years
　　condemn.
At the going down of the sun and in the
　　morning
We will remember them.

Binyon also translated Dante's 'Divina Commedia' (1933–43).

Biographia Literaria, a literary autobiography by S. T. Coleridge (q.v.) (1817).

The autobiographical thread is slender. The work consists in the main of a discussion of the philosophy of Kant, Fichte, and Schelling, and a criticism of Wordsworth's poetry.

Biography, the history of the life of an individual; recognized as a literary form from the earliest times. Asser's 'Life of Alfred' is perhaps the earliest biography in English. Other famous biographies are Harpsfield's 'Thomas More', Walton's 'Lives', Johnson's 'Lives of the Poets', Boswell's 'Johnson', Lockhart's 'Life of Scott', etc. In the 20th cent. Lytton Strachey (q.v.) brought a new method to the form, as expounded in his preface to 'Eminent Victorians', which had a lasting influence.

Bion (*fl. c.* 100 B.C.), a pastoral poet of Smyrna, an imitator of Theocritus. He died by poison. He is best known for his lament for Adonis, on which Shelley partly modelled his 'Adonais'. He is generally coupled with Moschus (q.v.).

Birmingham, GEORGE A., pen-name of the REVD. JAMES OWEN HANNAY (1865–1950), author of many light novels, mainly in an Irish setting, including 'Spanish Gold', 'General John Regah', etc.

Birnam Wood, see *Macbeth*.

Biron, see *Berowne*.

Birrell, AUGUSTINE (1850–1933), president of the Board of Education, 1905–7; chief secretary for Ireland, 1907–16; author of 'Obiter Dicta' (1884, 1887, 1924), 'William Hazlitt' (1902), 'Andrew Marvell' (1905). An acute literary critic.

Bishop Blougram's Apology, a poem by R. Browning (q.v.), included in 'Men and Women' (1855).

The poem is a casuistical apology for the position of a beneficed priest whose belief does not extend to all the doctrines of the Roman Catholic religion.

Bishop Hatto: a legend of the 10th cent. relates that Hatto, archbishop of Mainz, at a time of famine (970) assembled a company of poor people in a barn and burnt them to death. He was pursued by an army of mice and was devoured by them. The legend is told in 'Coryat's Crudities', and in a poem by Southey (q.v.).

The historical Bishop Hatto was not guilty of this atrocity.

Bismarck, OTTO EDUARD LEOPOLD, PRINCE VON (1815-98), known as 'The Iron Chancellor', became Prussian prime minister in 1862, and under his administration were fought the war against Denmark of 1864 and the war against Austria of 1866. In 1870-1 ensued the war with France, and the German Empire was constituted in 1871 with Bismarck as its first chancellor. Having incurred the displeasure of the Emperor William II, he resigned in 1890.

Black Beauty, see *Sewell.*

Black Bess, the mare of Dick Turpin (q.v.).

Black Book of Carmarthen, THE, a Welsh manuscript of the 12th cent., containing a collection of ancient Welsh poetry.

Black Death, THE, the bubonic plague which, coming from the East, devastated Europe near the middle of the 14th cent., and caused great mortality in England in 1348-9; sometimes also the recurrences of the epidemic in 1360 and 1379.

Black Douglas, see *Douglas (The Black).*

Black Dwarf, The, a novel by Scott (q.v.), in the first series of the 'Tales of My Landlord' (1816).

Black-eyed Susan, see *Gay (J.).*

Black Friars, members of the order of the Dominicans, founded at the beginning of the 13th cent. by St. Dominic, so called from the colour of their dress.

Blackfriars Theatre, THE, an apartment in the dissolved monastery of the Black Friars (q.v.) adapted for a play-house and purchased by James Burbage (q.v.) in 1596. It was handed over to the Children of the Chapel (see *Paul's, Children of*) but reverted to Richard Burbage (q.v.) in 1608. After this date Shakespeare acted there.

Black Hole of Calcutta, the punishment cell of the barracks in Fort William, Calcutta, into which, by order of Suraja Dowlah, 146 Europeans were thrust for a night in 1756, of whom only 23 survived till the morning.

Black Letter, type reproducing the *Jexbura* book-script used for liturgical and other formal writing from the 12th until the 15th cent., the most elaborate of the scripts known as 'Gothic'.

Black Michael, the king's wicked brother in 'The Prisoner of Zenda' (q.v.).

Black Monks, the Benedictines (q.v.), so called from the colour of their dress.

Blackmore, SIR RICHARD (*d.* 1729), physician to Queen Anne, produced some indifferent poems of great length, and 'The Creation, a philosophical poem' (1712), which was warmly praised by Dr. Johnson.

Blackmore, RICHARD DODDRIDGE (1825-1900), published some volumes of verse and a number of novels, of which the most famous was 'Lorna Doone' (q.v.) (1869).

Blackpool, STEPHEN, a character in Dickens's 'Hard Times' (q.v.).

Black Prince, THE, a name given to Edward, the eldest son of Edward III (1330-76).

Black Rod, the Chief Gentleman Usher of the Lord Chamberlain's department of the royal household, who is also usher to the House of Lords.

Blackstick, FAIRY, a character in Thackeray's 'The Rose and the Ring'.

Blackstone, SIR WILLIAM (1723-80), the first Vinerian professor of English law at Oxford. His fame rests on his 'Commentaries on the Laws of England' (1765-9).

Blackwood's Edinburgh Magazine, a monthly periodical started in 1817 by William Blackwood (1776-1834) the publisher, as a rival to the 'Edinburgh Review' (q.v.), of a less ponderous kind than the 'Quarterly' (q.v.). It had John Wilson, J. G. Lockhart, and James Hogg (qq.v.) on its staff. 'Blackwood's' was then

Tory in politics, and the avowed enemy, in literary matters, of the 'Cockney School', i.e. Lamb, Hazlitt, and in particular Leigh Hunt. De Quincey was among the early contributors.

Blair, ERIC, see *Orwell*.

Blair, HUGH (1718-1800), Scottish divine and professor of rhetoric, is remembered for his famous sermons (5 vols., 1777-1801), and 'Lectures on Rhetoric'.

Blair, ROBERT (1699-1746), published in 1743 'The Grave', a didactic poem of some 800 lines of blank verse, in which he celebrates death, the solitude of the tomb, and the anguish of bereavement. The poem compares favourably with the somewhat similar 'Night Thoughts' (q.v.) of Edward Young, with which it was almost exactly contemporary. It was later illustrated by William Blake (q.v.).

Blaize, FARMER, in Meredith's 'The Ordeal of Richard Feverel', Lucy Feverel's uncle.

Blake, WILLIAM (1757-1827), did not go to school, but was apprenticed to James Basire, engraver. His earliest poems are contained in 'Poetical Sketches', published, in 1783 at the expense of his friends, Flaxman and Mrs. Mathew. In 1789 he engraved and published his 'Songs of Innocence', in which he first showed the mystical cast of his mind. In 1790 Blake engraved his principal prose work, the 'Marriage of Heaven and Hell', in which he takes up his revolutionary position, of which the main features are the denial of the reality of matter, the denial of eternal punishment, and the denial of authority. The 'Songs of Experience' (1794) are in marked contrast with the 'Songs of Innocence'. The brightness of the earlier work gives place to a sense of gloom and mystery, and of the power of evil. They include the famous 'Tiger! Tiger! burning bright'. In 1804 Blake began to engrave his final symbolic works, 'Milton' and 'Jerusalem'. His later minor poems include some beautiful lyrics, such as 'The Morning' and 'The Land of Dreams'; also the fragmentary 'The Everlasting

Gospel', his own interpretation of the Gospel of Christ.

Blake made, and sometimes engraved, designs in illustration of many works besides his own poems, notably Young's 'Night Thoughts', Blair's 'The Grave', Gray's poems, the Book of Job, and the 'Divina Commedia'. The same symbolic and imaginative qualities are evident in his drawings as in his poems.

Blanchefleur or BLANCHEFLOUR, see *Flores and Blancheflour*.

Blandamour, in Spenser's 'Faerie Queene', Bk. IV, a 'jolly youthful knight', who consorts with Paridell and Duessa (qq.v.).

Blank verse, verse without rhyme, especially the iambic pentameter or unrhymed heroic, the regular measure of English dramatic and epic poetry. This metre was introduced into England in the 16th cent. by Surrey (q.v.), who translated two books of the 'Aeneid' in that form. Modelled on classical metres, his verse was formless and unnatural but is important historically. Blank verse was used in the early tragedies, e.g. in Kyd's 'The Spanish Tragedy' (q.v.). It still suffered from a rough monotony and a tendency to make a unit of each line. Marlowe's verse showed a great advance in this respect: under his influence blank verse rhythms became freer. This development, shared by Elizabethan drama generally, can be traced in Shakespeare's plays: from the 'end-stopped' (i.e. the sense ending with the line) verses of his early plays, to the 'over-flow' lines of his later tragedies where the unit of rhythm is the phrase within the line. With the Caroline dramatists, blank verse, though still pleasant, tended to become weaker and more formless.

Milton's use of blank verse, defended against the growing popularity of the heroic couplet in his preface to 'Paradise Lost', had a great influence on later poets. Its characteristics were a rigid iambic form, weighted with a heavily Latinized vocabulary and a large use of proper names, but saved from monotony by a great variation in the position of the caesura and by skilful onomatopoeic effects. The blank verse of Thomson and others which was popular throughout the 18th cent. is modelled on that of Milton, though less taut and strenuous in form. Wordsworth (in 'The Prelude', etc.) brought a new ease to the metre, more akin to Cowper's conversational verses, though capable of rhetorical passages. Tennyson's skill renewed the general popularity of blank verse: he often gave, by his use of onomatopoeia, a musical effect like that of rhymed verse. Bridges (q.v.), an expert in metrical theory and Miltonic prosody in particular, was responsible for new and individual developments in blank-verse technique.

Blarney, a village near Cork. In the Castle of Blarney there is an inscribed stone. The popular saying is that any one who kisses the 'Blarney stone' will ever after have 'a cajoling tongue and the art of flattery or of telling lies with unblushing effrontery'.

Blarney, LADY, a character in Goldsmith's 'The Vicar of Wakefield' (q.v.).

Blatant Beast, THE, in Spenser's 'Faerie Queene' (VI. xii), a monster, the personification of the calumnious voice of the world. Sir Calidore pursues it and chains it up. But finally it breaks the chain, 'and now he raungeth through the world again'.

Blattergowl, MR., in Scott's 'The Antiquary' (q.v.), the minister of Trotcosey.

Bleak House, a novel by Dickens (q.v.) (1852–3).

The book contains a vigorous satire on the abuses of the old court of Chancery. The tale centres in the fortunes of Richard Carstone, a futile youth, and his amiable cousin Ada Clare. They are wards of the court in the case of Jarndyce and Jarndyce, concerned with the distribution of an estate. They fall in love and secretly marry. The weak Richard, lured by the fortune that is to be his when the case is settled, sinks gradually to ruin and death, and the case of Jarndyce and Jarndyce

comes to an end when the costs have absorbed the whole estate in dispute.

Ada has for a companion Esther Summerson, a supposed orphan, and the narrative is written partly as though from her pen.

Sir Leicester Dedlock is devotedly attached to his beautiful wife, Lady Dedlock, who before her marriage has loved a certain Captain Hawdon and has become the mother of a daughter, whom she believes dead. Hawdon is supposed to have perished at sea. In fact the daughter lives in the person of Esther Summerson, and Hawdon in that of a penniless scrivener. Lady Dedlock discovers the fact of his existence, and her uneasiness awakens the cunning old lawyer Tulkinghorn to the existence of a mystery. Her former lover dies, but Tulkinghorn traces out the facts and tells Lady Dedlock that he is going to expose her next day to her husband. That night Tulkinghorn is murdered. Bucket, the detective, reveals to the baronet what Tulkinghorn had discovered, and arrests a former French maid of Lady Dedlock who has committed the murder. Lady Dedlock flies from the house in despair, and is found dead near the grave of her lover.

Much of the story is occupied with Esther's devotion to John Jarndyce; her acceptance of his offer of marriage from a sense of duty and gratitude, though she loves a young doctor, Woodcourt; and Jarndyce's surrender of her to Woodcourt.

There are interesting minor characters, Harold Skimpole (drawn 'in the light externals of character' from Leigh Hunt), who disguises his utter selfishness under an assumption of childish irresponsibility; Mrs. Jellyby, who sacrifices her family to her selfish addiction to professional philanthropy; Jo, the crossing-sweeper, who is chivied by the police to his death; Chadband, the pious, eloquent humbug; Turveydrop, the model of deportment; Miss Flite, the little lunatic lady who haunts the Chancery courts; and

Jarndyce's friend, the irascible and generous Boythorn (drawn from Walter Savage Landor).

Blenheim, BATTLE OF, in 1704. For poems on the battle see *Addison* and *Southey*.

Blenheim Palace, near Woodstock, Oxfordshire, erected by the nation for the duke of Marlborough after the victory of Blenheim. It was built on the designs of Sir John Vanbrugh (q.v.).

Blessed Damozel, The, a poem by D. G. Rossetti (q.v.), of which the first version appeared in 'The Germ' (q.v.) (1850), and many revised versions subsequently.

In this poem the maiden, 'one of God's choristers', leans out from the rampart of heaven, sees the worlds below and the souls mounting up to God, and prays that she may be united once more with the lover whom she has left on earth, and whose own comments are introduced parenthetically.

Blifil, a character in Fielding's 'Tom Jones' (q.v.), the extreme of hypocritical meanness.

Bligh, WILLIAM (1754–1817), the commander of H.M.S. 'Bounty' (q.v.).

Blimber, DR., and his daughter COR-NELIA, characters in Dickens's 'Dombey and Son' (q.v.).

Blind Beggar of Bethnal Green, see *Beggar's Daughter of Bednall Green*.

Blind Harry, see *Henry the Minstrel*.

Blondel de Nesle, French poet, in legend a friend of Richard Cœur de Lion. Richard was imprisoned by the duke of Austria in 1192. Blondel discovered him by singing under the walls of Richard's prison a song in French that he and the king had composed together; half-way through the song he paused, and Richard completed it. Blondel returned to England and reported where the king was.

Bloody Brother, *The, or Rollo, Duke of Normandy,* a play by J. Fletcher (q.v.), Jonson (q.v.), and perhaps other collaborators, produced about 1616.

Bloom, LEOPOLD, a character in James Joyce's 'Ulysses' (q.v.).

Bloomfield, ROBERT (1766–1823), worked as an agricultural labourer and then as a shoemaker in London, enduring extreme poverty. He is remembered as author of the poem, 'The Farmer's Boy' (1800) of which 26,000 copies were sold in three years. The similarity of his circumstances to those of John Clare (q.v.) leads to their being frequently compared, but the talent of Bloomfield was inferior to that of Clare.

Bloomsbury Group, the name given to a group of friends who began to meet about 1906 and included, among many others, John Maynard Keynes, Lytton Strachey, Virginia and Leonard Woolf, Vanessa and Clive Bell, David Garnett, Duncan Grant, E. M. Forster, and Roger Fry. The association derived its philosophy from the central passage of G. E. Moore's 'Principia Ethica': 'By far the most valuable things . . . are . . . the pleasures of human intercourse and the enjoyment of beautiful objects; . . . it is they . . . that form the rational ultimate end of social progress.'

Blot in the 'Scutcheon, A, a tragedy in three acts, by R. Browning (q.v.), performed at Covent Garden Theatre in 1843.

Blougram, BISHOP, see *Bishop Blougram's Apology*.

Blount, MARTHA (1690–1762), the friend of Pope to whom he dedicated his 'Epistle on Women' ('Moral Essays') and his Epistles 'To a Young Lady with the Works of Voiture' and 'To the same on her leaving the Town'.

Blouzelinda, a shepherdess in 'The Shepherd's Week' of J. Gay (q.v.).

Blue Beard, a popular tale in an oriental setting, from the French of Perrault (q.v.).

A man of great wealth, but of evil reputation because he has married several wives who have disappeared, asks for the hand of Fatima. She is prevailed on to marry him. Blue Beard leaves the keys of all his treasures to his young wife, but enjoins her not to make use of the key of a particular room. Overcome by curiosity, she opens this room and finds in it the bodies of Blue Beard's previous wives. Horror-struck, she drops the key, which becomes indelibly stained with blood. Blue Beard returns, discovers her disobedience, and orders her death. She begs for a little delay, 'Sister Anne' sees her brothers arriving, and Blue Beard is killed before he can execute the sentence.

Blue-coat School, a charity school of which the pupils wear the almoner's blue coat. Of these schools there are many in England, the most noted being Christ's Hospital (q.v.), formerly in London, founded by Edward VI.

Blue Stocking, a woman having or affecting literary tastes. The origin of the term is to be found in the evening parties held about 1750 in the houses of Mrs. Vesey, Mrs. Montagu, and Mrs. Ord, at which conversations on literary subjects took place in which eminent men of letters often took part. Many of those who attended, among them Benjamin Stillingfleet, habitually wore blue worsted, in lieu of black silk, stockings. Hannah More (q.v.) wrote a poem 'Bas Bleu, or Conversation' on the subject.

Blumine, in Carlyle's 'Sartor Resartus' (q.v.), the lady with whom Herr Teufelsdröckh falls in love.

Blunden, EDMUND CHARLES (1896–1974), poet and scholar. During the war of 1914–18 he served with the Royal Sussex and his 'Undertones of War' (1928) is an outcome of this experience. After his own poetry (collected edition, 1930; later poems, 1940), his greatest service to poetry has been the researches into and discovery and publication of hitherto unpublished poems of John Clare (q.v.). He also published the first adequate biography of Leigh Hunt (1930), and 'Shelley, a Life Story' (1946). He was professor of poetry at Oxford 1966–8.

Blunt, WILFRID SCAWEN (1840–1922), poet and publicist, author of 'The Love Sonnets of Proteus' (1880) and other poems (complete edition, 1914). His political life and writings were devoted to a defence of nationalism, Irish, Egyptian, and Indian, and to attacks on the methods of British imperialism.

Boadicea, BONDUCA, mis-spellings for BOUDICCA, queen of the Iceni in the east of Britain, who led a revolt against the Romans, but was defeated by Suetonius Paulinus in A.D. 61 and took her own life.

She is the subject of a poem in galliambics by Tennyson; also of a fine ballad by W. Cowper. See also *Bonduca*.

Boanerges, 'sons of thunder', the name given to James and John by Christ (Mark iii. 17).

Boar of the Ardennes, THE WILD, William Count de la Marck, who figures in Scott's 'Quentin Durward' (q.v.).

Boar's Head Inn, THE, celebrated in connection with Falstaff (in Shakespeare's 'Henry IV'), was in Eastcheap, where the statue of William IV now stands.

Bob and wheel: in prosody the *wheel* is a set of short lines forming the concluding part of a stanza, usually five in number, varying in form and length, but generally having the first line rhyming with the last, and often the intervening lines rhyming with each other; the first line in some types is very short, and is then called the *bob*.

Bobadill, CAPTAIN, in Jonson's 'Every Man in his Humour' (q.v.), an old soldier, vain, boastful, and cowardly.

Bobby, a slang nickname for a policeman after Robert Peel, who was home secretary when the Police Act was passed in 1828.

Boccaccio, GIOVANNI (1313–75), Italian writer and humanist, born at or near Florence. His formative years, from about 1325 until 1340, were spent in Naples. He returned to Florence in 1340 and from 1350 onwards was employed on various diplomatic missions by the municipality. His friendship with Petrarch (q.v.) gave a powerful impetus to his classical studies. He wrote a life of Dante (q.v.) and was the first to give a course of public lectures on the 'Divina Commedia' (1373–4). Boccaccio's chief works were: the 'Decameron' (q.v.); 'Filocolo', a prose romance embodying the story of 'Flores and Blancheflour' (q.v.); 'Filostrato', a poem on the story of Troilus and Cressida; and 'Teseida', a poem adapted by Chaucer for his 'Knight's Tale'.

Boccaccio is an important figure in the history of literature, particularly of narrative fiction, and among the poets who found inspiration in his works were Chaucer, Shakespeare, Dryden, Keats, Longfellow, and Tennyson.

Bodleian Library, see *Bodley.*

Bodley, SIR THOMAS (1545-1613), from 1588 to 1596 was English diplomatic representative at The Hague. He devoted the rest of his life and most of his resources to founding at Oxford the great library that bears his name. It was opened in 1602. In 1610 the Stationers' Company undertook to give to the library a copy of every book printed in England. It received also important gifts of books, in its early days, from Laud, Oliver Cromwell, Junius, and Robert Burton (author of 'The Anatomy of Melancholy'); also John Selden's library, given in 1659, and the Rawlinson MSS. in more recent times.

Boece, see *Boëthius.*

Boehme, JACOB (1575-1624), a peasant shoemaker of Görlitz in Germany, a mystic. The doctrines of Boehme strongly influenced W. Law (q.v.).

Boeotia (pron. 'Bē-ō´shia'), a country in central Greece. Its inhabitants were proverbial for dullness of intellect, and 'Boeotian' has come to be used as a derogatory adjective, synonymous with boorish, dull-witted.

Boëthius, ANICIUS MANLIUS SEVERINUS, frequently referred to as 'Boece' in the Middle Ages, born at Rome between A.D. 470 and 475, was consul in 510 and in favour with Theodoric the Great; but incurring his suspicion of plotting against the Gothic rule, was imprisoned and put to death in 525. In prison he wrote the celebrated work, 'De Consolatione Philosophiae', which was translated by King Alfred (q.v.). The 'De Consolatione' was also translated by Chaucer under the title 'Boethius', by Queen Elizabeth, and others.

Boffin, MR. and MRS., characters in Dickens's 'Our Mutual Friend' (q.v.).

Boggley Wallah, THE COLLECTOR OF, Jos Sedley, a character in Thackeray's 'Vanity Fair' (q.v.).

Bohemia, SEA COAST OF: in Shakespeare's 'The Winter's Tale', III. iii, Antigonus says, 'our ship hath touched upon the deserts of Bohemia'. Sometimes quoted as one of the rare instances where Shakespeare failed in general knowledge, since Bohemia is an entirely inland country, but it is possible that at one time the name covered territory bordering on the Adriatic.

Bohemia, Story of the King of, told by Corporal Trim in vol. viii of Sterne's 'Tristram Shandy' (q.v.).

Bohemian, frequently used in the sense of a gipsy of society, especially an artist, literary man, or actor, who leads a free, vagabond, or irregular life, and despises conventionalities. This meaning was introduced into English by Thackeray.

Bohn, HENRY GEORGE (1796-1884), publisher and author. Among Bohn's many publications may be specially mentioned his 'Antiquarian Library' and his famous series of translations of the classics.

Boiardo, MATTEO MARIA (1441?-94), an Italian poet who drew on the legends of Arthur and Charlemagne for his materials. His principal work was the unfinished 'Orlando Innamorato' (q.v.).

Boileau (DESPRÉAUX), NICOLAS (1636-1711), French critic and poet, the friend of Molière, La Fontaine, and Racine, who by his 'Satires', 'Épîtres', and 'Art Poétique', remarkable for discrimination and good sense, did much to form French literary taste, previously vitiated by Spanish and Italian influences. He was greatly admired by Pope, whose 'Essay on Criticism' is modelled on Boileau's 'Art Poétique'.

Bois-Guilbert, SIR BRIAN DE, the fierce Templar in Scott's 'Ivanhoe' (q.v.).

C

Boke of the Duchesse, The, a poem of some 1,300 lines by Chaucer, written in 1369. It is an allegorical lament on the death of Blanche of Lancaster, first wife of John of Gaunt. In a dream the poet joins a hunting party of the Emperor Octovien. He comes upon a knight in black who laments the loss of his lady. The knight tells of her virtues and beauty and their courtship, and in answer to a question declares her dead. The hunting party reappears, a bell strikes twelve, and the poet awakes, with the story of Ceyx and Halcyone, which he had been reading, in his hand.

Boldrewood, ROLF, pseudonym of T. A. BROWNE (q.v.).

Bold Stroke for a Wife, A, a comedy by Mrs. Centlivre (q.v.), produced in 1718.

Bolingbroke, son of John of Gaunt, the future Henry IV, figures in Shakespeare's 'Richard II' (q.v.).

Bolingbroke, HENRY ST. JOHN, *first Viscount* (1678-1751), a supporter of Harley and the Tory party in parliament, became secretary of state in 1710, and was in charge of the negotiations which led to the treaty of Utrecht (1713). He was dismissed from office on the accession of George I and attainted. He fled to France and was secretary of state to James the Pretender, from whose service he was dismissed in 1716. He was pardoned and returned to London in 1725, and settled at Dawley, Middlesex. It is to the following period that his principal political and philosophical writings belong. He contributed to the 'Craftsman' from 1727 to 1735 a number of virulent attacks on the Whig government. In 1736 he wrote 'A Letter on the Spirit of Patriotism', and in 1738 'The Idea of a Patriot King' (published 1749).

After Bolingbroke's death David Mallet published (1754) his collected works including a number of essays of a deistical tendency. These were probably written in connection with Pope's 'Essay on Man' (q.v.).

Bolton, FANNY, a character in Thackeray's 'Pendennis' (q.v.).

Bonduca (Boadicea), a tragedy by J. Fletcher (q.v.), produced some time before March 1619.

Bon Gaultier Ballads, a collection of parodies and light poems by W. E. Aytoun and Sir T. Martin (qq.v.) (1845).

Boniface, the landlord of the inn in Farquhar's 'The Beaux' Stratagem'; whence taken as the generic proper name of innkeepers.

Boniface, ABBOT, in Scott's 'The Monastery' (q.v.), the abbot of Kennaquhair.

Boniface, ST. (680-755), the apostle of Germany, was educated near Winchester. He proceeded to Rome in 718 and thence to Germany, where he organized the Church. He is commemorated on 5 June.

Bonnivard, see *Prisoner of Chillon*.

Bonny Dundee, Graham of Claverhouse (q.v.).

Bonthron, ANTHONY, in Scott's 'The Fair Maid of Perth', a villainous cut-throat.

Booby, SIR THOMAS and LADY, and SQUIRE BOOBY, characters in Fielding's 'Joseph Andrews' (q.v.).

Boojum, in Lewis Carroll's 'The Hunting of the Snark' (q.v.), a dangerous variety of the Snark.

Book of Kells, see *Kells*.

Book of Martyrs, see *Actes and Monuments*.

Book of St. Albans, The, issued (1486) from the press at St. Albans. It contains treatises on hawking, hunting, and heraldry attributed to Juliana Berners, perhaps prioress of the nunnery at Sopwell. The book is a compilation and probably not all by one hand.

Book of Snobs, The, see *Snobs of England*.

Book of the Duchess, The, see *Boke*.

Boone, DANIEL (1735-1820), American pioneer, explorer, and Indian fighter, who played a notable part in the opening up and settlement of Kentucky and Missouri. Byron devotes to him seven stanzas in the eighth canto of 'Don Juan'.

Booth, WILLIAM (1829-1912), popularly known as 'General' Booth, the founder of the Salvation Army (q.v.).

Booth, WILLIAM, the hero of Fielding's 'Amelia'.

Borachio, a large leather bottle used in Spain for wine; hence a drunkard. Shakespeare used it as the name of one of the characters in his 'Much Ado about Nothing' (q.v.), and it occurs in Congreve, Middleton, etc., to signify a drunkard.

Borderers, The, a tragedy by Wordsworth (q.v.), composed in 1795-6.

The gentle Marmaduke, leader (in the reign of Henry III) of a band of Borderers whom he has collected to protect the innocent, is induced by the perfidy of the villainous Oswald to cause the death of the blind old Baron Herbert, whose daughter Idonea he loves, being led to believe that her father intends to sell her into infamy.

Boreas, the north wind.

Borgia, CESARE (1476-1507), favourite son of Pope Alexander VI, notorious for his violence and crimes, yet a man of great military capacity, and an early believer in the unity of Italy.

Borgia, LUCREZIA (1480-1519), daughter of Pope Alexander VI and sister of Cesare Borgia. Her court became a centre for artists, poets, and men of learning, such as Ariosto, Titian, and Aldus Manutius (qq.v.).

Borgia, RODRIGO (1431-1503), Pope Alexander VI, a Spaniard by birth, the father of Cesare and Lucrezia Borgia (qq.v.), elected to the pontificate in 1492.

Boron or BORRON, ROBERT DE, a 12th-13th-cent. French poet, to whom is attributed the authorship of two important parts of the Arthurian cycle of legends.

Borough, The, a poem by Crabbe (q.v.) (1810), in twenty-four 'Letters' describing life and character as seen by the poet in Aldeburgh.

Borrow, GEORGE (1803-81), was articled to a solicitor, but adopted literature as a profession. He edited 'Celebrated Trials, and Remarkable Cases of Criminal Jurisprudence' (1825), and then travelled through England, France, Germany, Russia, Spain, and in the East, studying the languages of the countries he visited. Finally he settled near Oulton Broad in Suffolk. He published a number of books based in part on his own life and travels: 'The Bible in Spain' (q.v.) (1843), 'Lavengro' (q.v.) (1851), 'The Romany Rye' (q.v.) (1857), and 'Wild Wales' (1862). His novels have a peculiar picaresque quality, graphically presenting a succession of gipsies, rogues, and adventures of all kinds, the whole permeated with the spirit of the 'wind on the heath' and of the unconventional. The first three of the above works are largely autobiographical, but the border-line between autobiography and fiction in them is hard to trace.

Bosola, a character in Webster's 'The Duchess of Malfi' (q.v.).

Bossuet, JACQUES BÉNIGNE (1627-1704), a French divine and famous preacher, a controversialist of distinction, and author of many eloquent funeral orations.

Boswell, JAMES (1740-95), the son of Alexander Boswell, Lord Auchinleck, a Scottish judge. He reluctantly studied law at Edinburgh, Glasgow, and Utrecht, his ambition being directed to literature or politics. He made the acquaintance of Samuel Johnson (q.v.) in London in 1763. He travelled on the Continent in 1765-6 and was introduced to General Paoli in Corsica, became absorbed in Corsican affairs, and published 'An Account of Corsica' in 1768, and 'Essays in Favour of the Brave Corsicans' in 1769. Boswell paid frequent visits to Johnson in London (from Edinburgh, where he practised at the bar) between 1772 and 1784, and made a tour in Scotland and the Hebrides with Johnson in 1773. He was elected a member of the Literary Club in 1773 and succeeded to his father's estate in 1782. In 1789 he came to reside in London. His 'Journal of a Tour to the Hebrides' appeared in 1785. He had been storing up materials for his great work, the 'Life of Samuel Johnson', since 1763, and after Johnson's death in 1784 he applied himself to the task under pressure from Malone. The book appeared in 1791, and proved Boswell's extraordinary aptitude and talent as a biographer. While Johnson owes much to Boswell, Boswell's devotion to Johnson was the source of his own fame.

Botanic Garden, The, see *Darwin (E.).*

Botany Bay Eclogues, early poems by Southey (q.v.), written at Oxford in 1794. They take the form of monologues and dialogues by transported felons.

Bothie of Tober-na-Vuolich, The, a poem in English hexameters by Clough (q.v.) (1848), tells the story of the love of Philip Hewson, a young Oxford radical on a reading-party in Scotland, for Elspie, the daughter of a Highland farmer.

Bothwell, JAMES HEPBURN, *fourth earl of* (1536?-78), husband of Mary Queen of Scots, is the subject of a historical poem by W. E. Aytoun (q.v.) (1856), and of a tragedy by Swinburne (q.v.) (1874).

Bothwell, SERGEANT, in Scott's 'Old Mortality', a soldier in Claverhouse's force, who claims the name of Francis Stewart.

Botticelli, SANDRO (1447-1510), a Florentine painter who sought inspiration in the works of Dante and Boccaccio or the classics. His paintings are marked by the freshness of the early Renaissance.

Bottom, NICK, the weaver in Shakespeare's 'A Midsummer Night's Dream' (q.v.).

Bouillon, GODEFROI DE, leader of the First Crusade. He died in 1100. He figures in Scott's 'Count Robert of Paris'.

Bounderby, JOSIAH, a character in Dickens's 'Hard Times' (q.v.).

Bounty, The Mutiny and Piratical Seizure of H.M.S., a narrative by Sir J. Barrow (1831).

H.M.S. 'Bounty', which had been sent to the South Sea Islands to collect breadfruit trees, left Tahiti early in 1789. On April 28 Fletcher Christian and others placed Lt. Bligh, the commander, and 18 of the crew in an open boat and cast them adrift. These eventually reached Timor. The 'Bounty' then sailed to Tahiti, where 16 of the crew were put ashore. These were subsequently arrested and many of them were drowned in H.M.S. 'Pandora'. Fletcher Christian and 8 others with some Tahitians settled at Pitcairn Island. There they founded a colony which was subsequently taken under the protection of the British government. These events form in part the basis of Lord Byron's poem 'The Island' (q.v.).

Bouts-rimés '. . . were the favourites of the French nation for a whole age together . . . a List of Words that rhyme to one another, drawn up by another Hand, and given to a Poet, who was to make a poem to the Rhymes in the same Order.' Addison, 'Spectator', No. 60.

Bovary, Madame, the chief work of Flaubert (q.v.).

Bowdler, THOMAS (1754-1825), M.D., of Edinburgh, published his 'Family Shakespeare', an expurgated edition of the text, in 1818; and prepared on similar lines an edition of Gibbon's 'History'. His works gave rise to the term, 'to bowdlerize'.

Bower of Bliss, THE, in Spenser's 'Faerie Queene', II. xii, the home of Acrasia (q.v.), demolished by Sir Guyon.

Bowery, THE, a street in the south of New York, formerly notorious for its criminal population and distinctive dialect.

Bowge of Court, The, a poem satirizing court life by Skelton (q.v.).

Bowles, WILLIAM LISLE (1762-1850), is remembered chiefly for his 'Fourteen Sonnets' (1789), the first of any merit that had appeared for a long period. They stimulated Coleridge and Southey, and the former made many manuscript copies of them for his friends. In 1806 Bowles published an edition of Pope, which aroused a controversy, with Byron and Campbell as participants, as to the value of Pope's poetry.

Bowling, LIEUTENANT TOM, a character in Smollett's 'Roderick Random'.

Bowling, TOM, the subject of a well-known song by C. Dibdin (q.v.).

Bows, MR., in Thackeray's 'Pendennis' (q.v.), the first fiddler in the orchestra of Mr. Bingley's company.

Bowzybeus, a drunken swain, in the 'Shepherd's Week' of J. Gay (q.v.).

Box and Cox, a farce by J. M. Morton (q.v.) (1847). Box is a journeyman printer, Cox a journeyman hatter. Mrs. Bouncer, a lodging-house keeper, has let the same room to both, taking advantage of the fact that Box is out all night, and Cox out all day, to conceal from each the existence of the other. Discovery comes when Cox unexpectedly gets a holiday. Indignation follows, and complications connected with a widow to whom both have proposed marriage; and finally a general reconciliation. See also *Cox and Box*.

Boyle, CHARLES, *fourth earl of Orrery* (1676-1731), editor of the spurious 'Epistles of Phalaris' (see *Phalaris, Epistles of*).

Boyle, JOHN, *fifth earl of Orrery* (1707-62), son of Charles Boyle (q.v.), was an intimate friend of Swift, Pope, and Johnson (qq.v.). His 'Remarks on the Life and Writings of Dr. Jonathan Swift' were written in a series of letters to his son Hamilton at Christ Church, Oxford, and published in 1751. The letters give a critical account of Swift's character, his life, his relations with Stella and Vanessa, and his friendship with Pope and others, and a discussion of his works.

Boyle Lectures, THE, on religion, established in 1691 under the terms of the will of the Hon. Robert Boyle (1627-91), son of the first earl of Cork, natural philosopher and chemist, one of the founders of the Royal Society.

Boyne, BATTLE OF THE, fought in 1690 in Ireland. William III and the Protestant army defeated James II, who escaped to France.

Boythorn, a character in Dickens's 'Bleak House' (q.v.).

Boz, the pseudonym used by Dickens (q.v.) in his contributions to 'The Morning Chronicle' and in 'The Pickwick Papers'.

Brabantio, in Shakespeare's 'Othello' (q.v.), the father of Desdemona.

Bracegirdle, ANNE (1663?-1748), a famous actress, the friend of Congreve, to the success of whose comedies she largely contributed. She was finally eclipsed by Mrs. Oldfield in 1707 and retired from the stage.

Bracton, BRATTON, or BRETTON, HENRY DE (*d.* 1268), a judge and ecclesiastic, was author of the first attempt at a complete treatise on the laws and customs of England.

Bracy, SIR MAURICE DE, a character in Scott's 'Ivanhoe' (q.v.).

Bradamante, in the 'Orlando Innamorato' and 'Orlando Furioso' (qq.v.), a maiden warrior, sister of Rinaldo.

Braddon, MARY ELIZABETH (MRS. MAXWELL) (1837-1915), became famous by her novel 'Lady Audley's Secret' (1862).

Bradlaugh, CHARLES (1833-91), famous as an advocate of free thought, was elected M.P. for Northampton in 1880, but unseated, having been refused the right to affirm instead of swearing on the Bible. He was re-elected in 1881 and a prolonged struggle ensued, ending in 1886, when he was at last allowed to take his seat. Bradlaugh engaged in several lawsuits to maintain the freedom of the press, and during 1874-85 was associated with the work of Mrs. Besant (q.v.).

Bradley, ANDREW CECIL (1851-1935), brother of F. H. Bradley (q.v.), and literary critic, especially noted for his contributions to Shakespearian scholarship. His best-known works are 'Shakespearean Tragedy' (1904) and 'Oxford Lectures' (1909).

Bradley, EDWARD (1827-89), who wrote under the pseudonym CUTHBERT BEDE, was the author of the 'Adventures of Mr. Verdant Green, an Oxford Freshman' (1853-7).

Bradley, FRANCIS HERBERT (1846-1924), brother of A. C. Bradley (q.v.), published 'Ethical Studies' in 1876, and 'Principles of Logic' in 1883. His

'Appearance and Reality' (1893) was considered an important philosophical work of profound criticism of contemporary metaphysical thought.

Bradley, DR. HENRY (1845-1923), philologist, is principally remembered for his work on the 'Oxford English Dictionary' (q.v.). He succeeded Sir James Murray (q.v.) as chief editor.

Bradshaw's Railway Guide was first published in 1839 in the form of 'Railway Time Tables' by George Bradshaw (1801-53), engraver and printer. These developed into 'Bradshaw's Monthly Railway Guide' in 1841 and continued to be published until May 1961.

Bradstreet, ANNE (*c.* 1612-72), American poet, was born in England but emigrated to Massachusetts in 1630. Her volume of poems, published in England in 1650, was the first literary work of any significance to be produced in the New England colony.

Bradwardine, THE BARON OF, and ROSE, characters in Scott's 'Waverley' (q.v.).

Braes of Yarrow, THE, see *Yarrow*.

Braggadochio, in Spenser's 'Faerie Queene', the typical braggart. His adventures and final exposure and humiliation occur in Bks. II. iii; III. viii; and v. iii.

Brahms, JOHANNES (1833-97), born at Hamburg, a great composer, author of many beautiful songs, of examples of every kind of chamber music, and of four symphonies.

Brainworm, a character in Jonson's 'Every Man in his Humour'.

Bramble, MATTHEW and TABITHA, characters in Smollett's 'Humphry Clinker' (q.v.).

Bran, The Voyage of, an early Irish work, partly in prose, partly in verse, thought to have been originally written in the 7th cent. and copied in the 10th.

Brand, a lyrical drama by Ibsen (q.v.) (1866).

Brandan, ST., see *Brendan*.

Brandon, COLONEL, a character in Jane Austen's 'Sense and Sensibility' (q.v.).

Brandt, MARGARET, the heroine of Reade's 'The Cloister and the Hearth' (q.v.).

Branghtons, THE, in Fanny Burney's 'Evelina' (q.v.), the heroine's vulgar relations.

Branwen, see *Mabinogion*.

Brass, MAN OF, see *Talus*.

Brass, SAMPSON, and his sister SALLY, characters in Dickens's 'The Old Curiosity Shop' (q.v.).

Brave New World, a novel by A. Huxley (q.v.) (1932).

Brawne, FANNY, the lady whom Keats (q.v.) met in 1818 and with whom he fell in love. His passion is reflected in one or two of his sonnets, notably 'The day is gone', and 'I cry your mercy'. Her letters to his sister were published in 1937.

Bray, MADELINE, a character in Dickens's 'Nicholas Nickleby' (q.v.).

Bray, Vicar of, see *Vicar of Bray*.

Brecht, BERTOLT (1898-1956). German dramatist and lyric poet. After emigration from Nazi Germany he returned and settled in 1949 in East Berlin, where he founded the Berlin Ensemble. Brecht's early plays (e.g. 'Baal', 1922) show kinship with Expressionism. His theory of 'epic theatre' regarded a play as a series of loosely connected scenes, dispensed with the traditional 'dramatic' excitement, and used songs as an integral element. The theory is illustrated in 'The Life of Galileo' (1937-9), 'The Good Woman of Setzuan' (1938-41), 'Mother Courage' (1941), and 'The Caucasian Chalk Circle' (1948), plays which call for highly stylized acting. Some of Brecht's plays (like 'The Preventible Rise of Arturo Ui') combine an anti-capitalist theme with the theme of Hitlerism. The didactic plays of the period around 1930 are closely connected with the interests of the Communist Party, with which Brecht, although never a member, was intimately associated from the late 1920s.

Breck, ALAN, a character in R. L. Stevenson's 'Kidnapped' (q.v.) and 'Catriona'.

Breeches Bible, THE, the English Bible printed at Geneva in 1560, named in allusion to the version adopted of Gen. iii. 7, 'They sewed fig leaves together, and made themselves breeches'.

Brendan, BRANDAN, or BRENAINN, ST. (484-577), of Clonfert in Ireland, perhaps made a journey to the northern isles which formed the basis of the medieval legend of the 'Navigatio Sancti Brendani', now generally accepted as a Christianized *imram* or story of an adventurous sea-voyage, an old Irish literary genre which flourished between the 6th and 12th cents. and of which 'The Voyage of Bran' and 'Maeldune' (qq.v.) are representative. The story has been repeated in many languages at various times, and recently by Matthew Arnold and Sebastian Evans. The saint, sailing in search of the earthly Paradise, meets with fabulous adventures. Of these the best known is his meeting with Judas on a lonely rock on Christmas night, where the traitor is allowed once a year to cool himself in recompense for a single act of charity in his lifetime. He is commemorated on 16 May.

Brer Fox and Brer Rabbit, characters in 'Uncle Remus'. See *Harris* (*J. C.*).

Breton, NICHOLAS (1545?-1626?), author of a miscellaneous collection of satirical, religious, romantic, and pastoral writings in verse and prose. His best work is to be found among his short lyrics in 'England's Helicon' (q.v.), and in his pastoral volume 'The Passionate Shepheard' (1604).

Breton Lays, in English literature of the Middle English period, are short stories in rhyme, like those of Marie de France (q.v.), taken from Celtic stories. For an example see *Orfeo*.

Bretton, MRS. and JOHN, characters in Charlotte Brontë's 'Villette' (q.v.).

Brewer's Dictionary of Phrase and Fable, first published in 1870 (revised 1952 and subsequently), a work containing explanations of English phrases, cant and slang terms, characters of fiction and romance, etc., by the Revd. Ebenezer Cobham Brewer (1810-97).

Briana, in Spenser's 'Faerie Queene', VI. i, the mistress of a castle who takes a toll of ladies' locks and knights' beards to make a mantle for her lover Crudor.

Brian Boru (926-1014), having become king of Munster, started on a career of conquest, in which he defeated the Danes, and gradually extended his dominion until he became chief king of Ireland. He gained a great victory over the Danes at Clontarf in 1014, but was slain in his tent after the battle.

Briareus, in Greek mythology, one of the hundred-handed giants who supported the gods in their struggle with the Titans.

Bridal of Triermain, The, a poem by Sir W. Scott (q.v.) (1813).

Bridehead, SUE, a character in Hardy's 'Jude the Obscure' (q.v.).

Bride of Abydos, The, a poem by Lord Byron (q.v.) (1813).

Bride of Lammermoor, The, a novel by Sir W. Scott (q.v.) (1819) (in the third series of 'Tales of My Landlord').

Bridewell, originally a royal palace. It was afterwards converted into a house of correction.

Bridge of Sighs, THE, at Venice, connecting the Palace of the Doge with the State prison, across which prisoners were conducted from judgement to punishment.

Bridge of Sighs, The, a poem by T. Hood (q.v.) (1846), one of Hood's most popular works.

Bridges, ROBERT (1844-1930), studied, and for a time practised, medicine. His reputation as a poet was made by the successive volumes of his 'Shorter Poems', published in 1873, 1879, 1880, 1890, and 1893. He also published some longer poems: 'Prometheus, the Firegiver' (1884), 'Eros and Psyche' (1894), and 'Demeter' (1905). An edition of the 'Poetical Works of Robert Bridges' appeared in 1898-1905, which contained in addition his eight plays (published between 1885 and 1893). The Oxford Press edition of the 'Poetical Works' (1912) first made the author known to the world in general. In 1913 Bridges was appointed poet laureate. In 1914 he issued privately 'October, and other Poems', subsequently published, with some war poems added, in 1920. In 1916 he published 'The Spirit of Man', a collection of prose and verse extracts from various authors, having special bearing on the spiritual needs of the time, and in 1925 a volume of 'New Verse'. Bridges also wrote much prose, including essays on 'Milton's Prosody' (1893), 'John Keats' (1895), and on 'The Influence of the Audience on Shakespeare's Drama'. He was one of the founders of the Society for Pure English (q.v.) and edited its series of Tracts.

The author of many beautiful lyrics and a remarkable metrist, Bridges was perhaps too subtle and severe a poet to appeal to a very wide public. But his great philosophical poem in 'loose alexandrines', 'The Testament of Beauty' (1929), a compendium of the wisdom, learning, and experience of an artistic spirit, went through fourteen editions or impressions in its first year.

Bridget or BRIGIT or BRIDE, ST. (453-523), one of the patron saints of Ireland.

Bridie, JAMES, pen-name of OSBORNE HENRY MAVOR (1888-1951), playwright. His plays include 'The Anatomist' (1930), 'Tobias and the Angel' (1930), 'Mr. Bolfry' (1943), 'Dr. Angelus' (1947), and 'The Queen's Comedy' (1950).

Brieux, EUGÈNE (1858-1932), French dramatist, author of plays on social themes, made known to English readers in general by G. B. Shaw (q.v.), in an introduction to a translation by his wife of three of Brieux's plays (1911).

Briggs, MISS, a character in Thackeray's 'Vanity Fair' (q.v.).

Briseis fell into the hands of Achilles (q.v.) when her country was conquered by the Greeks, but was taken from him by Agamemnon. This was the occasion of the wrath of Achilles and of his withdrawal from the Trojan War.

Brisk, FASTIDIOUS, a character in Jonson's 'Every Man out of his Humour'.

Bristol Boy, THE, Chatterton (q.v.).

Britannia, by W. Camden (q.v.), was published in Latin in 1586, the sixth (much enlarged) edition appearing in 1607. It was translated in 1610 by Philemon Holland (q.v.). It is in effect a guidebook of the country, county by county, replete with information.

Britannia's Pastorals, see *Browne (W.)*.

British Academy, see *Academy (The British)*.

British Association for the Advancement of Science, THE, held its first meeting at York in 1831. Its object is the promotion and diffusion of science.

British Museum, THE, Bloomsbury, occupies the site of the old Montagu House, acquired in 1753 to house the library and curiosities of Sir Hans Sloane. These were enormously increased, notably by the purchase of the Harleian MSS., the gift by George II and George IV of royal libraries, the purchase of the Elgin Marbles (q.v.), and the acquisition of Egyptian antiquities. The new buildings were erected in 1823-47.

Britomart, the heroine of Bk. III of Spenser's 'Faerie Queene', the female knight of chastity. She has fallen in love with Artegall (q.v.), whose image she has seen in a magic mirror, and the poet recounts her adventures in her quest for him.

Britomartis, a Cretan deity, mistress of the fruits of the earth, who presided over hunting and fishing. She was also known as *Dictynna*.

Britten, BENJAMIN, *first Baron Britten* (1913-76), composer. His works include arrangements of folk-songs, orchestral compositions, the operas 'Peter Grimes' (1945), 'Albert Herring' (1947), a new version of 'The Beggar's Opera' (1948), 'Billy Budd' (with E. M. Forster and Eric Crozier, 1951), 'The Turn of the Screw' (1954), and his notable 'A War Requiem', with words from the *Missa pro Defunctis* and the poems of Wilfred Owen (1962).

Broadside, a sheet of paper printed on one side only, forming one large page; a term generally used of ballads, etc., so printed.

Broad Stone of Honour, The, a study of chivalry, by Kenelm Digby (1822).

Brobdingnag, see *Gulliver's Travels*.

Broceliande, in the Arthurian cycle, a legendary region, adjoining Brittany, where Merlin lies enchanted by Vivien.

Broken Heart, The, a tragedy by J. Ford (q.v.), printed in 1633. Its concluding scenes were highly praised by Lamb.

Brome, RICHARD (d. 1652?), playwright, was servant or perhaps secretary to Jonson, whose friendship he afterwards enjoyed. 'The Northern Lass', his first extant play, was printed in 1632. 'The Sparagus Garden', a comedy of manners, was acted in 1635; 'The Joviall Crew', his master-piece and latest play, in 1641. Some of the plays, particularly 'The City Witt' (printed 1653), show the marked influence of Jonson, others that of Dekker.

Bronté, DUKE OF, Lord Nelson.

Brontë, ANNE (1820-49), sister of Charlotte and Emily Brontë (qq.v.), was part author with her sisters of 'Poems, by Currer, Ellis, and Acton Bell', and author, under the pseudonym Acton Bell, of 'Agnes Grey' (1847), and of 'The Tenant of Wildfell Hall' (1848).

Brontë, CHARLOTTE, afterwards NICHOLLS (1816-55), daughter of Patrick Prunty or Brontë, an Irishman, perpetual curate of Haworth, Yorkshire, from 1820 till his death in 1861. Charlotte's mother died in 1821, leaving five daughters and a son. Four of the daughters were sent to a clergy daughters' boarding-school (of which Charlotte gives her recollection in the Lowood of 'Jane Eyre'). In 1831-2 Charlotte was at Miss Wooler's school at Roehead, whither she returned as a teacher in 1835-8. She was subsequently a governess, and in 1842 went with her sister Emily to study languages at a school in Brussels, where during 1843 she was employed as teacher. In the next year

Charlotte was back at Haworth, and in 1846 appeared a volume of verse entitled 'Poems by Currer, Ellis, and Acton Bell', the pseudonyms of Charlotte, Emily, and Anne. 'The Professor', Charlotte's first novel, was refused by Messrs. Smith Elder and other publishers, and was not published until 1857; while Emily's 'Wuthering Heights' (q.v.) and Anne's 'Agnes Grey' were accepted by Newby in 1847 and published in 1848. Charlotte's 'Jane Eyre' (q.v.) was published by Smith Elder in 1847 and achieved immediate success. Fresh sorrows now descended on the author: her brother, whose vicious habits had caused the sisters much distress, died in September 1848, Emily before the end of the same year, and Anne in the following summer, and Charlotte alone survived of the six children. She produced 'Shirley' in 1849, and 'Villette', founded on her memories of Brussels, in 1853; both stories, as well as 'Jane Eyre', appeared under the pseudonym Currer Bell. 'Emma', a fragment, appeared in the 'Cornhill Magazine' in 1860, after her death. Charlotte married in 1854 the Revd. A. B. Nicholls, her father's curate, but died a few months later.

Brontë, EMILY (1818-48), sister of Charlotte and Anne Brontë (qq.v.), was part author with her sisters of 'Poems by Currer, Ellis, and Acton Bell' (1846), and author, under the pseudonym of Ellis Bell, of 'Wuthering Heights' (q.v.). 'Last Lines' and 'Remembrance' are among her finest poems. She was, at her best, a great poet.

Brontë, (PATRICK) BRANWELL (1817-48), the brother of Charlotte, Anne, and Emily. He was a clerk on the Leeds and Manchester railway, and was dismissed for culpable negligence. He was subsequently tutor to a family. He took to opium and died of consumption.

Brook, MASTER, in Shakespeare's 'The Merry Wives of Windsor' (q.v.), the name assumed by Ford when Falstaff is making love to his wife.

Brooke, LORD, see *Greville* (*Fulke*).

Brooke, RUPERT CHAWNER (1887–1915), began to write poetry while at Rugby; his first volume of verse was published in 1911. During 1913–14 Brooke travelled in America and the South Seas. When the war broke out, he took part in the unsuccessful defence of Antwerp, and early in 1915 was sent to the Mediterranean. He died and was buried at Scyros on 23 April of that year. His 'Collected Poems' (1918), including the '1914' group of sonnets (published in 1915), caught the mood of romantic patriotism of the early war years. His 'Letters from America' appeared in 1916, with an introduction by Henry James.

Brooks's, a London club founded in the middle of the 18th cent., a noted gambling centre, much associated with the names of C. J. Fox and Sheridan.

Brother Jonathan, the nickname of the American nation, as John Bull is of the British. The origin is unknown.

Brougham, HENRY PETER, *Baron Brougham and Vaux* (1778–1868), rose to be Lord Chancellor. Best known as a parliamentary orator and the advocate of Queen Caroline, in the history of literature he is remembered principally as one of the founders, with Jeffrey and Sydney Smith, of 'The Edinburgh Review' (q.v.) in 1802.

The BROUGHAM, a one-horse closed carriage, with two or four wheels, was named after him.

Brougham Castle, Song at the Feast of, a poem by Wordsworth (q.v.), composed in 1807.

Broughton, RHODA (1840–1920), novelist. Her best-known books are: 'Cometh up as a Flower' (1867), 'Not Wisely but too Well' (1867), 'Doctor Cupid' (1886), and 'A Waif's Progress' (1905).

Browdie, JOHN, in Dickens's 'Nicholas Nickleby' (q.v.), a kind-hearted Yorkshireman.

Brown, CAPTAIN and JESSIE, characters in Mrs. Gaskell's 'Cranford' (q.v.).

Brown, CHARLES BROCKDEN (1771–1810), the first professional American author.

He is remembered for his four Gothic novels: 'Wieland' (1798), 'Arthur Mervyn' (1799), 'Ormond' (1799), and 'Edgar Huntly' (1799). They are of interest for their attempt to set the Gothic in the American scene.

Brown, FATHER, in G. K. Chesterton's detective stories, a Roman Catholic priest, highly successful in the detection of crime by intuitive methods.

Brown, GEORGE DOUGLAS (1869–1902), novelist. Under the name GEORGE DOUGLAS he published 'The House with the Green Shutters' (1901), written from the standpoint of realism in contrast to the sentimentalization of the 'Kailyard School' (q.v.).

Brown, JOHN 'of Osawatomie' (1800–59), the anti-slavery leader commemorated in the well-known marching song 'John Brown's body lies a-mouldering in the grave'.

The author of the song is unknown; it was set to an old Methodist hymn-tune and became the most popular marching-song of the Federal forces.

Brown, DR. JOHN (1810–82), author of essays published under the title 'Horae Subsecivae' ('odd hours', 1858–82), including in the second series the beautiful dog story 'Rab and his Friends'.

Brown, JOHN (1826–83), for over thirty years a favourite and devoted Scottish attendant of Queen Victoria, who became 'almost a State personage'.

Brown, LANCELOT (1716–83), landscape architect, called 'Capability Brown' because he was reputed to say, when consulted on the landscaping of an estate, that it had capabilities.

Brown, THOMAS (1663–1704), satirist, wrote the famous 'I do not love you, Dr. Fell' (see *Fell*). He settled in London as a hack-writer and translator. His collected works appeared in 1707.

Brown, THOMAS EDWARD (1830–97), published 'Betsy Lee, a Foc's'le Yarn' in 1873, 'Foc's'le Yarns' in 1881, and other books of verse. His collected poems were issued in 1900. The greater part of his poems are in the Manx dialect and deal with the life of the humble inhabitants of the island. They have found very warm admirers, who rank Brown high among the English poets of the 19th cent.

Browne, CHARLES FARRAR (1834-67), an American humorous moralist, who wrote under the pseudonym of ARTEMUS WARD. He purports to describe the experiences of a travelling showman, and like 'Josh Billings' (H. W. Shaw, q.v.) uses his own phonetic spelling. He contributed to 'Punch' and died in England.

Browne, HABLOT KNIGHT (1815-82), under the pseudonym 'Phiz', illustrated some of the works of Dickens, Surtees, Smedley, etc.

Browne, ROBERT, see *Brownists*.

Browne, SIR THOMAS (1605-82), studied medicine at Montpellier, Padua, and Leiden, and graduated at this last university as doctor. In 1637 he settled at Norwich, where he practised physic. His 'Religio Medici' (q.v.) appeared in 1643, though written some years earlier; his 'Pseudodoxia Epidemica', better known as 'Vulgar Errors' (q.v.), appeared in 1646; 'Urn Burial' (q.v.) and 'Garden of Cyrus' in 1658; his 'Christian Morals' was not published till 1716, after his death, and was later (1756) edited by Samuel Johnson. He is famous for his rich prose style and eloquent musings on mortality.

Browne, THOMAS ALEXANDER (1826-1915), best known under his pseudonym 'Rolf Boldrewood', an Australian squatter and police magistrate, author of the very popular 'Robbery under Arms' (1888), the story of a bush-ranger, Captain Starlight.

Browne, WILLIAM (1591-1645), published 'Britannia's Pastorals', a fluent but desultory narrative poem in couplets interspersed with lyrics, Bk. I in 1613, Bk. II in 1616; but Bk. III remained in manuscript till 1852. His poetry is characterized by a genuine love of nature, and influenced Milton, Keats, and Mrs. Browning.

Browning, ELIZABETH BARRETT (1806-61), married Robert Browning in 1846. Her 'Essay on Mind; with other Poems' appeared in 1826; a volume of 'Poems' (including 'The Cry of the Children') in 1844; 'Sonnets from the Portuguese' (privately printed in 1847) in 1850; 'Aurora Leigh' (q.v.) in 1857; and 'Poems before Congress' in 1860. 'Last Poems' appeared posthumously in 1862. After her marriage Mrs. Browning lived mostly in Italy, and died at Florence. Her best work is contained in the 'Sonnets from the Portuguese', where the form restricted her tendency to prolixity.

Browning, ROBERT (1812-89), was privately educated. His first poem, 'Pauline', appeared in 1833 and he first visited Italy in 1834. 'Paracelsus', which attracted the friendly notice of Carlyle, Wordsworth, and other men of letters, appeared in 1835. He next published 'Strafford', a tragedy, which was played at Covent Garden in 1837. 'Sordello' followed in 1840. 'Bells and Pomegranates' (including 'Pippa Passes', 'The Return of the Druses', 'A Blot in the 'Scutcheon', 'Colombe's Birthday', 'Luria', 'A Soul's Tragedy', and other pieces) appeared during 1841-6. In 1846 he married Elizabeth Barrett (see under *Browning, E. B.*), and lived with her mainly in Italy at Pisa, Florence, and Rome, until her death in 1861, after which Browning settled in London. In 1850 he published 'Christmas Eve and Easter Day', and in 1855 'Men and Women'. 'Dramatis Personae' appeared in 1864, and in 1868-9 the long poem 'The Ring and the Book' (q.v.). His chief remaining works appeared as follows: 'Fifine at the Fair' in 1872, 'Red Cotton Nightcap Country' in 1873, 'Dramatic Idyls' in two series in 1879-80, and 'Parleyings with certain People' in 1887. His last volume of poems, 'Asolando' (q.v.), was published on the day of his death.

Browning, though always esteemed by a small circle of readers, only achieved genuine fame late in life, when he came to be ranked with Tennyson. The characteristics of his poems were a strong psychological interest in human emotions and motives and a tendency to obscure or deliberately tortuous language. His lyrics by contrast are often delightfully simple and musical.

Brownists, adherents of the ecclesiastical principles of Robert Browne (1550?–1633?), who preached *c.* 1578 denouncing the parochial system and ordination, whether by bishops or by presbytery. He is regarded as the founder of Congregationalism.

Brownlow, MR., a character in Dickens's 'Oliver Twist' (q.v.).

Bruce, JAMES (1730–94), author of an interesting narrative of his 'Travels to discover the source of the Nile' (he discovered that of the Blue Nile), and of his visit to Abyssinia, published in 1790.

Bruce, The, an epic poem by Barbour (q.v.), written about 1375.

Brugglesmith, a short story by Kipling (q.v.), included in 'Many Inventions'.

Brummell, GEORGE BRYAN (1778–1840), called BEAU BRUMMELL, a friend of the prince regent (George IV) and leader of fashion in London. He died in poverty at Caen.

Brunanburh, a poem in Old English, included in the Anglo-Saxon Chronicle (q.v.) under the year 937, dealing with the battle fought in that year at Brunanburh between Æthelstan with an English army and the Northmen supported by the forces of Scotland and Wales. J. H. Frere (q.v.) and Tennyson wrote translations of the poem.

Brunhild, see *Nibelungenlied*.

Brut, meaning 'chronicle', is a transferred use of *Brut = Brutus*, the legendary founder of Britain, as in the French title, 'Roman de Brut', and in the 'Brut' of Layamon (q.v.).

Brut of Layamon, see *Layamon*.

Brute or BRUTUS, legendary founder of the British race. Geoffrey of Monmouth (q.v.) states that Walter, archdeacon of Oxford, gave him an ancient book containing an account of the kings of Britain from Brutus to Cadwallader. This Brutus was son of Sylvius, grandson of Ascanius and great-grandson of Aeneas. He collected a remnant of the Trojan race and brought them to England (uninhabited at the time 'except by a few giants'), landing at Totnes. He was the progenitor of a line of British kings including Gorboduc, Ferrex and Porrex, Cymbeline, Coel (Cole, the 'merry old soul'), Vortigern, and Arthur.

Brutus, DECIUS, a character in Shakespeare's 'Julius Caesar' (q.v.).

Brutus, LUCIUS JUNIUS, the legendary first consul of Rome. His brother was murdered by Tarquinius Superbus, and he escaped the same fate only by simulating idiocy—whence the name Brutus. After the death of Lucretia (see *Lucrece*), he stirred the Romans to expel the Tarquins and was elected to the consulship. He put to death his two sons for conspiring to restore the Tarquins.

Brutus, MARCUS JUNIUS (85–42 B.C.), joined Pompey in the civil war (49), but after the battle of Pharsalia was pardoned by Caesar. He nevertheless joined the conspirators who assassinated Caesar, in the hope of restoring republican government. On the occasion of Caesar's murder, the dying man uttered the famous words, '*Et tu, Brute*'. In the subsequent war between Brutus and Cassius on the one hand and Octavian and Antony on the other, the former were defeated at Philippi (42), and Brutus took his own life. His wife was Porcia, daughter of Cato of Utica.

Bryant, WILLIAM CULLEN (1794–1878), American poet. He was for fifty years editor of the New York 'Evening Post'. He began to make a name as a poet as early as 1817, with the publication of 'Thanatopsis', and confirmed his reputation as the leading American poet of the day with his 'Poems' (1821). He was a limited poet, deeply indebted to Wordsworth, but often wrote with great dignity and power, as in the well-known lyric 'To a Waterfowl'.

Bryce, JAMES (1838-1922), *Viscount Bryce*, Regius professor of civil law at Oxford, 1870-93, held a number of high political and diplomatic posts. His publications include two classical works: 'The Holy Roman Empire' (1864) and 'The American Commonwealth' (1888), besides a number of other writings on various subjects.

Brynhild, or BRUNHILD, see *Nibelungenlied.*

Bucephalus, a horse of Alexander the Great, whose head resembled that of a bull.

Buchan, JOHN (1875-1940), *first Baron Tweedsmuir*, author. Private secretary to the high commissioner of S. Africa, 1901-3; on H.Q. staff of British Army, France, 1916-17; director of information under the prime minister, 1917-18; governor-general of Canada, 1935-40. Among his writings are: 'Montrose' (1913, 1928), 'History of the Great War' (1921-2), 'Augustus' (1937). His novels of adventure include: 'The Thirty-Nine Steps' (1915), 'Greenmantle' (1916), 'Mr. Standfast' (1919), 'Midwinter' (1923), 'The Three Hostages' (1924), 'Dancing Floor' (1926).

Buchanan, GEORGE (1506-82), became tutor to a natural son of James V. He satirized the Franciscans and was imprisoned at St. Andrews. Escaping, he became a professor at Bordeaux, where he had Montaigne among his pupils, and in 1547 was invited to teach in the university of Coimbra, but was imprisoned by the Inquisition, 1549-51. He returned to Scotland and professed himself a Protestant. He became a bitter enemy of Mary, in consequence of the murder of Darnley, and vouched that the 'Casket Letters' (q.v.) were in her handwriting. He was tutor to James VI during 1570-8.

Buchanan, ROBERT WILLIAMS (1841-1901), poet and novelist, came to London in 1860, and made his reputation by 'London Poems' in 1866, and 'Ballads of Life, Love, and Humour' (1882). He satirized Swinburne and others in 'The

Session of the Poets' in 'The Spectator' (1866), and attacked the Pre-Raphaelites (q.v.) in a pseudonymous article entitled 'The Fleshly School of Poetry', which led to a prolonged controversy.

Bucket, INSPECTOR, the detective in Dickens's 'Bleak House' (q.v.).

Buckhurst, LORD, see *Sackville* (*T.*) and *Sackville* (*C.*).

Buckingham: the line, 'Off with his head! So much for Buckingham', occurs in Colley Cibber's version of Shakespeare's 'Richard III'.

Buckingham, Complaint of, see *Complaint of Buckingham.*

Buckingham, GEORGE VILLIERS, *first duke of* (1592-1628), the favourite of James I, figures in Scott's 'The Fortunes of Nigel' (q.v.). He was assassinated by John Felton.

Buckingham, GEORGE VILLIERS, *second duke of* (1628-87), a prominent figure in the reign of Charles II, was the Zimri of Dryden's 'Absalom and Achitophel' (q.v.). He was author of the burlesque 'The Rehearsal' (q.v.), 1671, and of other verses and satires. He figures in Scott's 'Peveril of the Peak'.

Bucklaw, THE LAIRD OF, Frank Hayston, a character in Scott's 'The Bride of Lammermoor'.

Buckle, HENRY THOMAS (1821-62), received no school or college training and devoted himself to travelling on the Continent. The first volume of his 'History of Civilization in England' appeared in 1857 and the second in 1861. Buckle criticized the methods of previous historians, and sought to adopt a more scientific basis, with special regard to the physical conditions of various countries, such as their climate and soil.

Bucolic (Greek βουκόλος, herdsman), pastoral; BUCOLICS, pastoral poems.

Buddha, 'the Enlightened', the title given to the founder of BUDDHISM, Sakyamuni, Gautama, or Siddartha, who flourished in northern India in the 5th cent. B.C. The principal doctrines of Buddhism are, that suffering is inseparable from existence;

that the suppression of suffering can be obtained by the suppression of desire, and this in turn by Buddhist discipline, of which *nirvana* is the reward. *Nirvana* is the extinction of individual existence and absorption into the supreme spirit.

Budgell, EUSTACE (1686-1737), a cousin of Addison, a miscellaneous writer who contributed to 'The Spectator' and is alluded to by Pope in 'The Dunciad'.

Buffalo Bill, the name under which William Cody (1846-1917) obtained a world-wide reputation. His fame as a scout, slayer of Indians, and terror of bandits was largely fictitious.

Buffon, GEORGES LOUIS LECLERC DE (1707-88), French naturalist, author of a remarkable 'Histoire Naturelle' in thirty-six volumes (1749-88).

Bukton, a friend of Chaucer to whom he addressed an 'Envoy'.

Bulbul, a bird of the thrush family, much admired in the East for its song; hence sometimes called the 'nightingale' of the East.

Bull, from Latin *bulla*, the leaden seal attached to the Pope's edicts, and hence a papal or episcopal edict.

Bull, an expression containing a manifest contradiction in terms or involving a ludicrous inconsistency unperceived by the speaker. The origin of the term is unknown. Often associated with the Irish.

Bull, JOHN, see *John Bull*.

Bulldog Drummond, see *Sapper*.

Bulstrode, MR., a character in George Eliot's 'Middlemarch' (q.v.).

Bultitude, MR. and DICK, characters in F. Anstey's 'Vice Versa' (q.v.).

Bumble, the beadle in Dickens's 'Oliver Twist' (q.v.).

Bumby, MOTHER, a fortune-teller frequently alluded to by the Elizabethan dramatists. Lyly (q.v.) wrote a play entitled 'Mother Bombie' (1594).

Bumper, SIR HARRY, a character in Sheridan's 'The School for Scandal' (q.v.), who sings the famous song:

'Here's to the maiden of bashful fifteen'.

Bunbury, an imaginary character introduced by Wilde (q.v.) in 'The Importance of being Earnest'.

Bungay, THOMAS, known as 'Friar Bungay' (*fl.* 1290), a Franciscan, divinity lecturer of his order in Oxford and Cambridge. He was vulgarly accounted a magician. See *Friar Bacon and Friar Bungay*.

Bungay and Bacon, the rival publishers in Thackeray's 'Pendennis' (q.v.).

Bunkum, BUNCOMBE, empty claptrap oratory, from *Buncombe*, the name of a county in N. Carolina, U.S. The use of the word originated in the 16th congress, when the member for this district rose to speak, declaring he was bound to *make a speech for Buncombe*.

Bunsby, CAPTAIN JOHN, a character in Dickens's 'Dombey and Son' (q.v.), a friend of Captain Cuttle.

Bunthorne, REGINALD, in Gilbert and Sullivan's comic opera 'Patience', 'a fleshly poet' in whose person the 'Aesthetic Movement' of the eighties was caricatured.

Bunyan, JOHN (1628-88), the son of a tinsmith, was early set to his father's trade. On completing his sixteenth year he was drafted into the parliamentary army, an experience perhaps reflected in his 'The Holy War'. He had profited by two religious books belonging to his first wife (who died *c.* 1656, leaving four young children) and devoted himself to reading the Bible. He married his second wife, Elizabeth, *c.* 1659, and was arrested in Nov. 1660 for preaching without a licence. He was kept in prison for twelve years, until Charles II's Declaration of Indulgence. During the first half of this period he wrote nine of his books, the principal of which was his 'Grace Abounding to the Chief of Sinners' (1666). In the same year appeared 'The Holy City, or the New Jerusalem', inspired by a passage in the book of Revelation. After his release in 1672 he was appointed pastor to the same church in Bedford, but was again imprisoned for a short period, during which he wrote the first part of 'The Pilgrim's Progress from this World to that which is to come' (q.v.). The second part, with the whole work, was published in 1684. His other principal works are 'The Life and Death of Mr. Badman' (1680), and 'The Holy War' (1682). He is remarkable in English literature for his simple and homely style, which can be at times both forceful and eloquent.

Burana Carmina, see *Carmina Burana*.

Burbage, JAMES (*d.* 1597), actor, one of the earl of Leicester's players in 1574. He leased land in Shoreditch (1576), on which he erected, of wood, the first building in England specially intended for plays. In 1596 he acquired a house in Blackfriars, and converted it into the 'Blackfriars Theatre' (q.v.).

Burbage, RICHARD (1567?-1619), actor, was son of James Burbage (q.v.). He acted as a boy at the theatre in Shoreditch and rose to be an actor of chief parts, 1595-1618, in plays by Shakespeare, Ben Jonson, and Beaumont and Fletcher. He excelled in tragedy.

Burchell, MR., in Goldsmith's 'The Vicar of Wakefield' (q.v.), the name assumed by Sir William Thornhill.

Burden of a song, from the Romanic *bourdon*, the continuous bass or 'drone' of a bagpipe, is the refrain or chorus, a set of words recurring at the end of each verse.

Burial of Sir John Moore, The, see *Wolfe* (C.).

Buridan, a French scholastic philosopher of the end of the 12th cent. 'Like Buridan's ass between two bundles of hay' is said of a person undecided between two courses of action, who adopts neither.

Burke, EDMUND (1729-97), educated at Trinity College, Dublin. He entered the Middle Temple in 1750. His first published works, 'A Vindication of Natural Society' and 'A Philosophical Inquiry into the Sublime and Beautiful', appeared in 1757. Burke entered parliament as member for Wendover in 1765, and first spoke in the House in 1766 on the American question. During the following years he vehemently attacked the Tory government. He published his 'Observations on "The Present State of the Nation"' in 1769, and 'Thoughts on the Present Discontents' in 1770. He became M.P. for Bristol on the invitation of the citizens in 1774, and made his speeches 'On American Taxation' and 'On Conciliation with the Colonies' in 1774 and 1775. His championship of free trade with Ireland and of Catholic emancipation lost him his seat at Bristol in 1780. He became M.P. for Malton in Yorkshire in 1781. By his attacks on the conduct of the American War he contributed powerfully to North's resignation of office. He opened the case for the impeachment of Warren Hastings in 1788, and supported Wilberforce in advocating the abolition of the slave-trade in 1788-9. His 'Reflections on the Revolution in France' (q.v.) appeared in 1790. He retired from parliament in 1794.

Burke's political life was devoted to five 'great, just, and honourable causes': the emancipation of the House of Commons from the control of George III and the 'King's friends'; the emancipation (but not the independence) of the American colonies; the emancipation of Irish trade, the Irish parliament, and the Irish Catholics; the emancipation of India from the misgovernment of the East India Company; and opposition to the atheistical jacobinism displayed in the French Revolution. He is one of the most eloquent and persuasive of English writers.

Burke, WILLIAM, a criminal executed at Edinburgh in 1829 for smothering many persons in order to sell their bodies for dissection. Hence 'to burke' is to murder, and, figuratively, to smother, 'hush up', suppress quietly.

Burke's Peerage, first compiled by John Burke in 1826. Since 1847 it has been published annually.

Burlesque, from Italian *burlo*, ridicule, mockery; literary composition or dramatic representation which aims at exciting laughter by the comical treatment of a serious subject or the caricature of the spirit of a serious work. Notable examples of burlesque in English literature are Butler's 'Hudibras', 'The Rehearsal', and Fielding's 'Tom Thumb' (qq.v.).

Burnand, SIR FRANCIS COWLEY (1836-1917), contributed to 'Punch' from 1863, and was editor, 1880-1906. He wrote the operetta 'Cox and Box' (q.v., 1867).

Burne-Jones, SIR EDWARD COLEY (1833-98), an eminent painter of the romantic school, a friend of D. G. Rossetti and W. Morris (qq.v.); famous for his pictures ('King Cophetua', etc.), designs for stained-glass windows, and other decorative work.

Burnell the Ass, the hero of the 'Speculum Stultorum' of Wireker (q.v.). Burnell, an ass who wishes to acquire a larger tail, goes to Salerno and to Paris to study, meets with various adventures, and finally loses his tail altogether.

Burnet, GILBERT (1643-1715), bishop of Salisbury in 1689 under William III. He published his account of the death-bed repentance of Rochester (q.v.) in 1680, and his 'History of the Reformation in England', vol. i in 1679, vol. ii in 1681, vol. iii in 1714; his best-known work, 'The History of My Own Times', appeared posthumously (1724-34).

Burnett, FRANCES ELIZA HODGSON (1849-1924), writer of popular stories, emigrated to the United States in her youth. Best known as the author of 'Little Lord Fauntleroy' (1886).

Burney, FRANCES ('FANNY'), MADAME D'ARBLAY (1752-1840), daughter of Dr. Burney, the historian of music, lived during her youth in the midst of that literary society which included Dr. Johnson and Burke. In 1778 she published her first novel 'Evelina' (q.v.) anonymously, but the revelation of its authorship brought her into prominence, and she was appointed second keeper of the robes to Queen Charlotte (1786). In 1793 she married General d'Arblay, a French refugee in England. Her second novel 'Cecilia' was published in 1782, 'Camilla' in 1796, 'The Wanderer' in 1814. She

edited her father's 'Memoirs' in 1832. Her 'Early Diary' (1768-78), with pleasant sketches of Johnson and Garrick, was published in 1889, and her later 'Diary and Letters' (1778-1840), which gives an interesting account of her life at court, in 1842-6. Miss Burney was the originator of the simple novel of home life, taking as her theme the entry into the world of a young girl of virtue and understanding, but inexperienced, and exposing her to circumstances and incidents that develop her character and display the various droll persons with whom she comes in contact.

Burning Babe, The, see *Southwell.*

Burns, ROBERT (1759-96), the son of a cottar, was educated by his father. Set to work as a farm labourer, he early developed an inclination for literature, and also a tendency to dissipation. From 1784 to 1788 he farmed, and during this period wrote some of his best work: 'The Cotter's Saturday Night', 'The Twa Dogs', 'Halloween', 'The Jolly Beggars', 'To a Mouse', 'To a Mountain Daisy', and some of his keenest satires. In 1786 he published the Kilmarnock edition of his early poems. It made him famous, and took him to Edinburgh, where his modesty and conviviality made him very popular. The second edition of his poems brought him £500 and enabled him to settle down on a small farm at Ellisland and to marry Jean Armour, one of his many loves. He also received an exciseman's place which was his principal means of support. Apart from songs, he now wrote little of importance ('Tam o' Shanter' and 'Captain Matthew Henderson' are the chief exceptions). He contributed some 200 songs to the successive volumes of James Johnson's 'Scots Musical Museum' (1787-1803), among others the famous 'Auld Lang Syne', 'Scots wha hae', 'A Red, Red Rose', and 'It was a' for our Richtfu' King'. Among his many beautiful lyrics may be mentioned 'John Anderson, my Jo', 'Comin' thro' the Rye', 'The Banks of Doon', and 'Mary Morison'. In a different category fall the humorous vernacular 'Address to the Deil', 'To a Louse', etc.

The sympathy that Burns had at first for the French revolutionaries nearly cost him his place; while his inclination to convivial living undermined his health, and he died in 1796. Revered as a national poet by the Scottish nation, he is a considerable lyric poet whose talents were largely based on a native ballad tradition.

Burton, SIR RICHARD FRANCIS (1821–90), joined the Indian Army in 1842. His Indian experiences are recorded in 'Scinde, or the Unhappy Valley' (1851); his experiences in Africa, where he travelled with Speke, in 'First Footsteps in East Africa' (1856) and 'The Lake Region of Central Africa' (1860). He was one of the first Englishmen to visit Mecca, making the pilgrimage in disguise, and published his narrative thereof in 1855-6. He translated the 'Lusiads' of Camoëns (q.v.) (1881), but is best known for his translation of the 'Arabian Nights' (q.v.) (1885-8) and of 'Kama Sutra' (1883), 'The Perfumed Garden' (1886), and other works of Arabian erotica.

Burton, ROBERT (1577-1640), author of 'The Anatomy of Melancholy' (q.v.).

Busby, RICHARD (1606-95), a famous headmaster of Westminster School from 1638 to 1695. Among his pupils were Dryden, Locke, Atterbury, and Matthew Prior.

Busirane, in Spenser's 'Faerie Queene', III. xi and xii, the 'vile Enchaunter' symbolizing unlawful love.

Busiris, a mythical king of Egypt, son of Poseidon, who sacrificed all strangers who came to the country. He was slain by Hercules. He is the subject of a tragedy by E. Young (q.v.).

Buskin, a word existing in many European languages, whose ultimate derivation is unknown. The special source of the English word is likewise uncertain. It is the word used for the high thick-soled boot (*cothurnus*) worn by actors in ancient Athenian tragedy, frequently contrasted with the 'sock' (*soccus*) or low shoe worn

by comedians. Hence it is applied figuratively to the style or spirit of tragedy, the tragic vein. *To put on the buskins*, to write tragedy.

Bussy D'Ambois, a tragedy by Chapman (q.v.) (1607), the most famous of the author's plays. It was severely criticized by Dryden.

The story is the same as that told by Dumas in 'La Dame de Montsoreau'.

Bussy D'Ambois, The Revenge of, a tragedy by Chapman (q.v.), composed in 1610 or 1611, printed in 1613. The play is a sequel to the tragedy 'Bussy D'Ambois'. The similarity of the play in certain respects to Shakespeare's 'Hamlet' is evident.

Busybody, The, a comedy by Mrs. Centlivre (q.v.), produced in 1709.

Butler, JOSEPH (1692-1752), bishop of Bristol, from which he was translated to Durham in 1750. In 1736 appeared his 'Analogy of Religion', a defence of the Christian religion against the Deists by showing that their natural religion is open to the same objections as revelation.

Butler, THE REVD. REUBEN, in Scott's 'The Heart of Midlothian' (q.v.); he marries Jeanie Deans.

Butler, SAMUEL ('Hudibras' Butler) (1612-80), the son of a farmer. As attendant on Elizabeth, countess of Kent, he became acquainted with Selden (q.v.). Nothing further is known of his life until 1661, when he was employed by the earl of Carbery. About 1673 he enjoyed the patronage of George Villiers, second duke of Buckingham, who is satirized in his 'Hudibras' (q.v.). Of this work, Pt. I was published in 1663, Pt. II in 1664, and Pt. III in 1678. It was highly approved by Charles II, who gave the author £300 and later a pension of £100 a year; but Butler was perhaps for a time neglected, and was said to have died in penury.

Butler, SAMUEL ('Erewhon' Butler) (1835-1902), the grandson of Dr. Samuel Butler (1774-1839), the great headmaster of Shrewsbury School and bishop of Lichfield. He went to New Zealand in

1859, where he succeeded as a sheep breeder, as recounted in his 'A First Year in Canterbury Settlement' (1863). He returned to England in 1864 and settled in Clifford's Inn. In 1872 he published 'Erewhon' (q.v.), and next wrote a series of works of scientific controversy. His general attitude in these was one of protest against the Darwinian banishment of mind from the universe; and he maintained the transmissibility, by heredity, of acquired habits. In 1896 appeared his 'Life and Letters of Dr. Samuel Butler', his grandfather. Meanwhile Butler had developed a keen interest in Homer, which led to his theory of the feminine authorship of the 'Odyssey' and its origin at Trapani in Sicily. On the latter subject he published 'The Authoress of the Odyssey' in 1897, and translations of the 'Iliad' and the 'Odyssey' into a vigorous homely prose in 1898 and 1900. 'Shakespeare's Sonnets Reconsidered' appeared in 1899, and 'Erewhon Revisited' in 1901. Butler's autobiographical novel, 'The Way of All Flesh' (q.v.), was published posthumously in 1903, and selections from his note-books in 1912, under the title, 'The Note-books of Samuel Butler'.

Butler was pre-eminently a satirist, who waged war against the torpor of thought, the suppression of originality, the hypocrisies and conventions, that he saw around him.

Button's Coffee-house, the rival of Will's (q.v.), in Russell Street, Covent Garden, was frequented by Dryden, Addison, Steele, and Pope.

Buzfuz, Mr. Serjeant, in Dickens's 'The Pickwick Papers' (q.v.), counsel for the plaintiff in Bardell v. Pickwick.

Bycorne, see *Chichevache.*

By-Ends, Mr., in Bunyan's 'The Pilgrim's Progress' (q.v.), 'a downright hypocrite'.

Byrhtnoth's Death, see *Maldon (Battle of).*

Byrom, John (1692-1763), wrote, besides a quantity of religious verse, a pleasant anapaestic 'Pastoral'. He was an enthu-

siastic admirer of W. Law (q.v.) and turned some of his teaching into verse. Byrom wrote the hymn, 'Christians, awake! Salute the happy morn', and the famous epigram (on Handel and Bononcini), 'Strange all this difference should be 'Twixt Tweedledum and Tweedledee!'

Byron, George Gordon, *sixth Baron* (1788-1824), son of Captain John Byron, a profligate, and Catherine Gordon of Gight, was born in London and came into the title when ten years old. He was educated at Harrow and Trinity College, Cambridge. While at Cambridge he printed his 'Hours of Idleness' (at first named 'Juvenilia'), published in 1807, which were severely criticized in 'The Edinburgh Review'. To this criticism he replied, in 1809, in 'English Bards and Scotch Reviewers'. From 1809 to 1811 he travelled abroad, visiting Portugal, Spain, Greece, and the Levant. On his return he published the first two cantos of 'Childe Harold' (q.v.). During the next four years appeared 'The Giaour' (q.v.), 'The Bride of Abydos', 'The Corsair' (q.v.), 'Lara' (q.v.), 'Parisina', 'The Siege of Corinth' (q.v.), and 'Hebrew Melodies' (q.v.); also 'The Dream', a beautiful visionary poem in blank verse. In 1815 Byron married Anne Isabella Milbanke, an heiress, from whom he was separated in 1816. He thereupon left England, never to return, embittered by the strictures of what he regarded as a hypocritical society. In company part of the time with the Shelleys, he travelled to Switzerland and Venice, which, with Ravenna, Pisa, and Genoa, became his headquarters. Canto iii of 'Childe Harold' appeared in 1816, canto iv in 1818. In 1817 appeared 'The Lament of Tasso', a dramatic soliloquy, expressing that poet's passionate love and regret, as he lies in prison, for Leonora d'Este. Byron wrote the first five cantos of 'Don Juan' (q.v.) in 1818-20; 'Beppo' appeared in 1818. At Ravenna and subsequently at Pisa he wrote his dramas, the principal of which are 'Manfred', 'Cain', 'Marino Faliero', 'The Two Foscari',

'Sardanapalus', 'Heaven and Earth'; also 'Mazeppa' (q.v.) and the later cantos of the unfinished 'Don Juan'. In 1822 Byron and Leigh Hunt joined in the production of 'The Liberal' magazine. The first number contained Byron's 'The Vision of Judgment' (q.v.), an outcome of his feud with Southey. In 1823 Byron set out to join the Greek insurgents, and died of fever at Missolonghi in April 1824. His last works include the tragedy 'Werner' (1822), the beautiful romantic verse tale 'The Island' (1823), 'The Age of Bronze' (1823), a satirical poem inspired by the Congress of Verona, and 'The Deformed Transformed', an unfinished drama (1824).

Byron's poetry, though much criticized on moral grounds, was immensely popular at home, and also abroad, where it exerted great influence on the Romantic movement. This popularity it owed to the author's persistent attacks on 'cant political, religious, and moral', to the novelty of his oriental scenery, to the romantic character of the Byronic hero (constantly reappearing in successive works), and to the ease and fluency, and (very frequently) the real beauty, of his verse.

Byron, HARRIET, the heroine of Richardson's 'Sir Charles Grandison' (q.v.).

Byron, JOHN (1723-86), as a midshipman on one of the ships of Lord Anson's squadron, was wrecked on an island off the coast of Chile in 1741. His 'Narrative' of the shipwreck, published in 1768, was used by his grandson, Lord Byron, in his description of the storm and wreck in 'Don Juan'.

Byron, *The Conspiracy and Tragedy of Charles Duke of*, a double play by Chapman (q.v.) (1608).

Byronic, characteristic of or resembling Lord Byron (q.v.) or his poetry, that is to say, contemptuous of and rebelling against conventional morality, or defying fate, or possessing the characteristics of Byron's romantic heroes, or imitating his dress and appearance.

Bywater, INGRAM (1840-1914), an eminent Greek scholar. He succeeded Jowett as Regius professor of Greek at Oxford in 1893. His monumental edition of the 'Poetics' of Aristotle appeared in 1909.

Byzantine, the word used to designate the art, and especially the architecture, developed in the Eastern division of the Roman Empire which endured from A.D. 395 to the capture of Constantinople, its capital, formerly known as Byzantium, by the Turks in 1453. The Byzantine architecture is distinguished by its use of the round arch, cross, circle, dome, and rich mosaic ornament.

C

Cabal (Hebrew, *qabbalah*), a secret intrigue or a small body of persons engaged in an intrigue; applied specially to the five ministers of Charles II who signed the treaty of alliance with France in 1672; these were Clifford, Arlington, Buckingham, Ashley, and Lauderdale, the initials of whose names thus arranged happened to form the word *cabal*.

Cabell, JAMES BRANCH (1879-1958), American novelist. His chief works are: 'The Cream of the Jest' (1917), 'Jurgen' (1919), 'The Silver Stallion' (1926), 'Something about Eve' (1927).

Cable, GEORGE WASHINGTON (1844-1925), American novelist, author of stories of the old Creole society of Louisiana, including 'Old Creole Days' (1879).

Cacodemon, from the Greek word meaning an evil spirit, in which sense it is used in Shakespeare's 'Richard III', I. iii.

Cacus, a famous robber in Roman legend, who stole the cattle of Hercules but was detected and slain.

Cade, JACK, REBELLION OF, a movement in 1450 by the men of Kent against the misrule of Henry VI. It was headed by Jack Cade, an Irish adventurer. With a large mob he marched on London, but after a fight on London Bridge, the insurgents deserted Cade, who was pursued into Sussex and slain. Shakespeare's '2 Henry VI' is largely occupied with the story of this rebellion.

Cadenus and Vanessa, a poem by Swift (q.v.), written in 1713 for Esther Vanhomrigh ('Vanessa'), and published after her death by her request. It is the narrative, in mock classical form, of the author's relations with 'Vanessa' and an apology for his conduct.

'Cadenus' is an anagram for Decanus, or Dean.

Cadmean victory, a victory involving one's own ruin, associated with Thebes or the Thebans. Cadmus (q.v.) was the founder of Thebes. Cf. *Pyrrhic victory*.

Cadmus, son of Agenor, king of Phoenicia, was sent by his father in search of his sister Europa (q.v.), whom Zeus had carried away. His companions were devoured by a dragon, which he overcame by the assistance of Athene. He sowed its teeth in the plain, upon which armed men sprang up. He threw a stone in the midst of them, whereupon they turned their arms against each other, till all perished except five, who helped Cadmus to found the city of Thebes in Boeotia. Cadmus was reputed the first to introduce the use of letters into Greece.

Cadwal, in Shakespeare's 'Cymbeline' (q.v.), the name borne by Arviragus while he lived in the woods.

Cadwallader, the last king of the Britons, who reigned in the 7th cent.

CADWALLADER is also the name of a character in Smollett's 'Peregrine Pickle',

and a MRS. CADWALLADER figures in George Eliot's 'Middlemarch'.

Cædmon (corruptly CEDMON) (*fl.* 670), entered the monastery of Streaneshalch (Whitby) between 658 and 680, when already an elderly man. He is said by Bede to have been an unlearned herdsman, who received suddenly the power of song. In 1655 François Dujon (Franciscus Junius) published at Amsterdam from the unique Bodleian MS. Junius 11 (*c.* 1000) long scriptural poems, which he took to be those of Cædmon. These are 'Genesis', 'Exodus', 'Daniel', and 'Christ and Satan' (qq.v.). Modern scholarship denies them to Cædmon. The only authentic fragment of his work that survives is his first Hymn, which Bede quotes.

Caelia, in Spenser's 'Faerie Queene' (q.v.), I. x, the Lady of the House of Holiness.

Caelica, a collection of sonnets and songs by Fulke Greville (q.v.).

Caerleon, see *Carlion*.

Caesar, the name of a patrician family of Rome, made famous by GAIUS JULIUS CAESAR (102?–44 B.C.). He was not only a great general and statesman, but an orator and historian. The only work of his that has come down to us is his history of the first seven years of the Gallic War, and of part of the Civil War. The name Caesar was assumed by his adopted son, Octavianus (Augustus), and by Tiberius as the adopted son of Augustus. Both names were used by successive emperors, and Caesar survived as a title in *Kaiser* and *Tsar*.

Caesar and Cleopatra, a play by G. B. Shaw (q.v.) (1901).

Caesar and Pompey, a Roman tragedy by Chapman (q.v.), published 1631.

Caesarion, son of Gaius Julius Caesar (q.v.) and Cleopatra (q.v.), put to death by order of Augustus.

Caesar's Wife: Julius Caesar divorced his wife Pompeia, who was accused of an intrigue with Clodius, not because he thought her guilty, but because Caesar's wife must be above suspicion.

Caesura, in Greek and Latin prosody, the division of a metrical foot between two words, especially in certain recognized places near the middle of the line; in English prosody, a pause about the middle of a metrical line, generally indicated by a pause in the sense.

Cain, The Wanderings of, see *Wanderings.*

Cain: A Mystery, a tragedy by Lord Byron (q.v.) (1821).

The audacity of the poem, which defends sin and incest, aroused intense indignation, and evoked many attacks on the author.

Cain-coloured, of the reputed colour of the hair of Cain, to whom, as to Judas Iscariot, a red or reddish-yellow beard was attributed.

> He hath but a little wee face, with a little yellow beard, a Cain-coloured beard. (Shakespeare, 'The Merry Wives of Windsor', I. iv. 22.)

Caine, SIR THOMAS HENRY HALL (1853-1931), was a friend of D. G. Rossetti (q.v.), whom he first met in 1880. For the last few months of Rossetti's life, Caine was his housemate. He was author of a number of novels of wide popularity, many of them centred in the Isle of Man, including 'The Shadow of a Crime' (1885), 'The Scapegoat' (1891), 'The Manxman' (1894), 'The Eternal City' (1901), 'The Prodigal Son' (1904). 'My Story', a narrative of the early years of Caine's literary career, appeared in 1908.

Caius, DR., a character in Shakespeare's 'The Merry Wives of Windsor' (q.v.).

Calantha, the heroine of Ford's 'The Broken Heart' (q.v.).

Calderón DE LA BARCA, PEDRO (1600-81), a great Spanish dramatist, and the successor of Lope de Vega (q.v.). Dryden, Goethe, Shelley, Bridges, among others, were under obligations to him. Besides some 120 plays, Calderón wrote more than 70 *autos,* dramatic presentations of the Mystery of the Holy Eucharist.

Caleb Balderstone, a character in Scott's 'The Bride of Lammermoor'.

Caleb Williams, Adventures of, a novel by W. Godwin (q.v.) (1794).

This work is interesting as an early example of the propagandist novel and the novel of crime and its detection.

Caledonia, the Roman name for the north of Britain, hence poetically for Scotland.

Calendar, the system according to which the beginning and length of the year are fixed.

The JULIAN CALENDAR is that introduced by Julius Caesar in 46 B.C., in which the ordinary year has 365 days, and every fourth year is a leap year of 366 days. This was known as 'Old Style' when the Gregorian Calendar was introduced.

The GREGORIAN CALENDAR is the modification of the preceding, introduced by Pope Gregory XIII in 1582 and adopted in Great Britain in 1752. It was known as 'New Style'. The error, due to the fact that the Julian year was 11 minutes 10 seconds too long, amounted in 1752 to 11 days, and in order to correct this, 2 Sept. was in that year followed by 14 Sept., while for the future the years 2000, 2400, 2800, were to be reckoned as leap years, but the other hundredth years, 1800, 1900, 2100, etc., were to be ordinary years. See *Year.*

THE FRENCH REPUBLICAN CALENDAR made the year begin at the autumnal equinox, and was in use in France from 22 Sept. 1792, date of the proclamation of the Republic, until 1 Jan. 1806.

The JEWISH CALENDAR combines solar years with lunar months, an additional month being intercalated in each of seven years in every cycle of nineteen years. It reckons from the creation of the world (3760 B.C.). The new year begins on the first day of the month *Tishri.* Thus A.D. 1932 = A.M. 5692-3, *Tishri* 1 of A.M. 5693 falling on 1 Oct. 1932.

In the MUSLIM CALENDAR the year consists of twelve lunar months dating from A.D. 622, the year of the Hijra.

See also *Calends, Nones, Ides,* and *Newgate Calendar.*

Calends or KALENDS, the first day of any month in the ancient Roman calendar.

See also *Greek Calends*.

Caliban, in Shakespeare's 'The Tempest' (q.v.), the monster son of the witch Sycorax.

Caliban upon Setebos, a poem by R. Browning (q.v.), included in 'Dramatis Personae'.

Calidore, SIR, the Knight of Courtesy, in Bk. VI of Spenser's 'Faerie Queene'. He pursues and chains the 'Blatant Beast' (q.v.).

Caligula, GAIUS CAESAR, son of Germanicus, so called from his wearing, when a boy, *caligae* or soldiers' boots, was Roman emperor A.D. 37-41. The cruelties and vices that marked his reign were perhaps due to his madness. He was finally murdered.

Caliphate, the rule of the Caliphs ('vice regents') who succeeded Mohammed (q.v.).

Calipolis, in Peele's 'The Battle of Alcazar', the wife of the Moorish king, frequently quoted as typical of a sweetheart (e.g. Shakespeare, '2 Henry IV', II. iv).

Calisto, see *Callisto*.

Callimachus, a celebrated poet of Alexandria, who was perhaps librarian of the library of that city about 260-240 B.C. His epitaph on his friend Heraclitus has been translated in a well-known poem by W. J. Cory (q.v.).

Calliope, the muse (q.v.) of epic poetry.

Callipolis, see *Calipolis*.

Callisthenes, a philosopher, and pupil of Aristotle, who accompanied Alexander the Great on his expedition. He was accused of being privy to a plot against him, and was put to death.

Callisto, a nymph, the companion of Artemis, was beloved by Zeus and became the mother of Arcas (the eponymous hero of Arcadia). She was metamorphosed into a she-bear by the jealous Hera, and, when about to be slain by her son in the chase, was turned by Zeus into the constellation, the Great Bear.

Call of the Wild, The, the story of a dog, by Jack London (q.v.) (1903).

Calvary, the name of the mount of the Crucifixion, near Jerusalem.

Calverley, CHARLES STUART (1831-84), published 'Verses and Translations' in 1862 and 'Fly Leaves' in 1866, becoming famous under the initials 'C.S.C.' for his parodies and for the wit and scholarship of his verse.

Calves' Head Club, an association formed at the end of the 17th cent. to ridicule Charles I, calves' heads being used to represent the monarch and his courtiers.

Calvin, JOHANNES (1509-64), the great French theological writer and reformer. He settled at Geneva in 1536, where he became dictator of a kind of theocracy. He was the spiritual father of John Knox and the originator of the doctrines of Scottish Presbyterianism.

Calypso, a nymph who reigned in the island of Ogygia. When Odysseus (q.v.) was shipwrecked on her coasts, she offered him immortality if he would remain with her. The hero refused, and after seven years' delay was allowed to depart.

Cam and Isis, the rivers on which Cambridge and Oxford stand, sometimes used to signify these universities.

Camballo or CAMBALO, one of the two sons of King Cambuscan, in Chaucer's 'The Squire's Tale' (see *Canterbury Tales*; see also *Cambell*).

Cambell or CAMBELLO, the name given by Spenser ('Faerie Queene', IV. iii) to Cambal (q.v.), whose tale he borrows from Chaucer, and completes. Cambell is brother of Canace, for whom there are many suitors. It is arranged that the strongest of these, three brothers, shall fight with Cambell, and the lady be awarded to the victor. Two of the brothers are defeated; the contest between the third, Triamond, and Cambell is undecided, each wounding the other. They are reconciled by Cambina, Triamond's sister; Canace is awarded to Triamond and Cambell marries Cambina. The magic ring of Canace in 'The Squire's Tale' reappears in the 'Faerie Queene', with the power of healing wounds.

Cambrensis, GIRALDUS, see *Giraldus de Barri.*

Cambridge (OE. *Grantebrycg*), was according to legend made the seat of a school by Sigebert, king of the East Angles, about 630. The first historical trace of Cambridge as a university (*studium generale*) is in 1209, its first recognition in a royal writ to the chancellor of Cambridge in 1230, the first papal recognition in 1233. The process of development of the prerogatives of the University was slow, the chancellor's jurisdiction reaching its full extension in 1383. (See H. Rashdall, 'Universities of Europe'.)

Cambridge (Mass., U.S.A.), near Boston, is the seat of Harvard University.

Cambridge Platonists, see *Platonists.*

Cambridge University Press. Books were first printed at Cambridge in 1521-2 by John Siberch, a friend of Erasmus. A charter was granted to the University in 1534 authorizing the printing of books there, but not until 1583 was the first university Printer, Thomas Thomas, appointed. The activity of the Press was developed under the influence of R. Bentley (1662-1742, q.v.), and many notable books were produced by it in the 18th cent. and in modern times.

Cambuscan, in Chaucer's 'The Squire's Tale' (see *Canterbury Tales*), a king of Tartary.

Cambyses, KING, subject of a tragedy (1569) by Thomas Preston (q.v.), which illustrates the transition from the morality play to the historical drama. It is founded on the story of Cambyses in Herodotus; its bombastic grandiloquence became proverbial (e.g. '1 Henry IV', II. iv. 425).

Camden, WILLIAM (1551-1623), antiquary and historian. He was appointed headmaster of Westminster School in 1593. He made tours of antiquarian investigation up and down England, and published his 'Britannia' (q.v.) in 1586,

of which the sixth (greatly enlarged) edition appeared in 1607. He wrote principally in Latin, but his 'Britannia' was translated into English by Philemon Holland (q.v.) in 1610, and his 'Annales' in 1625, 1628, and 1635 by other hands.

Camden Society, founded in 1838 in honour of W. Camden (q.v.), for the purpose of publishing documents relating to the early history and literature of the British Empire.

Camelot, in the Arthurian legend, the place where King Arthur held his court, is stated by Malory to be Winchester. But there was a Camelot in Somerset, which still survives in Queen's Camel, and Leland found traditions of Arthur there.

Cameronians, the followers of Richard Cameron (*d.* 1680), a noted Scottish Covenanter and field preacher. His followers afterwards constituted the body called the 'Reformed Presbyterian Church of Scotland'. They figure prominently in Scott's 'Old Mortality'.

Camilla, a Volscian princess. She was so fleet of foot that she could run over a field of corn without bending the blades. She marched to assist Turnus against Aeneas and died of a wound she received. *Camilla, or a Picture of Youth,* a novel by F. Burney (q.v.) (1796).

Camillo, a character in Shakespeare's 'The Winter's Tale' (q.v.).

Camoëns, LUIS DE (1524-80), a Portuguese poet, author of 'Os Lusiadas', the 'Lusiads', an epic poem (1572). There is a close translation in English by Aubertin, and Sir Richard Burton also wrote a version.

Camorra, a secret society of lawless malcontents in Naples during the 19th cent.

Campaign, The, see *Addison.*

Campaigner, THE, Mrs. Mackenzie in Thackeray's 'The Newcomes' (q.v.).

Campaspe, Alexander and, a prose comedy by Lyly (q.v.) (1584). The play includes the charming lyric, 'Cupid and my Campaspe play'd, At cards for kisses . . .'

Campbell, ROY (1902-57), poet, born

in Durban. His works include 'The Flaming Terrapin' (1924), 'Adamastor' (1930), and 'Light on a Dark Horse', autobiography (1951). His 'Collected Poems' were published in two volumes in 1949 and 1959.

Campbell, THOMAS (1777–1844), son of a Glasgow merchant, published 'The Pleasures of Hope' in 1799, 'Gertrude of Wyoming' in 1809, and 'The Pilgrim of Glencoe' and other poems in 1842. He is principally remembered for his splendid war-songs, 'Hohenlinden', 'The Battle of the Baltic', and 'Ye Mariners of England'; for 'The Soldier's Dream', 'Lord Ullin's Daughter', and 'Lochiel's Warning'. He was also a prominent reformer and one of the founders of London University.

Camperdown, a village on the coast of the Netherlands, off which in 1797 the British fleet under Duncan defeated the Dutch under De Winter.

Campion, EDMUND (1540–81), fellow of St. John's College, Oxford (1557), went to Douai in 1571 and graduated there, and joined the Jesuits in 1573. He returned to England in 1580, preached privately in London, was arrested in 1581, sent to the Tower, examined under torture, and executed.

Campion, THOMAS (1567–1620), physician, poet, and musician, published in 1595 a volume of Latin 'Poemata', and in 1602 'Observations in the Art of English Poesie' directed 'against the vulgar and unartificial custom of riming', to which Daniel (q.v.) replied. He wrote masques for presentation at court, a treatise on music, a volume of songs on the death of Prince Henry, and four 'Books of Ayres' (1610–12), containing pleasant lyrics (some set to music by Campion himself), including the beautiful 'There is a garden in her face'.

Campo-Basso, COUNT OF, an Italian captain, figures in Scott's 'Quentin Durward' and 'Anne of Geierstein'.

Camulodunon, the Old British name of Colchester.

Camus, ALBERT (1913–60), French writer, born in Algeria, author of two

notable novels: 'L'Étranger' (1942) and 'La Peste' (1947); a number of plays; also essays and other prose writings. His name is associated with a 'philosophie de l'absurde' bearing some resemblance to Existentialism (q.v.).

Canace (pron. Can′ăsē), the daughter of King Cambuscan (q.v.), in Chaucer's 'The Squire's Tale' (see *Canterbury Tales*), and in Spenser's 'Faerie Queene' (Bk. IV).

Cancel, in printing, a new page or sheet substituted for one cancelled or suppressed.

Cancer, (1) the zodiacal constellation of the Crab; (2) the fourth of the signs of the zodiac, which the sun enters on 21 June.

Candăcē, a legendary queen of Tarsus who, in the stories attaching to Alexander the Great (q.v.), lures the conqueror, by her fascination, to a life of sloth.

Candida, one of the 'pleasant' plays in G. B. Shaw's 'Plays, Pleasant and Unpleasant'.

It deals with the conflict between the poet Eugene Marchbanks and the Christian Socialist parson Morell. Candida is Morell's wife.

Candide, a romance by Voltaire (q.v.), satirizing optimistic philosophies.

Candlemas, 2 Feb., the feast of the Purification of the Virgin Mary.

Candour, MRS., one of the scandalmongers in Sheridan's 'The School for Scandal' (q.v.).

Canicular Days, the days about the heliacal rising of the dog-star (either Sirius or Procyon), about 11 Aug.; the dog-days.

Canicular Year, the ancient Egyptian year, reckoned from one heliacal rising of Sirius to the next.

Cannae, the site, in Apulia, of the memorable defeat of the Romans by Hannibal in 216 B.C.

Canning, GEORGE (1770–1827), statesman and author. He was appointed foreign secretary in 1822 and premier in 1827. Apart from his political speeches, he is remembered as founder of and contributor to 'The Anti-Jacobin' (q.v.); his

'Poems' (1823) include the well-known epigram:

> In matters of commerce the fault of the Dutch
> Is offering too little and asking too much.

Canongate, Chronicles of the, see *Chronicles of the Canongate.*

Canonical Hours, stated times of the day appointed by the canon of the Catholic Church for prayer and devotion.

Canon's Yeoman's Tale, The, see *Canterbury Tales.*

Canossa, in the district of Modena, where the Emperor Henry IV submitted to the penance imposed on him by Pope Gregory VII; hence 'to go to Canossa' means to submit to penance or humiliation.

Cantab, an abbreviation of CANTABRIGIAN, of or belonging to the University of Cambridge.

Canterbury Tales, The, Chaucer's greatest work, designed about 1387, and written for the greater part in heroic couplets (about 17,000 lines). The main *Prologue* is especially interesting for the vivid picture it presents of contemporary life. A party of twenty-nine[1] pilgrims are assembled at the Tabard Inn in Southwark, about to travel to the shrine of Becket at Canterbury, and of each of these the poet draws a striking portrait. They are the following:

1. Knight;
2. Squire;
3. Yeoman (servant);
4. Prioress;
5. Nun;
6, 7, 8. Three Priests;
9. Monk;
10. Friar;
11. Merchant;
12. Clerk of Oxford;
13. Sergeant of Law;
14. Franklin (freeman and freeholder);
15. Haberdasher;
16. Carpenter;
17. Webbe (weaver);
18. Dyer;
19. Tapicer (maker of tapestry);
20. Cook;
21. Shipman (sailor);
22. Doctor of Physic;
23. Wife of Bath;
24. Parson (parish priest);
25. Ploughman;
26. Miller;
27. Manciple (steward);
28. Reeve (bailiff);
29. Summoner (officer of ecclesiastical court);
30. Pardoner (seller of indulgences);
31. Chaucer himself.

After supper the host proposes that they shall shorten the way by telling each two stories on the way out and two on the way back. The teller of the best stories shall have a free supper on his return. The host will accompany them and act as guide. The pilgrims agree and the tales follow, each of them preceded by a prologue. But the poem was not completed and contains only twenty-three tales as follows:

1. *The Knight's Tale,* a version of the 'Teseida' of Boccaccio, the story of the love of Palamon and Arcite, prisoners of Theseus, king of Athens, for Emilia, sister of Hippolyta, queen of the Amazons, whom Theseus has married. The rivals compete for her in a tournament. Palamon is defeated, but Arcite at the moment of his triumph is thrown and injured by his horse and dies. Palamon and Emilia, after prolonged mourning for Arcite, are united.

2. *The Miller's Tale,* a ribald story of the deception, first of a husband (a carpenter) through the prediction of a second flood, and secondly of a lover who expects to kiss the lady's lips and avenges himself for his disappointment with a hot coulter.

3. *The Reeve's Tale,* connected with a French *fabliau* and the 'Decameron', an indecent story of two clerks who are

---

[1] So the prologue states, but there are, including Chaucer himself, thirty-one. It has been suggested that the words *and preestes three* (Prol. 164) are not Chaucer's. But evidently Chaucer changed his mind as the work proceeded, and left it unfinished when he died.

robbed by a miller of part of their meal, and revenge themselves on the miller's wife and daughter. (The Reeve, who had been a carpenter, thus retorts upon the Miller.)

4. *The Cook's Tale* (another tale of 'harlotrie' as Chaucer calls it) is imperfect and omitted in some manuscripts.

5. *The Man of Law's Tale*, related to a story in Gower's 'Confessio Amantis', is the story of Constance, daughter of a Christian emperor, married to the Soldan on condition that he shall become a Christian, and by the device of the Soldan's mother cast adrift on the sea.

6. *The Wife of Bath's Tale* is preceded by a long prologue, a condemnation of celibacy in the form of an account of her life with her five successive husbands. The tale is like Gower's story of Florent in 'Confessio Amantis', but is transferred to the court of King Arthur. It relates how a knight who is required, in order to avoid execution, to answer correctly within a twelvemonth the question, what do women love most, is told the right answer— 'sovereignty'—by a foul old witch on condition that he marries her. He reluctantly complies and finds the witch restored to youth and beauty.

7. *The Friar's Tale* tells how a summoner meets the devil dressed as a bailiff, who confides to him his methods in dealing with men. The summoner attempts to extort a gift from a widow, who commends him to the devil. The devil thereupon hales him off to hell.

8. *The Summoner*, in retaliation, relates how the manœuvres of a greedy and hypocritical friar by a sick-bed were unsavourily defeated.

9. *The Clerk's Tale*, which the poet states he learnt from Petrarch, was translated by the latter into Latin from the 'Decameron'. It tells how the Marquis of Saluces married the humble Griselda, and of her virtues and patience under trials. (Cf. Dekker's 'Patient Grissil'.)

10. *The Merchant's Tale*, of an old man and his young wife. The old man becomes blind; the wife and her lover take advantage of this in a pear-tree. Pluto suddenly restores the husband's sight, but Proserpine enables the wife to outwit him. The precise source of the story has not been traced.

11. *The Squire's Tale*, of Cambuscan, king of Tartary, to whom on his birthday an envoy from the king of Arabia brings magic gifts, including a ring for the king's daughter Canace, which enables her to understand the language of birds. A female falcon tells Canace the story of her own desertion by a tercelet. The poet promises the continuation of the tale, but it is incomplete. (See under *Cambell* for the continuation in Spenser's 'Faerie Queene'.) The tale is referred to by Milton in 'Il Penseroso'. The origin of the tale is unknown.

12. *The Franklin's Tale*, of a woman, Dorigen wife of Arveragus, who to escape the assiduity of her lover, the squire Aurelius, makes her consent depend upon an impossible condition, that all the rocks on the coast of Brittany be removed. When this condition is realized by the aid of a magician, the lover, from a generous remorse, releases her from her promise. Chaucer states that the tale is taken from a 'Breton Lay', but this is lost. Similar stories are found in Boccaccio.

13. *The Second Nun's Tale*, in rhyme-royal, is perhaps translated from the life of St. Cecilia in the Golden Legend of Jacobus de Voragine. It describes the miracles and martyrdom of the noble Roman maiden Cecilia and her husband Valerian.

A certain canon and his yeoman having joined the party at Boughton-under-Blee, we next have

14. *The Canon's Yeoman's Tale*, an exposure of the follies and rogueries of the Alchemists.

15. *The Doctor's Tale*, of the death of Virginia by her own wish at her father's hands, to save her from the designs of the wicked judge Apius, who has conspired to get possession of her. Chaucer quotes

Livy as the source, but has followed fairly closely the version of the story in the 'Roman de la Rose'.

16. *The Pardoner's Tale* has an analogue in an Italian miscellany. The Pardoner discourses on the evils of Gluttony and Drunkenness, Gambling and Swearing. This theme is illustrated by the story of three revellers who in plague-time set out on a search for Death, who has killed one of their comrades. An old man tells them they will find him under a certain tree. There they discover a heap of gold. Each designs to get sole possession of the treasure, but they only succeed in killing one another.

17. *The Shipman's Tale.* There is a similar story in the 'Decameron', D. viii, N. 1. The wife of a niggardly merchant asks the loan of a hundred francs from a priest to buy finery. The priest borrows the sum from the merchant and hands it to the wife, and the wife grants him her favours. On the merchant's return from a journey the priest tells him that he has repaid the sum to the wife, who cannot deny receiving it.

18. *The Prioress's Tale*, the source of which is unknown, is the legend of a widow's child living in 'a great city' in Asia, who is murdered by Jews because he sings 'O alma Redemptoris mater' when passing through the Jewish quarter on his way to school. The body is discovered owing to the fact that he miraculously continues his song after his throat is cut. The Prioress ends with an invocation to 'yonge Hugh of Lincoln', also reputed to have been a victim of Jewish ritual murder. This tale is in rhyme-royal.

19. Chaucer's own contribution follows, in the form of the *Tale of Sir Thopas*, in which he slyly ridicules the romances of knight-errantry by contemporary rhymers. It contains phrases from 'Isumbras', 'Li Beaus Desconus', and refers to Sir Bevis, Sir Guy, etc. It is soon interrupted, and Chaucer then gives the *Tale of Melibeus*, a prose translation of a French romance, 'a moral tale vertuous'. It is a long and (to

us) tedious disputation between Melibeus and his wife Prudence on the most judicious method of dealing with enemies who have done them grievous injuries.

20. *The Monk's Tale* is composed of a number of 'tragedies' of persons fallen from high estate, taken from different authors and arranged on the model of Boccaccio's 'De casibus virorum illustrium'. The tale is in eight-lined stanzas.

21. *The Nun's Priest's Tale*, perhaps developed from one of the episodes in the French story of Reynard the Fox, tells of a fox that beguiled a cock by praising his father's singing, and was beguiled in turn to let the cock escape.

22. *The Manciple's Tale* is the fable of the Crow, which had been treated by many authors from Ovid onwards. A certain Phebus has a crow that is white and can counterfeit any man's speech. It thus reveals to Phebus his wife's infidelity. Phebus in a fury kills his wife, and then, in remorse, plucks out the crow's white feathers, deprives it of its speech, and throws it out 'unto the devil', which is why crows are now black.

23. *The Parson's Tale*, a dissertation in prose on penitence, the character of each kind of sin, and the appropriate remedy. It is probably the raw material on which Chaucer proposed to work, rather than his finished tale.

Canute or CNUT, a Dane, king of England, 1016–35. The story of Canute and the sea is told in Holinshed. He sat down close to the rising tide and bade it go no further. When it advanced and wetted him, he said to his courtiers that he 'could not stay this small portion of water'. This he did to reprove their flattery.

Canute, The Song of, a famous early English ballad, stated to have been composed and sung by the king as he rowed past Ely. It begins:

Merie sungen the muneches binnen Ely
Tha Cnut cning reu ther by.

'Capability' Brown, see *Brown* (L.).

Capell, EDWARD (1713–81), Shakespearian commentator. His edition of

Shakespeare in ten volumes in 1768 was the first to be based on complete and careful collations of all the old copies, and it is his arrangement of the lines that is now usually followed.

Capet, the name of the French dynasty founded by Hugo Capet in 987, which ruled until 1328, when it was succeeded by the House of Valois.

Capgrave, JOHN (1393-1464), an Augustinian friar, wrote, in Latin, sermons, theological tracts, and commentaries on many books of scripture, also in English a chronicle of English history extending to A.D. 1417.

Capitol, THE, in ancient Rome, that summit of the Capitoline hill on which stood the magnificent temple of Jupiter. In this temple were kept the Sibylline books (q.v.), and here the consuls took the vows on entering upon office.

In Washington the Capitol is the seat of the National Congress.

Caponsacchi, CANON GIUSEPPE, one of the principal characters in Browning's 'The Ring and the Book' (q.v.).

Capricorn, (1) the zodiacal constellation of the He-goat, lying between Sagittarius and Aquarius; (2) the tenth of the signs of the zodiac, which the sun enters about 21 Dec.

Captain Kettle, see *Kettle*.

Captain Nemo, see *Nemo*.

Captain Singleton, Adventures of, see *Singleton*.

Capuchin, a friar of the order of St. Francis, of the new rule of 1528, so called from their sharp-pointed capuches or hoods.

Capulets, THE, in Shakespeare's 'Romeo and Juliet' (q.v.), the noble Veronese house to which Juliet belongs, hostile to the family of the Montagues.

Carabas, MARQUESS OF, a character in the fairy tale of 'Puss in Boots'; in B. Disraeli's 'Vivian Grey'; and in Thackeray's 'Book of Snobs'.

Caractacus or CARADOC, king of the Silures in the west of Britain during the reign of Claudius, was defeated by the

Romans and taken a prisoner to Rome in A.D. 51, where his noble spirit so pleased the emperor that he pardoned and released him. He figures as Caratach in Beaumont and Fletcher's 'Bonduca'. W. Mason (1724-97) wrote a play 'Caractacus'.

Caradoc, see *Caractacus*.

Carbonek, in the legend of the Holy Grail, the enchanted castle where the Grail is found.

Cardinall, The, a tragedy by James Shirley (q.v.), produced in 1641.

Cardinal's Snuff-Box, The, a novel by Henry Harland (q.v.) (1900).

Careless, a character in Sheridan's 'The School for Scandal' (q.v.); also in Congreve's 'The Double Dealer'.

Careless Husband, The, a comedy by Cibber (q.v.) (1715).

Carew (pron. 'Carey'), THOMAS (1598?-1639?), won the favour of Charles I, was appointed to an office at court, and received an estate from him. He was, in poetry, a disciple of Ben Jonson, and wrote a fine elegy on Donne. His principal works are a masque, 'Coelum Britannicum' (1634), 'The Rapture' (an amatory poem), and numerous graceful songs and lyrics.

Carey, HENRY (d. 1743), is remembered as the author of the burlesque 'Chrononhotonthologos' (1734), and principally as the author of the words and music of 'Sally in our Alley'. He also wrote a burlesque opera, 'The Dragon of Wantley' (1734).

Carker, surname of two brothers, in Dickens's 'Dombey and Son' (q.v.).

Carleton, Memoirs of Captain, see *Memoirs of Captain Carleton*.

Carleton, WILLIAM (1794-1869), was the author of a number of remarkable stories of Irish peasant life, of which he paints the melancholy as well as the humorous side. The best of his longer stories was 'Fardorougha, the Miser' (1839).

Carlion, in Malory's 'Morte Darthur' (q.v.), the city where Arthur was crowned and held his court, probably Caerleon-upon-Usk.

Carlos, DON, the deformed son of Philip

II of Spain. The marriage of the latter with Elizabeth of France, who had been affianced to Don Carlos, forms the subject of Otway's tragedy 'Don Carlos'.

Carlovingians or CAROLINGIANS, the second royal dynasty of the Franks. Pepin, the father of Charlemagne, was the first king (751).

Carlton Club, THE, founded in 1831 by the Duke of Wellington, a political club for men of Tory opinions.

Carlyle, JANE BAILLIE WELSH (1801–66), wife of Thomas Carlyle (q.v.). Collections of her letters were published in 1883, 1924, and 1931.

Carlyle, THOMAS (1795–1881), was born in Dumfriesshire, of peasant stock, educated at the parish school, and at the age of 15 entered Edinburgh University. He was subsequently a schoolmaster, but soon took to literary work, studying German literature, and writing his 'Life of Schiller', which appeared in the 'London Magazine' in 1823-4. In 1826 he married Jane Welsh, a Scottish lady of strong character and shrewd wit, one of the best letter-writers in the English language, and retired to her farm at Craigenputtock. He contributed essays on German literature to the 'Edinburgh' and other reviews, wrote 'Sartor Resartus' (q.v.), and the first part of 'The French Revolution' (q.v.). He removed to Cheyne Row, Chelsea, in 1834. The manuscript of the first volume of 'The French Revolution' was accidentally burnt while in J. S. Mill's keeping, but Carlyle re-wrote it and the work finally appeared in 1837. In the same and following years he gave several courses of popular lectures. In his 'Chartism' (1839) and 'Past and Present' (1843) he turned his attention to political problems of the day, and the present and future of Labour. Salvation, according to him, was to be sought in a return to medieval conditions and the rule of the strong just man, who was not to be got by popular election. The same views, in an exaggerated form, are to be found in his 'Latter-Day Pamphlets' (1850). Carlyle's second great work,

'Oliver Cromwell's Letters and Speeches', was published in 1845, and the 'Life of John Sterling' in 1851. After this he spent fourteen years on the preparation of the 'History of Frederick the Great' (1858-65). Mrs. Carlyle died in 1866, and after this he wrote little of importance. His 'Life' was written with more frankness than judgement by his friend and disciple, James Anthony Froude (q.v.). Several volumes of his letters have been published.

Carmelites, an order of mendicant friars (called also WHITE FRIARS) and nuns, who derive their origin from a colony founded on Mt. Carmel in the 12th cent.

Carmilhan, a spectre ship, in one of Longfellow's 'Tales of a Wayside Inn'. She brings disaster to whatever ship meets her.

Carmina Burana, a collection of Goliardic (q.v.) poems from the Benedictine monastery of Benedictbeuern in Bavaria.

Carnegie, ANDREW (1835–1919), was taken when a child to America by his parents. At the age of 13 he began work in a cotton factory. Later, by his energy and shrewd speculative investments, he became enormously rich and in 1901, retiring from business, set about the distribution of his surplus wealth. The most important of his benefactions from a literary standpoint was his provision of public libraries in Great Britain and the United States. He also instituted a trust for the universities of Scotland, and several trusts for the advancement of research and education in the United States.

Carol, originally (before about 1550) a song on any subject, composed of uniform stanzas and provided with a burden or refrain. This last qualification is important as often distinguishing it from other forms of medieval lyric and ballad: it connects it with the *Carole*, or song accompanied with a dance, from which it is derived. The great popularity of the carol in the medieval period and the influence on its forms of Latin accentual lyrics led to its use for religious purposes, particularly by the Franciscans. This has led in the modern period to the term 'carol' being applied to songs or hymns of religious joy, particularly in connection with Christmas festivities. The definition of the editors of 'The Oxford Book of Carols' is relevant: 'Carols are songs with a religious impulse that are simple, hilarious, popular, and modern.' The first collection of Christmas carols that we possess was printed by Wynkyn de Worde in 1521. (For the medieval forms see Greene, 'The Early English Carol', 1935.)

Caroline, a term applied to the dramatists, authors, etc., of the period of Charles I. As a literary period it was marked by an advance in lyrical poetry and prose writing but a decline in dramatic vigour. (See also *Caroline Drama, Metaphysical Poets, Cavalier Lyrics*.)

Caroline, QUEEN, (1) consort of George II, figures in Scott's 'The Heart of Midlothian' (q.v.) and is prominent in the memoirs of the time; (2) consort of George IV, figures in Byron's poems, etc.

Caroline Drama, the drama of the period of Charles I. In this period, the traditions of the Elizabethan stage were continued, without any great individuality or originality but with a good deal of technical skill. Massinger, Ford, and Shirley (qq.v.) were the most notable dramatists of the period but there were also many minor playwrights, e.g. Brome, Cartwright, Shackerley Marmion, etc. The tendency, based on popular demand, was toward comedy and masque and away from tragedy. On the whole, the stage was less popular and was supported more by aristocratic patronage. Prose was used more: blank verse tended to be softer and less rhythmical.

Caroline Minuscule, a style of writing developed at Tours under Charlemagne, and perpetuated in our modern hand.

Carolingians, see *Carlovingians*.

Carpet-bagger, in U.S. political slang, a scornful term applied after the American Civil War of 1861–5 to immigrants from the northern to the southern states, whose 'property qualification' consisted merely of the contents of the carpet-bag. Hence applied generally to any one interfering with the politics of a locality with which he is thought to have no genuine or permanent connection.

Carrasco, SAMSON, in 'Don Quixote' (q.v.), a bachelor of the University of Salamanca, who tries to cure Don Quixote of his folly.

Carroll, LEWIS, see *Dodgson*.

Carson, KIT (1809–68), famous American trapper and guide.

Carstone, RICHARD, one of the two wards in Chancery in Dickens's 'Bleak House' (q.v.).

Carter, ELIZABETH (1717–1806), a member of the Blue Stocking (q.v.) circle, was a friend of Richardson and of Dr. Johnson, to whose 'Rambler' she contributed two numbers. Her letters to Miss Talbot, Mrs. Vesey, and Mrs. Montagu, were published after her death (1809–17).

Cartesianism, see *Descartes*.

Carthage, a famous city of the ancient world. The Punic Wars (as the wars between Rome and Carthage were called), which lasted 265–242, 218–201, and 149–146 B.C., ended in the destruction of the latter city. See *Cato the Censor* and *Marius among the ruins of Carthage*.

Carthusians, an order of monks founded by St. Bruno in 1086, remarkable for the severity of their rule. See also under *Charterhouse*.

Carton, SYDNEY, a character in Dickens's 'A Tale of Two Cities' (q.v.).

Caruso, ENRICO (1873–1921), famous Italian opera singer.

Carvel, Hans, see *Hans Carvel*.

Cary, (ARTHUR) JOYCE (LUNEL) (1888–1957), novelist. He joined the Nigerian political service in 1913, and served with a Nigerian regiment in the Cameroons campaign, 1915–16. His early 'African' novels, 'Aissa Saved' (1932), 'An American Visitor' (1933), 'The African Witch' (1936), and 'Mister Johnson' (1939), show the relations between Africans and their

British administrators. His greatest work consists of two trilogies: 'Herself Surprised' (1941), 'To Be a Pilgrim' (1942), and 'The Horse's Mouth' (1944), concerned mainly with art; and 'Prisoner of Grace' (1952), 'Except the Lord' (1953), and 'Not Honour More' (1955), a study of politics.

Cary, HENRY FRANCIS (1772-1844), translated Dante's 'Divina Commedia' (1805-14), the 'Birds' of Aristophanes (1824), and Pindar (1832).

Caryll, JOHN (1625-1711), diplomatist, and author of 'Sir Solomon Single', a comedy. He was a friend and correspondent of Pope, to whom he suggested the subject of 'The Rape of the Lock' (q.v.).

Casabianca, LOUIS (1755-98), commanded the French vessel 'l'Orient' at the battle of Aboukir, where he is said to have blown up his ship to prevent its falling into the hands of the English, and perished with his little son. This incident is the subject of the well-known poem by Mrs. Hemans (q.v.).

Casanova de Seingalt, GIACOMO (1725-98), an Italian adventurer, whose memoirs, written in an imperfect but lively French, describe his rogueries and amours in most countries of Europe.

Casaubon, ISAAC (1559-1614), a French Huguenot scholar and theologian, published critical editions of a number of classical authors of the early Christian era. A life of Casaubon was written by Mark Pattison (q.v.) (1875).

Casby, CHRISTOPHER and FLORA, characters in Dickens's 'Little Dorrit' (q.v.).

Casca, one of the conspirators in Shakespeare's 'Julius Caesar' (q.v.).

Case is altered, The, a comedy by Jonson (q.v.), written before 1599.

Casket Letters, THE, letters supposed to have passed between Mary Queen of Scots and Bothwell, and to have established her complicity in the murder of Darnley.

Cask of Amontillado, The, a tale by Edgar Allan Poe (q.v.).

Caslon, WILLIAM (1692-1766), the first English typefounder to make a complete range of roman and italic types of his own design, besides cutting Greek and exotic scripts. His types are still in use.

Cassandra, daughter of Priam, king of Troy, received the gift of prophecy from Apollo. But as she slighted him, the god contrived that no trust should be placed in her predictions. After the fall of Troy she fell to the lot of Agamemnon, and was murdered by Clytemnestra (q.v.).

Cassibellaun (CASSIBELAN in Shakespeare's 'Cymbeline'), or CASSIVELAUNUS, the ruler of the country north of the Thames, who was given the chief command of the British forces that resisted Caesar's second invasion (54 B.C.). He was defeated and obliged to sue for peace.

Cassio, MICHAEL, in Shakespeare's 'Othello' (q.v.), the Moor's lieutenant.

Cassiodorus, MAGNUS AURELIUS (*c.* A.D. 480-575), a distinguished statesman who governed for many years the Ostrogothic kingdom, a man of exceptional learning for his period. He spent the last years of his life at the monastery at Viviers which he had founded. There he set his monks to copy classical (Latin) manuscripts; much would have been lost but for this. He was author of several works in Latin.

Cassiopeia, wife of Cepheus, king of Ethiopia, and mother of Andromeda (q.v.), who boasted herself more beautiful than the Nereids. She was changed into a northern constellation, the 'starr'd Ethiop queen' of Milton's 'Il Penseroso'.

Cassius, in Shakespeare's 'Julius Caesar' (q.v.), the friend of Brutus and leader of the conspiracy.

Castalia, the name of a spring on Mt. Parnassus, sacred to Apollo and the Muses, said to be so called from Castalia (daughter of Achelous), who plunged into it to escape the pursuit of Apollo.

Castalio, a character in Otway's 'The Orphan' (q.v.).

Castiglione, BALDASSARE (1478-1529), Italian humanist, chiefly known for his prose dialogue, 'Il Cortegiano' (1528), translated in 1561 into English by Sir Thomas Hoby (1530–66). In this dialogue all the qualifications of the ideal courtier are set out and discussed. The work had much influence on the literature of England, e.g. on Surrey, Wyatt, Sidney, and Spenser.

Castle Dangerous, a novel by Sir W. Scott (q.v.) (1831), in the fourth and last of the 'Tales of My Landlord'.

Castle of Indolence, The, a poem in Spenserian stanzas by J. Thomson (q.v.) (1748), the most beautiful and musical of Thomson's works.

Castle of Otranto, The, a Gothic Story, a novel by H. Walpole (q.v.) (1764).

This work purported in the first edition to be a translation from the Italian, but its authorship was acknowledged in the second edition. The events related are supposed to have occurred in the 12th or 13th cents. It set a fashion for 'Gothic' tales of mystery and horror. See *Gothic novels*.

Castle Perilous, in Malory's 'Morte Darthur', the castle of the Lady Lyones. See *Gareth and Lynette*.

Castle Rackrent, a novel by M. Edgeworth (q.v.) (1800).

The book gives a vivid picture of the reckless living which in the 18th cent. brought many Irish landlords to ruin.

Castlereagh, ROBERT STEWART, *second marquis of Londonderry*, better known as *Viscount Castlereagh* (1769–1822), was foreign secretary from 1812 to 1822, and took a leading part in the European settlement at the Congress of Vienna and after Waterloo, restraining the allies from retaliation on France. His mind became affected by work and responsibility and he committed suicide. Shelley (q.v.) in his 'Masque of Anarchy' (provoked by the Peterloo affair, q.v.) wrote:

I met Murder on the way—
He had a mask like Castlereagh.

Castlewood, THOMAS, *third Viscount*, and his wife ISABEL; FRANCIS, *fourth Viscount*, his wife RACHEL, and his daughter, BEATRIX; FRANCIS, *fifth Viscount*;

characters in Thackeray's 'Esmond' (q.v.). Also EUGÈNE, *earl of Castlewood*, in Thackeray's 'The Virginians' (q.v.), son of the last named.

Castor and Pollux, twin brothers, sons of Zeus by Leda (q.v.). They took part in the expedition of the Argonauts (q.v.). The twins were regarded as the friends of navigators, having the power to calm storms. They were made a constellation known as *Gemini* or the Twins.

Catachrēsis, application of a term to a thing it does not properly denote; misuse of words.

Cataian, variant of CATHAIAN, a man of Cathay or China; used also to signify a sharper, and so used by Shakespeare in 'The Merry Wives of Windsor', II. i.

Catalectic, said of a verse whose last foot is truncated and has only one syllable, or is altogether cut off; e.g. 'Best and brightest, come away'. Cf. *acatalectic*.

Catharine of Alexandria, ST., a princess of the 3rd cent.; she was beheaded in 307 after tortures which have given their name to the catherine wheel, a kind of firework.

Catharine of Genoa, ST. (*b.* 1447), an outstanding mystic, who wrote 'Dialogues of the Soul and Body' and a 'Treatise on Purgatory'.

Catharine of Siena, ST. (1347–80), an Italian saint. Her holiness of life and gift of diplomacy were so famous that she was called upon to mediate between Pope Urban VI and the Florentines in 1378.

Cathay ('Khitai'), the name by which China was known under the Mongol dynasty.

Cather, WILLA SIBERT (1876–1947), American novelist. Her chief books are: 'My Antonia' (1918), 'A Lost Lady' (1923), a moving lament for the passing of the pioneering era of the West, 'Death Comes for the Archbishop' (1927), and 'Shadows on the Rock' (1931).

Catherine, by Thackeray (q.v.) (1839–40), written under the pseudonym 'Ikey Solomons, junior', an ironical tale of a criminal life.

Catholic Church, a term first applied to

the whole body of Christian believers. After the separation of the Eastern and Western Churches, 'Catholic' was assumed by the latter as its descriptive epithet, and 'Orthodox' by the former. At the Reformation the term 'Catholic' was claimed as its exclusive right by the body remaining under the Roman obedience, in opposition to the Protestant or Reformed Churches. These, however, also retained the term, giving it, for the most part, a wider and more ideal and absolute sense. In order to distinguish the unreformed Latin Church, its chosen epithet of 'Catholic' was further qualified by 'Roman'. On this analogy 'Anglo-Catholic' has been used by some, since about 1835, of the Anglican Church, in preference to 'Protestant'. In the latter part of the 19th and in the 20th cents., the term Anglo-Catholic has been applied in a more special sense to the high church element in the Anglican Church, which was associated with the Oxford Movement (q.v.).

Catholic King, HIS CATHOLIC MAJESTY, a title assumed by the kings of Spain.

Catiline, a Roman tragedy by Jonson (q.v.), first acted in 1611. The play is based on the events of the year 63 B.C., when Catiline organized a conspiracy to overthrow the existing government. Cicero and Antonius were elected consuls, and Catiline, secretly encouraged by Caesar and Crassus, prepared for a rising. Cicero, however, warned by Fulvia, the mistress of Curius, summons the senate and accuses Catiline, who leaves Rome and joins the troops raised by his adherents at Faesulae. Cicero obtains evidence of the guilt of the conspirators through the ambassadors of the Allobroges, and submits it to the senate, which resolves that they shall be put to death. Catiline falls in the decisive engagement between his troops and those of the government commanded by Petreius.

Cato, a tragedy by Addison (q.v.), produced in 1713.

The political excitement at the moment

when the play was produced—the question of the succession was acute—contributed to the success of a drama dealing with Cato's last stand for liberty. It deals with the last phase of the life of M. Porcius Cato the republican, who is besieged in Utica by Caesar (46 B.C.). He takes his own life rather than surrender to the dictator.

Cato Street Conspiracy, a plot by a certain Arthur Thistlewood (1770-1820) and some thirty other persons in 1820 to murder the ministers of the Crown, provoked by the repressive measures taken by the government. The conspirators met in a stable in Cato Street near the Edgware Road. The conspiracy was betrayed and the leaders executed.

Cato the Censor (234-149 B.C.) was famous for his opposition to the prevalent fashions of luxury. He became convinced that Rome would never be safe until Carthage was destroyed. Whenever called upon to vote in the senate, and whatever the subject, his final words were 'Delenda est Carthago'.

Catriona, see *Kidnapped*.

Catullus, GAIUS VALERIUS (c. 84-c. 54 B.C.), a great Roman poet and epigrammatist, born in or near Verona. The Lesbia celebrated in his poems was Clodia, the notorious sister of Publius Clodius.

Caudine Forks, narrow passes in the mountains of Samnium where the Roman army surrendered to the Samnites in 321 B.C.

Caudle Lectures, see *Mrs. Caudle's Curtain Lectures*.

Cavalier, Memoirs of a, see *Memoirs of a Cavalier*.

Cavaliers, the adherents of the king in the Civil War of the 17th cent. The term was originally reproachful and given to the swashbucklers on the king's side, who hailed the prospect of war.

CAVALIER LYRICS, a term applied to the lyrical poetry of which there was a remarkable outburst during the reign of Charles I, and of which the court was the centre, though Robert Herrick, the chief of these lyrists, was not a courtier. The principal other Cavalier lyrists were Thomas Carew, Sir John Suckling, and Richard Lovelace (qq.v.). Their lyrics were notable for their sweetness and charm.

Cave, EDWARD (1691–1754), a London printer, published many journals and books, but is chiefly remembered as the founder of 'The Gentleman's Magazine' (q.v.), which he conducted from 1731 until his death.

Cavendish, HENRY (1731–1810), natural philosopher, discovered the constitution of water and atmospheric air, and experimented on electricity and the density of the earth. His name is commemorated in the CAVENDISH LABORATORY at Cambridge.

Cave of Adullam, see *Adullamites*.

Cave of Harmony, THE, in Thackeray's 'The Newcomes' (q.v.).

Cave of Mammon, see *Mammon*.

Cavour, CAMILLO BENSO, *Conte di* (1810–61), was prime minister in the Sardinian government 1852–9 and 1860–1. His statesmanship brought about, before his death, the unification of the greater part of Italy.

Cawdor, THANE OF, see *Macbeth*.

Caxon, JACOB, in Scott's 'The Antiquary' (q.v.), hairdresser at Fairport.

Caxton, WILLIAM (*c.* 1421–91), the first English printer, and a merchant and man of affairs. He was apprenticed to a London merchant and then spent thirty years in the Low Countries. In 1471 he was in Cologne where he probably worked in a printing house. He printed his translation, the 'Recuyell of the Historyes of Troye', *c.* 1475, on a press set up with Colard Mansion, a calligrapher. He also printed in Bruges 'The Game and Playe of the Chesse' (q.v.), *c.* 1475. He established a press at Westminster in 1476 and printed about 100 books, a number of them his own translations from the French. He used eight founts of type. His importance in the history of English literature is by no means confined to his

work as a printer, for he contributed by his translations to the formation in the 15th cent. of an English prose style.

Caxtons, The, a novel by Bulwer Lytton (q.v.) (1849).

Cecilia, ST., a Christian martyr who died at Rome in 230. She is said to have been forced to marry, in spite of her vows of celibacy, a certain Valerian. She converted him to Christianity, and both suffered martyrdom. When the Academy of Music was founded at Rome in 1584 she was adopted, perhaps inappropriately, as the patroness of Church Music. Her story is told in Chaucer's 'Second Nun's Tale' (see *Canterbury Tales*). Dryden (q.v.) wrote a 'Song for St. Cecilia's Day', and Pope (q.v.) an 'Ode for Music on Saint Cecilia's Day'. She is commemorated on 22 Nov.

Cecilia, or Memoirs of an Heiress, a novel by Fanny Burney (q.v.) (1782).

This was the second of Miss Burney's novels, and was at once successful.

Cecrops, the legendary first king of Attica, which he called CECROPIA after him, and founder of Athens. See *Athene*.

Cedilla, a mark (ҙ), derived through the letter *z* from the Arabic letter *sād*, written, especially in French and Portuguese words, under the letter *c*, to show that it has the soft sound in positions in which the hard sound would be normal, as before *a, o, u.*

Cedric the Saxon, one of the principal characters in Scott's 'Ivanhoe' (q.v.).

Ceix and Alceone, a tale in Bk. v of Gower's 'Confessio Amantis' (q.v.). See *Halcyone*. See also Chaucer's *Boke of the Duchesse*.

Celestial City, THE, in Bunyan's 'The Pilgrim's Progress' (q.v.), signifying Heaven.

Celestina, or the Tragi-Comedy of Calisto and Melibea, a novel in dialogue which has had several stage adaptations. The first known edition appeared about 1499, in sixteen acts, and a later version, in 1502, in twenty-one acts. It is reasonably certain that Acts II–XVI were written by the Spanish writer Fernando de Rojas (*c.* 1465-1541).

The work takes the form of a dialogue, but is essentially dramatic, and marks an important stage in the literary history of Spain and of Europe. It is an extremely vivid, entertaining work, one of the first to present romance in everyday life.

An excellent and racy, if exuberantly diffuse, translation into English prose, 'The Spanish Bawd', was made by James Mabbe (1572-1642?), and published in 1631. The early part of 'Celestina' was translated into English verse by John Rastell, provided with a happy ending, and published (*c.* 1530) as 'A new comodye in englysh in manner of an interlude', better known as 'An Interlude of Calisto and Melebea'. It is one of the first English dramatic works that approach true comedy.

Celia, one of the principal characters in Shakespeare's 'As You Like It' (q.v.).

Cellini, BENVENUTO (1500-71), a Florentine goldsmith and sculptor, and author of one of the most vivid and interesting autobiographies ever written. The first edition was published in 1730 (dedicated to Richard Boyle) at Naples. The best-known English translation is by J. A. Symonds (1888).

Celt, a name applied in modern times to peoples speaking languages akin to those of the ancient Galli or Gauls, including the Bretons in France, the Cornish, Welsh, Irish, Manx, and Gaelic of the British Isles.

Celtic Twilight, The, a collection of stories by Yeats (q.v.) (1893), illustrating the mysticism of the Irish. It has since become a generic phrase (slightly ironical) for the whole Irish literary revival movement.

Cenci, The, a tragedy by P. B. Shelley (q.v.) (1819).

Count Francesco Cenci, after a life of wickedness, conceived an implacable hatred against his children, which towards one daughter Beatrice took the form of an incestuous passion. Beatrice after vain attempts to escape, plotted with her step-mother Lucretia, and her brother Bernardo, the murder of their common tyrant. Circumstances having aroused suspicion against them, the Cenci were arrested, and by dint of examinations and torture, the facts were discovered, and the Cenci sentenced to death. These events occurred in the year 1599, and are made the subject of Shelley's play.

Written in blank verse, the play has considerable dramatic qualities. Beatrice's last speech before her death is famous.

Censorship. Proclamations against the publishing of seditious and heretical books were made in the reign of Henry VIII soon after the introduction of printing; in 1538 licensing by the Privy Council or other royal nominees was made a necessary requirement. When the Stationers' Company obtained a charter for incorporation in 1557 (see under *Copyright*), only members of the Company might print any work for sale in England. Further efforts to enforce State control were made in the time of Elizabeth, notably by Archbishop Whitgift, in an attempt to suppress Puritan pamphlets (see *Martin Marprelate*). The abolition by the Long Parliament in 1641 of the Court of Star Chamber (one of whose last measures was a stringent decree in 1637) did not bring any greater freedom. Milton's 'Areopagitica' (q.v.) is a noble appeal for a free press which was not, however, granted. Under the Restoration the control and licensing of the press continued, although there was greater liberty in practice. The licensing system came finally to an end in 1694, although prosecutions for seditious or other obnoxious publications were frequent in the 18th cent. The unsuccessful prosecution of Wilkes (q.v.) in 1763 brought a greater measure of freedom, which was increased by the responsibility of determining a libel being given to the jury and not to the judge (Fox's Libel Act, 1792). Executive interference with the press had on the whole declined throughout the 18th cent. and governments had come to rely on presenting their own case in rival publications. This freedom of the press has not been questioned in Great Britain in recent years—except perhaps by the rulers of totalitarian states anxious to remove sources of foreign criticism. The following are the chief heads under which the law today punishes the publication of illegal matter: (1) *Libel as a civil injury*, the publication of matter defamatory to the plaintiff. (2) *Libel as a criminal offence*, i.e. as calculated to provoke a breach of the peace or to outrage public feeling or morality, or to endanger the State. Under the Obscene Publications Act 1959 a book 'is deemed to be obscene if its effect . . . taken as a whole, is such as to tend to deprave and corrupt persons who are likely . . . to read . . . the matter contained . . . in it', but 'A person shall not be convicted of an offence [of publishing an obscene article] if it is proved that publication of the article in question is justified as being for the public good on the ground that it is in the interests of science, literature, art, or learning, or of other subjects of general concern.' Since 1959, for the first time, defendants have been allowed to bring witnesses to give evidence on the literary and moral qualities of a publication.

Control of the drama was exercised, in Elizabethan times by the Master of the Revels, from Restoration times onwards by the Lord Chamberlain. This control, which became more concerned with questions of public morality than with political matters, lasted until 1968, when the Lord Chamberlain's responsibility for licensing plays ceased.

Centaurs, a fabulous people of Thessaly, half men, half horses. See also *Cheiron*.

Centlivre, SUSANNAH (1667?-1723), actress and dramatist, married in 1706 Joseph Centlivre, cook to Queen Anne. She wrote eighteen plays, chiefly comedies, between 1700 and 1722. 'The Busybody' (1709) and 'A Bold Stroke for a Wife' (1718) are tolerably good.

Cent Nouvelles Nouvelles, Les, a collection of French tales, probably related to a real Court audience, licentious in character, and showing Italian influence (e.g. of the 'Decameron'). It was presented by its author to Philippe duke of Burgundy in 1462.

Cento (Latin *cento*, a garment of patchwork), a literary composition made up of scraps from various authors.

Cephalus, the husband of Procris. Eos (see *Aurora*) fell in love with him, and caused dissension between husband and wife. Artemis gave Procris a dog called Laelaps ('Storm') and a spear that never missed its aim. These Procris gave to Cephalus and a reconciliation followed. But Procris was still jealous, and watched her husband, hidden in a bush, when he was hunting. Cephalus thinking that he heard some animal stirring in the bush, hurled the spear and killed Procris. There is a reference to this myth in the 'Shafalus' and 'Procrus' of Pyramus and Thisbe (Shakespeare, 'A Midsummer Night's Dream', v. i). Milton refers to Cephalus as 'the Attic boy' in 'Il Penseroso' (q.v.).

Cerberus, the dog of Pluto (q.v.), who had fifty heads according to Hesiod, and three according to other authors. He was stationed at the entrance of hell. The heroes who in their lifetime visited Pluto's kingdom appeased him with a cake, whence the expression 'a sop to Cerberus'.

Ceres, see *Demeter*.

Cervantes Saavedra, MIGUEL DE (1547-1616), Spanish novelist and dramatist, was wounded and lost for life the use of his left hand at the battle of Lepanto (1571). He was taken by pirates in 1575, and spent the next five years as a prisoner at Algiers. His greatest work 'Don Quixote' (q.v.) was published, the first part in 1605, the second in 1615. He also wrote a number of plays, short stories, and a tale of adventure.

Cézanne, PAUL (1839-1906), French painter. At first closely connected with Impressionism (q.v.), Cézanne became more and more concerned with the rendering of solidity by the simplification of forms. His work was the starting-point for the development of Cubism (q.v.).

Chabot, The Tragedy of, a tragedy by Chapman (q.v.), probably revised and added to by Shirley, published in 1639. The date of its composition is uncertain.

Chadband, a character in Dickens's 'Bleak House' (q.v.).

Chainmail, MR., a character in Peacock's 'Crotchet Castle' (q.v.). He believes the 12th cent. to be the best period in English history.

Chaldean, a native of Chaldea, especially one skilled in occult learning, astrology, etc. Hence generally a seer, soothsayer, astrologer.

Chaldee MS., a famous satire on Edinburgh society published in 'Blackwood's Magazine' (q.v.) (1817).

Challenger, PROFESSOR GEORGE EDWARD, hero of 'The Lost World' and other stories by Sir A. Conan Doyle (q.v.), a distinguished zoologist and anthropologist of great vitality and violent temper.

Cham, an obsolete form of the word *Khan*, formerly applied to the emperor of China. Smollett, in a letter to Wilkes, 16 March 1759 (in Boswell), refers to Johnson as 'that great Cham of literature'.

Chambers, SIR EDMUND KERCHEVER (1866-1954), civil servant (Education) and literary critic. He is best known for the critical exactness and range of his history of the Elizabethan drama down to and including Shakespeare. His publications include: 'The Medieval Stage' (1903), 'The Elizabethan Stage' (1923), 'William Shakespeare' (1930).

Chambers, EPHRAIM (*d.* 1740), published his 'Cyclopaedia' (the first English Encyclopaedia, which has no connection with the current 'Chambers's Encyclopaedia') in 1728.

Chambers, ROBERT (1802-71), author and publisher. His 'Vestiges of Creation', published anonymously in 1844, is notable as an early statement of the theory of evolution.

Chambers's Encyclopaedia was begun in 1859 and completed in 1868, by the firm of W. and R. Chambers. There have been many subsequent editions.

Chamont, one of the principal characters in Otway's 'The Orphan' (q.v.).

Champion, The, a periodical issued thrice a week in 1739-41, mainly written by H. Fielding (q.v.).

Chances, The, a play by J. Fletcher (q.v.), with perhaps some contributions by another hand. The dialogue shows Fletcher at his best. The date of the play is uncertain.

Chandler, RAYMOND (1888-1959), American writer of mystery stories. His best-known books, distinguished for their style, are 'The Big Sleep' (1939), 'Farewell, My Lovely' (1940), and 'The Little Sister' (1949).

Changeling, The, a tragedy by T. Middleton and W. Rowley (qq.v.), printed in 1653, but acted as early as 1623.

Channing, WILLIAM ELLERY (1780-1842), an American Unitarian clergyman, who had a marked influence on American intellectual life. His 'Remarks on American Literature', calling for a literary Declaration of Independence, appeared in 1830.

Chansons de geste, epic poems in Old French embodying legends which had grown up about earlier historical figures. The earliest extant versions are of the 12th cent., and use the legends to embody problems and difficulties of feudal society: either the stresses within the feudal system itself caused by conflicting loyalties, or those caused by the impact of the crusades on feudalism, as in the 'Chanson de Roland' (see *Roland*). The earliest poems, such as the 'Roland', are heroic in tone; the 12th-cent. poems with William of Orange as their hero are more realist; the later poems have courtly and marvellous elements in them, and lose the tragic seriousness of the early works.

Chanticleer, the cock, in 'Reynard the Fox' (q.v.) and in Chaucer's 'Nun's Priest's Tale' (see *Canterbury Tales*).

Chap-book, a name applied by book-collectors to specimens of the popular literature which was formerly circulated by itinerant dealers, or chapmen, consisting chiefly of small pamphlets of popular tales, ballads, tracts, etc. They reproduced old romances or nursery rhymes and fairy tales. They were issued in great numbers throughout the 18th cent.

Chapel, CHILDREN OF THE, see *Paul's* (*Children of*).

Chapman, GEORGE (1559?-1634?), is chiefly known for his translation of Homer, commemorated in Keats's sonnet, 'Much have I travelled in the realms of gold'; but Swinburne and others have drawn attention to the remarkable quality of his dramatic works. He was renowned as a scholar and is perhaps the 'rival poet' of Shakespeare's 'Sonnets'.

He published the obscure poem 'The Shadow of Night' in 1594, and a continuation of Marlowe's 'Hero and Leander' in 1598. His principal tragedies were published at the following dates: 'Bussy D'Ambois' (1607), 'The Conspiracy and Tragedy of Byron' (1608), 'The Revenge of Bussy D'Ambois' (1613), 'Caesar and Pompey' (1631), 'The Tragedy of Chabot' (1639). His principal comedies were: 'An Humorous Day's Mirth' (1599), 'All Fools' (1605), 'May-Day' (1611), 'The Gentleman Usher' (1606), 'Eastward hoe' (1605). This last play, written in collaboration with Ben Jonson and Marston, gave offence at Court, and led to the temporary imprisonment of the authors. Chapman published a specimen of his rhyming fourteen-syllable version of the 'Iliad' in 1598, and the whole 'Iliad' in 1611, adding the 'Odyssey' (rhyming ten-syllable) in 1614-15, and the hymns, etc. in 1616.

Characteristics of Men, Manners, Opinions, Times, see *Shaftesbury*.

Character of a Trimmer, see *Savile* (*G.*).

Charge of the Light Brigade, THE, see *Balaclava*.

Charitie, The Balade of, see *Balade*.

Charivari (from 14th-cent. French and medieval Latin words of unknown origin), a serenade of 'rough music'. Hence a con-

fused medley of sounds. 'Charivari' was taken as the name of a satirical journal in Paris, and adopted in 1841 as part of the title of the London 'Punch' (q.v.).

Charlemagne (742-814), king of the Franks (768) and emperor of the West (800), the son of Pepin. He and his paladins are the subject of numerous *chansons de geste*, of which the 'Chanson de Roland' is the most famous (see *Roland*).

Charles I, king of England, 1625-49.

Charles II, king of England, 1660-85. He figures in Scott's 'Peveril of the Peak' and 'Woodstock', and many other works.

Charles XII, king of Sweden, 1682-1718, and a great military commander. His life was written by Voltaire. Johnson ('Vanity of Human Wishes') says of him:

He left the name at which the world grew pale,
To point a moral or adorn a tale.

See also *Mazeppa*.

Charles Edward Stuart (1720-88), the Young Pretender, figures in Scott's 'Waverley' and 'Redgauntlet'.

Charles's Wain, the constellation comprising the seven bright stars in *Ursa Major*, known also as 'The Great Bear', 'The Plough', and 'The Dipper' (U.S.A.).

Charles the Bold, duke of Burgundy (1467-77), figures in Scott's 'Anne of Geierstein' and 'Quentin Durward'.

Charley, CHARLIE, the name colloquially given in former times to a night-watchman.

Charley's Aunt, a highly popular farcical comedy by Brandon Thomas, produced in 1892 and still frequently played.

Charmian, in Shakespeare's 'Antony and Cleopatra' and Dryden's 'All for Love' (qq.v.), the attendant of Cleopatra. The name, given as Charmion, is in Plutarch's 'Antony'.

Charon, in Greek mythology, the ferryman who, for an obol, conveyed the souls of the dead over the river Styx to Hades.

Charterhouse, THE, near Smithfield, London, one of the houses of the Carthusian (q.v.) order in England, converted into a school and a house for the aged poor. The school became famous and numbered Steele, Addison, Wesley, Leech, and Thackeray among its pupils. It was removed to Godalming, Surrey, in 1872. The home for poor brethren is the scene of Colonel Newcome's last days and death in Thackeray's 'The Newcomes' (q.v.).

Chartist, one of the body of political reformers (chiefly of the working classes) who arose in 1837 and who made certain demands embodied in the 'People's Charter'. The 'Chartists', as such, disappeared after 1848.

Charybdis, in Greek legend, a dangerous whirlpool on the coast of Sicily, in the straits of Messina, opposite Scylla (q.v.).

Chastelard, a tragedy by Swinburne (q.v.) (1865) on the subject of Mary Queen of Scots, and Chastelard, who fell desperately in love with her and followed her to Scotland. He was discovered in her room, sentenced to death, and executed.

Chaste Maid in Cheapside, A, a comedy by T. Middleton (q.v.) (1630).

Chateaubriand, FRANÇOIS RENÉ, *Vicomte de* (1768-1848), one of the pioneers of the French Romantic Movement.

Chatterton, THOMAS (1752-70), published in 1768 a pseudo-archaic description of the mayor of Bristol's passing over the 13th-cent. bridge, and met William Barrett, an antiquarian surgeon, George Catcott, and Henry Burgum, for all of whom he fabricated documents, pedigrees, poems, of which he claimed to possess the originals. He also fabricated a number of poems purporting to be the work of an imaginary 15th-cent. Bristol poet, Thomas Rowley. He offered some of these to Dodsley, the publisher, and sent a history of painting in England (supposed to be by Rowley) to Horace Walpole, who was temporarily deceived. The fraud was exposed by T. Tyrwhitt in his 'Poems supposed to have been written . . . by Thomas Rowley', 1777 and 1778; but the poems are none the less the work of a poetical genius. In 1770 Chatterton came to London, and his burlesque opera 'The

Revenge' was successfully produced in that year. Reduced to despair by his poverty, he poisoned himself with arsenic, 24 Aug. 1770, at the age of 17. There are admiring references to him in poems by Wordsworth, Coleridge, Keats, etc.

Chaucer, GEOFFREY (prob. 1345-1400), was son of John Chaucer (*d.* 1366), vintner, of London. In 1357 he was employed in the service of Lionel, afterwards duke of Clarence. He entered military service in 1359, served in France, was taken prisoner, but shortly ransomed. He married Philippa, probably sister of John of Gaunt's third wife, and evidently enjoyed John of Gaunt's patronage. Philippa died apparently in 1387. Chaucer held various positions at court, and was sent on a mission to Genoa and Florence in 1372-3, when he perhaps met Boccaccio and Petrarch. In 1374 he was appointed controller of customs in the port of London and leased the dwelling-house over Aldgate. He was buried in Westminster Abbey, a monument being erected to him in 1555.

Chaucer's writings fall into three periods: (1) The period of French influence (1359-72), in which he uses the octosyllabic couplet. To this period belong 'The Boke of the Duchesse', 1369, and 'The Romaunt of the Rose', so far as written by Chaucer. (2) The period of Italian influence, especially of Dante and Boccaccio, 1372-86, in which he leaves off the octosyllabic couplet, uses mainly the 'heroic' stanza of seven lines, and begins to use the heroic couplet. To this period belong 'The Hous of Fame'; 'The Parlement of Foules'; 'Troylus and Cryseyde'; 'The Legende of Good Women'; and the first drafts of some of his tales. (3) The period of his maturity, 1386-1400, in which he uses the heroic couplet. To this period belong 'The Canterbury Tales', designed about 1387. His prose works include a translation of Boethius, and a 'Treatise on the Astrolabe' compiled for 'little Lewis my son', in English, 'for Latin ne canst thou yet but small, my little son'.

Chaucer's well-known portrait was made from memory by Occleve on the margin of one of his works. 'The Canterbury Tales' (q.v.) were first printed by Caxton in 1478(?); the collected works were first issued by W. Thynne in 1532. The fullest edition is that of W. W. Skeat, with introduction and notes, Oxford, 7 vols. (1894-7).

Chaucerians, SCOTTISH, see *Scottish Chaucerians.*

Chauvinism, an exaggerated and bellicose patriotism, derived from Nicholas Chauvin, a veteran French soldier of the First Republic and Empire, whose demonstrative patriotism was celebrated and at length ridiculed by his comrades.

Chaworth, MARY ANNE, later Mrs. Chaworth-Musters, the lady with whom Byron fell in love in his youth, and to whom he proposed in 1803. She is celebrated in Byron's poem, 'The Dream'.

Cheeryble Brothers, THE, Ned and Charles, characters in Dickens's 'Nicholas Nickleby' (q.v.).

Cheiron or CHIRON, a centaur (q.v.), famous for his knowledge of medicine, music, and archery. He was the instructor of many heroes and the friend of Hercules.

Cheke, SIR JOHN (1514-57), tutor to Edward VI, and subsequently professor of Greek at Cambridge. He was an eminent scholar, and was influential in promoting a simple style of English prose. He is referred to in Milton's Sonnet XI, 'A Book was writ of late'.

Chekhov, ANTON PAVLOVICH (1860-1904), Russian dramatist and short-story writer, whose gift of satirical humour has given a wide vogue to his works. His first successful play 'Ivanov' (1887) was followed by 'The Seagull' (1896), 'Uncle Vanya' (1897), 'The Three Sisters' (1901), and (what is generally considered the best) 'The Cherry Orchard' (1904). Chekhov's fame rests chiefly on these and on his short tales, but he also wrote a number of novels.

Chelsea. Here Sir Thomas More (q.v.) had his residence, where he received Erasmus. In the 17th and 18th cents. it was much patronized by Cockneys and was famous for its bun-house. See also Congreve's 'Love for Love', II. ii. Chelsea has a reputation as a home of painters: Rossetti, Whistler, and many others lived there.

Chelsea, SAGE OF, T. Carlyle (q.v.).

Chemos or CHEMOSH, a Moabite god (1 Kings ix. 7), ranks after Moloch in Milton's hierarchy of hell ('Paradise Lost', i. 406).

Chenier, ANDRÉ (1762-94), French poet and one of the early figures in the French Romantic movement.

Cherry and **Merry,** in Dickens's 'Martin Chuzzlewit' (q.v.), Pecksniff's daughters, Charity and Mercy.

Cherubim, a Hebrew word of uncertain derivation. Cherubim first appear in Gen. iii. 24, as guardians of the tree of life. Their inclusion among the angels appears to belong to Christian mysticism. According to Dionysius the Areopagite they form the second of the nine orders of angels. See *Angel.*

Cheshire Cat, *To grin like a*: no satisfactory explanation of the allusion has been put forward. The Cheshire Cat figures in Lewis Carroll's 'Alice in Wonderland' (q.v.).

Cheshire Cheese, THE, a hostelry in Wine Office Court, off Fleet Street, London, rebuilt shortly after the Restoration, frequented by Ben Jonson, and still in existence.

Chester, SIR JOHN, and EDWARD his son, characters in Dickens's 'Barnaby Rudge' (q.v.).

Chester Plays, see *Miracle Plays.*

Chesterfield, PHILIP DORMER STANHOPE, *fourth earl of* (1694-1773), statesman and diplomatist, was a wit and an orator, wrote political tracts, and contributed to the 'World', but is remembered principally for his 'Letters' to his natural son, Philip Stanhope. These were written almost daily from 1737 onwards and were designed for the education of the young man. They are full of sensible instruction, admirably expressed, but have been reprobated on account of a few passages contrary to good morals. The letters to his son were published (by the son's widow) in 1774. Chesterfield is also remembered in connection with Johnson's 'Dictionary'. Johnson had addressed the 'Plan' of that work to Chesterfield, but it was received with neglect. On the publication of the Dictionary, Chesterfield wrote two papers in the 'World' in commendation of it. Thereupon on 7 Feb. 1755 Johnson addressed to Chesterfield the famous letter, in which he bitterly rejected a notice which 'had it been early, had been kind; but it has been delayed till I am indifferent, and cannot enjoy it; till I am solitary and cannot impart it; till I am known, and do not want it'.

Chesterton, GILBERT KEITH (1874-1936), an essayist, critic, novelist, and poet, among whose best-known writings are: (novels and short stories) 'The Napoleon of Notting Hill', 'The Flying Inn', 'The Innocence of Father Brown'; (poetry) 'The Ballad of the White Horse', 'Wine, Water, and Song', 'Poems'; (essays) 'Generally Speaking', 'What's Wrong with the World'; (biography) 'Robert Browning', 'Charles Dickens'.

Chestre, THOMAS, see *Launfal*.

Chettle, HENRY (*d.* 1607?), a minor Elizabethan dramatist, for a time partner in a printing business. He is reputed the author of thirteen, and the joint-author of thirty-five plays, but most of his work has perished.

Chevalier, THE YOUNG, Charles Edward Stuart (1720-88), the Young Pretender.

Chevalier de St. George, James Francis Edward Stuart (1688-1766), the Old Pretender, called by the Jacobites 'King James III and VIII'.

Chevy Chase, The Ballad of, one of the oldest of the English ballads, probably dates from the 15th cent. Its subject is the rivalry of the Border families of Percy and Douglas. The two parties meet and fight, there is great slaughter on both sides, and both Percy and Douglas are killed.

Cheyne Row and **Walk**, in Chelsea. Carlyle lived in Cheyne Row; George Eliot, Count d'Orsay, D. G. Rossetti, Turner, in Cheyne Walk.

Chiaroscuro, meaning originally the style of pictorial art in which only the light and shade, and not the various colours, are represented, is used figuratively of poetic and literary treatment in the sense of mingled clearness and obscurity, light and gloom, praise and blame, etc.; but is still used chiefly for pictorial art.

Chiasmus, a figure of speech by which the order of the words in the first of two parallel clauses is reversed in the second, e.g. 'He saved others; himself he cannot save'.

Chichele or CHICHELEY, HENRY (1362?-1443), archbishop of Canterbury, founded the Chichele chest in Oxford University for the relief of poor students, built a house for Cistercians in Oxford, and was co-founder, with Henry VI, of All Souls College.

Chichevache, a perversion of the French *chiche face*, 'thin-face', a fabulous monster said to feed only on patient wives, and hence, from scarcity of the diet, to be always lean and hungry. Her spouse, the Bycorne, on the contrary, grew fat on his abundant diet of patient husbands. (Cf. Chaucer, 'Clerk's Tale', 1132.)

Child, FRANCIS JAMES (1825-96), American scholar, edited the poetical works of Spenser in 1855 and published his great collection of 'English and Scottish Popular Ballads' in 1883-98.

Childe, in 'Childe Harold', 'Childe Roland', etc., signifies a youth of gentle birth, and is used as a kind of title, a young noble awaiting knighthood.

Childe Harold's Pilgrimage, a poem in Spenserian stanzas by Lord Byron (q.v.), begun in Albania in 1809, of which the first two cantos appeared in 1812, canto iii in 1816, canto iv in 1818.

The poem purports to describe the travels and reflections of a pilgrim who, sated and disgusted with a life of pleasure and revelry, seeks distraction in foreign lands. The first two cantos take the reader to Portugal, Spain, the Ionian Isles, and Albania, and end with a lament on the bondage of Greece. In the third canto the pilgrim passes to Belgium, the Rhine, the Alps, and the Jura. The historical associations of each place are made the poet's theme, the Spanish war, the eve of Waterloo and Napoleon, and more especially Rousseau and Julie. In the fourth canto the poet abandons his imaginary pilgrim and speaks in his own person, of Venice, Arquà and Petrarch, Ferrara and Tasso, Florence and Boccaccio, Rome and her great men, from the Scipios to Rienzi.

Childe Roland, in an old Scottish ballad, a son of King Arthur.

> Child Rowland to the dark tower came,
> His word was still 'Fie, foh, and fum,
> I smell the blood of a British man.'
>
> (Shakespeare, 'King Lear', III. iv.)

Halliwell ('Nursery Rhymes') thinks that Shakespeare is here quoting from two different compositions, the first line from a ballad on Roland, the second and third from the story of Jack the Giant-killer (q.v.).

Childe Roland to the Dark Tower Came, a poem by R. Browning (q.v.), published in 'Men and Women' in 1855.

A brave knight is attempting an adventure, in which all who have previously undertaken it have failed. He reaches the tower just when he despairs of succeeding and sounds his horn to announce that he has come.

Childers, ERSKINE (1870-1922), Irish revolutionary and author of a fine novel of adventure, 'The Riddle of the Sands' (1903).

Children in the Wood, THE, the subject of an old ballad, included in Percy's and Ritson's collections. A gentleman of Norfolk on his death-bed leaves his property to his infant son and daughter, and gives the charge of them to his brother, who hires two ruffians to slay them in a wood. One of these repents and kills his fellow, and then abandons the children in the wood. The children perish and the robin-redbreast covers them with leaves.

Children of the Chapel, CHILDREN OF PAUL'S, see *Paul's (Children of).*

Chillip, DR., a character in Dickens's 'David Copperfield' (q.v.).

Chillon, The Prisoner of, see *Prisoner of Chillon.*

Chiltern Hundreds, hundreds (i.e. subdivisions of a county) which contain the Chiltern Hills. The manorial rights of these belonged to the Crown, which appointed over them bailiffs and stewards. No member of parliament may by law resign his seat so long as he is duly qualified; on the other hand a member who accepts an office of profit under the Crown must vacate his seat. Therefore a member who desires to resign applies for the 'Stewardship of the Chiltern Hundreds', which is held to be such an office; the appointment entails his resignation, and having thus fulfilled its purpose, is itself vacated.

Chimaera, according to Greek legend, a monster with the head of a lion, the body of a goat, and the tail of a dragon. It was overcome by Bellerophon (q.v.), mounted on Pegasus.

Chimes, The, a Christmas book by Dickens (q.v.) (1845).

The story of a nightmare in which Toby Veck, under the influence of the goblins of the church bells and a dish of tripe, witnesses awful misfortunes befalling his daughter, a vision happily dissipated at the end.

Chingachgook (pron. 'chi´ca´go'), the Indian chief in the tales of Indian life of J. F. Cooper (q.v.).

Chios, an island in the Aegean Sea, one of the reputed birthplaces of Homer. It was celebrated for its wine.

Chippendale, THOMAS (1718-79), a famous furniture-maker of London, noted for his light and elegant style.

Chivery, MR. and 'YOUNG JOHN', characters in Dickens's 'Little Dorrit' (q.v.).

Chloe, The Tale of, see *Tale of Chloe.*

Choice, The, see *Pomfret.*

Choliamb, see *Scazon.*

Chopin, FRÉDÉRIC FRANÇOIS (1809-49). He composed two concertos, and a large number of pianoforte solo compositions, études, mazurkas, preludes, nocturnes, etc. His romantic connection with George Sand (q.v.) is recorded in her 'Lucrezia Floriani', where Chopin figures as Prince Karol.

Chopine, a kind of shoe raised by a cork sole or the like, worn about 1600 in Spain and Italy, and on the English stage. (Cf. Shakespeare, 'Hamlet', II. ii.)

Choriamb, a metrical foot of four syllables, $\_\cup\cup\_$. A choree is a trochee (q.v.).

Chrétien de Troyes, a writer of courtly romances for the French feudal aristocracy in the second half of the 12th cent. His extant works are: 'Erec and Enide' (c. 1160), 'Cligès' (c. 1162), 'Yvain and Lancelot' or the 'Chevalier de la Charete' (c. 1170), and 'Perceval' or 'Le Conte du Graal' (c. 1180), which he left unfinished, and which was the starting-point for the cycle of Grail romances. His works were very popular, and exercised a great influence both in France and abroad.

Christ and Satan, an OE. poem, or perhaps three poems, contained in the Junius MS. (see *Cædmon*).

Christabel, a poem by S. T. Coleridge (q.v.) (1816). The first part was written in 1797, and the second in 1800.

The poem is unfinished. Christabel, daughter of Sir Leoline, praying at night in the wood for her betrothed lover, finds a lady in distress, the fair Geraldine, and brings her to the castle. She claims to be the daughter of Lord Roland de Vaux, once the friend of Sir Leoline before they were estranged by a quarrel. In reality she is a malignant supernatural creature, and Christabel has seen through her disguise, but is forced to silence by a spell. Sir Leoline sends his bard to Lord Roland to tell him that his daughter is safe and to offer reconcilement.

The poem, apart from introducing a new metre, is one of the most beautiful in English poetry.

Christ Church, Oxford, a college begun by Cardinal Wolsey (it was to be called 'Cardinal College'), and taken over after his fall and established by Henry VIII in 1546. Among famous men educated there were Locke, John Wesley, Dr. Pusey, and Gladstone.

Christian, the hero of Bunyan's 'The Pilgrim's Progress' (q.v.).

Christian, FLETCHER, see *Bounty.*

Christiana, in 'The Pilgrim's Progress' (q.v.), the wife of Christian.

Christian Hero, The. An Argument proving that no Principles but those of Religion are Sufficient to make a great Man, a treatise by Steele (q.v.) (1701).

Finding, as the author tells us, 'Military life exposed to much Irregularity', he wrote this little work. In it he inculcates the value of the Bible as a moral guide and the failure of the old philosophy. The work is important as one of the first signs of a change of tone in English literature.

Christianity, An Argument against abolishing, see *Swift.*

Christian Morals, see *Browne (Sir T.).*

Christian Year, The, a collection of sacred poems by Keble (q.v.) (1827). The book attained great popularity owing to its connection with the Oxford Movement (q.v.).

Christie, DAME AGATHA (LADY MALLOWAN) (1891-1976), prolific writer of detective fiction and plays, including 'The Mysterious Affair at Styles' (1920, which introduced the Belgian detective Hercule Poirot), 'Ten Little Niggers' (1939), 'The Mousetrap' (1952), etc.

Christie Johnstone, a novel by C. Reade (q.v.) (1853).

Christie's: Christie, Manson, and Woods, King Street, St. James, fine art auctioneers.

Christis Kirk on the Green, an old Scottish poem, doubtfully attributed to James I or James V of Scotland, in nine-lined stanzas with a 'bob' after the eighth line, descriptive of the rough fun, dancing, and love-making of a village festival or 'wappinshaw'. Two additional cantos were composed by Allan Ramsay (q.v.).

Christmas Carol, A, a Christmas book by Dickens (q.v.) (1843).

Scrooge, an old curmudgeon, receives on Christmas Eve a visit from the ghost of Marley, his late partner in business, and beholds a series of visions, including one of what his own death will be like unless he is quick to amend his ways. As a result of this he wakes up on Christmas morning an altered man.

Christmas Eve and Easter Day, two distinct poems under one title, by R. Browning (q.v.) (1850).

In the first the narrator recounts a spiritual experience, a vision in which he is taken first to a dissenting chapel, then to St. Peter's Church at Rome, then to a lecture-room where a German professor is investigating the origin of the Christian myth, and finally back to the dissenting chapel.

In 'Easter Day' a Christian and a sceptic are disputing. The Christian narrates a vision from which he has learnt the value of life, with its limitations, but with the hope remaining 'to reach one eve the Better Land'.

Christopher, St., meaning 'Christbearer', a Christian martyr of the 3rd cent., said to have lived in Syria and to have been a man of exceptional size and strength, who for a penance carried pilgrims, and on one occasion Jesus in the form of a child, across a river. The saint is commemorated on 25 July. He is the patron saint of wayfarers.

Christopher North, a pseudonym used by J. Wilson (1785–1854, q.v.).

Christopher Sly, see *Taming of the Shrew*.

Christ's Hospital, London, also known as the Bluecoat School (q.v.), founded under a charter of Edward VI. Here were educated Coleridge, Lamb, and Leigh Hunt. The school was removed to Horsham in 1902.

Christs Teares over Jerusalem, a tract by T. Nash (q.v.) (1593), in which he analyses with his usual vigour the vices and abuses of contemporary society.

Christs Victorie and Triumph, the principal poem of Giles Fletcher (q.v.).

Christy Minstrels, a troupe of minstrels imitating Negroes, originated in the 19th cent. by one George Christy of New York.

Chronicles, see under *Anglo-Saxon Chronicle, Annales Cambriae, Asser, Bede, Camden (William), Capgrave (John), Eadmer, Fabyan, Geoffrey of Monmouth, Gesta Francorum, Gildas, Giraldus Cambrensis, Hall (Edward), Harrison (William), Hayward (Sir John), Holinshed (Raphael), Hoveden (Roger), Jocelin de Brakelond, Nennius, Peterborough Chronicle, Richard III (History of), Robert of Gloucester, Speed (John), Stow (John), Vergil (Polydore), Wace of Jersey, William of Malmesbury, William of Newburgh, Wyntoun (Andrew of)*.

Chronicles of the Canongate, The, an inclusive title for certain of Sir W. Scott's novels, 'The Highland Widow', 'The Two Drovers', and 'The Fair Maid of Perth'.

Chrononhotonthologos, a burlesque of contemporary drama by Henry Carey (q.v.), acted in 1734.

Chrysal, or the Adventures of a Guinea, see *Adventures of a Guinea*.

Chrysaor, in Spenser's 'Faerie Queene', v. i. 9 and v. xii. 40, the sword of Justice, wielded by Sir Artegal.

Chryseis, daughter of Chryses, a priest of Apollo. She had been taken prisoner and allotted to Agamemnon. Thereupon the god sent a plague on the Greek host. To avert this, Achilles urged that Agamemnon should surrender the damsel. This he was obliged to do, but took from Achilles the girl Briseis (q.v.), thereby causing Achilles to retire for a time from the Trojan War.

Chrysostom, St. John (*c.* 345–407), one of the Greek Fathers of the Church. In his writings he emphasized the ascetic element in religion and the need for personal study of the Scriptures. His voluminous works include, notably, commentaries on the Gospel of St. Matthew and on the Epistles to the Romans and Corinthians. The name 'Chrysostom' means 'golden-mouthed' and refers to his eloquence.

Chuang-tzu, see *Taoism*.

Chucks, Mr., a character in Marryat's 'Peter Simple' (q.v.).

Chuffey, in Dickens's 'Martin Chuzzlewit', Anthony Chuzzlewit's old clerk.

Churchill, Charles (1731-64), became famous by his satire on contemporary actors, 'The Rosciad' (1761), and his violent satire on Bute and the Scots, 'The Prophecy of Famine' (1763). He attached himself to John Wilkes (q.v.) and contributed largely to his paper 'The North Briton'. He wrote other political and social satires but died young, at Boulogne, on his way to visit Wilkes in France.

Churchill, Frank, a character in Jane Austen's 'Emma' (q.v.).

Churchill, Rt. Hon. Sir Winston (Leonard Spencer) (1874-1965), eldest son of Lord Randolph Churchill (third son of the seventh duke of Marlborough); first lord of the Admiralty, 1911-15; secretary of state for war, 1918-21; for the colonies, 1921-2; chancellor of the exchequer, 1924-9; prime minister, 1940-5 and 1951-5. His works include 'Lord Randolph Churchill' (1906-7), 'The World Crisis' (4 vols. 1923-9), works on Marlborough, 'The History of the Second World War' (1948-54), and 'A History of the English-speaking Peoples' (4 vols., 1956-8). He was awarded the Nobel Prize for Literature in 1953.

Churchill, Winston (1871-1947), American novelist. Among his works are: 'Richard Carvel' (1899), 'The Crisis' (1901), 'The Crossing' (1904), and 'A Far Country' (1915).

Churchyard, Thomas (1520?-1604), published, before 1553, 'A Mirror for Man'. Between 1560 and 1603 he issued a multitude of broadsheets. His best-known works are 'Shore's Wife' (1563), in 'A Mirror for Magistrates' (q.v.).

Spenser in his 'Colin Clout' refers to Churchyard as 'Old Palaemon that sung so long until quite hoarse he grew'.

Cibber, Colley (1671-1757), became an actor in 1690. He brought out his first play 'Love's Last Shift' in 1696, in which he showed skill as a playwright rather than the qualities of a man of letters. One of the best of Cibber's plays was 'The Careless Husband' (1705). Cibber was made poet laureate in 1730, and was fiercely attacked in consequence by other writers. Pope made him the hero of 'The Dunciad' (q.v.) in the final edition of that poem. Cibber published in 1740 an autobiography, entitled 'Apology for the life of Mr. Colley Cibber, Comedian'.

Cicero, Marcus Tullius (106-43 B.C.), sometimes referred to in English literature as Tully, became consul in 63. Owing to the enmity of Clodius he was banished in 58 for a short time. In the civil war between Caesar and Pompey he joined the party of the latter, but after Pharsalia was pardoned by Caesar. After Caesar's assassination he took the lead of the republican party and vigorously attacked Mark Antony in his Philippic orations. On the formation of the triumvirate he was proscribed, and put to death in 43. His works consist of writings on the art of rhetoric; on political philosophy; on moral philosophy ('De Officiis', 'De Senectute', and 'De Amicitia'); and on theology; of a large number of orations (including the Verrines and the Philippics) and epistles (many of them to his friend Atticus).

Cicisbeo (pron. 'tchi-tchiz-bay´-o'), the name formerly given in Italy to the recognized gallant of a married woman.

Cid, The, the favourite hero of Spain, in the account of whom history and myth are difficult to disentangle. Rodrigo Diaz de Bivar, el Cid Campeador, of a noble Castilian family, was born *c.* 1030. He was banished and became a soldier of fortune, fighting at times for the Christians, at others for the Moors. His principal feat was the capture of Valencia from the Moors after a siege of nine months. He died of grief at the defeat of his force, in 1099. In myth his character has been glorified into a type of knightly and Christian virtue. His achievements are narrated in the 'Poema del Cid' of the 12th cent., in the Spanish Chronicle of the 13th cent., and in numerous ballads. The chronicles relating to him were translated by R. Southey (q.v.) (1808). The Cid is the subject of the most famous drama of Corneille (q.v.).

Cider, for J. Philips's poem, see *Cyder*.

Ci-devant, a French term meaning 'formerly', in the language of the French Revolution, a man of rank, i.e. one formerly such.

Cimabue, GIOVANNI (*c.* 1240-1302?), Italian painter of Florence, whose best-known work is the 'Madonna' in the Church of Santa Maria Novella there.

Cimmerian, of or belonging to the Cimmerii, a people fabled by the ancients to live in perpetual darkness; hence proverbially used as a qualification of dense darkness.

Cincinnatus, LUCIUS QUINCTIUS, a type of integrity and frugality in the Roman republic. He was called in 458 B.C. from the plough, with which he cultivated his own land, to deliver the Roman army from the peril in which it stood. Having done this and held the command for only sixteen days, he returned to his plough.

Cinderella, a fairy tale, from the French of Perrault (q.v.).

Cinderella is cruelly used by her stepmother and two stepsisters. Her stepsisters having gone to a ball, she is left crying at home. Her fairy godmother arrives and sends her to the ball, on condition that she returns before the stroke of twelve. The prince falls in love with her. She hurries away at midnight, losing one of her tiny glass slippers. The prince announces that he will marry her whom the slipper fits. To the discomfiture of the stepsisters the slipper is found to fit only Cinderella, who marries the prince. Analogous stories exist in the folklore of various countries.

Cinque Ports, a group of sea-ports (originally five, Hastings, Dover, Sandwich, Romney, Hythe, to which were added Rye and Winchelsea, and many associated towns) having jurisdiction along the south-east coast from Seaford in Sussex to Birchington in Kent.

Cinthio, GIAMBATTISTA GIRALDI (1504-73), the author of 'Hecatommithi' or hundred tales, told after the manner of Boccaccio's 'Decameron' (q.v.). Some of these were incorporated by Painter in his 'Palace of Pleasure' (q.v.) and provided the plots of Shakespeare's 'Othello' and 'Measure for Measure', and of plays by Beaumont and Fletcher and Shirley.

Circe, celebrated for her knowledge of magic and venomous herbs, inhabited an island called Aeaea. Odysseus, returning from the Trojan War, visited this island. His companions were changed by Circe's spells into swine. Odysseus, fortified against her enchantment by the herb called *moly*, demanded from Circe the restoration of his companions. Circe complied, and Odysseus remained with her for a year. See also *Scylla* and *Gryll*.

Circumlocution Office, THE, the type of a government department, satirized in Dickens's 'Little Dorrit' (q.v.).

Cistercians, the name of a monastic order, an offshoot of the Benedictines, founded at Cistercium or Cîteaux in 1098 by Robert, abbot of Molesme. St. Bernard (q.v.) was a Cistercian; his *Bernardines* were a branch of the Cistercians with reformed rules.

Cities of the Plain, THE, see *Sodom and Gomorrah*.

Citizen of the World, The, by Goldsmith (q.v.) (1762), a collection of letters purporting to be written by or to an imaginary philosophic Chinaman, Lien Chi Altangi, residing in London. They are a series of whimsical or satirical comments on English customs and peculiarities, together with character-sketches and episodes, the whole strung on a slender thread of narrative. The best-known character-sketches in the book are the 'Man in Black' and 'Beau Tibbs'.

City Heiress, The, a comedy by Aphra Behn (q.v.), produced in 1682.

City Madam, The, a comedy by Massinger (q.v.), acted in 1632 and printed in 1659.

City of Destruction, THE, in Bunyan's 'The Pilgrim's Progress' (q.v.), the state of the worldly and irreligious.

City of Dreadful Night, The, see under *Thomson* (*J.,* 1834-82) and *Kipling.*

City of Dreaming Spires: M. Arnold ('Thyrsis') refers to Oxford as 'that sweet city with her dreaming spires'.

City of Seven Hills, THE, Rome. The seven hills are the Palatine, Aventine, Capitoline, Caelian, Esquiline, Viminal, and Quirinal.

City of the Violet Crown, THE, Athens, so referred to by Pindar and Aristophanes.

City Witt, or the Woman wears the Breeches, a comedy by Brome (q.v.), printed in 1653.

Civil War, THE, the war between Charles I and Parliament, 1642-6. It was followed by the second Civil War of 1648-51, which was terminated by the battle of Worcester.

In American history, the Civil War or War of Secession (1861-5) was caused by the secession of the eleven southern or Confederate states and was terminated by the surrender of their armies.

Civil Wars between the two Houses of York and Lancaster, an epic poem by S. Daniel (q.v.) (1595, 1609). It contains some 900 eight-lined stanzas, of a philosophic cast, and marked by strong patriotism.

Clairmont, CLAIRE (CLARA MARY JANE) (1798-1879), daughter of Mary Clairmont, William Godwin's (q.v.) second wife. She accompanied Mary Godwin on her elopement with Shelley (q.v.), returned to London with the Shelleys, and in 1816 obtained an introduction to Byron, becoming so intimate with him that when he went to Switzerland the Shelleys were induced to follow him. Her child Allegra was born in 1817, and for nearly three years lived with Byron. In 1821

Allegra was placed in a convent near Ravenna much against the will of Claire, and died in 1822 as the result of a fever. Claire died in Florence in 1879.

Clandestine Marriage, The, a comedy by Colman the elder and Garrick (qq.v.), produced in 1766.

Clare, JOHN (1793-1864), the son of a Northamptonshire labourer, and himself at various times a herd-boy, militiaman, vagrant, and unsuccessful farmer, who became insane in 1837. He published in 1820 'Poems Descriptive of Rural Life', 'The Village Minstrel' in 1821, 'The Shepherd's Calendar' in 1827, and 'The Rural Muse' in 1835. Other poems of his were published after his death (ed. A. Symons, 1908), and an edition of more of his poems by E. Blunden and A. Porter appeared in 1920. An autobiography of his early years was edited by Blunden in 1931.

Clarendon, CONSTITUTIONS OF, enacted at a council summoned in 1164 by Henry II to meet at Clarendon in Wiltshire. Their object was to check the power of the clergy. After the murder of Becket, Henry was compelled to give up the Constitutions of Clarendon.

Clarendon, EDWARD HYDE, *earl of* (1609-74). As M.P. he at first sided with the opposition, but, as a strong Anglican, from 1641 onwards he was one of the chief supporters and advisers of the king. He followed the Prince of Wales in his exile, where he began his 'History'. He was lord chancellor and chief minister to Charles II from 1658, retaining this position at the Restoration. The future James II married his daughter Anne. Clarendon subsequently became unpopular, and being impeached, he fled to France in 1667. At Montpellier he composed his 'Life', part of which he incorporated with the 'History'.

The 'History'—'The True Historical Narrative of the Rebellion and Civil Wars in England'—was first printed from a transcript under the supervision of Clarendon's son in 1702-4.

Clarendon was chancellor of the University of Oxford from 1660 until his fall. His works were presented to the University by his heirs, and from the profits of the publication of the 'History' a new printing-house, which bore his name, was built for the University Press (q.v.).

Clarendon Press, see *Oxford University Press*.

Clarendon's History of the Rebellion and Civil Wars in England, see *Clarendon (Edward Hyde)*.

Clarissa Harlowe, a novel by Richardson (q.v.), of which two volumes were issued in 1747 and five in 1748.

This was the second of Richardson's novels and, as in the others, the story is told by means of letters, written by the heroine Clarissa to her friend Miss Howe, and by the other principal character, Robert Lovelace, to his friend John Belford. Clarissa, a young lady of good family, is wooed by Lovelace, an unscrupulous man of fashion. Clarissa's family oppose the match but he succeeds in carrying her off. Clarissa dies of shame, and Lovelace is killed in a duel by her cousin, Colonel Morden.

Clarke, CHARLES COWDEN- (1787–1877), schoolmaster and friend of Keats (q.v.), and author of 'Recollections of Writers' (with Mary Cowden-Clarke, 1878), etc.

Clarke, MARCUS ANDREW HISLOP (1846–81), wrote a number of plays and novels, of which the best known is 'For the Term of his Natural Life' (1874), a vivid and gloomy tale of a penal settlement in Australia.

Classic, in relation to literature, is defined by Sainte-Beuve as what is very good and is made to last. The OED. defines it as (1) 'Of the first class, of the highest rank or importance; approved as a model; standard, leading. (2) Of or belonging to the standard authors of Greek and Latin antiquity. (3) In the style of the literature of Greek and Latin antiquity.' Cf. *Romantic*.

Classicism, in English literature usually regarded as a quality of the Augustan Age

(q.v.), which affected a great admiration of the ancients and a rigid code of critical values and literary forms. The artificialities of the period, however—as exemplified, for instance, in Pope's translations from Homer—make the comparison true as regards aim rather than achievement. The term is used mainly by way of contrast with the Romantic Movement (q.v.) which followed.

Claudian (CLAUDIUS CLAUDIANUS), the last poet of ancient Rome, was a native of Alexandria. He is known to have lived in Rome *c*. A.D. 395–404.

Claudio, (1) the lover of Hero in Shakespeare's 'Much Ado about Nothing' (q.v.); (2) a character in his 'Measure for Measure' (q.v.).

Claudius, in Shakespeare's 'Hamlet' (q.v.), the king of Denmark.

Claus, see *Santa Claus*.

Claverhouse, GRAHAM OF, see *Graham of Claverhouse*.

Clavering, SIR FRANCIS and LADY, characters in Thackeray's 'Pendennis' (q.v.).

Claverings, The, a novel by A. Trollope (q.v.) (1867).

Clay, MRS., a character in Jane Austen's 'Persuasion' (q.v.).

Clayhanger, see *Bennett (E. A.)*.

Claypole, NOAH, in Dickens's 'Oliver Twist' (q.v.), a fellow apprentice of the hero; and subsequently one of Fagin's gang of thieves.

Cleanness, an alliterative poem of 1,800 lines, of the period 1300–60 or later, exalting purity and the delights of lawful love. It is attributed to the same author as 'Pearl' and 'Patience' (qq.v.).

Cleishbotham, JEDEDIAH, see *Tales of My Landlord*.

Cleland, JOHN (1709–89), novelist and journalist. His novel 'Memoirs of a Woman of Pleasure' (published in 2 vols., 1749) was suppressed as pornography in 1749, since when it has enjoyed a persistent surreptitious publication. Cleland's own expurgated edition, 'Memoirs of Fanny Hill', appeared in 1750. An unexpurgated edition published openly in England in 1963 was seized by the police. Cleland also wrote 'Memoirs of a Coxcomb' (1751) and other novels.

Clemens, SAMUEL LANGHORNE (1835–1910), wrote under the pseudonym MARK TWAIN, adopted from the leadsman's call which had become familiar to him on the Mississippi. He first came into prominence as a writer with his 'Jim Smiley and his Jumping Frog' in 1865, and shortly after became a popular lecturer. His best-known works are 'The Innocents Abroad' (q.v., 1869); 'The Adventures of Tom Sawyer' (1876); and 'The Adventures of Huckleberry Finn' (1884), a masterpiece of humorous fiction and an accurate picture of the old rough civilization of the Mississippi. His 'A Connecticut Yankee in King Arthur's Court' appeared in 1889.

Clementina Porretta, a character in Richardson's 'Sir Charles Grandison' (q.v.).

Clementine Vulgate, see *Vulgate*.

Clennam, ARTHUR and MRS., characters in Dickens's 'Little Dorrit' (q.v.).

Cleon, an Athenian demagogue, opponent of Pericles, famous for his capture of the Spartans at Sphacteria in the Peloponnesian War. He was subsequently defeated by Brasidas and killed in battle (422 B.C.).

Cleon, a character in Shakespeare's 'Pericles' (q.v.).

Cleon, a poem by R. Browning (q.v.) (1855).

Cleopatra, daughter of Ptolemy Auletes, king of Egypt, born in 68 B.C. She was named by her father heir of the kingdom, jointly with her brother, but was driven from the throne by his guardians. She was restored to the throne with her brother Ptolemy by Julius Caesar, by whom she had a son named Caesarion. After Caesar's death in 44 B.C. she met Antony and gained his heart by her beauty and fascination. In the war between Antony and Octavian the defection of her fleet at the battle of Actium (31 B.C.)

hastened her lover's defeat. Despairing of Antony's fortunes, she caused a report to be spread of her death. Thereupon Antony stabbed himself. To escape being carried captive to Rome by Octavian, Cleopatra took her own life (30 B.C.). The story of her relations with Antony has been made the theme of three famous plays, Shakespeare's 'Antony and Cleopatra' (q.v.), Dryden's 'All for Love' (q.v.), and Samuel Daniel's 'Cleopatra' (see below). Her relations with Caesar are the theme of a play by G. B. Shaw (q.v.), 'Caesar and Cleopatra'.

Cleopatra, a tragedy in blank verse by S. Daniel (q.v.) (1594). It is on the Senecan model, and deals with the story of Cleopatra after the death of Antony.

Cleopatra, in Dickens's 'Dombey and Son' (q.v.), the name by which Mrs. Skewton was known.

Clerihew, an epigrammatic verse-form invented by Edmund Clerihew Bentley (q.v.), consisting of two rhymed couplets, usually dealing with the character or career of a well-known person, e.g.

> Sir Christopher Wren
> Was dining with some men;
> He said: 'If anyone calls,
> Tell them I'm designing St. Paul's'.

Clerk of Chatham, THE, the schoolmaster in Shakespeare's '2 Henry VI', who is haled before Jack Cade.

Clerk's Tale, The, see *Canterbury Tales*.

Cleveland, JOHN (1613–58), one of the most popular poets of the mid 17th cent. He was an active royalist and much of his writing was political satire which is lost on the modern reader. His poetry shows extreme examples of metaphysical conceits.

Cliché, French, 'a stereotype block', a stock expression which by constant use has become hackneyed and lost its sharp edge.

Clifford, LORD, THE SHEPHERD, see *Shepherd (Lord Clifford, the)*.

Clio, the Muse (q.v.) of history.

C L I O were the letters with one or other of which Addison signed all his papers in the 'Spectator'.

Clitus or CLEITUS, a friend and general of Alexander the Great. At a banquet Alexander, who was heated with wine, killed him with a javelin, and was then inconsolable for his loss.

Clive, CATHERINE (1711–85), commonly known as KITTY CLIVE, actress, and friend of Horace Walpole, by whom she was pensioned.

Clive, ROBERT, *Baron Clive of Plassey* (1725–74), obtained an ensign's commission in the East India Company's service in 1747. He showed his military gifts by the capture of Arcot in 1751 and his subsequent defence of that city. In 1757 he avenged the tragedy of the Black Hole of Calcutta (q.v.) by the great victory of Plassey. He became governor of Bengal in 1758, and a second time in 1765. He resigned owing to ill health in 1767. His conduct was subjected in 1772–3 to a parliamentary inquiry, which resulted substantially in his favour.

Cloister and the Hearth, The, a historical romance by Reade (q.v.) (1861).

The story, which is laid in the 15th cent., was inspired by the author's reading of the 'Colloquies' and life of Erasmus, and the writings of Froissart and Luther. Gerard, the hero, is destined for the Church, but falls in love with Margaret Brandt the daughter of a poor scholar. He abandons his career and betroths himself to her, but is imprisoned. He escapes to Margaret, but is presently pursued and obliged to flee the country. The story now proceeds through a series of exciting incidents and vivid scenes as Gerard travels through the disturbed countries of Germany and Burgundy to Italy. Here he receives false news of the death of Margaret, and in despair takes the cowl. Meanwhile Margaret gives birth to a son. Finally, as a Dominican preacher, he returns to his native town, is astounded to discover Margaret alive, and is at length persuaded to return to her. His son, the story indicates, is the future Erasmus.

Clorin, the 'Faithful Shepherdess' in Fletcher's drama of that name (q.v.).

Cloten, a character in Shakespeare's 'Cymbeline' (q.v.).

Clotho, see *Parcae.*

Cloud-cuckoo-land, see *Nephelococcygia.*

Cloudesley, WILLIAM OF, see *Adam Bell.*

Clough, ARTHUR HUGH (1819–61), a fellow of Oriel, and, after throwing up his fellowship, principal of University Hall, London. He died at Florence, and Matthew Arnold's 'Thyrsis' was written to commemorate his death. He is chiefly remembered as the author of the hexameter poem, 'The Bothie of Tober-na-Vuolich' (q.v.) (1848), and of some fine lyrics, including the well-known 'Say not the struggle nought availeth', which bear the mark of the spiritual agitation caused by religious doubts.

Clove, a character in Jonson's 'Every Man out of his Humour' (q.v.), who makes a display of long words and abstruse terms.

Club, THE, see *Johnson (Samuel).*

Clutterbuck, CAPTAIN CUTHBERT, a fictitious personage supposed to be concerned with the publication of some of Sir W. Scott's novels.

Clym of the Clough, see *Adam Bell.*

Clym Yeobright, a character in T. Hardy's 'The Return of the Native' (q.v.).

Clytemnestra, daughter of Tyndareus, king of Sparta, and Leda (q.v.), and wife of Agamemnon (q.v.), king of Argos. On the return of Agamemnon from the Trojan War, she, with her paramour Aegisthus (q.v.), murdered her husband, and was in turn slain by Orestes, Agamemnon's son.

Cnut, see *Canute.*

Coal Hole, THE, a tavern in Fountain Court, Strand, from which Thackeray in part drew his 'Cave of Harmony' (q.v.).

Coavinses, in Dickens's 'Bleak House' (q.v.), see *Neckett.*

Cobbett, WILLIAM (1763–1835), enlisted as a soldier and served in New Brunswick from 1784 to 1791. He brought an accusation of peculation against some of his officers, and in 1792 retired to America to avoid prosecution. There he published pro-British pamphlets under the pseudonym of 'Peter Porcupine'. He returned to England in 1800 and became a Tory journalist, editing 'Cobbett's Political Register', a weekly newspaper, from 1802. Soon he adopted popular opinions and wrote from 1804 in the radical interest. From 1817 to 1819 he was in America. His 'History of the Protestant "Reformation" in England and Ireland' appeared in 1824; his 'Advice to Young Men' in 1829. He wrote with exceptional perspicuity and vigour, and showed good sense and sound observation in agricultural matters. His 'Rural Rides' (q.v.), collected in 1830, are today the most interesting of his writings.

Cobden, RICHARD (1804–65), a leader of the Anti-Corn Law League. He powerfully contributed to the repeal of the Corn Laws (1846), and negotiated the commercial treaty with France, 1859–60.

Cock-and-bull story, an expression that apparently had its origin in some tale or fable, means a long idle rambling story; or a concocted, incredible story.

Cock and Pie, used in asseverations, is perhaps for 'God and Pie', where 'Pie' is the table of rules of the Roman Catholic Church governing the offices for each day. Cf. Shakespeare, 'The Merry Wives of Windsor', I. i.

Cockatrice, a serpent identified with the basilisk (q.v.), fabled to kill by its mere glance, and to be hatched from a cock's egg. In heraldry, it is a hybrid monster with the head, wings, and feet of a cock, and the body of a serpent with a barbed tail.

Cockayne or COCKAIGNE, LAND OF, the name of a fabulous country, the abode of luxury and idleness. The origin of the term remains obscure.

Cocker, EDWARD (1631–75), a teacher of arithmetic and writing in London, whose treatise on arithmetic gave rise to the expression 'according to Cocker'.

Cock Lane Ghost, a supposed ghost to which were attributed mysterious noises

heard at No. 33 Cock Lane, Smithfield. They were discovered in 1762 to be due to an imposition practised by one William Parsons, his wife, and daughter. Dr. Johnson took part in the investigation of the mystery (see Boswell's 'Life', 1763). See D. Grant, 'The Cock Lane Ghost' (1965).

Cockney, from Middle English *cokeney*, 'cocks' egg', of which the original meaning was perhaps one of the small or misshapen eggs occasionally laid by fowls. It came to mean 'a cockered child', an effeminate fellow or milksop, and so was used derisively for a townsman, and finally for one born in the city of London. Hence it was extended to the London dialect or accent.

THE COCKNEY SCHOOL was a nickname given by Lockhart to a set of 19th-cent. writers belonging to London, of whom Leigh Hunt and Hazlitt were representative members.

Cock of the North, George, fifth duke of Gordon (1770–1836), who raised the regiment now known as the Gordon Highlanders and commanded it (1795–9) in Spain, Corsica, Ireland, and Holland.

Cockpit, THE, the name of a theatre in London in the 17th cent., referred to by Pepys (11 Oct. 1660 and 5 Jan. 1662–3).

The COCKPIT OF EUROPE is an expression applied to Belgium as the scene of many wars (a cockpit being the scene of cock-fights).

Cocles, PUBLIUS HORATIUS, a Roman who opposed the whole army of Porsena, king of Etruria, at the head of the bridge leading into Rome, while his companions behind him were breaking down the bridge to the other shore. When the bridge was destroyed, Cocles, though wounded, leapt into the Tiber and swam across in his armour. The feat is the subject of one of Macaulay's 'Lays of Ancient Rome'.

Cocytus, the river of lamentation', from κωκύω, 'I howl'; a river of Epirus, and by the poets regarded as a river of Hades. See *Styx*.

Codille, a term used in the game of ombre, when the adversaries of ombre win the game.

Codlin and **Short,** in Dickens's 'The Old Curiosity Shop' (q.v.), travel about the country with a Punch and Judy show.

Coelebs in Search of a Wife, a novel by Hannah More (q.v.) (1809), a collection of social sketches and precepts.

Coffee-houses were first introduced in London in the time of the Commonwealth and were much frequented in the 17th and 18th cents. for political and literary discussion, circulation of news, etc. There is an interesting description of them in Macaulay's 'History of England', c. iii. See *Button's, Will's, Grecian.*

Cogglesby, ANDREW and TOM, characters in Meredith's 'Evan Harrington'.

Coke, SIR EDWARD (1552–1634), a barrister of the Inner Temple, was advanced by Burghley's influence to be attorney-general, to the disappointment of Francis Bacon (q.v.), whose lifelong rival he was. Coke's fame as a legal author rests on his eleven volumes of 'Reports' (1600–15), and his 'Institutes' (1628–44) in which he recast, explained, and defended the common law rules.

Colbrand, in the romance of 'Guy of Warwick' (q.v.), the Danish giant slain by Sir Guy.

Cole, KING, the 'merry old soul' of the nursery rhyme, was Coel, one of the legendary kings of Britain enumerated by Geoffrey of Monmouth (q.v.) in his 'Historia Regum Britanniae'. There is a poem about him by Masefield (q.v.) in 'King Cole and other Poems' (1923).

Colenso, JOHN WILLIAM (1814–83), became bishop of Natal. Besides textbooks on arithmetic and algebra, he published a 'Commentary on the Epistle to the Romans' (1861), which attacked the sacramental system; and a 'Critical Examination of the Pentateuch' (1862–79), concluding that these books were post-exile forgeries. He was deposed and excommunicated by Bishop Gray of Capetown (who had no jurisdiction over

him), but confirmed in the possession of his see by the law courts (1866).

Coleridge, HARTLEY (1796–1849), eldest son of Samuel Taylor Coleridge (q.v.), was appointed a probationer fellow of Oriel College, Oxford, but dismissed in 1820 on a vague charge of intemperance. He contributed to the 'London Magazine' and 'Blackwood's', and lived mainly at Grasmere. His poems include some beautiful sonnets, and some pieces marked by a singular melancholy charm, such as 'She is not fair to outward view', and 'She pass'd away like morning dew'. His collected poems were issued in 1851, and his essays and some of his notable marginalia in the same year by his brother, Derwent.

Coleridge, MARY ELIZABETH (1861–1907) (her grandfather, Francis Coleridge, was the nephew of S. T. Coleridge (q.v.)), was author of some remarkable poetry. Her 'Poems Old and New' (1907) and 'Gathered Leaves' (1910) were published posthumously. Her first novel, 'The Seven Sleepers of Ephesus' (1893), was praised by R. L. Stevenson.

Coleridge, SAMUEL TAYLOR (1772–1834), son of the vicar of Ottery St. Mary, Devon, was educated at Christ's Hospital (Lamb, in his Elia essay, describes him there) and at Jesus College, Cambridge. He enlisted in the 15th Dragoons, but was discharged after a few months. He made the acquaintance of Robert Southey (q.v.), and the pair devoted themselves to 'Pantisocracy', a form of communism which they contemplated realizing on the banks of the Susquehanna. He married Sara Fricker in 1795, Southey marrying her sister.

He contributed verses to 'The Morning Chronicle' as early as 1793–5, and in 1794 wrote and published in conjunction with Southey 'The Fall of Robespierre'. In 1796 he started a journal, 'The Watchman', which lasted for only ten numbers. In 1795 he made the acquaintance of Wordsworth, and the two poets lived in close intercourse for about a year at Nether Stowey and Alfoxden in Somerset.

Their 'Lyrical Ballads' (q.v.) containing Coleridge's 'The Ancient Mariner' (q.v.) appeared in 1798. Coleridge wrote the first part of 'Christabel' (q.v.) and 'Kubla Khan' (q.v.) in 1797, and contributed some of his best poems to 'The Morning Post' during 1798-1802. 'Dejection' was written in 1802. After his visit to Germany in 1798-9 he published (1799-1800) his translations of Schiller. He settled for a time (1800-4) at Keswick, where he wrote the second part of 'Christabel'. In 1804 he travelled to Malta and Italy, returning in 1806 broken in health and a prey to the use of opium. In 1808 he gave lectures on the English poets at the Royal Institution, which were imperfectly reported, and in 1809 he launched his second periodical, 'The Friend', 'a literary, moral, and political weekly paper', subsequently rewritten and published as a book (1818). He spent much of the latter part of his life in the houses of friends, and, after 1816, lived with a kindly surgeon, James Gillman, at Highgate. In 1817 appeared his 'Biographia Literaria' (q.v.) or literary autobiography, and in 1825 his 'Aids to Reflection' (q.v.), in the first of which he did much to introduce German philosophy to English thinkers. He also wrote three plays, 'The Fall of Robespierre' (1794), 'Zapolya' (1817), and 'Osorio'. This last was acted, under the title 'Remorse', at Drury Lane in 1813. Coleridge's finest poems, 'The Ancient Mariner', 'Kubla Khan', and 'Christabel', are characterized by the sense of mystery that he suggests. His gift in a lighter mood is seen in such a poem as 'The Devil's Thoughts' (q.v.), written with Southey.

Apart from his poetry, Coleridge did valuable work in literary criticism, maintaining that the true end of poetry is to give pleasure 'through the medium of beauty'. The 'Biographia' contains much of this criticism, in particular of the poems of Wordsworth. In philosophy, he advocated a spiritual and religious interpretation of life, based on what he had learnt from Kant and Schelling. 'Anima Poetae' (q.v.), edited from his unpublished notebooks in 1895 by E. H. Coleridge, contains some of his most interesting work in this sphere. In political philosophy he declared himself the heir of Burke and an enemy of Jacobinism, though constructively he had little to offer.

Coleridge, SARA (1802-52), daughter of S. T. Coleridge (q.v.) and wife of Henry Nelson Coleridge, was author of 'Phantasmion' (1837), an elaborate romantic fairytale. She also helped her brother Derwent to edit their father's poems, and her husband to edit her father's philosophical writings.

Colet, JOHN (1467?-1519), dean of St. Paul's and the principal Christian humanist of his day in England. As dean of St. Paul's, he founded and endowed St. Paul's School, for which he wrote a Latin accidence, W. Lily supplying the syntax. This book, revised by Erasmus, ultimately developed into the 'Eton Latin Grammar'. Colet was a pioneer of the English Reformation, famous as a preacher and lecturer.

Colette, SIDONIE-GABRIELLE (1873-1954), the foremost French woman author of her day, wrote novels and other prose works notable for their sensitive understanding and descriptions of nature (human and animal) and of country life. The 'Claudine' series (1900-3) made her name, but her outstanding novels include: 'La Vagabonde', 'Chéri', 'La Chatte', etc.

Colin Clout, the name adopted by Edmund Spenser (q.v.) in 'The Shepheards Calender' and 'Colin Clouts come home againe'. COLIN CLOUT is also the name of a rustic in Gay's 'Shepherd's Week'. See also *Colyn Cloute*.

Colin Clouts come home againe, an allegorical pastoral written by Spenser (q.v.) on his return to Kilcolman after his visit to London of 1589-91. It was dedicated to Sir Walter Ralegh and describes in allegorical form how Ralegh visited Spenser in Ireland, and induced him to come to England 'his Cynthia to see'—i.e. the queen. Of the characters mentioned in the work, Cynthia is Queen Elizabeth, Hobbinol is G. Harvey (q.v.), Amyntas is T. Watson (q.v.), the Shepheard of the Sea is Sir W. Ralegh (q.v.).

Coliseum, THE, see *Colosseum*.

Colkitto, 'or MACDONNEL, or GALASP', in Milton's first 'Tetrachordon' sonnet, was the lieutenant-general of the marquess of Montrose in his campaign on behalf of Charles I. He figures in Scott's 'A Legend of Montrose'.

Collier, JEREMY (1650-1726), is chiefly remembered for his 'Short View of the Immorality and Profaneness of the English Stage' (1698), in which he particularly attacked Congreve and Vanbrugh (qq.v.). The work created a great, if temporary, impression. Several of the poets replied to it, though none of them very effectively.

Collins, WILLIAM (1721-59), was an exquisite lyrical poet, but his verse was small in quantity, and some of it is unfortunately lost. He published his 'Persian Eclogues' as an undergraduate in 1742, and in 1747 his 'Odes'. The best known of these are the 'Ode to Evening', the 'Ode to Simplicity', and the 'Ode written in 1746' ('How sleep the brave'). The charming 'Dirge in Cymbeline' must also be mentioned. His long 'Ode on the popular Superstitions of the Highlands', containing some magnificent verse, was written in 1749 and published posthumously. He became insane and died in his sister's house at Chichester.

Collins, WILLIAM, in Jane Austen's 'Pride and Prejudice' (q.v.), a pompous, silly, and self-satisfied young clergyman. The solemn letter of thanks that he addresses to Mr. Bennet (c. xxiii, though the text is not given) after his stay with the family has led to his name being colloquially associated with such letters.

Collins, (WILLIAM) WILKIE (1824-89), was called to the bar in 1851, but adopted literature as a profession. He made the acquaintance of Dickens and his contributions to 'All the Year Round' included in 1860 'The Woman in White' (q.v.), which

is remembered as the first example of detective fiction in English. He wrote several other novels of which 'No Name' (1862) and 'The Moonstone' (q.v., 1868) are best known.

Colman, GEORGE, the elder (1732-94), manager of the Covent Garden Theatre, 1767-74, and of the Haymarket Theatre, 1777-89, a friend of Garrick, with whom he collaborated in writing an excellent comedy, 'The Clandestine Marriage' (1766). He wrote or adapted some thirty dramatic pieces, edited Beaumont and Fletcher (1778), and translated Terence and Horace. He was celebrated for his charm and conversation.

Colman, GEORGE, the younger (1762-1836), dramatist, son of the above. His comedy 'The Heir-at-Law' (1797) is famous for its presentation of Dr. Pangloss, the greedy, pompous pedant.

Colmekill, in Shakespeare's 'Macbeth', II. iv, is *I-Colm-kill* (the island of Columba of the Church), the modern Iona (q.v.).

Cologne, THREE KINGS OF, or Wise Men of the East: the Magi, Gaspar, Melchior, and Balthazar, whose bones the Emperor Barbarossa is said to have brought from Milan and deposited in Cologne Cathedral.

Colombe's Birthday, a play by R. Browning (q.v.), published in 1844 and acted in 1853.

Colonel Jack, *The History and Remarkable Life of Colonel Jacque, Commonly Call'd*, a romance of adventure by Defoe (q.v.) (1722).

Colophon, from Gk. κολοφών, summit, 'finishing touch', the inscription or device, sometimes pictorial or emblematic, placed at the end of a book or manuscript, and containing the title, the scribe's or printer's name, the date and place of printing, etc.

Colosseum, THE, or Flavian amphitheatre, in Rome, was begun by Vespasian in A.D. 72 and inaugurated by Titus. It was the scene, during four centuries, of countless gladiatorial combats and of the martyrdom of many Christians.

Colossus of Rhodes, bronze statue of Apollo by the Greek sculptor Chares,

250 B.C., which passed for one of the seven wonders of the world. It is said by Pliny to have been seventy cubits high. It was demolished by an earthquake in 224 B.C.

Colum, PADRAIC (1881-1972), Irish poet and dramatist, associated with W. B. Yeats and Lady Gregory (qq.v.) in the Irish theatre movement; author of 'Wild Earth' (poems, 1907), etc.

Columba, ST., otherwise COLUMCILLE or COLUMBANUS (521-97), Irish abbot and missionary. He went to Scotland in 563, founded the monastery of Hy (Iona), and preached to the Picts. His relics were translated to Ireland in 878, but were destroyed by the Danes in 1127. Several books believed to have been written by him were long venerated in Ireland. He is commemorated on 9 June.

Columban, ST. (543-615), resided in Burgundy, 585-610. There he built monasteries, for which he drew up a monastic rule, afterwards common in France, until replaced by that of St. Benedict. He was expelled from Burgundy by Theodoric II and preached to the heathen Germans and Suabians. He founded the monastery of Bobbio in the Piedmont and died there. He is commemorated on 21 Nov.

Columbiad, The, an epic poem by Joel Barlow (q.v.), which surveys the panorama of early American history. First published as 'The Vision of Columbus' (1787), the poem was renamed 'The Columbiad' in 1807.

Columbine, a character in Italian comedy, the daughter of Pantaloon and mistress of Harlequin, which has been transferred to our pantomime or harlequinade.

Columbus, CHRISTOPHER (*c.* 1445-1506), in Spanish CRISTÓVAL COLÓN, a Genoese navigator, the discoverer of America. He obtained the favour of Queen Isabella of Castile and embarked on his first voyage in 1492. He met with much ingratitude and persecution, but made in all four voyages to the West Indies. His object was to reach the Cathay of Marco Polo, and he remained under the impression that the regions he discovered were the fringes of the Asiatic continent.

Columella, LUCIUS JUNIUS MODERATUS, a native of Gades in Spain, a contemporary of Seneca and the author of a work (*c.* A.D. 65) on the various forms of agriculture. The 'Columella' referred to by Jane Austen in 'Sense and Sensibility' is the hero of a tale by Richard Graves (q.v.).

Colyn Cloute, a satirical poem by Skelton (q.v.), directed against ecclesiastical abuses, and written about 1519. See also *Colin Clout.*

Combe, WILLIAM (1741-1823), is specially remembered for the verses that he wrote to accompany Rowlandson's drawings of the adventures of 'Dr. Syntax'. The first of these works, 'Dr. Syntax in search of the Picturesque', a parody of books of picturesque travels, appeared in 1809.

Comberback, SILAS TOMKYN, the name assumed by S. T. Coleridge (q.v.) on joining the Dragoons.

Comedy, a stage play of a light and amusing character with a happy conclusion to its plot (OED.). In Greece it originated in the festivals of Dionysus celebrated with song and merriment at the vintage; the Roman comedy of Plautus and Terence was imitated, with some native elements, from the Greek comedy of Menander and other dramatists of his period. Latin comedy continued to exercise an influence throughout the Middle Ages, particularly on the 'Saints Plays' which were often written to celebrate some merry saint and were largely comic with a concluding serious scene. The Miracle Plays (q.v.) of the later Middle Ages were also conducive to comedy rather than to tragedy, and as with the Morality Plays (q.v.) were most independent in their comic parts, which were often separated from the main theme of the play. In Morality Plays the gradual rise of a humorous element is noticeable and the Vice in particular came to be recognized as a stock comic character.

With the recovery in the 15th cent. of twelve lost plays of Plautus and a renewed study of Terence, comedies on classical models came to be written. The plays of John Heywood (q.v.) and Rastell retain more of the elements of the Morality, but Nicholas Udall's 'Ralph Roister Doister' (1553?) and 'Gammer Gurton's Needle' (1566), of uncertain authorship, are clearly based upon classical models. These two plays are the first recognizable examples of modern English comedy. Throughout the 16th cent. this type of college or university play became gradually more popular, while the Morality passed out of fashion. Elizabethan comedy was lightened by a romantic element, as exemplified in Lyly (q.v.) and Greene (q.v.), drawn from Italian and French romances. Lyly in particular explored the possibilities of prose dialogue and Greene showed great skill in his blending of plot and sub-plot. Shakespeare's comedies, which were nearly all written before 1600, owed much to these two predecessors. His comedies make no great attempt at moralizing or satirizing: their main essentials are a delightful story in some romantic setting arriving at a fortunate issue. The comedies of Ben Jonson (q.v.), which are written almost entirely in prose, have a definite moral and satirical vein running through them, but Beaumont and Fletcher (qq.v.) preserved the more romantic and less realistic tradition.

With the revival of drama after the Restoration, the influence of French comedy, and particularly of Molière, was predominant, while Jonson was regarded as the greatest English model. The characteristics of Restoration comedy, as exemplified in the plays of Wycherley, Etherege, Dryden, etc., are wit—rather than humour—a great measure of licentiousness, but at the same time considerable polish and elegance. Prose was by this time recognized as the natural vehicle for comedy. The Restoration comedy reached its greatest heights in the works of Congreve (q.v.) at the end of the century, while Vanbrugh and Farquhar (qq.v.)

continued the same tradition though with less wit and originality. After these, Steele (q.v.), deprecating the immoral tone of contemporary plays, popularized what is known as the 'sentimental comedy'. In such plays as his 'Conscious Lovers' (1722), the rewards attendant on virtuous behaviour are stressed and vices such as drinking and duelling are condemned. This type of play came to be dominant throughout the 18th cent. Steele and his followers had no doubt a salutary influence on the morals of their generation, but their plays on the whole lacked realism and dramatic intensity. Goldsmith in 'She Stoops to Conquer' (1773) and Sheridan in 'The School for Scandal' (1777) and 'The Critic' (1779) deliberately and successfully recaptured the best features of Restoration comedy. Their plays were successful, but they found no followers of any distinction and, in general, few comedies of the 18th or 19th cent. have any place in literary history. Examples from the end of the 19th cent. include Oscar Wilde's 'The Importance of Being Earnest', 'Lady Windermere's Fan', and 'A Woman of No Importance', the lighter plays of Shaw (e.g. 'You Never Can Tell'), and the better plays of Arthur Pinero. In modern times, a new type of comedy, which relies on greater realism and on subtleties of character as well as of plot, has been developed.

See also *Farce*, *Burlesque*.

Comedy, *The Divine*, see *Divina Commedia*.

Comedy of Errors, *The*, a comedy by Shakespeare (q.v.), acted in 1594 (and perhaps as early as 1592), and first printed in the folio of 1623, one of the earliest and crudest of Shakespeare's plays; in the main, an adaptation of the 'Menaechmi' of Plautus.

Syracuse and Ephesus being at enmity, any Syracusan found in Ephesus is put to death unless he can pay a ransom of a thousand marks. Aegeon, an old Syracusan merchant, has been arrested in Ephesus, and on the duke's order explains

how he came there. He and his wife
Aemilia had twin sons, exactly alike and
each named Antipholus; the parents had
purchased twin slaves, also exactly alike,
and each named Dromio, who attended on
their sons. Having in a shipwreck been
separated, with the younger son and one
Dromio, from his wife and the other son
and slave, Aegeon had never seen them
since. The younger son (Antipholus of
Syracuse) on reaching manhood had gone
(with his Dromio) in search of his brother
and mother and had no more been heard
of, though Aegeon had now sought him
for five years over the world, coming at
last to Ephesus.

The duke, moved by this tale, gives
Aegeon till evening to find the ransom.
Now, the elder Antipholus (Antipholus
of Ephesus), with one of the Dromios, has
been living in Ephesus since his rescue
from shipwreck and is married. Antipholus of Syracuse and the other Dromio have
arrived there that very morning. Each
twin retains the same confusing resemblance to his brother as in childhood.
From this the comedy of errors results.
Antipholus of Syracuse is summoned
home to dinner by Dromio of Ephesus;
he is claimed as husband by the wife of
Antipholus of Ephesus, the latter being
refused admittance to his own house, because he is supposed to be already within;
and so forth. Finally Antipholus of
Ephesus is confined as a lunatic, and Antipholus of Syracuse takes refuge from his
brother's jealous wife in a convent.

Meanwhile evening has come and
Aegeon is led to execution. As the duke
proceeds to the place of execution, Antipholus of Ephesus appeals to him for
redress. Then the abbess of the convent
presents Antipholus of Syracuse, also
claiming redress. The simultaneous presence of the two brothers explains the
numerous misunderstandings, Aegeon
recovers his two sons and his liberty, and
the abbess turns out to be his lost wife,
Aemilia.

Comedy of Manners, name applied to
the comedy of the late 17th cent. (Etherege,
Wycherley, Congreve, etc.), revived in the
18th cent. by Sheridan and Goldsmith,
where the emphasis is laid upon the social
follies of the characters rather than on
humours of plot and situation. (See also
Comedy.)

Comical Revenge, The, or Love in a Tub,
a comedy by Etherege (q.v.) acted in 1664,
important as the first example of English
prose comedy, as afterwards seen in Congreve and Sheridan; while the serious
portions are written in rhymed heroics.
The play shows acquaintance with the
early comedies of Molière.

Coming of Arthur, The, the first of
Tennyson's 'Idylls of the King' (q.v.)
(1869), though not the first to be published.

Arthur, newly crowned and setting out
to conquer his rebellious barons, sees and
falls in love with Guinevere, daughter of
King Leodegran of Cameliard; and after
his success sends to ask her hand. Lancelot
comes to fetch Guinevere, and Arthur and
she are married. An indication is given of
the purpose that Arthur sets before himself in his kingdom, to

Have power on this dark land to lighten
    it,
And power on this dead world to make it
    live.

Coming Race, The, a romance by Bulwer
Lytton (q.v.) (1871).

The narrator describes his visit to a sub-
terranean race in the bowels of the earth.
Owing to the discovery of Vril, a form of
energy, this race has reached a high degree
of civilization and scientific invention and
their country is a Utopia.

Commander of the Faithful, a title of
the Caliphs. See *Caliphate*.

Commedia dell'Arte, in Italian drama,
improvised drama of the 16th cent. having
its origin in the Atellan fables (q.v.).

Commines, PHILIPPE DE (*c.* 1445-1511),
first served Philip of Burgundy and his
son Charles the Bold, and then entered
the service of the French king Louis XI,
whose counsellor he became. He wrote

remarkable chronicles of Louis XI and Charles VIII, which inspired Sir W. Scott's 'Quentin Durward' (q.v.), in which Commines himself figures.

Common, DOL, a character in Jonson's 'The Alchemist' (q.v.).

Common Prayer, The Book of, was evolved in the 16th cent. to meet the popular need for aids to devotion and the demand for the use of the vernacular in church services. The reading in churches of a chapter of the Bible in English, and the Litany in English (probably the work of Cranmer, q.v.), were introduced in 1544, and an English communion service in 1548. About the same time the Primers were revised, and the King's Primer issued in 1545 in the interests of uniformity; it included the English Litany. Cranmer and a commission each drafted a scheme for a prayer book, and these were discussed in Edward VI's reign, leading to the successive issue of the Prayer Books of 1549 and 1552. In the latter the form of the Book of Common Prayer was practically settled, though a revision was made under Elizabeth (1559), minor changes under James I, and the final text is that of 1662. As it stands the Prayer Book represents largely the work of Cranmer; Nicholas Ridley (q.v.) may perhaps claim some share.

Common Prayer, The Revised Book of, embodied the proposals which, after prolonged discussion, the bishops, presided over by Archbishop Randall Davidson, laid before Convocation in 1927. It consisted of the Prayer Book of 1662 with a permissive alternative version as regards Holy Communion, Baptism, Confirmation, and Matrimony, and numerous additional occasional prayers. Opposition arose in regard to the revision of the office for Holy Communion, and when the Revised Book was submitted to Parliament at the end of 1927, it was rejected by the House of Commons though passed by the House of Lords. It was again submitted in the following year with certain modifications, but again rejected.

Though without formal authority, the 1928 Book is used in many churches.

Communism, a theory that advocates a state of society in which there should be no private ownership, all property being vested in the community and labour organized for the common benefit of all members, each working according to his capacity and receiving according to his wants.

For the social order established in Russia by the Bolshevik party, see *Lenin.*

Complaint, The, or Night Thoughts on Life, Death, and Immortality, see *Night Thoughts.*

Complaint of Buckingham, The, a poem by T. Sackville (q.v.), contributed by him to 'A Mirror for Magistrates' (q.v.).

Complaint of Deor, see *Deor.*

Compleat Angler, The, or the Contemplative Man's Recreation, a discourse on fishing by I. Walton (q.v.) (1653, second edition 1655). The fifth edition, containing Cotton's continuation, appeared in 1676.

It takes the form of a dialogue, at first between the author, Piscator (a fisherman), Auceps (a fowler), and Venator (a hunter), each recommending his own recreation, in which Auceps is silenced, and Venator becomes a pupil of the angle; then between Piscator and Venator alone. In the course of this, after a short spell with the otter-hounds, the author instructs his pupil in the mode of catching all the various kinds of fresh-water fish, with directions for dressing some of them for the table. The instruction is given as they fish along the river Lea near London, and there are pleasant interludes of verse and song. The continuation, supplied by Charles Cotton (q.v.), takes the form of conversations between Piscator and Viator (a traveller, who turns out to be Venator of the earlier part) as they fish along the river Dove. Piscator instructs Viator in fishing 'fine and far off' for trout and grayling; and opportunities are taken to indicate the rocky and picturesque scenery of the district.

Compton-Burnett, DAME IVY (1892–1969), a novelist whose stories are told within the strict conventions of her own style. The plots emerge mainly through the prolonged conversations of the characters. Her novels include 'Dolores' (1911), 'Pastors and Masters' (1925), 'A House and its Head' (1935), and 'Mother and Son' (1955).

Comte, AUGUSTE (1798–1857), French philosopher, was in early life secretary to the socialist C. H. de Saint-Simon by whom he was influenced, but whom he subsequently repudiated. He was the chief exponent of the positivist philosophy, which excludes metaphysics and revealed religion, and substitutes the religion of humanity and sociological ethics, based on history and designed for the improvement of the human race. His principal English disciple was F. Harrison (q.v.), but he also influenced J. S. Mill (q.v.).

Comus, A Masque, presented at Ludlow Castle, 1634, before the Earl of Bridgewater, Lord President of Wales, by Milton (q.v.). Though described as a 'masque', it is strictly a pastoral entertainment.

This work was, like the 'Arcades' (q.v.), written at the request of Henry Lawes, the musician, while Milton was at Horton. The occasion was the celebration of the earl of Bridgewater's entry on the presidency of Wales and the Marches. The name 'Comus' was not included in the title in the first three printed editions, but is taken from one of the characters, a pagan god invented by Milton, son of Bacchus and Circe, who waylays travellers and tempts them to drink a magic liquor which changes their countenances into the faces of wild beasts. A lady and her two brothers are benighted in a forest. The lady, separated from her companions, and attracted by the revelry of Comus and his rout, comes upon Comus, in the guise of a shepherd, who offers to lodge her in his cottage, and leads her off. The brothers appear and are told what has happened by the good Attendant Spirit, who has taken the form of the shepherd Thyrsis. He warns them of the magic power of Comus and gives them the root of the plant Haemony as a protection. The scene changes, and Comus, with his rabble round him, is discovered pressing the lady to drink from a glass, while she, strong in her purity, resists his enticements. The brothers burst in and disperse the crew. Unfortunately they have not secured the wand of Comus, and are unable to release the lady from the enchanted chair in which she sits. Thyrsis thereupon invokes Sabrina, goddess of the neighbouring river Severn, who comes attended by water-nymphs, and frees the lady. After an ode of thanks to Sabrina, the lady and her brothers return safely to Ludlow Castle.

Conceit, used as a literary term to mean a fanciful, ingenious, or witty notion or expression; and so, disparagingly, a strained or far-fetched comparison or literary figure. From being a mark of excellence throughout the 17th cent. it came, by Johnson's time, to be a term of reproach.

Conciliation with America, On, a speech by E. Burke (q.v.), made in the House of Commons on 22 March 1775.

This was a last effort by Burke to find a peaceful solution of the difference with the American colonies, and is one of his greatest speeches, and a literary masterpiece.

Concordat, an agreement between Church and State, especially between the Roman See and a secular government relative to matters that concern both. One of the most famous of such agreements was that made in 1801 between Napoleon and Pius VII.

Condell, HENRY, see *Heming.*

Conduct of the Allies . . ., The, title of a pamphlet by Swift (q.v.), composed in Nov. 1711 in favour of peace.

Confederacy, The, a comedy by Vanbrugh (q.v.), produced in 1705.

Confessio Amantis, the principal English poem of Gower (q.v.).

Confessions, see *Augustine* and *Rousseau.*

Confessions of an English Opium Eater, by De Quincey (q.v.) (1822, enlarged edition, 1856).

This book, which established De Quincey's literary reputation, after an account of his early years and his rambling life in Wales, relates how he was led by physical suffering and nervous irritation first to take opium, and then to increase his consumption of it, until he reached the large quantity of 8,000 drops of laudanum a day. He describes the fearful effects, chiefly in the form of tumultuous dreams, brought about by this abuse of the drug, continued during eight years, until, alarmed at the prospect of imminent death, he determined to conquer the habit. The narrative ends with the account of the gradual reduction that he effected in his daily dose, a reduction itself attended by great suffering, but finally in the main successful.

Confucius, the latinized form of K'ung Fu-tzu (551–479 B.C.), meaning 'Master K'ung', who has been revered by the Chinese as their greatest sage.

Little is known for certain about his life. He became a teacher of moral and political wisdom, mainly to young men who were potential statesmen. He has been revered not only for his lofty ideals, but also because he was traditionally (but mistakenly) regarded as author or editor of the oldest among the Thirteen Classics. This heterogeneous corpus of history, poetry, ethics, etc., includes the 'Analects', which contains the most authentic of the Master's sayings.

CONFUCIANISM became systematized during the Han dynasty (206 B.C. to A.D. 220). Despite the rivalry of Taoism (q.v.) and Buddhism (which entered China in the 1st cent. A.D.), it formed the dominant ideology of China throughout most of its history down to the close of the empire in 1911.

Congreve, WILLIAM (1670–1729), of English birth, was educated with Swift at Kilkenny school and Trinity College, Dublin. He entered the Middle Temple, but soon gave up law for literature, and in 1693 suddenly achieved fame by his comedy 'The Old Bachelor'. Of his other comedies, 'The Double Dealer' appeared in 1694, 'Love for Love' in 1695, and 'The Way of the World' in 1700. In these Congreve shows himself the supreme master of the artificial comedy or comedy of manners, displaying the narrow world of fashion and gallantry. His one tragedy 'The Mourning Bride' was produced in 1697. Congreve gave up writing for the stage in consequence, it is said, of the comparative failure of his last comedy. But he was then in moderately affluent circumstances, holding more than one government post, and enjoying general admiration and the friendship of men like Swift, Steele, and Pope. He was visited by Voltaire, and was closely attached to the duchess of Marlborough. He was throughout the friend of the enchanting Mrs. Bracegirdle (q.v.). He was buried in Westminster Abbey.

Coningsby, or The New Generation, a political novel by Disraeli (q.v.) (1844).

Connoisseur, The, a periodical conducted in 1754–6 by George Colman the elder and Bonnell Thornton, contained some early papers by W. Cowper (q.v.).

Connolly, CYRIL (1903–74), became a journalist and regular contributor to 'The New Statesman' and from 1942 to 1943 was literary editor of 'The Observer'. He founded the literary review 'Horizon' with Stephen Spender in 1939. He has published a novel and collections of essays.

Conquest of Granada, The, a heroic play in rhymed couplets, in two parts (the first being entitled 'Almanzor and Almahide; or, The Conquest of Granada), by Dryden (q.v.) (1672).

The play was very famous in its day, and besides much rant and bombast, contains some good verse and pleasant lyrics. It was one of the principal objects of satire in 'The Rehearsal' (q.v.).

Conrad, the pirate chief in Lord Byron's 'The Corsair' (q.v.).

Conrad, JOSEPH (1857–1924) (Teodor

Josef Konrad Korzeniowski), was born of Polish parents in the Ukraine. He accompanied his parents when they were exiled to northern Russia; was subsequently for a time at school at Cracow; and in 1874 became member of the crew of a French vessel, thus satisfying a long-felt craving for a seafaring life. In 1878 he joined an English merchant ship, and in 1884 was naturalized as a British subject. He left the sea in 1894 and devoted himself to literature.

The sea provides the setting of most of his works, and his devotion to it is seen at its best in his 'Mirror of the Sea' (1906). His earlier novels, 'Almayer's Folly' (1895) and 'An Outcast of the Islands' (1896), reveal Conrad struggling with the difficulties of a language and a technique unfamiliar to him. But he achieved success in 'The Nigger of the Narcissus' (1898), and 'Lord Jim' (1900), the tale of a young Englishman who in a moment of panic deserts his apparently sinking ship, loses his honour, and finally retrieves it by an honourable death. In 'Youth', 'Heart of Darkness', and 'Typhoon' (1902) Conrad produced three of his finest short stories.

Conrade of Montserrat, a character in Scott's 'The Talisman' (q.v.), based on the historical Conrad of Montferrat.

Conscience, MR., in Bunyan's 'The Holy War', the Recorder of the city of Mansoul, deposed from his office during the tyranny of Diabolus.

Conscious Lovers, The, a comedy by Steele (q.v.), based on the 'Andria' of Terence, produced in 1722. This was Steele's last play, and in it he illustrates his views on duelling, the proper attitude of men to women, etc.

Constable, HENRY (1562–1613), was educated at St. John's College, Cambridge, embraced Roman Catholicism, and withdrew to Paris. He published 'Diana', a volume of sonnets, in 1592. Verses by him were embodied in various collections, among others in 'England's Helicon' (q.v.).

Constable, JOHN (1776–1837), famous English landscape-painter.

Constance, (1) or CONSTAUNCE or CUSTANCE, the heroine of 'The Man of Lawe's Tale' in Chaucer's 'The Canterbury Tales' (q.v.); (2) in Shakespeare's 'King John' (q.v.), the mother of Arthur, the king's nephew.

Constance of Beverley, a character in Scott's 'Marmion'.

Constant Couple, The, or a Trip to the Jubilee, a comedy by Farquhar (q.v.), produced in 1700.

Constantine the Great, Roman emperor, A.D. 306–37. He was converted to Christianity, it is said, by seeing a luminous cross in the sky before the battle (312) in which he defeated his rival Maxentius. He transferred the capital of the empire to Byzantium, which he renamed Constantinople. See *Helena* (*Saint*).

Contarini Fleming, a Psychological Romance, by Disraeli (q.v.) (1832).

Conversation, A complete Collection of polite and ingenious, by Swift (q.v.) (1738).

In this entertaining work Swift good-humouredly satirizes the stupidity, coarseness, and attempted wit of the conversation of fashionable people as he had observed it. In three dialogues he puts into the mouth of various characters samples of questions and answers, smart sayings, and repartees. The work was published under the pseudonym of 'Simon Wagstaff, Esq.'

Cook, ELIZA (1818–89). Her complete collected poems were published in 1870. The most popular of these was 'The Old Arm Chair', which had appeared in 1837.

Cook, JAMES (1728–79), the celebrated circumnavigator, left records of his three principal voyages: the first, round the Horn and the Cape of Good Hope, 1768–71; the second, 'A Voyage towards the South Pole and round the World in 1772–5' (1777); the third, 'A Voyage to the Pacific Ocean in 1776–80' (1784). Cook touched at Hawaii in 1779, was driven off by a storm, and on putting back to refit was murdered by the natives.

Cook's Tale, The, see *Canterbury Tales*.

Cooper, JAMES FENIMORE (1789–1851) spent his youth partly on the family estate on Otsego Lake (N.Y.), partly in the merchant marine, partly in the American navy. He then settled down as a writer of novels. His second book, 'The Spy' (1821), a stirring tale of the American Revolution, brought him into prominence. His other best-known works are: 'The Pioneers' (1823), 'The Last of the Mohicans' (1826), 'The Prairie' (1827), 'The Pathfinder' (1840), and 'The Deerslayer' (1841). They furnish not only exciting incidents, but a vivid picture of the Red Indian and his surroundings in a period that has passed away.

Cooper's Hill, see *Denham*.

Copenhagen, THE BOMBARDMENT OF, by Nelson in 1801. It was in the course of this that Nelson, placing his telescope to his blind eye, declared that he could not see the signal of recall hoisted by Admiral Parker.

Copernicus, latinized form of the surname of MIKOLAI KOPERNIK (1473–1543), a native of Thorn in Prussian Poland, propounded the theory that the planets including the earth move in orbits round the sun as centre, in opposition to the theory of Ptolemy (q.v.) that the sun and planets move round the earth.

Cophetua, KING, a legendary king in Africa, who cared not for womankind, until he saw a beggar maid, with whom he fell in love. The tale is told in one of the ballads included in Percy's 'Reliques', where the maid's name is given as Penelophon. Shakespeare in 'Love's Labour's Lost' (IV. i) gives it as Zenelophon. There are other references to the story in Shakespeare's 'Romeo and Juliet' (II. i) and '2 Henry IV' (v. iii).

Copmanhurst, CLERK OF, otherwise Friar Tuck (q.v.) in Scott's 'Ivanhoe' (q.v.).

Copyright. The protection of literary property in some measure was ensured in early times either by a royal grant of privilege to publish or else by the activity of the Stationers' Company. (It should be noted that the ownership of the copyright in unpublished manuscripts, including letters, has always been assumed in English common law to rest with the author.) The Stationers' Company, incorporated in 1557, protected the rights of its different members to print particular books by domestic measures, fines, etc. It gave often little protection to authors (as witness the piracy of Elizabethan plays) but defended the rights of publishers in works to which they may or may not have had good title. The prerogative of the Crown remained—and remains to this day—in the granting of the right to publish Bibles, prayer-books, etc., which is reserved for the Queen's Printers and for the Oxford and Cambridge University presses.

The Act of 1709 gave to authors, and their assignees for the future, the sole right of publishing a book for a term of fourteen years, renewable for a further fourteen years if the author was alive at the end of the first term. The question whether or not the title to a perpetual literary property (e.g. Tonson and his descendants' ownership of 'Paradise Lost') had survived this Act was debated throughout the 18th cent. and finally settled against the publishers and authors. The author's period was increased to twenty-eight years or the term of his life in 1814, and with Macaulay's intervention, to forty-two years or seven years after death, whichever might be the longer, by the Act of 1842.

The Act of 1911 extended the period of copyright to the life of the author and fifty years after his death; made registration at Stationers' Hall no longer necessary; and included in the definition of 'copyright' the right to publish a hitherto unpublished work, the right thus becoming part of the personal property of the deceased author. The provisions of the Act of 1911 were incorporated and to some extent modified in the Act of 1956, which also recognized that scope should be given to certain libraries to make research and private study easier by providing students with copies of articles in periodicals, and copies of parts of published works.

International copyright has been obtained by a series of Conventions following the Berne Convention of 1885. A step forward in the sphere of international relations was taken with the passing of the Universal Copyright Convention, the product of UNESCO, in 1952. It brought in not only the U.S.A. but also a large number of states which had hitherto not entered into copyright relations with the European countries, e.g. most of the South American Republics.

Coranto, or current of news, the name applied to periodical news-pamphlets issued between 1621 and 1641 containing foreign intelligence taken from foreign papers. The Corantos were one of the first forms of English journalism, and were followed by the 'newsbook' (q.v.).

See also *Newspaper*.

Corbaccio, a character in Jonson's 'Volpone' (q.v.).

Corceca, in Spenser's 'Faerie Queene', I. iii. 18, 'blindness of heart', an old blind woman, mother of Abessa (Superstition).

Cordelia, in Shakespeare's 'King Lear' (q.v.), the youngest daughter of the king.

Corelli, MARIE, pen-name of MARY MACKAY (1855-1924), novelist. Her publications include: 'A Romance of Two Worlds' (1886), 'Barabbas' (1893), 'The Sorrows of Satan' (1895), 'The Mighty Atom' (1896).

Corflambo, in Spenser's 'Faerie Queene', IV. vii and viii, symbolizes lust. He carries off Amoret, who is released from him by Timias and Belphoebe. He is slain by Prince Arthur.

Coriat, THOMAS, see *Coryate*.

Corineus, see *Gogmagog*.

Corinna, (1) a Greek poetess of Boeotia of the 6th cent. B.C. She is said to have instructed Pindar; (2) Ovid's mistress.

Corinthian, from the proverbial luxury and licentiousness of ancient Corinth, a gay licentious man.

'I am . . . a Corinthian, a lad of mettle, a good boy.'
(Shakespeare, '1 Henry IV', II. iv. 13.)

In the first half of the 19th cent., 'Corinthian' was used for a man of fashion about town.

Corinthian Order, one of the orders of classical architecture, more ornate than Doric and Ionic.

Coriolanus, a Roman historical drama, by Shakespeare (q.v.), probably written about 1608. It was printed in the folio of 1623. The story is taken from North's Plutarch.

Caius Marcius, a proud Roman general, performs wonders of valour in a war against the Volscians, and captures the town Corioli, receiving in consequence the surname Coriolanus. On his return it is proposed to make him consul, but his outspoken contempt of the Roman rabble makes him unpopular, and the tribunes of the people have no difficulty in securing his banishment. He goes to the house of Aufidius, the Volscian general, is received with delight, and leads the Volscians against Rome to effect his revenge. The Romans send emissaries, old friends of Coriolanus, to propose terms, but in vain. Finally the mother, wife, and son of Coriolanus come and beseech him to spare the city. He yields, makes a treaty favourable to the Volscians, and returns with them to Antium, a Volscian town. Here Aufidius accuses him of betraying the Volscian interests, and with the assistance of his faction, slays Coriolanus.

Corneille, PIERRE (1606-84), French dramatist of the classical period. His severe and dignified style and strict classical tradition were much admired by contemporary English playwrights and critics. His most famous drama was 'Le Cid' (q.v., 1637).

Cornelia, 'Mother of the Gracchi' (2nd cent. B.C.), was mother of the famous tribunes, Tiberius and Caius. When a lady once made a show of her jewels at Cornelia's house, Cornelia produced her two sons, saying 'These are my jewels'.

Cornelia, the wife of Pompey in Kyd's tragedy, 'Pompey the Great'; also in Masefield's 'The Tragedy of Pompey the Great'.

Cornhill Magazine, The, a monthly periodical, founded in 1860 with Thackeray (q.v.) as first editor. His last two novels were published in it, as were also contributions from Ruskin and Matthew Arnold, Mrs. Gaskell, and Trollope. Sir Leslie Stephen (q.v.) was editor from 1871 to 1882.

Corn-law Rhymer, see *Elliott* (*E.*).

Corn Laws, THE, restricting the importation of foreign corn, were a subject of acute controversy during the first half of the 19th cent. The Corn Law was abolished by Peel in 1846, as a consequence of the agitation of the Anti-Corn Law League of Bright and Cobden, the distress prevalent in England, and the Irish famine of 1845.

Cornucopia, see *Amalthea*.

Cornwall, BARRY, see *Procter* (*B. W.*).

Corpus Christi, the Feast of the Blessed Sacrament or Body of Christ, observed on the Thursday after Trinity Sunday. It was instituted about 1264, and at many places was celebrated by the performance of sacred plays (see *Miracle Plays*).

Corsair, The, a poem in heroic couplets by Lord Byron (q.v.) (1814). It is a romantic tale of a pirate chief and his tragic loves.

Cortegiano, Il, see Castiglione.

Cortez, HERNANDO (1485–1547), the conqueror of Mexico. He entered Mexico City in 1519. It was not he, but Balboa (q.v.) who first of all Europeans gazed on the Pacific. His life has been made familiar by the writings of Prescott (q.v.).

Corvino, a character in Jonson's 'Volpone' (q.v.).

Corvo, BARON, see *Rolfe* (*F. W.*).

Cory, WILLIAM JOHNSON (1823–92), is remembered as the author of two volumes of poems, notably his 'Ionica' (1858) containing the well-known translation of the epigram on Heraclitus by the Alexandrian poet Callimachus, 'They told me, Heraclitus, they told me you were dead'.

Coryate, THOMAS (1577?–1617), travelled in 1608 through France, Italy, Switzerland, Germany, and Holland, mainly on foot. He published in 1611 a narrative of his travels, entitled 'Coryats Crudities' and 'Coryats Cramb'. In 1612 he set out overland to India, travelling through Constantinople, Palestine, Mesopotamia, and reaching Agra in 1616. He died at Surat. A letter of his from the court of the Great Mogul is printed by Purchas. Coryate wrote in a strange and extravagant style. See 'The Life and Adventures of Thomas Coryate', by M. Strachan (1962).

Corybantes, the priests of Cybele (q.v.), who in the celebration of their festivals beat their cymbals and behaved as if delirious.

Corycian Cave, THE, on Mt. Parnassus, named from a nymph Corycia, beloved of Apollo. The Muses are sometimes called Corycian Nymphs.

Corydon, a shepherd in Theocritus and in the Eclogues of Virgil, whose name has become conventional in pastoral poetry.

Coryphaeus, the leader of a chorus in the Attic drama.

Costard, a clown in Shakespeare's 'Love's Labour's Lost' (q.v.).

Costigan, CAPTAIN and EMILY (Miss Fotheringay), characters in Thackeray's 'Pendennis' (q.v.).

Cotgrave, RANDLE (*d.* 1634?), author of a famous French-English Dictionary published in 1611. Urquhart (q.v.) relied largely upon his dictionary for the translation of Rabelais.

Cotswold, LION OF, i.e. a sheep. John Heywood, in the 16th cent., refers to someone who was as fierce 'as a lion of Cotswold'.

Cotswold Games, public athletic contests held, from antiquity, on the open rounded hills of the Cotswolds. They were revived and organized about 1604 by Captain Robert Dover, and were made the subject of 'Annalia Dubrensia, or Celebration of Captain Robert Dover's Cotswold Games', a collection of poems by thirty-three writers, including Drayton, Ben Jonson, Randolph, and Heywood.

Cotter's Saturday Night, The, a poem by Burns (q.v.).

Cotton, CHARLES (1630–87), author of the dialogue written in 1676, which forms the second part in the fifth edition of Izaak Walton's 'The Compleat Angler' (q.v.). He also wrote many pleasant verses, and a translation of Montaigne's 'Essays' (1685).

Cotton, SIR ROBERT BRUCE (1571–1631), an antiquary and collector of manuscripts and coins. He gave the free use of his library to Bacon, Camden, Ralegh, Selden, Speed, Ussher, and other scholars, and sent a gift of manuscripts to the Bodleian Library on its foundation. The COT-TONIAN LIBRARY, largely composed of works rescued from the dissolved monasteries, was left to the nation by Sir John Cotton (1621–1701), grandson of Sir Robert; it suffered severely from fire in 1731 and was removed to the British Museum in 1753. It includes such treasures as the Lindisfarne Gospels, and the manuscripts of 'Beowulf', 'Pearl', and 'Sir Gawain and the Green Knight' (qq.v.).

Couch, SIR ARTHUR THOMAS QUILLER-, see *Quiller-Couch*.

Coué, ÉMILE (1857–1926), a chemist of Troyes in France, who developed a system by which he claimed that persons, through auto-suggestion, could counteract a tendency to disease. His formula, 'Every day, in every way, I am becoming better and better', had a wide vogue.

Council of Trent, an 'oecumenical' council of the Roman Catholic Church which sat at Trent in the Tyrol, 1545–63, settling in a coherent form the doctrines of that Church in opposition to those of the Reformation.

Counter-Reformation, a movement of reform in the Roman Catholic Church in opposition to the Protestant Reformation. It developed in the latter part of the 16th cent. In the course of the repressive measures which formed part of this movement, Giordano Bruno was burnt as a heretic.

Countess Cathleen, The, a play by Yeats (q.v.) (1892), one of the two plays with which the Irish Literary Theatre started on its course.

Count Julian, a tragedy by Landor (q.v.) (1812).

It deals with the story of the vengeance taken by Count Julian, a Spanish nobleman, on Roderigo the king, who has dishonoured Julian's daughter. The subject is also treated in Southey's 'Roderick'.

Count Robert of Paris, a novel by Sir W. Scott (q.v.) (1831). This was one of the 'Tales of My Landlord', fourth series, the last of the Waverley Novels. It was written in ill health and betrays the decline of his powers.

The scene is laid in Constantinople in the days of the Emperor Alexius Comnenus (1081–1118), and the story centres in the arrival there of the first crusaders. Anna Comnena figures largely in the novel and provides some of its best pages.

Country Wife, The, a comedy by Wycherley (q.v.) (1675).

This is one of the wittiest of Wycherleys plays, but the manners depicted are coarse and indecent. Mr. Pinchwife, having occasion to come to London for the marriage of his sister, Alithea, brings with him his artless young country wife, and the excess of his suspicion puts ideas into her head. Sparkish, who was to marry Alithea, loses her from the opposite excess of confidence and credulity at the last moment to a new wooer. While Horner, a witty young libertine, who has spread a false report about himself in order to facilitate his amours, is able to satisfy Pinchwife of his wife's innocence.

County Palatine, in England, a county of which the earl or lord had originally royal privileges, with the right of exclusive civil and criminal jurisdiction. The counties palatine are now Cheshire and Lancashire.

Coup de théâtre, an unexpected and sensational turn in a play.

Couplet, heroic, see *Heroic couplet*.

E

Courcy, LORD and LADY DE, and their sons and daughters, characters in A. Trollope's Barsetshire novels (q.v.), types of a worldly aristocracy.

Courier, The, a newspaper published in the early part of the 19th cent., under the management of Daniel Stuart (q.v.). Coleridge and Wordsworth were among its contributors. Galt (q.v.) was at one time its editor.

Courtier, The ('Il Cortegiano'), see *Castiglione.*

Courtly love, a conception of love which first developed in the feudal courts of the south of France in the first half of the 12th cent., and is the chief theme of the troubadours in their chansons; it is essentially aristocratic, its basic situation of humble lover, haughty lady, and tale-bearing slanderers being modelled on the relation of vassal to overlord in feudal society. Treated as an elegant and entertaining social and literary game of gallantry in the Midi, courtly love passed into the north of France in the second half of the 12th cent., where, in the hands of writers like Chrétien de Troyes (q.v.), it developed into a more serious code of social morality.

Court of Love, an institution said to have existed in Provence and Languedoc in the Middle Ages, a tribunal composed of lords and ladies for deciding questions of gallantry.

Court of Love, The, an allegory (1,400 lines in rhyme-royal) attributed doubtfully to Chaucer, in which the poet visits the Court of Venus, converses with those who frequent it, and reads its twenty statutes. Linguistic peculiarities suggest that this poem was of later date than Chaucer, or was extensively rewritten. In spirit it is thoroughly Chaucerian.

Courtship of Miles Standish, see *Miles Standish.*

Covenant, THE, or NATIONAL COVENANT, a protestation signed all over Scotland in 1638, in which the subscribers swore to defend the Protestant religion. A COVENANTER was a subscriber or adherent of the above.

Covenant, THE SOLEMN LEAGUE AND, a treaty (1643) between the English and Scottish nations.

Covent Garden, in London, the old Convent Garden of Westminster. Many celebrated people lived there (Sir Kenelm Digby, Sir Godfrey Kneller, Sir Peter Lely, Lady Mary Wortley Montagu, among others), and the Bedford Coffeehouse, and those of Will and Button (qq.v.) were in the neighbourhood. Covent Garden is frequently mentioned in 17th- and 18th-cent. literature, generally as a centre of dissipation. It is still the principal wholesale market in London for vegetables, fruit, and flowers.

The first COVENT GARDEN THEATRE was opened by Rich in 1732. It was burnt down in 1808, and its successor in 1856. The new theatre (by Barry) opened in 1858 has been the principal home in England of opera.

Covent Garden Journal, The, see *Fielding (H.).*

Coventry, To SEND TO, to exclude a person from the society of which he is a member, on account of objectionable conduct. The expression perhaps originated from a phrase in Clarendon's 'History' (see *Clarendon (E. H.)).*

Coventry Miracle Plays, see *Miracle Plays.*

Coverdale, MILES (1488-1568), studied at Cambridge, was ordained priest in 1514 and adopted Lutheran views. He was bishop of Exeter, 1551-3. He translated at Antwerp the Bible and Apocrypha from German and Latin versions with the aid of Tyndale's New Testament. A modified version was issued in 1537. Coverdale also superintended the printing of the 'Great Bible' of 1539 (see under *Bible, The English).* If he was in fact (which has been questioned) the translator of the version of the Bible attributed to him, he is entitled to the credit for much of the noble language of the Authorized Version, and in particular for the Prayer-book version of the Psalter.

Coverley, SIR ROGER DE, a character

described by Addison (q.v.) in 'The Spectator' (q.v.). He is a member of the Spectator Club, 'a gentleman of Worcestershire, of ancient descent, a baronet. . . . He is a gentleman that is very singular in his behaviour, but his singularities proceed from his good sense, and are contradictions to the manners of the world, only as he thinks the world is in the wrong.' He figures in a number of 'The Spectator' papers (by both Addison and Steele), being depicted at home, at church, at the assizes, in town, at the play, at Vauxhall, etc.

Coward, SIR NOËL (1899-1973), actor and dramatist, author of many plays, mostly sophisticated comedies, including 'Private Lives' (1930), 'Cavalcade' (1931), and 'Blithe Spirit' (1941).

Cowley, ABRAHAM (1618-67), was king's scholar at Westminster, and scholar and fellow of Trinity College, Cambridge. His amazing precocity is shown by the fact that when 10 years of age, he composed an epical romance (included) in 'Poetical Blossoms', 1633). 'Love's Riddle', a pastoral drama, appeared in 1638; and 'The Guardian', reissued as 'The Cutter of Coleman Street', a comedy directed against the Puritans, in 1641. Ejected from Cambridge as a result of the Civil War, he went in 1646 to Paris, where he became secretary to Queen Henrietta Maria and was employed on delicate diplomatic missions. After the Restoration, a competence was provided for him, and he received a grant of the manor of Oldcourt (Nethercot).

His principal works, besides those mentioned above, are 'The Mistress', a love-cycle, 1647; 'Miscellanies' including four books of the 'Davideis', an epic in decasyllabic couplets on the biblical history of David, 1656. In his 'Pindarique Odes', included in the 'Miscellanies', he introduced the fashion of the rhetorical ode, in irregular verse, imitated by Dryden and others. His prose works, marked by grace and simplicity of style, include some 'Essays', notably one 'Of Myself', con-

taining interesting particulars of his early life.

Cowley, MRS. HANNAH (1743-1809), *née* PARKHOUSE, wrote a number of comedies between 1776 and 1795, including 'A Bold Stroke for a Husband' (1783) and 'The Belle's Stratagem', produced in 1780.

Cowper (pron. 'Cooper'), WILLIAM (1731-1800), was educated at a private school (where he was bullied) and at Westminster School. He was then articled to a solicitor (1750-2) and was called to the bar in 1754. He suffered from fits of depression, which developed into mania, and he tried to commit suicide. From his mania he was cured, but he thereafter lived in retirement. In 1765 he became a boarder in the house of Morley Unwin at Huntingdon, where the cheerful simple life perfectly suited him. After Unwin's death, he removed with Mary, Unwin's widow, to Olney, coming under the influence of John Newton (q.v.), the evangelical curate of the place, at whose instance he contributed to the collection of 'Olney Hymns' (1779), his contributions including such well-known hymns as 'Hark, my soul! it is the Lord', and 'God moves in a mysterious way'. In 1779, the influence of the strenuous Newton being withdrawn, Cowper entered upon the most peaceful period of his life, and began to write much poetry. At the suggestion of Mrs. Unwin he wrote eight satires: 'Table Talk', 'The Progress of Error', 'Truth', 'Expostulation', 'Hope', 'Charity', 'Conversation', and 'Retirement'. These were published in 1782. The volume included some shorter poems, among others the well-known 'Boadicea' and 'Verses supposed to be written by Alexander Selkirk'. In 1782 he wrote 'John Gilpin' (q.v.) and in 1784 'The Task' (q.v.). In 1786 he moved, with Mrs. Unwin, to Weston, where he wrote some short poems published after his death, including the verses 'On the Loss of the Royal George', the sonnet 'To Mrs. Unwin', and the beautiful lines 'To Mary'. In 1785 he undertook the translation of Homer (1791), which was not successful. He received a pension in 1794. Mrs. Unwin died in 1796, and her loss left Cowper shattered in mind and body. He wrote the fine but gloomy poem 'The Castaway' shortly before his death.

Cowper's admirable letters, of which several editions have been published, throw light on his simple, gentle, and humane personality. His poetry is notable as heralding a simpler and more natural style than the classical style of Pope and his inferior imitators.

Cox and Box, an operetta by Sir F. Burnand, music by Sir A. Sullivan (qq.v.), produced in 1867. See also *Box and Cox*.

Crab, in Shakespeare's 'The Two Gentlemen of Verona' (q.v.), Launce's dog.

Crabbe, GEORGE (1754-1832), was apprenticed to a doctor, and subsequently practised medicine at Aldeburgh in Suffolk. He made the acquaintance of Sarah Elmy, whom he married ten years later. In 1780 he went to London, where he was generously befriended by Edmund Burke and published 'The Library' in 1781, a poem in the manner of Pope. He took orders and became curate of Aldeburgh, and from 1782 to 1785 was chaplain at Belvoir to the duke of Rutland. In 1783 appeared, after revision by Burke and Johnson, 'The Village', a poem in heroic couplets. A long interval followed during which Crabbe published nothing of importance. In 1807 appeared a volume containing among other poems 'The Parish Register', which first revealed the gifts of Crabbe as a narrative poet. The same volume contained 'Sir Eustace Grey', the terrible account, in eight-lined stanzas, by a patient in a madhouse, of his decline from happiness and prosperity. In 1810 he published 'The Borough', a poem in twenty-four 'letters', in which he illustrates by various stories the life of a country town. This was followed in 1812 by 'Tales', and in 1819 he published 'Tales of the Hall', stories again, terrible, humorous, or sad. The collected edition of his works issued by his son in 1834 con-

tained some fresh tales of considerable merit. Crabbe was a realistic describer of life as he saw it, in all its ugliness— 'Though nature's sternest painter yet the best', as Byron called him—and rarely rose to the higher flights of poetry.

Craftsman, The, a periodical started in Dec. 1726 to which Bolingbroke (q.v) contributed his 'Remarks upon the History of England'. Among other contributors were Dr. Arbuthnot, Swift, Budgell, and perhaps Pope. Its title was intended to indicate Sir Robert Walpole as a 'man of craft'.

Craigenputtock, see *Carlyle* (T.).

Craik, MRS., see *Mulock*.

Crane, HART (1899-1932), American poet. He published two volumes of verse, 'White Buildings' (1926) and 'The Bridge' (1930), in which the force of genius is fully apparent. 'Collected Poems', which contained some new work, appeared in 1933.

Crane, STEPHEN (1871-1900), American writer. He made his name with his brilliant novel 'The Red Badge of Courage: An Episode in the American Civil War' (1895). His other publications include two fine collections of short stories, 'The Open Boat' (1898) and 'The Monster' (1899).

Cranford, by Mrs. Gaskell (q.v.), published in 'Household Words' in 1851-3, republished in 1853.

'Cranford' is a prose idyll, in which the authoress, drawing in part on her experiences of Knutsford, describes with much tenderness, and a just blend of humour and pathos, life in a quiet Cheshire village in the early 19th cent. We have sketches of the stern Miss Deborah, who thinks 'Pickwick' by no means equal to Dr. Johnson, of the tragedy of the genial Captain Brown, run over by a train while deep in the perusal of a number of the obnoxious 'Pickwick'; of Miss Matty's unhappy little love story; of the panic caused in the village by a succession of purely imaginary robberies; and so forth, ending with the ruin of Miss Matty through the failure of a bank, and the fortunate return from India of her long-lost brother Peter, who describes how he once 'shot a Cherubim'.

Cranmer, THOMAS (1489-1556), archbishop of Canterbury. He propounded views in favour of the divorce of Henry VIII from Catharine of Aragon, was appointed to the archbishopric in 1533, and maintained the king's claim to be the supreme head of the Church of England. He supervised the production of the first prayer-book of Edward VI, 1549; prepared the revised prayer-book of 1552; and promulgated the forty-two articles of religion (afterwards reduced to thirty-nine) in the same year. In Queen Mary's reign he was condemned for heresy by Cardinal Pole, and degraded in 1556. He signed six documents admitting the truth of all Roman Catholic doctrines except transubstantiation, in vain, and was burnt at the stake on 21 March 1556 at Oxford, holding his right hand (which had written his recantation) steadily in the flames, that it might be the first burnt. His chief title to fame is that of being the principal author of the English liturgy.

For CRANMER'S BIBLE, which appeared in 1539, see under *Bible* (*The English*).

Crapaud or JOHNNY CRAPAUD, a derisive term at one time in use for a Frenchman.

Crashaw, RICHARD (1612?-49), the son of a noted anti-papal preacher, entered the Roman Catholic Church and went to Paris, and appears to have been introduced to Queen Henrietta Maria by his friend Cowley (q.v.), her secretary. She in turn introduced him to Cardinal Pallotto, the governor of Rome, who procured him a benefice in Loretto in 1649, where he died shortly after his arrival.

His principal poetical work was the 'Steps to the Temple' (1646), a collection of religious poems showing great devotional ecstasy, and the influence of Marino and also, as Gosse has pointed out, of the Spanish Mystics. To this was attached a secular section, the 'Delights of the Muses', containing the pretty 'Wishes.

To his (supposed) Mistresse', beginning 'Whoe'er she be'.

Cratchit, BOB, a character in Dickens's 'A Christmas Carol' (q.v.).

Crawford, LORD, a character in Scott's 'Quentin Durward' (q.v.).

Crawford, FRANCIS MARION (1854-1909), novelist, travelled extensively and his novels reflect his knowledge of foreign lands. Thus four have Rome for their scene; one has Constantinople; three have the East; and three have Germany, 'Dr. Claudius' (1883), 'Greifenstein' (1889), and 'The Cigarette-Maker's Romance' (1890); while the scene of others is laid in England or America.

Crawford, HENRY and MARY, characters in Jane Austen's 'Mansfield Park' (q.v.).

Crawley, THE REVD. JOSIAH, and his daughter GRACE, characters in A. Trollope's 'Framley Parsonage' and 'The Last Chronicle of Barset'.

Crawley, SIR PITT, his sister MISS CRAWLEY, his brother the REVD. BUTE, and MRS. BUTE, and his sons, PITT and RAWDON, leading characters in Thackeray's 'Vanity Fair' (q.v.).

Craye, COL. HORACE DE, a character in Meredith's 'The Egoist'.

Creakle, in Dickens's 'David Copperfield' (q.v.), the bullying headmaster.

Credo, 'I believe', the first word of the Apostles' and Nicene Creeds in Latin. Hence a name for either of these creeds.

Creevey, THOMAS (1768-1838), was whig M.P. successively for Thetford and Appleby. The 'Creevey Papers', published in 1903, are interesting for the light they throw on the characters of prominent persons and on the society of the later Georgian era.

Cresseid, *The Testament of*, the chief work of the Scottish poet Henryson (q.v.), was printed in 1593. It is written in rhyme-royal. The poet describes in the prologue how he took up a book

Written by worthie Chaucer glorious
Of fair Cresseid and lusty Troilus,

and proceeded to tell the retribution that came upon the fickle Cressida.

Cressida, see *Troilus and Cressida*, also *Cresseid*.

Creusa, (1) or GLAUCE, a daughter of Creon, king of Corinth. When about to marry Jason (q.v.) she put on a poisoned garment given her by Medea. It set her body on fire, so that she died in torment; (2) a daughter of Priam, king of Troy, and the wife of Aeneas (q.v.) and mother of Ascanius. In the flight after the fall of Troy she became separated from her husband, who never recovered her.

Crewler, THE REVD. HORACE and MRS., characters in Dickens's 'David Copperfield' (q.v.), the parents of SOPHY, whom Traddles marries.

Crichton, JAMES, 'THE ADMIRABLE' (1560–85?), travelled to Paris, 1577, where he is said to have disputed on scientific questions in twelve languages. He served in the French army, was a staunch Catholic, and a good swordsman. He was killed in a brawl at Mantua. His title of Admirable originated in Sir Thomas Urquhart's narrative of his career, 1652.

For the play 'The Admirable Crichton', see *Barrie*.

Cricket on the Hearth, The, a Christmas book by Dickens (q.v.) (1846).

John Peerybingle, carrier, and his much younger wife, Dot, are a happy couple, although the venomous old Tackleton, who himself is about to marry the young May Fielding, throws suspicion on Dot's sincerity. This suspicion appears to be verified when an eccentric old stranger takes up his abode with the Peerybingles and is discovered by John, metamorphosed into a bright young man by the removal of his wig. By the fairy influence of the Cricket on the Hearth John is brought to the decision to pardon her offence. But there turns out to be no occasion for forgiveness, for the bright young man is an old friend, the lover of May Fielding, believed dead, who has turned up just in time to prevent her marrying Tackleton.

Crisparkle, THE REVD. SEPTIMUS, a character in Dickens's 'Edwin Drood' (q.v.).

Crispin and **Crispinian**, SAINTS, brothers, members of a noble Roman family, who preached Christianity and were ordered by the Emperor Maximian to be put to death. They are the patron saints of shoemakers, and are commemorated on 25 Oct., date of the battle of Agincourt. See Shakespeare's 'Henry V', IV. iii. 40.

Crispinus, in Jonson's 'The Poetaster' (q.v.), represents the dramatist Marston.

Criterion, The, a literary periodical, founded by T. S. Eliot in 1922 and edited by him until it ceased publication in 1939.

Critic, The, or a Tragedy Rehearsed, a comedy by R. B. Sheridan (q.v.), produced in 1779.

In this play Sheridan satirized, after the manner of Buckingham's 'The Rehearsal' (q.v.), not only the sentimental drama, but also the malignant literary criticism of the day. We have first Dangle and Sneer, the venomous critics; Sir Fretful Plagiary, the poetaster (a caricature of Richard Cumberland, q.v.); and Puff, the unscrupulous advertiser of literary wares who has reduced the puff to a science. But Puff himself has written a tragedy, 'The Spanish Armada', to the rehearsal of which he takes Sneer and Dangle. This is an absurd historical drama with an admixture of the sentimental element, written in bombastic style, in which Sir Walter Ralegh, Sir Christopher Hatton, the earl of Leicester, and Lord Burleigh are presented, at the moment when the Armada is approaching; while Tilburina, the daughter of the governor of Tilbury Fort, is in love with Don Ferolo Whiskerandos, a Spanish prisoner. The discussion of the play by the author and the two critics makes a highly entertaining caricature of the dramatic art.

Critical Review, The, a paper founded in 1756 in opposition to 'The Monthly Review' (q.v.). It was edited during 1756–9 by Smollett (q.v.) and supported by Johnson and Robertson. It came to an end in 1817.

Criticism. The beginnings of English

literary criticism cannot be traced much before the Elizabethan period. Writers like Chaucer, e.g. in his 'Tale of Sir Thopas', which is a burlesque of the contemporary romance fashion, passed literary judgements, but these were given only incidentally. Wilson's 'Arte of Rhetorique' is one of the first English critical works, although it deals rather with modes of speech and address. It was followed by Gascoigne's 'Certain Notes of Instruction' and by the writings of Webbe and Puttenham. These are all works of rather pedestrian merit, though they contain some interesting contemporary judgements. Sidney's 'Apologie for Poetrie' (q.v.), evoked by the strictures of Gosson (q.v.), has distinct literary graces, and so too, though to a less degree, has Lodge's reply to Gosson. The works of these early critics were taken up with attempts to apply rules of classical criticism, often—as with the doctrine of 'Unities' (q.v.)—only half understood, to English literature. The parallel absurdities which this involved of introducing classical metres, etc., into English verse are seen in the letters of Gabriel Harvey (q.v.). Ben Jonson's prefaces, however, show a more intelligent and better informed knowledge of classicism.

English criticism showed no real advance until Dryden, the first great English critic. He used for the first time 'the pure language of criticism', observing what was written and refusing to be dominated by the ill-fitting theories of neo-classicism. His work is seen at its best in his 'Essay of Dramatick Poesie' and in the critical prefaces to his plays. Critics who followed him, e.g. Rymer, Dennis (qq.v.), continued, however, to be dominated by preconceived theories for the most part, though some writers, e.g. Addison in his essays on 'Paradise Lost', showed a greater degree of enlightenment. Pseudo-classical theories of literature and art continued to win a greater respect than their exponents deserved. The tradition persisted through Kames and others to Johnson. The latter's sturdy common sense, however, rescued him from the worst faults of these inherited prejudices. His judgements on Milton's minor poems have continued to shock posterity, but they should not allow the genuine fairness and clarity of his criticism to be obscured. His 'Lives of the English Poets' remains one of the great works of English criticism.

A welcome change towards a fresh bias is evidenced in the 18th cent. in the writings of the Wartons and others. This early appreciation of romanticism involved a widening of critical horizons and an appreciation, for example, of Spenser as well as Pope. It led ultimately to the critical work of Coleridge, associated first with Wordsworth in their prefaces to 'Lyrical Ballads' (q.v.) and afterwards in his great work, the 'Biographia Literaria'. With him should be grouped the other great critics of the romantic period, Lamb, Leigh Hunt, Hazlitt, and De Quincey (qq.v.). Their work tended to be subjective—and with the doubtful exception of Coleridge—based on no central body of theory; its merits were a depth of perception and a fine sensitivity.

In the modern period a great deal of criticism has been written. The only critic of the first order to arise is probably Matthew Arnold, who added to a dignified style of writing a very wide knowledge of contemporary foreign literature and a genuine appreciation of classical standards. Of lesser fame are charming essayists, such as Bagehot, Pater, Edmund Gosse, and Quiller-Couch (qq.v.), or literary historians such as Walter Raleigh and Saintsbury (qq.v.), who have succeeded him. In the 20th cent. T. S. Eliot (q.v.) has been regarded as the greatest critic since Matthew Arnold.

Croaker, a character in Goldsmith's 'The Good-natured Man'.

Croce, BENEDETTO (1866-1952), Italian philosopher, notable for his contributions to the theory of aesthetic.

Crockett, DAVID (1786-1836), American

politician. He was transformed by Whig journalists into an eccentric and humorous frontier hero, and has remained a mythical figure.

Crockford, 'Crockford's Clerical Directory', first published in 1857. A book of reference for facts relating to the clergy and the Church of England.

Crocodile's Tears: the crocodile was fabulously said to weep, either to allure a man for the purpose of devouring him, or while devouring him. Whence many allusions in literature.

Crocus, in mythology, the lover of the maiden Smilax. The pair were changed into the plants that bear their names.

Croesus, the last of the kings of Lydia, who passed for the richest of mankind. In conversation with Solon he claimed to be the happiest of men, but the philosopher replied that no man should be deemed happy until he had finished his life happily. When Croesus, conquered by Cyrus, was about to be burnt alive, he exclaimed 'Solon!' Cyrus, asking the reason for this, was moved at the explanation and released Croesus, whom he made his friend.

Croft, ADMIRAL and MRS., characters in Jane Austen's 'Persuasion' (q.v.).

Croker, JOHN WILSON (1780-1857), was secretary to the Admiralty and a prominent Tory politician. He is the supposed original of Rigby in Disraeli's 'Coningsby' (q.v.). He was a contributor to 'The Quarterly Review', and became notorious for his scathing criticism of Keats's 'Endymion'. He edited Boswell's 'Life of Johnson' (1831) and was severely criticized by Macaulay. The 'Croker Papers', published in 1884, are interesting for the light they throw on the political life of Croker's period of office (1808-32). It was Croker whom Macaulay said he 'detested more than cold boiled veal'.

Crome, JOHN (1768-1821), called 'Old Crome' to distinguish him from his son, was one of the greatest of English landscape-painters. He founded the Norwich school of painting.

Cromwell, OLIVER, Lord Protector, 1653-8. He figures in Scott's 'Woodstock'.

Cromwell, RICHARD, Lord Protector, 1658-9.

Cromwell, THOMAS, *earl of Essex* (1485?-1540), secretary to Cardinal Wolsey (q.v.) and subsequently to Henry VIII, the principal promoter of the dissolution of the monasteries. He negotiated Henry's marriage with Anne of Cleves. The failure of this match and of the policy that underlay it, led to his downfall. A bill of attainder was passed and Cromwell was executed.

Cromwell, The True Chronicle Historie of the whole life and death of Thomas Lord, a play (1602), stated in the title to have been 'written by W. S.'. It was included in the 3rd and 4th Shakespeare folios (1663 and 1685). The play has little merit and is certainly not by Shakespeare.

Cronos or KRONOS, in Greek mythology, one of the Titans, a son of Uranus and Ge, and father by Rhea of Hestia, Demeter, Hera, Hades, and Zeus. The children of Uranus conspired against their father, who immediately after their birth had confined them in Tartarus, and Uranus was castrated and divided from Ge by Cronos. Cronos succeeded Uranus as ruler of the universe, and was in turn dethroned by Zeus. The Saturn (q.v.) of the Romans was identified with him.

Crosbie, ADOLPHUS, a character in A. Trollope's 'The Small House at Allington'.

Crosby Hall, in Bishopsgate, London, built by alderman Sir John Crosby (*d.* 1475) about 1466. Sir Thomas More lived there about 1520, and the countess of Pembroke, 'Sidney's sister', in 1609. It is mentioned in Shakespeare's 'Richard III', I. iii, and III. i. The Hall, after a chequered career, was re-erected in 1908 on a site in Chelsea.

Crossjay Patterne, a character in Meredith's 'The Egoist' (q.v.).

Crotchet Castle, a novel by Peacock (q.v.) (1831). As in most of Peacock's novels, the story includes an assembly of oddities at a country house, Mr. Skionar (Coleridge), Mr. MacQuedy (a Scottish economist), Mr. Firedamp (a meteorologist), Mr. Chainmail (typifying medieval romance), and others.

Crown of Wild Olive, The, four lectures by Ruskin (q.v.), delivered in 1866; the first on 'War', delivered at the Royal Military Academy; the second on 'The Future of England', at the Royal Artillery Institution; the third on 'Work', to a working men's institute; the fourth, in the Bradford Town Hall, on 'Traffic' (in the sense of buying and selling).

A crown of wild olive was the only prize at the Olympic Games (q.v.). Ruskin used it as a title in allusion to the importance of not working for a false idea of reward.

Croyland or CROWLAND, a famous abbey in Lincolnshire, figures prominently in C. Kingsley's 'Hereward the Wake' (q.v.).

Croyland or *Crowland History, The,* a chronicle of the 14th or 15th cent., long erroneously attributed to Ingulf, abbot of Croyland (*d.* 1109). It was shown by Sir Francis Palgrave and others to be a forgery of the 15th cent.

Cruden, ALEXANDER (1701-70), a bookseller and corrector of the press, who in 1737 published his 'Biblical Concordance'.

Cruikshank, GEORGE (1792-1878), artist and caricaturist, illustrated a large number of literary works and periodicals, including Dickens's 'Sketches by Boz' and 'Oliver Twist', novels by Harrison Ainsworth, Thackeray's 'Legend of the Rhine', etc.

Crummles, MR. VINCENT, MRS., and NINETTA ('the infant phenomenon'), characters in Dickens's 'Nicholas Nickleby' (q.v.).

Cruncher, JERRY, a character in Dickens's 'A Tale of Two Cities' (q.v.).

Crusoe, ROBINSON, see *Robinson Crusoe.*

Cry of the Children, The, a poem by E. B. Browning (q.v.), published in 1843 in 'Blackwood's Magazine'. It is the lament of the children in factories and mines, victims of industrial development and the capitalist system.

Crystal Palace, see *Exhibition.*

Cubism, a movement in art developed by Picasso (q.v.) and Georges Braque (1882-1963): the first Cubist pictures were exhibited in 1907. In Analytical Cubism forms are broken down into simple geometric shapes, various views of an object being shown together. In Synthetic Cubism, which developed *c.* 1912, fragments of objects, such as newspapers and matches, are often incorporated in the paintings (collages).

Cuchulain (pronounced 'Cuhoo′lin'), one of the principal heroes of the Ulster cycle of Irish mythology. He is supposed to have lived in the first century of the Christian era.

A series of the legends about him have been translated by Lady Gregory (q.v.).

Cuckoo-Song, The, see *Sumer is icumen in.*

Cuddy, a herdsman or shepherd, in 'The Shepheards Calender' of Spenser, and in 'The Shepherd's Week' of Gay (qq.v.).

Cudworth, RALPH (1617-88), one of the leading members of the Cambridge Platonists (q.v.). The characteristic feature of the philosophy of Cudworth and the other Platonists is its reaction against the narrow Puritan dogmatism.

Cuff, SERGEANT, the detective in Wilkie Collins's 'The Moonstone' (q.v.).

Cullŏ′den, near Inverness, the site of the battle in which in 1746 the duke of Cumberland defeated the force of the Young Pretender.

Cumberland, RICHARD (1732-1811), author of a number of sentimental comedies, of which 'The West Indian' (1771) and 'The Brothers' (1769) are the best. Cumberland is caricatured by Sheridan as Sir Fretful Plagiary in 'The Critic' (q.v.).

Cumberland, WILLIAM AUGUSTUS, *duke of* (1726-65), second son of George II, in command of the English army at Culloden (1746); known as 'the Butcher' on account of the severity with which he stamped out disaffection among the High-landers. He figures in Scott's 'Waverley' (q.v.).

Cummings, E. E. (1894-1962), American poet. 'Tulips and Chimneys', the first of his many volumes of verse, appeared in 1924; 'Poems 1923-54' in 1954. Cummings's experiments with typography and punctuation helped to give his verse a greater air of modernity than it in fact possessed. 'The Enormous Room' (1922), an account of his imprisonment in a French military camp, is a masterpiece of its kind.

Cumnor, LORD and LADY, and their daughter, LADY HARRIET, characters in Mrs. Gaskell's 'Wives and Daughters'.

Cunctator, see *Fabius.*

Cunningham, ALLAN (1784-1842), published 'Traditional Tales of the English and Scottish Peasantry' in 1822 and 'The Songs of Scotland, Ancient and Modern' (including the famous 'A Wet Sheet and a Flowing Sea') in 1825. Many of Cunningham's short pieces and imitations of ancient ballads gained much popularity.

Cunninghame Graham, ROBERT BONTINE (1852-1936), a man of varied career, during which he was M.P., a leader of the Dock Strike in 1887, an anarchist, and a traveller in remote parts of the world, particularly in the interior of Spanish America. His writings include remarkable stories of travel and descriptions of strange scenes and people, and tales of Scotland, notably in 'Mogreb-el-Acksa' (Morocco, 1898), 'Thirteen Stories' (1900), 'Success' (1902), 'Hernando de Soto' (1903), 'Scottish Stories' (1914), 'The Horses of the Conquest' (1930).

Cunobelin (Cymbeline), a king of Britain in the early years of the Christian era, and father of Caractacus (q.v.).

Cupid, identified by the Romans with the Greek EROS, the god of Love. He is generally represented to be the son of Venus (Aphrodite), but his father is variously stated to be Jupiter, Mars, or Mercury. He is pictured as a winged infant, armed with a bow, a quiver full of arrows, and torches.

Cupid and Campaspe, see *Campaspe.*

Cupid and Psyche, an episode in the fable of the 'Golden Ass' (q.v.) of Apuleius. Cupid becomes enamoured of Psyche, daughter of a king, and visits her every night, but remains invisible and forbids her to attempt to see him. One night she takes a lamp and looks at Cupid while he sleeps, and agitated by the sight of his beauty lets fall a drop of hot oil on his shoulder. The angry god departs and Psyche wanders over the earth in search of her lover, until Jupiter makes her immortal and reunites her to Cupid.

This fable was the subject of a poem by Shackerley Marmion (q.v.), 1637; of another by William Morris in 'The Earthly Paradise'; and there is a version of it in Pater's 'Marius the Epicurean' and in the 'Eros and Psyche' of Bridges (q.v.).

Cure for a Cuckold, A, a comedy by J. Webster and W. Rowley (qq.v.), brought out in 1661.

Curius Dentatus, MARCUS, Roman consul in 290, 275, and 274 B.C., celebrated as a type of frugality and virtue. Compare *Cincinnatus.*

Curll, EDMUND (1675-1747), a book-seller and pamphleteer, chiefly remembered for the controversy about the publication of Pope's correspondence (see under *Pope, Alexander*), and on account of his literary frauds and indecent publications (Pope refers to 'Curl's chaste press' in 'The Dunciad', i. 40). Curll is also mentioned in Swift's poem 'On the Death of Dr. Swift'.

Currer Bell, see *Brontë* (*C.*).

Curse of Kehama, The, a poem by Southey (q.v.) (1810).

Cursor Mundi, a poem in Northern Middle English of some 30,000 lines, mainly in eight-syllabled couplets, of the early 14th cent. It recounts, with many divagations, the Bible history from the creation onwards. The author, whose name is unknown, shows skill in popularizing religious instruction. Many copies of the poem survive, indicating the favour in which it was held.

Curule Chair, in Roman antiquity, was a chair inlaid with ivory and shaped like a camp-stool, used by the highest magistrates.

Curzon, ROBERT, *fourteenth Baron Zouche* (1810-73), was author of a 'Visit to the Monasteries of the Levant' (1849), a fascinating record of travels; also of 'Armenia' (1854), and of an 'Account of the most celebrated Libraries in Italy' (1854).

Curzon of Kedleston, GEORGE NATHANIEL, *first marquess* (1859-1925), was viceroy of India from 1899 to 1905, and secretary of state for foreign affairs, 1918-22. Lord Curzon's immense powers of work, combined with a certain aloofness of demeanour and preference for splendour and formality, gave rise to numerous legends, many of them of a humorous character.

Custance, the widow in Udall's 'Ralph Roister Doister' (q.v.).

Custance or CONSTAUNCE, see *Constance*.

Custom of the Country, The, a romantic drama by J. Fletcher and P. Massinger (qq.v.), composed between 1619 and 1622.

Custos Rotulorum, the principal justice of peace in a county, who has the custody of the rolls and records of the sessions of the peace.

Cute, ALDERMAN, a character in Dickens's 'The Chimes' (q.v.), said to be intended for Sir Peter Laurie, the City magistrate.

Cuthbert, ST. (*d.* 687), entered the monastery of Melrose, of which he became prior. In 684, at a synod held under St. Theodore, archbishop of Canterbury, he was selected for the see of Lindisfarne. He is commemorated on 20 March.

Cutpurse, MOLL, see *Moll Cutpurse*.

Cutter of Coleman Street, The, see *Cowley* (*A.*).

Cuttle, CAPTAIN EDWARD, a character in Dickens's 'Dombey and Son' (q.v.).

Cutty Sark, the name of a famous clipper ship built in 1869 for the China tea trade.

Cutty Stool, formerly in Scotland, a particular seat in church where offenders against chastity, etc., had to sit during divine service and receive a public rebuke from the minister.

Cuvier, GEORGES (1769-1832), a great French naturalist, and a founder of the sciences of comparative anatomy and palaeontology.

Cybele, a goddess representing the fecundity of nature, worshipped in Phrygia. Thence her cult passed into Greece, where she was known as RHEA.

Cyclades, a group of islands in the Aegean sea, regarded as lying in a circle round Delos.

Cyclic poets, a group of Greek epic writers whose writings formed a sort of legendary history of the world from the earliest times, and supplied themes to Greek dramatic and lyric poets.

Cyclopes, a race of giants having but one eye, in the middle of the forehead, who inhabited the western part of the island of Sicily. When Odysseus visited the island, Polyphemus (q.v.) was chief among them.

Cyder, a poem in blank verse, in two books, by J. Philips (q.v.) (1708), on the manufacture and virtues of cider, written in imitation of Virgil's Georgics.

Cymbeline, a play by Shakespeare (q.v.), acted in 1610 or 1611, first printed in the folio of 1623, in which he combines a fragment of British history, freely adapted from Holinshed, with the story of Ginevra from Boccaccio's 'Decameron' (ii. 9).

Imogen, daughter of Cymbeline, king of Britain, has secretly married Leonatus Posthumus. The queen, Imogen's stepmother, desirous that her son Cloten should marry Imogen, reveals this secret marriage to the king, who banishes Posthumus. The latter, at Rome, enters into a wager with Iachimo that if he can win Imogen's favour he shall have a diamond ring that Imogen had given Posthumus. Iachimo, repulsed by Imogen, by a stratagem gets admission to her chamber at night, brings back to Post-humus evidence that convinces him of her infidelity, and receives the ring. Post-humus writes to Pisanio, his servant at the court, directing him to kill Imogen. Pisanio from compassion spares her, provides her with a man's apparel, and leaves her in a forest, where she is kindly entertained by Bellarius and the two sons of Cymbeline, whom he had stolen in their infancy. A Roman army invades Britain. Imogen falls into the hands of the Roman general and becomes his page. In the ensuing battle, Cymbeline is captured and then rescued, and the general and Imogen are taken prisoners, as also Iachimo, thanks to the valour of Bellarius, of the king's sons, and also of Posthumus, who has returned from Rome to fight for Cymbeline. He now surrenders himself for execution as having returned from banishment. The Roman general asks Cymbeline to spare Imogen. The king moved by something familiar in her appearance, spares her life and grants her a boon. She asks that Iachimo be forced to tell how he came by the ring that he wears on his finger. Iachimo discloses his treachery. Posthumus, learning that his wife is innocent and believing her dead, is in despair, till Imogen reveals herself. The king's joy at recovering his daughter is intensified when Bellarius restores to him his two lost sons, and the scene ends in a general reconciliation. The play contains the beautiful dirge, 'Fear no more the heat o' the sun'.

Cymochles, in Spenser's 'Faerie Queene', II. v, vi, and viii, 'a man of rare redoubted might', 'given all to lust and loose living', the husband of Acrasia and brother of Pyrochles. He is finally slain by Prince Arthur.

Cymodoce, one of the Nereids. Swin-burne's 'Island of Cymodoce' in 'Songs of the Springtides' is the island of Sark.

Cymry, the Welsh. The word, which is Welsh, probably means 'the compatriots'.

Cynewulf, probably a Northumbrian or Mercian poet of the late 8th or 9th cent.

Modern scholarship is inclined to restrict the canon of his works to four poems in Old English contained in the 'Exeter Book' and the 'Vercelli Book' (qq.v.). The epilogues of these are 'signed' with runic characters corresponding to the letters that compose the name Cynewulf. The poems are 'St. Juliana', 'Elene', the story of the discovery of the true cross by the Empress Helena, mother of Constantine, the 'Fates of the Apostles', a brief martyrology of the apostles, and a poem on the Ascension which is placed in the 'Exeter Book' between a poem on the Incarnation and one on the Last Judgement. Of the four, the finest is the 'Elene'.

Cynics, see *Antisthenes*.

Cynosure, 'dog's tail', the constellation *Ursa Minor*, which contains in its tail the Pole star; hence a centre of attraction.

Cynthia, (1) a surname of Artemis or Diana (q.v.), the moon; (2) Spenser, in 'Colin Clouts come home againe', uses the name to designate Queen Elizabeth; (3) in Congreve's 'The Double Dealer', the daughter of Sir Paul Plyant.

Cynthia's Revels, a comedy by Jonson (q.v.), printed in 1601, satirizing some court types. The plot is extremely slight, and the play is of little interest at the present day. The song of Hesperus in v. iii, 'Queen and huntress, chaste and fair', is one of Jonson's most beautiful lyrics.

Cypress, a coniferous tree, often regarded as symbolic of mourning.

In Shakespeare's 'Twelfth Night', II. iv ('in sad cypress let me be laid'), 'cypress' in the opinion of Aldis Wright means a coffin of cypress wood, or a bier strewn with cypress branches; but in III. i, of the same play, 'a cypress, not a bosom, hideth my heart', the word means 'cypress lawn' or crape. Cf. Milton, 'Il Penseroso', 'sable stole of cypress lawn'. In the latter sense the word is derived from the name of the island of Cyprus.

Cypress, Mr., a character in Peacock's 'Nightmare Abbey' (q.v.), a caricature of Byron.

Cypresse Grove, *The*, see *Drummond of Hawthornden*.

Cyprian, belonging to Cyprus, an island famous in ancient times for the worship of Aphrodite or Venus. Hence the word is used in the sense of 'lewd' or 'licentious', and in the 18th-19th cents. was used to signify a prostitute.

Cyprian, ST. (*c.* A.D. 200-58), bishop of Carthage and a Father of the Church, author of theological works, beheaded under the Emperor Valerian.

Cyrano de Bergerac, see *Bergerac*.

Cyrenaic School of philosophy, see *Aristippus*.

Cythera, an island (Cerigo) on the coast of the Peloponnese, sacred to Aphrodite, who was thence surnamed Cytherea.

D

Dacier, THE HON. PERCY, a character in Meredith's 'Diana of the Crossways'.

Dactyl, a metrical foot consisting of one long followed by two short syllables, or of one accented followed by two unaccented. See *Metre*.

Daedalus, an ingenious Athenian, said to be the inventor of the wedge and other mechanical devices. Having murdered his nephew Talus, he fled with his son Icarus to Crete, where he constructed the famous labyrinth for King Minos (q.v.), and was himself confined in the labyrinth. Thence he escaped with Icarus by means of wings. But Icarus flew too high, and the heat of the sun melted the wax wherewith the wings were fastened, so that he fell into the sea west of Samos (hence called the Icarian Sea) and was drowned.

Dagon, the national deity of the Philistines, represented as half man, half fish (Judges xvi. 23; 1 Sam. v. 1-5; Milton, 'Paradise Lost', i. 462).

Dagonet, in Malory's 'Morte Darthur', King Arthur's fool.

Daguerreotype, an early photographic process invented by Louis Jacques Daguerre in 1839.

Daily Courant, The, the first English daily newspaper, 1702-35. It contained foreign intelligence, translated from foreign newspapers.

Daily News, The, was founded by Dickens (q.v.), as a Liberal rival to 'The Morning Chronicle', in 1846. But Dickens soon abandoned the editorship to John Forster (q.v.). Among notable contributors and members of its staff at various times may be mentioned Harriet Martineau and Andrew Lang (qq.v.). It became 'The News Chronicle', having absorbed 'The Daily Chronicle' in 1930.

Daily Telegraph, The, founded in 1855, was the first daily paper to be issued in London at a penny. Its enterprising character proved so successful that for a time it enjoyed a larger circulation than any other English newspaper. It has since become more staid and conservative, and in 1937 absorbed 'The Morning Post' (q.v.).

Daisy, SOLOMON, see *Solomon Daisy*.

Daisy Miller, one of Henry James's (q.v.) most popular stories (1879), which recounts the adventures of a young American girl travelling in Europe.

Dale, LAETITIA, a character in Meredith's 'The Egoist'.

Dale, LILY, the heroine of Trollope's (q.v.) 'The Small House at Allington'. She figures also in 'The Last Chronicle of Barset'.

Dalgarno, LORD, a character in Scott's 'The Fortunes of Nigel' (q.v.).

Dalgetty, DUGALD, a character in Scott's 'A Legend of Montrose'.

Damien, FATHER JOSEPH (1841-89), a

Belgian priest at Honolulu, went in 1873 to the neglected leper settlement on the island of Molokai. There he spent the rest of his life ministering to the spiritual and material welfare of 700 lepers. In 1885 he contracted the disease, but continued at work until his death. R. L. Stevenson wrote an account of him in 1890.

Damocles, one of the flatterers of Dionysius the elder, tyrant of Syracuse. He pronounced Dionysius the happiest of men, whereupon Dionysius invited him to experience the happiness of a monarch. He placed him at a banquet, where presently Damocles perceived a naked sword hanging over his head by a single hair.

Damoetas, (1) a shepherd in Theocritus and in the 'Eclogues' of Virgil; (2) a character in Sidney's 'Arcadia'; (3) an old shepherd in Milton's 'Lycidas' (q.v.).

Damon, a shepherd singer in Virgil's eighth 'Eclogue'; a name adopted by poets for a rustic swain. Cf. 'Epitaphium Damonis' of Milton (q.v.), his Latin elegy on his friend Charles Diodati (q.v.).

Damon and Pythias, a rhymed play by R. Edwards (q.v.), acted probably in 1564, printed in 1571.

Dampier, WILLIAM (1652-1715), buccaneer and explorer, visited in the course of his activities many parts of the world. He published accounts, in a vivid and straightforward style, of his travels and observations, in his 'Voyages' (1697), 'Voyages and Descriptions' (1699), and 'A Voyage to New Holland' (1703-9).

Dana, RICHARD HENRY (1815-82), an American jurist and politician, shipped in 1834 as a sailor for reasons of health. He published in 1840 a record of this experience under the title 'Two Years before the Mast'.

Danae, the daughter of Acrisius, king of Argos. An oracle foretold that the king would be killed by his daughter's son, and Acrisius therefore confined her in a brazen tower. Zeus, who was enamoured of her, visited her there in a shower of gold. Their son was Perseus (q.v.). For the further story of Danae and Perseus, see *Perseus.*

Danaïdes, the fifty daughters of Danaus, king of Argos, were promised in marriage to their fifty cousins, the sons of Aegyptus. Danaus quarrelled with Aegyptus and made his daughters promise to slay their husbands on their wedding night. This they all did except Hypermnestra, who suffered her husband Lynceus to escape. The others were condemned to eternal punishment in hell.

Dance of Death, The, or *Danse Macabre,* of which most nations of Europe had a version, pictorial or written, embodies ideas prevalent especially in the 15th cent., as a consequence of the terrible plague known as the Black Death.

Dandie Dinmont, in Scott's 'Guy Mannering' (q.v.), a sturdy Liddesdale farmer, the owner of a special breed of terriers.

Danegeld, an annual tax imposed at the end of the 10th or in the 11th cent., originally (as is supposed) to provide funds for the protection of England from the Danes, and continued after the Norman Conquest as a land-tax.

Dane-law, the part of England over which Danish law prevailed, being the district NE. of Watling Street ceded by the treaty of Wedmore (878).

Dangle, a character in Sheridan's 'The Critic' (q.v.).

Daniel, an OE. poetical paraphrase of the biblical story, contained in the Junius MS. (see *Cædmon*).

Daniel, SAMUEL (1562-1619), became tutor to William Herbert, third earl of Pembroke, and later to Anne Clifford, daughter of the countess of Cumberland. He is mentioned in Spenser's 'Colin Clout' (q.v.) as the 'new shepherd late up sprong'. He published 'Delia', a collection of sonnets in 1592; 'The Complaynt of Rosamond', also in 1592; 'Cleopatra', a Senecan tragedy, in 1594; and the 'Defence of Rhyme' in 1602 (?), in which he maintained, in reply to Thomas

Campion's 'Art of English Poesy', the fitness of the English language for rhymed verse. He issued in 1609 a new edition of his 'Civil Wars' (q.v.), which had first appeared in 1595. He composed numerous masques for court festivities, and was inspector of the children of the queen's revels from 1615 to 1618. His poems were sharply criticized by Ben Jonson, but praised for their 'sweetness of ryming' by Drummond of Hawthornden, and for their purity of language by Sir John Harington and S. T. Coleridge. William Browne (q.v.) calls him 'well-languaged Daniel'.

Daniel come to judgement, A, a quotation from Shakespeare's 'The Merchant of Venice', IV. i, in allusion to Susanna, 45 et seq.

Daniel Deronda, a novel by G. Eliot (q.v.) (1876), the last of her novels.

Daniel in the lions' den, a reference to the story in Dan. vi of Daniel being cast, by order of King Darius, into the den of lions, and of their mouths being shut by the angel of God, so that they did not hurt him.

Dannisburgh, LORD, a character in Meredith's 'Diana of the Crossways', drawn from Lord Melbourne.

D'Annunzio, GABRIELE (1863-1938), Italian poet, novelist, and playwright. In 1919 he occupied Fiume, where he remained as dictator until 1922. His flamboyance, his grand passion for Eleonora Duse, the erotic and decadent aspects of some of his works, and their Nietzschean content, made him the subject of controversy, both as man and writer.

Dansker, a Dane.

Dante Alighieri (1265-1321), was born at Florence of a Guelph family. The circumstances of his early life are obscure, but we know that in 1277 he was formally betrothed to his future wife, Gemma Donati, and that in 1289 he took part in military operations against Arezzo and Pisa. During this early period of his life he fell in love with the girl whom he cele-

brates under the name of Beatrice in the 'Vita nuova' and the 'Divina Commedia'. Her identity has been much discussed, but the generally accepted view is that she was Bice Portinari, who became the wife of Simone de' Bardi. When she died, in 1290, Dante was grief-stricken and sought consolation in the study of philosophy. In 1295 he became active in the political life of Florence. In 1301 he was one of three envoys sent to Rome to negotiate with Boniface VIII. During his absence the Black faction seized power, and Dante (whose sympathies were with the Whites) went into exile. Thereafter he led a wandering existence, probably going as far afield as Paris. He died at Ravenna.

The first of Dante's works in order of composition (apart from his earliest lyric poems) was the 'Vita nuova', written in the period 1290-4. In it Dante brings together thirty-one poems, most of them relating to his love for Beatrice. A linking prose narrative and commentary tells the story of his love and interprets the poems from the standpoint of one who has come to see his beloved as the instrument of his spiritual salvation. The 'Convivio', or 'Banquet', is an unfinished philosophical work, planned as a series of fourteen treatises. The four completed treatises were written between 1304 and 1308. The first book contains a defence of the Italian language. The Latin treatise 'De vulgari eloquentia', begun shortly before the 'Convivio', is also unfinished. The completed part consists of an inquiry into the form of vernacular language most suitable for lofty poetry. It is a pioneering work in the field of linguistic history. The 'Monarchia', written in the period 1309-12, is a Latin treatise on the universal empire and the relations between emperor and pope. It is very uncertain when Dante began his masterpiece, the 'Divina Commedia' (q.v.). It may have been begun as early as 1307, or possibly not until 1314 or later. It was finished just before his death.

Dan to Beersheba, FROM, i.e. from one end of the land to the other, an expression said to be first used by Sterne (q.v.) in the 'Sentimental Journey' (cf. Judges xx. i).

Danton, JACQUES (1759–94), a celebrated French statesman of the Revolution. He finally came into conflict with Robespierre and was guillotined.

Daphnaïda, an elegy by Spenser (q.v.).

Daphne, a daughter of the river Peneus, of whom Apollo became enamoured. Daphne entreated the assistance of the gods, who changed her into a laurel. Hence the laurel became the favourite tree of Apollo.

Daphnis, a son of Hermes who became a shepherd, regarded as the inventor of pastoral poetry.

Daphnis and Chloe, a Greek pastoral romance, one of the earliest works of its kind, sometimes attributed to an author Longus, of whom nothing is known. Its date is uncertain, perhaps the 2nd cent. A.D. G. Moore (q.v.) wrote a translation, 'The Pastoral Loves of Daphnis and Chloe' (1924).

D'Arblay, MME, see *Burney (F.).*

Darby and Joan, a jocose appellation for an attached husband and wife, especially in advanced years and humble life.

Darcy, FITZWILLIAM, one of the principal characters in Jane Austen's 'Pride and Prejudice' (q.v.).

Dares Phrygius, in Homer's 'Iliad', v. 9, a priest of Hephaestus among the Trojans. A work in Latin, the 'De Excidio Trojae', purporting to be the translation of an account by him of the destruction of Troy, was popular in the Middle Ages. It dates perhaps from the 6th cent. A.D. See *Dictys Cretensis.*

Darius the Great, son of Hystaspes, was king of Persia 521–485 B.C. He greatly extended the Persian Empire and in his reign began the great war between the Persians and the Greeks. His army was defeated at Marathon, and before he was able to renew the struggle he died, leaving the execution of his schemes to his son Xerxes (q.v.).

Dark Ages, in modern use, refers to the period between the break-up of the Roman Empire and the end of the 10th cent.

Darley, GEORGE (1795–1846), an Irish poet and mathematician, a member of the staff of 'The London Magazine'; wrote the pleasant pastoral drama 'Sylvia' (1827) and the poem 'Nepenthe', besides a good deal of other verse.

Darling, GRACE, in 1838 gallantly put out in a coble in a heavy sea and rescued several passengers of the wrecked 'Forfarshire' steamer.

Darnay, CHARLES, a character in Dickens's 'A Tale of Two Cities' (q.v.).

D'Artagnan, one of the heroes of Alexandre Dumas's 'The Three Musketeers' (q.v.).

Dartle, ROSA, a character in Dickens's 'David Copperfield' (q.v.).

Darwin, CHARLES ROBERT (1809–82), originator of the theory of evolution (see also *Wallace, A. R.*), was grandson of Erasmus Darwin (q.v.), and embarked in 1831 as naturalist on the 'Beagle', bound for South America on a scientific expedition. He returned in 1836, and published in 1839 his 'Journal of Researches into the Geology and Natural History of the various countries visited by H.M.S. Beagle'. His great work, 'On the Origin of Species by means of Natural Selection', appeared in 1859. Darwin's book gave rise to intense opposition, but found distinguished supporters in Huxley, Lyell, and Sir Joseph Hooker.

Darwin, ERASMUS (1731–1802), embodied the botanical system of Linnaeus in a poem 'The Botanic Garden', of which Pt. II, 'The Loves of the Plants', appeared in 1789, and Pt. I, 'The Economy of Vegetation', in 1791. The poem is in heroic couplets, in imitation of Pope. The work was ridiculed by Canning and Frere in 'The Loves of the Triangles'. In his 'Zoonomia', published in 1794–6, Darwin expounds the laws of organic life on the evolutionary principle.

Dashwood, ELINOR and MARIANNE, the principal characters in Jane Austen's 'Sense and Sensibility' (q.v.). JOHN DASHWOOD is their step-brother.

Datchery, DICK, the name assumed by one of the characters in Dickens's 'Edwin Drood' (q.v.); his identity is not revealed when the fragment ends.

Daudet, ALPHONSE (1840–97), French novelist, perhaps best known in England as the creator of the amusing type of Provençal Frenchman, 'Tartarin de Tarascon'. Daudet wrote some charming short stories, and a number of novels which attained great popularity.

Dauphin, the title of the eldest son of the king of France from 1349 to 1830.

The edition of the Latin classics *ad usum Delphini* (1674) was prepared for the son of Louis XIV.

D'Avenant, SIR WILLIAM (1606–68), was born at Oxford and is said to have been Shakespeare's godson. His earliest drama 'The Tragedy of Albovine' was published in 1629, his comic masterpiece 'The Wits' 1636, and 'Love and Honour' in 1649 (acted in 1634). D'Avenant was made poet laureate in 1638. He actively supported the cause of Charles I, and was knighted by him in 1643 at the siege of Gloucester. He was imprisoned in the Tower, 1650–2, and is said to have been saved by Milton. His romantic epic 'Gondibert' (q.v.) appeared in 1651. He practically founded English opera by his 'The Siege of Rhodes' (1656). After the Restoration he and Thomas Killigrew (q.v.) obtained patents from Charles II giving them the monopoly of acting in London. In conjunction with Dryden he adapted Shakespeare's 'The Tempest' in 1667. With Dryden and others he is satirized in 'The Rehearsal' (q.v.).

David, in Dryden's 'Absalom and Achitophel' (q.v.), represents Charles II.

David, KING, the second king of Israel, the youngest son of Jesse of the tribe of Judah. In his youth he slew the Philistine, traditionally Goliath (1 Sam. xvii). On the death of Saul he became king of Judah, and after the murder of Ishbosheth, of the whole of Israel (2 Sam. ii and v). His last years were darkened by the rebellion and death of his son Absalom (2 Sam. xv–xviii). See also *David and Jonathan*.

David, ST. (6th cent.), the patron saint of Wales, is commemorated on 1 March.

David, Song to, see *Smart.*

David and Bethsabe, The Love of King, a play in blank verse by G. Peele (q.v.) (1599).

David and Jonathan, types of loving friends (1 Sam. xviii. 1). Jonathan was the son of Saul, David was Saul's appointed successor as king of Israel.

David Copperfield, a novel by Dickens (q.v.) (1849–50). 'Of all my books,' wrote Dickens, 'I like this the best.' It is (in some of its details) Dickens's veiled autobiography.

David Copperfield is born in Suffolk, after the death of his father. His mother, a gentle weak woman, marries again, and her second husband, Mr. Murdstone, by cruelty disguised as firmness, and abetted by Miss Murdstone his sister, drives her to an early grave. Young Copperfield is sent to school, where he is bullied by the headmaster, Creakle, but makes two friends in the brilliant and fascinating Steerforth and the good-humoured plodding Traddles. Thence he is sent to menial employment in London, where he lives a life of poverty and misery, enlivened by his acquaintance with the mercurial and impecunious Mr. Micawber and his family. He runs away and walks to Dover to throw himself on the mercy of his aunt, Betsey Trotwood, an eccentric old lady. He is kindly received and given a new home, which he shares with an amiable lunatic, Mr. Dick. Copperfield continues his education at Canterbury, living in the house of Miss Trotwood's lawyer, Mr. Wickfield, whose daughter, Agnes, exercises a powerful influence on the rest of his life. He then enters Doctors' Commons, being articled to Mr. Spenlow, of the firm of Spenlow and Jorkins. Meanwhile he has come again into touch with Steerforth, whom he introduces to the family of his old nurse, Clara Peggotty, married to Barkis, the carrier. This family consists of Mr. Peggotty, a Yarmouth fisherman, his nephew Ham, and Little Em'ly, a pretty simple girl whom Ham is about to marry. Steerforth induces Em'ly to run away with him. Mr. Peggotty sets out to find her, following her through many countries, and finally recovering her after she had been cast off by Steerforth. The tragedy finds its culmination in the shipwreck and drowning of Steerforth, and the death of Ham in trying to save him.

Meanwhile Copperfield marries Dora Spenlow, a pretty empty-headed child, and becomes famous as an author. Dora dies after a few years of married life, and Copperfield, at first disconsolate, gradually awakens to the mistake he has made in rejecting such a treasure as Agnes. Her father has fallen into the toils of a villainous and cunning clerk, Uriah Heep, who, under the cloak of fawning humility, has obtained complete control over him and nearly ruined him. Uriah also aspires to marry Agnes. But his misdeeds, which include forgery and theft, are exposed by Micawber, employed as his clerk, with the assistance of Traddles, now a barrister. Uriah is last seen in prison, under a life sentence. Copperfield marries Agnes. Mr. Peggotty and Em'ly are found prospering in Australia, where Mr. Micawber, relieved of his debts, appears as a much-esteemed colonial magistrate.

Davideis, an epic poem by A. Cowley (q.v.) (1656).

David Simple, The Adventures of, in Search of a Real Friend, a romance by Sarah Fielding (q.v.) (1744).

Davidson, JOHN (1857-1909), settled in London in 1889, having previously published 'Scaramouch in Naxos' (1889) and other plays. His 'Fleet Street Eclogues' (1893) proved his genuine poetic gift, followed by 'Ballads and Songs' in 1894, etc. Between 1901 and 1908 he wrote a series of 'Testaments' expounding (in blank verse) a materialistic and rebellious philosophy. He committed suicide in 1909, leaving an unfinished poem 'God and Mammon'.

Davies, JOHN (1565?-1618), poet and writing-master. He published 'Microcosmos' (1603), 'Wittes Pilgrimage (by Poeticall Essaies)' (1611), 'The Muse's Sacrifice', containing the author's famous 'Picture of an Happy Man' (1612), and 'Wit's Bedlam' (1617). He also issued an 'Anatomy of Fair Writing' (1633). Some of his epigrams, most of which are contained in 'The Scourge of Folly' (undated), are valuable for their notices of Ben Jonson, Fletcher, and other contemporary poets.

Davies, SIR JOHN (1569-1626), was appointed lord chief justice of the King's Bench in England, but died before taking up this office. His 'Orchestra', a poem in the school of Spenser, in which natural phenomena are reduced to an ordered motion, was published in 1596. 'Astraea', a collection of acrostics on the name Elizabeth, appeared in 1599, and 'Nosce Teipsum' (highly praised by Coleridge), a philosophical poem, in the same year.

Davies, WILLIAM HENRY (1871-1940), poet, after a wandering life of poverty and adventure became, in his own words, 'a poet at 34 years of age; been one ever since'. Some account of his life is given in his famous prose work, 'The Autobiography of a Super-tramp' (1908). His collected poems were published in 1943.

Davison, FRANCIS (1575?-1619?), secretary of state to Queen Elizabeth, issued, with his brother Walter, 'A Poetical Rapsody' in 1602.

Davy, SIR HUMPHRY (1778-1829), natural philosopher, was professor of chemistry at the Royal Institution, and greatly advanced the knowledge of chemistry and galvanism. He invented the miner's safety-lamp. His collected works, prose and verse, with a memoir by his brother, were published in 1839-40.

Davy Jones, in nautical slang, the spirit of the sea, the sailor's devil. DAVY JONES'S LOCKER, the grave of those who perish at sea.

Dawson, BULLY, a notorious character in the 17th cent. (Cf. Addison in 'The Spectator', No. 2.)

Day, DAYE, or DAIE, JOHN (1522–84), the foremost English printer of the reign of Elizabeth I. He published Protestant devotional books under Edward VI and was imprisoned by Queen Mary. He printed the first church-music book in English (1560) and the first English edition of Foxe's 'Martyrs' (1563). He was the first to print Old English, having type made for it.

Day, JOHN (*fl.* 1606), collaborated with Dekker and others in a number of plays. His best work, 'The Parliament of Bees', appeared perhaps in 1607, though the earliest extant copy is of 1641. See also *Parnassus Plays.*

Day, THOMAS (1748–89), a barrister of the Middle Temple, devoted himself largely to works of moral and social reform. He was the author of 'The History of Sandford and Merton' (1783–9, see *Sandford and Merton*), in which he attempted to reconcile Rousseau's naturalism with a sounder morality.

Day-Lewis, CECIL (1904–72), poet. He was professor of poetry at Oxford from 1951 to 1956, and was appointed poet laureate in 1968. His works include 'Collected Poems 1929–36' (1938) and 'Collected Poems' (1954), translations of Virgil, and a number of detective stories written under the pseudonym of NICHOLAS BLAKE.

Dead Souls, see *Gogol.*

Deane, MR. and LUCY, characters in G. Eliot's 'The Mill on the Floss' (q.v.).

Dean of St. Patrick's, THE, Swift (q.v.).

Deans, DAVID, and his daughters JEANIE and EFFIE, the principal characters in Scott's 'The Heart of Midlothian' (q.v.).

Death and Dr. Hornbook, a satirical poem by Burns (q.v.).

Death of Blanche, The, see *Boke of the Duchesse.*

Death's Jest-Book, or The Fool's Tragedy, a play by Beddoes (q.v.), begun by him in 1825 and altered and touched up by him until the end of his life. It was published, after his death, in 1850. Three distinct manuscript versions of the play exist. The play contains some fine blank verse and beautiful lyrics.

De Augmentis, see *Bacon (Francis).*

De Bourgh, LADY CATHERINE, a character in Jane Austen's 'Pride and Prejudice' (q.v.).

Debrett, the peerage of the United Kingdom first published (1802) by John Debrett, under the title 'Peerage of England, Scotland, and Ireland, containing an Account of all the Peers'. Now issued annually.

Decameron, The, a collection of tales by Boccaccio (q.v.), written probably over many years, but assembled in their definitive form between 1349 and 1351, and drawn from many sources. Florence being visited by the plague in 1348, seven young ladies and three young men leave the city for neighbouring villas, and spend part of each of ten days (whence the name) in diverting one another with stories. The work had much influence on English literature, notably on Chaucer, and many of the tales were incorporated in Painter's 'Palace of Pleasure' (q.v.).

Declaration of Independence, THE, the document signed 4 July 1776, whereby the American Congress declared the United States of North America to be independent of the British Crown.

Declaration of Indulgence, THE, was issued by Charles II in 1672 to give religious liberty to Roman Catholics and Dissenters. A fresh Declaration of Indulgence was issued by James II in 1687; and a third in April 1688. It was for refusing to compel their clergy to read the last that the seven bishops were brought to trial.

Decline and Fall of the Roman Empire, The History of the, a historical work by Gibbon (q.v.) (vol. i 1776, vols. ii and iii 1781, and the last three volumes 1788). A standard edition, ed. J. B. Bury, appeared in 1909–13.

This, the greatest of historical works in English literature, falls into three divisions, as defined by the author in the preface: from the age of Trajan and the Antonines to the subversion of the Western Empire; from the reign of Justinian in the East to the establishment of the second or German Empire of the West, under Charlemagne; from the revival of the Western Empire to the taking of Constantinople by the Turks. It thus covers a period of about thirteen centuries, and traces the connection of the ancient world with the modern.

The history is marked by lucidity, completeness, and substantial accuracy. The principal criticism to which it is open is a lack of proportion, and a want of sympathy with man in his nobler impulses.

Decretals, epistles of the popes on points of doctrine or ecclesiastical law.

De Croye, ISABELLE and HAMELINE, characters in Scott's 'Quentin Durward' (q.v.).

Dedalus, STEPHEN, a character in James Joyce's 'A Portrait of the Artist as a Young Man' and 'Ulysses' (q.v.).

Dedlock, SIR LEICESTER, LADY, and VOLUMNIA, characters in Dickens's 'Bleak House' (q.v.).

Deerslayer, The, a novel by James Fenimore Cooper (q.v.).

Defarge, M. and MME, characters in Dickens's 'A Tale of Two Cities' (q.v.).

Defence of All Learning, see *Musophilus*.

Defence of Poesie, see *Apologie for Poetry*.

Defence of Poetry, see *Shelley* (P. B.).

Defender of the Faith, DEFENSOR FIDEI, a title conferred on Henry VIII by Leo X in 1521, in recognition of Henry's 'Defence of the Seven Sacraments'.

Defoe, DANIEL (1660?-1731), born in London, the son of James Foe, a butcher. He changed his name to Defoe *c.* 1703. He took part in Monmouth's rebellion, and joined William III's army in 1688. In 1701 he published 'The True-born Englishman', a satirical poem combating the popular prejudice against a king of foreign birth. In 1702 appeared 'The Shortest Way with the Dissenters', a notorious pamphlet in which Defoe, himself a Dissenter, ironically demanded the total suppression of dissent, to show the absurdity of ecclesiastical intolerance.

For this he was fined, imprisoned (May-Nov. 1703), and pilloried; the sense of his unjust treatment appears to have affected his character. Under the influence of this and of pecuniary distress—he attributed his ruin to his imprisonment— he became shifty and mercenary in public affairs. He wrote his 'Hymn to the Pillory', a mock-Pindaric ode, while imprisoned, and started his newspaper 'The Review' (q.v.) in 1704. In 1706 appeared his 'True Relation of the Apparition of one Mrs. Veal', a vivid piece of reporting of a current ghost story. During the following years he was employed as a secret agent, largely in Scotland. Certain ironical anti-Jacobite pamphlets in 1712-13 led to his prosecution by the Whigs for treasonable publications and to a brief imprisonment. He now started a new trade journal, 'Mercator', in place of 'The Review'.

He published the first volume of his best-known work 'Robinson Crusoe' (q.v.) in 1719, the 'Farther Adventures' of his hero following a few months later. The next five years saw the appearance of his most important works of fiction: 'Captain Singleton' in 1720; 'Moll Flanders', 'A Journal of the Plague Year', and 'Colonel Jack' in 1722; 'Roxana' in 1724. His 'Tour through the Whole Island of Great Britain', a delightful guide-book, in three volumes, appeared in 1724-7. In addition to the works mentioned above, Defoe produced a vast number of pamphlets on all sorts of subjects; in all he published over 250 works. Defoe was not only extraordinarily prolific and versatile, but also a liberal and humane writer.

Deformed Transformed, The, an unfinished drama by Lord Byron (q.v.), written in 1822.

Deianira, a daughter of Oeneus of Claydon, and wife of Hercules, who won her by defeating the river-god Achelous. As they travelled together, they were stopped by the swollen stream of the Evenus, and the centaur Nessus offered to carry her safely to the opposite shore. When Nessus reached the opposite bank he offered violence to Deianira. Hercules shot a poisoned arrow and mortally wounded Nessus, who gave Deianira his tunic, stained with blood infected by the poisoned arrow, telling her that it had the power to reclaim a husband from unlawful loves. When Hercules was unfaithful to her, Deianira sent him the centaur's garment, which caused his death.

Deiphobus, a son of Priam of Troy, who married Helen (q.v.) after the death of his brother Paris. He was slain by Menelaus. He figures in Shakespeare's 'Troilus and Cressida' (q.v.).

Deirdre, the heroine of the tale of 'The Sons of Usnach', one of the 'Three Sorrowful Stories of Erin'. (See Lady Gregory, 'Cuchulain of Muirthemne', and the dramas on Deirdre by G. W. Russell, Synge, and Yeats.)

Deism, or 'natural religion', the belief in a Supreme Being as the source of finite existence, with rejection of revelation and the supernatural doctrines of Christianity.

The DEISTS, who came into prominence at the end of the 17th and during the 18th cents., were a group of writers holding the above belief, of whom the chief were Charles Blount (1654–93), John Toland (1670–1722), Matthew Tindal (1657–1733), and the third earl of Shaftesbury (q.v.). Their views derived from those of Lord Herbert of Cherbury (q.v.).

Dekker, THOMAS (1570?–1632), was born, and mainly lived, in London, the manners of which his writings vividly illustrate. He suffered from poverty and was in prison for debt, but appears to have been a man of happy temperament. He was engaged about 1598 by Philip Henslowe (q.v.) to write plays (most of which are now lost) in collaboration with Drayton, Ben Jonson, and many others. He published 'The Shoemaker's Holiday' and 'Old Fortunatus' (qq.v.), comedies, in 1600. His other principal plays are 'The Honest Whore', and 'The Witch of Edmonton' (qq.v.), written in collaboration with Ford and Rowley, 1623. He wrote a number of pamphlets: 'The Wonderful

Yeare 1603', containing a poignant description of London during the plague of that year; 'The Seuen deadly Sinnes of London'; and 'Newes from Hell', an imitation of Nash, 1606. He produced 'The Guls Hornebooke', 1609, and 'Fowre Birds of Noahs Arke', a prose devotional work, 1609. His writings are marked by a sunny simplicity and sympathy for the poor and oppressed (including animals tortured for man's amusement).

De La Mare, WALTER (1873–1956), the author of many poems in which dreams and reality, fairies and humble natural creatures, are blended. His works include 'The Listeners' (1912), 'Peacock Pie' (1913), 'The Veil' (1921), 'Winged Chariot' (1951), all poems; 'Collected Poems' (1942); 'The Return' (1910), 'Memoirs of a Midget' (1921), (novels). His early books were published under the name of Walter Ramal.

Delane, JOHN THADDEUS (1817–79), the famous editor of 'The Times' (q.v.), 1841–77.

Delany, MRS. MARY (1700–88), of the Granville family, the wife (after the death of her first husband) of Dr. Patrick Delany (the friend of Swift), has left a voluminous correspondence ('Autobiography and Correspondence', 1861–2) throwing much light on the mode of life among people of quality in the 18th cent. Mrs. Delany introduced Fanny Burney at court.

De La Ramée, MARIE LOUISE, see *Ouida.*

Delectable Mountains, THE, in Bunyan's 'The Pilgrim's Progress' (q.v.), 'Emmanuel's Land', within sight of the Celestial City.

Delenda est Carthago, see *Cato the Censor.*

Delia, a collection of sonnets by S. Daniel (q.v.) (1592).

Delilah (DALILA in Milton's 'Samson Agonistes' (q.v.)), in Judges xvi, a woman of the valley of Sorek, loved by Samson, who persuaded him to tell her the secret of his strength and (by cutting off his hair) betrayed him to the Philistines.

Della Crusca, ACCADEMIA, the name of an academy established at Florence in 1582, mainly with the object of sifting and purifying the Italian language. The first edition of its dictionary appeared in 1612.

The name Della Cruscan is also applied to a school of English poetry, at once silly and pretentious, started towards the end of the 18th cent. It was taken from the Florentine Academy, to which Robert Merry (1755–98), one of the members of the school, in fact belonged. The Della Cruscan poets were attacked by W. Gifford (q.v.) in his 'Baviad' and 'Maeviad'.

Deloney, THOMAS (1543?–1600?), ballad-writer and pamphleteer. His three chief works, written between 1596 and 1600, are prose narratives relating respectively to the clothier's craft ('Thomas of Reading'), the weaver's craft ('Jack of Newbury'), and the shoemaker's craft ('The Gentle Craft'). This last includes the story of 'Simon Eyre' (a story adapted by Dekker in 'The Shoemaker's Holiday' (q.v.)). In these works the author, with considerable humour, portrays the life of the middle classes of Elizabethan times, and gives vivid pictures of London scenes.

Deloraine, WILLIAM OF, a character in Scott's 'The Lay of the Last Minstrel' (q.v.).

Delos, an island in the Aegean, one of the Cyclades. It contained temples of Apollo and Latona. The whole island was declared sacred by the Greeks, and was made the treasury of the Greek confederacy against the Persians. It was the transfer of this treasury to Athens that provoked the jealousy of other Greek states, and led to the Peloponnesian War.

Delphi, situated in Phocis, on the slopes of Mt. Parnassus, was the seat of a temple to Apollo and of an oracle of world-wide fame. It was customary for those who consulted the oracle to give large presents to the god; whence were derived the immense treasures of the temple. The oracle was in existence in the Mycenaean age and did not finally disappear until the 4th cent. A.D. But its period of greatest influence was in the 8th to 5th cents. B.C.

Demeter, known as CERES to the Romans, was the Greek goddess of the corn-bearing earth and of agriculture. Persephone (Proserpine, q.v.) was her daughter. After the carrying off of Proserpine by Pluto (see under *Proserpine*), so great was her grief that Jupiter granted Proserpine to spend part of the year with her mother and the remainder with Pluto. This myth, symbolical of the sowing of the seed and growing of the corn, was celebrated in the great Eleusinian mysteries. The myth has been treated by Tennyson in his 'Demeter and Persephone', and in Bridges' masque 'Demeter' (1905).

Demetrius, (1) a character in Shakespeare's 'A Midsummer Night's Dream' (q.v.); (2) a character in Jonson's 'The Poetaster', where he represents the poet Marston.

Democritus, a celebrated Greek philosopher, born at Abdera about 460 B.C. His cheerfulness led to his being called the laughing philosopher. He advanced (with Leucippus) the theory that the world was formed by the concourse of atoms, the theory subsequently expounded by Lucretius, and confirmed and developed by recent scientific discovery.

Democritus Junior, pseudonym of Robert Burton (q.v.).

Demogorgon, the name of a mysterious and terrible infernal deity, described in the 'Genealogia Deorum' of Boccaccio as the primeval god of ancient mythology, and this appears to be the sense of the word in modern literature (Spenser, Milton, Shelley, etc.).

De Morgan, WILLIAM FREND (1839–1917), at first devoted his attention to art, working for a time in association with his friend William Morris (q.v.). In the latter part of his life he turned to the writing of fiction. 'Joseph Vance', his masterpiece, appeared in 1906, 'Somehow Good' in 1908, and 'A Likely Story' in 1911.

'The Old Madhouse' (1919) and 'The Old Man's Youth' (1921), left unfinished by De Morgan, were skilfully completed by his widow.

Demosthenes (*c.* 383-322 B.C.), the Athenian orator. His fame, won in spite of lack of wealth and position, rests principally on the orations delivered to rouse his countrymen to the danger of the subjugation of Greece by Philip of Macedon (hence the word 'philippic'). Demosthenes, pursued by the Macedonian emissaries, took poison and died.

Denham, SIR JOHN (1615-69), took part in public affairs on the king's side and was forced to surrender Farnham Castle, of which he was governor, to Sir William Waller in 1642. His chief poetical work is the topographical poem 'Cooper's Hill' (1642), combining description of scenery with reflections, and containing the well-known quatrain on the river Thames, which begins 'O could I flow like thee'.

Denis, ST., first bishop of Paris and patron saint of France, decapitated in 280 with two companions on the hill of Montmartre. Legend relates that they carried their heads in their hands to the spot where subsequently the abbey of Saint-Denis, near Paris, was built.

Denis Duval, an unfinished novel by Thackeray (q.v.) (1864), his last work of fiction.

Dennis, in Dickens's 'Barnaby Rudge' (q.v.), the hangman and one of the leaders of the No-Popery riots.

Dennis, JOHN (1657-1734), author of 'Rinaldo and Armida' (1699) and other tragedies, one of which, 'Appius and Virginia' (1709), was satirized for its bombast by Pope ('Essay on Criticism', iii. 585-8). He is best known for his critical works, which include 'The Advancement and Reformation of Modern Poetry' (1701), 'The Grounds of Criticism in Poetry' (1704), 'An Essay on the Genius and Writings of Shakespeare' (1712).

Dennison, JENNY, in Scott's 'Old Mortality' (q.v.), the attendant on Edith Bellenden.

Denouement, the unravelling of the plot, the final solution, in a drama or novel; Aristotle's λύσις.

De Nugis Curialium, see *Map*.

Deor, Complaint of, an OE. poem of 42 lines, divided into stanzas. It is included in the 'Exeter Book' (q.v.). Deor is a minstrel who has fallen out of favour and been supplanted by another minstrel, Heorrenda, and consoles himself by considering the misfortunes of others, Wayland the Smith, Theodoric, Hermanric, etc. Each stanza ends with the refrain 'That passed; this also may'.

De Profundis, the first two words of the Latin version of Psalm 130; the title of Oscar Wilde's (q.v.) apologia.

'Deputy', in Dickens's 'Edwin Drood' (q.v.), the nearest thing to a name acknowledged by the imp who attends on Durdles.

De Quincey, THOMAS (1785-1859), after leading for some time a rambling life, went to Worcester College, Oxford, but took no degree. He there first began opium-eating. He wrote 'Confessions of an English Opium Eater' (q.v.) for the 'London Magazine' while living in London, 1821-4, and contributed to 'Blackwood's Edinburgh Magazine' (q.v.), for which he wrote 'On Murder as one of the Fine Arts' (1827). De Quincey produced a great deal of miscellaneous literary work and a large number of essays on a great variety of subjects. Mention should be made of his 'Autobiographic Sketches' (1834-53), his articles on Wordsworth, Coleridge, Lamb, and others, and his tales, 'The Spanish Military Nun' and 'The Revolt of the Tartars'. Of his critical work, his essay 'On the Knocking at the Gate in Macbeth' is best remembered. He wrote an ornate prose, sometimes marked by splendid imagery and humour.

De Rerum Natura, the great philosophical poem by Lucretius (q.v.).

Dervish, a Muslim friar, who has taken vows of poverty.

Descartes, RENÉ (1596-1650), a French mathematician, physicist, and philosopher, the founder of the school of philosophy known as CARTESIAN. The starting-point of his philosophy, expounded in his chief work 'Le Discours de la Méthode' (1637), was the famous phrase *cogito, ergo sum*, 'I think, therefore I am', and the distinction between spirit and matter. He relied exclusively on reason, and adopted a quasi-mechanical conception of the universe. He did not, however, explain the interaction of spirit and matter, while some of his principal physical theories were upset by Newton's discoveries. But his influence on the development of philosophy and science was immense. It extended to literature, where the impulse he gave to the rule of reason is manifested in the writers of the Augustan Age.

Deschamps, EUSTACHE, surnamed MOREL (b. *c.* 1346), French poet and fabulist, one of the creators of the *ballade*. He addressed a complimentary poem to Chaucer, whom he styled 'great translator'.

Desdemona, the heroine of Shakespeare's 'Othello' (q.v.).

Deserted Village, The, a poem by Goldsmith (q.v.) (1770), of which the theme is the superiority of agriculture to trade in the national economy. The poet revisits Auburn, a village hallowed by early associations, and laments a state of society where 'wealth accumulates and men decay'. Boswell attributes the last four lines to Johnson. (Cf. the protest against Goldsmith's picture in Crabbe's 'The Village'.)

Despair, GIANT, in Bunyan's 'The Pilgrim's Progress' (q.v.), imprisons Christian and Hopeful in Doubting Castle.

Desperate Remedies, the first of Hardy's (q.v.) published novels (1871).

Destiny, a novel by S. E. Ferrier (q.v.) (1831).

De Sublimitate, the critical treatise attributed to Longinus (q.v.).

Detectives in Fiction, see *Alleyn, Brown (Father), Bucket, Cuff, Dupin, Fortune, French, Hanaud, Holmes, Lecoq, Lupin, Maigret, Poirot, Tabaret, Thorndyke, Trent, Vance, Wimsey (Lord Peter).*

Deucalion, a son of Prometheus (q.v.). Jupiter, angered by the impiety of mankind, covered the earth with a deluge. Deucalion and his wife Pyrrha saved their lives by making an ark for themselves. After the flood had subsided, Deucalion and Pyrrha consulted the oracle of Themis on the question how to repair the loss of mankind and were told to throw stones behind them. The stones thrown by Deucalion became men, and those thrown by Pyrrha women.

Deus ex machina, 'God from the machine', an unexpected event or intervention in a play or novel, which resolves a difficult situation. When a god was introduced in the ancient Greek drama, he was brought on to the stage by some mechanical device ($\mu\eta\chi\alpha\nu\dot{\eta}$).

Deuteronomy (from Greek $\delta\dot{\epsilon}\nu\tau\epsilon\rho\sigma$ second, and $\nu\dot{\sigma}\mu\sigma$ law), the title of the fifth book of the Pentateuch, originating in a mistranslation of the Hebrew words in Deut. xvii. 18, which mean 'a copy or duplicate of this law'.

Deva, the river Dee in Cheshire.

De Vere, AUBREY THOMAS (1814–1902), the son of Sir Aubrey de Vere (1788–1846, himself a poet), he came early under the influence of Coleridge and Wordsworth. He was a friend of Tennyson, and a lifelong friend and advocate of Sir Henry Taylor, as poet and dramatist. Later friends included Robert Browning and R. H. Hutton. He published 'The Waldenses and other Poems' in 1842, and 'English Misrule and Irish Misdeeds', displaying Irish sympathies, in 1848.

De Veritate, the principal philosophical work of Lord Herbert of Cherbury (q.v.).

Devil, THE (from the Greek $\delta\iota\dot{\alpha}\beta\sigma\lambda\sigma$), in Jewish and Christian theology, the name of the supreme spirit of evil, subordinate to the Creator, but possessing superhuman powers of access to, and influence over, men. The word 'devil' is also applied to malignant beings of supernatural powers, of whom Satan is the prince, clothed, in medieval conception, in grotesque and hideous forms, with horns, tails, and cloven hoofs, derived from figures of Greek and Roman mythology (Pan, the satyrs); thence it is transferred to malignantly wicked or cruel men. It is finally applied colloquially to a junior legal counsel who does professional work for his leader, a literary hack, and generally one who does work for which another receives credit.

Devil is an Ass, The, a comedy by Jonson (q.v.), first acted in 1616, ridiculing the 'projectors' or monopolists, and exposing the pretended demoniacs and witchfinders of the day.

Devil's Advocate, see *Advocatus Diaboli.*

Devil's Thoughts, The, a humorous satirical poem by S. T. Coleridge and Southey (qq.v.) describing the Devil going a-walking and enjoying the sight of the vices of men as they follow their several avocations. The poem was imitated by Byron in his 'Devil's Drive', and by Shelley in his 'Devil's Walk'.

Dewey, JOHN (1859-1952), American philosopher, one of the leaders of the Pragmatist school.

Dewy, DICK, the hero of Hardy's 'Under the Greenwood Tree' (q.v.).

Diacritic, from διακρίνειν to separate, a sign or mark above or under a letter used to distinguish its various sounds or values, e.g. ö, é, ç, å.

Diaeresis, from διαιρέειν to divide, (1) the separation of a diphthong into two separate vowels; (2) the sign [¨] placed over the second of two vowels, which otherwise make a diphthong or single sound, to indicate that they are to be pronounced separately.

Dialect, one of the subordinate forms or varieties of a language arising from local peculiarities of vocabulary, pronunciation, or idiom. Specially, a variety of speech differing from the standard or literary 'language', a provincial method of speech.

The fairly distinct forms of speech which were current in England during the Anglo-Saxon period—the broadest divisions were Wessex, Mercian, and Northumbrian—were preserved into the Middle English period. At that time, spoken and written English differed from place to place throughout the country. The gradual acceptance of London English as the standard form (see under *Standard English*) has not prevented the survival of these dialects into the modern period, although their incidence now tends to be a matter of class and education as much as of geography. It should be emphasized that a dialect is simply a 'language' within a smaller range, and that, for example, English and present-day German are merely 'dialects' in relation to the original Germanic branch of the Aryan language family. The selection of any particular dialect as the standard form of speech in a country does not imply any absolute merit.

Diall of Princes, the translation by Sir T. North (q.v.) of Guevara's 'El Relox de Principes' (1577), which provided much of the material for Lyly's 'Euphues' (q.v.).

Dialogues concerning Natural Religion, a treatise on natural theology, by Hume (q.v.) (1779).

There are three interlocutors in the Dialogues, whose attitudes are indicated by Hume when he contrasts 'the accurate philosophical turn of Cleanthes' with 'the careless scepticism of Philo' and 'the rigid inflexible orthodoxy of Demea'; the subject of the Dialogues is the nature of God.

Dialogues of the Dead, Four, by Prior (q.v.), written in 1721, imaginary conversations on the model set by Lucian (q.v.).

George, Lord Lyttelton (q.v.), also wrote 'Dialogues of the Dead' (1760).

Diamond Necklace, AFFAIR OF THE, a plot, successfully carried out in 1783-4, by Jeanne de St. Remy de Valois, the descendant of an illegitimate son of Henri II and wife of a self-styled Comte de Lamotte, to get possession of a diamond necklace from the jewellers who had made it, on the pretence that Queen Marie

Antoinette had consented to purchase it.
Jeanne got possession of the necklace. It
was broken up, and the Comte de Lamotte
fled to England with most of the jewels.
Jeanne was arrested, whipped, and
branded. She escaped, came to England,
wrote her memoirs, and died in 1791.
(See A. Lang, 'Historical Mysteries', and
T. Carlyle, 'The Diamond Necklace'.)

Diana, a Roman goddess identified with
the Greek ARTEMIS. She lived in perpetual celibacy and was the goddess of the
chase. She also presided over child-birth,
and in post-Homeric literature was identified with the moon, in which character she
frequently occurs in English literature.
'Great is Diana of the Ephesians' was the
cry of the silversmiths of Ephesus, when
they found their trade in shrines for Diana
threatened by the preaching of Paul
(Acts xix. 24 et seq.).

Diana, a character in Shakespeare's 'All's
Well that Ends Well' (q.v.).

Diana, a volume of sonnets by H.
Constable (q.v.) (1592).

Diana Enamorada, see *Montemayor*.

Diana Merion, the heroine of Meredith's
'Diana of the Crossways' (q.v.).

Diana of the Crossways, a novel by
Meredith (q.v.) (1885). The story has
some historical foundation, but not in
respect of the central incident of the
betrayal of a political secret with which
the name of the Hon. Mrs. Norton,
Sheridan's granddaughter, was falsely
connected.

Diary of a Country Parson, The, see
Woodforde.

Diary of a Nobody, The, by George and
Weedon Grossmith (1892). It is the diary
of Charles Pooter, of The Laurels, Hollo-
way, and recounts with an amusing
simplicity his domestic, social, and business troubles, and their satisfactory issue.

Dibdin, CHARLES (1745-1814), dramatist
and song-writer, is remembered for his
nautical songs, including 'Tom Bowling'.

Dick, MR., the amiable lunatic in
Dickens's 'David Copperfield' (q.v.).

Dickens, CHARLES (1812-70), the son of

a government clerk, underwent in early
life, as the result of his family's poverty
(his father was imprisoned in the Marshalsea), experiences similar to some of those
depicted in 'David Copperfield', and
received little education. He became
reporter of debates in the Commons to
the 'Morning Chronicle' in 1835, and contributed to periodicals articles subsequently republished as 'Sketches by Boz,
Illustrative of Every-Day Life and Every-
Day People' (1836-7). These were immediately followed by 'The Posthumous
Papers of the Pickwick Club', of which
the publication in twenty monthly numbers began in April 1836 (the author being
then 24). In this work Dickens suddenly
reached the plenitude of his powers as
a humorist and achieved success and
financial ease. 'Oliver Twist' (q.v.) (1837-
8) followed in 'Bentley's Miscellany', and
'Nicholas Nickleby' (q.v.) (1838-9) in
monthly numbers. His next two novels,
'The Old Curiosity Shop' (q.v.) and
'Barnaby Rudge' (q.v.), Dickens published as parts of the serial 'Master
Humphrey's Clock' (1840-1), an unnecessary device which he soon abandoned.
In 1842 he went to America, where he
advocated international copyright and the
abolition of slavery. The literary results
of the voyage were 'American Notes'
(1842) and 'Martin Chuzzlewit' (q.v.)
(1843-4). 'A Christmas Carol' appeared in
1843, a Christmas book that was followed
in each of the succeeding years by 'The
Chimes', 'The Cricket on the Hearth'
(q.v.), 'The Battle of Life', and 'The
Haunted Man', works which added greatly
to his popularity. He paid a long visit
to Italy in 1844, and to Switzerland in
1846, where he wrote 'Dombey and Son'
(q.v.), published in 1848. In 1850 Dickens
started the weekly periodical 'Household
Words', succeeded in 1859 by 'All the
Year Round', and this he carried on until
his death. 'David Copperfield' (q.v.) appeared in monthly numbers in 1849-50,
'Bleak House' (q.v.) in 1852-3, the unsuccessful 'Child's History of England' in

1852-4, 'Hard Times' (q.v.) in 1854, 'Little Dorrit' (q.v.) in 1855-7, 'A Tale of Two Cities' (q.v.) in 1859, 'Great Expectations' (q.v.) in 1860-1, and 'Our Mutual Friend' (q.v.) in 1864-5. Dickens had begun to give public readings in 1858, which he continued during his second visit to America in 1867-8. After his return he began, in 1870, 'Edwin Drood' (q.v.), but died suddenly before finishing it. The original biography of Dickens is that of John Forster (1872-4; memorial edition, 1911); see also that by Edgar Johnson (1953).

Dickens was one of the greatest of Victorian writers and perhaps of English novelists. His immense vitality and originality, his vivid power of characterization, compensate for a tendency to caricature and for occasional lapses into sentimentality.

Dickinson, EMILY (1830-86), American poet. Only two of her poems were published—without her consent—during her lifetime, but she left over a thousand in manuscript. Thomas H. Johnson's definitive edition (1955) first made it possible to assess the range of her extraordinary genius. Her lyrical, paradoxical, gnomic verse is marked as much by wit and a keen sense of domestic realities as by mysticism.

Diction, POETIC, see under *Poetic Diction*.
Dictionary of National Biography, see *National Biography*.
Dictionary of the English Language, *A*, by S. Johnson, see *Johnson's Dictionary*.
Dictys Cretensis, the reputed author of a diary of the Trojan War. A Latin translation of what purported to be a Greek version of this diary has come down to us. This and the narrative of Dares Phrygius (q.v.) are the chief sources of medieval Trojan legends.
Didactic, instructive, having the manner of a teacher. Applied in literary criticism particularly to poetry having a moral or religious tone, a type of work which was especially popular in the 18th cent. (e.g. Young's 'Night Thoughts', q.v.).

Diddler, JEREMY, the chief character in James Kenney's farce 'Raising the Wind' (1803). Jeremy's methods of raising money probably gave rise to the current sense of the verb 'diddle'—to cheat or victimize.
Diderot, DENIS (1713-84), French philosopher, dramatist, and critic, chiefly remembered in England as one of the founders (with D'Alembert) of the 'Encyclopédie' (q.v.). He was the author of sentimental comedies, of the amusing dialogue on literature, education, and many other things, 'Le Neveu de Rameau' (1773), of novels ('La Religieuse', 1760), and of much miscellaneous writing.
Dido, also called ELISSA, the legendary daughter of a Tyrian king. She was married to her uncle, Sychaeus, who was murdered for the sake of his wealth. But Dido sailed secretly from Tyre, and arriving on the coast of Africa, she founded Carthage. Virgil makes Dido a contemporary of Aeneas (q.v.). She falls in love with him when he is shipwrecked on the coast of Carthage. When Aeneas, by order of the gods, forsakes her, Dido kills herself. There is an opera, 'Dido and Aeneas', by Henry Purcell (q.v.).
Dido, The Tragedy of, a tragedy by Marlowe and Nash (qq.v.) (1594).
Die-hard, one that resists to the last; an appellation of the 57th Regiment of Foot, earned by their gallant conduct at the battle of Albuera; now frequently applied in a political sense to those who are ultra-conservative in their general views.
Dies Irae, 'day of wrath', the first words of the greatest among medieval Latin hymns, the authorship of which is attributed to Thomas of Celano (*fl. c.* 1225).
Dietrich of Bern, the name given in the 'Nibelungenlied' (q.v.) to Theodoric, a great king of the Ostrogoths (*c.* 454-526). He was the hero of the German 13th-cent. epics and of the Teutonic race in general, and the centre round which clustered many legends.
Dieu et mon droit, 'God and my right', said to be the password given by Richard I at the battle of Gisors (1198). It has been

the motto of the sovereigns of England since the time of Henry VI.

Digby, SIR KENELM (1603-65), an author, a naval commander, and a very rash diplomatist. He published a criticism of Sir T. Browne's 'Religio Medici' in 1643, and wrote 'Of Bodies' and 'Of the Immortality of Man's Soul' in the same year. His 'Private Memoirs' were published in 1827-8.

Dilettanti, SOCIETY OF THE, originally founded about 1732 as a dining society by some gentlemen of wealth and position who had travelled in Italy, soon devoted itself to the patronage of the fine arts. It has chiefly encouraged the study of classical archaeology.

Dilke, SIR CHARLES WENTWORTH (1843-1911), liberal statesman, was author of 'Greater Britain' (1868), the record of a tour through many parts of the British Empire. He was proprietor of the 'Athenaeum' and 'Notes and Queries'.

Dillon, WENTWORTH, *fourth earl of Roscommon* (1633?-85), author of a blank-verse translation of Horace's 'Ars Poetica' (1680) and an 'Essay on Translated Verse' (1684). He was the first critic who publicly praised Milton's 'Paradise Lost'.

Dimeter, see *Metre.*

Dinadan, SIR, in Malory's 'Morte Darthur', one of King Arthur's knights, 'the best joker and jester, and a noble knight of his hands'.

Dingley Dell, in 'The Pickwick Papers' (q.v.), the home of the hospitable Mr. Wardle.

Dinmont, see *Dandie Dinmont.*

Diocletian (245-313), born of obscure parents in Dalmatia, was proclaimed Roman emperor in 284. In 305 he abdicated and retired to Dalmatia, where he built the magnificent palace, the ruins of which, still to be seen at Spalato, inspired Robert Adam's design of the Adelphi. The Christians were subjected to severe persecution in his reign (303).

Diodati, CHARLES (d. 1638), son of an Italian Protestant who had settled in London, the schoolfellow and close friend

of Milton. Milton addressed to him two of his Latin elegies, and lamented his death in the pastoral 'Epitaphium Damonis'.

Diodorus Siculus, a Greek historian, who flourished in the latter half of the 1st cent. B.C. He wrote a history of the world in forty books, of which we possess i-v and xi-xx.

Diogenes the Cynic, a Greek philosopher born about 412 B.C., who, after a dissolute youth, practised at Athens the greatest austerity, finally taking up his residence, it is said, in a large earthenware jar. He was taken prisoner by pirates, and sold as a slave at Corinth, but soon received his freedom. Here occurred his famous interview with Alexander the Great, who asked him whether he could oblige him in any way, and was told 'Yes, by standing out of my sunshine'. It is said that Alexander was so struck with his independence that he said, 'If I were not Alexander, I should wish to be Diogenes.'

Diomedes, son of Tydeus and king of Argos, was one of the Greek princes who joined in the expedition against Troy, and, next to Achilles, was the bravest in the host.

Dione, according to Homer, the mother of Aphrodite by Zeus; according to Hesiod, the daughter of Oceanus. In early Greek mythology she was probably the supreme goddess, the female counterpart of Zeus.

Dionysius, the ELDER and YOUNGER, were tyrants of Syracuse (405-367 B.C., and 367-343 B.C. respectively). The elder, in his later years cruel and suspicious, encouraged literature and art, and gathered distinguished men about him, including Plato.

The younger was twice driven from the throne, and finally was, it is said, reduced to support himself at Corinth as a schoolmaster.

Dionysius of Halicarnassus (1st cent. B.C.), Greek rhetorician, author of a history of Rome and works of literary criticism.

Dionysius the Areopagite, a disciple of St. Paul (Acts xvii. 34). A 5th-cent. Neoplatonic writer claimed to be Dionysius the Areopagite, and successfully imposed on medieval Christendom.

Dionysus, a Greek god, also known as BACCHUS, the son of Zeus and Semele (q.v.), a god of the fertility of nature, a suffering god, who dies and comes to life again, particularly a god of wine, who loosens care and inspires man to music and poetry. Hence his connection with the dithyramb, tragedy, and comedy.

Dionyza, a character in Shakespeare's 'Pericles' (q.v.).

Dioscuri, or 'sons of Zeus', a name given to Castor and Pollux (q.v.).

Dipsychus, a poem by Clough (q.v.), published posthumously. The poem, which represents the 'conflict between a tender conscience and the world', takes the form of dialogues between Dipsychus and an attendant Mephistophelean spirit.

Discoverie of Witchcraft, The, see *Scott (Reginald)*.

Discoveries made upon Men and Matter, see *Timber*.

Dismal Science, THE, political economy; so named by T. Carlyle.

Dismas, or DYSMAS, or DIMAS, the legendary name of the Penitent Thief crucified by the side of Jesus Christ. The name of the Impenitent Thief was Gestas.

Dispensary, The, see *Garth*.

Disraeli, BENJAMIN, *first earl of Beaconsfield* (1804–81), eldest son of Isaac D'Israeli (q.v.), received his literary training chiefly in his father's library, and was never at a university. He entered Lincoln's Inn in 1824, and published his first novel 'Vivian Grey' in his twenty-second year (1826–7). He was much hampered by debt during his early years, but he made the grand tour. He published 'The Young Duke' in 1831, 'Contarini Fleming' in 1832, 'Henrietta Temple' in 1837, and 'Venetia' in the same year. In that year also he entered parliament as member for Maidstone. 'Coningsby' and 'Sybil' appeared in 1844 and 1845, 'Tancred' in 1847. For many years after this political affairs absorbed his energies, and it was not until 1870 that his next famous novel 'Lothair' was published. He was prime minister from Feb. to Dec. 1868; and again from 1874 to 1880. He became the intimate friend of Queen Victoria. He published his last novel, 'Endymion', in the latter year. His principal merit as a novelist is his skill in presenting political and social types and the motives by which they are actuated, as a rule with a kindly humour. Many of his characters are drawn from personages of his time.

D'Israeli, ISAAC (1766–1848), the father of Benjamin Disraeli (q.v.), was the author of several discursive collections of literary and historical anecdotes, of which the first, and best, was 'Curiosities of Literature' (1791–3 and 1823). He also wrote 'Calamities of Authors' (1812–13), and 'Amenities of Literature' (1841).

Dissertation upon Parties, A, by *Bolingbroke (Viscount)* (q.v.).

Distaff's or ST. DISTAFF'S **Day,** the day after Twelfth Day or the Feast of the Epiphany (7 Jan.), on which women resumed their ordinary employments after the holidays.

Dithyramb, a Greek choric hymn, originally in honour of Dionysus or Bacchus, vehement and wild in character.

Diurnalls, see *Newsbooks*.

Diversions of Purley, Ἔπεα πτερόεντα *or,* see *Tooke*.

Dives, a Latin word meaning 'rich man', which occurs in the Vulgate version of the parable of Lazarus (Luke xvi), and has come to be used generically for 'rich man'.

Divina Commedia (pron. 'commay´-dyah'), the greatest work of Dante (q.v.), comprising the 'Inferno', the 'Purgatorio', and the 'Paradiso', in *terza rima* (lines of eleven syllables, arranged in groups of three and rhyming a b a b c b c d c).

The 'Inferno' is a description of Hell, conceived as a graduated conical funnel, to the successive circles of which the various categories of sinners are assigned.

The 'Purgatorio' is a description of Purgatory, a mountain rising in circular ledges, on which are the various groups of repentant sinners. In his visit to Hell and Purgatory, Dante has for guide the poet Virgil. The 'Paradiso' is a vision of a world of beauty, light, and song, where the Poet encounters Beatrice.

Among well-known translations are those of Longfellow and H. F. Cary (qq.v.).

Divine Sarah, Sarah Bernhardt (q.v.).

Divorce, The Doctrine and Discipline of, the first of Milton's Divorce Tracts. See *Milton*.

Dixie, the name of an American national song, composed in 1859 by Daniel Decatur Emmett (1815-1904). 'Dixie' signifies the Southern States. It occurs in many other Southern songs which the Civil War produced. The origin of the name is obscure.

Dixon, RICHARD WATSON (1833-1900), the intimate friend of Burne-Jones, William Morris, R. Bridges, and G. M. Hopkins, held various preferments, and was canon of Carlisle for many years. He published an elaborate 'History of the Church of England from the Abolition of Roman Jurisdiction' (1877-1900) and several volumes of poems; the best are included in the selection of 'Poems' issued with a memoir by Bridges in 1909.

Dizzy, familiar abbreviation of the name of Benjamin Disraeli (q.v.).

Djinn, see *Jinn*.

Dobbin, CAPTAIN, afterwards COLONEL, WILLIAM, a character in Thackeray's 'Vanity Fair' (q.v.).

Dobbs, DOMINE, a character in Marryat's 'Jacob Faithful' (q.v.).

Dobell, SYDNEY THOMPSON (1824-74), published in 1850 'The Roman', a dramatic poem inspired by sympathy with oppressed Italy, and in 1854 'Balder'. Two volumes of his poetical works appeared in 1875. Dobell was a leading member of the 'Spasmodic School' ridiculed by Aytoun (q.v.).

Dobson, HENRY AUSTIN (1840-1921), an accomplished writer of verse of the lighter kind, some of his best work appearing in 'Vignettes in Rhyme' (1873), 'Proverbs in Porcelain' (1877), and in 'Old World Idylls' (1883). Dobson had a wide knowledge of the 18th cent., testified by his prose biographies of William Hogarth (1879, extended 1891), Steele (1886), Goldsmith (1888), Horace Walpole (1890), Samuel Richardson (1902), Fanny Burney (1903). He also published three series of 'Eighteenth-Century Vignettes' (1892-4-6), besides several volumes of collected essays.

Doctor, The, a miscellany by Southey (q.v.) (1834-47). It contains the nursery story of The Three Bears, and its humour is occasionally Rabelaisian.

Doctor ANGELICUS, Thomas Aquinas; INVINCIBILIS, William Ockham; IRREFRAGABILIS, Alexander of Hales; MIRABILIS, Roger Bacon; SUBTILIS, Duns Scotus; UNIVERSALIS, Albertus Magnus (qq.v.).

Doctor Faustus, The tragical history of, a drama in blank verse and prose by Marlowe (q.v.), published apparently in 1604, though entered in the Stationers' Register in 1601, and probably produced in 1588. It is perhaps the first dramatization of the medieval legend of a man who sold his soul to the Devil, and who became identified with a Dr. Faustus, a necromancer of the 16th cent. The legend appeared in the 'Volksbuch' published at Frankfurt in 1587, and was translated into English. Marlowe's play follows this translation, though not in the conception of the principal character, who, under the poet's hand, becomes a man athirst for infinite power, ambitious to be 'great Emperor of the world'.

Faustus calls up Mephistopheles, with whom he makes a compact to surrender his soul to the Devil in return for twenty-four years of life; during these Mephistopheles shall attend on him and give him whatsoever he demands. Then follow a number of scenes, notable among them the calling up of Helen of Troy, where Faustus addresses her in the well-known lines: 'Was this the face that launched a thousand ships . . .' The anguish of mind of Faustus as the hour for the surrender of his soul draws near is poignantly depicted. Both in its end and in the general conception of the character of Faustus, the play thus differs greatly from the 'Faust' (q.v.) of Goethe (q.v.). The work is notable for the free vigour of its blank verse.

Doctor Fell, see *Fell*.

Doctors' Commons, originally the common table and dining-hall of the College of Doctors of Civil Law in London; hence the name is applied to the buildings occupied by these, and now to their site, to the south of St. Paul's Cathedral. The society was dissolved in 1858 and the buildings taken down in 1867. Literary allusions to Doctors' Commons in later times generally relate to marriage licences, probate and registration of wills, and divorce proceedings, presumably because such matters were dealt with there.

Doctors of the Church, certain early 'fathers', distinguished by their learning and sanctity: especially, in the Western Church, Ambrose, Augustine, Jerome, Gregory; in the Eastern Church, Athanasius, Basil, Gregory of Nazianzus, and Chrysostom.

Doctor's Tale,The, see *Canterbury Tales.*

Dr. Syntax, see *Combe.*

Doctor Thorne, a novel by A. Trollope (q.v.) (1858), one of the Barsetshire group of novels.

Dr. Wortle's School, a novel by A. Trollope (q.v.) (1881).

Dodd, WILLIAM (1729-77), forged a bond for £4,200 in the name of his former pupil, the fifth Lord Chesterfield, and was executed, in spite of many petitions on his behalf, one of them written by Dr. Johnson. Dodd's numerous publications include 'Beauties of Shakespeare' (1752).

Doddridge, PHILIP (1702-51), a nonconformist divine, was a celebrated hymn-writer and author of 'The Rise and Progress of Religion in the Soul' (1745), a work notable for its literary quality.

Dodgson, CHARLES LUTWIDGE (1832-98), celebrated under his pseudonym LEWIS CARROLL, was mathematical lecturer at Oxford from 1855 to 1881. Dodgson wrote books for children that had the advantage of appealing by their humour, logic, and inventive absurdity to grown-up people also. His most popular works were 'Alice's Adventures in Wonderland' (1865), and 'Through the Looking-Glass' (1871), both illustrated by Sir John Tenniel. His other publications include 'The Hunting of the Snark' (1876), besides various mathematical treatises of which the most valuable is 'Euclid and his Modern Rivals' (1879).

Dodona, in Epirus, the seat of a celebrated oracle of Zeus, the oldest in Greece.

Dodsley, ROBERT (1703-64), while a footman, published 'Servitude, a Poem' (1729). He became a bookseller and wrote several plays, but he is chiefly remembered as the publisher of works by Pope, Johnson, Young, Goldsmith, and Gray, and of 'A Collection of Poems by Several Hands' (1748-58).

Dodson and Fogg, in Dickens's 'The Pickwick Papers' (q.v.), Mrs. Bardell's attorneys.

Doe, JOHN, see *John Doe.*

Dogberry and **Verges,** in Shakespeare's 'Much Ado about Nothing' (q.v.), constables. Dogberry is a precursor of Mrs. Malaprop in his gift for misapplying words.

Doggerel, comic or burlesque, or trivial, mean, or irregular verse. The derivation is unknown, but cf. *Dog-Latin.*

Dog-Latin, bad, unidiomatic Latin. '"Nescio quid est materia cum me", Sterne writes to one of his friends (in dog-Latin, and very sad dog-Latin too)'; Thackeray, 'The English Humourists of the Eighteenth Century' vi. Cf. *Doggerel.*

Dogs, famous in History, Myth, and Fiction:

Actaeon's hounds, see *Actaeon.*

Argos, q.v. (2).

Beau, Cowper's spaniel.

Boatswain, Byron's favourite dog; he

possessed 'Beauty without vanity, Strength without insolence, Courage without ferocity, and all the Virtues of man without his Vices'.

Bounce, a Danish dog belonging to Pope.

Boy, a favourite dog of Prince Rupert's, his companion in imprisonment at Lintz, suspected of being his master's familiar spirit, and famous in pamphlet warfare. His death at Marston Moor was greeted with exultation by the Puritans.

Bull's-eye, in Dickens's 'Oliver Twist', Bill Sikes's dog.

Cerberus, q.v.

Crab, q.v.

Dash, Thomas Hood's dog and later Charles Lamb's; he provides some amusing passages in Lamb's letters.

Diogenes, in Dickens's 'Dombey and Son', the dog that Toots gives to Florence Dombey.

Flush, Mrs. Browning's cocker spaniel.

Garryowen, the Citizen's mangy old mongrel in Joyce's 'Ulysses'.

Geist, a dachshund belonging to Matthew Arnold, celebrated in the poem 'Geist's Grave'. Geist was succeeded by other dachshunds, Max and Kaiser.

Gelert, according to tradition, a hound given by King John to Llewelyn. On his return from the chase one day Llewelyn found the hound smeared with blood, his child's bed in disorder, while the child was not to be seen. Thinking that the hound had devoured the child, Llewelyn killed Gelert. The child, awakened by the hound's dying yell, cried out from under a heap of coverings, and under the bed was found a wolf which Gelert had killed.

Jip, in Dickens's 'David Copperfield', Dora's dog.

Keeper, Emily Brontë's bulldog.

Laelaps, see *Cephalus*. This hound was fated to catch whatever it pursued. A difficulty seemed likely to arise when it was set to hunt an uncatchable fox which was devastating the Theban territory; but Zeus evaded the problem by turning both into stone.

Lufra, in Scott's 'The Lady of the Lake' (v. 25), Douglas's hound.

Maida, a favourite hound of Sir Walter Scott's.

Margarita, a hunting dog to which a tombstone, now in the British Museum, was erected by its Roman master and mistress.

Math, King Richard II's favourite greyhound.

Mauthe dog, a spectral dog, of which an account is given in a note to Scott's 'Peveril of the Peak', reputed to have haunted Peel Castle in the Isle of Man.

Music, a favourite dog of Wordsworth's, on which he wrote two poems.

Mustard and *Pepper*, in Scott's 'Guy Mannering', the terriers of Dandie Dinmont.

Peritas, a dog belonging to Alexander the Great, after which he is said to have named a city.

Pomero and *Giallo*, Pomeranian dogs belonging to W. S. Landor.

Quoodle, in Chesterton's 'The Flying Inn', 'a sort of mongrel bull-terrier'.

Roswal, in Scott's 'The Talisman' (q.v.), Sir Kenneth's hound.

Tartar, in Charlotte Brontë's 'Shirley', Shirley's dog, 'of a breed between mastiff and bull-dog'.

Theseus' hounds, in 'A Midsummer Night's Dream', 'bred out of the Spartan kind . . . slow in pursuit, but match'd in mouth like bells'.

Tobias's dog, which accompanies Tobias and Raphael on their journey (Tobit v. 16).

Xanthippus' dog, the dog of Xanthippus (the father of Pericles) which swam by his master's galley to Salamis when the Athenians were obliged to abandon their city, and was buried by his master on a promontory known as Cynossema (Dog's Grave).

Dog-star, the star Sirius, the brightest of the fixed stars.

The days about the time of the heliacal rising of the dog-star are known as the DOG-DAYS (in current almanacs 3 July to 11 Aug.).

Dolabella, a character in Shakespeare's 'Antony and Cleopatra' (q.v.), and in Dryden's 'All for Love' (q.v.).

Dolben, DIGBY MACKWORTH (1848-67), was educated at Eton and became an Anglican Benedictine monk in 1864. He was accidentally drowned in the river Welland in his twentieth year. His poems, many of them religious and devotional, were edited with a memoir by Robert Bridges in 1915.

Dol (or DOLL) **Common,** in Jonson's 'The Alchemist' (q.v.), the female confederate of Subtle and Face.

Dollalolla, QUEEN, a character in Fielding's 'Tom Thumb' (q.v.).

Dollar, the English name for the German *thaler*, a large silver coin, of varying value, current in the German states from the 16th cent.

DOLLAR is also the English name for the peso or *piece of eight* (i.e. eight reales), formerly current in Spain and the Spanish American colonies, and marked with the figure 8. The dollar is now the standard unit of coinage of the United States, and the name is also applied to various foreign coins of a value more or less approaching that of the Spanish or American dollar.

Doll Tearsheet, a character in Shakespeare's '2 Henry IV' (q.v.).

Dolly Dialogues, The, by Anthony Hope (see *Hawkins*) (1894). They are amusing and witty conversations, hung on a slight thread of story, in which figure Samuel Travers Carter, a middle-aged bachelor, and the attractive Dolly Foster.

Dolly Varden, a character in Dickens's 'Barnaby Rudge' (q.v.). Also the name of a picture hat.

Dolon, a Trojan who went up by night as a spy to the Greek camp and was slain by Odysseus and Diomedes ('Iliad', x). In Spenser's 'Faerie Queene', v. vi, Dolon is 'a man of subtill wit and wicked mind'.

Dolores, a poem in anapaests by Swinburne (q.v.) (first series of 'Poems and Ballads'). It is addressed to 'Our Lady of Pain' and in it the poet sings of for-bidden pleasures and the weariness and satiety that follow them.

Dom, a shortened form of the Latin *dominus*, prefixed to the names of Roman Catholic ecclesiastical and monastic dignitaries.

Dombey and Son, Dealings with the Firm of, a novel by Dickens (q.v.) (1847-8).

Mr. Dombey, the rich, proud head of the shipping house of Dombey and Son, has just been presented with a son, Paul, and his wife dies. The father's hopes are centred in the boy, a delicate, prematurely old child, who is sent to Dr. Blimber's school, under whose strenuous discipline he sickens and dies. Dombey neglects his daughter, Florence, and the estrangement is increased by the death of her brother. Walter Gay, a frank, good-hearted youth in Dombey's employment, falls in love with her, but is sent to the West Indies by Dombey, who disapproves of their relations. He is shipwrecked on the way and believed to be drowned. Dombey marries again—a young widow, Edith Granger, but his arrogant treatment drives her into relations with his villainous manager, Carker, with whom she flies to France. They are pursued, Carker meets Dombey in a railway station, falls in front of a train, and is killed. The house of Dombey fails; Dombey has lost his fortune, his son, and his wife; his daughter has married Walter Gay, who has survived his shipwreck. Thoroughly humbled, he lives in desolate solitude till Florence returns to him.

Among the other notable characters in the book are Solomon Gills, the nautical instrument-maker, and his friend Cuttle, the genial old sea-captain; Joe Bagstock, the gouty retired Major; and 'Cousin Feenix', the good-natured aristocrat.

Domesday Book, where 'Domesday' is a Middle English spelling of 'Doomsday', day of judgement, is the name applied since the 12th cent. to the record of the survey of the lands of England, made by order of William the Conqueror in 1086. It contains a record of the ownership, area, and value of these lands, and of the numbers of tenants, livestock, etc.

Domett, ALFRED (1811–87), a barrister of the Middle Temple, emigrated to New Zealand. He was a friend of R. Browning, who lamented his departure in his poem 'Waring'. Domett was author of 'Ranolf and Amohia, a South Sea Day Dream' (1872), a story of Maori life which contains beautiful descriptions of New Zealand scenery.

Dominicans, an order of mendicant friars instituted in 1215 by the Spanish ecclesiastic, Domingo de Guzman, also called St. Dominic, known in England as the Black Friars from the colour of their mantles.

Don Carlos, a tragedy by Otway (q.v.), in rhymed verse, produced in 1676.

Don John of Austria, see *John of Austria.*

Don Juan, according to a Spanish story, was Don Juan Tenorio, of Seville. Having attempted to ravish Doña Anna, the daughter of the commander of Seville, he is surprised by the father, whom he kills in a duel. A statue of the commander is erected over his tomb. Juan and his cowardly servant Leporello visit the tomb, when the statue is seen to move its head. Juan jestingly invites it to a banquet. The statue comes, seizes Juan, and delivers him to devils. Don Juan is the proverbial heartless and impious seducer. His injured wife is Elvira.

Don Juan is the theme of a play by Shadwell (q.v.), 'The Libertine'; and of a poem by Lord Byron (see below). Aspects of a similar character are dealt with in R. Browning's *Fifine at the Fair* and G. B. Shaw's *Man and Superman.*

Don Juan, an epic satire in *ottava rima,* in sixteen cantos by Lord Byron (q.v.) (1819–24).

Don Juan, a young gentleman of Seville, in consequence of an intrigue with Donna Julia, is sent abroad by his mother at the age of 16. The vessel in which he travels is wrecked and crew and passengers take to the long-boat. After much suffering,

Juan is cast up on a Greek island. He is restored to life by Haidée, the beautiful daughter of a Greek pirate, and the pair fall in love. The father returns, finds the lovers together, and places Juan in chains on one of his ships. Haidée goes mad and dies, and Juan is sold as a slave in Constantinople to a sultana who has fallen in love with him. He has the misfortune to arouse her jealousy, is menaced with death, but escapes to the Russian army which is besieging Ismail. In consequence of his gallant conduct at the capture of the town, he is sent with dispatches to St. Petersburg, where he attracts the favour of the Empress Catharine. The latter sends him on a political mission to England. The last cantos (the poem is unfinished) are taken up with a satirical description of social conditions in England, and in a less degree with the love-affairs of Juan. With the story are intermingled innumerable digressions on every sort of subject, treated in a mocking vein; and with attacks on the victims of Byron's scorn or enmity, Southey, Coleridge, Wellington, Lord Londonderry, and many others.

The hero himself, unlike the proverbial Don Juan, is a charming, handsome, and unprincipled young man, who delights in succumbing to the beautiful women he meets, until the whole poem becomes a species of worldly fantasy intershot with Byron's passionate wit.

Donne, JOHN (1571 or 1572–1631), the son of a London ironmonger and of a daughter of J. Heywood (q.v.), was in the early part of his life a Roman Catholic. He was secretary to Sir T. Egerton, keeper of the great seal from 1598 to 1602, but alienated his favour by a secret marriage with Anne More, niece of the lord keeper's wife. He sailed in the two expeditions of Essex, to Cadiz and to the Islands, in 1596 and 1597, an episode of which we have a reflection in his early poems 'The Storm' and 'The Calm'. He took Anglican orders in 1615 and preached sermons which rank among the best of the

17th cent. From 1621 to his death he was dean of St. Paul's and frequently preached before Charles I.

In verse he wrote satires, epistles, elegies, and miscellaneous poems, distinguished by wit, profundity of thought and erudition, passion, and subtlety, coupled with a certain roughness of form ('I sing not Syren-like to tempt; for I am harsh'). He was the greatest of the writers of 'metaphysical' poetry, in which passion is interwoven with reasoning. His best-known poems are some of the miscellaneous ones, 'The Ecstasie', 'Hymn to God the Father', the sonnet to Death ('Death, be not proud'), 'Go and catch a falling star', etc. They include also a fine funeral elegy (in 'Anniversaries') on the death of Elizabeth Drury. Thomas Carew described him as

> a king who ruled as he thought fit
> The universal monarchy of wit,

and Ben Jonson wrote of him that he was 'the first poet in some things'.

A biography of Donne was written by Izaak Walton (1640). His name is usually pronounced and was frequently spelt 'Dunne'. Most of his work, though known in manuscript in his lifetime, was not published until after his death.

Donnithorne, ARTHUR, a character in George Eliot's 'Adam Bede' (q.v.).

Don Quixote de la Mancha, a satirical romance by Cervantes (q.v.) (1605, second part, 1615).

Cervantes gave to this work the form of a burlesque of the romances of chivalry, but he soon ceased to write mere burlesque; the character of the hero gradually deepens and the work becomes a criticism of life, which Spaniards accept as permanent and universal. The substance of the story is as follows. Don Quixote, a poor gentleman of La Mancha, a man of amiable character, has had his wits disordered by devotion to such tales, and imagines himself called upon to roam the world in search of adventures, on his old horse (Rosinante), accompanied by his squire, the rustic Sancho Panza. He conforms to chivalric tradition in nominating a girl of a neighbouring village to be mistress of his heart, under the style of Dulcinea del Toboso, an honour of which she is entirely unaware. He is involved in the most absurd adventures with distressing consequences to himself. Finally one of his friends, the bachelor Samson Carrasco, disguises himself as a knight, overthrows Don Quixote, and requires him to abstain for a year from chivalrous exploits. This period Don Quixote resolves to spend as a shepherd, living a pastoral life, but, falling sick on his return to his village, after a few days he dies. The book was translated into English, as early as 1612, by Thomas Shelton, and in 1700-3 by Motteux (q.v.); and the plots of several 17th-cent. English plays have been traced to it.

Don Sebastian, a tragi-comedy, by Dryden (q.v.) (1690).

Dooley, MR., see *Dunne*.

Doolittle, HILDA, see *H. D.*

Doomsday Book, see *Domesday Book*.

Dorastus and Fawnia, see *Pandosto*.

Dorcas Society, a ladies' association, connected with a church, for the purpose of making clothes for the poor; called after the Dorcas mentioned in Acts ix. 36.

Dorian Mode, in music, one of the ancient Greek modes, of a simple and solemn character, appropriate to earnest or warlike melodies.

Doric, from the name of a small country in Greece, south of Thessaly, the home of the Dorians, one of the principal Hellenic races. The word is used to signify unrefined, as opposed to 'Attic' (q.v.), and also rustic.

DORIC ORDER, in architecture, one of the three Grecian orders (Doric, Ionic, Corinthian); of which it is the oldest, strongest, and simplest.

Dorigen, the heroine of the Franklin's Tale, in Chaucer's 'The Canterbury Tales' (q.v.).

Dorothea, ST., a Christian martyr who suffered in the persecution under Diocletian (303). She is commemorated on

6 Feb. Her story forms the subject of Massinger's 'The Virgin-Martyr' (1622).

Dorothea Brooke, the heroine of G. Eliot's 'Middlemarch' (q.v.).

D'Orsay, COUNT ALFRED GUILLAUME GABRIEL (1801–52), a Frenchman who, coming to London in 1821, soon made himself famous as a wit, a dandy, and an artist. In 1823 he travelled to Genoa, where he met Byron and made a rapid pencil sketch of the poet which has survived. He was prominent in the society of Gore House at which Lady Blessington entertained all literary, political, and artistic London.

Dorset, EARL OF, see under *Sackville* (*C.*) and *Sackville* (*T.*).

Dos Passos, JOHN (1896–1970), American novelist. His chief books are: 'Three Soldiers' (1921), 'Manhattan Transfer' (1925), and 'U.S.A.' (1938), a trilogy composed of 'The 42nd Parallel' (1930), '1919' (1932), and 'The Big Money' (1936). He has also published poetry, plays, essays, and books of travel.

Dostoevsky, FEODOR MIKHAILOVICH (1821–81), Russian novelist. His major novels are 'Crime and Punishment' (1866), 'The Idiot' (1866), 'The Devils' (1871), and 'The Brothers Karamazov' (1880). Dostoevsky's novels are notable for their depth of character analysis, preoccupation with abnormal psychology, and the humour of the absurd. In his socioreligious themes Dostoevsky advanced his own mystical view of Russian Christianity as an antidote to rationalism and socialism.

Dotheboys Hall, in Dickens's 'Nicholas Nickleby' (q.v.), the school conducted by Mr. Squeers.

Double Dealer, The, a comedy by Congreve (q.v.), produced in 1694.

Doubloon, a Spanish gold coin, originally double the value of a pistole (q.v.).

Doubting Castle, in Bunyan's 'The Pilgrim's Progress' (q.v.), the castle of Giant Despair.

Doucepers, see *Douzepers*.

Doughty, CHARLES MONTAGU (1843–1926), remembered for his remarkable

record of 'Travels in Arabia Deserta' carried out in 1876–8, first published in 1888 (republished in 1920 and 1921). It is notable for its style, Chaucerian and Elizabethan English mixed with Arabic. Doughty also wrote a number of poems: 'The Dawn in Britain' (6 vols., 1906), 'The Clouds' (1912), 'The Titans' (1916), etc.

Douglas, a romantic tragedy by J. Home (q.v.), acted in 1756.

Douglas, LORD ALFRED BRUCE (1870–1945), poet and friend of Oscar Wilde (q.v.), whose 'Salome' he translated from French into English. His published verse includes 'The City of the Sorel' (1899), 'Sonnets' (1909), 'In Excelsis' (1924), and 'Lyrics' (1935).

Douglas, ARCHIBALD, *fifth earl of Angus* (Bell-the-Cat, q.v.), figures in Scott's 'Marmion' (q.v.).

Douglas, THE BLACK, a name applied to two of the Douglases:

(1) Sir James Douglas (1286?–1330), who in 1319, in the days of Robert Bruce and Edward II, invaded England and plundered many towns and villages in the north.

(2) Sir William Douglas, Lord of Nithsdale (*d.* 1392?), illegitimate son of Archibald, third earl of Douglas. In 1388 he made a retaliatory raid on Ireland, burning Carlingford and plundering the Isle of Man.

Douglas, ELLEN, heroine of Scott's 'The Lady of the Lake' (q.v.).

Douglas, GAWIN or GAVIN (1474?–1522), Scottish poet and bishop of Dunkeld. He wrote two allegorical poems, 'The Palice of Honour' (first published 1553?) and 'King Hart' (first printed 1786); also a translation of the 'Aeneid' with prologues (printed 1553), which constitutes him the earliest translator of the classics into English.

Douglas, GEORGE, see *Brown* (*G. D.*).

Douglas, SIR JAMES and SIR WILLIAM, see *Douglas* (*The Black*, (1) and (2)).

Douglas, KEITH (1920–44), poet of the Second World War, killed during the invasion of Normandy. His poems, of which those written on active service in the Middle East are the most important, were not published in full until 1951.

Douglas, NORMAN (1868-1952), novelist and essayist. Among his works are 'Alone' (1921), 'South Wind' (1917), 'In the Beginning' (1928), 'Three of Them' (1930).

Douglas Tragedy, The, a ballad included in Scott's 'Border Minstrelsy', the story of the carrying off of Lady Margaret by Lord William Douglas. They are pursued by her father and seven brothers, who fall in the ensuing fight. Lord William dies of his wounds, and Lady Margaret does not survive him.

Dousterswivel, HERMAN, a character in Scott's 'The Antiquary' (q.v.).

Douzepers, or DOUCEPERS, in the Carlovingian romances, the twelve peers or paladins of Charlemagne, said to be attached to his person as being the bravest of his knights. Spenser in the 'Faerie Queene', III. x. 31, likens Braggadochio to 'a doughty Doucepere'.

Dove Cottage, a short distance from the NE. shore of Grasmere Lake, occupied by Wordsworth and his sister, 1799-1807.

Dover, CAPTAIN ROBERT, see *Cotswold Games.*

Dowden, EDWARD (1843-1913), educated at Trinity College, Dublin, became professor of English literature there in 1867. He was noted as a Shakespearian scholar, publishing in 1875 'Shakespere, his Mind and Art', and his 'Shakespere Primer' in 1877, followed by many editions of single plays, and a number of other volumes of criticism.

Dowel, Dobet, Dobest, characters in 'Piers Plowman' (q.v.), *passus* ix.

Dowland, JOHN (1563?-1626?), lutanist and composer, published three books of 'Songes or Ayres of Foure Partes with Tableture for the Lute' (1597, 1600, and 1603).

Downing, SIR GEORGE (1623?-84), soldier, diplomat, and politician.

DOWNING STREET, Westminster, No. 10 of which is the official residence of the prime minister, is named after him.

Down with Knavery, see *Hey for Honesty.*

Dowson, ERNEST (1867-1900), poet of the 'Nineties', author of a book of remarkable poems (1896), of which the best known are 'Non sum qualis eram . . .' with the refrain 'I have been faithful to thee, Cynara! in my fashion' and 'They are not long, the weeping and the laughter'.

Doyle, SIR ARTHUR CONAN (1859-1930), will be remembered chiefly for his creation of the amateur detective, Sherlock Holmes, embodied in a cycle of stories ('The Adventures of Sherlock Holmes' (1891), 'The Memoirs of Sherlock Holmes' (1894), 'The Hound of the Baskervilles' (1902), and others), and of his friend and foil Dr. Watson. Doyle's first work of fiction, 'A Study in Scarlet' (also a Holmes story), appeared in 1887, and was followed by a series of historical and other romances for half a century. Notable among them may be mentioned 'Micah Clarke' (1889), 'The White Company' (1891), 'The Exploits of Brigadier Gerard' (1896), 'Rodney Stone' (1896). 'The Lost World' (1912) was the first of the Professor Challenger (q.v.) stories. He wrote a 'History of Spiritualism' (1926), a subject in which during his later years he was much interested.

Doyle, SIR FRANCIS HASTINGS CHARLES (1810-88), became fellow of All Souls and professor of poetry at Oxford. He published several volumes of verse, including ballads on military subjects ('The Loss of the Birkenhead', 'The Red Thread of Honour', and 'The Private of the Buffs').

Doyle, RICHARD (1824-83), illustrator. He worked for 'Punch' (1843-50) and designed its cover. He illustrated chiefly fairy stories and published books of annotated drawings, including 'The Foreign Tour of Brown, Jones, and Robinson' (1854).

Draco, a celebrated lawgiver of Athens, whose code (621 B.C.) was noted for its severity, hence the adjective 'draconian' = 'severe'.

Dracula, the story of a vampire, written in 1897 by Bram Stoker (1847–1912). The fiendish activities of Count Dracula, told in dramatic diary form by the principal characters, begin and end in the mountains of Transylvania, the traditional home of vampire lore.

Dragon of Wantley, The, a humorous ballad, probably of the 17th cent., satirizing the old verse romances.

A burlesque opera called 'The Dragon of Wantley' by Henry Carey (q.v.) was produced in 1734. The inn at Barchester mentioned by Trollope (*passim*) is 'The Dragon of Wantley'.

Dragon's Teeth, see *Cadmus*.

Drake, Sir Francis (1540?–96), circumnavigator and admiral. In 1577 he set out in the 'Pelican' (afterwards renamed 'The Golden Hind') for the river Plate, sailed through the Straits of Magellan, plundered Valparaiso, rounded the Cape of Good Hope, and completed the circumnavigation of the world. He was knighted by Elizabeth on his return in 1581. In 1587 he destroyed a Spanish armament in the harbour of Cadiz. Drake, as vice-admiral, commanded one of the divisions of the English fleet against the Armada. He died in Jan. 1596 off Portobello in the course of an unsuccessful expedition with Sir John Hawkins to the W. Indies; Hawkins had died on the same expedition a few weeks before Drake. The narratives of some of his expeditions figure in Hakluyt and Purchas, and he became the hero of many legends.

Drama, see under *Theatre, Comedy, Tragedy, Heroic Drama*, etc.

Dramatic irony, or Tragic irony: a figure of speech in which what is said by the characters in a play has a different and more serious meaning to the audience who are more aware than are the characters concerned of the catastrophe which is either impending or has occurred. As, for example, Duncan's speech in 'Macbeth' on arriving at Macbeth's castle, where his murder has already been planned, or Macbeth's 'Fail not our feast' to Banquo when he has arranged Banquo's murder for that same evening.

Dramatis Personae, a collection of poems by R. Browning (q.v.) (1864). The collection includes 'Abt Vogler', 'Prospice', 'Rabbi Ben Ezra', and the longer pieces 'Caliban upon Setebos' and 'Mr. Sludge, "The Medium"'.

Draper, Mrs. Eliza (1744–78), wife of Daniel Draper (an official in the East India Company), with whom Sterne (q.v.) had one of his love-affairs. She is the 'Eliza' and the 'Bramine' of the 'Journal to Eliza' and of the 'Letters from Yorick to Eliza'.

Drapier's Letters, The, published by Swift (q.v.) in 1724. The word 'Drapier' = 'Draper'.

A patent had been granted to the duchess of Kendal for supplying copper coins for use in Ireland, and by her had been sold to a certain William Wood for £10,000. Swift, writing in the character of a Dublin draper, published a series of four letters in which he prophesied ruin to the Irish if 'Wood's half-pence' were admitted into circulation. The letters produced an immense effect, and the government was forced to abandon the project and compensate Wood.

Drawcansir, a character in Buckingham's 'The Rehearsal' (q.v.), parodying Almanzor in Dryden's 'The Conquest of Granada'.

Drawcansir, Sir Alexander, pseudonym of H. Fielding (q.v.).

Drayton, Michael (1563–1631), of the details of whose life little is known, produced a vast quantity of historical, topographical, and religious verse, besides odes, sonnets, and satires. In 1593 he published 'Idea, the Shepheards Garland', eclogues in the tradition of Spenser, and containing pleasant songs. Drayton's 'Ideas Mirrour', a series of sonnets, including the magnificent 'Since there's no help, come let us kiss and part', was published in 1594.

Drayton's great topographical poem on England, 'Polyolbion' (q.v.), was completed in 1622, and 'Poemes Lyrick and Pastorall', containing the splendid 'Ballad of Agincourt' ('Fair stood the wind for France'), *c.* 1605.

Drayton's chief historical poems were republished as 'The Barrons Wars', 1603; and in 1597 appeared his 'England's Heroicall Epistles', imaginary letters in verse exchanged by historical personages.

Dream, The, a poem by Lord Byron (q.v.), written in 1816 and inspired by his love for Mary Chaworth.

Dream of Fair Women, A, a poem by Lord Tennyson (q.v.).

Dream of Gerontius, The, see *Newman*.

Dream of the Rood, The, an OE. poem, formerly attributed by some to Cædmon (q.v.), by others to Cynewulf (q.v.). It consists of a narrative introduction, relating the vision of the cross, and the poet's emotions in its presence; followed by the address of the visionary cross to the poet.

The poem is included in the Vercelli Book (q.v.) and parts of it are inscribed in runes on the Ruthwell Cross (q.v.).

Dreiser, THEODORE (1871-1945), American novelist. His chief books are: 'Sister Carrie' (1900), 'The Financier' (1912), 'The "Genius"' (1915), 'An American Tragedy' (1925), an indictment of American business and society.

Dreme, The, see *Lindsay (Sir D.)*.

Dreyfus, ALFRED (1859-1935), an officer in the French army, famous owing to the judicial miscarriage which caused his imprisonment and the fierce controversy which preceded his rehabilitation. In the course of this controversy, Émile Zola published his famous letter, entitled 'J'accuse' (Jan. 1898), and was condemned in consequence to a year's imprisonment.

Drinkwater, JOHN (1882-1937), poet and dramatist, is perhaps best known for his fine historical play 'Abraham Lincoln' (1918). His published works include other historical plays, several volumes of verse, an edition of Sir Philip Sidney's poems, and a life of Pepys (1930).

Droeshout, MARTIN (*fl.* 1620-51), engraver; see *Shakespeare*.

Drolls, or DROLL-HUMOURS, in Commonwealth days, when various devices were employed to evade the ordinance of 2 Sept. 1642 forbidding stage plays, were farces or comic scenes adapted from existing plays or invented by the actors, and produced generally on extemporized stages at fairs and in taverns. Among the subjects of such 'drolls' were Falstaff, the grave-diggers' colloquy in 'Hamlet', and Bottom the Weaver.

Dromio, the name of the twin slaves in Shakespeare's 'The Comedy of Errors' (q.v.).

Drugger, ABEL, a character in Jonson's 'The Alchemist' (q.v.). One of Garrick's most famous parts.

Druidism, a religious system that prevailed among the ancient Celts of Gaul and Britain. According to Caesar the Druids were a learned and priestly class. They believed in the immortality and transmigration of the soul. Their rites were conducted in oak-groves, and the oak and mistletoe were objects of veneration to them.

Drummond of Hawthornden, WILLIAM (1585-1649), a friend of Drayton and an acquaintance of Ben Jonson, a Royalist and episcopalian. Mary Cunningham of Barns, to whom he was affianced, died on the eve of their wedding, and inspired many of his sonnets and songs. He also wrote elegies, satires, and hymns.

Drummond lamented Prince Henry in 'Tears on the Death of Mœliades' in 1613, and published 'The Cypresse Grove', his finest work, a prose meditation on death, in 1623. He also left manuscript notes (printed in 1832) of a visit that Ben Jonson paid him. The first collected edition of his poems was issued in 1656 and his complete works were printed in 1711.

Drum's Entertainment, JACK or TOM, a rough reception. The expression occurs in Shakespeare, 'All's Well that Ends Well', III. vi.

Drury Lane, London, named after the Drury family. The theatre of that name, originally a cockpit, was converted into a theatre in James I's time, and rebuilt by Thomas Killigrew (1612-83) (q.v.), again by Wren in 1674, and again in 1812. Booth, Garrick, Mrs. Siddons, Kemble, and Kean are among the famous actors who have been seen there. In the 19th cent. it was the great house of Christmas pantomimes.

Druses, or DRUZES, a political and religious sect, inhabiting the region round Mt. Lebanon, in Syria. Their religious tenets are sedulously veiled in obscurity. See also *Return of the Druses*.

Dryads and **Hamadryads**, in the belief of the Greeks and Romans, were the nymphs (q.v.) of trees, and were thought to die with the trees that had been their abode.

Dryasdust, DR. JONAS, a fictitious character, a prosy antiquarian, to whom Sir W. Scott addresses the prefaces of some of his novels.

Dryden, JOHN (1631-1700), was educated at Westminster, under Busby, and at Trinity College, Cambridge. In 1658 he wrote his remarkable 'Heroic Stanzas' (quatrains) on the death of Cromwell, 'Astraea Redux' in 1660, on the return of Charles II, in which he first showed his mastery of the heroic couplet; and a 'Panegyric' on the Restoration in 1661. His early plays, 'The Wild Gallant' (in prose, acted in 1663) and 'The Rival Ladies' (acted in 1664), are not of great importance, except that the latter is an early example of the use of the rhymed couplet in dramatic verse. 'The Indian Emperor' (1665) (a heroic play dealing with the conquest of Mexico by Cortez) was very popular and is one of the best of its kind. In 1667 Dryden published his 'Annus Mirabilis' (q.v.). He was appointed poet laureate in 1668 and historiographer in 1670, and wrote some fourteen plays between 1668 and 1681. Of these the most important are the following: 'The Conquest of Granada', 1672 (q.v.); 'Aurengzebe', his last rhymed tragedy, 1676; 'The Spanish Fryar', 1681, an attack on the papists. His best play and his first drama in blank verse, 'All for Love' (q.v.), a version of the story of Antony and Cleopatra, appeared in 1678. Of his earlier comedies the best is 'Marriage-à-la-Mode', produced in 1673. In 1679 he wrote an adaptation of 'Troilus and Cressida', 'which might', said George Saintsbury, 'much better have been left unattempted'.

In 1671 appeared 'The Rehearsal' (q.v.), attributed to Buckingham, satirizing the rhymed heroic plays of Dryden, D'Avenant, and others. In 1673 Dryden was engaged in a literary controversy with Elkanah Settle (q.v.). In 1679, having incurred the ill-will of John Wilmot, second earl of Rochester, he was attacked and beaten, it has been thought at Rochester's instigation, by masked men in Rose Alley, Covent Garden.

Dryden wrote a number of critical pieces which generally took the form of prefaces to his plays; but one, the 'Essay of Dramatick Poesie' (q.v.), was an independent work. The Dedication to 'Examen Poeticum' (vol. iii of 'Miscellany Poems') is another notable piece of critical work.

In 1680 began the period of Dryden's satirical and didactic poems. 'Absalom and Achitophel' (q.v.) appeared in 1681; 'The Medal' (q.v.) in 1682; 'Mac Flecknoe' (q.v.) (pirated ed. 1682, authorized ed. 1684, probably written *c*. 1679); 'Religio Laici' (q.v.) also in 1682; 'The Hind and the Panther' (q.v.) in 1687, after his conversion to Roman Catholicism in 1686. His Pindaric ode on the death of Charles II, 'Threnodia Augustalis', and his much finer 'Ode to the Memory of Mrs. Anne Killigrew' (pronounced by Johnson to be the finest in the language) appeared in 1685 and 1686. His later dramas include two operas, and 'Don Sebastian', a tragicomedy, and 'Amphitryon', a comedy, both of the year 1690. His last play was 'Love Triumphant', a tragi-comedy on the lines of 'Marriage-à-la-Mode', 1694.

Dryden refused to take the oaths at the Revolution and was deprived of the laureateship. The last part of his life was occupied largely with translations. He translated in verse Persius and the Satires of Juvenal (1693), the whole of Virgil (the complete work appeared in 1697), and parts of Horace, Ovid, Homer, Theocritus, and Lucretius. He wrote his famous second ode for St. Cecilia's day (the first 'Song for St. Cecilia's Day' was published in 1687), entitled 'Alexander's Feast', for a musical society in 1697; he thought it the best of all his poetry. His last great work was the collection of paraphrases of tales by Chaucer, Boccaccio, and Ovid, called 'Fables, Ancient and Modern', with a delightful preface, published late in 1699, shortly before his death in April 1700. He was buried in Westminster Abbey, in Chaucer's grave.

Dualism, a philosophical system that recognizes two ultimate and independent principles in the scheme of things, such as mind and matter, or good and evil. It is opposed to *monism* and to *pluralism*.

Du Barry, JEANNE BÉCU, *Comtesse* (1743-93), mistress of Louis XV, executed during the Terror.

Du Bartas, GUILLAUME SALLUSTE, *Sieur* (1544-90), French poet and soldier, published in 1578 an epic on the creation of the world called 'La Semaine', translated into English by Joshua Sylvester (1605). He may have influenced Spenser and Donne; and Milton, in writing the 'Paradise Lost', had perhaps, here and there, Sylvester's translation in mind.

Dubric or DUBRICIUS, ST. (*d.* 612), the reputed founder of the bishopric of Llandaff, said by Geoffrey of Monmouth to have crowned Arthur king of Britain. He is mentioned in Tennyson's 'The Coming of Arthur' (q.v.).

Ducat, from Italian *ducato*, late Latin *ducatus*, used as the name of a silver coin issued in 1140 by Roger II of Sicily. In 1284 the first gold ducat (worth about 9s.) was struck at Venice. The silver ducat was worth about 3s. 6d.

Ducdame, ducdame, ducdame, in Shakespeare's 'As You Like It', II. v, perhaps a transposition for *duc ad me*, 'bring to me', or mere jargon.

Duchess of Malfi, The, a tragedy by J. Webster (q.v.), published in 1623, but played before 1614.

The duchess, a widow, in a charming scene reveals her love for the honest Antonio, the steward of her court. They are secretly married, in spite of the warning of her brothers, the cardinal and Ferdinand, duke of Calabria; a warning induced by consideration for their 'royal blood of Arragon and Castile', and, as Ferdinand afterwards confesses, by desire to inherit her property. They place in her employment, to spy upon her, the ex-galley-slave Bosola, who betrays her to them. The duchess and Antonio fly and separate. The duchess is captured and is subjected by Ferdinand and Bosola to fearful mental tortures and finally strangled with two of her children. Retribution comes upon the murderers; Ferdinand goes mad, the cardinal is killed by the remorseful Bosola, and Bosola by the lunatic Ferdinand. Bosola has already killed Antonio, mistaking him for the cardinal. The often-quoted line 'Cover her face. Mine eyes dazzle. She died young', occurs in Act IV, sc. ii.

Duck, STEPHEN (1705-56), began his working life as a farm labourer. Almost entirely self-educated, he took to writing verse, and came to the notice of Queen Caroline, who gave him a pension. He took Holy Orders and became rector of Byfleet in 1752. His best-known poem 'The Thresher's Labour' was published in 1736.

Duenna, The, a comic opera by R. B. Sheridan (q.v.) (1775).

Duessa, in Spenser's 'Faerie Queene', the daughter of Deceit and Shame, Falsehood in general, in Book I signifies in particular the Roman Catholic Church, and in Book V, ix, Mary Queen of Scots (the reference causing great offence to the king of Scotland).

Dugdale, SIR WILLIAM (1605-86), antiquary, author of 'The Antiquities of

Warwickshire', a topographical history
(1656). Dugdale's 'Monasticon Anglicanum', written in collaboration with
Roger Dodsworth, an account of the
English monastic houses, appeared in
three volumes in 1655-73.

Duke of Milan, *The*, a tragedy by
Massinger (q.v.) (1623), one of his earliest
and most popular plays.

Duke's Children, *The*, see *Phineas
Finn*.

Dulcarnon, from an Arabic word meaning 'two-horned', a dilemma; *at dulcarnon*,
non-plussed. (Cf. Chaucer, 'Troylus and
Cryseyde', iii. 881.)

Dulcinea del Toboso, the name of Don
Quixote's (q.v.) chosen lady, hence frequently used by English poets as a name
for a sweetheart.

Dumaine, in Shakespeare's 'Love's
Labour's Lost' (q.v.), one of the three
lords attending on the king of Navarre.

Dumas, ALEXANDRE (1803-70), French
dramatist and novelist, known generally
as 'Dumas père', was the son of a mulatto
general of the Empire. His fame rests
mainly on the long series of romantic
novels in which he dealt with many periods
of European history. His backgrounds
are less solidly constructed than Scott's,
and his characters less elaborate, but in
vigour and vitality his work compares with
the best of Scott's historical novels. The
most famous are the d'Artagnan group
('Les Trois Mousquetaires', 'Vingt ans
après', 'Le Vicomte de Bragelonne', etc.).
In England his 'Comte de Monte-Cristo'
is perhaps as well known as the above, but
Dumas—and his assistants—wrote countless books of which the titles here given
are a very small selection.

Dumas, ALEXANDRE, known as 'Dumas
fils' (1824-95), son of A. Dumas the
novelist (q.v.), was the author of some
highly successful romantic dramas, of
which the best known is 'La Dame aux
camélias'.

Du Maurier, GEORGE LOUIS PALMELLA
BUSSON (1834-96), born in Paris, where
he was educated, was the author of three

novels, 'Peter Ibbetson' (1891), 'Trilby'
(1894), and 'The Martian' (published
posthumously in 1896). They are rendered
interesting by the author's recollections of
early days as an art student in Paris and
Antwerp, but are somewhat marred by
sentimentalism and melodrama.

Dumbello, LADY, in A. Trollope's
Barsetshire novels, the married name *of*
Griselda, daughter of Archdeacon Grantly.

Dumbiedikes, THE LAIRD OF, in Scott's
'The Heart of Midlothian (q.v.); (1) the
grasping landlord of the widow Butler and
Davie Deans; (2) Jock Dumbie, his son,
Jeanie Deans's silent suitor.

Dumb Ox of Cologne, Thomas Aquinas
(q.v.); so called because of his taciturnity.

Dunbar, WILLIAM (1460?-1520?),
Scottish poet, wrote 'The Thrissill and
the Rois', his first great poem, in 1503;
'The Dance of the Sevin Deidly Synnis'
between 1503 and 1508; 'The Goldyn
Targe', the 'Lament for the Makaris', and
'The Twa Maryit Women and the Wedo',
about 1508; and numerous minor pieces.
He is supposed by some to have fallen at
Flodden (1513), by others to have written
the 'Orisone' after 1517. The 'Lament for
the Makaris' (makers = poets) is a splendid
elegy, suggestive of Villon, with a refrain
Timor mortis conturbat me, in which he
bewails the deaths of his predecessors
(beginning with Chaucer) and contemporaries. His works show much Rabelaisian
humour, satirical power, and imagination.

Duncan, in Shakespeare's 'Macbeth'
(q.v.), the king of Scotland murdered by
Macbeth.

Duncan Gray, a poem by Burns (q.v.).

Dunciad, *The*, a satirical poem by Pope
(q.v.), of which three books were published anonymously in 1728. Its authorship was acknowledged in 1735. The
'New Dunciad' was published in 1742,
and this forms the fourth book of the complete work as it appeared in 1743. Theobald (q.v.) was made the hero of the poem
in its earlier form, but in the final edition
of 1743 Cibber (q.v.) was enthroned in his
stead. The satire is directed against Dul-

ness in general, and in the course of it all the authors who have earned Pope's condemnation are held up to ridicule. But the work is not confined to personal abuse, for literary vices receive their share of exposure. The argument of the poem is as follows.

Book I. The reign of Dulness is described. Bayes (i.e. Cibber) is carried off by the goddess and anointed king in the place of Eusden, the poet laureate, who has died.

Book II. This solemnity is graced by games, in which poets, critics, and booksellers contend.

Book III. The king is transported to the Elysian shades, where, under the guidance of Elkanah Settle (q.v.), he sees visions of the past triumphs of the empire of Dulness and of the future.

Book IV. The realization of these prophecies is described, and the subjugation of the sciences and universities to Dulness, and the consummation of all in the restoration of night and chaos.

Dun Cow, Book of the, an Irish manuscript of the 11th cent. containing mythological romances. A fragment of it survives, containing many of the feats of Cuchulain (q.v.).

Dun Cow of Dunsmore, a monstrous animal slain by Guy of Warwick (q.v.).

Dundreary, LORD, in 'Our American Cousin' (1858) by Tom Taylor, an indolent brainless peer. His long drooping whiskers became proverbial.

Dun in the Mire, where 'Dun' (originally a dun horse) is a quasi-proper name for any horse, is the name of an old Christmas game in which the horse in the mire is represented by a heavy log, and the players compete to lift and carry it off.

Dunne, FINLEY PETER (1867–1936), American author, remembered as the creator of 'Mr. Dooley', whose shrewd and humorous sayings helped to steady American public opinion during and after the Spanish-American War of 1898.

Dunsany, EDWARD JOHN MORETON DRAX PLUNKETT, *eighteenth Baron* (1878–1957),

writer of plays, prose, and verse, of fantasy and myth. His stories include 'The Gods of Pegana' (1905), 'Time and the Gods' (1906), 'A Dreamer's Tales' (1910), and 'The Book of Wonder' (1912). His first play, 'The Glittering Gate', was produced (1909) at the Abbey Theatre and was followed by many others.

Duns Scotus, JOANNES (1265?–1308?), known as the DOCTOR SUBTILIS, a Franciscan, who entered the order at Dumfries in 1278. He lectured on the 'Sententiae' of Peter Lombard at Oxford, probably 1300-4, and at Paris, 1304-7. He died at Cologne, probably on 8 Nov. 1308. Duns was the author of 'Quaestiones subtilissimae' on the Metaphysics of Aristotle, and of other works. An extreme realist in philosophy, he borrowed from Ibn Gebirol (*fl.* 1045) the theory of a universal matter, while he was one of the first to challenge the harmony of faith and reason, which was an essential point in the doctrine of Thomas Aquinas. He was a vigorous supporter of the doctrine of the Immaculate Conception, and of the freedom of the will.

His followers, the SCOTISTS, were a predominating scholastic sect until the 16th cent. when the system was attacked, first by the humanists, and then by the reformers. The DUNSMEN or DUNSES, on their side, railed against the 'new learning', and the name DUNS or DUNCE, already synonymous with 'cavilling sophist', soon passed into the sense of 'blockhead incapable of learning or scholarship'.

Dunstable, the name of a town in Bedfordshire, used in such expressions as 'plain as Dunstable way', apparently referring to the road from London to Dunstable, a part of the Roman road called Watling Street, notable for its long straight stretches.

Dunstan, ST. (924–88), born at Glastonbury. He became a favourite of King Æthelstan, but was expelled from the court on an accusation of being a wizard. Dunstan was restored to favour by King

Eadmund and appointed by him abbot of Glastonbury. He restored the abbey materially and spiritually and made it a famous school. When King Eadwig succeeded, he incurred his disfavour, but Eadgar recalled Dunstan to him and appointed him bishop of Worcester (957), bishop of London (959), and archbishop of Canterbury (961). He devoted his energies to restoring and reforming English monasteries and to making the Danes an integral part of the nation. His festival is kept on 19 May. There is a famous late story of the Devil appearing in the form of a woman to tempt Dunstan, who seized the apparition by the nose with red-hot smith's tongs.

Dunton, JOHN (1659-1733), a publisher and bookseller, who in 1690-6 issued the 'Athenian Gazette' (afterwards 'Athenian Mercury') dealing with philosophical and other abstruse matters, and was the author of a large number of political pamphlets.

Duodecimo, generally abbreviated '12mo', a book in which each leaf is one-twelfth of a whole sheet. Hence applied to a person or thing of diminutive size.

Dupin, the detective in the detective tales of Poe (q.v.).

Durdles, the stone-mason in Dickens's 'Edwin Drood' (q.v.).

Dürer, ALBRECHT (1471-1528), born in Nuremberg, spent most of his life there, but visited Italy and the Netherlands. He was not only a great painter, but also an engraver, sculptor, and architect, the greatest artist of the Renaissance in Germany.

D'Urfey, THOMAS (1653-1723), familiarly known as TOM DURFEY, wrote a large number of songs, tales, satires, melodramas, and farces. He was a scurrilous fellow, but the familiar friend of everyone, including Charles II and James II.

Durham, CONSTANTIA, a character in Meredith's 'The Egoist' (q.v.).

Durrell, LAWRENCE GEORGE (1912-), poet and novelist. His poetry includes 'Private Country' (1943), 'Cities, Plains, and People' (1946), 'On Seeming to Pre-

sume' (1948), 'The Tree of Idleness' (1955), and 'Selected Poems' (1956). 'The Alexandria Quartet' (completed in 1960) comprises four novels, 'Justine', 'Balthazar', 'Mountolive', and 'Clea'.

Dutch, MY OLD, a famous music-hall song; the word 'Dutch' is an abbreviation of 'Dutchess' (old spelling of 'Duchess') and is slang for 'wife'.

Dutch courage, courage induced by liquor, an allusion to the drinking habits ascribed to the Dutch.

Dutch Courtezan, The, a comedy by Marston (q.v.) (1605).

Duval, CLAUDE (1643-70), a highwayman notorious for his daring and gallantry.

Dwarf, in Scandinavian mythology, the name of a class of supernatural beings of diminutive form; they dwelt under the earth, and their nature partook of good and evil. They were particularly skilful in working metals.

Dyck, SIR ANTHONY VAN (1599-1641), Flemish painter. He began to work in Rubens's studio when a youth, and soon became his chief assistant. In 1632 he came to England as court painter to Charles I. He was knighted and had great success, painting many portraits of the royal family and the court. He set the style of the grand portrait for nearly two centuries. He died in England and was buried in Old St. Paul's.

Dyer, SIR EDWARD (d. 1607), poet, born in Somerset and introduced by the earl of Leicester at court, where he held various official positions. His most famous poem is the description of contentment, beginning, 'My mind to me a kingdom is'.

Dyer, GEORGE (1755-1841), educated at Christ's Hospital, author of poems and critical essays. He is remembered principally as the friend of C. Lamb (q.v.), who speaks of him as a gentle and kindly eccentric. See 'Amicus Redivivus' and 'Oxford in the Vacation' in 'The Essays of Elia'.

Dyer, JOHN (1699-1758), a Welshman remembered as the author of 'Grongar

Hill', a poem descriptive of the scenery of the river Towy (1726). His later didactic poems, 'The Ruins of Rome' (1740) and 'The Fleece' (1757), merit less notice.

Dynasts, The, An Epic-Drama of the War with Napoleon, in three Parts, nineteen Acts and one hundred and thirty Scenes, by Thomas Hardy (q.v.), was published, Part I in 1904, Part II in 1906, Part III in 1908.

This great work is written mainly in blank verse, partly in a variety of other metres, partly in prose. The stirring events of history with which it deals are recounted in the descriptive passages and stage directions. The whole centres round the tragic figure of Napoleon. Part I opens with the year 1805, and Napoleon's threat of invasion.

In Part II we have the defeat of the Prussians at Jena, the meeting of Napoleon and Alexander at Tilsit, the battle of Wagram, the fall of Godoy and the abdication of the king of Spain, the war in Spain (Coruña, Talavera, Torres Vedras), the divorce of Josephine, and Napoleon's marriage with Marie Louise.

Part III presents the Russian expedition of 1812, the British victories in the Pyrenees, the battle of Leipzig, Napoleon's abdication, his return from Elba, the ball in Brussels, Quatre-Bras, and Waterloo. By the side of the major scenes are little 'patches of life' seen at close quarters, episodes showing how these great events affected English rustics in Wessex, private soldiers, camp-followers, and other humble folk. And above them all, 'supernatural spectators of the terrestrial action', are 'certain impersonated abstractions or Intelligences, called Spirits'. At the head of them is the Immanent Will, the force, unconscious and heedless, that moves the world. They are introduced not 'as a systematized philosophy' but to give by their comments a universal signification to particular events.

Dysmas, see *Dismas*.

E

Eadgar, king of England, 959–75. In 957 Eadgar, the younger of the two brothers, divided the realm with Eadwig: Eadwig died in 959, and Eadgar united the whole realm till his death in 975.

Eadmer (*d.* 1124?), a monk of Canterbury, who wrote a Latin chronicle of the events of his own time down to 1122 ('Historia Novorum in Anglia'), and a biography of his friend Anselm.

Eadmund (841–70), see *Edmund*.

Eadmund, king of England, 940–6.

Eadmund Ironside, king of England in 1016. After dividing the realm with Canute the Dane, he died suddenly (probably murdered by Canute).

Eadred, king of England, 946–55.

Eadward the Confessor, king of England, 1042–66.

Eadward the Elder, king of England, 901–24.

Eadward the Martyr, king of England, 975–9.

Eadwig, king of England, 955–9 (but see *Eadgar*).

Eagle, SOLOMON, a crazy fanatic in Ainsworth's 'Old St. Paul's'.

Eames, JOHNNY, a character in A. Trollope's 'The Small House at Allington' and 'The Last Chronicle of Barset'.

Earle, JOHN, see *Microcosmographie*.

Early English Text Society, founded in 1864 by F. J. Furnivall (q.v.), for the publication of Early and Middle English texts.

Earnshaw, HINDLEY and HARETON, characters in Emily Brontë's 'Wuthering Heights' (q.v.).

Earthly Paradise, THE, see *Paradise*.

Earthly Paradise, The, a poem by W. Morris (q.v.) (1868-70), consisting of a prologue and twenty-four tales, in Chaucerian metres.

Easter Day, festival of the Christian Church, commemorating the Resurrection of Christ, and corresponding to the Jewish Passover, is celebrated on the first Sunday after the calendar full moon which happens on or after 21 March. The name is derived from the Saxon goddess EOSTRE, the dawn-goddess, whose festival was celebrated at the vernal equinox.

Easter Island, in the S. Pacific, is noted for its remarkable monolithic statues facing seawards, some of them 20 feet and more in height. The date of the idols is unknown. The inhabitants of the island also used a pictographic script engraved on wooden tablets.

Eastern Church, see *Orthodox Church*.

Eastern Empire, the more easterly of the two parts into which the Roman Empire was divided in A.D. 395. Its capital was Byzantium (Constantinople), taken by the Turks in 1453.

East India Company, THE, was incorporated in 1600, and from 1773 had the chief part in the political administration of Hindustan, until 1858. After the Mutiny the government was assumed by the Crown.

East Lynne, a novel by Mrs. H. Wood (q.v.).

Eastward hoe, a comedy by G. Chapman, Jonson, and J. Marston (qq.v.), printed in 1605. A passage derogatory to the Scots (III. iii. 40-7) gave offence at court, and the three authors were imprisoned, but released on the intercession of powerful friends. The play is particularly interesting for the light it throws on London life of the time. Like Dekker's 'The Shoemaker's Holiday', it gives a sympathetic picture of a tradesman.

Eatanswill, the scene of the parliamentary election in Dickens's 'The Pickwick Papers' (q.v.).

Ecce Homo, 'Behold the man' (John xix. 5), hence used for a picture representing Christ wearing the crown of thorns. See also *Seeley*.

Ecclesiastes (abbreviated *Eccles.*), one of the books of the O.T., formerly ascribed to Solomon, but now thought to be of later date, probably of the 3rd cent. B.C. The author exhorts to wisdom, industry, and the fear of God; but the book concludes, as it begins, sombrely: 'Vanity of vanities, saith the Preacher; all is vanity.'

Ecclesiastical History of Bede, see *Historia Ecclesiastica*.

Ecclesiastical Politie, Of the Laws of, see *Laws of Ecclesiastical Politie*.

Ecclesiastical Sonnets, by Wordsworth (q.v.) (1822).

Ecclesiasticus (abbreviated *Ecclus.*), a book of the Apocrypha. It is a collection of moral and practical maxims, dating probably from the first half of the 2nd cent. B.C.

Echidna, in Greek mythology, a monster, half woman and half snake. She was the mother of various other monsters of antiquity, such as Chimaera, Cerberus, the Sphinx (qq.v.), etc. In Spenser's 'Faerie Queene' (VI. vi), she is the mother of the Blatant Beast (q.v.).

Echo, according to Ovid was an Oread (q.v.) whose loquacity caused Juno to change her into an echo. She fell in love with Narcissus and pined away for love of him till only her voice remained.

Eckermann, JOHANN, see *Goethe*.

Eckhart or ECKHARD, JOHANNES (1260?-1327?), a German philosopher and mystic, regarded as the founder of German mysticism.

Eclectics, a class of philosophers who neither attached themselves to any school, nor constructed independent systems, but 'selected such doctrines as pleased them in every school'.

Eclogue, from Greek ἐκλογή, a selection, is a short poem, especially a pastoral dialogue, such as Virgil's 'Bucolics'.

Eclogue, Virgil's Fourth, see *Virgil*.

Eclogues, The, of A. Barclay (q.v.),

written about 1515, are interesting as the earliest English pastorals, anticipating Spenser.

Ector, SIR, in Malory's 'Morte Darthur' (q.v.), the knight to whom the infant King Arthur was entrusted. He was father of Sir Kay, the seneschal.

Ector de Maris, SIR, in Malory's 'Morte Darthur' (q.v.), brother of Sir Launcelot. It is he who, in the last chapter of the work, finds Sir Launcelot dead and utters his great lament over him.

Edda, an old Norse name of two distinct Icelandic books:

(a) The *Prose* or *Younger Edda*. A summary of Odinic mythology, followed by two treatises on poetic composition. This work is attributed to Snorri Sturlason (q.v., *c*. 1230).

(b) The *Poetic* or *Elder Edda*. A collection (made *c*. 1200) of old Norse poems on cosmogony, mythology, and traditions of Norse heroes.

The Eddas are the chief source of our knowledge of Scandinavian mythology.

Eddington, SIR ARTHUR STANLEY (1882–1944), professor of astronomy at Cambridge, noted for his researches into the motions of stars and the structure of the heavens; also for his contributions to the theory of Relativity and the popularization of modern physical theory.

Eddy, MRS. MARY BAKER GLOVER (1821–1910), born at Bow, New Hampshire, the founder of Christian Science, expounded in 'Science and Health' (1875).

Eden, in Dickens's 'Martin Chuzzlewit' (q.v.), a dismal pestilential settlement in the United States, promoted by swindlers, where even Mark Tapley finds it creditable to be jolly.

Eden, GARDEN OF, in the biblical narrative, the first abode of man (Gen. ii. 8 et seq.). The word Eden means 'delight', and the term is used figuratively to signify a paradise.

Eden Hall, LUCK OF, see *Luck of Eden Hall*.

Edgar, (1) a character in Shakespeare's 'King Lear' (q.v.); (2) master of Ravens-wood, the hero of Scott's 'The Bride of Lammermoor' (q.v.).

Edgar Huntly, a Gothic novel of the American frontier (1799), by C. B. Brown.

Edge-hill, see *Jago*.

Edgeworth, MARIA (1767–1849), a successful novelist, and a friend of Sir W. Scott, who admired her work. Her principal novels, devoted in great part to depicting Irish life, were 'Castle Rack-rent' (1800); 'Belinda' (1801), a picture of society at the end of the 18th cent., commended by Jane Austen in 'Northanger Abbey' (q.v.); 'The Absentee' (1812).

Edict of Nantes, issued by Henri IV of France in 1598, granting liberty of conscience and worship to the Protestants. The Edict was revoked by Louis XIV in 1685.

Edinburgh Review, *The*, a quarterly periodical established in October 1802 by Francis Jeffrey, Henry Brougham, and Sydney Smith (qq.v.). It initiated a new era in literary criticism, adopting a higher and more independent tone than its predecessors. Though Tories (including at first Sir W. Scott) wrote for it, it assumed gradually a completely Whig attitude. It was notable for its condemnation of the school of Lake poets. Among famous contributors to it were Macaulay, Carlyle, Hazlitt, Thomas Arnold, Arthur Stanley, Sir J. Stephen, and Gladstone. 'The Edinburgh Review' came to an end in 1929.

There was an earlier 'Edinburgh Review' of 1755, but only two numbers of it appeared.

Edith Plantagenet, THE LADY, kinswoman of Richard I, a character in Scott's 'The Talisman' (q.v.).

Edith Swan-neck, mistress of Harold II, king of England.

Edmund, or EADMUND (841–70), king of the East Angles, martyr and saint. He succeeded to Offa's throne in 855. He was defeated by the Danes at Hoxne, bound to a tree, scourged, shot at with arrows, and beheaded on refusing to renounce Christianity. He is commemorated on 20 Nov.

Edmund, in Shakespeare's 'King Lear' (q.v.), the bastard son of the earl of Gloucester.

Edward I, king of England, 1272-1307.

Edward II, king of England, 1307-27.

Edward II, a historical drama in blank verse by Marlowe (q.v.), produced in 1593. It deals with the recall by Edward II, on his accession, of his favourite, Piers Gaveston; the revolt of the barons, and the capture and execution of Gaveston; the estrangement of Queen Isabella from her husband; her rebellion, supported by her paramour Mortimer, against the king; the capture of the latter, his abdication of the crown, and his murder in Berkeley Castle. Shakespeare's 'Richard II' has many general resemblances to this play.

Edward III, king of England, 1327-77.

Edward III, The Raigne of, a historical play, published in 1596, of uncertain authorship, attributed by some, at least in part, to Shakespeare.

Edward IV, king of England, 1461-83.

Edward V, king of England in 1483, in which year he was deposed and murdered. See *Princes in the Tower*.

Edward VI, king of England, 1547-53.

Edward VII, king of England, 1901-10.

Edward VIII, king of England, 20 Jan.-11 Dec. 1936.

Edwardian, characteristic of the early years of the present century (roughly, the reign of Edward VII), a term frequently used in contrast with 'Victorian' (q.v.), as implying a reaction from some of the tendencies of the Victorian age, notably its self-satisfaction and unquestioning acceptance of authority in religion, morality, and literature. The Edwardian age is in the main an age of criticism and questioning, and of refusal to accept established institutions. This tendency is seen, for instance, in the works of G. B. Shaw, H. G. Wells, and Arnold Bennett. From another point of view the Edwardian age appears as a time of great prosperity and

glitter, of social stability and spacious ease, the halcyon period before the storm.

Edwards, JONATHAN (1703-58), the New England philosopher, ardent divine, and formidable preacher. His principal philosophical work, 'A Careful and Strict Enquiry into the Modern Prevailing Notions of . . . Freedom of Will' (1754), occasioned Johnson's aphorism, 'All theory is against freedom of the will; all experience for it'.

Edwards, RICHARD (1523?-66), was master of the children of the Chapel Royal, 1561. The 'Excellent Comedie of . . . Damon and Pithias', 1571, is his only extant play. He was the compiler of 'The Paradyse of Daynty Devises' (q.v.), published after his death (1576).

Edward the Confessor, see *Eadward*.

Edward the Martyr, see *Eadward*.

Edwin and Angelina, see *Hermit*.

Edwin Drood, The Mystery of, an unfinished novel by Dickens (q.v.) (1870).

The fathers of Edwin Drood and Rosa Bud have before their deaths betrothed their young children to one another. The orphan Rosa has been brought up in Miss Twinkleton's school at Cloisterham (Rochester), where Edwin, also an orphan, has an uncle, John Jasper, the precentor of the cathedral. Jasper, a sinister and hypocritical character, gives Rosa music-lessons and loves her passionately, but inspires her with terror and disgust. There now come upon the scene two other orphans, Neville and Helena Landless. Neville admires Rosa and is disgusted at Edwin's unappreciative treatment of her. This enmity is secretly fomented by Jasper and there is a violent quarrel between the young men. On the last of Edwin's visits to Cloisterham, Rosa and he recognize that their marriage will not be for their happiness, and break off the engagement. That same night Edwin disappears under circumstances pointing to foul play and suggestive of the possibility that he has been murdered by Neville Landless, a theory actively supported by Jasper. But Jasper receives with uncontrollable symptoms of dismay the intelligence that the engagement of Edwin and Rosa had been broken off before Edwin's disappearance. Neville is arrested, but as the body of Edwin is not found, is released untried. He is ostracized by public opinion and is obliged to hide himself as a student in London. The remainder of the fragment of the novel is occupied with the continued machinations of Jasper against Neville and his pursuit of Rosa, who in terror of him flies to her guardian in London. Of the solution or catastrophe intended by the author no hint exists, beyond the statement as to the broad lines of the plot given by John Forster, the biographer of Dickens. There have been many conjectures, turning mainly on whether Edwin Drood had in fact been murdered or had miraculously survived.

Besides the persons above referred to, mention should be made of some notable characters: the fatuous Mr. Sapsea, auctioneer and mayor; Mr. Honeythunder, the bullying 'philanthropist'; the grim stonemason Durdles, and his attendant 'Deputy'.

Egan, PIERCE, the elder (1772-1849), the author of 'Life in London; or the Day and Night Scenes of Jerry Hawthorn and his elegant friend Corinthian Tom', issued in monthly numbers from 1820, illustrated by George and Robert Cruikshank. The book is a description of the life of the 'man about town' of the day, interesting for the light it throws on the manners of the period and for the many slang phrases it introduces. His son, PIERCE EGAN, the younger (1814-80), was associated with him in several of his works and wrote a vast number of novels.

Egdon Heath, the scene of Hardy's 'The Return of the Native'.

Egerton, SIR THOMAS, *Baron Ellesmere* and *Viscount Brackley* (1540?- 1617), was lord chancellor from 1603 till his death. He befriended Francis Bacon. John Donne was his secretary for four years (1596-1601), and Samuel Daniel and John Owen addressed poems to him. He left judicial and legal treatises in manuscript.

Eglantine or EGLENTYNE, MADAME, the Prioress in Chaucer's 'Canterbury Tales' (q.v.).

Egoist, The, a novel by Meredith (q.v.) (1879).

It is 'a comedy in narrative' of which the central figure is Sir Willoughby Patterne, rich and handsome, with a great position in the county, but insufferably selfish and fatuously conceited.

Egoist, The, originally 'The New Freewoman: An Individualist Review', founded by Miss Harriet Shaw Weaver and Miss Dora Marsden. It published articles on modern poetry and the arts, and from being a feminist paper became, under the influence of Ezra Pound and others, a mouthpiece for the Imagist poets (see *Imagism*). It ran from 1914 to the end of 1919, with Richard Aldington as assistant editor, followed by T. S. Eliot in 1917. Joyce's 'Portrait of the Artist as a Young Man' was published serially in the magazine in 1914-15.

Eighteenth Century, an age associated in England, in a literary connection, with the names of Swift, Pope, Defoe, Goldsmith, Richardson, Sterne, Johnson, Bolingbroke, Berkeley, Burke, and Young; an age of prose rather than poetry, of lucidity, simplicity, and grace, rational and witty rather than humorous, and somewhat lacking in intensity.

Eikon Basilike, the Pourtraicture of His Sacred Majestie in His Solitudes and Sufferings, a book of which Dr. Gauden (q.v.) claimed authorship, purporting to be meditations by King Charles I, and accepted as such at the time, published about the date of his execution. The book appealed to the popular sentiment of the moment so strongly that forty-seven editions of it were published, and the parliament thought it necessary to issue a reply, which was Milton's 'Eikonoklastes' (1649).

Eikonoklastes, see *Eikon Basilike*.

Einstein, ALBERT (1879–1955), born at Ulm of German-Jewish parents, became in 1902 an engineer in the Swiss Patent Office, where he remained until 1909. It was during this period that he evolved some of his principal theories, the Special Theory of Relativity, the Inertia of Energy, etc. His General Theory of Relativity followed some years later (1915–17). He was expelled from Germany and went to live in America. He is chiefly famous for his revolutionary theory of the nature of space and time, known as the Theory of Relativity, which entirely upset the Newtonian conception of the universe; but he also did important work in other branches of physics.

Eisteddfod, a Welsh word meaning 'session', the congress of Welsh bards held annually.

Elaine, in Malory's 'Morte Darthur', (1) ELAINE LE BLANK, the FAIR MAID OF ASTOLAT, who falls in love with Launcelot and dies for love of him; (2) the daughter of King Pelles and the mother, by Launcelot, of Galahad.

Elder Brother, The, a drama by Fletcher (q.v.), assisted probably by Massinger (q.v.), and completed about 1635.

El Dorado, the name of a fabulous country or city, 'The Great and Golden City of Manoa', which was believed by the Spaniards and Sir Walter Ralegh (q.v.), to exist on the banks of the Amazon or the Orinoco.

Eleanor Crosses, crosses erected by Edward I at the places where the funeral cortège of his queen, Eleanor of Castile, who died in 1290 at Harby, Notts., rested between Lincoln and Westminster, where she was buried.

Eleatic, the name used to describe the philosophy of Parmenides (*d. c.* 450 B.C.) and Zeno (*fl. c.* 460 B.C.). They maintained that reality was one and indivisible, and that change and plurality were illusions.

Elector Palatine, the ruler of a state of the old German Empire. He was one of the seven original electors of the empire.

Electra, a daughter of Agamemnon (q.v.). She incited her brother Orestes (q.v.) to avenge their father's death by assassinating Clytemnestra (q.v.). Orestes gave her in marriage to his friend Pylades. She is the subject of plays by Sophocles and Euripides.

Elegiac, (1) in prosody, the metre consisting of a dactylic hexameter and pentameter (qq.v.), as being the metre appropriate to elegies; (2) generally, of the nature of an elegy, which according to Coleridge 'is the form of poetry natural to the reflective mind'. It may treat, he adds, of any subject, if it does so with reference to the poet himself. In a narrow sense, an elegy is a song of lamentation for the dead.

The term *elegy* is now most commonly used in this latter sense in English literature. Famous examples are Milton's 'Lycidas', Shelley's 'Adonais', Matthew Arnold's 'Thyrsis', and Tennyson's 'In Memoriam' (qq.v.).

Elegy in a Country Churchyard, a meditative poem in quatrains of ten-syllabled lines by Gray (q.v.) (1750); it was begun in 1742.

The churchyard referred to is perhaps that of Stoke Poges. The poet in a reflective and melancholy mood gives expression to the thoughts called up in his mind by the sight of the tombs of the 'rude forefathers of the hamlet', and compares their humble lot with the great careers from which their fate excluded them. The poem ends on a personal note, with the supposed death of the author, his burial in the churchyard, and the epitaph on his grave.

Elene, see *Cynewulf.*

Elephant in the Moon, The, a satire against the Royal Society by S. Butler ('Hudibras' Butler, q.v.).

Eleusinia, the Eleusinian mysteries, the most famous of the religious ceremonies of Greece, celebrated in honour of Demeter and Persephone, at Eleusis near Athens.

Elf, a class of supernatural beings, in Teutonic mythology supposed to possess magical powers and believed to be of dwarfish form. In modern literature *elf* is a synonym of *fairy*.

Elgin Marbles, THE, derived chiefly from the frieze and pediment of the Parthenon at Athens, the work of Phidias (*c.* 440 B.C.). They were collected by the earl of Elgin (1766-1841) and sold to the British government. They were placed in the British Museum in 1816. Byron attacked this 'vandalism', as he regarded it, in 'Childe Harold' (q.v.).

El Greco, see *Greco (El)*.

Elia, see *Essays of Elia*.

Elidure, a legendary king of Britain, the subject of a poem, 'Artegal and Elidure', by Wordsworth (q.v.).

Elijah, a Hebrew prophet in the reign of Ahab. He was miraculously fed by ravens; confuted the prophets of Baal; and was carried to heaven in a chariot of fire (1 Kings xvii et seq.).

Eliot, SIR CHARLES (1863-1931), a distinguished diplomatist, author of 'Turkey in Europe' (1901, under the pseudonym 'Odysseus'), a learned and entertaining account of Macedonia; of 'Letters from the Far East' (1907); and of 'Hinduism and Buddhism' (1921).

Eliot, GEORGE (MARY ANN CROSS, *née* EVANS) (1819-80). From somewhat narrow religious views she was freed by the influence of Charles Bray, a Coventry manufacturer, and devoted herself to completing a translation of Strauss's 'Life of Jesus' (1846). In 1850 she became a contributor to 'The Westminster Review' (q.v.) and in 1851 its assistant editor, resigning the post in 1853. In 1854 she joined George Henry Lewes (q.v.) in a union, without legal form, that lasted until his death. 'Amos Barton', the first of the 'Scenes of Clerical Life', appeared in 'Blackwood's Magazine' in 1857. 'Adam Bede' (q.v.) was published in 1859, 'The Mill on the Floss' (q.v.) in 1860, and 'Silas Marner' (q.v.) in 1861. In 1860 and 1861 she visited Florence, where the story of 'Romola' (q.v.) was conceived; it was published in the 'Cornhill' in 1862-3. 'Felix Holt', her only

novel that deals with English politics, appeared in 1866. 'Middlemarch' was published in instalments in 1871-2, and 'Daniel Deronda', her last great work, in the same way in 1874-6.

In May 1880 she married John Walter Cross, but died in December of the same year. Her novels reveal a sense of the humour and pathos of human life and wide and varied learning.

Eliot, THOMAS STEARNS, O.M. (1888-1965), a major figure in English literature since the 1920s. He was born at St. Louis, Missouri, and educated at Harvard, the Sorbonne, and Oxford. He settled in England in 1915. His first volume of verse 'Prufrock and Other Observations' was published in 1917, and was followed by 'Poems' in 1919. During this time he was assistant editor of 'The Egoist' (q.v.), to which he contributed some of his early criticism, and in 1922 he founded 'The Criterion' (q.v.), in which 'The Waste Land' was first published. This cryptic and allusive poem, the masterpiece of Eliot's earlier manner, expressed powerfully, through the use of ancient myths translated into contemporary social life, man's need for salvation.

In 1927 he became a British subject and a member of the Anglican Church, and in 'Ash Wednesday' (1930) and the series of Ariel Poems he developed a less taut, more lyrical style in which to treat the experience of the discovery of faith. The masterpiece of this new style was 'Four Quartets', first published as a whole in New York in 1943, the different parts having been published separately from 1936. In these highly original poems he first reached a wide public and succeeded in communicating in a modern idiom the fundamentals of Christian faith and experience. With 'Sweeney Agonistes' in 1932 Eliot began his attempt to revive poetic drama, continued with 'Murder in the Cathedral' (1935), 'The Family Reunion' (1939), and three 'comedies': 'The Cocktail Party' (1950), 'The Confidential Clerk' (1954), and 'The Elder Statesman' (1958).

He also produced a minor masterpiece in 'Old Possum's Book of Practical Cats' (1939), a classic among books of poetry for children.

Eliot was highly influential as a critic and in his combination of literary and social criticism may be called the Arnold of the 20th cent. Among his works may be mentioned: 'The Sacred Wood: Essays on Poetry and Criticism' (1920), 'The Use of Poetry and the Use of Criticism' (1933), 'Elizabethan Essays' (1934), 'The Idea of a Christian Society' (1940), 'Notes towards the Definition of Culture' (1948), 'Poetry and Drama' (1951), and 'Essays on Poets and Poetry' (1957).

Elisha, the successor as prophet of Elijah (q.v.); the children that mocked him were eaten by bears (2 Kings ii). For his miracles see 2 Kings iii et seq.

Elision, the suppression of a vowel or syllable in pronouncing.

Elissa, (1) a name borne by Dido (q.v.); (2) in Spenser's 'Faerie Queene', II. ii, one of the two 'froward sisters' of Medina (q.v.).

Eliza, in Sterne's writings, Mrs. Eliza Draper (q.v.).

Elizabeth I, queen of England, 1558-1603.

Elizabeth II, queen of England, 1952-   .

Elizabethan Age, THE, in English literature is regarded as roughly contemporary with Elizabeth I, 1558-1603, but its main literary activity did not begin until about 1580 and lasted with the same general characteristics until about 1620. Its two main characteristics were: (1) the nationalist fervour of the country, enhanced by a successful sea-war against Spain, and by the beginnings of world exploration, trade, and colonization, all of which were reflected in contemporary literature; (2) the influences of Renaissance learning and interest which began to be more generally felt. The English language was enriched at this time by extensive borrowings, particularly from Latin, Greek, Italian, and French. English verse was freed from the weak inflected endings which had been irregularly retained up to Wyatt's time and had prevented verse from being smooth or fluent. Verse forms such as the sonnet, blank verse, etc., introduced and experimented with throughout the 16th cent., became familiar, and writers used them with a new technical facility. Prose, greatly improved by the scholarly influences of the early part of the 16th cent., e.g. by the writings of More, Ascham, Elyot, became clear and lucid, as, for example, in Bacon and Hooker; although it retained, particularly in the works of Lyly and his followers, in the picaresque novels, and in the numerous pamphlets of the time, a greater richness often tending to extravagance and over-ornamentation.

In poetry the period is noted for the works of Spenser (his 'Shepheards Calender', 1579, is a notable landmark), Sidney, Daniel, Drayton, Chapman, and many others; as well as for the dramatists, of whom Marlowe, Shakespeare, Ben Jonson, Webster, Dekker, Massinger, and Beaumont and Fletcher are best known.

The completion in this period (1611) of the Authorized Version of the Bible, a genuinely Elizabethan work in language and conception, should be noted.

Elizabeth and her German Garden, an amusing novel by Elizabeth Mary, Countess Russell, by her first marriage Countess von Arnim (1898).

Elizabeth of Bohemia, daughter of James I, celebrated in a poem by Sir Henry Wotton (q.v.).

Ellen Alleyne, the pseudonym under which C. Rossetti (q.v.) produced her earlier poems.

Ellen Douglas, the 'Lady of the Lake' in Scott's poem of that name (q.v.).

Elliot, JANE (1727-1805), author of the most popular version of the old lament for Flodden, 'The Flowers of the Forest', beginning, 'I've heard them lilting at our ewe-milking'.

Elliot, SIR WALTER, his daughters ELIZABETH, ANNE, and MARY, and his heir presumptive WILLIAM WALTER ELLIOT, characters in Jane Austen's 'Persuasion' (q.v.).

Elliott, EBENEZER (1781-1849), became a master-founder at Sheffield, and is remembered as the 'Corn-law Rhymer'. As a poet he attracted the attention of Southey. He bitterly condemned the bread-tax, to which, in his 'Corn-Law Rhymes' (1828), he attributed all national misfortunes. He also wrote some lyrics of much beauty, and the well-known political 'Battle Song'.

Elliott, KIRSTIE, ROBERT, GILBERT, CLEMENT, and ANDREW, characters in R. L. Stevenson's 'Weir of Hermiston' (q.v.).

Ellipsis, the leaving out from a sentence words necessary to express the sense completely.

Ellis, GEORGE (1753-1815), was one of the founders with Canning of 'The Anti-Jacobin' (q.v.), after having previously taken a hand on the other side in the 'Rolliad' (q.v.). He published in 1805 his valuable 'Specimens of Early English Romances in Metre'. He was a friend of Sir W. Scott.

Ellis, (HENRY) HAVELOCK (1859-1939), writer and scientist. His principal works, in which he showed independence of thought and ardour for scientific social progress, were: 'The New Spirit' (1890), 'Man and Woman' (1894), 'Studies in the Psychology of Sex' (1897-1910), 'Affirmations' (1898, studies of Nietzsche, Zola, and other writers), 'The Soul of Spain' (1908), 'The Task of Social Hygiene' (1912), and some volumes of verse.

Ellwood, THOMAS (1639-1713), Quaker and friend of Milton (q.v.), to whom he claimed to have suggested by a chance remark the writing of 'Paradise Regained' (q.v.).

Eloi or ELOY (ELIGIUS), ST. (588-659), a skilful goldsmith, who became bishop of Noyon. He is the patron of craftsmen. He is commemorated on 1 Dec.

Eloisa or HÉLOÏSE, see *Abélard*.

Elphinstone, MOUNTSTUART (1779-1859), governor of Bombay from 1819 to 1827, was author of a classic 'History of India' (1841), and of 'The Rise of the British Power in the East' (1887).

Elshender the Recluse, CANNY ELSHIE, or the WISE WIGHT OF MUCKLESTANE-MOOR, the 'Black Dwarf' in Scott's novel of that name.

Elsinore, a seaport in Denmark, on the Sound, the scene of Shakespeare's 'Hamlet' (q.v.). Now called Helsingör.

Elton, OLIVER (1861-1945), author of 'The Augustan Ages' in 'Periods of European Literature' (1899), and of three 'Surveys of English Literature', viz. 1780-1830 (1912), 1830-80 (1920), and 1730-80 (1928).

Elton, THE REVD. PHILIP, in Jane Austen's 'Emma' (q.v.), the conceited young vicar of Highbury. He marries the rich ill-bred Miss Hawkins of Bristol, sister of Mrs. Suckling of Maple Grove.

Elvira, (1) the wife of Don Juan (q.v.); (2) the heroine of Dryden's 'The Spanish Fryar' (see under *Dryden*).

Elvire, the wife of Browning's 'Don Juan' in 'Fifine at the Fair'.

Elyot, SIR THOMAS (1499?-1546), author of the 'Boke named the Governour' (1531), a treatise on education and politics. He wrote a number of other works, including 'The Doctrine of Princes' (translated from Isocrates, 1534) and Platonic dialogues and compilations from the Fathers. His translations did much to popularize the classics in England. His 'Dictionary' (Latin and English, 1538) was the first book published in England to bear this title.

Elysium, a place or island in the western ocean, where, according to Greek mythology, the souls of the virtuous enjoy complete happiness.

Emathia, the original seat of the Macedonian monarchy. Hence 'Emathian conqueror' for Alexander the Great in Milton's sonnet, 'When the assault was intended to the City'.

Ember Days, four periods of fasting and prayer appointed by the Church. By the Council of Placentia (1095) they were appointed to be the Wednesday, Friday, and Saturday next following (1) the first Sunday in Lent, (2) Whit-Sunday, (3) Holy Cross Day, 14 Sept., (4) St. Lucy's Day, 13 Dec.

Emblem-book, a book containing pictorial representations whose symbolic meaning is expressed in words. This kind of literature was begun by Alciati, a Milanese, whose 'Emblematum Libellus' appeared in 1522. The best known of his English followers were Quarles and Wither (qq.v.). Emblematic verses sometimes also took the form of verses themselves shaped in various forms, such as crosses, altars, bottles, etc. Wither for instance wrote a rhomboidal dirge. See also *Emblems.*

Emblems, a book of short devotional poems by Quarles (q.v.) (1635).

The poems are in various metres, each based on some scriptural text, followed by appropriate quotations from the Fathers, and an epigram, and illustrated by quaint engravings.

A 'Collection of Emblemes' was also published by Wither (q.v.) in 1634-5. See also *Emblem-book.*

Emelye, see *Emilia.*

Emerald Isle, Ireland, so called on account of its verdure.

Emerson, RALPH WALDO (1803-82), American philosopher and poet, studied theology, was ordained, but resigned his charge owing to his views on the nature of the sacrament. He came to Europe and visited England in 1833, meeting Coleridge, Wordsworth, and Carlyle. On his return to America he lectured on literature, biography, history, and human culture. Emerson's prose essay 'Nature', on the relation of the soul to nature, was published in 1836, and earned for his philosophical doctrine the epithet 'transscendental' (q.v.), which signifies that he was an idealist with a tinge of mysticism. Emerson lectured on various reforms during 1838-9, and was editor of the idealist periodical 'The Dial' until 1844. In this appeared his poems, 'The Prob-

lem', 'Wood-Notes', 'The Sphinx', and 'Fate'. In 1841 was published the first volume of his 'Essays', the second in 1844, and a collection of poems in 1847. He again came to England in 1847 and delivered lectures in the following year. 'Representative Men' was published in 1850, and 'English Traits' in 1856. His 'Journals', published in 1909-14, contain records of his self-communion and observations on men and books, as well as chronicles of daily events.

Emilia, (1) the lady loved by Palamon and Arcite, the EMELYE of 'The Knight's Tale' (see *Canterbury Tales*), who figures also in Fletcher's 'Two Noble Kinsmen' (q.v.); (2) in Shakespeare's 'Othello' (q.v.), the wife of Iago.

Emilia in England, see *Sandra Belloni.*

Emilia Viviani, see *Epipsychidion.*

Em'ly, LITTLE, a character in Dickens's 'David Copperfield' (q.v.).

Emma, a novel by Jane Austen (q.v.), begun in 1814 and published in 1816.

Emma, a clever and very self-satisfied young lady, is the daughter, and mistress of the house, of Mr. Woodhouse, an amiable old valetudinarian. Emma takes under her wing Harriet Smith, the natural daughter of some person unknown, a pretty but foolish girl of 17. Emma's active mind sets to work on schemes for Harriet's advancement, and the story is mainly occupied with the mortifications to which Emma is subjected as a result of her injudicious attempts in this connection. But all ends well, and Harriet and Emma herself find suitable husbands.

Empedocles, a learned and eloquent philosopher, of Agrigentum in Sicily, who flourished about 444 B.C. It is said that his curiosity to visit the crater of Etna proved fatal to him, a legend to which Milton refers in 'Paradise Lost', iii. 471, Lamb in 'All Fools' Day', and Meredith in 'Empedocles'. Matthew Arnold (q.v.) also wrote a dramatic poem 'Empedocles on Etna' (first published anonymously in 1852), in which the philosopher climbs to the summit of the mountain resolved to die. He muses on man's mediocre lot and his own happier days, and speculates on the fate of the soul after death, before plunging into the crater.

Empedocles on Etna, see *Empedocles*.

Empire, (1) the ROMAN, a term applied to the period of the rule of, or to the territories ruled by, the Roman emperors, beginning with Augustus Caesar (27 B.C.). The Roman Empire was divided into Eastern (q.v.) and Western Empires in A.D. 395; see also *Holy Roman Empire*; (2) the FIRST, of France, Napoleon I emperor, 1804-15; (3) the SECOND, of France, Napoleon III emperor, 1852-70; (4) the INDIAN, instituted in 1876, when Queen Victoria was proclaimed Empress of India; and many others.

Empson, WILLIAM (1906–), poet and critic. He published two volumes of verse, 'Poems' (1935) and 'The Gathering Storm' (1940). His criticism includes 'Seven Types of Ambiguity' (1930), 'The Structure of Complex Words' (1951), and 'Milton's God' (1961). Empson's poetry is extremely difficult, making use of analytical argument and imagery drawn from modern physics and mathematics, but together with his criticism it has proved widely influential on younger writers.

Empyrean, THE, in ancient cosmology, the highest heaven, the sphere of the pure element fire (from the Greek ἐμπύριος, fiery). In Christian use, the abode of God and the angels.

Enceladus, in Greek mythology a son of Tartarus and Ge, one of the giants who made war on the gods.

Encyclopædia Britannica. The first 'Encyclopædia Britannica' was issued by a 'Society of Gentlemen in Scotland' in numbers (1768-71), the editor being William Smellie, a printer, afterwards secretary of the Society of Scottish Antiquaries. It was a dictionary of the Arts and Sciences. The undertaking was taken over by Constable in 1812, and the copyright sold after the failure of that house in 1826. After some further editions it

passed to Cambridge University for the publication in 1910-11 of the eleventh edition in twenty-eight volumes. The fourteenth edition, under the editorship-in-chief of Mr. J. L. Garvin, was published in London and New York in 1929. Since then a system of continuous revision has replaced the making of new editions. See also *Chambers's Encyclopaedia*.

Encyclopédie, L', an encyclopaedia published under the direction of Diderot and D'Alembert in thirty-five volumes, between 1751 and 1776. Its contributors (the 'Encyclopaedists') included Voltaire, Montesquieu, J. J. Rousseau, Buffon, Turgot, and other brilliant writers. It embodied the philosophic spirit of the 18th cent., and its attempt to give a rational explanation of the universe is marked by love of truth and contempt for superstition. Its sceptical tendencies brought upon it the hostility of the clergy and official classes, and its publication was twice prohibited.

Endimion, The Man in the Moone, an allegorical prose play by Lyly (q.v.) (1591).

Endor, THE WITCH OF, the woman with 'a familiar spirit' consulted by Saul, when forsaken of God and threatened by the Philistines. At his request she calls up Samuel, who prophesies the death of Saul and the destruction of his army (1 Sam. xxviii).

Endymion, a beautiful shepherd, of whom Selene (Diana) became enamoured when she saw him sleeping on Mt. Latmos. She caused him to sleep for ever that she might enjoy his beauty.

Endymion, a poem in four books, by Keats (q.v.) (1818).

The poem tells, and develops with a wealth of invention, the story of Endymion. With this story are mingled the legends of Venus and Adonis, of Glaucus and Scylla, and of Arethusa. The poem includes in Bk. I the great 'Hymn to Pan', and in Bk. IV the beautiful roundelay 'O sorrow'.

In his preface, Keats described this work as 'a feverish attempt rather than a deed accomplished'. The allegory, which is somewhat obscure, represents the poet pursuing ideal perfection and distracted from his quest by human beauty. The poem was violently attacked in 'Blackwood's Magazine' and the 'Quarterly'.

Endymion, a novel by Disraeli (q.v.) (1880).

England's Helicon, a miscellany of Elizabethan verse (1600), the best collection of lyrical and pastoral poetry of the Elizabethan age, includes pieces by Sidney, Spenser, Drayton, Greene, Lodge, Ralegh, Marlowe, and others.

England's Parnassus, a collection of extracts from contemporary poets, by R. Allot (1600).

English, originally the dialect of the Angles (the first to be committed to writing), and extended to all the dialects of the vernacular, whether Anglian or Saxon. OLD ENGLISH or ANGLO-SAXON is the English language of the period which ends about 1100–50; followed by MIDDLE ENGLISH during the period to about 1500; and after this by MODERN ENGLISH, which derives from the East Midland dialect, especially that of London. KING'S or QUEEN'S ENGLISH is correct grammatical English.

English, HISTORY OF THE ENGLISH LANGUAGE. The Anglo-Saxon language, from which Modern English developed, belonged to the West Germanic branch of the Aryan or Indo-Germanic family, and was closely allied to Low German, Frisian, etc. It was a highly inflected language, rich in consonantal combinations and diphthongs, and spoken in several dialects throughout England. (See *Anglo-Saxon Literature*; see also under *Dialect*.) After Alfred's time (9th cent.) West Saxon became the standard literary language. A gradual decay of inflexion persisted throughout the Anglo-Saxon period, encouraged by Danish and other influences, particularly in northern England. Many Danish words entered the language at this time.

After the Norman Conquest (1066), the language of the ruling and official classes was Norman-French. There was little writing in English until the late 13th and 14th cents. Norman influence, and the absence of a conserving force in literature, continued the process of breaking down inflexions and by Chaucer's time (late 14th cent.) these had nearly all been either lost or levelled to a weak ĕ. A large number of French words were introduced, particularly in the 14th and 15th cents.; these added to the vocabulary and simplified constructions, particularly by the adoption of French prepositions, conjunctions, and adverbs. (See also *Middle English*.)

'Standard English' (q.v.) in the late Middle-English period was London English, a Middlesex dialect with a mixture of East Midland and occasional Kentish forms. This composite dialect has developed into modern 'Standard English' (see also under *Dialect*).

Fifteenth-century English was still largely unformed as a language. Grammatical forms, constructions, and spelling were subject to wide variations. The weakening of inflexions and irregular survival of the final ĕ made verse particularly irregular and formless. The literature of the period reflects the uncouthness of the language.

During the 16th cent., late Renaissance influences of classical learning, and interest in French, Italian, and other European literatures, stimulated more carefully written forms of the language, and helped particularly in the development of a more regular prose style. Irregularities of plural forms, etc., were, with few exceptions, smoothed out during the Elizabethan period.

The language is regarded as virtually 'Modern English' from this period, or slightly earlier, onwards. The developments of the 17th, 18th, and 19th cents. have been: further word borrowings, particularly to be noticed in the tendency to latinization in the 17th and 18th cents., with effects on spelling and vocabulary;

conscious regularization of grammatical forms; normalization of spelling; decrease in illiteracy, and extended popular education increasing the numbers speaking 'standard English', as against dialectal or 'uneducated' English.

English Association, THE, founded in 1906 to promote the teaching and study of the English language and of English literature.

English Bards and Scotch Reviewers, a satirical poem in heroic couplets by Lord Byron (q.v.) (1809).

Nettled by a contemptuous criticism of his 'Hours of Idleness' in 'The Edinburgh Review', Byron wrote this satire, in which he attacks not only Jeffrey, the editor of the 'Review', but Southey, Scott, Wordsworth, and Coleridge, and all the poets and poetasters of the romantic school, while holding up to admiration Dryden and Pope, and their followers, Campbell and Rogers, in the classical tradition.

English Place-Name Society, THE, founded in 1923 to carry out the survey of English place-names. The Survey is published county by county.

English Poets, Lives of the, originally entitled 'Prefaces biographical and critical to the Works of the English Poets. By Samuel Johnson' (q.v.) (1779-81).

The work was undertaken at the request of certain London booksellers, to serve as biographical prefaces to a reprint, which they contemplated, of the works of the English poets. The selection of the poets was made by them and includes authors of very different merit, and no poet earlier than Milton. The 'Lives' contain much interesting biographical matter, but are not always trustworthy and have been superseded in this respect. The criticism is unequal. At its best, it is some of the finest in the language; it is at its worst when Johnson is dealing with authors with whom he is out of sympathy, such as Milton and Gray. His condemnation of Milton's 'Lycidas' on the grounds of its artificiality and insincerity is well known.

English Review, The, see Ford (*F. M.*).

English Traveller, The, a romantic drama by T. Heywood (q.v.), printed in 1633.

Enid, see *Geraint and Enid*.

Enitharmon, in the mystical poems of Blake (q.v.), conveys Urizen's moral laws to mankind.

Enjambment, a technical term in verse, signifying the carrying on of the sense of a line or couplet into the next.

Enna, the vale in Sicily in which Proserpine (q.v.) was gathering flowers when carried off by Pluto.

Enneads, name given to the works of Plotinus (q.v.).

Ennius, QUINTUS (239-169 B.C.), Roman tragedian and the originator of Roman epic poetry, introducing the hexameter and the Homeric mode of treatment, in which he was followed by Virgil. Only fragments of his works survive.

Enobarbus [Domitius Ahenobarbus], in Shakespeare's 'Antony and Cleopatra' (q.v.), a friend of Antony.

Enoch, the sixth in descent from Adam and father of Methuselah. To his authorship are ascribed two apocryphal works, the 'Book of Enoch' and the 'Book of the Secrets of Enoch'. The former is an important collection of Pharisaic fragments, dating from the 2nd or 1st cent. B.C. The second is of later date and was perhaps written by a Hellenistic Jew of Alexandria.

Enoch Arden, a poem by Lord Tennyson (q.v.) (1864).

Enoch Arden, Philip Ray, and Annie Lee are children together in a little seaport town. Both the boys love Annie, but Enoch wins her, and they live happily till Enoch, under temporary adversity, accepts an offer to go as boatswain in a merchantman. He is shipwrecked and for more than ten years nothing is heard of him. Annie is reduced to poverty, and Philip, who has faithfully loved her throughout, renews his wooing and finally makes her his wife. Then Enoch, rescued from a lonely island, returns. He witnesses, unknown, the happiness of Annie and his children and Philip. Broken-hearted, he finds strength to resolve that they shall not know of his return until after his death.

Enquiry concerning Human Understanding, by Hume, see *Treatise of Human Nature*.

Enquiry concerning the Principles of Morals, by Hume, see *Treatise of Human Nature*.

Enquiry into the Present State of Polite Learning, *An*, by Goldsmith (q.v.) (1759).

This was Goldsmith's first considerable piece of writing, but the subject was hardly suited to his genius. In it he examines the causes of the decline of polite learning from ancient times. He attributes the existing literary decay in England to the pedantry, solemnity, and lack of naturalness of poets, to the restrictions to which dramatic writers are subject, and to the defective system of the English universities.

Entail, The, a novel by Galt (q.v.) (1823).

Entelechy, an Aristotelian term meaning the realization of some function; used by later writers to signify that which gives perfection, the informing spirit, the soul.

Eolus, see *Aeolus*.

Eos, see *Aurora*.

Eōthen, see *Kinglake*.

Ephesians, inhabitants of Ephesus, a word used by Shakespeare ('2 Henry IV', II. ii, 'The Merry Wives of Windsor', IV. v) for boon companions.

Epic, a poem that celebrates in the form of a continuous narrative the achievements of one or more heroic personages of history or tradition. Among the great epics of the world may be mentioned the 'Iliad', 'Odyssey', and 'Aeneid' of classical, and the 'Mahabharata' and 'Ramayana' of Hindu literature; the 'Chanson de Roland'; the 'Poema del Cid'; Milton's 'Paradise Lost'; Boiardo's 'Orlando Innamorato'; Ariosto's 'Orlando Furioso'; Tasso's 'Gerusalemme Liberata'; and Camoëns's 'Lusiads' (qq.v.).

In English literature, the Anglo-Saxon poem 'Beowulf' is perhaps the only genuine epic, if an epic is defined as a long poem of a heroic age, based on anonymous lays and being impersonal and objective in its narrative.

Of 'literary epics', Spenser's 'Faerie Queene' and Milton's 'Paradise Lost' are most famous. There was much speculation among critics in the 17th cent. on the theory of epic poetry, and several attempts were made to write an epic in English comparable to the 'Iliad'. (Famous examples, both poor and unfinished, are Cowley's 'Davideis' and D'Avenant's 'Gondibert'.) Wordsworth's 'Prelude' has been termed an 'epic of the mind', and Byron's 'Don Juan' ranks as epic poetry. Some critics have claimed the same rank for Browning's 'The Ring and the Book'; it is perhaps more accurately classed as a 'novel in verse'.

Epicede or EPICEDIUM, a funeral ode.

Epicœne, *or The Silent Woman*, a comedy by Jonson (q.v.), first acted in 1609, and one of the most popular of his dramas. Morose, an egotistic bachelor, proposes to disinherit his nephew Sir Dauphine Eugenie, and to marry, if he can find a Silent Woman. Cutbeard, his barber, has found such a one in Epicœne. Immediately after the marriage Epicœne recovers the vigorous use of her tongue, to the dismay of Morose, which is increased by the arrival of his nephew and friends. Driven frantic by the hubbub, he accepts his nephew's offer to rid him of Epicœne for five hundred pounds a year and the reversion of his property. Whereupon Sir Dauphine reveals Epicœne as a boy whom he has trained for the part. (The word 'epicœne' means 'with characteristics of either sex'.)

Epic of Hades, The, a poem in blank verse by Sir L. Morris (q.v.) (1876–7).

Epic of the Wheat, The, see *Norris (F.)*.

Epictetus, Stoic philosopher (1st cent. A.D.), taught at Rome, and is said to have been lame and poor. He wrote nothing himself, and the 'Enchiridion', or collection of his principles, was compiled by his disciple Arrian. According to Epictetus, virtue consists in endurance and abstinence.

Epicurean, The, a prose romance by T. Moore (q.v.) (1827).

Epicurus (341-270 B.C.), the founder of the school of philosophy that bears his name. After teaching philosophy in various places, he finally established his school in Athens. His will and some fragments of his writings survive, but his philosophy may be best read in the 'De Rerum Natura' of Lucretius. He adopted the atomic theory of Democritus (q.v.), concerning the universe, and in ethics regarded the absence of pain—ἀταραξία, or repose of mind—as the greatest good. Since virtue produces this repose, it is virtue that we should pursue.

Epidaurus, a town on the NE. coast of the Peloponnese and a centre of the worship of Aesculapius (q.v.), whom Milton refers to as 'the God in Epidaurus' ('Paradise Lost', ix. 506).

Epigoni, 'the Descendants', the sons of the seven heroes who perished in the expedition against Thebes (see *Eteocles*). Ten years after this expedition the Epigoni, led by Adrastus (q.v.), attacked Thebes, and razed it to the ground. The name is also applied to the descendants of Alexander the Great's successors (the Diadochi).

Epigram, originally an inscription, usually in verse, e.g. on a tomb; hence a short poem ending in a witty or ingenious turn of thought; hence a pointed or antithetical saying. Bacon, Pope, and Macaulay are masters of epigrammatic expression.

Epimetheus, brother of Prometheus (q.v.). He married Pandora (q.v.) and opened her box, whence issued the train of evils which have since vexed mankind.

Epiphany, THE, the festival commemorating the manifestation of Christ to the Gentiles in the persons of the Magi; observed on 6 Jan.

Epipsychidion, a poem by P. B. Shelley (q.v.) (1821).

The poem is addressed to Emilia Viviani, a lady in whom the poet thought he had found the visionary soul in perfect harmony with his own. It is an exposition and defence of free love, not only Platonic but passionate.

Epistolae Obscurum Virorum, see Hutten.

Epitaph, words or verses, usually, but not necessarily, inscribed on a tombstone or monument, commemorating the dead person. Tradition has prescribed a terse and epigrammatic form, but in the 18th cent. they were often long and grandiloquent by preference. (See, for example, Arbuthnot's savage epitaph on Charteris in Aitken's 'Life and Works of Arbuthnot', pp. 137-8). Famous literary epitaphs are those of Gay on himself:

Life is a jest and all things show it;
I thought so once and now I know it.

And the line which Keats wished to have engraved on his tomb:

Here lies one whose name was writ in water.

Epithalamion, a splendid hymn by Spenser (q.v.), perhaps in celebration of his marriage with Elizabeth Boyle in 1594. The poem was printed with the 'Amoretti' (q.v.) in 1595. The name is Greek, 'upon the bridal chamber'.

Epode, (1) a kind of lyric poem invented by Archilochus, in which a long line is followed by a shorter one, in metres different from the elegiac (q.v.), as in Horace's 'Epodes'; (2) the part of a lyric ode sung after the strophe and antistrophe (q.v.).

Eponymous, that gives its name to anything, used especially of the mythical personages from whose names the names of places or peoples are reputed to be derived.

Epopee, an epic poem, or the epic species of poetry.

Eppie, in G. Eliot's 'Silas Marner' (q.v.), the daughter of Cass and adopted child of Silas.

Epstein, SIR JACOB (1880-1959), sculptor, born in New York of Russian-Polish parents. He settled in London in 1905. He modelled portraits in bronze and carved and modelled large figures, often of religious subjects.

Erasmus, DESIDERIUS (1466-1536), the great Dutch humanist, came more than once to England, where he was welcomed by the great scholars of the day, More, Colet, and Grocyn, and was induced by Fisher to lecture at Cambridge on Greek. His principal works were the 'Novum Instrumentum', a new Latin version of the N.T., with a commentary (1516); 'Encomium Moriae' ('The Praise of Folly', 1509, a satire written at the suggestion of Sir Thomas More, principally directed against theologians and Church dignitaries); 'Institutio Christiani Principis' ('Education of a Christian Prince'); the vivid and entertaining 'Colloquia' and letters furnishing autobiographical details and pictures of contemporary life, which have been drawn upon by C. Reade in 'The Cloister and the Hearth' (q.v.) and by Sir W. Scott (q.v.) in 'Anne of Geierstein'. Erasmus prepared the way for the Reformation by his writings—his version of the N.T., the scathing comments on Church abuses that accompanied it, and his 'Encomium Moriae'. With the movement itself he sympathized at first. But although invoked by both sides, he urged moderation on both and disclaimed sympathy with Luther's violence.

Erastian, a name applied to the doctrine, attributed to Erastus, of the subordination of the ecclesiastical to the secular power. Erastus was a physician of Heidelberg in the 16th cent.

Erato, one of the Muses (q.v.), who presided over love poetry.

Erceldoune, THOMAS OF, called also the RHYMER and LEARMONT (*fl.* 1220?-1297?), seer and poet, is said to have predicted the death of Alexander III, king of Scotland, and the battle of Bannockburn, and is the traditional fountain of many (fabricated) oracles. He is reputed author of a poem on the Tristram story, which Sir Walter Scott considered genuine.

Erebus, in Greek mythology, (1) a place of utter darkness, on the way to Hades; (2) the god of darkness.

Erechtheus, a mythical king of Athens,

Erechtheus killed Eumolpus, the son of Poseidon. Poseidon demanded in expiation the sacrifice of one of the daughters of Erechtheus and his wife Praxithea. The choice was made by lot, whereupon the two other sisters resolved to die also, and Erechtheus himself was killed by a thunderbolt at the request of Poseidon. Erechtheus is the subject of a tragedy in the Greek form by Swinburne (q.v.).

Erewhon (pronounced as three short syllables, 'ĕ-rĕ-whŏn'), a satirical romance by S. Butler (1835-1902, q.v.) (1872).

The narrator having crossed an unexplored chain of mountains in a remote part of a colony (Butler had in mind New Zealand), comes upon the land of Erewhon (an anagram of 'nowhere'). The institutions that he finds there and describes are a vigorous satire on the hypocrisy, compromise, and mental torpor that Butler was ever inveighing against. Finally the narrator escapes from the country in a balloon, accompanied by an Erewhonian lady with whom he has fallen in love.

Erewhon Revisited, a sequel to 'Erewhon' (q.v.) by S. Butler (1835-1902, q.v.) (1901).

Higgs (to adopt the name by which the narrator of Erewhon was known to the Erewhonians) revisits that country after an interval of twenty years, to discover that his ascent in a balloon has been held miraculous, that a religious myth has grown up round it, that he is himself now worshipped as the child of the sun, and that a great temple is on the point of being dedicated to him. Horrified at the mischief he has done, Higgs reveals himself, but is hustled away by friendly hands. An amusing conference follows between all concerned to decide what is to be done about 'Sunchildism', as the new religion is called; and Higgs is then smuggled out of the country.

Eric, or Little by Little, an edifying story of school life by Frederic William Farrar (1831-1903, dean of Canterbury), published in 1858.

Erigena, see *Scotus*.

Erin, the ancient name of Ireland.

Erin go bragh: 'Ireland for ever!', the refrain of 'The Exile of Erin', a poem by T. Campbell (q.v.).

Erinyes, see *Furies*.

Ermeline, in 'Reynard the Fox' (q.v.), Reynard's wife.

Ernani, see *Hernani*.

Ernest Maltravers, and *Alice, or the Mysteries*, a novel and its sequel by Bulwer Lytton (q.v.) (1837 and 1838).

Ernulf or ERNULPHUS (1040-1124), bishop of Rochester, and author of the 'Textus Roffensis', a collection of laws, papal decrees, and documents relating to the church of Rochester. The comprehensive curse of Ernulphus figures in Bk. III, chs. x, xi of Sterne's 'Tristram Shandy' (q.v.).

Eros, see *Cupid*. Eros in Shakespeare's 'Antony and Cleopatra' (q.v.) is the faithful attendant of Antony, who kills himself to avoid killing his master.

Erra-Pater, the assumed name of the author of an astrological almanac, published in 1535, referred to by Butler in 'Hudibras', I. i (q.v.), and by Congreve in 'Love for Love'.

Erse, a term used to designate (1) Irish Gaelic; (2) in 18th-cent. practice, the Gaelic language of Scotland (which is in fact of Irish origin).

Ervine, ST. JOHN GREER (1883-1971), dramatist and novelist, manager of the Abbey Theatre (q.v.) 1915. Among his many successful plays are 'Jane Clegg' (1911), 'Antony and Anna', 'The First Mrs. Fraser' (1928), and 'Robert's Wife' (1938). He is also the author of seven novels, and other miscellaneous works including some political studies on the Irish question.

Esau, see *Jacob and Esau*.

Esculapius, see *Aesculapius*.

Esdras, the reputed author of two of the books of the Apocrypha: the first mainly a compilation from Chronicles, Nehemiah, and Ezra; the second a record of angelic revelations and visions.

Esmond, BEATRIX, one of the principal characters in Thackeray's 'Esmond' and 'The Virginians' (qq.v.).

Esmond, The History of Henry Esmond, Esquire, a novel by Thackeray (q.v.) (1852).

The History is narrated by Henry Esmond himself. He is the son (supposed to be illegitimate) of the third Viscount Castlewood. Henry then comes under the protection of the fourth viscount, in whose household he serves as page. He is kindly treated by Lord Castlewood, and particularly by Lady Castlewood, for whom he conceives a profound devotion. He has the misfortune to bring the small-pox into the household, by which Lady Castlewood loses some of her beauty, and in consequence much of her husband's love. The unprincipled Lord Mohun takes advantage of the estrangement between them to attempt to seduce Lady Castlewood. A duel follows, in which Lord Castlewood is mortally wounded. On his death-bed he reveals to Henry that he is the rightful owner of the title and property. Henry decides to sacrifice himself and not claim his rights, so as not to injure Lady Castlewood and her son Frank. But Lady Castlewood bitterly upbraids Henry for allowing the duel to take place, and banishes him from her house.

Henry joins the army and serves with distinction in Marlborough's campaigns, from Blenheim to Malplaquet. In the course of his service he returns to England. Meanwhile Frank, the present viscount, and Beatrix his sister, have grown up. The latter is a girl of extraordinary beauty, but vain of her beauty and ambitious. Henry falls deeply in love with her, but she is too proud to consider an alliance with one whom she regards as of illegitimate birth. She becomes affianced to the duke of Hamilton, but he is murdered by Lord Mohun. Finally she causes the failure of a scheme for the proclamation of the Pretender, by flirting with the Prince and luring him to Castlewood at the moment when his presence in London.

is necessary. Completely disillusioned, Henry abandons her and marries Lady Castlewood. Henry and his wife migrate to Virginia and their subsequent history in that country is referred to in 'The Virginians' (q.v.). Thackeray gives a vivid picture of English society in the early years of the 18th cent., introducing Dick Steele and his Prue, Marlborough and his Duchess, Swift, and Addison.

Esop, see *Aesop*.

Esoteric, a word used by Lucian, who attributes to Aristotle a classification of his own works into 'esoteric', i.e. designed for, or appropriate to, an inner circle of advanced or privileged disciples, and 'exoteric', i.e. popular, untechnical. Later writers use the word to designate the secret doctrines said to have been taught by Pythagoras to a select few of his disciples.

Esperanto, a universal language introduced in 1887 by Dr. L. L. Zamenhof, a Polish physician.

Esprit d'escalier, French, a tardy wit, which thinks of a smart retort or witticism too late, when its owner is going downstairs, on his way out of the house.

Essay, usually a short prose composition, embodying the author's reflections on a particular subject. It has been a popular form of writing for critics and moralists from the earliest times. Famous English essayists have been Bacon, Cowley, Dryden (who published critical prefaces to his works), Addison, Steele, Johnson, Lamb, Hazlitt, De Quincey, etc. There have been many essayists in modern times, stimulated in part by the demand for journalistic and magazine writing of good quality. Among them may be mentioned Max Beerbohm, Hilaire Belloc, G. K. Chesterton, Aldous Huxley, E. V. Lucas, and Virginia Woolf.

Essay concerning Human Understanding, a philosophical treatise by Locke (q.v.) (1690; 2nd edition, 1694; 4th, 1700; 5th, 1706; each with large additions).

The Essay is an examination into the nature of knowledge, as calculated to guide us to the proper use of our under-standing. Locke begins by refuting the doctrine of 'innate ideas', and maintaining that all knowledge is of empiric origin. The materials or objects of understanding are termed by him *ideas.* The source of ideas is *experience*, the observation of external objects or the internal operations of the mind, i.e. sensation or reflection.

Knowledge consists in the perception of the agreement or disagreement of ideas. Knowledge in matters of real existence is limited to two certainties, of our own existence, by intuition, and of the existence of God, by demonstration.

We have a lesser degree of certainty of the existence of finite beings without us, of which the mind perceives nothing but its own ideas, and cannot know that they agree with the things themselves. The faculty that God has given us in place of clear knowledge is judgement, whereby the mind takes a proposition to be true or false without demonstration. Locke discusses the relations of faith and reason. Unlike Bacon and Hobbes, he holds that faith is nothing but the firm assent of the mind, which cannot be accorded to anything except on good reason. Revelation must be judged by reason. But the field of knowledge being so limited, it must be supplemented by faith, and this is the basis of Locke's 'Reasonableness of Christianity', 1695.

Essay of Dramatick Poesie, by Dryden (q.v.) (1668), probably written in Wiltshire during the plague.

It takes the form of a dialogue between four interlocutors, Eugenius (Dorset), Crites (Sir Robert Howard), Lisideius (Sir Charles Sedley), and Neander (Dryden himself). The four friends have taken a boat on the Thames on the day of the engagement between the English and Dutch fleets in the mouth of the river (3 June 1665). At first the friends are mainly occupied with this stirring event, but presently as the sound of firing becomes more distant, their talk turns to literary subjects, and they discuss the comparative merits of the English and

French drama, and of the old and the new English drama. The Essay is largely concerned with a defence of the use of rhyme in drama. It also contains an admirable appreciation of Shakespeare.

Essay on Criticism, a didactic poem by Pope (q.v.), in heroic couplets, published anonymously in 1711. It begins with an exposition of the rules of taste and the authority to be attributed to the ancient writers. The laws by which a critic should be guided are discussed, and instances are given of critics who have departed from them. The work is remarkable as having been written when Pope was only 21.

Essay on Man, a philosophical poem in heroic couplets by Pope (q.v.) (1732-4).

It consists of four epistles, addressed to Henry St. John, Lord Bolingbroke, and perhaps to some extent inspired by his fragmentary philosophical writings. It is part of a larger poem projected but not completed. Its object is to vindicate the ways of God to man; to prove that the scheme of the universe is the best in spite of appearances of evil, and that our failure to see the perfection of the whole is due to our limited vision. Epistle I treats of the nature and state of man with respect to the universe; Epistle II, of man with respect to himself as an individual; Epistle III, of man with respect to society; Epistle IV, of man with respect to happiness. Dr. Johnson's verdict was: 'Never were penury of knowledge and vulgarity of sentiment so happily disguised.'

Essays, or Counsels, Civill and Morall, The, of F. Bacon (q.v.), are collections of reflections and generalizations, and extracts from previous authors, woven together, for the most part, into counsels for the successful conduct of life and the management of men.

Three editions of the essays were published in Bacon's lifetime (1597, 1612, and 1625). Of the essays some deal with questions of state policy, such as the essay on 'Greatness of Kingdoms'; some with personal conduct, such as those on 'Wisdom for a Man's Self' and 'Cunning';

some on abstract subjects such as 'Truth', 'Death', and 'Unity'; while some reveal Bacon's delight in nature, such as the pleasant essay on 'Gardens'. They are famous for their aphoristic style.

Essays and Reviews, a collection of essays on religious subjects from a broad church standpoint (1860). The editor was the Revd. Henry Bristow Wilson, and the other contributors were Frederick Temple (the future archbishop), Mark Pattison (q.v.), Jowett (q.v.), Rowland Williams, Baden-Powell, and C. W. Goodwin.

The essays occasioned much offence. Wilson and Williams were tried in the Court of Arches and found guilty of heresy, but were acquitted on appeal.

Essays contributed to the Edinburgh Review, Critical and Historical, by T. B. Macaulay (q.v.), a collection published in 1843. They take, as a rule, the form, not so much of a review of the books named at the head of each, but of a general survey, biographical, political, or literary, of the subject of that book. They are occasionally truculent, as that on Croker's 'Boswell', and misleading (it is said), as those on Bacon and Hastings. The best are those on Chatham, Clive, and Sir William Temple.

Essays in Criticism, see *Arnold (M.)*.

Essays of Elia, The, miscellaneous essays by C. Lamb (q.v.), of which the first series appeared in 'The London Magazine' between 1820 and 1823, and were republished in a separate volume in the latter year. The second series was published in 1833. Lamb adopted the pseudonym Elia (which he appears to have pronounced 'Ellia') to save the susceptibilities of his brother John, still a clerk in the South-Sea House, which is the subject of the first of the 'Essays'. The name was that of an Italian clerk formerly in the service of that institution.

The 'Essays' are largely autobiographical; they deal with mankind at large as seen through the medium of Lamb's own experiences and impressions. They present, with exquisite humour and pathos, and in a brilliant and inimitable style, characters that the author has known, recollections of childhood, or of later life, and general comments and criticism.

Estella, a character in Dickens's 'Great Expectations' (q.v.).

Esther Waters, a novel by G. Moore (q.v.) (1894).

It is the story of the life of a religiously minded girl, driven from home into service at 17 by a drunken stepfather. She obtains a situation at Woodview, the house of the Barfields, where a racing-stable is kept, and all above and below-stairs (except Mrs. Barfield), are wrapped up in gambling on races. There, in a moment of weakness, she is seduced by a fellow servant and deserted. She has to leave her place, though kindly treated by Mrs. Barfield. Then follows a poignant tale of poverty, hardship, and humiliation: the lying-in hospital, service as wet-nurse, other miserable situations, even the workhouse, in the mother's brave struggle to rear her child. Her seducer re-enters her life, marries her, and makes a good husband. But he is a book-maker and public-house keeper; exposure to weather at the races ruins his health, and trouble with the authorities over betting at his house causes the latter to be closed. He dies, and leaves his wife and son penniless. Finally Esther returns to Woodview, where she finds peace at last, with Mrs. Barfield, now a widow, living alone and impoverished in a corner of the old house.

Estotiland, a mythical land in North America, mentioned by Milton, 'Paradise Lost', x. 686.

Estrildis, a German maiden brought to England by King Humber, loved by Locrine, king of Britain, and mother by him of Sabrina. She and her daughter were drowned in the Severn by Locrine's angry queen, Gwendolen. The story is told by Geoffrey of Monmouth and reappears in Spenser's 'Faerie Queene' (II. x), also in Swinburne's 'Locrine'.

Eteocles, son of Oedipus (q.v.) and Jocasta, and brother of Polyneices. It was agreed that the brothers should reign in Thebes in alternate years; but Eteocles refused to give up the throne at the appointed time. Polyneices, assisted by Adrastus, king of Argos, and the Argive army headed by seven heroes, marched against Thebes. After indecisive fighting, it was decided that the struggle should be settled by the brothers in single combat. In this they slew each other. The Argive chiefs were slain with the exception of Adrastus. This war was known as that of 'The Seven against Thebes', the subject of a tragedy by Aeschylus.

Ethelred, see *Æthelred*.

Ethelwold, St., see *Æthelwold*.

Etherege or ETHEREDGE, SIR GEORGE (1634?-91?), dramatist, produced 'The Comical Revenge, or Love in a Tub', in 1664. The serious portions are in rhymed heroics, setting a fashion that was followed for some years, while the comic underplot in prose with its lively realistic scenes was, as Sir Edmund Gosse has pointed out, the foundation of the English comedy of Congreve, Goldsmith, and Sheridan. In this, Etherege drew his inspiration from Molière. In 1668 he produced 'She would if she could', and in 1676 'The Man of Mode', two further comedies. Etherege was sent in 1685 as envoy to Ratisbon, where he remained for some years, a period of his life on which his manuscript 'Letter-book', discovered by Gosse (and since published), throws an interesting light.

Ethiop queen, THE STARR'D, in Milton's 'Il Penseroso' (q.v.), is Cassiopea (q.v.).

Eton College, near Windsor, was founded by Henry VI, as a preparatory school for King's College, Cambridge, the charter of foundation being dated 1440 and followed by various charters of endowment.

Among the many names eminent in literature, connected with Eton, may be mentioned those of Edward Hall, the historian, Thomas Tusser, Sir Henry Wotton, Edmund Waller, Henry More, Bolingbroke, Henry Fielding, Thomas Gray, Horace Walpole, Richard Porson,

Shelley, Praed, Gladstone, Hallam, Swinburne, and Robert Bridges (qq.v.).

Etruscans, THE, a people of whose origin nothing certain is known, who are found in early times established in what is now Tuscany. Thence they extended their dominion temporarily over a considerable part of Italy and developed a flourishing civilization of which many remains have been discovered. After 500 B.C. the political strength of the Etruscans began to decline, though the influence of their more highly developed art and civilization continued to be felt in Rome.

Ettarre, see *Pelleas and Ettarre*.

Ettrick Shepherd, THE, see *Hogg* (*J.*).

Euclid (EUCLEIDES), the celebrated geometrician, lived at Alexandria in the reign of the first Ptolemy (323-283 B.C.). His great work on elementary geometry retained its authority until the end of the 19th cent.

Eugene Aram, a novel by Bulwer Lytton (q.v.) (1832). It is based on the story of Eugene Aram, a schoolmaster, said to have been of unusual ability and gentle disposition, who in 1759 was tried and executed at York for murder.

In the novel, Eugene Aram is a romantic character, who under pressure of poverty consents to the murder, which is done by his accomplice Houseman. Aram suffers the torments of remorse. He settles in a remote village and falls in love with Madeline Lester, a woman of noble character. Their marriage is about to take place when Houseman reappears and betrays Aram, who is tried and sentenced to death, while Madeline succumbs to the shock.

Eugene Aram, The Dream of, a poem by Hood (q.v.), based on the same story as the preceding.

Eugenius, in Sterne's 'Tristram Shandy' (q.v.), the friend of Yorick, represents John Hall Stevenson.

Eulenspiegel, TILL, the name of a German, born according to tradition about 1300, the son of a peasant, and the subject of a collection of satirical tales, published in 1519 (Flemish version 1520-1). One of his adventures figures in Chaucer's 'Summoner's Tale'. The book was translated into many languages, among others into English in an abridged form by William Copland, under the title 'Howleglass', about 1560.

Eumaeus, the faithful swineherd of Odysseus (q.v.).

Eumenides, see *Furies*.

Euphemism, the substitution of a less distasteful phrase or word for a more accurate but more offensive one.

Euphrosyne, one of the Graces (q.v.).

Euphues, a prose romance by Lyly (q.v.), of which the first part, 'Euphues: the Anatomy of Wit', was published in 1578, and the second, 'Euphues and his England', in 1580. The plot of each is little but a peg on which to hang discourses, conversations, and letters, mainly on the subject of love.

'Euphues' is famous for its peculiar style, to which it has given the name 'Euphuism'. Its principal characteristics are the excessive use (1) of antithesis, which is pursued regardless of sense, and emphasized by alliteration and other devices; and (2) of allusions to historical and mythological personages and to natural history (probably drawn from the writings of Erasmus). Scott has satirized Euphuism in the character of Sir Piercie Shafton in 'The Monastery' (q.v.), and C. Kingsley has defended 'Euphues' in 'Westward Ho!' (q.v.).

The work is interesting for its place in the evolution of the English novel, and it had a stimulating effect on the writers of the age, such as Lodge and Greene.

Euphues Golden Legacie, see *Rosalynde*.

Euphuism, see *Euphues*.

Eureka!, a Greek word meaning 'I have found it', the exclamation uttered by Archimedes (q.v.) when he discovered, by observing in his bath the water displaced by his body, the means of testing (by specific gravity) whether base metal had been introduced in Hiero's crown.

Euripides (480-406 B.C.), the youngest and most 'modern-minded' of the three

G

great Attic tragedians. The characteristics of his plays are their human quality (men are represented in them as they are in everyday life), their poignant realism, and the frequent use of divine intervention, the *deus ex machina*, in their conclusion. Among his extant plays, the survivals of some ninety that he is said to have written, are the following: 'Alcestis', 'Medea', 'Hippolytus', 'Hecuba', the 'Suppliants', 'Iphigenia among the Tauri', the 'Trojan Women', the 'Phoenissae' (the story of Eteocles and Polyneices, with a chorus of Phoenician maidens), 'Electra', 'Orestes', 'Iphigenia at Aulis', the 'Bacchae' (the destruction of King Pentheus by the Bacchantes).

Europa, daughter of Agenor, king of Phoenicia, of whom Zeus became enamoured. He assumed the shape of a beautiful bull and carried her off to Crete, where she afterwards became the mother of Minos, Sarpedon, and Rhadamanthus.

Eurus, the East wind.

Euryalus, see *Nisus.*

Eurydice, see *Orpheus.*

Eurystheus, a king of Argos, for whom Hercules (q.v.) executed his twelve labours.

Eusden, LAURENCE (1688-1730), poet laureate from 1718 until his death. He had celebrated the marriage of the duke of Newcastle, who gave him the laureateship. Pope refers to him in 'The Dunciad' (q.v.):

> Know Eusden thirsts no more for sack or praise;
> He sleeps among the dull of ancient days.

Eusebius of Caesarea in Palestine (A.D. 265-340), bishop of Caesarea, and a celebrated historian and theologian, was one of the leaders at the Council of Nicaea. He was a voluminous writer, and a valuable authority on the early church.

Eustace, FATHER, a character in Scott's 'The Monastery' (q.v.), the energetic subprior of Kennaquhair.

Eustace Diamonds, The, a novel by A. Trollope (q.v.), reprinted from the 'Fortnightly Review' in 1873.

Euterpe, the Muse (q.v.) of lyric poetry.

Euxine, the ancient Greek name of the Black Sea.

Evadne, a character in Beaumont and Fletcher's 'The Maid's Tragedy'.

Evalak or EVELAKE, king of Sarras in the legend of the Grail (q.v.).

Evandale, LORD, a character in Scott's 'Old Mortality' (q.v.).

Evangelical, a term applied from the 18th cent. to that school of Protestants which maintains the doctrine of salvation by faith in the atoning death of Christ, lays more stress on faith than on works, and upholds the verbal inspiration of the Bible. As a distinct party designation, the term came into general use, in England, at the time of the Methodist revival.

Evangeline, a narrative poem in hexameters, by Longfellow (q.v.) (1847).

Gabriel Lajeunesse and Evangeline Bellefontaine, son and daughter of two peasants of Grandpré in Acadia (Nova Scotia) have recently been betrothed, when the inhabitants are driven from their homes for disaffection to the English rule. The lovers are carried to widely distant destinations. Gabriel and his father become prosperous farmers in Louisiana. Evangeline, her father having died of grief, travels to seek Gabriel, and at length reaches his farm, only to find that he has migrated to the western prairies. At length she finds Gabriel, at the point of death, in an almshouse, and the lovers are united as he dies. The poem is notable for its descriptions of American scenery and its idyllic simplicity.

Evan Harrington, a novel by Meredith (q.v.) (1861).

Evans, SIR ARTHUR JOHN (1851-1941), archaeologist, from 1893 was engaged on archaeological investigations in Crete, which resulted in the discovery of the pre-Phoenician script and an entire new civilization. He carried out the excavation of the Palace of Knossos, Crete.

Evans, SIR HUGH, a Welsh parson in Shakespeare's 'The Merry Wives of

Windsor' (q.v.). He is the 'Sir Hugh' referred to in Lamb's 'Amicus Redivivus' ('Essays of Elia').

Evans, MARY ANN, see *Eliot* (*G*.).

Evans's, in Covent Garden, became famous for its musical parties and suppers. Thackeray's 'Cave of Harmony' is partly drawn from it.

Eve, the name given by Adam to his wife (Gen. iii. 20), the first woman.

Evelina, a novel by Fanny Burney (q.v.) (1778).

Sir John Belmont, disappointed of the fortune which he expected to receive with his wife, abandons her and her child Evelina. Evelina goes to visit a friend, Mrs. Mirvan, in London, where she is introduced into society and falls in love with the handsome and dignified Lord Orville, but is exposed to much mortification by reason of her vulgar grandmother, Mme Duval, her ill-bred relatives, and the pursuit of her pertinacious lover, Sir Clement Willoughby. An attempt is made to induce Sir John Belmont to recognize Evelina as his daughter, which is met by the surprising announcement that his daughter had been conveyed to him by the woman who had attended Lady Belmont in her last illness and had been in his care since infancy. It is now discovered that this nurse had passed her own child off on Sir John. Evelina is recognized as his heir, and marries Lord Orville.

Evelyn, JOHN (1620–1706), a man of means, of unblemished character, and a cultured dilettante. He published books on engraving, and on practical arbori-culture, and a number of translations from the French on architecture, gardening, etc. He is remembered principally by his 'Diary', describing his travels on the Continent and containing brilliant por-traits of his contemporaries; it covers his whole life. It was first published in 1818, but not printed in full until the edition of 1955 by E. S. de Beer.

Evening, Ode to, see *Collins* (*William*).

Eve of St. Agnes, The, a poem by Keats (q.v.) written in 1819. Madeline has been told the legend that on St. Agnes' Eve maidens may have visions of their lovers. Her lover Porphyro is of hostile lineage, and she is surrounded by 'hyena foemen, and hot-blooded lords'. Yet he steals in on this night, and when she wakes from dreams of him, she finds him by her bed-side. Together they escape from the castle.

Tennyson (q.v.) also wrote a poem, 'St. Agnes' Eve', describing the rapture of a nun in her convent garden on that night.

Everard, COLONEL MARKHAM, a charac-ter in Scott's 'Woodstock' (q.v.).

Everyman, a popular morality (q.v.) of the 15th cent., of Dutch origin. The characters are God, Messenger, Death, Everyman, Fellowship, Kindred, Good Deeds, Goods, Knowledge, Beauty, Strength, and similar abstractions. The theme is the summoning of Everyman by Death. Everyman finds that no one of his friends except Good Deeds will accom-pany him.

Every Man in his Humour, a comedy by Jonson (q.v.), performed at the Curtain Theatre (with Shakespeare in the cast) in 1598.

Kitely, a merchant, is the husband of a young and pretty wife, and his 'humour' is jealousy. His house is resorted to by his young brother with a crowd of riotous but harmless gallants. One of these young men is Edward Knowell, whose father's 'humour' is excessive solicitude for his son's morals. Bobadill, one of Jonson's greatest creations, a 'Paul's man', is a boasting cowardly soldier. Out of these elements, by the aid of the devices and disguises of the mischievous Brainworm, Knowell's servant, an imbroglio is pro-duced in which Kitely and his wife are brought face to face at a house to which each thinks the other has gone for an improper purpose; Bobadill is exposed and beaten; young Knowell is married to Kitely's sister; and poetasters and 'gulls' are held up to ridicule. The misunder-standings are cleared up by the shrewd and kindly Justice Clement.

The prologue contains an exposition of Jonson's dramatic theory.

Every Man out of his Humour, a satirical comedy by Jonson (q.v.), first acted in 1599 at the Globe Theatre, in which the poet holds up to ridicule various absurd characters and fashions of the day: Fastidious Brisk, the spruce fashionably dressed courtier; Fungoso, a student, whose aim in life is to be a courtier, but who is always behind the fashion; Sordido, his father, a countryman, whose recreation is reading almanacs; Sogliardo, Sordido's brother, whose ambition is to be taken for a man of quality; Deliro, who dotes absurdly on his wife; Puntarvolo, a vainglorious knight, who makes a ridiculous insurance on the safe return of his cat and dog from a voyage to Constantinople. They are all put 'out of humour' with their various predilections.

Evidences of Christianity, see *Paley*.

Evil, THE, see *King's Evil*.

Ewing, MRS. JULIANA HORATIA (1841–85), *née* GATTY, a notably successful writer of books for the young, including 'The Miller's Thumb' (1873, republished as 'Jan of the Windmill', 1884).

Examiner, The, a Tory periodical started by Viscount Bolingbroke (q.v.) in the autumn of 1710, and conducted by Jonathan Swift until June 1711. Prior was a contributor. Some forty numbers appear to have been published. It engaged in controversy with Steele's 'Guardian' (q.v.) and Addison's 'Whig Examiner'.

Examiner, The, a weekly periodical launched in 1808 by John Hunt and his brother Leigh Hunt (q.v.), dealing with literature and politics, which exercised a considerable influence on the development of English journalism. From 1821 to 1849 it was edited by Albany Fonblanque, a radical; then by John Forster and Henry Morley. It lasted until 1880.

Excalibur, a corrupt form of 'Caliburn' (the name used in Geoffrey of Monmouth), was King Arthur's sword, which he drew out of a stone when no one else could draw it (Malory, I. iv), or which was given him by the Lady of the Lake (Malory, II. iii). When Arthur was mortally wounded in the last battle, he ordered Sir Bedivere to throw Excalibur into the water. A hand rose from the water, caught the sword, and vanished.

Excelsior, Latin 'higher', the motto adopted (in defiance of Latin grammar) by the state of New York in 1778; used by Longfellow (as an expression of incessant aspiration after higher attainment) for the refrain of a well-known poem.

Exchange, THE LONDON STOCK, for the sale and purchase of securities (shares, stocks, and bonds) was originally conducted at Jonathan's coffee-house in Change Alley. In 1801 joint stock capital was raised to provide premises on the present site of the Stock Exchange in Capel Court.

Exchange, THE NEW, a bazaar on the south side of the Strand, a popular resort in the 17th–18th cents., often referred to in the drama of the period.

Exchange, THE ROYAL, London, was originally founded by Sir T. Gresham (see *Gresham's Law*) in 1566 and opened by Queen Elizabeth. It was destroyed in the Great Fire of 1666. Its successor was likewise burnt in 1838. The present building was opened in 1844.

Excursion, The, a poem in nine books by Wordsworth (q.v.) (1814). This is the middle portion of a great philosophical poem 'on man, on nature and on human life', in three parts, designed by the author, but of which this alone was completed. The whole work was to be entitled 'The Recluse', 'as having for its principal subject the sensations and opinions of a poet living in retirement'. It was planned in 1798, when Wordsworth was living at Alfoxden, near Coleridge.

The story is very slight. The poet travelling with the Wanderer, a philosophic pedlar, meets with the latter's friend, the pessimistic Solitary. The source of the latter's despondency is traced to his want of religious faith and of confidence in the virtue of man, and is reproved in lengthy arguments. Another character, the Pastor, is introduced, who illustrates the harmonizing effect of virtue and religion by narratives of the lives of persons interred in his churchyard. They visit the Pastor's house, and the Wanderer draws his general philosophical and political conclusions from the discussions that have passed. The last two books deal in particular with the industrial expansion of the early part of the century and the degradation of the humbler classes that followed in its train. The remedy is found in the provision of proper educational facilities for the children. Book I embodies the beautiful 'Story of Margaret' or 'The Ruined Cottage', originally written as a separate poem.

Exeter Book, THE, a famous collection of Old English poems, copied about 975, given by Bishop Leofric (*d.* 1072) to Exeter Cathedral, where it still remains. The book contains many important poems, including 'Christ', 'Guthlac', 'The Phoenix', 'Juliana', 'The Wanderer' (q.v.), 'The Seafarer' (q.v.), 'Widsith' (q.v.), 'Deor' (q.v.), and the 'Riddles'.

Exhibition, THE GREAT, the first international exhibition, promoted by Prince Albert, and held in 1851 in Hyde Park in the Crystal Palace (afterwards removed to Sydenham).

Existentialism, the name commonly given to a group of somewhat loosely associated philosophical doctrines and ideas which have found contemporary expression in the work of such men as Sartre, Heidegger, Marcel, Camus, and Jaspers. Though the theories advanced by different existentialist writers diverge widely in many important respects, certain underlying themes can be singled out as characteristic. Existentialists tend, for example, to emphasize the unique and particular in human experience; they place the individual person at the centre of their pictures of the world, and are suspicious of philosophical or psycho-logical doctrines that obscure this essential individuality by speaking as if there were some abstract 'human nature', some set of general laws or principles, to which men are determined or required, by their common humanity, to conform. Each man is what he chooses to be or make himself. Sartre, in particular, insists upon the notion of the individual as the source of all value, and as being obliged to choose for himself what to do and what standards to adopt or reject: consciousness of such freedom is a condition of 'authentic' existence. Thus existentialists typically give priority to sincerity and creativity in the moral life, and sometimes appear to regard any decision as justified if it is made in perfect honesty and with absolute inner conviction. In their psychological explorations existentialists have often shown an impressive insight and introduced interpretative concepts which have greatly extended the area of moral self-knowledge and self-awareness. This, perhaps more than anything, explains the wide appeal of their writings.

Exodus, an OE. poetical paraphrase of the biblical story, contained in the Junius MS. (see *Cædmon*). The style is lively and vigorous, and there is a famous description of the Egyptians in the Red Sea.

Exoteric, see *Esoteric*.

Expansion of England, The, see *Seeley*.

Extravaganza, a composition, literary, musical, or dramatic, of an extravagant or fantastic character.

Eyck, JAN VAN (active 1422-41), Flemish painter. The existence of his elder brother Hubert is disputed. The discovery of oil painting has been attributed to the brothers, but probably Jan only developed a technique which was already in existence. Jan was court painter to the duke of Burgundy.

Eyrbyggya Saga, see *Saga*.

Eyre, SIMON, see *Simon Eyre*.

F

Faber, FREDERICK WILLIAM (1814–63), a friend of Coleridge and Newman, published many hymns (including 'Pilgrims of the Night' and 'The Land beyond the Sea') and devotional treatises.

Fabian, in Shakespeare's 'Twelfth Night' (q.v.), a servant of Olivia.

Fabian, ROBERT, see *Fabyan*.

Fabian Society, a society, founded in 1884, consisting of socialists who advocate a 'Fabian' policy (see *Fabius Maximus*) as opposed to immediate attempts at revolutionary action. The 'Fabian Essays' of the society were issued in 1889. The names of Sidney Webb and Mrs. Webb, and of G. B. Shaw (q.v.), are especially associated with it.

Fabius Maximus, QUINTUS, nicknamed *Cunctator* or 'the delayer', was appointed dictator at Rome in 217 B.C. He carried on a defensive campaign against Hannibal, avoiding direct engagements, and harassing the enemy. Hence the expressions, 'Fabian tactics', 'Fabian policy'.

Fable of the Bees, The, or Private Vices, Public Benefits, see under *Mandeville* (*B. de*).

Fables, Ancient and Modern, by Dryden (q.v.) (1699).

They are verse paraphrases of tales by Chaucer, Boccaccio, and Ovid.

Fabliau, a short tale in verse, almost invariably in octosyllabic couplets, dealing for the most part from a comic point of view with incidents of ordinary life. The *fabliau* was an important element in the French poetry of the 12th–13th cents.

Fabyan, ROBERT (d. 1513), chronicler, was sheriff of London in 1493. His chronicles are of importance with respect to the history of London.

Face, a character in Jonson's 'The Alchemist' (q.v.).

Factotum, see *Johannes Factotum*.

Faerie Queene, The, the greatest work of Spenser (q.v.), of which the first three books were entrusted to the printer in Nov. 1589, and the second three were published in 1596.

The general scheme of the work is expounded in the author's introductory letter addressed to Sir Walter Ralegh. By the Faerie Queene the poet signifies Glory in the abstract, and Queen Elizabeth in particular (who also figures under the names of Belphoebe, Mercilla, and Gloriana). Twelve of her knights, the 'patrons' or examples of twelve different virtues, undertake each an adventure, on the twelve successive days of the Queen's annual festival. Prince Arthur symbolizes 'Magnificence', in the Aristotelian sense of the perfection of all the other virtues. Arthur has a vision of the Faerie Queene, and, determining to seek her out, is brought into the adventures of the several knights and carries them to a successful issue. But this explanation, given in the introduction, does not appear from the poem itself; for the author starts at once with the adventures of the knights, intending to give his account of their origin in the last of the twelve books which the work was to contain, but this was never written. Spenser published only six books, of which the subjects are as follows:

(I) the adventures of the Red Cross Knight of Holiness (the Anglican Church), the protector of the Virgin Una (truth, or the true religion), and the wiles of Archimago and Duessa (qq.v.);

(II) the adventures of Sir Guyon, the Knight of Temperance, his encounters with Pyrochles and Cymochles, his visit to the cave of Mammon and the House of Temperance and his destruction of Acrasia (q.v.) and her Bower of Bliss. Canto x of this Book contains a chronicle of British kings from Brute to Elizabeth;

(III) the legend of Chastity, exemplified by Britomart and Belphoebe (qq.v.);

(IV) the legend of Triamond and Cambell (q.v.), exemplifying Friendship; together with the story of Scudamour and Amoret;

(V) the adventures of Artegall, the Knight of Justice, in which allegorical reference is made to various historical events of the reign of Queen Elizabeth: the defeat of the Spaniards in the Netherlands, the recantation of Henri IV of France, the execution of Mary Queen of Scots, and the administration of Ireland by Lord Grey de Wilton;

(VI) the adventures of Sir Calidore, exemplifying Courtesy.

We have also a fragment on Mutability, being the sixth and seventh cantos of the legend of Constance, which was to have formed the seventh Book. This fragment contains a charming description of the Seasons and the Months.

The work as a whole, modelled to some extent on the 'Orlando Furioso' of Ariosto, suffers from a certain monotony, and its chief beauties lie in the particular episodes with which the allegory is varied and in descriptions. The poem is written in the stanza invented by Spenser (and since utilized by Thomson, Keats, Shelley, and Byron), in which a ninth line of twelve syllables is added to the eight lines of ten syllables of the *ottava rima*, rhyming a b a b b c b c c.

Fag, a character in Sheridan's 'The Rivals' (q.v.).

Fagin, a character in Dickens's 'Oliver Twist' (q.v.).

Fainall and **Mrs. Fainall**, characters in Congreve's 'The Way of the World' (q.v.).

Fairchild Family, The, see *Sherwood*.

Fair Maid of Perth, Saint Valentine's Day, or the, a novel by Sir W. Scott (q.v.) (1828), the second of 'The Chronicles of the Canongate'. The scene is laid at Perth in the turbulent times at the close of the 14th cent.

Fair Maid of the West, The, or *A Girle worth Gold*, a comedy of adventure, in two parts, by Heywood (q.v.), printed in 1631.

Fair Penitent, The, a tragedy in blank verse by Rowe (q.v.), produced in 1703.

The plot of the play is that of Massinger and Field's 'The Fatal Dowry', shortened and somewhat modified at the end. The play was extremely successful and was constantly revived until the early 19th cent. The 'haughty, gallant, gay Lothario' has become proverbial, and was the model on which Richardson drew Lovelace in his 'Clarissa Harlowe' (q.v.).

Fair Quarrel, A, a comedy by Middleton and Rowley (qq.v.), published in 1617.

Fair Rosamond, see *Rosamond*.

Fairservice, ANDREW, in Scott's 'Rob Roy' (q.v.), a gardener at Osbaldistone Hall.

Faithful, in Bunyan's 'The Pilgrim's Progress' (q.v.) accompanies Christian on the first part of his journey; he is put to death at Vanity Fair.

Faithful, JACOB, see *Jacob Faithful*.

Faithful Shepherdess, The, a pastoral play by J. Fletcher (q.v.), printed not later than 1610. Though without much dramatic interest, the play is full of passages of poetic beauty, and ranks, as a pastoral, with Ben Jonson's 'Sad Shepherd' and Milton's 'Comus'.

Falconer, WILLIAM (1732–69), author of 'The Shipwreck' (1762), a poem in three cantos recounting the wreck of a ship on the coast of Greece, which had considerable vogue in its day. Falconer was drowned at sea.

Falernian, a wine celebrated among the ancient Romans, made from the grapes of Falernus in Campania.

Falkland, one of the principal characters in Godwin's 'Caleb Williams' (q.v.).

Fall of Robespierre, The, a drama (1794) written by Coleridge (Act I) and Southey (Acts II and III) in collaboration.

Falls of Princes, see *Lydgate*.

False One, The, a tragedy attributed to J. Fletcher (q.v.), in which Massinger may also have had a share, printed in 1647; the date of production is uncertain.

Falstaff, SIR JOHN, in Shakespeare's 'Henry IV' (q.v.), a fat, witty, good-humoured old knight, loving jests, self-indulgent, and over-addicted to sack; a braggart who, when exposed, has presence of mind and resource enough to find some shift to save his face; he seems to exaggerate and boast his vices in order to bring out their humorous side. The Falstaff of Shakespeare's 'The Merry Wives of Windsor' (q.v.), written to command, presents a very different character. A mere designing knave, he cuts a sorry figure in the indignities to which his vices expose him. The character was originally called Oldcastle, but objection was taken by Lord Cobham, a descendant of the original Sir John Oldcastle (q.v.), 'for he died a martyr'.

Falstaff, Original Letters of Sir John, and his Friends; now first made public by a Gentleman, a Descendant of Dame Quickly, by James White (1775-1820), a friend of C. Lamb, who collaborated in their production (1796).

Familiar Letters, see *Howell (J.)*.

Fancyfull, LADY, a character in Vanbrugh's 'The Provok'd Wife'.

Fanny, LORD, see *Hervey (John)*.

Fanny's First Play, a comedy by G. B. Shaw (q.v.) (1911).

Fanny's Way, PRETTY, a phrase from a poem by T. Parnell (q.v.).

Fanshawe, ANNE, LADY (1625-80), wife of Sir Richard Fanshawe, who was a devoted adherent to, and sufferer for, the Royalist cause, and after the Restoration was ambassador to Portugal and subsequently to Spain. Lady Fanshawe shared her husband's wanderings and wrote interesting 'Memoirs', first printed in 1829.

Fanshawe, CATHERINE MARIA (1765-1834), poetess, remembered on account of her riddle on the letter H, which has often been attributed to Byron. The opening line originally ran ' 'Twas in heaven pronounced, and 'twas muttered in hell'; but the accepted reading—and the alteration is generally assigned to James Smith (q.v.)—now is ' 'Twas whispered in heaven, 'twas muttered in hell'.

Faraday, MICHAEL (1791-1867), the eminent physicist, made notable contributions to nearly all branches of physical science; but his greatest achievement was the discovery of magneto-electricity. His 'Experimental Researches in Electricity', reprinted from 'Philosophical Transactions', were published in 1839-55; his 'Life and Letters' in 1870.

Farce (from a metaphorical use of the word *farce*, stuffing), was originally applied to explanatory or additional matter introduced into the liturgy; thence to the impromptu buffoonery which the actors were wont to insert in the text of religious dramas. It now means a dramatic work designed solely to excite laughter. It should be distinguished from Extravaganza (q.v.), with which it is sometimes confused.

Fardorougha, the Miser, a novel by W. Carleton (q.v.) (1839).

Far from the Madding Crowd, a novel by Hardy (q.v.) (1874).

Gabriel Oak, the shepherd, serves the capricious Bathsheba Everdene for many years with unselfish devotion. Sergeant Troy, the fascinating soldier, who deserts Fanny Robin, wins Bathsheba for his wife and then ill-treats her. Troy is murdered by Farmer Boldwood, who is impelled by a furious longing for Bathsheba. Boldwood becomes a lunatic, and Gabriel and Bathsheba are at last united.

Farmer George: George III was caricatured as 'Farmer George' on account of his interest in agriculture.

Farmer's Boy, The, see *Bloomfield*.

Farquhar, GEORGE (1678-1707), after being an officer in the army became an actor, took to writing comedies, and produced 'Love and a Bottle' in 1699, 'The Constant Couple, or a Trip to the Jubilee' in 1700, 'Sir Harry Wildair' in 1701, 'The Inconstant' and 'The Twin Rivals' in 1702, 'The Stage Coach' (with Motteux, q.v.) in 1704, 'The Recruiting Officer' in 1706, and 'The Beaux' Stratagem' in 1707. The last two are the best of his plays, and are marked by an atmosphere of reality and genial merriment very different from that of the artificial comedy of the period. Farquhar died in poverty.

Fascist (pron. 'fashist'), from Italian *fascisti*, which is derived from *fascio* (Latin *fascis*), a sheaf or bundle, used metaphorically in *fascio delle forze* in the sense of union or association of forces. In this sense the word *fascio* was adopted by the Italian socialists at the end of the 19th cent. Early in 1915 a group of Italian revolutionary socialists led by Mussolini and Corridoni separated themselves from the official party and formed a *Fascio interventista*, advocating intervention in the War. In March 1919, Mussolini formed at Milan a small group of men called *Fascio nazionale di combattimento*, with the object of resisting by every means, including violence, the communistic movement. At the end of 1921, when the government of the day seemed inclined to declare the *Fasci* to be unlawful armed bands, a party was formed (*Partito nazionale fascista*) which absorbed the old *Fasci di combattimento* and took as its symbol the Roman fasces. It was this party that in Oct. 1922 marched on Rome and accomplished the Fascist revolution. The term has since been applied, in Germany and elsewhere, to any party of the middle classes which aims at the suppression of communism, or sometimes democracy, by force.

Fashion, SIR NOVELTY and YOUNG, characters in Vanbrugh's 'The Relapse', who reappear in Sheridan's adaptation ('A Trip to Scarborough').

Fastidious Brisk, a character in Jonson's 'Every Man out of his Humour' (q.v.).

Fastolf, SIR JOHN (1378-1459), a distinguished warrior in the French wars of Henry V. The few coincidences between the careers of Fastolf and Shakespeare's Sir John Falstaff (q.v.) are accidental.

Fatal Curiosity, The, a tragedy by Lillo (q.v.), published in 1736, based on an old story of a Cornish murder.

Fatal Dowry, The, a tragedy by Massinger and Field (qq.v.), printed in 1632. The text as we have it is corrupt.

Rowe's 'The Fair Penitent' (q.v.) is founded on this play.

Fatal Marriage, The, or the Innocent Adultery, a tragedy by Southerne (q.v.), produced in 1694.

Fata Morgana, see *Morgan le Fay*. (The word *fata* in Italian means 'fairy'.)

Fat Boy, THE, Joe, Mr. Wardle's servant in Dickens's 'The Pickwick Papers' (q.v.).

Fates, THE, see *Parcae*.

Father Brown, see *Brown (Father)*.

Father O'Flynn, a popular Irish song, by A. P. Graves (q.v.).

Fathers, THE APOSTOLIC, the Fathers of the Church (q.v.) who were contemporary, or nearly contemporary, with the apostles, as Clement, Hermas, Barnabas, Polycarp, Papias, and Ignatius.

Fathers of the Church, the early Christian writers, a term usually applied to those of the first five centuries. Sometimes the Greek and Latin fathers are distinguished, the former including Cyprian, Athanasius, Basil the Great, Gregory Nazianzen, and Chrysostom; the latter Jerome, Ambrose, Augustine, Gregory (Pope Gregory I), and Bernard.

Fathom, FERDINAND COUNT, see *Ferdinand Count Fathom*.

Fatima, the daughter of Mohammed (q.v.) and the wife of the Caliph Ali. In fiction Fatima is the name of the last wife of Bluebeard (q.v.).

Faulconbridge, ROBERT and PHILIP THE BASTARD, his half-brother, characters in Shakespeare's 'King John' (q.v.).

Faulkland, a character in Sheridan's 'The Rivals' (q.v.).

Faulkner, WILLIAM (1897-1962), American novelist. In his masterpiece, 'The Sound and the Fury' (1929), Faulkner views the decline of the South. 'As I Lay Dying' (1930) illustrates his comic as well as his tragic vision. Among his important works are 'Light in August' (1932), 'Absalom, Absalom!' (1936), 'The Wild Palms' (1939), 'The Hamlet' (1940), 'Requiem for a Nun' (1951), and 'A Fable' (1954). His collected short stories were published in 1950.

Faunus, an ancient Italian nature-god, the patron of rural pursuits, developed from an earlier conception of a number of *Fauni*, spirits of the countryside, who were assimilated to the *Satyrs* (q.v.) of Greek mythology.

Faust, the subject of the great dramas of Marlowe and Goethe, was a wandering conjurer, who lived in Germany about 1488-1541 and is mentioned in various documents of the period. For Marlowe's play see *Doctor Faustus*. 'Faust', the drama (1808-31) by Goethe (q.v.), consists of two parts. It begins with a Prologue in Heaven, in which Mephistopheles obtains permission to try to effect the ruin of the soul of Faust. The play itself opens with a soliloquy by Faust, disillusioned with the world. Mephistopheles having presented himself, Faust enters into a compact to become his servant if Faust should exclaim, of any moment of delight procured for him, 'Stay, thou art so fair'. Then follow the attempts of Mephistopheles to satisfy Faust, culminating in the incident of Gretchen (Margaret), whom Faust seduces, bringing about her miserable death. This is the end of Pt. I, Faust being left remorseful and dissatisfied.

The story of Pt. II is extremely complex and its symbolism obscure. It consists in the main of two portions, of which the first is the incident of Helen, symbolizing perfect beauty. She is ardently pursued by Faust, but finally reft from him. Euphorion, their son, personifying poetry and the union of the classical and the romantic and at the end representing Lord Byron, vanishes in a flame. In the second portion (Acts IV and V), the purified Faust, pursuing the service of man, reclaims from the sea a stretch of submerged land. Finally satisfied in the consciousness of a good work done, he cries to the fleeting moment, 'Ah, stay, thou art so fair', and falls dead. Hell tries to seize his soul, but it is borne away by angels.

Faustus, Doctor, see *Doctor Faustus*.

Favonius, the Latin name of the zephyr or west wind.

Fawnia, see *Pandosto*.

Feast of Fools, a medieval festival originally of the sub-deacons of the cathedral, held about the time of the Feast of the Circumcision (i.e. 1 Jan.), in which the humbler cathedral officials burlesqued the sacred ceremonies. A lord of the feast was elected, styled bishop, cardinal, abbot, etc., according to the locality. The Feast of Fools had its chief vogue in the French cathedrals, but there are records of it in a few English cathedrals, notably at Lincoln, and at Beverley Minster.

Feathernest, Mr., in Peacock's 'Melincourt', a caricature of Southey.

Federal States, the northern States in the American War of Secession (1861-5) which resisted the attempt of the Southern or Confederate States to secede.

Feeble, in Shakespeare's '2 Henry IV', III. ii, one of the recruits brought up before Falstaff.

Feenix, Cousin, a character in Dickens's 'Dombey and Son' (q.v.), the nephew of Mrs. Skewton, and cousin of Edith, Dombey's second wife.

Felix Holt the Radical, a novel by G. Eliot (q.v.) (1866).

Felix Holt is a noble-minded young reformer who deliberately chooses the life of a humble artisan in order to bring home to his fellow workers that the hope of an improvement in their conditions lies in education and learning to think for themselves, and not in this or that legislative programme. The story is complicated by involved legal questions, and marred for many readers by melodramatic and improbable elements.

Fell, Dr. John (1625-86), successively dean of Christ Church, Oxford, and bishop of Oxford, remembered in a literary connection as an enthusiastic patron and promoter of the Oxford University Press (q.v.). He procured for the Press the matrixes and punches of the best types that could be found (from which the 'Fell types' are still cast), and arranged every year for the publication of some classical author. His name is associated with the widely known jingle,

I do not love you, Dr. Fell;
But why I cannot tell;
But this I know full well,
I do not love you, Dr. Fell.

a translation of Martial, Epigrams, i. 32, by Thomas Brown (q.v.), one of the undergraduates of his college. 'Doctor Fell' has thus unfairly come to be used to describe a type of vaguely unamiable person against whom no precise ground of dislike can be adduced.

Female Quixote, The, or The Adventures of Arabella (1752), a romance in imitation of 'Don Quixote' by Mrs. Charlotte Lennox (1720–1804), a lady who was flattered and befriended by Dr. Johnson.

Feminine ending, in blank verse, the unstressed eleventh syllable at the end of an iambic pentameter line, as in:

'Upon your charter and your city's free*dom*.'

A favourite Shakespearian device to avoid a monotonous regularity, particularly in his later blank verse. Cf. *Weak ending*.

Feminine rhyme, rhyme in which an unstressed syllable follows the rhyming stress, as *flatter, matter*. Also called *weak rhyme*. See *Masculine rhyme*.

Fénelon, FRANÇOIS DE SALIGNAC DE LA MOTHE- (1651–1715), French divine. 'The apostle of interior inspiration', as opposed to the inflexible dogmatism of Bossuet (q.v.), he expounded his Quietist doctrine in the 'Maximes des Saints' (1697). For the instruction of his pupil, the duc de Bourgoyne, he wrote 'Aventures de Télémaque' (1699), a graceful narrative in admirable prose, and 'Examen de la conscience d'un roi' (1734). His numerous other writings include some excellent critical works.

Fenians, originally a semi-mythical, semi-historical military body said to have been raised for the defence of Ireland against Norse raids; in modern times an association formed among the Irish in the United States and in Ireland in the middle of the 19th cent. for promoting the over-throw of the English government in Ireland.

Fenton, a character in Shakespeare's 'The Merry Wives of Windsor' (q.v.).

Ferdinand, (1) in Shakespeare's 'The Tempest' (q.v.), son of the king of Naples; (2) in Shakespeare's 'Love's Labour's Lost' (q.v.), the king of Navarre.

Ferdinand Count Fathom, The Adventures of, a romance by Smollett (q.v.) (1753).

Ferguson, SIR SAMUEL (1810–86), wrote a fine elegy on Thomas Davis, the Irish nationalist leader, in 1845, and his epic 'Congal' in 1872. 'Ogham Inscriptions in Ireland, Wales, and Scotland' (1887) is his most important antiquarian work.

Fergusson, ROBERT (1750–74), an Edinburgh clerk, published a volume of poems in 1773, which were much praised by Burns and Stevenson. His lyrics are interesting as an anticipation of the manner of Burns, and as giving a vivid picture of the life and amusements of the Edinburgh poor.

Ferney, a village near Geneva, where Voltaire (q.v.) spent the last twenty years of his life. He is frequently referred to as the 'Philosopher of Ferney'.

Fern seed: before the mode of reproduction of ferns was understood, they were popularly supposed to produce an invisible seed, which was capable of communicating its invisibility to any person who possessed it. Cf. Shakespeare, '1 Henry IV', II. i. 96.

Ferrar, NICHOLAS (1592–1637), fellow of Clare College, Cambridge, was a member of parliament, and active in the affairs of the Virginia Company. In 1625 he retired to Little Gidding, received holy orders, and acted as chaplain there to a small Anglican community who devoted their lives to contemplation and prayer. The community was dispersed by the parliamentary troops in 1646. A record of its activities survives in the 'Little Gidding Story Books', five manuscript volumes bound by Mary Collett, a member of the community, of which a part was printed in 1899, containing romances and pious discourses. An interesting picture of the community is given in 'John Inglesant' (q.v.). Crashaw (q.v.) was at one time greatly influenced by Ferrar.

Ferrers, GEORGE, see *Mirror for Magistrates*.

Ferrex and Porrex, see *Gorboduc*.

Ferrier, JAMES FREDERICK (1808–64), nephew of Susan Ferrier (q.v.), studied German philosophy at Heidelberg, and was successively professor of civil history at Edinburgh (1842–5) and of moral philosophy and political economy at St. Andrews (1845–64).

Ferrier's conclusions closely resemble those of Hegel (q.v.), though reached independently and from a different starting-point. They are well set out in his 'Introduction to the Philosophy of Consciousness' (1838–9) and in his 'Berkeley and Idealism' (1842). He is a vigorous and stimulating writer.

Ferrier, SUSAN EDMONSTONE (1782–1854), a friend of Sir W. Scott, and the authoress of three good novels of Scottish life, 'Marriage' (1818), 'The Inheritance' (1824), and 'Destiny' (1831), all marked by a sense of humour and high comedy.

Ferumbras or *Firumbras*, *Sir*, a Middle English metrical version of the French Charlemagne romance 'Fierabras'. The same story is told in the 'Sowdone of Babylon', a paraphrase (of about the year 1400) of a lost French poem.

Fesolè, the modern Fiesole, a hill and small town adjoining Florence. Cf. Milton, 'Paradise Lost', i. 288.

Feste, the fool in Shakespeare's 'Twelfth Night' (q.v.).

Festus, a poem by P. J. Bailey (q.v.) (1839). Successive editions appeared, and the poem gradually increased in length, until the fiftieth anniversary edition (1893) contained some 40,000 lines. The work was at one time immensely popular. It is written in blank verse, interspersed with couplets and lyrics, and takes the form of dialogues distributed over some fifty scenes. It is a philosophical poem with a story on the lines of that of Faust. Watts-Dunton claimed for it that it contains 'lovely oases of poetry' among 'wide tracts of ratiocinative writing'.

Festus, PORCIUS, Roman procurator of Judaea *c.* A.D. 60–2, before whom the apostle Paul was brought (Acts xxv and xxvi).

Feuchtwanger, LION (1884–1958), German novelist, best known as the author of 'Jud Süss' (1925, 'Jew Süss').

Feuilleton, a portion of French newspapers marked off by a rule and appropriated to light literature, criticism, etc. Also, incorrectly, used in England for a serial or short story in a daily paper.

Fezziwig, MR. and MRS., characters in Dickens's 'A Christmas Carol' (q.v.).

Fiammetta, the name given by Boccaccio (q.v.) to the lady whom he loved, one Maria, illegitimate daughter of Robert, king of Naples, and wife of a Count d'Aquino.

Fichte, JOHANN GOTTLIEB (1762–1814), German philosopher, a pupil of Kant (q.v.), from whose dualism he subsequently dissented. Fichte's philosophy is a pure idealism. This doctrine he expounded in his principal work, 'Wissenschaftslehre' (1794). Influenced by the humiliation of Prussia in 1806–7, he became increasingly interested in the idea of nationhood, and sought reality, not in the *ego*, but in the 'divine idea which lies at the base of all experience', and of which the world of the senses is the manifestation.

Fiction, see *Novel*.

Fidele, in Shakespeare's 'Cymbeline' (q.v.), the name assumed by Imogen when disguised as a boy.

Fidelio, Beethoven's opera, see *Leonora*.

Fidessa, in Spenser's 'Faerie Queene', I. ii, the name assumed by the companion of Sansfoy (q.v.), whom the Red Cross Knight takes under his protection. She turns out to be the false Duessa (q.v.).

Field, MICHAEL, the pseudonym adopted by Katharine Bradley (1846–1914) and her niece Edith Cooper (1862–1913).

They wrote several novels and some good poetry.

Field, NATHANIEL (1587-1633), actor and dramatist, acted in plays by Shakespeare, Ben Jonson, and Beaumont and Fletcher. His name is made synonymous with 'best actor' in Jonson's 'Bartholomew Fayre'. He wrote two comedies of some merit, but is remembered chiefly as having collaborated in Massinger's 'The Fatal Dowry'.

Fielding, MRS. and MAY, characters in Dickens's 'The Cricket on the Hearth' (q.v.).

Fielding, HENRY (1707-54), was educated at Eton (where he was contemporary with the elder Pitt and Fox), and studied law at Leyden. He supported himself in London by writing for the stage, mostly comedies and farces, which contain some spirited songs, but of which the only one that is remembered is his burlesque of the popular playwrights of the day, 'The Tragedy of Tragedies, or Tom Thumb' (1730). During 1739-41 he conducted the 'Champion' periodical. The publication of Richardson's 'Pamela' (q.v.) provoked Fielding to parody it and led to the publication in 1742 of 'The History of the Adventures of Joseph Andrews and his friend Mr. Abraham Adams'. Fielding was also perhaps the author of 'Shamela' (1741). In 1743 he published three volumes of 'Miscellanies', including his powerful satire 'Jonathan Wild the Great', and 'A Journey from this World to the Next'. He now took up political journalism and was made justice of the peace for Westminster. In 1749 appeared his great novel 'Tom Jones' (q.v.), and in 1751 'Amelia'. In 1752 he started 'The Covent Garden Journal' under the pseudonym Sir Alexander Drawcansir, which contains some of his best miscellaneous essays. His health now broke down, and in 1754, in an attempt to recover it, he made a voyage to Portugal, of which he has left a pleasant account in his 'Journal of a Voyage to Lisbon', published posthumously. He died at Lisbon. He contributed powerfully to determine the form of the English novel. An essentially honest, manly, and humane character, he poured contempt on hypocrisy, meanness, and vanity.

Fielding, SARAH (1710-68), sister of Henry Fielding (q.v.), and authoress of romances, including 'The Adventures of David Simple in search of a Faithful Friend' (1744). She translated Xenophon's 'Memorabilia' and 'Apologia' (1762).

Field of the Cloth of Gold, the meeting-place of Henry VIII and François I of France, near Calais, in 1520.

Fiennes, CELIA (1662-1741), granddaughter of the first Viscount Saye and Sele. Nearly all that is known about her life is to be found in her Journal, of which an incomplete version was published in 1888 under the title 'Through England on a Side Saddle in the Time of William and Mary'. A definitive edition, 'The Journeys of Celia Fiennes', edited by C. Morris, was published in 1947. Between 1685 and 1703 Celia Fiennes travelled into every county of England, and her journal provided the first comprehensive survey of the country since Harrison and Camden (qq.v.). She recorded throughout what interested her. Her style is breathless and her spelling erratic, but she communicates a lively enthusiasm.

Fierabras, see *Ferumbras.*

Fifine at the Fair, a poem by R. Browning (q.v.) (1872).

Fifteen, THE, the Jacobite rising of 1715.

Fifth Monarchy Men, English fanatics of the 17th cent. who believed that the second coming of Christ was at hand. The Fifth Monarchy is the last of the five great empires referred to in the prophecy of Daniel (Dan. ii. 44).

Figaro, the barber in Beaumarchais's 'Barbier de Séville' and the valet in his 'Mariage de Figaro', an ingenious rascal.

Fig Sunday, a dialectal name for Palm Sunday.

Filer, a canting churl in Dickens's 'The Chimes' (q.v.).

Filomena, *Santa*, a poem by Longfellow, in which the poet celebrated Florence Nightingale.

Filostrato, a poem in *ottava rima* on the story of Troilus and Cressida, by Boccaccio (q.v.), the source of Chaucer's 'Troylus and Cryseyde'.

Finch, ANNE, see *Winchilsea* (*Countess of*).

Fin de siècle, a French phrase usually applied to the art and literature of the end of the 19th cent., in those aspects of it which were characterized by disillusionment and decadence.

Fingal, the name given by Macpherson (q.v.) in his Ossianic poems to the hero Finn (q.v.). Fingal figures, chiefly as a righter of wrongs and defender of the oppressed, in many of the other Ossianic poems. It is noteworthy that Macpherson brings together Fingal and Cuthullin (the Irish Cuchulain), who according to legend were divided by centuries, and makes the Irish Finn into a Scot.

Finlay, GEORGE (1799-1875), studied law at Glasgow and Göttingen, and went to Greece in 1823, where he took part in the war of independence. His 'History of Greece' covers the period from its conquest by the Romans (146 B.C.) to modern times, thus covering the Byzantine Empire and the long period of Greece's subjugation. It appeared in sections between 1844 and 1861, and was published collectively in 1877.

Finn or FIONN, the principal hero of the southern or later cycle of Irish legends, also called the Fenian or Ossianic cycle.

Finnegans Wake, a prose work by James Joyce (q.v.), published in 1939. It is written in a unique and extremely difficult style, making use of puns and portmanteau words, and a very wide range of allusion. The central theme of the work is a cyclical pattern of fall and resurrection. This is presented in the story of H. C. Earwicker, a Dublin tavern keeper, and the book is apparently a dream-sequence representing the stream of his unconscious mind through the course of one night. In spite of its obscurity it contains passages of great lyrical beauty, and also much humour.

Finnsburh, the name given to a fragment (of 50 lines) of an Old English epic poem, dealing with a portion of the tale of Finn and Hildeburh which is told by the minstrel in the poem 'Beowulf' (q.v.).

Fiona Macleod, see *Sharp* (*W.*).

Firbank, (ARTHUR ANNESLEY) RONALD (1886-1926), author of the following novels: 'Vainglory' (1915), 'Inclinations' (1916), 'Caprice' (1917), 'Valmouth' (1919), 'The Flower beneath the Foot' (1923), 'Sorrow in Sunlight' (1925, published in New York as 'Prancing Nigger'), and 'Concerning the Eccentricities of Cardinal Pirelli' (1926). He was an aesthete whose work reflects a fastidious and sophisticated mind.

Firdusi or FIRDAUSI, ABUL KASIM MANSUR (*c.* 950-1020), Persian poet, and author of the 'Shahnameh', the great Persian epic.

Fire-drake, a fiery dragon of Germanic mythology, used in a transferred sense of a person with a fiery nose, as in Shakespeare, 'Henry VIII', v. iv. 46.

Fire of London, THE GREAT, in 1666 (2-6 Sept.) destroyed the buildings on some 400 acres, including St. Paul's and 87 churches, and over 13,000 houses.

Firmilian, see *Aytoun*.

Firmin, DR. GEORGE BRAND and PHILIP, the principal characters in Thackeray's 'The Adventures of Philip'; Dr. Firmin had previously figured in his 'A Shabby Genteel Story'.

First Gentleman of Europe, GEORGE IV, so called on account of his gracious manner and his deportment in public.

First of June, THE GLORIOUS, the date of the naval battle in which, in 1794, Lord Howe defeated a French fleet off Ushant.

Firth, SIR CHARLES HARDING (1857-1936), historian and literary critic; Regius professor of modern history at Oxford, 1904-25. His writings include 'Oliver

Cromwell' (1900) and other works on 17th cent. history.

Firumbras, Sir, see *Ferumbras.*

Fisher, ST. JOHN (1459-1535), became chancellor of Cambridge University and bishop of Rochester, 1504, and was president of Queens' College, Cambridge, 1505-8. He was a patron of Erasmus (q.v.) and induced him to lecture on Greek at Cambridge from 1511 to 1514. He wrote three treatises against the Lutheran reformation, and was deprived, attainted, and beheaded, 1535, for refusing to acknowledge the king as supreme head of the Church. His Latin theological works were issued in 1597 (republished in 1967); his English works, edited by J. E. B. Mayor, appeared in 1876. His English prose style showed a great advance in point of rhetorical artifice and effect. He was canonized in 1935 and is commemorated on 22 June.

Fitz-Boodle, GEORGE SAVAGE, a pseudonym assumed by Thackeray (q.v.) in the 'Fitz-Boodle Papers' contributed to 'Fraser's Magazine', 1842-3.

Fitz-Fulke, HEBE, *Duchess of,* a character in Byron's 'Don Juan' (q.v.).

FitzGerald, EDWARD (1809-83), lived a retired life in Suffolk and was a friend of Carlyle, Thackeray, and the Tennysons. His chief work was the English poetic version (from the Persian) of the 'Rubáiyát of Omar Khayyám' (q.v.), published in 1859 anonymously. In 1852 he published 'Polonius', a collection of aphorisms, and in 1853 'Six Dramas of Calderon', free translations in blank verse and prose. He likewise made English versions of the 'Agamemnon' of Aeschylus and of the two 'Oedipus' tragedies of Sophocles. His charming letters were published 1889-1901.

Fitzgerald, F. SCOTT (1896-1940), American novelist and short-story writer. He was the typical figure of the 'jazz age', as he called it, the decade of the 'lost generation' following the First World War. He sprang into fame with 'This Side of Paradise' (1920), a novel set in Princeton.

He published two collections of short stories, 'Flappers and Philosophers' (1920) and 'Tales of the Jazz Age' (1922), and another novel, 'The Beautiful and the Damned' (1922), before 'The Great Gatsby' (1925), the story of the tragic love affair of a shady financier, his finest work. 'All the Sad Young Men', short stories, appeared in 1926, and 'Tender is the Night', novel, in 1934. His last novel, 'The Last Tycoon' (1941), was unfinished.

Fitzralph, RICHARD (*d.* 1360), frequently referred to as 'Armachanus', was chancellor of Oxford (1333) and archbishop of Armagh (1347). He had great repute as a preacher, wrote a treatise against the friars' doctrine of obligatory poverty, 'De Pauperie Salvatoris', expressing the view on this subject that Wycliffe (q.v.) adopted.

Fitzroy, VICE-ADMIRAL ROBERT (1805-65), commanded the 'Beagle' in the surveying expedition to Patagonia and the Straits of Magellan (1828-36), having Darwin as naturalist for the last five years. With Darwin he wrote a narrative of the voyage.

Fitzstephen, WILLIAM (*d.* 1190?), author of a life of Thomas à Becket, which contains a valuable account of early London.

Five Nations, The, a collection of poems by Kipling (q.v.) (1903). The 'Five Nations' are the chief component parts of the British Empire.

Five Towns, THE, in the novels of Arnold Bennett (q.v.), Tunstall, Burslem, Hanley, Stoke-upon-Trent, and Longton. These are represented in the novels by Turnhill, Bursley, Hanbridge, Knype, and Longshaw.

Fizkin, HORATIO, a character in Dickens's 'The Pickwick Papers' (q.v.).

Flaccus, see *Horace.*

Flamborough, FARMER and the MISSES, characters in Goldsmith's 'The Vicar of Wakefield' (q.v.).

Flaming Tinman, THE, a character in Borrow's 'Lavengro' (q.v.).

Flanders, MOLL, see *Moll Flanders.*

Flanders Mare: Henry VIII's description of Anne of Cleves, his fourth wife.

Flatman, THOMAS (1637–88), fellow of New College, Oxford, much esteemed as a painter of miniatures. He also wrote poems, and some hymns ('Poems and Songs', 1674).

Flaubert, GUSTAVE (1821–80), French novelist, remarkable for his highly finished style and for his impersonal, objective method of narrative. His most famous novel is 'Madame Bovary', a realistic sordid tale of bourgeois life (1857).

Flavius, in Shakespeare's 'Timon of Athens', (q.v.), the faithful steward of Timon.

Fleance, in Shakespeare's 'Macbeth' (q.v.), the son of Banquo.

Flecker, (HERMAN) JAMES ELROY (1884–1915), poet and playwright. He entered the consular service and was posted first to Constantinople and then to Beirut. But his health broke down and he died of consumption in Switzerland. He published 'The Bridge of Fire' (1907), 'Forty-Two Poems' (1911), 'The Golden Journey to Samarkand' (1913), and 'The Old Ships' (1915). His two plays, 'Hassan' and 'Don Juan', were published posthumously in 1922 and 1925.

Flecknoe, RICHARD (d. 1678?), said to have been an Irish priest, printed privately several poems and prose works. He was the subject of a lampoon by Andrew Marvell (1645), which suggested to Dryden his satire on Shadwell, 'Mac Flecknoe' (q.v.).

Fledgeby, in Dickens's 'Our Mutual Friend' (q.v.), a cowardly villain.

Fleece, GOLDEN, see *Golden Fleece*.

Fleet Prison, THE, stood in the neighbourhood of the present Farringdon Street, London. After the abolition of the Star Chamber in 1640, it served mainly as a debtors' prison, until demolished in 1848. As a debtors' prison it figures in Dickens's novels, notably in 'The Pickwick Papers' (q.v.).

In the early part of the 18th cent. FLEET MARRIAGES were celebrated by accommodating clergymen imprisoned in its walls, without licence or banns, until the practice was stopped by the Marriage Act of 1753.

Fleet Street, now the headquarters of London journalism, is sometimes used to signify British journalism and journalistic writing.

Fleet Street Eclogues, see *Davidson*.

Fleming, MARJORY (1803–11), 'Pet Marjorie', a youthful prodigy. She wrote a quaint diary, a poem on Mary Queen of Scots, and other verses, and was the subject of an essay by Dr. John Brown (q.v.), though his story of the friendship of Sir Walter Scott and Marjory is now believed to be apocryphal.

Fleming, (1) ROSE and AGNES, characters in Dickens's 'Oliver Twist' (q.v.); (2) ARCHDEACON, in Scott's 'The Heart of Midlothian'; (3) LADY MARY, in Scott's 'The Abbot'; (4) SIR MALCOLM, in Scott's 'Castle Dangerous'; (5) PAUL, in Longfellow's 'Hyperion'; (6) FARMER, RHODA, and DAHLIA, in Meredith's 'Rhoda Fleming'.

Fleshly School of Poetry, The, the title of an article in 'The Contemporary Review' (Oct. 1871), in which Robert Buchanan (q.v.), under the pseudonym of 'Thomas Maitland', attacked the Pre-Raphaelites (q.v.), especially D. G. Rossetti. This attack was the prelude to a long and bitter controversy.

Fletcher, GILES, the Elder (1549?–1611), was sent as envoy to Russia in 1588. His book on Russia (1591), suppressed, and only partially printed in Hakluyt and Purchas, was published entire in 1856 (ed. Bond). 'Licia, or Poemes of Love' (1593), printed by Grosart, 1871, is of some importance as one of the first collections of sonnets that followed the appearance of Sidney's 'Astrophel and Stella'. He was uncle of John Fletcher (q.v.), the collaborator of Beaumont.

Fletcher, GILES, the Younger (1588?–1623), the younger son of Giles Fletcher the Elder (q.v.), was rector of Alderton, Suffolk, and a poet of the Spenserian school, who dealt with religious themes allegorically. His 'Christs Victorie and Triumph in Heaven and Earth' (1610) has been several times reprinted.

Fletcher, JOHN (1579-1625), was nephew of Giles Fletcher the Elder (q.v.) and cousin of Giles the Younger and Phineas Fletcher (qq.v.). He collaborated with Francis Beaumont from about 1606 to 1616 in the production of plays, the exact number of which is not known, but does not exceed fifteen. He was sole author of not less than sixteen plays, and collaborated with Massinger, Rowley, and others in yet other plays.

Among the principal plays of which Fletcher was author or part author are the following:

Probably by Fletcher alone: 'The Faithful Shepherdess', printed by 1610; 'Valentinian', acted before 1619; 'The Loyal Subject', acted in 1618; 'The Humorous Lieutenant', acted in 1619; 'The Wild Goose Chase', 1621, printed in 1652; 'The Pilgrim', a comedy, 1621, printed in 1647; 'Rule a Wife and Have a Wife', a comedy, acted in 1624; 'Monsieur Thomas', 1619, printed in 1639; 'The Chances', 1620, printed in 1647.

Certainly or probably by Beaumont and Fletcher: 'The Knight of the Burning Pestle' (q.v.), 1609, printed in 1613; 'The Scornful Lady', 1610, printed in 1616; 'Philaster', 1611, printed in 1620; 'The Maid's Tragedy' and 'A King and no King', 1611, printed in 1619; 'Bonduca', 1614, printed in 1647; 'Thierry and Theodoret', a tragedy, perhaps written with the collaboration of Beaumont and Massinger, printed in 1621.

Probably by Fletcher and some other dramatist: 'Love's Pilgrimage' and 'The Double Marriage', comedies, printed in 1647; 'Sir John van Olden Barnavelt', acted in 1619; 'The Custom of the Country', printed in 1647; 'The Spanish Curate' and 'The Beggars Bush', acted in 1622. In these Fletcher certainly or probably collaborated with Massinger. The romantic drama, 'The Lovers' Progress',

produced in 1623 and printed in 1647, was an adaptation by Massinger of an earlier play by Fletcher. 'The Elder Brother', printed in 1637, is thought to have been written by Fletcher and revised by Massinger. 'The Fair Maid of the Inn', printed in 1647, was probably the result of similar collaboration, with perhaps assistance from Jonson and Rowley. 'The Nice Valour', a comedy, printed in 1647, was probably written by Fletcher and Middleton. It contains the lyric 'Hence all you vain delights', which suggested 'Il Penseroso' to Milton. In 'The Bloody Brother, or Rollo, Duke of Normandy' Fletcher is supposed to have had the assistance of Jonson (in the astrological scene) and others; the tragedy was probably produced about 1616. It contains the lyric 'Take, oh take those lips away', which occurs with certain changes in Shakespeare's 'Measure for Measure'. 'The Noble Gentleman', a comedy acted in 1626, is by Fletcher with Beaumont, or perhaps Rowley. 'The Two Noble Kinsmen' (q.v.), printed 1634, was probably the work of Fletcher and Shakespeare. It is probable also that Fletcher had a share in the composition of Shakespeare's 'Henry VIII'.

Fletcher, PHINEAS (1582-1650), the elder son of Giles Fletcher the Elder (q.v.), was rector of Hilgay, Norfolk, 1621-50. Like his brother Giles, he was a poet of the Spenserian school. His chief work, 'The Purple Island', an allegorical poem on the human body, the mind, and the virtues and vices, was published in 1633. 'Britain's Ida', 1628, seems to be his.

Fleur and Blanchefleur, see *Flores and Blancheflour*.

Flibbertigibbet, probably in its original form 'flibbergib', which Latimer uses in a sermon for a chattering or gossiping person. Shakespeare in 'King Lear' III. iv has 'Flibbertigibbet', 'the foul fiend' who walks at night. Scott, in 'Kenilworth' (q.v.), gives the nickname 'Flibbertigibbet' to Dickie Sludge.

Flintwinch, a character in Dickens's 'Little Dorrit' (q.v.). His wife was known as Affery.

Flite, MISS, a character in Dickens's 'Bleak House' (q.v.).

Flodden or FLODDON **Field,** the battle of Flodden, in Northumberland, fought on 9 Sept. 1513, when the earl of Surrey on behalf of Henry VIII (then in France) defeated James IV of Scotland, the latter sovereign being killed on the field. It was made the subject of poems, of rejoicing or lament, on both sides of the border. Skelton's 'Against the Scots' is a rude song of exultation on the English victory. On the Scottish side there is the beautiful lament, 'The Flowers of the Forest', of which the most popular version is by Jane Elliot (q.v.). The battle is described in the 6th canto of Scott's 'Marmion, A Tale of Flodden Field' (q.v.).

Flora, the goddess of flowers and spring of the ancient Romans.

Florac, COMTE DE, in Thackeray's 'The Virginians' (q.v.), and in 'The New-comes' (q.v.) an *émigré* from France. His wife (who had been loved as a girl by Thomas Newcome), son, and daughter-in-law figure in the latter novel.

Florent or FLORENTIUS, the subject of a tale in Gower's (q.v.), 'Confessio Amantis' and of 'The Wife of Bath's Tale' in Chaucer's 'The Canterbury Tales' (q.v.).

Flores and Blancheflour, a metrical romance of the Middle English period, relating the adventures of Blancheflour, a Christian princess carried off by the Saracens and brought up with the Christian prince Flores. A version of this story forms the subject of Boccaccio's 'Filocolo'.

Florestan, KING, a character in Disraeli's 'Endymion'.

Florimell, in Spenser's 'Faerie Queene', Bks. III and IV, the type of chastity and virtue in woman. She is in love with the knight Marinell, who 'sets nought' by her. She takes refuge from her pursuers in the sea and is imprisoned by Proteus. Finally the heart of Marinell is touched by her complaint, and Neptune orders Proteus to release her.

Florin, the English name of a gold coin first issued at Florence in 1252, so called because it had a flower stamped upon it. The name was applied to two English gold coins (known also as 'leopards' and 'double leopards') of the value of 3s. and 6s., issued by Edward III. The English silver coin worth 2s. called a florin was first minted in 1849.

Florio, JOHN (1553?-1625), son of an Italian Protestant refugee, was reader in Italian to Anne of Denmark, wife of James I, 1603, and groom of the privy chamber, 1604. His great Italian-English dictionary appeared in 1598. He published a translation of Montaigne's 'Essays' in 1603, which had an important influence on English literature and philosophy. It is marked by a certain extravagance and eccentricity of language, but he loved his author and made a vivid work of the translation.

Florizel, a character in Shakespeare's 'The Winter's Tale' (q.v.), the lover of Perdita.

Florizel, PRINCE, the chief character in 'The New Arabian Nights' of R. L. Stevenson (q.v.).

Flosky, MR., a character in Peacock's 'Nightmare Abbey' (q.v.), who illustrates the transcendentalism of Coleridge.

Flower and the Leaf, The, an allegory of 600 lines in rhyme-royal, formerly attributed to Chaucer, in which the poet wandering in a grove sees the white company of knights and ladies of the leaf (Diana, goddess of chastity), and the green company of the flower (Flora), the 'folk that loved idleness' and had delight 'of no businesse, but for to hunt and hauke, and pley in medes', and witnesses their processions and sports.

Linguistic characteristics suggest that this poem is of later date than Chaucer or was extensively rewritten. The spirit of the poem is thoroughly Chaucerian.

Flowers of the Forest, see *Elliot (Jane)*.

Fludd, ROBERT (1574-1637), physician and Rosicrucian (q.v.), was as a writer a medical mystic of the school that looked to the Bible for secret clues to science.

Fluellen, in Shakespeare's 'Henry V' (q.v.), a brave, choleric, and pedantic Welsh officer.

Flute, in Shakespeare's 'A Midsummer Night's Dream' (q.v.), a bellows-mender, who takes the part of Thisbe in the play of 'Pyramus and Thisbe'.

Flutter, SIR FOPLING, a character in Etherege's 'The Man of Mode' (q.v.).

Flying Dutchman, The, a phantom ship, which, in consequence of a murder committed on board, is supposed to haunt the sea in a perpetual endeavour to make Table Bay. Capt. Marryat's novel 'The Phantom Ship' and a music-drama by R. Wagner (q.v.) are founded on this legend.

Foedera, Conventiones, et cujuscunque generis Acta Publica, a collection of public records in twenty volumes, by Rymer (q.v.) and Robert Sanderson (1704-35). The documents extend down to 1654, and provided for the first time a scientific basis for the writing of history.

Fogg, PHILEAS, the hero of Jules Verne's 'Round the World in Eighty Days'.

Foible, in Congreve's 'The Way of the World' (q.v.), Lady Wishfort's woman.

Foker, HARRY, a character in Thackeray's 'Pendennis' (q.v.).

Folio, a sheet of paper folded once only, or a volume made up of sheets so folded (consequently of the largest size).

Folio, TOM, a pedantic bibliophile, the subject of one of Addison's essays.

Folios and Quartos, SHAKESPEARIAN. The earliest published forms of Shakespeare's plays are referred to as folios or quartos according to the size of the book, folios being large tall volumes, and the quartos usually smaller and squarer (see *Folio* and *Quarto*). Of about 1,200 copies of the 'First Folio' printed by the Jaggards (q.v.) between Feb. 1622 and Nov. 1623, some 230 survive. The Second, Third, and Fourth Folios followed in 1632, 1663, and 1685 respectively. The First Folio contained thirty-six plays, eighteen printed

for the first time, arranged by Heming (q.v.) and Condell into sections of comedies, histories, and tragedies. F1, which was dedicated to William Herbert, earl of Pembroke, and Philip Herbert, earl of Montgomery, contains the Droeshout portrait, together with commendatory verses by contemporaries including Jonson (q.v.), who may also have written the address to the readers. 'An Epitaph on . . . Shakespeare' by Milton (q.v.), his first printed poem, was added to F2.

The nineteen texts which first appeared as quartos were divided by A. W. Pollard (1859-1944) into 'bad' (mutilated texts perhaps reconstructed from memory) and 'good' quartos (those based on authoritative manuscripts). The fullest accounts of F1 are by Sir W. W. Greg ('The Shakespeare First Folio', 1955) and C. Hinman ('The Printing and Proof-reading of the First Folio of Shakespeare', 1963).

Folklore, the traditional beliefs, legends, and customs current among the common people; and the study of them.

Folliott, THE REVD. DOCTOR, a character in Peacock's 'Crotchet Castle' (q.v.).

Fontarabia, now FUENTERRABIA, in Spain. Milton appears to have confused it with Roncesvalles, some forty miles away, where the rout of the rearguard of Charlemagne's army is generally supposed to have occurred (cf. 'Paradise Lost', i. 587).

Fool of Quality, The, a novel by Henry Brooke (1703-63), published in 1766-72.

It was highly admired by John Wesley, who edited it for Methodist use, and by Charles Kingsley (q.v.), who contributed a laudatory preface to the edition of 1859.

Foote, SAMUEL (1720-77), actor and dramatist, was particularly successful in comic mimicry; acting in his own plays, he caricatured his fellow actors and various well-known persons. He wrote a number of short dramatic sketches of two or three acts, depending largely for their success on topical allusions. He was known to his contemporaries as the English Aristophanes, counsel in a libel action having likened his client to Socrates and Foote to Aristophanes.

Foppington, LORD, a character in Vanbrugh's comedy 'The Relapse', and Sheridan's 'A Trip to Scarborough'; also in Colley Cibber's 'The Careless Husband'.

Ford and Mrs. Ford, characters in Shakespeare's 'The Merry Wives of Windsor' (q.v.).

Ford, FORD MADOX (formerly Ford Madox Hueffer) (1873-1939), author. In 1908 he founded 'The English Review', which he edited until the end of 1909 and which published the first stories of D. H. Lawrence and whose contributors included Hardy, Henry James, Galsworthy, and H. G. Wells (qq.v.). He collaborated with Conrad (q.v.) in the novels 'The Inheritors' (1901) and 'Romance' (1903). Of his own large output of novels the best known are 'The Good Soldier' (1915) and the Tietjens sequence, 'Some Do Not' (1924), 'No More Parades' (1925), 'A Man Could Stand Up' (1926), 'The Last Post' (1928), subsequently collected under the title 'Parade's End'. His work includes critical studies, verse, and reminiscences.

Ford, JOHN (*fl.* 1639), dramatist, was born in Devonshire, and was admitted at the Middle Temple in 1602. He probably spent his last years in Devonshire. Some of his plays have perished (four were destroyed by Warburton's (q.v.) cook). Of those which have survived, the chief are 'The Lover's Melancholy' (1629), ''Tis Pity she's a Whore' (1633), 'The Broken Heart' (1633), 'Perkin Warbeck' (1634). He collaborated with Dekker and Rowley in 'The Witch of Edmonton'. The principal characteristic of his work is the powerful depiction of melancholy, sorrow, and despair. A vivid little portrait of him has been preserved in the couplet, from the 'Time-Poets' ('Choice Drollery', 1656):

> Deep in a dump John Ford was alone got,
> With folded arms and melancholy hat.

Lamb greatly admired his work and describes him as 'the last of the Elizabethans'.

Forgers and Fabricators, LITERARY, and other **Impostors**, see under *Chatterton, Croyland History, Dodd, Ireland, Lauder, Mandeville, Munchausen, Psalmanazar*.

There is a remarkable invocation of forgers and impostors in ch. xx of Anatole France's 'M. Bergeret à Paris'.

Forrest, The, a collection of miscellaneous short poems by Jonson (q.v.), printed in the folio of 1616. It includes the beautiful songs: 'Drink to me only with thine eyes', and 'Come, my Celia, let us prove'.

Fors Clavigera, a collection of letters to the workmen of Great Britain, by Ruskin (q.v.), published in 1871-84.

This remarkable collection deals with a great variety of subjects, though the underlying motive—the redress of poverty and misery—is present throughout.

Forster, EDWARD MORGAN, O.M. (1879-1970), novelist. He lived for a time in Italy, the background of 'Where Angels Fear to Tread' (1905) and 'A Room with a View' (1908). 'The Longest Journey' (1907), which has a considerable element of autobiography, was followed by 'Howards End' (q.v., 1910) and 'A Passage to India' (q.v., 1924). Forster's experiences in India, where he went in 1912 and in 1921, are described in 'The Hill of Devi' (1953). He also wrote the short stories: 'The Celestial Omnibus' (1914) and 'The Eternal Moment' (1928), and essays. He wrote, with Eric Crozier, the libretto for Benjamin Britten's opera 'Billy Budd' (1951). 'Some Aspects of the Novel' is the title of his Clark lectures at Cambridge (1927).

Forster, JOHN (1812-76), edited the 'Foreign Quarterly Review' in 1842-3, the 'Daily News' in 1846, and the 'Examiner' in 1847-55. Forster wrote a number of biographical works: 'Life and Adventures of Oliver Goldsmith' (1848), 'Life of Walter Savage Landor' (1869), 'Life of Charles Dickens' (1872-4), and the first volume of a 'Life of Swift' (1876).

Forsyte Saga, see *Galsworthy*.

Fortescue, SIR JOHN (1394?-1476?), chief justice of the king's bench under Henry VI, and the earliest English constitutional lawyer. His principal works were a Latin treatise, 'De Natura Legis Naturae' (1461-3), distinguishing absolute from constitutional monarchy; an English treatise on the same subject; a Latin treatise, 'De Laudibus Legum Angliae' (1471); and an English work 'On the Governance of England'.

Fortescue, HON. SIR JOHN (1859-1933), author of a 'History of the British Army' (1899-1929), and other works of military history.

Forties, THE HUNGRY, a term applied to a period of acute distress in England, resulting from a series of bad harvests beginning in 1837, coupled with the taxation of imported wheat. This distress culminated in 1842, and was marked by the Chartist and Anti-Corn-Law agitations.

Fortnightly Review, The, was founded in 1865, as the organ of advanced liberalism, and edited successively by G. H. Lewes, John Morley (1867-83), and Frank Harris among others. It was at first issued fortnightly, but before long only once a month.

Fortunate Isles, THE, in the belief of the ancient Greeks and Romans, lay west of the Pillars of Hercules in the Atlantic Ocean. They are represented as the seat of the blessed, where the souls of the virtuous were placed after death.

Fortunate Mistress, The, see *Roxana*.

Fortunatus's purse, the subject of a European 15th-cent. romance, translated into many languages and dramatized by Dekker. For the story see *Old Fortunatus*.

Fortune, MR. REGINALD, in H. C. Bailey's detective stories, the adviser of the C.I.D.

Fortunes of Nigel, The, a novel by Sir W. Scott (q.v.) (1822).

The young Nigel Olifaunt, Lord Glenvarloch, threatened with the loss of his ancestral estate if he is unable promptly to redeem a heavy mortgage, comes to London to endeavour to recover from James I a sum of 40,000 marks advanced to the latter at a crisis in his fortunes by Nigel's father. The story concerns his adventures in London, their successful issue, and his marriage to Margaret Ramsay, the clockmaker's daughter.

The novel contains a number of interesting characters, including the pedantic freakish James I; Richard Moniplies, Nigel's conceited servant; Dame Ursula Suddlechop, milliner and secret agent; the miser Trapbois and his austere daughter; the rattling Templar, Lowestoffe; and the embittered courtier, Sir Mungo Malagrowther.

Forty-five, THE, the year 1745, and the Jacobite rebellion in that year.

Forty Thieves, THE, see *Ali Baba*.

Foscari, The Two, see *Two Foscari*.

Fosco, COUNT, a character in Wilkie Collins's 'The Woman in White' (q.v.).

Fosse Way, THE, a Roman road running across England from Bath to Lincoln.

Foster, ANTHONY, a character in Scott's 'Kenilworth' (q.v.).

Fotheringay, MISS, the stage name of Emily Costigan, in Thackeray's 'Pendennis' (q.v.).

Foulis, ROBERT (1707-76), a barber's apprentice at Glasgow. With his brother Andrew he visited Oxford and France in 1738-40 collecting rare books, and started as bookseller and printer at Glasgow. He printed for the university their first Greek book (1743) and a number of other remarkable books.

Foul Play, a novel by Reade (q.v.) (1869).

Fountain of Youth, *fontaine de jouvence*, in the 'Roman d'Alisandre' (see under *Alexander the Great*), a magic fountain in which Alexander and his army bathe, and are thereby restored to the prime of life.

The belief in a fountain possessing this magical property was widespread in the Middle Ages.

Four Dialogues of the Dead, see *Dialogues of the Dead*.

Four Georges, *The*, lectures on Kings George I–IV and their times, delivered by Thackeray (q.v.) in the United States and London in 1855-6, printed in 'The Cornhill Magazine', 1860.

Four Horsemen of the Apocalypse, *The*, a novel by B. Ibañez (q.v.); it was the basis of one of the earliest spectacular films.

Fourierism, a communistic system for the reorganization of society devised by Charles Fourier (1772-1837), a French author. Under it the population was to be grouped in *phalansteries*, or socialistic groups of about 1,800 persons, who would live together as one family and hold property in common.

Four Just Men, *The*, a well-known novel by Edgar Wallace (q.v.). The Four Just Men undertake a crusade for the destruction of noxious members of society.

Four P's, *The*, a famous interlude (q.v.) by J. Heywood (q.v.). It has no plot but considerable humour.

Fourteenth of July, see *Bastille*.

Fourth Estate, THE, the Press. The expression is attributed by Carlyle to Burke, but not traced in his speeches. A correspondent of 'Notes and Queries' (1st Series, xi. 452) attributes it to Brougham.

Fourth of June, an Eton College celebration.

Fourth of July, 'Independence Day', in the United States, the anniversary of the day on which, in 1776, was signed the Declaration of Independence, by which the original thirteen States of the union broke their allegiance to the British crown.

Fowler, HENRY WATSON (1858-1933) and Francis George (1870-1918), lexicographers and grammarians; joint authors of 'The King's English' (1906), 'The Concise Oxford Dictionary' (1911), and 'The Pocket Oxford Dictionary' (1924). 'A Dictionary of Modern English Usage' (1926; 2nd edition, 1965, ed. Sir E. Gowers) is the work of H. W. Fowler.

Fowler, KATHERINE, see *Philips (K.)*.

Fox, CHARLES JAMES (1749-1806), became M.P. for Midhurst in 1768, making his mark by his speeches against Wilkes in 1769, and was a lord of the Admiralty under Lord North in 1770; but his independent attitude brought him into disfavour with the king, and he was dismissed from the ministry in 1774. In 1782 he was appointed foreign secretary in Lord Rockingham's ministry, but was thwarted by Shelburne and resigned when the latter became premier. In 1783 he formed a coalition with North, but was dismissed in the same year. He was one of the managers of the proceedings against Warren Hastings, and was a constant opponent of the policy of Pitt (during the first long ministry of the latter). When Napoleon obviously threatened invasion, Fox was willing to serve with Pitt in the 1804 Ministry, but the prejudice of George III excluded him. After Trafalgar he held that the danger was over; he soon found out Napoleon's duplicity however, and his last act was to knit up close relations with Russia against France. Fox was a man of great personal charm, noted for his love of letters and his scholarship; also for his passion for gambling and for the influence he exercised over the Prince of Wales.

For the 'Early History of Charles James Fox' see under *Trevelyan (Sir George)*.

Fox, GEORGE (1624-91), founder of the Society of Friends (q.v.). His 'Journal', revised by a committee under William Penn's superintendence (1694), is a narrative, in simple and direct style, of his spiritual experiences and of the troubles to which he and his followers were exposed by persecution.

Foxe, JOHN (1516-87), the martyrologist, became a fellow of Magdalen College, Oxford, but resigned in 1545, being unwilling to conform to the statutes in religious matters. In 1554 he retired to the Continent, and issued at Strasburg his 'Commentarii' (the earliest draft of his 'Actes and Monuments'). On his return to England he was ordained priest by Grindal in 1560, and in 1564 joined John Day, the printer, who in 1563 had issued the English version of the 'Rerum in ecclesia gestarum . . . Commentarii' as 'Actes and Monuments' (q.v.), popularly known as the 'Book of Martyrs'. Four editions of the 'Actes and Monuments' (1563, 1570, 1576, and 1583) appeared in the author's lifetime; of the posthumous issues, that of 1641 contains a memoir of Foxe, attributed to his son, but of doubtful authenticity.

Fra Angelico, see *Angelico, Fra*.

Fra Diavolo ('Brother Devil'), the popular name of an Italian brigand, Michele Pezza (1771-1806), connected with political movements in southern Italy at the beginning of the 19th cent. He was leader of a troop of guerrillas, and was arrested and shot. He is the subject of the famous opera by Auber which bears his name.

Fradubio, in Spenser's 'Faerie Queene', I. ii. 32 et seq., 'the doubter', the lover of Fraelissa; he doubts whether her beauty is equal to that of Duessa. Duessa transforms Fraelissa into a tree, obtains Fradubio's love, and when he discovers her deformity, turns him also into a tree.

Fra Lippo Lippi, a poem by R. Browning (q.v.), in 'Men and Women' (1855).

The painter monk (Fra Filippo Lippi, *c.* 1406?-1469) narrates his life: his entry as a half-starved child into a Carmelite convent, and his present mode of life, painting under the influence of the prior's doctrine, but breaking bounds at times.

Framley Parsonage, a novel by A. Trollope (q.v.) (1861). The fourth of the Barsetshire series.

France, ANATOLE, the pseudonym of JACQUES ANATOLE FRANÇOIS THIBAULT (1844-1924), French man of letters, the son of a bookseller. His first book of stories 'Jocaste et le chat maigre' appeared in 1879, followed in 1881 by 'Le Crime de Sylvestre Bonnard', which established his reputation as a novelist. He thereafter produced a long series of witty, graceful, and satirical tales, of which the best known are the following: 'Le Livre de mon ami' (1885); 'Thaïs' (1890); 'Sur la pierre

blanche' (1905); four political satires with the figure of M. Bergeret as the centre; 'L'Île des pingouins' (1908); 'La Révolte des anges' (1914); 'Le Petit Pierre' (1918).

Francesca da Rimini, see *Paolo and Francesca*.

Franceschini, COUNT GUIDO, a character in Browning's 'The Ring and the Book' (q.v.).

Francis, SIR PHILIP (1740-1818), became a junior clerk in the office of the secretary of state in 1756, and clerk or amanuensis to General Edward Bligh, Lord Kinnoul, and the elder Pitt. From 1762 to 1772 he was a clerk in the War Office. He became one of the four newly appointed councillors of the governor-general of India in 1774. He opposed Warren Hastings and was wounded in a duel with him. He left India in 1780, became a member of parliament, and assisted Burke to prepare the charges against Hastings. He was intimate with the Prince Regent and was created a K.C.B.

There is strong evidence, but falling short of certainty, for identifying Francis with the author of the letters of 'Junius' (q.v.).

Franciscans, an order of friars founded by St. Francis of Assisi (q.v.) about 1209. Their rules require chastity, poverty, and obedience, and special stress is laid on preaching and ministry to the sick. They came to England about 1220, where they were known as Minors, Minorites, or Greyfriars (from the colour of their dress). See also *Capuchins*.

Francis of Assisi, ST., GIOVANNI FRANCESCO BERNARDONE (1181?-1226), experienced as a young man a spiritual crisis while on a military expedition, in consequence of which he lived for a time in solitude and prayer and devoted himself to the relief of the poor, the sick, and the lepers. He was joined by disciples, the first of the Franciscan order, for whom he drew up the rule. He preached in Italy, and went to the Holy Land and Spain. The special note of his teaching was joyousness and love of nature (St. Francis preaching to the birds is a favourite subject in art).

Frankenstein, or the Modern Prometheus, a tale of terror by Mary W. Shelley (q.v.) (1818).

Byron and the Shelleys spent part of a wet summer in Switzerland in reading and writing ghost stories. 'Frankenstein', developed into a long story at her husband's suggestion, was Mrs. Shelley's contribution.

Frankenstein learns the secret of imparting life to inanimate matter. Collecting bones from the charnel-houses he constructs the semblance of a human being and gives it life. The creature, endowed with supernatural size and strength, but revolting in appearance, inspires loathing in whoever sees it. Lonely and miserable, it is filled with hatred for its creator, and murders Frankenstein's brother and his bride. Frankenstein pursues it to the Arctic regions to destroy it, but dies in the pursuit. The monster looks at his dead body and claims him as its last victim, then disappears in order to end its own life.

Frankie and Johnny, or FRANKIE AND ALBERT, the most popular specimen of modern American balladry, of Negro origin and known to exist in more than two hundred variants.

Franklin, BENJAMIN (1706–90), born in Boston, Mass., and largely self-educated, was sent on a political mission to England in 1757. This was the beginning of his long diplomatic career in Europe as the agent of the American colonies, in the course of which he negotiated the alliance between them and France, and finally appeared as one of the signatories to the treaty of peace between the United States and Great Britain.

He wrote voluminously, on political, economic, and scientific subjects (he was an experimenter and inventor). He was a man of cool calculating reason and broad humanity in politics, rather than of high moral principle. Among his writings mention may be made of his ironical 'Edict

by the King of Prussia' and 'Rules by which a Great Empire may be reduced to a Small One', which appeared in the 'Gentleman's Magazine' in 1773; and of his 'Autobiography' (the first authentic edition was that of Bigelow, 1868; imperfect texts had appeared from 1793).

Franklin, SIR JOHN (1786–1847), Arctic explorer, was author of two remarkable 'Narratives' of voyages to the Polar Sea (1823 and 1828). Franklin started on his last voyage of discovery, with the 'Erebus' and 'Terror', in 1845, and never returned.

Franklin's Tale, The, see *Canterbury Tales*.

Fraser's Magazine, founded in 1830 by Maginn (q.v.) and Hugh Fraser. Among the notable early contributors to it were Carlyle, Lockhart, Theodore Hook, Hogg, Coleridge, Harrison Ainsworth, Thackeray, Southey, and Barry Cornwall. It was taken over by Longmans in 1863, and ceased to appear in 1882. It was edited by J. A. Froude (q.v.), 1860–74.

Frazer, SIR JAMES GEORGE (1854–1941), fellow of Trinity College, Cambridge, held the chair of social anthropology at Liverpool, 1907–22. His publications include: 'Totemism' (1887), 'The Golden Bough' (q.v.), of which the first volume appeared in 1890 and the twelfth and last in 1915, and a large number of other works on anthropology and folklore.

Frea, see *Freya*.

Frederick, the usurping duke in Shakespeare's 'As You Like It' (q.v.).

Frederick Barbarossa, see *Barbarossa*.

Frederick the Great, Friedrich II of Prussia (1712–86), son of Friedrich Wilhelm I and Sophia Dorothea, daughter of George I of England, ascended the throne in 1740. He engaged in prolonged wars with Austria, the dominions of which had passed to Maria Theresa by virtue of the Pragmatic Sanction; and was supported by England, mainly through subsidies, in the Seven Years War (1756). By his military talent he raised Prussia to the position of a powerful state, while his intellectual interests were shown by his long intimacy with Voltaire (q.v.). See also *Carlyle* (*T.*).

Freeman, MRS., the name under which the duchess of Marlborough corresponded with Queen Anne. The latter called herself Mrs. Morley.

Freeman, EDWARD AUGUSTUS (1823–92), Regius professor of modern history at Oxford from 1884 to 1892, was a historian of eminence (particularly in regard to the eleventh and twelfth centuries of English history). His principal works were the 'History of the Norman Conquest' (1867–79), 'Growth of the English Constitution' (1872), 'Methods of Historical Study' (1886), 'Chief Periods of European History' (1886), and the first volume of a 'History of Federal Government' (1863). In his historical works Freeman relied wholly on printed chronicles and knew nothing of manuscripts. Many of his conclusions have in consequence been upset.

Freeman, MARY E. WILKINS (1852–1930), American author, distinguished for her realistic stories of New England life. Her best-known books are: 'A Humble Romance and Other Stories' (1887), and 'A New England Nun and Other Stories' (1891).

Freemason, originally a member of a certain class of skilled workers in stone who had a system of secret signs and passwords by which they could be recognized. The term first occurs in the 14th cent. Early in the 17th cent. the societies of freemasons began to admit honorary members, known as ACCEPTED MASONS, who were admitted to a knowledge of the secret signs and instructed in the legendary history of the craft. In 1717, four of these societies or 'lodges' in London united to form a 'grand lodge', whose object was mutual help and the promotion of brotherly feeling among its members. The London 'grand lodge' became the parent of other lodges in Great Britain and abroad, and there are now powerful bodies of freemasons, more or less recognizing each other in most countries of the world.

French, INSPECTOR, in Freeman Wills Croft's detective stories, a member of the C.I.D.

French Revolution, THE, is generally regarded as beginning with the meeting of the States General in May 1789. The Bastille was stormed on 14 July 1789, and the royal family was removed from Versailles to Paris in October of the same year. The king's attempted flight from Paris took place in June 1791. The Legislative Assembly sat from Oct. 1791 to Sept. 1792, when, under the menace of the allied advance, it was replaced by the National Convention, and the Republic was proclaimed. The king was brought to trial in Dec. 1792, and executed 21 Jan. 1793. The institution of the Committee of Public Safety and of the Revolutionary Tribunal immediately followed. The Reign of Terror developed during the summer of 1793 and lasted until the fall of Robespierre, 27 July (9 Thermidor) 1794. The Convention in Oct. 1795 gave place to the Directory, which in turn gave place to the Consulate in 1799. Napoleon became emperor in May 1804.

French Revolution, The, A History, by T. Carlyle (1837).

The work was written in London. The manuscript of the first volume, while in the keeping of John Stuart Mill, was accidentally destroyed, but the author courageously set to work to re-write it. The history, beginning with the death of Louis XV in 1774, extends to 5 Oct. 1795, when Buonaparte quelled the insurrection of Vendémiaire. The work, said to be a very partial view of the Revolution, may be regarded as the poetic unrolling of a great historical drama, illustrating the nemesis that comes upon the oppression of the poor. It offers in addition a gallery of magnificent portraits (Mirabeau, Lafayette, Danton, Robespierre), and stamps upon the memory such episodes as the march to Versailles, the fall of the Bastille, and the flight to Varennes.

Frere, JOHN HOOKHAM (1769–1846), a friend of Canning and British envoy at

Lisbon (1800–2), at Madrid (1802–4), and with the Junta (1808–9). While at Eton, Frere wrote a translation of 'Brunanburh' (q.v.). He was one of the founders of 'The Microcosm' periodical (1786–7), and contributed to 'The Anti-Jacobin' (q.v.). He collaborated in Ellis's 'Specimens of the Early English Poets' (1801) and in Southey's 'Chronicle of the Cid' (1808), and was one of the founders of 'The Quarterly Review' (q.v.).

Freud, SIGMUND (1856–1939), born at Freiberg in Moravia, of a Jewish family, is known as the inventor of psycho-analysis. His studies led him to important conclusions as to the influence of a sub-conscious element in the mind and also as to the importance of the sexual motive in human behaviour. He was expelled from Austria in 1938.

Frey or FREYR, in Scandinavian mytho-logy, the god of fertility and dispenser of rain and sunshine.

Freya or FREYJA, in Scandinavian mytho-logy, the most beautiful of the goddesses, the northern Venus, the goddess of love and of the night.

Friar Bacon and Friar Bungay, The honorable historie of, a comedy in verse and prose by R. Greene (q.v.), acted in 1594. Bacon with the help of Friar Bungay makes a head of brass, and, conjuring up the Devil, learns how to give it speech. After watching day and night for three weeks, Bacon hands over to his servant Miles and falls asleep. The head speaks two words 'Time is'. Miles, thinking his master would be angry if waked for so little, lets him sleep. The head presently speaks again, 'Time was'; and finally 'Time is past', when it falls down and breaks. Bacon awakes, and heaps curses on Miles's head. The above is diversified with the pleasant story of the loves of Edward Prince of Wales (afterwards Edward I) and Lord Lacy for the fair Margaret, the keeper's daughter of Freshingfield, and the prince's surrender of her to Lacy.

Friar Bungay, see *Bungay* (*T.*).

Friars Minor, the Franciscans (q.v.).

Friar's or *Frere's Tale, The*, see *Canterbury Tales*.

Friar Tuck, one of the characters in the legend of Robin Hood (q.v.); the jovial and pugnacious father-confessor of the outlaw chief. He figures in Scott's 'Ivanhoe' and in Peacock's 'Maid Marian'.

Friday, MAN, see *Robinson Crusoe*.

Friends, SOCIETY OF, a religious society founded in 1648–50 by George Fox (q.v.), distinguished by peaceful principles and plainness of dress and manners. See *Quakers*.

Frigga, in Scandinavian mythology, the wife of Odin (q.v.), the goddess of married love and of the hearth. Our 'Friday' is named from her.

Friscobaldo, ORLANDO, see *Orlando Friscobaldo*.

Frith, MARY, see *Moll Cutpurse*.

Froissart, JEAN (1337?–*c.* 1410), a French chronicler, visited England after the peace of Brétigny (1360) and was received at the court of Edward III and Queen Philippa his countrywoman. His travels extended to Scotland, Italy, and Belgium. His 'Chroniques' cover the period 1325–1400. Three editions of them were issued at different periods of his life. They are the work of a literary artist rather than a trustworthy historian, but give a faithful picture of the broad features of his period, and are instinct with the spirit of chivalry. They were admirably translated into English by John Bourchier, Lord Berners (q.v.), 1523–5.

Fronde, THE, the name given to the rebellion which took place (1648–52) in France against Mazarin and the court during the minority of Louis XIV. The word *fronde* means a sling.

Frost, ROBERT (1874–1963), American poet. He farmed in England from 1912 to 1915, where his first two volumes of verse, 'A Boy's Will' (1913) and 'North of Boston' (1914), were published, and where he became a friend of Edward Thomas. On his return to New England he devoted himself to poetry, supporting himself by teaching. He became one of the most popular of modern American poets. Ten volumes of his verse were collected in 1949, and his last volume of lyrics, 'In the Clearing', appeared in 1962.

Froude, JAMES ANTHONY (1818-94), was educated at Oriel College, Oxford, where, like his brother, R. H. Froude (q.v.), he took part in the Tractarian Movement and came under the influence of Newman; but on the latter's secession he reacted towards scepticism. He became a friend of C. Kingsley, and made the acquaintance of Carlyle in 1849, subsequently becoming his chief disciple. In 1856-70 he published his 'History of England from the Fall of Wolsey to the Defeat of the Spanish Armada', which has been criticized on the score of inaccuracy and prolixity. In 1872-4 he published 'The English in Ireland in the Eighteenth Century', which met with severe criticism, from Lecky (q.v.) among others. From 1881 to 1884 he was engaged, as Carlyle's literary executor, in issuing biographical remains of Carlyle and his wife, the frankness with which he discharged this task provoking much indignation. Froude visited Australia in 1884-5, and published 'Oceana, or England and her Colonies' in 1886; he visited the West Indies in 1886-7, and published 'The English in the West Indies' in 1888. He was appointed Regius professor of modern history at Oxford in 1892.

Froude, RICHARD HURRELL (1803-36), brother of J. A. Froude (q.v.), was educated at Oriel College, Oxford, of which he became a fellow. He was intimate with Newman, with whom he wrote the poems contained in 'Lyra Apostolica' (1836), and greatly influenced the Tractarians, contributing three of the 'Tracts for the Times' (see under *Oxford Movement*). His 'Remains' (1838-9), including strictures on the Reformation, helped to rouse public hostility against the Tractarian Movement.

Fry, CHRISTOPHER (1907-), dramatist. His verse plays owe their success to his skill as a poet and his experience as an actor and producer. Among the best known are: 'A Phoenix too Frequent' (1946), 'The Lady's not for Burning' (1948), 'Venus Observed' (1950), and 'A Sleep of Prisoners' (1951). He has also translated plays by Anouilh and by Giraudoux (q.v.).

Fry, MRS. ELIZABETH (1780-1845), *née* GURNEY, a Quaker reformer and successful preacher, celebrated for her efforts to improve the state of the prisons.

Fudge Family in Paris, The, satirical verses by T. Moore (q.v.) (1818).

These light verses take the form of letters written by or to various members of the Fudge family when visiting Paris in 1817.

Fugger News-letters, a collection of letters, consisting of about 36,000 pages of manuscript, sent mostly to Count Philip Edward Fugger (1546-1618). The letters cover the period 1568-1605. Two series of the Letters have been published in English: the first series (1924) being translated from a Vienna edition by P. de Chary, the second (1926), never before published, translated by L. S. R. Byrne.

Fulgens and Lucrece, a 15th-cent. secular play by Henry Medwall (*fl.* 1486); important in dramatic history as the earliest known English secular play.

Fuller, MARGARET (1810-50), American author, whose name is associated with the New England Transcendentalists, and with the movement for 'women's rights', in which she was a pioneer.

Fuller, THOMAS (1608-61), became a prebendary of Salisbury in 1631, and rector of Broadwindsor, Dorset, in 1634. Shortly before the Civil War he was made preacher at the Savoy, and followed the war as chaplain to Sir Ralph Hopton. After the Restoration he resumed his canonry and lectureship at the Savoy and became 'chaplain in extraordinary' to the king. He published his 'History of the Holy Warre', viz. the crusades, in 1639; 'The Holy State and the Profane State' 1642; 'A Pisgah-sight of Palestine', 1650; his 'Church History of Britain', and 'History of Cambridge University', 1655. 'The Worthies of England' (q.v.), his best-known and most characteristic work, appeared after his death, in 1662. His 'Good Thoughts in Bad Times' (1645), followed by two sequels, contain much 'sound, shrewd good sense, and freedom of intellect' (Coleridge). His writings, which were highly approved by Southey, Coleridge, and Lamb, are marked by humour and a quaint wit, sometimes a little incongruous with the subject.

Funeral, The, or Grief à-la-Mode, a comedy by R. Steele (q.v.), produced in 1701.

Funeral Oration, The, of Pericles, at the celebration for the Athenians who had fallen in the first year of the Peloponnesian War (431 B.C.). It is given in Thucydides, ii. 35 et seq.

Fungoso, a character in Jonson's 'Every Man out of his Humour' (q.v.).

Furies, or EUMENIDES, or ERINYES, THE, in Greek mythology, the avenging deities, who executed the curses pronounced upon criminals, or inflicted famines and pestilences. The name 'Eumenides', 'the kindly ones', is a euphemism used with a propitiatory purpose.

Furnivall, FREDERICK JAMES (1825-1910), became in 1861 editor of the suggested English Dictionary, which developed into the 'Oxford English Dictionary' (q.v.). He was founder of the Early English Text Society, the Chaucer Society, the Ballad and New Shakespere Societies, and the Shelley, Wyclif, and Browning Societies. He edited Chaucer's works and the 'Percy Ballads'. He was an enthusiastic oarsman, and helped to found the Working Men's College in London (1854).

Fust, JOHANN (*d.* 1467), German goldsmith. He financed Gutenberg's (q.v.) experiments in printing, but the partnership between them was dissolved probably in 1455 and Fust carried on with his son-in-law Peter Schöffer.

Futhorc, the runic alphabet, so named from its first six letters (th = þ). See also *Rune*.

Futurism, a 20th-cent. movement in Italian art, literature, and music, promoted by Marinetti (q.v.) and others. Futurist painting was a development of Cubism (q.v.), designed to represent nature not in a static but a dynamic state, to give in other words a cinematographic effect. Sévérin's 'Bal Tabarin' (1912) is regarded as a good illustration of the method. The movement was so named as being a glorification of youth and the future as against the academic past.

G

Gaberlunzie, a wandering mendicant; in Scotland a licensed beggar. There is a ballad of 'The Gaberlunzie Man' in Percy's 'Reliques'.

Gaboriau, ÉMILE (1835-73), French novelist, a pioneer in the romance of crime and its detection, and the creator of Monsieur Lecoq and Père Tabaret. His best-known works are: 'L'Affaire Lerouge' (1866), 'Monsieur Lecoq' (1869), and 'Les Esclaves de Paris' (1869).

Gabriel, the name of one of the arch-angels (Dan. ix. 21 and Luke i. 19, 26). Milton makes him 'Chief of the angelic guards' ('Paradise Lost', iv. 550).

Gabriel Lajeunesse, a character in Longfellow's 'Evangeline' (q.v.).

Gadarene Swine, THE MIRACLE OF THE, in Mark v, was the subject of a controversy between Huxley and Gladstone (qq.v.), in 'The Nineteenth Century' (1890-1), echoed in Gladstone's 'Impregnable Rock of Holy Scripture' and Huxley's 'Science and Christian Tradition'.

Gadshill, near Rochester, the scene of Falstaff's famous exploit ('1 Henry IV', II. ii), and also the name of one of Falstaff's companions. Gadshill was the home of Dickens in his later years.

Gael, a Scottish Highlander or Celt. The word in more recent times has also been applied to the Irish branch of the Celtic race.

Gahagan, MAJOR, see *Major Gahagan*.

Gaheris, SIR, in Malory's 'Morte Darthur', brother of Gawain, Agravain, and Gareth; by mishap slain by Sir Launcelot.

Gainsborough, THOMAS (1727–88), painter. His early paintings are landscapes and conversation pieces, and he continued to paint landscapes all his life, though he became a fashionable portrait painter and rival of Reynolds (q.v.).

Gairdner, JAMES (1828–1912), was associated with J. S. Brewer in the preparation of the voluminous 'Calendar of Letters and Papers of the Reign of King Henry VIII' for the Rolls Series, and completed the work after Brewer's death. He published the standard edition of the Paston Letters (q.v.) in 1904, and lives of Richard III and Henry VII (1878 and 1889). In 1908 he began to publish his longest work, 'Lollardy and the Reformation in England', of which vol. iv was issued after his death.

Gai saber, Provençal, the gay science, the poetry of the troubadours (q.v.).

Galahad, SIR, in Malory's 'Morte Darthur', is (by enchantment) the son of Launcelot and Elaine, daughter of King Pelles. He is predestined by his immaculate purity to achieve the quest of the Holy Grail (see *Grail*).

Galahalt or GALAHAULT, SIR, described in Malory's 'Morte Darthur' as the 'haut prince' of Surluse and the Long Isles, is, in the story of the early loves of Launcelot and Guinevere, as told in a 13th-cent. French romance, the knight who introduces Launcelot to the queen.

Galatea, (1) a sea-nymph, loved by the Cyclops Polyphemus (q.v.); (2) also the name given to the statue wrought by Pygmalion (q.v.) and brought to life.

Galathea, a play by Lyly (q.v.).

Galen or GALENUS, CLAUDIUS (c. A.D. 129–99), a celebrated physician, and a friend of Marcus Aurelius. He is said to have written no fewer than 500 treatises, of which over a hundred survive. He wrote in Greek. Linacre (q.v.) translated six of his works, and there are references to him in Chaucer.

Galeotti, MARTIUS, in Scott's 'Quentin Durward' (q.v.), the astrologer of Louis XI.

Galileo Galilei (1564–1642), Italian astronomer and physicist, was born at Pisa of a Florentine family. He made important discoveries and experiments. His observations brought him into conflict with the Inquisition, and in 1633 he was compelled to repudiate the Copernican theory and was sent to prison, where Milton (q.v.) visited him.

Galliambic, the metre of the 'Attis' of Catullus, imitated by Tennyson in his 'Boadicea' and by G. Meredith in his 'Phaethon'.

Galligantus, a giant slain by Jack the Giant-killer (q.v.).

Gallio, in Acts xviii, the proconsul of Achaia (and brother of Seneca). 'A careless Gallio' is a term of reproach in the Puritan literature of the 17th century.

Galsworthy, JOHN (1867–1933), novelist and dramatist. His most important work is the series of novels, including 'The Man of Property' (1906), 'In Chancery' (1920), and 'To Let' (1921), collectively entitled 'The Forsyte Saga', of which the main theme is the possessive instinct, embodied to an exaggerated degree in Soames Forsyte. The record of the later Forsyte family extends over the later Victorian period, and is resumed in 'A Modern Comedy' (1929), containing 'The White Monkey' (1924), 'The Silver Spoon' (1926), and 'Swan Song' (1928). In these the author depicts a society whose foundations have been shattered by the Great

War, but in which the Victorianism of a glum Soames Forsyte here and there survives. Among Galsworthy's other best-known novels are 'The Island Pharisees' (1904), 'The Country House' (1907), 'Fraternity' (1909), 'The Patrician' (1911).

Of Galsworthy's plays the most notable are: 'The Silver Box', 1909; 'Strife' (an industrial dispute in which reconciliation is occasioned by the death of the wife of the men's leader), 1909; 'Justice' (a criticism of the existing prison system), 1910; 'The Skin Game' (a conflict between a parvenu manufacturer and an old-established aristocrat), 1920; and 'Loyalties', 1922.

Galt, JOHN (1779-1839), born in Ayrshire, was employed for some time in the custom-house at Greenock. While travelling on the Continent he made the acquaintance of Byron (of whom he published a life in 1830), and subsequently of Carlyle, by whom he was favourably noticed. In 1824 he visited Canada as secretary of a land company. Galt did a great amount of miscellaneous writing. His poems, dramas, historical novels, and travels call for no special notice. But he wrote three admirable studies of country life in Scotland, by which he is remembered: 'The Ayrshire Legatees' (1821), 'Annals of the Parish' (1821), and 'The Entail' (1823).

Gama, KING, in Tennyson's 'The Princess' (q.v.), the father of Princess Ida.

Gama, VASCO DA (c. 1469-1524), a great Portuguese navigator, who was the first to double the Cape of Good Hope (1497) and sail to India, the hero of the 'Lusiads' of Camoëns (q.v.).

Game and Playe of the Chesse, The, a translation by Caxton (q.v.) from Vignay's French version of the 'Liber de ludo scacchorum' of Jacobus de Cessolis, and probably the second book printed at Caxton's press in Bruges, c. 1475.

Game at Chesse, A, a comedy by T. Middleton (q.v.), produced in 1624 and chiefly interesting in its political connection.

It deals allegorically with the rivalry of England and Spain (the White House and the Black House), and the project of the 'Spanish Marriage' (1623). The play gave great offence to the Spanish Ambassador and to King James, and was prohibited.

Gamelyn, The Tale of, a verse romance of c. 1350, containing some 900 lines.

The piece is interesting because apparently Chaucer intended to make it his 'Cook's Tale of Gamelyn' in 'The Canterbury Tales' (q.v.); also as providing materials for Shakespeare's 'As You Like It', and as connected with the Robin Hood story.

Gamester, The, a comedy by James Shirley (q.v.), acted in 1633, printed in 1637.

Gammer Gurton's Needle, the second English comedy in verse (the first being 'Ralph Roister Doister', q.v.), was published in 1575, having previously been acted, in 1566, at Christ's College, Cambridge. Its authorship has been attributed to J. Still (q.v.), but the evidence is inconclusive and an alternative suggestion is that it may have been written by William Stevenson, a fellow of the College. It is written in rhymed long doggerel, and deals farcically with the losing and finding of the needle used to mend the garments of Hodge, Gammer Gurton's man. The play includes the famous old drinking-song with the refrain:

> Back and side go bare, go bare,
>   Both foot and hand go cold;
> But Belly, God send thee good ale
>   enough,
>   Whether it be new or old!

Gamp, SARAH, a character in Dickens's 'Martin Chuzzlewit' (q.v.). Her large cotton umbrella has given rise to the expression 'a gamp', for an umbrella, especially an untidy one; also for a midwife.

Gandercleugh, the imaginary place of residence of Jedediah Cleishbotham in Scott's 'Tales of My Landlord' (q.v.).

Gandish's, in Thackeray's 'The Newcomes' (q.v.), Professor Gandish's

'Academy of Drawing', where young Clive studies art.

Ganelon or GANO, in the Charlemagne romances, the traitor who schemes for the defeat of the rearguard at Roncesvalles. He figures in Dante's 'Inferno' (xxxii. 122) and Chaucer's 'Nun's Priest's Tale'.

Ganymedes or GANYMEDE, a beautiful youth of Phrygia, was carried up into heaven by an eagle at the command of Zeus, and became cup-bearer to the gods in place of Hebe.

Garamond, CLAUDE (*d.* 1561), French type-founder. His elegant roman types were widely adopted in France. His Greek type, cut for Francis I, was used by R. Estienne (1503-59).

Garden, The, a poem by Marvell (q.v.).

Garden of Cyrus, a treatise on the merits of the quincunx (: · :), by Sir Thomas Browne (q.v.), published (with 'Urn Burial', q.v.) in 1658.

This is a lighter work than its companion piece, treating quaintly of the Gardens of Antiquity and in particular of those of Cyrus as described by Xenophon, and of the garden of Paradise (with the Tree of Knowledge in the centre). From this the author passes to the use of the quincunx in a multitude of other connections, and certain mysterious properties of the number five, and concludes with a magnificent peroration.

Gardiner, COLONEL JAMES, a character in Scott's 'Waverley' (q.v.). The original of the character was the subject of a book by P. Doddridge (q.v.).

Gardiner, SAMUEL RAWSON (1829-1902), professor of modern history at King's College, London. The first instalment of his great 'History' of the first Stuarts and Cromwell appeared in 1863. Successive instalments followed, and in 1883-4 appeared a second edition of all these, entitled a 'History of England from the Accession of James I to the Outbreak of the Civil War, 1603-42'. The 'History of the Great Civil War' (1886-91) and the 'History of the Commonwealth and Protectorate' (1894-1901) carried the record

down to the year 1656 (an additional chapter was published posthumously). His writing shows minute accuracy and impartiality, but is lacking in picturesque quality.

Gareth, SIR, in Malory's 'Morte Darthur', nicknamed 'Beaumains' by Sir Kay the steward. See under *Gareth and Lynette* below.

Gareth and Lynette, one of Tennyson's 'Idylls of the King' (q.v.) (1872).

Gareth, son of Lot, king of Orkney, and Bellicent, obtains his mother's reluctant permission to go to the court on the condition that he will hire himself for a year there as a scullion. He presents himself in disguise and serves as a kitchen knave under Kay the Seneschal, until released from his vow by his mother. Lynette comes to the court to ask that Lancelot may release her sister Lyonors, besieged in her castle by four knights. The kitchen knave claims the adventure and to Lynette's disgust is granted it by the king. On the way she bitterly reviles him, but is gradually won over as he conquers the first three knights. Before his encounter with the fourth, named Death, she even trembles for his safety. But the fourth knight proves a mere boy masquerading in hideous armour.

> And he that told the tale in older times
> Says that Sir Gareth wedded Lyonors,
> But he, that told it later, says Lynette.

Gargantua, originally the name of a beneficent giant of French folklore, connected with the Arthurian cycle. It is probably to this folklore giant that Shakespeare refers in 'As You Like It', III. ii. 239. In Rabelais' 'La Vie très horrificque du Grand Gargantua', published in 1534, as a preliminary volume to 'Pantagruel' (q.v.), which had appeared in 1532, Gargantua is presented as a prince of gigantic stature and appetite, but also as studious, athletic, good-humoured, and peace-loving.

Gargery, JOE, a character in Dickens's 'Great Expectations' (q.v.).

Garibaldi, GIUSEPPE (1807-82), the celebrated Italian patriot and hero of the

Risorgimento (q.v.). He was enthusiastically received in England in 1864. Garibaldi's campaigns have been narrated by G. M. Trevelyan (q.v.).

Garland, Mr. and **Mrs.**, characters in Dickens's 'The Old Curiosity Shop' (q.v.).

Garland, Hamlin (1860-1940), American author, best known for his realistic studies of the Middle West.

Garnett, Constance (1861-1946), the daughter-in-law of Richard Garnett and mother of David Garnett (qq.v.), was a distinguished translator of the Russian classics. It was chiefly thanks to her that Russian literature exerted its influence in England in the first half of the 20th cent.

Garnett, David (1892-), novelist and critic, grandson of Richard Garnett (q.v.), author of 'Lady into Fox' (1923), 'The Man in the Zoo' (1929), etc.

Garnett, Richard (1835-1906), keeper of printed books in the British Museum, published in 1862 'Relics of Shelley', and in 1888 'The Twilight of the Gods' (pleasant apologues in Lucian's vein). He wrote brief biographies of Milton and Carlyle (1877), Emerson (1888), Edward Gibbon Wakefield (1898), and Coleridge (1904).

Garraway's, a celebrated coffee-house in Cornhill.

Garrick, David (1717-79), was S. Johnson's pupil at Edial, and accompanied him when he left Lichfield for London.

He first appeared as an actor at Ipswich in 'Oroonoko' in 1741, and in the same year made his reputation in the part of Richard III. He subsequently proved his versatility by many triumphs in both tragic and comic parts. In 1747 he joined Lacy in the management of Drury Lane, where he produced a large number of Shakespeare's dramas. He made his last appearance in 1776 and sold a moiety of his patent to Sheridan and two others for £35,000. He collaborated with Colman in writing 'The Clandestine Marriage' (q.v.), and also wrote a number of lively farces. He was a member of Johnson's Literary Club, and his portrait was painted by Reynolds, Hogarth, and Gainsborough. His interesting correspondence with many of the most distinguished men of his day was published in 1831-2, and, in a greatly enlarged collection, edited by D. M. Little and G. M. Kahrl, in 1963.

Garrick Club, The, founded in 1831, was much frequented by Thackeray, and possesses a famous collection of portraits of actors and actresses.

Garter, Order of the, the highest order of English knighthood. The institution of the order is attributed on the authority of Froissart to Edward III about the year 1344.

Garth, Sir Samuel (1661-1719), a physician, and a member of the Kit-Cat Club (q.v.), author of 'The Dispensary' (1699), a burlesque poem. Pope described him as 'the best good Christian without knowing it'.

Gascoigne, George (1525?-77), a man of a good Bedfordshire family, entered Gray's Inn and represented Bedfordshire in parliament. He is chiefly notable as a pioneer in various branches of literature. His 'Supposes', an adaptation of Ariosto's 'Suppositi', our earliest extant comedy in prose, was acted at Gray's Inn in 1566. In 1575 he issued 'The Posies of G. Gascoigne, corrected and completed', containing 'Jocasta' (paraphrased from the 'Phoenissae' of Euripides), the second earliest tragedy in English in blank verse. The book also contained 'Certain Notes of Instruction concerning the making of verse', the earliest English critical essay. He published his 'tragicall comedie', the 'Glasse of Government', a 'prodigal son' play, in 1575. His other works include 'The Steele Glas', a satire, published in 1576.

Gascoigne, Sir William (1350?-1419), appointed chief justice of the king's bench in 1400, figures in that capacity in Shakespeare's '2 Henry IV'. The story of his committing Henry V when Prince of Wales is without foundation.

Gashford, a character in Dickens's 'Barnaby Rudge' (q.v.).

Gaskell, ELIZABETH CLEGHORN (1810-65), novelist, daughter of William Stevenson, Unitarian minister, was brought up by her aunt at Knutsford in Cheshire, which is the original of Cranford, and of Hollingford (in 'Wives and Daughters'). In 1832 she married William Gaskell, minister at the Cross Street Unitarian chapel in Manchester. In 1848 she published 'Mary Barton', her first novel, based on the industrial troubles of the years 1842-3. It brought her into relations with Dickens, for whose 'Household Words' and 'All the Year Round' she subsequently wrote much. To the former of these she contributed in 1851-3 the famous series of papers subsequently republished under the title of 'Cranford' (q.v.). In 1853 appeared 'Ruth'; followed by 'North and South', in 1855, which reflects the easier industrial conditions that then prevailed. In 1857 Mrs. Gaskell produced her remarkable 'Life of Charlotte Brontë', some of the statements in which gave rise to complaint and were withdrawn. 'Wives and Daughters' appeared in 1864-6, but Mrs. Gaskell died before the work was quite completed. Her 'Letters', ed. J. A. V. Chapple and A. Pollard, were published in 1966.

Gaspar, one of the three Magi (q.v.) or 'Wise Men of the East'. He is represented as an Ethiopian, king of Tarshish.

Gauden, DR. JOHN (1605-62), bishop of Worcester. He claimed to be the author of 'Eikon Basilike' (q.v.).

Gauguin, PAUL (1848-1903), French painter. His exotic figure composition and landscapes, rendered in rich flat colours, were influential in the development of 20th-cent. art.

Gaunt, JOHN OF, see *John of Gaunt.*

Gautama, see *Buddha.*

Gautier, MARGUERITE, the heroine of 'La Dame aux Camélias' of Dumas fils (q.v.).

Gautier, (PIERRE JULES) THÉOPHILE (1811-72), French poet, novelist, and journalist, an extreme Romantic in youth, in later life an exponent of 'Art for art's sake'. As a novelist he is remembered by his 'Mademoiselle de Maupin' (1835) and his short stories.

Gawain (WALWAIN), is associated as a hero with King Arthur in the earliest of the Arthurian legends. He is the perfect knight, courageous, pure, and courteous. In the later developments of the story, however, his character shows deterioration. He is brother of Agravain, Gaheris, and Gareth. In Malory's 'Morte Darthur' he becomes the bitter enemy of Launcelot because the latter has killed his three brothers. He is killed when Arthur lands at Dover to recover his kingdom from Modred. The principal single adventure of Gawain is perhaps that described in 'Sir Gawain and the Green Knight' (q.v.). See also *Ywain and Gawain.*

Gawain and the Green Knight, Sir, an alliterative poem of 2,500 lines of the 14th cent. It is written in a north-west-midland dialect (for the author see under *Pearl*) and contains notable descriptive passages.

Gay, JOHN (1685-1732), published in 1708 an indifferent poem 'Wine'. He was secretary to the duchess of Monmouth during 1712-14. In 1713 he issued 'Rural Sports' on the model of Pope's 'Windsor Forest', and contributed to Steele's 'Guardian'. His 'Shepherd's Week', the first work that showed his real ability, appeared in 1714. His first play, 'What d'ye Call it', a satirical farce, was produced in 1715, and his 'Trivia' was published in 1716. With Pope and Arbuthnot he wrote 'Three Hours after Marriage', a comedy, which was acted in 1717. He became an inmate of the household of the duke and duchess of Queensberry, and in 1727 brought out the first series of his 'Fables', which were very popular. His 'Beggar's Opera' (q.v.) met with remarkable success in 1728, and was followed by the publication of its sequel 'Polly' (q.v.). The production of the latter on the stage was forbidden. These two plays contain many of Gay's pleasant ballads, but 'Sweet William's Farewell to Black-eyed Susan'

H

was published separately, and ''Twas when the seas were roaring' is from his first play. Some of his 'Eclogues' and the 'Epistles' deserve notice.

Gay, WALTER, a character in Dickens's 'Dombey and Son' (q.v.).

Gazette, from the Italian *gazzetta*, a news-sheet first published in Venice about the middle of the 16th cent. Similar news-sheets (see *Coranto*) appeared in England in the 17th cent., giving news from foreign parts.

The OXFORD GAZETTE was the first real newspaper, other than a newsletter, to be published in England. It appeared in Nov. 1665, the court being then at Oxford owing to the great plague, and was started by Henry Muddiman (q.v.) under the direction of Sir Joseph Williamson as a supplement to Muddiman's newsletters. It later became the 'London Gazette', which still survives. The 'London Gazette' is not now a newspaper, but a record of official appointments, notices of bankruptcies, etc., and in war time it is the official register of casualties.

Gazetteer, a geographical index or dictionary.

Ge or GAEA, in Greek mythology, the personification of the Earth, the wife of Uranus (q.v.), and mother of the Titans (q.v.).

Geber, an Arabian, thought to have been born at Seville at the end of the 8th cent. Certain Latin works on alchemy are regarded as translations from his Arabic text. Robert Burton speaks of him as 'that first inventor of Algebra', which implies an erroneous derivation of the latter word. *Gebir,* an epic poem by W. S. Landor (q.v.) (1798).

Geddes, JENNY, supposed name of the woman who threw a stool at Bishop Lindsay in St. Giles's, Edinburgh, when the new service was introduced, *temp.* Charles I.

Gehenna, originally a place-name, a valley near Jerusalem, which was at one time the scene of the idolatrous worship of the god Moloch. Thereafter it was used as a

place for casting refuse. Fires were kept burning there to prevent infection. Hence the name was used figuratively for hell.

Gelert, see *Dogs.*

Gellatley, DAVIE, a character in Scott's 'Waverley' (q.v.).

Gellius, AULUS, a Latin grammarian of the 2nd cent. A.D., author of twenty books of 'Noctes Atticae'. They form a miscel-lany, important as containing extracts from many lost authors, on many topics, literature, history, philosophy, philology, and natural science.

Gem, The, (1) a literary annual, edited by T. Hood (q.v.), 1829-32; (2) a weekly paper for boys, written by C. Hamilton (q.v.) under the pen-name Martin Clif-ford, 1907-39.

Gemini ('the twins'), a constellation, otherwise known as 'Castor and Pollux' (q.v.); also the third sign of the zodiac with which this constellation was anciently identical.

General, MRS., in Dickens's 'Little Dorrit' (q.v.), the lady-companion to Mr. Dorrit's daughters, remembered as the inventor of the formula 'prunes and prism'.

Genesis, meaning origin, creation, is the first in order of the books of the Bible, containing the account of the creation of the world. There is an OE. poetic para-phrase of the book, formerly attributed to Cædmon (q.v.). It contains an inter-polated section, which is translated from an Old Saxon original by another author.

Genesis and *Exodus,* poems in rhymed couplets, written about the middle of the 13th cent., relating scriptural history down to the death of Moses in popular form; and important as the first instance in English of the iambic dimeter frequently used by later poets, e.g. by Coleridge in 'Christabel'.

Genest, JOHN (1764-1839), author of 'Some Account of the English Stage from the Restoration in 1660 to 1830' (1832).

Geneva Bible, see *Bible (The English).*

Genevieve, the heroine of S. T. Cole-ridge's poem 'Love', first published in the 'Morning Post' (1799) and included in the second edition of 'Lyrical Ballads' (q.v.).

Geneviève, St. (c. 419-512), the patron saint of Paris. At the time of Attila's invasion (451) she encouraged the panic-stricken inhabitants and urged them to repentance; and Attila turned away from Paris towards Orléans.

Genghis Khan (1162-1227), the great Mongol conqueror, whose empire at his death extended from the shores of the Pacific to the northern shores of the Black Sea.

Genius, in classical pagan belief, the tutelary god or attendant spirit allotted to every person at his birth, to govern his fortunes and determine his character; also the spirit similarly connected with a place.

Gentilis, Albericus (1552-1608), an Italian, the most learned lawyer of his time, one of the founders of the system of international law. Grotius (q.v.) owed much to him.

Gentle Art of Making Enemies, The, a collection (1890) of the pungent letters and comments of J. McN. Whistler (q.v.). The first subject dealt with is Whistler's libel action against Ruskin in respect of a passage in 'Fors Clavigera' (q.v.).

Gentleman Dancing-Master, The, a comedy by Wycherley (q.v.), produced in 1673, the most entertaining of Wycherley's plays.

Gentleman's Journal, a periodical edited by Motteux (q.v.) from 1691 to 1694, containing the news of the month and miscellaneous prose and poetry. It was the germ of the modern magazine.

Gentleman's Magazine, The, a monthly periodical founded in 1731 by Cave (q.v.), originally to reproduce from the journals such news, essays, or other matter as appeared most interesting. Hence the use for the first time of the word 'magazine' in this sense. By Jan. 1739 original matter had largely replaced such extracts. The character of the paper was influenced by Samuel Johnson (q.v.), who at this time

became a regular contributor (until 1744). He at first edited, and subsequently wrote, the parliamentary reports. 'The Gentleman's Magazine' lasted until 1914.

Gentleman Usher, The, a tragicomedy, by Chapman (q.v.), printed in 1606, and probably acted c. 1602.

Gentle Shepherd, The, a pastoral drama by A. Ramsay (q.v.) (1725).

Geoffrey Crayon, the pseudonym of W. Irving (q.v.).

Geoffrey of Monmouth (1100?-1154), probably a Benedictine monk of Monmouth, studied at Oxford, and was attached to Robert, earl of Gloucester. He is said to have been archdeacon of Llandaff, and he was appointed bishop of St. Asaph in 1152.

In his 'Historia Regum Britanniae' he purports to give an account of the kings of Britain and especially of King Arthur. For this purpose he states that he drew upon a 'most ancient book in the British tongue' handed to him by Walter, archdeacon of Oxford, also known as Walter Calenius; but this book is unknown to any chronicler of the time. There is reason to suppose that this alleged work was in the main a mystification. Geoffrey drew on Bede and Nennius, on British traditions, perhaps on Welsh documents now lost, and probably for the rest on a romantic imagination. He is the creator of King Arthur as a romantic hero. His 'Historia' was translated into Anglo-Norman by Gaimar and Wace, and into English by Layamon and Robert of Gloucester; it was first printed in 1508 (Paris).

Geoffry Hamlyn, see *Kingsley (H.).*

George I, king of England, 1714-27.

George II, king of England, 1727-60.

George III, king of England, 1760-1820.

George IV, king of England, 1820-30.

George V, king of England, 1910-36.

George VI, king of England, 1936-52.

George, St., patron saint of England, Portugal, and formerly of Aragon and the republic of Genoa, is said to have been a native of Cappadocia, who rose to high military rank under Diocletian. He was arrested on account of his Christian religion, tortured, and executed at Nicomedia in A.D. 303. The legend is open to criticism, but it is probable that there was an officer of his name in the Roman army who suffered martyrdom under Diocletian. St. George's connection with the dragon is of much later date and its origin is obscure. The saint is perhaps the inheritor of some local myth, such as that of Perseus (q.v.). St. George has been recognized as the patron saint of England from the days of Edward III, perhaps because of having been regarded as the patron of the Order of the Garter. He is commemorated on 23 April.

George, HENRY (1839-97), American writer on political economy and sociology, author of 'Progress and Poverty' (1879), 'The Irish Land Question' (1882), 'Social Problems' (1884), 'Protection or Free Trade' (1886), an advocate of the nationalization of land and of the 'single tax' on its increment value.

George-a'-Green, the merry pinner or pinder (pound-keeper) of Wakefield. He is the subject of a play (licensed for publication, 1595) probably by Robert Greene (q.v.).

George and Vulture, THE, a hostelry in George Yard, Lombard Street, the temporary abode of Mr. Pickwick and Sam Weller ('The Pickwick Papers', ch. xxvi, xxxi, etc.). It is said to have been previously a coffee-house, frequented by Swift, Addison, and Steele, and at a later period by Hogarth and Wilkes.

George Barnwell, The History of, or The London Merchant, a domestic tragedy in prose by Lillo (q.v.), produced in 1731.

In this play, for the first time, everyday commercial life is made the theme of a tragedy. The play was a great success; it is based on an old ballad of 'George Barnwell', and deals with the seduction of an apprentice by the heartless courtesan Millwood. He becomes so infatuated that he robs his employer, Thorowgood, and is induced by Millwood to murder his uncle,

for which crime he and Millwood are brought to execution.

George Play, ST., see *Mummers' Play.*

George's, ST., HANOVER SQUARE, one of the fifty new churches built after the Fire of London, completed in 1724, frequently referred to as the scene of fashionable weddings.

Georgian Poetry, an anthology of contemporary verse initiated in 1912 by a group consisting of Rupert Brooke, John Drinkwater, Harold Monro, Wilfrid Wilson Gibson, Arundel del Ré, and Edward Marsh, of which five volumes appeared between 1912 and 1922, containing poems by Rupert Brooke, William H. Davies, W. de la Mare, John Drinkwater, John Masefield, Robert Graves, James Elroy Flecker, and others.

Georgics, The, a didactic poem by Virgil (q.v.) in four books, on agriculture, the care of domestic animals, and the keeping of bees.

Geraint and Enid, one of Tennyson's 'Idylls of the King', originally forming with 'The Marriage of Geraint' a single idyll, 'Enid' (1859).

In this idyll the baneful influence of the sin of Guinevere is first indicated. A word spoken by Enid to her husband Geraint provokes him to senseless suspicion of her fidelity. Her devotion to him in successive encounters gradually convinces him of her innocence and wins back his love.

Geraldine, THE FAIR, see *Surrey.*

Gerard, the hero of Reade's 'The Cloister and the Hearth' (q.v.).

Gerard, JOHN (1545-1612), author of the celebrated 'Herball or generall Historie of Plantes' (1597).

Gerbert of Aquitaine (c. 940-1003), Pope Sylvester II from 999 to 1003, the greatest figure in the 10th-11th cents., reckoned a magician for his knowledge; inventor, mathematician, scholar.

Gerhardie (originally GERHARDI), WILLIAM ALEXANDER (1895-1977), author, born of English parents in St. Petersburg and educated there and at Oxford. His novels were in a manner new to English imaginative literature and had much influence on younger writers. They include 'Futility: a Novel on Russian Themes' (1922), 'The Polyglots' (1925), 'Resurrection' (1934), and 'Of Mortal Love' (1936). His critical writings include 'Anton Chehov' (1923), 'Memoirs of a Polyglot' (1931, autobiographical), and 'The Romanoffs' (1940).

Germ, The, Thoughts towards Nature in Poetry, Literature, and Art, a periodical of which the first number appeared on 1 Jan. 1850. It was the organ of the 'Pre-Raphaelite Brotherhood' (q.v.). The title was changed in the third number to 'Art and Poetry, being Thoughts towards Nature'. Only four numbers in all appeared.

Géronte, in Molière's comedies, the typical old man whose absurdities are held up to ridicule.

Gerontius, Dream of, see *Newman*.

Gertrude, the queen of Denmark in Shakespeare's 'Hamlet' (q.v.).

Gertrude of Wyoming, a poem by T. Campbell (q.v.), in the Spenserian stanza (1809).

Gerusalemme Liberata, see *Jerusalem Delivered*.

Geryon, a monster with three bodies or three heads, who lived on an island in the West and was destroyed by Hercules (q.v.).

In Dante's 'Inferno' (xvii-xviii) he is the symbol of Fraud and guardian of the Eighth Circle of Hell, the place of punishment of traitors. He has the face of a just man, two hairy arms, and a forked tail.

Geryoneo, in Spenser's 'Faerie Queene', v. x and xi, a giant who represents Philip II of Spain, the Spanish power in the Netherlands, and the Inquisition.

Gessler, see *Tell*.

Gesta Francorum, a chronicle in medieval Latin, the first known to have been written by a layman. It gives the story of the First Crusade. Its actual author is unknown.

Gesta Romanorum, a collection of tales in Latin, some of Eastern origin, romances of chivalry, and legends of saints, originally compiled in England in the 14th cent. and first printed about 1472.

Gestas, see *Dismas*.

Gettysburg, in southern Pennsylvania, the scene of the defeat in 1863 of the confederate army under Gen. Robert E. Lee by the Federals under Gen. Meade. See *Lincoln (A.)*.

Ghibellines, see *Guelphs*.

Ghost of Abel, The, a dramatic dialogue by Blake (q.v.).

Ghost-words, a term used by Skeat (q.v.) to signify words which have no real existence, 'coinages due to the blunders of printers or scribes, or to the perfervid imaginations of ignorant or blundering editors'.

Giant Pope, in Bunyan's 'The Pilgrim's Progress' (q.v.), a giant by whose power and tyranny many men have in old time been cruelly put to death, but who is grown so crazy and stiff in his joints that he can now do little more than sit in his cave's mouth, grinning at the pilgrims as they go by, and biting his nails because he cannot come at them.

Giants or GIGANTES, THE, according to Greek mythology, were children of Ge (q.v.), frequently confused with the Titans (q.v.). They conspired to dethrone Zeus, and heaped Ossa on Pelion in order to scale the walls of heaven but were defeated and imprisoned in the earth.

Giaour, The, a poem by Lord Byron (q.v.) (1813).

The tale is of a female slave, Leila, who is unfaithful to her Turkish lord, Hassan, and is in consequence bound and thrown into the sea. Her lover, the Giaour, avenges her by killing Hassan.

Gibbie, GUSE, in Scott's 'Old Mortality' (q.v.), a half-witted lad, of very small stature.

Gibbon, EDWARD (1737-94), was educated at Westminster and Magdalen College, Oxford, but derived little benefit from either. At the age of sixteen he became a Roman Catholic, and was sent by his father to Lausanne, where he was reconverted to Protestantism and read widely. Here he became attached to Susanne Curchod (afterwards Madame Necker), but in deference to his father broke off the engagement. He returned to England in 1758 and published his 'Essai sur l'étude de la littérature' in 1761. In 1764, during a tour in Italy, he formed the plan of his 'History of the Decline and Fall of the Roman Empire' (q.v.). The death of his father, who had wasted his wealth, left him in some embarrassment, but enough remained from the wreck to enable him to settle in London in 1772 and proceed with his great work.

He entered parliament in 1774, voted steadily for Lord North, and was made a commissioner of trade and plantations. In 1776 appeared the first volume of his 'History', which was very favourably received; but his chapters on the growth of Christianity provoked criticisms. To his theological critics Gibbon replied in 1779 in 'A Vindication of some Passages in the Fifteenth and Sixteenth Chapters'. The second and third volumes appeared in 1781, but were less warmly received. He retired to Lausanne in 1783, where he completed the work, of which the last three volumes were published in 1788. His 'Memoirs', put together by Lord Sheffield from various fragments by Gibbon, were published in 1796, together with his 'Miscellaneous Works' (1796-1815).

Gibbons, GRINLING (1648-1721), woodcarver and sculptor. Evelyn (q.v.) describes in his 'Diary' how he discovered him in 1671 at Deptford and introduced him to Wren (q.v.), who employed him to carve decorative woodwork, principally in his houses and in St. Paul's Cathedral.

Gibbons, ORLANDO (1583-1625), composer, especially of madrigals.

Gibraltar, known to the ancients as Calpe, or, with Abyla on the opposite coast, as the Pillars of Hercules. It was captured by the British under Sir George Rooke in 1704.

Gibson, WILFRID (1878-1962), poet, published 'Collected Poems, 1905-1925', and other volumes.

Gide, ANDRÉ (1869-1951), French novelist, dramatist, and critic, author of 'L'Immoraliste' (1902), 'Les Caves du Vatican' (1914), 'Les Faux-Monnayeurs' (1926), 'Si le grain ne meurt' (1926, autobiography). He was awarded the Nobel Prize for literature in 1947.

Gifford, WILLIAM (1756-1826), published in 1794 and 1795 two satires, 'The Baviad' and 'The Maeviad', against the Della Cruscan (q.v.) school of poets and the contemporary drama. He became editor of 'The Anti-Jacobin' (q.v.) in 1797, and in 1809 first editor of 'The Quarterly Review' (q.v.). Gifford's rigorous adherence, as a literary critic, to the old school in literature and his hatred of radicals gave bitterness to his judgements of the rising authors. He translated Juvenal (1802) and Persius (1821), and edited some of the older English dramatists.

Gifford Lectures, on natural theology, founded in the universities of Edinburgh, Glasgow, Aberdeen, and St. Andrews by Adam, Lord Gifford (1820-87).

Gigadibs, MR., in R. Browning's 'Bishop Blougram's Apology', the bishop's interlocutor.

Gilbert, SIR HUMPHREY (1539?-83), halfbrother of Sir Walter Ralegh, made his first voyage of discovery with the latter in 1578. In 1583 he left Plymouth with five ships for Newfoundland, where he founded the first British colony in North America. On his return journey his ship the 'Squirrel' was lost in a storm off the Azores. Hakluyt (q.v.) gives a striking narrative of his end.

Gilbert, WILLIAM (1540-1603), physician to Queen Elizabeth and James I. His 'De Magnete' (1600) was the first great scientific book to be published in England.

Gilbert, SIR WILLIAM SCHWENCK (1836-1911), began his literary career in 1861 as a regular contributor to 'Fun'. He excelled as a writer of humorous verse, and his 'Bab Ballads' (q.v.) (published in volume form in 1869-73) were very popular. His first dramatic work was 'Dulcamara', a successful burlesque, in 1866. He wrote a blank-verse fairy comedy 'The Palace of Truth' (1870), 'Pygmalion and Galatea' (1871), and various serious dramas in verse. He collaborated with Sir Arthur Sullivan for D'Oyly Carte's opera company in a long series of comic operas (see *Gilbert and Sullivan Operas*).

Gilbert and Sullivan Operas, comic operas, including much social and topical satire, written in collaboration by Sir W. S. Gilbert and Sir A. Sullivan (qq.v.) for Richard D'Oyly Carte (1844-1901). The operas are: 'Trial by Jury' (1875), 'The Sorcerer' (1877), 'H.M.S. Pinafore' (1878), 'The Pirates of Penzance' (produced in New York, 1879, and in London, 1880), 'Patience' (1881), 'Iolanthe' (1882), 'Princess Ida' (1884), 'The Mikado' (1885), 'Ruddigore' (1887), 'The Yeomen of the Guard' (1888), 'The Gondoliers' (1889), 'Utopia, Limited' (1893), and 'The Grand Duke' (1896). They are known as the 'Savoy Operas' because from 'Iolanthe' onwards they were produced at the Savoy Theatre.

Gilbertian, a word derived from the name of Sir W. S. Gilbert (q.v.) to signify the kind of humorous absurdity which distinguishes many of the characters and situations in the Gilbert and Sullivan operas.

Gilbertines, see *Gilbert of Sempringham*.

Gilbert of Sempringham, ST. (1083?-1189), the founder of the Gilbertine order (*c.* 1135), with headquarters at Sempringham in Lincolnshire. He was held in great regard by Henry II and Queen Eleanor, lived to be over 100, and was canonized by Innocent III.

Gil Blas of Santillane, The Adventures of, a picaresque romance by Le Sage (q.v.) (1715-35).

The work gives an admirable satiric picture of Spanish life of the period, though Le Sage never saw Spain. It was translated into English (or the translation was revised) by Smollet (q.v.) in 1749.

Gildas, a British historian, who wrote in Latin shortly before 547 a sketch of the history of Britain, 'De Excidio et Conquestu Britanniae'. He says nothing of Arthur, but refers to the victory of Mount Badon.

Giles, BROTHER, of Assisi (*d. c.* 1261), convert and friend of St. Francis of Assisi (q.v.).

Giles (Aegidius), ST. (*fl.* 7th cent.), is said to have established himself in the wilderness near the mouth of the Rhône, in a dense forest, with a hind for sole companion. After a time he received disciples, and built a monastery. He came to be regarded as the patron of cripples and lepers. His festival is celebrated on 1 Sept.

Gilfil, THE REVD. MAYNARD, the parson in 'Mr. Gilfil's Love-Story', the second tale in George Eliot's (q.v.) 'Scenes of Clerical Life'.

Gillray, JAMES (1757-1815), caricaturist. He treated at first anonymously social subjects, turning to political themes after 1780. He depicted Pitt, Fox, Sheridan, and Burke; other caricatures dealt with Napoleon, Nelson, and the Revolution.

Gills, SOLOMON, a character in Dickens's 'Dombey and Son' (q.v.).

Gilpin, JOHN, see *John Gilpin*.

Ginn, see *Jinn*.

Gioconda, LA, or LA JOCONDE, names given to the famous portrait of Mona Lisa (q.v.) by Leonardo da Vinci.

Giotto's O: Giotto (1266?-1337), the painter, while studying with Cimabue, was summoned to Rome by Boniface VIII. When asked for some drawing which might be shown as proof of his skill, he, with a single sweep of his brush, drew a perfect circle on a panel, and gave this as sufficient testimony.

Giovanni, DON, Italian for Don Juan (q.v.).

Gipsy, a corruption of 'Egyptian', a member of a wandering race, by themselves called ROMANY, of Hindu origin, which first appeared in England about the beginning of the 16th cent. and was then believed to have come from Egypt.

Giraldus de Barri, called CAMBRENSIS (1146?-1220?), Welsh chronicler, archdeacon of Brecon. His works include 'Topographia', an account of the geography, fauna, marvels, and early history of Ireland; the 'Expugnatio', a narrative of the partial conquest of Ireland (1169-85); the 'Itinerarium' (the most important of his works), a description of the topography of Wales. See also *Glastonbury*.

Giraudoux, JEAN (1882-1944), French novelist, essayist, and dramatist. In 1928 his novel 'Siegfried et le Limousin' was successfully adapted for the stage, and thereafter he turned to drama. His plots are most frequently derived from biblical or classical legend. His plays include 'Amphitryon 38' and 'La Guerre de Troie n'aura pas lieu' (tr. C. Fry, q.v., 'Tiger at the Gates').

Girondists, the moderate republican party in the French Legislative Assembly of 1791-2 and the Convention of 1792-5, whose leaders were the deputies from the Gironde district.

Gisborne, MARIA (1770-1836), *née* James, a friend of Shelley (q.v.). She refused William Godwin and married John Gisborne in 1800. Shelley's 'Letter to Maria Gisborne' was written in 1820.

Gismond of Salerne, see *Sigismonda*.

Gissing, GEORGE ROBERT (1857-1903), was educated at Manchester, but left there in 1875 for London and subsequently for America, where he experienced the extreme poverty and misery reflected in many of his novels. After a short period at Jena, where he studied philosophy, he returned to London, and in 1880 published his first novel 'Workers in the Dawn'. He published 'The Unclassed' in 1884, 'Demos' in 1886, and other novels illustrating the degrading effects of poverty on character. 'The Emancipated' appeared in 1890, 'New Grub Street' in 1891, 'Born in Exile' in 1892, 'The Town Traveller' in 1898, 'The

Crown of Life' in 1899, 'Our Friend the Charlatan' in 1901, and 'Will Warburton' in 1905. Of a different character was 'The Private Papers of Henry Ryecroft' (1903), the imaginary journal of a recluse; it represents Gissing's own aspirations. Mention should also be made of his critical study of Charles Dickens, an author by whom Gissing had been deeply influenced (1898), 'Human Odds and Ends' (1898), a collection of short stories, and a second collection, 'The House of Cobwebs' (1906).

Gladstone, WILLIAM EWART (1809-98), the great Liberal statesman, is principally remembered in literary history for his 'Studies on Homer and the Homeric Age' (1858). 'Translations' by him and Lord Lyttelton appeared in 1863. His political writings include 'The State in its Relations with the Church' (1838), 'Letters to the Earl of Aberdeen' on the Neapolitan Government (1851), 'Vaticanism' (1875), 'Bulgarian Horrors and the Question of the East' (1876), and 'Lessons in Massacre' (1877).

Glanvill, JOSEPH (1636-80), was rector of the Abbey Church at Bath. He attacked the scholastic philosophy in 'The Vanity of Dogmatizing' (1661), a work that contains the story of the 'Scholar-Gipsy' (q.v.).

Glanville, RANULF DE (d. 1190), chief justiciar of England. The authorship of the first great treatise on the laws of England, 'Tractatus de Legibus et Consuetudinibus Angliae', has been doubtfully ascribed to him on the evidence of Roger of Hoveden.

Glasgow, ELLEN (1874-1945), American novelist, born in Virginia. She took her native region as her subject and attempted to show its social and political conflicts and development.

Glasse, HANNAH (*fl.* 1747), author of 'The Art of Cookery made Plain and Easy' (1747), 'The Compleat Confectioner' (1770), and 'The Servant's Directory or Housekeeper's Companion' (1770). She was habit-maker to the Prince of Wales.

Glastonbury, in Somerset, famous as the place where, according to legend, Joseph of Arimathea founded Glastonbury Abbey, and where, according to Giraldus Cambrensis (q.v.), the tomb of Arthur and Guinevere was discovered in the reign of Henry II.

Giraldus Cambrensis and Ralph of Coggeshall (*fl.* 1207) identify Glastonbury with Avalon.

Glatisant, in Malory's 'Morte Darthur' (q.v.), the name of the 'questing beast'.

Glaucé, in Spenser's 'Faerie Queene', III. ii. 30, etc., the nurse of Britomart.

Glaucus: (1) son of Sisyphus, grandson of Aeolus, and father of Bellerophon (qq.v.); (2) another legendary person, who lived at Potniae and was said to have been torn in pieces by his mares; (3) a fisherman of Boeotia who became a sea-god and assisted the Argonauts; (4) in Homer's 'Iliad', the grandson of Bellerophon, an ally of King Priam.

Glegg, MR. and MRS., characters in G. Eliot's 'The Mill on the Floss' (q.v.).

Gleig, GEORGE ROBERT (1796-1888), remembered as the author of 'The Subaltern', written for 'Blackwood's' in 1826.

Glenallan, EARL OF, a character in Scott's 'The Antiquary'.

Glenarvon, see *Lamb* (*Lady C.*).

Glencoe, in Argyllshire, memorable for the massacre of the inhabitants (Macdonalds) in 1692, under the orders of William III, obtained by Sir John Dalrymple, Master of Stair, their enemy. The massacre was carried out by Campbell of Glen Lyon and 120 soldiers.

Scott wrote a poem on the subject, and Talfourd a play (1840), and there is an echo of it in Campbell's 'Pilgrim of Glencoe'. Aytoun's 'Widow of Glencoe' is also well known.

Glendinning, HALBERT and EDWARD, characters in Scott's 'The Monastery' and 'The Abbot'.

Glendower, OWEN (1359?-1416?), the leader of the Welsh rebellion against Henry IV, who figures in Shakespeare's '1 Henry IV'.

Glenmire, LADY, a character in Mrs. Gaskell's 'Cranford' (q.v.).

Glenvarloch, LORD, the title borne by Nigel Olifaunt in Scott's 'The Fortunes of Nigel' (q.v.).

Globe Theatre, THE, the Burbages' theatre in Southwark, erected in 1599. It was a circular building, said to hold 1,200 spectators, and thatched. It was destroyed when the thatch caught fire in 1613, during a performance of Shakespeare's 'Henry VIII'. Shakespeare had a share in the theatre and acted there. It is the famous 'wooden O' referred to in 'Henry V'.

Gloria, a name for each of several formulae in Christian liturgical worship. (1) GLORIA PATRI, the doxology beginning 'Glory be to the Father'; (2) GLORIA TIBI, the response 'Glory be to thee, O Lord', following the announcement of the Gospel; (3) GLORIA IN EXCELSIS, the hymn 'Glory be to God on high' in the communion service or mass.

Gloriana, a name for Queen Elizabeth in Spenser's 'Faerie Queene'.

Glorious First of June, THE, see *First of June*.

Glorious John, a designation of Dryden (q.v.).

Glossin, GILBERT, a character in Scott's 'Guy Mannering'.

Gloucester, EARL OF, a character in Shakespeare's 'King Lear' (q.v.).

Glover, RICHARD (1712-85), published much blank verse: 'Leonidas' (1737) in nine books, and 'The Athenaid' in thirty, and produced two plays, 'Boadicea' and 'Medea', in 1753 and 1763. He is remembered only as the author of 'Hosier's Ghost', a ballad included in Percy's 'Reliques'.

Glover, SIMON and CATHARINE, two of the principal characters in Scott's 'Fair Maid of Perth'.

Glowry, CHRISTOPHER and SCYTHROP, characters in Peacock's 'Nightmare Abbey' (q.v.).

Glubbdubdrib, in Swift's 'Gulliver's Travels' (q.v.), the island of sorcerers, where Homer and Aristotle, Descartes and Gassendi, and many kings and generals are called up at Gulliver's request, and he learns the untrustworthy character of history.

Gluck, CHRISTOPH WILIBALD (1714-87), a famous operatic composer born in Bavaria. His great operas were 'Orfeo' (1762), 'Alceste' (1766), 'Iphigénie en Aulide' (1774), 'Armide' (1777), and 'Iphigénie en Tauride' (1779).

Glumdalclitch, in Swift's 'Gulliver's Travels' (q.v.), the farmer's daughter who attended on Gulliver during his visit to Brobdingnag.

Glyn, ELINOR (Mrs. Clayton Glyn) (1864-1943), authoress, born in Toronto, Canada. Among her novels were: 'The Visits of Elizabeth' (1900), 'Three Weeks' (1907), 'Man and Maid' (1922), 'Six Days' (1924).

Gnome, from modern Latin *gnomus*, used by Paracelsus, though perhaps not invented by him, to signify beings that have earth for their element. The word as generally used means one of a race of diminutive spirits fabled to inhabit the earth and to be guardians of its treasures.

Gnomic, from Gr. γνώμη, consisting of gnomes or general maxims, sententious.

Gnosticism, from Gr. γνῶσις knowledge, a religious movement of oriental origin which penetrated early Christianity, giving rise to a great variety of sects, prominent in the 2nd cent. A.D., who claimed special knowledge. They held the material world to be the work, not of the supreme Deity, but of an inferior Demiurge, antagonistic to what was truly spiritual. Gnosticism was allied to Manichaeism (q.v.).

Gobbo, LAUNCELOT, the clown in Shakespeare's 'The Merchant of Venice' (q.v.), servant to Shylock; OLD GOBBO is his father.

Goblin (Fr. *gobelin*, an obsolete word of uncertain derivation), a mischievous and ugly demon.

Goblin Market, a poem by C. Rossetti (q.v.) (1862).

The poem is a fairy tale, partly allegorical.

God and Mammon, The Triumph of Mammon, the first two parts of a blank verse trilogy (the third was never written) by Davidson (q.v.) (1907). It is an expression of materialistic idealism.

God from the machine, see *Deus ex machina*.

Godiva, the wife of Leofric, earl of Mercia, one of Edward the Confessor's great earls. According to legend, her husband, having imposed a tax on the inhabitants of Coventry, promised to remit it if she would ride naked through the streets at noonday. She agreed, directed the people to keep within doors and shut their windows, and complied with his condition. Peeping Tom, who looked out, was struck blind.

The story is told by Drayton in his 'Polyolbion' (q.v.), xiii; by Leigh Hunt; and by Tennyson in his 'Godiva'.

Godolphin, a novel by Bulwer Lytton (q.v.).

Godwin, MRS. MARY WOLLSTONECRAFT (1759-97), *née* Wollstonecraft, married William Godwin (q.v.) in 1797, and died at the birth of her daughter Mary, the future Mrs. Shelley. Her 'Vindication of the Rights of Women' (1792) was a courageous attack on the conventions of the day.

Godwin, WILLIAM (1756-1836), was at first a dissenting minister, but became an atheist and a philosopher of anarchical views. He believed that men acted according to reason, and that rational creatures could live in harmony without laws and institutions. He married Mary Wollstonecraft (see *Godwin, Mrs. M. W.*) in 1797, who died at the birth of her daughter, the future wife of Shelley. Godwin subsequently married Mrs. Clairmont, whose daughter by her first marriage, Claire Clairmont (q.v.), bore a daughter, Allegra, to Lord Byron (q.v.).

Godwin published in 1793 his 'Enquiry concerning Political Justice' in which he stated his philosophical and political views, in 1794 the 'Adventures of Caleb Williams', and in 1799 'St. Leon', novels designed to propagate these views. This last contains a portrait of Mary Wollstonecraft, of whom he also wrote a remarkable life. He exercised a great influence on Shelley and at one time on Wordsworth.

Goethe, JOHANN WOLFGANG VON (1749–1832), spent the greater part of his life in Weimar, occupying positions in the government of increasing importance until 1786. In 1791 he was appointed director of the ducal theatre, a post which he retained for twenty-two years. Throughout his life he devoted much time to the study of painting, for which he had only a mediocre gift. Apart from this, he divided his energies mainly between scientific research and literature.

In the sphere of literature, apart from his great dramatic poem 'Faust' (q.v.), his principal works were (i) 'Goetz von Berlichingen' (1771), a drama dealing with the story of a predatory knight of the German Empire in the 16th cent. The play was translated by Sir Walter Scott; (ii) 'The Sorrows of Young Werther' (first published 1774), a romance in epistolary form; (iii) 'Egmont', a play dealing with the revolt of the Netherlands against the power of Spain; (iv) 'Hermann und Dorothea', a poem (1797); (v) 'Dichtung und Wahrheit' ('Poetry and Truth'), completed in 1831, an autobiography in which those experiences are selected which had most influenced the author's development; (vi) 'Wilhelm Meister', written at intervals between 1777 and 1829, a romance of biographical interest. Part was translated by Carlyle (q.v.). Mention should also be made of Goethe's beautiful lyrics, ballads, and love-songs.

Goethe and Schiller came together in 1794, and were much associated until the latter's death in 1805. From 1823 to the end of his life Goethe was attended by Johann Eckermann, whose faithful record of Goethe's conversations has been translated into English.

Goetz von Berlichingen, see *Goethe.*

Gog and **Magog.** In Gen. x. 2, Magog is a son of Japhet. In Ezek. xxxviii and

xxxix, Gog is the chief prince of Meshech and Tubal. In Rev. xx. 7–9, Gog and Magog represent the nations of the earth that are deceived by Satan.

In the cycle of legends relating to Alexander the Great, Gog and Magog were allies of the Indian king Porus, in his resistance to that conqueror.

Gogh, VINCENT VAN (1853–90), Dutch Post-Impressionist painter who worked chiefly in France.

Gogmagog and **Corineus:** Gogmagog (called Goëmagot by Geoffrey of Monmouth and Spenser, 'Faerie Queene', III. ix. 50) was the chief of the giants of Albion whom Brute (q.v.) destroyed. Corineus was one of Brute's companions. He wrestled with Gogmagog and threw him into the sea, and Cornwall was assigned to him as a reward.

Gogol, NIKOLAI VASILEVICH (1809–52), Russian writer. His first major work, 'Evenings on a farm near Dikanka', appeared in 1831–2. Two collections of stories followed: 'Mirgorod' and 'Arabesques' (1835); and the well-known tales 'The Nose' (1835) and 'The Greatcoat' (1842). Gogol also wrote several plays, the best-known being 'The Inspector-General' (1836). His masterpiece is the novel 'Dead Souls' (first part, 1842). It was never finished and Gogol destroyed most of the second part.

Golconda, the old name of Hyderabad, formerly celebrated for its diamonds, a synonym for a mine of wealth.

Golden Age, THE, the first and best age of the world, in which, according to the Greek and Roman poets, man lived in a state of ideal happiness. It was thought to have occurred under the reign of Saturn (q.v.) on earth.

Golden Ass, The, a satire by Apuleius (q.v.). It takes the form of the supposed autobiography of the author, who is transformed into an ass by the mistake of the servant of an enchantress. He passes from master to master, observing the vices and follies of men, and finally recovers human form. The story includes a number of episodes, of which the best known is the beautiful fable of 'Cupid and Psyche' (q.v.).

Golden Bough, The, a comparative study of the beliefs and institutions of mankind, by Frazer (q.v.), in 12 volumes (1890-1915). His own abridged one-volume edition was published in 1922.

Golden Bowl, The, a novel by Henry James (q.v.) (1904).

Golden Fleece, THE, the name of an order of chivalry instituted by Philip the Good, duke of Burgundy, in 1429. See also under *Argonauts.*

Golden Grove, The, see *Taylor (Jeremy).*

Golden Hind, The, originally named 'The Pelican', the ship in which Drake circumnavigated the globe.

Golden Horn, THE, the harbour of Constantinople, a curved arm of the Bosphorus. The name dates from remote antiquity.

Golden Legend, The, a medieval manual of ecclesiastical lore: lives of saints, commentary on the church service, homilies for saints' days, etc. A version of this was published by Caxton (q.v.). One of its sources was the 'Legenda Aurea' of Jacobus de Voragine (1230-98).

Golden Legend, The, a poem by Longfellow (q.v.) (1852).

Golden Treasury of Songs and Lyrics, The, see *Palgrave (F. T.).*

Goldsmith, OLIVER (1730?-74), the second son of an Irish clergyman, entered Trinity College, Dublin, as a sizar in 1744, ran away to Cork, but returned, and graduated B.A. in 1749. He then studied medicine at Edinburgh and at Leyden, and wandered about France, Switzerland, and Italy, obtaining it is said a medical degree at some foreign university. He reached London in destitution in 1756, and supported himself with difficulty as a physician, an usher, and a hack-writer on Griffiths' 'Monthly Review'. He published in 1758 his notable translation of 'The Memoirs of a Protestant, condemned to the Galleys of France for his Religion' (Jean Marteilhe of Bergerac, a victim of

the revocation of the Edict of Nantes) and his 'Enquiry into the present State of Polite Learning' in 1759; about this time he became acquainted with Thomas Percy, afterwards bishop of Dromore. He published during Oct. and Nov. 1759 his little periodical 'The Bee', contributed to various magazines, and was also employed by John Newbery, the publisher, in whose 'Public Ledger' Goldsmith's 'Chinese Letters' appeared, subsequently republished as 'The Citizen of the World' (q.v.), in 1762.

He made the acquaintance of Samuel Johnson (q.v.) in 1761, and was one of the original members of 'The Club'. His poem 'The Traveller' (q.v.) (1764) was welcomed by the public; and in the same year appeared his 'History of England in a Series of Letters'. 'The Vicar of Wakefield', the publication of which had been delayed for unexplained reasons, appeared in 1766. He wrote a life of Voltaire (1761), a memoir of Beau Nash (1762), a 'History of Rome' (1769), lives of Parnell and Bolingbroke (1770), and an English history (1771). His first comedy 'The Goodnatur'd Man' was rejected by Garrick, but produced at Covent Garden in 1768 with moderate success. His second comedy, 'She Stoops to Conquer' (q.v.), was played at Covent Garden in 1773 with immense success. In 1770 appeared 'The Deserted Village' (q.v.); his 'History of Greece', and 'Animated Nature' (with 'tygers' in Canada), were his last works (1774). Boswell's 'Life of Johnson' contains many anecdotes about Goldsmith; Johnson, who was quite awake to his absurdities, had a high respect for his worth and literary abilities.

Golgotha, the hill of the Crucifixion near Jerusalem, from an Aramaic word meaning 'skull'.

Golias or GOLIARDUS, the name found attached in English manuscripts of the 12th and 13th cents. to Latin poems of a satirical and profane kind, the most famous of these being the so-called 'Apocalypse of Golias', for which no certain evidence of authorship can be claimed. According to F. J. E. Raby ('A History of Secular Latin Poetry in the Middle Ages'), the conception of Golias as 'Bishop' or 'Arch-poet' (q.v.) is a myth. The 'Goliards' are, it seems, to be linked with Golias, Goliath of Gath, the symbol of lawlessness and of evil, though the original derivation may have been from 'gula', on account of their gluttony.

Goliath, the Philistine giant slain by David, 1 Sam. xvii.

G.O.M., 'Grand Old Man', a current appellation for W. E. Gladstone from 1882, said to have been first applied to him by Lord Rosebery.

Goncourt, EDMOND and JULES DE (1822–96 and 1830–70), French authors, brothers, who wrote in close collaboration. Their earliest interests were art criticism and French social history. From 1851 they wrote novels of a closely documented type.

The famous Goncourt Diary is an almost day-to-day record of literary life in Paris. The Académie Goncourt, founded under the will of Edmond de Goncourt, awards an annual money prize (*Prix Goncourt*) for imaginative prose.

Gondibert, a romantic epic by D'Avenant (q.v.) (1651).

This work, which was never finished, consists of some 1,700 quatrains, and is a tale of chivalry.

Goneril and **Regan,** in Shakespeare's 'King Lear' (q.v.), the elder daughters of the king.

Gongorism, an affected type of diction and style introduced into Spanish literature in the 16th cent. by the poet Don Luis de Góngora y Argote (1561–1627), a style akin to Euphuism (q.v.) in England.

Goodfellow, ROBIN, see *Robin Good-fellow.*

Good-natur'd Man, The, a comedy by Goldsmith (q.v.), produced in 1768.

Good Thoughts in Bad Times, a collection of reflections by Fuller (q.v.) (1645), followed in 1647 by 'Good

Thoughts in Worse Times', and in 1660, at the Restoration, by 'Mixt Contemplations in Better Times'.

Googe, BARNABE (1504–94), a kinsman of Sir William Cecil, published 'Eglogs, Epytaphes, and Sonnetes', 1563, and translations. His eclogues are of interest as being, with those of Barclay (q.v.), the earliest examples of pastorals in English.

Goose, MOTHER, see *Mother Goose's Tales.*

Gorboduc, or *Ferrex and Porrex,* one of the earliest of English tragedies, of which the first three acts are by Thomas Norton (1532–84) and the last two by T. Sackville (q.v.). It was acted in the Inner Temple Hall in 1561. The play is constructed on the model of a Senecan tragedy, and the subject is taken from the legendary chronicles of Britain. Gorboduc and Videna are king and queen, Ferrex and Porrex are their two sons, and the dukes of Cornwall, Albany, Logres, and Cumberland are the other chief characters. Ferrex and Porrex quarrel over the division of the kingdom. Ferrex is killed by Porrex and Porrex is murdered in revenge by his mother. The duke of Albany tries to seize the kingdom and civil war breaks out. There is no action on the stage, the events being narrated in blank verse.

The legend of Gorboduc is told by Geoffrey of Monmouth, and figures in Spenser's 'Faerie Queene' (II. x. 34 and 35).

Gordius, the father of Midas (q.v.), a Phrygian peasant who became king, in consequence of an oracle which told the Phrygians that their troubles would cease if they appointed king the first man they met approaching the temple of Jupiter in a wagon. Gordius was the man thus chosen. He dedicated his wagon to Jupiter. The knot with which the yoke was fastened to the pole was so artful that the legend arose that whoever could untie it would gain the empire of Asia. Alexander the Great cut the *Gordian knot* with his sword and applied the legend to himself.

Gordon, ADAM LINDSAY (1833-70), Australian poet, born in the Azores and educated in England. He went to Australia in 1853, where he joined the mounted police. He spent most of his life in Australia among horses, and this is reflected in much of his poetry, for instance in his well-known pieces, 'The Sick Stockrider', 'How we beat the Favourite', 'The Ride from the Wreck', and 'Wolf and Hound'. Gordon committed suicide.

Gordon, CHARLES GEORGE (1833-85), commanded the Chinese forces against the Taiping rebels in 1863-4. He was sent by the British government in 1884 to rescue the Egyptian garrisons in the Sudan previous to abandonment, was hemmed in at Khartoum, and there killed. His Chinese diaries, Khartoum journals, and several volumes of his letters, have been published.

Gordon Riots, THE, in 1780, led by Lord George Gordon, were intended to compel parliament to repeal the Act of 1778 for the relief of Roman Catholics. They figure in Dickens's 'Barnaby Rudge' (q.v.).

Gore, MRS. CATHERINE GRACE FRANCES (1799-1861), née Moody, published about seventy works between 1824 and 1862, including the novels 'Mrs. Armytage' (1836) and 'Mothers and Daughters' (1831), which are her best.

Her novels were parodied by Thackeray in 'Lords and Liveries', one of the 'Novels by Eminent Hands'.

Gorgons, THE, three sisters, daughters of Phorcys and Ceto, whose names were Stheno, Euryale, and Medusa. Of these Medusa (q.v.) alone was mortal and is the most celebrated. According to the mythologists, their hair was entwined with serpents, their hands were of brass, and they turned to stone all on whom they fixed their eyes.

Gorky, MAXIM (ALEXEI MAXIMOVICH PESHKOV) (1868-1936), Russian writer. Obliged to work for his living from the age of 8, Gorky was self-educated. After the 1917 Revolution his independent views,

his emotional attitude to revolution, and increasing ill health led, in 1921, to his leaving Russia for Italy. In 1928 he returned to the Soviet Union as an enthusiastic supporter of the government. His best-known works are 'Twenty-six Men and a Girl' (1899), 'Foma Gordeev' (1899), 'The Mother' (1907), and his autobiographical masterpiece 'Childhood' (1913-14), 'In the World' (1915-16), 'My Universities' (1923). He also wrote plays.

Gosse, SIR EDMUND (1849-1928), the son of Philip H. Gosse, an eminent zoologist and a Plymouth Brother, his relations with whom are described in his 'Father and Son' (1907), entered the British Museum as assistant librarian in 1867, was translator to the board of trade, 1875-1904, and then became librarian to the House of Lords till 1914. He devoted much attention to the northern languages and wrote a life of Ibsen in 1908. He published the 'Life and Letters of John Donne' in 1899, lives of Gray (1882), Jeremy Taylor (1904), and Sir Thomas Browne (1905) for the English Men of Letters series; also lives of Congreve (1888) and Swinburne (1917). His collected poems appeared in 1911, and his 'Life and Letters', by the Hon. E. Charteris, in 1931. Gosse had known almost all his literary contemporaries, and was a specially close friend of Swinburne in earlier years, of Stevenson, and of Henry James (qq.v.). He is described by Somerset Maugham (q.v.) as one of the few great conversationalists of his time.

Gosson, STEPHEN (1554-1624). His plays are not now extant, but were ranked by Meres among 'the best for pastorall'. He was converted by Puritan censures and attacked poets and players in his 'Schoole of Abuse' (1579), etc. He evoked, by his unauthorized dedication of his 'Schoole of Abuse' to Sir Philip Sidney, Sidney's 'Apologie for Poetrie' (1595, q.v.).

Gotham, WISE MEN OF. For some reason, not clearly established, a reputation for folly was, from very early times, attributed to the inhabitants of Gotham, a village in

Nottinghamshire. There is reference to such a tradition in the Towneley 'Mysteries' (see *Miracle Plays*). The tradition once established, it seems probable that many new stories of folly were fathered on the village. These were collected in the 'Merrie Tales of the Mad Men of Gotam by A. B.' (perhaps Andrew Borde, physician, *c.* 1490–1549), of which a 1630 copy is extant. A reprint of a copy (prob. 1565) was published in 1965, ed. S. J. Kahrl.

Gothic, a style of architecture prevalent in Western Europe from the 12th to the 16th cents., of which the chief characteristic is the pointed arch. The most usual names for the successive periods of this style in England are EARLY ENGLISH, DECORATED, and PERPENDICULAR.

GOTHIC or BLACK-LETTER TYPE is that most commonly used for printing German. It is descended from the script used in the later Middle Ages.

Gothic novels, a class of novel dealing with the frightening and supernatural, and chiefly associated with Horace Walpole's 'The Castle of Otranto' (q.v., 1764), and the works of Ann Radcliffe, M. G. Lewis, and C. R. Maturin (qq.v.). Walpole, like some later writers, called his novel 'A Gothic [that is, medieval] Story' (on the title-page of the second edition, 1765). The popularity of such works, due in part to their supernatural element, led to the identification of 'Gothic' with 'supernatural', and many works with only a very slight 'medieval' element or none at all thus came to be called 'Gothic'. The Gothic novel specializes in ruins, haunted castles, frightening landscapes, magic. Some of its elements of atmosphere or characterization have been traced to other and earlier genres, such as Jacobean tragedy and 18th-cent. graveyard poetry. There are Gothic elements, too, in Smollett's novel 'Ferdinand Count Fathom' (1753). The Gothic novel and its readers are satirized in Jane Austen's 'Northanger Abbey' (q.v., 1818). Nineteenth-cent. exponents of the Gothic novel

(in one form or other) include Mary Shelley, Poe, and Sheridan Le Fanu (qq.v.).

Gothic Revival, the name given to architecture based on the Gothic style. It applies particularly to English architecture from *c.* 1840 when a scholarly study of Gothic was made, it being considered the only style for churches. Earlier exercises in Gothic, e.g. Horace Walpole's house, Strawberry Hill, were usually romantic in aim and used Gothic motifs to adorn buildings of contemporary plan.

Goths, THE, a Germanic tribe, who, in the 3rd, 4th, and 5th cents., invaded both the Eastern and the Western Empires. The Ostrogoths were the Eastern division of the tribe, which founded a kingdom in Italy; the Visigoths were the Western division, which founded a kingdom in Spain. The word 'Goth' is applied in a transferred sense to one who behaves like a barbarian, especially in the destruction or neglect of works of art.

Götterdämmerung, 'Twilight of the Gods', the last of Wagner's operas in the series of the 'Ring der Nibelungen' (q.v.). It follows the 'Siegfried' (q.v.).

Gould, NATHANIEL (1857–1919), known as Nat Gould, journalist and novelist, wrote about 130 novels, all concerned with horse-racing.

Gounod, CHARLES FRANÇOIS (1818–93), French musical composer. He wrote a number of operas, including 'Faust' (1859) and 'Roméo et Juliette' (1867).

Governour, The, a treatise on politics and education by Elyot (q.v.).

Gower, a character in Shakespeare's 'Henry V' (q.v.).

Gower, JOHN (1330?–1408), of a Kentish family and a man of some wealth. He was a friend of Chaucer, who called him 'moral Gower'. Of his chief poems the 'Speculum Meditantis' or 'Mirour de l'Omme' is written in French, the 'Vox Clamantis' (*c.* 1382?) in Latin, and the 'Confessio Amantis' (q.v., 1390) in English.

Goya y Lucientes, FRANCISCO (1746–1828), Spanish painter. He painted portraits and scenes of contemporary life with a brilliant and sometimes cynical realism. Among his portraits are two of the duke of Wellington.

Graal, HOLY, see *Grail*.

Grace Abounding to the Chief of Sinners, or the brief Relation of the exceeding Mercy of God in Christ to his poor Servant John Bunyan (q.v.) (1666), a homiletic narrative by Bunyan (q.v.) (1666).

The author relates his spiritual history with intense fervour and sincerity.

Graces, THE, called CHARITES by the Greeks, daughters of Zeus; Euphrosyne, Aglaia, and Thalia by name, goddesses of beauty and grace.

Gradgrind, MR., LOUISA, and TOM, leading characters in Dickens's 'Hard Times' (q.v.).

Graeme, or AVENEL, ROLAND, the hero of Scott's 'The Abbot'.

Grahame, KENNETH (1859-1932), author of 'The Golden Age' (1895), studies of childhood in an English countryside setting, which proved extremely popular. 'Dream Days', a sequel, followed in 1898. Grahame also wrote 'The Wind in the Willows' (1908), a book for children which many of their elders have also enjoyed.

Graham of Claverhouse, JOHN (1649?-89), *first Viscount Dundee*, executed the severities of the government in Scotland during the reigns of Charles II and James II. In 1688 he raised the Highlands for James and was killed at the battle of Killiecrankie. He figures prominently in Scott's 'Old Mortality' (q.v.).

Grail, THE HOLY, in medieval legend, the vessel used by Jesus at the Last Supper, in which Joseph of Arimathea received the Saviour's blood at the Cross.

In the earliest English poems on the subject, based on French prose versions, Joseph of Arimathea goes to Sarras, carrying the dish containing Christ's blood. He tells the story of Christ to Evalak, king of Sarras. Joseph aids him to defeat Tholomer, king of Babylon. Evalak and his brother-in-law are baptized by the names of Mordziens and Naciens (who figures in

later narratives). Joseph goes on a missionary journey, leaving the Grail in the care of two guardians, and is imprisoned in North Wales.

This narrative is in part reproduced and continued in Malory's 'Morte Darthur'. Launcelot is brought to the castle of King Pelles, and by enchantment has intercourse with the king's daughter Elaine, supposing her to be Guinevere. Their son is brought on the feast of Pentecost to the knights seated at the Round Table, and set in the vacant 'Siege Perilous'. In a burst of thunder and light the Holy Grail enters the hall, but none may see it. The knights, led by Gawain, vow to undertake its quest. The hermit Naciens warns them that none can achieve it who is not clean of his sins. Galahad obtains in an abbey a white shield with a red cross, which Joseph of Arimathea had given to King Evalak. Then follow numerous adventures by various knights in the course of their quest. Finally Galahad, Perceval, and Bors come to the castle of Carbonek, see a marvellous vision of the Saviour and partake of his body, receive the Grail from his hands, and convey it to Sarras. Galahad becomes king of Sarras, and after a year dies. The Grail is borne up to heaven and never seen again.

For Tennyson's idyll on this subject, see *Holy Grail*.

Grammar of Assent, *The*, a philosophical and religious treatise by Newman (q.v.) (1870), in which the author examines, on lines somewhat similar to those of Coleridge's 'Aids to Reflection' (q.v.), the nature of belief.

Grammont, see *Gramont*.

Gramont, *Mémoires de la Vie du Comte de*, an anonymous work published at Cologne in 1713, written by Anthony Hamilton (1646?-1720), the brother-in-law of the Comte de Gramont, who married Elizabeth Hamilton in 1663. The memoirs were edited (in French) by Horace Walpole and translated into English in 1714; and this translation, revised and annotated by Sir W. Scott, was reissued in 1811.

The first part of the memoirs deals with Gramont's life on the Continent down to the time of his banishment from the French court; the second part relates to the English court. It is an important source of information, but its trustworthiness on details is doubtful.

Granby, THE MARQUIS OF, in Dickens's 'The Pickwick Papers' (q.v.), the inn at Dorking kept by the second Mrs. Tony Weller.

Grand Cyrus, Le, see *Scudéry*.

Grandison, CARDINAL, a character in Disraeli's 'Lothair'.

Grandison, SIR CHARLES, see *Sir Charles Grandison*.

Grand Monarque, LE, Louis XIV.

Grand Old Man, see *G.O.M.*

Grand Question Debated, The, a poem by Swift (q.v.) (1729).

Grand Remonstrance, an indictment drawn up by the House of Commons in 1641 of the unconstitutional acts of Charles I, and a demand for ministers responsible to parliament.

Grand Siècle, LE, the age of Louis XIV of France, 1643-1715, signalized by military conquests and by literary and artistic splendour.

Granger, EDITH, in Dickens's 'Dombey and Son' (q.v.), the daughter of the Hon. Mrs. Skewton, and Dombey's second wife.

Grangerize, TO, to illustrate a book by the addition of prints, engravings, etc., especially such as have been cut out of other books. In 1769 James Granger (1723-76) published a 'Biographical History of England', with blank pages for the reception of engraved portraits; the filling up of the 'Granger' was for a short time a favourite hobby.

Granta, THE, the old name of the river Cam, which it retains above Cambridge.

Granta, The, a Cambridge University undergraduate periodical started in 1889.

Grantly, ARCHDEACON, a prominent character in A. Trollope's 'The Warden', 'Barchester Towers' (q.v.), and other novels of the Barsetshire series. Mrs.

Grantly is the elder daughter of Mr. Harding (the Warden); and Griselda, their daughter, marries Lord Dumbello.

Grantorto, in Spenser's 'Faerie Queene', v. xii, the tyrant from whom Sir Artegall rescues Irena (Ireland). He probably represents the spirit of rebellion.

Granville-Barker, HARLEY GRANVILLE (1877-1946), actor and dramatist, author of 'The Voysey Inheritance' (1905), and a number of other plays and publications, including four interesting series of Prefaces to plays of Shakespeare (1927, 1930, 1937, 1945).

Gratiano, a character in Shakespeare's 'The Merchant of Venice' (q.v.).

Grave Poem, a fragment of twenty-four lines in Old English, probably of the 12th cent., describing in gloomy terms the fate of the body committed to the grave. Longfellow's translation is well known.

For another poem on 'The Grave' see *Blair*.

Graves, ALFRED PERCEVAL (1846-1931), published volumes of Irish songs and ballads (including 'Father O'Flynn'), and an autobiography, 'To Return to All That' (1930).

Graves, RICHARD (1715-1804), novelist, author of 'The Spiritual Quixote' (1772); 'Columella, the Distressed Anchoret' (1776); 'Eugenius, or Anecdotes of the Golden Vale' (1785); 'Plexippus, or the Aspiring Plebeian' (1790); interesting less for their plots than for the picture they give of the social conditions of the time.

Graves, ROBERT RANKE (1895-   ), poet and novelist, son of A. P. Graves (q.v.). His first poetry appeared while he was serving in the First World War—'Over the Brazier' (1916), 'Fairies and Fusiliers' (1917)—and he has continued to publish poetry over the years. As a prose writer he is probably best known for his historical novels, 'I, Claudius' (1934), 'Claudius the God' (1934), and 'Count Belisarius' (1938). His autobiography, 'Good-bye to All That', appeared in 1929. His critical work includes 'The White Goddess: a historical grammar of poetic myth' (1948; amended and enlarged, 1952 and 1961). He was professor of poetry at Oxford from 1961 to 1966.

Graveyard School, the imitators of Robert Blair and Edward Young (qq.v.).

Gray, THOMAS (1716-71), educated at Eton with Horace Walpole, and at Cambridge. He accompanied Horace Walpole on a tour on the Continent in 1739-41, but they quarrelled in 1741 and returned home separately. Their friendship was renewed in 1744. Gray then resided at Cambridge, refused the laureateship in 1757, and was appointed professor of history and modern languages at Cambridge in 1768. He was buried at Stoke Poges in Bucks., a village with which the 'Elegy in a Country Churchyard' is traditionally identified.

His work as an English poet began in 1742, when he wrote his odes 'On Spring', 'On a Distant Prospect of Eton College', and 'On Adversity', and the 'Sonnet on the Death of West'. About the same year he began the 'Elegy in a Country Churchyard', which was finished in 1750. The 'Ode on the Death of a favourite Cat' (Walpole's) was written about 1747. In 1754 Gray finished his Pindaric ode on 'The Progress of Poesy' and in 1757 a second Pindaric ode 'The Bard'. These were published by Walpole in 1757. The popularity of his 'Elegy' led to his recognition as one of the foremost poets of the day and to the offer of the laureateship on the death of Colley Cibber. In his later years he devoted attention to Icelandic and Celtic verse and in imitation of this wrote the lays 'The Fatal Sisters' and 'The Descent of Odin' (1761). In 1769 he took a journey among the English Lakes, which is commemorated in the 'Journal' published in 1775, his most finished prose work. His letters are among the best in the language.

Gray's Inn, Holborn, one of the old inns of court. In its hall Shakespeare's 'The Comedy of Errors' was acted in Dec. 1594. Francis Bacon, Laud, and Southey were students there, and Tonson (qq.v.) lived there.

Great Cham, see *Cham*.

Great Commoner, THE, William Pitt the elder (q.v.).

Great Duke of Florence, *The*, a romantic comedy by Massinger (q.v.) (acted 1627, printed 1636); generally considered one of Massinger's best plays.

Great Expectations, a novel by Dickens (q.v.), which first appeared in 'All the Year Round' in 1860-1; published in book form in 1861.

It is the story of Philip Pirrip, commonly known as 'Pip', a village boy brought up by his termagant sister, the wife of the kindly blacksmith Joe Gargery. He is introduced to the house of Miss Havisham, a lady half-crazed by the desertion of her lover on her wedding day, who, in a spirit of revenge, has brought up the girl Estella to use her beauty as a means of torturing men. Pip falls in love with Estella, and aspires to become a gentleman. Expectations of wealth come to him from a mysterious source. He goes to London and meanly abandons the devoted Joe Gargery. His unknown benefactor proves to be an escaped convict, Abel Magwitch, to whom he, as a boy, had rendered a service; his great expectations fade away and he is penniless. Estella marries his sulky enemy, Bentley Drummle, by whom she is cruelly ill-treated. Taught by adversity, Pip returns to Joe Gargery and honest labour, and is finally reunited to Estella, who has also learnt her lesson. Other notable characters in the book are Joe's uncle, the impudent old impostor Pumblechook; Jaggers, the skilful Old Bailey lawyer, and his good-hearted clerk Wemmick; and Pip's friend in London, the 'dear boy' Herbert Pocket.

Great-heart, in Bunyan's 'The Pilgrim's Progress' (q.v.), the escort of Christiana and her children on their pilgrimage.

Great Nassau, William III.

Greats, in the University of Oxford, the colloquial name for the final examination for the degree of B.A., especially the examination for Honours in Literae

Humaniores. It was formerly known as GREAT GO.

Greaves, SIR LAUNCELOT, the hero of a novel of that name by Smollett (q.v.).

Grecian Coffee-house, THE, stood in Devereux Court, Essex Street, Strand, and was frequented by Addison, Steele, and Goldsmith. It was announced in No. 1 of 'The Tatler' that all learned articles would proceed from the Grecian.

Grecian Urn, Ode on a, see *Keats.*

Greco, EL, the name given to the painter, DOMENIKOS THEOTOKOPOULOS (1541–1614). He was born in Crete, probably studied under Titian, and settled in Toledo by 1577. He painted chiefly religious works and portraits, using distortion of form and livid colour for mystical and dramatic effect.

Greek Calends, a humorous expression for 'never', for the Greeks had no Calends, which were the first day of each month in the Roman calendar.

Greek Church, THE, see *Orthodox Church.*

Greeley, HORACE (1811–72), founder of the 'New York Tribune' (1841), and a prominent figure in the history of American journalism.

Green, JOHN RICHARD (1837–83), best known by his 'Short History of the English People' (1874). This work owed its great popularity to its simple style and generous outlook; the author includes in the scope of his work all the aspects, social, political, economic, and intellectual, of the national history. It was enlarged into 'The History of the English People' (1877–80). 'The Making of England' and 'The Conquest of England', in which he developed more fully certain parts of the 'History', appeared in 1881 and 1883.

Green, MATTHEW (1696–1737), author of 'The Spleen', a poem in praise of the contemplative life, written in witty, octosyllabic verse.

Green, THOMAS HILL (1836–82), philosopher. His publications began with a criticism of Locke, Hume, and Berkeley in the form of two very full introductions to a new edition of Hume's 'Treatise' (1874). His philosophical views are set forth in his 'Prolegomena to Ethics' (1883) and in his collected 'Works' (1885–8).

Green, VERDANT, the hero of a novel of that name by E. Bradley (q.v.) ('Cuthbert Bede'). It is a humorous account of the adventures of an innocent undergraduate.

Greenaway, KATE (1846–1901), illustrator of children's books, such as 'Kate Greenaway's Birthday Book' and 'Mother Goose', for which she often supplied the text. Her children, quaintly dressed in the costume of the early 19th cent., captured the public taste.

Greene, (HENRY) GRAHAM (1904–), novelist and dramatist. He early became a Roman Catholic convert and his religious views are reflected in many of his novels. These novels include 'Brighton Rock' (1938), 'The Power and the Glory' (1940), 'The Heart of the Matter' (1948), 'The End of the Affair' (1951), 'The Quiet American' (1956), and 'A Burnt-out Case' (1961). Others, described as 'entertainments', include 'Stamboul Train' (1932), 'A Gun for Sale' (1936), 'Loser Takes All' (1955), and 'Our Man in Havana' (1958). He has also written plays, essays, and short stories.

Greene, ROBERT (1560?–92), was educated at Cambridge, and was incorporated at Oxford in 1588. He appears from his own writings and the attacks of G. Harvey (q.v.) to have been a witty Bohemian, of good intentions but poor performance. He was assailed by G. Harvey in 'Foure Letters' as 'The Ape of Euphues', and defended by Nashe (q.v.) in 'Strange Newes'. He probably had some share in the authorship of the original 'Henry VI' plays, which Shakespeare revised or rewrote. Among his thirty-eight publications were pamphlets, romances, and five plays, including 'The Honorable Historie of Friar Bacon and Friar Bungay' (q.v.), acted in 1594. Of the romances, 'Menaphon' (1589), reprinted as 'Greene's Arcadia' (1599, etc.), 'Pandosto, or

Dorastus and Fawnia' (1588), and 'Philomela' (1592) contain lyrical passages of great charm. His numerous pamphlets include 'Euphues, his Censure of Philautus' (a continuation of Lyly, 1587), 'Greene's Mourning Garment' (1590), 'Never Too Late' (1590), 'Farewell to Folly' (1591), 'A Quip for an Upstart Courtier' (1592), and the autobiographical 'A Groatsworth of Wit bought with a Million of Repentance' (q.v.) (1592), in which occurs the attack on Shakespeare. His autobiographical sketches, and his tracts on 'Conny-catching' (1591 and 1592), in which he describes the methods of London rogues and swindlers, male and female, throw light on the low life of the times.

Green Knight, see *Gawain and the Green Knight*.

Green-sleeves, an inconstant lady-love, the subject of a ballad published in 1580. This, and the tune to which it was sung, became very popular, and both are mentioned by Shakespeare ('The Merry Wives of Windsor', II. i and v. v).

Greenwich Hospital stands beside the Thames on the site of a Tudor palace where Henry VIII and his daughters, Mary and Elizabeth, were born. A new palace was planned by Charles II, but only King Charles's Block was built (by John Webb). This was incorporated into the hospital for disabled seamen established by Queen Mary and built by Wren. Hawksmoor and Vanbrugh also contributed to the design.

Greenwich Observatory was erected by Charles II at the instance of Sir Jonas Moore, the mathematician, and Sir Christopher Wren. The meridian of Greenwich was adopted as the universal meridian at an international conference in Washington in 1884. (The work of the Observatory is now carried out at Herstmonceux Castle in Sussex.)

GREENWICH TIME is the mean time of the meridian of Greenwich.

Greg, SIR WALTER WILSON (1875-1959), bibliographer, general editor of the Malone Society's publications from 1906 to 1939. His writings include a great deal of editorial work on Shakespeare and on other Elizabethan texts.

Gregorian Calendar, see *Calendar*.

Gregorian chant, music, etc., the ancient system of ritual music, known as plain-chant or plain-song, characterized by free rhythm and a limited scale.

Gregory I, ST., 'The Great', Pope 590-604, one of the greatest of the early occupants of the see. It was he who sent Augustine (q.v.) to England. He was the author of the 'Cura Pastoralis' (see *Alfred*), 'Dialogues', 'Letters', homilies, etc.

Gregory VII, see *Hildebrand*.

Gregory, AUGUSTA, LADY (1852-1932), *née* Persse, married in 1881 Sir William Gregory. She co-operated with W. B. Yeats (q.v.) in the creation of the Irish National Theatre, for which she wrote many plays.

Gregory of Tours (*c*. 540-94), bishop of Tours, our chief authority for the early Merovingian period of French history.

Grendel, see *Beowulf*.

Grenfell, JULIAN HENRY (1888-1915), was killed early in the First World War. He is the author of the fine poem 'Into Battle'. The few other poems left by Grenfell are in a lighter vein.

Grenville, SIR RICHARD (1541?-91), the naval commander who, when his ship the 'Revenge' was isolated off Flores, fought fifteen Spanish ships for fifteen hours, and was mortally wounded. The exploit is celebrated in Tennyson's poem 'The Revenge'.

Gresham, FRANK, one of the principal characters in Trollope's 'Dr. Thorne'.

Gretchen, diminutive in German of Margaret, the principal female character in Pt. I of Goethe's 'Faust' (q.v.).

Gretna Green, a few miles NW. of Carlisle and just across the border, a spot celebrated for runaway marriages. The practice was in 1856 made illegal unless one of the parties had lived in Scotland for twenty-one days.

Grettla Saga, see *Saga*.

Greuze, JEAN-BAPTISTE (1725–1805), French painter of sentimental and moral scenes.

Greville, CHARLES CAVENDISH FULKE (1794–1865), was clerk to the council from 1821 to 1859, and intimate with statesmen of both political parties. This, and his remarkable insight into character, give exceptional interest to the three series of 'Greville Memoirs', of which the first, covering the reigns of George IV and William IV, was published in 1874. The second, dealing with the years 1837–52, and the third with the years 1852–60, appeared with some suppressions in 1885 and 1887. A complete edition appeared in 1938.

Greville, SIR FULKE, *first Baron Brooke* (1554–1628), came to court with Sir Philip Sidney, and became a favourite of Elizabeth. He was a member of the 'Areopagus' (see *Sidney*), a member of parliament, and held various important offices. He befriended Bacon, Camden, Coke, Daniel, and D'Avenant.

Except the tragedy of 'Mustapha' (1609) and one or two poems in 'The Phoenix Nest' and 'England's Helicon', Greville's works appeared only after his death. A collection of works 'written in his youth' was printed in 1633, his 'Life of Sidney' in 1652, and his 'Remains' in 1670. His complete works were reprinted by Grosart in 1870. Of these the principal are the tragedies of 'Mustapha' and 'Alaham', which Charles Lamb described as 'political treatises, not plays'; and 'Caelica', a collection of 'sonnets' and songs.

Grewgious, MR., a character in Dickens's 'Edwin Drood' (q.v.).

Grey Friars, Franciscans (q.v.).

Grey of Fallodon, EDWARD GREY, *Viscount* (1862–1933), foreign secretary, 1905–16; author of 'Fly-Fishing' (1899), 'The Charm of Birds' (1927), and his memoirs 'Twenty Five Years', which are valuable historically.

Gride, ARTHUR, a character in Dickens's 'Nicholas Nickleby' (q.v.).

Grieve, CHRISTOPHER MURRAY (1892–1978), poet and critic, was one of the founders of the Scottish Nationalist Party. Under the pseudonym 'Hugh McDiarmid' he became a leader of the Scottish literary renaissance, using Lowland Scots ('Lallans') in his poetry and seeking to revive the tradition of Henryson, Dunbar, and Burns (qq.v.) and the Scottish ballads. His 'Collected Poems' were published in 1962. His autobiography, 'Lucky Poet' (1943), expresses his passionate Anglophobia and desire for Scottish independence.

Griffin, GRIFFON, GRYPHON, a fabulous animal usually represented with the head and wings of an eagle and the body and hind-quarters of a lion.

Griffith Gaunt, or Jealousy, a novel by C. Reade (q.v.) (1866).

Grim, the fisherman in 'Havelok the Dane' (q.v.), the legendary founder of Grimsby.

Grimald, GRIMALDE, or GRIMVALD, NICHOLAS (1519–62), chaplain to Bishop Ridley, contributed to, and assisted in the compilation of, 'Tottel's Miscellany' (see *Tottel*). He published translations from Virgil and Cicero, and two Latin dramas.

Grimaldi, JOSEPH (1779–1837), a celebrated clown and pantomimist. His 'Memoirs' were edited by Dickens (2 vols., 1838).

Grimalkin, probably from *grey* and *malkin*, a name given to a cat, and contemptuously applied to a jealous or imperious old woman.

Grimbald, or GRIMBOLD, or GRYMBOLD, ST. (820?–903), a native of Flanders. Alfred summoned him to England for the promotion of learning, and appointed him abbot of the New Minster at Winchester. He is commemorated on 8 July.

Grimes, PETER, the subject of Letter xxii in Crabbe's 'The Borough' (q.v.). He was a villainous fellow who killed his apprentices by ill treatment. B. Britten's opera 'Peter Grimes' was produced in 1945.

Grimes, THOMAS, Tom's employer in Kingsley's 'The Water Babies' (q.v.).

Grimm, JACOB LUDWIG CARL (1785-1863), and WILHELM CARL (1786-1859), two German brothers, were authors of works on German philology and German folklore, and are chiefly known in England by their fairy tales ('Kinderund Hausmärchen', 1812-15), of which an English translation, illustrated by George Cruikshank, was published in 1823 under the title 'German Popular Stories'. There have been many later editions and selections in this country.

Jacob Grimm in his 'Deutsche Grammatik' formulated *Grimm's Law* of the mutations of the consonants in the several Aryan languages.

Grimwig, MR., a character in Dickens's 'Oliver Twist' (q.v.).

Gringolet, Gawain's horse (e.g. in the story of 'Sir Gawain and the Green Knight', q.v.). It has been said that the name belonged originally to the boat of the mythical hero Wade (q.v.); but it is found some centuries earlier as the name of Gawain's horse.

Grip, in Dickens's 'Barnaby Rudge' (q.v.), Barnaby's raven.

Griselda, see *Patient Grissil.*

Groat, a silver coin first issued in England by Edward I, and more permanently by Edward III, worth fourpence. None was struck after the time of Charles II, until the fourpenny piece was revived by William IV and continued to be issued until 1856.

Groatsettar, THE MISSES, characters in Scott's 'The Pirate'.

Groatsworth of Wit bought with a Million of Repentance, A, an autobiographical prose tract by R. Greene (q.v.) (1592). The tract ends with the curious 'Address' to his fellow playwrights, Marlowe, Lodge, and Peele, which contains the well-known passage about the 'Crow, beautified with our Feathers', the 'Johannes Factotum', who 'is in his owne conceit the only Shakescene in a Countrey', probably referring to Shakespeare, whose earliest plays were adaptations of works by his predecessors.

Grobian (German *Grobheit*, rudeness), the name of an imaginary personage, often referred to by writers of the 15th and 16th cents. in Germany as a type of boorishness.

Grocyn, WILLIAM (1446?-1519), educated at Winchester and New College, Oxford, held various ecclesiastical preferments. He studied in Italy with Linacre (q.v.) and was instrumental in introducing the study of Greek at Oxford.

Grongar Hill, see *Dyer (J.).*

Grosart, ALEXANDER BALLOCH (1827-99), author and editor, remembered for his reprints of rare Elizabethan and Jacobean literature.

Grosseteste, ROBERT (*d.* 1253), bishop of Lincoln, was the author of translations from the Greek, including Aristotle's Nicomachean Ethics and the works of Pseudo Dionysius Areopagita (see *Dionysius the Areopagite*); of works on philosophy, theology, and husbandry; and of an allegorical poem in French. He earned the commendation of Roger Bacon in the field of science, of Matthew Paris, of Wycliffe, and of Gower. Also he opposed the popes (especially Innocent IV) in their encroachments on the Church in England.

Grote, GEORGE (1794-1871), banker, was M.P. for the City of London from 1832 to 1841 and took an active part in favour of the Reform movement. He retired from parliament in order to devote himself to his famous 'History of Greece', which was published in 1846-56, and achieved immediate success.

Grotesque, apparently from *grotte*, grottoes, chambers of ancient buildings revealed by excavations and which contained those mural paintings which were typical examples of the 'grotesque' style; hence a kind of decorative painting or sculpture, consisting of representations of human and animal forms, fantastically combined and interwoven with foliage and flowers.

Grotius, Hugo (1583-1645), Dutch statesman and jurist. He wrote in 1601 a sacred drama in Latin, 'Adamus Exsul', with which Milton was probably familiar when he wrote 'Paradise Lost'. Grotius was Dutch ambassador in London in 1613, but was later condemned to imprisonment for life. From this he escaped, became the ambassador of Queen Christina of Sweden at the French court, and died, after shipwreck, in her service. He wrote a large number of works, but his principal title to fame is his great treatise of international law, the 'De jure Belli et Pacis' (1625).

Grove, Sir George (1820-1900), a writer on a great variety of subjects, is especially notable as having projected and edited the 'Dictionary of Music and Musicians' (4 vols. 1878-89, and later editions).

Growth of Love, The, a sonnet-sequence by R. Bridges (q.v.).

Grubbinol, a shepherd in Gay's 'The Shepherd's Week' (q.v.).

Grub Street, London, according to Samuel Johnson was 'originally the name of a street near Moorfields in London, much inhabited by writers of small histories, dictionaries, and temporary poems, whence any mean production is called *grubstreet*'. The name of the street was changed in the 19th cent. to Milton Street (Cripplegate). 'Grub Street' is current in modern usage as an epithet meaning 'of the nature of literary hackwork'.

Grub Street Journal, The, during 1730-8, vigorously attacked Pope's adversaries in the 'Dunciad' controversy. Pope probably had some part in its production.

Grueby, John, a character in Dickens's 'Barnaby Rudge' (q.v.).

Grundy, Mrs., the symbol of conventional propriety. See *Speed the Plough.*

Gryll, in Spenser's 'Faerie Queene', II. xii. 86, the hog in the Bower of Acrasia who repined greatly at being changed back into a man.

Gryll Grange, the last novel of Peacock (q.v.) (1860 or 1861).

Gryphon, see *Griffin.*

Guanhamara, see *Guinevere.*

Guardian, The, (1) a periodical started by Steele (q.v.) in March 1713. It professed to abstain from political questions, and Addison contributed fifty-one papers to it. It included also among its contributors Berkeley, Pope, and Gay. But Steele soon launched into political controversy, and owing to some disagreement with Tonson, the publisher, the 'Guardian' came to an end in Oct. 1713 and was succeeded by the 'Englishman'; (2) a national daily newspaper originally published as 'The Manchester Guardian' (q.v.).

Gubbins or Gubbings, a contemptuous name formerly given to the inhabitants of a district on the edge of Dartmoor, who are said to have been absolute savages.

Gudrun, (1) the subject of a German national epic of the 13th cent.; (2) in the 'Volsunga Saga' and in W. Morris's 'Sigurd the Volsung' (q.v.), the daughter of the king of the Nibelungs; (3) the heroine of the Laxdaela Saga.

Gudrun, The Lovers of, one of the tales in W. Morris's 'The Earthly Paradise', a translation of the Laxdaela Saga (see *Saga*).

Guelphs and the **Ghibellines,** The, the two great parties in medieval Italian politics, supporting respectively the popes and the emperors.

Guest, Stephen, a character in G. Eliot's 'The Mill on the Floss' (q.v.).

Guiderius, in Shakespeare's 'Cymbeline' (q.v.), the elder son of the king.

Guido da Colonna, or delle Colonne, a 13th-cent. Sicilian writer of Latin romances, author of a 'Historia Trojana' which was in fact a prose version of a poem of Benoît de Sainte-Maure (q.v.). His romance was translated in poems attributed to Barbour and Huchoun, and by Lydgate in his 'Troy Book'. The story of 'Troilus and Cressida', taken by Guido from Benoît de Sainte-Maure, was in turn developed by Boccaccio, Chaucer, Henryson, and Shakespeare (qq.v.).

Guido Franceschini, COUNT, one of the principal characters in R. Browning's 'The Ring and the Book' (q.v.).

Guignol, the chief character in the popular French puppet-show of that name, similar to our 'Punch and Judy'. GRAND GUIGNOL is a term applied to a theatre presenting plays of a gruesome character.

Guildenstern, a character in Shakespeare's 'Hamlet' (q.v.).

Guildford, JOHN OF, and NICHOLAS OF, see *Owl and the Nightingale*.

Guildhall, THE, the town hall of the city of London. The present Guildhall was built early in the 15th cent., replacing an earlier hall in Aldermanbury. The interior of the hall, burnt out in the Great Fire of 1666, was restored, but was severely damaged by an air-raid in 1940; the main hall and crypt have been restored.

Guillaume de Lorris, see *Roman de la Rose*.

Guillotin, JOSEPH IGNACE (1738–1814), a French physician, member of the Constituent Assembly, who supported the use of the guillotine, to which his name was given, though he did not invent it.

Guinea, originally an English gold coin. In 1663 the newly issued gold 20*s.* piece commanded a premium, and was generally taken for 21*s.* or 22*s.* Guinea gold money, struck from the intake from the African Company, was so prevalent at this time, that the coin which official documents still called a pound was usually nicknamed a 'guinea'. In 1816, when monometallism was adopted, the gold £1 was substituted for the 21*s.* guinea.

Guinea, Chrysal, or the Adventures of a, see *Adventures of a Guinea*.

Guinevere, the wife of King Arthur (q.v.) in the Arthurian legend. For her story see *Launcelot*. A more subtle and favourable view of her character than is found in the old romances is given in W. Morris's 'Defence of Guenevere' (1858) and in Tennyson's idyll 'Guinevere' (1859, q.v.).

Guinevere, one of Tennyson's 'Idylls of the King' (q.v.) (1859).

The poem describes how Guinevere bids Lancelot leave her and withdraw to his own lands. They meet for the last time, when the voice of the spying Modred is heard. Lancelot rushes out and hurls him headlong; then bids the queen fly with him. But she, declaring that she is shamed for ever, betakes herself to the nunnery at Almesbury. There she is visited by Arthur, and falls prostrate at his feet. He denounces the evil that she has wrought, and finally forgives her and bids her farewell. Heart-broken and contrite, she remains with the nuns, becomes their abbess, and after three years dies.

Guiscardo, see *Sigismonda*.

Guise, the name of a branch of the princely house of Lorraine. Mary of Guise was the queen of James V of Scotland and mother of Mary Stuart.

Guizot, FRANÇOIS (1787–1874), French statesman and historian, a minister under Louis Philippe. Among his historical works were the 'Histoire de la révolution d'Angleterre', 'Histoire de la civilisation en Europe', 'Histoire de la civilisation française', 'Essais sur l'histoire de France', etc.

Gulbeyaz, in Byron's 'Don Juan' (q.v.), the sultana to whom the hero is sold as a slave.

Gulistan, 'the rose garden', the name of the principal poem of the Persian poet Sadi (q.v.).

Gulliver's Travels, a satire by Swift (q.v.) (1726). Swift probably intended it to form part of the 'Memoirs of Scriblerus', and appears to have worked at the book from as early as 1720.

In the first part Lemuel Gulliver, a surgeon on a merchant ship, relates his shipwreck on the island of *Lilliput*, the inhabitants of which are six inches high, everything on the island being in the proportion of one inch to one foot as compared with things as we know them. Owing to this diminutive scale, the civil feuds of the inhabitants, the pomp of the emperor, the war with their neighbours across the channel, are made to look ridiculous. The English political parties and religious dissensions are satirized in the description of the wearers of high heels and low heels, and of the controversy on the question whether eggs should be broken at the big or small end.

In the second part Gulliver is accidentally left ashore on *Brobdingnag*, where the inhabitants are as tall as steeples, and everything else is in proportion.

The third part is occupied with a visit to the flying island of *Laputa*, and its neighbouring continent and capital *Lagado*. Here the satire is directed against philosophers, men of science, historians, and projectors, with special reference to the South Sea Bubble. In the Island of Sorcerers he is enabled to call up the great men of old, and discovers, from their answers to his questions, the deceptions of history. The *Struldbrugs*, a race endowed with immortality, so far from finding this a boon, turn out to be the most miserable of mankind.

The bitterness and misanthropy of Swift are accentuated in the fourth part, describing the country of the *Houyhnhnms*, or horses endowed with reason. Here the simplicity and virtues of the horses are contrasted with the disgusting brutality of the *Yahoos*, beasts in the shape of men.

The whole work, with the exception of certain passages, has the rare merit of appealing to both old and young, as a powerful satire on man and human institutions, and as a fascinating tale of travels in wonderland.

Guls Hornebooke, The, a satirical book of manners, by Dekker (q.v.) (1609). It is an attack on the fops and gallants of the day under the guise of ironical instructions.

Gummidge, MRS., a character in Dickens's 'David Copperfield' (q.v.).

Gunnar, in the 'Volsunga Saga' and W. Morris's 'Sigurd the Volsung' (q.v.), the king of the Nibelungs and the husband of Brynhild.

Gunpowder Plot, the plot of a few Roman Catholics to blow up the Houses

of Parliament on 5 Nov. 1605. The plot was devised by Robert Catesby, and Guy Fawkes was chosen to put it into execution. But it was betrayed, and Fawkes arrested on 4 Nov. The conspirators who were taken alive were executed; Catesby was killed while resisting arrest.

Guppy, a character in Dickens's 'Bleak House' (q.v.).

Gurney, THOMAS (1705-70), appointed shorthand-writer at the Old Bailey, 1737 (?1748), the first shorthand-writer to hold an official appointment. His grandson, William Brodie Gurney, shorthand-writer to the Houses of Parliament (1813), is referred to by Byron in 'Don Juan', i. 189.

Gurth, the Saxon swineherd in Scott's 'Ivanhoe' (q.v.).

Gustavus Adolphus (1594-1632), king of Sweden (1611-32). In 1630 he invaded Germany, and carried out his celebrated campaign, in which he defeated Tilly at Breitenfeld near Leipzig and Wallenstein at Lützen, but fell in the latter battle.

Guster, a character in Dickens's 'Bleak House' (q.v.).

Gutenberg, JOHANN (*c.* 1400-1468?), one of the earliest of German printers, inventor of movable printing types.

Guthlac, ST. (*d.* 714), a young nobleman of Mercia who became a hermit at Crowland or Croyland in Lincolnshire. His life is the subject of an Anglo-Saxon poem in the 'Exeter Book' (q.v.). There are frequent references to St. Guthlac and the abbey of Crowland in C. Kingsley's 'Hereward the Wake' (q.v.).

Guthrie, THOMAS ANSTEY, see *Anstey (F.)*.

Guy, THOMAS (1645?-1724), the founder of Guy's Hospital, set up as a bookseller in London in 1668 and was one of the Oxford University printers, 1679-92. He greatly increased his fortune by selling his South Sea stock, and was a liberal benefactor.

Guy Fawkes, see *Gunpowder Plot*.

Guy Livingstone, or Thorough, a novel by G. A. Lawrence (1857).

This novel shows a revolt against the

moral and domestic conventions of the period. The hero is an officer of the Life Guards, very wealthy, of colossal size and strength, and a great sportsman, who beats prize-fighters and performs other exploits, but whose lack of principle involves him in amatory difficulties.

This crude piece of melodrama was parodied by Bret Harte in his 'Guy Heavystone'.

Guy Mannering, a novel by Sir W. Scott (q.v.) (1815).

The story, laid in the 18th cent., centres in the fortunes of young Harry Bertram, son of the laird of Ellangowan, who is kidnapped by smugglers when a child, and carried to Holland. This is done at the instigation of Glossin, who has hopes of acquiring on easy terms the Ellangowan estate, in default of an heir male. Bertram, ignorant of his parentage, and bearing the name of Brown, goes to India, joins the army, and serves with distinction under Colonel Guy Mannering. Bertram (or Brown) is suspected by Mannering of paying attentions to his wife, and is wounded by him in a duel and left for dead. In reality Bertram is in love with Julia, Mannering's daughter. Recovering from his wound, he follows her to England and the neighbourhood of Ellangowan. Glossin, now in possession of the Ellangowan estate, is alarmed by the return of ᴗertram and the possibility, that he may learn the secret of his parentage. He plots with Dirk Hatteraick, the smuggler who had originally kidnapped the child, to carry him off once more and make away with him. But an old gipsy, Meg Merrilies, also recognizes Harry and devotes all her energies to secure his restoration. She frustrates the plot with the help of Bertram and Dandie Dinmont, a sturdy lowland farmer, but at the sacrifice of her own life. Hatteraick and Glossin are captured, and Hatteraick, after murdering Glossin in prison, takes his own life. Bertram is acknowledged and restored to

his property and to Mannering's favour, and marries Julia. The novel not only includes the notable characters of Meg Merrilies and Dandie Dinmont but also that of Dominie Sampson, the uncouth simple-minded tutor of the little Harry Bertram.

Guy of Warwick, a popular verse romance, containing some 7,000 lines, of the early 14th cent. Guy is the son of Siward, steward of Rohand, earl of Warwick. The poem recounts his exploits undertaken in order to win the hand of Felice, daughter of the earl.

The legend was accepted as authentic by the chroniclers and versified by Lydgate about 1450.

Guyon, SIR, in Spenser's 'Faerie Queene', the knight of Temperance. His various exploits, the visit to the cave of Mammon, the capture of Acrasia, and the destruction of her Bower of Bliss, are related in Bk. II, v–xii.

Guzman, DON, a character in Kingsley's 'Westward Ho!' (q.v.).

Gwyn, ELEANOR (1650–87), generally known as Nell Gwyn, orange-girl, actress, and mistress of Charles II. She was illiterate, but good in comedy, prologues, and epilogues. She figures in Scott's 'Peveril of the Peak'.

Gwynedd or GWYNETH, North Wales.

Gyges, a Lydian shepherd, who, according to Plato (Rep. ii. 359), descended into a chasm, where he found a brazen horse. Opening its side he saw within it the body of a man of unusual size. From his finger Gyges took a brazen ring, which, when he wore it, made him invisible. By means of this he introduced himself to the queen, murdered her husband, married her, and usurped the crown of Lydia.

According to Herodotus (i. 7 et seq.), the king, Candaules, boasted of his wife's beauty to Gyges, and allowed him to see her unveiled. She thereupon persuaded Gyges to murder her husband.

H

Habeas Corpus, a writ requiring the production in court of the body of a person who has been imprisoned, in order that the lawfulness of the imprisonment may be investigated. The HABEAS CORPUS ACT is the name commonly given to the Act of 1679 by which the enforcement of this writ was facilitated.

Habington, WILLIAM (1605-64), married Lucy Herbert, and celebrated her in 'Castara', a collection of love poems (1634). A later edition (1635) contained in addition some elegies on a friend, and the final edition of 1640 a number of sacred poems. In the latter year Habington also published a tragi-comedy, 'The Queene of Arragon'.

Habsburg, see *Hapsburg*.

Hades or PLUTO, in Greek mythology, the god of the nether world, the son of Cronos and Rhea, and brother of Zeus and Poseidon. Visiting the island of Sicily, after an earthquake, he beheld Proserpine, the daughter of Demeter (Ceres), gathering flowers in the plain of Enna, and becoming enamoured of her carried her away (see *Proserpine*). Proserpine accordingly became the queen of hell.

The name 'Hades' was transferred to his kingdom, a gloomy sunless abode, where, according to Homer, the ghosts of the dead flit about like bats. Its approach was barred by the rivers Styx, Cocytus, and Acheron with its tributary Phlegethon (see *Styx*). Tartarus was the region of Hades in which the most impious of men suffered retribution. The asphodel meadows were reserved for those who deserved neither bliss nor extreme punishment. The shades of the blessed were conveyed elsewhere (see *Elysium, Fortunate Isles*), but Virgil places Elysium in Hades.

Hadrian (PUBLIUS AELIUS HADRIANUS) (A.D. 76-138), Roman emperor 117-38. He was a patron of art and learning. He visited Britain and caused the wall to be built between the Solway and the mouth of the Tyne, known as HADRIAN'S WALL.

Haemony, in Milton's 'Comus', a herb 'more medicinal than moly' (q.v.) and potent against 'enchantments, mildew, blast, or damp, Or ghastly Furies' apparition'.

Hafiz, SHAMS-ED-DIN MUHAMMAD (*d. c.* 1390), a famous Persian poet and philosopher. He sang of love and flowers and nightingales, and the mutability of life. His principal work is the 'Diwan', a collection of short pieces.

Haggard, SIR HENRY RIDER (1856-1925), author of many popular romances, including 'King Solomon's Mines' (1885), 'She' (1887), 'Allan Quatermain' (1887), 'Ayesha, or the Return of She' (1905).

Haidée, a character in Byron's 'Don Juan' (q.v.).

Haj or HAJJ, the pilgrimage to Mecca, imposed as a moral obligation on all Muslims. HAJJI is a title conferred on those who have performed the pilgrimage.

Hakluyt, RICHARD (1552?-1616), was chaplain to Sir Edward Stafford, ambassador at Paris, 1583-8. Here he learnt much of the maritime enterprises of other nations, and decided to devote himself to collecting and publishing the accounts of English explorations, and to this purpose he gave the remainder of his life. In 1582 he published 'Divers Voyages touching the Discovery of America', in 1587 his 'Notable History, containing four Voyages made by certain French Captains into Florida'. His 'Principall Navigations, Voiages, and Discoveries of the English Nation' was issued in 1589, and, much enlarged, in three volumes, 1598-1600. He thus brought to light the hitherto obscure achievements of English navigators, and gave a great impetus to discovery and colonization. He left unpublished a number of papers which came into the hands of Purchas (q.v.).

Halcombe, MARIAN, a character in Wilkie Collins's 'The Woman in White' (q.v.).

Halcyone or ALCYONE, a daughter of Aeolus and the wife of Ceyx. Her husband perished in a shipwreck. Halcyone was warned in a dream of her husband's fate, and when she found, on the morrow, his body on the shore, she threw herself into the sea. Halcyone and Ceyx were changed into the birds that bear her name, which are fabled to keep the waters calm while they are nesting. Hence the expression 'halcyon days'.

The story is told in Gower's 'Confessio Amantis' and elsewhere.

Hale, SIR MATTHEW (1609-76), lord chief justice, and a voluminous writer on many subjects; but much of his best work was left in manuscript, and published long after his death. His principal legal work was a 'History of the Common Law of England' (1713).

Hales, ALEXANDER OF, see *Alexander of Hales*.

Haliburton, THOMAS CHANDLER (1796-1865), born at Windsor, Nova Scotia. Humorist, author of the shrewd sayings of the Yankee clock-maker 'Sam Slick', first series 1837, second 1838, and third 1840. Under its humorous disguise, the work is in reality a piece of political propaganda, designed to stimulate reform.

Halifax, MARQUESS OF, see *Savile*.

Halkett, COLONEL and CECILIA, characters in Meredith's 'Beauchamp's Career' (q.v.).

Hall, EDWARD (d. 1547), the author of a chronicle which is interesting for the account it gives of the times of Henry VIII.

Hall, JOSEPH (1574-1656), bishop of Exeter 1627-41, and Norwich 1641-7. He was expelled from his palace about 1647. He published his 'Virgidemiarum Sex Libri', vol. i in 1597, and vol. ii in 1598 (ed. A. B. Grosart, 1879). His 'Characters of Virtues and Vices' (1608)

are sketches on the model of Theophrastus (q.v.), designed with an educative and moral purpose. Hall claimed to be the first of English satirists, and although Lodge and Donne may in some respects have anticipated him, he certainly introduced the Juvenalian satire in English. (See also *Smectymnuus*.)

Hallam, ARTHUR HENRY (1811-33), the close friend of Lord Tennyson, died suddenly at Vienna at an early age. He is chiefly remembered as the subject of Tennyson's 'In Memoriam' (q.v.). His own 'Remains' (in verse and prose) appeared in 1834.

Hallam, HENRY (1777-1859), historian, spent some ten years on the preparation of his first published work, 'A View of the State of Europe during the Middle Ages' (1818). His best-known work is his 'Constitutional History of England' (1827).

Halley, EDMUND (1656-1742), the astronomer, originated by his suggestions Newton's 'Principia'. Famous for his accurate prediction of the return in 1758 of the comet (named after him) of 1531, 1607, and 1682.

Halliwell, afterwards **Halliwell-Phillipps,** JAMES ORCHARD (1820-89), a noted Shakespearian scholar.

Hallow-e'en, see *All-Hallows' Day*.

Hals, FRANS (c. 1580-1666), a celebrated Dutch portrait-painter.

Hamadryads, see *Dryads*.

Hamel, the cow in 'Reynard the Fox' (q.v.).

Hamilton, ANTHONY, see *Gramont*.

Hamilton, CHARLES (1875-1961), author, under many pseudonyms, of boys' weekly papers, of which the most famous were 'The Gem' (1907-39), written under the name MARTIN CLIFFORD, and 'The Magnet' (1908-40), under the name FRANK RICHARDS. 'The Magnet' introduced Billy Bunter of Greyfriars School.

Hamilton, EMMA, LADY (1761?-1815), *née* Lyon, married Sir William Hamilton (1730-1803), British ambassador at Naples, in 1791. She first saw Nelson in 1793, and became intimate with him in

1798. Owing to her extravagance, she died in obscurity and poverty, in spite of legacies from Nelson and Hamilton.

Hamilton, WILLIAM, OF BANGOUR (1704-54), author of the melodious 'Braes of Yarrow', and of the earliest Homeric translation into English blank verse.

Hamilton, SIR WILLIAM (1788-1856), the philosopher. His philosophical reputation was made by a number of articles which appeared in 'The Edinburgh Review' from 1829 to 1836.

A man of great philosophical erudition rather than a great philosophical thinker, Hamilton represents the influence of Kant upon the common-sense philosophy of the Scottish school as set forth by Reid. His philosophical views were vigorously attacked by J. S. Mill (q.v.).

Hamilton, SIR WILLIAM ROWAN (1805-65), famous mathematician. His fame rests principally on his discovery of the science of quaternions, a higher branch of the calculus. He had considerable poetical gifts, and was a close friend of Wordsworth.

Hamlet, a tragedy by Shakespeare (q.v.), probably produced before 1603-4, published imperfectly in quarto in 1603, and fully in quarto in 1604, and with some omissions in the first folio. The story is in Saxo Grammaticus and was accessible in Belleforest's 'Histoires Tragiques'. There was also an earlier play on the subject, not now extant.

A noble king of Denmark has been murdered by his brother Claudius, who has supplanted on the throne the dead man's son, Hamlet, and married with indecent haste the dead man's widow, Gertrude. Hamlet meets the ghost of his dead father, who relates the circumstances of the murder and demands vengeance. Hamlet vows obedience; but his melancholy, introspective, and scrupulous nature makes him irresolute and dilatory in action. He counterfeits madness to escape the suspicion that he is threatening danger to the king. His behaviour is attributed to love for Ophelia (daughter of Polonius, the lord chamberlain), whom he has previously courted but now treats rudely. He tests the ghost's story by having a play acted before the king reproducing the circumstances of the murder, and the king betrays himself. A scene follows in which Hamlet violently upbraids the queen. Thinking he hears the king listening behind the arras, he draws his sword and kills instead Polonius. The king now determines to destroy Hamlet. He sends him on a mission to England, with intent to have him killed there. But pirates capture Hamlet and send him back to Denmark. He arrives to find that Ophelia, crazed with grief, has perished by drowning. Her brother Laertes, a strong contrast to the character of Hamlet, has hurried home to take vengeance for the death of his father Polonius. The king contrives a fencing match between Hamlet and Laertes, in which the latter uses a poisoned sword, and kills Hamlet; but not before Hamlet has mortally wounded Laertes and stabbed the king; while Gertrude has drunk a poisoned cup intended for her son.

The play, and the character of Hamlet, have been the subject of much critical discussion.

Hamley, MR., MRS., OSBORNE, and ROGER, characters in Mrs. Gaskell's 'Wives and Daughters'.

Hammett, DASHIELL (1894-1961), American writer of detective stories. His best-known books are 'The Glass Key' (1931) and 'The Thin Man' (1932).

Hampden, JOHN (1594-1643), famous as the leader of the resistance to the imposition of ship-money (q.v.). He was impeached in 1642, but escaped the king's attempt to arrest him. He was mortally wounded in a skirmish at Chalgrove Field, near Oxford.

Hampton Court, on the Thames, was built by Cardinal Wolsey, and was ceded by him to Henry VIII. For two centuries it was a favourite residence of the English sovereigns. In William III's reign part of it was rebuilt by Wren.

Hampton Court Conference, a conference held in 1604 to settle points of dispute between the Church party and the Puritans, out of which arose the preparation of the Authorized Version of the Bible. See *Bible, The English*.

Hanaud, the detective in A. E. W. Mason's stories, 'At the Villa Rose', 'The House of the Arrow', 'The Prisoner in the Opal', etc.

Handel (originally HAENDEL), GEORGE FREDERICK (1685-1759), born in Saxony, came to England in 1710. His opera 'Rinaldo' was produced with great success at the Queen's Theatre, Haymarket, in 1711. He settled permanently in England in 1712, composed 'Esther', his first English oratorio (performed 1720), and 'Acis and Galatea' (performed 1720 or 1721). Handel was appointed court composer in 1727 and produced a number of operas at Covent Garden and Lincoln's Inn Fields, also musical settings for Dryden's 'Ode on St. Cecilia's Day' and 'Alexander's Feast'. His oratorio 'Israel in Egypt' was composed in 1738; the 'Messiah' was first heard (in Dublin) in 1741; his last oratorio, 'Jephthah', was produced at Covent Garden in 1752. He carried choral music to its highest point, but in instrumental did not advance beyond his contemporaries.

Handlyng Synne, a translation, in eight-syllabled verse, of the 'Manuel des Pechiez' of William of Wadington, by Robert Mannyng (1288-1338) of Brunne (Bourne in Lincolnshire), a Gilbertine monk, written between 1303 and 1338. Mannyng is a good story-teller, and his work throws much light on the manners of the time, notably on the tyranny and rapacity of the lords and knights.

Hand of Ethelberta, The, a novel by Hardy (q.v.) (1876).

Handy Andy, a novel by S. Lover (q.v.).

Hannay, J. O., see *Birmingham, George A.*

Hans Carvel, a *fabliau* by Matthew Prior (q.v.). The subject of it, a coarse jest on the method of retaining a wife's fidelity, has been treated in the 'Facetiae'

of Poggio, by Rabelais (III. xxviii), and other writers.

Hansard, the official reports of the proceedings of the Houses of Parliament, colloquially so called because they were for a long period compiled by Messrs. Hansard. They are now a regular publication of H.M. Stationery Office.

Hanse, THE, from a MHG. word meaning association, merchants' guild, was the name of a famous political and commercial league, also called the HANSEATIC LEAGUE, of Germanic towns, formed in 1241, their commerical object being to carry on trade between the east and west of Northern Europe. They had their own fleet and army, and waged war with Denmark.

Hapsburg or HABSBURG, HOUSE OF, the family to which the Imperial dynasty of Austria traced its descent. Charles VI, the last ruler of Austria of the male Hapsburg line, died in 1740. His daughter Maria Theresa became queen of Hungary, and from her and her husband the modern Hapsburgs are descended. The last of this line, the emperor Charles I, abdicated in 1918.

Harapha, in Milton's 'Samson Agonistes' (q.v.), the giant of Gath who comes to mock the blind Samson in prison.

Hard Cash, a novel by C. Reade (q.v.) (1863), perhaps the best known of the author's propagandist novels and designed to expose the abuses prevailing in lunatic asylums. It gave rise to lively protests in certain quarters.

Hardcastle, SQUIRE, MRS., and MISS, characters in Goldsmith's 'She Stoops to Conquer' (q.v.).

Hardenberg, FRIEDRICH LEOPOLD VON (1772-1801), German romantic poet and novelist, author of poems religious, mystic, and secular, who wrote under the pseudonym 'Novalis'.

Hardicanute, king of England, 1040-2, son of Canute.

Harding, THE REVD. SEPTIMUS, the principal character in A. Trollope's 'The Warden', and in its sequel 'Barchester

Towers' (q.v.). His death occurs in 'The Last Chronicle of Barset'.

Hard Times, a novel by Dickens (q.v.) (1854).

Thomas Gradgrind, a citizen of Coketown, an industrial centre, is a man who believes in facts and statistics, and nothing else, and brings up his children, Louisa and young Tom, accordingly. He marries Louisa to Josiah Bounderby, a manufacturer, thirty years older than herself. Louisa consents partly from the indifference and cynicism engendered by her father's treatment, partly from a desire to help her brother, who is employed by Bounderby. James Harthouse, a young politician, without heart or principles, is thrown into contact with her and attempts to seduce her. The better side of her nature is awakened by this experience, and she flees for protection to her father, who in turn is awakened to the folly of his system. He shelters her from Bounderby and the couple are permanently separated. But his son, young Tom, has robbed the bank of his employer, and though he contrives for a time to throw the suspicion on a blameless artisan, Stephen Blackpool, is finally detected and hustled out of the country. Among the notable minor characters are Sleary, the proprietor of a circus; Cissy Jupe, whose father had been a performer in his troupe; and Mrs. Sparsit, Mr. Bounderby's housekeeper.

Hardy, THOMAS (1840-1928), born at Upper Bockhampton, near Dorchester, Dorset, was the son of a builder. In early life he practised architecture. The underlying theme of much of Hardy's writing, of many of the novels, the short poems, and the great epic-drama 'The Dynasts', is the struggle of man against the force, neutral and indifferent to his sufferings, that rules the world. His strong sense of humour is seen principally in his rustic characters. Hardy's novels, according to his own classification, divide themselves into three groups.

I. *Novels of Character and Environment*—'Under the Greenwood Tree'
(1872); 'Far from the Madding Crowd' (1874); 'The Return of the Native' (1878); 'The Mayor of Casterbridge' (1886) (qq.v.); 'The Woodlanders' (1887); 'Wessex Tales' (1888); 'Tess of the D'Urbervilles' (q.v., 1891); 'Life's Little Ironies' (1894); 'Jude the Obscure' (q.v., 1896, in the edition of the 'Works' of that year).

II. *Romances and Fantasies*—'A Pair of Blue Eyes' (1873); 'The Trumpet-Major' (q.v., 1880); 'Two on a Tower' (1882); 'A Group of Noble Dames' (1891); 'The Well-Beloved' (published serially in 1892, revised and reissued in 1897).

III. *Novels of Ingenuity*—'Desperate Remedies' (1871); 'The Hand of Ethelberta' (1876); 'A Laodicean' (1881). 'A Changed Man, The Waiting Supper, and other Tales' (1913) is a reprint of 'a dozen minor novels' belonging to the various groups.

Hardy published a number of volumes of lyrics, and his great epic-drama 'The Dynasts' (q.v.) was published in three parts: Pt. I, 1904, Pt. II, 1906, Pt. III, 1908.

Hardy, SIR THOMAS MASTERMAN (1769-1839), Nelson's flag-captain in the 'Victory'. Nelson died in his arms.

Hare, WILLIAM, the accomplice of the murderer William Burke (q.v.).

Haredale, GEOFFREY and EMMA, characters in Dickens's 'Barnaby Rudge' (q.v.).

Harington or HARRINGTON, JAMES (1611-77), published in 1656 'The Commonwealth of Oceana' (q.v.), a political romance, and several tracts in defence of it.

Harington, SIR JOHN (1561-1612), godson of Queen Elizabeth, translated Ariosto's 'Orlando Furioso' (q.v.), by Queen Elizabeth's direction. His Rabelaisian 'Metamorphosis of Ajax' ('a jakes', 1596) and other satires led to his banishment from the court. He accompanied Essex to Ireland, and was deputed to appease the queen's anger against him, unsuccessfully. His letters and miscellaneous writings, in 'Nugae Antiquae', appeared in 1769.

Harland, HENRY (1861-1905), American author, became editor of the 'Yellow Book' in 1894, thereby figuring prominently in London literary life. He published several romances, the most successful being 'The Cardinal's Snuff-Box' (1900).

Harleian MSS., THE, were collected by Robert and Edward Harley, the first and second earls of Oxford (1661-1724, 1689-1741), and are now in the British Museum, having been purchased for the nation under an act of 1754.

Harleian Miscellany, a reprint of a selection of tracts from the library of Edward Harley, second earl of Oxford, edited by William Oldys, his secretary, and Samuel Johnson, published in 1744-6 by Thomas Osborne.

Harlequin, from the Italian *arlecchino*, originally a character in Italian comedy, a mixture of childlike ignorance, wit, and grace. In English pantomime a mute character supposed to be invisible to the clown and the pantaloon, the rival of the clown in the affections of Columbine.

Harleth, GWENDOLEN, the heroine of G. Eliot's 'Daniel Deronda' (q.v.).

Harley, the principal character in 'The Man of Feeling' of H. Mackenzie (q.v.).

Harley, ADRIAN, in Meredith's 'The Ordeal of Richard Feverel', the cynical tutor of Richard, drawn from Meredith's friend Maurice FitzGerald.

Harley Street, used allusively of medical specialists, from the fact that many medical specialists live in or near this street, which is in the West End of London.

Harmodius and **Aristogeiton:** when the brothers Hippias and Hipparchus, the sons of Peisistratus, were tyrants of Athens (527-514 B.C.), Harmodius and Aristogeiton, and some others, joined in a conspiracy to slay the tyrants at the festival of the Panathenaea. Owing to an error, Hipparchus was killed before Hippias arrived, Harmodius was immediately struck down by the guards, and Aristogeiton tortured to death. Subsequently Harmodius and Aristogeiton

came to be highly honoured as patriots and liberators of the state.

Harmon, JOHN, *alias* JOHN ROKESMITH, *alias* JULIUS HANDFORD, the hero of Dickens's 'Our Mutual Friend' (q.v.).

Harold I, son of Canute, king of England, 1035-40.

Harold II, son of Godwine, king of England in 1066, killed in that year at the battle of Hastings or Senlac. See *Harold, the Last of the Saxon Kings*.

Harold, a historical drama by Lord Tennyson (q.v.) (1876). It presents in dramatic form the events dealt with in Bulwer Lytton's romance of the same name (see below).

Harold, the Last of the Saxon Kings, a novel by Bulwer Lytton (q.v.) (1848).

The story deals with the latter years of the reign of Edward the Confessor and the short reign of Harold, from the visit of Harold to William, duke of Normandy, to his death at Senlac. With this is woven the romance of Harold's love for Edith the Fair, whom, owing to their relationship, he is forbidden by the Church to marry. For political reasons, and at Edith's behest, he marries Aldyth, sister of the northern earls Eadwine and Morcar. But when he lies dead on the field of Senlac, Edith seeks him out and dies beside him, thus fulfilling the saying of Hilda, the Saxon prophetess, that they should be united.

Harold, Childe, see *Childe Harold*.

Harold the Dauntless, a poem by Sir W. Scott (1817).

Haroun-al-Raschid (763-809), caliph of Baghdad, who figures in many tales of the 'Arabian Nights' (q.v.), together with Ja'far, his vizier, and Mesrour his executioner.

Harpagon, a character in Molière's (q.v.) 'L'Avare', the typical miser.

Harper's New Monthly Magazine, an American periodical, founded in 1850, originally to reproduce in America the work of distinguished English contributors (such as Dickens and Bulwer Lytton). It subsequently became American in character.

Harpier, in Shakespeare's 'Macbeth', IV. i. 3, apparently an error for Harpy.

Harpies, THE, in Greek HARPYIAE, ugly winged monsters, Aello, Ocypete, and Celaeno, who were supposed to carry off persons or things. They plundered Aeneas during his voyage to Italy. See also under *Phineus.*

Harpocrates, the Roman equivalent of the Egyptian HORUS (q.v.), in his character of the youthful sun, born afresh every morning, and represented sitting with his finger in his mouth, an attitude symbolical of childhood. From a misunderstanding of this attitude, he came to be regarded by the Greeks and Romans as the god of silence.

Harpur, CHARLES (1817–68), Australian poet, published a number of volumes of verse (collected edition, 1883). His best poem is 'The Creek of the Four Graves'.

Harriet Smith, a character in Jane Austen's 'Emma' (q.v.).

Harrington, see *Harington.*

Harris, MRS., in Dickens's 'Martin Chuzzlewit' (q.v.), the mythical friend of Mrs. Gamp.

Harris, FRANK (1856–1931), successively editor of the 'Fortnightly Review', the 'Saturday Review', and 'Vanity Fair'. His books include: 'The Man Shakespeare' (1909), 'The Women of Shakespeare' (1911), 'Oscar Wilde' (1920).

Harris, JOEL CHANDLER (1848–1908), American author of the famous 'Uncle Remus' series. These contain a great number of folklore tales with the rabbit as hero and the fox next in importance, told by a Negro to a little boy and interspersed with comments on many other subjects.

Harrison, DR., a character in Fielding's 'Amelia' (q.v.).

Harrison, FREDERIC (1831–1923), professor of jurisprudence and international law to the Inns of Court from 1877 to 1889, and from 1880 to 1905 president of the English Positivist Committee, formed to represent in this country the philosophic doctrines of Auguste Comte (q.v.). He was author of many works.

Harrison, WILLIAM (1534–93), author of the admirable 'Description of England' included in the 'Chronicles' of Holinshed (q.v.).

Harrowing of Hell, The, a poem of some 250 lines in octosyllabic couplets of the late 13th or 14th cent. It consists of a narrative introduction, followed by speeches, as in a drama. Christ reproves Satan and claims Adam, breaks in the door, binds Satan, and frees his servants.

Harrow School, at Harrow-on-the-Hill, Middlesex, founded and endowed by John Lyon (*c.* 1514–91), of Preston, under Letters Patent and a Charter granted by Queen Elizabeth. Rodney was the first of the many great men educated at Harrow, a list which includes Samuel Parr, Bryan Waller Procter (q.v.), Theodore Hook (q.v.), Lord Byron (q.v.), besides several prime ministers (Perceval, Sir Robert Peel, Lord Aberdeen, Lord Palmerston, Mr. Baldwin, and Sir Winston Churchill).

Harry Richmond, The Adventures of, a novel by G. Meredith (q.v.) (1871).

Harry the Minstrel, or BLIND HARRY, see *Henry the Minstrel.*

Harte, FRANCIS BRET (1836–1902), was taken to California when 18, where he probably saw something of mining life. But he worked on various newspapers and periodicals in San Francisco, to which he contributed the short stories which made him famous. Notable among these were 'The Luck of Roaring Camp' (1868), and 'Tennessee's Partner' and 'The Outcasts of Poker Flat' (included in the 1870 collection). His humorous-pathetic verse includes: 'Jim', 'Her Letter', and 'Plain Language from Truthful James'. Bret Harte was American consul at Crefeld in Germany (1878–80) and at Glasgow (1880–5), after which he lived in England.

Hartford, or CONNECTICUT, **Wits, THE,** a group of writers who flourished during the last two decades of the 18th cent. at Hartford and New Haven, Connecticut, U.S.A., now chiefly remembered for their vigorous political verse satires. Chief among them were Timothy Dwight, Joel Barlow, John Trumbull, and Theodore Dwight.

Harthouse, JAMES, a character in Dickens's 'Hard Times' (q.v.).

Hartley, DAVID (1705-57), philosopher. In his 'Observations on Man, his Frame, Duty, and Expectations' (1749), he repudiated the view of Shaftesbury and Hutcheson that the 'moral sense' is instinctively innate in us, and attributed it to the association of ideas, i.e. the tendency of ideas which have occurred together, or in immediate succession, to recall one another. His philosophy greatly influenced Coleridge (q.v.).

Harun-al-Rashid, see *Haroun-al-Raschid.*

Harvard, JOHN (1607-38), of humble origin, M.A. of Emmanuel College, Cambridge, settled in Charlestown, Massachusetts, and bequeathed half his estate and all his books to the newly founded educational institution at Cambridge, Massachusetts, known in memory of him as HARVARD COLLEGE.

Harvey, GABRIEL (c. 1550-1631), son of a rope-maker at Saffron Walden, became acquainted with Spenser, over whom he exercised some literary influence, not always for the best. He published satirical verses in 1579 which gave offence at court; attacked Robert Greene in 'Foure Letters' in 1592; wrote 'Pierce's Supererogation' and the 'Trimming of Thomas Nashe' (1593 and 1597) against Nashe. Harvey tried, with others, to introduce the classical metres into English, and claimed to be the father of the English hexameter. His literary judgement may be further gauged by his condemnation of the 'Faerie Queene'.

Harvey, WILLIAM (1578-1657), educated at Cambridge, and at Padua, expounded his theory of the circulation of the blood to the College of Physicians in 1616. But his treatise on the subject was not published until 1628.

Hastings, a character in Goldsmith's 'She Stoops to Conquer' (q.v.).

Hastings, WARREN (1732-1818), the first governor-general of British India. He left India in 1785, was impeached on the ground of corruption and cruelty in his administration, and acquitted after a trial of 145 days, extending, with long intervals, from 1788 to 1795. Burke and Fox were among the prosecutors.

Hatchway, LIEUTENANT, a character in Smollett's 'Peregrine Pickle' (q.v.).

Hathaway, ANNE (1557?-1623), the wife of Shakespeare (q.v.).

Hatter, THE MAD, a character in Lewis Carroll's 'Alice in Wonderland' (q.v.).

Hatteraick, DIRK, the smuggler captain in Scott's 'Guy Mannering' (q.v.).

Hatto, see *Bishop Hatto.*

Hatton, SIR CHRISTOPHER (1540-91), the favourite of Queen Elizabeth. He was the friend and patron of Spenser and Churchyard, and wrote Act IV of the play 'Tancred and Gismund' (see *Wilmot (R.)*).

Haunch of Venison, The, a poetical epistle to Lord Clare, by Goldsmith (q.v.), written about 1770.

Haunted Man and the Ghost's Bargain, The, a Christmas book by Dickens (q.v.) (1848).

Redlaw, a learned man in chemistry, is haunted by the memories of a life blighted by sorrow and wrong. His Evil Genius makes a bargain with him by which he shall forget them; but on condition that he communicates this power of oblivion to all with whom he comes in contact. He discovers with horror that he blots out from his own life and the lives of those about him (in particular the delightful Tetterbys), gratitude, repentance, compassion, and forbearance. He is released from his bargain by the influence of the good angel, Milly Swidger.

Haut-ton, SIR ORAN, the orang-outang in Peacock's 'Melincourt'.

Havelok the Dane, The Lay of, one of the oldest verse romances in English, dating from the early 14th cent. and containing 3,000 lines. It tells the story of Havelok, son of Birkabeyne, king of Denmark, and of Goldborough, daughter of

Æthelwold, king of England. These are excluded from their rights by their respective guardians, Godard and Godrich. Godard hands Havelok over to a fisherman, Grim, to drown; but the latter, warned by a mystic light about the boy's head, escapes with him to England and lands at the future Grimsby. Havelok, taking service as scullion in Earl Godrich's household, is chosen by him as husband for Goldborough, whom Godrich seeks to degrade. The mystic flame reveals to her the identity of her husband. Havelok with Grim returns to Denmark, where, with the help of the Earl Ubbe, he defeats Godard and becomes king. Godard is hanged and Godrich burnt at the stake.

Havisham, MISS, a character in Dickens's 'Great Expectations' (q.v.).

Hawes, STEPHEN (d. 1523?), a poet of the school of Chaucer and Lydgate, was groom of the chamber to Henry VII. His 'Passetyme of Pleasure, or History of Graunde Amoure and la Bel Pucel' was first printed by Wynkyn de Worde, 1509. He is author of the well-known couplet:

'For though the day be never so long
At last the bells ringeth to evensong.'

Hawk, SIR MULBERRY, a character in Dickens's 'Nicholas Nickleby' (q.v.).

Hawker, ROBERT STEPHEN (1803-75), is remembered principally for his 'Song of the Western Men' (rewritten from an old Cornish ballad, with the refrain 'And shall Trelawny die?'). But he wrote other fine poems, and in 1864 he published part of a long poem, 'The Quest of the Sangraal'.

Hawkesworth, JOHN, see *Adventurer*.

Hawkeye, the name under which Natty Bumppo (q.v.) appears in J. F. Cooper's 'The Last of the Mohicans' (q.v.).

Hawkins, MR., the fighting naval chaplain in Marryat's 'Mr. Midshipman Easy' (q.v.).

Hawkins, SIR ANTHONY HOPE (1863-1933), author (as 'Anthony Hope') of 'The Prisoner of Zenda' (q.v.) (1894), 'Rupert of Hentzau' (1898), 'The Dolly Dialogues' (q.v.) (1894), and other novels and plays.

Hawkins, JIM, the narrator and hero of Stevenson's 'Treasure Island' (q.v.).

Hawkins, SIR JOHN (1719-89), a lawyer and magistrate who devoted much of his time to music and literature. His 'History of Music' (5 vols., 1776) is of particular antiquarian interest. He was a friend of Dr. Johnson and wrote his 'Life' in 1787.

Hawksmoor or HAWKESMORE, NICHOLAS (1661 or 1666-1736), architect. He was employed by Wren from the age of 18 and later by Vanbrugh. He designed six London churches under the act of 1711 and the west front of Westminster Abbey.

Hawkwood, SIR JOHN (d. 1394), the famous condottiere, leader of the body of English mercenaries known as the White Company (a similar company is the subject of Sir A. Conan Doyle's novel of that name); he fought for one Italian city or another, and for pope or prince, from 1360 to 1390.

Hawthorne, NATHANIEL (1804-64), was American consul at Liverpool. He subsequently visited Italy, where he wrote the romance 'Transformation' or 'The Marble Faun' (1860). But he is best known as the author of 'The Scarlet Letter' (1850) and 'The House of the Seven Gables' (1851).

Haydn, FRANZ JOSEF (1732-1809), the composer, was born in Austria, the son of a wheelwright who was also organist of his village church. He has been described as 'the father of modern instrumental music', and it may be noted that Beethoven received lessons from him. He composed three oratorios, a number of masses, cantatas, and songs, more than 100 symphonies, and many concertos, quartets, etc.

Haydon, BENJAMIN ROBERT (1786-1846), a historical painter, and the author of 'Lectures on Painting and Design' (1846), is principally remembered for his sincere and delightful autobiography, edited by Tom Taylor in 1853; also on account of the severe strictures passed on him by Ruskin in 'Modern Painters', and as the object of Keats's youthful enthusiasm. There is a sonnet on him by Wordsworth.

Hayley, WILLIAM (1745-1820), poet; friend of Cowper, Blake, Romney, and Southey; author of lives of Milton, Cowper, and Romney, and of an amusing autobiography.

Haymarket, THE, London, so called from the Hay Market established there in 1664, and maintained until 1830. Her Majesty's Theatre, Haymarket (called also the Opera House), was the first opera house in London (1705).

Hayraddin, the Maugrabin or gipsy, a character in Scott's 'Quentin Durward' (q.v.).

Hayston, FRANK, the laird of Bucklaw, in Scott's 'The Bride of Lammermoor'.

Hayward, SIR JOHN (1564?-1627), was the author of various historical works, in which he emulated the style of the great Roman historians. His 'First Part of the Life and Raigne of Henrie the IIII' (1599), dedicated to Essex, gave offence to Elizabeth and led to his imprisonment.

Haywood, MRS. ELIZA (1693?-1756), *née* Fowler, after writing plays and libellous memoirs, issued in 1744-6 the periodical 'The Female Spectator', followed by 'The Parrot' (1747), and subsequently produced two novels.

Hazlitt, WILLIAM (1778-1830), the son of a Unitarian minister of strong liberal views, spent most of his youth at the secluded village of Wem near Shrewsbury. His early relations with S. T. Coleridge and Wordsworth are described in his essay 'My First Acquaintance with Poets'. He was a quarrelsome and unamiable man, and almost as much an artist as a thinker and writer. At first he showed an inclination for painting, but he soon gave this up for literature. In London he became the friend of Lamb and other literary men, and in 1808 married Sarah Stoddart, a friend of Mary Lamb, from whom he was divorced in 1822. In 1824 he married Mrs. Bridgewater. From 1812 onwards he wrote abundantly for various periodicals, including 'The Edinburgh Review', on the Liberal side. His chief writings divide

themselves into three classes: (1) those on art and the drama, including the pleasant 'Notes on a Journey through France and Italy' (1826), written after his second marriage; the 'Conversations of James Northcote' (1830, republished with an introductory essay by E. Gosse in 1894); and 'A View of the English Stage' (1818-21). (2) The essays on miscellaneous subjects, which contain some of his best work (e.g. 'The Feeling of Immortality in Youth', 'Going a Journey', 'Going to a Fight'). (3) The essays in literary criticism, which in the opinion of some are his chief title to fame. The best of these are included in his 'Characters of Shakespeare's Plays' (1817-18), 'Lectures on the English Poets' (1818-19), 'English Comic Writers' (1819), 'Dramatic Literature of the Age of Elizabeth' (1820), and 'Table Talk, or Original Essays on Men and Manners' (1821-2); while 'The Spirit of the Age' (1825) contains interesting appreciations of his contemporaries. Mention should be made of his 'Characteristics', containing some notable aphorisms, and of the 'Liber Amoris' (1823), the record of a miserable love-affair. Of his ability in controversy his famous 'Letter to William Gifford' (1819) is an example.

Hazlitt, WILLIAM CAREW (1834-1913), bibliographer, grandson of William Hazlitt (q.v.), was author of a 'Handbook to the Popular, Political, and Dramatic Literature of Great Britain . . . to the Restoration' (1867), and of three series of 'Bibliographical Collections and Notes' (1876-89). His 'Confessions of a Collector' appeared in 1897.

H. D., pen-name of HILDA DOOLITTLE (1886-1961), American poet. She came to Europe in 1911 and became one of the leading members of the Imagist group (see *Imagism*). She married Richard Aldington (q.v.).

Headlong Hall, a novel by Peacock (q.v.) (1816).

It contains hardly any plot, but is enlivened by burlesque incident, and a number of good songs.

Headrigg, CUDDIE and MAUSE, in Scott's 'Old Mortality' (q.v.), ploughman to Lady Bellenden, and his old covenanting mother.

Headstone, BRADLEY, a character in Dickens's 'Our Mutual Friend' (q.v.).

Hearn, LAFCADIO (1850-1904), worked as a journalist in America, and resided for a time at St. Pierre, Martinique, an experience recorded in his 'Two Years in the French West Indies' (1890). In 1891 he moved to Japan, where he married a Japanese wife. His power of communicating impressions is shown in his remarkable 'Glimpses of Unfamiliar Japan' (1894). His 'Japan: an attempt at interpretation' (1904) was less successful. 'Karma', and other short stories, appeared in 1921. Hearn died in Japan.

Hearne, THOMAS (1678-1735), historical antiquary, author of 'Reliquiae Bodleianae' (1703), and editor of a valuable collection of early English chronicles, of Leland's 'Itinerary', Camden's 'Annales', and other works. He was the 'Wormius' of Pope's 'Dunciad'.

Heartbreak House, a play by G. B. Shaw (q.v.).

Heart of Midlothian, The, a novel by Sir W. Scott (q.v.) (1818), the second series of 'Tales of My Landlord' (q.v.).

The novel takes its name from the old Edinburgh Tolbooth or prison, known as the 'Heart of Midlothian', and opens with the story of the Porteous riot of 1736. With these substantially historical events Scott links the story of Jeanie and Effie Deans, which also has some basis in fact. Robertson, whose real name is George Staunton, a reckless young man of good family, is the lover of Effie Deans, who is imprisoned in the Tolbooth on a charge of child-murder, and the attack on the Tolbooth is partly designed by him with a view to the flight of Effie. But Effie refuses to escape. She is tried, and as her devoted half-sister Jeanie, in a poignant scene, refuses to give the false evidence which would secure her acquittal, is sentenced to death. Thereupon Jeanie sets out on foot for London, and through the influence of the duke of Argyle, obtains an interview with Queen Caroline and her sister's pardon. Effie marries her lover, and becomes Lady Staunton, and it comes to light that her child, whom she was accused of having murdered, is in fact alive. He had been sold to a vagrant woman by Meg Murdockson (who had charge of Effie during her confinement) presumably in revenge against Robertson (alias Staunton) for having seduced her daughter 'Madge Wildfire'. Staunton, in his efforts to recover his son, encounters a band of ruffians and is killed by a boy who turns out to be his own son.

Among the notable minor characters of the story are the officious Bartoline Saddletree, the law-loving harness-maker; and the Laird of Dumbiedikes, Jeanie's taciturn suitor. The novel contains the beautiful lyric 'Proud Maisie', which Madge Wildfire sings on her death-bed.

Heartwell, the 'Old Bachelor' in Congreve's comedy of that name.

Heathcliff, the central figure in Emily Brontë's 'Wuthering Heights' (q.v.).

Heathen Chinee, THE, in Bret Harte's humorous poem, 'Plain Language from Truthful James'.

Heaven, THE SEVENTH. In the cosmographies based on the Ptolemaic system, the realms of space round the earth were divided into successive spheres or heavens, in which the sun, moon, and planets severally revolved. Their number varied in different computations from seven to eleven. These conceptions have given rise to the expression *in the seventh heaven,* signifying 'supremely happy'.

Heaven and Earth, a drama by Lord Byron, published in the second number of 'The Liberal' (1822). It deals with the biblical legend of the marriage between angels and the daughters of men.

Heavenly Twins, THE, Castor and Pollux (q.v.). Also the title of a novel (1893) by Sarah Grand (1862-1943).

Hebe, the daughter of Zeus and Hera, and the goddess of youth. She attended on Hera and filled the cups of the gods.

Heber, REGINALD (1783–1826), wrote some well-known hymns and other verses and a pleasant 'Narrative of a Journey' in India (1828, 1844).

Heber, RICHARD (1773–1833), half-brother of Reginald Heber (q.v.), travelled widely to collect his library of 150,000 volumes, and edited Persius and other classical authors.

Hebrew Melodies, a collection of short poems by Lord Byron (q.v.) (1815). They were written in the autumn of 1814, when Byron was engaged to marry Miss Milbanke, and were set by I. Nathan to favourite airs sung in the religious services of the Jews. Most of them deal with scriptural subjects, but they include some love-songs, such as

She walks in Beauty, like the night
Of cloudless climes and starry skies.

Hebrides, The Journal of a Tour to the, see *Journal of a Tour to the Hebrides.* See also *Journey to the Western Islands of Scotland.*

Hecate, a goddess associated in Greek literature with the lower world and with night, the queen of ghosts and magic, sometimes identified with Artemis. In statues she was often represented in triple form.

Hector, a son of Priam and Hecuba (qq.v.), the most valiant of the Trojans who fought against the Greeks. He married Andromache (q.v.), and was father of Astyanax. He was slain by Achilles (q.v.). In medieval romance he is the great hero of the Trojan War.

Hector de Mares, see *Ector de Maris.*

Hecuba, the wife of Priam, king of Troy, and mother of Hector, Paris, and Cassandra (qq.v.) among other children. After the capture of Troy she fell to the lot of Odysseus. Her daughter Polyxena was sacrificed on the tomb of Achilles, and Hecuba had the further grief of seeing the body of her son Polydorus washed up by the sea. She was finally metamorphosed into a dog, and threw herself into the sea. She is the subject of a play by Euripides.

Hedonism, from the Greek word meaning pleasure, the doctrine in which plea-

sure is regarded as the chief good, or the proper end of action.

Heep, URIAH, a character in Dickens's 'David Copperfield' (q.v.).

Hegel, GEORG WILHELM FRIEDRICH (1770–1831), professor of philosophy at Heidelberg and at Berlin. His first important work was the 'Phaenomenology of Spirit' (1807), followed by his 'Logic' (1812–16), and later by the 'Philosophy of Right' (1820) embodying his political views.

Kant (q.v.) had left an essential dualism in his philosophy, nature opposed to spirit, object opposed to subject, the outer world composed of isolated unrelated substances whose nature is beyond the reach of knowledge. Hegel endeavours to bridge the gulf, and reduce duality to unity. He shows that all difference presupposes a unity, that a definite thought cannot be separated from its opposite, that the idea of fullness, e.g., cannot be separated from that of emptiness, that they are identical in difference. Duality and unity are thus blended in consciousness and the boundaries between mind and matter set aside. Hegel's central idea is the dialectic of thesis—antithesis—synthesis which he applied to the problem of historical evolution. He did this in a very abstract way, utilizing the concept of *Weltgeist,* and in such a manner incidentally that the rise of Prussia was seen as the consummation of the process.

Hegira, see *Hijra.*

Heimskringla, a history of Norse kings from mythical times to 1177 by Snorri Sturlason (q.v.), containing graphic pictures of the domestic and adventurous life of the Vikings.

Heine, HEINRICH (1797–1856), the German poet, migrated to Paris after the revolution of 1830 and there spent his remaining days. His political works show him a radical and a cosmopolitan (he wrote both in German and French and many of his prose works exist in both languages). He was an acute critic of philosophy. But he was most famous as a lyrical poet, pre-eminent in wit and raillery, and the Romantic movement in Germany was in part checked by his irony. His chief works include the poems in the 'Buch der Lieder' (1827); the travel sketches in his 'Reisbilder' (1826-31); 'Zur Geschichte der Religion und Philosophie in Deutschland' (1834) and 'Die Romantische Schule' (1836); and among his later writings 'Atta Troll' (1847).

Heinsius, DANIEL (1580-1655), Dutch scholar. His son NICOLAAS HEINSIUS (1620-81) published critical editions of Roman poets; his Virgil is the most famous.

Heir of Redclyffe, The, a novel by Charlotte M. Yonge (q.v.) (1853).

In this simple romance, Sir Guy Morville, the generous young heir of Redclyffe, falls in love with Amy, his guardian's daughter, but is suspected of gambling by his malevolent cousin Philip. In fact, he has paid the debts of a disreputable uncle, but sacrifices his own character. He is banished from his guardian's household until his uncle's intervention rehabilitates him. Guy and Amy are married, and on their honeymoon in Italy find Philip ill with fever. Guy nurses him through his illness, catches the fever himself, and dies; and Philip, reduced to contrition, inherits Redclyffe.

Hejira, see *Hijra.*

Hel, see *Hell.*

Helen, according to Greek legend, the most beautiful woman of her age, was daughter of Zeus and Leda (q.v.). She selected Menelaus (q.v.), king of Sparta, for her husband, and was subsequently seduced by Paris (q.v.), son of Priam, king of Troy, and carried off to Troy. Menelaus assembled the Greek princes who had been her suitors, and these resolved to make war on Troy for her recovery. After the fall of Troy she was reconciled to Menelaus.

Helena, (1) the heroine of Shakespeare's 'All's Well that Ends Well' (q.v.); (2) a character in his 'A Midsummer Night's Dream' (q.v.); (3) Helen of Troy in Goethe's 'Faust' (q.v.).

Helena, ST., the mother of the Emperor Constantine (q.v.), converted to Christianity by her son. It is said that she discovered the True Cross, having instituted a search for it in consequence of the Emperor Constantine's vision of the sign of a cross in the sky, with the inscription 'In hoc signo vinces'. This is the *Invention of the Cross,* commemorated on 3 May. St. Helena is the 'Elene' of Cynewulf (q.v.).

The ISLAND OF SAINT HELENA in the S. Atlantic was the place of Napoleon's captivity from 1815 until his death in 1821.

Helen of Kirkconnell, the subject of an old ballad (included in Scott's 'Border Minstrelsy' and the 'Golden Treasury'), who dies to save her lover.

Heliand, The, an Old Saxon paraphrase of the N.T., dating from the 9th cent. Fragments also survive of a paraphrase of the O.T. by the author of the 'Heliand'.

Helicon, a mountain of Boeotia sacred to the Muses, who had a temple there. The fountains Hippocrene and Aganippe flowed from this mountain.

Helinore, see *Hellenore.*

Helios, the Greek name of the sun-god, the son of (and sometimes identified with) Hyperion, and father of Phaeton (qq.v.).

Hell, a word derived from Old Norse *Hel,* 'the coverer up or hider', the Proserpine of northern mythology, the goddess of the infernal regions. The word 'hell' is used in the Authorized Version of the N.T. as a rendering of the Greek words *Hades, Gehenna,* and *Tartarus* (qq.v.).

For Dante's 'Hell' see *Divina Commedia.*

Hellas, the name used by the Greeks to signify the abode of the HELLENES, which the Romans called GRAECIA, and we call Greece.

Hellas, a lyrical drama by P. B. Shelley (q.v.) composed at Pisa in 1821 and published in 1822. It was inspired by the Greek proclamation of independence, followed by the war of liberation from the Turks. In form it follows the 'Persae' of Aeschylus. The Sultan Mahmud learns from successive messengers of the revolt in various parts of his dominions, and the old Jew Ahasuerus calls up a vision of the fall of Stamboul. The poet puts some of his finest lyrics in the mouths of the chorus of captive Greek women.

Hellen, HELLENES, see *Hellas*.

Hellenistic, a term applied to the civilization, language, and literature, Greek in its general character, but pervading people not exclusively Greek, current in Asia Minor, Egypt, Syria, and other countries after the time of Alexander the Great.

Hellenore, in Spenser's 'Faerie Queene', III. x, the wife of Malbecco, who elopes with Paridell.

Hellespont, see under *Hero*.

Hell-fire Clubs, associations of profligate young ruffians who were a nuisance to London chiefly in the early 18th cent. There is information about them in Charles Johnstone's 'Adventures of a Guinea' (q.v.). There was a later Hell-fire Club, founded about 1745. See under *Medmenham Abbey*.

Héloïse, see *Abélard*.

Helot, a class of serf in ancient Sparta.

Helps, SIR ARTHUR (1813–75), became clerk of the privy council in 1860. Besides revising (at Queen Victoria's request) Prince Albert's speeches (published in 1862) and preparing for the press the Queen's 'Leaves from the Journal of Our Life in the Highlands' (1868), he acquired popularity by his 'Friends in Council' (four series, 1847–59), dialogues on ethical and aesthetic questions.

Helvetia, Switzerland, the country formerly of the HELVETII.

Helvétius, CLAUDE ARIEN (1715–71), see *Philosophes*.

Hemans, MRS. FELICIA DOROTHEA (1793–1835), *née* Browne, poetess. Her collected works (issued in 1839) include 'Translations from Camoens and other Poets', 'Lays of Many Lands', 'The Forest Sanctuary', and 'Songs of the Affections'. She is perhaps chiefly remembered as the author of 'Casabianca' ('The boy stood on the burning deck'), 'The

Landing of the Pilgrim Fathers', 'England's Dead', and 'The Better Land'.

Heming or HEMINGES, JOHN (*d.* 1630) and **Condell**, HENRY (*d.* 1627), fellow actors of Shakespeare, who jointly edited the first folio of his plays (1623) (see *Folios and Quartos, Shakespearian*). Heming is said to have been the first actor of Falstaff.

Hemingway, ERNEST (1898–1961), American short-story writer and novelist. He made his name with the novel 'The Sun Also Rises' (1926, U.K. 'Fiesta', 1927), in which he exactly caught the post-war mood of disillusion, and made a great impression with the economy of his style and the 'toughness' of his attitude of mind. 'A Farewell to Arms' (1929) confirmed his position as one of the most influential writers of the time. He was a finer writer of short stories than a novelist, and his collections, 'Men Without Women' (1927) and 'Winner Take Nothing' (1933), are especially notable. His growing dissatisfaction with contemporary culture was shown by his deliberate cultivation of the brutal and the primitive; he celebrated bull-fighting in 'Death in the Afternoon' (1932) and big-game hunting in 'The Green Hills of Africa' (1935). He actively supported the Republicans during the Spanish Civil War, and his powerful novel 'For Whom the Bell Tolls' (1940) is set against its background. The failure of his novel 'Across the River' (1950) was to some extent redeemed by the success of his long short story 'The Old Man and the Sea' (1952). He was awarded a Nobel Prize in 1954.

Hemistich, half of a line of verse.

Henchard, MICHAEL, the principal character in Hardy's 'The Mayor of Casterbridge' (q.v.).

Hendecasyllabic, a verse of eleven syllables, a metre used by Catullus and imitated by Tennyson:

O you chorus of indolent reviewers.

Hendiadys, from the Greek words meaning 'one by means of two', a figure of speech by which a single complex idea is expressed by two words joined by a conjunction, e.g. 'Such as sit in darkness and in the shadow of death, being fast bound in misery and iron' (Ps. cvii. 10).

Hengist and **Horsa**, the traditional leaders of the Jutes who landed at Ebbsfleet in or about 449, and were given by Vortigern the Isle of Thanet for a dwelling-place. The names may be those of real warriors.

Henley, JOHN (1692-1756), generally known as 'Orator Henley', a contributor to 'The Spectator', published works on oratory, theology, and grammar, was caricatured by Hogarth and ridiculed by Pope ('Dunciad', iii. 203).

Henley, WILLIAM ERNEST (1849-1903), a pupil of T. E. Brown (q.v.), was a cripple from boyhood. He did a great deal of miscellaneous literary work, as editor at various times of the 'Magazine of Art', the 'National Observer', the 'New Review', etc. He was a friend of R. L. Stevenson (q.v.), with whom he collaborated in plays. He compiled 'Lyra Heroica' (1891), a book of verse for boys, and was joint compiler of the 'Slang Dictionary' (1894-1904). His poetical work includes the 'Book of Verses' (1888), 'The Song of the Sword' (1892, revised 1893), etc., and the remarkable volume entitled 'In Hospital' (1903), written in an Edinburgh infirmary. His collected works were published in 1908. Among his best-known pieces are 'Invictus' ('Out of the night that covers me'), the ballad with the refrain

I was a king in Babylon
And you were a Christian slave,

and 'England, my England'.

Henri IV, king of France, 1589-1610. He had been king of Navarre since 1570 and had married Marguerite de Valois, sister of Charles IX. He figures in Macaulay's lay, 'Ivry'.

Henrietta Temple, a novel by Disraeli (q.v.) (1837).

Henry I, king of England, 1100-35.

Henry II, king of England, 1154-89. This was a period of (Latin) literary

eminence: see *Glanville, Map, Giraldus Cambrensis.*

Henry III, king of England, 1216-72.

Henry IV, king of England, 1399-1413.

Henry IV, King, Parts I and II, a historical drama by Shakespeare (q.v.), produced about 1597, and printed in quarto, Pt. I in 1598, and Pt. II in 1600.

The subject of Pt. I is the rebellion of the Percys, assisted by Douglas, and in concert with Mortimer and Glendower; and its defeat by the king and the Prince of Wales at Shrewsbury (1403). Falstaff (q.v.) first appears in this play. The Prince of Wales associates with him and his boon companions, Poins, Bardolph, and Peto, in their riotous life. Poins and the prince contrive that the others shall set on some travellers at Gadshill and rob them, and be robbed in their turn by themselves. The plot succeeds, and leads to Falstaff's well-known fabrication to explain the loss of the booty, and his exposure. At the battle of Shrewsbury, Falstaff finds the body of the lately slain Hotspur, and pretends to have killed him.

Pt. II deals with the rebellion of Archbishop Scroop, Mowbray, and Hastings; while in the comic underplot, the story of Falstaff's doings is continued, with those of the prince, Pistol, Poins, Mistress Quickly, and Doll Tearsheet. Falstaff, summoned to the army for the repression of the rebellion, falls in with Justices Shallow and Silence in the course of his recruiting, makes a butt of them, and extracts a thousand pounds from the former. Henry IV dies, and Falstaff conceives that the prince's accession to the throne will make himself all-powerful. He is rudely disabused when he encounters the new king, is banished from his presence, and thrown into prison.

The play is notable, among other things, for the memories of Shakespeare's early life in Warwickshire interwoven in the story.

Henry V, king of England, 1413-22.

Henry V, King, a historical drama by Shakespeare (q.v.), performed in 1599, an imperfect draft being printed in 1600, the corrected text appearing in the first folio (1623).

The play deals with the arrest of Lord Scroop, Sir Thomas Grey, and the earl of Cambridge for treason; the invasion of France and siege and capture of Harfleur; the battle of Agincourt (1415); and Henry's wooing of Katharine of France. The knaves Nym and Bardolph and the braggart Pistol, who is made to eat the leek by the choleric Welshman Fluellen, provide relief from the more serious theme. The death of Falstaff is related by Mistress Quickly (II. iii).

Henry VI, king of England, 1422-61, restored for six months, 1470-1, and then murdered in the Tower of London in 1471.

Henry VI, King, Parts I, II, and III, a historical drama ascribed to Shakespeare (q.v.). The extent to which it was actually written or revised by him is uncertain. The three parts were acted about 1592; the first part was published in 1623, the second part anonymously in 1594 as 'The first part of the contention betwixt the two famous houses of Yorke and Lancaster', and the third part in 1595, as 'The True Tragedie of Richard, Duke of Yorke, and the death of good King Henrie the Sixt'. The second and third parts (with modifications of the text) appeared, together with the first part, in the folio of 1623. Various commentators have found the hands of Marlowe, Kyd, Peele, Greene, Lodge, and Nash, as well as Shakespeare, in different passages of the play, but the question of authorship remains undecided. The play probably evoked Greene's famous censure of Shakespeare in his 'A Groatsworth of Wit bought with a Million of Repentance' (q.v.).

Pt. I deals with the wars in France during the early years of Henry VI, the relief of Orleans by the French and the gradual expulsion of the English from a large part of France. The French are guided and inspired by Joan of Arc, who in accordance with the ideas of the time, is represented as a 'minister of hell' and a wanton. On the English side, the commanding figure of Talbot, until his death near Bordeaux, throws the other leaders into the shade. At home, the play deals with the dissensions between the nobles, and the beginning of the strife of York and Lancaster.

Pt. II presents the marriage of Henry to Margaret of Anjou, the intrigues of the Yorkist faction, and the other chief historical events, including Jack Cade's rebellion, down to the battle of St. Albans (1455) and the death of Somerset.

Pt. III takes us from Henry's surrender of the succession to the crown to the duke of York, and Queen Margaret's revolt against the disinheriting of her son, to the battle of Tewkesbury in 1471, concluding with the murder of Henry VI by Richard, duke of Gloucester, whose ambitious and unscrupulous character (as subsequently developed in 'King Richard III') is here first indicated.

Henry VII, king of England, 1485-1509. His life was written by Francis Bacon (q.v.).

Henry VIII, king of England, 1509-47. His life was written by Lord Herbert of Cherbury (q.v.). His book, 'A defence of the Seven Sacraments' (1521), directed against Luther's teaching, was presented to Leo X, who conferred on Henry the title 'Defender of the Faith'.

Henry VIII, a historical drama by Shakespeare (q.v.), with parts perhaps written by a collaborator, probably Fletcher. It was acted in 1613 and included in the folio of 1623.

It deals with the accusation and execution of the duke of Buckingham; the question of the royal divorce; the pride and fall of Cardinal Wolsey and his death; the advancement and coronation of Anne Boleyn; the triumph of Cranmer over his enemies; and the christening of the Princess Elizabeth. The firing of the cannon at the end of Act I caused the burning of the Globe Theatre in 1613.

Henry, O., pseudonym of WILLIAM SYDNEY PORTER (1862-1910), American short-story writer. He had a chequered early career, which included a term in prison for embezzlement (1896). He began to write short stories in prison, and published the first of his many collections, 'Cabbages and Kings', in 1904. He was prolific, humorous, and highly ingenious, especially in his use of coincidence, and became the most famous writer of his kind of the day.

Henry and Emma, see *Prior*.

Henry of Huntingdon (1084?-1155), archdeacon of Huntingdon, compiled a 'Historia Anglorum', which in its latest form extends to 1154.

Henryson or HENDERSON, ROBERT (1430?-1506), a Scottish poet of the school of Chaucer. He was probably a clerical schoolmaster attached to Dunfermline Abbey. His 'Tale of Orpheus' was first printed in 1508. His 'Testament of Cresseid' (q.v.) was attributed to Chaucer till 1721, though printed as his own in 1593.

Henry the Minstrel, or BLIND HARRY or HARY (*fl.* 1470-92), Scottish poet, wrote a spirited poem on the life of Sir William Wallace, containing some 12,000 lines in heroic couplets, inspired by violent animosity against the English. Its chronology and general accuracy have been questioned, but in some instances corroborated. William Hamilton of Gilbertfield's modern version (1722) became more familiar than the original.

Henslowe, PHILIP (*d.* 1616), a theatrical manager who rebuilt and managed till 1603 the Rose playhouse on Bankside, and subsequently managed other theatres. He employed a number of the minor Elizabethan dramatists, including Munday, Chettle, Day, Samuel Rowley, and Drayton, and his diary contains valuable information as to their works.

Henty, GEORGE ALFRED (1832-1902), writer for boys, who also published some twelve orthodox novels, including 'Dr. Thorndyke's Secret' (1898).

Heorot, in 'Beowulf' (q.v.), the palace of Hrothgar.

Hephaestus, the Greek god of fire, called by the Romans VULCAN (q.v.).

Hepplewhite, GEORGE (*d.* 1786), cabinet-maker. His designs, published in 'The Cabinet Maker and Upholsterer's Guide', 1788, include the 'shield-back' chair.

Heptameron, The, a collection of love stories, resembling Italian *novelle*, composed, according to the explicit statement of Brantôme, by Marguerite, sister of François I and queen of Navarre (1492-1549).

Heptarchy, THE, the seven kingdoms reckoned to have been established in Britain by the Angles and Saxons (5th-9th cents.).

Hera, known as JUNO by the Romans, was the daughter of Cronos and Rhea and the sister and wife of Zeus or Jupiter. She is represented in mythology as pursuing with inexorable jealousy the mistresses of Zeus and their children, Ino, Semele, Hercules, etc. She was mother of Ares (Mars), Hebe, and Hephaestus (Vulcan).

Heracles, see *Hercules*.

Heraclitus, of Ephesus, a philosopher who wrote, about 500 B.C., a work 'Concerning Nature' ($\pi\epsilon\rho\grave{\iota}$ $\phi\acute{\upsilon}\sigma\epsilon\omega\varsigma$), in which he maintained that all things are in a state of flux. The melancholy view of Heraclitus as to the changing and fleeting character of life led to his being known as the 'weeping philosopher'.

Heralds' College or COLLEGE OF ARMS, a royal corporation, founded in 1483, exercising jurisdiction in matters armorial, and now recording proved pedigrees, and granting armorial bearings.

Herball or general historie of Plantes, see *Gerard* (*J.*).

Herbert, ALAN PATRICK, 'A. P. H.' (1890-1972), contributor to 'Punch' from 1910, author of 'The Water Gipsies' (1930), 'Holy Deadlock' (1934), collections of light verse, essays, etc.; advocate of divorce law reform.

Herbert, EDWARD, *first Baron Herbert of Cherbury* (1583-1648), philosopher, historian, poet, and diplomatist, was the elder brother of the poet, G. Herbert (q.v.). He had a career full of incident as a diplomatist, traveller, and soldier. His 'Autobiography' (which extends only to 1624) was first printed by Horace Walpole in 1764 and edited by Sir Sidney Lee in 1886. His 'De Veritate' in Latin (Paris 1624, London 1625), the chief of his philosophical works, is the first purely metaphysical work by an Englishman, and important as advancing a theory of knowledge substantially the same as that later adopted by the Cambridge Platonists (see *Platonists*). He is known as the 'Father of Deism'. His 'Life of Henry VIII' was published in 1649. His poems, which show grace and freshness, were edited by G. C. Moore Smith in 1923. They are noteworthy for his use of the metre subsequently adopted by Tennyson in his 'In Memoriam'.

Herbert, GEORGE (1593-1633), the younger brother of Lord Herbert of Cherbury (q.v.), was educated at Cambridge, where he was public orator from 1619 to 1627. He took orders and accepted in 1630 the living of Bemerton, where he died. His verse is almost entirely included in 'The Temple' (1633), a collection of 160 poems of a religious character, marked by quaint and ingenious imagery, and occasionally marred by extravagant conceits and bathos. His chief prose work 'A Priest to the Temple', set forth with fervent piety, was first printed in his 'Remains', 1652. I. Walton (q.v.) wrote a life of George Herbert, which appeared in 1670. He was one of the first and greatest of the Metaphysical poets (q.v.).

Herbert, MARY, see *Pembroke*.

Hercules, or in Greek HERACLES, was the son of Zeus and Alcmena (see *Amphitryon*). Hera's jealousy of Alcmena extended to her son. She sought to destroy the infant by sending two serpents to devour him, but he seized and crushed them in his hands. He became the most valiant and accomplished of men. After various exploits he married Megara, the daughter of Creon, but being driven mad by Hera, killed his wife and children. By direction of an oracle he submitted himself to the authority of Eurystheus, king of Argos and Mycenae, and at the order of the latter undertook a number of enterprises, known as the twelve 'LABOURS OF HERCULES'. These were as follows: (1) the destruction of the lion of Nemea, which Hercules strangled, and whose skin he afterwards wore; (2) the destruction of the Lernaean hydra, a creature with many heads, each of which when cut off gave place to two new ones; (3) the capture of an incredibly swift stag; (4) the capture of a destructive wild boar; (5) the cleansing of the stables of Augeas (q.v.); (6) the destruction of the carnivorous birds near lake Stymphalus; (7) the capture of the Cretan wild bull; (8) the capture of the mares of Diomedes, which fed on human flesh; (9) the obtaining of the girdle of the queen of the Amazons; (10) the destruction of the monster Geryon, king of Gades, and the capture of his flocks; (11) the obtaining of apples from the garden of the Hesperides (q.v.); (12) the bringing from hell of the three-headed dog, Cerberus (q.v.). For his destruction by the cloak of Nessus, see under *Deianira*. After his death he obtained divine honours, having devoted the labours of his life to the benefit of mankind.

Hercules, PILLARS or COLUMNS OF, a name given to two mountains opposite one another at the entrance of the Mediterranean, called Calpe (Gibraltar) and Abyla, supposed to have been parted by the arm of Hercules.

Herder, JOHANN GOTTFRIED (1744-1803), German philosopher and critic, who decisively influenced Goethe (q.v.). He was an ardent student and collector of folksong, an investigator of problems of language, a critic of Shakespeare, and a philosopher of history. As a philosopher Herder's great contribution lay in his recognition of historical evolution, which helped to bridge the gap between the Enlightenment and Romanticism.

Hereward the Wake (*fl.* 1070), an outlaw, a legendary account of whose wanderings is given by the 15th-cent. forger who called himself Ingulf of Croyland in his 'Gesta Herewardi'. He headed a rising of English against William the Conqueror at Ely in 1070, and with the assistance of the Danish fleet plundered Peterborough in the same year. He was joined by Morcar and other refugees, and escaped when his allies surrendered to William. He is said to have subsequently been pardoned by William, and, according to Geoffrey Gaimar, to have been slain by Normans in Maine.

The last of the completed novels of C. Kingsley (q.v.) bears this name, and was published in 1866. It is based on the legends of Hereward's exploits and extraordinary strength. See also *Swallow*.

Hergesheimer, JOSEPH (1880–1954), American writer. His best-known books are 'The Three Black Pennys' (1917), 'Java Head' (1919), and 'Linda Condon' (1919).

Hergest, RED BOOK OF, a Welsh manuscript of the 14th–15th cents. containing the 'Mabinogion' (q.v.), the 'Triads' (q.v.), Welsh translations of British chronicles, etc.

Hermann und Dorothea, see *Goethe*.

Hermaphroditus, a son of Hermes and Aphrodite, was beloved by a nymph, Salmacis. She closely embraced him and prayed the gods to make the twain one body, which they did. Hence 'Hermaphrodite', a name for a being combining both sexes in a single body.

Hermes, called MERCURY by the Romans, was the son of Zeus and Maia, the inventor of the lyre (he placed strings across the shell of a tortoise), and the messenger and herald of the gods. He was regarded as the patron of travellers and merchants, and of thieves, pickpockets, and all dishonest persons. He is generally represented as equipped with the *caduceus*, a winged rod entwined by two serpents, the *petasus* or winged cap, and *talaria* or winged sandals.

Hermes Trismegistus, the 'thrice great Hermes' of Milton's 'Il Penseroso', the name given by the Neoplatonists and the devotees of mysticism and alchemy to the Egyptian god THOTH. From the 3rd cent. onwards the name was applied to the author of various Neoplatonic writings, some of which have survived, notably the Ποιμάνδρης. Hence HERMETIC PHILOSOPHY, alchemy; HERMETIC BOOKS, the philosophical, theosophical, and other writings ascribed to Hermes Trismegistus.

Hermia, a character in Shakespeare's 'A Midsummer Night's Dream' (q.v.).

Hermione, (1) daughter of Menelaus and Helen, and the wife, first of Neoptolemus, then of Orestes; (2) in Shakespeare's 'The Winter's Tale' (q.v.), the wife of Leontes.

Hermit, The, a poem by T. Parnell (q.v.).

Hermit, The, or *Edwin and Angelina*, a ballad by Goldsmith (q.v.), written in 1764, and included in 'The Vicar of Wakefield' (q.v.).

Hermit of Hampole, THE, Richard Rolle (q.v.).

Hernani, a tragedy (1830) by V. Hugo (q.v.). Verdi's opera 'Ernani' is founded on Hugo's drama.

Herne the Hunter, a spectral hunter of medieval legend, said to have been originally a keeper in Windsor Forest, who figures in Shakespeare's 'The Merry Wives of Windsor', IV. iv, and in Harrison Ainsworth's 'Windsor Castle'.

Hero, (1) a beautiful priestess of Aphrodite at Sestos on the European shore of the Hellespont, beloved of Leander, a youth of Abydos on the opposite shore. Leander at night used to swim across to Hero, who directed his course by holding up a lighted torch. One tempestuous night Leander was drowned, and Hero in despair threw herself into the sea. The story has been made the subject of poems by Marlowe and T. Hood (qq.v.), and of a burlesque by T. Nashe (q.v.) in his 'Prayse of Red Herring'; (2) the heroine of Shakespeare's 'Much Ado about Nothing' (q.v.).

Herod, To OUT-HEROD, to outdo Herod (represented in the old miracle plays as a blustering tyrant) in violence; a Shakespearian expression ('Hamlet', III. ii) which has come into current use.

Herod Agrippa I (*d.* A.D. 44), grandson of Herod the Great (q.v.), ruler of the tetrarchies of north-eastern Palestine. He persecuted the Christians and died a horrible death (Acts xii).

Herod Agrippa II (*c.* A.D. 27-100), son of Herod Agrippa I, sided with the Romans in the Jewish war. It was before him that Paul was brought (Acts xxv; the Bernice there referred to was his sister).

Herodas or HERONDAS, a Greek writer of mimes (q.v.) of the 3rd cent. B.C.

Herodias, the sister of Herod Agrippa I, granddaughter of Herod the Great, the wife of Herod Philip and afterwards of his half-brother Herod Antipas, whom she caused to imprison and execute John the Baptist. She was the mother of Salome (q.v.).

Herodotus (*c.* 480–*c.* 425 B.C.), a Greek historian, known as the father of history, for he was the first to collect his materials systematically, test their accuracy so far as he was able, and arrange them agreeably. His work, the first masterpiece of Greek prose, is divided into nine books, each called after one of the Muses. He travelled widely in Europe, Asia, and Africa. The main theme of his work is the enmity between Asia and Europe. He traces it from mythical times, through the reign of Croesus in Lydia, the rise of the Persian monarchy, the expedition of Cambyses into Egypt (with details of Egyptian history), that of Darius against the Scythians, the Ionian revolt, and the struggle between Persia and Greece.

Herod the Great, king of Judaea, 40–4 B.C. According to Matt. ii, he ordered the slaughter of all the children in Bethlehem, of 2 years old and under, in order that the infant Jesus should be destroyed.

Heroes and Hero-Worship, a series of lectures by T. Carlyle (q.v.) (1841).

Heroic couplet, English heroic verse, iambic pentameters, rhyming in pairs, aa bb cc etc. It was a familiar verse form from Chaucer's time onwards, and used by the Elizabethans, though their preference for blank verse or more elaborate verse forms prevented it from being generally popular. In the 17th cent. it was regarded by Dryden and others as the true form for English heroic verse and most suitable for tragic or heroic drama (q.v.). Throughout the 18th cent. the heroic couplet, as perfected by Pope, was a standard measure for all forms of poetry; and the reaction of Wordsworth and Coleridge in 'Lyrical Ballads' was partly against its dominance. (The controversy between Byron, Bowles, and others on the merits of Pope also concerned itself with the use of this verse form.) In modern times it has been used freely, though not with such persistence; it has tended to be associated with light verse, satire, etc.

Heroic drama, a term applied to the tragedies of the Restoration period. They were usually written in rhymed heroic couplets, but this was not essential to the concept: Dryden's 'All for Love' and Otway's 'Venice Preserv'd' (qq.v.) are examples of blank verse tragedies which preserved nearly all the ingredients of the 'heroic' play.

The essentials of this type of play were that it should present in dramatic form all the qualities of the heroic poem or epic. 'The work of an heroic poem', wrote Hobbes (q.v.), 'is to raise admiration, principally for three virtues, valour, beauty, and love.' The characters were exaggerated and spoke habitually in terms of bombast and rant; plays were produced —following D'Avenant's lead—with a lavish regard to spectacle and splendour; the plots were simple but involved usually the actions of kings and queens, a background of war, love, and jealousy, and more often than not, after certain preliminary slaughter, a happy ending for the hero and heroine. In this last respect the plays were not strictly tragedies: the Restoration audience on the whole preferred to avoid the spectacle of ultimate disaster; Elizabethan tragedies were often emended to give them a happy ending, e.g. Waller's version of Beaumont and Fletcher's 'The Maid's Tragedy'.

The heroic drama was parodied, notably in 'The Rehearsal' (q.v.) and later in Fielding's 'Tom Thumb'; its absurdities and habitual exaggerations have prevented any modern revival in popularity. At its best, in plays like Dryden's 'Aurengzebe', in the plays of Lee or Otway (qq.v.), it had a certain grandeur, nearer perhaps to grand opera than to ordinary tragedy, but nevertheless not entirely to be despised.

Heroic poetry, the same as epic (q.v.).

Heroic verse, that used in epic poetry: in Greek and Latin poetry, the hexameter; in English, the iambic of five feet or ten syllables; in French, the Alexandrine of twelve syllables.

Herrick, ROBERT (1591-1674), incumbent of Dean Prior, in Devonshire, from 1629 to 1647, when he was ejected; after which he lived in Westminster, until restored to his living in 1662. He was a devoted admirer of Ben Jonson. His chief work is the 'Hesperides' (1648), a collection of some 1,200 poems. His 'Noble Numbers' (published in one book with 'Hesperides', but bearing on its separate title-page the date 1647) is a collection of short poems dealing with sacred subjects. His poems show great diversity of form, from imitations of Horace and Catullus, epistles, eclogues, and epigrams, to love-poetry and simple folk-songs. He possessed a great lyrical facility and was an apt and charming exponent of the Horatian way of life.

Herrick, ROBERT (1868-1938), American author. Among his principal novels are: 'The Common Lot' (1904), 'The Memoirs of an American Citizen' (1905), 'Together' (1908), and 'The Master of the Inn' (1908).

Herschel, SIR JOHN FREDERICK WILLIAM (1792-1871), astronomer, son of Sir W. Herschel (q.v.), discovered a great number of double stars and nebulae, and did a vast amount of work in connection with these and other branches of astronomical science.

Herschel, SIR WILLIAM (1738-1822), astronomer, began to construct optical instruments in 1773 and to observe stars. He discovered Uranus in 1781, and later many stars and nebulae, and contributed greatly to the knowledge of astronomy.

Hertha or NERTHUS, according to Tacitus, a goddess of some ancient Germanic tribes, representing the earth or fertility.

'Hertha' is the title of one of Swinburne's 'Songs before Sunrise' (q.v.).

Hervé Riel, the subject of a poem by R. Browning (q.v.), a Breton sailor who piloted a French squadron to safety in St. Malo harbour after the defeat of the fleet at La Hogue in 1692.

Hervey, JAMES (1714-58), was prominent in the early Methodist movement. His 'Meditations among the Tombs', 'Reflections in a Flower Garden', and 'Contemplations on the Night' (1746-7) were extremely popular, but are marked by a pompous and affected style.

Hervey, JOHN, *Baron Hervey of Ickworth* (1696-1743), as vice-chamberlain exercised great influence over Queen Caroline. He was a close friend of Lady Mary Wortley Montagu (q.v.) and engaged in controversy with Pope, by whom he was attacked in 'The Dunciad' and 'Bathos' as 'Lord Fanny', and as the 'Sporus' of 'An Epistle to Arbuthnot'. His 'Memoirs of the Reign of George II' give a vivid satirical picture of the court. .

Hesiod (8th cent. B.C.?), one of the earliest of Greek poets, author of 'Works and Days', a poem addressed to his brother Perses, urging him to toil, and descriptive of agricultural life in Boeotia; probably of the 'Theogony', containing a mythical account of the origin of the world and the genealogy of the gods; and of a 'Catalogue of Women', who, being beloved by the gods, had become mothers of heroes. Of this last work only fragments survive.

Hesione, daughter of Laomedon, king of Troy, and sister of Priam. She was chained by her father on a rock to be devoured by a monster in order to appease the anger of Apollo and Poseidon. Hercules promised to deliver her, for a reward of Laomedon's wonderful horses, and killed the monster. But Laomedon then refused to surrender the horses. Hercules besieged and captured Troy, and gave Hesione to his friend Telamon, by whom she became the mother of Teucer.

Hesperia, the western land, for the Greek poets was Italy. The Roman poets similarly gave the name to Spain.

Hesperides, nymphs appointed to guard the golden apples that Ge gave to Hera on the day of her nuptials with Zeus.

Hesperides, the title of the collection of secular poems written by Herrick (q.v.).

Hesperus, the Evening Star, the planet Venus.

Hewlett, MAURICE (1861-1923), novelist, poet, and essayist, became known by his romantic novel of the Middle Ages, 'The Forest Lovers' (1898). He subsequently wrote historical novels and 'Song of the Plow' (1916), a long poem in which the history of the 'governed race' in England and particularly of Hodge, the agricultural labourer, from the Norman Conquest, is made the subject of pungent comments; and a number of other volumes of fiction, poetry, and essays.

Hexameter (see *Metre*), a verse of six metrical feet, which in the typical form consists of five dactyls and a trochee or spondee; for any of the dactyls a spondee may be substituted. The hexameter is the Greek and Latin heroic metre. Longfellow's 'Evangeline' and Clough's 'Bothie' are examples of English hexameter poems.

Hexham, LIZZY, a character in Dickens's 'Our Mutual Friend' (q.v.).

Hey for Honesty, Down with Knavery, a comedy by T. Randolph (q.v.), printed in 1651. The play is a free adaptation of Aristophanes' 'Plutus', and contains interesting allusions to current events and

recent plays, including mentions of Falstaff, Hamlet's ghost, and Shakespeare himself.

Heylyn, PETER (1600-62), a notable controversial writer, chiefly on ecclesiastical history. He was also author of 'Microcosmus: a little Description of the Great World', reissued in an enlarged form in 1652 as 'Cosmographie', a compilation of descriptions of the various countries of the world.

Heywood, JOHN (1497?-1580?), married Elizabeth Rastell, niece of Sir T. More. Under Henry VIII he was a singer and player on the virginals. He was much favoured by Queen Mary, and on her death withdrew to Malines, and afterwards to Antwerp and Louvain. He published interludes, substituting the human comedy of contemporary types for the allegory and instructive purpose of the morality; but he did this in the form of narrative and debate rather than of plot and action. His principal works were 'The Four P's' (see *Interludes*), first printed in 1545(?), the 'Play of the Wether' (1533), in which Jupiter takes the conflicting opinions of various persons regarding the kind of weather to be supplied, and 'A Play of Love' (1534). He may also have been the author of 'The Pardoner and the Frere' and 'Johan the husbande Johan Tyb the wife & syr Jhān the preest', comedies of a wider scope. Heywood also wrote 'A Dialogue concerning Witty and Witless', and collections of proverbs and epigrams.

Heywood, THOMAS (1574?-1641), dramatist. He was a member of the lord admiral's company in 1598, and later one of the queen's players, and a retainer of the earl of Southampton and the earl of Worcester. He wrote a large number of plays, many of which are lost; his chief strength lay in the domestic drama. His best plays are 'A Woman Kilde with Kindnesse' (acted 1603, printed 1607), 'The Fair Maid of the West' (printed 1631), and 'The English Traveller' (printed 1633). He also published 'An Apology for Actors'

(1612), and poems (including 'Hierarchy of the Blessed Angels', 1635), translations, and compilations.

Hiawatha, a poem in trochaic dimeters by H. W. Longfellow (q.v.), published in 1855, reproducing American Indian stories which centre in the life and death of Hiawatha, son of the beautiful Wenonah and the West Wind, who marries Minnehaha ('laughing water'), the Dacota maiden.

The original legendary Hiawatha (Haion 'hwa 'tha) was a Mohawk chief, statesman, and reformer, the advocate of a League of Nations among the Indians.

Hibernia, one of the Latin names for Ireland.

Hickey, WILLIAM (1749?-1830), the author of entertaining 'Memoirs', 1749-1809 (first published 1913-25), in which he describes his numerous voyages and, with great frankness, his weakness for women and claret.

Hieroglyphics, the characters used in writing by the ancient Egyptians, consisting of figures of objects representing (directly or figuratively) words or parts of words. The term is also used of the picture-writing of other peoples.

Hieronimo, the principal character in Kyd's 'The Spanish Tragedy' (q.v.).

Hieronymus, see *Jerome* (*St.*).

Higden, MRS. BETTY, a character in Dickens's 'Our Mutual Friend' (q.v.).

Higden, RANULF (*d.* 1364), a Benedictine of St. Werburg's, Chester. He wrote the 'Polychronicon', a universal history down to his own days, in Latin prose.

High-Heels and **Low-Heels**, in Swift's 'Gulliver's Travels' (q.v.), the name of two political parties in Lilliput.

Highland Widow, *The*, a short tragic tale, by Sir W. Scott (q.v.), one of the stories in 'The Chronicles of the Canongate' (1827).

Hijra or HEGIRA or HEJIRA, the flight of Mohammed from Mecca to Medina in A.D. 622, from which the Muslim era is reckoned.

Hildebrand (*c.* 1020-85), Pope Gregory VII, became archdeacon of Rome in 1059,

and from that time exercised great influence on the policy of the papal see, whose temporal power he endeavoured consistently to magnify. He was elected pope in 1073.

Hill, AARON (1685-1750), dramatist, satirized by Pope, whom he attacked in his 'Progress of Wit' (1730). He wrote the words of Handel's 'Rinaldo' (1711).

Hill, GEORGE BIRKBECK NORMAN (1835-1903), editor of Boswell's 'Life of Johnson' (6 vols., 1887) and other Johnsoniana.

Hill, SIR ROWLAND (1795-1879), originator of penny postage and other postal reforms.

Hind and the Panther, *The*, a poem by Dryden (q.v.) (1687).

Dryden was converted to Roman Catholicism in 1685, and this poem is an outcome of his change of view. It is divided into three parts. The first is occupied with a description of the various religious sects under the guise of the different beasts, and particularly the Church of Rome (the 'milk-white Hind, immortal and unchanged') and the Church of England (the fierce and inexorable Panther). The second part is occupied with the arguments between the two Churches. The third passes to a satirical discussion of temporal and political matters.

Hindenburg Line, known to the Germans as the SIEGFRIED LINE, the line to which, in the Great War, the German forces retreated in Feb.-March 1917, the line of the Somme having proved hardly tenable in the fighting of the previous September.

Hindi, the great Aryan vernacular language of Northern India.

Hippo, THE BISHOP OF, St. Augustine (q.v.).

Hippocrates (*c.* 460-357 B.C.), the most celebrated physician of antiquity. Of the 'Corpus Hippocraticum' or collection of Greek medical works of various dates which have come down to us, only a small portion can be attributed to Hippocrates himself.

Hippocrene, a fountain on Mt. Helicon in Boeotia, sacred to the Muses. It rose from the ground when struck by the hoof of the horse Pegasus (q.v.).

Hippodamia, (1) the wife of Peirithous, king of the Lapithae; at their wedding occurred the famous battle of the Centaurs and Lapithae; (2) the daughter of Oenomaus (see *Pelops*).

Hippogriff, a fabulous animal, the front part like a winged griffin, the hind part like a horse. It is on a beast of this kind that Rogero rescues Angelica from the Orc, and that Astolpho visits the moon (see *Orlando Furioso*).

Hippolyta, a queen of the Amazons (q.v.), given in marriage to Theseus (q.v.) by Hercules, who had conquered her and taken away her girdle, the achievement being one of his twelve labours. She had a son by Theseus called Hippolytus (q.v.). According to another story she was slain by Hercules, and it was her sister Antiope who was the wife of Theseus.

She figures in Shakespeare's 'A Midsummer Night's Dream' (q.v.).

Hippolytus, a son of Theseus and Hippolyta (qq.v.), famous for his virtue and misfortunes. His stepmother Phaedra fell in love with him, and, when he repulsed her advances, accused him to her husband Theseus. Hippolytus fled from his father along the sea-shore; his horses took fright at a sea-monster sent there by Poseidon at the prayer of Theseus, so that they ran away, the chariot was broken among the rocks, and Hippolytus was killed. He is the subject of a play by Euripides. (See also Browning's 'Artemis Prologizes'.)

Hippotades, Aeolus (q.v.), the son of Hippotes, and ruler of the winds.

Hiren, a corruption of Irene, the name of a female character in Peele's lost play 'The Turkish Mahamet and Hyren the fair Greek' (*c.* 1594), used allusively by Shakespeare ('2 Henry IV', II. iv) and early 17th-cent. writers as meaning a seductive woman, a harlot.

Historia Britonum, see *Nennius*.

Historia Ecclesiastica Gentis Anglorum, by Bede (q.v.), was completed in 731.

It is a Latin history of the English people, in five books, from the invasion of Julius Caesar to the year 731, beginning with a description of Britain and ending with an account of the state of the country in 731. The author draws on Pliny and other Latin authors, and on Gildas (q.v.) and probably the 'Historia Britonum' of Nennius (q.v.). It was later translated into Anglo-Saxon (see under *Alfred*).

Historians, the first English historians are to be found in the Anglo-Saxon period, notably Bede, Gildas, and Nennius (all of whom wrote in Latin). The 'Anglo-Saxon Chronicle' (q.v.), begun by Alfred in the 9th cent., has many notable descriptive passages. Similar qualities distinguish many of the medieval chroniclers (e.g. William of Malmesbury, Henry of Huntingdon, and Matthew Paris, qq.v.), but their history lacks as a rule any critical faculty. The beginnings of historical method and principle are to be found in some 16th- and 17th-cent. writings, notably in More's 'Richard III' and Bacon's 'Henry VII'. Clarendon's 'History of the Rebellion' (q.v.) (1702-4) is perhaps the first great English historical work. It was followed in the 18th cent. by the histories of Hume and of Gibbon (qq.v.). The 19th cent. saw a great development in historical research, full value being placed for the first time on contemporary records and authorities, many of which were published during this period. Famous historians of this period were Macaulay, whose prejudices and picturesque qualities do not conceal a genuine historical ability, J. A. Froude, Freeman, Green, and Gardiner. The modern period has produced a great deal of detailed research, much very competent historical writing, and some brilliant biography.

Historical Society, THE ROYAL, was founded towards the end of the year 1868.

Historic Doubts on . . . Richard III, a work by H. Walpole (q.v.).

History of the Decline and Fall of the Roman Empire, see *Decline and Fall of the Roman Empire*.

Histriomastix, see *Prynne*.

Hoadly, BENJAMIN (1676-1761), bishop successively of Bangor, Hereford, Salisbury, and Winchester, famous as the initiator of the 'Bangorian Controversy' (q.v.). He was high in the favour of Queen Caroline.

Hobbema, MEINDERT (1638-1709), Dutch landscape-painter.

Hobbes, JOHN OLIVER, pseudonym of Mrs. P. M. T. CRAIGIE (1867-1906), novelist and playwright.

Hobbes, THOMAS (1588-1679), philosopher. For a great part of his life he was in the service of the Cavendish family, and in 1647 was appointed mathematical tutor to the Prince of Wales. At some time (probably between 1621 and 1626) he was in contact with Bacon, translated some of his essays into Latin and took down his thoughts from his dictation. On three occasions he travelled on the Continent with a pupil, and met Galileo, Gassendi, Descartes, and Mersenne (the French mathematician). On his return to England in 1652 he submitted to the Council of State, and was pensioned after the Restoration. He was intimate with Harvey, Ben Jonson, Cowley, and Sidney Godolphin.

As a philosopher Hobbes resembles Bacon in the practical or utilitarian importance that he attaches to knowledge. The basis of all knowledge, according to him, is sensation, and the causes of all sensations are the several motions of matter. Motion is the one universal cause, and our appetites are our reactions, in the direction of self-preservation, to external motions. Accordingly man is essentially a selfish unit. Upon this theory Hobbes bases the political philosophy which is expounded in his 'Leviathan' (q.v.) (1651). Hobbes was a master of English prose. Without Bacon's profusion of imagery, his style, by its economy and invariable choice of the right

and striking word, is most vivid and effective.

Hobbididance, the name of a malevolent sprite or fiend, one of those introduced into the morris-dance, and one of the five fiends that pestered Poor Tom in Shakespeare's 'King Lear', IV. i.

Hobbinol, in Edmund Spenser's writings, was the poet's friend G. Harvey (q.v.).

Hobgoblin, a mischievous tricksy imp or sprite, another name for Puck or Robin Goodfellow.

Hobson, a Cambridge carrier, who died in Jan. 1630-1. Milton wrote two epitaphs on him, and his name survives in 'Hobson's Choice', which refers to his custom of letting out his horses in rotation, and not allowing his customers to choose among them. (See 'The Spectator', No. 509.)

Hobson-Jobson, the well-known dictionary of Anglo-Indian colloquial words and phrases by Sir H. Yule (q.v.) and Arthur Coke Burnell (1886). The title 'Hobson-Jobson' is an Anglo-Indian vernacular term for a native festal excitement.

Hoby, SIR THOMAS (1530-66), the translator of the 'Cortegiano' of Castiglione (q.v.).

Hoccleve, see *Occleve*.

Hocktide, Hock Monday and Tuesday, the second Monday and Tuesday after Easter, on which, in pre-Reformation times, money was collected for church and parish expenses, with various festive and sportive customs.

Hock-Tuesday Play, an early English mimetic performance, perhaps of ritual origin, representing the defeat of the Danes by the English. It was revived during the festival given to Queen Elizabeth at Kenilworth, and our knowledge of it is chiefly based on descriptions of this. See *Hocktide*.

Hocus-pocus, originally, it appears, the assumed name of a 17th-cent. conjurer, derived from the sham Latin formula employed by him. The notion that this is a corruption of *hoc est corpus*, the words used in the Eucharist, rests merely on a conjecture.

Hodge, a familiar adaptation of Roger, used as a typical name for the English rustic. Also the name of Dr. Johnson's cat.

Hodgson, RALPH (1871-1962), poet, whose chief works are 'The Bull', 'A Song of Honour', and 'Eva' (all 1913). His work, though slight in quantity, has great lyrical and descriptive qualities.

Hödur or HÖDR, in Scandinavian mythology, a son of Odin, a blind god, who by the machination of Loki (q.v.) kills his twin brother Balder (q.v.).

Hoel, see *Howell*.

Hofer, ANDREAS (1767-1810), the son of a Tyrolese innkeeper, was a leader of the insurrection of his compatriots against Bavarian rule, when in 1805 the Tyrol was transferred from Austria to Bavaria. He twice liberated the Tyrol, but was each time deserted by Austria and the country ceded afresh to Bavaria. A further attempt to renew the revolt led to the capture of Hofer by Italian troops. He was executed at Mantua in 1810.

Hoffmann, ERNST THEODOR AMADEUS (originally WILHELM) (1776-1822), German romantic writer and music critic. His stories provided the inspiration for Offenbach's 'Les Contes d'Hoffmann'.

Hoffmann, HEINRICH (1809-74), German physician, author of the immortal 'Struwwelpeter' ('Shock-headed Peter', 1847), written for the amusement of his children, and translated into several languages.

Hogarth, DAVID GEORGE (1862-1927), archaeologist, and authority on Near Eastern affairs. He was a close friend and adviser of T. E. Lawrence (q.v.). His publications include: 'A Wandering Scholar in the Levant' (1896), 'The Penetration of Arabia' (1904), 'The Life of C. M. Doughty' (1928).

Hogarth, WILLIAM (1697-1764), painter and engraver. He established his reputation by the illustrations which he engraved for Butler's 'Hudibras' (1726). The

'Harlot's Progress' (1732) was the first of his series of engravings on moral subjects; it was followed by the 'Rake's Progress', 'Marriage à la Mode', the 'Election', and other social and political caricatures. For many of these he first painted pictures in oils. He was the author of 'The Analysis of Beauty' (1753).

Hogg, JAMES (1770-1835), the 'Ettrick Shepherd', was born in Ettrick Forest, and early became a shepherd. His poetical gift was discovered by Scott, to whom he furnished material for the 'Border Minstrelsy'. His early ballads were published by Constable as 'The Mountain Bard' in 1807. He went to Edinburgh in 1810 and obtained poetical reputation by 'The Queen's Wake' (1813), making the acquaintance of Byron, Wordsworth, Southey, Prof. John Wilson, and John Murray. He published the 'Forest Minstrel' in 1810, 'Pilgrims of the Sun' in 1815, 'Queen Hynde' in 1826, but is remembered as a poet chiefly on account of 'The Queen's Wake' and particularly the verse tale of 'Kilmeny' included therein; also for a few of his songs and 'The Jacobite Relics of Scotland' (with music) (1819). Hogg was a contributor to 'Blackwood's Magazine' (q.v.), and is impersonated as the 'Ettrick Shepherd' in its 'Noctes Ambrosianae' (q.v.).

Hogg, THOMAS JEFFERSON (1792-1862), educated at University College, Oxford, with Shelley (q.v.), and sent down on the publication of the latter's 'The Necessity of Atheism'. He was the friend and biographer of the poet, publishing two volumes of his life in 1858.

Hoggarty Diamond, The Great, a novel by Thackeray (q.v.) (1841), the story of the struggles and misfortunes of Mr. Samuel Titmarsh.

Hoggins, MR., a character in Mrs. Gaskell's 'Cranford' (q.v.).

Hogmanay, the name given in Scotland and some parts of the north of England to the last day of the year, also called 'Cake-Day'.

Hohenlinden, in Bavaria, the scene of

a great battle in 1800, in which the French revolutionary general, Moreau, defeated the Austrians; celebrated by T. Campbell (q.v.) in his 'Battle of Hohenlinden'.

Holbach, PAUL HENRI, *Baron d'* (1723-80), one of the Philosophes (q.v.).

Holbein, HANS (1497/8-1543), the Younger, son and pupil of Hans Holbein the Elder (c. 1465-1524), an Augsburg painter. In 1526 he visited Sir Thomas More in London, with an introduction from Erasmus. He became court painter to Henry VIII c. 1536, painting portraits, often from drawings, and designing architectural decorations and goldsmith's work.

Holcroft, THOMAS (1745-1809), successively stable-boy, shoemaker, tutor, actor, and author, and a friend and associate of Thomas Paine and William Godwin (qq.v.), wrote an entertaining autobiography ('Memoirs', edited and completed by Hazlitt, after his death, 1816), and a number of sentimental plays, of which the best known is 'The Road to Ruin' (1792). Holcroft also wrote some novels, including 'Alwyn, or the Gentleman Comedian' (1780), and translated Goethe's 'Hermann und Dorothea' (1801) and other works.

Holger Danske, the tutelary hero of Denmark, who is supposed to be sleeping under the Kronenborg at Elsinore, his long beard grown into the table, waiting to arise in the hour of Denmark's peril. He is the subject of one of Hans Andersen's tales. See *Ogier the Dane*.

Holinshed, RAPHAEL (*d.* 1580?), came to London early in the reign of Elizabeth, and was employed as a translator by Reginald Wolfe, the printer and publisher. While in his employ he planned the 'Chronicles' (1577) which are known by his name and are by several hands. The 'Historie of England' was written by Holinshed himself. The 'Description of England', a vivid account not devoid of humour, of English towns, villages, crops, customs, etc., of the day, was written by William Harrison (q.v.). The 'Chronicle'

was utilized by Shakespeare and other dramatists.

Holland, PHILEMON (1552-1637), celebrated for his translations of Livy (1600), Pliny's 'Natural History' (1601), Plutarch's 'Moralia' (1603), Suetonius (1606), Camden's 'Britannia' (1610), and Xenophon's 'Cyropaedia' (1632). His knowledge of Greek and Latin was accurate and profound, and his renderings are made in a vivid, familiar, and somewhat ornate English.

Holland House, Kensington, built at the beginning of the 17th cent. In 1767 it was acquired by Henry Fox, first Baron Holland, who entertained Horace Walpole and George Selwyn there. In the time of his grandson, the third Baron Holland (1773-1840), Holland House became a great political, literary, and artistic centre, and many eminent authors, such as Sheridan, Moore, Thomas Campbell, Macaulay, Grote, and Dickens, were among the guests received there.

Holme, CONSTANCE (1881-1955), novelist, author of 'The Lonely Plough' (1914), 'The Splendid Fairing' (1919), 'The Trumpet in the Dust' (1921), etc.

Holmes, OLIVER WENDELL (1809-94), was professor of anatomy and physiology at Harvard University from 1847 to 1882. His 'The Autocrat of the Breakfast-Table' appeared in 'The Atlantic Monthly' in 1857-8, 'The Professor at the Breakfast-Table' in 1860, 'The Poet at the Breakfast-Table' in 1872, and 'Over the Tea-Cups' in 1891. He also wrote novels, some volumes of poems and essays, and memoirs of R. W. Emerson and J. L. Motley. His essays in the 'Breakfast-Table' series are notable for their kindly humour and general sagacity. His poems include a few good lyrics and familiar verses.

Holmes, SHERLOCK, the famous private detective who figures in a number of works by Sir A. Conan Doyle (q.v.). (The character was in part suggested by an eminent Edinburgh surgeon, Dr. Joseph Bell (1837-1911), under whom Doyle studied medicine.) His assistant and foil is Dr. Watson, his great enemy Prof. Moriarty.

Holofernes, (1) Nebuchadnezzar's general, who was killed by Judith (Judith iv. 1, etc.); (2) the great doctor in theology (Thubal Holoferne) who instructed the youthful Gargantua (Rabelais, I. xiv); (3) the pedantic schoolmaster in Shakespeare's 'Love's Labour's Lost'. This character has been thought to represent John Florio (q.v.), 'Holofernes' being a partial anagram of his name.

Holt, FATHER, in Thackeray's 'Esmond' (q.v.), a Jesuit priest and Jacobite intriguer.

Holy Alliance, THE, an alliance formed in 1815, after the fall of Napoleon, between the sovereigns of Russia, Austria, and Prussia, with the professed object of uniting their governments in a Christian brotherhood. Great Britain refused to be a party; and Castlereagh called it 'a piece of sublime mysticism and nonsense'. It virtually came to an end in 1822, and entirely in 1825.

Holy Bottle, THE ORACLE OF THE, the object of a search in Rabelais's 'Pantagruel' (q.v.).

Holy Cross Day, the festival of the exaltation of the Cross, 14 Sept., on which the Jews in Rome were obliged formerly to go to church and hear a sermon. It is the subject of a satirical poem by R. Browning.

Holy Grail, THE, see *Grail*.

Holy Grail, The, one of Tennyson's 'Idylls of the King' (q.v.) (1869).

Sir Percivale, having left the court of Arthur for the cowl, recounts to a fellow monk the story of the quest of the Holy Grail (q.v.) and the success of Sir Galahad.

Holy Living and *Holy Dying,* see *Taylor* (*Jeremy*).

Holy Mountain, see *Athos*.

Holy Office, THE, see *Inquisition*.

Holy Roman Empire, the name given to the realm of the sovereign who claimed to inherit the authority of the ancient Roman emperors in the West. It comprised, in general, the German-speaking states of Central Europe. There is a classic work on the Holy Roman Empire by J. Bryce (q.v.).

Holy State and Profane State, The, a series of characters and essays, by Fuller (q.v.) (1642), one of Fuller's most popular works.

Holy War, The, an allegory by Bunyan (q.v.) (1682).

The author narrates how Diabolus gets possession by his wiles of the city Mansoul (i.e. soul of man). Thereupon King Shaddai, the builder of the city, sends Boanerges and three other captains to recover it, and finally his own son Emmanuel to lead the besieging army. The vicissitudes of the siege are recounted with much spirit. Bunyan in this allegory evidently drew upon his experience as a soldier in the parliamentary war.

Holy Willie's Prayer, a poem by Burns (q.v.).

Home, DANIEL DUNGLAS (1833–86), a spiritualistic medium, whose seances in England in 1855 and subsequent years were attended by well-known people. Browning, who witnessed them, remained sceptical (see his 'Mr. Sludge "The Medium"'). Home published 'Incidents of my Life' (1863 and 1872).

Home, HENRY, *Lord Kames* (1696–1782), a Scottish judge and psychologist. His 'Introduction to the Art of Thinking' (1761) and 'Elements of Criticism' (1762) were widely read in his day.

Home, JOHN (1722–1808), a Scottish minister and, after his resignation from the ministry, secretary to Lord Bute and tutor to the Prince of Wales, and a friend of Hume, Robertson, and Collins. He was the author of a tragedy 'Douglas' produced in 1756, which enjoyed much popularity. Home was a friend of Macpherson (q.v.) and a firm believer in 'Ossian'.

Homer, the great Greek epic poet, who was regarded by the ancients (though the belief has in modern times been contested) as the author of the 'Iliad' and the 'Odyssey' (qq.v.). There is doubt as to both his birthplace and his date, the latter being variously placed between 1050 and 850 B.C. The seven cities that claimed to be his birthplace were 'Smyrna, Rhodus, Colophon, Salamis, Chios, Argos, Athenae'. Tradition represents him as blind and poor in his old age. The origin of the epics, whether by the enlargement and remodelling of earlier material by one or more hands or as a direct composition from traditional material, is disputed. Recent scholarship tends to recur to the view of 'One Homer'.

The origin and date of the 'HOMERIC HYMNS' are also uncertain. The Hymns are preludes to epic poems, addressed to various deities, and recounting legends relating to them.

Home, Sweet Home, a song by John Howard Payne (q.v.), an American dramatist and song-writer. It formed part originally of the opera 'Clari' (1823). The music is by Sir Henry Rowley Bishop (1786-1855).

Homilies, BOOKS OF, in the Church of England, two books of homilies, published in 1547 and 1563, appointed to be read in the churches.

Homonym, the same name or word used to denote different things; or a person or thing having the same name as another, a namesake. Cf. *Synonym*.

Homophone, a word having the same sound as another, but a different meaning.

Hone, WILLIAM (1780-1842), author and bookseller, who published political satires on the government illustrated by Cruikshank, and was prosecuted for his 'Political Litany' (1817). He published his 'Every-Day Book' (dedicated to Lamb and praised by Scott and Southey) in 1826-7.

Honest Whore, The, a play by Dekker (q.v.), in two parts, of which the first was printed in 1604 and the second in 1630. It appears from Henslowe's (q.v.) diary that Middleton collaborated in writing the first part.

In Pt. I Count Hippolito, making the acquaintance of Bellafront, a harlot, converts her to honesty. She falls in love with Hippolito, who repels her and marries Infelice, daughter of the duke of Milan. Bellafront is married to Matheo, who had caused her downfall.

In Pt. II we find the converted Bellafront as the devoted wife of the worthless Matheo. Hippolito, now falling in love with her, tries to seduce her. She stoutly resists temptation, and is finally rescued from misery by her father, Orlando Friscobaldo. The painful character of the play, one of the great dramas of the age, heightened by Dekker's powerful treatment and by scenes in Bedlam and Bridewell, is somewhat alleviated by the comic underplot, dealing with the eccentricities of the patient husband, Candido the linen-draper.

Honeycomb, WILL, in Addison's 'Spectator' (q.v.), one of the members of the club by which that periodical is described as being conducted.

Honeyman, CHARLES, in Thackeray's 'The Newcomes' (q.v.), brother-in-law of Colonel Newcome, a self-indulgent clergyman, incumbent of Lady Whittlesea's fashionable chapel. His worthy sister, MARTHA HONEYMAN, keeps lodgings at Brighton.

Honeythunder, LUKE, a character in Dickens's 'Edwin Drood' (q.v.).

Honi soit qui mal y pense, the motto of the order of the Garter (q.v.).

Honorificabilitudinitatibus, the long word in Shakespeare's 'Love's Labour's Lost' (v. i), in which Baconians (see *Baconian Theory*) see a cryptogram indicating that Bacon was the author of the works attributed to Shakespeare.

Hood, ROBIN, see *Robin Hood*.

Hood, THOMAS (1799-1845), the son of a bookseller, became sub-editor of 'The London Magazine', 1821-3, and made the acquaintance of Lamb, Hazlitt, and De Quincey. He edited various periodicals at different times: 'The Gem' (1829), in which his 'Eugene Aram' appeared; the 'Comic Annual' (1830); the 'New Monthly Magazine' (1841-3); and 'Hood's

Magazine' (1843). In addition to the humorous work for which he is perhaps chiefly remembered, Hood wrote a number of serious poems: the popular 'Song of the Shirt' (published anonymously in 'Punch' in 1843) and 'The Bridge of Sighs', and shorter pieces such as the 'Time of Roses' and 'The Death-bed'.

Hood, THOMAS, the Younger (1835-74), known as Tom Hood, was the son of Thomas Hood (q.v.). He was editor of a comic paper 'Fun' (1865), and in 1867 began 'Tom Hood's Comic Annual' which was continued after his death. His works, which are mainly humorous, include 'Pen and Pencil Pictures' (1857) and 'Captain Master's Children' (1865).

Hook, CAPTAIN, the one-armed and villainous pirate captain in Barrie's 'Peter Pan' (q.v.).

Hook, THEODORE EDWARD (1788-1841), is remembered as a wit, a writer of light verses, and a successful editor (chiefly of the Tory 'John Bull').

Hooker, RICHARD (1554?-1600), theologian, was born at Exeter of poor parents, and by Bishop Jewel's patronage sent to Corpus Christi College, Oxford, where he remained till 1579, becoming a fellow and deputy professor of Hebrew. He was appointed to the living of Drayton-Beauchamp in 1584, master of the Temple 1585, rector of Boscombe in Wiltshire, and of Bishopsbourne in Kent, where he died. Of his great prose classic, the defence of the Church of England as established in Queen Elizabeth's reign, entitled 'Of the Laws of Ecclesiastical Politie' (q.v.), four books appeared in 1594, the fifth in 1597. A pleasant biography of Hooker was written by Izaak Walton and published with the 1665 edition of his 'Ecclesiastical Politie'. There is some reason to credit Hooker with the first steps towards making known in England the theory of 'original contract' as a basis of sovereignty; it was already popular in France.

Hope, ANTHONY, see *Hawkins* (*Sir A. H.*).

Hope Theatre, THE, on Bankside, Southwark, built in 1613 by Henslowe (q.v.) as a bear-garden, with a movable stage on which plays could be performed. Jonson's 'Bartholomew Fayre' was acted there in 1614.

Hopkins, GERARD MANLEY (1844-89), educated at Balliol College, Oxford, the pupil of Jowett and Pater, numbered Bridges and Dolben (and later in life Coventry Patmore) among his friends, and was a disciple of Pusey and Liddon, and, after his conversion in 1866 to the Church of Rome, of Newman. He entered the Jesuit novitiate in 1868, and in 1884 was appointed to the chair of Greek at Dublin University. He was a poet of much originality and a skilful innovator in rhythm. His poems, none of which was published in his lifetime, were collected by Robert Bridges, who published a small selection in Miles's 'Poets and Poetry of the Century'. The first edition of the poems, edited by Bridges, appeared in 1918 and a substantially enlarged new edition, edited by W. H. Gardner and N. H. Mackenzie, was published in 1967. His letters to Bridges, Dixon, and Patmore have been edited by C. C. Abbott (1935-8, 1955-6); his 'Notebooks and Papers' by H. House (1937, 1959).

Hopkins, MATTHEW (*d.* 1647), the witchfinder, made journeys for the discovery of witches in the eastern counties in 1644-7. He published his 'Discovery of Witches' in 1647. He was exposed and hanged as a sorcerer. He is referred to in Butler's 'Hudibras' (q.v.).

Hopkinson, JOSEPH (1770-1842), American poet, remembered as author of the national hymn, 'Hail, Columbia!'.

Hop-o'-my-thumb, a name applied generically to a dwarf or pigmy, occurring as early as the 16th cent. See also below.

Hop o' my Thumb, *Little Thumb*, a fairy tale, from the French of Perrault (q.v.), translated by Robert Samber (1729?).

Hop o' my Thumb (*Le petit Poucet*) is the youngest of seven children of a woodman and his wife, who are forced by poverty to get rid of the children by losing them in the forest. Hop o' my Thumb fills his pocket with white pebbles, which he drops along the way, and by means of these leads his brothers home again. The parents once more lose them, Hop o' my Thumb this time using bread-crumbs to mark the way. But the birds eat up the bread-crumbs, and the children arrive at the house of an ogre, who is deluded by Hop o' my Thumb into killing his own children instead of the woodman's. Hop o' my Thumb steals his seven-league boots, and with the help of these obtains enough wealth to set his parents at ease.

Horace (QUINTUS HORATIUS FLACCUS, 65-8 B.C.), the Roman poet, was born at Venusia in Apulia, was present on the losing side at the battle of Philippi, but obtained his pardon and returned to Rome; here he became the friend of Maecenas (q.v.), who bestowed on him a Sabine farm. His poems include the 'Satires', 'Odes' and 'Epodes', 'Epistles', and the 'Ars Poetica'. His peculiarly terse lyrical gift and his whimsically epicurean philosophy of life make him one of the greatest of classical poets.

Horae, in classical mythology, originally the goddesses of the seasons, generally three in number. According to Homer they control the weather and grant the rain. According to Hesiod they are daughters of Zeus and Themis, and give laws, justice, and peace.

Horatii and the Curiatii, THE, three Roman brothers and three Alban brothers, a battle between whom, according to legend, led to the subjection of Alba to Rome.

Horatio, in Shakespeare's 'Hamlet' (q.v.), the friend of Hamlet.

Horatius Cocles, see *Cocles*.

Horizon, a literary magazine founded by Cyril Connolly (q.v.) in 1939 to provide a medium for contemporary literature in wartime, and edited by him until it ceased publication in 1950.

Horn, CAPE, the southernmost point of America, on the last island of the Fuegian archipelago, discovered by the Dutch navigator Schouten in 1616.

Horn, King, see *King Horn*.

Horn-book, a leaf of paper, containing the alphabet (often with the addition of the ten digits, the Lord's Prayer, etc.) protected by a thin plate of translucent horn, and mounted on a tablet of wood with a projecting piece for a handle, used for teaching children to read. A simpler and later form of this, consisting of the tablet without the horn covering, or a piece of stiff cardboard varnished, was also called a battledore.

Hornbook, DR., see *Death and Dr. Hornbook*.

Horn Childe, a verse romance of the early part of the 14th cent., containing some 1,100 lines. The general plot is similar to that of 'King Horn' (q.v.), but is different in details. The poem is inferior to 'King Horn', and is one of those referred to by Chaucer in his 'Tale of Sir Thopas', see *Canterbury Tales* (19).

Horne, JOHN, see *Tooke*.

Horne, RICHARD HENRY or HENGIST (1803-84), led an adventurous life until he was 30, when he took up literature. He is remembered chiefly as the author of the epic 'Orion', which he published in 1843 at a farthing 'to mark the public contempt into which epic poetry had fallen'. Abandoning poetry, he went to Australia from 1852 to 1869, where he was a commissioner for crown lands, commanded the gold escort from Ballarat to Melbourne, etc. He published in 1859 his entertaining 'Australian Facts and Prospects', with his 'Australian Autobiography' as preface, in which he gives a stirring account of his experiences. E. B. Browning collaborated with him in his 'A New Spirit of the Age' (1844).

Horner, a character in Wycherley's 'The Country Wife' (q.v.).

Horner, JACK, see *Jack Horner*.

Horniman, ANNIE ELIZABETH FREDERICKA (1860-1937), a pioneer supporter of the modern English drama, founder of the Manchester Repertory Theatre.

By her generous assistance, the Irish National Theatre Society was provided with a permanent home in the Abbey Theatre (q.v.).

Horse, THE TROJAN or WOODEN, the artifice by which the Greeks got possession of Troy. They constructed a large wooden horse and filled it with armed men, and then withdrew, leaving Sinon behind. He declared himself to the Trojans as a deserter, and professed to them that the horse was an offering to Athene and if brought within the city it would render it impregnable. When the horse was within the walls, Sinon at dead of night released the armed men, who made themselves masters of the city.

Horses, FAMOUS, see *Bayard*, *Black Bess*, *Bucephalus*, *Gringolet*, *Hrimfaxi*, *Marocco*, *Pegasus*, *Rosinante*, *Skinfaxi*, *Swallow*, *White Surrey*.

Hortensio, a character in Shakespeare's 'The Taming of the Shrew' (q.v.).

Horus, the Egyptian god of light, the son of Osiris and Isis (qq.v.). He was regarded as the rising sun, born afresh daily, the symbol of renewed life. See also *Harpocrates*.

Hosier's Ghost, Admiral, a ballad by R. Glover (q.v.).

Hospitallers of St. John of Jerusalem, KNIGHTS, also called KNIGHTS OF ST. JOHN, KNIGHTS OF RHODES, and KNIGHTS OF MALTA, a military religious order, originally an association that provided a hostel at Jerusalem for the reception of pilgrims. The Knights of St. John defended Acre in 1290, took Rhodes in 1310, and defended it against the Saracens until 1525; then retired to Candia and Sicily, and finally in 1530 were given Malta by the Emperor Charles V. This they were obliged to surrender to Buonaparte in 1798; it was taken by the British in 1800 and ceded by the Treaty of Paris in 1814.

Hotspur: SIR HENRY PERCY (1364-1403), called 'Hotspur', eldest son of the first earl of Northumberland, figures in Shakespeare's 'I Henry IV' (q.v.), a gallant fiery character.

Houghton, LORD, see *Milnes*.

Houghton, WILLIAM STANLEY (1881-1913), the son of a Manchester merchant, devoted from early life to the drama, wrote a number of plays of Lancashire life, strongly influenced by the Ibsen tradition, including 'The Dear Departed', 'Independent Means', 'The Younger Generation', and 'Hindle Wakes'.

Hound of Heaven, The, see *Thompson* (F.).

Hours, Book of, a book containing the prayers or offices of the Roman Catholic Church to be said at the seven times of the day appointed for prayer.

House, THE, a familiar name for (1) the House of Commons; (2) Christ Church, Oxford; (3) the Stock Exchange; (4) the workhouse.

House, ASTROLOGICAL, a twelfth part of the heavens as divided by great circles through the north and south points of the horizon. A special signification was attached to each house. They were numbered eastwards beginning with the HOUSE OF THE ASCENDANT. THE ASCENDANT was the degree of the zodiac which at any moment, e.g. that of the birth of a child, is rising above the eastern horizon. The 'house of the ascendant' included five degrees of the zodiac above this point and twenty-five degrees below it. The LORD OF THE ASCENDANT was any planet within the house of the ascendant. The ascendant and its lord were supposed to exercise a special influence on the life of a child according to the moment of its birth.

Household Words, a weekly periodical started in 1850 by Dickens (q.v.), from which politics were ostensibly excluded and which was adapted to a more popular standard of taste than such magazines as 'Blackwood's'. It received contributions from such noted writers (besides Dickens himself) as Bulwer Lytton, Lever, Wilkie Collins, and Mrs. Gaskell.

House of Life, The, a sonnet-sequence by D. G. Rossetti (q.v.), published partly in 1870, partly in 1881. The sonnets are records of the poet's spiritual experiences,

inspired by love of his wife and sorrow for her death, and permeated with mysticism.
House of the Seven Gables, The, a novel by N. Hawthorne (q.v.) (1851).
House of Usher, The Fall of the, one of the 'Tales of Mystery and Imagination' of Poe (q.v.).
House that Jack Built, The, a nursery accumulative tale of great antiquity, probably based on an old Hebrew original.
House with the Green Shutters, The, a novel by G. D. Brown (q.v.), written under the pen-name GEORGE DOUGLAS (1901).
Housman, ALFRED EDWARD (1859-1936), a distinguished classical scholar, professor of Latin at Cambridge University, the author of three volumes of lyrics, remarkable for economy of words and simplicity, 'A Shropshire Lad' (1896), 'Last Poems' (1922), and 'More Poems' (ed. L. Housman, 1936). His essay on 'The Name and Nature of Poetry' (1932) is a remarkable piece of critical writing, and occasioned considerable discussion when it was first published.
Housman, LAURENCE (1865-1959), brother of the above, author and artist. His plays on Queen Victoria achieved a remarkable success.
Hous of Fame, The, a poem by Chaucer of 1,080 lines composed probably between 1372 and 1386. In a dream the poet visits the Temple of Venus, where he sees graven the story of the flight of Aeneas after the fall of Troy, and of his reception by, and betrayal of, Dido. He is then carried by an eagle to the House of Fame, full of a great company of aspirants for renown and adorned with the statues of historians and poets; and sees the queen, Fame, distributing fame and slander. He is then taken to the House of Rumour, crowded with shipmen, pilgrims, and pardoners, and other bearers of false tidings. The poem is unfinished.
Houyhnhnms, the talking horses in Swift's 'Gulliver's Travels' (q.v.).
Hoveden or HOWDEN, ROGER OF (*d.* 1201?), a Yorkshireman and a chronicler who lived in the reign of Henry II. He

was the author of both the main chronicles of the reigns of Henry II and Richard I, the 'Gesta Regis Henrici' and the 'Chronica'.
Howard, HENRY, see *Surrey*.
Howards End, a novel by E. M. Forster (q.v.) (1910). It deals with personal relationships and conflicting values. On the one hand are the Schlegel sisters, Margaret and Helen, and their brother Tibby, who care about civilized living, music, literature, and conversation with their friends; on the other, the Wilcoxes, Henry and his children, Charles, Paul, and Evie, who are concerned with the business side of life and distrust emotions and imagination. Helen Schlegel is drawn to the Wilcox family, falls briefly in and out of love with Paul, and thereafter reacts away from them. Margaret becomes more deeply involved. She is stimulated by the very differences of their way of life and acknowledges the debt of the intellectuals to the men of affairs who guarantee stability. She marries Henry Wilcox, to the consternation of both families. In the ensuing strains and misunderstandings her marriage cracks but does not break. At last, torn between her sister and her husband, she succeeds in bridging the mistrust that divides them. Howards End, where the story begins and ends, is the house that belonged to Henry Wilcox's first wife, and is a symbol of human dignity and endurance.
Howe, MISS, a character in Richardson's 'Clarissa Harlowe' (q.v.).
Howell, JAMES (1594?-1666), held diplomatic and administrative posts under Charles I, and wrote a number of historical and political pamphlets; but is chiefly remembered for his 'Epistolae Ho-elianae: Familiar Letters'. Some of these are political or historical and deal with various countries, others are essays on literary and social topics.
Howells, WILLIAM DEAN (1837-1920), American novelist, editor of the 'Atlantic Monthly', 1871-81, and associate editor of 'Harper's Magazine', 1886-91, to which

periodicals he contributed many articles on literary subjects. His numerous romances include 'The Rise of Silas Lapham' (1885) and 'Indian Summer' (1886).

Howleglass, see *Eulenspiegel.*

How they brought the Good News from Ghent to Aix, a poem by R. Browning (q.v.), included in 'Dramatic Romances', published in 'Bells and Pomegranates' (1842-5).

This, one of the most popular of the author's poems, is a vivid imaginary tale of three horsemen galloping to save their town, one horse falling dead on the way, the second within sight of the town, the third reaching the market-place, where the town's last measure of wine is poured down its throat.

Hoyle, EDMOND (1672-1769), author of a 'Short Treatise on Whist' (1742 and later editions). Hoyle's 'Laws' of 1760 ruled whist till 1864.

Hrimfaxi ('dewy-mane'), in Scandinavian mythology, the horse of Night.

Hrothgar, the Danish king in 'Beowulf' (q.v.).

Hrotsvitha or ROSWITHA, a Benedictine abbess, in the 10th cent., of Gandersheim in Saxony, who adapted the comedies of Terence for the use of her convent, an example of the survival of classical influence in the Middle Ages.

Hubbard, MOTHER, see *Mother Hubberd's Tale.*

Huchoun (*fl.* 14th cent.), Scottish author of romances in alliterative verse. Among the poems attributed to him, with various degrees of probability, are the alliterative 'Morte Arthure', 'The Awntyrs of Arthure', 'Sir Gawain and the Green Knight', 'The Pistyl of Susan', 'Patience', 'Pearl', and 'Cleanness'. He is perhaps to be identified with Sir Hugh of Eglintoun, a statesman of the reigns of David II and Robert II.

Huckleberry Finn, a novel by S. L. Clemens (q.v.), published in 1884 as a sequel to 'Tom Sawyer', under the pseudonym MARK TWAIN. It is accepted as his masterpiece and one of the greatest works of American fiction.

Hudibras or HUDDIBRAS, in Spenser's 'Faerie Queene', II. ii. 17, the lover of Elissa.

Another Huddibras in II. x. 25 of the same poem is a legendary king of Britain. *Hudibras,* a satire in octosyllabic couplets, and in three parts, each containing three cantos, by S. Butler (1612-80) (q.v.), published, Pt. I in 1663, Pt. II in 1664, and Pt. III in 1678.

The satire takes the form of a mock-heroic poem, in which the hypocrisy and self-seeking of the Presbyterians and Independents are held up to ridicule. It is externally modelled on 'Don Quixote', while there are Rabelaisian touches, and the influence of Scarron on the style has been pointed out. The name 'Hudibras' is taken from the 'Faerie Queene' (see above). The character has been thought to represent the Puritan Sir S. Luke. He is pictured as a pedantic Presbyterian, setting forth 'a-colonelling', a grotesque figure on a miserable horse, with rusty arms but ample provisions. He is accompanied by his squire Ralpho, an Independent, and the satire is largely occupied with their sectarian squabbles.

Hudibrastic, in the metre or after the manner of Butler's 'Hudibras' (q.v.), burlesque-heroic.

Hudson, WILLIAM HENRY (1841-1922), born of American parents near Buenos Aires, came to England in 1869, where he at first, and indeed till nearly the end of his life, suffered much from poverty and loneliness. He was naturalized a British subject in 1900. He has left an admirable picture of his early life in the Argentine in 'Far Away and Long Ago' (1918). From his youngest days he was an intense observer of nature, and a large proportion of his writings was devoted to birds. His most remarkable work is probably 'A Shepherd's Life' (1910), in which he depicts the humble folk of the Wiltshire downs. He also wrote a striking romance of the S. American forest, 'Green Mansions' (1904), of which the central figure 'Rima', the semi-human embodiment of the spirit of the forest, has been made familiar by Epstein's sculpture. His other writings include: 'The Purple Land' (1885), 'El Ombu' (1902), 'A Crystal Age' (1906), 'Afoot in England' (1909), 'A Hind in Richmond Park' (1922).

Hudson's Bay Company: the company received a charter from Charles II in 1670, for trade and 'to discover a passage leading to the Pacific Ocean'. Prince Rupert was the company's first governor. Hudson Bay is named after Henry Hudson, the explorer, who was turned adrift there with his son and some companions by a mutinous crew, and perished in 1611.

Hueffer, F. M., see *Ford* (*F. M.*).

Hugh, in Dickens's 'Barnaby Rudge' (q.v.), the ostler of the Maypole Inn.

Hughes, RICHARD ARTHUR WARREN (1900-76), novelist and short-story writer. He published the novels 'A High Wind in Jamaica' (1929), 'In Hazard' (1938), and 'The Fox in the Attic' (1961), the first volume of a long historical novel of his own times. He also published collections of short stories.

Hughes, THOMAS (1822-96), educated at Rugby and Oriel College, Oxford, was a follower of Frederick Denison Maurice (q.v.). He published in 1857, over the signature 'An Old Boy', his chief work, 'Tom Brown's Schooldays', the story of an ordinary schoolboy at Rugby under Dr. Arnold's headmastership. In this he depicted, with a didactic purpose, schoolboy cruelties and loyalties, and considerably influenced English ideas on public schools. The sequel, 'Tom Brown at Oxford' (1861) has less merit.

Hugh of Lincoln, ST. (? 1246-55), a child supposed to have been crucified by a Jew at Lincoln, after having been starved and tortured. The body is said to have been discovered in a well and buried near that of Grosseteste in the cathedral, and to have been the cause of several miracles. The story, a frequent theme for poets, is referred to by Chaucer

('The Prioress's Tale') and by Marlowe in 'The Jew of Malta'. See also the ballad of 'The Jew's Daughter' in Percy's 'Reliques'.

Hugo, VICTOR-MARIE (1802-85), French poet and novelist, the leader of the French Romantic movement. He entered political life after the revolution of 1848, and showed himself an eloquent defender of liberty. He spent the years 1851-70 in exile. Hugo introduced flexibility, sonority, and melody into the rigid verse that had prevailed during many generations. His important plays were: 'Hernani' (1830), 'Marion de Lorme' (1831), 'Le Roi s'amuse' (1832), and 'Ruy Blas' (1838). His most famous novels are 'Notre Dame de Paris' (1831), 'Les Misérables' (1862), 'Les Travailleurs de la Mer' (1866), and 'Quatre-vingt-treize' (1873).

Huguenot, a member of the Reformed or Calvinistic communion of France in the 16th and 17th cents.

Hulme, THOMAS ERNEST (1883-1917), an anti-romantic whose advocacy of the 'hard dry image' in poetry influenced Imagism (q.v.). He published a series of articles on Bergson (q.v.) in 1911 in the 'New Age', a political and literary weekly, which also published five short poems called 'The Complete Poetical Works of T. E. Hulme'. His 'Speculations: essays on humanism and the philosophy of art' were published in 1924 (ed. Herbert Read).

Humanists, THE, in English literary history, a term usually applied to the 'Oxford scholars' of the early 16th cent., Erasmus, More, Grocyn, Colet, etc., who were leading figures in the Revival of Learning in England and devoted themselves to the study of the language, literature, and antiquities of Greece and Rome. In general, one who follows these studies, a lover of the 'humanities'.

Human Nature, Treatise of, see *Treatise of Human Nature*.

Hume, DAVID (1711-76), born at Edinburgh, developed early in life a passion for philosophy. He spent three years (1734-7) with the Jesuits at La Flèche, and in 1739 published anonymously 'A Treatise of Human Nature' (q.v.) in two volumes, a third volume appearing in 1740. The work aroused little interest, but his 'Essays Moral and Political' (1741-2) were more successful. His 'Enquiry concerning Human Understanding' (originally entitled 'Philosophical Essays') appeared in 1748 and his 'Enquiry concerning the Principles of Morals' in 1751 (for these two works see *Treatise of Human Nature*). In 1752 he published his 'Political Discourses', which were translated into French and made Hume famous on the Continent. In 1754 appeared the first volume of his 'History of Great Britain' (see below), followed by further volumes in 1757, 1759, and 1761. The first two volumes were translated into French. From 1763 to 1765 Hume was secretary to the Embassy in Paris. He brought back Rousseau to England and befriended him, but Rousseau's suspicious nature presently led to a quarrel. Hume was under-secretary of state in 1767-8, and after this finally settled in Edinburgh. After his death, his friend Adam Smith (q.v.) published his autobiography (1777). Hume's 'Dialogues concerning Natural Religion' (q.v.) were published in 1779 by his nephew.

Hume's philosophical works are dealt with under the heading 'Treatise of Human Nature'. His views on religion are contained in the essay 'Of Miracles' (included in the 'Enquiry concerning Human Understanding'), in 'The Natural History of Religion', and in the 'Dialogues concerning Natural Religion' (q.v.). They may be described as an 'attenuated theism' (Prof. Campbell Fraser), the view 'that the cause or causes of order in the universe probably bear some remote analogy to human intelligence'.

Hume's political opinions as expressed in his various writings show a process of development. He appears to have abandoned the view that men are naturally equal and that society is established by contract. He finally seems to have regarded political society as evolved from the family and existing for the purpose of administering justice; and in contrast to his Tory attitude in the 'History' (see below), in his later essays he regards liberty as an ideal limiting the sphere of authority of government.

As a political economist Hume attacked the mercantile system, and in general anticipated the views of later economists (including Adam Smith).

Hume's Enquiry concerning Human Understanding, see *Treatise of Human Nature*.

Hume's History of Great Britain (see *Hume*), containing the reigns of the Stuarts (1754-7). Two further volumes on the Tudor reigns appeared in 1759, and two on the period from Julius Caesar to Henry VII in 1761.

Hume's object was to trace the steps by which the nation had arrived at its present system of government, and he started with the reign of James I as the period in which the revolt against the prerogative of the crown commenced. The work is criticized as superficial and as containing many misstatements, and the author is said to show Tory prejudice. But it was the first great English history, and, however imperfect, a fine conception. The first volume was coldly received, but the work subsequently became popular, and for long was regarded as a standard history.

Humgudgeon, CORPORAL GRACE-BE-HERE, a character in Scott's 'Woodstock' (q.v.).

Humorous Lieutenant, The, a comedy by J. Fletcher (q.v.), produced about 1620.

Humours, COMEDY OF, a term applied especially to the type of comic drama written by Ben Jonson (q.v.), where a 'humour' is a personification of some individual passion or propensity.

Humphrey, DUKE OF GLOUCESTER (1391-1447), youngest son of Henry IV, 'the Good Duke Humphrey', gave the first books for a library at Oxford. His original library, built in the 15th cent., forms the oldest part of the Bodleian.

Humphrey's Clock, Master, see *Master Humphrey's Clock.*

Humphry Clinker, The Expedition of, a novel by Smollett (q.v.) (1771).

This is the last and the pleasantest of Smollett's novels. It relates, in the form of letters, the adventures of Mr. Matthew Bramble's family party as they travel through England and Scotland. The party consists of Bramble himself, an outwardly misanthropical but really kind-hearted old valetudinarian bachelor; his sister Tabitha, a virago bent on matrimony; his nephew Jery, an amiable young spark, and his sister Lydia; Mrs. Winifred Jenkins, the maid; and Humphry Clinker, a ragged ostler whom they pick up *en route* as postilion, and who turns out a creature of much resource and devotion.

Humpty-Dumpty, a short dumpy, hump-shouldered person. In the well-known nursery rhyme or riddle the name is commonly explained as signifying an egg. The riddle is found in one form or another in many parts of Europe.

Huncamunca, in Fielding's 'Tom Thumb, a Tragedy' (q.v.), the daughter of King Arthur and the wife of Tom Thumb.

Hundred Days, THE, the period in 1815 between Napoleon's arrival in Paris after his escape from Elba and the restoration of Louis XVIII after Waterloo.

Hundreth good pointes of husbandrie, see *Tusser* (*T.*).

Hungry Forties, see *Forties.*

Huns, an Asiatic race of warlike nomads who invaded Europe *c.* A.D. 375. In the middle of the 5th cent. under their king, Attila (q.v.), they overran and ravaged a great part of Europe. The name is used in a transferred sense (like 'Vandals') of uncultured devastators.

Hunt, (JAMES HENRY) LEIGH (1784–1859), was educated at Christ's Hospital. He began to edit 'The Examiner' in 1808 and 'The Reflector' in 1810, and was sentenced with his brother to a fine and two years' imprisonment in 1813 for reflections in the former paper on the Prince Regent.

He continued editing 'The Examiner' while in gaol, where he was visited by Byron, Moore, Bentham, and Lamb. Subsequently he brought about the meeting of Keats and Shelley, and introduced the two poets to the public in 'The Examiner'. He published his chief poetical work 'The Story of Rimini' (based on the story of Paolo and Francesca) in 1816. He joined Byron at Pisa in 1822 and there for a time carried on with him 'The Liberal' magazine (see under *Byron*). In 1847 he received a civil list pension. His poetical work, which was far less extensive than his prose writings, includes the lines entitled 'Abou Ben Adhem' and 'Jenny kissed me'. In addition to the two periodicals already mentioned, Leigh Hunt at various times conducted and largely wrote 'The Indicator' (1819–21), 'The Companion' (1828), a new 'Tatler' (1830–2), and 'Leigh Hunt's London Journal' (1834–5).

The importance of Leigh Hunt lies chiefly in his development of the light miscellaneous essay, in his recognition of the genius of Shelley and Keats, and in the wide range of his critical work. He was depicted by Dickens as Skimpole (in 'Bleak House', q.v.), at any rate as regards 'the light externals of character', that is to say a certain vagueness and irresponsibility.

Hunter, SIR WILLIAM WILSON (1840–1900), a distinguished civil servant in India and a man of wide culture, was appointed by Lord Mayo to compile a statistical survey of the Indian Empire, which he condensed in 'The Imperial Gazeteer of India' (1881). He published 'Annals of Rural Bengal' in 1868, and two charming lighter works, 'The Old Missionary' (1890) and 'The Thackerays in India' (1897). Of his 'History of British India' (1899) only two volumes had been completed at his death.

Huntingdon, ARTHUR and HELEN, leading characters in Anne Brontë's 'The Tenant of Wildfell Hall'.

Huntingdon, HENRY OF, see *Henry of Huntingdon.*

Huntingdon, ROBERT, *Earl of*, a noble-man born about 1160, and, according to Ritson, the original of Robin Hood (q.v.).

Huntinglen, EARL OF, a character in Scott's 'The Fortunes of Nigel' (q.v.).

Hunting of the Snark, The, a mock-heroic nonsense poem by Lewis Carroll (see *Dodgson*) (1876). The Snark is an imaginary animal of elusive character. On this occasion, it turns out to be a Boojum, a highly dangerous variety.

Huon of Bordeaux, the hero of a French 13th-cent. *chanson de geste*. Huon is the son of Seguin of Bordeaux. He has the misfortune to kill Charlot, son of the Emperor Charlemagne, in an affray, not knowing who his assailant is. He is there-upon condemned to death by the emperor, but reprieved on condition that he will go to the court of Gaudisse, amir of Babylon, bring back a handful of his hair and four of his teeth, kill his doughtiest knight, and kiss Esclarmonde his daughter. By the help of the fairy Oberon, Huon achieves the adventure. The work was translated by Lord Berners (q.v.) and printed by Wynkyn de Worde in 1534. Huon's adventure is the theme of Weber's opera 'Oberon'.

Hurlothrumbo, a popular burlesque (1729) by Samuel Johnson (1691-1773), a Manchester dancing-master.

Husbandrie, Hundreth good pointes of, see *Tusser* (*T.*).

Husband's Message, The, an OE. poem included in the 'Exeter Book' (q.v.). It takes the form of a message to a woman from her husband, who has had to leave his home owing to a vendetta, telling her that he has obtained wealth and position in another land, and asking her to sail and join him when spring comes.

Hussites, followers of John Huss (1373-1415), the Bohemian preacher of the Reformation, who was convicted of heresy by the Council of Constance (1414-18) and burnt alive.

Hutcheson, FRANCIS (1694-1746), pro-fessor of moral philosophy at Glasgow from 1729 until his death. Hutcheson, in his ethical system, developed the ideas of Shaftesbury (q.v.), but elaborated the theory of the moral sense.

Hutchinson, ARTHUR STUART-MENTEITH (1879-1971), novelist, author of 'If Winter Comes' (1921), a novel of the war period.

Hutchinson, MRS. LUCY (*b.* 1620), daughter of Sir Allen Apsley, and wife of John Hutchinson. She was author of 'The Memoirs of the Life of Colonel Hutchin-son', her husband, and of a fragment of a 'Life' of herself. The 'Memoirs' give an interesting picture, from the Puritan standpoint, of the state of the country at the outbreak of the Civil War and of the conflict in the vicinity of Nottingham.

Hutten, ULRICH VON (1488-1523), soldier, humanist, and supporter of Luther. To him is attributed the author-ship of the major part of the 'Epistolae Obscurorum Virorum' (1515-17), an anonymous collection of letters in medieval Latin in support of the new learning.

Hutton, RICHARD HOLT (1826-97), principal of University Hall, London. With Walter Bagehot (q.v.) he was joint-editor of 'The National Review' from 1855 to 1864. His works, mainly of literary and theological criticism, include a volume on Cardinal Newman.

Huxley, ALDOUS (LEONARD) (1894-1963), novelist and essayist. His best-known books are: 'Crome Yellow' (1921), 'Antic Hay' (1923), 'Those Barren Leaves' (1925), 'Point Counter-Point' (1928), 'Brave New World' (1932), 'Eyeless in Gaza' (1936), 'After Many a Summer' (1939), 'Time Must Have a Stop' (1944), 'The Genius and the Goddess' (1955), 'Island' (1962), all novels. Also 'Leda' (1920), a poem; and 'On the Margin' (1923), 'Jesting Pilate' (1926), 'Beyond the Mexique Bay' (1934), 'The Olive Tree' (1936), 'Ape and Essence' (1948), 'Heaven and Hell' (1956), essays.

Huxley, THOMAS HENRY (1825-95), studied at Charing Cross Hospital and from 1846 to 1850 was assistant surgeon on H.M.S. 'Rattlesnake'. Apart from a large number of papers on technical subjects, he influenced English thought by many addresses and publications on philosophical and religious subjects. Among these may be mentioned 'Man's Place in Nature' (1863), 'Lay Sermons, Addresses and Reviews' (1870), 'Science and Morals' (1886), in which he defines the relation of science to philosophical and religious speculation, 'Essays upon some Controverted Questions' (1892), and his Romanes Lecture, 'Ethics and Evolution' (1893). In this last he refuses to see in the struggle of evolution a basis for morality, of which the criterion is to be sought elsewhere. Huxley coined the word 'agnostic' to express his own philosophical attitude. He was a powerful but discriminating supporter of Darwinism, and a vigorous disputant. A controversy between him and Gladstone, carried on in the magazines, on the subject of the Gadarene swine, is celebrated.

Hyacinthus, in Greek mythology, a youth beloved by Apollo and Zephyrus. He returned the love of the former, and Zephyrus, incensed at his preference of his rival, resolved to punish him. As Apollo was playing at quoits with Hyacinthus, Zephyrus blew the quoit thrown by Apollo so that it struck the boy and killed him. Apollo changed his blood into the flower that bears his name.

Hyacinthus de Archangelis, DOMINUS, a character in R. Browning's 'The Ring and the Book' (q.v.).

Hyades, daughters of Atlas (q.v.), who were so disconsolate at the death of their brother Hyas, killed by a wild boar, that they pined away and died, and were placed among the stars (cf. *Pleiades*). The rising of the group of stars simultaneously with the sun was supposed to indicate rainy weather whence probably its name (from ὕειν, to rain).

Hybla, a town in Sicily, on the slope of Mt. Etna, where thyme and odoriferous herbs grew in abundance, famous for its honey.

Hyde, DOUGLAS (1860–1949), Irish writer, a pioneer of the movement for the revival of the Irish language and literature. He was one of the founders of the Abbey Theatre (q.v.). He was the first president of Eire (1938–45).

Hyde Park, London, the ancient manor of Hyde, passed into the possession of the Crown at the dissolution of the monasteries. The corner near the Marble Arch is the favourite pitch of HYDE PARK ORATORS, popular exponents of various causes, social, political, and religious.

Hyde Park, a comedy by Shirley (q.v.), acted in 1632 on the occasion of the opening of Hyde Park to the public. It was printed in 1637. The plot is very slight, and the chief interest is in the representation of contemporary manners.

Hydra, a many-headed monster that infested the neighbourhood of the lake Lerna in the Peloponnese. It was one of the labours of Hercules to destroy it, but as soon as one head was struck off, two arose in its place. This difficulty was overcome with the help of Iolaus, who applied a burning brand to the wound as each head fell. Hercules dipped his arrows in the Hydra's blood, so that the wounds they gave were incurable.

Hydriotaphia, see *Urn Burial.*

Hygieia, the goddess of health, and daughter of Aesculapius (q.v.).

Hylas, a beautiful youth, stolen away by Hercules and carried on board the ship 'Argo' to Colchis. On the Asiatic coast, the Argonauts (q.v.) landed to take a fresh supply of water, when Hylas fell into the fountain and was drowned, or according to the poets was carried away by the nymphs for love of his beauty. Hercules, disconsolate, abandoned the Argonautic expedition.

Hymen, in Greek and Roman mythology, the god of marriage, represented as a young man carrying a torch and veil.

Hymettus, a mountain in Attica celebrated for its honey and for its marble.

Hymns, Ancient and Modern, a collection promoted and edited by the Revd. Sir Henry Williams Baker (1821–77), vicar of Monkland, near Leominster, who contributed to it many original hymns and translations from the Latin. The collection first appeared in 1861. Supplements were added in 1889 and 1916, edited respectively by C. Steggall and S. H. Nicholson. A revised edition appeared in 1950.

Hypallage (Greek = exchange), a transference of epithet, as Spenser's 'Sansfoy's dead dowry' for 'dead Sansfoy's dowry'.

Hypatia, or New Foes with an Old Face, a historical novel by C. Kingsley (q.v.), published in 'Fraser's Magazine' in 1851 and in book form in 1853.

The time of the story is the 5th cent., when the Western Empire was rapidly succumbing before the Teutonic advance, and the scene is Alexandria.

The historical Hypatia was daughter of the Alexandrian mathematician Theon; she was a Neoplatonic philosopher, and perished as described in the novel.

Hyperbole, the use of exaggerated terms to emphasize the importance or extent of something; e.g. Shakespeare's 'Our house is hell and thou, a merry devil, Didst rob it of some taste of tediousness'. Cf. *Meiosis*.

Hyperboreans, THE, in Greek legends connected with the worship of Apollo, a happy and peaceful people, worshippers of that god, who lived in a land of perpetual sunshine and plenty. This came to be conceived as lying in the extreme north, 'beyond the influence of the north wind', perhaps from the derivation of their name, now generally rejected, from ὑπὲρ Βορέας.

Hyperion, a son of Uranus and Ge, one of the Titans, and father of the Sun, or the Sun itself. In Greek the word was pronounced Hyperíon, but Shakespeare and most English poets accent it Hyper´ion. The phrase 'Hyperion to a satyr' is in 'Hamlet', I. ii.

Hyperion, a poem by Keats (q.v.), written in 1818–19.

Keats wrote two versions of the poem and each remains an uncompleted fragment. In the first the story of Hyperion is told in simple narrative; in the other in the form of an allegorical vision granted to the poet. In the former, Saturn is presented mourning his fallen realm, and debating with the Titans how he may recover it. They look in vain to Hyperion, the sun-god, who is still undeposed, to help them. Then the young Apollo is introduced, the god of music, poetry, and knowledge. At this point the fragment ends.

In the other form of the poem, the poet in a dream passes through a garden towards a shrine, of which the approach is granted to none

But those to whom the miseries of the world
Are misery, and will not let them rest.

Then the fate of Hyperion, the last of the Titans, who is dethroned by Apollo, is revealed to him by Moneta, the mournful goddess of the 'wither'd race' of Saturn; but the tale is uncompleted.

Hyperion, a prose romance by Longfellow (q.v.) (1839).

Hypermnestra, see *Danaïdes*.

Hypocorism, a childish or pet name, used endearingly or euphemistically.

Hyrcania, a region adjoining the Caspian or Hyrcanian sea. It was reputed to abound in wild beasts, serpents, etc.

Hysteron proteron, in grammar and rhetoric, a figure of speech in which the word or phrase that should properly come last is put first; in general, 'putting the cart before the horse'.

Hythloday, RAPHAEL, in More's 'Utopia' (q.v.), the traveller in whose mouth the author places the criticisms of English institutions, etc.

I

Iachimo, a character in Shakespeare's 'Cymbeline' (q.v.).

Iago, a character in Shakespeare's 'Othello' (q.v.).

Iambic, verse consisting of, or based on, iambuses, that is feet consisting of a short followed by a long syllable (see *Metre*). The IAMBIC TRIMETER is a verse of six iambuses, the first, third, and fifth of which may be replaced by a tribrach or a spondee or a dactyl. This was the principal metre of the Greek drama. In modern use, an iambic verse of six feet is known as an Alexandrine (q.v.).

The basic measure of English verse is the iambic pentameter, which, with variations to avoid monotony, is the standard measure of blank verse and of the heroic couplet (qq.v.).

Ianthe, (1) the heroine of D'Avenant's 'The Siege of Rhodes'; (2) the young lady to whom Byron dedicated his 'Childe Harold's Pilgrimage', Lady Charlotte Mary Harley (1801–80); (3) the lady whom Landor addressed in a series of poems, Sophia Jane Swifte, an Irishwoman, who became Countess de Molandé; (4) the name of the daughter of Shelley and his wife Harriet; (5) in Shelley's 'Queen Mab', the maiden to whom the fairy grants a vision of the world.

Ibáñez, VICENTE BLASCO (1867–1928), Spanish novelist, whose best-known works (translated into English) are: 'La Catedral' (1903, 'The Shadow of the Cathedral'), 'Los Cuatro Jinetes del Apocalipsis' (1916, 'The Four Horsemen of the Apocalypse'), 'Mare Nostrum' (1918, 'Our Sea').

Iberia, the Greek name for Spain, from the river *Iberus*, the Ebro.

Ibsen, HENRIK (1828–1906), Norwegian dramatist, whose satirical problem plays, directed to social reforms, obtained wide fame and exerted a powerful influence.

Ibsen's early work consisted of historical romantic dramas.

Then, in a moment of pecuniary distress, and embittered by disappointment at the attitude taken by his country in the Dano-German war, Ibsen gave vent to his despondency in his two great lyrical dramas 'Brand' and 'Peer Gynt' (1866 and 1867). There followed the series of problem plays, of which the general subject is the relation of the individual to his social environment, the shams and conventions that hinder his self-expression, and especially the case of woman in the state of marriage. These plays included 'A Doll's House' (1879), 'Ghosts' (1881), 'Rosmersholm' (1886), 'Hedda Gabler' (1890), and 'When we Dead awake' (1900).

Icarus, see *Daedalus*.

Ichabod, 'inglorious', the name that the wife of Phinehas gave to her child, saying, 'The glory is departed from Israel'. (1 Sam. iv. 21.)

Ichor, in Greek mythology, the ethereal fluid supposed to flow like blood in the veins of the gods. Thus R. Bentley (q.v.) in his edition of Milton substituted 'ichorous' for 'nectarous' in 'Paradise Lost', vi. 332.

Ichthys, the Greek word for 'fish', used in early Christian times as a symbol of Christ, as being composed of the initials of the words *I*esous *CH*ristos *TH*eou *U*ios *S*oter, Jesus Christ, son of God, Saviour.

Icknield Way, an ancient road dating probably from pre-Roman times, crossing England in a wide curve from Norfolk (the country of the *Iceni*, from whom the name is perhaps derived) to Cornwall. An account of it by Edward Thomas (q.v.) is one of his most pleasant works.

Icon Basilike, see *Eikon Basilike*.

Ictus, Latin 'beat', the stress on particular syllables that marks the rhythm of a verse.

Ida, the name of a mountain in Phrygia near Troy, where the Simoïs and Scamander had their sources. From its summit the gods watched the Trojan War. There was another Mt. Ida in Crete; in a cave on this mountain Zeus (q.v.) was said to have been brought up.

The IDAEAN MOTHER was Cybele (q.v.), who was particularly connected with Mt. Ida in Crete and the Phrygian Ida.

Ida, PRINCESS, the heroine of Tennyson's 'The Princess' (q.v.), which is the basis of the Gilbert and Sullivan opera 'Princess Ida'.

Idea, the Shepheards Garland, nine pastorals by M. Drayton (q.v.), issued, 1st ed. 1593, 3rd revision (entitled 'Pastorals') 1619.

Idealism, in philosophy, any system of thought in which the object of external perception is held to consist of ideas, whether of the perceiving mind or of the universal mind; or in which no independent reality is held to underlie our ideas of external objects. The principal exponents of idealistic philosophies include Kant, Fichte, Schelling, and Hegel (qq.v.). In common use the word means the representation of things in an ideal form, or as they might be; the imaginative treatment of a subject in art or literature.

Iden, ALEXANDER, in Shakespeare's '2 Henry VI', a Kentish man, who slew Jack Cade.

Ides, in the ancient Roman calendar, the 15th of March, May, July, and October, and the 13th of all the other months. The *Ides of March* was the day on which Julius Caesar was assassinated. See Shakespeare, 'Julius Caesar', I. ii and III. i.

Idler, The, a series of papers contributed by S. Johnson (q.v.) to the 'Universal Chronicle, or Weekly Gazette', between 15 April 1758 and 5 April 1760. These papers are shorter and lighter than those of 'The Rambler' (q.v.), but their general character is the same. They include the well-known sketches of Dick Minim, the critic, of Mr. Sober (the author himself), Jack Whirler (John Newbery), and Tom Restless.

Idyll, from a Greek word meaning a little picture, a short poem, descriptive of some picturesque scene, chiefly in rustic life; e.g. the 'Idylls' of Theocritus (q.v.).

Idylls of the King, The, a series of connected poems by Lord Tennyson (q.v.), of which the first fragment, 'The Morte d'Arthur', subsequently incorporated in 'The Passing of Arthur', was published in 1842. In 1859 appeared 'Enid', 'Vivien', 'Elaine', and 'Guinevere'. In 1869 were added 'The Coming of Arthur', 'The Holy Grail', 'Pelleas and Ettarre', and 'The Passing of Arthur'. 'The Last Tournament' appeared in 1871, 'Gareth and Lynette' in 1872, 'Balin and Balan' in 1885.

These poems form parts in a general presentment of the story of Arthur, of his noble design of the Round Table, and of its failure under the ever-widening influence of evil, in the shape of the sin of Lancelot and Guinevere. It is a story of bright hope (in 'The Coming of Arthur' and 'Gareth and Lynette'), followed by growing disillusionment, of which the protagonists are the melancholy characters of Arthur and Guinevere, Lancelot and Elaine. The chief criticism which has been passed on it relates to the shadowy and unreal, almost symbolical, character of Arthur himself.

Ierne, IVERNA, HIBERNIA, ancient names of Ireland.

Igdrasil, see *Yggdrasil.*

Igerne, see *Igraine.*

Ignatius, ST. (*c.* 35–*c.* 107), bishop of Antioch, said to have been martyred under the Emperor Trajan. He is the author of famous epistles from which we derive the little that is known about him.

Ignatius Loyola, see *Loyola.*

Ignis fatuus, meaning 'foolish fire', is a phosphorescent light seen hovering or flitting over marshy ground, and supposed to be due to the spontaneous combustion of an inflammable gas derived from decaying vegetable matter, popularly called Will-o'-the-wisp, Jack-o'-lantern, etc.

Ignoramus, a famous university farcical play by George Ruggle (1575-1622), produced in 1615 before James I.

Ignoratio elenchi, a logical fallacy which consists in apparently refuting an opponent while actually disproving some statement other than that advanced by him.

Igraine, or IGERNE, or YGERNE, in the Arthurian legend, the wife of Gorlois of Cornwall, whom Uther Pendragon, assuming the likeness of her husband by the help of Merlin's magic, won for his wife. Of their union Arthur (q.v.) was born.

Iliad, The, a Greek epic poem attributed to Homer (q.v.), describing the war waged by Achaean princes against Troy for the purpose of recovering Helen, wife of Menelaus, whom Paris, son of Priam, king of Troy, had carried away. In particular it deals with the wrath of Achilles, the special hero of the poem, at the slight put upon him by Agamemnon, leader of the host, and his final return to the field and slaying of Hector. See *Achilles*.

Ilium, see *Troy*.

Illuminati, a name applied to, or assumed by, various societies or sects because of their claim to special enlightenment in religious or intellectual matters.

Il Penseroso, see *Penseroso*.

Imaginary Conversations, by Landor (q.v.) (1824-9), followed by 'Imaginary Conversations of Greeks and Romans' (1853).

These represent the bulk of Landor's prose work. Some of the conversations are dramatic, some idyllic, some satirical, while others treat of political, social, or literary questions; action and incidents are occasionally interposed, which add to their variety. There are some 150 of these dialogues. Their form is admirable, but the matter is unequal; for Landor made use of them to express his personal views, which were sometimes ill-judged, on a multitude of subjects.

Imagism, a movement of English and American poets in revolt from romanticism, seeking clarity of expression through the use of precise images. It flourished from 1910 to 1918 and its first anthology, 'Des Imagistes' (1914), included poems by 'H. D.' (Hilda Doolittle), Amy Lowell, James Joyce, Ezra Pound, and Ford Madox Hueffer (Ford) (qq.v.). The principles of the Imagist manifesto were laid down by Pound in 1913, but the official credo was not prepared until the 1915 anthology, 'Some Imagist Poets', edited by Amy Lowell.

Imitation of Christ, or *De Imitatione Christi*, see *Thomas à Kempis*.

Imitations of Horace, see *Pope (A.)*.

Imlac, a character in Johnson's 'Rasselas' (q.v.).

Immortals, THE (LES IMMORTELS), the forty members of the French Academy (q.v.), so called because the place of each member is filled as soon as he dies. The name was also given in ancient times to a body of 10,000 Persian infantry whose number was kept constantly full.

Imogen, in Shakespeare's 'Cymbeline' (q.v.), the wife of Posthumus.

Imp, originally a young shoot of a plant or tree; hence a scion, especially of a noble house. It came to be used specifically of a child of the devil; a little devil, a mischievous child.

Impressionism, the name given in derision (from a painting by Monet called '*Impression, soleil levant*') to the work of a group of French painters who held their first exhibition in 1874. Their aim was to render the effects of light on objects rather than the objects themselves. Claude Monet (1840-1926), Alfred Sisley (1839-99), and Camille Pissarro (1831-1903) carried out their aims most completely; Auguste Renoir (1841-1919), Edgar Degas (1834-1917), and Cézanne (q.v.) were also associated with the movement. The term is used by transference in literature and music.

Imprimatur, meaning 'let it be printed', the formula signed by an official licenser authorizing the printing of a book. Hence generally, an authorization.

Inca, the title of the emperor or king of Peru before its conquest by the Spaniards.

Inchbald, MRS. ELIZABETH (1753–1821), *née* Simpson, was a novelist, dramatist, and actress. She is chiefly remembered for her two prose romances 'A Simple Story' (1791) and 'Nature and Art' (1796). Her play 'Lovers' Vows' (q.v.) was acted in 1798.

Inchcape Rock, THE, a rock in the North Sea, off the Firth of Tay, dangerous to mariners, near which the abbot of Arbroath or Aberbrothock fixed a warning bell on a float. In Southey's ballad on the subject, Sir Ralph the Rover, to plague the abbot, cuts the bell from the float, and later, on his homeward way, is himself wrecked on the rock.

Incunabula (Latin = swaddling-clothes), is used to signify books produced in the infancy of the art of printing, especially those printed before 1500.

Independence Day, 4 July, see *Fourth of July*.

Index Expurgatorius, strictly, an authoritative specification of the passages to be expunged or altered in works otherwise permitted to be read by Roman Catholics. The term is frequently used in England to cover the 'Index Librorum Prohibitorum', or list of forbidden books (not authors, as sometimes thought). The 'Index Expurgatorius' and the 'Index Librorum Prohibitorum' were abrogated in 1966.

Indian summer, the name given to a period of the autumn in the United States when the atmosphere is dry and hazy, the sky cloudless, and the temperature mild.

Indo-European, the name applied to the great family of cognate languages (also called Indo-Germanic and Aryan) spoken over the greater part of Europe and extending into Asia as far as northern India.

Iñez, DONNA, in Byron's 'Don Juan' (q.v.), the mother of the hero.

Inferno, The, of Dante, see *Divina Commedia*.

Inge, THE VERY REVD. WILLIAM RALPH (1860–1954), dean of St. Paul's Cathedral, London, 1911–34. He published many works of a philosophical character. On account of his outlook on contemporary life he was jocularly termed 'The Gloomy Dean'.

Ingelow, JEAN (1820–97), poetess. Her works include three series of poems (1871, 1876, and 1885), and stories for children. Her most remarkable poems are 'Divided' and 'The High Tide on the Coast of Lincolnshire, 1571' (1863), and 'A Story of Doom' (1867).

Ingoldsby Legends, The, see *Barham*.

Ingres, JEAN AUGUSTE DOMINIQUE (1780–1867), a celebrated French painter, mainly of historical pieces.

Ingulf, see *Croyland History*.

Inheritance, The, a novel by S. E. Ferrier (q.v.) (1824).

In Memoriam A.H.H., a poem by Lord Tennyson (q.v.) written between 1833 and 1850, and published in the latter year. The poem was written in memory of Arthur H. Hallam, the son of Henry Hallam, the historian, a young man of extraordinary promise and an intimate friend of Tennyson, who died in 1833 at Vienna when 22 years old. It is written in stanzas of four octosyllabic lines rhyming a b b a. (See under *Quatrain*.)

'In Memoriam' is not so much a single elegy as a series of poems written at different times, inspired by the changing moods of the author's regret for his dead friend. The series describes, broadly speaking, the 'Way of the Soul', as Tennyson sometimes called it, in presence of a great loss, the gradual transformation of the regret felt by the living for the dead and of the longing for his bodily presence, into a sense of spiritual contact and possession and a wider love of God and humanity.

Inn Album, The, a poem by R. Browning (q.v.) (1875).

Innisfail, a poetical name for Ireland.

Innocents Abroad, The, an autobiographical account by S. L. Clemens (q.v.), published (1869) under the pseudonym of MARK TWAIN, of a cruise to the Mediterranean with a company of Americans in 1867. The fun consists in seeing Europe viewed through the eyes of an American 'innocent'.

Inns of Court and of **Chancery** were the earliest settled places of residence, resembling colleges, of associations of law students in London, and date from the 13th and 14th cents. The Inns of Court are the four sets of buildings belonging to the four legal societies that have the exclusive right of admitting persons to practise at the bar. They are: Lincoln's Inn, Inner Temple, Middle Temple, and Gray's Inn. The Inns were the frequent scenes of masques and revels in the 16th and 17th cents.

In petto, Italian, in contemplation, undisclosed; used, in the phraseology of the Roman Curia, for nomination of a cardinal which is not yet to be disclosed.

In principio, Latin, in the beginning; the first words of Genesis and of St. John's Gospel in the Vulgate.

Inquisition, THE, in the Roman Catholic Church, an ecclesiastical tribunal directed to the suppression of heresy and punishment of heretics. The Congregation of the Inquisition (the Holy Office) was the final court of appeal. The Inquisition was abolished in France in 1772, and finally in Spain in 1820.

Instauratio Magna, the title of Francis Bacon's (q.v.) great projected work, of which his 'Novum Organum' is the second part.

Institutes of Justinian, The, an elementary treatise on Roman Law compiled by order of the Emperor Justinian in A.D. 533.

Instructions to a Painter, Last, see *Marvell*. The title was adopted for a number of political satires (by Denham and others) in the latter half of the 17th cent. The original 'Instructions' were those of Waller for the celebration of the duke of York's victories over the Dutch.

Intelligencer, The, see *L'Estrange*.

Interludes were plays performed at court, in the halls of the nobles, at the Inns of Court, and in colleges, generally but not exclusively by professional actors, dealing with a short episode and involving a limited number of characters. That interludes were sometimes performed by villagers we know from 'Pyramus and Thisbe' in 'A Midsummer Night's Dream' (q.v.). Their vogue was chiefly in the 15th and 16th cents. They succeeded 'moralities' (q.v.) in the history of the drama, and are not always clearly distinguishable from them. The characters are still frequently allegorical, but the comic or farcical element is more prevalent. The versification tends to doggerel and they are shorter than the moralities. A notable producer of interludes was J. Heywood (q.v.), author of 'The Four P's', etc. Interludes were revived during the Commonwealth period when plays were prohibited.

In the Midst of Life, a collection of short stories by Ambrose Bierce (q.v.), originally entitled 'Tales of Soldiers and Civilians'.

Invention of the Cross, THE, see *Helena (St.)*.

Invincible Doctor, THE, William of Ockham (q.v.).

Io, a daughter of Inachus, king of Argos, who was loved by Zeus. To escape the jealousy of Hera, Zeus changed his mistress into a beautiful heifer. Hera sent a gadfly to torment Io, so that she wandered over the face of the earth, swimming the Bosporus (i.e. passage of the ox), and reaching the banks of the Nile, where she recovered her human shape and bore a son, named Epaphus.

Iona or ICOLMKILL, an island of the Inner Hebrides, where St. Columba (q.v.) founded a monastery about 563, an important centre of Celtic missions.

Ionian mode, one of the modes of ancient Greek music, characterized as soft and effeminate.

Ionic dialect, the most important branch of ancient Greek, the language of that part of the Hellenic race which occupied

Attica and the northern coast of the Peloponnese and founded colonies in Italy, Sicily, and especially Asia Minor. Attic was a development of Ionic.

Ionic Order, one of the three orders of classical architecture (Doric, Ionic, Corinthian), characterized by a capital with volutes.

Iphigenia, a daughter of Agamemnon and Clytemnestra (qq.v.). When the Greeks on their way to the Trojan War were detained by contrary winds at Aulis, they were told that Iphigenia must be sacrificed to appease the wrath of Diana. Agamemnon consented, but, as the priest was about to strike the fatal blow, Iphigenia disappeared. The goddess had borne her away to Tauris and entrusted her with the care of her temple. Here Iphigenia was obliged to sacrifice all strangers who came to the country. When Orestes (q.v.) and Pylades came to Tauris, Iphigenia discovered that one of the strangers she was about to immolate was her brother. Thereupon she conspired with them to escape and to carry away the statue of the goddess, as the oracle had directed; and this they accomplished.

The story of Iphigenia was made the subject of plays by Aeschylus, Sophocles, and notably by Euripides; also in modern times by Racine and Goethe.

Iran, the Persian name for Persia. IRANIAN in comparative philology is the name of one of the two Asiatic families of Indo-European languages, comprising Zend and Old Persian and their modern descendants or cognates.

Iras, in Shakespeare's 'Antony and Cleopatra' (q.v.), one of Cleopatra's attendants.

Ireland, WILLIAM HENRY (1777–1835), son of Samuel Ireland the engraver, is remembered as a forger of Shakespeare manuscripts. He had access to Elizabethan parchments in the lawyer's chambers where he was employed, and in 1794–5 forged deeds and signatures of, or relating to, Shakespeare. He also fabricated in forged handwriting the pseudo-Shake-spearian plays 'Vortigern and Rowena' and 'Henry II', which deceived many experts and men of letters. Ireland subsequently made an avowal of his fraud.

Irena, in Spenser's 'Faerie Queene' (Bk. v), personifies Ireland, oppressed by Grantorto, and righted by Sir Artegall.

Irene, a tragedy by S. Johnson (q.v.).

Iris, according to mythology, the messenger of the gods, and particularly of Zeus and Hera. The rainbow was the path by which she travelled between the gods and men.

Irish National Theatre, see *Abbey Theatre.*

Irish R.M., Experiences of an, see *Somerville (E. Œ.).*

Iron, RALPH, pseudonym of OLIVE SCHREINER (q.v.).

Iron Duke, a popular name for the duke of Wellington (1769–1852).

Iron Mask, THE MAN IN THE, a state prisoner in the reign of Louis XIV, confined finally in the Bastille, whose name was concealed and who wore a mask covered with black velvet. His identity has never been established. Alexandre Dumas wrote a novel with this title.

Ironside, IRONSIDES, a name given to Edmund, king of England (1016), and Oliver Cromwell. 'Ironsides' was also applied to Cromwell's troopers in the Civil War.

Irony, a figure of speech in which one's meaning is expressed by language of an opposite or different tendency, especially by the simulated adoption of another's point of view for purpose of ridicule: e.g. Job's 'No doubt ye are the people and wisdom shall die with you.' See also *Dramatic Irony.*

Iroquois, a confederacy of North American Indians, known in English as the 'Five Nations'.

Irredentist, from (*Italia) irredenta,* unredeemed, in Italian politics (from 1878) a member of the party that advocated the freedom and union of Italy. Hence the general application.

Irrefragable Doctor, THE, Alexander of Hales (q.v.).

Irving, EDWARD, see *Irvingites*.

Irving, SIR HENRY (1838–1905), whose original name was JOHN HENRY BRODRIBB, became famous by his acting in the melodrama 'The Bells' (1871-2), and afterwards scored successes in a large number of Shakespearian and other parts, his impersonation of Tennyson's 'Becket' being one of his chief triumphs.

Irving, WASHINGTON (1783–1859), born at New York, the son of an Englishman, first came into literary repute by his humorous 'History of New York to the end of the Dutch Dynasty, by Diedrich Knickerbocker' (1809). His writings include 'The Sketch-Book' (1820), 'Bracebridge Hall' (1822), 'Tales of a Traveller' (1824), 'Oliver Goldsmith' (1849), and 'Life of George Washington' (1855-9). This last is his greatest work; but he is perhaps best known by his pleasant collections of essays and tales, 'The Sketch-Book', which includes 'Rip van Winkle' (q.v.).

Irvingites, a religious body founded about 1835 on the basis of principles promulgated by Edward Irving (1792-1834), a minister of the Church of Scotland, excommunicated in 1833. Edward Irving was a friend and encourager of Carlyle; both Carlyle and Hazlitt have left us descriptions of him.

Irwine, THE REVD. ADOLPHUS, the rector in George Eliot's 'Adam Bede' (q.v.).

Isaac of York, in Scott's 'Ivanhoe' (q.v.), the father of Rebecca.

Isabella, a character in (1) Kyd's 'The Spanish Tragedy' (q.v.); (2) Shakespeare's 'Measure for Measure' (q.v.); (3) Southerne's 'The Fatal Marriage'.

Isabella, or the Pot of Basil, a poem by Keats (q.v.), published in 'Lamia . . . and other Poems' in 1820.

The poem is based on Boccaccio's 'Decameron', IV. v. The proud brothers of Isabella, a Florentine lady, having discovered the love of Lorenzo and their sister, decoy Lorenzo away, murder him, and bury his body in a forest. Isabella, apprised by a vision, finds his body,

places the head in a flower-pot, and sets a plant of basil over it. Her brothers, observing how she cherishes the basil, steal the pot, discover the head, and fly conscience-stricken; and Isabella pines and dies.

Isaiah, the greatest of the prophets of the O.T. He prophesied in Judah during the latter part of the 8th cent. B.C. Chapters XL–LXVI of the biblical book that bears his name are of much later date; chapters XL–LV were written in Babylon.

Isegrym or ISENGRIN, the wolf in 'Reynard the Fox' (q.v.).

Isenbras, Sir, see *Isumbras*.

Iseult (ISOUD, YSOLDE, or YSOUDE), LA BEALE, in the Arthurian legend, is the sister or daughter of the king of Ireland. For her story see *Tristram*.

Iseult (ISOUD, YSOLDE, or YSOUDE), LA BLANCHE MAINS, in the Arthurian legend, is the daughter of the duke of Britanny and the wife of Tristram (q.v.).

Isherwood, CHRISTOPHER WILLIAM BRADSHAW (1904–   ), novelist, since 1946 an American citizen. His novels include 'The Memorial' (1932), 'Mr. Norris Changes Trains' (1935), 'Goodbye to Berlin' (1939), 'Prater Violet' (1945), 'The World in the Evening' (1954), and 'Down There on a Visit' (1962). The earlier books give an interesting picture of Berlin on the eve of Hitler's rise. He also wrote plays in collaboration with W. H. Auden (q.v.).

Ishmael, the son of Abraham by Hagar, hence allusively an outcast.

'Call me Ishmael' is the opening sentence of 'Moby Dick' (q.v.).

Ishtar, see *Astarte*.

Isidore of Seville (*c.* 560–636), archbishop of Seville, an encyclopaedic writer esteemed in the Middle Ages, author of 'Originum seu Etymologiarum libri xx', etc.

Isis, one of the great Egyptian deities, the sister and wife of Osiris (q.v.), and mother of Horus (q.v.). Her worship as a great nature-goddess spread to Greece and Rome.

Isis, a name for the Thames at Oxford.

Islam, an Arabic word meaning 'resignation', signifies the religion revealed through the Prophet Mohammed (q.v.), or the Muslim world.

Island, The, a poem by Byron (q.v.) (1823).

The poem is based on the narrative of the mutiny on H.M.S. 'Bounty' (q.v.), and the life of the mutineers on Tahiti.

Isle of Saints, a medieval name for Ireland.

Isocrates (436–338 B.C.), an Attic orator and teacher of rhetoric. He is 'that old man eloquent' referred to by Milton in the sonnet to the Lady Margaret Ley.

Isthmian Games, games similar to the Olympic Games (q.v.).

Isumbras, or *Isenbras, Sir*, a popular verse tale of the 14th cent. Isumbras is strong, handsome, and prosperous, but proud and arrogant. A bird sent by God gives him the choice between suffering in youth or in old age. He chooses the former. Extreme misfortunes befall him, which he bears patiently. He loses wife, children, and possessions, and for twenty-one years suffers among the Saracens, doing deeds of prowess; after which an angel announces that his sins are forgiven, and he is restored to his family and happiness.

Millais's picture 'Sir Isumbras at the Ford' was painted in 1857.

Italic type, a compact sloping type based on an Italian 15th-cent. style of cursive writing, introduced by Aldus Manutius (q.v.) in 1501 for use in his small editions of the classics.

Ithaca, the kingdom of Odysseus (q.v.), a small island in the Ionian sea.

Ithuriel, in Milton's 'Paradise Lost', IV. 788 et seq., one of the cherubim charged by Gabriel to search for Satan in Paradise. Touched by Ithuriel's spear, which 'no falsehood can endure', the Fiend starts up in his own shape.

Itinerary of Antoninus, an official list of the roads in the Roman Empire, probably an early 3rd-cent. compilation. Nothing is known of the author.

It is Never too Late to Mend, a novel by Reade (q.v.) (1856). The novel combines, rather loosely, two distinct stories: first, that of a young farmer who emigrates to Australia. Secondly, that of a thief sentenced to jail and transportation, in the course of which the author exposes the brutalities and abuses of the English prison system.

Itylus, the son of Aedon, who was wife of Zethus, king of Thebes. Aedon, jealous of Niobe, the wife of her brother, who had six sons and six daughters, determined to kill one of these sons, but by mistake killed Itylus. She was changed by Zeus into a nightingale, whose song is Aedon's lament for her son. Swinburne (q.v.) wrote a poem on this subject ('Itylus' in 'Poems and Ballads', First Series).

Itys, see *Philomela*.

Ivanhoe, a novel by Sir W. Scott (q.v.), (1819). This was the first of the author's novels in which he adopted a purely English subject.

Wilfred of Ivanhoe, son of Cedric, of noble Saxon birth, loves his father's ward, the lady Rowena, who traces her descent to King Alfred, and who returns his love. For this reason Cedric, who is passionately devoted to the cause of the restoration of the Saxon line to the throne of England and sees the best chance of effecting this in the marriage of Rowena to Athelstane of Coningsburgh, also of the Saxon blood royal, has in anger banished his son. Ivanhoe has joined Richard Cœur de Lion at the crusade and there won the king's affection. In Richard's absence, his brother John has found support among the lawless and dissolute Norman nobles for his design of ousting Richard from the throne, a design favoured by Richard's imprisonment in Austria on his return from Palestine.

The story centres in two chief events: a great tournament at Ashby-de-la-Zouche, where Ivanhoe aided by Richard, who unknown to all has returned to England, defeats all the knights of John's party, including the fierce Templar, Sir

Brian de Bois-Guilbert; and the siege of Front-de-Bœuf's castle of Torquilstone, whither Cedric and Rowena, with the wounded Ivanhoe, Athelstane, the Jew Isaac, and his beautiful and courageous daughter Rebecca, have been carried captives by the Norman nobles. After an exciting fight, the castle is carried by a force of outlaws and Saxons, led by Locksley (otherwise Robin Hood) and King Richard himself. The prisoners are rescued, with the exception of Rebecca whom the Templar carries off to the Preceptory of Templestowe. Here the unexpected arrival of the Grand Master of the order, while relieving Rebecca from the dishonourable advances of Bois-Guilbert, exposes her to the charge of witchcraft, and she escapes sentence of death only by demanding trial by combat. Ivanhoe appears as her champion, and in the encounter between him and Bois-Guilbert, the latter falls dead, untouched by his opponent's lance, the victim of his own contending passions. Ivanhoe and Rowena are united; the more interesting Rebecca, suppressing her love for Ivanhoe, leaves England with her father.

Among the many characters in the story, besides Robin Hood and Friar Tuck,

mention may be made of the poor fool Wamba, who imperils his life to save that of his master Cedric; Gurth, the swineherd; and Isaac the Jew, divided between love of his shekels and love of his daughter. Thackeray's 'Rebecca and Rowena' is an amusing sequel to, and critical reinterpretation of, Scott's tale.

Ivry, in France, the scene of a battle in which Henri IV of France defeated the Leaguers under the duke of Mayenne (1590), the subject of a lay by T. B. Macaulay (q.v.) (1824).

Ixion, a king of Thessaly, who having married Dia, daughter of Deïoneus, refused his father-in-law the present he had promised him; so that Deïoneus had recourse to violence and stole some of Ixion's horses. Ixion invited Deïoneus to a feast, and threw him into a pit filled with burning coals. As a consequence Ixion was shunned by men. Zeus carried him to heaven, where instead of showing gratitude, he became enamoured of Hera, attempted to seduce her, and boasted that he had done so. Angered at his insolence, Zeus banished him to hell and ordered him to be tied to a perpetually revolving wheel. Browning wrote a poem on this subject ('Ixion' in 'Jocoseria', 1883).

J

Jabberwock, a fictitious monster, the subject of the poem 'Jabberwocky' in Lewis Carroll's 'Through the Looking-Glass' (q.v.). The story, told in an invented vocabulary, begins: ''Twas brillig and the slithy toves'.

J'accuse, see *Dreyfus.*

Jack, COLONEL, see *Colonel Jack.*

Jack-a-Lent, a figure of a man, set up to be pelted. Hence figuratively a butt for every one to throw at (Shakespeare, 'The Merry Wives of Windsor', v. v. 137).

Jack and the Bean-stalk, a nursery tale

based on a world-wide myth, found e.g. among the North American Indians and the native tribes of S. Africa. The beanstalk is said to be derived from the ash, the world-tree of northern mythology (see *Yggdrasil*).

Jack, the son of a poor widow, exchanges his mother's cow for a hatful of beans. His mother in anger throws the beans out of the window. The next morning a beanstalk has grown up into the clouds. Jack climbs up and finds himself in a strange country, where a fairy directs him to the house of a giant who has killed his father. He robs the giant of a hen that lays golden eggs, a self-playing harp, and bags of diamonds, and is finally discovered by the giant and pursued down the bean-stalk. Jack reaching the ground first, cuts the bean-stalk with an axe, and the giant falls and is killed.

Jackdaw of Rheims, The, one of the best known of Barham's 'Ingoldsby Legends' (see *Barham*) which tells how a jackdaw stole the ring of the cardinal-archbishop of Rheims.

Jack Drum's Entertainment, see *Drum's Entertainment.*

Jacke Wilton, The Life of, see *Unfortunate Traveller.*

Jack Horner, the subject of a nursery rhyme ('Little Jack Horner sat in a corner', etc.), which occurs in an 18th-cent. chapbook. The origin of the rhyme is attributed to a Jack Horner who was steward to the abbot of Glastonbury in the reign of Henry VIII and by a trick acquired the deeds of the manor of Mells; the family still holds the manor.

Jack-in-office, a consequential petty official.

Jack of Dover, in the Prologue to Chaucer's 'Cook's Tale', is probably some sort of pie.

Jack-o'-Lantern or JACK-A-LANTERN, see *Ignis Fatuus.*

Jack-pudding, a clown or buffoon.

Jack Robinson, 'before one can say Jack Robinson', i.e. very quickly, a phrase whose origin is unknown. The earliest quotation given for it in the OED. is from Fanny Burney's 'Evelina' (II. xxxvii).

Jack Sprat, of the nursery rhyme, who 'would eat no fat', figures in a rhyme given by James Howell, in the collection of proverbs annexed to his 'Tetraglotton' (1659), as 'Archdeacon Pratt'.

Jack Straw, the leader of a party of insurgents from Essex in the Peasants' Rising of 1381.

Jack the Giant-killer, a nursery tale of Northern origin, known in England from very early times.

Jack was the son of a Cornish farmer, and lived in the days of King Arthur. He acquired from a giant a coat that made him invisible, shoes that gave him extraordinary speed, and a sword of magic potency. With the help of these he destroyed all the giants in the land.

Jack the Ripper, the name assumed by an unknown man who claimed to be the perpetrator of a series of murders in the East End of London in 1888-9.

Jacob and Esau, the twin sons of Isaac and Rebecca. Esau, coming in faint from the field, sold his birthright to Jacob for a mess of pottage (Gen. xxv).

Jacob Faithful, a novel by Marryat (q.v.) (1834).

Jacob Faithful is born on a Thames lighter, and as lighterman and wherryman meets with various adventures and entertaining characters, until he is pressed on a frigate and carried to sea. From this life he is soon rescued by the inheritance of a fortune from an old gentleman who has befriended him and whom he has saved from drowning.

Jacobin, originally a name of the French friars of the order of St. Dominic, then of the members of a French political club established in 1789, in Paris, in the old convent of the Jacobins, to maintain the principles of extreme democracy and absolute equality. It was applied about 1800 as a nickname for any political reformer.

Jacobite, a partisan of the Stuarts after the revolution of 1688.

Jacobs, WILLIAM WYMARK (1863-1943), writer of short stories, principally of two kinds, those of macabre invention, of which 'The Monkey's Paw' is the best known, and those of a humorous nature, particularly concerning seafaring men and the famous 'Night-watchman'; they have been collected, e.g., in 'Many Cargoes' (1896), 'Night Watches' (1914). 'The Monkey's Paw' and others of his stories have been dramatized.

Jacob's Ladder, the ladder that Jacob saw in a dream, set up on earth and reaching to heaven, with the angels of God ascending and descending on it (Gen. xxviii. 12).

Jacob's Staff, a pilgrim's staff, derived from St. James (*Jacobus*), whose symbols in religious art are a staff and a scallop shell (see Spenser, 'Faerie Queene', I. vi).

Jacobus de Voragine, see *Golden Legend*.

Jacquerie, LA, a bloody insurrection of the peasantry of northern France in 1358.

Jaffier, one of the principal characters in Otway's 'Venice Preserv'd' (q.v.).

Jaggard, WILLIAM (*fl.* 1594–1623), and **ISAAC** (*fl.* 1613–27). London printers and principal publishers of the Shakespeare First Folio (see *Folios and Quartos, Shakespearian*).

Jaggers, MR., a character in Dickens's 'Great Expectations' (q.v.).

Jago, RICHARD (1715–81), the author of 'Edge-Hill', a poem in four books describing, with many moral and other digressions, the views seen at morning, noon, afternoon, and evening, as he looks from that famous spot over Warwickshire.

Jakin, BOB, a character in G. Eliot's 'The Mill on the Floss' (q.v.).

James I (1394–1437), king of Scotland, was captured while on his way to France by an English ship, probably in 1406. He was detained in England for nineteen years and well educated. While in England he composed his poem, 'The Kingis Quair' (q.v.). James I was assassinated at Perth. One or two other poems, 'The Ballad of Good Counsel', 'Christis Kirk on the Green', have been doubtfully attributed to him. He is the subject of D. G. Rossetti's poem 'The King's Tragedy'.

James I (James VI of Scotland), king of England, 1603–25. He is reputed the author of 'The True Law of Free Monarchies' (1603); 'Basilikon Doron' (1599), precepts on the art of government); 'A Counterblaste to Tobacco' (1604), in which the alleged virtues of the plant are refuted; and a good many mainly theological works.

James II, king of England, 1685–8. In 1688 he was driven out by an aristocratic revolution and was succeeded in 1689 by William and Mary, the throne being declared vacant. He lived until 1701.

James, HENRY (1843–1916), born in New York, and after a desultory education in New York, London, Paris, and Geneva, entered the law school at Harvard in 1862. He settled in Europe in 1875. From 1865 he was a regular contributor of reviews and short stories to American periodicals, and owed much to his friendship with the novelist Howells (q.v.). For more than twenty years he lived in London, and in 1898 moved to Lamb House, Rye, where his later novels were written. He at first chiefly concerned himself with the impact of the older civilization of Europe upon American life, and to this period belong his more popular novels, e.g. 'The American' (1877) and the exquisite 'Portrait of a Lady' (1881). He next turned to a more exclusively English stage in 'The Tragic Muse' (1890) and 'The Awkward Age' (1899), in which he analysed English character with extreme subtlety. In his last three great novels, 'The Wings of the Dove' (1902), 'The Ambassadors' (1903), and 'The Golden Bowl' (1904), he returned to the 'international' theme of the contrast of American and European character.

Besides nearly a hundred short stories (including the well-known ghost story, 'The Turn of the Screw', 1898), James wrote several volumes of sketches of travel and literary criticism; a number of plays, of which the few that were acted were not successful; and a life of Nathaniel Hawthorne.

James, MONTAGUE RHODES (1862–1936), medievalist and provost of Eton. As well as editing a great number of bibliographical and palaeographical works he edited and translated 'The Apocryphal New Testament' (1924). His ghost stories are well known and have been collected in one volume (1931).

James, WILLIAM (1842–1910), American philosopher, elder brother of Henry James (q.v.). His views are embodied in his 'Principles of Psychology' (1890), and show a tendency to subordinate logical proof to intuitional conviction.

Jameson Raid: in 1895 a 'reform committee' in Johannesburg was making plans for the forcible overthrow of the S. African republic. It was supported by Cecil Rhodes, and to Leander Starr Jameson (1853–1917), administrator of Mashonaland, was allotted the task of raising a mounted force in Rhodesia. Jameson decided to take the initiative, and on 29 Dec. marched his force across the Transvaal frontier. He was surrounded by the Boers, and his band was forced to surrender to the Boer commandant on 2 Jan. 1896. Alfred Austin, the newly appointed poet laureate, wrote a curiously bad poem in praise of the raid.

Jamieson, THE HON. MRS., a character in Mrs. Gaskell's 'Cranford' (q.v.).

Jane, a small silver coin of Genoa (Fr. *Gênes*) introduced into England towards the end of the 14th cent. The word is used by Chaucer and Spenser.

Jane Eyre, a novel by C. Brontë (q.v.) (1847).

The heroine, a penniless orphan, has been left to the care of her aunt, Mrs. Reed, who consigns her to Lowood Asylum, a charitable institution, where after some miserable years she becomes a teacher. Thence she passes to be a governess at Thornfield Hall to a little girl, the natural daughter of Mr. Rochester, a man of grim aspect and sardonic temper. Rochester is fascinated by her elfish wit and courageous spirit, and falls in love with her, and she with him. Their marriage is prevented at the last moment by the revelation that he has a wife living, a raving lunatic, kept in seclusion at Thornfield Hall. Jane flees from the Hall, and is taken in and cared for by the Revd. St. John Rivers and his sisters. Under the influence of Rivers, she nearly consents to marry him and accompany him to India. She is prevented by a telepathic appeal from Rochester, and sets out for Thornfield Hall, to learn that the place has been burnt down, and that Rochester, in vainly trying to save his wife from the flames, has been blinded and maimed. She finds him in utter dejection, becomes his wife, and restores him to happiness.

Jane Shore, see *Shore.*

Janet's Repentance, one of the tales in G. Eliot's 'Scenes of Clerical Life' (q.v.).

Janissaries or JANIZARIES, a body of Turkish infantry, first organized in the 14th cent., mainly recruited from Christian subjects of the Turks and constituting the sultan's guard.

Jansenism, the doctrine of a school that developed in the Roman Catholic Church holding the doctrines of Cornelius Jansen (1585–1638), which approximated to those of predestination and were closely analogous to Calvinism. But Jansen maintained that the personal relation of the human soul with God was possible only through the Roman Church.

January and May, the title of a version by Pope of Chaucer's 'Merchant's Tale' (see *Canterbury Tales*).

Janus, an ancient Roman deity, the god of the doorway (*janua*); the guardian of the state during war, when the gates of his temple were left open (being closed in peace time). He was represented with two faces, looking before and behind.

Jaquenetta, a country maid in Shakespeare's 'Love's Labour's Lost' (q.v.).

Jaques, a character in Shakespeare's 'As You Like It' (q.v.).

Jarley, MRS., in Dickens's 'The Old Curiosity Shop' (q.v.), the proprietor of a travelling wax-works show.

Jarndyce, JOHN, a character in Dickens's 'Bleak House' (q.v.).

Jarvie, BAILIE NICOL, a character in Scott's 'Rob Roy' (q.v.).

Jason, a celebrated hero of antiquity, son of Aeson, king of Iolcos. He was entrusted to the care of Cheiron the centaur (q.v.), by whom he was educated. Returning to Iolcos by the direction of the oracle, he boldly demanded from Pelias the restoration of the kingdom, and to obtain it undertook the expedition to Colchis to recover the Golden Fleece (see under *Argonauts*). This he accomplished successfully with the help of Medea (q.v.), whom he married, but subsequently deserted in order to marry Glauce or Creusa (q.v.).

Jason, The Life and Death of, a poem in heroic couplets by W. Morris (q.v.) (1867).

The story is that of Jason and Medea, the Argonauts and the Golden Fleece.

Jasper Packlemerton, 'of atrocious memory', in Dickens's 'The Old Curiosity Shop' (q.v.), a notable figure in Mrs. Jarley's wax-works.

Javan, a son of Japhet, Gen. x. 2, also Ezek. xxvii. 13, where he represents the Ionians of Asia Minor, in which sense Milton speaks of 'Javan's issue'.

Jeames de la Pluche, The Diary of, a short story by Thackeray (q.v.), published in 'Punch' (1845-6), reprinted in 'Miscellanies' (1856).

Jean de Meun(g), see *Roman de la Rose*.

Jean Jacques, a current abbreviation of the name of Jean Jacques Rousseau (q.v.).

Jean Paul, pen-name of J. P. F. RICHTER (q.v.).

Jeans, SIR JAMES HOPWOOD (1877-1946), astronomer and popular writer on the universe. His work 'The Mysterious Universe' appeared in 1930.

Jebb, SIR RICHARD CLAVERHOUSE (1841-1905), was professor of Greek at Glasgow in 1875, and at Cambridge in 1889. He is remembered for his critical editions and translations of Sophocles (1883-96) and Bacchylides (1905), and other works on classical subjects.

Jebusites, in Dryden's 'Absalom and Achitophel' (q.v.), and generally in the 17th cent., the Roman Catholics.

Jeeves, in many of P. G. Wodehouse's (q.v.) stories, the omniscient and resourceful valet.

Jefferies, RICHARD (1848-87), the son of a Wiltshire farmer, and a writer with a remarkable power of observing nature and representing it in combination with a strain of poetry and philosophy. He first attracted notice by his 'Gamekeeper at Home' (1878). There followed 'Wild Life in a Southern County' (1879), 'Wood Magic' (1881), 'Bevis' (1882), 'The Life of the Fields' (1884); also his remarkable spiritual autobiography, 'The Story of my Heart' (1883). His novels were less successful.

Jeffers, ROBINSON (1887-1962), American poet. He made his name with a narrative poem, based on the biblical story of Tamar, 'Tamar and Other Poems' (1924).

Jeffrey, FRANCIS, *Lord Jeffrey* (1773-1850), remembered as the founder, with Sydney Smith, of 'The Edinburgh Review' (q.v.), as its editor until 1829, and for his unsparing criticism of the authors (notably the Lake school) of whom he disapproved.

Jeffreys, GEORGE, *first Baron Jeffreys* (1644-89), lord chief justice, 1682. He presided at the trial of Titus Oates, and is chiefly notorious for his brutality and as the judge who held the 'Bloody Assizes' after Monmouth's rebellion in 1685.

Jehovah, the English representation of the Hebrew principal name of God in the O.T.

Jehu, a fast and furious driver; a coachman; in humorous allusion to 2 Kings ix. 20.

Jekyll and Mr. Hyde, The Strange Case of Dr., a novel by R. L. Stevenson (1886).

Dr. Jekyll, a physician, discovers a drug by means of which he can create for himself a separate personality that absorbs all his evil instincts. This personality, repulsive in appearance, he assumes from time to time and calls Mr. Hyde, and in it he gives rein to his evil impulses. It gradually gains a greater ascendancy, and Hyde commits a horrible murder. Jekyll now finds himself from time to time involuntarily transformed into Hyde, while the drug loses its efficacy in restoring his original form and character. On the point of discovery and arrest, he takes his own life.

Jellyby, MRS., a character in Dickens's 'Bleak House' (q.v.).

Jenghis Khan, see *Genghis Khan*.

Jenkins, MRS. WINIFRED, a character in Smollett's 'Humphry Clinker' (q.v.).

Jenkinson, EPHRAIM, an old swindler in Goldsmith's 'The Vicar of Wakefield' (q.v.).

Jenkins's Ear, an allusion to an incident which precipitated the war with Spain in 1739. Robert Jenkins, a master mariner, produced to a committee of the House of Commons what he declared to be his ear, cut off by a Spanish captain at Havana.

Jenkyns, DEBORAH, MATILDA, and PETER, characters in Mrs. Gaskell's 'Cranford' (q.v.).

Jennings, MRS., (1) a character in Jane Austen's 'Sense and Sensibility' (q.v.); (2) the mother of John Keats (q.v.), as she became by her second marriage.

Jenny Wren, see *Wren* (*J.*).

Jenyns, SOAME (1704–87), author of 'Poems' (1752) and of 'A Free Enquiry into the Nature and Origin of Evil' (1757). The latter was vigorously criticized by Johnson in 'The Literary Magazine'. Jenyns also wrote a 'View of the Internal Evidence of the Christian Religion' (1776), which had considerable vogue.

Jephthah's daughter, see Judges xi. 30 et seq. When Jephthah went out against the Ammonites he vowed to sacrifice, if victorious, whatever came forth from his house to meet him. This proved to be his daughter. She figures in Tennyson's 'A Dream of Fair Women'.

The ballad in Percy's 'Reliques' entitled 'Jephthah Judge of Israel' is that which Hamlet quotes in Shakespeare's play (II. ii).

Jeremiad, a doleful complaint in allusion to the Lamentations of Jeremiah in the O.T.

Jerome, ST. (HIERONYMUS) (*c.* 342–420), born in Dalmatia of a Christian family, was educated at Rome, adopted the practice of asceticism, and after living for some years, first in the desert, then at Rome, settled in 386 in Bethlehem, where he spent the rest of his life. His great work was the Latin version of the Scriptures, known as the Vulgate.

Jerome, JEROME KLAPKA (1859–1927), novelist and playwright, author of the amusing narrative 'Three Men in a Boat' (1889) and of a famous play 'The Passing of the Third Floor Back' (1908).

Jerrold, DOUGLAS WILLIAM (1803–57), remembered as the contributor to 'Punch' of 'Mrs. Caudle's Curtain Lectures' (q.v.), which added greatly to that periodical's popularity and appeared in book form in 1846. He was also author of 'Black-ey'd Susan' (1829), and other successful plays.

Jerusalem, for the poem of that name by William Blake, see *Blake.*

Jerusalem, THE NEW, the celestial city (Rev. xxi. 2).

Jerusalem Delivered (*Gerusalemme Liberata*), a poem by Tasso (q.v.), published without his consent in 1580 and in authorized form in 1581. (Tasso later rewrote the poem, changing the title to 'Gerusalemme Conquistata'. The new work, published in 1593, was inferior to the original.)

The poem is the epic of a crusade, with the addition of romantic and fabulous elements. It was translated into English in 1594 by R. Carew, and by Edward Fairfax in 1600 (under the title 'Godfrey of Bulloigne'). Spenser's description of Acrasia's Bower of Bliss ('Faerie Queene', II. xii) was modelled on the gardens of Armida in Tasso's poem.

Jesse, a genealogical tree representing the genealogy of Christ from 'the root of Jesse', used in churches in the Middle Ages as a decoration of windows, walls, etc.

Jessica, Shylock's daughter in Shakespeare's 'The Merchant of Venice' (q.v.).

Jesuits, see *Loyola.*

Jew, THE WANDERING, see *Wandering Jew.*

Jew of Malta, The, a drama in blank verse by Marlowe (q.v.), produced about 1592 but not published until 1633.

The Grand Seignior of Turkey having demanded the tribute of Malta, the governor of Malta decides that it shall be paid by the Jews of the island. Barabas, a rich Jew, who resists the edict, has all his wealth impounded and his house turned into a nunnery. In revenge he indulges in an orgy of slaughter, and finally is killed in one of his own traps.

Jezebel, the proud and infamous wife of Ahab, king of Israel, hence used allusively of an impudent or abandoned woman.

Jihad or JEHAD, a religious war of Muslims against unbelievers in Islam.

Jingle, ALFRED, a character in Dickens's 'The Pickwick Papers' (q.v.).

Jingo. The word appears first about 1670 as a piece of conjurer's gibberish. Later it was adopted as a nickname for those who supported the policy of Lord Beaconsfield in 1878, from the refrain of a music-hall song of the period ('We don't want to fight, but by Jingo if we do'). It is extended to advocates in general of bellicose nationalism in dealing with foreign powers.

Jiniwin, MRS., in Dickens's 'The Old Curiosity Shop' (q.v.), the mother of Mrs. Quilp.

Jinn or DJINN, in Muslim demonology, an intermediate order of beings between angels and men.

Jo, the crossing-sweeper in Dickens's 'Bleak House' (q.v.).

Joan, POPE, a mythical female pope, supposed to have intervened as John VIII between Leo IV and Benedict III in the 9th cent.

Joan of Arc, ST. (1412-31), JEANNE D'ARC, or more correctly JEANNE DARC, an illiterate girl who contributed powerfully to liberate France from the English in the reign of Charles VII. Her mission was a double one, (1) to raise the siege of Orléans; (2) to conduct Charles to his coronation at Rheims. She accomplished both these tasks and then wished to return home; but she yielded to the demands of the French patriots and was taken prisoner by the Burgundians, who handed her over to the English. But it was a French court of ecclesiastics (with the help of the Inquisition) who sentenced her as a witch, and the English who burned her at Rouen. She was canonized in 1920. She is the subject of Voltaire's 'La Pucelle', of a tragedy by Schiller, of a poem by Southey, and of dramas by G. B. Shaw and Anouilh.

Job, the hero of the O.T. book that bears his name, a wealthy and prosperous man suddenly overtaken by dire calamities, the typical example of patience under misfortune.

Jocasta, see *Oedipus.*

Jocasta, a tragedy in blank verse, translated from an Italian adaptation of the 'Phoenissae' of Euripides, by George Gascoigne (q.v.).

Jocelin de Brakelond (*fl.* 1200), a monk of Bury St. Edmunds, whose chronicle of his abbey (1173-1202) inspired Carlyle's 'Past and Present'.

Jockey of Norfolk, in Shakespeare's 'Richard III', v. iii. 305-6, was Sir John Howard, first duke of Norfolk, who commanded Richard's vanguard at the battle of Bosworth, and was slain.

Jock o' Hazeldean, a ballad, of which one stanza is ancient, the rest by Sir W. Scott.

Joe, 'the fat boy' in Dickens's 'The Pickwick Papers' (q.v.).

Joe Miller's Jests, a jest-book by John Mottley (1692-1750), published in 1739. The name is taken from Joseph Miller (1684-1738), an actor and reputed humorist. A 'Joe Miller' is a stale jest.

Johannes Factotum, 'John Do-everything', a Jack of all trades, a would-be universal genius. The phrase is found in the 16th cent. It occurs in Greene's 'A Groatsworth of Wit bought with a Million of Repentance' (q.v.).

John, king of England, 1199-1216.

John, DON, a character in Shakespeare's 'Much Ado about Nothing' (q.v.).

John, PRESTER, see *Prester John.*

John Anderson, my Jo, a lyric by Burns (q.v.), suggested to him by an older song.

John-a-Nokes, a fictitious name for one of the parties in a legal action, usually coupled with JOHN-A-STILES as the name of the other.

John Barleycorn, see *Barleycorn.*

John Bull, *The History of*, a collection of pamphlets by Arbuthnot (q.v.), issued in 1712, and rearranged and republished in Pope and Swift's 'Miscellanies' of 1727.

The pamphlets, of which the first appeared on 6 March 1712, were designed to advocate, in the form of humorous allegories, the cessation of the war with France, the various parties concerned being designated under the names of John Bull, Nicholas Frog (the Dutch), Lord Strutt (Philip of Spain), Lewis Baboon (the French king).

John Buncle, *Esq.*, *The Life of*, a work of fiction by Amory (q.v.) (1756–66, 2 vols.).

This strange book takes the form of an autobiography, and the hero, in the words of the 'illustrious Miss Noel', his first love, is 'an odd compound of a man'. He marries seven wives in succession, each of them dying within a couple of years, and each of them surpassingly beautiful and clever. The story of his matrimonial ventures is varied with digressions on religious, literary, and scientific subjects, and a good deal of eating and drinking.

John Company, a name for the East India Company (q.v.).

John Doe and **Richard Roe**, legal fictions in old actions of ejectment, adopted to simplify the old procedure under which a number of irrelevant matters had to be proved. All this was swept away by the Common Law Procedure Act, 1852.

John Gilpin, *The Diverting History of*, a poem by Cowper (q.v.), first published anonymously in the 'Public Advertiser', reprinted in chapbook form, and included in the same volume as 'The Task' in 1785.

John Gilpin, a 'linen-draper bold' of Cheapside, and his wife, decide to celebrate their twentieth wedding-day by a trip to the Bell at Edmonton, he on a borrowed horse, she, her sister, and the children in a chaise and pair. But when John's horse begins to trot John loses control; and the poem describes his headlong career to Edmonton, and ten miles beyond it to Ware, and then back again.

John Halifax, *Gentleman*, a novel by Dinah Mulock (q.v.) (1857).

This is the plain domestic tale of a poor but honest and hard-working boy, who by his own exertions and with the help of Phineas Fletcher, the son of one of his employers, improves his education, achieves a good position, and marries the heroine, Ursula March.

John Inglesant, a historical novel by Shorthouse (q.v.) (1881).

The story is set in the time of Charles I and the Commonwealth. John Inglesant, a high-souled gentleman, of a serious and mystical cast of mind, is brought in his early years under the influence of a Jesuit emissary and becomes the tool of the Jesuit body in the political intrigues that attended the latter years of Charles I. After the death of Charles I he passes to Italy. The story presents a picture of the Italian life of the period, and of the religious factions and political intrigues, culminating in the long-drawn-out election of a pope on the death of Innocent X.

John of Austria, DON (1547–78), illegitimate son of the Emperor Charles V, a Spanish commander, famous, among other achievements, for his naval victory over the Turks at Lepanto (1571).

John of Gaunt (1340–99), fourth son of Edward III, born at Ghent ('Gaunt'), a notable figure in political history, a patron of Wycliffe and Chaucer, and a character in Shakespeare's 'Richard II'.

John of Salisbury (d. 1180), studied at Paris under Abélard (q.v.) and at Chartres, returning to England about 1150. He became bishop of Chartres in 1176. He was not only an able politician and ecclesiastic but the most learned classical writer of his time.

Johnson, *Anecdotes of the late Samuel*, by Mrs. Piozzi (see *Thrale*) (1786).

Johnson, ESTHER, Swift's 'Stella', see *Swift*.

Johnson, LIONEL PIGOT (1867–1902), a scholar-poet and critic. He became a Roman Catholic. His chief works are 'Postliminium' (essays and critical papers,

1912), 'The Art of Thomas Hardy' (1896), and two books of verse, 'Poems' (1895) and 'Ireland' (1897).

Johnson, RICHARD (1573-1659?), was a freeman of London, and author of 'The Nine Worthies of London' (1592), the 'Famous Historie of the Seven Champions of Christendom' (*c.* 1597), etc.

Johnson, THE REVD. SAMUEL (1649-1703), a Whig divine, figures in 'Absalom and Achitophel' (q.v.) as 'Ben-Jochanan'.

Johnson, SAMUEL (1709-84), born at Lichfield, the son of a bookseller of that town, educated at Lichfield Grammar School and at Pembroke College, Oxford, where he spent fourteen months but took no degree. His father died in 1731 and left his family in poverty, and Johnson's career for a time is not clearly known. In 1735 he published anonymously a condensed translation of a French version of Father Lobo's 'Voyage to Abyssinia'. In the same year he married Mrs. Elizabeth Porter, a widow considerably older than himself, and started a private school at Edial, near Lichfield. This was not successful, and in 1737, accompanied by one of his pupils, David Garrick (q.v.), he set out for London. He entered the service of Edward Cave, the printer (q.v.), who had founded 'The Gentleman's Magazine' (q.v.) in 1731. To this he contributed essays, poems, Latin verses, biographies, and reports of parliamentary debates. In 1738 he published his poem 'London'. In 1744 appeared his notable 'Life of Mr. Richard Savage' (see under *Savage, Richard*). In 1747 he issued the 'Plan' of his 'Dictionary' (see *Johnson's Dictionary*), addressed to Lord Chesterfield, with results referred to under the name of that nobleman. In 1749 he published 'The Vanity of Human Wishes', his longest and best poem, and in the same year his tragedy 'Irene' was produced by Garrick. In 1750 he started 'The Rambler' (q.v.), a periodical written almost entirely by himself, which ran until 1752 (when his wife died), appearing twice a week. From March 1753 to March 1754 Johnson

contributed regularly to Hawkesworth's 'Adventurer'. The 'Dictionary' was published in 1755, and an abridgement in 1756. During 1758-60 he contributed the 'Idler' series of papers to the 'Universal Chronicle'. In 1759 appeared his 'Rasselas, Prince of Abyssinia' (q.v.). In 1762 Johnson received, on Wedderburn's application, a pension of £300 a year from Lord Bute, and in 1763 made the acquaintance of James Boswell (q.v.), his biographer. It was in the next year that 'The Club', later known as the 'Literary Club', was founded, including among its original members, besides Johnson, Reynolds, Burke, and Goldsmith, to whom Garrick, C. J. Fox, and Boswell were shortly added. Besides a number of writings of minor importance, he worked at his edition of Shakespeare, which after much delay was published in 1765. In 1773 Johnson undertook a journey with Boswell to the Scottish Highlands and the Hebrides, recorded in his 'Journey to the Western Islands of Scotland' (1775) and in Boswell's 'Journal of a Tour to the Hebrides' (1785). In 1777 he undertook, at the request of a number of booksellers, to write the 'Lives of the Poets' (q.v.), published in 1779-81. In 1784, after two melancholy years, he died at his house in Bolt Court and was buried in Westminster Abbey. Johnson's literary output bears no proportion to his reputation. The latter is due in great measure to the fortunate accident by which an ideal biographer was found in Boswell to record for us the humour, wit, and sturdy common sense of his conversation, and a kindness of heart sometimes concealed under a gruff exterior.

Apart from Boswell's 'Life', much information about Johnson is to be found in Mrs. Piozzi's (Mrs. Thrale's) 'Anecdotes of the late Samuel Johnson' (1786) and in his 'Life' by Sir John Hawkins (1787). *Johnson, The Life of Samuel*, by Boswell (q.v.) (1791).

Boswell informed Johnson in 1772 of his intention to write his life, and had collected materials for the purpose ever since he first met him in 1763. After Johnson's death in 1784 he set to work arranging and adding to the 'prodigious multiplicity of materials', a task which, he writes in 1789, involved him in great labour, perplexity, and vexation. The final edition, after Boswell's death, was revised by Edmund Malone. The standard edition, that of G. B. Hill, has been revised by L. F. Powell (1934-50; 1964).

Johnson's Dictionary, *A Dictionary of the English Language*, by S. Johnson (q.v.) (1755).

The prospectus of the Dictionary was issued in 1747 (see under *Chesterfield, earl of*). In his collection of words he does not go back further than the works of Sidney, holding that 'from the authors which rose in the time of Elizabeth a speech might be formed adequate to all the purposes of use or elegance'. His derivations suffer from the scantiness of etymological knowledge in his day. But the dictionary is principally remarkable for the definitions of the meanings of words, and for the quotations in illustration of their use.

Johnson's 'Dixonary' was Miss Pinkerton's invariable present to departing scholars. Becky Sharp threw her copy into the garden as the coach drove off ('Vanity Fair', ch. i).

Johnstone, CHARLES, see *Adventures of a Guinea*.

Joinville, JEAN DE (1224-1317), a witness of the events of the disastrous crusade of Louis IX, wrote an account of the latter in his 'Histoire de Saint Louis'.

Jolly Beggars, *The*, a cantata by Burns (q.v.), written in 1785.

Jolly Roger, the pirates' black flag.

Jonah, A, a bearer of ill-luck, an allusion to the O.T. story.

Jonathan, see *David and Jonathan*.

Jonathan, BROTHER, see *Brother Jonathan*.

Jonathan's, a coffee-house in Change Alley, Cornhill, referred to in 'The Tatler' (No. 38) and 'The Spectator' (No. 1) as a mart for stockjobbers.

Jonathan Wild the Great, *The Life of*, a satirical romance by H. Fielding (q.v.) (1743). See also *Wild*.

It relates the career of a consummate rogue, from his birth and his baptism by Titus Oates, to his arrival at the 'tree of glory', the gallows. The hero becomes the chief of a gang of robbers, contriving their exploits, taking the largest share of the booty, keeping himself out of the clutches of the law, and maintaining discipline by denouncing any of the gang who contest his authority. But his trickery is exposed, and he meets his end with the 'greatness' that has distinguished him throughout.

Jones, DAVID (1895-1974), writer and artist. 'In Parenthesis' (1937), based on his experiences in the First World War, is written partly in prose and partly in free verse. 'Anathemata' (1952) is a religious poem which combines references to the Catholic Mass with images from the author's personal and racial past.

Jones, HENRY ARTHUR (1851-1929), dramatist. Among his successful plays were: 'The Silver King' (1882), 'The Dancing Girl' (1891), 'The Crusaders' (1891), and his masterpiece 'The Liars' (1897).

Jones, INIGO (1573-1652), architect, who introduced into England the fully realized Renaissance style based on Palladio and Roman antiquities, which he had studied in Italy. He designed settings for court masques by Ben Jonson and others, introducing the proscenium arch and movable scenery. He quarrelled with Ben Jonson, who satirized him as 'In-and-In Medlay' in 'A Tale of a Tub'. In 1615 he was made royal surveyor and designed the Queen's House at Greenwich and the Banqueting House, Whitehall. He built a classical façade to old St. Paul's, and worked on the layout of Covent Garden piazza and Lincoln's Inn Fields.

Jones, JOHN PAUL (1747-92), naval

adventurer of Scottish birth. After some years spent in the slave trade, smuggling, and trading to the W. Indies, he entered the American navy in 1775. While in command of the 'Ranger' he took the fort at Whitehaven and captured the 'Drake' off Carrickfergus (1778). Jones afterwards served in the French navy.

Jonson, BENJAMIN (1572–1637) ('Ben Jonson'), was educated at Westminster School under William Camden, and was for a time in the business of his stepfather, a bricklayer. His occupation from 1591/2 to 1597 is uncertain, but included some voluntary military service in Flanders. In 1597 he began to work for Henslowe's company. His 'Every Man in his Humour' (q.v.), with Shakespeare in the cast, was performed in 1598, and 'Every Man out of his Humour' (q.v.) at the Globe, 1599; his 'Cynthia's Revels', 1600, and 'The Poetaster' (attacking Dekker and Marston), 1601. In 1600-1 he was writing additions to Kyd's 'Spanish Tragedy' (q.v.). His first extant tragedy, 'Sejanus', was given at the Globe by Shakespeare's company, 1603; his first court masque 'of Blackness' (with scenery by Inigo Jones, q.v.) was given on Twelfth Night, 1605. He was temporarily imprisoned for his share in 'Eastward hoe', a play reflecting on the Scots. His 'Volpone' was acted both at the Globe and the two universities in 1606. 'Epicœne, or the Silent Woman' followed in 1609; 'The Alchemist' in 1610; 'Bartholomew Fayre' in 1614; and 'The Devil is an Ass' in 1616. Though not formally appointed the first poet laureate, the essentials of the position were conferred on him in 1616, when a pension was granted to him by James I. In 1618 he went to Scotland, where he was entertained by Drummond of Hawthornden (q.v.), who recorded their conversation. He produced 'The Staple of News', his last great play, in 1625. From 1605 onwards he was constantly producing masques (q.v.) for the court, a form of entertainment that reached its highest elaboration in Jonson's hands. He intro-

duced into it the 'antimasque', sometimes a foil to the principal masque, sometimes a dramatic scene, frequently of Aristophanic comedy. Jonson quarrelled with Inigo Jones after production of the masque 'Chloridia', 1630, and lost court patronage. He was buried in Westminster Abbey and celebrated in a collection of elegies entitled 'Jonsonus Virbius' (1637-8). His friends included Bacon, Selden, Chapman, Beaumont, Fletcher, Donne, and Shakespeare, and of the younger writers (his 'sons') Herrick, Suckling, Sir Kenelm Digby, and Lord Falkland. Among his patrons were the Sidneys, the earl of Pembroke, and the duke and duchess of Newcastle. His poems include 'Epigrammes' (containing the epitaph on Salathiel Pavy, the boy actor) and 'The Forrest' (1616), 'Underwoods' (1640), and translations. His chief prose work is 'Timber; or Discoveries made upon Men and Matter' (q.v., 1640).

As a man Jonson was arrogant and quarrelsome, but fearless, warm-hearted, and intellectually honest. The estimate of him formed by his contemporaries is summed up in the inscription upon his tomb, 'O rare Ben Jonson'.

Jordan, DOROTHY (1761–1816), actress, *née* Phillips, much praised by Hazlitt, Lamb, Leigh Hunt, etc.

Jorkins, see *Spenlow and Jorkins*.

Jorrocks, JOHN, 'a great city grocer of the old school' and a natural born sportsman, is, with Mr. Sponge and Mr. Facey Romford, among the celebrated characters of the novels of R. S. Surtees (q.v.).

José, DON, the father of the hero in Byron's 'Don Juan' (q.v.).

Joseph Andrews and his Friend Mr. Abraham Adams, The History of the Adventures of, a novel by H. Fielding (q.v.) (1742).

This was the first of Fielding's novels and was begun as a skit on Richardson's 'Pamela' (q.v.). As the latter had related the efforts of Pamela Andrews, the servingmaid, to escape the attentions of her master, so here her brother Joseph, also in service, is exposed to attacks on his virtue. Mr. B. of 'Pamela' becomes young Squire Booby, and mild fun is made of Pamela herself. But presently the satire is in the main dropped, Joseph sinks rather into the background, and the real hero of the remainder of the novel is Parson Adams, the simple, good-hearted, slightly ridiculous but lovable curate in Sir Thomas Booby's family.

Joseph of Arimathea. For the legend of Joseph and the Holy Grail, see *Grail.* According to fable, St. Philip sent twelve disciples into Britain to preach Christianity, of whom Joseph of Arimathea was the leader. They founded at Glastonbury the first primitive church, which subsequently was developed into Glastonbury Abbey.

Josephus, FLAVIUS (A.D. 37–*c.* 98), a Jewish statesman and soldier. He came to Rome with Titus, was honoured with Roman citizenship, and devoted himself to study. He wrote in Greek a 'History of the Jewish War', and 'Jewish Antiquities', which is a history of the Jews down to A.D. 66.

Joseph Vance, a novel by De Morgan (1906).

Josh Billings, see *Shaw* (*H. W.*).

Journalese, the style of language supposed to be characteristic of daily newspapers: marked by verbose and tautological *clichés* and phrases; the use of pompous and pedantic circumlocution.

In this respect 'journalese' has tended to become characteristic of, for the most part, more old-fashioned newspapers. Modern sensational journalism has tended to cultivate a style, strongly influenced by American models, which while not always elegant, is more direct and realistic.

Journalism, see *Newspaper.*

Journal of a Tour to the Hebrides, The, by Boswell (q.v.) (1785). It is a narrative of the journey taken by Boswell and Dr. Johnson in Scotland and the Hebrides in 1773. Boswell's manuscript, which Johnson and others read, was discovered at Malahide Castle with other manu-

scripts and private papers and was published in 1936, edited by F. A. Pottle and C. H. Bennett; it is longer by about a third than the earlier publication.

Journal of the Plague Year, A, see *Plague Year.*

Journey from this World to the Next, A, a Lucianic (see *Lucian*) narrative by H. Fielding (q.v.) (1743).

After a lively satirical account by the author of his spirit's journey, in company with those of other persons recently dead, in a stage-coach to Elysium, we have a long discourse by the spirit of Julian the Apostate. This is followed by a fragment containing a similar narrative by the spirit of Anne Boleyn.

Journey to the Western Islands of Scotland, A, by S. Johnson (q.v.) (1775), a narrative of the tour undertaken by Johnson and Boswell in 1773.

Jove, a poetical equivalent of Jupiter (q.v.).

Joviall Crew, A, or The Merry Beggars, a romantic comedy by Brome (q.v.), produced in 1641.

Jowett, BENJAMIN (1817–93), became fellow of Balliol in 1838, Regius professor of Greek at Oxford in 1855, and master of Balliol in 1870. He contributed to 'Essays and Reviews' (q.v.) an essay on 'The Interpretation of Scripture' (1860), and published translations of Plato (1871), Thucydides (1881), and Aristotle's 'Politics' (1885). Jowett was an Oxford figure and the subject of innumerable stories.

Joyce, JAMES AUGUSTINE ALOYSIUS (1882–1941), novelist, educated at University College, Dublin. Dissatisfied with the narrowness and bigotry of Irish Catholicism, as he saw it, he went for a year to Paris in 1902 and after returning to Dublin for a short time left Ireland for good. He spent the rest of his life abroad, chiefly in Trieste, Zürich, and Paris, supporting himself by teaching English, contending for many years with poverty, and suffering latterly from severe eye trouble. His first published work was a volume of verse, 'Chamber Music' (1907), followed by 'Dubliners' (short stories, 1914), 'Exiles' (a play, 1918), 'A Portrait of the Artist as a Young Man' (a novel, largely autobiographical, first published serially in 'The Egoist' (q.v.), 1914-15), and 'Pomes Penyeach' (verse, 1927). His novel 'Ulysses' (q.v.) was first published in Paris in 1922, and 'Finnegans Wake' (q.v.), extracts of which had already appeared as 'Work in Progress', was published in its complete form in 1939. These last two works revolutionized the form and structure of the novel in the development of the stream of consciousness technique, and in 'Finnegans Wake', especially, language was pushed to the extreme limits of communication.

Joyous Gard, Launcelot's castle in the Arthurian legend. Malory says that 'some men say it was Anwick, and some men say it was Bamborow'.

Juan, DON, see *Don Juan.*

Juan Fernandez, an island off the coast of Chile, discovered by Juan Fernandez, a Spaniard, about 1565. See *Robinson Crusoe.*

Jubal, 'father of all such as handle the harp and the organ' (Gen. iv. 19-21). He is the subject of a poem by G. Eliot (1874).

Judas Iscariot, the disciple who betrayed Christ (Matt. xxvi. 14-15) for thirty pieces of silver. He repented, brought back the thirty pieces, and hanged himself (Matt. xxvii. 3). The legend that he is once a year, on Christmas eve, allowed to cool himself for a day on an iceberg is treated by M. Arnold (q.v.) in his 'Saint Brandan'.

Judas Maccabaeus (*d.* 160 B.C.), leader of the Jews in their revolt against Antiochus Epiphanes (see *Maccabees*).

Jude the Obscure, a novel by Hardy (q.v.), reprinted in revised form from 'Harper's Magazine' in the 1895 edition of his 'Works'.

It is a story, in the author's words, 'of a deadly war waged with old Apostolic desperation between flesh and spirit', and tells how the intellectual aspirations of Jude Fawley, a South Wessex villager, are thwarted by a sensuous temperament, lack of character, and the play of circumstances, and end in utter tragedy.

Judith, the heroine of the book of the Apocrypha that bears her name, a widow of Bethulia who, when the army of Nebuchadnezzar was threatening her town, adventured herself in the camp and tent of Holofernes, the enemy general, and cut off his head. She figures in Lascelles Abercrombie's (q.v.) 'Emblems of Love'. The story was dramatized by E. A. Bennett (q.v.).

Judith, a fragment of 350 lines of a poem in Old English. It relates the deeds of Judith of the Apocrypha.

Judy, a familiar pet-form of the name JUDITH, the name of the wife of Punch in the puppet-show 'Punch and Judy' (q.v.).

Juggernaut or JAGANNATH, in Hindu mythology, a title of Krishna, the eighth avatar of Vishnu; also specifically the uncouth idol of this deity at Pūrī in Orissa, annually dragged in procession on an enormous car, under the wheels of which many devotees are said formerly to have thrown themselves to be crushed. Hence JUGGERNAUT CAR is used of practices, institutions, etc., to which persons blindly sacrifice themselves.

Julia, a character in Shakespeare's 'The Two Gentlemen of Verona' (q.v.).

Julia, DONNA, in Byron's 'Don Juan' (q.v.), a lady of Seville, whose love for the hero is the first incident in his career.

Julian and Maddalo, A Conversation, a poem by P. B. Shelley (q.v.), written on the occasion of his visit to Venice in 1818.

The poem takes the form of a conversation between Julian (the author) and Maddalo (Lord Byron) on the power of man over his mind, followed by a visit to a Venetian madhouse, where a maniac, whose mind has been unhinged by unfortunate love, recounts his story.

Juliana of Norwich (*c.* 1342-after 1413), anchoress; she wrote 'XVI Revelations of Divine Love'.

Julian the Apostate, Roman emperor A.D. 361-3, was brought up compulsorily as a Christian, and on attaining the throne proclaimed himself a pagan. He made a great effort to revive the worship of the old gods.

Julie, the heroine of the 'Nouvelle Héloïse' of Rousseau (q.v.), loved by Saint-Preux.

Juliet, the heroine of Shakespeare's 'Romeo and Juliet' (q.v.).

Julius Caesar, a Roman tragedy by Shakespeare (q.v.), probably produced in 1599, and printed in the 1623 folio. The plot is taken from North's translation of Plutarch's 'Lives', and deals with the events of the year 44 B.C., after Caesar, already endowed with the dictatorship, had returned to Rome from a successful campaign in Spain.

Distrust of Caesar's ambition gives rise to a conspiracy against him among Roman lovers of freedom, notably Cassius and Casca; they win over to their cause Brutus, who reluctantly joins them from a sense of duty to the republic. Caesar is slain by the conspirators in the Senate-house. Antony, Caesar's friend, stirs the people to fury against the conspirators by a skilful speech at Caesar's funeral. Octavius, nephew of Julius Caesar, Antony, and Lepidus, united as triumvirs, oppose the forces raised by Brutus and Cassius. The quarrel and reconciliation of Brutus and Cassius, with the news of the death of Portia, wife of Brutus, provide one of the finest scenes in the play. Brutus and Cassius are defeated at the battle of Philippi (42 B.C.), and kill themselves.

Jung, CARL GUSTAVE (1875-1961), Swiss psychiatrist. His 'The Psychology of Dementia Praecox' appeared in 1906 and 'Studies in Word Association' in 1916. The terms 'extrovert' and 'introvert' which he introduced into his study of psychological types have become part of everyday language. In his later work Jung developed his theory of the 'collective unconscious', based upon the evidence provided by mythology and by the dreams and phantasies of his patients, which seemed to derive from the common experience of primitive society rather than from the personal experience of the individual.

Jungle, The, a novel by Upton Sinclair (q.v.), which exposed the life and evil practices of the Chicago stockyards (1906). Its effect was so great that many Americans refused for a time to eat meat from Chicago, and an investigation of the yards was instituted by the U.S. government, much to the annoyance of the author, who was concerned more with the social conditions of the workers than with the reactions of Americans to the quality of their tinned meat.

Jungle Book, The, and *The Second Jungle Book,* stories by Kipling (q.v.) (1894-5), which tell how the child Mowgli was brought up by wolves and was taught by Baloo, the bear, and by Bagheera, the black panther, the law and business of the jungle.

Junius, the pseudonym of the author of a series of letters that appeared in the 'Public Advertiser' from 1769 to 1771, attacking, among others, the duke of Grafton, the duke of Bedford, Lord North, and Lord Mansfield, while George III is not spared the irony of the writer. Junius also takes an active part on behalf of Wilkes. The identity of Junius, which he concealed with great skill, has never been definitely established; but there are strong reasons for attributing the letters to Sir Philip Francis (q.v.). An authorized edition of the 'Letters of Junius' appeared in 1772.

Junius, FRANCIS, or DU JON, FRANÇOIS (1589-1677), philologist and antiquary. He was librarian to Thomas Howard, second earl of Arundel, and tutor to his son. He presented Anglo-Saxon manuscripts and philological collections to the Bodleian Library, and published an edition of Cædmon in 1655, and other works. He took an active interest in the Oxford University Press (q.v.) and presented it with materials for Gothic, Runic, Anglo-Saxon, and Roman printing.

Juno, see *Hera.*

Jupe, Cissy, a character in Dickens's 'Hard Times' (q.v.).

Jupiter, originally the elemental god of the Romans, came to be identified with the Greek Zeus (q.v.), the myths concerning whom were transferred to Jupiter.

Justinian I, emperor of Constantinople 527-65, famous for his successful wars (Belisarius and Narses were his generals), and for the code of Roman law that he caused to be drawn up. Famous also for building St. Sophia at Constantinople.

Jutes, a Low German tribe that invaded Great Britain (according to tradition under Hengist and Horsa, qq.v.) in the 5th cent. Their connection with Jutland is disputed.

Juvenal (DECIMUS JUNIUS JUVENALIS, *c.* A.D. 60-*c.* 130), the great Roman satirical poet. His extant works consist of sixteen satires, depicting contemporary society and denouncing its vices. They have served as models to many English poets.

The references to 'The English Juvenal' in Scott's 'Waverley' (q.v.) and 'The British Juvenal' in his 'The Heart of Midlothian' (q.v.) are to George Crabbe (q.v.). The title 'English Juvenal' has also been applied to John Oldham (q.v.).

K

Kafka, FRANZ (1883-1924), German novelist (of Czech origin). He made little or no mark during his lifetime, but has since achieved a position and influence of outstanding importance. He is the author of three novels ('The Trial', 'The Castle', and 'America') and of a large number of short stories, of which 'The Transformation' and 'The Judgement' are among the best known. He also wrote many very short prose-pieces, often suggestive of parables, and the fragmentary philosophic items in his published notebooks are of great interest. Characteristic of Kafka's work is the portrayal of an enigmatic reality, in which the individual is seen as lonely, perplexed, and threatened, and guilt is one of his major themes. His work is difficult because it resists any single interpretation. Much of it was published posthumously.

Kaikhosru, see *Khusrau I.*

Kaikobad, known to history as Qubad I, king of Iran. He is celebrated in the 'Rubáiyát' of Omar Khayyám (q.v.).

Kailyard School, from 'kail-yard', a cabbage patch such as is commonly attached to a small cottage, a term applied to writers of a class of fiction which flourished in the eighteen-nineties describing, with much use of the vernacular, common life in Scotland, e.g. J. M. Barrie (q.v.), 'Ian Maclaren' (John Watson, 1850-1907), and S. R. Crockett (1860-1914).

Douglas's sombre novel 'The House with the Green Shutters' (q.v.) was written as a counterblast to works of this type.

Kalends, see *Calends.*

Kalevala ('Land of Heroes'), the national epic poem of Finland, compiled from popular lays transmitted orally until the 19th cent., when a collection was published by Zacharias Topelius (1822). The poem is concerned with the myths of Finland, which are of great antiquity, perhaps dating, according to internal evidence, from the time when Finns and Hungarians were still one people.

Kames, LORD, see *Home* (*H.*).

Kant, IMMANUEL (1724-1804), of Königsberg in Prussia, was educated at the university of that town, and supported himself as a tutor. He published his first considerable work, 'A General Natural History and Theory of the Heavens', in 1755, and in that year became a lecturer at Königsberg, where he remained for fifteen years, during which he published a number of minor philosophical treatises. In 1770 he became professor of logic and metaphysics at Königsberg, retaining the appointment until his death. He remained unmarried. His 'Critique of Pure Reason' appeared in 1781, 'Prolegomena to any future Metaphysics' in 1783, 'Fundamental Principles of the Metaphysic of Ethics' in 1785, the second edition of the 'Critique of Pure Reason' in 1787, the 'Critique of Practical Reason' in 1788, and the 'Critique of Judgement' in 1790. His 'Religion within the Boundaries of Pure Reason' (1793) called down on him the censure of the government.

Kant's philosophy was developed and profoundly modified by Fichte, Schelling, and Hegel (qq.v.).

Kate Barlass, see *King's Tragedy*.

Katharina, a character in Shakespeare's 'The Taming of the Shrew' (q.v.).

Katharine, (1) a character in Shakespeare's 'Love's Labour's Lost' (q.v.); (2) in his 'Henry V' (q.v.), the daughter of the king of France.

Katharine of Aragon, QUEEN, the wife of Henry VIII, whose divorce is one of the principal incidents in Shakespeare's 'Henry VIII'.

Katinka, in Byron's 'Don Juan' (canto VI), one of the beauties of the harem.

Kay, SIR, in Malory's 'Morte Darthur' (q.v.), King Arthur's seneschal, son of Sir Ector (q.v.).

Kean, CHARLES JOHN (1811?-68), actor, second son of Edmund Kean (q.v.).

Kean, EDMUND (1789-1833), the son of an itinerant actress, deserted by his mother, was an unrivalled tragic actor. His numerous successes included Shylock, Richard III, Hamlet, Othello, Iago, Macbeth, and Lear.

Kearney, CAPTAIN, a character in Marryat's 'Peter Simple' (q.v.).

Keats, JOHN (1795-1821), the son of a livery-stable keeper in London, acquired a knowledge of Latin and history, and some French, but no Greek. He was apprenticed to an apothecary, but his indentures were cancelled that he might qualify for a surgeon. He passed his examinations but abandoned surgery owing to his passion for literature. He became intimate with Hazlitt and Leigh Hunt, who printed a sonnet for him in the 'Examiner' in May 1816, and in whose house he met Shelley. His sonnet on Chapman's 'Homer' was printed in the 'Examiner' in Dec. 1816. With the help of Shelley he published in 1817 'Poems by John Keats', which were financially a failure. They include 'Sleep and Poetry', an expression of the author's own poetic aspirations. In the course of 1818 Keats wrote 'Endymion' (q.v.), which was savagely criticized in 'Blackwood's Magazine' and the 'Quarterly'; and commenced 'Hyperion' (q.v.). In the same year he nursed his brother Tom until his death. He began 'The Eve of St. Agnes' early in 1819, and wrote 'La Belle Dame sans Merci' and the unfinished 'Eve of St. Mark'. About the same time he wrote his great odes 'On a Grecian Urn', 'To a Nightingale', and 'To Autumn'; and those 'On Melancholy', 'On Indolence', and 'To Psyche'. His dramatic experiments, 'Otho the Great' and 'King Stephen', also belong to 1819, and a little after them the burlesque poem 'Cap and Bells'. He had meanwhile fallen deeply in love with Fanny Brawne. His 'Lamia and other Poems', including 'The Eve of St. Agnes' and 'Isabella, or the Pot of Basil', appeared in 1820 and was praised by Jeffrey (q.v.) in 'The Edinburgh Review'. Keats was by now seriously ill with consumption. He sailed for Italy in Sept. 1820, reached Rome in Nov., and died there, desiring that there should be engraved on his tomb the words, 'Here lies one whose name was writ in water'. He was lamented by Shelley in 'Adonais' (q.v.). Of Keats's letters, which throw a valuable light on his poetical development, the most complete edition is that of H. E. Rollins, 1958.

Keble, JOHN (1792-1866), fellow and tutor of Oriel College (where Newman and Pusey were also fellows), and pro-

fessor of poetry at Oxford. In 1833 he
initiated the Oxford Movement (q.v.),
which he supported by seven of the 'Tracts
for the Times' (q.v.). He also edited
Hooker's works (1836) and helped Newman with R. H. Froude's 'Remains'.
Keble was eminent as a writer of sacred
verse. His poetical work is contained in
'The Christian Year' (1827), which
obtained immense popularity, 'Lyra
Innocentium' (1846), and 'Miscellaneous
Poems' (1869).

Keble College, Oxford, was founded in
1870 as a memorial to John Keble.

Kedar, a son of Ishmael (Gen. xxv. 13),
whose reputed descendants were a tribe
of nomadic Arabs.

Kehama, The Curse of, see *Curse of
Kehama.*

Kells, Book of, an 8th- to 9th-cent. manuscript of the four Gospels, with Prefaces,
Summaries, and Canon Tables; seven
charters of the abbey of Kells have been
added on blank pages. It is written in
Irish majuscule and has magnificent
illustrations consisting of intricate patterns
made up of abstract and animal forms. It
was probably written at Kells in County
Meath, the headquarters of the Columban
community after the sack of Iona in 806.
It was collated by James Ussher (q.v.) in
1621 and presented to Trinity College,
Dublin, after the Restoration.

Kelly, a name applied to the series of
directories published by Kelly's Directories, Ltd. The Post Office directory
was first published in 1799.

Kelly, HUGH (1739-77), an Irishman
who came to London in 1760. He wrote
three comedies, 'False Delicacy' (produced by Garrick in 1768), 'A Word for
the Wise' (1770), and 'The School for
Wives' (1773).

Kelmscott Press, see *Morris* (W.).

Kelpie or KELPY, the Lowland Scottish
name of a fabled water-spirit or demon.

Kelvin, LORD, see *Thomson* (Sir W.).

Kemble, CHARLES (1775-1854), an actor
of great range and pre-eminent in comic
parts, younger brother of John Philip

Kemble and Mrs. Siddons (qq.v.). He
was the father of Fanny Kemble (q.v.).

Kemble, FRANCES ANNE, afterwards MRS.
BUTLER, generally known as FANNY
KEMBLE (1809-93), daughter of Charles
Kemble (q.v.), an actress who appeared
with great success as Juliet, and subse-
quently as Lady Macbeth, Portia, Beatrice,
Queen Katharine, and in many other
parts.

Kemble, JOHN PHILIP (1757-1823), an
eminent actor, elder brother of Charles
Kemble and Mrs. Siddons (qq.v.).

Kemp, WILLIAM (*fl.* 1600), a comic actor
and dancer, who acted in plays by Shakespeare and Jonson. He danced a morris-
dance from London to Norwich, of which
an account, 'Kemps Nine Daies Wonder',
written by himself (1600), has been twice
reprinted.

Kempenfelt, RICHARD (1718-82), the
son of a Swede in the service of James II,
rose to be a rear-admiral. He was flying
his flag on the 'Royal George' when this
ship went down at Spithead, as commemorated in Cowper's poem.

Kempis, THOMAS À, see *Thomas à
Kempis.*

Kendall, HENRY CLARENCE (1841-82),
Australian poet, published several volumes
of verse, of which the most notable are:
'Poems and Songs' (1862) and 'Songs
from the Mountains' (1880).

Kenelm Chillingly, a novel by Bulwer
Lytton (q.v.) (1873).

Kenilworth, a novel by Sir W. Scott
(q.v.)(1821).

The novel is based on the tradition of
the tragic fate, in the reign of Elizabeth,
of the beautiful Amy Robsart, daughter of
Sir John Robsart (called Sir Hugh in the
novel). She has been enticed, by the
designs of the villainous Richard Varney,
into a secret marriage with his patron, the
earl of Leicester, Elizabeth's favourite.
Varney, by misrepresenting the relations
of Amy and Tressilian, induces Leicester
to believe her guilty of infidelity to him.
In a passion Leicester orders Varney to
remove Amy to Cumnor Place and to kill

her. The true facts are revealed too late, and Tressilian arrives at Cumnor Place only to find that Amy, by Varney's machinations, has fallen through a trap-door and perished.

Among the many interesting features in the novel are the glimpses of the court of Elizabeth, where the young Walter Ralegh is just coming into favour; the description of the revels at Kenilworth; and the adaptation of the legend of Wayland Smith (q.v.) the skilful farrier and physician, who aids Tressilian in his attempts to recover the unfortunate Amy. Dickie Sludge, or Flibbertigibbet, the impish friend of Wayland Smith, also deserves mention.

Kennedy, JOHN PENDLETON (1795-1870), American author and statesman; his writing was much influenced by Washington Irving, whose friend and admirer he was. His best-known books are 'Swallow Barn' (1832) and 'Horse-Shoe Robinson' (1835).

Kennedy, MARGARET (1896-1967), novelist, author of 'The Constant Nymph' (1924) and its sequel 'The Fool of the Family' (1930).

Kennedy, WALTER (1460?-1508?), Scottish poet, the rival of William Dunbar (q.v.) in 'The Flyting of Dunbar and Kennedie' (1508), of whose poems only a few survive.

Kenneth, SIR, or the KNIGHT OF THE LEOPARD, the hero of Scott's 'The Talisman' (q.v.).

Kensington Gardens, originally the gardens of Kensington Palace (q.v.), thrown open to the public in the 18th cent.

Kensington Palace was built *c.* 1605, sold to Sir Heneage Finch, earl of Nottingham in 1661, and bought by William III and enlarged by Wren, 1689-1721. It was a royal residence until the death of George II, after which it was assigned to various members of the royal family. Queen Victoria was born there.

Kensington Square became fashionable in the days of William III. Thackeray (who lived near by in Young Street)

placed the residence of Lady Castlewood (see *Esmond*) there. It is associated with the names of Steele, Addison, J. S. Mill, and J. R. Green.

Kent, EARL OF, a character in Shakespeare's 'King Lear' (q.v.).

Kentish Fire, a prolonged and ordered salvo of applause, or disapproval, said to have originated in meetings held in Kent in 1828-9 in opposition to the Catholic Emancipation Bill.

Kenwigs, MR. and MRS., a genteel couple in Dickens's 'Nicholas Nickleby' (q.v.).

Kepler, JOHANN (1571-1630), the celebrated German astronomer, whose three laws of planetary motion provided the basis for much of Newton's work.

Ker, WILLIAM PATON (1855-1923), professor of poetry at Oxford, and Quain professor of English literature in London; author of many learned critical books on English, Scottish, and Scandinavian literature.

Kester, the old farm servant in Mrs. Gaskell's 'Sylvia's Lovers'.

Ketch, JACK (*d.* 1686), executioner, probably from 1663. The name is used allusively for an official executioner.

Kettle, CAPTAIN, the hero of many adventures in stories by C. J. Cutcliffe Wright Hyne (1865-1944). The stories were published in book form from 1898 to 1932.

Kettledrummle, THE REVD. MR., in Scott's 'Old Mortality' (q.v.), a fanatical covenanting divine.

Kew, COUNTESS OF, a character in Thackeray's 'The Newcomes' (q.v.).

Kew Gardens, Richmond, since 1841 the Royal Botanic Gardens, are the principal national botanical gardens. Originally the gardens of Kew House and Richmond Lodge, they were laid out as a botanic garden by the mother of George III.

Key, FRANCIS SCOTT (1779-1843), American lawyer and poet, author of the national anthem, 'The Star-Spangled Banner' (q.v.).

Keyes, SIDNEY (1922-43), a poet of originality and promise, killed in the

Second World War. 'The Iron Laurel' was published in 1942, 'The Cruel Solstice' in 1943, and his 'Collected Poems' in 1946.

Keynes, JOHN MAYNARD, *first Baron* (1883-1946), a distinguished economist and man of wide cultural interests, author of 'The Economic Consequences of the Peace' (1919), 'A General Theory of Employment, Interest, and Money' (1936), etc. He founded and endowed the Arts Theatre at Cambridge and was chairman of C.E.M.A. (Council for the Encouragement of Music and the Arts) in 1942 and the first chairman when it became the Arts Council of Great Britain in 1945.

Khusrau I (CHOSROES, KAIKHOSRU), king of Iran, A.D. 531-79, who took the name of ANUSHIRVAN, and extended the Persian dominions from the Indus to the Red Sea. Under the name of Kaikhosru he is mentioned in the 'Rubáiyát' of Omar Khayyám (q.v.).

Kid, THOMAS, see *Kyd*.

Kidd, WILLIAM (*d.* 1701), pirate; imprisoned for piracy, 1699; sent to England under arrest, 1700; hanged, 1701.

Kidnapped and *Catriona*, a novel and its sequel by R. L. Stevenson (q.v.) (1886 and 1893).

The central incident in the story is the murder of Colin Campbell, the 'Red Fox' of Glenure, the king's factor on the forfeited estate of Ardshiel. This is a historical event. The young David Balfour, whose uncle Ebenezer unlawfully detains his estate, being left in poverty on the death of his father, goes to Ebenezer for assistance. Ebenezer, a miserly old villain, has him kidnapped on a ship to be carried off to the Carolinas. On the voyage Alan Breck is picked up from a sinking boat. He is a Jacobite, 'in trouble about the years forty-five and six'. The ship is wrecked on the coast of Mull, and David and Alan journey together. They are witnesses of the murder of Colin Campbell, and suspicion falls on them. After a perilous journey across the Highlands, they escape across the Forth, and the first novel ends

with the discomfiture of Ebenezer and David's recovery of his rights.

'Catriona' is principally occupied with the unsuccessful attempt of David Balfour to secure, at the risk of his own life and freedom, the acquittal of James Stewart of the Glens, who is falsely accused, from political motives, of the murder of Colin Campbell; with the escape of Alan Breck to the Continent; and with David's love-affair with Catriona Drummond, the daughter of the renegade James More.

Kierkegaard, SØREN AABYE (1813-55), Danish philosopher and theologian. His life was tortured and unhappy, but within its short span he wrote a large number of books on a wide variety of topics. Thus, although he is now chiefly remembered as having initiated much that is characteristic of existentialist trends in modern philosophy (e.g. in 'Concluding Unscientific Postscript', tr. W. Lowrie and D. F. Swenson, 1941), he was also the author of works whose themes were primarily religious, psychological, or literary; moreover, his satirical gifts made him a formidable social critic, witness his essay on 'The Present Age' (tr. A. Dru, 1962). For all their diversity of subject, his writings have certain distinctive common features: a distrust of abstract dogma and a correlative emphasis upon the particular case or concrete example; an acute concern with the forms under which human character and motivation may manifest themselves; and a passionate belief in the value of individual choice and judgement as contrasted with tame acquiescence in established opinions and norms. It was his insistence upon the importance of personal decision that lay at the root of his rejection of Hegel. For he saw in Hegelianism a philosophy which tended to obliterate the element of subjective commitment and 'risk' implicit in every valid act of faith, and which sought to submerge the unique consciousness of the individual beneath a welter of universal categories. Some of Kierkegaard's most penetrating psychological observations occur in his descriptions of the 'leap of faith' and in his analyses of the state of 'dread' (*Angst*) which precedes and accompanies it; in such passages, too, one is made aware of the peculiar significance he attached to the notion of freedom. The stress upon freedom in his sense, as an inescapable condition of life and action and as something which both fascinates and repels the choosing individual, represents perhaps the clearest link between his philosophical ideas and the doctrines of his existentialist successors.

Kilkenny Cats, TO FIGHT LIKE. The origin of the allusion is said to be as follows: During the rebellion of 1798 (or it may be of 1803) Kilkenny was garrisoned by a regiment of Hessian soldiers whose custom it was to tie together two cats by their tails and throw them across a clothes-line. The cats fought until one or both died.

Killigrew, HENRY (1613–1700), brother of T. Killigrew (q.v.), the elder, was the author of one play, 'The Conspiracy' (1638). He was the father of Anne Killigrew (1660–85; see *Dryden*).

Killigrew, Mrs. Anne, Ode to the Memory of, see *Dryden*.

Killigrew, THOMAS, the elder (1612–83), was page to Charles I, and a favourite companion of Charles II. He built a playhouse on the site of the present Drury Lane Theatre, London, in 1663, and was master of the revels in 1679. His most popular play, 'The Parson's Wedding', a comedy whose coarseness is not redeemed by any notable wit or humour, was played between 1637 and 1642, and printed in 1664.

Killigrew, THOMAS, the younger (1657–1719), son of T. Killigrew the elder (q.v.), and gentleman of the bedchamber to George II when Prince of Wales. He was author of 'Chit Chat', a comedy (1719).

Killigrew, SIR WILLIAM (1606?–95), brother of T. Killigrew the elder (q.v.), and author of several comedies.

Killing No Murder, a pamphlet advocating the assassination of Oliver Cromwell,

printed in Holland in 1657, when it was believed that Cromwell would accept the crown. It was written by Edward Sexby (*d.* 1658), who had been one of Cromwell's troopers, and revised by Capt. Silas Titus.

Killingworth, Birds of, one of Longfellow's (q.v.) 'Tales of a Wayside Inn'.

Kilmansegg, see *Miss Kilmansegg and her precious Leg*.

Kilmeny, the subject of the thirteenth bard's song in 'The Queen's Wake' of James Hogg (q.v.), and Hogg's chief title to fame as a poet.

Kilvert, ROBERT FRANCIS (1840–79), was a curate at Clyro in Radnorshire for seven years and later vicar of Bredwardine on the Wye. His Diary (1870–9) gives a lively picture of contemporary rural life, and of a young clergyman diligent in his parochial duties and at the same time keenly enjoying the beauties of nature and the diversions of social intercourse. A selection from his notebooks (ed. W. Plomer) was published in 3 vols. (1938–40; new edn. 1969).

Kim, a novel by Kipling (q.v.) (1901).

Kim, by his proper name Kimball O'Hara, the orphaned son of a sergeant in an Irish regiment, spends his childhood as a vagabond in Lahore, until he meets an old lama from Tibet, and accompanies him in his travels. He falls into the hands of his father's old regiment, and is adopted. Colonel Creighton of the Ethnological Survey remarks his aptitude for secret service, and on this he embarks under the direction of the native agent, Hurree Babu. The book presents a vivid picture of India, its teeming population, religions and superstitions, and the life of the bazaars and the road.

Kinde Hart's Dream, a pamphlet by Chettle (q.v.), licensed in 1592(?), noteworthy for its allusion to Shakespeare.

King, EDWARD (1612–37), friend of Milton (q.v.); commemorated in 'Lycidas' (q.v.).

King, HENRY (1592–1669), bishop of Chichester and the friend of Izaak Walton,

Donne, and Jonson. He published verses sacred and profane, including the pleasant piece, 'Tell me no more how fair she is'.

King, WILLIAM (1663-1712), the holder of various minor posts in England and Ireland, and a clever and amusing writer. His 'Dialogue concerning the way to Modern Preferment' was published in 1690, and his 'Dialogues of the Dead', in which (with Charles Boyle) he joined in the attack on Bentley (see *Battle of the Books*), in 1699. He wrote a number of other burlesques and light pieces.

King Alisaunder, see *Alisaunder*.

King and no King, A, a romantic drama by Beaumont and Fletcher (see *Fletcher, J.*), acted in 1611, printed 1619.

King Charles's Head, in 'David Copperfield' (q.v.), a subject that intruded into everything that Mr. Dick wrote or talked about; hence, generally, an obsession.

King Horn, the earliest of the extant English verse romances, dating from the late 13th cent. and containing some 1,500 lines. Horn is a beautiful child, the son of King Murray and Queen Godhild of Suddene (Isle of Man). A host of invading Saracens slay the inhabitants, including the king. Horn's beauty saves him from the sword, and he is turned adrift in a boat with his companions, Athulf and Fikenhild. They reach the coast of Westernesse, where King Almair's daughter, Rymenhild, falls in love with Horn. Fikenhild betrays the lovers to the king. Horn is banished and goes to Ireland, and enters the service of the king under the name of Cutberd. He slays the champion of the Saracens, who are attacking the country. The king offers his realm and daughter to Horn, who postpones acceptance. Meanwhile Rymenhild sends word that she is sought in marriage by a powerful suitor. Horn arrives disguised as a palmer and makes himself known to Rymenhild by means of the ring she had given him. With the help of Athulf he slays the rival suitor. He now reveals his birth to the king, and returns to Suddene

to recover his kingdom, leaving Rymenhild with her father. He presently learns that Rymenhild is wedded to Fikenhild. Disguised as a harper he makes his way into the castle and slays Fikenhild, thereafter living happily with Rymenhild in Suddene.

See also *Horn Childe*.

Kingis Quair, The, a poem of some 200 stanzas, in rhyme-royal, by James I of Scotland (q.v.), written in 1423 and 1424 while he was a prisoner in England and about the time of his marriage with Lady Jane Beaufort, the heroine of the poem. The poem shows the influence of Chaucer. Rossetti quotes from the poem in 'The King's Tragedy' (q.v.).

The word 'Quair' means 'quire' or 'book'.

King John, a historical play by Shakespeare (q.v.), adapted by him before 1598 from an earlier work, 'The Troublesome Raigne of King John', and not printed until 1623.

The play, with some departures from historical accuracy, deals with various events in King John's reign, and principally with the tragedy of young Arthur. It ends with the death of John at Swinstead abbey. The tragic quality of the play, the poignant grief of Constance, Arthur's mother, and the political complications depicted, are relieved by the wit, humour, and gallantry of the Bastard Faulconbridge.

King John, a historical drama (*c.* 1547) by Bale (q.v.), of interest as an early example of the chronicle play from which the later Elizabethan historical plays developed.

Kinglake, ALEXANDER WILLIAM (1809-91), published in 1844 'Eōthen', a charming narrative of his travels in the Near East, and undertook, at the request of Lady Raglan, the history of the Crimean War to the death of Lord Raglan. The first two volumes of this long and exhaustive work appeared in 1863, and the remaining six volumes at intervals down to 1887.

King Lear, a tragedy by Shakespeare (q.v.), was performed in 1606 and two slightly different versions of it were printed in 1608. For the origin of the name 'Lear' see *Llyr*. The story of Lear and his daughters is given by Geoffrey of Monmouth and by Holinshed. 'King Lear' resembles in certain respects an older play 'Leir', which had been 'lately acted' in 1605.

Lear, king of Britain, a petulant and unwise old man, has three daughters: Goneril, wife of the duke of Albany; Regan, wife of the duke of Cornwall; and Cordelia, for whom the king of France and duke of Burgundy are suitors. Intending to divide his kingdom among his daughters according to their affection for him, he bids them say which loves him most. Goneril and Regan make profession of extreme affection, and each receives one-third of the kingdom. Cordelia, self-willed, and disgusted with their hollow flattery, says she loves him according to her duty, not more nor less. Infuriated with this reply, Lear divides her portion between his other daughters. Burgundy withdraws his suit for Cordelia, and the king of France accepts her without dowry. The earl of Kent, taking her part, is banished. Goneril and Regan reveal their heartless character by grudging their father the maintenance that he had stipulated for, and finally turning him out of doors in a storm. The earl of Gloucester shows pity for the old king, and is suspected of complicity with the French, who have landed in England. His eyes are put out by Cornwall, who receives a death-wound in the affray. Gloucester's son Edgar, who has been traduced to his father by his bastard brother Edmund, takes the disguise of a lunatic beggar, and tends his father till the latter's death. Lear, whom rage and ill-treatment have deprived of his wits, is conveyed to Dover by the faithful Kent in disguise, where Cordelia receives him. Meanwhile Goneril and Regan have both turned their affections to Edmund. Embittered by this rivalry, Goneril poisons Regan, and takes her own life. The English forces under Edmund and Albany defeat the French, and Lear and Cordelia are imprisoned; by Edmund's order Cordelia is hanged, and Lear dies from grief. The treachery of Edmund is proved on him by his brother Edgar. Albany, who has not abetted Goneril in her cruel treatment of Lear, takes over the kingdom.

King Log and King Stork, in the fable of the frogs who asked for a king. Jupiter sent them a log, and they complained of its inertness. He then sent them a stork, which devoured them.

King-maker, THE, Richard Neville, earl of Warwick (1428–71), so named for his influence on the fortunes of Henry VI and Edward IV. See also *The Last of the Barons*.

King of Bath, R. Nash (q.v.).

King of Misrule, see *Misrule*.

King's Bench Prison, a gaol in Southwark which was appropriated to debtors and criminals confined by order of the supreme courts.

King's College, Cambridge, founded in 1441 by Henry VI. Its great Chapel is famous as a fine example of ornate Perpendicular. Giles Fletcher, Sir W. Temple, E. Waller, and Horace Walpole (qq.v.) were educated at this college.

King's Evil, or THE EVIL, scrofula, which the king was popularly supposed to be able to cure by touching the diseased person.

King's Friends, THE, the members of parliament who under the administrations of Lord Bute and Lord North voted subserviently as George III required. So named in allusion to 1 Maccabees ii. 18.

Kingsley, CHARLES (1819–75), became curate and subsequently, in 1844, rector of Eversley in Hampshire and held the living for the remainder of his life. He was professor of modern history at Cambridge from 1860 to 1869, and after this held canonries at Chester and Westminster. He came much under the influence of F. D. Maurice and the writings of Carlyle, and took a vigorous interest in the movement for social reform of the middle of the century, though disapproving of the violent policy of the Chartists. His literary activities were large and varied. In 'The Heroes' (1856) he tells for young readers the stories of Perseus, Theseus, and the Argonauts. His poetry included the 'Saint's Tragedy' (1848); 'Andromeda' (1859), dealing with the classical myth; and many pleasant songs and ballads. His principal novels were 'Yeast' (1850) and 'Alton Locke' (1850), showing his sympathy with the sufferings of the working classes; 'Hypatia' (1853); 'Westward Ho!' (1855); 'The Water Babies' (1863); and 'Hereward the Wake' (1866). In 1864 he became engaged in controversy with J. H. Newman (q.v.) which was the occasion of the latter's 'Apologia'.

Kingsley, HENRY (1830–76), younger brother of C. Kingsley (q.v.), went to Australia, where he spent five years (1853–8), and was for a time a trooper in the Sydney mounted police. His experiences with bushrangers while in this force are reflected in some of his novels. On his return he published 'Geoffry Hamlyn' (1859), a somewhat melodramatic story of the life of early settlers in Australia, in which bushfires, attacks of bushrangers, etc., provide exciting incidents. This was followed three years later by 'Ravenshoe' (1862), and a number of less known novels.

Kings of Cologne, THE THREE, see *Cologne*.

King's or **Queen's Printer**, the printer of royal proclamations, etc., appointed under royal patent. The earliest known patent was granted in 1530. At the present day the controller of the Stationery Office (under Letters Patent) is the Queen's Printer of Acts of Parliament, and in him is vested the copyright in all government publications. Messrs. Eyre & Spottiswoode are also termed the Queen's Printers; their privilege is the printing of the Bible and Prayer Book, a privilege shared with the University Presses of Oxford and Cambridge. (See under *Copyright*.)

Kingston, WILLIAM HENRY GILES (1814–80), writer of boys' stories: 'Peter the Whaler' (1851), 'The Three Midshipmen' (1862), and many others.

King's Tragedy, The, a poem by D. G. Rossetti (q.v.), included in 'Ballads and Sonnets' (1881).

It is the story, which purports to be told by Catherine Douglas ('Kate Barlass'), of the ominous incidents which preceded the attack on the life of King James I of Scotland, and of her attempt to save him by barring the door with her arm against his murderers.

Kipling, RUDYARD (1865–1936), son of John Lockwood Kipling, the illustrator of 'Beast and Man in India', was born in Bombay and educated at the United Services College, Westward Ho! He was engaged in journalistic work in India from 1882 to 1889. His fame rests principally on his short stories, dealing with India, the sea, the jungle and its beasts, the army, the navy, and a multitude of other subjects; and in a less degree on his verse, which is variously judged, and as diversified in subject as his tales. His publications include 'Departmental Ditties' (1886); 'Plain Tales from the Hills', 'Soldiers Three' (1888); 'The City of Dreadful Night', 'The Light that Failed' (1890); 'Life's Handicap' (1891); 'Barrack-Room Ballads' (1892); 'Many Inventions' (1893); 'The Jungle Book' (q.v., 1894); 'The Second Jungle Book' (1895); 'The Seven Seas' (1896); 'Captains Courageous' (1897); 'The Day's Work' (1898); 'Stalky & Co.' (1899); 'Kim' (q.v., 1901); 'Just So Stories' (1902); 'The Five Nations' (1903); 'Traffics and Discoveries' (1904); 'Puck of Pook's Hill' (1906); 'Actions and Reactions' (1909); 'Rewards and Fairies' (1910); 'A Diversity of Creatures' (1917); 'The Years Between' (1919); 'Debits and Credits' (1926); 'Thy Servant a Dog' (1930).

Kipps, a novel by H. G. Wells (q.v.) (1905).

L

Arthur Kipps is a little, vulgar, un-educated draper's assistant at Folkestone, who unexpectedly inherits twelve hundred a year. After the first days of delirious joy, he finds his troubles begin. He be-comes engaged to a young lady of the superior classes, who has ambitions and sets firmly about Kipps's social education. At last, driven desperate, he bolts, and hastily marries Ann, his boyhood's love, now in domestic service. But even then he is not out of his troubles; for his wealth, with its trail of social obligations, threatens his happiness. So that the loss of nearly the whole of it—by the embezzlement of a solicitor—comes as a positive relief, and real happiness begins only when he starts life again as a shopkeeper. The description of Kipps's early life as a draper's apprentice is interesting for its auto-biographical character.

Kirke, EDWARD (1553–1613), a friend of Edmund Spenser, wrote the preface, the arguments, and a verbal commentary to Spenser's 'The Shepheards Calender', under the initials 'E. K.', 1579.

Kirkrapine, in Spenser's 'Faerie Queene', I. iii, 'a stout and sturdy thief' of the church, who was destroyed by Una's lion.

Kismet, a Turkish word meaning fate, destiny.

Kit-Cat Club, founded in the early part of the 18th cent. by leading Whigs, includ-ing (according to Pope) Steele, Addison, Congreve, Garth, and Vanbrugh (qq.v.). Jacob Tonson (q.v.), the publisher, was for many years its secretary.

Kite, SERGEANT, one of the chief charac-ters in Farquhar's 'The Recruiting Officer'. One of his songs is the well-known 'Over the hills and far away'.

Kitely, a character in Jonson's 'Every Man in his Humour' (q.v.).

Kit Nubbles, a character in Dickens's 'The Old Curiosity Shop' (q.v.).

Klopstock, FRIEDRICH GOTTLIEB (1724–1803), German poet, famous for his patriotic odes and his great religious epic 'Messias' ('The Messiah') (1748, 1773).

He was visited by Wordsworth and Coleridge when they were in Germany.

Knag, MISS, in Dickens's 'Nicholas Nickleby' (q.v.), Mme Mantalini's fore-woman.

Knickerbocker, DIEDRICH, the pseu-donym under which W. Irving (q.v.) wrote his 'History of New York', and 'Rip van Winkle' and 'The Legend of Sleepy Hollow' (in 'The Sketch-Book').

Knickerbocker Magazine, The, founded in New York City, 1 Jan. 1833. From that date until it was discontinued in 1865, it numbered many of the foremost American writers among its contributors, including Washington Irving, H. W. Longfellow, W. C. Bryant, O. W. Holmes, J. R. Lowell, Horace Greeley, and J. F. Cooper.

Knightley, GEORGE, and JOHN, his brother, characters in Jane Austen's 'Emma' (q.v.).

Knight of the Burning Pestle, The, a comedy by Beaumont and Fletcher (see *Fletcher, J.*), printed in 1613. It is prob-ably in the main the work of Beaumont.

The play is at once a burlesque of knight-errantry and of T. Heywood's (q.v.) 'The Four Prentices of London' and thus the first of English parody plays —and a comedy of manners. The plot is very slight. A grocer and his wife in the audience insist that their apprentice, Ralph, shall have a part in the play. He therefore becomes a Grocer Errant, with a Burning Pestle portrayed on his shield, and undertakes various absurd adven-tures. These are interspersed in the real plot, in which Jasper, a merchant's appren-tice, is in love with his master's daughter Luce.

Knight of the Leopard, Sir Kenneth of Scotland, hero of Scott's 'The Talis-man' (q.v.).

Knight of the Rueful Countenance, Don Quixote (q.v.).

Knight of the Swan, THE, Lohengrin (q.v.).

Knightsbridge, in the West End of London, at the end of the 17th cent. was a place of some notoriety, with two taverns of questionable reputation, referred to in Congreve's 'Love for Love' (q.v.).

Knights Hospitallers, see *Hospitallers of St. John of Jerusalem.*

Knights of Malta, see *Hospitallers of St. John of Jerusalem.*

Knights of Rhodes, see *Hospitallers of St. John of Jerusalem.*

Knights of the Bath, an order of British knighthood, instituted in 1399.

Knights of the Garter, see *Garter.*

Knights of the Golden Fleece, see *Golden Fleece.*

Knights of the Round Table, see *Round Table.*

Knight's Tale, The, see *Canterbury Tales.*

Knights Templars, see *Templars.*

Knockdunder, THE CAPTAIN OF, a character in Scott's 'The Heart of Midlothian' (q.v.).

Knolles, RICHARD (1550?-1610), author of a 'General Historie of the Turkes' (1603), interesting for the influence which Byron acknowledges that it had upon himself.

Knossos, see under *Minoan.*

Knowell, a character in Jonson's 'Every Man in his Humour' (q.v.).

Knowles, JAMES SHERIDAN (1784-1862), playwright, author of 'Caius Gracchus' (produced 1815), 'Virginius' (produced 1820), 'William Tell' (1825); and comedies, 'The Beggar's Daughter of Bethnal Green' (1828), etc.

Knox, EDMUND GEORGE VALPY (1881-), editor of 'Punch', 1932-49, has written under the pen-name of 'Evoe' many volumes of light verse, essays, etc.

Knox, FLURRY, the M.F.H. in the 'Experiences of an Irish R.M.' by E. Œ. Somerville (q.v.) and Martin Ross.

Knox, JOHN (1505-72), began preaching for the reformed religion in 1547. He went abroad at the accession of Mary Tudor, wrote his 'Epistle on Justification by Faith' in 1548, met Calvin at Geneva in 1554, was pastor of the English congregation at Frankfort-on-the-Main, 1554-5, and from 1556 to 1558 lived at Geneva. Thence he addressed epistles to

his brethren in England suffering under the rule of Mary Tudor, and in Scotland under the regency of Mary of Lorraine. It was this situation which led to the publication of his 'First Blast of the Trumpet against the Monstrous Regiment of Women' (1558), of which the title, Saintsbury remarks, was the best part. In 1559 appeared the 'First Book of Discipline', of which Knox was part-author, and his 'Treatise on Predestination' in 1560. His 'History of the Reformation of Religion within the realme of Scotland' was first printed in 1587.

Knox, THE RT. REVD. MONSIGNOR RONALD ARBUTHNOTT (1888-1957), brother of E. G. V. Knox (q.v.), was received into the Church of Rome in 1917. He was Catholic chaplain at the University of Oxford from 1926 to 1939. He published a new translation of the Bible, based on the Vulgate text (New Testament, 1945; Old Testament, 2 vols., 1949). His works include 'A Spiritual Aeneid' (1918, autobiographical), 'The Belief of Catholics' (1927), 'Essays in Satire' (1928), 'Let Dons Delight' (1939), 'God and the Atom' (1945), 'Enthusiasm' (1950), 'On Translation' (Romanes Lecture, 1957). He also wrote six detective stories.

Knyvett, THOMAS (1596-1658), a Royalist in sympathy during the Civil War. His letters to his wife, which have been preserved, throw an interesting light on the life of the period.

Koestler, ARTHUR (1905-), author, born in Budapest and educated at the University of Vienna. He worked as a foreign correspondent in the Middle East, Paris, and Berlin, was imprisoned by Franco during the Spanish Civil War, served in the French Foreign Legion, 1939-40, and settled in England in 1940. His publications include 'Spanish Testament' (1938), 'Darkness at Noon' (1940), 'The Trail of the Dinosaur and other essays' (1955), 'Reflections on Hanging' (1956), 'The Sleepwalkers: a history of man's changing view of the universe'

(1959), and 'The Act of Creation: a study in the history of scientific discovery and an essay in the analysis of literary and artistic creation' (1964). 'Scum of the Earth' (1941) and 'Arrow in the Blue' (1952) are autobiographical.

Koh-i-noor, an Indian diamond, famous for its size and history, which became one of the British crown jewels on the annexation of the Punjab in 1849.

Koran or QURÂN, THE, from the Arabic verb signifying 'to read', the sacred book of the Muslims, consisting of revelations orally delivered from time to time by Mohammed, taken down by scribes, and collected and put in order after his death by Abu Bakr.

Kosciusko, TADEUS (1746–1817), Polish patriot and general, who led the Polish insurrection of 1794.

Kottabos, a Trinity College, Dublin, magazine started in 1868. It ran for some twenty years in all, and excelled in light verse and parodies.

Its contributors included Edward Dowden, Oscar Wilde, Standish O'Grady, and John Todhunter.

Kotzebue, AUGUST VON (1761–1819), a German dramatist, author of a large number of sentimental plays which had considerable vogue in their day and influenced the English stage. 'Lovers' Vows' (q.v.), made famous by Jane Austen's 'Mansfield Park' (q.v.), was adapted from his 'Das Kind der Liebe'.

Kraken, a mythical sea-monster of enormous size, said to have been seen at times off the coast of Norway. Tennyson wrote a short poem about it.

Kreutzer Sonata, The, a famous sonata for piano and violin by Beethoven (q.v.), dedicated to Rodolphe Kreutzer (1766–1831), a French composer. Also the title of a work by Tolstoy (q.v.).

Kriemhild, see *Nibelungenlied*.

Krishna, a great deity of later Hinduism, an incarnation of Vishnu (q.v.).

Kronos, see *Cronos*.

Krook, a character in Dickens's 'Bleak House' (q.v.).

Ku-Klux-Klan, a widespread secret society, which arose in the Southern States of North America after the civil war of 1861–5, beginning with an effort to overawe the Negro population by whipping and arson, and developing into a system of political outrage and murder. Though suppressed in 1871 by an act of Congress, a kindred organization still survives.

Kubla Khan, a Vision in a Dream, a poem by S. T. Coleridge (q.v.) (1816).

The poet, in 1797, living at a lonely farmhouse on the confines of Somerset and Devon, fell asleep in his chair when reading a passage in 'Purchas his Pilgrimage' relating to the Khan Kubla and the palace that he commanded to be built. On awaking he was conscious of having composed in his sleep two or three hundred lines on this theme, and immediately set down the lines that form this fragment. He was then unfortunately interrupted, and, on returning to his task an hour later, found that the remainder of the poem had passed from his memory. All that remains to us is the vision of the scene amid which Kubla's palace was built. See *Xanadu*.

Kyd or KID, THOMAS (1558?–94?), dramatist. His 'The Spanish Tragedy' (q.v.) was printed in 1594(?), and 'Pompey the Great, his faire Corneliaes Tragedy' in 1595. He was perhaps the author of a pre-Shakespearian play (now lost) on the subject of Hamlet. He was one of the best-known tragic poets of his time, and his work shows an advance in the construction of plot and development of character.

Kýrie Eléison, Greek words meaning 'Lord, have mercy', a short petition used in various offices of the Eastern and Roman churches; also a musical setting of these words.

Kyrle, JOHN, the MAN OF ROSS (1637–1724), lived very simply on his estates at Ross and devoted his surplus income to works of charity. He was celebrated by Pope in the 'Moral Essays' (q.v.), Epistle III.

L

La Balue, CARDINAL (1421-91), a minister of Louis XI, figures in Scott's 'Quentin Durward' (q.v.).

La Belle Dame sans Merci, see *Belle Dame sans Merci.*

La Bruyère, JEAN DE (1645-96), French ethical writer, author of 'Caractères' on the model of Theophrastus.

Labyrinth of Crete, THE, a maze constructed by Daedalus (q.v.) for Minos (q.v.), king of Crete. In it the Minotaur (q.v.) and Daedalus himself were confined.

Lachesis, see *Parcae.*

Lachmann, KARL KONRAD FRIEDRICH WILHELM (1793-1851), a German philologist, distinguished in both the German and classical spheres. His 'Lucretius' was his greatest work, and a landmark in the history of textual criticism.

Laconic, following the Laconian (i.e. Spartan, q.v.) manner, especially in speech and writing; brief, concise, sententious.

La Creevy, MISS, the cheerful miniature-painter in Dickens's 'Nicholas Nickleby' (q.v.).

Ladon, the dragon that guarded the apples of the Hesperides (q.v.).

Lady Bountiful, in Farquhar's 'The Beaux Stratagem', a 'country gentlewoman, that cures all her neighbours of their distempers' and lays out half her income in charitable uses.

Lady Day, a day kept in celebration of some event in the life of the Virgin Mary; now used only of 25 March, the Feast of the Annunciation.

Lady Margaret foundations at Oxford and Cambridge were instituted by Margaret Beaufort, wife of Edmund Tudor, and mother of Henry VII. She was an early patron of Caxton and Wynkyn de Worde.

Lady of Christ's, Milton's nickname at Cambridge.

Lady of Lyons, The, or Love and Pride, a romantic comedy by Bulwer Lytton (q.v.), produced in 1838.

Lady of Shalott, The, a poem by Lord Tennyson (q.v.) (1852), of which the story finds fuller development in the author's 'Lancelot and Elaine' (q.v.), one of the 'Idylls of the King'.

Lady of the Idle Lake, see *Phaedria.*

Lady of the Lake, THE, in the Arthurian legends, a somewhat indistinct supernatural character. In Malory's 'Morte Darthur', she first appears as giving Arthur the sword Excalibur and is killed by Balin. But Nimue is spoken of later in the same work as the Lady of the Lake. Nimue befriends Arthur and rescues him in peril, and marries Pelleas. She is one of the three queens in the ship in which Arthur is borne away to be healed of his wounds. These may perhaps be taken as different aspects of one figure, the lake lady Morgen, who appears also as Morgan le Fay (q.v.). Nimue is also called Vivien, the two names arising from miscopyings by successive scribes.

Lady of the Lake, The, a poem in six cantos by Sir W. Scott (q.v.) (1810).

A knight, who gives his name as James Fitz-James, receives hospitality in the home of Roderick Dhu, the fierce Highland chief, on Loch Katrine, where he falls in love with Ellen, daughter of the outlawed Lord James of Douglas. Roderick himself and the young Malcolm Graeme are also suitors for her hand, and Ellen loves the latter. Under threat of an attack by the royal forces, Roderick summons his clans. Douglas, regarding himself as the cause of the attack, sets out for Stirling to surrender himself to the king. Meanwhile James Fitz-James returns and proposes to carry Ellen off to safety. She refuses, confessing her love for another. Fitz-James generously withdraws, giving her a signet-ring which will enable her to obtain from the king any boon she may ask. On his way back to Stirling he falls in with Roderick. A fierce quarrel springs up between them and they fight. Fitz-James's skill prevails, and the wounded Roderick is carried prisoner to Stirling. Ellen appears at the king's court, presents her signet-ring, asks for her father's pardon, and discovers that Fitz-James is the king himself. The king and Douglas are reconciled, Roderick dies of his wounds, and Ellen marries Malcolm Graeme. The poem includes the beautiful *coronach* 'He is gone on the mountain', and Ellen's song 'Soldier, rest, thy warfare o'er'.

Lady of the Lamp, The, a name given to Florence Nightingale (1820–1910), famous for her services as a nurse during the Crimean War.

Lady or the Tiger, The, a famous short story by Frank Stockton (1882).

Laelaps, see *Cephalus*.

Laertes, (1) the father of Odysseus (q.v.); (2) in Shakespeare's 'Hamlet' (q.v.) the brother of Ophelia.

Lafeu, a character in Shakespeare's 'All's Well that Ends Well' (q.v.).

La Fontaine, JEAN DE (1621–95), a French poet of great versatility, who wrote dramas, satires, and light verse, but is chiefly famous for his 'Contes et Nouvelles' (1664–74), a collection of verse-tales in which he recast the popular *fabliaux* of Europe; and for his 'Fables' (1668, 1678–9, and 1694).

Lagado, see *Gulliver's Travels*.

Laïs, the name of two celebrated Greek courtesans, of the 5th and 4th centuries B.C., respectively.

Lake Poets, LAKE SCHOOL, THE, terms applied to the three poets, Coleridge, Southey, and Wordsworth, who resided in the neighbourhood of the English Lakes. 'Lake School' first appears in this sense in 'The Edinburgh Review', Aug. 1817.

Lake Regillus, near Rome, memorable for the victory of the Romans over the Latins and Tarquin *c.* 496 B.C., cele-brated by T. B. Macaulay (q.v.) in his lay, 'The Battle of Lake Regillus'.

Lallans, the vernacular speech of the Lowlands of Scotland. Its use for literary purposes has been revived by C. M. Grieve (q.v.), Tom Scott, S. Goodsir Smith, and others.

Lalla Rookh, a series of oriental tales in verse, connected together by a story in prose, by T. Moore (q.v.) (1817).

The prose story relates the journey of Lalla Rookh, the daughter of the Emperor Aurungzebe, from Delhi to Cashmere, to be married to the young king of Bucharia. On the way, she and her train are diverted by four tales told by Feramorz, a young Cashmerian poet, with whom she falls in love, and who turns out, on her arrival at her destination, to be the king of Bucharia himself.

The first of the tales is written in heroic couplets, the others in stanzas of varied metre, mostly octosyllabic.

L'Allegro, see *Allegro*.

La Mancha, an ancient province of Spain, from which Don Quixote (q.v.) took his title.

Lamarck, JEAN BAPTISTE, *Chevalier de* (1744–1829), French biologist and botanist. Darwin adopted from Lamarck the theory of the transmissibility of acquired characteristics, but in other respects their views were not in harmony.

Lamartine, ALPHONSE DE (1790–1869), one of the chief poets of the early Romantic Movement in France, and a diplomat by profession until about 1830, best known for his 'Méditations poétiques' (1820), meditative poems of a religious and mystical cast. He subsequently turned to politics, and for a brief period in 1848 held office in the provisional government.

Lamb, LADY CAROLINE (1785–1828), daughter of the third earl of Bessborough, married William Lamb, afterwards second Viscount Melbourne. She became passionately infatuated with Byron. Her first novel 'Glenarvon', published anonymously in 1816, after his rupture with her (republished as 'The Fatal Passion',

1865), contained a caricature portrait of him. Her accidental meeting with Byron's funeral procession on its way to Newstead in 1824 permanently affected her mind.

Lamb, CHARLES (1775-1834), was born in London. His father, the Lovel of the 'Essays of Elia' ('The Old Benchers of the Inner Temple'), was the clerk and confidential attendant of Samuel Salt, a lawyer, whose house in Crown Office Row was Lamb's birthplace and his home during his youth. Lamb was educated at Christ's Hospital, where he formed an enduring friendship with S. T. Coleridge. After a few months' employment at the South Sea House, he obtained at 17 an appointment in the East India House, where he remained from 1792 to 1825. In 1796 his mother was killed by his sister Mary in a fit of insanity. Lamb undertook the charge of his sister, who remained subject to periodic seizures, and she repaid him with her sympathy and affection. He himself was for a short time (1795-6) mentally deranged, and the curse of madness acted as a shadow on his life. A volume of poems by S. T. Coleridge published in 1796 contains four sonnets by Lamb, and in 1798 appeared 'Blank Verse' by Charles Lloyd and Charles Lamb, which includes 'The Old Familiar Faces'. In the same year appeared 'The Tale of Rosamund Gray and Old Blind Margaret', a simple tragic tale of a young girl, the victim of an undeserved misfortune. In 1802 Lamb published 'John Woodvil' (first called 'Pride's Cure'), a tragedy in the Elizabethan style; in 1806 his farce 'Mr. H——' proved a failure at Drury Lane. With his sister he wrote 'Tales from Shakespear' (1807), designed to make Shakespeare familiar to the young; also 'Mrs. Leicester's School' (1809), a collection of ten stories, reminiscences of childhood supposed to be told by the pupils at a Hertfordshire school, containing autobiographic details of the authors. 'The Adventures of Ulysses' (1808) is a successful attempt by Lamb to do for the 'Odyssey' what, with his sister, he had done

for Shakespeare. In 1808 he also published his 'Specimens of English Dramatic Poets contemporary with Shakespeare, with Notes'. Between 1810 and 1820 his literary output was small. It includes the essays on 'The Tragedies of Shakespeare' and 'On the Genius and Character of Hogarth' (1811). He wrote for Leigh Hunt's 'Reflector' and for the 'Examiner', and in 1814 contributed to 'The Quarterly Review' an article (much altered editorially) on Wordsworth's 'Excursion'. A collection of his miscellaneous writings in prose and verse appeared in 1818. From 1820 to 1823 Lamb was a regular contributor to the 'London Magazine', in which appeared the first series of miscellaneous essays known as the 'Essays of Elia' (q.v.), published in a separate volume in 1823. The second series was published in 1833. Of his poems the best known are 'The Old Familiar Faces' (referred to above), the lyrical ballad 'Hester' (1803), and the elegy 'On an Infant dying as soon as born' (1827); but 'Album Verses', published in 1830, also includes many charming lyrics and sonnets. He died in 1834. His sister survived him for thirteen years.

Lamb, MARY ANN (1764-1847), the sister of Charles Lamb (q.v.). Besides 'Tales from Shakespear' (her share in which was the comedies), she wrote the greater part of 'Mrs. Leicester's School' (1809), to which her brother contributed three tales.

Lambert, GENERAL, MRS., THEO, and HETTY, characters in Thackeray's 'The Virginians' (q.v.).

Lambeth, was in 1197 acquired by the archbishop of Canterbury. Of the palace an important part was built by Hubert Walter, who was archbishop in 1193-1205, and other parts were added at various times. It is on the Thames, $1\frac{1}{2}$ miles south-west of St. Paul's Cathedral, London.

Lamia, a poem by Keats (q.v.), written in 1819.

The story was taken by Keats from Burton ('Anatomy of Melancholy', III.

ii. 1. 1), who quotes it from Philostratus ('De Vita Apollonii'). Lamia, a witch, is transformed by Hermes from a serpent into a beautiful maiden. She loves the young Corinthian Lycius, and he, spellbound by her beauty, takes her secretly to his house. Not content with his happiness, he makes a bridal feast and summons his friends. Among them comes the sage Apollonius, who pierces through Lamia's disguise, and calls her by her name, whereupon with a frightful scream she vanishes.

Lammas, from OE. *hlafmæsse*, loafmass, 1 Aug., in the early English Church observed as a harvest festival. In Scotland one of the quarter-days.

Lammeter, NANCY, a character in G. Eliot's 'Silas Marner' (q.v.).

Lammle, ALFRED and SOPHRONIA, characters in Dickens's 'Our Mutual Friend' (q.v.).

Lamorak de Galis, SIR, in Malory's 'Morte Darthur' (q.v.), son of Sir Pellinore and brother of Sir Percival. He was slain by Gawaine, Agravaine, Gaheris, and Modred because of his adultery with their mother, King Lot's wife.

Lamplighter, The, a novel by the American authoress Maria Susanna Cummins (1827–66), published in 1854.

Lampman, ARCHIBALD (1861–99), Canadian poet, published two volumes of verse, 'Among the Millet' (1888) and 'Lyrics of Earth' (1896). A third volume 'Alcyone' was in preparation when he died. It contained one of his finest works 'The City of the End of Things', a sombre allegory of human life.

Lampoon, a virulent or scurrilous satire, according to French etymologists derived from *lampons*, let us drink, a drunken song.

Lancaster, JOSEPH (1778–1838), the founder of a system of education, based 'on general Christian principles', described in 'Improvements in Education' (1803). The proposal which he put forward gave rise to the 'voluntary system' of elementary schools that endured until 1870.

Lancelot, see *Launcelot of the Lake.*

Lancelot and Elaine, one of Lord Tennyson's 'Idylls of the King' (q.v.) (1859).

In this idyll we see the beginning of the retribution for the sin of Lancelot and Guinevere. Lancelot, the guilty lover of the queen, leaves the court so as to attend the 'diamond jousts' unknown, and goes to the castle of Astolat. The events that follow, ending with the death of Elaine, 'the lily maid of Astolat', and Lancelot's remorse, are given under *Launcelot of the Lake.*

Lancelot du Lake, Sir, a ballad included in Percy's 'Reliques'. Falstaff sings a snatch from this ballad in Shakespeare's '2 Henry IV', II. iv.

Landfall, a New Zealand quarterly review, established in 1947 and edited by Charles Brasch.

Land League, an association of Irish tenant farmers organized in 1879 by Charles Stewart Parnell and suppressed by the government in 1881.

Landless, NEVILLE and HELENA, characters in Dickens's 'Edwin Drood' (q.v.).

Landon, LETITIA ELIZABETH (1802–38), afterwards Mrs. Maclean, wrote under the initials L. E. L. She published a number of poems between 1824 and her death. She also wrote novels, of which the best is 'Ethel Churchill', published in 1837.

Landor, ROBERT EYRES (1781–1869), youngest brother of Walter Savage Landor (q.v.), was author of a tragedy, 'The Count of Arezzi' (1823), which was attributed to Byron, of a poem 'The Impious Feast' (of Belshazzar, 1828), etc.

Landor, WALTER SAVAGE (1775–1864), was educated at Rugby and at Trinity College, Oxford, whence he was rusticated, an intractable temper frequently involving him in trouble throughout his life. He married in 1811 Julia Thuillier, with whom he quarrelled in 1835, lived in Italy (Como, Pisa, and Florence) from 1815 to 1835, at Bath from 1838 to 1858, and the last part of his life in Florence. His principal prose work took the form of 'Imaginary Conversations' (q.v.) (1824–9);

his 'Pericles and Aspasia' appeared in 1836, and 'The Pentameron' in 1837. These show an elaborate and finished style of great charm. Landor's verse was spread over most of his life, and includes 'Gebir' (1798); 'Count Julian', a tragedy (1812); 'The Hellenics' (1846-7), short tales or dialogues in verse on Greek mythical or idyllic subjects; and among shorter pieces the various verses addressed to 'Ianthe' (q.v.), the beautiful 'Dirce', 'Rose Aylmer', and 'The Three Roses'. Boythorn, in Dickens's 'Bleak House', is a genial caricature of some peculiarities of Landor.

Landseer, SIR EDWIN HENRY (1802-73), animal-painter. He visited Sir W. Scott at Abbotsford in 1824 and drew the poet and his dogs. He had enormous popular success and enjoyed the favour of Queen Victoria and the Prince Consort. He modelled the lions for the Nelson monument in Trafalgar Square.

Lane, EDWARD WILLIAM (1801-76), Arabic scholar, published in 1836 his 'Account of the Manners and Customs of the Modern Egyptians' and in 1838-41 a translation of 'The Thousand and One Nights'.

Lanfranc (1005?-89), archbishop of Canterbury from 1070, a man educated in the secular learning of the time and in Greek, reputed as a teacher.

Lang, ANDREW (1844-1912), born at Selkirk, was educated at St. Andrews University and Balliol College, Oxford, and became a fellow of Merton. In 1875 he settled down in London to a life of journalism and letters.

Lang's first book was of verse, 'Ballads and Lyrics of Old France' (1872); followed by many others. Many of his poems were written in the old French forms of ballade, rondeau, triolet, virelai, etc. His 'Collected Poems' were published in 1923.

Lang valued himself most as an anthropologist. His first book on folklore, 'Custom and Myth', did not appear until 1884, but contained papers written and printed much earlier. It was followed

by 'Myth, Ritual, and Religion' dealing chiefly with totemism (1887), and 'The Making of Religion' (1898). Mention should be made in this connection of Lang's 'Perrault's Popular Tales' (1888, see *Perrault*), in which he discusses the origins of many of our nursery tales.

Lang, as a Greek scholar, devoted himself to Homer. He was one of the joint authors (with S. H. Butcher) of the admirable prose versions of the 'Odyssey' (preceded by his best sonnet, 1879) and (with W. Leaf and E. Myers) of the 'Iliad' (1883), and also published three books on the Homeric question.

Lang's novels, with the exception of 'The Mark of Cain' (1886) and 'The Disentanglers' (1902), were less remarkable.

Langland, WILLIAM (1330?-1400?), poet, details of whose life are chiefly supplied from the work generally attributed to him, 'The Vision of William concerning Piers the Plowman' (q.v.). He was a native of the western Midlands, was probably educated at the monastery of Great Malvern, went to London, and was engaged on his great work, which appeared in three versions (in 1362, 1377, and 1392). But recent critical discussion of these three versions has left the question of their authorship undecided. It is now thought unlikely that Langland was the author of 'Richard the Redeless' (see *Mum, Sothsegger*).

Langue d'oïl, the language of the north of France during the medieval period, so called to distinguish it from the langue d'oc (see *Provençal*), the distinction being based on the particle of affirmation; Late L. 'hoc ille' for 'yes' became 'o il' in the North and 'oc' in the South. The distinction of language corresponded to a difference of culture and literature, the langue d'oïl being the literary medium of the trouvères (q.v.), the langue d'oc or Provençal that of the troubadours (q.v.).

Languish, LYDIA, the heroine of Sheridan's 'The Rivals' (q.v.).

Lanier, SIDNEY (1842-81), American poet and critic. He published his 'Poems' in 1877; a complete 'Poems' appeared in

1884, with further additions in subsequent editions. His critical writings include 'The Science of English Verse' (1880) and 'The English Novel' (1883).

Laocoön, according to legend a Trojan priest of Apollo, who, when he was offering a sacrifice to Poseidon, saw two serpents issue from the sea and attack his sons. He rushed to their defence, but the serpents wreathed themselves about him and crushed him. This was said to be a punishment for his temerity in dissuading the Trojans from admitting the wooden horse into Troy.

For Lessing's essay see *Laokoon*.

Laodamia, the wife of Protesilaus, who was the first of the Greeks to land and be slain before Troy. Visited by the spectre of her dead husband, she could not bear to part with it, and took her own life. Wordsworth wrote a poem on her.

Laodicean, one who has the fault for which the Church of Laodicea is reproached in Rev. iii. 15, 16; lukewarm, indifferent in religion or politics.

Laodicean, A, a novel by Hardy (q.v.) (1881).

Laokoon, an essay in literary and artistic criticism by Lessing (q.v.) (1766). It takes its title from the celebrated group of statuary disinterred at Rome in the 16th cent. representing Laocoön (q.v.) and his sons in the coils of a serpent. Adopting this group as the initial subject of discussion, Lessing examines the divergence in the treatment of the scene by the artist and by Virgil who described it, and develops the essential differences between the art of poetry and the plastic arts. The work was left unfinished.

Laomedon, see *Hesione*.

Laon and Cythna, see *Revolt of Islam*.

Lao-tzu, see *Taoism*.

Laputa, see *Gulliver's Travels*.

Lara, a poem in heroic couplets by Lord Byron (q.v.) (1814), a sequel to 'The Corsair' (q.v.). Lara is Conrad, the pirate chief, returned to his domains in Spain, accompanied by his page, Kaled, who is Gulnare in disguise. He lives aloof

and a mystery hangs over him. He is recognized, and involved in a feud in which he is finally killed. But the interest of the poem lies not in the story but in the character of Lara, in which one may see the author's conception of himself.

Lares, Roman tutelary deities of the home.

La Rochefoucauld, FRANÇOIS DE MARSILLAC, *Duc de* (1613-80), famous for his 'Réflexions, Sentences, et Maximes Morales' (1665), pithy maxims, embodying a cynical philosophy that finds in self-love the prime motive of all action.

Larousse, PIERRE ATHANASE (1817-75), French lexicographer, compiler of the 'Grand Dictionnaire universel du xixe siècle', a vast encyclopaedia (1866-76).

Larynx, THE REVD. MR., a character in Peacock's 'Nightmare Abbey' (q.v.).

La Saisiaz, a poem by R. Browning (q.v.), written in 1877 under the influence of the sudden death of a friend. In it the poet examines afresh the basis of his faith in a future life.

Lassalle, FERDINAND, a German Socialist, who appears as Alvan in 'The Tragic Comedians' of G. Meredith (q.v.).

Last Chronicle of Barset, The, a novel by A. Trollope (q.v.) (1866-7).

Last Days of Pompeii, The, a novel by Bulwer Lytton (q.v.) (1834).

The scene is laid at Pompeii, shortly before its destruction, and deals with the love of two young Greeks, Glaucus and Ione, and the villainous designs of Arbaces, the girl's guardian, who is enamoured of his ward. The work gives an interesting picture of Roman life at the time of the catastrophe (A.D. 79).

Last of the Barons, The, a historical novel by Bulwer Lytton (q.v.) (1843).

The 'Last of the Barons' is Warwick the king-maker, and the historical events described in the novel occurred between 1467 and the death of Warwick at the battle of Barnet in 1471, that is to say in the last years of the feudal period.

Last of the Mohicans, The, a novel by J. F. Cooper (q.v.) (1826).

Last of the Tribunes, The, see *Rienzi.*

Last Ride Together, The, a short poem by R. Browning (q.v.), published in 'Men and Women' in 1855.

Last Tournament, The, one of Tennyson's 'Idylls of the King' (q.v.), privately printed in 1871, and published in 1889.

At the last tournament held at Arthur's court, Tristram wins the prize, a carcanet (necklace) of rubies. Disloyal to his wife, Iseult of Brittany, he carries this to his paramour, Iseult, the wife of Mark. He finds her alone at Tintagel, and, as he clasps it round her neck, he is killed by Mark.

Lateran, a locality in Rome, the site of the palace of the popes and the cathedral church known as St. John Lateran. The LATERAN COUNCILS were five general councils of the Western Church held in the church of St. John Lateran (1123, 1139, 1179, 1215, 1512-17).

Latimer, DARSIE, in Scott's 'Redgauntlet' (q.v.), the name borne by the hero, Sir Arthur Darsie Redgauntlet.

Latimer, HUGH (1485?-1555), was educated at Cambridge, took priest's orders, and became known as a preacher. He was accused of heresy, brought before convocation, and absolved on making a complete submission, in 1532. He was appointed bishop of Worcester in 1535, but resigned his bishopric. His famous sermon 'of the plough' was preached in 1548. Latimer was committed to the Tower on Mary's accession, 1553; and was condemned as a heretic and burnt at Oxford with Ridley on 16 Oct. 1555. His extant writings are notable for a simple vernacular style and for their graphic and vivid illustrations.

Latin Quarter, in Paris, on the left bank of the Seine, the quarter where students live and the university is situated.

Latinus, the legendary king of the ancient inhabitants of Latium, who, after at first opposing Aeneas when he landed, was reconciled with him and gave him his daughter Lavinia in marriage.

Latitudinarians, a name applied to those divines of the English Church in the 17th cent. who, while attached to episcopal government and forms of worship, regarded them as things indifferent. Hence applied to those who, though not sceptics, are indifferent to particular creeds and forms of worship.

Latona, Latin form of the Greek LETO, was the daughter of a Titan, and beloved by Zeus. She was the mother of Apollo and Artemis.

Latter-Day Pamphlets, see *Carlyle* (T.).

Latter-day Saints, the Mormons (q.v.).

Laud, WILLIAM (1573-1645), became archbishop of Canterbury (1633). He supported the king in his struggle with the Commons and adopted the policy of enforcing uniformity in the Church of England. He was impeached of high treason by the Long Parliament in 1640, committed to the Tower in 1641, tried in 1644, condemned and beheaded in 1645. A few of his sermons were published in 1651, and a collected edition of his works in 1695-1700. Laud gave some 1,300 manuscripts in eighteen different languages, and his collection of coins, to the Bodleian Library.

Lauder, WILLIAM (d. 1771), literary forger, a good classical scholar, was proved to have interpolated in the works of Masenius and Staphorstius (17th-cent. Latin poets) extracts from a Latin verse rendering of 'Paradise Lost' in an attempt to convict Milton of plagiarism. Incidentally he proved that Milton had deeply studied the works of modern Latin poets.

Dr. Johnson (q.v.), who was at first deceived by these forgeries, insisted on their being made public.

Laughing Philosopher, THE, see *Democritus.*

Launce, a character in Shakespeare's 'The Two Gentlemen of Verona' (q.v.).

Launcelot Gobbo, in Shakespeare's 'The Merchant of Venice' (q.v.), servant to Shylock.

Launcelot of the Lake, appears only late in the series of English Arthurian romances, though he is the subject of a great French prose-work, 'Lancelot', of the 13th cent. His story is first dealt with at length in English in the 14th-cent. poem 'Le Morte Arthur' (not Malory's). In this, Launcelot, a knight of the Round Table, is the lover of Queen Guinevere. King Arthur having proclaimed a tournament at Winchester, Launcelot goes secretly to the jousts. Elaine the Fair Maid of Astolat (or Ascolot) falls in love with him; though faithful to the queen, he wears the maid's sleeve at the tournament. There he takes the weaker side and is wounded by his kinsman, Sir Ector de Maris. He is carried to Ascolot and gives his own armour as a keepsake to Elaine before returning to the court. The Maid of Ascolot is brought dead in a barge to Arthur's palace, a letter in her purse declaring that she has died for love of Launcelot. Agravain (brother of Gawain) betrays Launcelot and Guinevere to the king, and with twelve knights surprises the lovers. Launcelot slays all except Modred, escapes and carries off the queen. Arthur and Gawain besiege Launcelot and the queen in Launcelot's castle, Joyous Gard. Launcelot restores the queen to Arthur and retires to Brittany, where Arthur and Gawain pursue him. Launcelot wounds Gawain. Modred seizes Arthur's kingdom, and tries to get possession of Guinevere. Arthur, returning, lands at Dover, where Gawain is slain. After several battles, Modred retreats to Cornwall. In the final battle all the knights are slain except Arthur, Modred, and two others. Arthur and Modred mortally wound each other, the sword Excalibur is thrown into the river, and Arthur is borne off to Avalon. Launcelot arrives to aid Arthur, and, finding him dead, seeks the queen, but finds that she has taken the veil. Launcelot becomes a priest and helps to guard Arthur's grave. On his death he is carried to Joyous Gard, and visions indicate that he has been received into heaven. The queen is buried with Arthur, and the abbey of Glastonbury rises over their graves.

The story as told in Malory's 'Morte Darthur' is substantially similar, but fuller, and more exploits are attributed to Launcelot.

Launfal, Sir, see *Sir Launfal.*

Laura, (1) see *Petrarch*; (2) the wife of Beppo, in Byron's poem 'Beppo'.

Laurence, FRIAR, a character in Shakespeare's 'Romeo and Juliet' (q.v.).

Laurence, ST., an early Christian martyr, who, according to a tradition, was roasted alive at Rome in the 3rd cent.

Laurentian Library, THE, had its origin in the private collections of Cosimo and Lorenzo de' Medici (q.v.) in the 15th cent., subsequently purchased by Leo X, taken to Rome, and enlarged by him, with the intention that it should ultimately be returned to Florence. This intention was carried out by Clement VII.

Laurie, ANNIE (1682-1764), the subject of the famous Scottish song that bears her name. She married Alexander Ferguson. The song was written by her rejected lover, William Douglas. It was revised and set to music by Lady John Scott in 1835.

Laus Veneris, see *Swinburne* (*A. C.*) and *Tannhäuser.*

Lavater, JOHANN KASPAR (1741-1801), a Swiss divine and poet, a student of physiognomy.

Lavengro, the Scholar—the Gypsy—the Priest, a novel by Borrow (q.v.) (1851). 'Lavengro', in gipsy language, means 'philologist'. The name was applied to Borrow in his youth by Ambrose Smith, the Norfolk gipsy, who figures in this work as Jasper Petulengro.

In this book, as in 'The Romany Rye' and 'The Bible in Spain', autobiography is inextricably mingled with fiction. It purports to be the story, told by himself, of the son of a military officer, a wanderer from his birth, at first accompanying his father from station to station, and later under the impulse of his own restless spirit. In the course of his wanderings he makes the acquaintance of a family of gipsies, with whom he becomes intimate, and of many other strange characters, an Armenian, an old apple-woman, a tinker (the Flaming Tinman with whom he has a memorable fight), pickpockets and sharpers, and the like. In London he experiences the hardships of the life of a literary hack. He is much given to the comparative study of languages, of which the reader is told a good deal, and he shows his aversion to the Roman Catholic Church. The book closes in the midst of the romantic episode of Belle Berners, the sturdy wandering lass, which is resumed in the sequel, 'The Romany Rye' (q.v.).

Lavinia, (1) the daughter of King Latinus (q.v.), who, though betrothed to Turnus, was given in marriage to Aeneas; (2) a character in Shakespeare's 'Titus Andronicus' (q.v.).

Law, WILLIAM (1686-1761), was elected a fellow of Emmanuel College, Cambridge, but, declining to take the oath of allegiance to George I, lost his fellowship. Edward Gibbon made him the tutor of his son, the father of the historian, in 1728, and he remained as the friend of the family until 1740, when he returned to his native King's Cliffe and became the centre of a small spiritual community.

Law's earlier writings are of a controversial character, but his chief claim to be remembered rests on his treatises of practical morality, 'A Practical Treatise on Christian Perfection' (1726), and more particularly his 'Serious Call to a Devout and Holy Life' (1729), of which Wesley admitted that it sowed the seed of Methodism. Dr. Johnson attributed to his reading of it his first earnest attention to religion. The work contains admirable portraits of typical characters, such as the man of affairs and the woman of fashion.

In his later life Law's writing assumed a mystical character. He was strongly influenced by Boehme (q.v.).

Law is a Bottomless Pit, a political pamphlet included in 'The History of John Bull', see *Arbuthnot*.

Lawless, EMILY (1845-1913), daughter of Lord Cloncurry, was author of the successful Irish novels 'Hurrish' (1886) and 'Grania' (1892).

Lawrence, DAVID HERBERT (1885-1930), novelist. He was the son of a Nottinghamshire miner, was educated at University College, Nottingham, and was for a time a schoolmaster before turning to writing as a profession. Apart from the years in England during the First World War, he lived mostly abroad, in Italy, Australia, and New Mexico. Among his best-known novels are 'The White Peacock' (1911), 'Sons and Lovers' (1913), 'The Rainbow' (1915), 'Women in Love' (1920), 'Aaron's Rod' (1922), 'Kangaroo' (1923), 'The Plumed Serpent' (1926), 'Lady Chatterley's Lover' (expurgated edition 1928; unabridged, Paris, 1929; first published in full in England, 1960). His short stories include 'The Prussian Officer' (1914), 'England, My England' (1922), and 'The Woman who Rode Away' (1928). His essay 'Fantasia of the Unconscious' appeared in 1922. Lawrence published several volumes of poems; a collected edition appeared in 1928. His 'Collected Letters', edited by H. T. Moore, were published in 1962.

Lawrence, GEORGE ALFRED (1827-76), the author of 'Guy Livingstone' (q.v.) (1857), a novel that enjoyed great popularity, but was denounced in some quarters for its exaltation of the muscular blackguard.

Lawrence, SIR THOMAS (1769-1830), painter. His works are distinguished for their courtliness and social elegance.

Lawrence, THOMAS EDWARD (1888-1935), as an archaeologist travelled and excavated in Syria. In the First World War he was one of the British officers sent from Egypt to help the Sherif of Mecca in his revolt against the Turks. He gained a position of great influence with the Arabs, performed many daring exploits, and entered Damascus in 1918 with the leading Arab forces. His narrative of these experiences, 'The Seven Pillars of Wisdom', was printed for private circulation in a limited edition in 1926 (made public 1935); a shortened version, 'Revolt in the Desert', was published in 1927. After the War he joined the Royal Air Force as an aircraftman, changing his name to Shaw by deed-poll in 1927. He was killed in a motor-cycling accident in 1935. His modern and almost colloquial translation of the 'Odyssey' was published in the same year.

Laws of Ecclesiastical Politie, Of the, by Hooker (q.v.), a philosophical and theological treatise of which four books appeared in 1594, the fifth in 1597. The last three books, as we have them, were not published until after Hooker's death, and do not represent work prepared by him for the press. The whole was reissued with a life of Hooker by Izaak Walton in 1666.

The work is a defence, written in a dignified and harmonious prose, of the position of the Anglican Church against the attacks of the Puritans. The principal characteristics of the work are its breadth of outlook and tolerant spirit, and its advocacy of intellectual liberty against the dogmatism of Calvin and the ecclesiastical despotism recommended by the Puritans.

Laxdaela Saga, see *Saga*.

Lay, a short lyric or narrative poem intended to be sung; originally applied specifically to the poems, usually dealing with matter of history or romantic adventure, which were sung by minstrels.

The general theory of epic poetry (q.v.) sees it as originating in a series of lays which were then welded into single epic poems. The ballad (q.v.) is a later and romanticized version of the lay.

Layamon or LAWEMON (meaning Lawman) (*fl.* 1200), according to his own statement a priest of Ernley (Arley Regis, Worcester), author of a 'Brut' or history of England from the arrival of the legendary Brutus to Cadwallader (A.D. 689), based directly or indirectly on Wace's French version of the 'Historia Regum Britanniae' of Geoffrey of Monmouth (q.v.), with additions from Breton or Norman sources. It is especially interesting as giving for the first time in English not only the story of Arthur, but also that of Lear and Cymbeline and other personages dealt with in later English literature. It is the first considerable work in Middle English and shows no little literary power. It is written in the OE. alliterative line of two short sections, but the alliteration is frequently abandoned and rhyme is occasionally introduced.

Lay of the Last Minstrel, The, a poem in six cantos by Sir W. Scott (q.v.) (1805). It is in irregular stanzas of lines of four accents and seven to twelve syllables. This was Scott's first important original work. It is a metrical romance, put in the mouth of an ancient minstrel, the last of his race, based on an old Border legend. The period of the tale is the middle of the 16th cent.

The lady of Branksome Hall, the seat of the Buccleuchs, has lost her husband in an affray in which Lord Cranstoun was one of his opponents. Lord Cranstoun and Margaret, the lady's daughter, are in love, but the feud renders their passion hopeless. The lady commissions Sir William Deloraine to recover from the tomb of the wizard Michael Scott in Melrose Abbey the magic book which is to help her in her vengeance. As Deloraine returns, he encounters Lord Cranstoun and is wounded by him. At Lord Cranstoun's bidding, his elfin page carries the wounded man to Branksome Hall, and, impelled by the spirit of mischief, lures away the lady's little son, the heir of the house, who falls into the hands of her English enemy, Lord Dacre. The latter, with Lord William Howard, intends to storm Branksome, alleging Deloraine's misdeeds as a Border thief. The Scots army is on its way to relieve Branksome. A single combat is suggested between Sir William Deloraine, now lying wounded, and Sir Richard Musgrave, whose lands Deloraine has harried; the lady's little son to be the prize. The challenge is accepted and Musgrave defeated. It is discovered that the victor is Lord Cranstoun, who with his page's assistance has assumed the form and arms of Deloraine. This service rendered to the house of Buccleuch heals the feud, and Lord Cranstoun marries Margaret.

Lays of Ancient Rome, by Macaulay (q.v.) (1842).

These are attempts to reconstruct, in English form, the lost ballad-poetry of Rome out of which its traditional history was at one time thought to have grown. The lays are: 'Horatius', dealing with the valiant defence by Horatius Cocles of the bridge leading to Rome against the Tuscan bands; 'The Battle of Lake Regillus', in which the Romans, aided by the gods Castor and Pollux, defeated the Latins; 'Virginia', the story of the slaying of a young Roman maiden by her father Virginius, to save her from the lust of the patrician, Appius Claudius; and 'The Prophecy of Capys' the blind seer, who foretells the great future of the Roman race.

In the edition of 1848 there were added: 'Ivry', a ballad of the victory of the Huguenots under Henry of Navarre at that place in 1590; and the fragment, 'The Armada', describing the scenes in England on the arrival of the news that the Spanish fleet was coming.

Lays of the Scottish Cavaliers, a collection of ballads by Aytoun (q.v.) (1849).

They are ballad-romances, in the style of those of Scott, dealing with such subjects as the pilgrimage of Sir James Douglas to the Holy Land to bury there the heart of Bruce, and—the best of them —'The Island of the Scots', an exploit of the company of old officers of Dundee's army serving the French king against the Germans.

Leacock, STEPHEN BUTLER (1869-1944), political economist, but better known as a writer of humorous stories, 'Nonsense Novels' (1911), 'Frenzied Fiction' (1917), 'Winsome Winnie' (1920), etc.

Leander, see *Hero*.

Lear, EDWARD (1812-88), artist and traveller, as well as author, wrote 'The Book of Nonsense' (1846) for the grandchildren of his patron, the earl of Derby, which did much to popularize the 'Limerick' (q.v.).

Lear, KING, see *King Lear* and *Llyr*.

Learoyd, JOHN, with Terence Mulvaney and Stanley Ortheris, the three privates in Rudyard Kipling's 'Soldiers Three'.

Leatherstocking, a nickname of Natty Bumppo, the hero of the five novels of American frontier life by J. F. Cooper (q.v.), which are in consequence called the 'Leatherstocking' novels.

Leavis, FRANK RAYMOND (1895-   ), critic and fellow of Downing College, Cambridge. He was editor and co-founder of 'Scrutiny' (1932-53), a critical quarterly review. His publications include 'Mass Civilization and Minority Culture' (1930), 'New Bearings in English Poetry' (1932; a study of Hopkins, Eliot, and Pound), 'Tradition and Development in English Poetry' (1936), 'The Great Tradition: George Eliot, James, and Conrad' (1948), 'The Common Pursuit' (1952), and 'D. H. Lawrence, Novelist' (1955).

Lecky, WILLIAM EDWARD HARTPOLE (1838-1903), published anonymously in 1860 'The Religious Tendencies of the Age', and in 1862 'Leaders of Public Opinion in Ireland', which at the time met with little success. After travelling in Spain and Italy he published his 'History of Rationalism' (1865). The work first brought him into fame. In 1869 he published his 'History of European Morals from Augustus to Charlemagne', describing man's changing estimate of the various virtues and its effect on happiness. Lecky next set himself to collect materials for his 'History of England in the Eighteenth Century', of which the first two volumes appeared in 1878, and the others at various dates to 1890.

Lecoq, the professional detective in Gaboriau's stories of crime. See *Tabaret*.

Le Corbusier, the name by which the Swiss-born French architect C.-E. JEANNERET (1888-1965) was known. His books, such as 'Vers une Architecture'

(1923), and his buildings, such as the 'Unité d'Habitation' at Marseilles (1952), have profoundly influenced architecture.

Leda, wife of Tyndareus, king of Sparta. She was seen bathing in the river Eurotas by Zeus, who became enamoured of her and took the form of a swan in order to approach her. Of their union were born Castor and Pollux, and Helen (qq.v.).

Lee, SIR HENRY, COLONEL ALBERT, and ALICE, characters in Scott's 'Woodstock' (q.v.).

Lee, NATHANIEL (1653?-92), failed as an actor and became a playwright, producing 'Nero' in 1675, and 'Gloriana' and 'Sophonisba', in heroics, in 1676. His best-known tragedy 'The Rival Queens; or The Death of Alexander the Great', in blank verse, appeared in 1677. He collaborated with Dryden in 'Oedipus' (1679) and 'The Duke of Guise' (1682). He lost his reason and was confined in Bedlam from 1684 to 1689. He produced 'The Massacre of Paris' in 1690, and went mad once more, escaped from his keepers, and perished. His plays, which are marked by rant and extravagance, were long popular.

Lee, SIR SIDNEY (1859-1926), a member of the editorial staff of the 'D.N.B.' (see *National Biography*) from the beginning, joint editor in 1890, and sole editor from 1891. His publications include 'Life of William Shakespeare' (1898), 'Life of Queen Victoria' (1902), 'Great English-men of the 16th Century' (1904), 'Eliza-bethan Sonnets' (1904), etc.

Lee, VERNON, pseudonym of VIOLET PAGET (1856-1935), English essayist and novelist.

Leech, JOHN (1817-64), contributed drawings to 'Punch' from 1841 till his death, among them 600 cartoons.

Le Fanu, (JOSEPH) SHERIDAN (1814-73), great-grand-nephew of R. B. Sheridan (q.v.). His principal novels and stories, in which he successfully introduced the element of the mysterious and the terrible, include 'Uncle Silas' (1864), 'The House by the Churchyard' (1863), and 'In a Glass Darkly' (1872).

Le Fevre, the hero of an episode in vol. vi of Sterne's 'Tristram Shandy' (q.v.).

Lefroy, EDWARD CRACROFT (1855-91), author of remarkable sonnets, 'Echoes from Theocritus, and other Sonnets' (1885).

Le Gallienne, RICHARD (1866-1947), poet and essayist, of Channel Island descent. 'The Romantic Nineties' (1926, new ed. 1951) is a first-hand account of the literary and artistic group of which Beardsley, Symons, and Wilde (qq.v.) were the chief figures. 'The Lonely Dancer' (1913) is a book of verse.

Legenda Aurea, see *Golden Legend*.

Legend of Good Women, The, written by Chaucer (q.v.) probably between 1372 and 1386, was his first experiment in the heroic couplet.

The poem begins with an allegorical prologue (of which there are two versions extant) in which the god of love rebukes the poet for the reflections on the fidelity of women contained in the 'Romaunt of the Rose' and 'Troylus and Cryseyde'. Alceste, his queen, defends the poet, but directs that he shall write henceforth in praise of women. The poet accordingly narrates nine stories of good women, classical heroines: Cleopatra, Thisbe, Dido, Hypsipyle and Medea, Lucrece, Ariadne, Philomela, Phyllis, and Hypermnestra. The matter is taken from the 'Heroides' of Ovid, and various authors.

Legend of Montrose, A, a novel by Sir W. Scott (q.v.) (1819), in the third series of 'Tales of My Landlord'.

It is the story of the campaign of 1644, in which the Highland clans, having risen in favour of Charles I and against the Covenanters of their own country, inflicted a succession of defeats on their opponents, thanks in great measure to the skilful generalship of their great commander, the earl of Montrose, whose character the author strongly contrasts with that of his rival, the marquess of Argyle.

Legion of Honour, an order instituted in 1802 by Buonaparte, when First Consul, to reward civil and military services.

Lehmann, JOHN FREDERICK (1907-), poet and essayist, is best known as the editor of 'New Writing' (q.v.) and 'The London Magazine' (from its foundation in 1954 to 1961). 'The Age of the Dragon', a collection of his poems, appeared in 1951. His autobiography, 'The Whispering Gallery' (vol. i, 1951) and 'I am my Brother' (vol. ii, 1960), describes the birth and development of 'New Writing' and his work with Virginia and Leonard Woolf at the Hogarth Press from 1931 to 1946.

Leibniz, GOTTFRIED WILHELM (1646-1716), German philosopher and mathematician. He discovered the infinitesimal calculus at about the same time as Newton, but by a different method. As a philosopher he was inspired by Descartes, Spinoza, and Hobbes (qq.v.), but broke away from Descartes's mechanical conception of the universe. He was one of the chief forces in the German Enlightenment movement.

Leicester, ROBERT DUDLEY, *earl of*, the favourite of Queen Elizabeth, figures in Scott's 'Kenilworth' (q.v.) as the husband of the unfortunate Amy Robsart.

Leif Eriksson, Icelandic discoverer of America, *c.* A.D. 1000. See *Vinland*.

Leigh, AMYAS, the hero of C. Kingsley's 'Westward Ho!' (q.v.).

Leigh, AUGUSTA, half-sister of Lord Byron (q.v.), being the daughter of his father by the latter's earlier marriage with Lady Conyers. Her relations with Lord Byron were the object of Lady Byron's jealousy and occasioned their separation.

Leila, (1) in Byron's 'Don Juan' (q.v.), the Muslim child whom Juan rescues at the siege of Ismail; (2) in Byron's 'The Giaour', the unfortunate heroine.

Leinster, Book of, an Irish manuscript of the 12th cent., containing stories of Gaelic mythology, in particular the feats of Cuchulain (q.v.).

L.E.L., see *Landon* (*L. E.*).

Leland or LEYLAND, JOHN (1506?-52), the earliest of modern English antiquaries, studied at Paris, took holy orders, became library-keeper to Henry VIII before 1530,

and king's antiquary, 1533. He made an antiquarian tour through England, 1534-43, intending his researches to be the basis of a great work on the 'History and Antiquities of this Nation', but he left in fact merely a mass of undigested notes. 'Leland's Itinerary' was first published at Oxford in nine volumes (1710), and his 'Collectanea' in six (1715).

Lemnos, one of the largest islands in the Aegean. Hephaestus (Vulcan) is said to have fallen there when hurled from Olympus by Zeus.

Lemon, MARK (1809-70), is remembered as one of the founders and first joint-editors, and subsequently sole editor, of 'Punch' (q.v.). He also published farces, melodramas, and operas.

Lemprière, JOHN (*d.* 1824), classical scholar; author of 'Bibliotheca Classica', a famous classical dictionary (1788).

Lenclos, ANNE, known as NINON DE LENCLOS (1620-1705), a Frenchwoman noted for her beauty and wit, which she retained to a very advanced age, depicted by Mlle Scudéry as 'Clarisse' in her 'Clélie'. She had many celebrities for her lovers, and her *salon* was frequented by St. Évremond, Molière, the youthful Voltaire, etc.

Lenin (real name UL'YANOV), VLADIMIR IL'ICH (1870-1924), a lawyer by training, in 1893 became a professional revolutionary. He was active for the Marxists against the Populists, and in 1895 led the St. Petersburg Union of Struggle for the Liberation of the Working Class. Arrested that year, he spent two years in prison and three in Siberia, publishing 'The Development of Capitalism in Russia' (1899). Upon release he set out to gain control of the Social-Democratic Labour Party. In the pamphlet 'What Is To Be Done?' (1902) he laid down his views on political strategy, tactics, and organization, the basis of Communist practice ever since. From 1900 to 1917 (except during the 1905-7 revolution) he was an *émigré* in Western Europe, whence he tried to direct the activities in Russia of the Social-Democratic Party. He constantly insisted

on Marxist orthodoxy (though his interpretation of Marxism was challenged by
other leaders) and on the priority of the
political struggle against the government
over the workers' struggle against the
employers.

After the fall of the monarchy in March
1917, Lenin returned and led his supporters, now organized in a separate
Bolshevik Party (later renamed Communist), towards the seizure of power
from the half-socialist Provisional Government, arguing (in 'Imperialism as the
Last Stage of Capitalism') that Russia
was ripe for a socialist revolution and (in
'State and Revolution') that such a revolution should bring about a 'dictatorship of
the proletariat'. The régime established
after the *coup* in Nov. 1917 was in fact a
dictatorship of the Party. The Communist government headed by Lenin con-
fiscated privately owned land and most
industry, dispersed the Constituent Assembly, concluded a separate peace
treaty with Germany, and won the Civil
War (1918–20). In 1921 Lenin inaugurated the 'New Economic Policy' of
concessions to the peasants and the per-
mitting of some private trade and industry,
though at the same time he suppressed
the socialist parties and rival factions
within the Communist Party.

Lennox, Mrs. Charlotte (1720–1804),
author of a novel, 'The Female Quixote'
(1752), and a 'Shakespeare Illustrated',
to both of which Dr. Johnson wrote
dedications. She also wrote a comedy,
'The Sister', acted in 1769.

Lenore, the heroine of a celebrated ballad
by Gottfried August Bürger (1747–94), a
German poet. Lenore is carried off on
horseback by the spectre of her lover after
his death and married to him at the grave's
side. Sir W. Scott's translation or imitation of the ballad was one of his first
poetical works.

Leo, the 5th sign of the zodiac; also a
constellation.

Leo Hunter, Mrs., a character in
Dickens's 'The Pickwick Papers' (q.v.).

Leonardo da Vinci (1452–1519),
Florentine painter, sculptor, and engineer.
The range of Leonardo's genius is revealed
in his notebooks and drawings, which include studies of clouds, water, and other
physical phenomena, engineering projects
and inventions, such as aeroplanes and
weapons, and anatomical research, as well
as studies for unfinished works of art, now
lost. He made notes for a treatise on
painting which were first published in
1651 as 'Trattato della Pittura'. See also
Mona Lisa.

Leonato, in Shakespeare's 'Much Ado
about Nothing' (q.v.), the father of Hero
and uncle of Beatrice.

Leonidas, king of Sparta (491–480 B.C.),
the hero of the defence of the pass of
Thermopylae in 480 B.C. against the
invading army of Xerxes.

Leonine City, the part of Rome in which
the Vatican stands.

Leonine verse, a kind of Latin verse
much used in the Middle Ages, consisting of hexameters, or alternate hexameters and pentameters, in which the
last word rhymes with that preceding the
caesura; for instance:

His replicans clare tres causas explico
     quare

  More Leonino dicere metra sino.

The term is applied to English verse of
which the middle and last syllable rhyme.

Leonora, (1) 'the unfortunate jilt', an
episode in Fielding's 'Joseph Andrews'
(q.v.); (2) the original name of Beethoven's
one opera, produced as 'Fidelio' in 1805;
(3) Bürger's ballad, see *Lenore.*

Leontes, in Shakespeare's 'The Winter's
Tale' (q.v.), the husband of Hermione.

Leopardi, Giacomo (1798–1837), Italian
poet and scholar, an invalid from his
youth, the author of some of the finest
poetry in modern Italian literature, imbued with melancholy and pessimism.

Leprechaun, a fabulous creature of Irish
folklore, who makes shoes for the fairies
and knows where treasures lie hidden.

Lêr, in Gaelic mythology, the sea-god,
one of the *Tuatha Dé Danann*; perhaps

to be identified with Llyr (q.v.) the British sea-god.

Le Sage, ALAIN RENÉ (1668–1747), a French novelist and dramatist, whose first important work was 'Le Diable Boiteux' (1707), followed in 1715–35 by the famous picaresque romance 'Gil Blas' (q.v.), which gives a wonderful picture of Spanish life.

Lesbia, the name under which the poet Catullus celebrated the lady whom he loved. She was the beautiful but infamous Clodia, sister of Publius Clodius, and wife of Metellus Celer.

Lesbos, an island in the Aegean, famous, in a literary connection, as the birthplace of Terpander, Alcaeus, Sappho, and Arion (qq.v.). Hence 'Lesbian' is sometimes used to signify pertaining to or resembling Sappho in the perverted character attributed to her.

Lesly, LUDOVIC, 'Le Balafré', a character in Scott's 'Quentin Durward' (q.v.).

Lessing, GOTTHOLD EPHRAIM (1729–81), German critic and dramatist, in the words of Macaulay, 'beyond all dispute, the first critic in Europe', who emancipated German literature from the narrow conventions of the French classical school, and one of the principal figures of the 'Aufklärung' or 'Enlightenment'. His critical essay 'Laokoon' (q.v.) was published in 1766.

L'Estrange, SIR ROGER (1616–1704), one of the earliest of English journalists and writers of political pamphlets. He was an active Royalist and was obliged to flee the country during the parliamentary wars. He wrote a number of pamphlets in favour of the monarchy and against the army leaders and Presbyterians. After the Restoration, in 1663, he was appointed surveyor of printing presses and licenser of the press. He issued the 'Intelligencer' and 'The News' during 1663–6. He also perhaps projected the 'City Mercury' in 1675.

Lethe, a Greek word meaning 'oblivion', the name of a river in Hades; its waters were drunk by souls about to be rein-carnated so that they forgot their past lives.

Leto, see *Latona*.

Letters on a Regicide Peace, see *Regicide Peace*.

Letters to Archdeacon Singleton, by Sydney Smith (q.v.) (1837).

In these three letters the author argues against the attempts of the Reformed Government to interfere with the incomes of the clergy.

Letter to a Noble Lord on the attacks made upon him and his pension in the House of Lords by the Duke of Bedford and the Earl of Lauderdale, by E. Burke (q.v.) (1796).

Burke retired from parliament in 1794 and received a pension from the government of Pitt. This grant was criticized in the House of Lords, principally by the peers above named, as excessive in amount and inconsistent with Burke's own principles of economical reform. Burke replied in one of the greatest masterpieces of irony and feeling in the English language, comparing his own services to the State with those rendered by the duke of Bedford and his house, which had been the recipient of enormous grants from the Crown.

Letter to Sir William Wyndham, A, written in 1717 by Viscount Bolingbroke (q.v.) while in exile, was his first important contribution to political literature. It is intended to vindicate his conduct during the period 1710–15, and to persuade the Tories to renounce all idea of a Jacobite restoration.

Letter to the Sheriffs of Bristol, A, by E. Burke (q.v.) (1777).

The American War had at this time followed its disastrous course for two years. In this letter Burke defends the course that he has taken. Asserting his zeal for the supremacy of parliament, he defines the problem which the exercise of this supremacy involves. The scheme of taxing America is incompatible with his conception of imperial policy, and Burke has consequently voted for the pacification of 1766, and even for the surrender of the whole right of taxation.

Leucothea, the name of the sea-goddess into whom Ino, a daughter of Cadmus (q.v.), was changed.

Lever, CHARLES JAMES (1806-72), contributed much of his early work to the 'Dublin University Magazine', which he edited during 1842-5. His 'Harry Lorrequer' appeared there in 1837, 'Charles O'Malley' in 1840. 'Tom Burke of Ours' in 1844, etc. He then settled at Florence, where he wrote 'The Dodd Family Abroad' (1853-4), and other books. His vivid rollicking pictures of military life and of the hard-drinking fox-hunting Irish society of his days were very popular. There are amusing parodies of Lever by Thackeray and Bret Harte.

Leviathan, a Hebrew word of uncertain origin, the name of some aquatic animal (real or imaginary) frequently mentioned in Hebrew poetry. It is used in English in this and various figurative senses, e.g. a ship of great size, a man of formidable power, etc.

Leviathan, The, or the Matter, Form, and Power of a Commonwealth, Ecclesiastical and Civil, a treatise of political philosophy by Hobbes (q.v.) (1651).

By 'The Leviathan', the author signified sovereign power. The basis of his political philosophy is that man is not, as Aristotle held, naturally a social being, recognizing the claims of the community upon him and sharing in its prosperity, but a purely selfish creature, seeking only his own advantage and resisting the competing claims of others. The result is 'contention, enmity, and war'. There is 'continual fear; and the life of man is solitary, poor, nasty, brutish and short'. To escape from these intolerable conditions man has adopted certain 'articles of peace' restricting individual liberty.

To enforce these covenants it is necessary to establish an external power, which shall punish their infraction; accordingly all individuals must enter into a contract 'to confer all their power and strength

upon one man, or upon an assembly of men'. This person or assembly is the sovereign.

The absolute power thus given to the sovereign is, however, subject to certain limits. There is liberty to refuse obedience if the command of the sovereign frustrates the end for which the sovereignty was ordained.

Levin, CONSTANTINE, a character in Tolstoy's 'Anna Karenina'.

Lewes, GEORGE HENRY (1817-78), a versatile writer, was the author of a popular 'Biographical History of Philosophy' (1845-6), a 'Life of Goethe' (1855), 'Physiology of Common Life' (1859), and 'Problems of Life and Mind' (1873-9), this last a philosophical work of considerable importance. Lewes collaborated with Thornton Leigh Hunt in the 'Leader' in 1850 and edited the 'Fortnightly Review' in 1865-6. He made the acquaintance in 1851 of Mary Ann Evans ('George Eliot', q.v.) and in 1854 formed a lifelong union with her.

Lewesdon Hill, a descriptive poem (1788) somewhat in the style of Thomson and Cowper, by William Crowe (1745-1829).

Lewis, ALUN (1915-44), a promising poet of the Second World War, who died in the Burma campaign. His work includes 'Raider's Dawn' (1942), 'Ha! Ha! Among the Trumpets' (1945), and 'In the Green Tree' (1948).

Lewis, CECIL DAY, see *Day-Lewis.*

Lewis, CLIVE STAPLES (1898-1963), literary scholar and critic, professor of Medieval and Renaissance English at Cambridge, 1954-63. His critical works include 'The Allegory of Love' (1936) and 'English Literature in the Sixteenth Century' (vol. iii in the Oxford History of English Literature, 1954). His religious and moral writings include 'The Pilgrim's Regress' (1933), 'The Problem of Pain' (1940), 'The Screwtape Letters' (1942), and 'The Four Loves' (1960). 'Out of the Silent Planet' (1938) is science fiction with a strong moral flavour. He also wrote a number of children's books. 'Surprised by Joy' (1955) is autobiographical.

Lewis, MATTHEW GREGORY (1775-1818), the author of the novel 'The Monk' (q.v., 1796). He wrote numerous dramas, and his verses had a considerable influence on Scott's earlier poetry.

Lewis, (PERCY) WYNDHAM (1884-1957), artist, novelist, and critic. He was a leader of the Vorticist movement and, with Ezra Pound, edited 'Blast, the Review of the Great English Vortex' (1914-15). His writing, which is mainly satirical, includes the novels 'Tarr' (1918), 'The Childermass', Book I (1928) of a trilogy entitled 'The Human Age', of which Books II and III, 'Monstre Gai' and 'Malign Fiesta' were published in 1955 (a projected fourth Book, 'The Trial of Man', was not completed), 'The Apes of God' (1930), 'Self Condemned' (1954), 'The Red Priest' (1956); short stories: 'Rotting Hill' (1951); essays and criticism: 'The Art of Being Ruled' (1926), 'Time and Western Man' (1927), 'The Writer and the Absolute' (1952), and verse: 'One Way Song' (1933). 'Blasting and Bombardiering' (1937) and 'Rude Assignment' (1950) are autobiographies.

Lewis, SINCLAIR (1885-1951), American novelist and journalist. His first important novel was 'Main Street', which scored an enormous success upon its appearance in 1920. In it he described with realism and satire the dullness of life in a small midwestern town, called Gopher Prairie. He strengthened his reputation as the most widely read and controversial of American writers with 'Babbitt' (q.v., 1922) and 'Arrowsmith' (1925). 'Elmer Gantry' (1927) was followed by 'The Man Who Knew Coolidge' (1928) and 'Dodsworth' (1929). Lewis was awarded a Nobel Prize in 1930, the first American writer to be so honoured. His later novels lack the strength and originality of those with which he made his reputation.

Lewis and Short, the well-known Latin-English dictionary, the work of Charlton T. Lewis and Charles Short (1879).

Lewis Baboon, in Arthuthnot's 'The History of John Bull' (q.v.), represents Louis XIV of France.

Li Beaus Desconus (= *le bel inconnu*), a 14th-cent. verse romance attributed to Thomas Chestre, the author of 'Sir Launfal' (q.v.).

This is one of the romances referred to by Chaucer in his 'Tale of Sir Thopas' (see under *Canterbury Tales* (19)).

Libel of English Policy, The, a political poem written *c.* 1436, in which the author exhorts his countrymen to regard the sea as the source of the national strength. The poem was included by Hakluyt. It is perhaps the work of Adam Moleyns or Molyneux, clerk of the king's council. 'Libel' in the title means 'a little book'.

Liberal, The, magazine, see *Byron* (*Lord*).

Liber Amoris, see *Hazlitt* (*W.*).

Liberty, On, an essay by J. S. Mill (q.v.) (1859).

In this work Mill examines from the standpoint of Utilitarian philosophy the proper relations of society to the individual, and criticizes the tyranny of the custom-ridden majority that is concealed under such expressions as 'self-government' and 'the power of the people over themselves'. In his view 'the sole end for which mankind are warranted, individually or collectively, in interfering with the liberty of action of any of their number, is self-protection'. But Mill is careful to point out that this doctrine is reconcilable with the State's interference in trade and industry.

Liberty Hall, a place where one may do as one likes. 'This is Liberty Hall, gentlemen,' says Squire Hardcastle (in 'She Stoops to Conquer') to Marlow and Hastings, who have mistaken his house for an inn.

Liberty of Prophesying, see *Taylor* (*Jeremy*).

Libra or THE BALANCE, one of the zodiacal constellations; also the seventh sign of the zodiac.

Library, The, a magazine of bibliography and literature. In 1920 it was merged with the 'Transactions' of the Bibliographical Society, though retaining its original title.

Libri, THE BOOK THIEF, whose full name was Guglielmus Brutus Icilius Timoleon, Count Libri-Carucci dalla Somaja (1803-69), belonged to an old Florentine family. He migrated to France in 1830, where he obtained professional posts, was highly esteemed by Guizot, and was appointed to inspect libraries and archives. His visits to these were found to be followed by the disappearance of valuable books and manuscripts. Libri fled to England, where he protested his innocence, but sold books and manuscripts purloined from French and Italian libraries, and acquired a fortune.

Libya, the ancient Greek name for the continent of Africa.

Liddell, HENRY GEORGE (1811-98), headmaster of Westminster School, 1846-55, and dean of Christ Church, Oxford, 1855-91, is remembered as the author, with Robert Scott (1811-87), of the famous 'Greek-English Lexicon'.

It was for Alice Liddell, his daughter, that Dodgson (q.v.) wrote 'Alice in Wonderland'.

Liddon, HENRY PARRY (1829-90), a disciple of Pusey and Keble, became canon of St. Paul's (1870), where his sermons for twenty years were an important factor in London life. Many volumes of his sermons were published, and he left at his death a 'Life of Pusey' ready for publication (1893-7).

Lien Chi Altangi, in Goldsmith's 'Citizen of the World' (q.v.), the Chinaman who studies English customs.

Life and Death of Jason, The, see *Jason* (*Life and Death of*).

Life in London, see *Egan.*

Life on the Mississippi, by Mark Twain (see *Clemens, S. L.*) (1883), an autobiographical account of the author's early years.

Ligea, one of the Nymphs (q.v.), mentioned by Milton in 'Comus' (l. 880).

Lightfoot, JOSEPH BARBER (1828-89), bishop of Durham, published many valuable works on biblical criticism and early Christian history and literature.

Light of Asia, or The Great Renunciation, a poem in eight books of blank verse, by Sir E. Arnold (q.v.) (1879).

In it the author, to use his own words, seeks 'by the medium of an imaginary Buddhist votary to depict the life and character and indicate the philosophy of that noble hero and reformer, Prince Gautama of India, founder of Buddhism'.

Lilith, an Assyrian demon, associated with the night, a vampire. In Rabbinical literature Lilith was the first wife of Adam, and was dispossessed by Eve.

Lilli-Burlēro Bullen-a-la! These 'are said to have been the words of distinction used among the Irish Papists at the time of their massacre of the Protestants in 1641' (Percy). They were made the refrain of a song, written by Lord Wharton satirizing the earl of Tyrconnel on the occasion of his going to Ireland in Jan. 1686-7 as James II's papist lieutenant. The song is given in Percy's 'Reliques'.

Lilliput, see *Gulliver's Travels.*

Lillo, GEORGE (1693-1739), was the author of the famous prose domestic tragedy 'The London Merchant, or the History of George Barnwell' (see *George Barnwell*), produced in 1731. Very little is known about him. He wrote several other plays and is important as a pioneer; his introduction of domestic tragedy had an influence which extended beyond English literature.

Lilly, WILLIAM (1602-81), a noted astrologer, who published almanacs yearly from 1644 until his death, and pamphlets of prophecy.

Lillyvick, MR., a character in Dickens's 'Nicholas Nickleby' (q.v.).

Lily, WILLIAM (1468?-1522), was the first high-master of St. Paul's School. He contributed a short Latin syntax, with the rules in English, under the title 'Grammatices Rudimenta', to Colet's 'Æditio' (1527).

Limbo (from Latin *limbus,* an edge), a region supposed to exist on the border of hell as the abode of the just who died before Christ's coming, and of un-baptized infants. (See also *Paradise of Fools*.)

Limehouse, used of virulent political abuse, in allusion to a celebrated speech at Limehouse, London, by Lloyd George (30 July 1909), directed against territorial and financial magnates.

Limerick, a form of facetious jingle, usually of five lines, rhyming *a a b b a* with the third and fourth lines half the length of the others, of which the first instances occur in 'Anecdotes and Adventures of Fifteen Young Ladies' and the 'History of Sixteen Wonderful Old Women' (1820), subsequently popularized by Edward Lear (q.v.) in his 'Book of Nonsense'. In Lear's limericks the first and last lines were usually the same: as it developed, the last line has tended to have an epigrammatic conclusion.

Linacre, THOMAS (1460?-1524), physician and classical scholar. He was Latin tutor to the Princess Mary, for whom he composed a Latin grammar, 'Rudimenta Grammatices'. He wrote grammatical and medical works, and translated from the Greek, mainly from Galen.

Lincoln, ABRAHAM (1809-65), was president of the United States, 1861-5, and political leader of the Northern States in the American Civil War. He was assassinated in 1865. In a literary connection he is remarkable as an interpreter of the American theory of democracy and as a framer of political aphorisms. Notable among his speeches was his 'Gettysburg Address', given in Nov. 1863. John Drinkwater (q.v.) made Abraham Lincoln the subject of a successful drama.

Lincoln Green, a bright green stuff made at Lincoln, used for woodmen's jackets and the like.

Lincoln's Inn, named after the third earl of Lincoln, who had a mansion there in Edward I's reign. It became an Inn of Court in 1310.

Lind, JOHANNA MARIA, known as JENNY LIND (1820-87), the 'Swedish Nightin-gale', born at Stockholm, was remarkable for the combination of the histrionic gift with a magnificent voice and great musical talent. She first appeared in England in 1847 with immense success.

Lindisfarne, Holy Island, off the coast of Northumberland. See *Cuthbert* (*St.*).

Lindisfarne Gospels, a manuscript of the four Gospels in the Vulgate text, probably written in honour of the canonization of St. Cuthbert (q.v., 698). The script is Anglo-Saxon majuscule and there are magnificent illuminations and decorative capitals. An Anglo-Saxon gloss was added in the 10th cent. with a colophon stating that the text was written by Eadfrith, bishop of Lindisfarne, 698-721. The manuscript is in the Cottonian collection in the British Museum.

Lindor, a conventional poetical name for a shepherd lover.

Lindsay, LADY ANNE (1750-1825), daughter of the fifth earl of Balcarres, wrote in 1771 the popular ballad 'Auld Robin Gray'. She became by marriage Lady Anne Barnard, and accompanied her husband to S. Africa.

Lindsay or LYNDSAY, SIR DAVID (1490-1555), Scottish poet and Lyon king-of-arms; usher to Prince James (afterwards James V). His first poem, 'The Dreme', written in 1528, but not printed till after his death, is an allegorical lament on the misgovernment of the realm, followed by a vigorous exhortation to the king. In 1529 he wrote the 'Complaynt to the King'. The 'Testament and Complaynt of our Soverane Lordis Papyngo' (1530) combines advice to the king, put in the mouth of his parrot, with a warning to courtiers. Lindsay's principal poem, 'Ane Pleasant Satyre of the Thrie Estaitis', a morality, was produced in 1540 before the king and court.

Lindsay, (NICHOLAS) VACHEL (1879-1931), American poet. Among his best-known poems are 'General William Booth enters into Heaven' (1913) and 'The Congo' (1914).

Linet, see *Lynet(te)*.

Lingard, JOHN (1771-1851), the author of a 'History of England' (1819-30) which remains a principal authority from the point of view of enlightened Roman Catholicism.

Lingua franca, a mixed language or jargon used in the Levant, consisting largely of Italian words deprived of their inflexions. The term is extended to any mixed jargon formed as a medium of intercourse between people speaking different languages.

Linkinwater, TIM, in Dickens's 'Nicholas Nickleby' (q.v.), clerk to the brothers Cheeryble.

Linklater, ERIC (1899-1974), novelist. As a Commonwealth Fellow to America, 1928-30, he collected material for his book, 'Juan in America' (1931), an amusing satire on contemporary America. Amongst his other books, the best known are 'Poet's Pub' (1929), 'Magnus Merriman' (1934), 'Ripeness is All' (1935), 'The Wind on the Moon' (a children's book, 1944), 'Private Angelo' (1946), 'The Faithful Ally' (1954), and 'Position at Noon' (1958). He has also written short stories and plays.

Linton, EDGAR, ISABELLA, and CATHERINE, characters in E. Brontë's 'Wuthering Heights' (q.v.).

Lintot, BARNABY BERNARD (1675-1736), published many poems and plays by Pope, Gay, Farquhar, Steele, and Rowe. His uncouth appearance was compared by Pope, in 'The Dunciad', ii. 63, to that of a dabchick.

Lion, THE BRITISH, the lion as the national emblem of Great Britain, used figuratively for the British nation, perhaps derived from the royal arms.

Lion of the North, Gustavus Adolphus (q.v.).

Lionesse, see *Lyonesse.*

Lismahago, LIEUTENANT OBADIAH, a character in Smollett's 'Humphry Clinker' (q.v.).

Lister, JOSEPH, *first Baron Lister* (1827-1912), the founder of modern surgery by his antiseptic treatment of wounds.

Literary Anecdotes of the Eighteenth Century, by J. Nichols (1745-1826).

Literary Club, THE, see *Johnson (S.).*

Literary Magazine, The, or Universal Review, a periodical started in 1756 and edited in 1756-7 by Samuel Johnson (q.v.), to which he contributed many articles.

Literature, THE ROYAL SOCIETY OF, was founded in 1823 under the patronage of George IV. The Society has published Transactions and a certain number of separate works.

Litotes, a figure of speech in which an affirmative is expressed by the negative of the contrary, e.g. 'a citizen of no mean city'; an ironical understatement.

Littimer, in Dickens's 'David Copperfield' (q.v.), the valet of James Steerforth.

Little, THOMAS, see *Moore (T.).*

Little Billee, a humorous ballad of three sailors of Bristol, of whom Little Billee is the youngest. When provisions fail he narrowly escapes being eaten by the other two. Thackeray wrote a version of the ballad. Du Maurier uses 'Little Billee' as the nickname of the hero of 'Trilby' (q.v.).

Little Dorrit, a novel by Dickens (q.v.), published in monthly parts, 1855-7.

William Dorrit has been so long in the Marshalsea prison for debtors that he has become the 'Father of the Marshalsea'. He has had the misfortune to be responsible for an uncompleted contract with the Circumlocution Office (a satirical presentment of the government departments of the day). His lot is alleviated by the devotion of Amy, his youngest daughter, 'Little Dorrit'. Amy has a snobbish sister Fanny, a theatrical dancer, and a scapegrace brother, Tip. Old Dorrit and Amy are befriended by Arthur Clennam, the middle-aged hero, for whom Little Dorrit conceives a deep passion, at first unrequited. The unexpected discovery that William Dorrit is heir to a fortune raises the family to affluence. Clennam, on the other hand, is brought in turn to the debtors' prison, and is found in the Marshalsea, sick and despairing, by Little Dorrit, who tenderly nurses and consoles him. He has meanwhile learnt the value of her love, but her fortune stands in the way of his asking her hand. The loss of this makes their union possible, on Clennam's release.

With this main theme is wound the thread of an elaborate mystery. Clennam has long suspected that his mother has done some wrong to Little Dorrit. Through the agency of a stagy villain, Rigaud *alias* Blandois, this is brought to light, and it appears that Mrs. Clennam is not Arthur's mother, and that she has suppressed a codicil in a will that benefited the Dorrit family.

There are a host of minor characters in the work, of whom the most notable are the worthy Pancks, rent-collector to the humbug Casby; Merdle, the swindling financier, and Mrs. Merdle, who 'piques herself on being society'; Affery, the villain Flintwinch's wife; and the Meagles and Gowan households. The Marshalsea scenes have more reality than the rest of the story, for Dickens's father had been immured in that prison.

Little-endians, in 'Gulliver's Travels' (q.v.), the orthodox party in Lilliput, as opposed to the Big-endians, on the question at which end an egg should be broken.

Little Gidding Community, see *Ferrar*.

Little-go, the popular name at Cambridge for the matriculation examination, and at the University of Dublin for the final Freshman examination taken at the end of the second year.

Little John, one of the companions of Robin Hood in the legends relating to that outlaw. He figures in Sir W. Scott's 'Ivanhoe' (q.v.).

Littlejohn, HUGH, John Hugh Lockhart, the grandson of Sir Walter Scott, to whom 'The Tales of a Grandfather' are dedicated.

Little Lord Fauntleroy, see *Burnett* (*F. E. H.*).

Little Musgrave and Lady Barnard, an ancient ballad, given in Percy's 'Reliques'. It is referred to in Beaumont and

Fletcher's 'The Knight of the Burning Pestle' (q.v.), Act v.

Little Nell (TRENT), the heroine of Dickens's 'The Old Curiosity Shop' (q.v.).

Little Red Ridinghood, see *Red Ridinghood*.

Little Women, one of the most popular juvenile books ever written, by L. M. Alcott (q.v.) (1868). The story is concerned with the daily lives of four girls— Jo, Meg, Beth, and Amy—in a New England family of the mid-19th cent.

Littré, MAXIMILIEN PAUL ÉMILE (1801–81), French scholar, philosopher, and lexicographer, began his great dictionary of the French language in 1844. It was published in four volumes (1863–72) with a supplementary volume in 1877. The whole work was reprinted in 1950.

Lityerses, in Greek legend, son of Midas, king of Phrygia. He used to require all comers to help in the harvest, and if they did not surpass him in activity, to kill or beat them. Probably, in origin, a harvest deity. Arnold alludes to him in 'Thyrsis'.

Livery Companies, the London City companies, descended from the old City Guilds, so called because they formerly had distinctive costumes for social occasions.

Lives of the Poets, The, a biographical and critical work by S. Johnson (q.v.) (1779–81).

Johnson was invited in 1777 by a deputation of London booksellers to undertake the preparation of biographical notices for an edition of the English poets that they were contemplating. When the work was completed, these notices were issued without the texts, under the above title. It had originally been intended to include all important poets from Chaucer onwards, but the scheme was curtailed and Cowley was taken as the point of departure. Fifty-two poets were included and it is significant of the taste of the age that Herrick and Marvell are not among them. The facts of each life are given and the character of the man brought out; and then Johnson passes to an estimate of his poems. In this respect the work is now considered unequal. The severe stric- tures, for instance, on Milton's 'Lycidas' and Gray's 'Odes' would not be endorsed at the present day. But the work as a whole is outstanding in the history of English criticism.

Livingstone, DAVID (1813-73), the great African missionary and explorer, embarked for the Cape of Good Hope in 1840. He made a number of journeys into the interior in the following years, discovered Lake Ngami in 1849, and the Zambesi in the interior of the continent in 1851. Livingstone published 'Missionary Travels in S. Africa' in 1857, and 'The Zambesi and its Tributaries' in 1865. In that year he started on an expedition to discover the sources of the Nile, returned almost dying to Ujiji, where he was rescued by H. M. Stanley (q.v.), resumed his explorations, and finally died in a village in the country of Ilala.

Livy (TITUS LIVIUS) (59 B.C.–A.D. 17), the Roman historian, born at Patavium (Padua). He was a friend of the Emperor Augustus in spite of his republican lean- ings. His great work was the history of Rome ('Ab Urbe Condita') from the foundation of the city to the death of Drusus (9 B.C.). Of the 142 books in which it was contained we have 35, and epitomes of the greater part of the rest. See *Patavinity*.

Lloyd's, an association in London of shipowners, merchants, and underwriters, which had its origin in a coffee-house kept by Edward Lloyd in Lombard Street early in the 18th cent. It is principally con- cerned with marine insurance and the col- lection of shipping intelligence.

Lludd or NUDD, one of the chief gods of the ancient Britons, who survived in later times as the mythical King Lud, and perhaps as the Arthurian King Lot (q.v.).

Llyr, the sea-god of the ancient Britons; his name survived as that of a British king in Shakespeare's 'King Lear'.

Lochiel, the title of the chief of the clan Cameron. T. Campbell (q.v.) wrote a poem called 'Lochiel's Warning'.

Lochinvar, the hero of a ballad included in the fifth canto of Scott's 'Marmion'.

Locke, JOHN (1632-1704), held various academic posts at Oxford, and became physician to Anthony Ashley Cooper (first earl of Shaftesbury). He held official positions and subsequently resided at Oxford and then lived in Holland, where he became known to the Prince of Orange. He was commissioner of appeals and member of the council of trade under William III.

His principal philosophical work is the 'Essay concerning Human Understand- ing' (q.v.) (1690), which led John Stuart Mill to call him the 'unquestioned founder of the analytic philosophy of mind'. He was a strong advocate of religious liberty. He published an essay on the 'Reasonable- ness of Christianity' in 1695, maintaining that, as our understanding is not com- mensurate with reality, knowledge must be supplemented by religious faith.

Locke published in 1690 two 'Treatises of Government' designed to combat the theory of the divine right of kings and to justify the Revolution. He finds the origin of the civil state in a contract, involving reciprocal obligations on the government and the governed. He published treatises on education in 1693, and on the rate of interest and the value of money in 1691 and 1695.

Locke, WILLIAM JOHN (1863-1930), a successful writer of fiction. His 'Morals of Marcus Ordeyne' (1905), and still more 'The Beloved Vagabond' (1906), enjoyed a very wide popularity. Locke also wrote a few plays.

Locker, FREDERICK (1821-95), who took the name of LOCKER-LAMPSON in 1885, published in 1857 a volume of light verse entitled 'London Lyrics', and in 1879 'Patchwork', a miscellany of verse and prose. 'My Confidences', in prose, ap- peared posthumously in 1896.

Locket, LUCY, see *Lucy Locket*.

Locket's, a fashionable ordinary or tavern in Charing Cross, frequently alluded to in the drama of the 17th-18th cents.

Lockhart, JOHN GIBSON (1794-1854), was called to the Scottish bar, and became one of the chief contributors to 'Blackwood's Magazine' (q.v.) in 1817. His fierceness as a critic earned him the nickname of 'The Scorpion'. In 1820 he married Sir W. Scott's elder daughter Sophia, and from 1825 to 1853 was editor of the 'Quarterly Review' (q.v.). He published his famous 'Life of Scott' in 1837-8. He wrote four novels, of which the most notable is 'Some Passages in the Life of Adam Blair' (1822). Lockhart was an early admirer of Wordsworth and Coleridge, though he condemned Keats and Shelley.

Lockit, and his daughter LUCY, characters in Gay's 'The Beggar's Opera' (q.v.).
Locksley, the name under which Robin Hood figures in Scott's 'Ivanhoe' (q.v.).
Locksley Hall, a poem by Lord Tennyson (q.v.) (1842).

It takes the form of a monologue, in which the speaker, revisiting Locksley Hall, the home of his youth, recalls his love for his cousin Amy, 'shallow-hearted', who abandoned him for a worldly marriage in deference to her parents. This leads him to conjure up again his youthful vision of the progress of the world, in which he finally expresses his confidence.

A sequel, 'Locksley Hall Sixty Years After', appeared in 1886.
Locrine or LOGRIN, according to Geoffrey of Monmouth and Spenser ('Faerie Queene', II. x), was the eldest son of Brute (q.v.), and the father of Sabrina.
Locrine, The Lamentable Tragedie of, a play (1595) included in the third Shakespeare folio. The authorship is unknown; modern opinion is inclined to attribute it to Peele (q.v.).
Lodbrog, or LODBROK, RAGNAR, see *Ragnar Lodbrog.*
Lodge, SIR OLIVER (1851-1940), physicist. After 1910 he became known as a leader in psychic research, and among his writings dealing with this subject are: 'The Survival of Man' (1909), and 'The Reality of a Spiritual World' (1930).

Lodge, THOMAS (1558?-1625), son of Sir Thomas Lodge, lord mayor of London. He was a student of Lincoln's Inn in 1578. He abandoned law for literature, and published 'A Defence of Plays', a reply to the 'Schoole of Abuse' of S. Gosson (q.v.), in 1580; and in 1584 'An Alarum against Usurers', depicting the dangers that money-lenders present for young spendthrifts.

His first romance, 'The Delectable Historie of Forbonius and Priscilla' appeared in 1584, and 'Scillaes Metamorphosis' in 1589 (reissued in 1610 as 'Glaucus and Scilla'). This work is interesting as the first romantic treatment in verse of a classical subject, the prototype of Shakespeare's 'Venus and Adonis'. Lodge sailed on a freebooting expedition in 1588, and again in 1591. In the course of the former voyage he wrote his second and best-known romance, 'Rosalynde. Euphues Golden Legacie' (q.v.) (1590). His chief volume of verse, 'Phillis', a cycle of amorous sonnets, largely translations or imitations of French and Italian poems, with songs and lyrics, was issued in 1593. He published 'A Fig for Momus', containing satires and epistles in verse on the Horatian model, in 1595. Lodge excelled as a lyric poet and was the best of the imitators of the style of 'Euphues' (q.v.).
Loeb, JAMES (1867-1933), an American banker, founded in 1912 the Loeb Classical Library of Greek and Latin authors, which gives the original text and the translation on opposite pages.
Logic, A System of, ratiocinative and inductive, a treatise by J. S. Mill (q.v.) (1843, revised and enlarged in the editions of 1850 and 1872).

The importance of Mill's 'Logic' lies in the fact that it supplied, to use the author's own words ('Autobiography'), 'a text-book of the opposite doctrine [to the *a priori* view of human knowledge put forward by the German school]—that which derives all knowledge from experience, and all moral and intellectual qualities principally from the direction given to the associations'. In this work Mill formulated the inductive procedure of modern science, while, unlike Bacon, giving its proper share to deduction.

In attributing to experience and association our belief in mathematical and physical laws, he came into conflict with the intuitional philosophers, and gave his own explanation 'of that peculiar character of what are called necessary truths'. This conflict with the intuitional school is further developed in Mill's 'Examination of Sir William Hamilton's Philosophy' (1865).

Logrin, see *Locrine.*

Lohengrin, the son of Perceval (q.v.). According to legend he is summoned from the temple of the Grail at Montsalvatch and borne in a swan-boat to Antwerp, where he defends the Princess Elsa of Brabant against Frederick of Telramund. He overcomes Frederick and consents to marry Elsa on condition that she shall not ask his race. But she fails to abide by this condition, and the swan-boat comes and carries Lohengrin back to the castle of the Grail. Lohengrin is the subject of Wagner's music-drama 'Lohengrin', produced in 1850.

Lois the Witch, a novel by Mrs. Gaskell (q.v.) (1859), telling how the fanatical frenzy of the people of New England caused an innocent English girl to be hanged as a witch.

Loki, in Norse mythology, one of the Æsir, the spirit of evil and mischief. It is he who contrives the death of Balder (q.v.).

Lolah, one of the beauties of the harem in Byron's 'Don Juan' (q.v.), vi.

Lollards, from a Dutch word meaning 'mumbler', a name of contempt given in the 14th cent. to certain heretics, who were either followers of Wycliffe (q.v.) or held opinions similar to his. See also *Oldcastle.*

Lollius, an unknown author mentioned by Chaucer twice in 'Troylus and Cryseyde' (i. 394 and vi. 1667), and once in 'The Hous of Fame' (iii. 378).

Lombard, PETER, see *Peter Lombard.*

Lombard Street, London, a financial centre of the city, as indicated in the expression, 'All Lombard Street to a China orange'.

London: the name *Londinium* is first mentioned by Tacitus ('Annals', 14, 33, A.D. 61) as that of a place notable for its concourse of merchants; but the earlier existence of the town is proved by coins (of Cunobelin) and other Celtic objects found on the site. After evacuation by the Romans, conquest by the Saxons, and plundering by the Danes in the 9th cent., London was resettled by Alfred in 886.

London, a poem by S. Johnson (q.v.) (1738), in imitation of the Third Satire of Juvenal.

Thalēs (perhaps Richard Savage, q.v.), disgusted with London and its vices, leaves it for the fields of Wales, and as he does so utters his indignant reflections on the degeneracy of the times, the oppression of the poor, and the arrogance of wealth.

London, JACK (1876-1916), an American novelist who began life as a common sailor, and took part in the Klondike gold rush (1897). Besides his semi-autobiographical 'Martin Eden' (1909) and 'John Barleycorn' (1913), London is remembered for his novels 'The Call of the Wild' (1903), 'The Sea-Wolf' (1904), and 'White Fang' (1906), based upon life in the Far North. London also published several collections of tales, including 'The Son of the Wolf' (1900) and 'South Sea Tales' (1911).

London, Survey of, see *Stow.*

London Bridge. There is evidence in Dio Cassius of the existence of a bridge at London in A.D. 43. No further mention of a bridge is found until the 10th cent. The wooden bridge that existed in 1136 was burnt down in that year. The great medieval stone bridge was begun in 1176 by Peter the Bridge Master and curate of St. Mary Colechurch (*d.* 1205) and finished in 1209. The houses on the bridge were demolished in 1758-62, and the old bridge itself was taken down in

1831. There is a good description of the bridge in its last phase in 'Lavengro', ch. xxxvi.

London Cuckolds, The, a rollicking farce by Edward Ravenscroft (*fl.* 1671–97), which was produced in 1682 and annually revived on lord mayor's day for nearly a century.

London Gazette, see *Gazette*.

London Library, THE, was founded in 1840, largely at the instance of T. Carlyle (q.v.), and opened in 1841.

London Lickpenny, see *Lydgate*.

London Magazine, The, a periodical which ran from 1732 to 1785, founded in opposition to the 'Gentleman's Magazine' (q.v.).

A magazine bearing the same name had a distinguished career from 1820 to 1829, in opposition to 'Blackwood's' (q.v.), with Lamb, Hazlitt, De Quincey, Hood, and Miss Mitford on its staff. The tragic outcome of the hostility between the 'London Magazine' and 'Blackwood's' was a duel, in which John Scott, first editor of the 'London', was killed.

A new 'London Magazine' was founded in 1954 with John Lehmann (q.v.) as editor.

London Merchant, The, or The History of George Barnwell, see *George Barnwell*.

London Prodigal, The, a comedy published in 1605, attributed to Shakespeare in the title of the quarto of that year and included in the 3rd and 4th folios, but undoubtedly by some other hand.

The play is a comedy of London manners, and deals with the reclaiming of the prodigal young Flowerdale by the fidelity of his wife.

London Spy, The, see *Ward* (E.).

Longaville, a character in Shakespeare's 'Love's Labour's Lost' (q.v.).

Longfellow, HENRY WADSWORTH (1807–82), American poet, educated at Bowdoin (where he was the class-mate of Hawthorne, q.v.), and at Harvard, became professor of modern languages at Bowdoin and in 1836 at Harvard. He travelled in France, Spain, Italy, and Germany after leaving Harvard, and again went to Europe (Sweden, Denmark, and Holland) before taking up his professorship at Harvard.

Longfellow's prose romance, 'Hyperion', appeared in 1839, the tale of a young man who seeks to forget sorrow in travel, a thread on which are hung philosophical discourses, poems, and legends. In the same year was published 'Voices of the Night', including his didactic pieces, 'The Psalm of Life', 'Footsteps of the Angels', and 'The Reaper and the Flowers'. In 1841 appeared 'Ballads and other Poems', containing 'The Wreck of the Hesperus', 'Excelsior', and 'The Village Blacksmith'. Longfellow visited London in 1842, and was the guest of Dickens. On the return voyage he wrote his 'Poems on Slavery'. In 1845 appeared 'The Belfry of Bruges and other Poems'; in 1847, 'Evangeline' (q.v.); in 1855, 'Hiawatha' (q.v.); in 1858 'The Courtship of Miles Standish' (q.v.); in 1863, the first series of 'Tales of a Wayside Inn', including 'Paul Revere's Ride' and 'The Saga of King Olaf'. In 1872 appeared his 'Christus', a trilogy which Longfellow regarded as his greatest achievement. In 1872 he also published 'Three Books of Song', including further 'Tales of a Wayside Inn'. Longfellow's last volumes were 'Ultima Thule' (1880) and 'In the Harbor', published in 1882, after his death.

Longinus, CASSIUS, a Greek philosopher and critic of the 3rd cent. A.D. The author, conventionally called Longinus, of the treatise of literary criticism 'On the Sublime', was probably of earlier date.

Longinus or LONGIUS, the traditional name of the Roman soldier who pierced with his spear the side of our Lord at the crucifixion.

Long John Silver, a character in Stevenson's 'Treasure Island' (q.v.).

Long Meg, see *Meg of Westminster*.

Long Melford, in Borrow's 'Lavengro' (q.v.), the expression that Belle Berners uses for Lavengro's long right arm.

Long Parliament, THE, the second of the two parliaments summoned by

Charles I in 1640. In 1642 hostilities broke out between this parliament and the king. The Long Parliament was dissolved by Cromwell in 1653.

Longus, the reputed author of 'Daphnis and Chloe' (q.v.), of whom nothing is known.

Looking Backward, a Utopian novel by Edward Bellamy (q.v.) (1888).

Lope de Vega, see *Vega.*

Lord of Burleigh, The, a poem by Lord Tennyson (q.v.), of a country girl who marries a landscape-painter and discovers that he is a wealthy noble.

Lord of the Ascendant, see *House* (*Astrological*).

Lord of the Isles, The, a poem in six cantos by Sir W. Scott (q.v.) (1815).

The poem, founded on the chronicles of the Bruce, deals with the return of Robert Bruce in 1307 to Scotland, and the period of his subsequent struggle against the English, culminating in the battle of Bannockburn.

Lord Ormont and his Aminta, a novel by G. Meredith (q.v.) (1894).

Lords and Liveries, in Thackeray's 'Novels by Eminent Hands', is a parody of the novels of Mrs. C. G. F. Gore (q.v.).

Lord Strutt, in Arbuthnot's 'History of John Bull' (q.v.), represents King Philip of Spain.

Lord Ullin's Daughter, a ballad by T. Campbell (q.v.).

Lorelei, a cliff on the Rhine, where, according to German legend, dwelt a siren of the same name, who lured boatmen to destruction by her song. It is the subject of a poem by Heine.

Lorenzo, a character in Shakespeare's 'The Merchant of Venice' (q.v.).

Lorna Doone, a novel by R. D. Blackmore (q.v.) (1869). The story is set in the times of Charles II and James II, and has a slight historical background, for Monmouth's rebellion and Judge Jeffreys figure in it, and John Ridd and the highwayman Tom Faggus have some traditional foundation.

John Ridd is a young Exmoor yeoman

of herculean strength and stature. His father has been killed by the Doones, a clan of robbers and murderers who inhabit a neighbouring valley. The vengeance which John and his neighbours finally exact from the Doones for their numerous crimes, complicated by John's love for Lorna Doone, provides the main theme of the book and the occasion for many thrilling and romantic adventures.

Lorris, GUILLAUME DE, see *Roman de la Rose.*

Lorry, JARVIS, a character in Dickens's 'A Tale of Two Cities' (q.v.).

Los, a character in the mystical books of Blake (q.v.).

Lost Leader, The, a poem by R. Browning (q.v.), on the desertion by a poet (Wordsworth?) of the cause of liberty and progress.

Lot or LOTH, in the Arthurian legend, is king of Orkney and the husband of Arthur's sister, and the father of Gawain and, in the earlier version, of Modred.

Lot, PARSON, the pseudonym of C. Kingsley (q.v.).

Lothair, a novel by Disraeli (q.v.) (1870). This is one of Disraeli's last two novels, written while out of office, and, though containing many references to politics, has no political purpose.

Lothario, (1) the heartless libertine (proverbial as 'the Gay Lothario') in Nicholas Rowe's 'The Fair Penitent' (q.v.); (2) a character in the episode of 'The Curious Impertinent' in 'Don Quixote'; (3) a character in Goethe's 'Wilhelm Meister'.

Loti, PIERRE, pseudonym of JULIEN VIAUD (1850–1923), French naval officer and author. He is seen at his best in some of his earlier works, such as 'Pêcheur d'Islande' (1886), and 'Le Mariage de Loti' (1880).

Lotophagi or LOTUS-EATERS, according to the 'Odyssey', a people inhabiting a coast visited by Odysseus, who fed on a fruit called the lotus. Those who ate it lost all desire to return to their native country. 'The Lotos-Eaters' is the title of one of Tennyson's best-known poems, founded on the Homeric story, in Spenserian stanzas, followed by a choric ode of the sailors.

Lotus-eaters, see *Lotophagi.*

Louis XI, king of France (1461-83), figures in Scott's 'Quentin Durward' and 'Anne of Geierstein' (qq.v.).

Lourdes, a town in the Hautes-Pyrénées, France, one of the chief centres of Roman Catholic pilgrimage. Lourdes is the subject of Zola's (q.v.) novel of that name (1894).

Lousiad, The, a mock-heroic poem by Wolcot (q.v.) (1785).

Louvre, THE, the ancient palace of the kings of France in Paris. It now houses the MUSÉE DU LOUVRE, the principal art museum in France, containing a number of collections, of which the most important are those of pictures and of sculpture.

Love for Love, a comedy by Congreve (q.v.) (1695).

The comedy is enlivened by its witty dialogue and its humorous characters. Among these are Sir Sampson, with his 'blunt vivacity'; Ben, the rough young sea-dog, who intends to marry whom he chooses; and Foresight, the gullible old astrologer.

Love in a Tub, see *Comical Revenge.*

Lovel, the name assumed by the hero in Scott's 'The Antiquary' (q.v.).

Lovel the dog, see *Rat, the Cat,* etc.

Lovel the Widower, a short story by Thackeray (q.v.) (1860).

Lovelace, RICHARD (1618-58), was the heir to great estates in Kent. Wealthy, handsome, and of graceful manners, he had a romantic career. He was a courtier and served in the Scottish expeditions of 1639. In 1642 he was thrown into the Gatehouse prison, where he wrote the song, 'To Althea'. He rejoined Charles I in 1645 and served with the French king in 1646. It being reported that he was killed, his betrothed Lucy Sacheverell—'Lucasta'—married another man. He was again imprisoned in 1648, and in prison prepared for the press his 'Lucasta; Epodes, Odes, Sonnets, Songs, etc.', which includes the beautiful lyric 'On going to the wars'. He died in extreme want.

Lovelace, ROBERT, a character in Richardson's 'Clarissa Harlowe' (q.v.).

Lover, SAMUEL (1797-1868), Irish novelist and song-writer, is remembered for his ballad, and the novel developed out of it, 'Rory O'More' (1836), which deal with the tragic events in Ireland in 1798, and also for his novel 'Handy Andy' (1842) in which he depicts the whimsical aspects of Irish character.

Lover's Melancholy, The, a romantic comedy by J. Ford (q.v.), acted in 1628.

Lovers of Gudrun, The, see *Gudrun (The Lovers of).*

Lovers' Progress, The, a romantic drama by J. Fletcher (q.v.), revised by P. Massinger (q.v.), produced in 1623 and printed in 1647.

Lovers' Vows, a play by Mrs. Inchbald (q.v.), adapted from 'Das Kind der Liebe' of Kotzebue (q.v.), acted in 1798. The play would be of little interest but for the place it occupies in the story of Jane Austen's 'Mansfield Park' (q.v.).

Love's Cruelty, a tragedy by James Shirley (q.v.), produced in 1631, printed in 1640.

Love's Labour's Lost, a comedy by Shakespeare (q.v.), on internal evidence one of his earliest works, probably produced about 1595, printed in quarto in 1598.

The king of Navarre and three of his lords have sworn for three years to keep from the sight of woman and to live studying and fasting. The arrival of the princess of France on an embassy, with her attendant ladies, obliges them 'of mere necessity' to disregard their vows. The king is soon in love with the princess, his lords with her ladies, and the courting proceeds amidst disguises and merriment, to which the other characters contribute, viz. Don Adriano de Armado, the Spaniard, a master of extravagant language, Holofernes the schoolmaster, Dull the constable, Sir Nathaniel the curate, and Costard the clown. News of the death of the princess's father interrupts the wooing, and the ladies impose a year's ordeal on their lovers. The play ends with the beautiful owl and cuckoo-song, 'When icicles hang by the wall'.

Loves of the Angels, The, a poem by T. Moore (1823). This was Moore's last long poem, and it had a very wide vogue. It was translated into several languages.

Loves of the Plants, The, see *Darwin (E.)*.

Loves of the Triangles, The, a parody by Canning and J. H. Frere in the 'Anti-Jacobin' (q.v.) of E. Darwin's (q.v.) 'The Loves of the Plants'.

Love's Sacrifice, a tragedy by J. Ford (q.v.), printed in 1633.

Lowell, AMY (1874-1925), American poet. She was an Imagist and so active in the movement (see *Imagism*) that Ezra Pound (q.v.) spoke of 'Amy-gism'. Among her collections of verse are 'Men, Women, and Ghosts' (1916) and 'Can Grande's Castle' (1918). She also published several books of criticism, among them a notable life of Keats (1925).

Lowell, JAMES RUSSELL (1819-91), succeeded Longfellow as professor of belles-lettres at Harvard in 1855, and was American minister in Spain, 1877-80, and in England, 1880-5. He was editor of the 'Atlantic Monthly' magazine in 1857. His works include several volumes of verse, the satirical 'Biglow Papers' (1848 and 1867), and memorial odes after the Civil War; and prose essays.

Lowell, ROBERT TRAILL SPENCE (1917-77), American poet, great-grandson of J. R. Lowell (q.v.). His volumes of verse include 'Land of Unlikeness' (1944), 'Lord Weary's Castle' (1946), 'The Mills of the Kavanaughs' (1951), 'Life Studies: New Poems and an Autobiographical Fragment' (1959), 'Imitations' (1961), and 'For the Union Dead' (1964). His play 'Old Glory' was published in 1965.

Low-heels and **High-heels**, in 'Gulliver's Travels' (q.v.), the name of two political parties in Lilliput.

Lowry, (CLARENCE) MALCOLM (1909-57), novelist, whose books include 'Ultramarine' (1933), 'Under the Volcano' (1947), and 'Hear Us O Lord from Heaven Thy Dwelling-place' (1962).

Loyal Subject, The, a drama by J. Fletcher (q.v.), produced in 1618.

Loyola, ST. IGNATIUS (1491-1556), a page to Ferdinand V of Aragon, and subsequently an officer in the Spanish army, was wounded in both legs at the siege of Pampeluna (1521), and thereafter devoted himself to religion. He constituted himself the Knight of the Blessed Virgin, went on a pilgrimage to the Holy Land, and on his return in 1534 founded in Paris the Society of Jesus (Jesuits), authorized by papal bull in 1540.

Lucan (MARCUS ANNAEUS LUCANUS) (A.D. 39-65), a Roman poet born at Corduba (Cordova) in Spain. His chief work is the 'Pharsalia', a heroic poem describing the struggle between Caesar and Pompey.

Lucas, EDWARD VERRALL (1868-1938), an essayist of remarkable charm, at one time assistant editor of 'Punch', published, among numerous works, a standard life of Charles Lamb (1905, 5th ed., 1921), editions of the works and letters of Charles and Mary Lamb (1903-35), and two pleasant anthologies, 'The Open Road' (1899, revised 1905), and 'The Friendly Town' (1905).

Lucasta, see *Lovelace (Richard)*.

Lucentio, a character in Shakespeare's 'The Taming of the Shrew' (q.v.).

Lucia, a character in Addison's 'Cato' (q.v.).

Lucian (*c*. A.D. 115-*c*. 200), a Greek writer, author of 'Dialogues of the Gods', 'Dialogues of the Dead', and many other fantastic tales, in which mythology, philosophers, and the society of the time are satirized. His 'Veracious ·History' is a narrative of imaginary travels, the prototype of 'Gulliver's Travels'.

Lucifer, the morning star; the Phosphorus of the Greeks, the planet Venus when it appears in the sky before sunrise.

The application of the name to Satan, the rebel archangel who was hurled from heaven, arises from a mistaken interpretation of Isa. xiv. 12, 'How art thou fallen from heaven, O Lucifer, son of the morning'.

Lucifera, in Spenser's 'Faerie Queene', I. iv. 12, the symbol of pride and worldliness.

Lucina, 'She who brings to light', the Roman goddess who presided over childbirth. She was identified with both Juno and Diana.

Lucius, (1) a mythical king of Britain, supposed to have been the first, to receive Christianity. See Spenser, 'Faerie Queene', II. x. 53; (2) in the legend of Arthur (q.v.), Lucius is the Roman emperor against whom Arthur wages war; (3) Brutus's page in Shakespeare's 'Julius Caesar' (q.v.); (4) a character in his 'Timon of Athens' (q.v.); (5) a character in his 'Titus Andronicus' (q.v.); (6) in his 'Cymbeline' (q.v.), Caius Lucius is 'General of the Roman Forces'.

Luck of Eden Hall, a goblet of enamelled glass long kept at Eden Hall in Cumberland; the subject of a ballad by the German poet Uhland, translated by Longfellow.

Luck of Roaring Camp, The, one of the best known of Bret Harte's (q.v.) short stories (1868).

Lucrece or LUCRETIA, a celebrated Roman lady, daughter of Lucretius, and wife of Tarquinius Collatinus, whose beauty inflamed the passion of Sextus (son of Tarquin, king of Rome), who used threats and violence to satisfy it. Lucretia, after informing her father and husband of what had passed, took her own life. The outrage committed by Sextus, coupled with the oppression of the king, led to the expulsion of the Tarquins from Rome, and the introduction of republican government.

Lucrece, The Play of, see *Fulgens and Lucrece*.

Lucrece, The Rape of, a poem in seven-lined stanzas by Shakespeare (q.v.) (1594),

dedicated to Henry Wriothesley, earl of Southampton. For the subject of the poem see *Lucrece*, above.

Lucretius (TITUS LUCRETIUS CARUS) the Roman poet, lived during the 1st cent. B.C., probably *c*. 99-55 B.C. His chief work is a philosophical poem in hexameters, in six books, 'De Rerum Natura'. He adopts the atomic theory of the universe of Epicurus (q.v.), and seeks to show that the course of the world can be explained without resorting to divine intervention, his object being to free mankind from terror of the gods. The work is marked by passages of great poetical beauty.

Lucretius, a dramatic monologue by Lord Tennyson (q.v.) (1868).

This, perhaps the greatest of Tennyson's poems on classical subjects, presents the philosopher, his mind distraught, and his 'settled, sweet, Epicurean life' deranged, by a love potion that Lucilia, his wife, has administered, mingling visions of atoms and of gods, lamenting his subjugation to 'some unseen monster', and finally taking his own life.

Lucrezia Borgia, see *Borgia (L.)*.

Lucullus, LUCIUS LICINIUS (*b. c.* 110 B.C.), Sulla's quaestor and subsequently consul, who for eight years (74-67) carried on the war with Mithridates. After his return to Rome, having amassed much wealth, he became famous for his magnificence and luxury. He was also a patron of literature.

Lucy, in Spenser's 'Faerie Queene', V. iv, the dowerless maid abandoned by Amidas and married by Bracidas.

Lucy, the subject of several poems by Wordsworth (q.v.) written about 1799, has been taken for a real person and was made the heroine of a story by the Baroness von Stockhausen. But nothing is known to suggest that she really existed. Coleridge surmised that one of the poems, 'A slumber did my spirit seal', referred to Dorothy Wordsworth.

Lucy Locket and **Kitty Fisher** (in the nursery rhyme about Lucy Locket losing her pocket) were, according to Halliwell,

M

celebrated courtesans in the time of Charles II.

For LUCY LOCKIT see *Beggar's Opera*.

Lud, a mythical king of Britain, originally a god of the ancient Britons. See also *Ludgate, Lludd*.

Luddites, English mechanics, who, under the pressure of the economic disturbance caused by the introduction of machinery to replace handicraft in the period 1811–16, set themselves to destroy machinery in the Midlands and north of England. The Luddites figure in C. Brontë's 'Shirley'. Byron's 'Song for the Luddites' was written in 1816 and published in 1830.

Ludgate, the name of one of the ancient gates of London, traditionally connected with King Lud.

Ludlow, EDMUND (1617?–92), Puritan general and regicide, author of famous 'Memoirs' (1698–9).

Luggnagg, a kingdom visited by Gulliver in his third voyage (see *Gulliver's Travels*). It was here that the Struldbrugs lived.

Luke, ST., the evangelist, the patron saint of medicine and painting. His festival is kept on 18 Oct., whence a period of fine weather about that day is called 'St. Luke's Summer'.

Lulli or LULLY, JEAN BAPTISTE (1633–87), French composer; the founder of the French grand opera.

Lully, RAYMOND (RAIMON LULL) (*c.* 1235–1315), a Catalan, became a Franciscan, a mystic, a philosopher, a missionary to the Arabs, an author of controversial treatises, and a poet.

Lumpkin, TONY, a character in Goldsmith's 'She Stoops to Conquer' (q.v.).

Lupercal, a cave on the Palatine hill in ancient Rome, sacred to LUPERCUS, or Faunus in the form of a wolf-deity. The 'Lupercalia' was the annual festival of Lupercus, when his priests (*Luperci*) ran about the city striking the women whom they met, a ceremony supposed to make them fruitful. (Cf. Shakespeare, 'Julius Caesar', I. ii.)

Lupin, ARSÈNE, the hero of Maurice Leblanc's novels of crime, a criminal skilled in detective methods.

Luria, a poetical drama by R. Browning (q.v.) (1846).

The play deals with an episode of the struggle between Florence and Pisa in the 15th cent.

Lusiads, The, see *Camoëns*.

Lusitania, (1) the Roman name of Portugal and western Spain; (2) the name of the Cunard liner that was sunk by a German submarine in the Atlantic on 7 May 1915, with the loss of over a thousand lives.

Lutetia or LUTETIA PARISIORUM, the modern Paris, on an island in the Sequana (Seine), was the capital of the Parisii, a Gallic tribe.

Luther, MARTIN (1483–1546), the leader of the Reformation in Germany. As a monk he visited Rome, and his experience of the corruption in high ecclesiastical places influenced his future career. He attacked the principle of papal indulgences, and as a consequence the papal ban was pronounced on him (1521) at the Diet of Worms. He left the monastic order and married, and devoted himself to forming the League of Protestantism. Beside polemical treatises and hymns, he made a translation into German of the Old and New Testaments, known as the Lutheran Bible (1534; portions had appeared earlier).

Luther's power lay in his revival of the doctrine of justification by the faith of the individual, implying religious liberty and attacking the scandal of indulgences.

Luttrell, HENRY (1765?–1851), author of an admirable light verse poem, 'Advice to Julia' (1820).

Lux Mundi, a collection of essays on the Christian faith, by various hands, edited by C. Gore, principal of Pusey House (1889).

The collection is an attempt to present the central ideas and principles of the Catholic faith in the light of contemporary thought and current problems. It was written by a group of Oxford men engaged in university tuition.

LXX, the Septuagint (q.v.).

Lyall, EDNA, the pseudonym of ADA ELLEN BAYLY (1857-1903), novelist and ardent supporter of women's emancipation and of all political liberal movements. Her best-known novels were 'Donovan' (1882, admired by Gladstone), its sequel 'We Two' (1884), and 'In the Golden Days' (1885).

Lyceum, THE, a gymnasium outside the city of Athens, sacred to Apollo Lyceus, where Aristotle taught philosophy.

Lyceum Theatre, THE, in London, at first known as the English Opera House, was originally built in 1794, and rebuilt, after being destroyed by fire, in 1834. It is especially associated with the name of Sir Henry Irving.

Lycidas, a poem by Milton (q.v.), written in 1637, while at Horton.

It is an elegy, in pastoral form, on the death of Edward King, a fellow of Christ's College, Cambridge, who had been a student there at the same time as Milton. King was drowned while crossing from Chester Bay to Dublin, his ship having struck a rock and foundered in calm weather.

Lycurgus, the legendary legislator of Sparta. Little is known about him, but the reforms attributed to him are now dated about 600 B.C.

Lydgate, JOHN (1370?-1451?), probably of the Suffolk village of which he bears the name, and a monk of Bury St. Edmunds. He enjoyed the patronage of Duke Humphrey of Gloucester (q.v.). He was a most voluminous writer of verse. His chief poems are: 'Troy Book' (q.v.), written between 1412 and 1420, first printed in 1513; 'The Story of Thebes', written *c*. 1420, first printed *c*. 1500; 'Falls of Princes', founded on Boccaccio's 'De Casibus Virorum Illustrium', some 36,000 lines in rhyme-royal, written between 1430 and 1438, first printed in 1494. A minor poem, 'London Lickpenny' (edited for the Percy Society by Halliwell), which gives a vivid description of contemporary manners in London and Westminster,

was long ascribed to Lydgate but modern scholarship denies it to him. Lydgate wrote also devotional, philosophical, scientific, historical, and occasional poems, besides allegories, fables, and moral romances.

Lydia, a part of Asia Minor, adjoining the Aegean Sea.

Lydian mode, one of the three principal modes of ancient Greek music, a minor scale appropriate to soft pathos.

Lyell, SIR CHARLES (1797-1875), geologist, published his famous works 'The Principles of Geology' in 1830-3, 'The Elements of Geology' in 1838, and (after the appearance of Darwin's 'Origin of Species') 'The Antiquity of Man' in 1863. He completely revolutionized the prevailing ideas of the age of the earth, and substituted for the old conception of 'catastrophic' change the gradual process of natural laws.

Lyle, ANNOT, a character in Scott's 'A Legend of Montrose' (q.v.).

Lyly, JOHN (1554?-1606), was M.P. successively for Hindon, Aylesbury, and Appleby (1589-1601), and supported the cause of the bishops in the Martin Marprelate controversy in a worthless pamphlet, 'Pappe with an Hatchet' in 1589. The first part of his 'Euphues' (q.v.), 'The Anatomy of Wit', appeared in 1578, and the second part, 'Euphues and his England', in 1580. Its peculiar style (see *Euphues*) received the name 'Euphuism'. Lyly's best plays are 'Alexander and Campaspe' (1584, see *Campaspe*), 'Endimion' (1591), 'Midas' (1592), and 'The Woman in the Moone' (1597). For his 'Mother Bombie' see *Bumby*. His 'Sapho and Phao' was acted in 1584; 'Endimion' in 1591. The plays contain attractive lyrics, which were first printed in Blount's collected edition of the plays (1632). Lyly as a dramatist is important as the first English writer of what is essentially high comedy, and as having adopted prose as the medium for its expression.

Lyndsay, SIR DAVID, see *Lindsay (Sir D.)*.

Lynet(te) or LYONET or LINET, in the 'Morte Darthur', the sister of dame Lyones (q.v.). She marries Sir Gaheris. See also *Gareth and Lynette*.

Lyon King of Arms, the title of the chief herald in Scotland, so named from the lion on the royal shield.

Lyones or LYONESSE in Malory's 'Morte Darthur', the lady of the castle Perilous, whom Sir Gareth rescues and marries.

Lyonesse or LYONES or LYONAS, in the Arthurian legends, the country of Tristram's birth, is supposed to be a tract between Land's End and the Scilly Isles, now submerged.

Lyonors, see *Gareth and Lynette*.

Lyons Mail, The, originally 'The Courier of Lyons', a melodrama by C. Reade (q.v.), produced in 1854. It kept the stage and furnished one of Sir H. Irving's successful parts.

Lyra Apostolica, a collection of sacred poems contributed originally to the 'British Magazine' by Keble, Newman, R. H. Froude, Wilberforce, and I. Williams, and reprinted in a separate volume in 1836.

Lyric, a short poem, of a musical and rhythmical nature, expressing directly the poet's own feelings. Palgrave (q.v.) in his preface to the 'Golden Treasury' wrote: 'Lyrical has here been held essentially to imply that each poem shall turn on some single thought, feeling, or situation', a definition which is now generally accepted.

Lyrical Ballads, a collection of poems by Wordsworth and S. T. Coleridge (qq.v.), of which the first edition appeared in 1798, the second with new poems and a preface in 1800, and a third in 1802.

Coleridge in his 'Biographia Literaria' (q.v.), ch. xiv, describes how Wordsworth and he decided to divide the field between them: 'it was agreed that my endeavours should be directed to persons and characters supernatural or at least romantic. . . . Mr. Wordsworth, on the other hand, was to propose to himself as his object, to give the charm of novelty to things of every day. . . .' Coleridge's con-

tributions to the first edition were three, increased in the second to five ('The Ancient Mariner', 'The Foster-Mother's Tale', 'The Nightingale', 'The Dungeon', and 'Love'). Wordsworth contributed such simple tales as 'Goody Blake and Harry Gill' and 'Simon Lee the Old Huntsman'. His fine meditative poem 'Lines composed above Tintern Abbey' was also included.

The 'Lyrical Ballads', with their sudden revolt from the artificial literature of the day to the utmost simplicity of subject and diction, were unfavourably received; and the hostility of the critics was even increased by the appearance in the second edition of a preface in which Wordsworth expounded his poetical principles, and by his additional essay on 'Poetical Diction'.

Lysander, (1) a famous Spartan commander, who captured the Athenian fleet off Aegospotami in 405 B.C., and fell at the battle of Haliartus, 395 B.C.; (2) a character in Shakespeare's 'A Midsummer Night's Dream' (q.v.).

Lysias (*c.* 459–*c.* 380 B.C.), Athenian rhetorician and pleader.

Lyttelton, GEORGE, *first Baron Lyttelton* (1709–73), a political opponent of Walpole and for a short time chancellor of the exchequer (1756), was a friend of Pope and Fielding and a liberal patron of literature. It is he whom James Thomson addresses in 'The Seasons' (q.v.). He published, among numerous works, 'Dialogues of the Dead' (1760) and 'The History of the Life of Henry the Second' (1767–71). Of the 'Dialogues', Mrs. Montague (q.v.) was the author of the last three.

Lytton, BULWER, see *Lytton* (*E. G. E. L. B*-).

Lytton, EDWARD GEORGE EARLE LYTTON BULWER-, *first Baron Lytton* (1803–73), was secretary for the colonies in 1858–9, and was created Baron Lytton of Knebworth in 1866. The principal novels of this versatile author, written under the name Bulwer Lytton, were published at the following dates: 'Pelham' (1828), 'The Disowned' (1829), 'Eugene Aram' (q.v.,

1832), 'The Last Days of Pompeii' (q.v., 1834), 'Rienzi' (1835), 'The Last of the Barons' (q.v., 1843), 'Harold' (1848), 'The Caxtons' (1849), 'My Novel' (1853). In addition Lytton produced three plays, 'The Lady of Lyons' and 'Richelieu' (1838), and 'Money' (1840). His poem 'The New Timon' (1846) contained an incidental sarcasm on Tennyson, to which the latter replied in verse.

Lytton, EDWARD ROBERT BULWER, *first earl of Lytton* (1831-91), son of Edward Bulwer-Lytton, first Baron Lytton (q.v.), became viceroy of India (1876-80), where his 'Forward' policy was the subject of much opposition. He published a number of volumes of verse, at first under the pseudonym 'Owen Meredith'. His poetry in general is marred by prolixity, but has some good lyrics.

M

Mab, QUEEN, see *Queen Mab*.

Mabillon, JEAN (1632-1707), a Benedictine monk of St. Maur (see *Maurists*), author of 'De re diplomatica' (1681, with supplement 1704), in which he created the science of Latin palaeography and laid down the principles for the critical study of medieval archives.

Mabinogion, The, a collection of Welsh tales (*mabinogi* = instruction for young bards). Four 'Mabinogi' are contained in the 'Red Book of Hergest', compiled in the 14th and 15th cents. They deal with old Celtic legends and mythology, in which the supernatural and magical play the chief part. They are, said Matthew Arnold, the '*detritus* of something far older'. The four Mabinogi are concerned respectively with: (1) Pwyll, prince of Dyved; (2) Branwen, daughter of Llyr; (3) Manawyddan, son of Llyr; and (4) Math, son of Mathonwy; and they are to some extent interconnected.

Lady Charlotte Guest published in 1838-49 a collection of eleven Welsh tales, with translation and notes, including the Mabinogi, under the title of 'Mabinogion'.

There is no mention of Arthur in the four Mabinogi, but among Lady Charlotte Guest's other seven Welsh tales from the 'Red Book of Hergest' there are five that deal with him.

Macabre, DANSE, see *Dance of Death*.

Macaroni, an exquisite of a class which arose in England about 1760 and consisted of young men who had travelled and affected foreign tastes and fashions.

Macaronic verse, a burlesque form of verse in which vernacular words are introduced into a Latin context with Latin terminations and in Latin constructions; also applied loosely to any form of verse in which two or more languages are mingled together.

Macaulay, DAME ROSE (1881-1958), novelist, whose works include: 'Potterism' (1920), 'Told by an Idiot' (1923), 'Orphan Island' (1924), 'Going Abroad' (1934), 'The World My Wilderness' (1950), and 'The Towers of Trebizond' (1956). She wrote a study of Milton in 1933.

Macaulay, THOMAS BABINGTON, *first Baron Macaulay* (1800-59), son of Zachary Macaulay, the philanthropist. His first article (on Milton) was published in 1825 in 'The Edinburgh Review' (q.v.), of which he became a mainstay. He was a member of the supreme council of India from 1834 to 1838. There he exerted his influence in favour of the choice of an English, instead of an oriental, type of education in India. He returned to London and engaged in literature and politics; he was secretary of war in 1839-41, and paymaster of the forces in 1846-7. He published his 'Lays of Ancient Rome' (q.v.) in 1842, and a collection of his 'Essays' (q.v.) in 1843 (enlarged in later editions). Volumes i and ii of his 'History of England' (see below) appeared in 1849, iii and iv in 1855 (vol. v, published in 1861, was edited by his sister, Lady Trevelyan). He also contributed to the 'Encyclopaedia Britannica' a remarkable series of articles on Atterbury, Bunyan, Goldsmith, Johnson, and the younger Pitt.

Macaulay's History of England from the Accession of James II, by T. B. Macaulay (q.v.), in five volumes (1849-61).

Macaulay had hoped to write the history of England from the reign of James II to the time of Sir Robert Walpole; but the work does not go beyond the death of William III, and, as regards the reign of the latter king, is incomplete. The 'History' is written on a vast scale, involving immense research, and presents a detailed and vivid picture of the age. The hero is William III, and the work, written from a Whig and Protestant point of view, is criticized as showing partiality. Nevertheless, it was, and remains, extremely popular, and is one of the great literary works of the 19th cent.

Macaulay's New Zealander, whom the author imagines, in the distant future, visiting London when it is a ruined city.

Macaulay's Schoolboy: Macaulay was apt to attribute to schoolboys a range of historical and literary knowledge not usually found among them. With regard to some abstruse statement he would assert that 'any schoolboy of fourteen' knew better.

Macbeth, a tragedy by Shakespeare (q.v.), founded on Holinshed's 'Chronicle of Scottish History', and probably finished in 1606; it was no doubt designed as a tribute to King James I. First printed in the folio of 1623.

Macbeth and Banquo, generals of Duncan, king of Scotland, returning from a victorious campaign against rebels, encounter the three weird sisters, or witches, upon a heath, who prophesy that Macbeth shall be thane of Cawdor, and king thereafter, and that Banquo shall beget kings though he be none. Immediately after comes the news that the king has created Macbeth thane of Cawdor. Stimulated by the prophecy, and spurred on by Lady Macbeth, Macbeth murders Duncan while on a visit to his castle. Duncan's sons, Malcolm and Donalbain, escape, and Macbeth assumes the crown. To defeat the prophecy of the witches regarding Banquo, he contrives the murder of Banquo and his son Fleance, but the latter escapes. Haunted by the ghost of Banquo, Macbeth consults the weird sisters, and is told to beware of Macduff, the thane of Fife; that none born of woman has power to harm Macbeth; and that he never will be vanquished till Birnam Wood shall come to Dunsinane. Learning that Macduff has joined Malcolm, who is gathering an army in England, he surprises the castle of Macduff and causes Lady Macduff and her children to be slaughtered. Lady Macbeth loses her reason and dies. The army of Malcolm and Macduff attacks Macbeth; passing through Birnam Wood every man cuts a bough and under this 'leavy screen' marches on Dunsinane. Macduff, who was 'from his mother's womb untimely ripped', kills Macbeth. Malcolm is hailed king of Scotland.

Maccabaeus, JUDAS, see *Judas Maccabaeus*.

Maccabees, THE, a family of Jews who led the revolt of their compatriots against the oppression of the Syrian king, Antiochus Epiphanes (175-164 B.C.). They afterwards established a dynasty of priest-kings.

McCarthy, JUSTIN (1830-1912), Irish politician, historian, and novelist, author of the 'History of Our Own Times' (published in several editions, 1879-1907). His best-known novels are: 'Dear Lady Disdain' (1875) and 'Miss Misanthrope' (1878).

McDiarmid, HUGH, see *Grieve* (*C. M.*).

Macdonald, FLORA (1722-90), a Jacobite

heroine who helped Prince Charles Edward to escape after Culloden (q.v.) by disguising him as her female servant.

Macdonald, GEORGE (1824-1905), poet and novelist, author of 'Within and Without' (1855, a narrative poem admired by Tennyson); 'David Elginbrod' (1863), 'Alec Forbes' (1865), and 'Robert Falconer' (1868), prose fiction, the first mystical in character, the others descriptive of Scottish humble life.

Macduff and **Lady Macduff,** characters in Shakespeare's 'Macbeth' (q.v.).

Mac Flecknoe, or A Satyr upon the True-Blew-Protestant Poet, T.S., a satire against Shadwell (q.v.) by Dryden (q.v.), probably written *c.* 1679 (authorized ed. 1684).

Shadwell had replied to Dryden's 'Medal' (q.v.) by the 'Medal of John Bayes', and moreover had called Dryden an atheist. Dryden thereupon dealt with the political character of Shadwell in the second part of 'Absalom and Achitophel' (q.v.), and with his literary character in this work. Flecknoe, an Irish writer of verse, who had been satirized by Marvell, is represented as passing on to Shadwell his pre-eminence in the realm of dullness.

McGill University, THE, in Canada, commemorates James McGill (1744-1813), who left £30,000 for the foundation of a university. A charter was granted in 1821, but it was not until the middle of the century that the institution became prosperous. It has its headquarters at Montreal, with affiliated colleges in certain other centres.

Macgregor, ROB ROY, see *Rob Roy*.

Machaon, a son of Aesculapius (q.v.), and one of the two surgeons of the Greek army in the Trojan War.

Machaut or MACHAULT, GUILLAUME DE (*c.* 1300-77), French poet. He was author of ballades and of several long poems, of interest because of their influence on Chaucer, notably in 'The Boke of the Duchesse' (q.v.).

Macheath, CAPTAIN, the hero of Gay's 'The Beggar's Opera' (q.v.).

Machiavelli, NICCOLÒ (1469-1527), a Florentine statesman and political theorist. He wrote his 'Art of War' between 1517 and 1520 (translated into English in 1560-2) and his 'Florentine History' in 1520-5 (translated in 1595). But his best-known work was the 'Prince' (written in 1513), a treatise on statecraft by an acute observer of the contemporary political scene with an idealistic vision of an Italian saviour who should expel all foreign usurpers. He teaches that the lessons of the past should be applied to the present, and that the acquisition and effective use of power may necessitate unethical methods. Although manuscript English versions of the work were circulating earlier, the first published translation was that of Edward Dacres in 1640. It is none the less repeatedly referred to in the Elizabethan drama, and influenced the policy of Thomas Cromwell, Cecil, and Leicester. There is a sketch of Machiavelli's character in George Eliot's 'Romola' (q.v.).

'The New Machiavelli' is a novel (1911) by H. G. Wells (q.v.).

M'Intyre, CAPTAIN HECTOR and MARIA, in Scott's 'The Antiquary' (q.v.), nephew and niece of Jonathan Oldbuck.

Mac-Ivor, FERGUS, of Glennaquoich, or VICH IAN VOHR, a character in Scott's 'Waverley' (q.v.).

Mackenzie, SIR COMPTON (1883-1972), author, among whose chief works are: 'Carnival' (1912), 'Sinister Street' (2 vols., 1913-14), 'Guy and Pauline' (1915), 'Vestal Fire' (1927), 'Our Street' (1931), 'The Four Winds of Love' (6 vols., 1937-45), 'Whisky Galore' (1947), all novels; 'Gallipoli Memories' (1929), 'First Athenian Memories' (1931), 'My Life and Times. Octave 1. 1883-91; Octave 2. 1891-1900' (1963); 'Octave 3. 1900-1907' (1964); 'Octave 4. 1907-1915' (1965); 'Octave 5. 1915-1923' (1966); 'Octave 6. 1923-1930' (1967), 'Octave 7. 1930-38' (1968), 'Octave 8. 1938-46' (1969), 'Octave 9. 1946-52' (1970), and 'Octave 10. 1953-63' (1971), autobiography.

Mackenzie, HENRY (1745-1831), the author of 'The Man of Feeling' (1771), in which the hero is presented in a series of sentimental sketches loosely woven together, somewhat after the manner of Addison's Sir Roger. This book was one of Burns's 'bosom favourites'. It was followed in 1773 by 'The Man of the World'; and in 1777 by 'Julia de Roubigné', a novel after the manner of Richardson's 'Clarissa' (q.v.). Mackenzie was sometimes spoken of as the 'Addison of the North'.

Mackenzie, MRS. and ROSEY, characters in Thackeray's 'The Newcomes' (q.v.).

McKerrow, RONALD BRUNLEES (1872–1940), bibliographer and Elizabethan scholar. Was joint secretary of the Bibliographical Society; editor of the 'Review of English Studies' from 1925 until his death.

Mackintosh, SIR JAMES (1765–1832), the author of 'Vindiciae Gallicae' (1791), a reasoned defence of the French Revolution and an answer to Burke's 'Reflections on the Revolution in France'. Mackintosh subsequently recanted, and finally summed up in 1815 in his 'On the State of France'. His 'Dissertation on the Progress of Ethical Philosophy' (1830) provoked James Mill's 'Fragment on Mackintosh'. He also wrote the first three volumes of a 'History of England' (1830–1), and an unfinished 'History of the Revolution in England in 1688' (1834).

Macklin, CHARLES (1697?–1797), an actor who made his reputation by his impersonation of Shylock. He was author of the comedies 'The Man of the World', produced in 1781, and 'Love à la Mode', produced in 1759.

MacLeish, ARCHIBALD (1892–   ), American poet and dramatist. He was one of the American expatriates in Paris in the 1920s, and was strongly influenced by T. S. Eliot and Ezra Pound (qq.v.). Among his early volumes of verse are 'The Pot of Earth' (1924) and 'The Hamlet of A. MacLeish' (1928). His 'Collected Poems 1917–1952' appeared in 1953. His verse dramas include 'Panic' (1935), 'The Fall of the City' (1937), and 'J. B.' (1958).

Macmorris, CAPTAIN, in Shakespeare's 'Henry V' (q.v.), the only Irishman presented in Shakespeare's plays.

Macmurray, JOHN, originally the name of John Murray (q.v.).

MacNeice, LOUIS (1907–63), poet, born in Belfast. During the 1930s he was associated as a poet with Auden and Spender but was more detached politically than they. In 1941 he joined the staff of the B.B.C. and wrote many radio scripts and features. His work includes 'Poems' (1935), 'The Earth Compels' (1938), 'Autumn Journal' (1939), 'Plant and Phantom' (1941), and other volumes of verse, as well as translations of Aeschylus' 'Agamemnon' and Goethe's 'Faust'. He also wrote a study of Yeats (1941). His collected poems appeared in 1949.

Macpherson, JAMES (1736–96), a man of considerable literary ability, with some knowledge of Gaelic poetry. In 1760 he published 'Fragments of Ancient Poetry collected in the Highlands of Scotland, and translated from the Gaelic or Erse language'. Then with the assistance of 'several gentlemen in the Highlands' he produced in 1762 'Fingal, an ancient epic poem in six books' (see under *Fingal*), and in 1763 'Temora', another epic, in eight books, purporting to be translations from the Gaelic of a poet called Ossian (q.v.). They were much admired for their romantic spirit, but their authenticity was challenged, notably by Dr. Johnson. Called upon to produce his originals, Macpherson was obliged to fabricate them. A committee appointed after his death to investigate the Ossianic poems, reported that Macpherson had liberally edited traditional Gaelic poems and inserted passages of his own.

Macready, WILLIAM CHARLES (1793–1873), first achieved eminence as an actor by his impersonation of Richard III (1819), and subsequently of King Lear. Tennyson wrote a sonnet on his retirement from the stage in 1851.

MacStinger, MRS., in Dickens's 'Dombey and Son' (q.v.), Captain Cuttle's termagant landlady.

Macwheeble, BAILIE DUNCAN, a character in Scott's 'Waverley' (q.v.).

Madame Bovary, the chief work of Gustave Flaubert (q.v.).

Madge Wildfire, see *Murdockson*.

Mad Hatter, THE, see *Hatter*.

Madoc, a poem by Southey (q.v.) (1805).

Madvig, JOHANN NICOLAI (1804–86), Danish scholar and philologist, professor at Copenhagen of Latin, and later of classical philology, and author of a celebrated Latin grammar (1841).

Maeander, a river of Phrygia, remarkable for its numerous windings; the origin of our verb 'to meander'.

Maecenas, GAIUS CILNIUS (*c.* 70–8 B.C.), a Roman knight who became celebrated for his patronage of learning and letters in the time of Augustus.

Maeldune or MAILDUN, the hero of an ancient Irish legend, who sets out in a ship to avenge his father, slain by plunderers shortly before his birth. After visiting many lands, he is persuaded by a holy man to forgive his enemy, as God has forgiven him. Maeldune finds his enemy and they are reconciled. The legend forms the subject of Tennyson's 'The Voyage of Maeldune'.

Maelstrom, a famous whirlpool in the Arctic Ocean off the west coast of Norway. Poe (q.v.) wrote an imaginative description of 'A Descent into the Maelström'.

Maenads, a name of the Bacchantes (q.v.) or priestesses of Bacchus.

Maeonia, an early name for Lydia (q.v.). The epithet *Maeonian* is sometimes applied to Homer.

Maeterlinck, MAURICE (1862–1949), Belgian poetic-dramatist and essayist. His Symbolist dramas include: 'La Princesse Maleine' (1889), 'Pelléas et Mélisande' (1892), 'Monna Vanna' (1902). 'L'Oiseau bleu' (1909) is a fairy play. His essays, of a philosophical character, include 'Le Trésor des humbles' (1896), 'La Vie des abeilles' (1901), and 'La Mort' (1912). He received the Nobel Prize for

literature in 1911. His early works show a more sombre imagination than his later essays: death and love and dark mysteries governing men's lives.

Maeviad, The, see *Gifford*.

Maffick, To, to indulge in extravagant demonstrations of exultation on occasions of national rejoicing. A word originally used of the behaviour of the crowds in London on the occasion of the relief of Mafeking (17 May 1900).

Maga, a familiar name for 'Blackwood's Edinburgh Magazine' (q.v.).

Magazine, originally a place where goods are laid up, has come also to mean a periodical publication containing articles by different authors. Thus 'The Gentleman's Magazine' in the introduction to its first number (1731) described itself as 'a Monthly Collection to store up, as in a Magazine, the most remarkable Pieces on the Subjects above-mentioned'. But the word had been used before this for a storehouse of information.

Magdalen, MAGDALENE (pron. 'Maudlen' in the names of Magdalen College, Oxford, and Magdalene College, Cambridge), the appellation (signifying a woman of Magdala) of a disciple of Christ named Mary. She has commonly been supposed to be identical with the unnamed 'sinner' of Luke vii. 37. The word is used to signify one whose history resembles that of the Magdalene.

MAGDALEN HOSPITAL, a home for refuge and reformation of prostitutes.

Magdeburg, CENTURIATORS OF, a number of Protestant divines who in the 16th cent. compiled a Church History in thirteen volumes.

Magellan, the English form of the name of the Portuguese navigator Fernão de Magalhães (1470?–1521), the first European to pass through the straits that bear his name.

Magi, the ancient Persian priestly caste, the priests of Zoroastrianism.

THE (THREE) MAGI, the three wise men who came from the East, bearing offerings to the infant Christ, named according to tradition, Gaspar, Melchior, and Balthazar. (See also *Cologne*.)

Magic Flute, The, 'Die Zauberflöte', a famous opera by Mozart (q.v.); also a book by G. Lowes Dickinson (1920).

Maginn, WILLIAM (1793–1842), one of the principal early contributors to 'Blackwood's Edinburgh Magazine' (q.v.) under the pseudonym of Ensign O'Doherty, and perhaps the originator of the 'Noctes Ambrosianae' (q.v.). He settled in London in 1823 and wrote for various periodicals. But his best work is contained in his shorter stories and verses, which are marked by humour, wit, and pathos. He was the original of Captain Shandon in Thackeray's 'Pendennis' (q.v.).

Magna Carta, the Great Charter of the liberties of England, granted by King John under pressure from the Barons, at Runnymede in Surrey, on 15 June 1215.

Magnet, The, a weekly paper for boys written by C. Hamilton (q.v.) under the pen-name Frank Richards, 1908–40.

Magnetic Lady, The, or *Humours Reconciled*, a comedy by Jonson (q.v.), produced in 1632.

Magnus, MR. PETER, a character in Dickens's 'The Pickwick Papers' (q.v.).

Magog, see *Gog*.

Magog Wrath and **Bully Bluck**, in Disraeli's 'Coningsby' the hired leaders of the two political parties in the Darlford constituency.

Magwitch, ABEL, a character in Dickens's 'Great Expectations' (q.v.).

Mahābhārata, The, one of the two great epics (the other being the 'Rāmāyana') of the Hindus. They are believed to have been composed before 500 B.C., but, in the form in which we have it, the 'Mahābhārata' probably dates from 200 B.C.

Mahatma, meaning 'great-souled'; in 'esoteric Buddhism', one of a class of persons with preternatural powers imagined to exist in India and Tibet. The word is also used by Theosophists.

Mahdi, a spiritual and temporal leader expected by the Muslims. The title is especially applied to Mohammed Ahmed (1843–85), who destroyed General Hicks's army in 1883, besieged Gordon (q.v.) in Khartoum, and overthrew the Egyptian power in the Sudan.

Mahomet, see *Mohammed*. 'Mahomet' is the title of a drama by Voltaire (q.v.).

Mahony, FRANCIS SYLVESTER (1804–66), best known by his pseudonym of FATHER PROUT, a Jesuit (dismissed from the order in 1830) and author of many entertaining papers and poems contributed to 'Fraser's Magazine' and 'Bentley's Miscellany'. The contributions were collected in 1836 as 'The Reliques of Father Prout'. He is best remembered for his 'Bells of Shandon'.

Mahound, the 'false prophet' Mohammed; in the Middle Ages often vaguely imagined to be worshipped as a god.

Mahu, the fiend of stealing, one of the five that pestered 'poor Tom' in Shakespeare's 'King Lear' (IV. i).

Maia, a daughter of Atlas, one of the Pleiades, and the mother by Zeus of Hermes.

Maid Marian, a female personage in the May-game and Morris-dance. In the later forms of the story of Robin Hood she appears as the companion of the outlaw.

Maid Marian, a novel by Peacock (q.v.) (1822). It is a gay parody of medieval romance, based on the story of Robin Hood, and contains some excellent songs.

Maid of Athens, THE, in Byron's poem is said to have been the daughter of Theodore Macri, who was a consul at Athens.

Maid of Honour, The, a romantic drama by Massinger (q.v.), published in 1632.

Maid of Orleans, Joan of Arc (q.v.).

Maid of Saragoza, THE, Agustina, whose bravery in the defence of Saragossa against the French in 1808-9 was celebrated by Byron in his 'Childe Harold' (I. liv–lvi).

Maid's Tragedy, The, a tragedy by Beaumont and Fletcher (see *Fletcher, J.*) (1619), generally accounted the best of their dramas.

Maigret, Le Commissaire, the detective-superintendent in the crime stories of G. Simenon (q.v.).

Maildun, see *Maeldune*.

Maimonides (1135-1204), a Jew of Cordova, rationalist and philosopher. His chief work was 'The Guide for the Perplexed', of which there are English, French, and German translations.

Main Street, a novel by Sinclair Lewis (q.v.) (1920).

Maitland, Frederic William (1850-1906), became reader in English law at Cambridge and, from 1888 until his death, Downing professor. His first important work was 'Bracton's Note-Book' (1887), followed by the 'History of English Law before the time of Edward I' (1895), in collaboration with Sir Frederick Pollock. His Essays on 'Domesday Book and Beyond' (1897), his Ford lectures on 'Township and Borough' (1898), his Rede lecture on 'English Law and the Renaissance' (1901), were other notable productions.

Major or Mair, John (1469-1550), 'the last of the schoolmen'. He studied at Cambridge and Paris, where he became doctor of theology. He lectured at Glasgow and St. Andrews and then returned to Paris, where he was regarded as the most eminent exponent of medieval learning. He published between 1509 and 1517 a Latin 'Commentary on the Sentences of Peter Lombard', and in 1521 a Latin 'History of Greater Britain, both England and Scotland' in which he advocated the union of the two kingdoms.

Major Gahagan, Some Passages in the Life of, and *Historical Recollections by*, an early work by Thackeray (q.v.), published in the 'New Monthly Magazine' in 1838-9.

Majuscule, a large letter or script, used in palaeography to denote the scripts of Greek or Roman antiquity, uncial (q.v.) or capital.

Malagrowther, Sir Mungo, a character in Scott's 'The Fortunes of Nigel' (q.v.).

Malaprop, Mrs., in Sheridan's 'The Rivals' (q.v.), the aunt and guardian of Lydia Languish, noted for her aptitude for misapplying long words, e.g. 'as headstrong as an allegory on the banks of the Nile'. Hence a 'malapropism', an error of this kind.

Malbecco, in Spenser's 'Faerie Queene' (iii. ix. x), a 'cancred crabbed carle', jealous and avaricious, married to the lovely Hellenore. Paridell elopes with her, and Malbecco, unable to escape from his jealous thoughts, throws himself from a rock.

Malbrouk s'en va-t-en guerre, the first line of an old French song, perhaps, but not very probably, referring to the campaigns of the duke of Marlborough. The tune resembles that of 'We won't go home till morning'.

Maldon, Battle of, a poem in Old English, perhaps of the 10th cent., dealing with the raid of the Northmen under Anlaf, at Maldon in Essex, in 991. The Northmen are drawn up on the shore of the Blackwater. The ealdorman Byrhtnoth, friend of Ælfric, exhorts his men to stand firm. An offer by the herald of the Northmen that their attack shall be bought off by payment of tribute is scornfully rejected. The fight is delayed by the rising tide which separates the two armies. Then Byrhtnoth is slain with a poisoned spear and some of his men flee. A fresh attack is led by Ælfwine, son of Ælfric. Godric falls. The end of the poem is lost. The poem is remarkable for the way in which, at this late period in Anglo-Saxon literature, it recaptures the purity of the epic tradition.

Maldon, Jack, in Dickens's 'David Copperfield' (q.v.), the scapegrace cousin of Mrs. Strong.

Male or Masculine **Rhymes**, see *Rhyme*.

Male Règle, La, see *Occleve*.

Malebolge, the name given by Dante to his eighth circle in Hell.

Malecasta, 'unchaste', in Spenser's 'Faerie Queene', iii. i, the lady of Castle Joyeous.

Maleger, in Spenser's 'Faerie Queene', II. xi, the captain of twelve troops, the seven deadly sins and the evil passions that assail the senses.

Malengin, in Spenser's 'Faerie Queene', v. ix, the personification of guile.

Mall, THE, a walk along the N. side of St. James's Park, London, originally a 'mall' where the game of 'pall mall' was played. It was a fashionable promenade in the 17th-18th cents.

Mallarmé, STÉPHANE (1842-98), French poet, the leader of the Symbolist movement at its height, author of the poem 'L'Après-midi d'un faune'.

Mallet (or MALLOCH), DAVID (1705?-65), author of the well-known ballad of 'William and Margaret'. He collaborated with J. Thomson (1700-48, q.v.) in the masque of 'Alfred', which contains 'Rule, Britannia'; but that song is generally attributed to Thomson. Mallet was the literary executor of Bolingbroke (q.v.).

Malleus Maleficarum, or *Hexenhammer*, the 'Hammer of Witches' (1484), by Jakob Sprenger and Heinrich Krämer. It was the textbook of the day on witchcraft, setting forth how it may be discovered and how it should be punished.

Malloch, DAVID, see *Mallet*.

Mallock, WILLIAM HURRELL (1849-1923), best known as author of 'The New Republic' (1877), a lively satire on English society and ideas, in which Ruskin figures as Mr. Herbert, and Jowett, Matthew Arnold, Pater, Huxley, Tyndall, etc., figure under thin disguises among the other characters. Mallock's other works include various studies of social and economic science directed against the doctrines of socialism.

Malmesbury, THE SAGE OF, Hobbes (q.v.).

Malmesbury, WILLIAM OF, see *William of Malmesbury*.

Malone, EDMOND (1741-1812), literary critic and Shakespearian scholar. He published in 1778 his 'Attempt to ascertain the Order in which the Plays of Shakespeare were written', and an edition of the works in 1790. A member of The Club and a friend of Boswell, he revised the 'Tour to the Hebrides', 1785, while it was going through the press, and gave great assistance with 'The Life of Johnson', 1791.

Malone Society, THE, was founded in 1906 for the purpose of making accessible materials for the study of early English drama.

Malory, SIR THOMAS (d. 1471), author of 'Le Morte Darthur' (q.v.), is identified by E. Vinaver with Sir Thomas Malory, Knight of Newbold Revel (Warwicks.) and Winwick (Northants.) who succeeded to his estates in 1433 or 1434. In 1450 he was charged with attempted murder, and he later suffered terms of imprisonment for various major crimes. He sat for his shire in Parliament in 1456, with the earl of Warwick followed Edward IV to Northumberland, and, probably with Warwick, joined the Lancastrians, for he is excluded by name from two pardons granted them by Edward. Three 'prayers for deliverance' occurring in his manuscript suggest that he wrote most of it to occupy himself while in prison, attracted by the adventurous content of the French Arthurian material.

Malperdy (*Malpertuis*), the castle of 'Reynard the Fox' (q.v.).

Malraux, ANDRÉ (1901-76), French novelist, essayist, and art-historian, whose outstanding works include: 'La Condition humaine' (1933), a novel of early Communism in China; 'L'Espoir' (1937), a novel about the Spanish Civil War of 1936; 'Psychologie de l'art' (1948-50, 3 vols.), art history. Phases in Malraux's career have been his early sympathy with Communist ideals, anti-Nazi and Resistance activities, and, under the Fifth Republic, ministerial responsibility for the furtherance of culture.

Malta, KNIGHTS OF, see *Hospitallers of St. John of Jerusalem*.

Malthus, THOMAS ROBERT (1766-1834), became curate of Albury in Surrey in 1798. In that year he published 'An

Essay on the Principle of Population', in which he argued that population would soon increase beyond the means of subsistence and that checks on this increase are necessary. The 'Essay' was recast in the second edition (1803); in this the author somewhat modifies his conclusions. The work aroused a storm of controversy and exerted a powerful influence on social thought in the 19th cent.

Malvolio, a character in Shakespeare's 'Twelfth Night' (q.v.).

Mamelukes, a military body, originally composed of Caucasian slaves of the Sultan of Egypt. They seized the government of Egypt in 1254 and Mameluke sultans reigned from 1254 to 1517. Subsequently Egypt was governed, under the nominal rule of a Turkish viceroy, by twenty-four Mameluke beys. In 1811 the remaining Mamelukes were massacred by Mohammed Ali, pasha of Egypt.

Mammet or MAUMET, a corruption of Mahomet, a false god, an idol, a doll.

Mammon, the Aramaic word for 'riches'. The name was taken by medieval writers as the proper name of the devil of covetousness. This use was revived by Milton in 'Paradise Lost', i. 678 and ii. 228.

Mammon, SIR EPICURE, in Jonson's 'The Alchemist' (q.v.), an arrogant, avaricious, voluptuous knight.

Mammon, THE CAVE OF, in Spenser's 'Faerie Queene', II. vii, is the treasurehouse of the god of wealth, visited by Sir Guyon.

Mammon, The Triumph of, see *God and Mammon.*

Man and Superman, a comedy by G. B. Shaw (q.v.) (1903); 'a stage projection of the tragi-comic love chase of the man by the woman'.

Manchester Guardian, The, founded in 1821 as a weekly, and in 1855 as a daily, paper; the principal liberal organ outside London, edited 1872-1929 by Charles Prestwich Scott (1846-1932). It became a national paper after the Second World War and in 1959 its title was changed to 'The Guardian'.

Manchester Massacre, THE, see *Peterloo.*

Manchester School, the name first applied by Disraeli to the political party, led by Cobden and Bright, who advocated the principles of free trade.

Manciple's Tale, The, see *Canterbury Tales.*

Mancus, an old English money of account worth thirty pence. See *Peter's Pence.*

Mandaeans, a body of pagan Gnostics of whom a small community survives south of Baghdad.

Mandeville, BERNARD DE (1670-1733), author of a satire in octosyllabic verse, entitled 'The Grumbling Hive, or Knaves turned Honest' (1705), reissued with a prose commentary as 'The Fable of the Bees, or Private Vices, Public Benefits' (1714), designed to illustrate the essential vileness of human nature. Society, like a hive of bees, thrives on a system of mutual rapacities. The paradox was widely controverted, among others by W. Law (q.v.), and by Berkeley in his 'Alciphron' (q.v.).

Mandeville, SIR JOHN, was the ostensible author of a book of travels bearing his name, composed soon after the middle of the 14th cent., purporting to be an account of his own journeys in the East, but really a mere compilation. The work was written originally in French, from which English, Latin, German, and other translations were made.

The writer of this remarkable literary forgery remains unknown, but probability points to a certain Jean d'Outremeuse, a writer of histories and fables, who lived at Liège at the time in question.

The 'Voiage of Sir John Maundevile' purports to be a guide to pilgrims to the Holy Land, but carries the reader a good deal farther, to Turkey, Tartary, Persia, Egypt, and India. It is an entertaining work combining geography and natural history with romance and marvels, such as the fountain of youth and ant-hills of gold dust.

Manes, the deified souls of the departed, whom the ancient Romans thought it desirable to propitiate.

Manette, Dr. and Lucie, characters in Dickens's 'A Tale of Two Cities' (q.v.).

Manfred, a dramatic poem by Lord Byron (q.v.) (1817).

Manfred, guilty of some inexpiable and mysterious crime, living among the Alps an outcast from society, is tortured by remorse. He calls up the spirits of the universe; they offer him everything but the one thing he seeks—oblivion. He visits the Hall of Arimanes (Ahriman) and has a vision of Astarte, the woman whom he has loved. She foretells his death on the morrow. At the appointed time, demons appear to summon him. He denies their power over him; they disappear, and Manfred expires.

Manichaeism, a religious system widely accepted from the 3rd to the 5th cent. Like Mithraism, which it replaced, it was of Iranian origin, and was composed of Gnostic, Christian, and pagan elements.

The essential feature of the system is its dualistic theology, of which the principal elements are light and darkness, God and Satan, the soul and the body. A conflict is in progress between the demons and the angels of light for the possession of mankind.

Manilius, the name given to the author of 'Astronomica', a Latin poem in five books on astrology and astronomy, written in the time of Augustus and Tiberius. An edition of the poem was published by A. E. Housman (5 vols., 1903-30).

Man in Black, The, (1) a character in Goldsmith's 'Citizen of the World' (q.v.), a man generous to profusion, who wishes to be thought a prodigy of parsimony; (2) the Jesuit priest in Borrow's 'Romany Rye' (q.v.).

Man in the Iron Mask, The, see *Iron Mask.*

Man in the Moon, The, a fancied figure, with a bundle of sticks on his back, made by the shadows on the moon. The nursery tale is that he is a man banished to the moon for gathering sticks on the Sabbath (an allusion to Num. xv. 32 et seq.).

Manitou, one of the American Indian deities or spirits, both good and bad, which dominate nature.

Manley, Mrs. Mary de la Rivière (1663-1724), avenged herself on society for an unhappy life by her 'New Atalantis' (1709), in which Whigs and persons of note were slandered. She was arrested but escaped punishment. She wrote other scandalous memoirs and several plays, and succeeded Swift as editor of 'The Examiner' in 1711.

Mann, Thomas (1875-1955), German novelist and essayist. He went into emigration in the Nazi period. 'Buddenbrooks', a novel with autobiographical features, appeared in 1901 and quickly made him famous. It was followed by 'Tonio Kröger' (1903), 'Der Tod in Venedig' (1912), 'Der Zauberberg' (1924), and the Joseph novels (in four parts, 1933-43). Constantly concerned about the role and character of the artist, he linked this theme with the problem of Nazism in his novel 'Dr. Faustus' (1947), and elaborated the subject in a book about this novel 'Die Entstehung des Dr. Faustus' (1949). His last full-length novel, 'Die Bekenntnisse des Hochstaplers Felix Krull' (1954), derived from the picaresque tradition. He was awarded a Nobel Prize in 1929.

Manning, Henry Edward (1808-92), became archdeacon of Chichester in 1840. In 1851 he joined the Roman Catholic Church, and became archbishop of Westminster in 1865 and cardinal in 1875. He published many religious and polemical works, including 'The Vatican Decrees' (1875) in reply to W. E. Gladstone. He was a great preacher and ecclesiastical statesman, of ascetic temper, and a subtle controversialist. He was a contemporary and in his career a rival of Newman (q.v.).

Mannyng, Robert, of Brunne, see *Handlyng Synne.*

Manoa, see *El Dorado.*

Man of Blood, THE, (1) David, king of Israel (2 Sam. xvi. 7, R.V.); (2) Charles I, so called by the Puritans.

Man of Brass, see *Talus*.

Man of Destiny, Napoleon I.

Man of Feeling, The, a novel by H. Mackenzie (q.v.).

Man of Law's Tale, The, see *Canterbury Tales*.

Man of Mode, The, or *Sir Fopling Flutter*, a comedy by Etherege (q.v.), produced in 1676. The play has no plot. It is a picture of a society living exclusively for pleasure, a slight web of love-affairs providing the occasion for brilliant dialogue and character-drawing.

Man of Ross, see *Kyrle*.

Man of the World, The, (1) a novel by H. Mackenzie (q.v.) (1773); (2) a comedy by Macklin (q.v.), produced in 1781.

Man of Wrath, THE, the husband in 'Elizabeth and her German Garden' (q.v.).

Manon Lescaut, Histoire du Chevalier des Grieux et de, a famous novel by the Abbé Prévost (1731).

Mansfield, KATHERINE, pen-name of KATHLEEN MANSFIELD BEAUCHAMP (1888–1923), short-story writer, born in New Zealand, and educated there and in London, where she went in 1903. Apart from a stay in New Zealand from 1906 to 1908, she spent the rest of her life in Europe, writing stories and continually seeking higher standards in her art, while at the same time battling with persistent ill health. Her work includes 'Bliss and Other Stories' (1920), 'The Garden Party' (1922), and 'The Dove's Nest' (1923). Her 'Collected Stories' were published in 1945. Her 'Journal' (1927) and 'Letters' (1928) were edited by her husband, John Middleton Murry (q.v.).

Mansfield Park, a novel by Jane Austen (q.v.), begun in 1812 and published in 1814.

Sir Thomas Bertram of Mansfield Park, a pompous baronet, has two sons, Tom and Edmund, and two daughters, Maria and Julia. His wife, a selfish, indolent woman, has two sisters, the widow Mrs. Norris, selfish and spiteful, a near neighbour, and Mrs. Price, wife of an impecunious officer of marines, with a large family of young children. In order to assist the latter, the Bertrams undertake the charge of Fanny Price, a girl of 9. In spite of her humble situation and the constant bullying of Mrs. Norris, Fanny, by her honesty and modest disposition, gradually becomes an indispensable part of the household. Her sterling character is especially shown during Sir Thomas's absence in the West Indies, when the family discipline is relaxed, private theatricals are indulged in, and there is some unseemly flirtation between Maria Bertram, who is engaged to marry Mr. Rushworth, 'a heavy young man, with not more than common sense', and Henry Crawford, the attractive but unprincipled brother-in-law of the local parson. Against all this Fanny resolutely sets her face. Loving her cousin Edmund, she grieves to see him fascinated by the worldly-minded Mary Crawford, Henry's sister. Maria having become Mrs. Rushworth, Henry Crawford turns his attention to Fanny, falls in love with her, and proposes. Fanny unhesitatingly rejects him, incurring the grave displeasure of Sir Thomas by what he regards as a piece of ungrateful perversity. During a visit paid by Fanny to her own home, matters come to a crisis. Henry, accidentally thrown again into contact with Mrs. Rushworth, runs away with her; and Julia elopes with an ineligible suitor, Mr. Yates. Mary Crawford's failure to reprobate her brother's conduct, coupled with her aversion to marrying a clergyman (Edmund has now taken orders), finally opens Edmund's eyes to her lack of principle. He turns for comfort to Fanny, falls in love with her, and marries her.

Mansoul, see *Holy War*. Also the title of a poem by Doughty (q.v.).

Mantalini, MADAME, in Dickens's 'Nicholas Nickleby' (q.v.), a fashionable dressmaker. Her husband, Mr. Mantalini, a selfish, affected fop, lives on her earnings and ruins her.

Mantuan or MANTUANUS (1448-1516), Johannes Baptista Spagnolo, a Carmelite of Mantua who wrote Latin eclogues.

Mantuan Poet, THE, Virgil (q.v.).

Manutius, ALDUS, see *Aldus Manutius.*

Manzoni, ALESSANDRO (1785-1873), Italian novelist, dramatist, and poet, chiefly famous for his historical novel 'I Promessi Sposi' (first version, 1825-7, final form, 1840-2), praised by Sir W. Scott as 'the best ever written'.

Map or MAPES, WALTER (*fl.* 1200), a Welshman, archdeacon of Oxford under Henry II, author of a satirical miscellany 'De nugis curialium' (Chaucer refers to this in the Prologue of the Wife of Bath).

Satirical poems on Bishop Golias (q.v.) have been doubtfully attributed to him; also a lost Latin original of the prose romance of 'Lancelot du Lac'.

Maranatha, an Aramaic phrase (1 Cor. xvi. 22) meaning 'Our Lord has come', often erroneously regarded as forming with 'anathema', which precedes it, an imprecation.

Marathon, a plain near the east coast of Attica, the scene of the defeat of the Persian army by Miltiades in 490 B.C.

MARATHON RACE, a long-distance race, named after the exploit of a Greek messenger who ran from Marathon to Athens with the news of the defeat.

Marble Faun, The, a novel by Hawthorne (q.v.), published in 1860 (under the title in England of 'Transformation').

Marchioness, THE, a character in Dickens's 'The Old Curiosity Shop' (q.v.).

Marcian, see *Martianus Capella.*

Marco Polo, see *Polo.*

Marconi, GUGLIELMO (1874-1937), Italian physicist who established wireless telegraphy on a commercial basis. Communication across the English Channel was established in 1899, and across the Atlantic in 1902.

Marcus Aurelius Antoninus (A.D. 121-80), Roman emperor A.D. 161-80, and religious philosopher, was author of twelve books of 'Meditations' in Greek, imbued with a Stoic philosophy.

Mardi, a fantastic South Sea romance by Herman Melville (q.v.) (1849).

Margaret, (1) in Shakespeare's 'Much Ado About Nothing' (q.v.), the gentlewoman attending on Hero; (2) in Goethe's 'Faust' (q.v.), the principal female character ('Gretchen') of Pt. I, a girl of humble station, simple, confiding, and affectionate.

Margaret, LADY, see *Lady Margaret.*

Margaret of Anjou (1430-82), 'the she-wolf of Anjou', queen consort of Henry VI of England; she played a prominent part in the Wars of the Roses. She figures in Shakespeare's 'Henry VI' (q.v.) and in Scott's 'Anne of Geierstein'.

Margaret of Navarre, see *Heptameron.*

Margites, 'The Booby', the name of a lost Greek comic poem, of unknown date and authorship, regarded by Aristotle as the germ of comedy and attributed by him to Homer.

Maria, a character in (1) Shakespeare's 'Twelfth Night' (q.v.); (2) Sterne's 'Tristram Shandy' (vol. vii) and 'A Sentimental Journey' (qq.v.); (3) Sheridan's 'The School for Scandal' (q.v.).

Mariamne, wife of Herod the Great, executed by him in a fit of jealousy, the subject of tragedies by Voltaire and others.

Marian, MAID, see *Maid Marian.*

Mariana, in Shakespeare's 'Measure for Measure' (q.v.), the lady betrothed to Angelo and cast off by him, who lives, dejected, at the moated grange.

Mariana, and *Mariana in the South,* two poems by Tennyson, suggested by the Mariana of the preceding entry.

Marianne, a familiar name given to the government of the French Republic.

For a Frenchman, *Marianne* still signifies the republican form of government, and not France. By foreigners, it is used as a name for France, as John Bull for England.

Marie Celeste, see *Mary Celeste.*

Marie de France, a late-12th-cent. French poetess, of whom little that is certain is known. She appears to have been born in France and to have done much or all of her literary work in England.

She wrote 'Lays', tales of love and adventure, in some of which Arthur and Tristram figure; a collection of Aesopic fables, to which she gave the name 'Isopet'; and a French version of the Latin legend of St. Patrick's Purgatory. (See also *Breton Lays*.)

Marie Roget, *The Mystery of*, a detective story by Poe (q.v.).

Maries, THE QUEEN'S, see *Queen's Maries*.

Marina, in Shakespeare's 'Pericles' (q.v.), the daughter of Pericles.

Marinell, see *Florimell*.

Marinetti, FILIPPO TOMMASO (1876–1944), Italian dramatist, novelist, and poet, who launched the Futurist movement in 1909. In his poems he anticipated the Dadaist technique of juxtaposing words without syntactical links. In his plays he abandoned verisimilitude and traditional methods of characterization and plot development.

Marino, GIAMBATTISTA (1569–1625), Neapolitan poet, best known for his 'Adone' (1623), a long poem on the love of Venus and Adonis. The term *marinismo* denotes the flamboyant style of Marino and his 17th-cent. imitators, with its extravagant imagery, excessive ornamentation, and verbal ingenuity.

Marino Faliero, *Doge of Venice*, a historical tragedy by Lord Byron (q.v.) (1821), produced in the same year at Drury Lane (against Byron's wish).

The conspiracy of the doge was likewise the subject of a tragedy, 'Marino Faliero', by Swinburne (q.v.) (1885).

Mariolatry, the idolatrous worship of the Virgin Mary attributed by opponents to Roman Catholics.

Marius among the ruins of Carthage, an allusion to an incident in the life of Gaius Marius, the great Roman general (157–86 B.C.). Overcome by his rival Sulla, he fled in 88 to Africa and landed at Carthage. The Roman governor sent to bid him leave the country. His only reply was, 'Tell the praetor you have seen Gaius Marius a fugitive sitting among the ruins of Carthage.'

Marius the Epicurean, a philosophical romance by Pater (q.v.) (1885).

This is the story of the life, in the time of the Antonines, of a grave young Roman. Against a background of the customs and modes of thought of that fortunate period, the author traces the reactions of Marius to the various spiritual influences to which he is subjected. Finally the quiet courage and enthusiasm of the young Christian community make a growing impression on him, and his end comes as a result of an act of self-sacrifice undertaken in order to save a Christian friend.

Marivaux, PIERRE CARLET DE CHAMBLAIN DE (1688–1763), French author of prose comedies and romances, marked by a delicate analysis of sentiment, and a subtle affected style which has given rise to the term *Marivaudage*.

Mark, a money of account, originally representing the value of a mark weight (usually regarded as equivalent to 8 oz.) of silver.

Mark, KING, in the Arthurian legend king of Cornwall, and husband of La Beale Isoud (see *Tristram*). He is held up to ridicule as a treacherous coward.

Mark, ST., the evangelist, represented in art accompanied by a winged lion, and commemorated on 25 April. Keats left, unfinished, a poem on the Eve of St. Mark, with which day certain superstitions were connected.

Markham, MRS., pseudonym of Mrs. Elizabeth Penrose (1780–1837), *née* Cartwright, who wrote well-known school histories of England (1823) and France (1828).

Markham, GERVASE (1568–1637), after a military career of some years in the Netherlands, became a writer on country pursuits, on the art of war, but especially on horsemanship and the veterinary art. He also wrote plays and poems.

Markleham, MRS., a character in Dickens's 'David Copperfield' (q.v.), familiarly known as the 'Old Soldier'.

Mark Tapley, in Dickens's 'Martin Chuzzlewit' (q.v.), servant at the Dragon Inn, who leaves it to find some position in which it will be a credit to show his indomitable good humour. He becomes the devoted attendant of Martin during his American tour, and finally marries the hostess of the Dragon.

Marley, in Dickens's 'A Christmas Carol' (q.v.), Scrooge's late partner, whose ghost appears.

Marlow, SIR CHARLES, and his son, characters in Goldsmith's 'She Stoops to Conquer' (q.v.).

Marlowe, CHRISTOPHER (1564–93), attached himself to the earl of Nottingham's theatrical company, which produced most of his plays. He was acquainted with the leading men of letters, including Ralegh. He wrote not later than 1587 'Tamburlaine' (q.v.), which was published in 1590 and gave a new development to blank verse. His 'Tragedy of Dr. Faustus' (q.v.) was first entered on the 'Stationers' Register' in 1601, but not apparently published till 1604. At some date after 1588 he wrote 'The Jew of Malta' (q.v.), which was first published in 1633; and about 1593 his best play, 'Edward II' (q.v., first published in 1594); also two inferior pieces, the 'Massacre at Paris' (probably published in 1600) and 'The Tragedy of Dido' (joint work of Marlowe and Nash), published in 1594. It has been suggested from internal evidence that he was part author of Shakespeare's 'Titus Andronicus'. He perhaps also wrote parts of 'Henry VI', which Shakespeare revised and completed, and of 'Edward III' (qq.v.). He translated Ovid's 'Amores' (*c.* 1597), 'The First Book of Lucan['s Pharsalia]' (1600); and wrote the song 'Come live with me and be my love' (published in 'The Passionate Pilgrim', 1599, and in 'England's Helicon'). Marlowe held and propagated atheistical opinions, and a warrant was issued for his arrest in 1593. He was killed, by one Ingram Frisar, at a tavern in Deptford, according to the inquiry held at the time, as the result of a quarrel about the score, but later researches have suggested that he was a government agent, and that his death had a political complexion. Marlowe was spoken of with affection by Edward Blount, Nashe, and Chapman, and Jonson referred to his 'mighty line'. He was quoted and apostrophized by Shakespeare in 'As You Like It', and praised by Drayton ('To Henery Reynolds, Esq., of Poets and Poems').

Marmion, A Tale of Flodden Field, a poem in six cantos by Sir W. Scott (q.v.) (1808).

The story relates to the year 1513. Lord Marmion, a fictitious character, a favourite of King Henry VIII and a compound of villainy and noble qualities, seeks to marry the wealthy Lady Clare, who is affianced to Sir Ralph de Wilton. To effect his purpose he accuses de Wilton of treason, and proves it by a forged letter. Marmion and de Wilton fight in the lists, and the latter is defeated and left for dead, but survives. The Lady Clare betakes herself to a convent to escape Marmion. De Wilton, disguised as a palmer, meets with the Abbess of St. Hilda, who has received proofs of Marmion's crime. The Abbess entrusts these proofs to de Wilton who escapes to the English camp, where he is rehabilitated. Marmion joins the English forces at the battle of Flodden, where he is killed. De Wilton and Clare are finally united. The poem contains the two well-known songs, 'Where shall the lover rest', and 'Lochinvar', and beautiful introductions to each canto.

Marmion, SHACKERLEY (1603–39), the author of several plays, of which the best is 'The Antiquary' (1641), and of a poem in heroic couplets 'Cupid and Psyche'.

Maro, the family name of the Roman poet Virgil (q.v.).

Marocco, the wonderful performing horse trained by Bankes, the Scottish showman (*fl.* 1588–1637). Its power of counting is referred to in Shakespeare's

'Love's Labour's Lost' (I. ii), and by other authors of the day.

Marot, CLÉMENT (1496-1544), French Protestant poet, whose sonnets and pastorals and translations of the Psalms influenced Spenser and the contemporary school of English poetry.

Marprelate Controversy, see *Martin Marprelate*.

Marquis of Granby, THE, in Dickens's 'The Pickwick Papers' (q.v.), the inn at Dorking kept by the second Mrs. Tony Weller.

Marriage, a novel by S. E. Ferrier (q.v.) (1818).

Marriage-à-la-Mode, a comedy by Dryden (q.v.), produced in 1673.

Marrow of Modern Divinity, The, title of a book advocating Calvinistic views, written by E. F. (Edward Fisher) in 1645, the condemnation of which (in 1718) by the general assembly of the Church of Scotland led to a prolonged controversy, known as the MARROW CONTROVERSY.

Marryat, FREDERICK (1792-1848), a captain in the Royal Navy, in which he served with distinction, was the author of a series of novels of sea-life, of which the best known are 'Frank Mildmay' (1829), 'Peter Simple' (1834), 'Jacob Faithful' (1834), and 'Mr. Midshipman Easy' (1836). Mention should also be made of 'Snarleyyow' (1837), the story of a mysterious and indestructible cur. 'Masterman Ready' (1841), 'The Settlers in Canada' (1844), and others, were specially intended by the author for boys.

Mars, the god of war of the ancient Romans, identified by them with the ARES of the Greeks.

Marseillaise, The, the French national anthem, was composed by a young French engineer officer, Rouget de Lisle, at Strasbourg in 1792, on the declaration of war against Austria. It was suppressed by Napoleon and at the restoration of the Bourbons.

Marsh, SIR EDWARD (1872-1953), was editor of 'Georgian Poetry' (q.v.) and a friend and biographer of Rupert Brooke

(q.v.). He translated the fables of La Fontaine (1931).

Marsh, DAME NGAIO (pron. 'Ny-o') EDITH (1899-), writer of detective stories, born in New Zealand. Her hero is Chief Detective Inspector Alleyn and her titles include 'A Man Lay Dead' (1934), 'Died in the Wool' (1945), and 'Spinsters in Jeopardy' (1954).

Marshalsea, a prison in Southwark, abolished in 1842. See *Little Dorrit*.

Marston, JOHN (1575?-1634), the dramatist. He renounced the drama in 1607 and took orders. He quarrelled with Ben Jonson, who attacked him in 'Every Man out of his Humour', 'Cynthia's Revels', and 'The Poetaster', where he is presented as Crispinus. But the pair made friends again. Marston published 'The Metamorphosis of Pigmalion's Image' (an erotic poem) 'and certain Satyres' in 1598, and further satires under the title 'The Scourge of Villanie' in the same year. Some of these were studies in social vices and others were directed against literary rivals, including Bishop Hall (q.v.). His dramatic works include the 'History of Antonio and Mellida', a tragedy (1602) ('Antonios Revenge' is the second part of this play); 'The Malcontent', a comedy, with additions by Webster (1604); 'Eastward hoe', a comedy, written with Jonson and Chapman, for which they were imprisoned (1605); 'The Dutch Courtezan', a comedy (1605); 'The Parasitaster', a comedy (1606); and 'What you Will', a comedy (1607).

Marston, PHILIP BOURKE (1850-87), son of John Westland Marston, the dramatist, a blind poet, author of some beautiful sonnets.

Marsyas, in Greek mythology, a celebrated player on the pipe, who had the imprudence to challenge Apollo to a musical contest. The victory having with difficulty been adjudged to Apollo by the Muses, Apollo tied Marsyas to a tree and flayed him alive.

Martext, SIR OLIVER, the vicar in Shakespeare's 'As You Like It' (q.v.).

Martial (MARCUS VALERIUS MARTIALIS) (*c.* A.D. 40-104), born in Spain, whence he came to Rome. He left a collection of short poems or epigrams, 1,500 in number, witty but frequently coarse, which throw a valuable light on Roman life and manners.

Martians, in H. G. Wells's 'The War of the Worlds' (1898), inhabitants of Mars, who, driven by the progressive cooling of their planet to seek a warmer world, invade the earth. They devastate England by means of a terrible heat-ray and an asphyxiating gas; but soon fall victims to diseases caused by the bacteria against which they have no power of resistance.

Martianus Capella, or MARCIAN, a N. African writer celebrated in the Middle Ages who lived in the latter part of the 5th cent. He was author of 'De Nuptiis Philologiae et Mercurii'. Marcian is referred to by Chaucer in 'The Merchant's Tale', ll. 488 et seq., and in 'The Hous of Fame', l. 985.

Martin, in 'Reynard the Fox' (q.v.), the ape. His wife is Dame Rukenawe.

Martin, in Dryden's 'The Hind and the Panther' (q.v.) symbolizes the Lutheran party; and in Swift's 'A Tale of a Tub' (q.v.) the Anglican Church, the allusion being to Martin Luther.

Martin, ST., bishop of Tours about 371, the patron saint of tavern-keepers. He is commemorated on 11 Nov., known as MARTINMAS or MARTLEMAS. ST. MARTIN'S SUMMER is a period of fine mild weather sometimes occurring about this date.

Martin, SIR THEODORE (1816-1909), contributed, under the pseudonym 'Bon Gaultier', humorous pieces to 'Tait's' and 'Fraser's' magazines, some of which attracted the attention of W. E. Aytoun (q.v.). Martin and Aytoun collaborated in the 'Bon Gaultier Ballads' (q.v., 1845), parodying verse of the day.

Martin Chuzzlewit, The Life and Adventures of, a novel by Dickens (q.v.) (1843-4).

Martin, the hero, is the grandson of old Martin Chuzzlewit, a wealthy gentleman who has been rendered misanthropical by the greed of the members of his family. The old man has bred up Mary Graham, a young orphan, to tend him, and regards her as his daughter. Young Chuzzlewit is in love with Mary; but the grandfather, distrusting his selfish character, repudiates him and gets him dismissed from his position as pupil to his cousin, Mr. Pecksniff, an architect and an arch-hypocrite. Thrown nearly penniless on the world, young Martin, accompanied by the indomitably cheerful Mark Tapley as his servant, sails for America to try his fortunes. He goes as an architect to the settlement of the Eden Land Corporation, a fraudulent affair, where he loses his money and nearly dies of fever. (This part gave great offence in the United States.) Martin then returns to England, purged by his experiences of his earlier selfishness. Meanwhile his grandfather has established himself and Mary in Pecksniff's household, and pretends to place himself under the latter's direction. By this means he becomes satisfied of Pecksniff's meanness and treachery (Pecksniff tries to inveigle and bully Mary into marrying him), exposes the hypocrite, restores his grandson to favour, and gives him the hand of Mary.

A second plot runs through the book, concerned with the doings of Jonas Chuzzlewit, the son of Anthony, old Martin's brother, a character of almost incredible villainy. He murders his father (in intention if not in fact); marries Mercy, one of Pecksniff's daughters, and treats her with the utmost brutality; murders the director of a bogus insurance company, by whom he has been inveigled and blackmailed; is detected; and finally poisons himself.

Besides the finished portraits of Pecksniff and Mark Tapley, the book contains many pleasant characters: Tom Pinch, Pecksniff's gentle loyal assistant, and his sister Ruth; Charity and Mercy (Cherry and Merry), Pecksniff's daughters; and Mrs. Gamp, the disreputable old nurse;

while in 'Todgers's', the author depicts the humours of a London boarding-house.

Martineau, HARRIET (1802-76), sister of J. Martineau (1805-1900), the philosopher. She was a Unitarian, and began as a writer on religious subjects. But she was chiefly successful in stories designed to popularize economic subjects, which show her as an ardent advocate of social reform. She published a novel, 'Deerbrook', in 1839; a historical romance, 'The Hour and the Man', in 1841; also a series of stories for young people. Her later writings display anti-theological views. Miss Martineau wrote an 'Autobiographical Memoir', published posthumously which contains interesting comments on the great literary figures of her day.

Martin Marprelate, the name assumed by the author of a number of anonymous pamphlets (seven are extant) issued in 1588-9 from a secret press, containing attacks in a railing rollicking style on the bishops and defending the Presbyterian system of discipline.

The importance of the Marprelate tracts lies in the fact that they are the best prose satires of the Elizabethan age. They called forth replies from such noted writers as Lyly and Nash, and Gabriel and Richard Harvey were presently involved in the controversy. But the replies show less literary ability than the original tracts.

The suspected authors of these, a Welshman named Penry and a clergyman named Udall, were arrested. The latter died in prison, the former was executed. Job Throckmorton, probably the real author, escaped punishment.

Martinus Scriblerus, Memoirs of, a satirical work, directed against 'false tastes in learning', initiated by the Scriblerus Club (q.v.), and written mainly by Arbuthnot (q.v.). It was printed in the second volume of Pope's prose works in 1741. The work is incomplete, and we have only the first book of it.

The name 'Martinus Scriblerus' was occasionally used by Pope as a pseudonym; and under it George Crabbe wrote some of his earlier poems.

Martyn, EDWARD (1859-1924), one of the founders of the Irish Literary Theatre (see *Yeats*). His best-known plays are 'The Heather Field' and 'Maeve'. He is one of the central figures in G. Moore's (q.v.) 'Hail and Farewell'.

Martyr, PETER, see *Peter Martyr*.

Marvell, ANDREW (1621-78), spent four years on the Continent, part of the time at Rome, and in 1650 became tutor to the daughter of Lord Fairfax, at Nun Appleton in Yorkshire. Here he wrote poems in praise of gardens and country life, including 'The Hill and Grove at Billborow' and 'Appleton House'. These tastes are again shown in his well-known poem 'The Garden'. In 1653 he became tutor to Cromwell's ward, William Dutton, and in 1657 Milton's assistant in the Latin secretaryship to the council. He wrote several poems in the Protector's honour, including the 'Horatian Ode upon Cromwell's Return from Ireland' (1650), and the elegy upon his death. After the Restoration he entered parliament and became a violent politician and wrote satires and pamphlets, attacking first the ministers, but afterwards Charles II himself. His principal verse satire is 'The last Instructions to a Painter' on the subject of the Dutch War. Marvell vigorously defended Milton, and wrote lines in praise of 'Paradise Lost', which were included with the second edition of that poem. From 1660 to 1678 he wrote a series of newsletters to his constituents at Hull, which are of historical importance. The bulk of his poems were not published until 1681, the satires not until 1689, after the revolution.

Marvellous Boy, THE, a name given by Wordsworth to Chatterton (q.v.).

Marx, KARL (1818-83), of Jewish descent, was editor of the 'Rheinische Zeitung' at Cologne in 1842. His extreme radical views led to the suppression of the paper, and Marx went to Paris, where he came into touch with Friedrich Engels and collaborated with him in works of political philosophy. He was expelled from Paris, moved to Brussels, and at the time of the revolutionary movement of 1848 returned to Cologne. His revolutionary views caused him to be once more expelled, and he finally settled in London. In 1867 appeared the first volume of his treatise 'Das Kapital', in which he propounded his theory of political economy. This was completed from his papers by Engels after the death of Marx. It is a criticism of the capitalistic system under which a diminishing number of capitalists appropriate the benefits of improved industrial methods, while the labouring class are left in increasing dependency and misery. The remedy for this state of things is the total abolition of private property, to be effected by the class war. When the community has acquired possession of all property and the means of production, it will distribute work to each individual and provide him with the means of sustenance.

Mary, in Dickens's 'The Pickwick Papers' (q.v.), Mr. Nupkins's pretty housemaid.

Mary I, queen of England, 1553-8. She married Philip of Spain in 1554. Tennyson made her the subject of a drama.

Mary II, eldest child of James II, queen of England, 1689-94, and consort of William III, whom she married in 1677. Her little-known 'Memoirs' were edited in 1886.

Mary Barton, a Tale of Manchester Life, the first novel by Mrs. Gaskell (q.v.) (1848). It was written soon after, and under the influence of, the death of her infant son.

The background of the story is Manchester in the 'hungry forties' of the 19th century, a period of acute distress in the industrial districts. The author's emphasis on the lack of sympathy shown by the employers for their workers was unpopular, but the literary merits of the work were fully recognized.

Mary Celeste, The, an American brig bound from New York to Genoa, picked up in the North Atlantic by a British barque on 5 Dec. 1872, derelict but in perfect condition. The ship's boats were missing and the fate of the crew is unknown.

Mary Graham, a character in Dickens's 'Martin Chuzzlewit' (q.v.).

Mary Magdalene, St., see *Magdalen.*

Mary Magdalene, Play of, the single surviving English drama of the late ME. period that is based on the legend of a saint (see *Miracle Plays*). It presents events in the saint's life both before the Resurrection and during her subsequent legendary residence in Provence.

Mary Morison, of Burns's song, was possibly Alison Begbie, an early love of the poet.

Mary Queen of Scots (MARY STUART) (1542-87), daughter of James V of Scotland, married to Francis II of France (1558), to Lord Darnley (1565), and to Bothwell (1567). She was imprisoned by Elizabeth and finally beheaded on a charge of conspiring against the latter's life. She figures in Scott's 'The Abbot', and is the subject of a tragedy by Schiller (q.v.), of a trilogy of plays by Swinburne (q.v.), and of the novel 'The Queen's Quair' by Maurice Hewlett.

Marys, THE QUEEN'S, see *Queen's Maries.*

Marys, THE THREE, AT THE CROSS, were Mary the mother of Jesus, Mary the wife of Cleophas, and Mary Magdalene (John xix. 25).

Masculine or MALE **rhymes,** see *Rhyme.*

Masefield, JOHN, O.M. (1878-1967), ran away to sea early in life (an experience of which there are reminiscences in his narrative-poem 'Dauber', 1913), went to America, and on his return to England became a journalist on the staff of the 'Manchester Guardian'. He then settled in London and during the first ten years of this century wrote poems ('Salt-Water Ballads', 1902, containing the well-known 'I must go down to the sea again', 'Ballads and Poems', 1910); collections of short stories; plays ('The Tragedy of Nan', 1909; 'The Tragedy of Pompey the Great',

1910); and essays. In 1911 appeared his remarkable poem 'The Everlasting Mercy', the realistic story of the conversion of the ruffianly Saul Kane, followed by 'The Widow in the Bye Street' (1912), 'The Daffodil Fields' (1913), and 'Reynard the Fox' (1919). Among his other works may be mentioned the novels, 'Captain Margaret' (1908), 'Sard Harker' (1924), 'Odtaa' (1926); his nativity play, 'The Coming of Christ' (1928); the poems, 'Lollingdon Downs' (1917), 'A Tale of Troy' (1932), 'A Letter from Pontus' (1936), 'Land Workers' (1942), and 'Collected Poems' (1946); his edition of the 'Chronicles of the Pilgrim Fathers' (1910); also the account of the evacuation of Dunkirk, 'The Nine Days Wonder' (1941), and 'So Long to Learn' (1952), which is autobiographical. He was appointed poet laureate in 1930.

Mas John or MESS JOHN, a term applied jocularly or contemptuously to a Scottish Presbyterian clergyman (shortened from Master John).

Masks, see *Masques*.

Maskwell, the 'Double Dealer' in Congreve's comedy of that name.

Mason, ALFRED EDWARD WOODLEY (1865-1948), author of many novels of adventure or detection, including 'The Four Feathers', 'At the Villa Rose', 'The House of the Arrow', 'No other Tiger', 'Running Water'. His detective is Hanaud.

Masques or MASKS, dramatic entertainments, involving dances and disguises, in which the spectacular and musical elements predominated over plot and character. They were acted by amateurs, and were popular at court and among the nobility. They were perhaps of Italian origin, but assumed a distinctive character in England in the 16th and 17th cents. Many of the great dramatic writers, Beaumont, Middleton, Chapman, wrote masques, and they reached their highest degree of elaboration in the hands of Ben Jonson (q.v.), who introduced the 'anti-masque' and an element of Aristophanic comedy. The great architect Inigo Jones (q.v.), designed the machinery and decorations for some of them. Ben Jonson's 'The Sad Shepherd', Fletcher's 'The Faithful Shepherdess', Randolph's 'Amyntas', and Milton's 'Comus' (q.v.), though sometimes described as masques, are strictly pastoral dramas.

Massacre of St. Bartholomew, see *Bartholomew* (*Massacre of St.*).

Massinger, PHILIP (1583-1640). His father had been in the service of the Herbert family, to members of which the poet addressed various dedications and other pieces. He soon became a famous playwright, collaborating frequently with Fletcher, and also with Nathaniel Field and Dekker (qq.v.).

The principal surviving plays entirely written by him are 'The Duke of Milan' (1623), 'The Bondman' (1624), 'The Roman Actor' (q.v., 1629), 'The Maid of Honour' (1632), 'A New Way to pay Old Debts' (q.v., 1633), 'The Guardian' (1655), 'The Bashful Lover' (1655), and 'The City Madam' (1658). Some see his hand also in portions of 'Henry VIII' and of 'Two Noble Kinsmen' (q.v., 1634), in both of which a share is attributed to Shakespeare. In collaboration with Dekker he wrote 'The Virgin-Martyr' (1622). His principal field was the romantic drama, of which his best examples are perhaps 'The Duke of Milan', 'The Great Duke of Florence', and 'The Fatal Dowry'. His best-known work is the fine comedy 'A New Way to pay Old Debts'. His political views in favour of the popular party, and his religious views in sympathy with the Church of Rome, are freely indicated in his plays.

Masson, DAVID (1822-1907), professor of rhetoric and English literature at Edinburgh University, 1865-95. His most important published work was his standard 'Life of Milton' (1859-80).

Master Humphrey's Clock, the framework, soon abandoned, in which Dickens set his novels 'The Old Curiosity Shop' and 'Barnaby Rudge' (qq.v.).

Master of Ballantrae, The, a novel by R. L. Stevenson (q.v.) (1889).

It is the story of the lifelong feud between the Master of Ballantrae, violent and unscrupulous, and his younger brother Henry, at the outset a quiet, honest fellow. The Master joins Prince Charles Edward in the '45, disappears after Culloden, and is believed dead. After many adventures the Master returns, with a price on his head, to find that Henry has succeeded to his place and to the woman whom he was to have married. Embittered by misfortune, he enters on a course of persecution, first in Scotland, then America, which finally drives Henry mad, and brings both brothers to an untimely grave.

Master of the Sentences, Peter Lombard (q.v.).

Masters, EDGAR LEE (1869-1950), American poet and novelist. His best-known work, 'The Spoon River Anthology' (1916), is a series of confessions and revelations from beyond the grave by the former inhabitants of a Middle Western village.

Matchless Orinda, THE, see *Philips* (*K.*).

Materialism, in philosophy, the opinion that nothing exists except matter and its movements and modifications.

Mathias, the chief character in 'The Bells' (q.v.).

Mathias, THOMAS JAMES (1754?-1835), became librarian at Buckingham Palace. His 'Pursuits of Literature' (1794), a vigorous satire on contemporary authors, went through sixteen editions and provoked many replies.

Matthew Paris, see *Paris* (*M.*).

Matty, MISS (Matilda Jenkyns), a character in Mrs. Gaskell's 'Cranford' (q.v.).

Maturin, CHARLES ROBERT (1782-1824). He was one of the principal writers of the terror or mystery novels called 'Gothic novels' (q.v.). In 1816 his tragedy 'Bertram' was produced by Kean at Drury Lane, on the recommendation of Scott and Byron, with great success. His masterpiece was 'Melmoth the Wanderer' (q.v.) (1820).

Maud, a poem by Lord Tennyson (q.v.) (1855).

The poem is a monodrama in sections of different metres, in which the narrator, a man of morbid and unbalanced temperament, gives voice to his feelings at various stages of the story: first lamenting his family's ruin by the contrivance of the old lord of the Hall; then expressing the gradual development of his love for Maud, the old lord's daughter; his triumph at winning the love of Maud; the fatal encounter with the brother; his own flight abroad and the madness that follows the blighting of his hopes; and his final re-awakening to life in the service of his country. The poem contains several of Tennyson's best love-lyrics ('I have led her home', 'Come into the garden, Maud', etc.); but some of the opinions expressed or implied in it, notably the approval of war in certain circumstances, were distasteful to many.

Maugham, (WILLIAM) SOMERSET (1874-1965), author, among whose chief works are: 'Liza of Lambeth' (1897), 'Of Human Bondage' (1915), 'The Moon and Sixpence' (1919), 'The Painted Veil' (1925), 'Cakes and Ale' (1930), 'The Razor's Edge' (1944), all novels; 'A Man of Honour' (1904), 'Lady Frederick' (1907), 'Home and Beauty' (1919), 'The Circle' (1921), 'East of Suez' (1922), 'Our Betters' (1923), 'The Constant Wife' (1927), 'For Services Rendered' (1932), 'Sheppey' (1933), plays; 'The Trembling of a Leaf' (1921), 'On a Chinese Screen' (1923), 'Ashenden' (1928), short stories. Several of his short stories have been dramatized.

Maul, in Pt. II of Bunyan's 'The Pilgrim's Progress' (q.v.), a giant slain by Mr. Greatheart.

Maumet, see *Mammet*.

Maundy, from Latin *mandatum*, a commandment, the ceremony of washing the feet of a number of poor people, performed by royal or other eminent persons, or ecclesiastics, on the Thursday before Easter.

Maupassant, GUY DE (1850-93), French novelist of the naturalistic school, a master of the short story, and a disciple of Gustave Flaubert (q.v.). His most remarkable work is the short story 'Boule de Suif', an audacious tale of an episode in the Franco-Prussian war. His 'Une Vie' (1883), 'Bel Ami' (1885), 'Pierre et Jean' (1888), are notable works, marred by a certain morbidity.

Mauretania, in ancient geography, the western part of North Africa, having Numidia on the east, and Gaetulia on the south; the country of the *Mauri* or Moors. It became a Roman province in A.D. 40.

Mauriac, FRANÇOIS (1885-1970), French novelist, dramatist, and critic, author of: 'Thérèse Desqueyroux' (1927), and other short psychological tales; 'Le Nœud de Vipères' (1932) and 'Le Mystère Fontenac' (1933), longer studies of family life; 'Asmodée' (1938) and 'Les Mal Aimés' (1945), dramas, etc.

Maurice, JOHN FREDERICK DENISON (1805-72), the son of a Unitarian minister, and educated at Trinity Hall, Cambridge. He took orders in the Church of England and felt himself called to the pursuit of religious unity. He was professor of English literature and history at King's College, London, 1840-53, and was dismissed in the latter year because of his unorthodoxy. He was appointed professor of moral philosophy at Cambridge in 1866. His religious views are principally contained in his 'The Religions of the World' (1847) and 'Theological Essays' (1853). Tennyson's lyric to him is well known.

Maurists, a congregation of French Benedictine monks. Under the impulse of its first superior-general, Dom Tarisse, it carried out an immense amount of historical and critical work in connection with patristic and biblical literature, monastic and ecclesiastical history, collections of documents, palaeography, and other branches of technical erudition.

Maurois, ANDRÉ (1885-1967), French author of biography: 'Ariel' (Shelley, 1923), 'Disraëli' (1927), 'Byron' (1930), 'A la recherche de Marcel Proust' (1949), 'Lélia' (George Sand, 1952), etc.; histories of England (1937) and the United States (1948); novels: 'Climats' (1929), 'Le Cercle de famille' (1932), etc.; also of 'Les Silences du Colonel Bramble' (1918), a brilliant analysis of the English character.

Mause Headrigg, see *Headrigg*.

Mausolus, a king of Caria (377-353 B.C.) and husband of Artemisia (q.v.), who erected to his memory a magnificent monument called the MAUSOLEUM, which was accounted one of the seven wonders of the world.

Mavor, O. H., see *Bridie (J.)*.

Max Müller, FRIEDRICH (1823-1900), son of the German poet Wilhelm Müller, was a naturalized British subject. He came to England in 1846 and was commissioned by the directors of the East India Company to bring out an edition of the Sanskrit 'Rigveda' (see *Veda*) (1849-73). He settled at Oxford in 1848 and was professor of comparative philology at Oxford from 1868 till his death. He devoted much attention to comparative mythology and the comparative study of religions. He edited, from 1875, the 'Sacred Books of the East', a series of English translations of the oriental religious classics.

May, THOMAS (1595-1650), adopted the parliamentary cause and was secretary for the parliament (1646). He was author of two narrative poems on the reigns of Edward III and Henry II, and of a 'History of the Long Parliament' (1647). He also wrote translations (which were praised by Ben Jonson), two comedies (c. 1620), and tragedies on classical subjects.

Maya, an ancient race of Central American Indians, noted for their architecture, stone-carving, pottery, and textiles.

Mayakovsky, VLADIMIR VLADIMIROVICH (1893-1930), Russian Futurist poet. He joined the Bolshevik Party at the age of

14, and political and social themes are prominent in his work. In 1912 he signed the Cubo-Futurist Manifesto, rejecting the language and literature of the past. In 1923 he attempted, with little success, to found a Soviet school of Futurism ('Left Front'). His best-known poems are 'A Cloud in Trousers' (1915), '150,000,000' (1922), and 'About This' (1923). He also wrote plays, the most notable being 'The Bedbug' (1928).

May Day, the 1st of May, celebrated with garlands and dancing, the choice of a queen of the May, the erection of a May-pole to dance round, etc. Perhaps derived from the Roman *Floralia*. May Day was adopted in 1889 as the international Labour holiday.

Mayfair, the fashionable west end of London; hence allusively for fashionable society.

Mayflower, The, the ship in which the Pilgrim Fathers sailed from Plymouth in 1620 to Cape Cod, Massachusetts.

Mayhew, HENRY (1812-87), one of the original proprietors of 'Punch' (q.v.) and co-editor with Mark Lemon during its first year. His great sociological study, 'London Labour and the London Poor', which began with a series of articles (1849-50) for 'The Morning Chronicle' (q.v.), was published in four volumes, 1861-2.

Maylie, MRS. and HARRY, characters in Dickens's 'Oliver Twist' (q.v.).

Mayor of Casterbridge, The, a novel by Hardy (q.v.) (1886).

Michael Henchard, a hay-tresser, when drunk at a fair, sells his wife and child for five guineas to a sailor, Newson. Returning to his senses he takes a solemn vow not to touch intoxicants for twenty-one years. By his energy he becomes rich, respected, and the mayor of Casterbridge (Dorchester). After eighteen years his wife returns, Newson being then supposed dead, and is reunited to her husband; she brings with her her daughter, Elizabeth-Jane, and Henchard is led to believe that Elizabeth-Jane is his child, whereas she is

Newson's. Henchard quarrels with his capable assistant in his corn business, Donald Farfrae. Mrs. Henchard dies, and Henchard learns the truth about the girl. Farfrae becomes Henchard's successful rival in business and marries the woman that Henchard had hoped to win. Henchard is ruined, the story of the sale of his wife is revealed, and he takes to drink. His stepdaughter is his only comfort, and Newson returns and claims her. Henchard becomes lonelier and more desolate, and dies wretchedly in a hut on Egdon Heath.

Mazarin, JULES (1602-61), an Italian, entered the French service, and was made a cardinal in 1641. He succeeded Richelieu as prime minister, and governed France during the minority of Louis XIV. His internal administration provoked the civil wars of the Fronde. He founded a splendid library in Paris, the *Bibliothèque Mazarine*.

Mazarin Bible, THE, the first printed Bible, and probably the first book to be printed with movable type, *c.* 1455, attributed to Gutenberg (q.v.) but perhaps by Fust (q.v.) and Schöffer. The first known copy was discovered in the Mazarine Library (see preceding entry) in Paris. It is also known as the 'forty-two line Bible' from the number of lines to the column.

Mazeppa, a poem by Lord Byron (q.v.) (1819).

The poem is founded on a passage in Voltaire's 'Charles XII'. Ivan Stepanovich Mazeppa, a Polish nobleman, tells a tale of his early life, when he was a page to Casimir V, king of Poland. Being detected in an intrigue with the wife of a local magnate, he had been bound naked on the back of a wild horse of the Ukraine, which was then loosed and lashed into madness. The horse galloped off, through forest and river, carrying his torn and fainting rider, never stopping till he reached the plains of the Ukraine, where he fell dead. Mazeppa, himself at the point of death, was rescued by peasants.

Mazzini, Giuseppe (1805?-72), Italian patriot and revolutionary agitator, was imprisoned in 1830 on a charge of political conspiracy, and subsequently resided in France and later in London, where he actively plotted for the liberation of Italy and its union under a republican government. He fomented risings in Italian cities, but his activities impeded rather than assisted the policy of Cavour (q.v.) and contributed little directly to the liberation. Mazzini remained a republican and refused allegiance to Victor Emmanuel.

Meagles, Mr., Mrs., and their daughter Pet, characters in Dickens's 'Little Dorrit' (q.v.).

Meal-tub Plot, The, the pretended conspiracy of the duke of Monmouth in 1679.

Meanjin Quarterly, a review of literature and art in Australia, founded in 1940 and edited by C. B. Christesen. The title (pron. 'Me-an´-jin') is taken from the aboriginal name for Brisbane, where the magazine was first published.

Measure for Measure, a comedy by Shakespeare (q.v.), probably first acted in 1604, but not printed till the folio of 1623. The plot is taken from Cinthio (q.v.) (translated by Whetstone, q.v.).

The duke of Vienna, on the pretext of a journey to Poland, hands over the government to Angelo, that he may escape the odium of enforcing laws against unchastity that have long been disregarded. Angelo at once sentences to death Claudio as guilty of seduction. Claudio sends word of his position to his sister Isabella, a novice, and begs her to intercede with Angelo. Isabella's prayers fail to win her brother's pardon, but her beauty awakens Angelo's passion, and, at a second interview, he offers her her brother's life if she will sacrifice to him her honour. Isabella indignantly refuses; and there follows the famous scene in the prison, when Isabella tells her brother of Angelo's offer, and he, momentarily weakening, pleads with her for his life. Meanwhile the duke, who has not left Vienna, but assumed the disguise

of a friar, and thus learnt the infamous conduct of Angelo, contrives the saving of Claudio as follows. He bids Isabella consent to go to Angelo's house at midnight, and obtains that Mariana, who had been betrothed to Angelo and loves him, but had been cast off by him, shall go there in Isabella's place. The ruse is successful; but none the less Angelo orders Claudio's execution at dawn. The provost of the prison disobeys. The duke, laying aside his friar's robes and simulating an unexpected return to Vienna, hears the complaint of Isabella and the suit of Mariana, and confutes Angelo, who denies their stories. Angelo is pardoned at the instance of Mariana and Isabella, and married to the former; and the duke reveals his love for Isabella. The play contains the beautiful song, 'Take, O take those lips away'.

Mecca, in Arabia, the birthplace of Mohammed (q.v.), and the chief place of pilgrimage of the Muslims.

Medal, The, a satirical poem by Dryden (q.v.) (1682).

The grand jury of Middlesex having thrown out the bill for high treason against the earl of Shaftesbury in 1681, the triumph of the Whigs was celebrated by the striking of a medal with the legend 'Laetamur'. Thereupon Dryden wrote his poem. It is a bitter attack on Shaftesbury and ridicules the policy of demagogic appeal to the people. It was prefaced by a prose 'Epistle to the Whigs'.

These attacks called forth a number of replies, including 'The Medal of John Bayes' by Shadwell (q.v.), and 'The Medal Revers'd' by Samuel Pordage.

Medea, a celebrated magician, daughter of Aeetes, king of Colchis. When Jason (q.v.) came to Colchis in quest of the golden fleece, he and Medea fell in love and were betrothed. On their return to Iolcos, Medea restored Jason's father Aeson to youth by her magic. The daughters of Pelias, king of Iolcos, were also desirous to see their father rejuvenated, and, encouraged by Medea, who wished to revenge the injuries that her husband's family had suffered from Pelias, they killed Pelias and boiled his flesh in a cauldron; but Medea refused to restore him. Driven in consequence from Iolcos, Jason and Medea fled to Corinth, where Jason deserted her for Glauce, the daughter of the king. Medea avenged herself by killing the two children she had had by Jason and destroying Glauce. She then married Aegeus, the father of Theseus, plotted to poison the latter for fear of his influence, and finally escaped to Asia. One of the tragedies of Euripides has Medea for its subject.

Medes, THE, the earliest Iranian inhabitants of Persia. The 'Law of the Medes and Persians' is proverbially immutable (Dan. vi. 8).

Medici, THE, the family that were rulers of Florence from 1434 and grand dukes of Tuscany from 1569 to 1737. The earlier Medici were great patrons of art and literature, chief among them Cosimo (1389-1464) and Lorenzo 'The Magnificent' (c. 1449-92).

Medina, in Arabia, the second great city of the Muslims, to which Mohammed went at the Flight or *Hijra* (q.v.), and where he died and was buried.

Medina, in Spenser's 'Faerie Queene', II. ii, represents the golden mean, her sisters Elissa and Perissa represent the extremes, of sensibility.

Medmenham Abbey, a ruined Cistercian abbey on the bank of the Thames near Marlow, notorious in the 18th cent. as the meeting-place of a convivial club known as the Franciscans or the Hell-fire Club. This was founded by Sir Francis Dashwood, and Wilkes and Bubb Dodington were among its members. See Johnstone's 'Chrysal, or the Adventures of a Guinea' (III. ii, chs. 17 et seq.).

Medora, a character in Byron's 'The Corsair' (q.v.).

Medusa, one of the three Gorgons (q.v.), and the only one that was mortal. For her destruction by Perseus, see under the name of the latter.

Medwall, HENRY, see *Fulgens and Lucrece*.

Megaera, one of the Furies (q.v.).

Megatherium, THE, a club mentioned in several of Thackeray's novels.

Meg Merrilies, see *Merrilies*.

Meg Murdockson, see *Murdockson*.

Meg of Westminster, LONG, the subject of ballads and pamphlets that appeared in 1582, 1590, and 1594, and referred to in Middleton and Dekker's 'The Roaring Girle', and by Nash, Harvey, and other authors of the period. Her biography appeared in 1635. She was a Lancashire girl who came to London, served in an alehouse, included among her acquaintance Will Sommers, Henry VIII's fool, and Skelton, assumed man's clothes and went to the wars, married a soldier and set up a public house at Islington.

Meiosis, an understatement, sometimes ironical or humorous and intended to emphasize the size, importance, etc., of what is belittled. Except in *litotes* (q.v.), which is a form of meiosis, this use of meiosis is chiefly colloquial; e.g. the use of 'rather' as a strong affirmative, 'I should rather think so'.

Meistersinger, a title taken in the 15th cent. by certain professional German poets of high skill and culture, to distinguish themselves from the wandering gleemen. They represent a phase of the development of German verse from the minnesang (see *Minnesingers*). The Meistersang and singer were governed by an elaborate set of rules and organization, which are depicted in Wagner's opera on the subject, 'Die Meistersinger von Nürnberg', produced in 1868.

Mel, THE GREAT, Melchizedek Harrington, the father of Evan Harrington in Meredith's novel of that name.

Melampus, the son of Amythaon, was regarded by the ancients as the first mortal to receive prophetic powers and to practise medicine, and as the founder of the worship of Dionysus in Greece. He is the subject of a poem by G. Meredith (q.v.).

Melanchthon, the graecized name of PHILIP SCHWARTZERD (1497-1560), German humanist who was professor of Greek at Wittenberg University; one of the principal advocates of the Reformation.

Melba, DAME NELLIE, the great singer, whose original name was Helen Porter Mitchell (1859-1931), was born in Australia. Her first appearance on the operatic stage took place in 1887 at Brussels in the part of Gilda in 'Rigoletto'. In England she first appeared in 1888 in 'Lucia di Lammermoor'. The wonderful purity of her voice and her engaging personality won her immense fame and popularity.

Melchior, one of the three Magi (q.v.) or 'Wise men of the East'. He is represented as a king of Nubia.

Melchizedek, in Gen. xiv. 18, king of Salem and the priest of the most high God. He is sometimes quoted as the type of self-originating power with reference to Heb. vii. 3-4.

Meleager, son of Oeneus, king of Calydon, and Althaea. The Parcae were present at his birth: Clotho said that he would be courageous, Lachesis that he would be strong, Atropos that he would live as long as the brand that was on the fire was not consumed. Althaea snatched the brand from the fire and kept it with jealous care. Meleager took part in the expedition of the Argonauts (q.v.) and subsequently in the hunt of the Calydonian boar that was ravaging his father's country. He slew the boar and gave the head to Atalanta (q.v.), who had first wounded it. The brothers of Althaea endeavoured to rob Atalanta of the prize. Meleager defended her and slew his uncles. As Althaea was going to the temple to give thanks for her son's victory over the boar, she learnt that he had killed her brothers, and in a moment of resentment threw into the fire the fatal brand, and as soon as it was consumed Meleager died.

Swinburne's play, 'Atalanta in Calydon', deals with this subject.

Meliagraunce, SIR, in Malory's 'Morte Darthur' (XIX. ii), the knight who captures Queen Guinevere and carries her off to his castle.

Melibeus, The Tale of, see *Canterbury Tales* (19).

Melincourt, or Sir Oran Haut-ton, a novel by Peacock (q.v.) (1817).

The plot is, as in Peacock's other novels, slight and unimportant, but brings together the usual collection of odd characters and gives occasion for much discussion of slavery in the West Indies, rotten boroughs, the Lake poets, etc. The book includes a virulent and unjustified attack on Southey (Mr. Feathernest), while Gifford (Mr. Vamp), Coleridge (Mr. Mystic), and Wordsworth (Mr. Paperstamp) come in for a share of the author's satire. See also under *Monboddo*.

Meliodas or MELIADUS, in Malory's 'Morte Darthur' (q.v.), king of Lyonesse and father of Tristram.

Melisande or MELISINDA, a name sometimes apparently confused with *Melusina*. In Spanish romance the daughter of Charlemagne. 'Pelléas et Mélisande' is one of the earlier plays of Maeterlinck (q.v.).

Mell, MR., in Dickens's 'David Copperfield' (q.v.), the poor usher at Creakle's school.

Melmoth the Wanderer, a novel by Maturin (q.v.) (1820).

This is one of the most powerful of the tales of mystery and terror of which a number were produced in the early part of the 19th cent. (see *Gothic novels*). The theme is the sale of a soul to the devil in return for prolonged life, the bargain being transferable if any one else can be persuaded to take it over.

About 1898 Oscar Wilde (q.v.) adopted the name Sebastian Melmoth—Melmoth from the romance of Maturin, a connection of his mother, Lady Wilde; Sebastian suggested by the arrows on his prison dress. He had contributed some information to the 1892 edition of 'Melmoth the Wanderer'.

Melodrama, in early 19th-cent. use, a stage play (usually romantic and sensational in plot and incident) in which songs and music were interspersed. In later use the musical element gradually ceased to be an essential feature, and the name now denotes a dramatic piece characterized by sensational incident and violent appeals to the emotions, but with a happy ending.

Melpomene, the Muse (q.v.) of tragedy.

Melville, HERMAN (1819–91), American writer. After the bankruptcy and early death of his father he was a clerk for a time and later a schoolmaster, and shipped as a cabin boy to Liverpool in 1839. In 1841 he sailed in the whaler 'Acushnet' for the South Seas. He jumped ship at the Marquesas, lived for a time with the savages, and eventually made his way home as an ordinary seaman on the U.S. frigate 'United States', being discharged in 1843. These experiences were the basis of his early and popular books. 'Typee' (1846) described his life among the savages, 'Omoo' (1847) continued the story of his wanderings among the islands, 'Redburn' (1849) was based on his voyage to Liverpool, and 'White Jacket' (1850) was a remarkable account of life on the naval frigate. He used his experience of whaling in his masterpiece 'Moby Dick' (q.v., 1851). He began to lose his popularity with 'Moby Dick', whose metaphysics and allegorical method had been foreshadowed in his earlier work—especially in 'Mardi' (1849), a discursive novel of the South Seas—and the process was hastened by his novel 'Pierre, or, The Ambiguities' (1852), which did not suit the public taste. His later work, which included novels, short stories, and verse, was disregarded, and Melville died in obscurity. His long short story 'Billy Budd' (q.v.) was published posthumously in 1924.

Melville, JULIA, a character in Sheridan's 'The Rivals' (q.v.).

Memnon, the son of Tithonus (q.v.) and Eos (Aurora), leader of the Ethiopians at the siege of Troy. He was killed by Achilles. The reference in Milton's 'Il Penseroso' to 'Prince Memnon's sister' is obscure; there is a reference to such a character in the History of the Trojan War of Dictys Cretensis.

Memoirs of a Cavalier, a historical romance attributed with good reason to Defoe (q.v.) (1724).

The pretended author, 'Col. Andrew Newport', a young English gentleman born in 1608, travels on the Continent, starting in 1630, goes to Vienna and accompanies the army of the emperor. He then joins the army of Gustavus Adolphus. After his return to England he joins the king's army, first against the Scots, then against the forces of parliament.

Memoirs of Captain Carleton, a narrative published in 1728, whose authorship has been contested, and attributed by some to Defoe (q.v.), by others to Swift (q.v.). Captain Carleton, who unquestionably existed, is the subject of an attractive story of soldierly adventure. Sir W. Scott, who regarded the 'Memoirs' as Carleton's own work, brought out a new edition in 1808.

Menaechmi, a celebrated comedy of Plautus (q.v.). It probably suggested Shakespeare's 'The Comedy of Errors'.

Menander (*c.* 342–292 B.C.), an Athenian dramatic poet, was the most distinguished writer of New Comedy, which, with its trend towards realistic fiction based on contemporary life, gave a pattern for much light drama from the Renaissance onwards, making its influence felt through Latin adaptations by Plautus and Terence (qq.v.). No play survived the Dark Ages; but 'Dyskolos' (or 'Misanthrope'), a light-hearted early play, and large parts of others have been recovered from papyri in the 20th cent.

Men and Women, a collection of poems by R. Browning (q.v.) (1855). These were redistributed in the collection of 1868, and only thirteen (most of them dramatic monologues) of the original fifty pieces were retained under the heading of 'Men and Women'. The original issue contained many of Browning's finest love-poems. It also included 'Bishop Blougram's Apology' (q.v.), 'Fra Lippo Lippi' (q.v.), 'Cleon', and 'Andrea del Sarto' (q.v.).

Menaphon, a prose romance, with interludes of verse, by R. Greene (q.v.) (1589); it was reprinted as 'Greene's Arcadia' in 1599. Among other pleasant lyrics, it contains the charming cradle-song, 'Weepe not, my wanton, smile upon my knee'.

Mencken, HENRY LOUIS (1880–1956), American journalist, born at Baltimore. He was a satirist of the 'cruder' manifestations of American civilization, and held strong views about European 'patronage' of America. His chief works are: 'George Bernard Shaw—His Plays' (1905), 'In Defense of Women' (1917), 'Prejudices' (6 series, 1919–27), and especially his scholarly 'The American Language' (1919). See also *Nathan (G. J.).*

Mendelism, the law or theory of heredity worked out by Gregor Johann Mendel (1822–84), abbot of Brünn, from his experiments on the cross-fertilization of garden peas.

Mendelssohn-Bartholdy, FELIX (1809–47), German composer, born at Hamburg, the son of a Jewish banker. His works include oratorios and cantatas, the music to 'A Midsummer Night's Dream', etc.

Menelaus, king of Sparta, according to Homer, son, but according to Hesiod and others, grandson, of Atreus (q.v.), and brother of Agamemnon (q.v.). He was the successful suitor of Helen (q.v.), but was robbed of her by Paris. Thereupon he assembled the princes who had been suitors of Helen, and the expedition against Troy was undertaken. After the fall of Troy he was reunited to Helen.

Mentor, a faithful friend of Odysseus. Hence 'a mentor' is frequently used for 'an adviser'.

Mephistopheles, a word of unknown origin, the name of the evil spirit to whom

Faust (q.v.) was said in the German legend to have sold his soul. Shakespeare in 'The Merry Wives of Windsor' (I. i) mentions 'Mephostophilus'.

Mercantile System, DOCTRINE, or THEORY, a term used by Adam Smith (q.v.) and later political economists for the system of economic doctrine based on the principle that money alone constituted wealth.

Mercator, GERARDUS, the latinized form of the name of Gerhard Kremer (1512–94), a Flemish geographer who devised the form of map known as 'MERCATOR'S PROJECTION', in which the meridians of longitude are at right angles to the parallels of latitude.

Mercator, a trade journal edited by Defoe (q.v.). It succeeded the 'Review' (q.v.) in 1713 and continued till the following year.

Merchant Adventurers, THE, originally merchants engaged independently in oversea trade, who combined in guilds in different areas (Germany, the Netherlands, Scandinavia) in the 15th cent. Henry VII gave them their first official 'patent', but not a regular charter. Then they were incorporated as a single company in 1564. Throughout the reign of Elizabeth this enjoyed a monopoly of the trade carried on by English subjects with the Low Countries and Germany, and became the greatest financial power in the country. It attacked the Hanse (q.v.) and finally drove it from England, and invaded the territory of the Hanse itself, contributing largely to its ultimate dissolution.

Merchant of Venice, The, a comedy by Shakespeare (q.v.), probably written about 1596, printed in quarto in 1600. It is based on material in Giovanni Fiorentino's collection of Italian novels, and perhaps on works in which this material was rehandled.

Bassanio, a noble but poor Venetian, asks Antonio, his friend, a rich merchant, for three thousand ducats to enable him to prosecute fittingly his suit of the rich heiress Portia. Antonio, whose money is all employed in foreign ventures, undertakes to borrow the sum from Shylock, a Jewish usurer, whom he has been wont to upbraid for his extortions. Shylock consents to lend the money against a bond by which, in case the sum is not repaid at the appointed day, Antonio shall forfeit a pound of flesh. Bassanio prospers in his suit. By her father's will Portia is to marry that suitor who selects of three caskets (one of gold, one of silver, one of lead) that which contains her portrait. He makes the right choice—the leaden casket —and is wedded to Portia, and his friend Gratiano to her maid Nerissa. News comes that Antonio's ships have been wrecked, that the debt has not been repaid when due, and that Shylock claims his pound of flesh. The matter is brought before the duke. Portia disguises herself as an advocate, and Nerissa as her clerk, and they come to the court to defend Antonio, unknown to their husbands. Failing in her appeal to Shylock for mercy, Portia admits the validity of his claim, but warns him that his life is forfeit if he spills one drop of blood, since his bond gives him right to nothing beyond the flesh. Pursuing her advantage, she argues that Shylock's life is forfeit for having conspired against the life of a Venetian citizen. The duke grants Shylock his life, but gives half his wealth to Antonio, half to the State. Antonio surrenders his claim if Shylock will turn Christian and make over his property on his death to his daughter, Jessica, who has run away and married a Christian and been disinherited; to which Shylock agrees. Portia and Nerissa ask as rewards from Bassanio and Gratiano the rings that their wives have given them, which they have promised never to part with. Reluctantly they give them up, and are taken to task accordingly on their return home. The play ends with news of the safe arrival of Antonio's ships.

Merchant's Tale, The, see *Canterbury Tales*.

Mercia, a kingdom founded in the 6th cent. by the Anglian invaders known as Mercians, between Wessex, Northumbria, and Wales.

Mercilla, in Spenser's 'Faerie Queene', v. viii, 'a mayden Queene of high renowne' (Queen Elizabeth).

Mercury, see *Hermes*.

Mercutio, a character in Shakespeare's 'Romeo and Juliet' (q.v.).

Mercy, in Bunyan's 'The Pilgrim's Progress' (q.v.), a companion of Christiana.

Merdle and **Mrs. Merdle**, characters in Dickens's 'Little Dorrit' (q.v.).

Meredith, GEORGE (1828-1909), was grandson of Melchizedek Meredith, a prosperous tailor and naval outfitter of Portsmouth (a circumstance reflected in his novel 'Evan Harrington'). In London, after being articled to a solicitor, he turned to journalism, published 'Poems' (dedicated to Peacock) in 1851, and the burlesque fantasy 'The Shaving of Shagpat: an Arabian Entertainment' (1856). His first great novel, 'The Ordeal of Richard Feverel', appeared in 1859, and he became acquainted with Swinburne, Rossetti and the Pre-Raphaelite group, and other notable people. But his book did not sell and for long his means were scanty and precarious. 'Evan Harrington' appeared serially during 1860. During 1861-2 he lodged for a time with Swinburne and Rossetti in Chelsea, and in the latter year published his chief tragic poem 'Modern Love' (q.v.). In 1864 appeared 'Emilia in England' (subsequently renamed 'Sandra Belloni'). He published 'Rhoda Fleming' in 1865, 'Vittoria' in 1866, 'The Adventures of Harry Richmond' (1871), 'Beauchamp's Career' (1876), and 'The Tale of Chloe' and 'The Egoist' (his greatest novel) in 1879. He delivered in 1877 a characteristic lecture on 'The Idea of Comedy and the Uses of the Comic Spirit' (separately published in 1897). Meredith obtained general popularity for his work for the first time by 'Diana of the Crossways' (q.v., 1885). His last three novels were, 'One of our Conquerors' (1891), 'Lord Ormont and his Aminta' (1894), and 'The Amazing Marriage' (1895). His tortuous and difficult style has prevented his later popularity, but the skill and penetration of his character drawing are widely recognized.

Meredith, OWEN, the pseudonym under which E. R. B. Lytton (q.v.), first earl of Lytton, published some of his earlier works.

Meres, FRANCIS (1565–1647), author of 'Palladis Tamia, Wit's Treasury' (1598), containing quotations and maxims from various writers. In this, Meres reviewed all literary effort from the time of Chaucer to his own day. He commemorates 125 Englishmen; and his list of Shakespeare's works with his commendation of the dramatist's 'fine filed phrase', and his account of Marlowe's death, are notable elements in English literary history.

Merlin. The germ of the story of Merlin is found in Nennius's 'Historia Britonum'. The British king, Vortigern, is building a citadel against Hengist and the Saxons, but the foundations are swallowed up as they are laid. Ambrosius, a boy without mortal sire, explains that beneath the site of the citadel there live two dragons, one red and one white. The dragons are found, they fight, and the white dragon is defeated. The boy interprets this as an omen that the Saxons will be expelled by the Britons.

Geoffrey of Monmouth identifies this Ambrosius with Merlin and recounts the same story. In 'Arthour and Merlin', a poem of the late 13th cent., the story is developed. Merlin's birth is narrated (the devil is his father) and he aids Arthur to defeat his foes by his counsel and magic. Reference is made to the beguiling of Merlin by Nimiane (Nimue or Vivien, see *Lady of the Lake*). In Malory's 'Morte Darthur' it is Merlin who makes the Round Table for Uther Pendragon. He dotes upon Nimiane, who, to get rid of him, inveigles him under a great stone.

In Welsh vernacular literature there is a group of poems of a patriotic character attributed to a bard Merlin (Myrddhin),

alluded to in Shakespeare ('1 Henry IV', III. i. 150, and 'King Lear', III. ii. 95). There is perhaps some connection between this bard and the Merlin of the Arthurian legend.

Merlin and Vivien, one of Tennyson's 'Idylls of the King' (q.v., 1859).

Vivien, the wily and malignant daughter of a man killed fighting against King Arthur, sets herself to win the aged enchanter Merlin, accompanies him to Broceliande, and there extracts from him the knowledge of a charm, which she immediately uses to leave him shut up for ever in an old oak.

Mermaid Tavern, THE, a tavern that stood in Bread Street (with an entrance in Friday Street), London. One of the earliest of English clubs, the Friday Street Club, started by Sir Walter Ralegh, met there, and was frequented by Shakespeare, Selden, Donne, Beaumont, and Fletcher. It is celebrated by Beaumont in his 'Master Francis Beaumont to Ben Jonson'.

Keats also wrote 'Lines on the Mermaid Tavern'.

Merope, (1) one of the daughters of Atlas, and one of the Pleiades (q.v.); (2) the daughter of Cypselus, wife of Cresphontes and mother of Aepytus.

Matthew Arnold's tragedy 'Merope' is concerned with the latter. It deals with the revenge of Aepytus on Polyphontes, who has killed Cresphontes, king of Messenia, the father of Aepytus, and has for reasons of state proposed marriage to Merope, the widowed mother of Aepytus.

Merovingian, the name of the first dynasty of Frankish kings, derived from Merwig, its legendary founder in the 5th cent. It rose to importance under Clovis I (481–511), but declined until the Merovingians were finally ousted by Pepin the Short in 751.

Merrilies, MEG, the old gipsy woman in Scott's 'Guy Mannering' (q.v.). She is the subject of a poem by Keats, 'Old Meg she was a gipsy'.

Merriman, HENRY SETON, pseudonym of HUGH STOWELL SCOTT (1862-1903), novelist, author of 'Young Mistley' (published anonymously, 1888), 'The Slave of the Lamp' (1892), 'The Sowers' (1896), etc.

Merry, ROBERT, see *Della Crusca.*

Merry Devil of Edmonton, The, a romantic comedy (1608), whose authorship is unknown. Charles Lamb, who praised it highly, suggested Drayton as the possible author.

Merry Monarch, THE, Charles II.

Merry Wives of Windsor, The, a comedy by Shakespeare (q.v.), probably of 1600-1. An imperfect text was printed in 1602, the corrected text in the folio of 1623. It is said by Dennis to have been written by command of Queen Elizabeth to show Sir John Falstaff in love.

Falstaff (q.v.), who is 'out at heels', determines to make love to the wives of Ford and Page, two gentlemen dwelling at Windsor. Nym and Pistol, the discarded followers of Falstaff, warn the husbands. Falstaff sends identical love-letters to Mrs. Ford and Mrs. Page, who contrive the discomfiture of the knight. At a first assignation at Ford's house, on the arrival of the husband, they hide him in a basket, cover him with foul linen, and have him tipped into a muddy ditch. At a second assignation, they disguise him as the 'fat woman of Brentford', in which character he is soundly beaten by Ford. The jealous husband having also been twice befooled, the plot is now revealed to him, and a final assignation is given to Falstaff in Windsor Forest, where he is beset and pinched by mock fairies and finally seized and exposed by Ford and Page.

The underplot is concerned with the wooing of Anne, the daughter of Page, by three suitors, Doctor Caius, a French physician, Slender, the foolish cousin of Justice Shallow, and Fenton, a wild young gentleman, whom Anne loves, and whom she finally runs away with.

Merygreek, MATTHEW, a character in Udall's 'Ralph Roister Doister' (q.v.).

Mesmer, FRIEDRICH ANTON (1733-1815), an Austrian physician, who popularized the doctrine or system known as *Mesmerism.*

Messalina, the wife of the Roman emperor Claudius, proverbial for her profligacy.

Messiah, the Hebrew title (meaning 'anointed') applied in the O.T. prophetic writings to a promised deliverer of the Jewish nation, and hence applied to Jesus of Nazareth as the fulfilment of that promise.

Messiah, The, (1) a sacred eclogue by Pope (q.v.), published in 'The Spectator' in May 1712, embodying in verse the Messianic prophecies of Isaiah; (2) a famous oratorio by Handel (q.v.); (3) a religious epic ('Messias') by Klopstock (q.v.).

Mess John, see *Mas John.*

Metamorphoses, The, a series of mythological tales in verse by the Roman poet Ovid (q.v.).

Metaphor, the transfer of a name or descriptive term to an object different from, but analogous to, that to which it is properly applicable, e.g. 'abysmal ignorance'. MIXED METAPHOR is the application of two inconsistent metaphors to one object.

Metaphysical Poets, a term invented by Dryden and adopted by Johnson as the designation of certain 17th-cent. poets (chief of whom were Donne and Cowley) addicted to 'witty conceits' and far-fetched imagery. But modern opinion does not endorse Johnson's condemnation of these poets. The virtue of the highly intellectual conventions in which they worked and of the genuine poetic qualities of such poets as Donne, Herbert, Vaughan, Crashaw, etc., has been widely recognized.

Metathesis, the transposition of letters or sounds in a word, as *ask*, OE. *acsian* (surviving in the dialect 'ax'). When the transposition is between the letters or sounds of two words, it is popularly known as a 'Spoonerism', of which a well-known specimen (attributed to the Revd. W. A. Spooner (1844-1930), Warden of New College, Oxford) is 'Kinquering congs their titles take'.

Methodism, a movement of reaction against the apathy of the Church of England that prevailed in the early part of the 18th cent. Its leaders were J. and C. Wesley and Whitefield (qq.v.).

The name 'Methodist' was originally applied to the members of a religious society established at Oxford in 1729 by the Wesleys and other members of the University, having for its object the promotion of piety and morality. It was subsequently extended to those who took part in or sympathized with the movement above described.

Methuselah, proverbial for the long life attributed to him in Gen. v. 27.

Metonymy, the figure of speech in which the name of an attribute is used for that of the thing meant, e.g. 'crown' for 'king'. Cf. *synecdoche*.

Metre, from Gk. μέτρον measure, any specific form of verse, determined by the number and character of the feet which it contains. In the compounds DIMETER, TRIMETER, etc., it is the unit which is repeated a certain number of times in a line of verse. This unit consists of two iambuses, trochees, or anapaests, or of one dactyl (qq.v.). Thus an iambic dimeter consists of four iambuses, a hexameter (q.v.) of six dactyls (or equivalents). In English (accentual) verse stressed syllables replace the long syllables, and unstressed syllables the short syllables, of Greek and Latin (quantitative) verse.

Meun(g), JEAN DE, see *Roman de la Rose*.

Meynell, ALICE (1847-1922), poet, essayist, and critic. Her rare gifts, both in prose and poetry, may be seen in her volumes of essays: 'The Rhythm of Life' (1893), 'The Children' (1896), 'The Spirit of Peace' (1898); and in her early volume of 'Preludes' (1875), 'Poems' (1893), and 'Last Poems' (1923). A complete edition of her poems was published in 1923. See also *Thompson* (*F.*).

Micawber, WILKINS and MRS., characters in Dickens's 'David Copperfield' (q.v.).

Michael, a pastoral poem by W. Wordsworth (q.v.) (1800).

Michael, ST., the archangel, mentioned as the leader of the angels against the dragon and his host in Rev. xii. 7, and described by Milton ('Paradise Lost', vi. 44) as 'of celestial armies prince'. His feast is celebrated on 29 Sept., known as MICHAELMAS.

Michael Angelo Titmarsh, the pseudonym adopted by Thackeray (q.v.) in many of his early works.

Michaelmas Terme, a comedy by T. Middleton (q.v.), printed in 1607.

Michal, in Dryden's 'Absalom and Achitophel' (q.v.), is the queen of Charles II, Catharine of Portugal, accused by Oates of conspiracy against the king's life.

Michelangelo Buonarroti (1475-1564), Italian painter, sculptor, architect, and poet. His early works (e.g. the 'David', 1504) express the humanistic ideals of the High Renaissance. His later work, such as the 'Last Judgement' in the Sistine Chapel, reveals a disillusionment which echoes the instability of Church and State after the Reformation and the Sack of Rome. His first patron was Lorenzo de' Medici, and he worked for the Medici family for much of his life. Pope Julius II commissioned him to carve his tomb and then interrupted the work by requiring him to paint the ceiling of the Sistine Chapel. In 1546 Michelangelo became chief architect to St. Peter's and designed the dome. He wrote a number of sonnets and madrigals, some addressed to his friend Vittoria Colonna (1490-1547).

Miching malicho, a phrase of uncertain meaning occurring in Shakespeare's 'Hamlet', III. ii. 148. 'Miching' is probably from the ME. verb 'to miche', meaning to pilfer, skulk, play truant. 'Malicho' perhaps represents the Spanish *malhecho*, misdeed. Lord Miching Malicho in

Peacock's 'Gryll Grange' represents Lord John Russell.

Microcosm of London, The, a well-known archaeological and topographical work, the text by William Combe, the figures drawn by Rowlandson, and the architecture by Augustus Charles Pugin (1808).

Microcosmographie, a collection of character sketches on the model of Theophrastus (q.v.), chiefly by John Earle (1601?-65), bishop of Salisbury (1628). The author analyses inconspicuous types, such as the plain country fellow, a modest man, and a poor man. The sketches are interesting in the evolution of the English essay.

Midas, a king of Phrygia, who, having hospitably entertained Silenus, the tutor of Bacchus, when he had lost his way, was permitted by the god to choose his recompense. He asked that whatever he touched might be turned to gold. His prayer was granted, but when he found that the very meat he attempted to eat became gold in his mouth, he entreated Bacchus to relieve him of the gift. On another occasion Midas declared that Pan was a superior flute-player to Apollo, whereupon the offended god changed his ears to those of an ass, to indicate his stupidity. This Midas attempted to conceal; but one of his servants saw the length of his ears and whispered the fact to some reeds, and these, whenever agitated by the wind, repeated it to the world.

Midas, a prose play by Lyly (q.v.) (1592), on the legend of Midas (see above).

Middle Ages, THE, the period of time from the Roman decadence (5th cent. A.D.) to the Renaissance (about 1500). The notion is that of an interval between two periods of advancing knowledge (cf. Bacon, 'Novum Organum' 1, § 78). The earliest use of *Middle Age*, in this sense, yet discovered, is in one of Donne's sermons (1621), but the corresponding Latin terms, *media aetas*, *medium aevum*, etc., are found at various dates in the 16th

cent. The term is no longer used in a pejorative sense and may include only the 11th-15th cents., the earlier period being called the Dark Ages.

Middle English, English language and literature from the 12th to the 15th cents., usually divided into 'early ME.', 1100-1250; 'ME.', 1250-1400; 'late ME.', 1400-1500.

The first period, following on the Norman Conquest and the neglect of English as a literary language, marked the end of Anglo-Saxon traditions. Layamon's 'Brut' (q.v.) is one of the last extant poems of the period to be written in the alliterative forms; internal rhyme and assonance are common throughout it. During the 13th cent. French influence predominated: rhyme was favoured and alliteration became a secondary ornament. New and elaborate rhyming forms were popular; continental traditions of romance and lyricism were successfully borrowed.

In the 14th cent. there was a revival of alliterative forms, particularly in the west of England; 'Piers Plowman' and 'Sir Gawain and the Green Knight' are famous examples. In this period, the north and north-west of England enjoyed a great literary productivity, producing notably Rolle, Minot (qq.v.), the poet of 'Gawain' and 'Pearl', Robert Mannyng, Wycliffe, and the unknown authors of the York and Towneley miracle cycles.

With Chaucer, the Renaissance influence of Italy and France was definitely established in England: his poetry looks forward through his 15th-cent. imitators to the main course of English literature. His contemporary, Gower (q.v.), on the other hand, represents the end of a purely medieval tradition.

Besides the works of 'Chaucerians' which dominate the 15th cent., there are also many traces of earlier influences. The alliterative technique was still used, e.g. in the 'Morte Arthure' (q.v.); the miracle play developed into the morality; ballads of the period are directly descended from 13th- and 14th-century verse tales, and

Skelton's octosyllabic verses are nearer to Gower than to Chaucer.

Modern English literature is—like the language—usually dated from the late 15th or early 16th cent. In poetry it begins perhaps with Wyatt and Surrey; in prose with More, Ascham, and Elyot.

Middlemarch, a Study of Provincial Life, a novel by G. Eliot (q.v.) (1871-2).

The scene is laid in the provincial town of Middlemarch in the first half of the 19th cent. The story is concerned principally with Dorothea Brooke, a St. Theresa, ardent, puritanical, with a high ideal of life. She marries the elderly pedant Mr. Casaubon, possessed of an archangelical manner, for whom she feels 'the reverence of a neophyte entering on a higher grade of initiation'. The marriage is intensely unhappy. Parallel with this runs the story of the unhappy marriage of Tertius Lydgate, an ambitious young doctor, with the beautiful but commonplace Rosamond Vincy, whose materialism brings about the failure of his hopes.

Middleton, CLARA and DR., characters in Meredith's 'The Egoist' (q.v.).

Middleton, CONYERS (1683-1750), fellow of Trinity College, Cambridge, was involved in the disputes with Bentley, the master. His chief works were his 'Life of Cicero' (1741) and a latitudinarian 'Free Inquiry into Miracles' (1748). His conclusion as to the unreality of postapostolic miracles aroused much criticism.

Middleton, THOMAS (1570?-1627), dramatist, wrote satirical comedies of contemporary manners, and later, under the influence of W. Rowley, romantic comedies. Much of his work was done in collaboration with Dekker, Rowley, Munday, and others. He also wrote pageants and masques for city ceremonials, and was appointed city chronologer in 1620. In 1624 he wrote a political drama 'A Game at Chesse' (q.v.) for which he and the actors were summoned before the Privy Council. His other plays (which were very popular) include 'Michaelmas Terme' (1607), 'A Mad World, my

Masters' (1608), 'The Roaring Girle' (1611, with Dekker), 'A Fair Quarrel' (1617, with Rowley), 'The Changeling' (1623, with Rowley), 'The Spanish Gipsy' (1623, with Rowley), 'A Chaste Maid in Cheapside' (1630), 'Women beware Women' (1657), 'Anything for a Quiet Life' (1662), 'The Widdow' (1652, with Ben Jonson and Fletcher). He is supposed to have also written some miscellaneous verse and prose.

Midshipman Easy, Mr., a novel by Marryat (q.v.) (1836).

Jack Easy is the son of Mr. Nicodemus Easy, a rich country gentleman, who believes all men are equal, and instils these ideas into his son. When Jack Easy goes to sea as a midshipman his insistence on these ideas, and his inclination to argument, bring him into conflict with naval discipline. His adventurous disposition leads him into a number of exciting incidents; their fortunate outcome is largely due to the devotion of the resourceful Ashantee, Mesty, and of his fellow midshipman, Edward Gascoigne. Among the many amusing naval characters in the book may be mentioned the bellicose chaplain, Hawkins, Mr. Biggs, the boatswain ('Duty before decency'), and Mr. Pottyfar, the lieutenant who kills himself with his own universal medicine.

Midsummer Night's Dream, A, a comedy by Shakespeare (q.v.), probably written in 1595 or 1596, and printed in 1600.

Hermia, ordered by her father, Egeus, to marry Demetrius, refuses, because she loves Lysander, while Demetrius has formerly professed love for her friend Helena, and Helena loves Demetrius. Under the law of Athens, Theseus, the duke, gives Hermia four days in which to obey her father; else she must suffer death. Hermia and Lysander agree to leave Athens secretly in order to be married where the Athenian law cannot pursue them, and to meet in a wood a few miles from the city. Hermia tells Helena of the project, and the latter tells Demetrius. Demetrius pursues Hermia to the wood, and Helena Demetrius, so that all four are that night in the wood. This wood is the favourite haunt of the fairies.

Oberon and Titania, king and queen of the fairies, have quarrelled, because Titania refuses to give up to him a little changeling boy for a page. Oberon tells Puck, a mischievous sprite, to fetch him a certain magic flower, of which he will press the juice on the eyes of Titania while she sleeps, so that she may fall in love with what she first sees when she wakes. Over-hearing Demetrius in the wood reproach-ing Helena for following him, and desirous to reconcile them, Oberon orders Puck to place some of the love-juice on Deme-trius's eyes, but so that Helena shall be near him when he does it. Puck, mistaking Lysander for Demetrius, applies the love-charm to him, and it chances that Helena is the first person that Lysander sees, to whom he at once makes love, enraging her because she thinks she is made a jest of. Oberon discovering Puck's mistake, now places some of the juice on Demetrius's eyes, and he on waking first sees Helena, so that both Lysander and Demetrius are now making love to Helena. The ladies fall to high words and the men go off to fight for Helena.

Meanwhile Oberon has placed the love-juice on Titania's eyelids, who wakes to find Bottom the weaver near her, wearing an ass's head (Bottom and a company of Athenian tradesmen are in the wood to rehearse a play for the Duke's wedding, and Puck has put an ass's head on Bottom); Titania at once becomes ena-moured of him, and toys with his 'amiable cheeks' and 'fair large ears'. Oberon, finding them together, reproaches Titania for bestowing her love on an ass, and again demands the changeling boy, whom she in her confusion surrenders; whereupon Oberon releases her from the charm. Puck at Oberon's orders throws a thick fog about the human lovers, and brings them all together, unknown to one another, and they fall asleep. He applies a remedy to their eyes, so that when they awake they return to their former loves. Theseus and Egeus appear on the scene, the runaways are forgiven, and the couples married. The play ends with the scene of 'Pyramus and Thisbe', comically acted by Bottom and his fellow tradesmen, to grace these nuptials and those of Theseus and Hippolyta.

Miggs, MISS, in Dickens's 'Barnaby Rudge' (q.v.), the shrewish servant of Mrs. Varden.

Migne, JACQUES PAUL (1800-75), French priest and publisher, who issued the great 'Patrologiae Cursus Completus', a col-lection of patristic writings.

Mignon, in the 'Wilhelm Meister's Ap-prenticeship' of Goethe (q.v.), a fairy-like child who from hopeless love and longing for her Italian home pines away and dies. She is the prototype of Fenella in Scott's 'Peveril of the Peak'. Ambroise Thomas wrote the opera 'Mignon', founded on the above.

Mikado, THE, the title of the emperor of Japan. For the comic opera, 'The Mikado', see *Gilbert and Sullivan Operas.*

Milesian Tales, a collection of short Greek stories of love and adventure, of a generally licentious character, by Aristides of Miletus of the 2nd cent. B.C., now lost.

Miles Standish, The Courtship of, a poem in hexameters by Longfellow (1858).

Miles Standish, a blunt old Puritan in the land of the Pilgrim Fathers, having lost his wife, sends his friend John Alden to make an offer of marriage on his behalf to the fair Priscilla. She indignantly replies that if she is worth winning she is worth wooing. John Alden himself loves her but is faithful to his trust. He tells Miles Standish the result of his mission, and the latter departs in anger. News comes of his death in battle, after which John and Priscilla are married. On the completion of their wedding, Standish reappears, repentant, and is reconciled to his friend.

Mill, JAMES (1773-1836), was educated for the ministry, but came to London in 1802 and took up journalism. He published in 1818 a 'History of British India', which obtained him a high post in the East India Company's service. He was closely associated with Bentham and Ricardo (qq.v.), whose views in philosophy and political economy, respectively, he adopted. He published his 'Elements of Political Economy' in 1821, his 'Analysis of the Human Mind' in 1829, and his 'Fragment on Mackintosh' in 1835. In the 'Analysis' he provided, by his theory of association, a psychological basis for Bentham's utilitarianism. Mill helped to found, and contributed to, 'The Westminster Review' (q.v.).

An interesting picture of Mill's rather grim personality is given in the 'Autobiography' of his son J. S. Mill (q.v.).

Mill, JOHN STUART (1806-73), son of James Mill (q.v.), formed the Utilitarian Society, which met during 1823-6 to read essays and discuss them, and in 1825 edited Bentham's 'Treatise upon Evidence'. But he gradually departed in some degree from the utilitarian doctrine expounded by Bentham, as is shown by his essay on that philosopher published in 'The London and Westminster Review' in 1832, and later in his 'Utilitarianism' (1861). In 1843 he published his chief work, the 'System of Logic', and his 'Principles of Political Economy' in 1848. In 1859 appeared his essay on 'Liberty'. His interesting 'Autobiography' appeared in 1873.

Millais, SIR JOHN EVERETT (1829-96), a precocious and brilliant painter. He was a member of the Pre-Raphaelite Brotherhood (q.v.), painting romantic and literary subjects, e.g. 'Isabella' (from Keats), and illustrating magazine stories. After *c.* 1860 he became a fashionable painter of portraits and genre scenes.

Millamant, the heroine of Congreve's 'The Way of the World' (q.v.), the author's most vivid creation.

Millay, EDNA ST. VINCENT (1892-1950), American poet. Her works include 'Renascence and other Poems' (1917), 'The Harp-Weaver and Other Poems'

(1923), and the play 'The Princess Marries the Page' (1932). Her 'Collected Sonnets' appeared in 1941 and her 'Collected Lyrics' in 1943.

Miller, ARTHUR (1915-), American dramatist. His plays include 'All My Sons' (1947), 'Death of a Salesman' (1949), which established him as a leading dramatist, 'The Crucible' (1953), 'A View from the Bridge' (1955), 'After the Fall' (1963), and 'The Price' (1968).

Miller, HUGH (1802-56), by trade a stonemason, was author of geological and other works, including 'The Old Red Sandstone' (1841); 'Footprints of the Creator' (1847); the pleasant autobiography, 'My Schools and Schoolmasters' (1854); and 'The Testimony of the Rocks' (1857).

Miller of the Dee, the subject of a song in the comic opera 'Love in a Village' by Bickerstaffe.

Miller of Trumpington, THE, the miller in 'The Reeve's Tale' in Chaucer's 'Canterbury Tales' (q.v.).

Miller's Tale, The, see *Canterbury Tales.*

Mill on the Floss, The, a novel by G. Eliot (q.v.) (1860).

Tom and Maggie, the principal characters in the story, are the children of the honest but ignorant and obstinate Mr. Tulliver, the miller of Doricote Mill on the Floss. Tom is a prosaic youth, narrow of imagination and intellect. Maggie is a far nobler type, highly strung and intelligent, of intense sensibility, and artistic and poetic tastes. She finds in Philip Wakem, the deformed son of a neighbouring lawyer, a temperament like her own, and they are mutually attracted. Unfortunately lawyer Wakem is the object of Mr. Tulliver's suspicion and dislike, which develop into intense hatred. Tom, loyal to his father, discovers the relations of affectionate friendship secretly maintained between Maggie and Philip. Maggie yields to her brother's authority and ceases to see Philip. Maggie leaves the Mill for a visit at St. Ogg's to her cousin Lucy Deane, who is to marry the cultivated and agreeable Stephen Guest. Stephen, though loyal in intention to Lucy, is attracted by Maggie's beauty; she, though similarly loyal to Philip, is drawn to Stephen. A boating expedition on the tidal river leads to Maggie's being innocently but irremediably compromised. Her brother turns her out of his house; the society of St. Ogg's ostracizes her. A great flood descends upon the town, in the course of which Maggie courageously rescues Tom from the mill. There comes a moment of revelation to the spirit of the awestruck Tom before the boat is overwhelmed, and brother and sister, reconciled at last, are drowned.

The tragedy of the story is somewhat relieved by a number of entertaining characters, notably Mrs. Tulliver's sisters, the strong-minded Mrs. Glegg and the melancholy Mrs. Pullet, with their respective spouses, and the ingenious packman Bob Jakin.

Mills, Miss, in Dickens's 'David Copperfield' (q.v.), Dora's friend.

Millwood, see *George Barnwell*.

Milly Swidger, the good angel in Dickens's 'The Haunted Man' (q.v.).

Milman, Henry Hart (1791-1868), professor of poetry at Oxford (1821-31), and dean of St. Paul's (1849). He wrote a number of dramas, but is chiefly remembered for his historical writings: his principal work is 'The History of Latin Christianity' (1854-5).

Milne, Alan Alexander (1882-1956), journalist and playwright, author of books of children's stories and verse, 'Winnie-the-Pooh', 'When We Were Very Young', etc., which enjoyed great popularity; and also of plays including 'Mr. Pim Passes By' and 'The Truth about Blayds'.

Milnes, Richard Monckton (1809-85), *first Baron Houghton*, was educated at Trinity College, Cambridge, where he was intimate with Tennyson, Hallam, and Thackeray. He became an active politician. Of his songs and other poems ('Poetical Works', 1876), those best known are 'The Brookside' and 'Strangers Yet'.

He also wrote on political and critical subjects and wrote a Life of Keats (1848); he was the first open champion of Keats as a poet of the first rank.

Milo, a celebrated athlete of Crotona in Italy, who attained immense strength. He was one of the disciples of Pythagoras. In attempting to tear down a tree in his old age, Milo's hands were caught in a cleft in the wood; being unable to escape, he was eaten up by wild beasts.

Milton, a symbolic poem by Blake (q.v.), which he began to engrave in 1804.

Milton, John (1608-74), son of John Milton the elder (a scrivener and composer of music), was educated at St. Paul's School and Christ's College, Cambridge, becoming B.A. in 1629 and M.A. in 1632. While at Cambridge he wrote the poems 'On the Death of a Fair Infant' and 'At a Vacation Exercise', and some Latin elegies and epigrams; but he first struck a distinctive note in the stately ode 'On the Morning of Christ's Nativity' (1629), the fragmentary 'Passion', and the poem 'On Shakespeare' (1630). After leaving Cambridge, Milton lived at Horton in Bucks. with his father, reading the classics and preparing himself for his vocation as a poet, from 1632 to 1637. Here he composed 'L'Allegro' and 'Il Penseroso' (qq.v.) in 1632, and at the invitation of Henry Lawes (who wrote the music for them) the 'Arcades' (part of a masque, 1633?) and the masque 'Comus' (q.v., 1634, published 1637). In 1637 he wrote 'Lycidas' (q.v.). During the twenty years that elapsed between this and his composition of 'Paradise Lost', Milton wrote no poetry but the sonnets and some Latin and Italian pieces. From 1637 to 1639 he travelled abroad, chiefly in Italy, and visited Grotius and Galileo. In 1641 he published a series of pamphlets against episcopacy, engaging in controversy with Bishop Hall. These were followed in 1642 by his 'Apology against a pamphlet . . . against Smectymnuus' (see *Smectymnuus*), containing some interesting autobiographical details. Milton married Mary

Powell, daughter of Royalist parents, probably in June 1642 (not 1643 as has been generally supposed). Within six weeks he consented to her going home to her parents on condition that she returned by Michaelmas. She did not do so, perhaps for reasons connected with the outbreak of the Civil War. Milton published in 1643 his pamphlet on the 'doctrine and discipline of divorce' which made him notorious. In 1644-5 he published three further pamphlets on divorce, his 'Tractate of Education', and the 'Areopagitica' (q.v.) on the liberty of the press. His wife rejoined him in 1645. After the execution of Charles I he published the 'Tenure of Kings and Magistrates' (1649), and was appointed Latin secretary to the newly formed Council of State. He replied officially to 'Eikon Basilike' (q.v.) in 'Eikonoclastes' (1649), and to Salmasius (q.v.) in 'Pro Populo Anglicano Defensio' (1651), and also to Du Moulin's 'Clamor' in 'Defensio Secunda' (1654), which contains autobiographical passages (the two 'Defensiones' were in Latin). Having become blind, he was assisted in his secretarial duties successively by G. R. Weckherlin, Philip Meadows, and Marvell (q.v.). His first wife died in 1652, leaving three daughters, and in 1656 he married Catherine Woodcock, who died in 1658. He retained his post as Latin secretary until the Restoration. At the Restoration he was arrested and fined, but released; he lost the greater part of his fortune. He returned to poetry and set about the composition of 'Paradise Lost' (q.v.), the first sketch of which can be dated as early as 1642. He married his third wife, Elizabeth Minshull (who survived him), in 1662. The 'Paradise Lost' is said by Aubrey to have been finished in 1663, but the agreement for his copyright was not signed till 1667. His last poems, 'Paradise Regained' (q.v.), and 'Samson Agonistes' (q.v.), were published together in 1671.

Of Milton's Latin poems, the finest is the 'Epitaphium Damonis', written in 1639, on the death of his friend Charles Diodati (q.v.); while the address to 'Mansus' (Manso, the intimate friend of Tasso and Marini) has great interest.

The 'State Papers' that he wrote as Latin secretary are mostly concerned with the routine work of diplomacy, but include an interesting series of dispatches on the expulsion of the Protestant Vaudois. The Latin prose writings include his 'De Doctrina Christiana', printed in 1825, which served as the occasion for Macaulay's essay on Milton.

Mime, a kind of simple farcical drama among the Greeks and Romans, characterized by mimicry and the ludicrous representation of familiar types of character; or a dialogue written for recital in a performance of this kind. The term is also occasionally applied to similar performances or compositions in modern times. But in the modern usage the word generally means dumb acting.

Minerva, the Roman goddess of wisdom and of arts and trades, subsequently identified with the Greek Athene (q.v.), which led to her being regarded also as the goddess of war. She was further held to have invented musical instruments.

Minerva, Jahrbuch der gelehrten Welt, a reference book of the universities, libraries, museums, etc., of the whole world, published by Walter de Gruyter & Co., Berlin and Leipzig.

Ming, the dynasty that ruled in China, 1368-1643. The porcelain of this period is highly esteemed.

Minim, DICK, a character sketched in Johnson's 'Idler' (q.v.). Inheriting a fortune, he turns man of wit and sets up as a critic. He has his own seat in a coffeehouse and heads a party in the pit, where he prudently spares the well-established authors and censures the unknown.

Minnehaha, see *Hiawatha.*

Minnesingers, German lyrical poets and singers of the 12th, 13th, and 14th cents., so called because love (*minne*) was the chief theme of their songs. They corresponded to the French *troubadours.*

Minoan, the name given by Sir A. Evans (q.v.), to the civilization revealed by his excavations at the Palace of Minos at Knossos in Crete, so called after the legendary King Minos (q.v.). Knossos was, in classical tradition, the seat of King Minos and the home of the Minotaur.

Minorites, Franciscan friars.

Minos, a legendary king of Crete, son of Zeus and Europa (q.v.), who was made a judge in the infernal regions. According to Athenian legend, Minos, after conquering the Athenians, caused a yearly tribute of seven youths and seven maidens to be brought to Crete to be devoured by the Minotaur (q.v.). He caused Daedalus (q.v.) to be confined in the labyrinth which he had constructed, and when Daedalus escaped, pursued him to Sicily, and was there slain by Cocalus, the king.

Minot, LAURENCE, probably a soldier, the author, about 1352, of English war-songs in various metres. Though not of a high poetical order, the songs are spirited, giving a vivid idea of medieval warfare, and marked by keen patriotism.

Minotaur, THE, a Cretan monster. Minos (q.v.) refused to sacrifice to Neptune a white bull. The god to punish him caused his wife Pasiphaë to become enamoured of the bull, and she gave birth to this monster. Minos confined it in the labyrinth made by Daedalus (q.v.), where it consumed the youths and maidens paid by the conquered Athenians as a tribute, until Theseus (q.v.) delivered his country and destroyed the monster.

Minstrel, The, a poem in Spenserian stanzas by Beattie (q.v.).

Minuscule, a small letter or script, a term used in palaeography to denote the scripts developed in the early Middle Ages. The best known is Caroline minuscule, the ancestor of 'Roman' type.

Mirabell, in Congreve's 'The Way of the World' (q.v.), the lover of Millamant.

Miracle Plays, medieval dramatic representations based on sacred history or on legends of the saints. Whether they were evolved from alternating songs sung in church (e.g. at the service on Easter Eve, between the three women approaching the grave and the Angel who guards it), or were spontaneous expressions of the dramatic instinct, is a point on which the authorities are not agreed. What is perhaps the earliest English miracle play, 'The Harrowing of Hell' is of the late 13th or 14th cent., though such plays existed in France much earlier. They reached their fullest development in the 15th and 16th cents. The four great collections of extant English 'miracles' or 'mysteries' are known by the names of the towns where they were, or are supposed to have been, performed, York, Chester, Coventry, and Wakefield (the last being also known as the 'Towneley' plays). Their performance was supervised by the corporation of the town, the several episodes being generally distributed among the guilds of handicrafts, and acted on wheeled stages moved processionally from one open place to another, or only in one place. The scenes varied in length from 180 to 800 lines, and were written in different metres, sometimes rhymed, sometimes alliterative, sometimes both. They were played principally on festivals, Corpus Christi day, Christmas, Whitsuntide, Easter. See also *Mary Magdalene* (*Play of*).

Not only is there no dearth of humour in these plays, but they are notable in the history of the drama for the introduction of comic by-play and episode.

Sir E. K. Chambers's 'The Mediaeval Stage' is the classic work on this subject.

Miranda, in Shakespeare's 'The Tempest' (q.v.), the daughter of Prospero.

Mirobolant, MONSIEUR, in Thackeray's 'Pendennis' (q.v.), the French cook at Clavering Park.

Mirror for Magistrates, A, a work planned by George Ferrers, Master of the King's Pastimes in the reign of Henry VIII, and William Baldwin of Oxford, in which divers illustrious men, most of them characters in English history, recount in verse their downfall, after the manner of Lydgate's version of Boccaccio's 'Fall of Princes'. It was licensed for publication in 1559, and contained twenty tragedies by various authors. Thomas Sackville contributed the 'Induction' and 'The Complaint of Buckingham' to the enlarged edition of 1563. Sackville's contribution is the only part having literary merit.

Mirror of Fools, 'Speculum Stultorum', see *Wireker*.

Mirvan, CAPTAIN, and MRS., and their daughter MARIA, characters in Fanny Burney's 'Evelina' (q.v.).

Mirza, The Vision of, see *Vision of Mirza*.

Misanthrope, Le, one of the greatest comedies of Molière (q.v.), produced in 1666, in which he represents the conflict between the noble but cross-grained Alceste and the worldly coquettish Célimène whom he loves.

Misfortunes of Elphin, The, a novel by Peacock (q.v.) (1829), an entertaining parody of the Arthurian legends.

Mishnah, the collection of binding precepts which forms the basis of the Talmud (q.v.) and embodies the contents of the oral law of the Jews.

Misrule, KING, LORD, or ABBOT OF, at the end of the 15th and beginning of the 16th cents., an officer appointed at court to superintend the Christmas revels. Lords of Misrule were also appointed in some of the university colleges and Inns of Court.

Miss Kilmansegg and her precious Leg, A Golden Legend, a tragi-comic poem by T. Hood (q.v.).

Mr. Clutterbuck's Election, a novel by H. Belloc (q.v.).

'**Mr. F's Aunt**', an eccentric character in Dickens's 'Little Dorrit' (q.v.).

Mr. Gilfil's Love-Story, see *Scenes of Clerical Life*.

Mr. Polly, The History of, a novel by H. G. Wells (q.v.) (1910).

Alfred Polly is a dyspeptic inefficient shopkeeper with a literary turn, who after a small legacy, and an injudicious marriage, has bought an unprofitable little shop in a small seaside town. After fifteen years of passive endurance he finds bankruptcy approaching and prepares for suicide. Instead, he sets his shop on fire and bolts. He chances upon a situation as man of all work at the Potwell Inn, but the landlady's ferocious nephew terrorizes and persecutes his aunt and threatens destruction to Polly. Polly, nobly conquering his innate timidity, in three murderous encounters defeats and finally ousts the villain, and is left completely happy.

Mr. Sludge, the 'Medium', a poem by R. Browning (q.v.) included in 'Dramatis Personae' (1864).

The poet puts into the mouth of Sludge, the detected cheat, a confession and defence of his profession of fraudulent medium.

Browning distrusted mediums, and was strongly antagonistic to the American spiritualist, Daniel D. Home (q.v.).

Mistletoe, a parasitic plant growing on various trees. The mistletoe of the oak was regarded by the Druids as a sacred plant. A trace of this belief is to be found in our use of mistletoe in Christmas decorations.

Mrs. Caudle's Curtain Lectures, by D. W. Jerrold (q.v.), appeared in 'Punch', 1845.

Mr. Caudle is a 'toyman and doll-merchant' and his wife is a voluble and jealous scold. The lectures, addressed to him when he wants to go to sleep, are reproofs for his mildly convivial habits, exhortations to take the family to the seaside, etc.

Mrs. Lirriper's Lodgings, and *Mrs. Lirriper's Legacy,* Christmas stories by Dickens (q.v.) (1863 and 1864). Mrs. Lirriper lets lodgings in Norfolk Street, Strand, and her lodgers and past lodgers tell their stories.

Mrs. Perkins's Ball, one of Thackeray's (q.v.) 'Christmas Books' (1847).

Mrs. Warren's Profession, a play by G. B. Shaw (q.v.), included in 'Plays Pleasant and Unpleasant' (q.v.).

Mitchel, JOHN (1818-75), an Irish nationalist, was editor of the 'Nation', and was tried for sedition and transported in 1848 to serve a sentence of fourteen years. He has left in his 'Jail Journal, or Five Years in British Prisons' (1856) a vivid account of his experiences. He escaped to America, where he engaged in journalistic work.

Mitford, MARY RUSSELL (1787-1855), is remembered for her charming collection of essays, 'Our Village, sketches of rural life, character, and scenery'. The scene of these is Three Mile Cross, near Reading. She also published a novel, 'Atherton' (1854), various plays, and 'Recollections of a Literary Life' (1852), which is of value for its chapters on some of her contemporaries.

Mitford, WILLIAM (1744-1827), the author of a 'History of Greece' (1785-1810), down to the death of Alexander, written at the suggestion of Gibbon, which enjoyed great popularity.

Mithraism, the religion of the worshippers of Mithras, one of the chief gods of the ancient Persians, in later times often identified with the sun. His worship was introduced among the Romans under the empire, and spread over most of northern and western Europe during the first three centuries A.D., the principal rival of Christianity.

Mitre Tavern, THE, frequented by Dr. Johnson, stood in Mitre Court, Fleet Street, over against Fetter Lane, not to be confused with the Mitre in Fleet Street of the days of Shakespeare and Jonson, which stood further west.

Mnemosyne, the mother by Zeus of the nine Muses (q.v.). The name signifies 'Memory'.

Moabite Stone, THE, a monument erected by Mesha, king of Moab, about 850 B.C., which furnishes the earliest-known inscription in the Phoenician alphabet.

Moby Dick, a romance of the sea, by H. Melville (q.v.) (1851).

Moby Dick is the name of a particularly cunning and ferocious whale, which has been the cause of so many disasters to its pursuers that it has become an object of fear and superstition. It has bereft Captain Ahab of his leg, and he has vowed revenge, and the story is that of the voyage of the ship 'Pequod' in pursuit of it. The author paints a vivid gallery of pictures of the strange characters aboard the 'Pequod', and, strangest of all, of the monomaniac Ahab. After a search round three-quarters of the globe, Moby Dick is found, and a thrilling contest, drawn out through three days, ends in its triumphant victory. It breaks Ahab's neck, crunches up or swamps all the boats, and finally sinks the 'Pequod' herself, with all hands, save one survivor.

Mock-heroic, a burlesque of the epic or tragic manner. Famous examples are Pope's 'Rape of the Lock' in which trivial incidents are invested with dignified and grandiloquent language; Gray's 'Ode on the Death of a favourite Cat'; or Fielding's 'Tom Thumb' which ridicules the bombast and rant of the heroic drama.

Modern Love, a series of fifty connected poems, each of sixteen lines, by G. Meredith (q.v.) (1862). It is the tragic tale of passionate married love giving place to discord, jealousy, and intense unhappiness.

Modern Painters, a treatise by Ruskin (q.v.), of which vol. i was published in 1843, vol. ii in 1846, vols. iii and iv in 1856, and vol. v in 1860.

The first volume, written when the author was only twenty-four, was conceived in a mood of indignation at the artistic ignorance of England, and written in particular to defend Turner against the attacks on his paintings.

Vol. ii 'expresses the first and fundamental law respecting human contemplation of the natural phenomena under whose influence we exist—that they can only be . . . interpreted . . . when they are accepted as the work and the gift of a Living Spirit greater than our own'.

The third volume, after an essay on the

Grand Style and a discussion of Idealism, passes to a history of the appreciation of landscape through the ages.

The fourth volume contains the famous passage on the tower of Calais church, and chapters on colour and illumination; followed, in this and the last volume, by a study of natural landscape in its various details.

The fifth volume proceeds to discuss the four orders of landscape painters— Heroic (Titian), Classical (Poussin), Pastoral (Cuyp), Contemplative (Turner); Dürer and Salvator Rosa; Wouvermans and Angelico. The work closes with a final lament for Turner.

Modest Proposal, A, a satirical pamphlet by Swift (q.v.).

Modo, in Shakespeare's 'King Lear', IV. i, the fiend of murder, one of the five that possess 'poor Tom'.

Modred or MORDRED, in the earliest Arthurian legends is the nephew of King Arthur. In Geoffrey of Monmouth he is the son of Arthur and his sister Morgawse. He traitorously seized the kingdom and Guinevere during Arthur's absence, and was killed by Arthur in the final battle in Cornwall.

Mogul, the Muslim Mongol empire in Hindustan. This was founded by Baber (a descendant of Tamerlane) in 1526. It reached its height under Akbar, Jehangir, Shah Jehan, and Aurungzebe, was broken up after the death of the last named, and finally disappeared in 1857. The GREAT MOGUL was the common designation among Europeans of the Mogul emperor.

Mohammed or MAHOMET (*c*. 570-632), the founder of the Muslim religion.

He declared himself a prophet about 611, and made known from time to time to his disciples the revelations that he claimed to receive, known as the Koran. His favourite wife was Ayesha, his favourite daughter Fatima.

Legend records that Mohammed, invited to show his miraculous powers, summoned Mt. Safa to come to him. He attributed its failure to do so to the mercy of Allah, for if it had come it would have overwhelmed him and the bystanders. Therefore, said Mohammed, he must go to the mountain, a proverbial example of bowing to the inevitable.

Mohican (pron. 'Mohēcan'), a warlike tribe of North American Indians.

For 'The Last of the Mohicans' see *Cooper* (*J. F.*).

Mohock, one of a class of aristocratic ruffians who infested the streets of London at night in the early years of the 18th cent.

Mohun (pron. 'Mo͞on'), CHARLES, *fifth Baron* (1675?-1712), a noted duellist; he figures prominently in Thackeray's 'Esmond' (q.v.).

Moidore, a gold coin of Portugal current in England in the first half of the 18th cent. It was worth about 27*s*. 6*d*.

Molière, the name assumed by JEAN BAPTISTE POQUELIN (1622-73), French comic dramatist. He became an actor and subsequently manager of a perambulating company. His real genius was first shown in 'Les Précieuses ridicules', acted in Paris in 1659. In this, abandoning imitations of Plautus and Terence, he introduced the ridicule of actual French society. His most famous plays were, besides that above mentioned: 'L'École des femmes' (1662), 'Le Tartuffe' (1664), 'Le Misanthrope' (1666), 'George Dandin' (1668), 'L'Avare' (1668), and 'Le Malade imaginaire' (1673).

Moll Cutpurse, Mary Frith, a notorious thief, fortune-teller, and forger, who lived about 1584-1659. She is the heroine of Middleton and Dekker's 'The Roaring Girle'.

Moll Flanders, The Fortunes and Misfortunes of the famous, a romance by Defoe (q.v.) (1722).

This purports to be the autobiography of the daughter of a woman who had been transported to Virginia for theft soon after her child's birth. The story relates her seduction, her subsequent marriage and liaisons, and her visit to Virginia, where she finds her mother and discovers that she has unwittingly married her own brother. Returning to England, she becomes a successful pickpocket and thief, but is presently transported to Virginia, in company with one of her former husbands, a highwayman. With the funds that each has amassed, they set up as planters, and spend their declining years in an atmosphere of penitence and prosperity.

Moloch or MOLECH, the name of a Canaanite idol, to whom children were sacrificed as burnt-offerings, represented by Milton ('Paradise Lost', i. 392) as one of the chief of the fallen angels.

Moly, a fabulous herb endowed with magic properties, said by Homer to have been given by Hermes to Odysseus as a charm against the sorceries of Circe ('Odyssey', x).

Momus, the god of mockery among the ancients, who turned to ridicule whatever the gods did. He was expelled from heaven for his criticisms.

Mona, an island between Britain and Ireland, anciently inhabited by Druids, supposed by some to be Anglesey, by others the Isle of Man.

Mona Lisa ('La Joconde', 'La Gioconda'), a portrait by Leonardo da Vinci (q.v.) of the wife of Francesco del Giocondo. It was taken to France by Francis I and is now in the Louvre. It is famous for its technical virtuosity and its enigmatic smile.

Monastery, The, a novel by Sir W. Scott (q.v.) (1820).

The story centres in the monastery of Kennaquhair, of which the prototype is Melrose Abbey on the Tweed, and the period chosen is the reign of Elizabeth, when the reformed doctrines were first making their way in Scotland and raising up troubles for the religious community that gives its title to the work.

Monasticon Anglicanum, see *Dugdale.*

Monboddo, JAMES BURNETT, LORD (1714–99), a Scottish judge and a pioneer in anthropology, who published 'Of the Origin and Progress of Language' (1773–92) and 'Antient Metaphysics' (1779–99).

He is perhaps chiefly remembered for his orang-outang, who figures in both these works, and suggested to Peacock the character of Sir Oran Haut-ton in his 'Melincourt' (q.v.).

Moneta, JUNO, 'Juno the admonisher', a goddess in whose temple at Rome money was coined; the origin of our word 'money'.

Monica, ST. (332–87), the mother of St. Augustine of Hippo (q.v.).

Monimia, the heroine of Otway's 'The Orphan' (q.v.).

Moniplies, RICHIE, a character in Sir W. Scott's 'The Fortunes of Nigel' (q.v.).

Monism, in philosophy, a general name for those theories which deny the duality (i.e. the existence as two ultimate kinds of substance) of matter and mind; opposed to dualism or pluralism.

Monk, The, a novel by M. G. Lewis (q.v.) (1796), a famous 'novel of terror and mystery'. (See *Gothic novels.*)

The mixture of the supernatural, the horrible, and the indecent makes the book unreadable today. But it has power, contains some notable verses ('Alonzo the Brave and the Fair Imogine'), and attained a considerable vogue.

Monkbarns, LAIRD OF, Jonathan Oldbuck, the principal character in Sir W. Scott's 'The Antiquary' (q.v.).

'Monk Lewis', soubriquet of M. G. Lewis (q.v.), author of 'The Monk' (q.v.).

Monks, a character in Dickens's 'Oliver Twist' (q.v.).

Monk's Tale, The, see *Canterbury Tales.*

Monologue, a scene in a drama in which one person speaks by himself; a long speech by one person.

For *dramatic monologue,* see under *Soliloquy.*

Monophysites, Christians who believe that there is only one nature in the person of Jesus Christ. They include at the present day the Coptic, Armenian, Abyssinian, and Jacobite Churches.

Monotheists, those who believe that there is only one God.

Monro, HAROLD (1879–1932), poet. He

wrote several volumes of poetry but is chiefly remembered as the founder of the 'Poetry Review' in 1912 and the Poetry Bookshop which he opened in London in 1913 and ran until his death. The Bookshop became a centre for anyone interested in poetry and a place where poetry readings could be given.

Monroe Doctrine, a political doctrine derived from a message of President Monroe (1823) in which he stated that interposition by any European power in the affairs of the Spanish-American republics would be regarded as an act unfriendly to the United States, and that the American continents were no longer open to European colonial settlement.

Monsieur D'Olive, a comedy by Chapman (q.v.), published in 1606 and acted a few years before. The plot is of little interest, but the play is enlivened by the remarkable character, D'Olive, 'the perfect model of an impudent upstart'.

Montagu, BASIL (1770–1851), legal and miscellaneous writer, intimate with Coleridge and Wordsworth. He published 'Essays' and edited Bacon (1825–37).

Montagu, MRS. ELIZABETH (1720–1800), well known as one of the leaders of the Blue Stocking (q.v.) circles. She combined beauty with wit and learning, and her conversation was highly praised by Dr. Johnson. She was author of the last three of the dialogues included in Lord Lyttelton's 'Dialogues of the Dead' (1760), and of an 'Essay on the Writings and Genius of Shakespeare' (1769), in which she defended the poet against the strictures of Voltaire.

Montagu, LADY MARY WORTLEY (1689–1762), wife of Edward Wortley Montagu, ambassador to Constantinople in 1716. She wrote from there some charming 'Turkish Letters' (published in 1763 after her death), and introduced into England the practice of inoculation against the small-pox. She is also remembered for her quarrels with Pope, who attacked her outrageously in his verse.

Montague, CHARLES EDWARD (1867–1928), joined the staff of the 'Manchester Guardian' in 1890 and later became assistant editor. He wrote novels, of which 'Right Off the Map' (1927) is probably the best known, short stories, and literary criticism. Some of his best work, such as the novel 'Rough Justice', was written during and about the First World War.

Montagues, THE, in Shakespeare's 'Romeo and Juliet' (q.v.), the Montecchi, a noble house of Verona, to which Romeo belongs, enemies of the Capulets (Cappelletti).

Montaigne, MICHEL EYQUEM DE (1533–92), educated at Bordeaux, where he had among other teachers George Buchanan (q.v.), was the author of the famous 'Essais', of which Bks. I and II appeared in 1580, an enlarged edition with Book III in 1588, and a posthumous edition in 1595. The first English translations were those of John Florio (q.v., 1603) and Charles Cotton (q.v., 1685). The essays reveal the author as a man of insatiable intellectual curiosity. The general conclusion of the essays is the recognition of the fallibility of the human reason and the relativity of human science.

Monte Cristo, Count of, a novel by Dumas (q.v.) the elder (1844–5). Edmond Dantès, falsely denounced by a personal enemy as a Bonapartist conspirator in 1815, is imprisoned in the Château d'If for many years, escapes, recovers a concealed treasure in the Island of Monte Cristo, and devotes years to the pursuit of his revenge under various names, including that of Count of Monte Cristo.

Montemayor, JORGE DE (c. 1521–61), a Portuguese poet, who wrote in Spanish. His chief work is his prose pastoral, the 'Diana Enamorada'. It was translated into English by Bartholomew Young (1598), and was perhaps used by Shakespeare in his 'Two Gentlemen of Verona'.

Montesquieu, CHARLES LOUIS DE SECONDAT DE (1689–1755), French political philosopher, best known for his 'Lettres persanes' (1721); and his greatest work, 'De l'Esprit des lois' (1748), in which he analysed various political constitutions, denounced the abuses of the French monarchical system, and advocated a liberal and beneficent type of government.

Montezuma (1466-1520), the ruler of Mexico at the time of the Spanish conquest. Dryden's play 'The Indian Emperor' has Montezuma for its subject.

Montfaucon, BERNARD DE (1655-1741), entered the Maurist (q.v.) community of Benedictines, working in various abbeys and at Rome on the study of manuscripts. His chief publication is 'Palaeographia Graeca' (1708), which did for the science of Greek palaeography what the 'De re diplomatica' of Mabillon (q.v.) had done for Latin palaeography.

Montgomerie, ALEXANDER (1556?-1610?), a Scottish poet, who held office in the Scottish court in 1577 and became laureate of the court, but got into trouble and was dismissed. His principal work is 'The Cherry and the Slae' (1597), a long allegorical poem. He also wrote a 'Flyting betwixt Montgomery and Polwart', published in 1621, and sonnets and miscellaneous poems.

Montgomery, ROBERT (1807-55), poetaster, author of religious poems ('The Omnipresence of the Deity', 1828, and 'Satan', 1830) which were extravagantly praised in the press, and severely criticized by Macaulay.

Monthly Review, The, founded in 1749 by the bookseller Ralph Griffiths. Oliver Goldsmith contributed to it articles of literary criticism in 1757. It was conducted by Griffiths until 1803, by his son until 1825, and expired in 1845. It was a rival to 'The Critical Review' (q.v.).

Montmartre, a district in the north of Paris, a haunt of artists and the site of many famous cafés and cabarets.

Montrose, JAMES GRAHAM, *first marquess and fifth earl of* (1612-50), the great general and rival of the marquess of Argyle, took a prominent part in Scottish history in the period immediately preceding the downfall of Charles I. He is the principal figure in Scott's 'A Legend of Montrose' (q.v.).

Monumenta Germaniae Historica, a series of the medieval texts bearing on the history of Germany, begun in 1816 and still continuing. Its editors have included many famous scholars.

Monumentum Ancyranum, a famous inscription in Greek and Latin in the temple of Augustus at Ancyra (modern Angora), a copy of the record of the chief events of the life of Augustus.

Moody and Sankey, Dwight Lyman Moody (1837-99) and Ira David Sankey (1840-1908), American evangelists. The compilation of the well-known 'Sacred Songs and Solos' was due to Sankey.

Moon, MAN IN THE, see *Man in the Moon.*

Moonstone, The, a novel by Wilkie Collins (q.v.) (1868).

The moonstone is an enormous diamond. At the siege of Seringapatam it had come into the possession of an English officer John Herncastle, who had killed its three Brahmin guards. It proved a dangerous acquisition, for other Brahmins set to work, with the utmost determination, to recover it. The moonstone is handed to Miss Verinder, on her eighteenth birthday, and mysteriously disappears the same night. Suspicion falls on three Indian jugglers who have been seen in the neighbourhood of the house. It has in fact been taken from Miss Verinder's cabinet, unconsciously, by her lover Franklin Blake, while under the influence of opium. From Franklin Blake, while still unconscious, the villain Godfrey Ablewhite has obtained it; and the story is occupied with the contest of cunning between Godfrey and the three Indians, ending in the murder of the former, the recovery of the diamond by the latter, and the revelation of the mystery. Sergeant Cuff, one of the first detectives in English fiction, figures in the story.

Moore, GEORGE (1852-1933), Anglo-Irish novelist, dramatist, and short-story writer. He studied painting in Paris from 1872 to

1882 and the knowledge of French writing he gained there stood him in good stead when, returning to England, he set about revitalizing the Victorian novel with naturalistic and, later, realistic techniques borrowed from Zola, Flaubert, the Goncourts, and Balzac (qq.v.). His first novel was 'A Modern Lover' (1883), followed by 'A Mummer's Wife' (1885), 'Esther Waters' (q.v., 1894), 'Evelyn Innes' (1898) and its sequel 'Sister Teresa' (1901). In his later novels, e.g. 'The Brook Kerith' (1916) and 'Ulick and Soracha' (1924), he aimed at epic effect. His 'Untilled Field' (1903), a group of short stories of outstanding merit, is strongly evocative of Turgenev and Dostoevsky (qq.v.). 'Confessions of a Young Man' (1888), 'Memoirs of my Dead Life' (1906), and 'Hail and Farewell' ('Ave', 1911, 'Salve', 1912, 'Vale', 1914), are all autobiographical. The last named is an important, though unreliable, source for the Irish literary movement associated with Yeats, 'AE', Lady Gregory (qq.v.), and others. He collaborated in the planning of the Irish National Theatre (see *Yeats*), a work which, in the words of Yeats, 'could not have been done at all without Moore's knowledge of the stage'.

Moore, GEORGE EDWARD (1873–1958), professor of philosophy in the University of Cambridge (1925–39). His first book, 'Principia Ethica' (1903), inaugurated a new era in British moral philosophy and had great influence outside academic philosophy, particularly on the Bloomsbury group (q.v.).

Moore, HENRY (1898–   ), sculptor, son of a Yorkshire miner. His figures and groups show, on the one hand, a deep humanity and, on the other, an interest in the forms and rhythms of natural objects.

Moore, SIR JOHN (1761–1809), became commander-in-chief in the Peninsula on the recall of Sir Harry Burrard (1808). He led the historic retreat to Coruña during the winter of 1808–9. Moore was mortally wounded, and buried at midnight of 16 Jan. 1809, in the citadel of Coruña. For the poem on this subject see *Wolfe*.

Moore, THOMAS (1779–1852), born in Dublin, the son of a grocer, issued in 1801 a volume of 'Poetical Works' under the pseudonym of 'Thomas Little', by which Byron refers to him in 'English Bards and Scotch Reviewers'. He became the national lyrist of Ireland (Moore was a musician as well as a poet) by the publication of his 'Irish Melodies' (1807–35). In 1813 he issued 'The Twopenny Post Bag', a collection of satires directed against the Regent. He acquired a European reputation by his 'Lalla Rookh' (q.v., 1817). His 'Loves of the Angels' (1823) excited much reprobation. He received in 1835 a literary pension, to which a civil list pension was added in 1850. Among his other works may be mentioned his novel, 'The Epicurean' (1827), 'The Fudge Family in Paris' (1818), and his lives of Sheridan (1825) and Lord Byron (1830). Moore was an intimate friend of the latter and Byron left him his memoirs (these were destroyed by Moore).

Mopsa, a character in Sidney's 'Arcadia' (q.v.).

Moral and Political Philosophy, *Principles of*, by Paley (q.v.) (1785).

An exposition of theological utilitarianism, largely based on the doctrine of Abraham Tucker, to which it gives method and clarity. The happiness of the individual is always the motive of his conduct. It is brought into conformity with the general happiness by the incentives of the Christian religion. Posthumous rewards and penalties are an essential part of Paley's ethical system; and the evidence for these is marshalled in his later works.

Moral Essays, four ethical poems by Pope (q.v.) (1731–5).

They were inspired by Lord Bolingbroke (q.v.) and take the form of four Epistles. Epistle I, addressed to Viscount Cobham, deals with the knowledge and characters of men; it sets forth the difficulties in judging a man's character and finds their solution in the discovery of the ruling passion, which 'clue once found unravels all the rest'. Epistle II, addressed to Martha Blount, deals with the characters of women, the most interesting of these being Atossa, intended for Sarah, duchess of Marlborough. Epistle III, to Lord Bathurst, deals with the use of riches. The Epistle contains the famous characters of the 'Man of Ross' (see *Kyrle*) and 'Sir Balaam' (q.v.). Epistle IV, to Lord Burlington, treats of the same subject as Epistle III, giving instances of the tasteless use of wealth. The epistle ends with indications as to the proper use of wealth.

Moralities, medieval dramatic pieces in verse, in which the biblical personages of the Miracle Plays (q.v.) gave place to personified abstractions, such as the vices and virtues. The action was simple and the purpose edifying. They belong mainly to the 15th cent., developing alongside of the 'Miracles'. Well-known examples are 'Everyman' (q.v.) and Skelton's 'Magnificence'.

Moral Ode, see *Poema Morale*.

Moral Sentiments, *Theory of*, see *Theory of Moral Sentiments*.

Moravians, the 'Unity of Moravian brethren', a Protestant sect founded early in the 18th cent. in Saxony by emigrants from Moravia. It obtained many adherents in England and the American colonies. They strongly influenced John Wesley (q.v.).

Morddure, in Spenser's 'Faerie Queene', II. viii. 20–1, the name of the sword made by Merlin for Prince Arthur. Its more general name is 'Excalibur'.

Mordecai, in the book of Esther, the foster-father of Esther, who sat at the gate and frustrated the design of the king's chamberlains to lay hands on the king, Ahasuerus. Hence 'a Mordecai at the gate'.

Mordred, see *Modred*.

More, HANNAH (1745–1833), in 1773 published 'The Search after Happiness',

a pastoral play for schools. She came to London in 1774, where she became intimate with Garrick and his wife, and obtained the friendship of Burke, Horace Walpole, Reynolds, Dr. Johnson, Mrs. Montagu, and the other ladies of the Blue Stocking (q.v.) coterie. Her tragedy 'Percy' was successfully produced by Garrick in 1777. After Garrick's death, Hannah More turned her attention to other subjects, and published tracts for the reformation of the poor, which proved very successful. In 1809 she published a popular novel, 'Cœlebs in Search of a Wife'. Her letters were published in 1834.

More, HENRY (1614–87), one of the leaders of the Platonist movement at Cambridge, author of many theological works. For an account of the chief members of this group see under *Platonists*.

More, SIR THOMAS (St.) (1478–1535), educated at Oxford, where he was the pupil of Linacre and Grocyn. He was for a time in youth in the household of Cardinal Morton, and it was probably from Morton's information that he derived his knowledge of Richard III. He devoted his leisure to literature, becoming intimate (1497) with Colet, Lily, and Erasmus, who afterwards stayed frequently at his house. He entered parliament in 1504. During an absence as envoy to Flanders he sketched his description (in Latin) of the imaginary island of 'Utopia' (q.v.), which he completed and published in 1516. He was Lord Chancellor, 1529–32.

Although willing to swear fidelity to the new Act of Succession, More refused to take any oath that should impugn the pope's authority; he was therefore committed to the Tower of London with John Fisher, bishop of Rochester. During the first days of his imprisonment he prepared a 'Dialogue of Comfort against Tribulation' and treatises on Christ's passion. He was indicted of high treason, found guilty, and beheaded in 1535.

More was a critic and a patron of art, and Holbein is said to have stayed three years in his house at Chelsea, and painted portraits of More and his family.

More's other chief English works are his 'Life of John Picus, Earl of Mirandula' (printed by Wynkyn de Worde, 1510), his 'History of Richard III' (printed imperfectly in Grafton's 'Chronicle', 1543, used by Hall, and printed fully by Rastell in 1557). His Latin publications (collected 1563, etc.) included, besides the 'Utopia', four dialogues of Lucian, epigrams, and controversial tracts in divinity.

More, Sir Thomas, a play written *c.* 1595-6 by Munday, Chettle, and probably Heywood, and further revised *c.* 1600-1 by a professional scribe (Hand C), Dekker, and Shakespeare (qq.v.). It was not performed. The three pages in which More's oratory quells the mob are the only known examples of Shakespeare's original composition.

The play is based on some of the chief events in the life of More, as recorded in Hall's Chronicle: his rise to favour as a result of his successful handling of an insurrection in London, his friendship with Erasmus, his refusal to support Henry VIII's policy, and his consequent imprisonment and execution.

Moresque, the Moorish Arabesque style of decoration (see *Arabesque*).

Morgan, in Thackeray's 'Pendennis' (q.v.), Major Pendennis's valet.

Morgan, MR., a character in Smollett's 'Roderick Random' (q.v.).

Morgan, CHARLES LANGBRIDGE (1894–1958), dramatic critic and author of the following novels: 'Portrait in a Mirror' (1929), 'The Fountain' (1932), 'Sparkenbroke' (1936), 'A Voyage' (1940), 'The Empty Room' (1941), 'The Judge's Story' (1947), and 'The River Line' (1949; adapted as a play, 1952).

Morgan, WILLIAM DE, see *De Morgan*.

Morgan le Fay, one of King Arthur's sisters, possessing magic powers, who married King Uriens. According to one version of the legend, she reveals to Arthur the intrigue of Launcelot and Guinevere. In the 'Morte Darthur' of Malory she

endeavours to kill Arthur. She is one of the three queens in the ship in which Arthur is carried off to be healed of his wounds. See also *Lady of the Lake*.

Morgann, MAURICE (1726–1802), author of an 'Essay on the Dramatic Character of Sir John Falstaff', a vindication of Falstaff's courage (1777).

Morgante Maggiore, a poem by Pulci (q.v.), a recasting, with humorous additions and alterations, of the popular epic 'Orlando'. Orlando (Roland) encounters three giants. He slays two and subdues the third, Morgante, converts him, and makes him his brother in arms. Byron translated the first canto.

Morgawse or MARGAWSE, in Malory's 'Morte Darthur', sister of King Arthur, wife of King Lot, and mother of Modred, Gawaine, Agravaine, Gaheris, and Gareth.

Morgiana, a character in the story of 'Ali Baba and the Forty Thieves' (q.v.).

Morglay, the name of the sword of Bevis of Hampton (q.v.). It is sometimes used allusively for a sword in general.

Morland, CATHERINE, the heroine of Jane Austen's 'Northanger Abbey' (q.v.).

Morland, GEORGE (1763–1804), genre painter, son of a painter, Henry Robert Morland (1716–97). He first exhibited at the Royal Academy at the age of 10. His vast output of country scenes, popular but superficial, failed to keep him out of debt and he died in a sponging-house.

Morley, CHRISTOPHER (1890–1957), American novelist and journalist. His chief works are: 'Where the Blue Begins' (1922), 'Parsons' Pleasure' (1923), 'Thunder on the Left' (1925), 'Kitty Foyle' (1939).

Morley, JOHN, *first Viscount Morley of Blackburn* (1838–1923), was twice chief secretary for Ireland (1886 and 1892-5), secretary of state for India (1905–10), and lord president of the council (1910–14). His chief publications were: 'Edmund Burke; an historical Study' (1867), 'Critical Miscellanies' (1871, second series, 1877), 'Life of Gladstone' (1903), 'Politics and History' (1914), 'Recollections' (1917).

He was also editor of the English Men of Letters series.

Morley, MRS., the name under which Queen Anne corresponded with the duchess of Marlborough (Mrs. Freeman).

Mormons, the popular name for 'The Church of Jesus Christ of Latter-day Saints', founded at Manchester, New York, in 1830 by Joseph Smith (1805-44). The 'Book of Mormon', it is claimed, was revealed to him in 1827. Its doctrines are in general harmony with those of the Bible. An additional revelation in favour of polygamy, which Smith claimed to have received in 1843, aroused general hostility to the sect. Under the leadership of Brigham Young, who succeeded Smith as president of the Mormon church in 1844, they made a remarkable pilgrimage to Utah, where they founded Salt Lake City in 1847. Polygamy was prohibited by the constitution of Utah in 1896.

Morning Chronicle, The, a Whig journal founded in 1769, rose to importance when James Perry became chief proprietor and editor in 1789. Its staff then included Sheridan, C. Lamb, Thomas Campbell, Sir James Mackintosh, Henry Brougham, Thomas Moore, and David Ricardo. Perry was followed by John Black in 1821. Among his contributors were James and John Stuart Mill; Charles Dickens was among his reporters, and Thackeray his art critic. 'The Morning Chronicle' came to an end in 1862.

Morning Post, The, a London daily newspaper, was founded in 1772. S. T. Coleridge was enlisted in its service at the end of the 18th cent., and Southey, Wordsworth, and Arthur Young also wrote for it. It was amalgamated with 'The Daily Telegraph' in 1937.

Morning Star of the Reformation, THE, Wycliffe (q.v.), so named by Daniel Neal in his 'History of the Puritans' (1732).

Morose, the principal character in Jonson's 'Epicœne' (q.v.).

Morpheus, the Greek god of dreams.

Morris, DINAH, a character in G. Eliot's 'Adam Bede' (q.v.).

Morris, SIR LEWIS (1833-1907), contributed actively to the establishment of the University of Wales. His principal poetical works were the 'Songs of Two Worlds' (1871) and the 'Epic of Hades' (1876-7). His simplicity of expression, melodious verse, cheerful optimism, and occasional exaltation made his work extremely popular, in spite of its poetic mediocrity.

Morris, WILLIAM (1834-96), was distinguished not only as a poet and artist, but also as a decorator, manufacturer and printer, and as a socialist. He was articled to the architect G. E. Street, and in 1858 he worked with Rossetti, Burne-Jones (qq.v.), and others on the frescoes in the Oxford Union. In 1858 he published his 'Defence of Guenevere, and other Poems'. The Red House, Bexley, designed for him by Philip Webb, was an important turning-point in the development of domestic architecture. Failing to find suitable furniture for it, Morris and a number of artists, including Rossetti, Burne-Jones, Madox Brown, and Webb, founded the firm of Morris, Marshall, Faulkner & Co. in 1861, which produced furniture, printed textiles, tapestries, wallpapers, and stained glass; his and his colleagues' designs brought about a complete revolution in the taste of the English public. In 1867 he published the 'Life and Death of Jason', and in 1868-70 'The Earthly Paradise' (q.v.). 'Love is enough' (a morality) appeared in 1872, a verse translation of the 'Aeneids of Virgil' in 1875, 'Three Northern Love Songs' in the same year, and the epic 'Sigurd and Volsung' (q.v.), perhaps his greatest work, in 1876. In 1883 he joined the Social Democratic Federation, the doctrine of which, largely under his leadership, developed into socialism. On its disruption in 1884 he became head of the seceders, who organized themselves as the Socialist League. In 1887 he published a verse translation of the 'Odyssey'. His later works, with the exception of

'Poems by the Way' (ballads and lyrics, 1891), were mainly in prose. Two of them, 'The Dream of John Ball' (mixed prose and verse, 1888) and 'News from Nowhere' (1891), were romances of socialist propaganda. Morris started in 1890, at Hammersmith, the Kelmscott Press, for which he designed founts of type and ornamental letters and borders, and from which were issued fifty-three books.

Morris twice visited Iceland, and the influence of the Sagas (many of which he translated in collaboration with Magnusson), as well as that of Chaucer, is apparent in his writings.

Morris-dance, a grotesque dance performed by persons in fancy costume, usually representing characters in the Robin Hood legend, especially Maid Marian and Friar Tuck. Maid Marian sometimes appears as Queen of May. The Morris-dance is referred to as early as the 15th cent. See also *Revesby Play*.

Morte Arthur, Le, a late 14th-cent. poem of 3,800 lines, in eight-lined rhyming stanzas, dealing with the loves of Launcelot and the Maid of Astolat, with Launcelot's love for Queen Guinevere, and with the last battles of Arthur and his bearing away to Avalon. See *Arthur* and *Launcelot*.

Morte Arthure, a 14th-cent. poem of 4,300 alliterative lines, dealing with the later history of King Arthur. The poem was written in northern England or southern Scotland.

Morte Darthur, Le, a prose translation made from the French, with adaptations from other sources, by Malory (q.v.), in twenty-one books, and finished between March 1469 and March 1470. It was edited and printed by Caxton in 1485. The work is a skilful selection and blending of materials taken from the mass of Arthurian legends. The central story consists of two main elements: the reign of King Arthur ending in catastrophe and the dissolution of the Round Table; and the quest of the Holy Grail, in which

Launcelot fails by reason of his sin, and Galahad succeeds. See under *Grail* and the names of the various characters in the book.

A manuscript contemporary with Caxton and considerably fuller than his text was found in Winchester College Library in 1934. It was edited by E. Vinaver and published under the title 'The Works of Sir Thomas Malory' (3 vols., 1947; second edition, 1967).

Morte d'Arthur, The a poem by Lord Tennyson (q.v.) (1842), subsequently incorporated in 'The Passing of Arthur' (q.v.), one of the 'Idylls of the King'.

Morton, HENRY, OF MILNWOOD, the hero of Scott's 'Old Mortality' (q.v.).

Morton, JOHN MADDISON (1811-91), wrote farces and showed a special gift for adaptations from the French. His most successful piece was 'Box and Cox' (q.v., 1847).

Morton, THOMAS (1764?-1838), the author of the successful comedies, 'The Way to get Married' (1796) and 'Speed the Plough' (1798). The last of these introduced the name of 'Mrs. Grundy' into England.

Morton's Fork, the dilemma that Cardinal Morton, Henry VII's chancellor, proposed to merchants and others whom he invited to contribute to benevolences. Either their handsome way of life manifested their opulence; or, if their course of living was less sumptuous, they must have grown rich by their economy.

Mosca, a character in Jonson's 'Volpone' (q.v.).

Moschus (*fl. c.* 150 B.C.), a pastoral poet of Syracuse, a pupil of Bion, a pathetic lament for whose untimely death is doubtfully attributed to him.

Moth, (1) in Shakespeare's 'Love's Labour's Lost' (q.v.), Armado's page, connected by Sir S. Lee with La Mothe, the French ambassador long popular in London; (2) a fairy in 'A Midsummer Night's Dream' (q.v.).

Mother Bumby, Mother Shipton, see under those names.

Mother Goose's Tales, and *Mother Goose's Melody*, nursery tales and verses published by Newbery (q.v.).

Mother Hubberd's Tale, or *Prosopopoia*, a satire in rhymed couplets, by Spenser (q.v.), included in the volume of 'Complaints' (1590). The ape and the fox, 'disliking of their hard estate', determine to seek their fortunes abroad, and assume the disguises first of an old soldier and his dog, then of a parish priest and his clerk, then of a courtier and his groom; their knaveries in these characters are recounted.

The poem is a vigorous satire on the abuses of the church and the evils of the court.

Mothering Sunday, Mid-Lent Sunday.

Motherwell, WILLIAM (1797–1835), published his 'Minstrelsy, Ancient and Modern' (1827), a collection of ballads, and in 1832 his 'Poems, Narrative and Lyrical', of which the best known and least characteristic is 'Jeanie Morrison'. With Hogg (q.v.) he published an edition of Burns's works in 1834-5.

Motion, the name given to puppet-plays in the 16th and 17th cents. These dealt originally with scriptural subjects, but their scope was afterwards extended. Shakespeare in 'The Winter's Tale' (IV. ii) refers to a 'motion of the Prodigal Son', and we have references to 'motions' in Jonson's 'Bartholomew Fayre', 'A Tale of a Tub', and 'Every Man out of his Humour'.

Motley, JOHN LOTHROP (1814–77), was American minister to Austria, 1861-7, and to Great Britain, 1869-70. His principal work was 'The Rise of the Dutch Republic' (1856).

Motteux, PETER ANTHONY (1660–1718), was born at Rouen and came to England in 1685. He edited 'The Gentleman's Journal' (q.v.), and completed Sir T. Urquhart's translation of Rabelais (1693-4).

Mouldy, RALPH, in Shakespeare's '2 Henry IV' (q.v.), III. ii, one of Falstaff's recruits.

Mountain, THE, the extreme democratic party led by Danton and afterwards by Robespierre in the first French Revolution.

Mount Zion or SION, the hill on which Jerusalem was built, used sometimes figuratively for the Christian Church, or (e.g. in 'The Pilgrim's Progress') for heaven. The name has often been given to dissenting chapels, as in Browning's 'Christmas Eve'.

Mourning Bride, The, a tragedy by Congreve (q.v.), produced in 1697. This was the author's only attempt at tragedy, and was received with enthusiasm.

The play contains lines that are widely known, such as the first in the play:

Music has charms to soothe a savage breast,

and those which close the third act:

Heaven has no rage, like love to hatred turned,

Nor hell a fury, like a woman scorned.

Mowcher, MISS, a character in Dickens's 'David Copperfield' (q.v.).

Mowgli, the child in Rudyard Kipling's 'The Jungle Book' (q.v.).

Moxon, EDWARD (1801–58), publisher and verse-writer, set up as a publisher in 1830, his first publication being Lamb's 'Album Verses'. He married Lamb's adopted daughter Emma Isola. He published for Southey, Wordsworth, Tennyson, Browning, Landor, and other well-known authors.

Mozart, WOLFGANG AMADEUS (1756–91), composed his first oratorio in 1767 (when eleven years old), and his first opera was produced in 1769. His work met with great success, but he was improvident and died in destitution. His principal operas were 'Le Nozze di Figaro', 'Don Giovanni', 'Così fan tutte', and 'Die Zauberflöte'. Besides these, he wrote church music, songs, forty-one symphonies, concertos, pianoforte sonatas, and much chamber music.

Mucedorus, The Comedie of, a play (1598), of uncertain authorship included in a volume with the title of 'Shakespeare' in

Charles II's library (but not by Shakespeare).

Much, in the Robin Hood legend, a miller's son, one of the outlaw's companions.

Much Ado about Nothing, a comedy by Shakespeare (q.v.), probably produced in the winter of 1598-9, and printed in 1600. The trick played by Borachio is in Bandello and Ariosto.

The Prince of Arragon, with Claudio and Benedick in his suite, visits Leonato, duke of Messina, father of Hero, and uncle of Beatrice. Claudio falls in love with Hero and their marriage is arranged. Beatrice, a mirthful, teasing creature, and the wild and witty Benedick, are ever engaged in wordy warfare. A plot is devised to make them fall in love. It is contrived that Benedick shall overhear the Prince and Claudio speak of the secret love of Beatrice for him; and Beatrice is made to overhear a like account of Benedick's love for her. The scheme is successful and they are brought to a mutual liking.

Don John, the soured and malignant brother of the prince, in order to wreck Claudio's marriage, contrives with a follower, Borachio, that Claudio shall be brought to doubt of Hero's honour. Borachio converses at midnight with Margaret, Hero's maid, dressed as Hero, at Hero's window, and the prince and Claudio, who have been posted near, are deceived by the trick.

At the wedding ceremony, Claudio and the prince denounce Hero, who falls in a swoon. By the advice of the Friar, who is sure of Hero's innocence, Leonato gives out that she is dead. Benedick, at the instance of Beatrice, challenges Claudio for slandering her cousin. At this moment Borachio, overheard boasting of his exploit, is arrested and confesses. Claudio offers to make Leonato any amends in his power, and is required to marry a cousin of Hero in her place. This lady when unmasked turns out to be Hero herself. Benedick asks to be married at the same time, and Beatrice 'on great persuasion,

and partly to save your life, because I was told you were in a consumption', consents.

Mucklebackit, ELSPETH, STEENIE, etc., characters in Scott's 'The Antiquary' (q.v.).

Mucklewrath, HABAKKUK, a fanatical preacher in Scott's 'Old Mortality' (q.v.).

Muddiman, HENRY (*b.* 1629), was authorized as a journalist by the Rump Parliament, in 1659, in which year he started 'The Parliamentary Intelligencer' and 'Mercurius Publicus'. He became the most famous of 17th-cent. journalists, and his newsletters in manuscript, sent twice a week to subscribers all over the kingdom, were an important political feature of the day. One of his principal rivals was L'Estrange (q.v.), whose papers however he drove from the field.

Muggletonians, a sect founded about 1651 by Lodowicke Muggleton and John Reeve. The belief of the sect rested on the personal inspiration of the founders, who claimed to be the 'two witnesses' of Rev. xi. 3-6.

Muggleton v. Dingley Dell, the cricket-match in ch. vii of 'The Pickwick Papers' (q.v.).

Mugwump, from an American Indian word meaning 'great chief', is used to signify one who stands aloof from party politics, professing disinterested and superior views.

Muir, EDWIN (1887-1959), novelist, poet, and critic, born and educated in Orkney. He was director of the British Institute at Rome in 1949, and professor of poetry at Harvard University, 1955-6. His novels are 'The Marionette' (1927), 'The Three Brothers' (1931), and 'Poor Tom' (1932). His poetry includes 'First Poems' (1925), 'The Chorus of the Newly Dead' (1926), 'Variations on a Time Theme' (1934), and 'The Voyage' (1946); 'Collected Poems, 1921-51' was published in 1952. He also published a number of critical works. With his wife, Willa, he translated Kafka's 'The Castle' and 'The Trial'. 'The Story and the Fable' (1940) is the first part of an autobiography completed in 1954.

Mulcaster, RICHARD (1530?-1611), headmaster of Merchant Taylors' School and high-master of St. Paul's School, author of two books on the education of children of the middle classes, 'The Positions' and 'The Elementarie' (1581 and 1582).

Mulciber, a name of Vulcan (q.v.), meaning 'the smelter' of metals.

Mulgrave, EARL OF, see *Sheffield*.

Mulla, frequently referred to in Spenser's poems, is the river Mulla, a tributary of the Blackwater in Ireland, near Kilcolman Castle, his residence when he composed the 'Faerie Queene'.

Mullah, THE MAD, a fanatical Muslim teacher, of Surat on the Indian frontier, who incited risings in 1897-8.

Müller, FRIEDRICH MAX, see *Max Müller*.

Mulliner, MR., (1) in Mrs. Gaskell's 'Cranford' (q.v.), the Hon. Mrs. Jamieson's butler; (2) the teller of some of the stories by P. G. Wodehouse (q.v.).

Mulock, DINAH MARIA (Mrs. Craik) (1826-87), author of 'John Halifax, Gentleman' (q.v.).

Mulvaney, TERENCE, see *Learoyd* (*J.*).

Mumbo Jumbo, a grotesque idol said to have been worshipped by certain Negro tribes in Africa. The term is used in English to signify an object of unintelligent veneration and the ceremonies connected with it.

Mummers' Play, THE, or **ST. GEORGE PLAY,** a folk-play evolved from the sword-dance (q.v.), widely spread through England, Scotland, Ireland, and Wales. The play, in its characters and detailed action, varies in different localities, but the main lines are as follows. The principal characters are St. George, the Turkish knight, Captain Slasher, and the Doctor. After a brief prologue, the several fighting characters advance and introduce themselves, or are introduced, in vaunting rhymes. A duel or several duels follow, and one or other of the combatants is killed. The Doctor then enters, boasts his skill, and resuscitates the slain. The central incident of the play is doubtless connected with the celebration of the

death of the year and its resurrection in the spring.

Mum, Sothsegger, 'Hush, Truth-teller', the title of an alliterative poem of the time of 'Piers Plowman' (q.v.). The title has long been known. The identification of the poem with a fragment which occurs in one of the manuscripts of the B-text of 'Piers Plowman', named 'Richard the Redeless' by Skeat, has been rendered possible by the discovery of a manuscript, published in 1936. The fragment, which deals with the misrule of Richard II, was ascribed by Skeat and Jusserand to the author of 'Piers Plowman', but internal evidence makes the ascription doubtful.

Munchausen, Baron, Narrative of his Marvellous Travels, by Rudolph Erich Raspe (1785).

The original Baron Münchhausen is said to have lived in 1720-97, to have served in the Russian army against the Turks, and to have been in the habit of grossly exaggerating his experiences. Raspe (1737-94) was a German adventurer who published in English a version of the Baron's narratives. They include such stories as that of the horse who was cut in two, drank of a fountain, and was sewn up again, etc.

Munday, ANTHONY (1553-1633), wrote or collaborated in a number of plays, and was ridiculed by Ben Jonson as Antonio Balladino in 'The Case is Altered'. Munday wrote ballads, which are lost, unless the charming 'Beauty sat bathing by a spring' in 'England's Helicon' (q.v.) is his. He also translated popular romances, including 'Amadis of Gaul' (q.v., 1590?), and wrote City pageants.

Munera, THE LADY, in Spenser's 'Faerie Queene', v. ii, the daughter of the Saracen Pollente, the personification of ill-gotten wealth.

Munera Pulveris, chapters by Ruskin (q.v.) of an unfinished treatise on political economy contributed to 'Fraser's Magazine' in 1862-3, the remainder of which was suppressed by popular clamour.

Munin and **Hugin,** the two ravens (thought and memory) who attend on Odin (q.v.).

Munro, HECTOR HUGH (1870-1916), writer of fiction, was correspondent in Russia and subsequently in Paris to 'The Morning Post'. 'Reginald', his first characteristic collection of short stories, was published under the pseudonym 'Saki' in 1904, and was followed by 'Reginald in Russia' (1910), 'The Chronicles of Clovis' (1911), and 'Beasts and Superbeasts' (1914). 'The Unbearable Bassington', a novel, appeared in 1912.

Murdockson, MEG, and her daughter MAGDALEN, called 'Madge Wildfire', characters in Scott's 'The Heart of Midlothian' (q.v.).

Murdstone, EDWARD and JANE, characters in Dickens's 'David Copperfield' (q.v.).

Murillo, BARTOLOMÉ ESTEBAN (1617-82), Spanish painter, chiefly of devotional subjects.

Murphy, ARTHUR (1727-1805), a playwright of the Garrick era, of more industry than originality. Among his best comedies are 'Three Weeks after Marriage', produced in 1764; and 'The Way to Keep Him' (1760).

Murray, GEORGE GILBERT AIMÉ (1866-1957), classical scholar, born at Sydney, N.S.W., Regius professor of Greek at Oxford 1908-36. A distinguished interpreter of Greek ideas, both by his editions and translations of the Greek dramatists, and special studies like 'The Rise of the Greek Epic' (1907), 'Aeschylus, the Creator of Tragedy' (1940), and 'Greek Studies' (1946). In 1952 he became President of the Society of Australian Writers.

Murray, SIR JAMES AUGUSTUS HENRY (1837-1915), became a schoolmaster and showed great activity in the acquirement of languages and in the study of antiquities. In 1879 he was appointed editor of the 'Oxford English Dictionary' (q.v.), of which work he laid down the lines and with which his name is principally associated.

Murray, JOHN (1745-93), the first of the famous publishing house of that name. He was succeeded by his son JOHN MURRAY (1778-1843), who started 'The Quarterly Review' (q.v.) in 1809. The latter became acquainted with Byron, whose works he published. He also published for Jane Austen, Crabbe, Borrow, and many others. His son JOHN MURRAY (1808-92), succeeded his father in the business. Among the third John Murray's publications were works of Layard, Grote, Milman, Darwin, and Dean Stanley.

Murry, JOHN MIDDLETON (1889-1957), critic. He met Katherine Mansfield (q.v.) in 1913 and later married her, and his writing was influenced both by her and by their friend D. H. Lawrence (q.v.). After the First World War he became editor of the 'Athenaeum' (1919-21) and in 1923 he founded the 'Adelphi' (1923-48). His works of literary criticism include 'The Problem of Style' (1922), 'Keats and Shakespeare' (1925), 'Son of Woman, the Story of D. H. Lawrence' (1931), 'The Life of Katherine Mansfield' (1933), 'William Blake' (1933), and 'Swift' (1954).

Musaeus, (1) a legendary pre-Homeric poet, said to have been a pupil of Orpheus; (2) a Greek poet, who perhaps lived about A.D. 500, the author of a poem on the story of Hero and Leander (q.v.).

Muses, THE, the nine daughters of Zeus and Mnemosyne, born in Pieria at the foot of Mt. Olympus, who presided over the various kinds of poetry, arts, and sciences. Their names were Clio, Euterpe, Thalia, Melpomene, Terpsichore, Erato, Polyhymnia, Urania, and Calliope (qq.v.). Helicon was sacred to them, and Parnassus, with its Castalian spring, was one of their chief seats.

Muse's Looking-Glasse, The, a defence of the drama, in the form of a play, by T. Randolph (q.v.), printed in 1638.

Musgrave, LITTLE, see *Little Musgrave and Lady Barnard.*

Musgrave, SIR RICHARD, a character in Scott's 'The Lay of the Last Minstrel' (q.v.).

Musgrove, MR. and MRS., their son CHARLES and his wife MARY (*née* ELLIOT), and their daughters HENRIETTA and LOUISA, characters in Jane Austen's 'Persuasion' (q.v.).

Musidorus, a character in Sidney's 'Arcadia' (q.v.).

Musophilus, or Defence of all Learning, a poem in six- and eight-lined stanzas by S. Daniel (q.v.) (1599). It is a discussion between Musophilus and Philocosmus, in which the former defends the merits of knowledge and virtue against the more worldly unlettered arts, and it shows Daniel's gift for moral reflection at its best.

Musset, ALFRED DE (1810–57), French poet of the romantic school, who wrote some sparkling comedies, tragedies, a long, partly autobiographical, novel 'La Confession d'un enfant du siècle' (1836), and much passionate lyrical verse. The episode of his journey to Italy with George Sand in 1833–4 and their rupture had considerable notoriety.

Mustapha, a tragedy by Sir F. Greville (q.v.) (1609).

Myers, LEOPOLD HAMILTON (1881–1944), novelist. His novels are concerned with social and ethical problems and the conflict between material and spiritual values. Apart from 'The Orissers' (1922), 'The "Clio"' (1925), and 'Strange Glory' (1936), the novels are set in 16th-cent. India and were all collected under the title 'The Near and the Far' in 1943.

My Mind to me a Kingdom is, the first line of a philosophical song, popular in the 16th cent. It is referred to by Jonson in his 'Every Man out of his Humour', I. i. Bartlett attributes it to Edward Dyer

(q.v.), with alternative versions by other authors.

Myrmidons, the name borne by a people on the southern borders of Thessaly who accompanied Achilles to the Trojan War.

Myrrha, the daughter of Cinyras, king of Cyprus, who became by him mother of Adonis (q.v.).

'Myrrha' is also the name of a character in Byron's 'Sardanapalus' (q.v.).

Mysie Happer, the miller's daughter in Scott's 'The Monastery' (q.v.).

Mysteries, a term used by modern writers as a name for 'miracle plays' (q.v.). A. W. Ward in 'English Dramatic Literature', i. 23, draws a distinction between 'mysteries' as dealing with Gospel events only, and 'miracle plays' as concerned with legends of the saints. But this is not generally accepted.

Mysteries of Udolpho, The, a novel by Mrs. Radcliffe (q.v.) (1794), which attained a wide fame.

The period of the story is the end of the 16th cent. Emily de St. Aubert, the beautiful daughter of a Gascon family, loses her parents, and comes under the despotic guardianship of an aunt, Madame Cheron. An affection has sprung up between Emily and Valancourt. The aunt, who has married a sinister Italian, Signor Montoni, carries off Emily to the sombre castle of Udolpho in the Apennines. Here, with all the apparatus of sliding panels, secret passages, abductions, and a suggestion of the supernatural, dark dealings are carried on. Emily escapes, meets Valancourt again, and after further vicissitudes, is finally united to him. Montoni, who proves to be the chief of a robber band, is captured and suffers the penalty of his crimes.

Mystic, MR., a character in Peacock's 'Melincourt', a caricature of Coleridge.

N

Nabokov, VLADIMIR (1899-1977), Russian emigré novelist, poet, and critic, sometimes using the pseudonym 'Vladimir Sirin'. His early work was written in Russian. Much of it has been translated, often by the author himself. Later work, in English, includes 'The Real Life of Sebastian Knight' (1941), 'Bend Sinister' (1947), 'Conclusive Evidence' (1951), 'Lolita' (1955), 'Prin' (1957), and 'Pale Fire' (1962). Nabokov also wrote a study of Pushkin's 'Eugene Onegin' (1964), and translations of poems by Pushkin, Lermontov, and Tyutchev.

Naboth's Vineyard, the vineyard of Naboth the Jezreelite, coveted by Ahab. Jezebel caused Naboth to be put to death that Ahab might have it (1 Kings xxi).

Naciens, in the legend of the Grail (q.v.), the brother-in-law of King Evalak of Sarras. In the 'Morte Darthur', NACIEN is the hermit who tells how the quest of the Grail should be made.

Naiads, see *Nymphs*.

Naiads, Hymn to the, a poem by Akenside (q.v.).

Nairne, CAROLINA, *Baroness* (1766-1845), *née* Oliphant, the author of some spirited Jacobite songs, of which the best known are 'Will ye no come back again?' and 'Charlie is my Darling'; also of humorous and pathetic ballads, such as 'The Land o' the Leal'.

Namancos, in Milton's 'Lycidas', is a place in Galicia, near Cape Finisterre, shown in Mercator's Atlas of 1623. The Castle of Bayona is shown near it.

Namby-Pamby, see *Philips (A.)*.

Nancy, in Dickens's 'Oliver Twist' (q.v.), the companion of Bill Sikes.

Nandy, JOHN EDWARD, in Dickens's 'Little Dorrit' (q.v.), the father of Mrs. Plornish.

Nansen, FRIDTJOF (1861-1930), Norwegian explorer and statesman. His 'The First Crossing of Greenland' appeared in 1892. He sailed in the 'Fram' in 1893 with Johansen for the Arctic regions and reached on foot 86° 14′ N., a voyage recorded in his 'Farthest North' (1897). After the First World War he was instrumental in organizing a relief bureau for refugees in connection with the League of Nations.

Nantes, EDICT OF, see *Edict of Nantes*.

Napier or **Neper,** JOHN (1550-1617), devoted himself for a time to the invention of instruments of warfare. He then set himself to facilitate arithmetical operations, and devised logarithms, explained in his 'Mirifici Logarithmorum Canonis Descriptio' (1614). His 'Rabdologia' (1615) explains the use of numerating rods, commonly called 'Napier's bones'—the earliest form of calculating machine. He also invented the present notation of decimal fractions.

Napier, SIR WILLIAM FRANCIS PATRICK (1785-1860), served in Sir John Moore's campaign in Spain (1808), and in the subsequent war in the Peninsula. He published in 1828-40 his 'History of the Peninsular War', which placed him high among historical writers.

Napoleon I, NAPOLEON BONAPARTE (BUONAPARTE) (1769-1821), of a Corsican family, first came into prominence as an artillery officer at the recapture of Toulon from the English in 1793. He was general-in-chief of the French army of Italy 1796-7, and was then sent to conquer Egypt, whence he returned in 1799. By a *coup d'état* at the end of that year he became master of the government and was named First Consul. Then followed the series of his European conquests. In 1804 he proclaimed himself emperor. The tide turned against him with the disastrous Russian campaign of 1812, followed by the defeat at Leipzig and by

Wellington's victories. In 1814 Napoleon abdicated and was sent to Elba. He returned in 1815 and was in that year finally defeated at Waterloo. He died at St. Helena. He married in 1795 Joséphine, widow of the Comte de Beauharnais, divorced her, and married in 1810 Marie Louise, daughter of the Austrian Emperor Francis II, by whom he had a son, the duke of Reichstadt (d. 1832).

Napoleon III, (CHARLES) LOUIS NAPOLEON BONAPARTE (1808–73), was the nephew of Napoleon I (q.v.). In 1836 and 1840, while living in exile, he made two unsuccessful attempts, at Strasburg and Boulogne, to stir up Bonapartist risings. In Dec. 1848, after the fall of Louis Philippe, he was elected president of the French Republic, became, as a result of a *coup d'état*, president for ten years in 1851, and was proclaimed emperor in 1852. Under him, France was Britain's ally in the Crimean War, and played an important part in the liberation of Italy by fighting with Sardinia against Austria in 1859. In the Franco–Prussian War of 1870–1 he was taken prisoner at Sedan in Sept. 1870, and, after a period of captivity, spent the remainder of his life at Chiselhurst.

Narcissa, see *Oldfield (A.)*.

Narcissus, a beautiful youth, son of the river god Cephissus and the nymph Liriope. He saw his image reflected in a fountain and became enamoured of it, thinking it to be the nymph of the place. His fruitless attempts to approach this beautiful object drove him to despair and death. He was changed into the flower that bears his name.

Narrenschiff, see *Ship of Fools*.

Nash, JOHN (1752–1835), architect, planned Regent Street and laid out Regent's Park.

Nash, RICHARD, 'Beau Nash' (1674–1762), supported himself in London as a gamester, and went to Bath in 1705, where he established the Assembly Rooms, drew up a code of etiquette and dress, and became unquestioned autocrat of society.

The gambling laws of 1740–5 deprived him of his source of income, and his popularity waned after 1745. A biography of Nash was written by Oliver Goldsmith.

Nash or **Nashe**, THOMAS (1567–1601), satirist, born at Lowestoft. After touring France and Italy he settled in London before 1588. His first publication was an acrid review of recent literature (prefixed to Greene's 'Menaphon', 1589), which he discussed at greater length in the 'Anatomie of Absurditie' (1589). He was attracted to the Martin Marprelate controversy (q.v.) by his hatred of Puritanism. Under the pseudonym of 'Pasquil' he wrote several pamphlets. Nash replied in 1591 to the savage denunciations of Richard Harvey, the astrologer and brother of G. Harvey (q.v.), and in 1592 wrote 'Pierce Pennilesse his Supplication to the Divell'. Nash avenged Gabriel Harvey's attack on Greene (q.v.) with 'Strange Newes of the Intercepting certaine Letters' (1593). Being subsequently troubled with religious doubts, he published his repentant reflections under the title 'Christes Teares over Jerusalem' in 1593. 'The Terrors of the Night' appeared in 1594, and in the same year 'The Unfortunate Traveller, or the Life of Jacke Wilton', a spirited romance of adventure. Nash further satirized Harvey in 'Haue with you to Saffron-Walden' (1596), to which Harvey replied, the government subsequently ordering the two authors to desist. He attacked so many current abuses in the state in his lost comedy 'The Isle of Dogs' (1597), that he was sent to the Fleet prison for some months. He published in 1599 'Lenten Stuffe', a burlesque panegyric of the red herring, written to repay hospitality enjoyed at Yarmouth, and a comedy still extant, called 'Summers Last Will' (1600). Nash's original personality gives him a unique place in Elizabethan literature, and his writings have something of the fascination of Rabelais. His romance of 'Jacke Wilton' inaugurated the novel of adventure in England.

Naso, see *Ovid.*

Nathan, GEORGE JEAN (1882-1958), American essayist and critic, born in Indiana, co-founder with H. L. Mencken (q.v.) of 'The American Mercury', of which he remained an editor until 1930. Among his chief works are 'The Popular Theatre' (1918), 'The American Credo', with H. L. Mencken (1920), 'The Critic and the Drama' (1922), 'The Auto- biography of an Attitude' (1925).

Nathaniel, SIR, in Shakespeare's 'Love's Labour's Lost' (q.v.), a curate.

National Anthem, THE. The first recorded public performance of 'God save the King' took place at Drury Lane Theatre on 28 Sept. 1745, during the excitement and alarm caused by the Jacobite invasion of that year. It was an unannounced addition by the actors to the ordinary programme of the day. The score was prepared by Thomas Augustine Arne (1710-78), leader of the orchestra at the theatre and composer of 'Rule, Britannia' (q.v.). The example set at Drury Lane was followed at other theatres and the song was soon very popular. It became customary about 1747 or 1748 to greet the king with it when he entered a place of public entertainment. The description of it as the National Anthem appears to have been adopted early in the 19th cent.

The remoter origin of 'God save the King' is obscure. Before being sung at Drury Lane in 1745, words and tune, with slight differences, had appeared in 'Thesaurus Musicus', a song collection published in 1744. There is good evi- dence that the song was originally written in favour of James II in 1688 or possibly of Charles II in 1681; but the author is unknown. As regards the melody, various 17th-cent. tunes of the same rhythm more or less resemble that of 'God save the King'. The closest resemblance is that of a galliard composed by Dr. John Bull (1563?-1628) in the early 17th cent. But this may be the keyboard setting of some folk tune or other well-known air of the time, and the tune of 'God save the King' may have been drawn directly from the original.

National Biography, Dictionary of, designed and published by George Smith (q.v.), was begun in 1882 with Sir Leslie Stephen (q.v.) as editor. It included in its original form biographies of all national notabilities from earliest times to 1900. The work has been continued by the publishing of decennial supplements. The 'Concise D.N.B.' is in two parts: Part I, epitome of the D.N.B. from earliest times to 1900, and Part II, epitome of the sup- plements, 1901-50. Sir Leslie Stephen was succeeded in the editorship by Sir Sidney Lee (q.v.). In 1917 the Dictionary was transferred to the Oxford University Press.

National Library of Scotland, see *Advocates' Library.*

Natty Bumppo, the hero of the 'Leather- stocking' novels of J. F. Cooper (q.v.).

Natural Religion, Dialogues on, see *Dia- logues on Natural Religion.*

Nature, a periodical founded in 1869, with Norman Lockyer as editor. Charles Darwin, Huxley, Tyndall, and Lubbock were among its distinguished early sup- porters.

Nausicaa, in Homer's 'Odyssey', the daughter of Alcinous, king of Phaeacia. She finds Odysseus (q.v.) shipwrecked on the coast, and brings him to her father's court. Samuel ('Erewhon') Butler (q.v.) argues that she was herself the authoress of the 'Odyssey'.

Navarino, a bay in the Peloponnese where in 1827 the British fleet, with the French and Russian squadrons, defeated the combined Turkish and Egyptian fleets and rendered possible the liberation of Greece.

Nazarene, (1) a native of Nazareth; (2) a follower of Jesus of Nazareth, a Christian; (3) in the plural, an early Jewish Christian sect, who accepted the divinity of Christ while conforming to the Mosaic law; (4) the name given to a group of German religious painters who settled in Rome in 1810.

Nazi, abbreviation of German 'National-sozialist', a member of the German National-Socialist party.

Nazirites (A.V. NAZARITES), the name given among the Hebrews to such as had taken certain vows of abstinence (see Num. vi).

Neaera, a conventional name among the Roman poets for a lady-love, referred to as such in Milton's 'Lycidas' (q.v.).

Neale, JOHN MASON (1818-66), a man of much versatility, was the founder of the Cambridge Camden Society (1839). He was author of a 'History of the Holy Eastern Church' (1847-50) and of many well-known hymns, including 'Jerusalem the Golden', 'Brief life is here our portion', several of them translated from the 'Rhythm' of Bernard of Morlaix (q.v.), others from hymns of the Eastern Church. He also wrote a historical novel, 'Theodora Phranza'.

Neanderthal, near Düsseldorf in Germany, gives its name to an early type of the human race, from a skull-cap and certain other bones found there in deposits of the Middle Pleistocene period. Modern man is not descended from him. He was succeeded by Aurignacian man.

Nebuchadnezzar, the king of Babylonia 605-562 B.C., who built the walls of Babylon, and perhaps the famous 'Hanging Gardens' also attributed to Cyrus. He captured Jerusalem and carried the Jews into the Babylonian captivity.

Necker, MADAME (SUSANNE CURCHOD) (1739-94), a Swiss woman, at one time engaged to Gibbon the historian (q.v.); she became the wife of Jacques Necker, the French financier and statesman. Her daughter was the celebrated Mme de Staël (q.v.).

Neckett, MR., the sheriff's officer in Dickens's 'Bleak House' (q.v.), generally referred to as COAVINSES, the name of the sponging-house which he keeps. He has three children, Tom, Emma, and Charlotte.

Nectabanus, the dwarf in Scott's 'The Talisman' (q.v.).

N.E.D., the 'New English Dictionary', known now as the 'Oxford English Dictionary' (q.v.).

Negus, (1) the title of the ruler of Abyssinia; (2) a mixture of wine, hot water, and sugar called *Negus*, so named after its inventor, Colonel Francis Negus (*d.* 1732).

Nekayah, in Johnson's 'Rasselas' (q.v.), the sister of the hero.

Nemea, a town in Argolis, the neighbourhood of which was infested by the famous Nemean lion, killed by Hercules (q.v.). The scene also of great periodical games.

Nemesis, in classical mythology daughter of Night, was in early Greek thought a personification of the Gods' resentment at, and punishment of, insolence (*hubris*) towards themselves.

Nemo, the law-writer in Dickens's 'Bleak House' (q.v.).

Nemo, CAPTAIN, the hero of Jules Verne's 'Twenty Thousand Leagues under the Sea'.

Nennius (*fl.* 796), the traditional author, but probably only the reviser, of the 'Historia Britonum'. There are several versions of the 'Historia', which is a collection of notes, drawn from various sources, on the history and geography of Britain, and is chiefly interesting for the account it purports to give of the historical Arthur. It is one of the sources on which Geoffrey of Monmouth (q.v.) drew.

Neoplatonism, a philosophical and religious system, combining Platonic ideas with oriental mysticism, which originated at Alexandria in the 3rd cent., and is especially represented in the writings of Plotinus, Porphyry, and Proclus. The works of St. Augustine show its influence.

Neoptolemus, the son of Achilles (q.v.), also called PYRRHUS on account of his yellow hair.

Nepenthe, a drug supposed to banish sorrow. Also the title of a poem (1839) by George Darley (q.v.).

Nephelococcygia, 'cloud-cuckoo-land', in the 'Birds' of Aristophanes (q.v.), an imaginary city built in the air by the birds.

Nepos, CORNELIUS (*c.* 99–*c.* 24 B.C.), Roman historian, a friend of Atticus and Catullus.

Neptune, the Roman god of the sea, identified with the Poseidon (q.v.) of the Greeks.

Nereids, THE, in Greek mythology, the daughters of Nereus, a deity of the sea; the nymphs (q.v.) of the Mediterranean.

Nerissa, in Shakespeare's 'The Merchant of Venice' (q.v.), Portia's waiting-maid.

Nero, a Roman emperor (A.D. 54–68), the last of the Julio-Claudian dynasty, proverbial for his tyranny and brutality. Some ancient authors assert that the burning of Rome in 64 was due to his order and that he fiddled while it burnt. His subjects revolted against his oppression in 68, and Nero took his own life.

Nerthus, see *Hertha*.

Nesbit, EDITH (MRS. HUBERT BLAND, later MRS. BLAND-TUCKER) (1858–1924), aspired to be a poet but achieved fame in writing books for children. She and her husband, Hubert Bland, were founder members of the Fabian Society (q.v.). Although for many years she wrote potboilers for various journals, her gift as a writer of children's stories did not appear until the publication of 'The Treasure Seekers' in 1899. Of the thirty or so that followed, the best known are: 'The Wouldbegoods' (1901), 'The Phoenix and the Carpet' (1904), 'The Railway Children' (1906), and 'The Enchanted Castle' (1907). The stories, with their direct appeal to the imagination of children, were at once immensely popular and have continued to be read by children of succeeding generations.

Nessus, see *Deianira*.

Nestor, king of Pylos and Messenia, led his subjects to the Trojan War, where he distinguished himself among the Grecian chiefs, as an aged statesman, by his wisdom, justice, and eloquence.

Nestorians, followers of Nestorius, patriarch of Constantinople in A.D. 428, who held that Christ had distinct human and divine persons. Nestorius was con-demned by the Councils of Ephesus in 431 and Chalcedon in 451. A remnant of Nestorian Christians survives in the mountains of E. Anatolia and Kurdistan (driven into Iraq during the War of 1914–18).

Neville, MISS, a character in Goldsmith's 'She Stoops to Conquer' (q.v.).

New Atalantis, see *Manley*.

New Atlantis, The, a treatise of political philosophy in the form of a fable, by Francis Bacon (q.v.) (1626).

It is an account of a visit to an imaginary island of Bensalem in the Pacific and of the social conditions prevailing there; and also of 'Solomon's House', a college of natural philosophy 'dedicated to the study of the works and creatures of God'.

New Bath Guide, see *Anstey (C.)*.

Newbery, JOHN (1713–67), a publisher and bookseller, who established himself in 1744 in St. Paul's Churchyard, London, and originated the publication of children's books. Goldsmith (q.v.) was among those who worked for him. Newbery figures in 'The Vicar of Wakefield' (q.v.) and as 'Jack Whirler' in Johnson's 'The Idler' (q.v.).

Newbolt, SIR HENRY JOHN (1862–1938), poet, author of many patriotic songs, including 'Drake's Drum', 'Clifton Chapel', etc.

Newcastle, MARGARET, DUCHESS OF (1624?–74), wrote a multitude of verses, essays, and plays (1653–68), and a biography of her husband. She is principally remembered for Pepys's condemnation of her as 'a mad, conceited, ridiculous woman'.

Newcomes, The, a novel by Thackeray (q.v.) (1853–5).

The story, told by Pendennis (q.v.), centres in the career of young Clive Newcome, the son of Colonel Thomas Newcome, an officer of the Indian army. Clive Newcome falls in love with his cousin, Ethel Newcome, daughter of the wealthy banker Sir Brian Newcome. But she is destined for a more exalted match by her grandmother, the countess of Kew, and by her other relatives. The most vigorous opponent of Clive's suit is Ethel's brother, Barnes Newcome, a mean, venomous little snob. Ethel, a fine and honourable girl, though influenced by ambition and her worldly surroundings, engages herself first to her cousin, Lord Kew, and then to Lord Farintosh; but both these matches she breaks off. Meanwhile Clive allows himself to be married to a pretty nonentity, Rosey Mackenzie, the daughter of a scheming widow. The marriage turns out miserably. Colonel Newcome loses his fortune; and his household, including Clive and his wife and Mrs. Mackenzie, are reduced to poverty. Mrs. Mackenzie subjects the Colonel to a long martyrdom by her taunts and reproaches, until he takes refuge in the Greyfriars [Charterhouse] almshouse. The pathos of the story reaches its climax with the scene of the Colonel's death-bed. Rosey having meanwhile died, we are left to infer that Clive and Ethel are finally united.

New English Bible, The, see *Bible (The English)*.

New English Dictionary, The, more generally known as the 'Oxford English Dictionary' (q.v.).

Newgate, the principal west gate of the ancient city of London. Its gate-house was a prison from the 12th cent. It was finally demolished in 1902, when the Central Criminal Court was built on its site.

Newgate Calendar, The, or Malefactors' Bloody Register, was published (the original series) about 1774, and dealt with notorious crimes from 1700 to that date. Later series were issued about 1826 by Andrew Knapp and William Baldwin.

New Grub Street, a novel by Gissing (q.v.) (1891), depicts the struggle for life, the jealousies and intrigues of the literary world of his time, and the blighting effect of poverty on artistic endeavour.

New Holland, a former name of Australia.

New Inne, The, a comedy by Jonson (q.v.),

first acted in 1629, when it was a complete failure, not being heard to the conclusion.

Newman, JOHN HENRY (1801–90), became a fellow of Oriel College, Oxford, where he came in contact with Keble and Pusey, and later with R. H. Froude (qq.v.). In 1832 he went to the south of Europe with R. H. Froude, and with him wrote in Rome much of the 'Lyra Apostolica' (1836), sacred poems. In 1833 he composed the hymn 'Lead, kindly Light'. In the same year he resolved with William Palmer, R. H. Froude, and A. P. Perceval to fight for the doctrine of apostolical succession and the integrity of the Prayerbook, and began 'Tracts for the Times' (see *Oxford Movement*), in which he found a supporter in Dr. Pusey. In 1837–8 he published a number of treatises in defence of the Anglo-Catholic view, and in 1841 his famous Tract XC, on the compatibility of the Articles with Catholic theology; this tract brought the Tractarians under the official ban. He joined the Church of Rome in 1845. In 1847 he established the Oratory at Birmingham. In 1854 he was appointed rector of the new Catholic University of Dublin, and in 1852, previous to his formal appointment, delivered his lectures on 'The Scope and Nature of University Education'. He found the Irish clergy and the 'New Catholic University' quite intractable and soon gave up his appointment.

In 1864 appeared his 'Apologia pro Vita sua', in answer to Charles Kingsley, who in 'Macmillan's Magazine', misrepresenting Newman, had remarked that Newman did not consider truth as a necessary virtue. The 'Apologia' came out serially, and when it was published as a book much of the controversial matter was omitted. It is an exposition, written with the utmost simplicity and sincerity, and in a style of limpid clearness, of his spiritual history, and has obtained recognition as a literary masterpiece. In 1866 appeared his poem, 'The Dream of Gerontius', a dramatic monologue of a just soul leaving the body at death, which made a wide appeal to religious minds. Mention should also be made of his religious novels, 'Loss and Gain' (1848) and 'Callista' (1856). He was created a cardinal in 1879.

Newnes, GEORGE (1851-1910), publisher and magazine proprietor. He founded in particular 'The Strand Magazine' (in which Conan Doyle's 'Adventures of Sherlock Holmes' first appeared) and 'Tit-Bits'.

New Republic, The, see *Mallock.*

News, The, see *L'Estrange.*

Newsbooks, or DIURNALLS, the successors of the 'Corantos' (q.v.) in the evolution of the newspaper. Newsbooks, consisting of one printed sheet (8 pages) or later of two printed sheets (16 pages), and containing domestic intelligence and the principal features of the modern newspaper, were issued, by various journalists and under various titles, during the period 1641-65. They then gave place to the 'Oxford' (later 'London') 'Gazette' (see *Gazette*).

Newsletters, a term specially applied to the manuscript records of parliamentary and court news, sent twice a week to subscribers from the London office of Muddiman (q.v.) in the second half of the 17th cent.

Newspaper. Examples can be found before the 17th cent. in England of personal newsletters and news pamphlets (condemned by Burton in 'The Anatomy of Melancholy' in 1614) with titles such as 'Newes from Spaine', etc.; but the first regular periodical was not issued till May 1622. (See under *Coranto.* Nathaniel Butter, Nicholas Bourne, and Thomas Archer were its leading promoters.) In the development of the periodical through the century, L'Estrange (q.v.) played an important part; and during the political disturbances of the time, fresh periodicals were continually being produced. Most of these papers were thrice weekly, but in 1703 the 'Daily Courant', the first daily paper, appeared. In Queen Anne's time, a remarkably talented group of writers

gave their services to periodical literature, including Defoe, the first great English journalist, Steele, Swift, and Addison. The political importance of papers increased and was not lessened by a stamp duty which was imposed. Walpole spent £5,000 a year on subsidizing newspapers; Henry Fielding was one of his journalistic opponents; Johnson reported parliamentary debates for 'The Gentleman's Magazine'.

Throughout the 18th cent. the circulation of any newspaper was seldom above 5,000. A change came with the introduction of cheaper and faster printing processes, initially sponsored by John Walter, who founded 'The Times' in 1788. (The 'Morning Post' was founded by Daniel Stuart in 1772; Stuart's reminiscences give a valuable account of journalism in the period, including sidelights on Coleridge, whom he employed at one time.) By 1834 the circulation of 'The Times' was 10,000; by 1844, 23,000; and in 1854, 51,000. Sir John Stoddart edited it for several years and was succeeded in 1816 by Thomas Barnes. It was one of the first papers to employ foreign correspondents, one of whom was Crabb Robinson (q.v.).

A further great change in English journalism came towards the end of the 19th cent. with the spread of literacy and the growth of a cheap (at one time a halfpenny) popular press. In this Alfred Harmsworth was a prime mover. Lords Beaverbrook and Rothermere were the direct inheritors of his tradition, and in the 20th cent. the tendency has been for the number of national papers to have been reduced by means of mergers and for the circulation to have increased, in some cases to over 4,000,000 per day. (See also under *Newsbooks, Newsletters, Gazette.*)

New Statesman, The, a weekly journal of politics, art, letters, and science, originally planned as an organ of Fabianism (see *Fabian Society*), socialist in standing but independent of party. It was first published in 1913 with Clifford Sharp as editor, J. C. Squire as literary editor, and the Webbs and G. B. Shaw as regular contributors. From that time it has maintained its policy 'of dissent, of scepticism, of inquiry, of non-conformity'.

Newton, SIR ISAAC (1642-1727), the philosopher, made his first communication to the Royal Society on his theory of light and colours in 1672. His researches on this subject were summed up in his 'Optics', published in 1704, to which was appended his 'Method of Fluxions', his great mathematical discovery, and the source of a bitter quarrel with Leibniz as to the priority of the invention. The first book of his 'Philosophiae Naturalis Principia Mathematica', embodying his laws of motion and the idea of universal gravitation, was exhibited at the Royal Society in 1686, and published in 1687.

Newton, JOHN (1725-1807), clergyman and friend of Cowper (q.v.), with whom he published the 'Olney Hymns' in 1779. 'An Authentic Narrative', first published anonymously in 1764, is an account of his early adventurous life at sea and his religious conversion.

New Way to pay Old Debts, A, a comedy by Massinger (q.v.) (1633), perhaps the best known of his works.

The cruel and rapacious Sir Giles Overreach, having got possession of the property of his prodigal nephew Frank Wellborn, treats him with contumely. Lady Allworth, a rich widow, to whose husband Wellborn had rendered important services, consents to help him by giving ground for the belief that she is about to marry him. Overreach changes his attitude, and gives Wellborn assistance. Tom Allworth, Lady Allworth's stepson, and page to Lord Lovell, is in love with Overreach's daughter Margaret.

Lord Lovell consents to help Allworth to win Margaret, and a trick is played on Overreach by which he facilitates the marriage, thinking that Lord Lovell is to be the bridegroom. Overreach becomes crazy on discovering the deceit and on finding that, by the device of one of his satellites,

his claim to Wellborn's property cannot be maintained; he is sent to Bedlam.

New Writing, a book-periodical edited by John Lehmann (q.v.), first published in 1936 and afterwards at approximately half-yearly intervals until 1940. It published imaginative writing, mainly by young authors, and particularly by those whose work was too unorthodox for the established magazines. In 1940 it came out as 'Folios of New Writing', which became 'New Writing and Daylight' in 1942 and lasted until 1946. Meanwhile 'Penguin New Writing' appeared in 1940, first as a monthly paperback and then in 1942 as a quarterly. It reprinted some work from 'New Writing', but relied more and more on new material.

New Yorker, The, an American weekly established in 1925 by Harold Ross. It is sophisticated, satirical, and cultivated, and is distinguished for its short stories, articles, and cartoons.

Nibelung (NIBLUNG, NIEBELUNG), in the Norse sagas and German 'Nibelungenlied' (q.v.), a mythical king of a race of dwarfs, the Nibelungs, who dwelt in Norway. The Nibelung kings and people figure in W. Morris's 'Sigurd the Volsung' (q.v.).

Nibelungen, Ring des, see *Ring des Nibelungen.*

Nibelungenlied, a German poem of the 13th cent. embodying a story found in primitive shape in both forms of the Edda (q.v.). In the latter the story is substantially as told by William Morris in his 'Sigurd the Volsung' (q.v.), Sigurd being the Siegfried of the German poem.

In the 'Nibelungenlied' the story is somewhat different. Siegfried, son of Siegmund and Sieglind, king and queen of the Netherlands, having got possession of the Nibelung hoard guarded by Alberich, rides to woo Kriemhild, a Burgundian princess, sister of Gunther, Gernot, and Giselher. Hagen, their grim retainer, warns them against Siegfried, but the match is arranged, and the hoard is given to Kriemhild as marriage portion. Siegfried undertakes to help Gunther to win Brunhild, queen of Issland, by defeating her in trials of skill and strength, which he succeeds in doing. The double marriage takes place, but Brunhild remains suspicious and ill-humoured, and Siegfried, called in by Gunther to subdue her, does so in Gunther's semblance and takes away her ring and girdle, which he gives to Kriemhild. The two queens quarrel, and Kriemhild reveals to Brunhild the trick that has been played on her. Hagen, who thinks his master's honour injured by Siegfried, treacherously kills the latter at a hunt.

Kriemhild later marries Etzel (Attila), king of the Huns, and in order to avenge her husband and secure the hoard, which her brothers have seized and sunk in the Rhine, persuades them to visit Etzel's court. There they are set upon and overcome, but refuse to betray the hiding-place of the hoard, and are slain. Hagen, the last survivor of the party who knows the secret, is killed by Kriemhild with Siegfried's sword; and Kriemhild herself is slain by Hildebrand, a knight of Dietrich of Bern.

Nice Valour, The, or *The Passionate Madman,* see *Fletcher (J.).*

Nicholas, St., said to have been bishop of Myra in Asia Minor about A.D. 300, is the patron saint of Russia. His festival is 6 Dec. See also *Santa Claus* and *Nicholas's Clerk.*

Nicholas Nickleby, a novel by Dickens (q.v.) (1838–9).

Nicholas, a generous, high-spirited lad of 19, his mother, and his gentle sister Kate, are left penniless on the death of his father. They appeal for assistance to his uncle, Ralph Nickleby, a griping usurer, of whom Nicholas at once makes an enemy by his independent bearing. He is sent as usher to Dotheboys Hall, where Wackford Squeers starves and maltreats forty urchins under pretence of education. His special cruelty is expended on Smike, a half-witted lad left on his hands and employed as a drudge. Nicholas, infuriated by what he witnesses, thrashes Squeers and escapes with Smike, who becomes his devoted friend. For a time he supports himself and Smike as an actor in the provincial company of Vincent Crummles; he then enters the service of the brothers Cheeryble, whose benevolence and good humour spread happiness around them. Meanwhile Kate, apprenticed to Madame Mantalini, dressmaker, is by her uncle's designs exposed to the gross insults of Sir Mulberry Hawk, one of his associates. From this persecution she is released by Nicholas, who breaks Sir Mulberry's head and makes a home for his mother and sister. Nicholas himself falls in love with Madeline Bray, the support of a selfish father, and the object of a conspiracy of Ralph Nickleby and another revolting old usurer, Gride, to marry her to the latter. Ralph, whose hatred for Nicholas has been intensified by the failure of his plans, knowing Nicholas's affection for Smike, conspires to remove the latter from him; but Smike succumbs to failing health and terror of his enemies. All Ralph's plots are baffled by the help of Newman Noggs, his eccentric clerk. Confronted with ruin and exposure, and finally shattered by the discovery that Smike was his own son, Ralph hangs himself. Nicholas, befriended by the Cheerybles, marries Madeline, and Kate marries the Cheerybles' nephew, Frank. Squeers is transported, and Gride is murdered.

Nicholas's Clerk, St., a highwayman, thief, also used to signify a poor scholar.

Nick, Old, see *Old Nick.*

Nicolette, see *Aucassin and Nicolette.*

Niebelung, see *Nibelung.*

Niebuhr, Barthold Georg (1776–1831). His great 'History of Rome', which originally took the form of lectures delivered at Berlin in 1810–12, appeared in 1827–8. Niebuhr was the first historian to deal with the subject in a scientific spirit, discussing critically the early Roman legends and paying more attention to the development of institutions and to social characteristics than to individuals and incidents.

Nietzsche, FRIEDRICH WILHELM (1844–1900), German philosopher and poet, appointed very young to a professorship of classical philology at Basel. He resigned because of ill health and in 1889 suffered a mental breakdown from which he never properly recovered. His basic ideas are the affirmation of the Superman, the rejection of Christian morality, the doctrine of power, and the 'revision of all values'. He began as a disciple of Schopenhauer (q.v.), but later rejected his pessimism and quietism. For some time he was an admirer of Wagner (q.v.), but was eventually unable to accept the Schopenhauerian elements in his outlook, and the breach with Wagner was one of the main episodes in Nietzsche's career. His influence on modern German literature has been enormous.

Nightingale, Ode to a, see *Keats.*

Nightmare Abbey, a novel by Peacock (q.v.) (1818).

The book is an entertaining satire on Byronism, Coleridgian transcendentalism, and pessimism in general. There is, as usual in Peacock's novels, little plot, but the house-party of amusing characters brings together Mr. Glowry, his son Scythrop, and Mr. Toobad, pessimists of various shades; Mr. Flosky, a caricature of Coleridge, and Mr. Cypress, of Byron. Scythrop, in his inability to fix his affections on one or other of two charmers, resembles Shelley.

Night Thoughts on Life, Death, and Immortality, The Complaint or, a didactic poem of some 10,000 lines of blank verse, in nine books, by E. Young (q.v.) (1742–5).

The first book is occupied, as the title suggests, with the poet's reflections during the night on the vicissitudes of life, death, and immortality. The next seven form a soliloquy, partly argumentative, partly reflective, addressed to a certain worldly infidel, named Lorenzo, who is exhorted to turn to faith and virtue. The ninth book, entitled 'The Consolation', contains a vision of the last day and of eternity.

The poem for a time enjoyed great popularity.

Nihilism (Latin *nihil,* nothing), originally a movement in Russia repudiating the customary social institutions. The term was introduced by the novelist Turgenev (q.v.). It was subsequently extended to a secret revolutionary movement which developed in the middle of the 19th cent.

Nimrod, 'the mighty hunter' (Gen. x. 9), of whom Milton says (basing himself on the Targum) 'and men not beasts shall be his game' ('Paradise Lost', xii. 30).

Nimue, NIMIANE, or VIVIEN, see *Lady of the Lake,* and *Merlin.*

Nineteen Eighty-four, a novel by George Orwell (q.v.), published in 1949. It is a nightmare story of totalitarianism of the future and one man's helpless struggle against it and final defeat by acceptance.

Nine Worthies, The, see *Worthies.*

Ninian, ST. (*d.* 432?), was sent on a mission to convert the pagans in the northern parts of Britain and evangelized the Southern Picts. He is commemorated on 16 Sept. He is also called St. Ringan (see, e.g., Scott's 'The Pirate'), and is frequently invoked as St. Treignan in Rabelais.

Ninon de Lenclos, see *Lenclos.*

Ninus, see *Semiramis.*

Niobe, a daughter of Tantalus (q.v.), and wife of Amphion. She was the mother of six sons and six daughters, and this so increased her pride, that she boasted herself superior to Latona, the mother of Apollo and Artemis. For this arrogance the sons of Niobe were immediately slain by the darts of Apollo, and the daughters by Artemis; and Niobe herself was changed into a stone, and still wept for her children in streams that trickled down the rock. Hence 'Niobe all tears' (Shakespeare, 'Hamlet', I. ii. 149).

Nipper, SUSAN, a character in Dickens's 'Dombey and Son' (q.v.).

Nirvana, in Buddhist theology, the extinction of individual existence and the absorption of the soul in the supreme spirit, or the extinction of all desires and passions and the attainment of perfect beatitude.

Nisroch, an Assyrian deity. Milton calls him 'of Principalities the prime' in the council of Satan ('Paradise Lost', vi. 446).

Nisus, a Trojan, who accompanied Aeneas to Italy. He was united in closest friendship to Euryalus, another Trojan, and together at night they penetrated the enemy camp. Euryalus fell into the enemies' hands. Nisus in endeavouring to rescue his friend perished with him, and their great friendship has become proverbial.

Njala Saga, see *Saga.*

Nobel Prizes, THE, were established under the will of Alfred Bernhard Nobel (1833-96), a Swedish chemist distinguished in the development of explosives, by which annual prizes are given for the most important discoveries in the sciences, to the author of the most important literary work of an idealist tendency, and to the person who shall have most promoted the fraternity of nations.

Noble, in 'Reynard the Fox' (q.v.), the name of the lion.

Noble, a former English gold coin, first minted by Edward III, issued as the equivalent of 6s. 8d. silver.

The ANGEL, called more fully at first the ANGEL-NOBLE, being originally a new issue of the noble, was first coined by Edward IV in 1465, when its value was 6s. 8d. It was last coined by Charles I.

The ROSE-NOBLE or RYAL was a gold coin first issued by Edward IV, as the equivalent of 10s. silver.

Noble Numbers, the title of the collection of religious poems written by Herrick (q.v.).

Noctes Ambrosianae, a series of papers that appeared in 'Blackwood's Magazine' (q.v.), 1822-35. They were by several hands, Prof. John Wilson's, Lockhart's, Hogg's, and Maginn's (qq.v.); but of the 71, 41 were by the first of these, Wilson ('Christopher North'), and have been reprinted in his works. The 'Noctes' take the form of imaginary conversations, of a boisterous, convivial kind, at Ambrose's tavern between the Ettrick Shepherd, Christopher North, and others. The novelty, wit, and humour of the conversations added greatly to the popularity of the magazine.

Noggs, NEWMAN, in Dickens's 'Nicholas Nickleby' (q.v.), Ralph Nickleby's clerk.

Noh or **Nō Plays,** THE, a form of traditional, ceremonial, or ritualistic drama peculiar to Japan, symbolical and spiritual in character. It was evolved from religious rites of Shinto worship, was perfected in the 15th cent., and flourished during the Tokugawa period (1652-1868). It has since been revived. About two hundred Noh Plays are extant. In various respects the Noh Plays are comparable with the early Greek drama.

Noli me tangere, Latin, 'touch me not', a phrase occurring in the Vulgate, John xx. 17, applied to paintings representing the appearance of Christ to Mary Magdalene at the sepulchre.

Noll or **OLD NOLL,** a nickname of Oliver Cromwell.

Nominalism, the view of those schoolmen and later philosophers who regard universals or abstract conceptions as mere names without corresponding reality.

Nonce-word, a term employed in the OED. to describe a word which is apparently used only for the nonce, coined for the occasion.

Nones, in the ancient Roman calendar, the 7th of March, May, July, and October, and the 5th of all the other months.

Nonjurors, the beneficed clergy who refused in 1689 to take the oath of allegiance to William and Mary.

N or M, the first answer in the Catechism of the English Church. The most probable explanation is that N stood for *nomen* (name), and that *nomen vel nomina* (name or names) was expressed by 𝔑 *vel* 𝔑𝔑, afterwards corrupted into 𝔑 or 𝔐.

Norman, the style of Romanesque (q.v.) architecture developed by the Normans and employed in England from the mid-11th to the end of the 12th cent., characterized by the use of the round arch.

Norns, in Scandinavian mythology, the three fates, Urd, Verdandi, and Skuld.

Norris, MRS., a character in Jane Austen's 'Mansfield Park' (q.v.).

Norris, FRANK (1870-1902), an American novelist whose early death interrupted a promising career, is chiefly remembered as the author of 'The Octopus' (1901) and 'The Pit' (1903), parts of an unfinished trilogy, an 'Epic of the Wheat'.

North, CHRISTOPHER, a pseudonym used by J. Wilson (1785-1854, q.v.).

North, SIR THOMAS (1535?-1601?), famous for his translations, which include the 'Diall of Princes' (1557) from Guevara's 'El Relox de Principes', 'The Morall Philosophie of Doni', from Italian (1570), and Plutarch's 'Lives' from the French of Amyot (1579), to which he made additions from other authors (1595). His Plutarch, written in a noble and vivid English, formed Shakespeare's chief storehouse of classical learning, and exerted a powerful influence on Elizabethan prose.

North and South, a novel by Mrs. Gaskell (q.v.), published in 'Household Words' in 1854-5. The book is a study in the contrast between the inhabitants of the North and of the South of England. It is also a study of the relations of employers and men in industry.

Northanger Abbey, a novel by Jane Austen (q.v.), begun in 1798, prepared for the press in 1803, but not published until 1818, when it appeared with 'Persuasion'. The origin of the story is the desire to ridicule tales of romance and terror such as Mrs. Radcliffe's 'Mysteries of Udolpho' and to contrast with these life as it really is.

Catherine Morland, the daughter of a well-to-do clergyman, is taken to Bath for the season by her friends, Mr. and Mrs. Allen. Here she makes the acquaintance of Henry Tilney, the son of the eccentric General Tilney, and his pleasant sister Eleanor. Catherine falls in love with Henry, and has the good fortune to obtain his father's approval. Catherine is invited

to Northanger Abbey, the medieval seat of the Tilneys. Somewhat unbalanced by assiduous reading of Mrs. Radcliffe's novels, Catherine here conjures up a gruesome mystery in which she persuades herself that General Tilney is criminally involved, and suffers severe humiliation when her suspicions are discovered. Presently General Tilney, having received a report representing Catherine's parents as in an extremely humble situation, packs her off back to her family. Henry follows Catherine to her home, proposes, and is accepted. General Tilney's consent is before long obtained, when he discovers the true situation of Catherine's family.

The main plot is complicated by a flirtation between Captain Tilney, Henry's elder brother, and the vulgar Isabella Thorpe, who is engaged to marry Catherine's brother; the consequent rupture of the engagement and of the friendship between Catherine and Isabella; and the latter's failure to secure Captain Tilney, who has formed a just estimate of Isabella's character, and pays his attentions in a spirit of mischief.

North Briton, The, a weekly political periodical founded in 1762 by Wilkes (q.v.), in opposition to 'The Briton', which Smollett was conducting in the interests of Lord Bute. In this venture Wilkes was assisted by Charles Churchill (q.v.). In No. 45 of 'The North Briton', Wilkes exposed himself to prosecution for libel, and 'The North Briton' was suppressed.

Northcliffe, ALFRED CHARLES WILLIAM HARMSWORTH, VISCOUNT (1865-1922), laid the foundation of his career as a newspaper proprietor by starting in 1888 'Answers to Correspondents', which, as 'Answers', and with other weekly periodicals owned by him and his brother Harold (first Viscount Rothermere), became extremely popular. In 1894 the brothers acquired the 'Evening News' and in 1896 Alfred started the 'Daily Mail', a halfpenny morning paper, the pioneer of a new phase of journalism, which was followed in 1903 by the illustrated 'Daily Mirror'. In 1908 he acquired 'The Times', which he controlled for some years. Through the influence which his newspapers exerted, Northcliffe took an important part in the First World War; and in 1918 was appointed to have charge of propaganda in foreign countries.

Northern Farmer, The ('Old Style' and 'New Style'), two poems in Lincolnshire dialect by Lord Tennyson (q.v.).

Northern Lass, The, a comedy by Brome (q.v.), printed in 1632.

Northward Hoe, a comedy by Webster and Dekker (qq.v.), printed in 1607.

North-West Passage, a passage for ships round the N. coast of the American continent from the Atlantic to the Pacific which it was long the object of Arctic explorers to discover. When found, as the result of the explorations of Franklin, Parry, and McClure, it proved of no practical utility.

Norumbega, a region on the Atlantic coast of North America, variously shown in 16th- and 17th-cent. maps. It is mentioned, with 'the Samoed shore', by Milton, 'Paradise Lost', x. 696.

Nosey, a nickname applied to Oliver Cromwell, the Duke of Wellington, and others.

Notes and Queries, a periodical founded in 1849 by Thoms, designed to furnish a means for the interchange of thought and information among those engaged in literature, art, and science.

Notre Dame de Paris, the cathedral church of Paris. Also the title of a romance by Victor Hugo.

Notus, the classic name for the south wind, synonymous with Auster.

Nouvelle Héloïse, La, see *Rousseau*.

Novalis, pseudonym of Hardenberg (q.v.).

Novel (Ital. *novella*), originally a short tale, as in Boccaccio's 'Decameron', a short story of this kind. Now, a prose narrative or tale of a fictional character of greater length than the 'short story'. (In the 17th and 18th cents. *novel* was

often contrasted with *romance* as being something shorter and having more relation to real life.)

In England, the beginnings of the novel can be traced in the long romances, mostly in verse, which were popular in the Middle Ages. (In the sense that a novel describes a development of character through a narrative, it has been argued that Chaucer's 'Troylus and Cryseyde' is the first true English novel.) Prose romances of this kind became very popular. Caxton, for example, printed several of them. In the 16th cent., under Italian influences, several collections of short tales were produced, e.g. Painter's 'Palace of Pleasure', in which he writes, 'In these histories (which by another terme I call Novelles)'. Lyly's 'Euphues' (q.v., 1579) shows no advance in technique of character drawing though it exercised a great influence on the prose style of the period. Similarly Sidney's 'Arcadia', the other famous romance of the time, has only stylistic attractions. Robert Greene and Thomas Lodge (qq.v.) wrote good stories within the romance conventions. Thomas Nash's picaresque novel, 'The Unfortunate Traveller or the Life of Jacke Wilton' (1594), introduced a welcome note of realism, which was to be taken up by Defoe and after him by Smollett (see below). Throughout the 17th cent. the romance type of fiction continued to be popular. The works of Aphra Behn are good examples.

Defoe can justly be described as the first real English novelist. His works (for which see under *Defoe*) have a quality, new in English literature, of an imaginative realism, and his characters are true to life. The 18th cent., beginning with Defoe, proved the great age of the novel. (It should be noted that there are elements of this development in the 'Coverley' papers of Steele and Addison with their skilful character drawing.) Samuel Richardson, with his delicate though rather sentimental and elaborate way of writing, gave place to Fielding, whose

'Tom Jones' (q.v., 1749) is often said to be the greatest English novel. Sterne, whose wit and skilful characterization compensate for a complete lack of plot, and Smollett, who recaptured crudely but vigorously the virtues of the picaresque novel, are also among the great novelists of the period.

A new element, noticeable towards the end of the 18th cent., was the 'novel of terror' (see *Gothic novels*) which had been inaugurated rather clumsily by Horace Walpole with his 'Castle of Otranto' (1764). To this time also belongs the didactic novel of which Godwin's 'Caleb Williams' (1794) is a good example.

Both these tendencies, embodying characteristics of the romantic revival, were eclipsed by the success of Sir Walter Scott, whose novels had a new breadth of historical writing with a much greater skill in character drawing. Jane Austen, writing at the same time, belongs in subject-matter to the 18th cent., though her skilful penetration and thoughtfulness have many of the elements of more modern periods.

In the interval between the dominance of Scott and the first productions of the great Victorian novelist, Marryat, a milder successor of Smollett, Bulwer Lytton, in the Byronic tradition, and Benjamin Disraeli, popularizer of the political novel, were widely read.

The modern popularity of the novel, which began with Scott, was continued with the writings of Dickens and Thackeray. Indeed, the greatness of the Victorian age was more fully exemplified in this branch of literature than in any other. George Borrow, Kingsley, Charles Reade, George Eliot, Meredith, and Trollope (qq.v.) are some of the more distinguished names from a wide field. Untroubled by considerations of length, since the appetite of the reading public seemed insatiable, authors used the novel form and its conventions for many purposes, including satire and social reform. The works of Dickens, Charles Reade, and Kingsley are noteworthy in this latter respect.

The Victorian novel lacked often the distinction of the greatest 18th-cent. novels; on the other hand it cultivated breadth, and often, as in the hands of Meredith, a greater subtlety. In the period of transition between the Victorian and the 20th-cent. novel Henry James and Conrad were major figures, bringing, from very different backgrounds, new style and shapeliness and eliminating much of the over-elaborate detail and padding that went with the lengthy novel. Thomas Hardy can claim an almost epic distinction in his best novels, akin to the Russians, though with a more self-conscious philosophy, and Arnold Bennett, notably in 'The Old Wives' Tale', has the same distinction.

The first half of the 20th cent. was a period of experimentation. In particular James Joyce and Virginia Woolf explored new methods of communication and conventions of writing, developing in different ways the stream-of-consciousness or interior monologue technique. The writings of D. H. Lawrence burn with his passionate desire to reform society and set up new ideals in place of the false values he exposed. Since the middle of the century the tendency has been to reject experiment and, except for some 'eccentrics' such as Samuel Beckett, Ivy Compton-Burnett, and Henry Green, to return to the more traditional style of the 19th cent.

Novel, PICARESQUE, see *Picaresque*, and also under *Novel*.

Novels by Eminent Hands, see *Prize Novelists*.

Novum Organum, a philosophical treatise in Latin by Francis Bacon (q.v.) (1620).

The ambition of Bacon was to extend to the utmost the dominion of man over nature by means of knowledge. The 'Novum Organum' describes, in a series of aphorisms, the *method* by which knowledge was to be universalized.

Experience is the source, and induction is the method, of knowledge. The rational processes of the mind must be applied to the fruits of experience by the method of induction. But the mind is subject to defects, which Bacon picturesquely classifies. This analysis of the sources of error leads to the 'just and methodical process' of interpreting nature by three inductive methods.

This procedure of investigation is to be applied to the facts of nature. Bacon claimed only to have provided the 'machine'. But although his method was defective, and in practice useless for purposes of scientific discovery, his principles of investigation were correct, and gave a great impulse to experimental science.

Noyes, ALFRED (1880–1958), a poet whose favourite topics were the sea and fairyland. His best-known works are 'Drake' (1908), a sea epic, 'Tales of the Mermaid Tavern' (1913), and 'The Torchbearers' (1922–30). His collected poems were published in 1950.

Nubbles, MRS. and KIT, characters in Dickens's 'The Old Curiosity Shop' (q.v.).

Numa, the legendary second king of Rome, revered as the founder of the Roman religious system.

Nun of Gandersheim, see *Hrotsvitha.*

Nun's Priest's Tale, The, see *Canterbury Tales.*

Nupkins, MR., a character in Dickens's 'The Pickwick Papers' (q.v.).

Nut-Brown Maid, The, a 15th-cent. poem, in praise of woman's fidelity. The lover, to prove the Maid, tells her that he must to the greenwood go, 'alone, a banyshed man', and live the life of an outlaw. She declares her intention of accompanying him, nor can be dissuaded by the prospect of hardships. The lover finally reveals that he is an earl's son 'and not a banyshed man'. The poem is included in Percy's 'Reliques'. It is the foundation of Prior's 'Henry and Emma' (see *Prior*).

Nym, in Shakespeare's 'The Merry Wives of Windsor' and 'Henry V' (qq.v.), a follower of Falstaff.

Nymphidia, a fairy poem by Drayton (q.v.) (1627).

Nymphs, in Greek mythology, female personifications of various natural objects, mountains, springs, rivers, and trees. The water nymphs were the OCEANIDES (the daughters of Oceanus, nymphs of the Ocean), NEREIDS (nymphs of the Mediterranean Sea), and NAIADS (nymphs of lakes, rivers, and fountains). The OREADS were nymphs of the mountains. The DRYADS and HAMADRYADS were nymphs of trees.

Nyren, JOHN (1764–1837), a famous early cricketer and cricket chronicler. His recollections were published in 'The Young Cricketer's Tutor' (edited by Charles Cowden Clark, 1833).

O

Oak, GABRIEL, a character in Thomas Hardy's 'Far from the Madding Crowd' (q.v.).

Oak-apple Day, 29 May, the anniversary of the restoration of Charles II, when oakleaves are worn in memory of his hiding in the oak at Boscobel on 6 Sept. 1651.

Oates, TITUS (1649–1705), the fabricator of the Popish Plot (1678), figures in

Scott's 'Peveril of the Peak'. He is the 'Corah' of Dryden's 'Absalom and Achitophel' (q.v.).

Obadiah, in the O.T. is (1) the minister of Ahab who protected the prophets of the Lord (1 Kings xviii), and (2) the author of the prophetic book which bears his name; in Sterne's 'Tristram Shandy' (q.v.), a servant of Mr. Walter Shandy.

Obelisk or OBELUS, a straight horizontal stroke, either simple or with a dot above and below, used in ancient manuscripts to indicate a spurious or corrupt word or passage. Hence to *obelize*. In modern use the word *obelisk* is applied to the mark † used in printing for reference to footnotes, etc.

Oberammergau, a village in Upper Bavaria, noted for the performances there of the Passion Play.

Obermann, a psychological romance by Étienne Pivert de Sénancour (1770–1846), French novelist, describing the sentimental speculations and aspirations of a melancholy egoist. Matthew Arnold (q.v.), in his 'Stanzas in Memory' of its author, compares its message with that of Wordsworth and Goethe. See also M. Arnold's 'Obermann once more'.

Oberon, in Shakespeare's 'A Midsummer Night's Dream' (q.v.), the king of the Fairies and husband of Titania.

Obidicut, in Shakespeare's 'King Lear', v. i, the fiend of lust, one of the five that harassed 'poor Tom'.

Obol, OBOLUS, a small coin of ancient Greece, worth about 1½*d*. (see *Charon*).

Obscurorum Virorum, *Epistolae*, see *Hutten*.

Observations on the Present State of the Nation, see *Present State of the Nation*.

O'Casey, SEAN (1884–1964), Irish playwright, educated, according to himself, in the streets of Dublin. His plays are informed with his own experience of poverty and violence, and show a strong sense of tragic irony as well as humour. The best known are 'The Shadow of a Gunman' (1925), 'Juno and the Paycock' (1925), 'The Plough and the Stars' (1926), 'The Silver Tassie' (1928), 'Red Roses for Me' (1942), 'Cock-a-Doodle Dandy' (1949), and 'The Bishop's Bonfire' (1955). He wrote an autobiography in six volumes (1939–54).

Occam, see *Ockham*.

Occleve or HOCCLEVE, THOMAS (1370?–1426), for many years a clerk in the office of the Privy Seal. His principal work, 'De

Regimine Principum', written *c*. 1411–12, is an English version in rhyme-royal of a Latin treatise by Aegidius (a disciple of St. Thomas Aquinas) on the duty of a ruler, addressed to Henry, Prince of Wales. The proem of 2,000 lines contains a eulogy of Chaucer and other interesting material. In 1406 he wrote a curious autobiographical poem 'La Male Règle'. He also wrote two verse-stories from the 'Gesta Romanorum', a manly 'Ars Sciendi Mori', a 'Complaint' and a 'Dialogue', and some shorter poems.

Oceana, see *Froude* (*J. A.*).

Oceana, *The Commonwealth of*, a political romance by James Harington (q.v.) (1656).

The work depicts the author's conception of an ideal government, 'Oceana' being England. The scheme is in contrast to that of Hobbes's 'Leviathan' (q.v.), published a few years previously.

Oceanus, according to the oldest Greek legends, the god of the river that was supposed to encircle the earth.

Ochiltree, EDIE, a character in Scott's 'The Antiquary' (q.v.).

Ockham or OCCAM, WILLIAM (*d*. 1349?), 'Doctor invincibilis', studied at Oxford, became a Franciscan, and graduated in Paris. He entered into the Franciscan controversy concerning poverty, was imprisoned at Avignon on a charge of heresy (1328), but escaped and spent the remainder of his life at Munich, where he died and was buried.

His principal importance lies in his philosophical work. He condemned the doctrine of Realism without accepting the extravagances of Nominalism. He thus approaches the point of view of Roger Bacon. Instead of reasoning from universal premisses, received from authority, we must generalize from experience of the natural order, the doctrine which we find advocated later by F. Bacon, Hobbes, and Berkeley.

Ocnus, in Roman fable, a man remarkable for his industry, who had a wife remarkable for her prodigality. He is represented as twisting a rope, which an ass standing by eats up as fast as he makes it; whence the CORD OF OCNUS, proverbial for wasted labour.

O'Connor, FRANK, the pseudonym of MICHAEL O'DONOVAN (1903-66), who was born and educated in Cork. His work includes novels, plays, and criticism, but he is best known for his short stories, such as 'Bones of Contention' (1936), 'Crab-Apple Jelly' (1944), 'The Common Chord' (1947), and 'Traveller's Samples' (1950). 'Kings, Lords, and Commons' (1961) is an anthology of translations from the Irish.

O'Connor, RT. HON. THOMAS POWER (1848-1929), M.P. and founder and first editor of 'The Star', 'The Sun', etc.; author of a life of Beaconsfield, etc. In parliament he was an active supporter of Parnell (q.v.).

Octavia, sister of Octavian and Mark Antony's wife, figures in Shakespeare's 'Antony and Cleopatra' and Dryden's 'All for Love' (qq.v.).

Octavo, the size of a book in which the sheets are so folded that each leaf is one-eighth of a whole sheet. Cf. *folio*.

Octosyllabic, consisting of eight syllables, usually applied to the eight-syllabled rhyming iambic metre of, e.g., 'The Lady of the Lake'.

Ode, in ancient literature, a poem intended or adapted to be sung; in modern use, a rhymed (rarely unrhymed) lyric, often in the form of an address, generally dignified or exalted in subject, feeling, and style, but sometimes (in earlier use) simple and familiar (though less so than a *song*): usually not more than 150 lines in length.

The different forms of the Greek ode have been variously imitated in English literature. 'Pindaric' odes, imitated from the choric odes of Pindar, were first attempted by Abraham Cowley (q.v.), and a fashion was set which lasted until the time of Gray—cf. his 'Progress of Poesy' and 'The Bard'. These odes were normally divided into strophe, antistrophe, and epode, a series of three

stanzas of which the third differed in metrical form from the first two. But the early view of Pindar assumed a greater irregularity of metre than actually existed, a supposed irregularity which is imitated, for example, in Dryden's 'Alexander's Feast'.

The alternative type of personal ode, e.g. the odes of Sappho and Anacreon, imitated by Horace (cf. Marvell's Horatian ode), consisted of a number of uniform stanzas with an elaborate metrical scheme. This type of ode has been more usually followed in shorter odes, cf. Keats's 'Ode on a Grecian Urn', Shelley's 'Ode to the West Wind', etc.

Besides those mentioned above, other famous odes in English literature are Wordsworth's 'Ode on the Intimations of Immortality'; Keats's 'Ode to a Nightingale', 'To Autumn', and 'To Melancholy'; and Tennyson's 'Ode on the Death of the Duke of Wellington'.

Ode on a Grecian Urn, see *Keats*.

Ode to Evening, see *Collins (William)*.

Ode to the West Wind, see *Shelley*.

Odets, CLIFFORD (1906-63), American playwright. He was a leading figure in the Group Theatre, which followed the naturalistic methods of the Moscow Arts Theatre. His first plays, 'Waiting for Lefty' (1935) and 'Awake and Sing' (1935), are his best.

Odin, the Norse form of the OE. *Woden* (whence our 'Wednesday'), in northern mythology the supreme god and creator.

O'Donovan, MICHAEL, see *O'Connor (F.)*.

O'Dowd, MAJOR, MRS., and GLORVINA, characters in Thackeray's 'Vanity Fair' (q.v.).

Odysseus, or, according to his Latin name, ULYSSES, son of Laertes, and king of the island of Ithaca. He became one of the suitors of Helen (q.v.), but despairing of success married Penelope (q.v.). When Helen was carried off to Troy, Odysseus joined the other Greek princes in the expedition to recover her. During the Trojan War he was distinguished for his prudence and sagacity no less than for his valour. After the war he embarked to return home, but was delayed by a series of adventures recounted in Homer's 'Odyssey'. He was thrown upon the coast of Africa and visited the country of the Lotus-eaters (q.v.); narrowly escaped destruction by the Cyclops, Polyphemus (q.v.); received a bag of winds from Aeolus (q.v.); was detained a year by Circe (q.v.), and for seven years by Calypso (q.v.); visited Hades to consult Tiresias (q.v.); was cast on the island of the Phaeacians, where he was kindly entertained by Nausicaa and her father Alcinous; and finally after an absence of twenty years reached Ithaca, where with the assistance of his son Telemachus, and the swineherd, Eumaeus, he destroyed the importunate suitors of Penelope.

In a dramatic monologue, Tennyson presents Odysseus, in his last years, setting out 'to sail beyond the sunset'. The episode is not in Homer, but in Dante ('Inferno', xxvi).

Odyssey, The, a Greek epic poem attributed to Homer (q.v.), describing the adventures of Odysseus (q.v.) in the course of his return from the Trojan War to his kingdom of Ithaca.

Oedipus, son of Laius, king of Thebes, and Jocasta. Laius had brought a curse upon his family and was informed by an oracle that he must perish at his son's hands, and consequently ordered the destruction of the child. Oedipus was exposed, hung to a tree by a twig passed through his feet (whence his name, 'swollen-foot'), but was rescued by a shepherd. In ignorance of his parentage, Oedipus later slew Laius his father, and having solved the riddle of the Sphinx (q.v.), obtained Jocasta, his mother, for his wife, by whom he had two sons, Polyneices and Eteocles, and two daughters, Ismene and Antigone. Having discovered the facts of his parentage, Oedipus, in horror at his crimes, put out his own eyes, while Jocasta hanged herself. He retired, led by his daughter

Antigone, to Colonos in Attica, where he died. The story of Oedipus is the theme of tragedies by Sophocles (q.v.).

Oedipus complex, in psycho-analysis, a manifestation of infantile sexuality in the relations of the child to its parents.

Oenone, a nymph of Mt. Ida, who became enamoured of the youthful shepherd, Paris (q.v.). Having the gift of prophecy, she foretold to him the disasters which would ensue from his voyage into Greece. When Paris had received his fatal wound, he had himself carried to Oenone, whom he had scurvily abandoned, and sought her help to cure him. She refused, but later, when she learnt that he was dead, took her own life. The story of Oenone is the theme of 'The Death of Paris' in Morris's 'The Earthly Paradise' (q.v.), and of two poems by Lord Tennyson, 'Oenone' and 'The Death of Oenone'.

Offa's Dyke, an entrenchment running from near the mouth of the Wye to near the mouth of the Dee, built by Offa, king of Mercia (757-95), as a boundary between Mercia and Wales.

Offenbach, JACQUES (1819-80), the 'creator of French burlesque opera', a composer of sprightly humorous music which has enjoyed great popularity. His best-known operas are 'Orphée aux enfers' and 'The Tales of Hoffmann'.

O'Flaherty, LIAM (1897-   ), novelist and master of the short story, born in the Aran Islands. His novels include 'The Informer' (1925), 'The Puritan' (1931), and 'Famine' (1937). His volumes of short stories include 'Spring Sowing' (1926), 'The Mountain Tavern' (1929), 'The Wild Swan' (1932), and 'Two Lovely Beasts' (1948).

Og, in Dryden's 'Absalom and Achitophel' (q.v.), represents Thomas Shadwell (q.v.), in allusion to his stoutness (Deut. iii. 11).

Ogham or OGAM, an alphabet of twenty characters used by the ancient British and Irish, and consisting of strokes upright or sloping, and dots, in various numbers.

Ogier the Dane, a hero of the Charlemagne cycle of legends, identified with a Frankish warrior Autgarius who fought against Charlemagne. He is included in some of the lists of Charlemagne's paladins (q.v.). He became the subject of Danish folk-song and a Danish national hero.

Ogre, a man-eating monster of fairy-tale, usually represented as a hideous giant.

Ogygia, in the 'Odyssey', the mythical island of Calypso. It is represented as being far away to the west of Greece.

O'Hara, JOHN HENRY (1905-70), American novelist. The first of his many novels, 'Appointment in Samarra' (1934), brought him fame. Other titles are 'Butterfield 8' (1935), 'A Rage to Live' (1949), and 'From the Terrace' (1958).

O. Henry, see *Henry (O.)*.

Oisin, the legendary Gaelic warrior, son of Finn, also known as Ossian (q.v.), the subject of a poem by Yeats (q.v.).

Olaf, ST., son of King Harald Grenske, was king of Norway, 1015-28. In his youth he is said to have gone to England as an ally of Æthelred. Like his cousin and predecessor, Olaf Tryggvesson, St. Olaf was active in the diffusion of Christianity in his kingdom. He was expelled from Norway by Canute in 1028, and, returning in 1030, met the rebels at Stiklestad, where he " fell mortally wounded.

Olaf Tryggvesson, king of Norway, 995-1000, not to be confused with Olaf Haraldson (St. Olaf, q.v.). He invaded England, and attacked London in 994. He was defeated and killed in 1000 by the kings of Denmark and Sweden, aided by his disaffected subjects. The story of his last great seafight, of the capture of his ship the 'Long Serpent', and of his leap to death in the sea, makes one of the most stirring narratives in the 'Heimskringla'.

Olaus Magnus (1490-1558), Swedish ecclesiastic and historian, was archbishop of Uppsala. His 'Historia de Gentibus Septentrionalibus' (1555) contains interesting information on the early Norsemen.

Old Bachelor, The, the first comedy of Congreve (q.v.), produced in 1693.

Oldbuck, JONATHAN, *Laird of Monkbarns*, the principal character in Sir W. Scott's 'The Antiquary' (q.v.). MISS GRISELDA ('GRIZZY') OLDBUCK is his sister.

Oldcastle, SIR JOHN (*d.* 1417), Lord Cobham in right of his wife, a leader of the Lollards (q.v.), after heterodox declarations of faith, was declared a heretic in 1414 and imprisoned in the Tower. He escaped, was outlawed, captured near Welshpool, and 'hung and burnt hanging' in St. Giles's Fields. There is a poem by Tennyson on the subject.

Oldcastle, The First Part of Sir John, a play (1600) of unknown authorship, included in the 3rd and 4th Shakespeare folios, but certainly not by him.

It deals with the proceedings in Henry V's reign against Sir John Oldcastle (q.v.), as the chief supporter of the Lollards.

Old Curiosity Shop, The, a novel by Dickens (q.v.), published in 1841.

Little Nell (Trent) lives in the gloomy atmosphere of the old curiosity shop kept by her grandfather. Reduced to poverty, he has borrowed money from Daniel Quilp, a hideous dwarf, and this money he secretly expends in gambling, in the vain hope of retrieving his fortunes, for Little Nell's sake. Quilp, who believes him a rich miser, at last discovers where the borrowed money has gone, and seizes the shop. The old man and the child flee and wander about the country, suffering great hardships, and haunted by the fear of being discovered by Quilp, who pursues them with unremitting hatred. They at last find a haven in a cottage by a country church, which they are appointed to look after. The grandfather's brother, returning from abroad, and anxious to relieve their needs, has great difficulty in tracing them. At last he finds them, but Nell, worn out with her troubles, has just died, and the grandfather soon follows her.

The novel contains a number of well-known characters: Quilp's associates, the attorney Sampson Brass and his grim sister Sally; the honest lad Kit Nubbles, devoted to Little Nell; Mr. and Mrs. Garland, the kindly old couple who befriend Kit; Dick Swiveller, the disreputable facetious friend of Fred Trent; 'the Marchioness', the half-starved drudge in the Brass household (who marries Dick in the end); Codlin and Short, the Punch and Judy men; and Mrs. Jarley, of the wax-works.

Old English, see *English*, and *Anglo-Saxon*.

Oldfield, ANNE (1683–1730), an actress who excelled both in tragedy and comedy. She is the 'Narcissa' of Pope's 'Moral Essays'.

Old Fortunatus, a comedy by Dekker (q.v.) (1600).

The beggar Fortunatus, encountering Fortune, is offered the choice between wisdom, strength, health, beauty, long life, and riches, and chooses the last. He receives a purse from which he can at any time draw ten pieces of gold. He goes on his travels, but at the height of his success Fortune steps in and puts an end to his life. His son Andelocia, refusing to take warning by his father's fate, and equipped with the purse, goes through a series of adventures at the court of Athelstane, is finally deprived of his talisman, and meets a miserable death.

Oldham, JOHN (1653–83), published several Pindaric odes, but is chiefly remembered for his ironical 'Satire against Virtue' and 'Satires against the Jesuits' (1681). He also wrote imitations of Horace, Bion, Moschus, and Boileau. Dryden addressed some beautiful lines to his memory.

Old Man Eloquent, THAT, Isocrates (q.v.), so called by Milton in his sonnet to Lady Margaret Ley.

Old Man of the Sea, see *Sindbad*.

Oldmixon, JOHN (1673–1742), a Whig historian and pamphleteer. By his 'Essay on Criticism', prefixed to the third edition (1727) of his 'Critical History of England' (1724–6), he incurred the hostility of Pope, who pilloried him in 'The Dunciad'.

Old Moore, Francis Moore (1657–1715), physician, astrologer, and schoolmaster, who in 1699 published an almanac containing weather predictions in order to promote the sale of his pills. There are now several almanacs called 'Old Moore', and the predictions range far beyond the weather.

Old Mortality, a novel by Sir W. Scott (q.v.) (1816) (in the first series of the 'Tales of My Landlord').

The title is taken from the nickname of a certain Robert Paterson, who towards the end of the 18th cent. wandered about Scotland cleaning and repairing the tombs of the Cameronians. The story, by a fiction of Scott, is said to be based on the anecdotes told by this supporter of their cause, and covers the period from the military operations undertaken against them in 1679 to the more peaceful days of William III. It is particularly concerned with the fortunes of Henry Morton of Milnwood, a young man of courage and high character, and a moderate Presbyterian, who, at the outset of the tale, is arrested by the dragoons of Claverhouse for having harboured an old friend of his father, John Balfour of Burley. Morton narrowly escapes immediate execution, and this act of oppression induces him to throw in his lot with the Covenanters. He accordingly becomes one of their leaders. This brings him into violent antagonism with Lady Margaret Bellenden, the Royalist owner of Tillietudlem Castle, with whose granddaughter Edith he is in love. But the final defeat of the Covenanters at Bothwell Bridge, and his own capture and banishment, sever him for years from Edith, who believes him dead; and she is on the point of yielding to the patient suit of her other suitor, Lord Evandale, when Morton, after the accession of William III, returns to England. Evandale is killed in a skirmish with a few fanatics, and Morton marries Edith.

Old Nick, the Devil, where Nick is probably the familiar abbreviation of Nicholas, though the reason for the appellation is obscure.

Old Pretender, THE, James Francis Edward Stuart (1688-1766), son of James II and Mary of Modena, served with the French army and distinguished himself at Oudenarde (1708) and Malplaquet (1709). He took a part in the unsuccessful rising in Scotland of 1715, and gave money for the rising of 1745.

Old Style, see *Calendar.*

Old Vic, THE, a theatre in the Waterloo Bridge Road, London, opened in 1818 as the 'Royal Coburg'; it declined into a music-hall with a promenade. It was started afresh in 1880 on more respectable lines. Miss Lilian Baylis became manager in 1912, and made it famous by her notable productions of Shakespeare plays.

Old Wives' Tale, The, a play in prose by G. Peele (q.v.) (1595).

The play is a satire on the romantic dramas of the time, the first English work of this kind. Two brothers are searching for their sister Delia, who is held captive by the magician Sacrapant. The brothers also fall into his hands. They are all rescued by the knight Eumenides aided by Jack's Ghost, who is impelled by motives of gratitude, because the knight had borne the expense of Jack's funeral.

The plot has interesting parallels to 'Comus' (q.v.).

Old Wives' Tale, The, a novel by E. A. Bennett (q.v.) (1908).

It is the long chronicle of the lives of two sisters, Constance and Sophia Baines, daughters of a draper of Bursley (Burslem, one of the 'Five Towns', q.v.), from their ardent girlhood, through disillusionment, to death. The drab life of the draper's shop, its trivial incidents, are made interesting and important. Constance, a staid and sensible young woman, marries the insignificant Samuel Povey, the chief assistant in the shop, and spends all her life in Bursley. The more passionate and imaginative Sophia elopes with the fascinating Gerald Scales, an unprincipled

blackguard, who carries her to Paris, where she is exposed to indignities, and finally deserts her. She struggles to success as a lodging-house keeper in Paris, where she lives through the siege of 1870. The sisters are reunited, and spend their last years together in Bursley.

Oliphant, LAURENCE (1829-88), after a desultory education and extensive travels, became in 1853-4 secretary to Lord Elgin at Washington, and then accompanied Lord Stratford de Redcliffe to the Crimea. He next accompanied Lord Elgin to China as private secretary. He is then heard of as plotting with Garibaldi in Italy, as secretary of legation in Japan, and in other parts of the world. He was 'Times' correspondent during the Franco-German War. In 1867 he had come under the subjection of the American 'prophet', Thomas Lake Harris, by whom he was commercially employed in America, an experience which led to the publication, in 1876, of 'The Autobiography of a Joint-Stock Company', exposing the methods of American financiers. He wrote several mystical works at Haifa in Palestine, where, with his second wife, he founded a community of Jewish immigrants. His many experiences provided materials for 'Episodes of a Life of Adventure' which appeared in 1887, not long before his death.

Oliphant, MARGARET OLIPHANT (1828-97), *née* Wilson, published many novels, of which the best known are the 'Chronicles of Carlingford', issued anonymously between 1863 and 1876. Of these the best are 'Salem Chapel' (which depicts the narrow and intolerant piety of a dissenting community) and 'Miss Marjoribanks'. She wrote a number of stories of which Scotland is the scene, and also published lives of Edward Irving (1862) and Laurence Oliphant (1892).

Oliver, in the Charlemagne cycle of legends, is the son of Renier, duke of Genoa. He is one of Charlemagne's paladins (q.v.), the close friend of Roland, with whom he has a prolonged and undecided single combat (the origin of their comradeship, see *Roland for an Oliver*). At the battle of Roncesvalles (see *Roland*) he urges Roland to summon help by sounding his horn, but Roland postpones doing so till too late.

Oliver, a character in Shakespeare's 'As You Like It' (q.v.).

Oliver Dain (OLIVIER LE DAIN), barber and counsellor of Louis XI; figures in Scott's 'Quentin Durward' (q.v.).

Oliver Twist, a novel by Dickens (q.v.) (1837–8).

Oliver Twist is a child of unknown parentage born in a workhouse and brought up under the cruel conditions to which pauper children were exposed, the tyrant at whose hands he especially suffers being Bumble, the parish beadle. After experience of an unhappy apprenticeship, he runs away, reaches London, and falls into the hands of a gang of thieves, at the head of which is the old Jew Fagin, and whose other members are the burglar, Bill Sikes, his companion Nancy, and 'the Artful Dodger', an impudent young pickpocket. Every effort is made to convert Oliver into a thief. He is temporarily rescued by the benevolent Mr. Brownlow, but kidnapped by the gang, whose interest in his retention has been increased by the offers of a sinister person named Monks. Oliver is now made to accompany Bill Sikes on a burgling expedition, in the course of which he receives a gunshot wound, and comes into the hands of Mrs. Maylie and her protégée Rose, by whom he is kindly treated and brought up. After a time, Nancy, who develops some redeeming traits, reveals to Rose that Monks is aware of Oliver's parentage, and wishes all proof of it destroyed; also that there is some relationship between Oliver and Rose herself. Inquiry is set on foot. In the course of it Nancy's action is discovered by the gang, and she is brutally murdered by Bill Sikes. A hue and cry is raised; Sikes, trying to escape, accidentally hangs himself, and the rest of the gang are secured and Fagin executed. Monks, found and threatened with exposure, confesses what

remains unknown. He is the half-brother of Oliver, and has pursued his ruin, to retain the whole of his father's property. Rose is the sister of Oliver's unfortunate mother. Oliver is adopted by Mr. Brownlow. Monks emigrates and dies in prison.

Olivia, (1) one of the principal characters in Shakespeare's 'Twelfth Night' (q.v.); (2) a character in Wycherley's 'The Plain Dealer'; (3) the elder daughter of Dr. Primrose, in Goldsmith's 'The Vicar of Wakefield' (q.v.).

Olney Hymns, see *Cowper* and *Newton* (*J.*).

Olor Iscanus, a collection of poems by Vaughan (q.v., 'The Swan of Usk') (1651). The poem which gives its title to the book is in praise of the river Usk.

Olympia, a small plain in the north-west of the Peloponnese, where the Olympic Games (q.v.) were celebrated. Here stood the famous statue of the Olympian Zeus by Phidias, and here was found the statue of Hermes by Praxiteles.

Olympiad, see *Olympic Games.*

Olympian Odes, THE, of Pindar, written to celebrate victories at the Olympic Games (q.v.).

Olympic Games, THE, were held every fourth year at Olympia in Elis in the Peloponnese. Their origin is lost in antiquity, but legend attributes it to Hercules. The intervals of four years between the successive celebrations were known as *Olympiads* and were reckoned in Greek chronology from the year 776 B.C., when Coroebus won the foot-race. The Olympic Games were revived in 1896 on an international basis.

Olympus, a lofty mountain standing at the eastern extremity of the range that divided Greece from Macedonia, regarded in Greek mythology as the home of the gods, who met in conclave on the summit.

The MYSIAN OLYMPUS was a lofty chain of mountains in the north-west of Asia Minor.

Omar Khayyám, The Rubáiyát of, a translation of the *rubais* or quatrains of the Persian poet of that name, by Edward

FitzGerald (q.v.), first published anonymously in 1859 (75 quatrains), remodelled and enlarged (110 quatrains) in 1868, and further modified and reduced (101 quatrains) in 1872 and 1879.

Omar Khayyám ('Khayyám' means 'tent-maker'), an astronomer and poet, was born at Naishapur in Khorassan in the latter half of the 11th cent. The original 'rubáiyát' or quatrains are independent stanzas, of which the form is reproduced in the translation; but the translator has woven them together in a connected train of thought. The stanzas contain the poet's meditations on the mysteries of existence, and his counsel to drink and make merry while life lasts.

Ombre (from Spanish *hombre*, man), a card game played by three persons with forty cards. It figures prominently in Pope's 'The Rape of the Lock' (q.v.).

Omoo, a Narrative of Adventures in the South Seas, a romance by Melville (q.v.) (1847), a continuation of the adventures begun in 'Typee' (see under *Melville*).

Omphale, a queen of Lydia. When Hercules (q.v.) committed a murder in a fit of madness, the Delphic oracle bade him go into servitude for three years. Omphale bought him, and he is represented as spinning by her side among her women, while Omphale wears his lion's skin.

O'Neill, EUGENE GLADSTONE (1888–1953), American dramatist. After writing several one-act plays, he scored his first big success with 'Beyond the Horizon' (1920). His reputation as America's leading and most original dramatist, however influenced by Ibsen and Strindberg, was confirmed with the production of the expressionistic 'Emperor Jones' (1920), and 'Anna Christie' (1921), a naturalistic study of a prostitute of the New York waterfront and her redemption. Among other important plays of this period were 'The Hairy Ape' (1922), 'All God's Chillun Got Wings' (1924), and 'Desire Under the Elms' (1924). O'Neill's criticism of contemporary values was powerfully and poetically expressed in 'The Fountain' (1925), 'The Great God Brown' (1926), 'Lazarus Laughed' (1927), and 'Marco Millions' (1927). He experimented with the stream-of-consciousness in 'Strange Interlude' (1928), and adapted a Greek theme to the aftermath of the American Civil War in 'Mourning Becomes Electra' (1931). Among his later plays was 'The Iceman Cometh' (1946). He was awarded a Nobel Prize in 1936.

One of our Conquerors, a novel by G. Meredith (q.v.) (1891).

Only Way, The, a play (1890) adapted by F. Wills from Dickens's 'A Tale of Two Cities'.

Onomatopoeia, the formation of a word by an imitation of the sound associated with the object or action designated; as 'hurly-burly'.

O.P., 'opposite the prompter's side' of the stage in a theatre; that is, the right-hand side (when facing the auditorium).

o.p., in booksellers' catalogues, 'out of print'.

Open, Sesamè! the magic formula in 'Ali Baba and the Forty Thieves' (q.v.).

Opera, a dramatic performance in which music forms an essential part, consisting of recitatives, arias, choruses, etc.

Opera first won popularity in Italy at the end of the 16th cent. It shared many features of stage display, etc., with the masque (q.v.), which was popularized in England at the beginning of the 17th cent. under Italian influence. D'Avenant's 'Siege of Rhodes' was first presented in operatic form, and Evelyn, writing in 1659, says, 'I went to see a new Opera, after the Italian way, in recitative music and sceanes, much inferior to the Italian composure and magnificence.' Dryden wrote the libretto for several operas including 'The State of Innocence', a rhymed version of 'Paradise Lost'. About the year 1730 the popularity of Italian opera and Italian singers was so great as to threaten the 'legitimate' stage. To this period belongs Gay's 'Beggar's Opera', a ballad-opera written by way of a parody on the prevailing fashion.

In later periods the opera has generally been disregarded by English writers as a field for their efforts, and German or Italian opera has flourished as an alien form of entertainment. Mention, however, should be made of the highly successful comic operas of W. S. Gilbert and Arthur Sullivan (qq.v.) in the 19th cent.

COMIC OPERA or LIGHT OPERA—opera of a lighter kind, e.g. Rossini's 'Barber of Seville'.

GRAND OPERA—opera in the grand or tragic tradition, e.g. the operas of Wagner, etc.

OPERA BOUFFE—comic opera, especially of a farcical character.

Ophelia, in Shakespeare's 'Hamlet' (q.v.), the daughter of Polonius.

Ophir, in O.T. geography, the place from which the ships of King Solomon brought gold and precious stones (1 Kings x. 11). It has been variously identified, and was probably in south-eastern Arabia.

Opie, MRS. AMELIA (1769-1853), *née* Alderson, wife of John Opie the painter. She was a novelist and poet, and intimate with Sydney Smith, Sheridan, and Mme de Staël.

Opium Eater, Confessions of an English, see *Confessions of an English Opium Eater*.

Ops, a Roman goddess of fertility and agriculture.

Orange, a name applied to the ultra-Protestant party in Ireland, in reference to the secret Association of Orangemen formed in 1795. The exact origin of this use of 'Orange' is obscure, but probably had reference to William of Orange.

Oran Haut-ton, SIR, the amiable orang-outang in Peacock's 'Melincourt' (q.v.).

Orbilius, the schoolmaster of Horace, a flogger.

Orc, in the mystical poems of Blake (q.v.), the symbol of rebellious anarchy, the opponent of Urizen.

Orcades, the Orkney Islands.

Orcus, a Roman name for the god of the Lower World.

Orczy, THE BARONESS (Mrs. Montagu Barstow, 1865-1947), playwright and novelist, author of the famous adventure story 'The Scarlet Pimpernel' (1905) and its many sequels, dealing with the French Revolution.

Ordeal of Richard Feverel, The, a novel by G. Meredith (q.v.) (1859).

Order, in classical architecture, a mode of architectural treatment founded upon the proportions of columns and the form of their capitals, with the relative proportions and amount of decoration used in their entablatures.

The FIVE ORDERS OF CLASSICAL ARCHITECTURE are the Doric, Ionic, Corinthian (qq.v.), Tuscan, and Composite, of which the first three are the original Greek orders, the other two Roman varieties.

An ATTIC ORDER has a square column of any of the five above orders.

Orders, RELIGIOUS, see *Benedictines, Capuchins, Dominicans, Franciscans, etc.*

Oreads, nymphs (q.v.) of the mountains.

Orestes, a son of Agamemnon and Clytemnestra (qq.v.). When his father was murdered by Clytemnestra and Aegisthus, young Orestes was saved from his mother's dagger by his sister Electra. When Orestes reached manhood, he, with the assistance of his friend Pylades, avenged his father's death by assassinating Aegisthus and Clytemnestra. To obtain purification from this murder Orestes was directed by the oracle at Delphi to bring to Greece a statue of Artemis from the Tauric Chersonese. Orestes and Pylades undertook the enterprise, and, having reached the Chersonese, were brought before Thoas, the king of the place, and ordered to be sacrificed. Iphigenia (q.v.) was then priestess of the temple of Artemis and it was her office to immolate these strangers. Having discovered that one of them was her brother, she resolved to fly with them from the Chersonese, carrying away the statue of Artemis. This they accomplished. Orestes became king of Argos, gave his sister Electra to Pylades, and himself married Hermione, daughter of Menelaus.

Orfeo, Sir, see *Sir Orfeo*.

Orgoglio (Ital., signifying haughtiness), in Spenser's 'Faerie Queene', I. vii. 9 and 10, captures the Red Cross Knight, and is slain by Prince Arthur.

Oriana, see under *Amadis of Gaul*. Oriana is (1) a name frequently applied by the Elizabethan poets to Queen Elizabeth; (2) the heroine of Fletcher's 'The Wild-Goose Chase'; (3) the subject of a ballad by Tennyson.

Oriflamme, said to be derived from *aurea flamma*, 'golden flame', a small silk three-pointed banner of the abbots of Saint-Denis, which became the French royal banner.

Origen (*c.* 185–*c.* 253), the second great Christian thinker and scholar of the Alexandrian school (Clement was the first). He combined with his orthodox Christianity personal theories as to reincarnation which were rejected by the Church. He was author of many theological works, and compiler of the famous *Hexapla* versions of the Old Testament.

Origin of Species, The, the great work of C. Darwin (q.v.), of which the full title was 'On the Origin of Species by means of Natural Selection, or the Preservation of Favoured Races in the Struggle for Life' (1859).

Orinda, THE MATCHLESS, see *Philips* (*K.*).

Orion, a giant and hunter of Boeotia, the subject of various legends. After his death he was placed among the stars. His constellation used to set about November, whence it was associated with storms and rain.

Orion, an allegorical poem by R. H. Horne (q.v.), published in 1843 at one farthing, as a satirical comment on the current estimation of poetry.

Orlando, (1) the Italian form of Roland (q.v.), a hero of the Charlemagne romances (see also *Orlando Furioso* and *Orlando Innamorato*); (2) in Shakespeare's 'As You Like It' (q.v.), the lover of Rosalind; (3) the title of a novel by V. Woolf (q.v.).

Orlando Friscobaldo, in Dekker's 'The Honest Whore' (q.v.), the father of Bellafront.

Orlando Furioso, a poem by Ariosto (q.v.) (1532) designed to continue the story of Orlando's love for Angelica begun by Boiardo in the 'Orlando Innamorato' (q.v.).

The main theme of the poem is this: Saracens and Christians, in the days of Charlemagne, are at war for the possession of Europe. The Saracens under Agramante, king of Africa, are besieging Charlemagne in Paris with the help of Marsilio, the Moorish king of Spain, and two mighty warriors, Rodomont and Mandricardo. Orlando, chief of the paladins, a perfect knight, is lured by Angelica's beauty to forget his duty and pursue her. Angelica meets with various adventures, finally coming upon the wounded Moorish youth Medoro, whom she tends, falls in love with, and marries. Orlando, learning their story, is seized with a furious and grotesque madness, runs naked through the country, and at last returns to Charlemagne's camp, where he is finally cured of his madness, and in a great final battle kills Agramante.

Although the madness of Orlando gives the poem its name, a not less important theme in it is the love of Rogero for Bradamant, a maiden warrior, and the many adventures and vicissitudes that interrupt the course of true love. Other notable episodes in the work are the voyage of Astolfo on the hippogriff to the moon, and the self-martyrdom of Isabella to escape the attentions of the pagan king, Rodomont.

The best translation of the 'Orlando Furioso' into English is that of Sir John Harington (q.v.).

Orlando Innamorato, a poem by Boiardo (q.v.) (1487), on the subject of the falling in love of Orlando (the Roland of the Charlemagne cycle) with Angelica, daughter of Galafron, the king of Cathay.

The poem, which was left unfinished, was refashioned by Berni, but its true sequel is in the 'Orlando Furioso' (q.v.) of Ariosto.

Orley Farm, a novel by A. Trollope (q.v.) (1862).

Ormond, a novel by M. Edgeworth (q.v.) (1817), a tale of life in Ireland, and in a minor degree in fashionable Paris society in the 18th cent.

Ormulum, The, a poem of some 10,000 lines in the vernacular, written in the first half of the 13th cent., by one Orm or Ormin, an Augustinian monk who probably lived in the east of England. It consists of paraphrases of the gospels for the year as arranged in the mass book, supplemented by a homily on each; but the scheme was not completed. It is composed of lines of fifteen syllables without rhyme or alliteration. The author has his own system of spelling, important for the light it throws on the evolution of the English language.

Ormuz or HORMUZ, an ancient city on an island at the mouth of the Persian Gulf; referred to by Milton, 'Paradise Lost', II. 2.

Oroonoko, or the History of the Royal Slave, a novel by Aphra Behn (q.v.) (*c.* 1688). The novel is remarkable as the first expression in English literature of sympathy for the oppressed Negroes. It no doubt reflects the authoress's memories of her early days in Surinam. It was made the subject of a tragedy by Southerne (q.v.), 'Oroonoko: A Tragedy', produced in 1695.

Orosius, a priest of Tarragona in Spain, *fl.* A.D. 500, disciple of St. Augustine and friend of St. Jerome, author of the 'Historia adversus Paganos', a universal history and geography, which King Alfred translated.

Orphan, The, a tragedy in blank verse by Otway (q.v.), produced in 1680.

The play proved a great success, and was frequently revived. Monimia, the orphan heroine, was one of Mrs. Barry's (q.v.) most celebrated parts.

Orpheus, a son of the muse Calliope, received from Apollo a lyre on which he played with such skill that the wild beasts, and also rocks and trees, came to listen to his song. He assisted the Argonauts (q.v.) in their expedition. He loved his wife Eurydice, and, when she died, determined to recover her. He entered the infernal regions and charmed Pluto and Persephone with his music. They consented to restore Eurydice to him on condition that he forebore to look behind him until he had emerged from hell. Orpheus was already in sight of the upper regions when he forgot the condition and turned back to look at Eurydice. She instantly vanished from his sight, and his attempts to rejoin her were vain. He now separated himself from the society of mankind, and the Thracian women, whom he had offended by his coldness, tore him in pieces and threw his head, which still uttered the name 'Eurydice', into the river Hebrus.

Orphicism, a mystic religion of ancient Greece, of which Orpheus (q.v.) was the centre. It appears to have developed in the 6th cent. B.C., when there was an abundant Orphic literature, little of which has survived. It sank to the level of a sectarian superstition in the 5th cent., but the profound thoughts which underlay it affected Pindar and Plato. The Orphics taught the transmigration of souls, retribution in a future life, and the final liberation of man by the observation of strict purity.

Orrery, EARLS OF, see *Boyle*.

Orsino, in Shakespeare's 'Twelfth Night' (q.v.), the duke of Illyria.

Orson, see *Valentine and Orson*.

Ortelius, ABRAHAM (1527-98), a geographer of Antwerp, who came to England and became friendly with Camden (q.v.). He published his atlas, 'Theatrum Orbis Terrarum', in 1570.

Ortheris, STANLEY, see *Learoyd* (*J.*).

Orthodox Church or GREEK CHURCH, THE, the Eastern Church which recognizes the headship of the Patriarch of Constantinople, together with the national Churches of Russia, Rumania, etc., which hold the same 'orthodox' creed.

Orville, LORD, the hero of Fanny Burney's 'Evelina' (q.v.).

Orwell, GEORGE, the pen-name of ERIC BLAIR (1903-50), who was born in Bengal, brought to England at an early age and educated at Eton. He served with the Indian Imperial Police in Burma from 1922 to 1927, and his experiences are reflected in his first novel, 'Burmese Days' (1934). Later he worked in Paris and London in a series of ill-paid jobs (see 'Down and Out in Paris and London', 1933). 'Homage to Catalonia' (1938) is an autobiographical record of the Spanish Civil War, in which he fought for the Republicans. He considered himself a democratic socialist, but he hated totalitarianism and became more and more disillusioned with the aims and methods of Communism. His political satires, 'Animal Farm' (q.v., 1945) and 'Nineteen Eighty-four' (q.v., 1949) were immensely popular. His other writings include the novels, 'Keep the Aspidistra Flying' (1936) and 'Coming Up for Air' (1939), and essays and studies such as 'The Road to Wigan Pier' (1937), an account of unemployment.

Osbaldistone, MR., FRANCIS, RASHLEIGH, and SIR HILDEBRAND, characters in Scott's 'Rob Roy' (q.v.).

Osborne, MR., GEORGE, his son, and MARIA and JANE, his daughters, characters in Thackeray's 'Vanity Fair' (q.v.).

Osborne, DOROTHY (1627-95), married Sir W. Temple (q.v.) in 1655. Her letters to him during the period 1652-4 were published in 1888.

Osborne, JOHN JAMES (1929-), playwright, whose play 'Look Back in Anger' (1957) helped to give currency to the phrase 'angry young man' in reference to certain writers of the fifties. ('Angry Young Man' was the title of a work by Leslie Paul, 1951.) Other plays by Osborne include 'The Entertainer' (1957), 'The World of Paul Slickey' (1959), and 'Luther' (1961).

O'Shaughnessy, ARTHUR WILLIAM EDGAR (1844-81), poet and friend of D. G. Rossetti (q.v.). He is remembered for his poem, 'Ode', which begins:

We are the music makers,
And we are the dreamers of dreams.

Osiris, a great deity of the ancient Egyptians, identified by the Greeks with Dionysus.

Osler, SIR WILLIAM (1849-1919), born in Canada, a great physician. His 'Principles and Practice of Medicine' appeared in 1891; his essays and addresses have been collected.

Osorius, JEROME (d. 1580), a Portuguese associate of Loyola (q.v.). In 1562 he wrote an attack on the English Reformation, which was answered by Haddon, and by John Foxe (1577, English translation 1581). His library was seized on the occasion of Essex's expedition of 1596 and subsequently given to the newly founded Bodleian Library.

Ossa, a lofty mountain in Thessaly, which the Giants (q.v.) heaped on Pelion in their endeavour to reach heaven.

Ossian, the name commonly given to *Oisin*, a legendary Gaelic warrior and bard, the son of Finn (Fingal), supposed to have lived in the 3rd cent. For the poems attributed to him, see under *Macpherson*.

Oswald, ST. (d. 992), was nephew of Archbishop Odo (d. 959). On St. Dunstan's initiative he was appointed bishop of Worcester in 961, and co-operated with him and with St. Æthelwold (q.v.) in the revival of religion and learning in the land, bringing scholars from the Continent, among them the distinguished Abbo of Fleury. He founded monasteries at Westbury, Worcester, Winchcombe, and in the Isle of Ramsey. He is commemorated on 28 Feb.

Othello, The Moor of Venice, a tragedy by Shakespeare (q.v.), acted in 1604, printed in quarto in 1622. The story is drawn from Cinthio (q.v.).

Desdemona, daughter of the Venetian senator, Brabantio, has secretly married the Moor, Othello, a gallant general in the service of the Venetian state. Haled before the duke, Othello is accused by Brabantio of carrying off his daughter; simultaneously comes news of an impending attack on Cyprus by the Turks, against whom Othello is needed to lead the Venetian forces. Brabantio reluctantly hands his daughter over to the Moor, who at once sets out with Desdemona for Cyprus.

Othello had lately promoted to the lieutenancy Cassio, a young Florentine whom he trusted. By this promotion he had deeply offended Iago, an older soldier who thought he had a better claim, and who now plots his revenge. By a device he first discredits Cassio, as a soldier, with Othello, so that Cassio is deprived of his lieutenancy. He instigates the latter to ask Desdemona to plead in his favour with Othello, which Desdemona warmly does. At the same time he craftily instils in Othello's mind suspicion of his wife's fidelity, and jealousy of Cassio. Finally by a trick he arranges that a handkerchief given by Othello to Desdemona shall be found on Cassio. He stirs Othello to such jealousy that the Moor smothers Desdemona in her bed. Shortly afterwards Cassio, whom Iago had set Roderigo, one of his associates and dupes, to assassinate, is brought in wounded. But Roderigo has failed in his purpose, and has been killed by Iago to prevent discovery of the plot; on him are found letters revealing the guilt of Iago and the innocence of Cassio. Othello, thunderstruck by the discovery that he had murdered Desdemona without cause, kills himself from remorse.

Otho the Great, a play written in 1819 by Keats (q.v.) in collaboration with his friend Charles Armitage Brown (1786–1842), who planned its construction.

O'Trigger, SIR LUCIUS, a character in Sheridan's 'The Rivals' (q.v.).

Ottava rima, an Italian stanza of eight eleven-syllabled lines, rhyming a b a b a b c c, employed by Tasso, Ariosto, etc. The English adaptation, as used by Byron, has English heroic lines of ten syllables.

Otterbourne, The Battle of, one of the earliest of English ballads; in Percy's 'Reliques'.

Ottoman Empire, the Turkish Empire, so called from its founder Othman or Osman (whence *Osmanli*), who flourished *c.* 1300.

Otway, THOMAS (1652–85), playwright. He appeared unsuccessfully on the stage, being given a part by the kindness of Mrs. Aphra Behn (q.v.). He for many years cherished an unrequited passion for Mrs. Barry (q.v.), the actress. He died in destitution at the early age of 33.

Of his three great tragedies, 'Don Carlos', in rhymed verse, was produced in 1676; 'The Orphan' (q.v.), in blank verse, in 1680; 'Venice Preserv'd' (q.v.), also in blank verse, in 1682. He also wrote prologues, epilogues, and a few poems.

Ouida (MARIE LOUISE DE LA RAMÉE) (1839–1908). Her pseudonym, 'Ouida', was a childish mispronunciation of her name Louise. Her forty-five novels deal chiefly with fashionable life and show a spirit of rebellion against the moral ideals reflected in much of the fiction of the time. She incurred a good deal of ridicule on account of the languid guardsmen, miracles of strength, courage, and beauty, whom she frequently presented as her heroes, and of her amusing mistakes in matters of men's sports and occupations. But these faults were redeemed by her gift for stirring narrative and other merits.

Oulton, THE OLD MAN OF: Borrow (q.v.).

Our Mutual Friend, a novel by Dickens (q.v.), published in monthly parts between May 1864 and Nov. 1865.

John Harmon returns from the exile to which he has been sent by a harsh father, a rich dust-contractor; he expects to receive the inheritance to which his father has attached the condition that he shall marry a certain girl, Bella Wilfer. Bella is unknown to him, and he confides to a mate of the ship which is bringing him home his intention of concealing his identity until he has formed some judgement of his allotted wife. The mate lures him to a riverside haunt, attempts to murder him, and is in turn murdered. The two bodies are thrown into the river. Harmon recovers and escapes; the mate's body is found after some days, and, owing to Harmon's papers found upon it, it is taken to be that of Harmon. Harmon's intention of remaining unknown is thus facilitated, and he assumes the name of John Rokesmith, and becomes the secretary of the kindly, disinterested Mr. Boffin, old Harmon's foreman, who, in default of young Harmon, inherits the property. He is thrown into close contact with Bella, a flighty minx, who is adopted by Boffin, and who is turned by her first taste of wealth into an arrogant mercenary jade. Rokesmith nevertheless falls in love with her and is contemptuously rejected. Harmon's identity is now discovered by the amiable Mrs. Boffin, and the Boffins, devoted to their old master's son and convinced of Bella's soundness of heart, contrive a plot to prove her. Boffin pretends to be transformed by his wealth into a hard and griping miser, and heaps indignities on Harmon, who is finally dismissed with contumely. Bella, awakened to the evils of wealth and to the merits of Rokesmith, flies from the Boffins and marries her suitor. His identity presently comes to light, and with his assistance the scheme of the one-legged old villain, Silas Wegg, to blackmail Boffin is exposed.

Concurrently with this main theme we have the story of the love of Eugene Wrayburn, a careless insolent young barrister, for Lizzy Hexam, daughter of a disreputable boatman. His rival for her affections, Bradley Headstone, a schoolmaster, attempts to murder Wrayburn. The latter is saved by Lizzy and marries her. Among the notable characters in the book are the Veneerings, types of social parvenus; the good Jew Riah; the blackmailing waterside villain, Rogue Riderhood; Jenny Wren, the dolls' dressmaker; Bella Wilfer's grotesque father, mother, and sister; and the spirited Betty Higden,

an old woman with a haunting dread of the workhouse.

Overbury, SIR THOMAS (1581-1613), opposed the marriage of his patron, Robert Carr (afterwards earl of Somerset), with the divorced countess of Essex, and on the pretext of his refusal of diplomatic employment was sent to the Tower, where he was slowly poisoned by agents of Lady Essex. Four of these were hanged; Somerset and his wife were convicted and pardoned. The prosecution was conducted by F. Bacon (q.v.). Overbury is chiefly remembered for his 'Characters', on the model of those of Theophrastus (q.v.)—not all of which, however, were written by Overbury himself.

Overreach, SIR GILES, a character in Massinger's 'A New Way to pay Old Debts' (q.v.).

Ovid (PUBLIUS OVIDIUS NASO) (43 B.C.–A.D. 18), the Roman poet. His works include (in rough chronological order) the 'Amores', 'Heroides', 'Ars Amatoria', 'Metamorphoses', 'Fasti', 'Tristia', and 'Epistulae ex Ponto'. Ovid wrote in elegiacs (q.v.), and was the favourite Latin poet of the Middle Ages.

Owen, ROBERT (1771-1858), socialist and philanthropist, was a successful owner of cotton-spinning mills in Manchester. He became famous for his 'institution for the formation of character', and for other proposals of social reform. His example was largely instrumental in bringing about the Factory Act of 1819.

Owen, WILFRED (1893-1918), poet of the First World War, killed just before the Armistice and before he was able to complete the book of poetry he had planned, of which he said in the preface 'My subject is War and the pity of War'. His Collected Poems were published in 1920 by his friend Siegfried Sassoon, a new edition appeared in 1931 by Edmund Blunden, and a third in 1963 by C. Day Lewis, with a memoir by Blunden.

Owl and the Nightingale, The, a poem of some 2,000 lines, in octo-syllabic couplets, probably of the early 13th cent. It is a debate between the grave Owl and the gay Nightingale as to the benefits they confer on man, symbolizing perhaps respectively the religious poet and the poet of love. The poem is attributed to one Nicholas of Guildford (*fl.* 1250), who is stated in the poem to have lived at Portisham in Dorset; but John of Guildford (probably *fl.* 1225), who is known to have written verse about this time, is also possibly the author.

Owlglass, see *Eulenspiegel*.

Ox, THE DUMB, a name for Aquinas (q.v.).

Oxford English Dictionary, The. The scheme of 'a completely new English Dictionary' was conceived in 1858, and Herbert Coleridge (1830-61), succeeded by Dr. F. J. Furnivall (1825-1910), were the first editors. Their work, which covered twenty years, consisted only in the collection of materials, and it was not until Dr. J. A. H. Murray (q.v.) took the matter up in 1878 that the preparation of the Dictionary began to take active form. The first part was published in 1884. The work was finished in 1928, seventy years from the inception of the undertaking. Dr. (afterwards Sir James) Murray was succeeded by Dr. H. Bradley, Dr. (later Sir) William Alexander Craigie (1867-1957) and Dr. Charles Talbut Onions (1873-1965). The essential feature of the Dictionary is its historical method. It contains a record of 414,825 words, whose history is illustrated by 1,827,306 quotations. An important supplement appeared in 1933. The original title of the work was 'A New English Dictionary on Historical Principles' (abbreviated as NED.). The title 'The Oxford English Dictionary' first appeared in a section published in 1895.

Oxford Gazette, The, see *Gazette*.

Oxford Movement or TRACTARIAN MOVEMENT, THE, a movement initiated in 1833 in revival of a higher conception than was generally prevalent of the position and functions of the Church, as 'more than a merely human institution' and as pos-

sessing 'privileges, sacraments, a ministry, ordained by Christ'. The movement began with a sermon preached in July 1833 at Oxford by Keble (q.v.). The principal leaders of the movement were, besides Keble, Newman, R. H. Froude, and Pusey (qq.v.). In course of time, new forces came into play, which had a disruptive effect on the movement, while public feeling was roused against it by the issue of the first volumes of the 'Literary Remains of Richard Hurrell Froude' (1838), with its strictures on the Reformation. Newman's famous Tract XC on the compatibility of the Thirty-nine Articles with Roman Catholic theology intensified the general hostility.

A remarkable history of the Oxford Movement was written by Dean Church (1891), while much light is also thrown on it by the 'Autobiography' of I. Williams and Newman's 'Apologia'.

Oxford Sausage, The, see *Warton* (*T.*).

Oxford University was organized as a *studium generale* soon after 1167, perhaps as a result of a migration of students from Paris. Roger Bacon and Duns Scotus testify to its importance in the 13th cent. University College, the first of its colleges, was founded in 1249, Balliol about 1263, Merton in 1264. Oxford was the home of Wycliffism in the 14th cent. Erasmus lectured there, and Grocyn, Colet, and More (qq.v.) were among its famous scholars in the 15th-16th cents. The University sided with the king in the Civil War.

Oxford University Press, THE, a publishing and printing business owned by the University and directed by its Delegates of the Press, of whom the Vice-Chancellor is *ex officio* chairman. Its aims are to produce books of religious, scholarly, and educational value, and its surplus profits are devoted to financing the editing and production of unremunerative works of this kind.

Printing in Oxford by independent craftsmen began in the 15th cent., and in 1584 one of these was appointed 'Printer to the University'. This title was borne by a succession of printers in the 17th cent. and was revived in 1925 for the head of the printing department of the Press. One press at Oxford was excepted from the prohibition of printing outside London by a decree of the Star Chamber in 1586, and in 1632 a royal charter allowed the University three presses and to print and sell 'all manner of books'. Archbishop Laud in 1634 bound the University to provide itself with a printing house; but a press under its immediate control did not come into being until 1690. In the meantime John Fell (q.v.) had won an international reputation for Oxford books by his exercise of the University's privilege of printing, let to him in 1672.

The copyright in Lord Clarendon's (q.v.) works, once very profitable, is secured to the University in perpetuity, and in his honour the building to which the Press moved in 1829 was named 'The Clarendon Press'. This address is the imprint given to learned books whose production is supervised by the Secretary to the Delegates at Oxford. The publication of a larger class of books with the imprint of 'Oxford University Press, London' has been undertaken since 1880 by the Delegates' London office.

Oxymoron, from two Greek words meaning 'sharp', 'dull', a rhetorical figure by which two contradictory terms are united in an expression so as to give it point; e.g. 'Faith unfaithful kept him falsely true'.

Ozymandias, a sonnet by P. B. Shelley (q.v.)

P

Pacolet, in the tale of 'Valentine and Orson' (q.v.), a dwarf in the service of the Lady Clerimond.

'Pacolet' is the name of Mr. Bicker-staff's 'familiar' in Steele's 'The Tatler' (No. 15), and of Norna's dwarf in Scott's 'The Pirate'.

Pacuvius (*b.c.* 220 B.C.), Roman tragic poet. Only fragments of his work survive.

Paean, in Greek antiquity an invocation or thanksgiving addressed to Apollo (later to other gods also), so called from its refrain 'Iē Paiōn'; especially a song of triumph after victory. The word is now used for a song of praise or thanksgiving, or a shout or song of triumph.

Paeon, a metrical foot of four syllables, one long and three short, named, according to the position of the long syllable, a first, second, third, or fourth paeon.

Paetus, CAECINA, was sentenced to death in A.D. 42 on a charge of conspiracy against the Emperor Claudius. When he hesitated to take his own life in accordance with the sentence, his wife Arria stabbed herself and handed him the dagger, saying, 'Paetus, it does not hurt' (Plin. Ep. iii. 16).

Pagan, ISOBEL (*Tibby*) (*d.* 1821), hostess of an Ayrshire inn, the reputed author of the songs 'Ca' the Yowes to the Knowes' and 'The Crook and Plaid', in which there is an anticipation of the genius of Burns.

Paganini, NICOLO (1782–1840), famous Italian violinist.

Page, MRS. PAGE, and ANNE PAGE, their daughter, characters in Shakespeare's 'The Merry Wives of Windsor' (q.v.).

Pahlavi or PEHLEVI, the name given by the followers of Zoroaster to the character in which are written the ancient translations of their sacred books; also the name for Middle Persian speech (the language transitional from Old Persian to Modern Persian) written in Aramaic script. The word is used in this sense in FitzGerald's translation of Omar Khayyám.

Pain, BARRY ERIC ODELL (1864–1928), British novelist, author of 'The One

Before' (1902), 'Eliza' (1900), 'Exit Eliza' (1912), etc.

Paine, THOMAS (1737-1809), son of a small farmer of Thetford. He became an excise officer, but was dismissed from the service in 1772 in connection with an agitation for an increase of excisemen's pay. He sailed for America, where he published in 1776 his pamphlet, 'Common Sense', a history of the transactions that had led to the war with England, and in 1776-83, a series of pamphlets, 'The Crisis', encouraging resistance to England. He held various posts under the American government until 1787, when he returned to England. In 1791 he published the first part of his 'Rights of Man' (q.v.) in reply to Burke's 'Reflections on the Revolution in France' (q.v.), and the second part in 1792. He fled to France to avoid prosecution, and was there warmly received and elected a member of the Convention. He published in 1793 the 'Age of Reason', a defence of Deism against Christianity and Atheism, written in a tone of arrogance and coarse violence. He returned to America in 1802, where his 'Age of Reason' and his opposition to Washington and the federalists made him unpopular. He died at New York.

His connection with the American struggle and afterwards with the French Revolution gave him a unique position, and his writings, which show him a shrewd political thinker, became a textbook for the extreme radical party in England.

Painter, WILLIAM, see *Palace of Pleasure*.

Pair of Blue Eyes, *A*, a novel by Hardy (q.v.) (1873).

Palace of Pleasure, a collection of translations into English (1566-7) of 'pleasant histories and excellent novels' 'out of divers good and commendable authors', made by William Painter (1540?-1594), master of Sevenoaks school in Kent. It served as a storehouse from which the Elizabethan dramatists drew many of their plots. Many of the translations are from Boccaccio and Bandello, but the compiler draws also on Herodotus and Livy.

Paladins, THE, in the cycle of Charlemagne legends, were the twelve peers who accompanied the king. The origin of the conception is seen in the 'Chanson de Roland' (see *Roland*), where the twelve peers are merely an association of particularly brave warriors, under the leadership of Roland and Oliver, who all perish at Roncesvalles. From the Spanish war the idea was transported by later writers to other parts of the cycle, and Charlemagne is often found surrounded by twelve peers. In England the word 'douceper' (see *Douzepers*) in the singular was even adopted to signify a paladin. The names of the twelve are differently stated by different authors, but Roland and Oliver figure in all the enumerations. Among the best known are Fierabras or Ferumbras and Ogier the Dane.

Palaeologi, a Byzantine dynasty which furnished rulers of the Eastern empire from 1261 (Michael Palaeologus) to the fall of Constantinople (1453).

Palafox, in Wordsworth's sonnet ('Sonnets to Liberty', 1810), was José de Palafox y Melzi, a Spanish general, who defended Saragossa against the French in 1808.

Palamedes, a Grecian chief, son of Nauplius, king of Euboea, sent by the Greek princes to oblige Odysseus to join the expedition to Troy. Odysseus, reluctant to leave his wife Penelope, feigned madness, but Palamedes exposed the deceit. Odysseus in consequence conceived a bitter enmity against him, and caused him to be convicted of treason and stoned to death. Palamedes is credited with much learning and ingenuity.

Palamides, SIR, in the Arthurian legend, a Saracen. His constant occupation is the pursuit of the 'Questing Beast'.

Palamon and Arcite, the subject of 'The Knight's Tale' in Chaucer's 'The Canterbury Tales' (q.v.). This tale was paraphrased in heroic couplets by John Dryden (q.v.) under the title 'Palamon and Arcite'. It is also the subject of Fletcher's 'The Two Noble Kinsmen'.

Palatine, see *County Palatine, Elector Palatine.*

Pale, THE ENGLISH, also simply THE PALE, in Ireland, that part of Ireland (varying in extent at different times) over which English jurisdiction was established.

Pales, in Roman religion, a rustic spirit, supposed to protect shepherds and their flocks.

Palestrini, GIOVANNI PIERLUIGI DA (1524?-1594), the great composer of sacred music for the Roman Catholic Church.

Paley, WILLIAM (1743-1805), one of the principal exponents of theological utilitarianism, of which his 'Moral and Political Philosophy', published in 1785, is the textbook. In his 'Evidences of Christianity' (1794), and 'Natural Theology' (1802), he finds proof of the existence of God in the design apparent in natural phenomena. For his utilitarian theory of morality see *Moral and Political Philosophy*.

Palgrave, SIR FRANCIS (1788-1861), author of 'The Rise and Progress of the English Commonwealth' (1832), etc. He rendered great service in promoting the critical study in England of medieval history.

Palgrave, FRANCIS TURNER (1824-97), son of Sir F. Palgrave (q.v.), a close friend of Tennyson. From 1885 to 1895 he was professor of poetry at Oxford. He is chiefly remembered for his anthology, 'The Golden Treasury of Songs and Lyrics' (1861; second series, 1896), but was also himself a poet, and published several volumes of lyrics.

Palimpsest, from πάλιν 'again', and ψηστός 'rubbed smooth', a manuscript in which a later writing is written over an effaced earlier writing. Of frequent occurrence in the early Middle Ages because of the cost of parchment.

Palindrome, from παλίνδρομος, 'running back again', a word, verse, or sentence that reads the same forwards or backwards, e.g.:

Lewd did I live & evil I did dwel
(Phillips, 1706).

Palinode, from παλινῳδία, 'singing over again', a recantation. 'Palinode' is the name of the Catholic shepherd in the fifth eclogue of Spenser's 'The Shepheards Calender' (q.v.).

Palinurus, the pilot of Aeneas, who fell into the sea and, after reaching the shore, was murdered by the inhabitants of the place.

Palladis Tamia, see *Meres.*

Palladium, a statue of Pallas Athene, which was supposed to confer security on the town that contained it and was accordingly kept hidden. The most celebrated statue of this kind was that at Troy, where it was retained until carried off by Odysseus and Diomedes, or, according to another version, by Aeneas.

Pallas, a name of *Athene* (q.v.).

Palliser, PLANTAGENET, and his wife LADY GLENCORA, characters in several of A. Trollope's (q.v.) novels.

Pall Mall Gazette, The, was founded in 1865 by Frederick Greenwood (1830-1909) and George Smith (q.v.), to combine the features of a newspaper with the literary features of the 'Spectator' and 'Saturday Review'. Its name was taken from Thackeray's 'Pendennis' (q.v.), where Captain Shandon prepares the prospectus of 'The Pall Mall Gazette', 'written by gentlemen for gentlemen'.

Palmerin of England (*Palmeirim de Inglaterra*), a chivalric romance of uncertain authorship, attributed to the Portuguese, Francisco de Moraes (c. 1500-72) or the Spaniard, Luis Hurtado (1530-1579?).

Southey (q.v.) published a revised translation of this romance (1807).

'Palmerin of England' and 'Amadis of Gaul' were two romances of chivalry specially excepted from the holocaust of such works in 'Don Quixote' (q.v.).

Palm Sunday, the Sunday next before Easter Day, observed in commemoration of Jesus Christ's triumphal entry into Jerusalem.

Pamēla, a character in Sidney's 'Arcadia' (q.v.).

Pamela, or Virtue Rewarded, a novel by Richardson (q.v.) (1740).

This was the author's first work of fiction, and the first example of what may be called the modern English novel of character. The story is told in a series of letters from the heroine, Pamela Andrews, a young maid-servant, whose mistress has just died when the story opens. The lady's son, Mr. B., becomes enamoured of Pamela, and, taking a dishonourable advantage of her position, pursues her with his advances. She indignantly repels them, leaves the house, is pursued by B., and shows considerable astuteness in defending herself. Finally B., being much in love with her, comes to terms and decides to marry her.

The second part of the book (1741), which is less interesting, presents Pamela married, suffering with dignity and sweetness the burden of a profligate husband.

The novel was made the object of several skits. The most famous of these were 'An Apology for the Life of Mrs. Shamela Andrews' (1741), of which the authorship is uncertain (it was perhaps by Fielding), and Fielding's 'Joseph Andrews' (q.v.).

Pamphlet, a small unbound treatise, especially on a subject of current interest. The word is apparently a generalized use of *Pamphilet*, a familiar name of the 12th-cent. Latin amatory poem or comedy called 'Pamphilus, seu de Amore', a highly popular opuscule in the 13th cent.

Pan, the Greek god of shepherds and huntsmen, represented as a monster, with two small horns on his head, flat nose, ruddy complexion, and the legs and feet of a goat. Plutarch mentions that in the reign of Tiberius a ship with passengers was driven near the coast of the Isles of Paxi. A loud voice was heard calling to one Thamus that the great god Pan was dead. The incident in Christian legend is associated with the birth of Christ.

PANIC FEAR is the fear that seizes people without obvious cause.

Pancks, a character in Dickens's 'Little Dorrit' (q.v.).

Pandarus, a son of Lycaon, who assisted the Trojans in their war with the Greeks. The part which he played in the tale of Troilus and Cressida (q.v.) has no foundation in classical antiquity. In Chaucer's 'Troylus and Cryseyde' and in Shakespeare's 'Troilus and Cressida' he is the uncle of Cressida and the go-between in her relations with Troilus; hence the word 'pander'.

Pandects, The, or *Digest*, of Justinian, a compendium in fifty books of Roman civil law, made by order of the Emperor Justinian in the 6th cent.

Pandemonium, the abode of all the demons; a place represented by Milton ('Paradise Lost', i. 756) as the capital of Hell, containing the council-chamber of the Evil Spirits.

Pandora, according to Hesiod, the first woman that ever lived. She was made of clay by Hephaestus at the request of Zeus, who wished to be revenged on Prometheus. When this woman of clay had received life, she was endowed by the gods with every gift, and Zeus gave her a box, which she was directed to present to the man who married her. Hermes then conducted her to Prometheus, but he, distrustful of Zeus, sent her away. His brother, Epimetheus, married her and opened the box, whereupon there issued from it all the evils that have since afflicted the human race. Hope alone remained at the bottom of the box.

Pandosto, or *Dorastus and Fawnia*, a prose romance by Greene (q.v.) (1588), is chiefly memorable as the basis of Shakespeare's 'The Winter's Tale' (q.v.).

Panem et circenses, 'bread doles and circus-shows', the only things that, according to Juvenal (x. 78-81), the degenerate Roman populace cared about.

Pangloss, DR., in the 'Candide' of Voltaire (q.v.), an optimistic philosopher who holds that all is for the best in the best of all possible worlds. The intended object of the satire was Leibniz (q.v.).

Panjandrum: from the farrago of nonsense composed by Foote to test the memory of Macklin (qq.v.). Hence 'Panjandrum' is used as a mock title for an imaginary personage of great pretensions.

Panope, one of the Nereids (q.v.), whom mariners invoked in a storm.

Pantagruel, the second book (in chronological order of the narrative) of Rabelais's (q.v.) great work, but the first to be written and published (1532). Pantagruel is presented as the son of Gargantua (q.v.) and Badebec, daughter of the king of the Amaurotes of Utopia (a reference to Sir Thomas More's work). The book tells of his birth, education, and life, satirizing the ancient learning and mingling serious and pious advice with burlesque. The narrative, which is continued in three further books, provides occasion for abundant satire directed against monks and schoolmen, the Papacy, and the magistrature.

Pantaloon, adapted from the Italian *pantalone,* 'a kind of mask on the Italian stage, representing the Venetian', of whom *Pantalone* was a nickname, supposed to be derived from *San Pantaleone,* formerly a favourite saint of the Venetians. The Venetian character in Italian comedy was represented as a lean and foolish old man, wearing slippers, pantaloons, and spectacles. In modern pantomime or harlequinade he is represented as a foolish and vicious old man, the butt of the clown's jokes.

Pantheism, (1) the doctrine that God and the universe are identical, that God is every thing, and every thing is God (implying a denial of the personality and transcendence of God); (2) the heathen worship of all the gods.

Pantheon, originally a temple dedicated to all the gods, especially that at Rome built by Agrippa *c.* 25 B.C., and transformed in A.D. 609 into a Christian church.

Pantisocracy, see *Coleridge (S. T.).*

Pantomime, (1) originally a Roman actor, who performed in dumb show, representing by mimicry various characters and scenes; (2) an English dramatic performance, originally consisting of action without speech, but in its further development consisting of a dramatized traditional fairy-tale, with singing, dancing, acrobatics, clowning, topical jokes, a transformation scene, and certain stock roles, especially the 'principal boy' (i.e. hero) acted by a woman and the 'dame' acted by a man.

Panurge, one of the principal characters in Rabelais's 'Pantagruel' (q.v.), a cunning, voluble, witty, and cowardly buffoon.

Panza, SANCHO, see *Don Quixote.*

Paolo and Francesca: Francesca, daughter of the count of Ravenna, was given in marriage by him to Giovanni Malatesta, of Rimini. She fell in love with Paolo, her husband's handsome brother, and, their relations being discovered, the two lovers were put to death in 1289. Dante, at the end of the fifth canto of his 'Inferno', relates his conversation with Francesca.

The story of Paolo and Francesca was made by Leigh Hunt (q.v.) the subject of his poem 'The Story of Rimini'; it was also the subject of a play that had a temporary vogue, by Stephen Phillips (1864-1915).

Paperstamp, MR., in Peacock's 'Melincourt' (q.v.), a caricature of Wordsworth.

Paphos, a city of Cyprus sacred to Aphrodite. Hence PAPHIAN, a courtesan.

Pappe with an hatchet, the title of a tract contributed in 1589 by Lyly (q.v.) to the Marprelate controversy (see *Martin Marprelate*) on the side of the bishops.

Paracelsus, a dramatic poem by R. Browning (q.v.) (1835), based on the actual life of Paracelsus, summarized below.

Paracelsus, PHILIPPUS AUREOLUS (THEOPHRASTUS BOMBASTUS AB HOHENHEIM, 1493-1541), wandered from country to country, practising magic, alchemy, and astrology, and visiting the universities of Germany, France, and Italy. He returned to Germany, effected there many remarkable cures, and was appointed to a chair of physic and surgery at Basel. He was, however, presently pronounced a quack, resumed his wandering life, and died. He initiated modern chemistry.

Paraclete (3 syllables), THE, from a Greek word meaning advocate, intercessor, a title of the Holy Spirit (John xiv. 16, etc.).

Paradise, derived from an old Persian word meaning enclosure or park, was used in its Greek form by the Septuagint translators for the Garden of Eden; and in the N.T. for the abode of the blessed. It is now used (1) in the sense of the Garden of Eden; (2) by some theologians in the sense of an intermediate place where the souls of the righteous await the Last Judgement; (3) in that of Heaven, the final abode of the righteous; and also (4) figuratively as a place of surpassing delight or bliss. See also *Paradise of Fools*.

Paradise, THE EARTHLY: the belief in the existence of a terrestrial paradise was widespread in the Middle Ages, and references to it are found in manuscripts and maps of the time. For W. Morris's poem see *Earthly Paradise* (*The*).

Paradise Lost, an epic poem by Milton (q.v.) originally in ten books, subsequently rearranged in twelve, first printed in 1667.

Milton formed the intention of writing a great epic poem, as he tells us, as early as 1639. A list of possible subjects, some of them scriptural, some from British history, written in his own hand about 1640-1, still exists, with drafts of the scheme of a poem on Paradise Lost. The work was not, however, begun in earnest until 1658, and it was finished, according to Aubrey, in 1663.

Book I. The general subject is briefly stated: man's disobedience and the loss thereupon of Paradise, with its prime cause, Satan, who, having revolted from God, has been driven out of Heaven. Satan is presented, with his angels, lying on the burning lake of Hell. He awakens his legions, comforts them, and summons a council. Pandemonium, the palace of Satan, is built.

Book II. The council debates whether another battle for the recovery of Heaven shall be hazarded, but decides to examine the report that a new world, with new creatures in it, has been created. Satan undertakes alone the search. He passes through Hell-gates, guarded by Sin and Death, and passes upward through the realm of Chaos.

Book III. God sees Satan flying towards our world, and foretells his success and the fall and punishment of Man. The Son of God offers himself a ransom for Man, is accepted, and exalted. Satan alights on the outer convex of our universe, the future Paradise of Fools (q.v.). He finds the stairs leading up to Heaven, descends to the Sun, and is directed by Uriel to this Earth, alighting on Mount Niphates.

Book IV. The Garden of Eden is described, where Satan first sees Adam and Eve, and overhears their discourse regarding the Tree of Knowledge, of which they are forbidden to eat the fruit. He decides to found his enterprise upon this, and proceeds to tempt Eve in a dream; but is discovered by Gabriel and Ithuriel, and ejected from the garden.

Book V. Eve relates her disquieting dream to Adam. Raphael, sent by God, comes to Paradise, warns Adam of his enemy, and enjoins obedience. At Adam's request he relates how and why Satan incited his legions to revolt.

Book VI. Raphael continues his narrative, how Michael and Gabriel were sent to fight against Satan. After indecisive battles the Son of God himself, causing his legions to stand still, alone attacked the hosts of Satan, and, driving them to the edge of Heaven, forced them to leap down into the deep.

Book VII. Raphael relates how thereafter God decided on the creation of another world with new creatures to dwell therein, and sent his Son to perform the creation in six days.

Book VIII. Adam inquires concerning the motions of the heavenly bodies, and is answered ambiguously. [The controversy regarding the Ptolemaic and Copernican systems was at its height when the 'Paradise Lost' was written, and Milton was unable to decide between them, as seen in Bk. X, 668 et seq.] Adam relates what he remembers since his own creation, and discourses with the angel regarding the relations of man with woman. Raphael departs.

Book IX. Satan enters into the serpent, and in this form finds Eve alone. He persuades her to eat of the Tree of Knowledge. Eve relates to Adam what has passed and brings him some of the fruit. Adam, perceiving that she is lost, from extreme love for her resolves to perish with her, and eats the fruit. This robs them of their innocence; they cover their nakedness, and fall to recriminations.

Book X. God sends his Son to judge the transgressors. He passes sentence on the man and on the woman. Sin and Death resolve to come to this world and make a broad highway thither from Hell. Satan returns to Hell and relates his success; he and his angels are temporarily transformed into serpents. Adam and Eve confer how to evade the curse upon their offspring, and finally approach the Son of God with repentance and supplication.

Book XI. The Son of God intercedes for Adam and Eve. God decides on their expulsion from Paradise. Michael comes down to carry out the decree. Eve laments, Adam pleads but submits. The angel leads him to a high hill and shows him in a series of visions the future misery of man and what shall happen till the Flood.

Book XII. Michael relates what shall follow, and explains the future coming of the Messiah, his incarnation, death, resurrection, and ascension, and foretells the corrupt state of the Church till his second coming. Adam and Eve, submissive, are led out of Paradise.

Paradise of Dainty Devices, see *Paradyse of Daynty Devises*.

Paradise of Fools: Milton in 'Paradise Lost', III. 448 et seq., describes, on the outer edge of our universe, a 'Limbo . . . , since called The Paradise of Fools', to which are consigned 'all who in vain things | Built their fond hopes of glory' (see *Limbo*).

Paradise Regained, an epic poem in four books by Milton (q.v.) (1671). See *Ellwood*.

It is a sequel to 'Paradise Lost', and deals exclusively with the temptation of Christ in the wilderness. According to the poet's conception, Paradise was lost by the yielding of Adam and Eve to Satan's temptation, and was regained by the resistance of the Son of God to the temptation of the same spirit. Satan is here represented not in the majestic lineaments that we find in the 'Paradise Lost', but as a cunning, smooth, and dissembling creature, a 'Spirit unfortunate', as he describes himself. There is a comparative scarcity of similes and ornament, and only a vivid and ingenious expansion of the biblical texts.

Paradiso, Il, of Dante, see *Divina Commedia*.

Paradyse of Daynty Devises, The, a collection of works by poets of the second rank who wrote in the early part of the 16th cent. Compiled by Richard Edwards (q.v.) and published in 1576.

Parcae or FATES, THE, the MOIRAE of the Greeks, goddesses who presided over the birth and life of men. They were sisters, Clotho, Lachesis, and Atropos. Clotho, the youngest, presided over the moment of man's birth and held a distaff in her hands. Lachesis with her spindle spun out the events and actions of his life. Atropos, the eldest, cut the thread of human life with her shears.

Pardiggle, MRS., in Dickens's 'Bleak House' (q.v.), a lady 'distinguished for rapacious benevolence'.

Pardoner's Tale, The, see *Canterbury Tales*.

Parian Chronicle, THE, included in the Arundel Marbles (q.v.), a marble inscription in which are recorded the chief events of Greek history from the reign of the mythical Cecrops to 354 B.C.

Paridell, in Spenser's 'Faerie Queene', a false and libertine knight who consorts with Duessa (q.v.), and elopes with Hellenore, the wife of Malbecco.

Paris, also known as ALEXANDER, was a son of Priam, king of Troy, and of Hecuba. Soothsayers foretold the calamities that her son would bring upon his country. Priam accordingly ordered his destruction; but the slave exposed the child on Mt. Ida, where the shepherds brought him up as their own son. He won the favour of the nymph Oenone, with whom he lived happily until appointed by the gods to adjudge the prize of beauty among the three goddesses, Hera, Aphrodite, and Athene. Aphrodite offered him the fairest woman in the world for wife, and to her he awarded the prize. Paris soon after visited Sparta, where he persuaded Helen, the wife of Menelaus, the fairest woman of her age, to elope with him. This brought about the expedition of the Greek princes against Troy. In the course of the war Paris was mortally wounded by an arrow shot by Philoctetes, and sought Oenone's help in vain (see *Oenone*).

Paris, COUNT, a character in Shakespeare's 'Romeo and Juliet' (q.v.).

Paris, MATTHEW (*d.* 1259), historian and monk, entered the monastery of St. Albans in 1217. He succeeded Roger of Wendover in his office of chronicler to the monastery, 1236, and carried on the 'Chronica Majora' from the summer of 1235. He expanded the scope of the chronicle, introducing narratives and accounts of events in foreign countries as well as in England, which he obtained from kings and all manner of great persons who came to St. Albans. He carried his greater chronicle down to May 1259, where he ends abruptly, and certainly died about that time. In vigour and brightness of expression he stands before every other English chronicler; and his writing possesses peculiar historic value.

Paris Garden, a place for bull- and bear-baiting on Bankside, Southwark, referred to in Shakespeare's 'Henry VIII', v. iv.

Parish Register, The, a poem by Crabbe (q.v.) (1807).

A country parson relates the memories awakened in him as he looks through the entries in his registers of births, marriages, and deaths.

Parisina, a poem by Lord Byron (q.v.) (1816).

Paris Sketch Book, The, a collection of six short stories, with essays and criticisms, by Thackeray (q.v.) (1840).

Park, MUNGO (1771-1806), a surgeon in the mercantile marine. He explored the course of the Niger and became famous by his 'Travels in the Interior of Africa' (1799). He perished at Boussa in 1806 in a conflict with the natives.

Parker, MATTHEW (1504-75), was licensed to preach by Cranmer in 1533, and in 1535 appointed chaplain to Anne Boleyn. He was deprived of his preferments by Queen Mary, and fled to Frankfort-on-the-Main during the persecution. He reluctantly accepted the archbishopric of Canterbury on Elizabeth's accession. He identified himself with the party (afterwards known as the Anglican party) which sought to establish a *via media* between Romanism and Puritanism. From 1563 to 1568 he was occupied with the production of the 'Bishops' Bible', his most distinguished service to the theological studies of the day. To his efforts we are indebted for the earliest editions of Gildas, Asser, Ælfric, the 'Flores Historiarum', Matthew Paris, and other important early chroniclers.

Parkinson, JOHN (1567-1650), king's herbalist, author of 'Paradisi in sole Paradisus terrestris' (1629); also of a great herbal, 'Theatrum botanicum' (1640).

Parlement of Briddes, see *Parlement of Foules*.

Parlement of Foules, The, or *The Parlement of Briddes*, a poem of 700 lines in rhyme-royal by Chaucer, probably written between 1372 and 1386. In a vision the poet sees the Court of Nature on St. Valentine's day, 'when every fowl cometh there to choose his mate'. Three tiercel eagles advance their claims to a beautiful 'formel' (female), and a debate of the fowls follows. Nature decides that the formel shall make election, and the formel asks for a year's respite 'to advise' her. The poem probably refers to some lady sought by royal lovers, perhaps Anne of Bohemia, and is noteworthy, *inter alia*, for its fine opening lines and its descriptive catalogues of trees and birds.

Parliament of Bees, The, a dramatic allegory or masque by J. Day (*fl.* 1606), published, it appears, in 1607, though the earliest extant copy is of the year 1641.

Parmenides (*b. c.* 513 B.C.), of Elea in Italy, the founder of the Eleatic school of philosophy. He rejected utterly the views of Heraclitus (q.v.), and regarded the universe as a continuous, unchanging, indivisible whole, and changing phenomena as illusions.

Parnassian School, THE, the name given to a group of French poets of the latter half of the 19th cent. who reflected the scientific spirit of the age. The name is taken from the title, 'Le Parnasse contemporain', of three collections of their poems published in 1866–76. Leconte de Lisle (1818–94) was their leader. Others were Heredia, Catulle Mendès, Sully Prudhomme, etc.

Parnassus, a mountain in Greece, a few miles north of Delphi, sacred to the Muses. One of its peaks was sacred to Apollo; the other to Dionysus.

Parnassus Plays, The, the name given to a trilogy, produced about the year 1600 by the students of St. John's College, Cambridge, consisting of 'The Pilgrimage to Pernassus' and 'The Returne from Pernassus', the latter in two parts, with 'The Scourge for Simony' as sub-title of the second. They have been attributed to J. Day (*fl.* 1606, q.v.), but their authorship is doubtful.

The second part of the 'Return' con-

tains an interesting review of the merits of certain contemporary poets, including Shakespeare and Jonson; and introduces Kemp and Burbage. Some of the scenes deal with the feud between town and gown at Cambridge, and hold up to obloquy Brackyn, the recorder of Cambridge.

Parnell, CHARLES STEWART (1846–91), entered parliament as M.P. for Meath in 1875 and by his extreme attitude won the confidence of the Fenians. He was elected chairman of the Home Rule party in the House of Commons in 1880 and, in spite of his being a Protestant, exerted an extraordinary sway over his supporters and enormous influence outside the house. With the help of the Liberal party he overthrew the Tory government in 1886, and converted Gladstone to his home-rule scheme. He vindicated himself in 1888–9 of the charge of connivance with outrage and crime brought in the articles on 'Parnellism and Crime' which were published in 'The Times' in 1887. His career was ruined by his appearance as co-respondent in a suit for divorce by Capt. O'Shea against his wife in 1890.

Parnell, THOMAS (1679–1718), was archdeacon of Clogher and a friend of Swift and Pope (to whose 'Iliad' he contributed an introductory essay). His works, which were published posthumously by Pope, include 'The Night Piece on Death', 'The Hymn to Contentment', and 'The Hermit', the two first being octosyllabic odes of great fluency, and the last a narrative poem in heroic couplets. Parnell's life was written by Goldsmith. His 'Homer's Battle of the Frogs and Mice with the Remarks of Zoilus', satirizing Theobald and Dennis, was published in 1717.

Parody, a form of literary composition in which an author's characteristics are ridiculed by imitation and exaggeration. True parody, it has been said, implies a sound and valid criticism of the original. Swinburne, for example, was able to parody effectively his own excessive use of alliteration. Famous English parodists have been James and Horace Smith (qq.v.) in their

P

'Rejected Addresses'; C. S. Calverley, Owen Seaman, and Sir John Squire.

Parolles, a character in Shakespeare's 'All's Well that Ends Well' (q.v.).

Paronomasia, a play on words, a pun.

Parsees, descendants of those Persians who fled to India in the 7th and 8th cents. to escape Muslim persecution, and who still retain their religion (Zoroastrianism, q.v.).

Parsifal, the title of a music-drama by R. Wagner (q.v.). See *Parzival* and *Perceval.*

Parson's Tale, The, see *Canterbury Tales.*

Parthenon, The, a temple at Athens sacred to Athene.

Parthenophil and Parthenope, a collection of sonnets by B. Barnes (q.v.), issued in 1593, notable as one of the first of such collections to appear after Sidney's 'Astrophel and Stella'.

Parthians, The, a people of Scythian origin who lived SE. of the Caspian Sea and came into conflict with the Romans. They were celebrated as mounted archers, who poured in a shower of arrows, and then fled, avoiding close contact, and still shooting their arrows as they retreated. Whence the expression 'a Parthian shot'.

Particularism, the dogma that Divine Grace is provided for a selected part, not the whole, of the human race.

Partington, Mrs., referred to by Sydney Smith (q.v.) in his speech in 1831 on the rejection of the Reform Bill. He compares the attempts of the House of Lords to stop the progress of reform to the efforts of Mrs. Partington, who lived close to the beach at Sidmouth, to keep out the Atlantic with a mop when a great storm in 1824 caused a flood in that town.

Partlet or Pertelote, the hen in 'Reynard the Fox' (q.v.) and in Chaucer's 'Nun's Priest's Tale' (see *Canterbury Tales*). 'Sister Partlet with her hooded head' in Dryden's 'The Hind and the Panther' (q.v.) stands for the Roman Catholic nuns.

Partridge, a character in Fielding's 'Tom Jones' (q.v.).

Partridge, John, the victim of a mystification by Swift. See *Bickerstaff.*

Parzival, an epic by Wolfram von Eschenbach, composed early in the 13th cent. on the subject of the legend of Perceval (q.v.) and his search for the Holy Grail.

Pascal, Blaise (1623-62), French mathematician, physicist, and moralist, came early under the influence of Jansenism (q.v.). His famous 'Pensées' (issued posthumously in 1670) were fragments of an uncompleted defence of the Christian religion, directed principally against the free-thinkers.

Pasiphaë, see *Minotaur.*

Pasquil, Pasquin: *Pasquino* or *Pasquillo* was the name popularly given to a mutilated statue disinterred at Rome in 1501, and set up by Cardinal Caraffa at the corner of his palace near the Piazza Navona. It became the custom to salute Pasquin on St. Mark's day in Latin verses. In process of time these *pasquinate* or pasquinades tended to become satirical, and the term began to be applied, not only in Rome, but in other countries, to satirical compositions and lampoons, political, ecclesiastical, or personal.

Pasquin, Anthony, see *Williams (J.).*

Passage to India, A, a novel by E. M. Forster (q.v.), published in 1924. It is a picture of society in India under the British Raj, of the clash between East and West, and of the prejudices and misunderstandings that foredoomed goodwill. Criticized at first for anti-British and possibly inaccurate bias, it has been praised as a superb character study of the people of one race by a writer of another. The story is told in three parts, *I, Mosque, II, Caves, III, Temple,* and concerns Aziz, a young Muslim doctor, whose friendliness and enthusiasm for the British turn to bitterness and disillusionment when his pride is injured. A sympathy springs up between him and the elderly Mrs. Moore, who has come to visit her son, the City Magistrate. Accompanying her is Adela Quested, young, earnest, and charmless, who longs to know the 'real' India and tries to disregard the taboos and snobberies of the British circle. Aziz organizes an expedition for the visitors to the Caves of Marabar, where an unforeseen development plunges him into disgrace and rouses deep antagonism between the two races. Adela accuses him of insulting her in the Caves, he is committed to prison and stands trial. Adela withdraws her charge, but Aziz turns furiously away from the British, towards a Hindu-Muslim *entente*. In the third part of the book he has moved to a post in a native state, and is bringing up his family in peace. He is visited by his friend Mr. Fielding, the former principal of the Government College, an intelligent, hard-bitten man. They discuss the future of India and Aziz prophesies that only when the British are driven out can he and Fielding really be friends. Among the many characters is Professor Godbole, who was the innocent cause of the contretemps, and who makes his final appearance in supreme tranquillity at the festival of the Hindu temple.

Passetyme of Pleasure, or the Historie of Graunde Amoure and La Belle Pucel, an allegorical poem in rhyme-royal and decasyllabic couplets by Hawes (q.v.), written about 1506 and first printed by Wynkyn de Worde in 1509.

Passing of Arthur, The, one of Tennyson's 'Idylls of the King' (q.v.) (1869). Sir Bedivere, the last surviving of Arthur's knights, relates the final scenes of the king's life; the great battle when all but Arthur, Bedivere, and Modred are killed; the slaying of Modred by Arthur and his own mortal wound; the throwing of Excalibur into the mere; and the coming of the black barge with the three queens, who bear off Arthur.

The poem incorporates the 'Morte d'Arthur', the earlier fragment (1842).

Passion, THE, the sufferings of Jesus Christ on the Cross (also often including the Agony in Gethsemane). PASSION WEEK was, until the middle of the 19th cent., generally used to signify the week

immediately before Easter. Since then this period has been designated *Holy Week*.

Passionate Pilgrim, A, a story by H. James (q.v.), his earliest work, written in 1870 and published in 1875.

Passionate Pilgrim, The, an unauthorized anthology of poems by various authors, published by William Jaggard in 1599, and attributed on the title-page to William Shakespeare.

Passion Play, a miracle play (q.v.) representing the Passion of Christ. See also *Oberammergau*.

Passover, THE, the name of a Jewish feast, held on the evening of the 14th day of the month Nisan, commemorative of the 'passing over' of the houses of the Israelites whose doorposts were marked with the blood of the lamb, when the Egyptians were smitten with the death of their firstborn (Exod. xii). It is extended to include the seven following days.

Pasternak, BORIS LEONIDOVICH (1890-1960), Russian novelist and poet. He originally intended to be a composer, but at the age of 18 turned to writing poetry and published 'My Sister Life' in 1922 and 'Themes and Variations' in 1923. Although an admirer of Mayakovsky's (q.v.) early work, he was not a Futurist, but a poet of the whole movement for liberation and a new life. He is best known outside Russia for his novel, 'Dr. Zhivago' (1958). He regarded the novel as his most important work (see his 'Essay in Autobiography', 1959). Pasternak also made several fine translations of plays of Shakespeare. He was awarded, but declined, the Nobel Prize.

Pasteur, LOUIS (1822-95), a famous French chemist and biologist, the founder of the science of bacteriology, and the discoverer of the method of inoculation for hydrophobia.

Pastiche, a literary composition made up from various authors or sources, or in imitation of the style of another author; or a picture made up of fragments pieced together or copied with modification from an original, or in professed imitation of the style of another artist.

Paston Letters, a collection of letters preserved by the Pastons, a well-to-do Norfolk family, written between *c.* 1420 and 1503.

They concern three generations of the family and most were written under the reigns of Henry VI, Edward IV, and Richard III. They are unique as materials for history, and interesting as showing the violence and anarchy that prevailed in the land, and the domestic conditions in which a family of this class lived.

Pastoral poetry was, in its origin, distinctively Dorian and especially Sicilian. Theocritus (q.v.) was its principal Greek representative. Pastoral romances and plays were developed in England in the 16th and 17th cents. from Italian and Spanish works, notably from the 'Diana' of Jorge de Montemayor (translated into English by Bartholomew Young, 1598), which inspired Sidney's 'Arcadia' (q.v.); also from Tasso's 'Aminta' (1581) and 'Il Pastor Fido' of Guarini (1590), translated in 1596 and 1602 respectively, the latter of which served as a model for Fletcher's 'The Faithful Shepherdess' (q.v.). The essence of the pastoral is simplicity of thought and action in a rustic setting. The most important examples of this kind of composition in English include, besides the two works mentioned above, Lodge's 'Rosalynde' (q.v.), Shakespeare's 'As You Like It' (q.v.), Jonson's 'Sad Shepherd', and Milton's 'Comus' (q.v.).

Pastorella, in Spenser's 'Faerie Queene', VI. ix–xii, a shepherdess.

Pastor Fido, Il, see under *Pastoral.*

Patavinity, provincialism in style. The word originally means the dialectal peculiarities of Patavium (Padua), as shown in the writings of Livy (q.v.).

Pater, WALTER HORATIO (1839–94), a fellow of Brasenose, became associated with the Pre-Raphaelites, and began his literary career by contributing in 1867 to 'The Westminster Review' an essay on 'Winckelmann', subsequently embodied

in his volume of 'Studies in the History of the Renaissance' (1873). This work first made Pater's fame. It was followed in 1885 by 'Marius the Epicurean', a philosophical romance; 'Imaginary Portraits' (1887), 'Appreciations' (1889), etc. His style was highly polished and his outlook predominantly 'aesthetic'.

Pathetic fallacy, a figure of speech by which emotions and feelings are attributed to inanimate objects, e.g. waves are said to weep, etc. The expression is Ruskin's who wrote, 'All violent feelings . . . produce . . . a falseness in . . . impressions of external things, which I would generally characterize as the "Pathetic fallacy".'

Pathfinder, The, one of the 'Leatherstocking' novels of J. F. Cooper (q.v.), and a nickname of the hero, Natty Bumppo.

Path to Rome, The, see *Belloc.*

Patience, an alliterative poem of 500 lines, of the later 14th cent., of which the story of Jonah is the subject, attributed to the same author as 'Pearl' and 'Cleanness' and 'Sir Gawain and the Green Knight' (qq.v.).

Patience, an opera by Gilbert and Sullivan (q.v.), produced in 1881, ridiculing the aesthetic movement (q.v.).

Patient Grissil, a comedy by Dekker (q.v.) in collaboration with Chettle and Haughton, printed in 1603. The play contains the beautiful song: 'Art thou poor, yet hast thou golden slumbers, O sweet content.'

The subject of this play is also treated in Chaucer's 'Clerk's Tale' (see *Canterbury Tales*). It was taken originally from the 'Decameron' (X. x).

Patmore, COVENTRY KERSEY DIGHTON (1823–96), was an assistant in the printed book department of the British Museum. He was a friend of Tennyson and Ruskin, and made the acquaintance of the Pre-Raphaelite (q.v.) group, to whose organ, 'The Germ', he contributed. His early work was collected in 'The Angel in the House', a long work designed to be the apotheosis of married love. Patmore became a Roman Catholic in 1864. In 1877 he published 'The Unknown Eros', odes on high themes very different from the domesticity of his previous poems.

Patrick, St. (*c.* 389-*c.* 461), the patron saint of Ireland, apparently of mixed Roman and British parentage, was born probably in Ailclyde (now Dumbarton). Feeling a supernatural call to preach to the heathen Irish, he landed in Wicklow in 405 (432?), proceeding thence to Strangford Lough, where he converted all the Ulstermen. He subsequently journeyed through Ireland and founded his first mission settlement near Armagh. His festival is on 17 March.

Patrick's, The Dean of St., Swift (q.v.).

Patrick Spens, Sir, see *Sir Patrick Spens*.

Patriot King, The Idea of a, a political treatise by Viscount Bolingbroke (q.v.), written in 1738, and published in 1749.

This treatise is generally accounted the best, as it was practically the last, of Bolingbroke's political writings.

Patroclus, one of the Grecian warriors during the Trojan War, and the close friend of Achilles (q.v.). Achilles lent Patroclus his armour. Patroclus was slain by Hector with the aid of Apollo. Achilles set about avenging the death of his friend. He slew Hector, who had increased his wrath by appearing in the armour taken from the body of Patroclus.

Patrologiae, see *Migne*.

Patterne, Sir Willoughby, Eleanor and **Isabel, Lieutenant**, and **Crossjay**, characters in Meredith's 'The Egoist' (q.v.).

Patti, Adelina (1843-1919), a famous soprano opera-singer.

Pattieson, Peter, a schoolmaster, the imaginary author of the 'Tales of My Landlord' (q.v.) of Sir W. Scott.

Pattison, Mark (1813-84), was for a time an ardent follower of Newman, but gradually separated himself from the high church party. He wrote a life of Isaac Casaubon (1875), and a life of Milton (1879); contributed to the E.B. articles on Erasmus, More, and Grotius, and edited certain works of Milton and Pope.

Paul Clifford, a novel by Bulwer Lytton (q.v.) (1830). The work was written with the object of securing an improvement of English penal discipline and law. It is interesting as one of the first novels of philanthropic purpose.

Paul Emanuel, Monsieur, one of the principal characters in C. Brontë's 'Villette' (q.v.).

Paulina, a character in Shakespeare's 'The Winter's Tale' (q.v.).

Pauline, the first published poem of R. Browning (q.v.). It appeared anonymously in 1833, and was an obscure and incoherent confession of the young poet's sentiments, largely it would seem of admiration for Shelley.

Paul's, Children of, a company of boy actors, recruited from the choristers of St. Paul's Cathedral, whose performances enjoyed great popularity at the end of the 16th and beginning of the 17th cents. The **Children of the Chapel**, recruited from the choristers of the Chapel Royal, was another company enjoying popular favour at the same time. Their rivalry with men actors is alluded to in 'Hamlet', II. ii.

Paul's Cathedral, St., was founded early in the 7th cent. by Mellitus, who was sent to England from Rome in 601 and consecrated bishop of London by St. Augustine in 604. The cathedral that preceded the present edifice, now spoken of as old St. Paul's, was begun in the 11th cent. after the great fire of 1087, and not finished until 1314. It lost much of its sacred character, and there are frequent references in the 16th and 17th cents. to the secular uses to which it was put.

Old St. Paul's was destroyed in the Fire of London (1666), and the cathedral as we know it was built by Sir C. Wren (q.v.).

Paul's School, St., was founded in 1512 by Colet (q.v.). Lily (q.v.) was its first high-master.

Paul the Deacon (Paulus Diaconus), a Lombard of the 8th cent.; one of the best chroniclers of the Dark Ages.

Pausanias, traveller and geographer, perhaps a native of Lydia, wrote in the reign of Marcus Aurelius (A.D. 161-180) his 'Periegesis' (Itinerary) of Greece, in which he describes the legends and objects of antiquity connected with the places that he visited.

Payne, JOHN HOWARD (1791-1852), American actor and playwright, famous as author of the song, 'Home, Sweet Home' (q.v.).

Peacham, HENRY (1576?-1643?), an author and a man of very varied talents. He published 'The Compleat Gentleman', the work by which he is best known, in 1622.

Peachum, and his daughter POLLY, characters in Gay's 'The Beggar's Opera' (q.v.).

Peacock, THOMAS LOVE (1785-1866), novelist and poet, was the son of a London merchant. He found mercantile occupation uncongenial, and for a time lived on his private means, producing some verse, and his satirical romances, 'Headlong Hall' (1816), 'Melincourt (q.v., 1817), and 'Nightmare Abbey' (q.v., 1818). He entered the East India Company's service in 1819, published another satirical novel, 'Crotchet Castle' (q.v.), in 1831, and late in life, in 1860 or 1861, the last of these, 'Gryll Grange'. The above works are a curious mixture of satire (personal, social, and political) and romance. In Peacock's other novels, 'Maid Marian' (1822) and 'The Misfortunes of Elphin' (1829), the satire is veiled under a more simply romantic form.

Pearl, an alliterative poem in twelve-lined octosyllabic stanzas, of the period 1350-80. The author is unknown. The two poems, 'Patience' and 'Cleanness' (qq.v.) are attributed to the same author, and also 'Sir Gawain and the Green Knight' (q.v.).

Pearl is the author's daughter, an only child, whom he has lost when she was less than 2 years old. Wandering disconsolate in the garden where she is buried, he has a vision of a river beyond which lies Paradise. Here he sees a maiden seated, in whom he recognizes his daughter grown

to maturity. She upbraids him for his excessive grief, and explains her blessed state. He strives to join her and plunges into the river, and awakes from his trance, comforted and resigned to his lot.

Pearson, JOHN (1613-86), a Royalist chaplain during the Civil War, and after the Restoration Master of Jesus College, and subsequently of Trinity College, Cambridge. In 1654 he preached the series of sermons which he published in 1659 as an 'Exposition of the Creed'. This work, on which his reputation still mainly rests, has long been a standard book in English divinity. He was probably the ablest scholar and best systematic theologian among Englishmen of the 17th cent.

Pecksniff, MR., a character in Dickens's 'Martin Chuzzlewit' (q.v.).

Pecock, REGINALD (1395?-1460?), a Welshman by birth and bishop successively of St. Asaph and Chichester. He distinguished himself by his writings against the Lollards, notably by his 'Repressor of over much Blaming of the Clergy' (1455). His 'Book of Faith' was issued in 1456. He alienated by his writings every section of theological opinion in England, and was obliged to resign his bishopric. His work is important from a literary standpoint for its development of the English vocabulary.

Pedro, DON, the Prince of Aragon in Shakespeare's 'Much Ado About Nothing' (q.v.).

Peel, JOHN, the hero of the well-known hunting song, 'D'ye ken John Peel', was born at Caldbeck, Cumberland, in 1776, and for over forty years ran the famous pack of hounds that bore his name. He died in 1854.

Peele, GEORGE (1558?-1597?), led a dissipated life, and in 1579 was turned out of his father's dwelling, within the precincts of Christ's Hospital, by the governors of the institution. He was almost certainly a successful player as well as playwright, and his lyrics were popular in literary circles. His works, which are very numerous, fall under three heads, plays, pageants, and miscellaneous verse. Among his plays may be mentioned 'The Arraignment of Paris' (*c.* 1581), 'The Battle of Alcazar' (printed in 1594), 'The Old Wives' Tale' (q.v., 1595), and 'David and Bethsabe' (1599). The lyrics in Peele's plays are particularly attractive.

Peeping Tom, see *Godiva.*

Peer Gynt, a lyrical drama by Ibsen (q.v.) (1867). Peer Gynt was intended by the author as the embodiment of certain aspects in the character of his countrymen at the end of the romantic period, and the work is an indictment of the half-heartedness, lack of character, and egoism that Ibsen reproved.

Peerybingle, JOHN and DOT, characters in Dickens's 'The Cricket on the Hearth' (q.v.).

Peg-a-Ramsey, the heroine of an old song popular in Shakespeare's day. He refers to her in 'Twelfth Night', II. iii.

Pegasus, a winged horse sprung from the blood of Medusa, when Perseus cut off her head. By striking Mt. Helicon with his foot, Pegasus gave rise to the fountain Hippocrene sacred to the Muses.

Peggotty, DANIEL, CLARA, and HAM, characters in Dickens's 'David Copperfield' (q.v.).

Pegler, MRS., in Dickens's 'Hard Times' (q.v.), Bounderby's mother.

Peg Woffington, a novel by Reade (q.v.) (1853).

It deals with an episode in the life of the famous Irish actress, Margaret Woffington (q.v.).

Peisistratus (*d.* 527 B.C.) became tyrant of Athens in 560 B.C., was twice expelled, but returned to power. It was probably under his auspices that dramatic contests were introduced at Athens, and he is said to have commissioned some learned men to collect the poems of Homer.

Pelagian, derived from *Pelagius,* the latinized form of the name of a British monk, Morgan, of the 4th and 5th cents. The Pelagians, his followers, denied the Catholic doctrine of original sin, and maintained that the human will is of itself capable of good without the assistance of divine grace.

Peleus, son of Aeacus, king of Phthia in Thessaly. He married Thetis, a Nereid. Of their union was born Achilles (q.v.).

Pelham, or The Adventures of a Gentleman, a novel by Bulwer Lytton (q.v.) (1828).

This was Lytton's second novel, and is generally considered his best.

Pelias, a king of Iolcos, whom his daughters put to death and boiled at the instigation of Medea (q.v.), in order to restore him to youth. Alcestis (q.v.) was one of his daughters.

Pelican, The, see *Golden Hind.*

Pelion, a mountain in Thessaly, on which the Giants (q.v.) in their war with the gods heaped Mt. Ossa, in order to scale the heights of heaven.

Pell, SOLOMON, in Dickens's 'The Pickwick Papers' (q.v.), an attorney in the Insolvent Court.

Pelleas, SIR, in the Arthurian legend, the lover of Ettard or Ettarre.

Pelleas and Ettarre, one of Tennyson's 'Idylls of the King' (q.v.) (1869).

Pelles, KING, in Malory's 'Morte Darthur', 'cousin nigh unto Joseph of Arimathie', and intimately connected with the story of the Holy Grail. He was father of Elaine, who became the mother of Galahad by Sir Launcelot.

Pellinore, KING, in Malory's 'Morte Darthur', the father of Sir Lamorak, Sir Percival, and Sir Tor.

Peloponnesian War, THE, between Athens and Sparta and their respective allies, 431-404 B.C. It ended in the surrender of Athens and the brief transfer of the leadership of Greece to Sparta.

Pelops, the son of Tantalus (q.v.) and founder of the Pelopid dynasty from which the Peloponnese took its name. By Hippodamia Pelops was father of Atreus (q.v.) and Thyestes.

Pembroke, MARY HERBERT, COUNTESS OF (1561-1621), Sir Philip Sidney's sister. She is referred to as 'Sidney's sister, Pembroke's mother' in her epitaph attributed to W. Browne (q.v.). She suggested the composition of her brother's 'Arcadia' (q.v.), which she revised and added to. She was a patron of Samuel Daniel, Nicholas Breton, Jonson, and other poets.

Penates, Roman household gods, cf. *Lares.*

Pendennis, The History of, a novel by Thackeray (q.v.), published serially in 1848-50.

Leaving school at 16 on the death of his father, Arthur Pendennis falls in love with an actress, Emily Costigan, the daughter of Captain Costigan, a wild tipsy Irishman. The engagement is broken off and Arthur goes to the university, where he is idle and extravagant, and involves himself and his mother in financial difficulties from which they are rescued by Laura Bell, an amiable girl, the daughter of a former unfortunate lover of his mother whom she has adopted. Laura also enables Arthur to start on a literary career in London. Here he shares chambers with George Warrington (a descendant of the Warringtons of 'The Virginians', q.v.), a fine character, one of the good influences in Arthur's life. His mother hopes that Arthur shall marry Laura, but when he in deference to his mother's wish proposes half-heartedly to Laura, she indignantly refuses him. Arthur's second entanglement is with Blanche Amory, daughter of Lady Clavering by her first husband. Blanche, though outwardly pretty and accomplished, is in reality a selfish little shrew. Old Major Pendennis, Arthur's uncle, is so actuated by worldly ambition on his nephew's behalf as to favour the match strongly, although aware that Blanche's father, an escaped convict, is, unknown to Lady Clavering, still alive.

After a flirtation with Fanny Bolton, the porter's daughter of Shepherd's Inn, and a period during which Laura is in love with Warrington (who in fact has had his life ruined by an imprudent early marriage), Laura and Arthur are finally united. But this occurs only after the latter has narrowly escaped from marriage with Blanche Amory.

Among the many amusing characters in the story may be mentioned Capt. Shandon, the first editor of the 'Pall Mall Gazette'; the rival publishers Bungay and Bacon; the vulgar but amiable 'Begum', Lady Clavering; and Morgan, the Major's blackmailing servant.

Penelope, daughter of Icarius, wife of Odysseus, and mother of Telemachus. When, at the close of the Trojan War, her husband did not return to Ithaca, she was beset by suitors. She received their addresses coldly; but declared that she would make choice of one of them when she had completed a piece of tapestry. To prolong the period she undid at night the work that she had done during the day, whence the proverb of *Penelope's web* for a labour that is never ended. The return of Odysseus after twenty years delivered her from the suitors.

Penelophon, the name of the beggar maid loved by King Cophetua. Shakespeare ('Love's Labour's Lost', IV. i) gives it as 'Zenelophon'.

Penguin New Writing, see *New Writing.*

Penn, WILLIAM (1644-1718), a Quaker and the founder of Pennsylvania. He was committed to the Tower of London in 1668 and there wrote 'No Cross, no Crown' (1669), an eloquent dissertation on the Christian duty of self-sacrifice. Religious persecution led him to look to America as a refuge for his co-religionists, and in 1682 he obtained grants of East New Jersey and Pennsylvania, and framed, in concert with Algernon Sydney, a constitution for the colony. In the same year he sailed for America.

Pennant, THOMAS (1726-98), naturalist, antiquarian, and traveller, published his 'Tour in Scotland' in 1771, 'A Tour in Wales' in 1778-81, etc. He figures in Gilbert White's 'Selborne' as one of the author's correspondents.

Penseroso, Il, a poem by Milton (q.v.), written at Horton in 1632 with its companion piece 'L'Allegro' (q.v.).

The poem is an invocation to the goddess Melancholy, bidding her bring Peace and Quiet, and Leisure and Contemplation. It describes the pleasures of the studious, meditative life, of tragedy, epic poetry, and music.

Pentameron, *The,* one of the longer prose works of Landor (q.v.) (1837).

Pentameter, in Greek and Latin prosody, a form of dactylic verse of which each half consists of two feet and a long syllable. In English literature, a line of verse of five feet, e.g. the English 'heroic' or iambic verse of ten syllables, as used for instance in 'Paradise Lost', or in the rhymed couplets of Dryden.

Pentateuch, THE (Greek πέντε five, τεῦχος implement or vessel), the first five books of the O.T. traditionally ascribed to Moses.

Pentecost, from the Greek word meaning fiftieth [day], a name for the Jewish harvest festival. Also a festival of the Christian Church, observed on the seventh Sunday after Easter, Whit-Sunday.

Penthea, a character in Ford's 'The Broken Heart' (q.v.).

Penthesilea, a queen of the Amazons. She came to the aid of the Trojans, and was slain by Achilles.

Pentheus, a king of Thebes, who resisted the introduction of the worship of Dionysus. He was driven mad by the god, his palace destroyed, and himself torn to pieces by the Bacchanals.

Pepys, SAMUEL (1633-1703) (pron. 'Peeps' or 'Pĕpўs'), son of John Pepys, a London tailor, married Elizabeth St. Michel, a girl of 15, and entered the household of Sir Edward Montagu, his father's first cousin, in 1656. His subsequent successful career was largely due to Montagu's patronage. His famous 'Diary' opens on 1 Jan. 1660, when Pepys was living in Axe Yard, Westminster, and was very poor. Soon after this he was appointed 'clerk of the King's ships' and clerk of the privy seal. In 1665 he became surveyor-general of the victualling office. Owing to failing eyesight he closed his diary on 31 May 1669, and in the same year his wife died. In 1672 he was appointed secretary to the Admiralty. In 1683 he was sent to Tangier with Lord Dartmouth and wrote an interesting diary while there. In 1684 he was reappointed secretary to the Admiralty, a post which he held until the revolution, labouring hard to provide the country with an efficient fleet. His 'Diary' remained in cipher (a system of shorthand) at Magdalene College, Cambridge, until 1825, when it was deciphered by John Smith and edited by Lord Braybrooke. It is a document of extraordinary interest, on account both of the light that its sincere narrative throws on the author's own lovable character, and of the vivid picture that it gives of contemporary everyday life, of the administration of the navy, and of the ways of the court.

Perceval. The legend of Perceval, of great antiquity as a folk-tale, is first found in poetical form in the French 'Perceval' of Chrétien de Troyes (q.v.). In English it was treated in 'Sir Percyvelle of Galles' and by Malory. The former, a 15th-cent. verse romance, contains no mention of the Holy Grail. Malory's 'Morte Darthur' makes Percivale a son of King Pellinore, and narrates his adventures in the course of his quest of the Grail (q.v.).

Percy, THOMAS (1729-1811), bishop of Dromore in 1782. He published in 1765 his 'Reliques of Ancient English Poetry' (see *Percy's 'Reliques'*). This work did much to promote the revival of interest in the older English poetry.

Percy Folio, THE, a manuscript in mid-17th-cent. handwriting, the most important source of our ballad literature and the basis of Child's collection. From it T. Percy (q.v.) drew the ballads included in Percy's 'Reliques' (q.v.).

Percy's 'Reliques' of *Ancient English Poetry*, a collection of ballads, historical songs, and metrical romances, published in 1765 by T. Percy (q.v.). The majority of them were extracted from the Percy Folio (q.v.) and were edited and 'restored' by Percy. They were of very different periods, some of great antiquity, others as recent as the reign of Charles I.

Perdita, a character in Shakespeare's 'The Winter's Tale' (q.v.). 'Perdita' was a name given to the actress Mary Robinson (1758–1800), who took the part. She attracted the attention of the Prince of Wales (afterwards George IV) and became his mistress for a short time.

Père Goriot, Le, the title of one of the greatest of Balzac's (q.v.) novels.

Peregrine Pickle, The Adventures of, a novel by Smollett (q.v.) (1751).

The hero is a scoundrel and a swashbuckler, with little to his credit except wit and courage; and the book is mainly occupied with his adventures in England and on the Continent, many of them of an amatory character. In the course of these he visits Paris, is imprisoned in the Bastille, visits the Netherlands, hoaxes the physicians of Bath, sets up as a magician, endeavours to enter parliament, is confined in the Fleet and released on inheriting his father's property, finally marrying Emily Gauntlet, a young lady whom he has, from the outset of the story, intermittently pursued with his attentions.

Pericles, the great Athenian statesman and military commander, who controlled the affairs of the state from 460 B.C. until his death in 429 B.C., including the earlier period of the Peloponnesian War. See also *Aspasia*, *Pericles and Aspasia*, and *Funeral Oration*.

Pericles, Prince of Tyre, a romantic drama by Shakespeare (q.v.), produced probably about 1608, and first printed (in a mangled form) in 1609, and in the third folio of 1664. Internal evidence suggests that the play was not written entirely by Shakespeare. The story is drawn from the 'Apollonius of Tyre' in Gower's 'Confessio Amantis' (q.v.). Gower himself appears as Chorus.

Pericles, prince of Tyre, having guessed the secret infamy of Antiochus, emperor of Greece, and his life being threatened in consequence, leaves his government in the hands of his honest minister, Helicanus,

and sails from Tyre. His ship is wrecked on the coast of Pentapolis, Pericles alone being saved. Here he defeats in the lists the other suitors for the hand of Thaisa, daughter of King Simonides, whom he weds. Shortly after, Helicanus makes known to him that Antiochus is dead and the people are clamouring to make him (Helicanus) king. Pericles and Thaisa set off for Tyre, but a storm arising, Thaisa falls in travail with fear, and gives birth to a daughter. A deep swoon gives the impression that Thaisa is dead, and she is committed to the waves in a chest. The chest is cast ashore near Ephesus, where Cerimon, a physician, opens it and restores Thaisa to life. She, thinking her husband drowned, becomes a priestess in the temple of Diana. Pericles carries his daughter Marina to Tarsus, where he leaves her with Cleon, the governor, and his wife, Dionyza. When the child grows up, Dionyza, jealous of her superior accomplishments, designs to kill her; but Marina is carried off by pirates and sold in Mitylene into a brothel, where her purity and piety win the admiration of Lysimachus, the governor of Mitylene, and the respect of even the brothel-keeper's brutal servant, and secure her release. Pericles, mourning the supposed death of his daughter, comes to Mitylene, where he discovers her, to his intense joy. A dream directs him to go to the temple of Diana at Ephesus and there recount the story of his life. This he does, with the result that the priestess Thaisa, his lost wife, recognizes him, and is reunited to her husband and daughter. Marina is married to Lysimachus. Cleon and Dionyza are burnt as a penalty for their intended crime.

Pericles and Aspasia, one of the longer prose works of Landor (q.v.) (1836).

Perilous Chair, THE, the 'Siege Perilous' at the Round Table (q.v.).

Peripatetics, the name given to the school of Aristotle from his habit of discoursing while walking up and down (περιπατῶν) in the shady paths of the Lyceum.

Periphrasis, a roundabout form of statement, a circumlocution.

Perissa, in Spenser's 'Faerie Queene', see *Medina*.

Perker, MR., in Dickens's 'The Pickwick Papers' (q.v.), Mr. Pickwick's attorney.

Perkin Warbeck, a historical play by J. Ford (q.v.) (1634).

The play is entirely unlike Ford's other work, and is a good historical drama.

Perrault, CHARLES (1628-1703), a French poet, critic, and member of the Academy, chiefly known in England for the fairy tales alleged to have been repeated to him by his little son and published by him under the title 'Histoires et Contes du Tems Passé (1697). They were translated into English by Robert Samber (1729?).

Persant of Inde, SIR, in Malory's 'Morte Darthur', one of the knights who kept the approach to Castle Perilous.

Persephone, see *Proserpine*.

Persepolis, the capital of the Persian empire, not far from the modern Shiraz, laid in ruins by Alexander. It occurs in Marlowe's famous line from 'Tamburlaine', 'And ride in triumph through Persepolis'.

Perseus, the son of Zeus and Danae. His early story will be found under *Danae*. Polydectes, having received the mother and child, became enamoured of Danae. Wishing to get rid of Perseus, Polydectes sent him to fetch the head of the Medusa (q.v.). But Pluto lent him a helmet that would make him invisible, Athene a buckler resplendent as a mirror (so that he did not need to look directly at the Medusa), and Hermes the *talaria* or wings for the feet. He was thus enabled to cut off the Medusa's head. In his further course, Perseus discovered Andromeda (q.v.) exposed on a rock to a dragon that was about to devour her. Having obtained from Cepheus, her father, the promise of her hand, Perseus slew the dragon. But Phineus, Andromeda's uncle, attempted to carry away the bride, and, with his attendants, was changed into stones by the Medusa's head. Perseus then returned to Seriphos, just in time to save Danae

from the violence of Polydectes, whom he likewise destroyed. At Larissa he took part in some funeral games, and when throwing the quoit, had the misfortune to kill a man in the throng, who turned out to be Acrisius, his grandfather. He refused to ascend the throne of Argos to which he became heir by this calamity, but founded the new city of Mycenae.

Persius (AULUS PERSIUS FLACCUS) (A.D. 34-62), Roman satirist, author of six satires, which show the influence of Horace and of the Stoic philosophy.

Persuasion, a novel by Jane Austen (q.v.), finished in 1816 and published in 1818.

Sir Walter Elliot, a foolish spendthrift baronet and a widower, with an overweening sense of his social importance and personal elegance, is obliged to retrench, and lets his seat, Kellynch Hall, to Admiral and Mrs. Croft. His eldest daughter Elizabeth, haughty and unmarried, is now 29; the second, Anne, intelligent, and of an amiable disposition, had some years before been engaged to a young naval officer, Frederick Wentworth, the brother of Mrs. Croft, but had been persuaded by her trusted friend, Lady Russell, to break off the engagement on the ground of his lack of fortune and from a misunderstanding of his sanguine temper. The breach had produced deep unhappiness in Anne and intense indignation in Wentworth. Anne is now 27 and the bloom of her beauty gone. The youngest daughter of Sir Walter, Mary, is married to Charles Musgrove, the heir of a neighbouring landed proprietor. Capt. Wentworth, who has had a successful career and is become rich, is now thrown again into Anne's society by the letting of Kellynch to the Crofts; and the story is concerned with the gradual revival of Wentworth's passion for Anne. The course of the reconciliation is, however, hindered by various impediments. Charles Musgrove has two sisters, Louisa and Henrietta. Wentworth is at first attracted by them both, and presently becomes entangled with Louisa, though no explicit declaration passes. A crisis arrives during a visit of the party to Lyme Regis, when Louisa, being 'jumped down' from the Cobb by Capt. Wentworth, falls and is dangerously injured. Wentworth's partial responsibility for the accident makes him feel an increased obligation to Louisa at the very time that his heart is being drawn back to Anne. Fortunately, during her convalescence and Wentworth's absence, Louisa becomes engaged to Capt. Benwick, a brother officer of Wentworth's, and the latter is free to proceed with his courtship. He goes accordingly to Bath, where Sir Walter is now established with his two elder daughters and Mrs. Clay, an artful woman with matrimonial designs on Sir Walter. But at Bath Wentworth finds the field occupied by another suitor for Anne's hand, in her cousin William Elliot, the heir presumptive to the Kellynch estate, who is paying assiduous attention to Anne and at the same time carrying on an intrigue with Mrs. Clay, so as to detach her from Sir Walter. Anne, however, is awakened to the duplicity of Mr. Elliot, and indeed her affection for Wentworth has remained unshaken. Being accidentally made aware of Anne's constancy, Wentworth takes courage to renew his offer of marriage and is accepted.

In this, her last work, satire and ridicule take a milder form, the tone is graver and more tender, and the interest lies in a more subtle interplay of the characters.

Pertelote, see *Partlet*.

Perugino (active 1469-1523), PIETRO VANNUCCI, Italian painter and master of Raphael.

Pervigilium Veneris, the name of a short Latin poem by an unknown author, perhaps of the 2nd cent. A.D.

Pétaud, KING, the king formerly elected by the community of beggars in France, so named facetiously from the Latin *peto*, I beg.

Peter Bell, a poem by Wordsworth (q.v.), published in 1819 with dedication to Southey, but written long before at

Alfoxden, in 1798, the year of the 'Lyrical Ballads'.

The ludicrous character of parts of the poem diverted attention from its merits, and it was made the subject of many parodies (among others one by Shelley).

Peterborough Chronicle, The, a version of the 'Anglo-Saxon Chronicle' (q.v.), written at Peterborough and including annals up to 1154.

Peterloo, the name (a burlesque adaptation of Waterloo) given to a charge of cavalry and yeomanry on the Manchester reform meeting held in St. Peter's Field, Manchester, on 16 Aug. 1819, as a result of which eleven persons are said (the figures are doubtful) to have been killed and about 600 injured.

Peter Lombard (*c.* 1100–*c.* 1160), *Magister Sententiarum*, or master of the sentences, became professor of theology, and subsequently in 1159 bishop of Paris. He wrote his 'Sententiae' between 1145 and 1150. They are a collection of opinions of the Fathers. The work was very popular and became a theological textbook.

Peter Martyr (PIETRO VERMIGLI) (1500-62), born in Florence, an Augustinian monk, who accepted the Reformed faith, fled from Italy, and became Regius professor of divinity at Oxford (1548). He helped Cranmer in the preparation of the second Prayer Book.

Peter Pan, or the Boy who wouldn't grow up, a dramatic fantasy by Barrie (q.v.), produced in 1904. The story of the play was published in 1911 under the title 'Peter and Wendy'.

It is a story of the three children of Mr. and Mrs. Darling, Wendy, John, and Michael, the nurse Nana (who is a Newfoundland dog), and the motherless Peter Pan, who, with the fairy Tinker Bell, takes the children off to Never-Never Land, where they encounter Redskins and pirates, including the notable Capt. Hook and the agreeable Smee.

Peter Plymley, Letters of, see *Plymley*.

Peter Porcupine, see *Cobbett*.

Peter's, ST., Rome, the metropolitan church of the Roman see, near the site of the old basilica of St. Peter and the traditional place of crucifixion of the saint.

Peter Simple, a novel by Marryat (q.v.) (1834), generally considered his masterpiece.

The hero is sent to sea as the 'fool of the family', and his simplicity at first exposes him to several ludicrous adventures. But he soon shows himself a gallant and capable officer, sees many exciting naval actions, is taken prisoner and escapes, rises in the service, and wins a charming wife.

Peterson, CARL, see *Sapper.*

Peter's Pence, an annual tax or tribute of a penny from each householder having land of a certain value, paid before the Reformation to the papal see at Rome.

Peter the Great (1672-1725) became Tsar jointly with his half-brother Ivan in 1682.

Peter the Hermit (PETER OF AMIENS) (*c.* 1050-1115), preached the first crusade, and led a multitude of followers into Asia Minor (1096). Nearly all these died or were killed by the Turkish garrison of Nicaea before the real 'Crusaders' arrived. Peter, however, survived and accompanied these Crusaders eastwards in 1097.

Petition of Right, a demand put forward by the Commons in 1628 that there should be no imprisonment without cause shown, no forced loans or taxes, no martial law or enforced billeting. The Petition was reluctantly accepted by Charles I and became law.

Pet Marjorie, see *Fleming.*

Peto, a character in Shakespeare's '1 and 2 Henry IV' (q.v.).

Petowker, HENRIETTA, a character in Dickens's 'Nicholas Nickleby' (q.v.). She marries Mr. Lillyvick.

Petrarch (FRANCESCO PETRARCA) (1304-74), Italian poet and humanist, devoted himself to the study of classical antiquity. This enthusiasm he shared with his friend Boccaccio. In 1341 he was crowned poet laureate at Rome. His famous 'Ode to Italy' reveals his ardent patriotism. His works, besides the Laura love-poems, include a large number of letters and treatises in Latin, among others an 'Epistle to Posterity' and a Latin epic, 'Africa', on the contest between Rome and Carthage.

Petrarch is justly regarded as the father of Italian humanism, the initiator of the revived study of Greek and Latin literature.

Petrarchan sonnet, see *Sonnet.*

Petronius, GAIUS, one of the emperor Nero's companions, and director of the pleasures of the imperial court (*arbiter elegantiae*). He was the author of 'Petronii Arbitri Satyricon', a prose satirical romance interspersed with verse, which has survived in a fragmentary state. Tacitus mentions that Petronius committed suicide (about A.D. 65) to avoid being killed by Nero.

Petruchio, in Shakespeare's 'The Taming of the Shrew' (q.v.), the husband of the termagant Katharina.

Petty, SIR WILLIAM (1623-87), political economist, studied on the Continent and became the friend of Hobbes. He published economic treatises, the principal of which was entitled 'Political Arithmetic' 1690, a term signifying what we now call statistics.

Petulengro, JASPER, the principal gipsy character in Borrow's 'Lavengro' and 'The Romany Rye' (qq.v.).

Peveril of the Peak, a novel by Sir W. Scott (q.v.) (1823).

The story is in the main concerned with the times of the pretended Popish Plot (1678), though it is only in the 14th chapter that the principal theme is reached.

The author draws elaborate portraits of Charles II and Buckingham, and gives glimpses of such historical characters as Titus Oates, Colonel Blood (the impudent revolutionary who tried to steal the crown jewels from the Tower), and Sir Geoffrey Hudson (Henrietta Maria's dwarf).

Pew, the blind beggar in Stevenson's 'Treasure Island' (q.v.).

Phaeacians, THE, in the 'Odyssey', the inhabitants of the island *Scheria*, on which Odysseus was cast ashore.

Phaedra, a daughter of Minos (q.v.) and Pasiphaë, and wife of Theseus (q.v.). She became enamoured of Hippolytus (q.v.), the son of Theseus by the amazon Hippolyta. Her advances being rejected, she accused Hippolytus to Theseus of attempts upon her virtue and caused his death. This story is the subject of tragedies by Euripides, Seneca, and Racine.

Phaedria, in Spenser's 'Faerie Queene', II. vi, the Lady of the Idle Lake.

Phaedrus, a Thracian slave who became a freedman of Augustus. He was author of a collection of Latin fables, based on those attributed to Aesop (q.v.).

Phaeton or PHAETHON, a son of Phoebus, the sun, by Clymene, begged his father to allow him to drive the chariot of the sun. He soon betrayed his incapacity and threatened the earth with a conflagration. Zeus, perceiving the disorder, hurled a thunderbolt and struck Phaeton, who fell into the river Eridanus (Po).

Phalaris, a tyrant of Agrigentum in Sicily, probably in the first half of the 6th cent. B.C., said to have been a cruel ruler. The people of Agrigentum revolted *c.* 554 B.C. and put Phalaris to death.

For the 'Phalaris controversy' see *Phalaris (Epistles of)*.

Phalaris, Epistles of, certain letters attributed to Phalaris (q.v.), which were praised by Sir William Temple (q.v.) and edited by Charles Boyle (q.v.) in 1695. Richard Bentley (q.v.) was able to show that they were spurious. There is an echo of the controversy in Swift's 'Battle of the Books' (q.v.).

Phantasmion, see *Coleridge (Sara)*.

Phantom Ship, THE, see *Flying Dutchman.*

Phaon, a boatman of Mitylene in Lesbos. According to an unfounded legend, Sappho, the poetess, fell in love with him,

and when he received her advances coldly, threw herself into the sea. Lyly (q.v.) wrote a play on the subject, 'Sapho and Phao'.

Pharamond, the legendary first king of the Franks. Also the name of a character in Beaumont and Fletcher's 'Philaster'.

Pharaoh, the generic appellation of the ancient Egyptian kings, especially used of those of the time of Joseph and the Exodus.

Pharisees, from a Hebrew word meaning 'separated', an ancient Jewish sect distinguished for their strict observance of the law. The word is applied to self-righteous or hypocritical persons.

Pharos, a small island in the bay of Alexandria. On it was erected a tower which was accounted one of the seven wonders of the world. It stood about 400 feet high and on the top fires were kept burning to direct sailors. Hence the word is often used as a synonym for a lighthouse.

Pharsalia, the epic poem of Lucan (q.v.) on the civil war between Pompey and Caesar; so named from the battle of Pharsalus (48 B.C.), in which the latter was victorious.

Phebe, a shepherdess in Shakespeare's 'As You Like It' (q.v.).

Pheidippides, the best runner in Greece, was sent from Athens to Sparta to announce the arrival of the invading Persians in 490 B.C. He covered the distance between the two cities, 150 miles, in two days.

Phidias (*c.* 490–*c.* 448 B.C.), Greek sculptor. His bronze Athena Promachos (460–450), some 30 feet high, stood on the Acropolis at Athens. He was commissioned by Pericles to design the sculptures of the Parthenon (447–432) and he made the chryselephantine statues of Athena Parthenos for the Parthenon and Zeus for Olympia. He fell a victim to the enemies of Pericles and went into exile.

Philander, TO, to play the Philander or trifling and even promiscuous lover. Philander, in an old ballad, was the lover of Phillis; and in Beaumont and Fletcher's 'Laws of Candy', the lover of Erota.

Philaster, or Love lies a-bleeding, a romantic drama by Beaumont and Fletcher (see *Fletcher, J.*), produced in 1611 and printed in 1620.

Philemon and **Baucis**, an aged couple who lived in a poor cottage in Phrygia when Zeus and Hermes travelled in disguise over Asia. They entertained the gods hospitably, and Zeus transformed their dwelling into a splendid temple, of which the old couple were made the priest and priestess. Having lived to extreme old age, they died in the same hour, according to their request, and were changed into trees, whose boughs intertwined. They are the subject of a poem by Swift (q.v.).

Philip, The Adventures of, the last complete novel of Thackeray (q.v.), published in 'The Cornhill Magazine' in 1861-2.

Philip drunk to Philip sober, APPEAL FROM: Valerius Maximus (vi. 2) relates that a foreign woman undeservedly condemned by Philip of Macedon, father of Alexander the Great, in his cups, declared that she would appeal to Philip, 'sed sobrium', 'but when he was sober'.

Philippi, a town in Macedonia, famous as the site of the battle in 42 B.C. in which Octavianus and Antony defeated Brutus and Cassius. This defeat figures in Shakespeare's 'Julius Caesar' (q.v.).

Philippics, see *Demosthenes* and *Cicero*.

Philips, AMBROSE (1675?-1749), poet, is principally remembered on account of a quarrel between him and Pope about the relative merits of their pastorals. Pope drew, in the 'Guardian', 'a comparison of Philips's performance with his own, in which, with an unexampled and unequalled artifice of irony, . . . he gives the preference to Philips' (Johnson). Philips's adulatory verses, in a seven-syllabled measure, earned him the nickname of 'Namby-Pamby'.

Philips, JOHN (1676-1709), author of 'The Splendid Shilling' (1705) and 'Cyder' (1708) (qq.v.). He was employed by Harley and Bolingbroke to write verses on the battle of Blenheim as a Tory counterpart to Addison's 'Campaign'.

Philips, KATHERINE (1631-64), the 'Matchless Orinda', *née* Fowler, married in 1647 James Philips of Cardigan and instituted a 'Society of Friendship', a literary salon for the discussion of poetry and similar topics, in which she assumed the pseudonym 'Orinda', to which her contemporaries added the epithet 'Matchless'. Her earliest verses were prefixed (1651) to the 'Poems' of Henry Vaughan (q.v.). Her collected verses appeared in 1667. Jeremy Taylor (q.v.) dedicated to her his 'Discourse on the Nature of Friendship', and Cowley (q.v.) mourned her death in an elegy.

Philip Sparrow, see *Phylyp Sparowe*.

Philip van Artevelde, a historical drama in two parts, in blank verse, by Sir H. Taylor (q.v.), published in 1834.

Philistine, the name of an alien warlike people, of uncertain origin, who in early times constantly harassed the Israelites. The name is applied to persons deficient in liberal culture and enlightenment. In this sense the word was introduced into English by Matthew Arnold ('Essays in Criticism', 'Heine').

Phillips, EDWARD (1630-96?), elder nephew of Milton, by whom he was educated. He was a hack-writer in London, and tutor (1663) to the son of John Evelyn (q.v.) and (1665) to Philip Herbert, afterwards seventh earl of Pembroke. His 'New World of Words' (1658), a philological dictionary, was very popular.

Phillips, JOHN (1631-1706), younger nephew of Milton, by whom he was brought up, wrote a scathing attack on Puritanism in 1655 in his 'Satyr against Hypocrites'. He was employed as a translator and hack-writer.

Philoclea, a character in Sidney's 'Arcadia' (q.v.).

Philoctetes, one of the Greek heroes of the Trojan War, a great archer. He was the subject of a play by Sophocles.

Philomela, a daughter of Pandion, king of Athens. Her sister Procne, having married Tereus, king of Thrace, pined for the company of Philomela. Tereus obtained Pandion's permission to conduct Philomela to her sister, but became enamoured of her, and after having offered violence to her, cut off her tongue that she might not be able to reveal his ill-usage. He then told Procne that her sister was dead. But Philomela in captivity depicted her misfortunes on a piece of tapestry and privately conveyed this to Procne. Procne murdered her son Itys in revenge and served up his flesh to Tereus. Tereus drew his sword to punish Procne and Philomela, but at that moment he was changed into a hoopoe, Philomela into a nightingale, Procne into a swallow.

Philosophes, LES, a name given in France to a group of 18th-cent. authors, sceptical in religion, materialist in philosophy, and hedonist in ethics, of whom the principal were Diderot (q.v.), D'Alembert, the Baron d'Holbach, Helvétius, and Condorcet. The 'Encyclopédie' (q.v.) embodied their ideas.

Philosophical Enquiry into the Origin of our Ideas of the Sublime and Beautiful, A, see *Sublime and Beautiful.*

Philosophical Essays concerning Human Understanding, see *Hume.*

Philosophy, ENGLISH. From the end of the 8th cent. down to the middle of the 14th cent., there was an almost constant succession of scholars of British birth among the writers who contributed to the development of philosophy in Europe. These philosophers wrote in Latin; they belonged to an international rather than to a national cultural system. The most important names in the succession are John Scotus Erigena, John of Salisbury, Alexander of Hales, Robert Grosseteste, Roger Bacon, John Duns Scotus, William of Ockham, and Thomas Bradwardine.

English philosophy in the national sense began with Francis Bacon (q.v.) who, nevertheless, wrote a great part of his philosophical and scientific works in Latin. Contemporary with him was Lord Herbert of Cherbury (q.v.), a forerunner of the Cambridge platonists and mystics, Henry More, Cudworth, and others. Hobbes (q.v.) was perhaps the first great English philosopher. His mechanical theory of reality as a whole was a complete and original philosophical system. He was followed by John Locke (q.v.) who, influenced by Descartes, put forward the doctrine of ideas as the objects of the understanding, having their origin in sensation or reflection. Bishop Berkeley (q.v.) took the 'idealist' position a stage further. A main stream of 18th-cent. thought was concerned with 'Deism', the doctrine of a rational world, ruled over by an impersonal God, 'the first great cause'. Bernard Mandeville, Toland, Tindal, and Bolingbroke were distinguished exponents of the belief. But the two great figures of the century were Hume and Adam Smith. Hume, with his passion for literature and wide learning, followed the theory of causation into the issue of scepticism which has ever since been a main philosophical problem. Adam Smith, with his belief in the 'ethics of sympathy', concentrated rather on the social and economic philosophy of mankind.

They were followed by lesser philosophers, such as Thomas Reid (who answered Hume with 'principles of common sense') and Hartley, whom Coleridge admired.

In the 19th cent. Bentham and the Utilitarians carried on the work of Adam Smith. James Mill, Godwin, and Malthus (qq.v.) are to be associated with this school. John Stuart Mill, diverging from them in some respects, did his finest work in a re-examination of logical theory.

There was in general a decline in speculative interest during the Victorian era, an age taken up with rationalist and religious controversy—best represented by John Grote and Newman (q.v.)—or scientific argument, evidenced in the writings of Herbert Spencer and T. H. Huxley, and the philosophy of evolution. A revival of interest in metaphysics came at the end of the century when, under the influence of post-Kantian speculation, and particularly of Hegel, a new group of

English 'idealists' arose, of whom T. H. Green, Edward Caird, and F. H. Bradley are best known. In the modern period, Bertrand Russell (q.v.), working first over the mathematical philosophies of Leibniz and further formulating his own philosophy, has been most eminent.

English philosophers have not on the whole been great builders of systems but rather general contributors to a line of thought. They have, however, been distinguished by very great literary abilities. Bacon and Hobbes were men of letters as well as philosophers; Locke and Berkeley were accomplished stylists; Hume famous as an essayist and historian; Adam Smith and J. S. Mill considerable literary figures.

Philotas, a Senecan tragedy in blank verse by Samuel Daniel (q.v.) (1605).

Philotime, in Spenser's 'Faerie Queene', II. vii. 48, 49, the daughter of Mammon, symbolizes ambition.

Philtra, in Spenser's 'Faerie Queene', v. iv, a self-seeking damsel in the episode of Amidas and Brasidas.

Phineas Finn, Phineas Redux, The Prime Minister, and *The Duke's Children*, novels of parliamentary life by A. Trollope (q.v.), published respectively in 1869, 1873, 1875, and 1880.

Phineus, son of Agenor and king of Thrace, a soothsayer blinded by the gods on account of his cruelty to his sons. He was constantly harassed by the Harpies (q.v.). When the Argonauts (q.v.) visited Thrace, he was delivered from these and in return instructed them regarding their way to Colchis.

Phiz, see *Browne* (*H. K.*).

Phlegethon or PYRIPHLEGETHON, a river of Hades, whose waters were flames. See *Styx*.

Phoebe and **Phoebus,** names given respectively to Diana (the moon) and Apollo (the sun), signifying bright, radiant.

Phoenix, a fabulous bird, of golden and red plumage, which, according to a tale reported by Herodotus (ii. 73), came to Heliopolis every 500 years, on the death of his father, and there buried his body in the temple of the sun. According to another version, the phoenix, after living 500 years, built himself a funeral pile and died upon it. From his remains a fresh phoenix arose.

'The Phoenix and the Turtle', a poem attributed to Shakespeare, was included in 1601 in Robert Chester's 'Love's Martyr'.

Phoenix, The, an OE. poem of 677 lines, contained in the 'Exeter Book' (q.v.).

Phoenix, THE, a theatre that stood in the parish of St. Giles-in-the-Fields, London, in the 16th and 17th cents.

Phoenix Nest, The, a poetical miscellany (1593), containing, amongst others, poems by Lodge and Breton (qq.v.).

Phonetic Spelling, a system of spelling in which each letter represents invariably the same spoken sound, e.g. the system proposed for the reform of English spelling, as opposed to the traditional (historical or etymological) system.

Phorcys, a sea deity, father of the Gorgons (q.v.) and the Graiae, and other monsters.

Phosphorus, 'the light-bringer', the morning star of the Greeks, corresponding to the Lucifer of the Romans.

Phrygian mode, one of the three modes of ancient Greek music, a minor scale appropriate to passion (Jebb).

Phryne, a celebrated Greek courtesan.

Phunky, MR., in Dickens's 'The Pickwick Papers' (q.v.), Serjeant Snubbin's junior in the case of Bardell *v.* Pickwick.

Phylyp Sparowe, a poem by Skelton (q.v.).

Physiocrat, one of a school of political economists founded by François Quesnay (1694–1774) in France in the 18th cent. They maintained that society should be governed according to an inherent natural order, that the soil is the sole source of wealth, etc. Adam Smith was strongly influenced by the sounder doctrines of the school.

Physiologus, see *Bestiaries*.

Picaresque, from the Spanish *picaro*, a rogue, a term applied to a class of romances that deal with rogues and knaves, of which the earliest important examples, such as 'Lazarillo de Tormes' and 'Guzman de Alfarache', were written in Spanish. 'Gil Blas' (q.v.) is the most famous picaresque story in French. (See under *Novel*.)

Picasso, PABLO RUIZ Y (1881–   ), Spanish painter. He settled in Paris in 1901 and first painted the characters of the Paris slums with a predominantly blue palette, then actors and clowns in warmer colours. In 1907 Picasso and Braque developed Cubism (q.v.). In 1917 he designed ballets for Diaghilev; then came the period of monumental nudes which developed in the 1930s into terrifyingly distorted forms. Latterly he has designed ceramics. A brilliant draughtsman, Picasso has produced an enormous number of etchings and lithographs, and has illustrated books.

Pickle-herring, a clown or buffoon. This application of the term originated in Germany, where it was the name of a humorous character in an early 17th-cent. play.

Pickwickian sense, IN A, applied to uncomplimentary language which in the circumstances is not to be interpreted in its strictly literal meaning; from the scene in ch. i of 'The Pickwick Papers'.

Pickwick Papers, The (*The Posthumous Papers of the Pickwick Club*), a novel by Dickens (q.v.), first issued in twenty monthly parts from April 1836 to Nov. 1837, and as a volume in 1837.

Mr. Samuel Pickwick, general chairman of the Pickwick Club which he has founded, Messrs. Tracy Tupman, Augustus Snodgrass, and Nathaniel Winkle, members of the Club, are constituted a Corresponding Society of the Club to report to it their journeys and adventures, and observations of character and manners. This is the basis on which the novel is constructed, and the Club serves as a connecting link for a series of detached incidents and changing characters, without elaborate plot. The principal elements in the story are: (1) the visit

of Pickwick and his friends to Rochester, and their falling in with Jingle, who gets Winkle involved in the prospect of a duel. (2) The visit to Dingley Dell, the home of the hospitable Mr. Wardle; the elopement of Jingle with Wardle's sister, their pursuit by Wardle and Pickwick, and the recovery of the lady. (3) The visit to Eatanswill, where a parliamentary election is in progress. (4) The visit to Bury St. Edmunds, where Mr. Pickwick and Sam Weller are fooled by Jingle and his servant, Job Trotter. (5) The pursuit of Jingle to Ipswich, where Mr. Pickwick inadvertently enters the bedroom of a middle-aged lady at night. (6) The Christmas festivities at Dingley Dell. (7) The misapprehension of Mrs. Bardell, Mr. Pickwick's landlady, regarding her lodger's intentions, which leads to the famous action of Bardell *v.* Pickwick for breach of promise of marriage. (8) The visit to Bath, in which Winkle figures prominently. (9) The period of Mr. Pickwick's imprisonment in the Fleet in consequence of his refusal to pay the damages and costs of his action. (10) The affairs of Tony Weller (Sam's father) and the second Mrs. Weller, ending in the death of the latter and the discomfiture of the pious humbug Stiggins. (11) The affairs of Bob Sawyer and Benjamin Allen, medical students and subsequently struggling practitioners. The novel ends with the happy marriage of Allen's sister, Arabella, to Winkle.

Pico della Mirandola, GIOVANNI (1463–94), an Italian humanist and philosopher. He spent part of his short life at Florence in the circle of Lorenzo de' Medici. In 1486 he published 900 theses, offering to maintain them at Rome, but some were pronounced heretical, and the public debate did not take place. The famous oration 'De dignitate hominis', with which he intended to introduce the debate, is one of the most important philosophical works of the 15th cent. Pico was a daring syncretist, who vainly tried to make a synthesis of Christianity, Platonism,

Aristotelianism, and the Jewish Cabbala. His life ('Life of John Picus, Erle of Myrandula, Greate Lorde of Italy'), and some of his pious writings, were translated by Sir Thomas More. John Colet (q.v.) was influenced by Pico's writings.

Pidgin, a Chinese corruption of the English word 'business'. Hence PIDGIN ENGLISH, the jargon used for inter-communication between Chinese and Europeans in China.

Piece of Eight, see *Dollar*.

Pied Piper of Hamelin, The, A Child's Story, a poem by R. Browning (q.v.), included in 'Dramatic Romances' (1845), based on an old legend.

Pierce Pennilesse, His Supplication to the Divell, a fantastic prose satire by T. Nash (q.v.) (1592). The author, in the form of a humorous complaint to the Devil, discourses on the vices of the day, throwing interesting light on the customs of his time.

Pierian, PIERIDES, names applied to the Muses (q.v.), from Pieria near Mt. Olympus, where they were worshipped.

Pierre, a character in Otway's 'Venice Preserv'd' (q.v.).

Pierrot, a typical character in French pantomime; now, in English, applied to a buffoon or itinerant minstrel, having, like the stage Pierrot, a whitened face and loose white fancy dress.

Piers Plowman, The Vision of William concerning Piers the Plowman, the most important work in Middle English with the exception of Chaucer's 'Canterbury Tales', is an alliterative poem of which the three versions, of very different length (2,500 to 7,300 lines), are attributed to William Langland, 'Long Will' as he calls himself. He is supposed to have written them between 1360 and 1399. But recent critical discussion has left the question of the authorship of the three versions (known as the A, the B, and the C texts) undecided. As to the details in the poem regarding the life of the author, the whole subject remains involved in obscurity.

Taking first the A text, the work may be very briefly summarized as follows:

Wandering on the Malvern Hills, the poet sees a vision of a high tower (Truth), a deep dungeon (Wrong), and a 'fair field full of folk' (the earth) between. There follows a vision in which Lady Meed (bribery), Reason, Conscience, and other abstractions are confronted. Then we have Conscience preaching to the people, and Repentance moving their hearts, the confession of the seven deadly sins, and 'a thousand of men' moved to seek St. Truth. Here Piers Plowman makes his appearance, and offers to guide the pilgrims if they will help him plough his half-acre. Some help him, but some are shirkers. Then follows a discussion of the labour problem of the day.

This takes us to the end of *passus VIII*. With *passus IX* the poem passes to a search for 'Do-well', 'Do-bet', and 'Do-best', who are vainly looked for among the friars, the priests, and in Scripture, with the help of Thought, Wit, and Study.

The additions contained in the B and C texts, though characterized by sincerity and power of impression, are too incoherent to be easily summarized. Their author is specially concerned with the corruption in the Church and with the merits of poverty. The seven new visions include a long disquisition on wealth and learning; a theological discussion between Reason, Conscience, Clergy, and a doctor of divinity; a conversation between Patience and 'Activa-Vita', the humble worker; narratives of Christ's life in which Christ and Piers Plowman blend one into the other; and finally the attack of Antichrist and Pride upon the house 'Unity', and of Death upon Mankind.

Pilgrimage of Grace, THE, a rising in Yorkshire in 1536 in protest against the dissolution of the monasteries. It is the subject of Wordsworth's poem, 'The White Doe of Rylstone'.

Pilgrimage to Pernassus, see *Parnassus Plays*.

Pilgrim Fathers, THE, the English Puritans who in 1620 set out from Delft Haven and Plymouth in the 'Mayflower', and who founded the colony of Plymouth in New England.

Pilgrim's Progress, The, from this World to that which is to come, an allegory by Bunyan (q.v.) (Part I 1678, Part II 1684).

The allegory takes the form of a dream by the author. In this he sees Christian, on the advice of Evangelist, fleeing from the City of Destruction. Pt. I describes his pilgrimage through the Slough of Despond, the House Beautiful, the Valley of Humiliation, the Valley of the Shadow of Death, Vanity Fair, the Delectable Mountains, the country of Beulah, to the Celestial City.

Pt. II relates how Christian's wife, Christiana, moved by a vision, sets out with her children on the same pilgrimage, accompanied by her neighbour Mercy.

The work is remarkable for the beauty and simplicity of its language (Bunyan was permeated with the English of the Bible), the vividness and reality of the impersonations, and the author's sense of humour and feeling for the world of nature.

Pillars of Hercules, see *Hercules (Pillars of).*

Pilot that weathered the storm, THE, William Pitt the younger, in a song by George Canning (q.v.).

For 'Dropping the Pilot', see *Tenniel.*

Piltdown, a down near Lewes, in Sussex, where prehistoric remains of a human skull and ape-like lower jaw and of worked flints and bone implements were discovered in 1912; they were claimed as belonging to the early pleistocene period, but scientific tests made in 1953 proved them to be forgeries.

Pinch, a schoolmaster in Shakespeare's 'A Comedy of Errors' (q.v.).

Pinch, TOM and RUTH, characters in Dickens's 'Martin Chuzzlewit' (q.v.).

Pinchwife, a character in Wycherley's 'The Country Wife' (q.v.).

Pindar (*c.* 522–442 B.C.), the great Greek lyric poet, acquired fame at an early age and was employed by many winners at the Games to celebrate their victories. The only complete poems of his that are extant are his 'Epinicia' or triumphal odes (see *Olympian Odes*); but he wrote many kinds of verse, and fragments of these survive. He exercised a great influence on Latin poetry (especially Horace).

For 'Pindaric ode' see under *Ode.*

Pindar, PETER, see *Wolcot.*

Pinero, SIR ARTHUR WING (1855–1934), dramatist. His first notable play, 'The Money Spinner', was produced in 1881, and was followed by three successful farces. He then turned to more serious dramatic works, of which the most important were 'Sweet Lavender' (1888), 'The Second Mrs. Tanqueray' (1893), and 'Trelawny of the Wells' (1898).

Pinkerton, THE MISSES, managers of an academy for young ladies in Thackeray's 'Vanity Fair' (q.v.).

Pinner of Wakefield, THE, see *George-a'-Green.*

Pinter, HAROLD (1930–   ), playwright, whose plays—including 'The Birthday Party' (1960), 'The Caretaker' (1960), and 'The Homecoming' (1965)—are especially notable for portraying, by means of dialogue which realistically reproduces the nuances of colloquial speech, the inability of people to communicate satisfactorily with one another.

Pinto, FERNÃO MENDES (1509?–1583), a Portuguese traveller in the East, who left a narrative of his voyages. Cervantes calls him the 'Prince of Liars' and Congreve in 'Love for Love' cites him as a typical liar.

Piozzi, MRS., see *Thrale.*

Pip, in Dickens's 'Great Expectations' (q.v.), the name by which the hero, Philip Pirrip, is commonly known.

Pipchin, MRS., in Dickens's 'Dombey and Son' (q.v.), a boarding-house keeper at Brighton.

Pippa Passes, a dramatic poem by R. Browning (q.v.) (1841) (the first of the series entitled 'Bells and Pomegranates').

Pirandello, LUIGI (1867–1936), Italian

dramatist, novelist, and short-story writer. His best-known works are: 'Così è (se vi pare)' (1917), 'Sei personaggi in cerca di autore' ('Six Characters in Search of an Author') (1921), 'Enrico IV' (1922), plays; 'Il fu Mattia Pascal' (1904), novel. His typical plays are built upon the theoretical presuppositions that truth is relative and that the personality of the individual is not single and unchanging, but multiform and fluid.

Pirate, The, a novel by Sir W. Scott (q.v.) (1821). The scene is laid principally in Zetland (or Shetland) in the 17th cent.

Pisces, the Fishes, the twelfth sign of the zodiac; also a constellation.

Pisistratus, see *Peisistratus*.

Pistol, ANCIENT, in Shakespeare's '2 Henry IV', 'Henry V', and 'The Merry Wives of Windsor' (qq.v.), one of Falstaff's associates, a braggart with a fine command of bombastic language.

Pistole, a name applied specifically from *c.* 1600 to a Spanish gold coin equivalent to four silver *pieces of eight* (see *Dollar*).

Pistyl of Susan, The, an alliterative poem of the 14th cent., which relates the story of Susannah and Daniel. It is attributed by some to Huchoun (q.v.). 'Pistyl'= Epistle.

Pitman, SIR ISAAC (1813–97), the inventor of phonography, a system of shorthand.

Pitt, WILLIAM, *first earl of Chatham* (1708–78), a great Whig statesman and orator. He was secretary of state in 1756-7, but his fame as a great administrator rests chiefly on the period of the Seven Years War that immediately followed, when Pitt and Newcastle were the chief ministers in coalition. Pitt resigned in 1761. He strenuously opposed from 1774 onwards the harsh measures taken against the American colonies.

Pitt, WILLIAM (1759–1806), second son of the above, became chancellor of the exchequer in his twenty-second, and prime minister in 1783 in his twenty-fifth year, and retained the position until 1801, during the troubled years which followed

the outbreak of the French Revolution, forming the great European coalitions that opposed French military aggression. He returned to office in 1804, formed the third coalition, and died in Jan. 1806, shortly after the battle of Austerlitz, his last words being, 'Oh, my country! How I leave my country!'

Placebo, Latin, 'I shall be pleasing', occurring in Ps. cxiv. 9 (*Placebo Domino in regione vivorum*), is used allusively in such phrases as 'sing placebo' to signify 'play the sycophant'. Chaucer uses Placebo in 'The Merchant's Tale' as a proper name for a flatterer, one of the brothers of old January.

Place-Name Society, THE, see *English Place-Name Society*.

Plagiary, SIR FRETFUL, a character in Sheridan's 'The Critic' (q.v.), a caricature of Richard Cumberland (q.v.).

Plague of London, THE GREAT, the epidemic of bubonic plague that visited London in 1665.

Plague Year, A Journal of the, a historical fiction by Defoe (q.v.) (1722).

It purports to be the narrative of a resident in London during 1664-5, the year of the Great Plague, and embodies much information that Defoe received from one source or another, including official documents. It is a good example of his realistic and factual writing.

Plain Dealer, The, a comedy by Wycherley (q.v.), produced in 1677.

This, perhaps the best of Wycherley's plays, a remote adaptation of Molière's 'Le Misanthrope', shows the author at his fiercest as a satirist.

Plato (*c.* 427-348 B.C.), the great Greek philosopher, was born at Athens, or, according to some, at Aegina. He became a pupil and devoted admirer of Socrates, and after his death in 399 retired to Megara, and subsequently resided for a time in Sicily. He returned to Athens about 386 B.C. and began to teach in the Academy (q.v.). The remainder of his life was mainly occupied with instruction and the composition of the Dialogues in some of which Socrates figures as conducting the discussions. All these Dialogues are extant. They have their origin in the teaching of Socrates (q.v.) but indicate an evolution in Plato's thought.

One of his principal contributions to philosophical thought is his 'theory of ideas'—divine types or forms of material objects, which ideas are alone real and permanent, while individual material things are but their ephemeral and imperfect imitations.

Plato's principal Dialogues were the 'Protagoras', 'Gorgias', 'Phaedo', 'Symposium', 'Republic', 'Phaedrus', 'Parmenides', 'Theaetetus', 'Sophist', 'Philebus', 'Timaeus', 'Laws', and the 'Apology'. Jowett's (q.v.) classic translation of the Dialogues appeared in 1871.

Platonic love, love of a purely spiritual character, free from sensual desire.

Platonic year, a cycle imagined by some ancient astronomers, in which the heavenly bodies were to return to their original relative positions; sometimes identified with the period of the revolution of the equinoxes (about 25,800 years).

Platonists, THE CAMBRIDGE, a group of philosophers, whose headquarters were Cambridge University, and who flourished in the middle of the 17th cent. The principal members of the group were Ralph Cudworth, Henry More, John Smith (1618-52), and Culverwel. They strongly influenced the poet Crashaw (q.v.).

Plautus, TITUS MACCIUS (*c.* 254-184 B.C.), the celebrated Roman comic poet. We possess twenty of his comedies, some of them imitations of Menander's plays. Several of his plays have been imitated by Molière, Shakespeare, and other modern writers. (See *Comedy of Errors.*)

Playboy of the Western World, The, a comedy by Synge (q.v.) (1907).

Plays for Puritans, a collection of three plays by G. B. Shaw (q.v.) (1901). The plays are 'The Devil's Disciple', 'Caesar and Cleopatra', and 'Captain Brassbound's Conversion'.

Plays, Pleasant and Unpleasant, a collection of seven plays (in two volumes) by G. B. Shaw (q.v.) (1898). The plays are (pleasant): 'Arms and the Man', 'Candida', 'The Man of Destiny', and 'You Never Can Tell'; (unpleasant): 'Widowers' Houses', 'The Philanderer', 'Mrs. Warren's Profession'.

Pleasant Satyre of the Thrie Estaitis in Commendatioun of Vertew and Vituperatioun of Vyce, Ane, a morality play by Sir D. Lindsay (q.v.), produced in 1540.

The play, which is extremely long, is written in various metres, eight- and six-lined stanzas and couplets. It is, as a dramatic representation, in advance of all contemporary English plays, and gives an interesting picture of the Scottish life of the time.

Pleasures of Hope, The, a poem by T. Campbell (q.v.) (1799).

The poem contains single lines that have become proverbial, such as

'Tis distance lends enchantment to the view,

and

Like angel-visits, few and far between.

Pleasures of Imagination, The, a didactic poem by Akenside (q.v.) (1744); it was completely rewritten and issued as 'The Pleasures of the Imagination' in 1757.

Akenside is indebted to Addison, Shaftesbury, and Hutcheson for the philosophical groundwork of his poem.

Pleasures of Memory, The, see *Rogers* (*S.*).

Pléiade, LA, a group of French poets of the latter part of the 16th cent., of whom Pierre de Ronsard and Joachim du Bellay were the most famous, animated by a common veneration for the writers of antiquity, and a desire to improve the quality of French verse. Their inauguration in France of the sonnet stimulated the interest in England in this form of verse. They had some influence on Spenser and others.

Pleiades, seven daughters of Atlas, who after their death were placed in heaven and form a group of stars. Their names were Alcyone, Merope, Maia, Electra, Taygete, Sterope, and Celaeno. The rising of the constellation was in May and its setting in November. Hence the connection with the showers of spring, the autumn seed-time, and autumn storms.

Pleydell, MR. COUNSELLOR PAULUS, a character in Scott's 'Guy Mannering' (q.v.).

Pliable, in Bunyan's 'The Pilgrim's Progress' (q.v.), one of Christian's companions, who turns back at the Slough of Despond.

Pliant, DAME, a character in Jonson's 'The Alchemist' (q.v.).

Pliny the Elder (GAIUS PLINIUS SECUNDUS) (A.D. 23-79), the author of the 'Historia Naturalis', and the intimate friend of Vespasian.

Pliny the Younger (GAIUS PLINIUS CAECILIUS SECUNDUS) (*b.* A.D. 61), nephew of the above, an advocate who held many public offices, was author of a 'Panegyricus' of Trajan, and of a number of delightful letters.

Plornish, MR. and MRS., characters in Dickens's 'Little Dorrit' (q.v.).

Plotinus (*c.* A.D. 203-62), born in Egypt, was the chief exponent of the Neoplatonic philosophy. After studying at Alexandria, he opened his school at Rome. He is generally described as a 'mystic', who developed Plato's teaching, and appears to have had some knowledge of oriental philosophies.

Plough-Monday, the first Monday after Epiphany. See *Plough Monday Play*.

Plough Monday Play, a folk-drama of the East Midlands. Like the St. George play, the Plough Monday play probably symbolizes, in its central incident, the death and resurrection of the year.

Plumdamas, PETER, a character in Scott's 'The Heart of Midlothian' (q.v.).

Plummer, CALEB and BERTHA, characters in Dickens's 'The Cricket on the Hearth' (q.v.).

Plutarch, the Greek biographer; the date of his birth is unknown, but according to

his own statement he was studying philosophy in A.D. 66. His great work is the 'Parallel Lives' of twenty-three Greeks and twenty-three Romans, arranged in pairs. These biographies are the source of the plots of many of our dramas, including some of Shakespeare's.

Sir Thomas North's version of them (1579) is a translation of the French rendering of Jacques Amyot. It is not a strictly accurate version, but is embellished by North's vivid English.

Pluto, another name of the god Hades (q.v.).

Plutus, the son of Demeter (q.v.), and the god of wealth.

Plymley, Peter, Letters of, by S. Smith (q.v.), published in 1807-8.

Plymouth Brethren, a religious body that arose at Plymouth, *c.* 1830. They have no formal creed (though believing in Christ) or official order of ministers.

Pocahontas or MATOAKA (1595-1617), an American-Indian princess. According to the untrustworthy account of Capt. John Smith (q.v.), one of the Virginia colonists, he was rescued by her when her father was about to slay him in 1607 (she was then only 12). In 1612 she was seized as a hostage by the colonists, became a Christian, and married a colonist, John Rolfe. She was brought to England in 1616, where she at first attracted considerable attention, but died neglected and in poverty in 1617. She is introduced by Ben Jonson in his 'The Staple of News' (q.v.), II. i. George Warrington, in Thackeray's 'The Virginians', composes a tragedy on her.

Pocket, HERBERT, a character in Dickens's 'Great Expectations' (q.v.).

Podsnap, MR., a character in Dickens's 'Our Mutual Friend' (q.v.), a type of self-satisfaction and self-importance.

Poe, EDGAR ALLAN (1809-49), born at Boston, Mass., was brought to England and sent to school at Stoke Newington, and was subsequently at the university of Virginia for a year. His first publication, 'Tamerlane, and other Poems', belongs to the year 1827. His poems met with no success and he turned to journalism. His 'Tales of the Grotesque and Arabesque' appeared in 1839; 'The Murders in the Rue Morgue' in 1841; 'The Gold Bug', dealing with the solution of a cryptogram, in 1843; 'The Raven', the first poem that brought him wide popularity, in 1845. His 'Ulalume' appeared in 1847; 'Annabel Lee', and 'The Bells', in 1849. Among his other remarkable tales may be mentioned 'The House of Usher', 1839; 'A Descent into the Maelstrom', 1841; 'The Masque of the Red Death' and 'The Mystery of Marie Roget', 1842; and 'The Cask of Amontillado', 1846. Poe also wrote much literary criticism.

Poeana, in Spenser's 'Faerie Queene', IV. viii. 49 et seq., the daughter of the giant Corflambo (q.v.).

Poema Morale, or *Moral Ode*, a poem in English of the period 1200-50, chiefly interesting for its metrical form, rhymed couplets of fourteen syllables.

Poems and Ballads, see *Swinburne* (*A. C.*).

Poetaster, The, a satirical comedy by Jonson (q.v.), produced in 1601. The scene is the court of Caesar Augustus, but the play deals with the quarrels and rivalries of the poets of Jonson's own day.

To the attack on Marston and Dekker the latter replied in 'Satiromastix' (q.v.).

Poetical Rapsody, A, a collection of Elizabethan verse, published by F. Davison (q.v.) and his brother Walter in 1602, and edited by Bullen in Arber's 'English Scholar's Library'. It includes 'The Lie', attributed to Sir Walter Ralegh, and poems by Greene, Wotton, Sidney, Spenser, Donne, and others.

Poetic diction, language and usage peculiar to poetry. The doctrine of a distinction between poetic and other language is of comparatively modern growth in English literature. Spenser, for example, was condemned for his use of archaisms in the 'Faerie Queene' by Jonson, who said that 'he writ no language': and in Elizabethan times the language of the dramas was at least likely to be used in prose if not in ordinary conversation. A conscious demarcation between the language of prose and poetry can be traced throughout the 17th cent. and was crystallized in the doctrine of 'correctness' of Pope and his followers. Though the language of the 'correct' school of poetry was not far divorced from that of prose, it did draw a definite line between the two. The vocabulary of poetry became highly standardized and remote from ordinary usage as a result, and the revolt of Wordsworth, as expressed in his early poems and in his prefaces to the 'Lyrical Ballads', was largely against this; though, in fact, his own poetic language was not always simply the 'language of ordinary men'. His views in this matter were repudiated by Coleridge and never consistently followed by Wordsworth; and, though poetry became less stilted in its language, its vocabulary remained on the whole distinctive throughout the Romantic and Victorian periods. A tendency to enlarge the poetic vocabulary, and to make it less remote from ordinary speech, has characterized poetry of the 20th cent.

Poet Laureate, the title given to a poet who receives a stipend as an officer of the Royal Household, his duty (no longer enforced) being to write court-odes, etc.

The first poet laureate in the modern sense was Ben Jonson, followed by D'Avenant, whose successor Dryden was the first to be given the title officially. The other laureates in chronological order are as follows: Shadwell, Tate, Rowe, Eusden, Cibber, Whitehead, T. Warton, Pye, Southey, Wordsworth, Tennyson, A. Austin, Bridges, Masefield, Day-Lewis, Betjeman (qq.v.).

Poetry Bookshop, see *Monro* (*H.*).

Poets' Corner, part of the south transept of Westminster Abbey containing the tombs or monuments of Chaucer, Spenser, Shakespeare, Ben Jonson, Milton, Drayton, Samuel Butler, and many later distinguished poets and authors.

Poggio Bracciolini, GIAN FRANCESCO

(1380-1459), Italian humanist, recovered many lost works of Roman literature.

Poins, in Shakespeare's '1 and 2 Henry IV' (q.v.), one of Falstaff's companions.

Poirot, HERCULE, the Belgian detective in Agatha Christie's (q.v.) stories of crime.

Polack, an obsolete name for a Pole, used by Shakespeare in 'Hamlet'.

Polite Learning, An Enquiry into the Present State of, see *Enquiry into the Present State of Polite Learning*.

Politian, see *Poliziano*.

Political Arithmetic, see *Petty*.

Politick Would-be, SIR and LADY, characters in Jonson's 'Volpone' (q.v.).

Polixenes, a character in Shakespeare's 'The Winter's Tale' (q.v.).

Poliziano, ANGELO (in English POLITIAN) (1454-94), the name assumed by AGNOLO AMBROGINI, Italian humanist and friend of Lorenzo the Magnificent (see *Medici*). He was one of the founders of modern textual criticism.

Pollente, in Spenser's 'Faerie Queene', v. ii, the 'cruel sarazin', slain by Sir Artegall.

Pollexfen, SIR HARGRAVE, the villain in Richardson's 'Sir Charles Grandison' (q.v.).

Pollux, see *Castor*.

Polly, a musical play by J. Gay (q.v.) (1729). Its production on the stage was prohibited by the lord chamberlain for its allusions to Walpole. The play is a sequel to 'The Beggar's Opera' (q.v.).

The principal characters are the Macheath and Polly Peachum of the earlier play, transported to the West Indies.

Polly, The History of Mr., see *Mr. Polly*.

Polo, MARCO (1254-1324), a member of a patrician family of Venice, accompanied his father and uncle in 1271 on an embassy from the Pope to Kublai, Grand Khan of Tartary, where Marco was employed on services of importance. After seventeen years in the territories of the Grand Khan, the Polos obtained permission to return home, eventually reaching Venice after an absence of twenty-four years. Marco

Polo's account of his travels was written while imprisoned by the Genoese. The work became very popular and was translated into many languages.

Polonius, a character in Shakespeare's 'Hamlet' (q.v.).

Poltergeist (from the German *polter*, noise, *geist*, spirit), a spirit that makes its presence known by noises.

Polybius (*c*. 204-122 B.C.), the friend of P. Cornelius Scipio Africanus Minor. He was enabled through his patronage to obtain access to materials for his great historical work (written in Greek). This begins at 264 B.C. with the Punic Wars, and extends to 146 B.C.

Polychronicon, The, see *Higden*.

Polydore, (1) in Shakespeare's 'Cymbeline' (q.v.), the name borne by Guiderius while in the Welsh forest; (2) a character in Otway's 'The Orphan' (q.v.).

Polydore Vergil, see *Vergil (P.)*.

Polyglot Bible, THE, edited in 1654-7 by Brian Walton (1600?-1661), bishop of Chester, with the help of many scholars. It contains various oriental texts of the Bible with Latin translations, and a critical apparatus.

Polyhymnia or POLYMNIA, the Muse (q.v.) of sacred song.

Polyhymnia, a poem by Peele (q.v.) written in 1590. It contains at the end the beautiful song 'His golden locks time hath to silver turned . . .' made widely known by Thackeray's quotation of it in 'The Newcomes'.

Polyneices, see *Eteocles*.

Poly-Olbion, The (this is the spelling of the first edition), the principal work of Drayton (q.v.). It was written between 1613 and 1622 and consists of thirty 'Songs' each of 300-500 lines, in hexameter couplets, in which the author endeavours to awaken his readers to the beauties and glories of their country. The first eighteen songs were annotated by John Selden (q.v.).

Polyphemus, one of the Cyclopes (q.v.), a son of Poseidon (q.v.). Odysseus and twelve companions returning from the

Trojan War, were seized by Polyphemus, who confined them in his cave. Odysseus intoxicated the Cyclops, put out his eye with a firebrand while he slept, and escaped from the cave by concealing himself in the wool under the belly of one of the rams of Polyphemus as they were let out to feed.

Polyxena, a daughter of Priam (q.v.) and Hecuba, who was loved by Achilles. When the Greeks were returning from the siege of Troy, the ghost of Achilles appeared to them and demanded her. Polyxena was accordingly sacrificed.

Pomfret, JOHN (1667-1702), chiefly remembered as the author of a poem, 'The Choice' (1700), which describes the kind of life and modest competence that the author would choose.

Pomona, an Italian goddess of gardens and fruit-trees.

Pompadour, MARQUISE DE (1721-64), mistress of Louis XV of France, believed to have exercised a great influence on French politics.

Pompeii, The Last Days of, see *Last Days of Pompeii.*

Pompey, naval slang for Portsmouth.

Pompey (GNAEUS POMPEIUS) (106-48 B.C.), surnamed 'The Great', a famous Roman general, formed with Julius Caesar and Crassus the first triumvirate in 60; became the leader of the aristocracy and conservative party, and began the civil war with Caesar in 49. He was defeated at Pharsalus in 48, and was shortly afterwards murdered in Egypt.

Pompey the Great, his faire Corneliaes Tragedy, a Senecan tragedy in blank verse by Kyd (q.v.) (1595).

'The Tragedy of Pompey the Great' is the title of a play by Masefield (q.v.).

Pompilia, in R. Browning's 'The Ring and the Book' (q.v.), the murdered wife of Count Guido Franceschini.

Pons Asinorum (Latin, the bridge of asses), a name given to the fifth proposition of the first book of Euclid, owing to the difficulty that beginners find in 'getting over' it.

Pooh-Bah, a character in Gilbert and Sullivan's opera, 'The Mikado'.

Poor Richard's Almanack, a series of almanacs, with maxims, issued by B. Franklin (q.v.), 1732-57. They attained remarkable popularity and were translated into many languages.

Poor Robin, the name of a facetious almanac, first published in 1661 or 1662.

Poor Tom, a name assumed by Edgar in Shakespeare's 'King Lear', III. iv.

Pooter, CHARLES, see *Diary of a Nobody.*

Pope, ALEXANDER (1688-1744), was the son of a Roman Catholic linen-draper of London. His health was ruined and his figure distorted by a severe illness at the age of 12. He showed his precocious metrical skill in his 'Pastorals' (1709), written, according to himself, when he was 16. He became intimate with Wycherley (q.v.), who introduced him to London life. His 'Essay on Criticism' (q.v., 1711), made him known to Addison's circle, and his 'Messiah' was published in 'The Spectator' in 1712. His 'Rape of the Lock' (q.v.) appeared in Lintot's 'Miscellanies' in the same year and was republished, enlarged, in 1714. His 'Ode for Music on St. Cecilia's Day' (1713), one of his rare attempts at lyric, shows that his gifts did not lie in this direction. In 1713 he also published 'Windsor Forest', which appealed to the Tories by its references to the Peace of Utrecht. He drifted away from Addison's 'little senate' and became a member of the 'Scriblerus Club', an association that included Swift, Gay, Arbuthnot, Atterbury (qq.v.), and others. He issued in 1715 the first volume of his translation in heroic couplets of Homer's 'Iliad'. This work, completed in 1720, though not an accurate version of the original, is one of the great poems of the age. It was supplemented in 1725-6 by a translation of the 'Odyssey', in which he was assisted by William Broome and Elijah Fenton.

In 1717 had appeared a collection of his works including the 'Verses to the Memory of an Unfortunate Lady' and 'Eloisa to

Abelard'. About this time he became strongly attached to Martha Blount (q.v.), with whom his intimacy continued throughout his life, and to Lady Mary Wortley Montagu (q.v.), whom in later years he assailed with bitterness.

Pope assisted Gay in writing the comedy 'Three Hours after Marriage' (1717). In 1723, four years after Addison's death, appeared Pope's portrait of Atticus, a satire on Addison, probably written some years earlier. An extended version of this appeared as 'A Fragment of a Satire' in a 1727 volume of the 'Miscellanies' (by Pope, Swift, Arbuthnot, and Gay), and it took its final form in 'An Epistle to Dr. Arbuthnot' (1735). In 1725 Pope published an edition of Shakespeare, the errors in which were pointed out in a pamphlet by Theobald (q.v.). This led to the selection of Theobald by Pope as the hero of his 'Dunciad' (q.v.), a satire on Dullness, in three books, of which the first edition appeared anonymously in 1728. A further enlarged edition was published in 1729, and the complete 'Dunciad' in four books appeared in 1743. In this Cibber replaces Theobald as the hero. Influenced by the philosophy of his friend Bolingbroke, Pope published a series of moral and philosophical poems, 'An Essay on Man' (q.v., 1733-4), consisting of four Epistles; and 'Moral Essays' (q.v.). In 1733 Pope published the first of his miscellaneous satires, 'Imitations of Horace'. The year 1735 saw the appearance of the 'Epistle to Dr. Arbuthnot', the prologue to the above Satires, one of Pope's most brilliant pieces of irony and invective, mingled with autobiography.

He was partly occupied during his later years with the publication of his earlier correspondence. He employed artifices to make it appear that it was published against his wish. Thus he procured the publication by Curll (q.v.) of his 'Literary Correspondence' in 1735, and then endeavoured to disavow him.

Pope, GIANT, see *Giant Pope*.
Pope Joan, see *Joan (Pope)*.

Popish Plot, THE, a plot fabricated in 1678 by Titus Oates. The existence of the plot was widely believed and great excitement prevailed. Many persons were falsely accused and executed.

Porch, THE, a name given to the Stoic school of Greek philosophy (see *Stoics*).

Pordage, SAMUEL (1633-91?), author of 'Azaria and Hushai' (1682), a feeble reply to Dryden's 'Absalom and Achitophel' (q.v.), and of 'The Medal Revers'd' (1682).

Porphyrius (233-*c*. 301), a Neoplatonic philosopher and opponent of Christianity.

Porrex, see *Gorboduc*.

Porsenna or **PORSENA, LARS** (6th cent. B.C.), a king of Etruria, who according to legend declared war against the Romans because they refused to restore Tarquin (q.v.) to the throne. He would have entered Rome but for the bravery of Horatius Cocles (q.v.) at the bridge.

Porson, RICHARD (1759-1808), Regius professor of Greek at Cambridge. He edited four plays of Euripides. 'His finest single piece of criticism' (Jebb) was his supplement to the preface to his 'Hecuba'. He advanced Greek scholarship by his elucidation of Greek idiom and usage, by his knowledge of Greek prosody, and by his emendation of texts. He was also famous as a lover of wine.

Porte, THE SUBLIME, the official title of the central office of the Ottoman government under the rule of the Sultans.

Porter, ENDYMION (1587-1649), became groom of the bed-chamber to Prince Charles and accompanied him and Buckingham on the visit to Spain in 1623. He was the friend and patron of poets, including Jonson, Herrick, D'Avenant, and Dekker (qq.v.), and the subject of their encomiums.

Porter, KATHERINE ANNE (1890-   ), American short-story writer. Her collections include 'Flowering Judas' (1930), 'Pale Horse, Pale Rider' (1939), and 'The Leaning Tower' (1944). Her powerful novel, 'Ship of Fools', appeared in 1962.

Porter, WILLIAM SYDNEY, see *Henry (O.)*.

Porthos, see *Three Musketeers*.

Portia, (1) the heroine of Shakespeare's 'The Merchant of Venice' (q.v.); (2) in his 'Julius Caesar' (q.v.), the wife of Brutus.

Portrait of a Lady, The, a novel by H. James (q.v.) (1881), one of the best of James's early works, in which he presents various types of American character transplanted into a European environment.

Poseidon, called NEPTUNE by the Romans, was according to Greek mythology a son of Cronos and Rhea, and brother of Zeus and Hades. He shared with them his father's empire, receiving as his portion the kingdom of the sea.

Positivist Philosophy, see *Comte.*

Posthumus Leonatus, a character in Shakespeare's 'Cymbeline' (q.v.).

Post-Impressionism, a term invented by Roger Fry (1866–1934) to cover the work of painters, particularly Cézanne, Gauguin, and van Gogh (qq.v.), who were opposed to the aims of Impressionism (q.v.).

Pot of Basil, The, see *Isabella, or the Pot of Basil.*

Pott, MR., in Dickens's 'The Pickwick Papers' (q.v.), editor of the 'Eatanswill Gazette'.

Potter, BEATRIX (MRS. WILLIAM HEELIS) (1866–1943), wrote and illustrated little story books for children, which became known as the 'Peter Rabbit' series. 'The Tale of Peter Rabbit' began with a letter to a small boy in 1893, was privately printed and sold in 1900, and published in its present form in 1902. It was followed by 'The Tailor of Gloucester' (her own favourite) in 1903, 'The Tale of Squirrel Nutkin', 'The Tale of Benjamin Bunny', and many others. The stories are the result of Beatrix Potter's love and knowledge of the countryside, combined with fantasy and humour. The animal characters are drawn sympathetically and shrewdly, never sentimentally. The illustrations are perfectly matched to the stories. Her 'Journal, 1881–1897' written in code was transcribed by Leslie Linder and published in 1966.

Pottyfar, MR., a character in Marryat's 'Midshipman Easy' (q.v.).

Poulter's measure, a fanciful name for a metre consisting of lines of twelve and fourteen syllables alternately, popularized by Gascoigne (q.v.) and others in the 16th century.

Pounce, PETER, a character in Fielding's 'Joseph Andrews' (q.v.).

Pound, EZRA LOOMIS (1885–1972), American poet. He came to Europe in 1908 and published his first volume of poems, 'A Lume Spento', in Italy. He then settled in London, where he became prominent in literary circles. He published several other volumes of verse including 'Personae' (1909), 'Canzoni' (1911), and 'Ripostes' (1912). With Richard Aldington and H. D. (Hilda Doolittle) he founded the so-called Imagist school of poets (see *Imagism*). Pound also championed the work of *avant-garde* writers and artists like Joyce and Eliot and Wyndham Lewis (qq.v.), whom he was always ready to assist critically and materially. Further volumes included the Chinese translations, 'Cathay' (1916), and 'Hugh Selwyn Mauberley' (1920). In 1920 he left England for Paris, and subsequently settled in Italy. There he worked on his long poem, the 'Cantos', of which the first thirty appeared between 1925 and 1930. He became increasingly preoccupied with economics, embraced Social Credit theories, and was persuaded that usura, or credit capitalism, lay at the root of all social and spiritual evils. His interpretations of these theories led him into anti-Semitism, and at least partial support for Mussolini's social programme in Italy. During the Second World War he broadcast over the Italian Radio: after giving himself up to American troops in 1945 he was charged with treason, but was found unfit to plead and confined to a mental institution. After his release in 1961 he returned to Italy. His critical writings are collected in 'Literary Essays of Ezra Pound' (1954).

Poundtext, THE REVD. PETER, in Scott's 'Old Mortality', a Presbyterian divine.

Povey, SAMUEL, a character in Bennett's 'The Old Wives' Tale' (q.v.).

Powell, ANTHONY DYMOKE (1905-), novelist. Much of his work is satirical, especially the early novels, 'Afternoon Men' (1931), 'Venusberg' (1932), 'From a View to a Death' (1933), 'What's Become of Waring?' (1939). 'The Music of Time' is a novel sequence: 'A Question of Upbringing' (1951), 'A Buyer's Market' (1952), 'The Acceptance World' (1955), 'At Lady Molly's' (1957), 'Casanova's Chinese Restaurant' (1960), 'The Kindly Ones' (1962), 'The Valley of Bones' (1964), 'The Soldier's Art' (1966), 'The Military Philosophers' (1968), 'Books do Furnish a Room' (1971), 'Temporary Kings' (1973), and 'Hearing Secret Harmonies' (1975).

Powys, JOHN COWPER (1872-1963), author and poet, the brother of Llewelyn and Theodore Francis (qq.v.). His writing expresses an individualistic philosophy, which interprets the meaning of life through ancient myths and elemental forces. His epic novel, 'A Glastonbury Romance' (1933), gives the legend of the Grail a modern context. His other works include the novels 'Wood and Stone' (1915), 'Ducdame' (1925), and 'Wolf Solent' (1929); critical and philosophical essays: 'The Meaning of Culture' (1930), 'The Pleasures of Literature' (1938), and 'The Art of Growing Old' (1948); poetry: 'Wolfsbane Rhymes' (1916), 'Mandragora' (1917), and 'Samphire' (1922). His 'Autobiography' was published in 1934.

Powys, LLEWELYN (1884-1939), essayist and novelist, brother of John Cowper and Theodore Francis (qq.v.). His essays and stories include 'Confessions of Two Brothers' (with J. C. Powys, 1916), 'Thirteen Worthies' (1923), 'Black Laughter' (1924), 'Ebony and Ivory' (1925), 'The Pathetic Fallacy' (a study of Christianity, 1930), 'A Pagan's Pilgrimage' (1931), and 'Dorset Essays' (1935). 'Apples be Ripe' (1930) and 'Love and Death' (1939) are novels.

Powys, THEODORE FRANCIS (1875-1953), novelist, brother of John Cowper and Llewelyn (qq.v.). In 1905 he settled for life in Dorset, the rural background of his allegorical stories of love and death, God and evil. His novels include 'Mr. Tasker's Gods' (1925), 'Mr. Weston's Good Wine' (1927), and 'Unclay' (1931). He also wrote short stories.

Poyser, MARTIN and MRS., characters in G. Eliot's 'Adam Bede' (q.v.).

Praed, WINTHROP MACKWORTH (1802-39), was called to the Bar and then entered parliament. He is remembered principally as a humorous poet, though like Hood, with whom he is naturally compared, he sometimes uses humour to clothe a grim subject.

Praeterita, Outlines of scenes and thoughts perhaps worthy of memory in my past life, an uncompleted autobiography by Ruskin (q.v.) (1885-9).

It tells of the influence on Ruskin of Copley Fielding (1787-1855) and Turner, of his childhood, of his first visit to the 'Gates of the Hills' (the Alps), of his travels in France and Italy, and of his friends, Dr. John Brown and Charles Eliot Norton.

Praetorian Guard, THE, at Rome, originally the *praetoria cohors* or select troops which attended the person of the praetor or general of the army; subsequently the force instituted by Augustus for the protection of Italy (where no legion was stationed). They acquired great political power, often, especially in the 3rd cent., deposing and elevating emperors.

Pragmatic sanction, the technical name given to some imperial and royal ordinances issued as fundamental laws. In more recent history it is applied particularly to the ordinance of the Emperor Charles VI in 1724, settling the succession to the territories of the House of Hapsburg.

Pragmatism, in philosophy, the doctrine that the test of the value of any assertion lies in its practical consequences.

Pratt, EDWIN JOHN (1882-1964), Canadian poet. He has published several narrative poems of considerable interest and power. Chief among them are 'The Roosevelt and the Antinoe' (1930), a story of a rescue at sea, 'The Titanic' (1935), 'Brébeuf and his Brethren' (1940), and 'Towards the Last Spike' (1952), an account of the building of the Canadian Pacific Railway.

Praxiteles (*b. c.* 390 B.C.), a great Greek sculptor, one of the leaders of a school which succeeded that of Phidias (q.v.).

Prayer, THE BOOK OF COMMON, see *Common Prayer.*

Précieuse, the French equivalent of our Blue Stocking (q.v.).

Prelude, The, an autobiographical poem, in fourteen books, by Wordsworth (q.v.), commenced in 1799 and completed in 1805, but not published until 1850, after the author's death.

It was meant to serve as a personal analysis and introduction to a long poem of which the 'Excursion' (q.v.) is a part. It is addressed to his friend Coleridge (q.v.). Wordsworth successively recalls his childhood, schooldays, his years at Cambridge, his first impressions of London, his first visit to France and the Alps, his residence in France during the Revolution (but not his connection with Annette), and his reaction to those various experiences. The full text, showing the alterations made by Wordsworth to it in his later years, was published by E. de Sélincourt (1926).

Pre-Raphaelite Brotherhood, a group of artists and critics—William Holman Hunt, John Everett Millais, Dante Gabriel Rossetti, William Michael Rossetti, Thomas Woolner, Frederick George Stephens, and James Collinson—who sought to infuse art with moral qualities through a scrupulous study of nature and the depiction of uplifting subjects. They published their doctrines in 'The Germ' (q.v.). The name of the group indicated that they considered that art from Raphael onwards was degenerate. The initials PRB were first used on Hunt's picture exhibited in 1849, and were adopted by the brotherhood.

Presbyterianism, a system of church government (the National Church of Scotland) in which no higher order than that of presbyter or elder is recognized, and all elders are ecclesiastically of equal rank. Each congregation is governed by its session of elders; these are subordinate to provincial Presbyteries, and these again are subordinate to the General Assembly of the Church.

Prescott, WILLIAM HICKLING (1796-1859), educated at Harvard, devoted himself to the study of ancient and modern literatures. His first work, 'The History of Ferdinand and Isabella', appeared in 1838. It was followed by the 'History of the Conquest of Mexico' (1843), and the 'History of the Conquest of Peru' (1847).

Present Discontents, Thoughts on the cause of the, a political treatise by E. Burke (q.v.) (1770).

In it Burke expounds for the first time his constitutional creed. He attributes the convulsions in the country to the control of parliament by a system of favouritism. He thinks the first requirement is the restoration of the right of free election, and looks for the restoration of party government.

Present State of the Nation, Observations on a late publication intituled the, a political treatise by E. Burke (q.v.) (1769), his first controversial publication on political matters. It is a reply to an anonymous pamphlet attributed to George Grenville.

Prester John, i.e. 'Priest John', the name given in the Middle Ages to an alleged Christian priest and king, originally supposed to reign in the extreme Orient, beyond Persia and Armenia, but from the 15th cent. generally identified with the king of Ethiopia.

Preston, THOMAS (1537-98), wrote 'A Lamentable Tragedy mixed full of Mirth conteyning the Life of Cambises, King of Percia' (1569), which illustrates the transition from the morality play to historical drama. The bombastic grandiloquence of the piece became proverbial.

Pretenders: THE OLD, James Francis Edward Stuart (1688–1766), son of James II; THE YOUNG, Charles Edward Stuart (1720–88), son of the Old Pretender.

Pretenders, The, an early play by Ibsen (q.v.).

Prévost D'Exiles, ANTOINE FRANÇOIS (1697–1763), generally known as the ABBÉ PRÉVOST, an industrious writer principally remembered for his novel, 'Histoire du Chevalier des Grieux et de Manon Lescaut' (1731).

Priam, the last king of Troy, was son of Laomedon, husband of Hecuba, and father of many sons (fifty according to Homer) and daughters, of whom the most famous were Hector, Paris, and Cassandra (qq.v.). Priam was slain by Neoptolemus (or Pyrrhus), the son of Achilles, after the fall of Troy.

Priapus, a god of fertility whose cult spread from the East to Greece and Italy. He was said to be the son of Aphrodite and Dionysus.

Price, FANNY, the heroine of Jane Austen's 'Mansfield Park' (q.v.).

Price, RICHARD (1723–91), a Unitarian minister in London, philosopher and writer on financial and political questions. He was the intimate friend of Franklin, and in 1778 was invited by Congress to transfer himself to America. He was denounced by Burke for his approbation of the French Revolution.

Pride and Prejudice, a novel by Jane Austen (q.v.). It was begun in 1796, and in its early form entitled 'First Impressions'. It was offered to Cadell, the publisher, in 1797, and refused. In its revised form it was published in 1813.

Mr. and Mrs. Bennet live with their five daughters at Longbourn in Hertfordshire. In the absence of a male heir, the property will pass by entail to a cousin, William Collins (q.v.), who has been presented to a rectory in the immediate vicinity of Lady Catherine de Bourgh's seat, Rosings, in Kent. Charles Bingley, a rich bachelor, takes a house near Longbourn, and brings there his two sisters and his friend, Fitzwilliam Darcy, nephew of Lady Catherine. Bingley and Jane, the eldest Bennet girl, fall mutually in love. Darcy, though attracted to her next sister, Elizabeth, offends her by his insolent behaviour. The aversion is intensified when Darcy and Bingley's sisters, disgusted with the impropriety of Mrs. Bennet and her younger daughters, effect the separation of Bingley and Jane.

Meanwhile Mr. Collins proposes to Elizabeth and is rejected. He promptly transfers his affections to Charlotte Lucas, a friend of the latter, who accepts him. Staying with the newly married couple at the parsonage, Elizabeth is again thrown into contact with Darcy. Strongly attracted to her in spite of himself, Darcy proposes to her in terms that do not conceal his pride. Elizabeth indignantly rejects him.

On a trip to the north of England with her uncle and aunt, Mr. and Mrs. Gardiner, Elizabeth visits Pemberley, Darcy's place in Derbyshire. Darcy welcomes the visitors, showing greatly improved manners. News reaches Elizabeth that her sister Lydia has eloped with Wickham, son of the steward of the Darcy property, an unprincipled adventurer. By Darcy's help the fugitives are traced, their marriage is brought about, and they are suitably provided for. The attachment between Bingley and Jane is renewed and leads to their engagement. In spite of the insolent intervention of Lady Catherine, Darcy and Elizabeth also become engaged.

Priestley, JOHN BOYNTON (1894–   ), novelist, playwright, and critic. His best-known novels are 'The Good Companions' (1929) and 'Angel Pavement' (1930). He contributed lives of Meredith and Peacock to the English Men of Letters series in 1926–7. His later work includes several successful plays, 'Laburnum Grove', 'Time and the Conways', etc.

Priestley, JOSEPH (1733–1804), published in 1768 his 'Essay on the First Principles of Government', advocating the view that the happiness of the majority is 'the great standard by which everything relating to' social life 'must finally be determined', the theory taken up and developed by Bentham.

Priestley was also a chemist. He was the discoverer of oxygen ('dephlogisticated air'), and author of 'The History and present State of Electricity' (1767) and of other works recording valuable investigations.

Prig, BETSEY, a character in Dickens's 'Martin Chuzzlewit' (q.v.).

Primas, the name given to Hugh of Orleans, a 12th-cent. poet who excelled in the writing of Latin lyrics which reveal both his scholarship and his love of wine, women, and gambling. Although he taught in Paris and Orleans and was admired by his contemporaries, his career was erratic and failed to bring a permanent position of honour.

Prime Minister, The, a novel by A. Trollope, see *Phineas Finn*.

Primrose, DR., the hero of Goldsmith's 'The Vicar of Wakefield' (q.v.). The other principal members of the family are: DEBORAH his wife; GEORGE their eldest son, who wanders about the Continent, much as Goldsmith himself did, seeking his fortune, then returns home, becomes a captain, and finally marries Miss Wilmot, an heiress; MOSES, the second son, a simpleton and a pedant, who, when sent to the fair to sell a horse, comes home with a gross of green spectacles in exchange; OLIVIA, the elder daughter, sprightly and commanding, who wished for many lovers; and SOPHIA, her sister, 'soft, modest, and alluring', who wished to secure one. All four children were 'equally generous, credulous, simple, and inoffensive'.

Primrose League, THE, was formed in 1883, in memory of Lord Beaconsfield, for the maintenance of Conservative principles. The anniversary of Lord Beaconsfield's death (19 April) is celebrated as 'Primrose Day'.

Primrose path, way to destruction; probably from two phrases of Shakespeare: 'primrose path of dalliance', 'Hamlet', I. iii. 47, and 'primrose way to the everlasting bonfire', 'Macbeth', II. iii. 22.

Primum Mobile (Latin, 'first moving thing'), the supposed outermost sphere, added in the Middle Ages to the Ptolemaic system of astronomy, and supposed to revolve round the earth from east to west in twenty-four hours, carrying with it the contained spheres.

Prince of the Power of the Air, Satan (Eph. ii. 2).

Princes in the Tower, THE, Edward V and Richard, duke of York, his brother. They were lodged in the Tower in 1483 and were there murdered, probably by order of their uncle, Richard III.

Prince's Progress, The, an allegorical poem by C. Rossetti (q.v.) (1866).

Princess, The, A Medley, a poem by Lord Tennyson (q.v.) (1847). The lyrics in it were added in the third edition, 1853.

A prince has been betrothed in childhood to the Princess Ida, daughter of the neighbouring King Gama. But the princess becomes a devotee of the rights of women, abjures marriage, and founds a university to promote her ideal. The prince and two companions, Cyril and Florian, gain admission to the university in the disguise of girl students. The deceit is detected by Princess Ida, and the three comrades are in peril of their lives, when the arrival of the prince's father with his army is announced. To decide the matter, a combat is arranged between fifty warriors led by the prince, and fifty led by King Gama's mighty son Arak. The latter are victorious, and the three comrades are laid wounded on the field. The university is turned into a hospital, the wounded are kindly tended, and the princess's heart is won.

The poem provided the plot for Gilbert and Sullivan's opera 'Princess Ida'.

Princesse de Clèves, La, a French romance (1678) by Mme de La Fayette

(1633-93). It initiated a new era in the history of the romance, and may be regarded as one of the first examples of the novel of character.

Princeton University, founded as a college for the middle American colonies (corresponding to Harvard and Yale for New England) under a charter of 1746, first at Elizabeth, N.J., transferred to Princeton in 1754.

Principall Navigations, Voiages and Discoveries of the English Nation, The, see *Hakluyt*.

Principia Mathematica, Philosophiae Naturalis, see *Newton*.

Principles of Moral and Political Philosophy, by Paley, see *Moral and Political Philosophy*.

Principles of Morals, Enquiry concerning the, by Hume, see *Treatise of Human Nature*.

Principles of Morals and Legislation, An Introduction to the, see *Bentham*.

Pringle, THOMAS (1789-1834), a friend of Sir Walter Scott (q.v.), and editor of 'The Edinburgh Monthly Magazine'. In 1819, the year in which his first volume of poems was published, he emigrated to South Africa, and is remembered chiefly as a poet of that country.

Prior, MATTHEW (1664-1721), was appointed secretary to the ambassador at The Hague and employed in the negotiations for the treaty of Ryswick. He joined the Tories and in 1711 was sent to Paris as a secret agent at the time of the peace negotiations, the subsequent treaty of Utrecht (1713) being popularly known as 'Matt's Peace'. He was recalled on Queen Anne's death and imprisoned for two years. A folio edition of his poems was brought out by his admirers after his release, by which he gained four thousand guineas. He was one of the neatest of English epigrammatists, and in occasional pieces and familiar verse he had no rival in English. Among his longer poems may be mentioned 'Henry and Emma', a paraphrase (or travesty) of the old ballad 'The Nut-Brown Maid'; 'Alma, or the Progress of the Mind', a dialogue, in three cantos, in the metre and manner of 'Hudibras'. He joined with Charles Montagu (Halifax) in writing 'The Hind and the Panther Transvers'd to the Story of the Country and City Mouse' (1687), a satire, after the manner of Buckingham's 'The Rehearsal' (q.v.), on Dryden's 'The Hind and the Panther' (q.v.). His more important prose works include 'Four Dialogues of the Dead' (q.v.).

Prioress's Tale, The, see *Canterbury Tales*.

Priscian, a Roman grammarian, who lived in the 6th cent. A.D., and taught at Constantinople. So 'to break Priscian's head' is to commit a grammatical fault.

Priscilla, the heroine of Longfellow's 'The Courtship of Miles Standish' (see *Miles Standish*).

Prisoner of Chillon, The, a poem by Lord Byron (q.v.) (1816).

The poem deals with the imprisonment of Bonnivard in the castle of Chillon, on the Lake of Geneva. François de Bonnivard was born in 1496, and conspired with a band of ardent patriots of Geneva to establish a free republic. For this he was twice imprisoned by the duke of Savoy.

Prisoner of Zenda, The, and its sequel 'Rupert of Hentzau', successful novels by Anthony Hope (see *Hawkins*) (1894 and 1898).

They deal with the perilous and romantic adventures of Rudolf Rassendyll, an English gentleman, in Ruritania, where, by personating the king at his coronation, he defeats a plot to oust him from the throne.

Pritchett, VICTOR SAWDON (1900-), author and critic, director of the 'New Statesman and Nation'. His stories show a shrewd understanding of the quirks of human behaviour and his criticism is fresh and stimulating. His novels include 'Clare Drummer' (1929), 'Dead Man Leading' (1937), and 'Mr. Beluncle' (1951). His short stories were published in a collected edition in 1956.

Private Presses are distinguished by aims that are aesthetic rather than commercial and by printing for the gratification of their owners rather than to order. Many such have been set up since the 17th cent. by amateurs of books or printing: that of Horace Walpole (q.v.) at Strawberry Hill (1757-97) is a well-known example. At the end of the 19th cent. presses of the kind were intended as a protest against the low artistic standards and degradation of labour in the printing trade. William Morris (q.v.) set up the Kelmscott Press with this object in 1891; and others, notably C. H. St. John Hornby (the Ashendene Press, 1895), Charles Ricketts (the Vale Press, 1896), and T. J. Cobden-Sanderson and Emery Walker (the Doves Press, 1900), followed him. In the 20th cent. the expression 'private press' has been applied, perhaps unjustifiably, to businesses specializing in producing books in the tradition of craftsmanship established by Morris.

Prize Novelists, Mr. Punch's, by Thackeray (q.v.), published in 'Punch' in 1847, and reissued as 'Novels by Eminent Hands' in 'Miscellanies' (1856), are parodies of Disraeli, Lever, Lytton, Mrs. Gore, G. P. R. James, and Fenimore Cooper.

Procne, see *Philomela*.

Procris, see *Cephalus*.

Procrustes, meaning 'the Stretcher', the surname of Polypemon or Damastes, a famous robber of Attica, who was killed by Theseus. He tied travellers on a bed, and if their length exceeded that of the bed, he cut short their limbs; but if the bed proved longer, he stretched them to make their length equal to it.

Procter, ADELAIDE ANNE (1825-64), daughter of B. W. Procter (q.v.), was author of 'Legends and Lyrics' (including 'A Lost Chord') (1858-61), etc.

Procter, BRYAN WALLER (1787-1874), was intimate with Leigh Hunt, Charles Lamb, Hazlitt, and Dickens, and had a considerable reputation as a writer, under the pseudonym of 'Barry Cornwall', of pretty songs.

Prodigal Son, THE, the subject of a group of plays written about 1540-75, showing the influence of the continental neo-classic writers of the period. The chief of these are 'Misogonus', written about 1560 (author unknown), and Gascoigne's 'Glasse of Government' (1575). The parable of the Prodigal Son is in Luke xv. 11-32.

Professor, The, a novel by C. Brontë (q.v.), written in 1846 (before 'Jane Eyre' and 'Shirley'), but not published until 1857.

The story, based on the authoress's experiences in Brussels, is in subject the same as that more successfully told in 'Villette' (q.v.).

Progress of Poesy, a Pindaric ode by Gray (q.v.), written in 1754 and published in 1757.

Prometheus, a son of Iapetus by Clymene (one of the Oceanides), and brother of Atlas and Epimetheus. Prometheus outwitted Zeus, climbed the heavens, and stole fire for men from the chariot of the sun. To avenge himself Zeus sent Pandora (q.v.) and her box to earth. Zeus, moreover, caused Prometheus to be chained to a rock on Mt. Caucasus, where during the daytime a vulture fed on his liver, which was restored each succeeding night. From this torture Prometheus was rescued by Hercules. To Prometheus mankind was believed to be indebted for many useful arts.

Prometheus Bound, a tragedy by Aeschylus, translated by E. B. Browning (q.v.).

Prometheus, the Firegiver, a poem by Bridges (q.v.).

Prometheus Unbound, a lyrical drama in four acts, by P. B. Shelley (q.v.) (1820).

Prometheus, the champion of mankind, is chained to a rock and subjected to perpetual torture. He remains unyielding to the threats of Jupiter (Zeus), the spirit of evil and hate. He is supported by Earth, his mother, and the thought of Asia, his bride, the spirit of Nature. Demogorgon, the Primal Power of the world, drives Jupiter from his throne, and Prometheus is released. The reign of love follows, when 'Thrones, altars, judgement-seats, and prisons' are things of the past.

Promos and Cassandra, see *Whetstone*.

Propertius, Sextus (*c.* 50–*c.* 16 B.C.), Roman elegiac poet, whose four extant books are concerned mainly with the successive phases of the poet's infatuation for a certain 'Cynthia'.

Proserpine, or, according to her Greek name, Persephone, was a daughter of Zeus and Demeter. She was carried off by Pluto (Hades) and made queen in the lower world. Demeter wandered over the earth seeking her. Finally Zeus allowed Persephone to spend six months of the year on earth and the remainder with Pluto, a myth symbolical of the burying of the seed in the ground and the growth of the corn.

Prosopopoia, the sub-title of Spenser's 'Mother Hubberd's Tale' (q.v.).

Prospero, in Shakespeare's 'The Tempest' (q.v.), the duke of Milan and father of Miranda.

Proteus, an old man of the sea, who tended the flocks of Poseidon. He had received the gift of prophecy from the god, but those who wished to consult him found him difficult of access, for he assumed various shapes at will.

Proteus, one of the 'Two Gentlemen of Verona' (q.v.) in Shakespeare's play of that name.

Prothalamion, a 'spousal verse' written by Spenser (q.v.) (1596) in celebration of the double marriage of the Lady Elizabeth and the Lady Katherine Somerset, daughters of the earl of Worcester.

Protomartyr, the first (Christian) martyr, St. Stephen.

Proudfute, Oliver, the bonnet-maker in Scott's 'The Fair Maid of Perth'.

Proudie, Dr. and Mrs., characters in A. Trollope's Barsetshire series of novels.

Proust, Marcel (1871–1922), French novelist. His famous novel, 'À la recherche du temps perdu', was published in seven sections, the last three appearing posthumously. It springs from a particular metaphysical conception of the unreality and reversibility of time, the power of sensation rather than intellectual memory to recover the past, and the subject's consequent power to cheat time and death. In earlier life, before anyone took Proust very seriously as an author, he published collections of essays and short stories as well as translations of Ruskin's 'Bible of Amiens' and 'Sesame and Lilies'. Fragments of a novel, 'Jean Santeuil', which contains much of 'À la recherche . . .' in embryo, and other fragments were found and published after his death (1952 and 1954).

Prout, Father, see *Mahony*.

Provençal or Langue d'oc, the language of the southern part of France (cf. *Langue d'oïl*), and the literary medium of the troubadours (q.v.). Their language was a class language, avoiding marked regional features. Provençal literature in the medieval period consisted chiefly of the lyric poetry composed by the troubadours for the feudal courts of the Midi, northern Italy, and Spain. The *canso*, the love song in the courtly style which was the troubadours' special achievement, was known all over western Europe, and gave rise to the courtly poetry of northern France, the Minnesang of Germany, and the Petrarchan poetry of Italy. This poetic flowering came to an end with the decline, after the Albigensian crusade, of the aristocratic society which had produced it.

An attempt made by the municipal authorities of Toulouse in the 14th cent. to revive Provençal as a literary language was unsuccessful. A more successful revival made in the 19th cent. by Frédéric Mistral (1830–1914) and others has led to a continuous production of literature in Provençal into the 20th cent., but the modern literary language is not unified and is based on peasant, not aristocratic usage.

Proverb, a short pithy saying in common or recognized use, often metaphorical or alliterative in form, held to express some truth ascertained by experience and familiar to all.

Examples occur in English literature from the Anglo-Saxon period onwards (cf. the A-S. collections of Gnomic verses). The use of proverbial sayings for learning either to read or write a language was a medieval as well as a modern custom, as is exemplified by early textbooks of rhetoric, etc. Collections of proverbs were popular, e.g. the 'Proverbs of Alfred' (q.v.), Erasmus's 'Adagia' (1500); and the Elizabethan period delighted in them and in the constant use of proverbs both in conversation and in writing. The greater sophistication of later periods has tended on the whole to displace them from literature and to regard proverbs as hackneyed forms of expression savouring of the 'cliché'.

Collections of proverbs were made by John Heywood (1546), William Camden, George Herbert ('Outlandish Proverbs', 1640), and John Ray (1670), among others. The standard work on the subject is the 'Oxford Dictionary of Proverbs' (1935, 2nd ed. 1948), with an introduction on the history and nature of proverbs by Janet Heseltine.

Proverbial Philosophy, see *Tupper*.

Proverbs of Alfred, a poem dating, in the form which has reached us, from the 13th cent., though much older in substance, containing instruction of various kinds, shrewd proverbs of popular origin, and religious teaching. The connection of the proverbs with King Alfred is more than doubtful.

Provok'd Husband, The, or a Journey to London, a comedy written by Vanbrugh (q.v.) and finished by Cibber (q.v.), produced in 1728.

Provok'd Wife, The, a comedy by Vanbrugh (q.v.), produced in 1697.

Prue: 'dear Prue' was Steele's (q.v.) familiar name for his second wife, Mary Scurlock.

Prunes and prism: 'Father is rather vulgar . . . Papa . . . gives a pretty form to the lips. Papa, potatoes, poultry, prunes, and prism, are all very good for the lips, especially prunes and prism.' (Dickens's 'Little Dorrit', II. v.)

Prynne, HESTER, the heroine of Hawthorne's 'The Scarlet Letter' (q.v.).

Prynne, WILLIAM (1600-69), Puritan pamphleteer, wrote against Arminianism from 1627, and endeavoured to reform the manners of his age. He published 'Histriomastix', an enormous work directed against stage-plays, in 1632. He was sentenced by the Star Chamber, in 1634, to be imprisoned during life. He was released by the Long Parliament, and his sentences declared illegal in Nov. 1640. He continued an active paper warfare, attacking Laud, then the independents, then the army (1647), then the government. In 1660 he asserted the rights of Charles II, and was thanked by him. He published altogether about two hundred books and pamphlets.

Psalmanazar, GEORGE (1679?-1763), a literary impostor, who gradually passed from ridicule to obscurity, although he still found patrons. He renounced his past life after a serious illness in 1728, became an accomplished Hebraist, and contributed to the 'Universal History'. Psalmanazar was regarded with veneration by Dr. Johnson.

Psalms, The, one of the books of the O.T. The Psalms were the basis of the medieval church services, probably the only book in the Bible on the use of which, by the laity, the medieval church imposed no veto at all. For the Prayer Book version of them, see *Coverdale*. A *Metrical Version* of the Psalms was begun by Sternhold (q.v.) and Hopkins (2nd ed., 1551). The complete *Old Version* (metrical) was published in 1562. The *New Version* by Dr. Nicholas Brady and Nahum Tate (q.v.) appeared in 1696.

Pseudodoxia Epidemica, see *Vulgar Errors*.

Psyche, see *Cupid and Psyche*.

Ptolemy (CLAUDIUS PTOLEMAEUS), who lived at Alexandria in the 2nd cent. A.D., was a celebrated mathematician, astronomer, and geographer. He devised the system of astronomy (according to which the sun, planets, and stars revolved round the earth) which was generally accepted until displaced by that of Copernicus. His work on this subject is generally known by its Arabic name of 'Almagest'.

Ptolemy Philadelphus (309-246 B.C.), king of Egypt, the son of Ptolemy Soter (the first king of the Ptolemaic dynasty, 323-285), is important in a literary connection as a patron of learning. In his reign Alexandria was the resort of the most distinguished men of letters of the time, and the celebrated Alexandrian Library, begun by his father, was increased. According to tradition the Septuagint (q.v.) version of the O.T. was made at his request.

Puccini, GIACOMO (1858-1924), a popular opera composer, born at Lucca. His most successful works were 'La Bohème' (1896), 'Tosca' (1899), 'Madame Butterfly' (1904).

Pucelle, La ('The Maid', i.e. Joan of Arc), a burlesque epic by Voltaire (q.v.) on the subject of Joan of Arc (q.v.), published in 1755. Joan is called 'la Pucelle' in Shakespeare's '1 King Henry VI' (q.v.).

Puck, originally an evil or malicious spirit or demon of popular superstition; from the 16th cent. the name of a fancied mischievous or tricksy goblin or sprite, called also Robin Goodfellow and Hobgoblin. In this character he figures in Shakespeare's 'A Midsummer Night's Dream' (II. i. 40) and Drayton's 'Nymphidia' (xxxvi).

Puff, a character in Sheridan's 'The Critic' (q.v.).

Pulci, LUIGI (1432-84), Florentine poet of the circle of Lorenzo de' Medici. His poem 'Morgante Maggiore' (q.v.) was the first romantic epic to be written by an Italian *letterato*.

Pulitzer Prizes, annual prizes established under the will of Joseph Pulitzer (1847-1911), an American newspaper proprietor of Hungarian birth, who used sensational journalism for the correction of social abuses. The prizes are confined to American citizens and offered in the interest of letters.

Pullet, MR. and MRS., characters in G. Eliot's 'The Mill on the Floss' (q.v.).

Pumblechook, MR., a character in Dickens's 'Great Expectations' (q.v.).

Pumpernickel, the name under which Thackeray satirizes the minor German principalities, particularly in 'Vanity Fair'.

Punch, or the London Charivari, an illustrated weekly comic periodical, founded in 1841.

Punch and Judy, a puppet-show drama probably introduced into England from the Continent towards the end of the 17th cent. Punch is generally a hump-backed, hook-nosed creature, dissipated, violent, and cunning. In a fit of anger he kills his child. His wife Judy, discovering the murder, attacks him with a bludgeon, but he wrests the weapon from her and kills her. The dog Toby seizes him by the nose, and he kills it. He is visited by a doctor when ill, kicks him, and when the doctor retaliates, bludgeons him to death. He is arrested and sentenced to death. He beguiles the hangman into putting his own head in the noose and promptly hangs him. Finally he is visited by the devil, whom he likewise vanquishes. The character of Punch may be in part derived from the Vice of the old Moralities.

Punch's Prize Novelists, Mr., see *Prize Novelists*.

Punic Faith, faithlessness. The Carthaginians were proverbial among the Romans for perfidy.

Puntarvolo, in Jonson's 'Every Man out of his Humour' (q.v.), a vainglorious knight.

Puppet-play, see *Motion*.

Purānas, THE, sacred mythological works in Sanskrit containing the mythology of the Hindus.

Purcell, HENRY (1658?-1695), one of the greatest of English composers. About

1690 he produced the music of 'Dido and Aeneas' (Nahum Tate (q.v.) composing the words), his best-known work. He wrote the incidental music for many plays and much church music.

Purchas, SAMUEL (1575?-1626), was rector of St. Martin's, Ludgate, London, 1614-26. In 1613 he published 'Purchas his Pilgrimage, or Relations of the World and the Religions observed in all Ages'; in 1619 'Purchas his Pilgrim, Microcosmus or the Histories of Man'; and in 1625 'Hakluytus Posthumus, or Purchas his Pilgrimes, contayning a History of the World in Sea Voyages and Land Travell by Englishmen and others'. This last is in part based on manuscripts left by Hakluyt (q.v.) and is a continuation of the latter's work.

Purgatorio, The, of Dante, see *Divina Commedia.*

Puritan, a member of that party of English Protestants who regarded the reformation of the Church under Elizabeth as incomplete, and called for its further 'purification'. In later times the term has become historical, without opprobrious connotation; but is also often used of one who affects extreme strictness in morals.

Puritan, The, or the Widow of Watling-Street, a comedy published in 1607 as 'written by W.S.' and included in the 3rd and 4th Shakespeare folios, but certainly by some other hand, perhaps John Marston (q.v.).

Puritans, Plays for, see *Plays for Puritans.*

Purley, The Diversions of, see *Tooke.*

Purple Island, The, a philosophical poem on the body, written in a Spenserian manner, by Phineas Fletcher (q.v.).

Pusey, EDWARD BOUVERIE (1800-82), was elected in 1822 a fellow of Oriel College, Oxford, where Keble and Newman (qq.v.) were also fellows. He joined them in the production of 'Tracts for the Times' (1833, see *Oxford Movement*), contributing tracts on baptism (1835) and the holy eucharist (1837). He supported Newman's explanation of the Thirty-nine Articles in the famous 'Tract XC', and in 1843 was

suspended from the office of university preacher for heresy. He continued to maintain high Anglican views while endeavouring to hinder secessions to the Church of Rome among his supporters. Later he attempted to bring about the union of the English and Roman churches.

Pushkin, ALEXANDER SERGEYEVICH (1799-1837), the national poet of Russia. A liberal aristocrat, he was exiled for some time from St. Petersburg for his political and atheistic writings. Though Pushkin's style reflects his classical education, his themes are largely Romantic, containing Byronic and folklore elements. His work consists of a large amount of lyric poetry; long narrative poems in various styles; one 'novel in verse', 'Eugenii Onegin' (1823-31) (his greatest work); one blank-verse historical drama, 'Boris Godunov' (1825). After 1830 Pushkin turned more to prose writing: 'The Tales of Belkin' (1830), 'The Queen of Spades' (1834), 'The Captain's Daughter' (1836), and 'The History of the Pugachov Rebellion' (1834).

Puttenham, RICHARD (1520?-1601?), author of 'The Arte of English Poesie', a critical discussion of English poetry, chiefly in its formal aspect, published anonymously in 1589. The work is sometimes assigned to his brother George.

Pye, HENRY JAMES (1745-1813), became poet laureate in 1790, and was the constant butt of contemporary ridicule.

Pygmalion, a king of Cyprus and a sculptor. He became enamoured of a beautiful statue that he had made of a woman, and at his request Aphrodite gave it life. The story is told in Ovid's 'Metamorphoses', in William Morris's 'Earthly Paradise' (q.v.), and is the subject of a comedy by W. S. Gilbert. 'Pygmalion' is also the title of a play by G. B. Shaw (q.v.).

Pygmies, a race of men of very small size, mentioned by ancient writers as inhabiting parts of Africa. In the last quarter of the 19th cent. dwarf races were ascertained to exist in equatorial Africa, who may be the 'pygmies' of Homer and Herodotus. According to ancient fable, the cranes came annually from Scythia and made war on them.

Pyke and **Pluck**, in Dickens's 'Nicholas Nickleby' (q.v.), the toadies of Sir Mulberry Hawk.

Pylades, see *Orestes*.

Pyramus, a youth of Babylon, who became enamoured of Thisbe. The two lovers, whom their parents forbade to marry, exchanged their vows through a chink in the wall which separated their two houses. They agreed to meet at the tomb of Ninus, outside the walls of Babylon. Thisbe came first to the appointed place, but being frightened by a lioness fled into a cave, dropping her veil, which the lioness covered with blood. Pyramus, arriving, found the bloody veil, and, concluding that Thisbe had been devoured, stabbed himself with his sword. Thisbe, emerging from the cave, distraught at the sight of the dying Pyramus, fell upon his sword. The story is the subject of the 'tedious brief scene' played by Bottom and his friends in 'A Midsummer Night's Dream' (q.v.).

Pyrochles, in Spenser's 'Faerie Queene', symbolizes rage.

Pyrocles, one of the chief characters in Sidney's 'Arcadia' (q.v.).

Pyrrhic, in ancient Greek and Latin verse, a foot consisting of two short syllables. In modern accentual verse, the term is sometimes applied to a group of two unstressed syllables.

Pyrrhic victory, a victory gained at too great a cost; in allusion to Pyrrhus (q.v.) and the battle of Asculum in which he routed the Romans but with the loss of the flower of his army.

Pyrrhus, (1) see *Neoptolemus*; (2) king of Epirus (318–272 B.C.), a great military adventurer, who carried on a series of campaigns against Rome, 280–275.

Pythagoras, the Greek philosopher, a native of Samos, lived in the 6th cent. B.C. He assigned a mathematical basis to the universe, and musical principles were also prominent in his system. He adopted the Orphic doctrine of metempsychosis or the transmigration of souls from man to man, or man to animal, or animal to man, in a process of purification or punishment. There are references to this Pythagorean doctrine in the dialogue between Feste and Malvolio ('Twelfth Night', IV. ii), in 'The Merchant of Venice', IV. i, and in 'As You Like It', iii. 2.

Pythia, the priestess of Apollo at Delphi (q.v.).

Pythian Games, see *Python* and *Delphi*.

Pythias, see *Damon and Pythias*.

Python, a serpent which was said to have guarded the ancient shrine at Delphi; it was slain by Apollo, who established the Pythian Games to celebrate the event.

Q

'Q', see *Quiller-Couch*.

Quadrille, a card game played by four persons with forty cards (the eights, nines, and tens being discarded). It replaced ombre (q.v.) as the fashionable game about 1726, and was in turn superseded by whist. The square dance called *quadrille* is of French origin.

Quadrivium, in the Middle Ages, the higher division of the seven liberal arts, the mathematical sciences (arithmetic, geometry, astronomy, and music); see *Trivium*.

Quakers, members of the religious society (the Society of Friends) founded by George Fox in 1648–50.

Quaritch, BERNARD (1819–99), bookseller and author of the valuable bibliographical work, 'A General Catalogue of Old Books and MSS.' (1887-9; index, 1892).

Quarles, FRANCIS (1592-1644), metaphysical poet, went abroad in the suite of the Princess Elizabeth, daughter of James I, on her marriage with the Elector Palatine. He wrote pamphlets in defence of Charles I, which led to the sequestration of his property. He is chiefly remembered for his 'Emblems' (q.v., 1635).

Quarterly Review, The, was founded in Feb. 1809 by J. Murray (q.v.), as a Tory rival to 'The Edinburgh Review' (q.v.). The liberal, conciliatory, and impartial lines on which it should be run were indicated by Sir W. Scott, in a letter to Gifford (q.v.), the first editor. Gifford was succeeded by Sir J. T. Coleridge (nephew of the poet) and Lockhart (q.v.). Among famous contributors to it have been Sir W. Scott, Canning, Southey, Rogers, Lord Salisbury, and Gladstone. Sir J. Barrow was a pillar of the Review during the years 1809-48. Special interest attaches to Scott's favourable review in it of Jane Austen's 'Emma', and to Scott's review (Jan. 1817) of his own 'Tales of My Landlord'; also to Croker's article (in 1818) on Keats's 'Endymion', which was supposed to have hastened the poet's death in 1821.

Quarto, the size of a volume in which the sheets are folded twice, so that each leaf is a quarter of the sheet.

Quatrain, a four-lined stanza. The most common arrangement of lines is that of four iambic pentameters, rhyming a b a b —the stanza of Gray's 'Elegy'. This has been called the *heroic quatrain* (cf. *heroic couplet*) although the term has no recognized currency. Tennyson's 'In Memoriam' quatrain, rhyming a b b a, adapted from Herbert of Cherbury (q.v.), is less familiar and less successful. FitzGerald's Omar Khayyám quatrain, rhyming a a b a, was brilliantly successful for its one particular occasion but has never been generally used.

Queen Anne's Bounty, a fund formed out of the first-fruits and tenths of clerical livings, vested by Queen Anne in trustees for the augmentation of poor livings.

Queen Mab, in Shakespeare's 'Romeo and Juliet' (q.v.), I. iv, 'the fairies' midwife'. In Drayton's 'Nymphidia' (q.v.) she is Oberon's wife and queen of the fairies. For Shelley's poem 'Queen Mab', see below.

Queen Mab, a poem by P. B. Shelley (q.v.), surreptitiously published in 1813.

This poem, written by Shelley when he was eighteen, is a crude and juvenile production. The fairy, Queen Mab, carries off in her celestial chariot the spirit of the maiden Ianthe, and shows her the past history of the world and expounds to her the causes of its miserable state. The fairy finally reveals the future state of a regenerate world.

Queen Mary, a historical drama by Lord Tennyson (q.v.) (1875).

The play presents the principal events of the reign of Mary Tudor.

Queen of Cornwall, The Famous Tragedy of the, a drama by Hardy (q.v.) on the story of King Mark, the two Iseults, and Tristram, produced in 1923.

Queen of the May, see *May Day*.

Queen's Maries or MARYS, THE, the four ladies named Mary, attendant on Mary Queen of Scots. The list is variously given, including: Mary Seton, Mary Beaton, Mary Livingstone, Mary Fleming, Mary Hamilton, and Mary Carmichael. They are frequently mentioned in Scottish ballads.

Queen's Wake, The, a poem by J. Hogg (q.v.), published in 1813.

Quentin Durward, a novel by Sir W. Scott (q.v.) (1823).

The scene is laid in the 15th cent. and the principal character is Louis XI of France. With him is contrasted his vassal and enemy, Charles the Bold of Burgundy. The story is concerned with the intrigues by which Louis attempts to procure, with the assistance of William de la Marck, the Wild Boar of the Ardennes, the revolt of Liège against Charles; and with the famous visit of Louis to Charles at Peronne and their temporary reconciliation. The romance of Quentin Durward (a young Scot of good family) is subordinate to these.

Questing Beast, THE, in Malory's 'Morte Darthur' (q.v.), pursued by Palamedes the Saracen.

Quickly, MISTRESS, in Shakespeare's 'The Merry Wives of Windsor' (q.v.), the servant of Dr. Caius.

Quickly, MISTRESS NELL, in Shakespeare's '2 Henry IV' and 'Henry V' (qq.v.), hostess of the Boar's Head Tavern in Eastcheap.

Quietism, a form of religious mysticism (originated prior to 1675 by Miguel Molinos, 1640–96), consisting in passive devotional contemplation. One of the best-known exponents of Quietist doctrines was Fénelon (q.v.).

Quiller-Couch, SIR ARTHUR THOMAS (1863–1944), became professor of English literature at Cambridge in 1912. His publications (most of them under the pseudonym 'Q') include: 'Dead Man's Rock' (1887), 'Troy Town' (1888), 'The Oxford Book of English Verse' (1900,

1939), 'Studies in Literature' (1918, 1922), etc. He wrote the conclusion of Stevenson's unfinished 'St. Ive's' (chs. 31 to the end) in 1899.

Quilp, DANIEL and MRS., characters in Dickens's 'The Old Curiosity Shop' (q.v.).

Quin, JAMES (1693–1766), an actor who took leading parts in tragedy. He was the last of the old school of actors, which gave place to that of Garrick.

Quinapalus, invented by the clown in Shakespeare's 'Twelfth Night' (q.v.) (I. v), as authority for a saying of his own.

Quince, PETER, in Shakespeare's 'A Midsummer Night's Dream' (q.v.), a carpenter.

Quintilian (MARCUS FABIUS QUINTILIANUS) (*c*. A.D. 35–*c*. 100), a great Roman rhetorician. His chief work was the 'De Institutione Oratoria', the tenth book of which contains a history of Greek and Roman literature.

Quinze Joyes de Mariage, Les, a famous 15th-cent. French satire on women, of uncertain authorship.

Quixote, see *Don Quixote*.

Quos ego . . ., from Virgil's 'Aeneid', i. 139, words proverbial for an implied threat.

R

Ra, in Egyptian mythology, the sun-god and supreme deity, generally represented as a hawk.

Rab and his Friends, see *Brown (Dr. J.)*.

Rabbi Ben Ezra, a poem by R. Browning (q.v.) included in 'Dramatis Personae' (q.v.). It is an exposition of the author's religious philosophy through the mouth of a learned Jew.

Rabelais, FRANÇOIS (1494?–1553), French humanist, satirist, and physician, took his medical degrees at Montpellier,

and practised and lectured on medicine at Lyons. He published 'Pantagruel' (q.v.) in 1532, 'Gargantua' (q.v.) in 1534, the 'Third Book' in 1546, part of the 'Fourth Book' in 1548, and the whole in 1552. The posthumous 'Fifth Book' is probably not authentic.

The first three books of his chief work were translated into English by Urquhart (q.v., two being published in 1653, the third in 1693); the last two by Motteux (q.v.) in 1693–4.

Racine, JEAN (1639-99), French dramatic poet. As a tragedian, he presented his characters in a more human and natural form than did Corneille, and depicted the society around him. 'Phèdre' (1677) and 'Athalie' (1691) were his greatest works.

Radcliffe, MRS. ANN (1764-1823), *née* Ward, a novelist whose fame rests on her 'Romance of the Forest' (1791), 'The Mysteries of Udolpho' (q.v., 1794), and 'The Italian' (1797). Mrs. Radcliffe's method, which found a number of imitators, was to arouse terror and curiosity by events apparently supernatural, but afterwards explained by natural means.

Radigund, in Spenser's 'Faerie Queene', v. iv-vii, a queen of the Amazons.

Raeburn, SIR HENRY (1756-1823), a Scottish portrait-painter, sometimes called the 'Scottish Reynolds'.

Ragnar Lodbrog, The Death-Song of, an old Icelandic poem translated by T. Percy (q.v.). Its publication exerted a great literary influence and stimulated the study in England of ancient Norse writings.

Ragnarök, in Scandinavian mythology, the day of the great battle between the gods and the powers of evil, in which both are to be destroyed.

Ragnel, a devil in medieval mystery plays.

Ralegh or RALEIGH, SIR WALTER (1552?-1618), son of a Devonshire gentleman, served in the Huguenot army (1569), and was engaged in various voyages of discovery and expeditions to the American continent. He obtained the favour of Queen Elizabeth, but forfeited it and was committed to the Tower (1592). After a most unfair trial he was condemned to death, respited, and again sent to the Tower in 1603 on a charge of conspiring against James I. He lived there with his wife and son until 1616, when he was permitted to undertake an expedition to the Orinoco in search of gold. On the failure of the expedition, Ralegh was arrested, and executed at Westminster on 29 Oct. 1618. Much of his poetry is lost. About thirty short pieces survive, the principal of which is a fragment of a long elegy entitled

'Cynthia, the Lady of the Sea', expressing devotion to Elizabeth. The well-known short pieces, 'The Lie', and 'The Pilgrimage', were probably written during his imprisonments. In prose he published 'A Report of the Truth of the Fight about the Isles of the Azores' (1591), which contains a narrative of the famous encounter of Sir Richard Grenville with the Spanish fleet. His 'History of the World' (1614) was designed for Prince Henry, who showed sympathy with Ralegh and visited him in the Tower. The first volume, which alone was completed, deals with the history of the Jews, early Egyptian history, and with Greek and Roman times down to 130 B.C. In addition he wrote many essays on political subjects, some of which were published after his death.

Raleigh, SIR WALTER (1861-1922), professor of English literature at Oxford from 1904. Among his critical works are lives of Milton (1900), Wordsworth (1903), Shakespeare (1907); 'Some Authors' (posthumous, 1923), etc.

Ralpho, the squire in Butler's 'Hudibras' (q.v.).

Ralph Roister Doister, the earliest known English comedy, by Udall (q.v.), probably written about 1553 and printed about 1567, and perhaps played by Westminster boys while Udall was headmaster of that school. The play, in short rhymed doggerel, represents the courting of the widow Christian Custance, who is betrothed to Gawin Goodluck, an absent merchant, by Roister, a swaggering simpleton, instigated thereto by the mischievous Matthew Merygreek. Roister is repulsed and beaten by Custance and her maids; and Goodluck, after being deceived by false reports, is reconciled to her. The play shows similarity to the comedies of Plautus and Terence.

Ralph the Rover, see *Inchcape Rock.*

Ram, THE, or ARIES, one of the zodiacal constellations, and the zodiacal sign entered by the sun on 21 April.

Rāma, see *Rāmāyana.*

Ramadan, one of the months of the

Arabian year, during which Muslims fast from sunrise to sunset.

Rāmāyana, The, one of the two great Hindu epic poems, the other being the 'Mahābhārata' (q.v.), composed, it is thought, not later than 500 B.C.

Rambler, The, a periodical in 208 numbers issued by S. Johnson (q.v.) from 20 March 1749/50 to 14 March 1751/2.

The contents are essays on all kinds of subjects, character-studies, allegories, criticism, etc., and were, with the exception of five, all written by Johnson himself. Their object was the instruction of his readers in wisdom or piety, and at the same time the refinement of the English language.

Ramsay, ALLAN (1686-1758), a Scottish poet, and subsequently bookseller by trade. He wrote elegies, partly pathetic, partly humorous, and satires. In 1724-32 he issued collections of old Scottish and English songs, with some by himself and contemporary poets.

Ramsay, MARGARET, a character in Scott's 'The Fortunes of Nigel' (q.v.).

Randolph, THOMAS (1605-35), made the acquaintance of Ben Jonson and, after becoming famous in Cambridge as a writer of English and Latin verse, went to London in 1632. His principal plays are 'Amyntas', a pastoral comedy, and 'The Muse's Looking-Glasse', printed in 1638; and 'Hey for Honesty', printed in 1651. He was also the author of a pleasant eclogue included in 'Annalia Dubrensia' (see *Cotswold Games*).

Ranke, LEOPOLD VON (1795-1886), a celebrated German historian. Of his numerous works his history of 'The Popes of Rome' (1834-6) is best known in England.

Rape of the Lock, The, a poem by Pope (q.v.), in two cantos, published in Lintot's 'Miscellany' in 1712; subsequently enlarged to five cantos and thus published in 1714.

Lord Petre having forcibly cut off a lock of Miss Arabella Fermor's hair, the incident gave rise to a quarrel between the families. With the idea of allaying this, Pope treated the subject in a playful mock-heroic poem, on the model of Boileau's 'Le Lutrin'. He presents Belinda at her toilet, a game of ombre, the snipping of the lock while Belinda sips her coffee, the wrath of Belinda and her demand that the lock be restored, the final wafting of the lock, as a new star, to adorn the skies. The poem was published in its original form with Miss Fermor's permission. Pope then expanded the sketch by introducing the machinery of sylphs and gnomes, and its renewed publication gave offence to the lady, who thought that her affairs had been sufficiently brought before the public.

Raphael, one of the archangels (see *Angel*).

Raphael (RAFFAELLO SANZIO) (1483-1520), Italian painter. He worked in Perugino's studio and then in Florence. He succeeded Bramante as architect of St. Peter's. Seven of his cartoons for tapestries for the Sistine Chapel were bought by Charles I. He employed assistants to cope with the great number of commissions he received.

Rashdall, THE VERY REVD. HASTINGS (1858-1924), philosopher, theologian, and historian. His philosophical works include 'The Theory of Good and Evil' (1907). 'The Universities of Europe in the Middle Ages' (1895, new edition, ed. Powicke and Emden, 1936) is a standard work.

Raspe, RUDOLPH ERICH, see *Munchausen.*

Rasselas, Prince of Abyssinia, The History of, a didactic romance by S. Johnson (q.v.) (1759).

It was composed in the evenings of a week to defray the expenses of the funeral of Johnson's mother and to pay her debts. It is an essay on the 'choice of life' and consists mainly of dissertations strung on a thin thread of story. Rasselas, a son of the emperor of Abyssinia, weary of the joys of the 'happy valley', escapes to Egypt, accompanied by his sister Nekayah and the much-travelled old philosopher Imlac. Here they study the various conditions of men's lives, and, after a few incidents of no great interest, return to Abyssinia. The charm of the work lies in the wisdom, humanity, and melancholy of the episodes and disquisitions, enlivened with a few gleams of humour.

Ratcliffe, JAMES, a character in Scott's 'The Heart of Midlothian' (q.v.).

Rat, the Cat, and Lovel the dog, THE, in the political rhyme, refers to three adherents of Richard III: Sir Richard Ratcliffe (killed at Bosworth, 1485), Sir John Catesby (d. 1486), and Francis, first Viscount Lovell (1454-88?).

Rattlin the Reefer, a novel of the sea by Edward Howard (d. 1841), published in 1836, and wrongly attributed to Marryat.

Ravel, MAURICE (1875-1937), one of the most prominent French composers of his time.

Raven, The, a poem by Poe (q.v.).

Ravenshoe, a novel by H. Kingsley (q.v.) (1861).

Ravenswood, EDGAR, MASTER OF, the hero of Scott's 'The Bride of Lammermoor'.

Rawlinson, GEORGE (1812-1902), a fellow of Exeter College, Oxford, was Camden professor of ancient history, 1861-89. He was author of 'The History of Herodotus' (1858-60), a translation accompanied by valuable historical and ethnological notes.

Rawlinson, SIR HENRY CRESWICKE (1810-95), is remembered chiefly as an Assyriologist. He deciphered the great Behistun inscription in 1846.

Rawlinson, THOMAS (1681-1725), a book-collector, whose manuscripts are in the Bodleian Library. He was satirized by Addison in the 'Tatler' (No. 158) as 'Tom Folio'.

Read, SIR HERBERT (1893-1968), poet and critic of art and literature. After distinguished war service he was Assistant Keeper at the Victoria and Albert Museum, 1922-31, and professor of fine art at Edinburgh, 1931-3. His poetry includes 'Naked Warriors' (1919; a collection of war poems), 'Collected Poems 1913-25' (1926), 'The End of a War' (1933), 'Poems 1914-34' (1935), and 'Collected Poems' (1946, 2nd edn. 1953). His critical writing includes 'English Prose Style' (1928), 'Form in Modern Poetry' (1932), 'Art and Industry' (1934), 'Education through Art' (1943), and 'The True Voice of Feeling' (1953). 'The Innocent Eye' (1933) and 'Annals of Innocence and Experience' (1940; enlarged edn., including 'The Innocent Eye' and 'In Retreat', 1946) are autobiographical.

Reade, CHARLES (1814-84), began his literary career as a dramatist, his most successful play 'Masks and Faces' appearing at the Haymarket in 1852. This he turned into a novel with the title 'Peg Woffington' (1853). The pleasant romance 'Christie Johnstone' and the propagandist novel 'It is Never too Late to Mend' appeared also in 1853, and were followed by 'The Course of True Love never did run Smooth' (1857) and 'Jack of all Trades' (1858), stories of strange avocations, in the manner of Defoe; 'The Cloister and the Hearth' (q.v., 1861), Reade's greatest work; 'Hard Cash' (1863); 'Griffith Gaunt' (1866); 'Foul Play' (1869); 'Put Yourself in his Place' (1870); and 'A Terrible Temptation' (1871). Reade also wrote with Tom Taylor 'The Courier of Lyons' (1854), the well-known melodrama frequently produced by Sir H. Irving under the name of 'The Lyons Mail'.

Reade was an admirable story-teller and an ardent social reformer.

Reade, WILLIAM WINWOOD (1838-75), traveller, novelist, and controversialist, nephew of Charles Reade (q.v.). He made exploratory voyages in West and South-West Africa in 1861 and 1869, and was special correspondent of 'The Times' in the Ashanti War. He published 'Savage Africa' in 1863 and 'The African Sketchbook' in 1873. 'The Martyrdom of Man' (1872, and many subsequent editions) contains his criticism of religious beliefs.

Ready-to-Halt, MR., a pilgrim who follows Mr. Greatheart in Bunyan's 'The Pilgrim's Progress' (q.v.).

Realism, in scholastic philosophy, the doctrine that attributes objective or absolute existence to universals, of which Thomas Aquinas (q.v.) was the chief exponent. Also in the arts a term meaning truth to the observed facts of life.

Reasonableness of Christianity, see *Essay concerning Human Understanding.*

Rebecca, a character in Scott's 'Ivanhoe' (q.v.).

Rebecca and Rowena, a Romance upon Romance, by Mr. Michael Angelo Titmarsh, a humorous sequel to Scott's 'Ivanhoe' (q.v.), by Thackeray (q.v.), published in 1850.

Recluse, The, see *Excursion.*

Record Office, PUBLIC: before the construction of the present office in Fetter Lane, the national records were kept in the Tower of London and Rolls House. Among important keepers of the records may be mentioned Selden, Prynne, and Sir F. Palgrave (qq.v.).

Recruiting Officer, The, a comedy by Farquhar (q.v.), produced in 1706.

Red Badge of Courage, The, by Stephen Crane (q.v.) (1895), is the author's best-known work, a study of an inexperienced soldier's reactions to the ordeal of battle during the American Civil War.

Red Book of Hergest, see *Hergest.*

Redburn, by H. Melville (q.v.) (1849), a largely autobiographical narrative dealing with the period of the author's voyage to Liverpool in 1837.

Red Cotton Night-Cap Country, or, Turf and Towers, a poem by R. Browning (q.v.) (1873).

Red Cross Knight, THE, in Bk. I of Spenser's 'Faerie Queene' is Saint George, the patron saint of England. He is the 'patron' or champion of Holiness, and represents the Anglican Church.

Redgauntlet, a novel by Sir W. Scott (q.v.) (1824).

The story is concerned with an apocryphal return of Prince Charles Edward to England some years after 1745, to try once more his fortunes, an attempt that meets with inglorious failure. Though not generally accounted one of the three or four greatest Waverley novels, 'Redgauntlet' (written in the last years of Scott's prosperity) contains some of his finest writing, notably in 'Wandering Willie's Tale', a perfect example of the short story.

Redlaw, a character in Dickens's 'The Haunted Man' (q.v.).

Red Riding-Hood, Little, a popular tale, translated from the French of Perrault (q.v.) by Robert Samber (1729?).

Reeve, CLARA (1729–1807), a disciple of Horace Walpole as a novelist, published 'The Champion of Virtue, a Gothic Story', her best-known work, in 1777. The title was changed to 'The Old English Baron' in the second edition.

Reeve's Tale, The, see *Canterbury Tales.*

Reflections on the Revolution in France, see *Revolution in France.*

Reformation, THE, the great religious movement of the 16th cent., having for its object the reform of the doctrines and practices of the Church of Rome, and ending in the establishment of the various Reformed or Protestant churches of central and north-western Europe. Its principal leaders were Luther in Germany, Calvin in Geneva, Zwingli in Zürich, and Knox in Scotland.

Reformation, History of the, see *Knox (J.).*

Reform Bill, a bill for widening the parliamentary franchise and removing inequalities and abuses in the system of representation, introduced by Lord John Russell (a member of Lord Grey's government) in 1831 and carried after an acute struggle in 1832.

Regan, in Shakespeare's 'King Lear' (q.v.), the second of Lear's daughters.

Regency, THE, in English history, the period (1811–20) during which George, Prince of Wales, acted as Regent, owing to the insanity of George III.

Regicide Peace, Letters on a, by E. Burke (q.v.), the first two published in 1796, the third in 1797, the fourth posthumously in the collected works.

By the end of 1796 France had reached a dominating position on the Continent. In Oct. 1796 Pitt sent Lord Malmesbury to Paris to negotiate a peace, but his proposals were scornfully rejected. It was in these circumstances that Burke wrote these letters, which purport to be addressed to a member of parliament. Their theme is the necessity for stamping out the Jacobin government of France; the futile and humiliating character of the negotiations undertaken; and the ability of England from an economic standpoint to carry on the struggle.

Regillus, Lake, see *Lake Regillus*.

Regulus, MARCUS ATILIUS, Roman consul in 267 and 256 B.C. Having been taken prisoner by the Carthaginians, he was allowed to accompany an embassy to Rome on condition that he should return if the Carthaginian proposals were not accepted. He advised the senate not to consent to peace, and when he returned to Carthage, was put to death with torture. (See Horace, 'Odes', III. v.)

Rehearsal, The, a farcical comedy attributed to George Villiers, second duke of Buckingham, but probably written by him in collaboration with others, among whom is mentioned S. Butler (q.v.). It was printed in 1672.

The play is designed to satirize the heroic tragedies of the day, and consists of a series of parodies of passages from these, strung together in an absurd heroic plot. The author of the mock play is evidently a laureate (hence his name 'Bayes'), and D'Avenant (q.v.) was probably intended; but there are also hits at Dryden (q.v.) (particularly his 'Conquest of Granada') and his brothers-in-law, Edward and Robert Howard.

Reid, THOMAS (1710-96), professor of moral philosophy at Aberdeen (1751) and at Glasgow University (1764). He published his 'Inquiry into the Human Mind' in 1764, his essay on the 'Intellectual Powers' in 1785, and that on the 'Active Powers' in 1788. He is the leading representative of the school of 'common sense',

and contested the view of Locke, Berkeley, and Hume (qq.v.).

Reid, THOMAS MAYNE (1818-83), novelist; author of 'The Rifle Rangers' (1850), 'The Scalp-Hunters' (1851), 'The Headless Horseman' (1866), etc.

Reign of Terror, THE, or THE TERROR, the period of ruthless executions during the First French Revolution from March (or according to another view June) 1793 to July 1794.

Rejected Addresses, a collection of parodies by James and Horace Smith (q.v.) (1812).

On the occasion of the opening of the present Drury Lane Theatre, which replaced Sheridan's building destroyed by fire, the committee in charge advertised for a suitable address to be spoken at the opening. The two Smiths composed imaginary addresses submitted by a number of the popular poets of the day, parodying their style. These include Wordsworth, Byron, Moore, Southey, Coleridge, Crabbe, and Sir Walter Scott.

Relapse, The, or Virtue in Danger, a comedy by Vanbrugh (q.v.), produced in 1696.

The play was adapted by Sheridan and produced as 'A Trip to Scarborough'.

Relations, a name applied to printed news-pamphlets of the early part of the 17th cent., recording domestic events.

Relativity, a theory of the physical universe evolved by Einstein (q.v.).

Religio Laici, a poem by Dryden (q.v.) (1682).

The poet argues for the credibility of the Christian religion and against Deism, and (perhaps with less conviction) for the Anglican Church against that of Rome. See *Hind and the Panther (The)*.

Religio Medici, a work by Sir T. Browne (q.v.), first printed without his sanction in 1642, reissued with his approval in 1643.

It is a confession of Christian faith (qualified by an eclectic and generally sceptical attitude), and a collection of opinions on a vast number of subjects more or less connected with religion, expressed with a wealth of fancy and wide erudition. The work contains two beautiful prayers in verse.

Reliques of Ancient Poetry, see *Percy* (*T.*).

Remarks on the Life and Writings of Dr. Jonathan Swift, see *Boyle* (*J.*).

Remarque, ERICH MARIA (1898-), German novelist, author of 'Im Westen nichts Neues' ('All Quiet on the Western Front', 1929) and 'Der Weg zurück' ('The Road Back', 1931).

Rembrandt van Ryn (1606-69), Dutch painter and etcher. His output was enormous: paintings, including many portraits and self-portraits; etchings of biblical subjects, landscapes, portraits, and genre subjects; and drawings; all searching studies of character and form, infused with profound feeling.

Remorse, a blank verse tragedy by S. T. Coleridge (q.v.), produced at Drury Lane in 1813.

Renaissance, THE, the great revival of art and letters, under the influence of classical models, which began in Italy in the 15th cent., culminating in the High Renaissance at the end of the century and spreading to northern Europe in the 16th and 17th cents. Among English writers who have dealt with the subject may be mentioned Symonds, Ruskin, and Pater (qq.v.).

Renan, ERNEST (1823-92), a learned French writer, philologist, and historian. The result of his studies of Christianity is embodied in the famous 'Origines du Christianisme' (1863-81), in which he applied the method of the historian to the biblical narrative.

Renaud, see under *Rinaldo*.

Renault, a character in Otway's 'Venice Preserv'd' (q.v.).

René of Provence (1408-80), titular king of Naples, the two Sicilies, and Jerusalem. His daughter, Margaret of Anjou, was wife of Henry VI. There is a picture of his court in Scott's 'Anne of Geierstein'.

He figures in Shakespeare's 'Henry VI' as 'Reignier'.

Representative Men, by Emerson (q.v.), a series of studies of Plato, Swedenborg, Montaigne, Shakespeare, Napoleon, Goethe (1850).

Repressor of over much Blaming of the Clergy, a work by Pecock (q.v.).

Republic, The, one of the dialogues of Plato (q.v.), in which Socrates is represented as eliciting, in the course of a discussion on justice, the ideal type of state.

Republic of Letters, THE, the collective body of those engaged in literary pursuits. The expression occurs first in Addison's 'Dialogues upon Ancient Medals', i. 19.

Restoration, THE, the re-establishment of monarchy in England with the return of Charles II (1660); also the period marked by this event, of which the chief literary figures are Dryden, Etherege, Wycherley, Congreve, Vanbrugh, Farquhar, Rochester, Bunyan, Pepys, and Locke (qq.v.). Its characteristics are a love of wit and gaiety, often of immorality, but at the same time a genuine revival of interest, particularly in scientific discovery.

Retaliation, an unfinished poem by Goldsmith (q.v.) (1774), consisting of a string of humorous and critical epitaphs on David Garrick, Reynolds, Burke, and other friends.

Retort courteous, THE, the first of Touchstone's seven causes of quarrel (Shakespeare's 'As You Like It', v. iv).

Returne from Pernassus, The, see *Parnassus Plays*.

Return of the Druses, The, a tragedy in blank verse by R. Browning (q.v.) (1843).

Return of the Native, The, a novel by Hardy (q.v.), published in 1878.

The scene is the sombre Egdon Heath, typical of the country near Wareham in Dorset. Damon Wildeve, engineer turned publican, after playing fast and loose with two women by whom he is loved—the gentle, unselfish Thomasin Yeobright and the selfish, capricious Eustacia Vye—marries the former to spite the latter;

while Thomasin rejects her humble adorer, the reddleman, Diggory Venn. Her cousin, Clym Yeobright, a diamond merchant in Paris, disgusted with the uselessness of his occupation, returns to Egdon with the intention of becoming a schoolmaster in his native county. He falls in love with Eustacia, and she in a brief infatuation marries him, in the hope of inducing him to return to Paris. His sight fails and he becomes a furze-cutter on the heath, to Eustacia's despair. She is the cause of estrangement between Clym and his mother, and unintentionally of her death. This, and the discovery that Eustacia's relations with Wildeve have not ceased, lead to a violent scene between Clym and his wife, and ultimately to Eustacia's flight with Wildeve, in the course of which both are drowned. Clym, attributing to himself some responsibility for the death of his mother and his wife, becomes an itinerant preacher. Thomasin marries Diggory Venn.

Revels, MASTER OF THE, an officer appointed to superintend masques and other entertainments at court. He is first mentioned in the reign of Henry VII. The first permanent Master of the Revels was Sir Thomas Cawarden, appointed in 1545.

Revenge, The, (1) the name of Sir R. Grenville's ship; (2) the title and subject of a ballad by Tennyson (q.v.) describing its famous fight with 53 Spanish ships; (3) a tragedy by E. Young (q.v.), of which the plot is akin to that of Shakespeare's 'Othello'.

Revenge of Bussy D'Ambois, The, see *Bussy D'Ambois (The Revenge of)*.

Revenger's Tragedy, The, see *Tourneur*.

Revere, PAUL (1735–1818), American patriot; remembered for his famous midnight ride from Charlestown to Lexington (18–19 April 1775) to give warning of the approach of British troops—the subject of Longfellow's poem in 'Tales of a Wayside Inn'.

Revesby Play, THE, a folk-drama acted by morris-dancers at Revesby in Lincoln-

shire at the end of the 18th cent. See E. K. Chambers, 'The Mediaeval Stage'.

Review, The, a periodical started by Defoe (q.v.) in 1704 and continued until 1713. It was written, practically in its entirety, by Defoe himself, who expressed in it his opinion on all current political topics.

Review of English Studies, The, a quarterly journal devoted to English scholarship, started in 1925.

Revised Version, THE, see *Bible (The English)*.

Revolt of Islam, The, originally entitled *Laon and Cythna*, a poem by P. B. Shelley (q.v.) in Spenserian stanzas (1818).

This poem was written in 1817, at a time when the reaction that followed the fall of Napoleon had brought much misery among the poorer classes, and had stirred Shelley's revolutionary instincts. It is a symbolic tale, in some respects obscure. Cythna, a heroic maiden, united with Laon in a common ideal, rouses the spirit of revolt among the people of Islam against their tyrants. The revolt is temporarily successful, but the tyrants return. Laon and Cythna are burnt at the stake, at the instigation of a priest. But the poem closes with an indication of 'the eternity of genius and virtue'.

Revolution in France, Reflections on the, by Burke (q.v.) (1790).

This treatise was provoked by a sermon preached by Dr. Richard Price, a nonconformist minister, in Nov. 1789, in which he exulted in the French Revolution. Burke contrasts the inherited rights of which the English are tenacious with the 'rights of man' of the French revolutionaries, inconsistent, says Burke, with an ordered society and leading to poverty and chaos. His general conclusion is that the defective institutions of the old régime should have been reformed, not destroyed. The work led to the subsequent breach between Burke and Fox and the splitting of the Whig party.

Reynard the Fox, the hero of various popular satirical fables or 'bestiaries' (q.v.) collected in France under the title of

'Roman de Renart'. The first part of this was written about 1200 and was followed by other parts during the 13th cent. Goethe wrote a free translation, called 'Reinecke Fuchs' in 1794. The fox in these fables is used to symbolize the man who, under various characters, preys upon and deludes society, is brought to judgement, but escapes by his cunning. We have an example of this type of fable in Chaucer's 'Nun's Priest's Tale' (see *Canterbury Tales*, 21).

The principal characters in the English version are, besides Reynard, King Noble the lion, Isegrym the wolf, Courtoys the hound, Bruin the bear, Tybert the cat, Grymbert the badger, Coart or Cuwaert the hare, Bellyn the ram, Martin and Dame Rukenawe the apes, Chanticleer the cock, and Partlet the hen. Ermeline is Reynard's wife, and Malperdy (*Malpertuis*) his castle.

Reynolds, SIR JOSHUA (1723-92), portrait painter and first President of the Royal Academy of Arts. He was a friend of Johnson, Burke, and Goldsmith, and one of the founders of 'The Club' (see *Johnson, Samuel*). In his 'Fifteen Discourses', delivered to the students of the Royal Academy between 1769 and 1790, he sought to encourage history painting as the noblest form of art.

Rhadamanthus, a son of Zeus and Europa, and brother of Minos, king of Crete. He became after death one of the judges in the infernal regions.

Rhapsody, originally an epic poem or part of one, sung by a 'rhapsodist' (meaning a stitcher together of song). It is applied also to an exalted or exaggeratedly enthusiastic expression of sentiment, or a speech, letter, or poem marked by extravagance of idea and expression.

Rhea, an ancient Greek nature-goddess, known also as CYBELE, the wife of Cronos (Saturn) and the mother of Zeus, Poseidon (Neptune), Pluto, Demeter, Hera, etc.

Rheims, The Jackdaw of, see *Jackdaw of Rheims*.

Rhine Gold, THE, the hoard of the Nibelungs (see under *Nibelungenlied*) of which Siegfried got possession and which, after Siegfried's death, the brothers of Kriemhild concealed by sinking it in the Rhine.

Rhoda Fleming, a novel by G. Meredith (q.v.) (1865).

Rhodes, CECIL JOHN (1853-1902), famous for his political and colonizing activities in South Africa. By his will he left about £6,000,000 to the public service, endowing some 170 scholarships at Oxford for students from various parts of the Empire, from the United States, and from Germany.

Rhodes, COLOSSUS OF, see *Colossus*.

Rhodes, KNIGHTS OF, see *Hospitallers of St. John of Jerusalem*.

Rhodope or RHODOPIS, a Greek courtesan, said to have been a fellow slave of Aesop (q.v.).

Rhopálic verse (from the Greek ῥόπαλον, a cudgel), verse of which each word contains one more syllable than the last, e.g.:

Spes Deus aeternae stationis conciliator.
(Ausonius.)

Rhyme: MALE or MASCULINE rhymes or endings are those having a final accented syllable, as distinguished from FEMALE or FEMININE rhymes or endings in which the last syllable is unaccented.

Rhymer, THOMAS THE, see *Erceldoune*.

Rhyme-royal, the seven-lined decasyllabic stanza, rhymed a b a b b c c. Its first appearance in English is in Chaucer's 'Complaint unto Pity'. Its name derives probably from the French *chant royal*, not from its adoption by James I in 'The Kingis Quair' (q.v.). It was used by Shakespeare in 'The Rape of Lucrece' (q.v.).

Rhyming Poem, The, included in the 'Exeter Book' (q.v.) and therefore of not later date than the 10th cent., is important as being arranged in rhymed couplets, with rhymes in the verses. It is a disquisition on the vicissitudes of life, contrasting the misfortunes of a fallen king with the days of his past glory. It has been suggested that it is a paraphrase of Job xxix and xxx.

Riah, the Jew in Dickens's 'Our Mutual Friend' (q.v.).

Rialto, THE (the 'Ponte di Rivo Alto' or bridge of the 'deep stream', on which Venice was founded), a beautiful single-span marble bridge in Venice, built at the end of the 16th cent., in the centre of the mercantile quarter of old Venice.

Ricardo, DAVID (1772–1823), made a fortune on the London Stock Exchange, and then devoted himself to the study of economics. Encouraged by James Mill (q.v.), he published in 1817 his chief work, 'Principles of Political Economy and Taxation', which is mainly occupied with the causes determining the distribution of wealth. In this his famous theory of rent played an important part.

Rice, ELMER (1892–1967), American dramatist. Among his many plays are 'The Adding Machine' (1923) and 'Street Scene' (1929). He also wrote several novels.

Rice, JAMES (1843–82), remembered for his collaboration in a number of novels with Besant (q.v.).

Rich, BARNABE (1540?–1617), fought in Queen Mary's war with France (1557–8) and in the Low Countries, and from 1574 onwards devoted himself to the production of romances in the style of Lyly's 'Euphues' (q.v.), pamphlets, and reminiscences. Notable among these are his 'Farewell to the Military Profession' (1581, which includes the source of the plot of Shakespeare's 'Twelfth Night'), and 'The Honesty of this Age'.

Rich, JOHN (1682?–1761), theatrical producer. He opened the New Theatre at Lincoln's Inn Fields, and the theatre at Covent Garden. In 1728 he produced Gay's 'Beggar's Opera'.

Rich, PENELOPE (1562?–1607), daughter of Walter Devereux, the first earl of Essex. Her charms were celebrated by Sir P. Sidney (q.v.) in his 'Astrophel and Stella' sonnets. She married Lord Rich, was

divorced by him, and married Lord Mountjoy.

Richard I, 'Cœur de Lion', king of England, 1189–99. He is introduced in two of Scott's novels, 'The Talisman' and 'Ivanhoe' (qq.v.); and is also the hero of Hewlett's (q.v.) 'Richard Yea-and-Nay'.

Richard II, king of England, 1377–99.

Richard II, King, a historical tragedy by Shakespeare (q.v.), produced probably about 1595, printed in 1597, and based on Holinshed. The play shows the influence of Marlowe, and is comparable with the latter's 'Edward II' (q.v.).

It deals with the arbitrary exile of Henry Bolingbroke and the duke of Norfolk by King Richard; the death of John of Gaunt. and the confiscation of his property by the king; the invasion of England by Bolingbroke during the king's absence in Ireland; the king's return and withdrawal to Flint Castle; his surrender to Bolingbroke; the latter's triumphal progress through London with Richard in his train; Richard's removal to Pomfret and his murder. The contrast of the characters of Richard and Bolingbroke is a notable feature. The play contains practically no comic element.

Richard III, king of England, 1483–5.

Richard III, King, a historical tragedy by Shakespeare (q.v.), produced probably in 1594, printed in 1597, and based on Holinshed. Shakespeare perhaps had before him an earlier play, 'The True Tragedie of Richard III'.

The play centres in the character of Richard of Gloucester, afterwards King Richard III, ambitious and sanguinary, bold and subtle, treacherous, yet brave in battle, a murderer and usurper of the crown. The principal incidents of the play are the imprisonment and murder of Clarence procured by his brother Richard; the wooing of Anne, widow of Edward Prince of Wales, by Richard as she accompanies the bier of her dead father-in-law; the death of Edward IV and the machinations of Richard to get the crown; the execution of Hastings, Rivers, and

Grey; the accession of Richard; the murder of the princes in the Tower; Richard's project of marrying his niece, Elizabeth of York; Buckingham's rebellion in support of the earl of Richmond, his capture and execution; Richmond's invasion, and the defeat and death of Richard at Bosworth (1485).

Richard Coeur de Lion, a spirited verse romance of the 14th cent. The author is unknown.

Richard Feverel, see *Ordeal of Richard Feverel*.

Richard Roe, see *John Doe*.

Richards, FRANK, see *Hamilton* (C.).

Richards, IVOR ARMSTRONG (1893-   ), critic and authority on semantics. He was the founder with C. K. Ogden of Basic English. Among his writings 'The Meaning of Meaning' (with C. K. Ogden, 1923), 'Principles of Literary Criticism' (1924), and 'Practical Criticism' (1929) are the best known.

Richardson, DOROTHY MILLER (1873-1957), novelist, was a pioneer in the 'stream-of-consciousness' method in the novel. Her novels, written between 1915 and 1938, form a single sequence entitled 'Pilgrimage'.

Richardson, HENRY HANDEL, pen-name of ETHEL FLORENCE RICHARDSON (MRS. J. G. ROBERTSON) (1870-1946), novelist, born in Melbourne. Her novels include 'Maurice Guest' (1908), 'The Getting of Wisdom' (1910), 'The Fortunes of Richard Mahony' (a trilogy consisting of 'Australia Felix', 1917, 'The Way Home', 1925, and 'Ultima Thule', 1929), and 'The Young Cosima' (1939).

Richardson, SAMUEL (1689-1761), received little education, and set up a printing business in London. At the request of two other printers he prepared 'a little volume of letters, in a common style, on such subjects as might be of use to country readers'. Out of the preparation of this book arose Richardson's first novel, 'Pamela' (q.v.), of which two volumes appeared in 1740 and two in 1741. This was followed by 'Clarissa

Harlowe' (q.v., 1747-8), which surpassed the success of 'Pamela', and won Richardson European fame. His 'Sir Charles Grandison' (q.v.), which appeared in 1753-4, though it never held so high a position as 'Clarissa', was received also with enthusiasm. The three works had a marked influence on subsequent writers of fiction, both in England and abroad.

Richard the Redeless, see *Mum, Sothsegger*.

Richard the Thirde, The History of, a work first printed in 1534, and questionably attributed to Sir T. More and to Cardinal Morton. It is distinguished from earlier English chronicles by its unity of scheme and dramatic effectiveness.

Richelieu, ARMAND JEAN DU PLESSIS, CARDINAL and DUC DE (1585-1642), one of the greatest of French statesmen, became prime minister of Louis XIII in 1624. He figures in 'The Three Musketeers' of Dumas (q.v.).

Richelieu, or The Conspiracy, a historical play in blank verse by Bulwer Lytton (q.v.), produced in 1839.

Richter, JOHANN PAUL FRIEDRICH (1763-1825), German romantic novelist, who wrote under the name 'Jean Paul'. He was at his best in idyllic representations of the village life he knew, and had also a certain gift of humour, which earned the enthusiastic praise of Carlyle.

Ridd, JOHN, see *Lorna Doone*.

Riddle of the Sands, The, a novel by Erskine Childers (q.v.) (1903). It deals with the discovery of a threatened invasion of England by a continental power.

Riderhood, ROGUE, a character in Dickens's 'Our Mutual Friend' (q.v.).

Ridley, NICHOLAS (1500?-55), became one of Cranmer's chaplains and began gradually to reject many Roman doctrines. As bishop of London he exerted himself to propagate reformed opinions. In Sept. 1555 he was condemned on the capital charge of heresy and burnt alive with Latimer (q.v.) at Oxford on 16 Oct. He wrote several theological treatises, which appeared after his death.

Rienzi, *or The Last of the Tribunes*, a novel by Bulwer Lytton (q.v.) (1835).

Rigaud, a character in Dickens's 'Little Dorrit' (q.v.).

Rigby, MR., a character in Disraeli's 'Coningsby' (q.v.).

Rights, BILL OF, a measure adopted by the Convention Parliament of 1689 condemning the interference by the Crown with civil liberty and the execution of the law.

Rights of Man, *The*, a political treatise by Paine (q.v.), in two parts (1791, 1792).

Pt. I is in the main a reply to Burke's 'Reflections on the Revolution in France' (q.v.). Condemning its unhistorical and unbalanced violence, Paine repudiates Burke's doctrine of prescription and denies that one generation can bind another as regards the form of government. Paine justifies the French Revolution, of which he traces the incidents to the adoption of the Declaration of the Rights of Man by the National Assembly.

In Pt. II Paine passes to a comparison of the principles of the new French and American constitutions with those of British institutions, to the disadvantage of the latter. The most interesting part of the work, however, consists in Paine's constructive proposals. Notable among these are: a large reduction of administrative expenditure and taxation; provision for the aged poor; family allowances; allowances for the education of the poor; maternity grants; funeral grants; a graduated income tax; and limitation of armaments by international agreement.

Rights of Woman, *Vindication of the*, see *Godwin* (*Mrs. M. W.*).

Rig-Veda, see *Veda*.

Rilke, RAINER MARIA (1875–1926), German lyric poet. The subjective emotionalism of his early poetry began to give way to poetry of a more objective type, the transition to which is seen in 'The Book of Pictures' (1902) and which finds its mature expression in 'New Poems' (1907–8). In 'Sketches of Malte Laurids Brigge' (1910), a prose work, Rilke explored the relationship between a sensitive poet and a threatening environment. The 'Duino Elegies', begun shortly before the First World War and completed not long afterwards, arose from his endeavour to discover for himself as a poet a satisfactory spiritual position amid the decay of reality; and the 'Sonnets to Orpheus' (1923) are the jubilant outcome of that endeavour. Rilke's extensive correspondence is of great literary interest.

Rima, see *Hudson* (*W. H.*).

Rimini, FRANCESCA DA, see *Paolo and Francesca*.

Rimini, *The Story of*, see *Hunt* (*J. H. L.*).

Rimmon, an Assyrian divinity (2 Kings v. 18). Milton makes him one of the fallen angels.

Rinaldo or RENAUD, first figures under the latter name in the Charlemagne cycle of legends, as the eldest of the four sons of Aymon, with his famous steed Bayard.

As Rinaldo, the hero figures in the 'Orlando Innamorato' and 'Orlando Furioso' (qq.v.). There he is the cousin of Orlando, the lord of Montalban, and one of the suitors for the hand of Angelica. He is the brother of Bradamante.

Ringan, ST., see *Ninian*.

Ring and the Book, *The*, a poem by R. Browning (q.v.) (1868–9).

The poem is based on the story of a Roman murder-case related in an old parchment-covered volume that Browning picked up one day in a Florentine market stall. This provided the raw material of the story, which is briefly as follows.

Count Guido Franceschini, an impoverished nobleman of Arezzo, marries Pompilia Comparini, a young girl of obscure family, but possessed of some slight wealth. Violante Comparini, Pompilia's supposed mother, confesses that Pompilia is not really her daughter, but a supposititious child. Guido thereupon determines to get rid of his base-born wife, and so harasses her that she persuades a certain Canon Caponsacchi, to carry her off from her husband's house at Arezzo to her old home. Guido pursues them and has them arrested. Pompilia is tried for adultery and is sent to a convent; Caponsacchi is banished for three years. Pompilia, being about to become a mother, is moved from the convent to her old home, where, after giving birth to a son, she is one night murdered, together with her putative parents, by her husband, assisted by four ruffians. Guido is arrested, tried, and on the Pope's final decision, executed.

The poem, after the preface, is occupied first with the opinion on the case of 'Half-Rome', then with the opinion of 'The Other Half-Rome', and then of 'Tertium Quid', who takes an impartial attitude. Count Guido next tells his story, which is followed by that of Caponsacchi; then come the pleadings of the advocates. After these we have the Pope's reflections and Guido's scornful and ferocious defiance, collapsing into abject cowardice when he finally knows his fate.

Ring des Nibelungen, Der, the series of four musical dramas by Richard Wagner (q.v.), 'Das Rheingold', 'Die Walküre', 'Siegfried', and 'Götterdämmerung' (see *Nibelungenlied*), and composed in 1853-70 (produced 1869-76).

Rintherout, JENNY, in Scott's 'The Antiquary' (q.v.), servant to Jonathan Oldbuck.

Rip Van Winkle, a story by W. Irving (q.v.), attributed to 'Diedrich Knickerbocker' (q.v.), and included in 'The Sketch Book' (1820).

Rip Van Winkle, taking refuge from a termagant wife in a solitary ramble in the Catskill mountains, falls asleep, and awakens after twenty years, to find his wife dead, his house in ruins, and the world completely changed.

Rise of Silas Lapham, The, the best known of W. D. Howells's (q.v.) novels (1885).

Risorgimento, an Italian word meaning 'resurrection', a name given to the movement for the union and liberation of Italy which took place in the middle of the 19th cent. See also *Cavour*, *Garibaldi*, *Mazzini*.

Ritchie, ANNE ISABELLA THACKERAY, Lady (1837-1919), elder daughter of Thackeray (q.v.), author of a number of novels and of some volumes of essays.

Ritson, JOSEPH (1752-1803), literary antiquary, a zealous student of English literature, attacked (1782) the 'History of English Poetry' of Thomas Warton (q.v.), and also Johnson and Steevens's edition of Shakespeare. In 1783 he published a 'Select Collection of English Songs' containing strictures on Percy's 'Reliques'.

Rival Queens, The, a tragedy by N. Lee (q.v.), produced in 1677.

Rivals, The, a comedy by R. B. Sheridan (q.v.), produced in 1775. This was the first of Sheridan's plays, and he was only 23 when he wrote it. The play was not a success on the first night, owing to the indifferent performance of the part of Sir Lucius O'Trigger.

Captain Absolute, son of Sir Anthony Absolute, is in love with Lydia Languish, the niece of Mrs. Malaprop (q.v.). As the romantic Lydia prefers a half-pay lieutenant to the heir of a baronet, he has assumed the character of Ensign Beverley, in order to pay his court, which has been favourably received. But Lydia loses half her fortune if she marries without her aunt's consent, and Mrs. Malaprop will have nothing to say to a beggarly ensign.

Sir Anthony arrives at Bath, ignorant of his son's proceedings, to propose a match between the said son and Lydia Languish, a proposal welcomed by Mrs. Malaprop. Capt. Absolute is afraid of revealing his deception to Lydia; while he has a rival in Bob Acres, who has heard of Ensign Beverley's courtship, and at the instigation of the fire-eating Sir Lucius O'Trigger, asks Capt. Absolute to carry a challenge to Beverley. Sir Lucius himself, who has been deluded into thinking that some amatory letters received by him from Mrs. Malaprop are from Lydia, likewise finds Capt. Absolute in his way and challenges him. But when Acres finds that Beverley is his friend Absolute (his courage had already been 'oozing out at the palms of his hands') he declines to fight and resigns all claim to Lydia. Sir Lucius is disabused by the arrival of Mrs. Malaprop, and Lydia, after a pretty quarrel with her lover for shattering her hopes of an elopement, finally forgives him.

Rizpah, a poem by Tennyson (q.v.), included in 'Ballads and other Poems' (1880).

Roaring Boys, a cant term used in the 16th to 18th cents. for riotous, quarrelsome blades, who abounded in London and took pleasure in annoying its quieter inhabitants.

Roaring Girle, The, or Moll Cut-Purse, a comedy by T. Middleton and Dekker (qq.v.), produced in 1611.

Robbery under Arms, a novel by R. Boldrewood; see *Browne (T. A.)*.

Robert Elsmere, see *Ward (M. A.)*.

Robert of Gloucester (*fl.* 1260-1300), the reputed author of a metrical chronicle from earliest times down to 1272, written in long lines, running to fourteen syllables and more. It contains among passages of special interest the account of a town and gown riot at Oxford in 1263, and a famous description of the death of Simon de Montfort at the battle of Evesham.

Robertson, FREDERICK WILLIAM (1816-53), acquired during his short life great influence among all ecclesiastical parties, and his sermons (five series), published at various dates, posthumously, had a wide circle of readers.

Robertson, THOMAS WILLIAM (1829-71), began life as an actor, but became a dramatist. His plays introduced a new and more natural type of comedy to the English stage than had been seen during the first half of the century.

Robertson, WILLIAM (1721-93), a Presbyterian minister, came into fame by the publication in 1759 of his 'History of Scotland during the Reigns of Queen Mary and of James VI'. This was followed in 1769 by his 'History of Charles V'. His

work, in style and method, shows a resemblance to that of Hume (q.v.), but is somewhat more animated and popular, and is based on more careful investigation.

Robert the Devil, sixth duke of Normandy, and father of William the Conqueror, a personage about whom many legends gathered, in consequence of his violence and cruelty.

Robespierre, ISIDORE MAXIMILIEN DE (1758-94), one of the most prominent figures in the French Revolution, a leader of the 'Mountain' or extreme party. He was overthrown in July 1794 and executed. See also *Sea-green Incorruptible*.

Robin and Makyne, an old Scottish pastoral by Henryson (q.v.), included in Percy's 'Reliques'.

Robin Goodfellow, a 'shrewd and knavish sprite' (Shakespeare, 'A Midsummer Night's Dream', II. i), Puck or Hobgoblin, at times a domestic spirit who renders services to the family (as in Milton's 'L'Allegro', ll. 105-10), at others a mischievous elf.

Robin Gray, Auld, see *Lindsay (Lady A.)*.

Robin Hood, a legendary outlaw. His historical authenticity is ill-supported. He is mentioned in 'Piers Plowman' (q.v.). As a historical character Robin Hood appears in Wyntoun's 'Chronicle of Scotland' (*c.* 1420), and is referred to as a ballad hero by Bower, Major, and Stow. The first detailed history, 'Lytell Geste of Robyn Hoode' (printed *c.* 1495) locates him in south-west Yorkshire; later writers place him in Sherwood, and finally make him earl of Huntingdon. Ritson says that he was born at Locksley, Nottinghamshire, about 1160, that his true name was Robert Fitz-Ooth, and that he was commonly reputed to have been earl of Huntingdon. There is a pleasant account of the activities of his band in Drayton's 'Polyolbion', song 26. According to Stow, there were about the year 1190 many robbers and outlaws, among whom were Robin Hood and Little John, who abode in the woods, robbing the rich, but killing none but such as would invade them, suffering no woman to be molested, and sparing poor men's goods. He is the centre of a whole cycle of ballads, one of the best of which is 'Robin Hood and Guy of Gisborne', and his legend shows affinity with 'The Tale of Gamelyn' (q.v.) and with the tales of other legendary outlaws such as Clym of the Clough and Adam Bell (q.v.). Popular plays embodying the legend appear to have been developed out of the village May game, the king and queen of the May giving place to Robin and Maid Marian.

Robin Hood, *A Tale of*, sub-title of Jonson's 'The Sad Shepherd'.

Robinson, EDWIN ARLINGTON (1869–1935), American poet. The following are among his works: 'The Torrent and the Night Before' (1896), 'Collected Poems' (1921), 'The Man Who Died Twice' (1924), 'Matthias at the Door' (1931).

Robinson, (ESMÉ STUART) LENNOX (1886–1958), Irish dramatist. He was manager of the Abbey Theatre (q.v.) from 1910 to 1914 and from 1919 to 1923, when he became director. Among his best-known plays are 'The Clancy Name' (1908), 'The Lost Leader' (1918), 'The White-headed Boy' (1920), 'Crabbed Youth and Age' (1924), and 'The Far-off Hills' (1928). He also edited several anthologies of Irish verse.

Robinson, HENRY CRABB (1775–1867), after spending some years in a solicitor's office in London, travelled in Germany, where he met Goethe and Schiller, and studied at Jena University. He became a foreign correspondent (in 1807, one of the first of the class), and subsequently foreign editor, of 'The Times', and its special correspondent in the Peninsula in 1808–9. He was acquainted with many notable people of his day. Part of his famous diary and correspondence, throwing light on many literary characters, such as Wordsworth, Coleridge, Lamb, and Hazlitt, was published in 1869; new editions of his letters were published in 1927 and 1929; 'Henry Crabb Robinson on Books and Their Writers' (3 vols.,

1938) is compiled by Edith J. Morley from his diary, travel journals, and reminiscences.

Robinson Crusoe, *The Life and strange surprising Adventures of*, a romance by Defoe (q.v.) (1719).

The story is based on the experiences of Alexander Selkirk (q.v.) on the uninhabited island of Juan Fernandez. Defoe embellished the narrative with many incidents of his imagination and presented it as a true story. The extraordinarily convincing account of the shipwrecked Crusoe's successful efforts to make himself a tolerable existence in his solitude first revealed Defoe's genius for vivid fiction. Defoe was nearly sixty when he wrote it.

The book had immediate and permanent success, was translated into many languages, and inspired many imitations. It was followed, also in 1719, by Defoe's 'The Farther Adventures of Robinson Crusoe', in which, with his man Friday, he revisits his island, is attacked by a fleet of canoes on his departure, and loses Friday in the encounter. 'The Serious Reflections . . . of Robinson Crusoe', 'with his vision of the Angelick World', appeared in 1720.

Robot, derived from a Slav word meaning 'work'. It was popularized by a play 'R.U.R.' (Rossum's Universal Robots) written by the Czech dramatist, Karel Čapek, in which society is represented as dependent on mechanical men. The latter revolt against their employers and destroy them.

Rob Roy, a novel by Sir W. Scott (q.v.) (1817).

The period of the story is that immediately preceding the Jacobite rising of 1715. Francis Osbaldistone, the son of a rich London merchant, on refusing to adopt his father's profession, is banished to Osbaldistone Hall in the north of England, the home of his uncle, Sir Hildebrand Osbaldistone. Here he is brought into contact with Sir Hildebrand's five boorish sons, a sixth son, Rashleigh, and Sir Hildebrand's niece, the high-spirited Diana Vernon. Rashleigh is deeply involved in Jacobite intrigues, has evil designs on Diana, and becomes the bitter enemy of Francis, who falls in love with Diana and is received by her with favour. The story is occupied with the attempts of Rashleigh to destroy Francis, and to rob and ruin Francis's father, attempts that are defeated partly by Diana, and partly by the singular Scotsman, Rob Roy Macgregor, from whom the novel takes its title. This historical character is a powerful and dangerous outlaw, the opponent of the government's agents, but capable of acts of justice and even generosity. In the outcome, Rashleigh is forced to surrender the funds that he has misappropriated, and is ultimately killed by Rob Roy. Francis is restored to his father's favour, becomes the owner of Osbaldistone Hall, and marries Diana. His rascally servant, Andrew Fairservice, is one of Scott's great characters.

Robsart, AMY, daughter of Sir John Robsart, married to Sir Robert Dudley, afterwards earl of Leicester, in 1549; she figures in Scott's 'Kenilworth' (q.v.).

Robyne and Makyne, see *Robin and Makyne*.

Roc, a mythical bird of Eastern legend, imagined as being of enormous size and strength. In the 'Arabian Nights' story of Sindbad the Sailor, the Roc carries Sindbad out of the valley of diamonds.

Rochester, MR., the hero of Charlotte Brontë's 'Jane Eyre' (q.v.).

Rochester, JOHN WILMOT, *second earl of* (1648-80), a poet of genius and a notorious libertine. He fought at sea in the Dutch War, and showed conspicuous gallantry. Rochester was attractive in person and manners and a favourite of Charles II, who frequently banished him from the court and as frequently pardoned him. He was a patron of Elizabeth Barry (q.v.) and temporarily of several poets, including Dryden, whom, however, it is said that he caused to be waylaid and beaten on account of a passage in Mulgrave's anonymous 'Essay on Satire', which he attributed to Dryden. His best literary work was satirical, notably in 'A Satire against Mankind' (1675), and among his amorous lyrics there are some marked with sincerity and feeling. But the wit and finish of his writing are frequently marred by obscenity.

Rockefeller, JOHN DAVISON (1839-1937), organized the Standard Oil Co. in 1870, substituting combination for the previous competition among the American oil companies, and became immensely rich. From 1890 he undertook the philanthropic distribution of his fortune, and by the end of 1927 is said to have bestowed some £100,000,000 on such purposes. The principal institutions that he set up were the 'Rockefeller Institute for Medical Research'; the 'Rockefeller Foundation' for medical education and the control of certain diseases; and the 'General Education Board' and 'International Education Board' for the development of teaching and research in the U.S.A. and the rest of the world respectively. His son (1874-1960), who bore the same names, continued to give large sums for education, research, and kindred purposes.

Rococo, apparently a fanciful formation on the stem of *rocaille*, shell- or pebble-work. The term is used for the style of interior decoration introduced into France in the first half of the 18th cent. The effect was of lightness and gaiety, achieved by the use of intricate gilded carving framing mirrors or against a light background, refined in detail and asymmetrical in design. It spread to Germany and Austria but was too frivolous for English taste.

Roderick, the last of the Goths, a poem by Southey (q.v.) (1814).

Roderick, Vision of Don, a poem by Sir W. Scott (q.v.) (1811).

Roderick Dhu, a character in Sir W. Scott's 'The Lady of the Lake' (q.v.).

Roderick Hudson, the first novel of H. James (q.v.) (1876).

Roderick Random, The Adventures of, a picaresque novel by Smollett (q.v.) (1748).

This was the first important work by Smollett. It is modelled on Le Sage's 'Gil Blas', and is a series of episodes, told with vigour and vividness, strung together on the life of the selfish and unprincipled hero, who relates them. Its chief interest is in the picture that it gives, drawn from personal experience, of the British navy and the British sailor of the day. But much of the story is repulsive.

Roderigo, a character in Shakespeare's 'Othello' (q.v.).

Rodin, AUGUSTE (1840-1917), French sculptor. A replica of his 'Burghers of Calais' stands near the Houses of Parliament. He presented a number of his works to the Victoria and Albert Museum.

Rodney Stone, a novel by Sir A. Conan Doyle (q.v.).

Rodomont, in the 'Orlando Innamorato' and the 'Orlando Furioso' (qq.v.), the king of Sarza, arrogant and valiant, the doughtiest of the followers of Agramant. His boastfulness gave rise to the word *rodomontade*.

Roger, the name of the Cook in Chaucer's 'The Canterbury Tales' (q.v.).

Roger de Coverley, SIR, see *Coverley*.

Rogero or RUGGIERO, the legendary ancestor of the house of Este, extolled in the 'Orlando Furioso' (q.v.).

Rogers, BRUCE (1870-1957), born in the United States, an eminent designer of books.

Rogers, SAMUEL (1763-1855), the son of a banker and a man of wealth, published in 1792 his 'The Pleasures of Memory', a piece of pleasant verse, which achieved popularity. He attained a position among men of letters, at a time when the poetical standard was not high. He was offered, but declined, the laureateship in 1850. His 'Recollections', dealing with a long life and a wide acquaintance, were published in 1859.

Rogers, WOODES (*d.* 1732), commander of a privateering expedition (1708-11) in which William Dampier (q.v.) was pilot, and in the course of which Alexander Selkirk (q.v.) was discovered on the island of Juan Fernandez. These incidents are described in Rogers's entertaining journal, 'A Cruizing Voyage round the World' (1712).

Roget's Thesaurus of English Words and Phrases, first published by Dr. Peter Mark Roget (1779-1869) in 1852 (enlarged edition, completed by his son, 1879, and many subsequent editions), contains words and phrases 'classified and arranged so as to facilitate the expression of ideas and assist in literary composition'.

Roi d'Yvetot, LE, the subject and title of a song by Béranger (q.v.), the type of easygoing, pleasure-loving monarch, the ruler of a very small but peaceful and contented territory. There is an excellent rendering by Thackeray.

Rois Fainéants, LES, a name given to the later Merovingian kings who were mere figure-heads.

Rokeby, a poem in six cantos by Sir W. Scott (q.v.) (1813).

The scene is laid chiefly at Rokeby near Greta Bridge in Yorkshire, and the time is immediately after the battle of Marston Moor (1644).

The poem includes the beautiful songs, 'A weary lot is thine, fair maid', and 'Brignal Banks'. It is interesting for the fact that Scott now recognized his own comparative failure as a poet, and thereupon turned to his true vocation as a romantic novelist.

Rokesmith, JOHN, in Dickens's 'Our Mutual Friend' (q.v.), the name assumed by John Harmon.

Roland, the most famous of the paladins (q.v.) of Charlemagne. His legend has some basis of fact. In Aug. 778 the rearguard of the French army of Charlemagne was surprised in the valley of Roncesvalles by the Basque inhabitants of the mountains; the baggage was looted and all the rearguard killed, including Hrodland, count of the Breton marches. The story of this disaster was developed by the imagination of medieval writers. For the Basques were substituted the Saracens. Roland becomes the commander of the rearguard, appointed to the post at the instance of the traitor Ganelon, who is in league with the Saracen king, Marsile. Oliver is introduced, Roland's companion in arms. Oliver thrice urges Roland to summon aid by sounding his horn, but Roland from excess of pride defers doing so till too late. Charlemagne returns and destroys the pagan army. Ganelon is tried and executed.

The legend has been handed down in three principal forms: in the fabricated Latin chronicle of the 12th cent. erroneously attributed to Archbishop Turpin (*d. c.* 800); in the 'Carmen de proditione Guenonis' of the same epoch; and in the 'Chanson de Roland', in medieval French, also of the 12th cent. According to tradition Taillefer, a *jongleur* in the army of William the Conqueror, sang a poem on Roncesvalles at the battle of Hastings (1066), possibly an earlier version of the extant 'Chanson'.

Roland, as Orlando, is the hero of Boiardo's 'Orlando Innamorato' and Ariosto's 'Orlando Furioso' (qq.v.).

Roland, Childe, see *Childe Roland*.

Roland de Vaux, (1) the baron of Triermain, in Scott's 'Bridal of Triermain'; (2) in Coleridge's 'Christabel' (q.v.), the name of the estranged friend of Christabel's father.

Roland for an Oliver, A, tit for tat, with reference to the evenly matched combat between Roland and Oliver (qq.v.).

Rolfe, FREDERICK WILLIAM (1860–1913), who liked to call himself 'Baron Corvo', was by turns schoolmaster, painter, and writer. He was a convert to Roman Catholicism and an unsuccessful candidate for the priesthood. His most outstanding work, 'Hadrian the Seventh' (1904), is a novel with a strong feeling of autobiography in the early chapters. It was made into a play by Peter Luke in 1967 (published 1968). His other writings include 'Stories Toto Told Me' (published in 1898 after first appearing in 'The Yellow Book' (q.v.)), 'Chronicles of the House of Borgia'

(1901), and 'The Desire and Pursuit of the Whole' (written in 1909, but considered too libellous at the time and not published until 1934). The story of Rolfe's frustrated life and unhappy death is told by A. J. A. Symons in 'The Quest for Corvo' (1934).

Rolland, ROMAIN (1866–1944), French historian and critic of music, novelist, biographer, and dramatist; author of 'Jean Christophe' (1905–12, novel in ten volumes), etc.

Rolle of Hampole, RICHARD (*c.* 1300–49), lived at various places in Yorkshire, finally at Hampole, where he died, near a Cistercian nunnery in which he had disciples. Among these was Margaret Kirkeby, who became an anchoress and was enclosed in his neighbourhood. Rolle wrote a number of scriptural commentaries, meditations, and other religious works, in Latin and English.

Rolliad, Criticisms on the, a collection of Whig political satires directed against William Pitt and his followers after their success at the election of 1784. The authors, members of the 'Esto Perpetua' club, are not known with certainty.

Rolls Series, otherwise 'Chronicles and Memorials of Great Britain and Ireland from the Invasion of the Romans to the Reign of Henry VIII'. Their publication was authorized by government in 1857 on the suggestion of Joseph Stevenson, the archivist, and the recommendation of Sir John Romilly, master of the rolls. Before 1914, ninety-nine chronicles, etc., had appeared in the series, most of them edited by the greatest historical scholars of the time.

Roman Actor, The, a tragedy by Massinger (q.v.), printed in 1629. The play is based on the life of the Emperor Domitian as told by Suetonius and Dio Cassius.

Romance languages, generally used as the collective name for the group of languages descended from Latin, the chief of which are French, Italian, Spanish, and Provençal.

Roman de la Rose. The first 4,058 lines of this allegorical romance were written *c.* 1240 by Guillaume de Lorris; the last 18,000 lines were composed about forty years later by Jean de Meung. The story in the first part of the poem is an allegorical presentation of courtly love (q.v.), substantially as presented in 'The Romaunt of the Rose' (q.v.). In the second part, Jean de Meung shows love in the real world and links it to an exposition of the new rationalist philosophy of the 13th cent. The 'Roman' remained a powerful influence all through the later Middle Ages, both inside and outside France.

Roman de Renart, see *Reynard the Fox.*

Roman Empire, THE HOLY, see *Holy Roman Empire.*

Romanesque, the style of architecture, based on Roman methods of building (i.e. using the round arch), used in Europe from, very roughly, A.D. 600 to 1150. The form used in England from the 11th cent. is called Norman.

Roman Father, The, a play by W. Whitehead (q.v.).

Romantic, a word for which, in connection with literature, there is no generally accepted definition. The OED. says 'Characterized . . . by, invested . . . with, romance or imaginative appeal', where romance appears to mean 'redolence or suggestion of, association with, the adventurous and chivalrous', something remote from the scene and incidents of ordinary life.

Romantic Movement, THE, in European literature began in the late 18th cent. (though there are earlier isolated examples of the romantic spirit) and lasted into the 19th cent. In literature and art the classical, intellectual attitude gave place to a wider outlook, which recognized the claims of passion and emotion and the sense of mystery in life, and in which the critical was replaced by the creative spirit, and wit by humour and pathos.

In English literature it was marked by a revolt against the conventionalized language and metres of Augustan poetry.

The revolt is usually dated from the publication of 'Lyrical Ballads' (q.v.) in 1798; but its beginnings can be traced much earlier, e.g. in the antiquarian researches of the Wartons (q.v.), the poems of Collins, Ossian, the neo-Gothic affectations of Horace Walpole, etc.

On the prose side, the Romantic movement is connected with the vogue for novels of mystery and terror, and with the historical romances of Sir W. Scott and others.

Roman type, the form normally used today, developed by early printers from humanist script, itself deriving from the capitals of Roman monumental inscriptions and the small letters of 9th-cent. (Carolingian) script, which Italian scholars of the 15th cent. preferred for classical texts.

Romany Rye, The, a novel by Borrow (q.v.) (1857). 'Romany Rye', in gipsy language, means 'Gipsy Gentleman', a name applied to Borrow in his youth by Ambrose Smith, the Norfolk gipsy. This book is a sequel to 'Lavengro' (q.v.), and continues in the same style the story of the author's wanderings and adventures.

Romaunt of the Rose, The, a poem of 7,700 lines in short couplets, attributed to Chaucer, but of which part only was probably written by him. It is a translation, with amplifications, of so much of the French 'Roman de la Rose' (q.v.) as was written by Guillaume de Lorris, and of parts of the continuation by Jean de Meung.

Romeo and Juliet, the first romantic tragedy of Shakespeare (q.v.), based on an Italian romance by Bandello, frequently translated into English. Shakespeare's play was probably written in 1595, first printed in corrupt form in 1597 (authentic second quarto, 1599).

The Montagues and the Capulets, the two chief families of Verona, are at bitter enmity. Romeo, son of old Lord Montague, attends, disguised by a mask, a feast given by old Lord Capulet. He sees and falls in love with Juliet, daughter of

Capulet, and she with him. After the feast he overhears, under her window, Juliet's confession of her love for him, and wins her consent to a secret marriage. With the help of Friar Laurence, they are wedded next day. Mercutio, a friend of Romeo, meets Tybalt, of the Capulet family, and they quarrel. Romeo comes on the scene, and attempts to reason with Tybalt, but Tybalt and Mercutio fight, and Mercutio falls. Then Romeo draws and Tybalt is killed. The duke with Montague and Capulet come up, and Romeo is sentenced to banishment. Early next day, after passing the night with Juliet, he leaves Verona for Mantua, counselled by the friar, who intends to publish Romeo's marriage at an opportune moment. Capulet proposes to marry Juliet to Count Paris, and when she seeks excuses to avoid this, peremptorily insists. Juliet consults the friar, who bids her consent to the match, but on the night before the wedding drink a potion which will render her apparently lifeless for 40 hours. He will warn Romeo, who will rescue her from the vault on her awakening and carry her to Mantua. Juliet does his bidding. The friar's message to Romeo miscarries, and Romeo hears that Juliet is dead. Buying poison, he comes to the vault to have a last sight of Juliet. He chances upon Count Paris outside the vault; they fight and Paris is killed. Then Romeo, after a last kiss on Juliet's lips, drinks the poison and dies. Juliet awakes and finds Romeo dead by her side, and the cup still in his hand. Guessing what has happened, she stabs herself and dies. The story is unfolded by the friar and Count Paris's page, and Montague and Capulet, faced by the tragic results of their enmity, are reconciled.

Romney, GEORGE (1734-1802), portrait painter. His numerous portraits of Lady Hamilton are well known. He is the subject of Tennyson's poem 'Romney's Remorse'.

Romola, a novel by G. Eliot (q.v.) (1863). The background of the novel is Florence at the end of the 15th cent., the troubled period, following the expulsion of the Medici, of the expedition of Charles VIII, of distracted counsels in the city, of the excitement caused by the preaching of Savonarola, and of acute division between the popular party and the supporters of the Medici. The story is that of the purification by trials of the noble-natured Romola, devoted daughter of an old blind scholar. Into their lives comes the clever, adaptable young Greek, Tito Melema. He robs, and abandons in imprisonment the benefactor of his childhood, Baldassare. He cruelly goes through a mock marriage ceremony with the innocent little contadina Tessa. After marrying Romola he wounds her deepest feelings by betraying her father's solemn trust. Nemesis pursues and at last overtakes him in the person of old Baldassare. Romola, with her love for her husband turned to contempt, and her trust in Savonarola destroyed, is rescued by the discovery of her duty in self-sacrifice. Concurrently with this termination the author relates the undermining of Savonarola's influence over the city, his trial, condemnation, and execution.

Romulus, the legendary founder of Rome, a son of Mars and Ilia, the daughter of Numitor, king of Alba. Remus was his twin brother. These two children were thrown into the Tiber, by order of Amulius, who had usurped the throne of his brother Numitor. But they were preserved and suckled by a she-wolf. In due course they put Amulius to death and restored Numitor to the throne. They afterwards undertook to build a city, the future Rome, and the omens having given the preference to Romulus, he began to lay the foundations. But Remus, in ridicule, leapt over them. This angered Romulus, who slew his brother.

Roncesvalles or RONCEVAUX, a valley in the western Pyrenees, celebrated as the scene of the defeat of the rearguard of Charlemagne's army and the death of Roland (q.v.) in 778 (see also *Fontarabia*).

Rondeau, a poem consisting of ten (or in stricter sense, of thirteen) lines, having only two rhymes throughout, and with the opening words used twice as a refrain.

Rondel, a RONDEAU (q.v.), or a special form of this.

Ronsard, PIERRE DE (1524-85), French lyric poet, the principal figure in the 'Pléiade' (q.v.). He contributed powerfully to the reform of French literature, creating a new poetic language, and exercised considerable influence on the English sonnet-writers of the 16th cent., and on Spenser.

Roper, MARGARET (1505-44), daughter of Sir T. More (q.v.). According to Stapleton (1535-98) she purchased the head of her dead father a month after it had been exposed on London Bridge and preserved it in spices till her death. It is believed that it was buried with her. Tennyson alludes to this:

Her, who clasped in her last trance
Her murdered father's head.

('Dream of Fair Women.')

Rosa Bud, a character in Dickens's 'Edwin Drood' (q.v.).

Rosalind, (1) in Spenser's 'Shepheards Calender' and 'Colin Clouts come home againe' (qq.v.), an unknown lady celebrated by the poet as his love; (2) a character in Shakespeare's 'As You Like It' (q.v.).

Rosaline, (1) a character in Shakespeare's 'Love's Labour's Lost' (q.v.); (2) in Shakespeare's 'Romeo and Juliet' (q.v.), a Capulet, with whom Romeo was in love before he saw Juliet.

Rosalynde, Euphues Golden Legacie, a pastoral romance in the style of Lyly's 'Euphues' (q.v.), diversified with sonnets and eclogues, by Thomas Lodge (q.v.) (1590). The story is borrowed in part from 'The Tale of Gamelyn' (q.v.) and was dramatized with little alteration by Shakespeare in his 'As You Like It' (q.v.).

Rosamond, FAIR, Rosamond Clifford (*d.* 1176?), daughter of Walter de Clifford, probably acknowledged as mistress of Henry II in 1174, and according to legend murdered by Queen Eleanor. The story is told in a ballad by Deloney (q.v.); and S. Daniel (q.v.) published in 1592 'The Complaint of Rosamond', a poem in rhyme-royal; Addison wrote an opera 'Rosamond' (1707).

Rosamund, Queen of the Lombards, a play by Swinburne (q.v.) (1861).

Rosciad, The, see *Churchill (C.).*

Roscius, whose full name was QUINTUS ROSCIUS GALLUS (*d.* 62 B.C.), the most celebrated of Roman comic actors.

Roscommon, EARL OF, see *Dillon.*

Rose, Romaunt of the, see *Romaunt of the Rose* and *Roman de la Rose.*

Rose and the Ring, The, a humorous fairy-tale by Thackeray (q.v.) (1855).

Rose Aylmer, an elegy by W. S. Landor (q.v.) on the daughter of Lord Aylmer. She was an early love of Landor's, but on her mother's second marriage was sent out to her aunt at Calcutta, where she died, aged twenty.

Rosebery, ARCHIBALD PHILIP PRIMROSE, *fifth earl of* (1847-1929), foreign secretary in the Gladstone governments of 1886 and 1892, prime minister in 1894-5, an eloquent and witty speaker. He was author of the works: 'Pitt' (1891), 'Napoleon—the Last Phase' (1900), etc.

Rose Mary, a poem by D. G. Rossetti (q.v.), included in 'Ballads and Sonnets', published in 1881.

Rose Mary, looking into a magic beryl, in which only the pure can see the truth, sees, as she thinks, the peril to which her lover is exposed, and he is warned. But Rose Mary has sinned and her sin has admitted into the beryl evil spirits, who have concealed the truth from her. Her lover is faithless and is killed. She takes her father's sword and breaks the beryl, thus releasing her soul from destruction.

Rosenberg, ISAAC (1890-1918), a poet of promise, killed in the First World War. His work was experimental in character, strongly influenced by his Jewish background, and his best-known poems deal with his experiences in the trenches. His collected works were published in 1937.

Rosencrantz and **Guildenstern,** characters in Shakespeare's 'Hamlet' (q.v.).

Rose-noble, see *Noble.*

'Rose-red city—half as old as time', in Dean J. W. Burgon's poem, 'Petra', the ancient capital of Arabia Petraea, now in ruins, discovered by Burckhardt in 1812.

Rose Tavern, THE, in Russell Street, Covent Garden, was a favourite place of resort in the latter part of the 17th and early 18th cents.

Rose Theatre, THE, on Bankside, Southwark, opened in 1592 and was managed by P. Henslowe (q.v.). Shakespeare acted there.

Rosetta Stone, a piece of black basalt found by Napoleon's soldiers near the Rosetta mouth of the Nile, bearing an inscription in Egyptian hieroglyphics, demotic characters, and Greek, which proved to be the key to the interpretation of hieroglyphics. It is now in the British Museum.

Rosicrucian, a member of a supposed society or order, reputedly founded by one Christian Rosenkreuz in 1484, but first mentioned in 1614, whose members were said to claim various forms of secret and magic knowledge. No Rosicrucian society appears to have actually existed. The Rosicrucians of the 17th cent. seem to have been moral and religious reformers, who covered their views with a cloak of mysticism and alchemy. There is a good deal on the subject in Shorthouse's 'John Inglesant' (q.v.).

Rosinante or ROZINANTE, the horse of Don Quixote (q.v.).

Ross, SIR JAMES CLARK (1800–62), Arctic and Antarctic explorer, was author of 'A Voyage in the Southern and Antarctic Regions (1839–43)' (1847).

Ross, SIR JOHN (1777–1856), uncle of the above, Arctic explorer, was author of two narratives of voyages in search of the North-West Passage (1819, 1835).

Ross, MARTIN, see under *Somerville* (E. Œ.).

Ross, THE MAN OF, see *Kyrle.*

Rossetti, CHRISTINA GEORGINA (1830–94), the sister of D. G. Rossetti (q.v.), contributed to 'The Germ' (q.v.) under the pseudonym 'Ellen Alleyne', and published her first work in book form, 'Goblin Market and other Poems', in 1862. 'The Prince's Progress' appeared in 1866, 'Sing-Song' in 1872, and 'A Pageant and other Poems' in 1881. Notable among her contributions to 'The Germ' is the lyric entitled 'The Dream'. Her work ranged from poems of fantasy and verses for the young to religious poetry, which constituted the greater part of her writings. They are in general pervaded by a spiritual and melancholy cast, and marked by a high degree of technical perfection. Her 'Monna Innominata' is a series of sonnets of unhappy love.

Rossetti, DANTE GABRIEL (1828–82), the son of Gabriele Rossetti, an Italian patriot who came to England in 1824. He formed with Holman Hunt, John Everett Millais, and others, part of the Pre-Raphaelite Brotherhood (q.v.). For many years he was known only as a painter, though he began to write poetry very early (from 1847). 'The Blessed Damozel', one of his earliest works, subsequently more than once revised, appeared in 'The Germ' (q.v.). In 1860 he married Miss Eleanor Siddal, and in 1861 he published his first volume, 'The Early Italian Poets', a collection of scrupulous translations from Dante (including the 'Vita Nuova' and the sonnets) and his predecessors and contemporaries. His wife died in 1862 and a manuscript containing a number of his poems was buried with her. These were subsequently disinterred and published in 'Poems by D. G. Rossetti' in 1870. They include 'Sister Helen', 'Eden Bower', 'The Stream's Secret', and 'Love's Nocturn'. 'Ballads and Sonnets' appeared in 1881, completing the sequence of love-sonnets called 'The House of Life', of which part had appeared in the earlier volume, and including such notable poems as 'Rose Mary', 'The White Ship', and 'The King's Tragedy' (qq.v.).

In 1871 Rossetti was attacked by Robert Buchanan under the pseudonym 'Thomas

Maitland' in an article entitled 'The Fleshly School', to which Rosseti published a convincing reply.

Rossetti, WILLIAM MICHAEL (1829-1919), brother of D. G. Rossetti (q.v.), a man of letters and art-critic. He was one of the Pre-Raphaelites and edited 'The Germ' (q.v.). His works include a blank-verse translation of Dante's 'Inferno' (1865), a 'Life of Keats' (1887), and a study of 'Dante and his Convito' (1910).

Rossini, GIOACHINO ANTONIO (1792-1868), Italian operatic composer. His best-known operas are 'The Barber of Seville' (1816) and 'William Tell' (1829).

Rostand, EDMOND (1868-1918), French dramatist, whose best-known work is 'Cyrano de Bergerac' (1898, see *Bergerac*).

Roswitha, see *Hrotsvitha*.

Rouget de L'Isle, CLAUDE JOSEPH (1760-1836), an engineer officer in the French army, who in 1792 composed the 'Marseillaise' (words and music), the French national hymn.

Roundabout Papers, The, a series of discursive essays by W. M. Thackeray (q.v.), published in 'The Cornhill Magazine', 1860-3.

Roundheads, members or adherents of the parliamentary party in the Civil War of the 17th cent., so called from the Puritan custom of wearing the hair cut close.

Round Table, THE, in the Arthurian legend, was made (according to one version by Merlin) for Uther Pendragon and given by him to King Leodegrance of Cameliard. The latter gave it as a wedding gift, with 100 knights, to Arthur when he married Guinevere, his daughter. It would seat 150 knights, and all places round it were equal. The 'Siege Perilous' was reserved for the knight who should achieve the quest of the Grail (q.v.). In Layamon's 'Brut', however, the table was made for Arthur by a crafty workman. It is first mentioned by Wace (q.v.).

Round Table, The, a Collection of Essays on Literature, Men, and Manners, consists of forty essays by William Hazlitt (q.v.) and twelve by Leigh Hunt (q.v.), published in two volumes, 1817.

Rousseau, JEAN-JACQUES (1712-78), was born at Geneva, son of a watch-maker. He led a wretched erratic life which he has described in his masterpiece, the 'Confessions' (published after his death).

He came early into notice by the works in which he expounded his revolt against the existing social order. 'La Nouvelle Héloïse', a novel in which the question of the return to nature was discussed in its relation to the sexes and the family, appeared in 1761. 'Du Contrat social', setting forth his political philosophy, was published in 1762, and 'Émile', his views on education, in the same year. The 'Contrat Social' had a profound influence on French thought, especially after 1789.

Rousseau attributed evil, not to sin, but to society, as a departure from the natural state, in which man is both good and happy. In political philosophy Rousseau held the view that society is founded on a contract, and that the head of the state is the people's mandatary, not their master.

Routh, MARTIN JOSEPH (1755-1854), president of Magdalen College, Oxford, for sixty-three years, edited the 'Gorgias' and 'Euthydemus' of Plato, and 'Reliquiae Sacrae' (1814-43), a collection of writings of ecclesiastical authors of the 2nd and 3rd cents. His long life and literary experience lend weight to his famous utterance: 'I think, Sir, you will find it a very good practice *always to verify your references.*' A life of Routh by R. D. Middleton was published in 1938.

Rowe, NICHOLAS (1674-1718), became a barrister of the Middle Temple; but abandoned the legal profession for that of playwright, and made the acquaintance of Pope and Addison. He produced at Lincoln's Inn Fields his tragedies, 'The Ambitious Stepmother' (1700), 'Tamerlane' (q.v., 1702), and 'The Fair Penitent' (q.v.) (adapted from Massinger's and Field's 'Fatal Dowry', 1703), and 'Jane

Shore' and 'Lady Jane Grey' in 1714 and 1715 respectively, at Drury Lane. The moral tone of his plays is in strong contrast to the licentiousness of the drama of the preceding fifty years. Rowe became poet laureate in 1715. His poetical works include a famous translation of Lucan (1718), and he did some useful work as editor of Shakespeare's plays (1709), dividing them into acts and scenes, supplying stage directions, and generally making the text more intelligible.

Rowena, (1) the legendary daughter of Hengist; (2) a character in Scott's 'Ivanhoe' (q.v.; see also *Rebecca and Rowena*).

Rowland, Child, see *Childe Roland*.

Rowlandson, THOMAS (1756-1827), caricaturist and painter of humorous low-life subjects. Among his illustrations were those for 'Dr. Syntax' (see *Combe*).

Rowley, in Sheridan's 'The School for Scandal' (q.v.), the old servant of the Surfaces.

Rowley, WILLIAM (1585?-1642?), dramatist and actor. His best dramatic work was done in collaboration with T. Middleton (q.v.). He collaborated in 'A Fair Quarrel' (1617), 'The Changeling' (performed 1621), and other plays, with Middleton; in 'Fortune by Land and Sea' (printed 1655) with Heywood; and in other pieces with Ford, Massinger, and Dekker (qq.v.).

Rowley Poems, see *Chatterton*.

Rowley Powley, THE REVD., in Byron's 'Don Juan', xi. 57, was G. Croly (1780-1860).

Roxana, the daughter of a Persian satrap, who was taken captive by Alexander the Great, and became his wife. Later, Alexander took a second wife, Barsine, daughter of Darius and Statira. On this has been based the story of the jealousy of Roxana and her vengeance on her rival. It forms the basis of Nathaniel Lee's (q.v.) tragedy, 'The Rival Queens', where the second wife is called Statira.

Roxana, or the Fortunate Mistress, a romance by Defoe (q.v.) (1724).

This purports to be the autobiography of Mlle Beleau, the beautiful daughter of French Protestant refugees who enters upon a career of prosperous wickedness.

Roxburghe, JOHN KER, *third duke of* (1740-1804), an ardent bibliophile. His splendid library was dispersed in 1812. In that year was inaugurated the ROXBURGHE CLUB, consisting of twenty-four members, with T. F. Dibdin as its first secretary. The Club, at first rather convivial in character, began its valuable literary work with the printing of the metrical romance of Havelok the Dane (1828).

Roxburghe Club, see *Roxburghe (J. K.)*.

Royal Academy, THE, see *Academy of Arts*.

Royal Exchange, THE, see *Exchange (The Royal)*.

Royal Historical Society, see *Historical Society*.

Royal Martyr, THE, (1) Charles I; (2) see *Tyrannic Love*.

Royal Society, THE, originated in the Philosophical Society, which was founded in 1645. Its meetings in London were resumed at the Restoration, and it received its charter as the Royal Society in 1662. Among its principal projectors were Abraham Cowley (q.v.) and Robert Boyle the chemist (see under *Boyle Lectures*). The remarkable feature of the Royal Society among scientific academies was that it took the whole field of knowledge for its province and included among its early members such men of letters as Dryden, Waller, Evelyn, and Aubrey. Its first historian was Bishop Sprat (q.v.), who describes its aims. Among these was the improvement of English prose.

Royal Society of Literature, see *Literature*.

Rozinante, see *Rosinante*.

Rubáiyát of Omar Khayyám, The, see *Omar Khayyám*.

Rubens, PETER PAUL (1577-1640). Flemish painter, the chief northern exponent of the baroque. He visited England in 1629 and was commissioned to paint the ceiling of the Banqueting House, Whitehall. He was an enormously prolific painter. His style was based on the great Italian masters, but in later life he painted for his own pleasure landscapes with a new feeling for the country.

Rubicon, a small river rising in the Apennines and flowing into the Adriatic; it separated Italy from Cisalpine Gaul. By crossing it with an army and thus overstepping the boundaries of his province, Julius Caesar committed himself to war against the Senate and Pompey (49 B.C.).

Rugby, JACK, in Shakespeare's 'The Merry Wives of Windsor' (q.v.), servant to Dr. Caius.

Rugby Chapel, a poem by M. Arnold (q.v.).

Rugby School, founded by Laurence Sheriff in 1567. T. Arnold (q.v.) was its headmaster from 1828 to 1842. A vivid picture of school-life at Rugby in his days is given in 'Tom Brown's Schooldays' by Thomas Hughes (q.v.).

Ruggiero, see *Rogero*.

Ruggle, GEORGE, see *Ignoramus*.

Ruin, The, an Old English poem of some thirty-five lines included in the 'Exeter Book' (q.v.), describing the result of the devastation by the Saxons of a Roman settlement (perhaps Bath), and showing, with deep feeling, the contrast of past splendour with present desolation.

Ruined Cottage, The, or *The Story of Margaret*, a poem by Wordsworth (q.v.), written in 1797, and subsequently embodied in Bk. I of 'The Excursion' (q.v.).

It is a harrowing tale of misfortune befalling a cottager and his wife. The husband leaves his home and joins a troop of soldiers going to a distant land. The wife stays on, pining for his return, in increasing wretchedness, till she dies and the cottage falls into ruin.

Ruines of Time, The, a poem by Spenser (q.v.), included in the 'Complaints' (1591). It is an allegorical elegy on the death of Sir P. Sidney (q.v.), which had also been the occasion of his earlier elegy 'Astrophel'.

Rukenaw, DAME, the ape's wife in 'Reynard the Fox' (q.v.).

Rule a Wife and Have a Wife, a comedy by J. Fletcher (q.v.), produced in 1624.

Rule, Britannia: for the words see *Thomson (James*, 1700-48); the air was composed by Thomas Augustine Arne (1710-78) for Thomson and Mallet's masque, 'Alfred'.

Rune, a letter or character of the earliest Teutonic alphabet, which was most extensively used (in various forms) by the Scandinavians and Anglo-Saxons. Also a similar character or mark having magical or mysterious powers attributed to it. The earliest runic alphabet dates from at least the 2nd or 3rd cent., and was formed by modifying the letters of the Roman or Greek alphabet so as to facilitate cutting them upon wood or stone.

Rupert of Hentzau, a novel by Anthony Hope, a sequel to 'The Prisoner of Zenda' (q.v.).

Rural Rides, by Cobbett (q.v.), collected in 1830, descriptive of various parts of England, with agricultural and political comments. A committee in 1821 had proposed certain remedies for the agricultural distress that followed the war. Cobbett disapproved of these and 'made up his mind to see for himself'.

Ruritania, an imaginary kingdom in central Europe, the scene of Anthony Hope's 'The Prisoner of Zenda' (q.v.) and its sequel 'Rupert of Hentzau'. The name connotes, more generally, make-believe romance, chivalry, intrigue, at a royal court in a modern European setting.

Ruskin, JOHN (1819-1900), the son of John James Ruskin, a partner in a wine business. He published in 1843 anonymously the first volume of the famous 'Modern Painters' (q.v.), of which five volumes in all were issued over a period of seventeen years. He made the acquaintance of Turner in 1840 and of Millais in 1851. In 1849 he published his 'Seven Lamps of Architecture' (q.v.) and 'Stones of Venice' (q.v.) in 1851-3. As 'Modern Painters' was begun in defence of Turner,

R

so in 1851 he wrote letters to 'The Times' and pamphlets conscientiously defending the Pre-Raphaelites (q.v.). His mind turned to economics, and some essays which he published on this subject in 'The Cornhill Magazine' in 1860 and in 'Fraser's Magazine' in 1862-3 aroused strong opposition by their heterodoxy. They were subsequently republished as 'Unto this Last' (1862) and 'Munera Pulveris' (qq.v.) (1872). These and other treatises and pamphlets advocated a system of national education, the organization of labour, and other social reforms. His interest in social reform is again shown in his most popular work 'Sesame and Lilies' (q.v., 1865), and in 'The Crown of Wild Olive' (q.v., 1866). In 1871 he settled at Coniston, and in that year began his monthly letters in 'Fors Clavigera' (q.v.), 'to the workmen and labourers of Great Britain'. He also engaged in several industrial experiments, including the revival of the hand-made linen industry in Langdale. His 'Praeterita', an autobiography which was never completed, was published at intervals during 1885-9.

Russell, LADY, a character in Jane Austen's 'Persuasion' (q.v.).

Russell, BERTRAND ARTHUR WILLIAM, *third Earl Russell* (1872-1970), philosopher. He wrote voluminously on philosophy, logic, education, economics, and politics. 'The Principles of Mathematics' (1903) and 'Principia Mathematica' (the latter in collaboration with A. N. Whitehead, 1910) are already classics of mathematical logic. Other important philosophical works include 'The Analysis of Mind' (1921), 'An Inquiry into Meaning and Truth' (1940), and 'Human Knowledge, its Scope and Limits' (1948).

Russell, GEORGE WILLIAM (1867-1935), an Irish poet and artist, widely known under his pseudonym 'Æ', 'A E', or 'A.E.'. His poems, the work of a mystic, were described by Yeats as 'the most delicate and subtle that any Irishman of our time has written'. The production of his drama 'Deirdre' by an amateur company in 1902 was one of the early steps towards the formation of the Irish National Theatre. Russell was editor of 'The Irish Statesman' from 1923 to 1930.

Russell, LORD JOHN, *first Earl Russell* (1792-1878), entered parliament in 1813, and was a strenuous advocate of parliamentary reform. He was prime minister 1846-52, and on the death of Palmerston, once more became prime minister, 1865-6. He published a 'Life of William, Lord Russell' (1819), 'Memoirs of Affairs of Europe' (1824-9), 'Life and Times of Charles James Fox' (1859-60), etc.

Russell, WILLIAM CLARK (1844-1911), wrote some sixty tales of nautical adventure. His writings led to improved conditions in the merchant service.

Rustem or RUSTUM, the great Persian national hero. He is represented as living during several centuries, a constant conqueror. He overcomes dragons and demons, and unwittingly fights with and kills his son Sohrab. This last episode is the subject of M. Arnold's 'Sohrab and Rustum' (q.v.).

Ruth, in the O.T. Book of Ruth, a Moabitess, the widowed daughter-in-law of Naomi of Bethlehem who gleaned corn in the fields of Boaz and became his wife.

Ruth, a novel by Mrs. Gaskell (q.v.) (1853).

Rutherford, MARK, see *White* (*W. H.*).

Ruthwell Cross, a stone monument in Dumfriesshire, dating perhaps from the 8th cent., on which are inscribed, in runes, extracts from 'The Dream of the Rood' (q.v.).

Rymenhild, see *King Horn*.

Rymer, THOMAS (1641-1713), is chiefly remembered for his valuable collection of historical records, 'Foedera' (1704-35). He wrote a play in rhymed verse, but is better known for his 'Tragedies of the last age considered' (1678), in which he discussed some of Beaumont and Fletcher's plays, and for his 'Short View of Tragedy' (1692), in which he condemned 'Othello'.

S

Sabbath, WITCHES', a midnight meeting of demons, sorcerers, and witches, presided over by the Devil, supposed to have been held annually as an orgy or festival.

Sabbath day's journey, the distance (2,000 *ammoth* = 1,125 yards) which (according to Rabbinical prescription in the time of Christ) was the utmost limit of permitted travel on the Sabbath.

Sabbatical Year, the seventh year, which according to Mosaic law was to be observed as a 'Sabbath', the land remaining untilled, and all debtors and Israelitish slaves being released; in modern use, a year of absence from duty for the purposes of study and travel, granted to teachers in universities, etc.

Sabellianism, the doctrine concerning the coequality and consubstantiality of the Trinity held by the followers of Sabellius, a heresiarch of Ptolemais who lived in the 3rd cent. Sabellianism came to be used as a term covering such of the unitarian doctrines as recognize the divinity of Christ.

Sabines, THE, an ancient people of Italy, whose lands were in the neighbourhood of Rome. They are celebrated in legend as having taken up arms against the Romans, to avenge the carrying off of their women by the latter at a spectacle to which they had been invited. Subsequently they are said to have made peace and migrated to Rome, where they settled with their new allies.

Sabrina, a poetic name for the river Severn (see under *Estrildis*). In Milton's 'Comus' (q.v.), which was presented at Ludlow Castle, Sabrina is the nymph of the Severn.

Sacharissa, see *Waller*.

Sachs, HANS (1494–1576), shoemaker of Nuremberg, and author of a vast quantity of verse. He figures in Wagner's opera 'Die Meistersinger von Nürnberg'.

Sack, adapted from the French *vin sec*, 'dry wine', i.e. wine 'free from sweetness and fruity flavour'. The word was used as a general name for a class of white wines imported from Spain and the Canaries. Sack was the favourite drink of Falstaff (Shakespeare, '2 Henry IV', IV. iii).

Sackville, CHARLES, *Lord Buckhurst*, and later *sixth earl of Dorset* (1638–1706), a friend and patron of poets, who was himself eulogized as a poet by Dryden and Prior. His poems include some pleasant songs (the best known is the ballad 'To all you Ladies now at Land') and mordant satires.

Sackville, THOMAS, *first earl of Dorset* and *Baron Buckhurst* (1536–1608), was raised to the peerage in 1567, and held a number of high official positions. He wrote the 'Induction' and 'The Complaint of Buckingham' for 'A Mirror for Magistrates' (q.v.), and collaborated (probably writing only the last two acts) with Thomas Norton in the tragedy 'Gorboduc' (q.v.).

Sackville-West, HON. VICTORIA (1892–1962), poet and novelist, daughter of third Baron Sackville. Her published works include 'The Land' (1927), 'Collected Poems' (1933), and 'The Garden' (1946), poetry; 'The Edwardians' (1930), 'All Passion Spent' (1931), and 'The Easter Party' (1953), novels; 'Knole and the Sackvilles' (1923) and 'Pepita' (1937), studies of her family and origins. 'The Eagle and the Dove' (1943) is a study of St. Teresa of Avila and St. Theresa of Lisieux. With her husband, Sir Harold Nicolson, she edited 'Another World Than This' (1945), an anthology.

Sacred Nine, THE, the Muses (q.v.).

Sacripant, in the 'Orlando Innamorato' and the 'Orlando Furioso' (qq.v.), the king of Circassia and a lover of Angelica. SACRAPANT figures as a magician in Peele's 'The Old Wives' Tale' (q.v.).

Saddletree, BARTOLINE, a character in Scott's 'The Heart of Midlothian' (q.v.).

Sadducees, one of the three sects (the others being the Pharisees and the Essenes) into which the Jews were divided in the time of Christ.

Sade, DONATIEN ALPHONSE, *Count* (generally known as *Marquis*) *de* (1740–1814), a French author whose licentious writings have given his name to SADISM, a form of sexual perversion marked by a love of cruelty.

Sadi, a celebrated Persian poet, said to have lived *c.* 1200.

Sadler's Wells, in north London, originally a hydropathic establishment at a mineral spring, developed by a Mr. Sadler in 1683. A place of entertainment was added, and in 1765 a theatre was opened. Here the pantomimist, Joseph Grimaldi (q.v.), gave his earliest performances. From 1844 to 1859 it was under the management of Mrs. Warner and Mrs. Phelps, whose Shakespeare productions are historic. The theatre was rebuilt, to a large extent by means of a grant from the Carnegie Trust, and reopened in 1931, to be for north London what the 'Old Vic' (q.v.) is for south London—a theatre where good plays can be seen at 'popular prices'.

Sad Shepherd, The, or, A Tale of Robin Hood, the last and unfinished play of Jonson (q.v.), a pastoral drama.

Saga, an Old Norse word meaning 'story', applied to the narrative compositions in prose that were written in Iceland or Norway during the Middle Ages. In English use it is often applied specially to those which embody the traditional history of the Icelandic families or of the kings of Norway. The Icelandic sagas divide themselves into two groups, the more historical, of which the 'Heimskringla' (q.v.) of Snorri and the 'Sturlunga Saga' of Sturla (q.v.) are the principal examples; and the less historical, of which the chief are: the 'Laxdaela' (of which we have a version in W. Morris's 'Earthly Paradise'); the 'Eyrbyggya', legends; the 'Egla'; the

'Njala' (translated by Sir George Dasent); and the 'Grettla', or the story of Grettir the Strong (translated by William Morris and Eirikr Magnusson).

Sagittarius, the zodiacal constellation of the *Archer*, according to myth, the centaur Cheiron (q.v.); the ninth sign of the zodiac, which the sun enters about 22 Nov.

Saint, for names with this prefix see, with the following exceptions, the names themselves.

Sainte-Beuve, CHARLES AUGUSTIN (1804–69), the first great French critic to break away from the dogmas of the classical school. Some of his early criticisms, notably the 'Tableau . . . de la poésie française . . . au XVIᵉ siècle' (1828), did much to promote the Romantic movement (q.v.) in France by the attention he drew to the poetry of the 16th cent., though his own sympathy with the Romantics did not last. He also wrote some poetry and an introspective, partly autobiographical, novel, 'Volupté' (1834).

Sainte-Maure, BENOÎT DE, see *Benoît*.

Saint-Évremond, CHARLES DE MARGUETEL DE SAINT-DENIS DE (1614?–1703), a French author, who was exiled from his own country for political reasons, and came to England, where he spent the years 1662–5 and from 1670 to his death. He was on intimate terms with the wits and courtiers of the day, and wrote critical essays on a variety of literary subjects, including one on English comedy (1685). Some of these were translated into English (with a character of St.-Évremond by Dryden) in 1692.

St. Irvyne, or the Rosicrucian, see *Shelley* (*P. B.*).

St. James's Palace was built by Henry VIII. After Stuart times it superseded Whitehall as the principal royal residence in London, and gave the official title to the 'Court of St. James'.

St. John, HENRY, *first Viscount Bolingbroke,* see *Bolingbroke* (*Viscount*).

St. Juliana, see *Cynewulf.*

Saint-Pierre, JACQUES HENRI BERNARDIN

DE (1737-1814), a French writer and follower of Rousseau (q.v.), chiefly known as the author of 'Paul et Virginie' (1787), a poetic romance of naïve and virtuous love, which obtained immense popularity.

St. Ronan's Well, a novel by Sir W. Scott (q.v.), published in 1823.

In this work the author for once chose a scene of contemporary life, in the Scottish spa of St. Ronan's Well, whose idle fashionable society is satirically described.

Saintsbury, GEORGE EDWARD BATEMAN (1845-1933), a distinguished literary critic and historian, and professor of rhetoric and English literature at Edinburgh University, 1895-1915. He was the author of a large number of works on English and European literature, and lives of Dryden, Sir Walter Scott, and Matthew Arnold and also of the interesting and entertaining 'Notes on a Cellar Book' (1920), etc.

Saki, see *Munro* (*H. H.*).

Saladin (SALA-ED-DIN YUSUF IBN AYUB) (1137-93), became Sultan of Egypt about 1174, invaded Palestine, defeated the Christians, and captured Jerusalem. He was attacked by the Crusaders under Richard Cœur-de-Lion and Philip II of France. He figures prominently in Scott's 'The Talisman' (q.v.).

Salamander, see *Sylph*.

Salanio and **Salarino**, characters in Shakespeare's 'The Merchant of Venice' (q.v.).

Salerno, in Italy, the seat of a medical school famous in the Middle Ages.

Salic Law, originally, a code of law of the Salian Franks, written in Latin, and extant in five recensions of Merovingian and Carolingian date. In early use, and still in popular language, the Salic Law is the alleged fundamental law of the French monarchy by which females were excluded from succession to the crown.

Sallust (GAIUS SALLUSTIUS CRISPUS) (86-35 B.C.), a Roman historian and an adherent of Caesar in the civil war. After the African war Caesar made him governor of Numidia. He wrote 'Catilina', a history of the conspiracy of Catiline; 'Bellum Jugurthinum', a history of the Roman war against Jugurtha (111-106 B.C.); and 'Histories' covering the period 78-67 B.C. Of the last very little survives.

Sally in our Alley, a ballad by Carey (q.v.).

Salmasius (CLAUDE DE SAUMAISE) (1588-1653), an eminent scholar, professor at Leyden University in 1649. He was commissioned by Charles II to draw up a defence of his father and an indictment of the regicide government. This took the form of the Latin 'Defensio Regia', which reached England at the end of 1649. Milton (q.v.) was ordered by the Council in 1650 to prepare a reply to it, and in 1651 issued his 'Pro Populo Anglicano Defensio', also in Latin. In this, instead of defending the people of England, as he purports to do, he merely heaps invective on his adversary. To this Salmasius rejoined in his 'Responsio', which is similarly composed mainly of personal abuse.

Salome, the daughter of Herodias (q.v.) by her first husband Herod Philip. Herod Antipas, her stepfather, enchanted by her dancing, offered her a reward 'unto the half of my kingdom'. Instructed by Herodias, Salome asked for the head of John the Baptist in a charger (see Matt. xiv). The story is the subject of a drama by Wilde (q.v.), 'Salomé' (1893), written in French, a marvel of mimetic power. The licenser of plays in the summer of 1893 refused to sanction the performance of this. It was translated into English by Wilde's friend, Lord Alfred Douglas (q.v.), in 1893 (with ten pictures by Aubrey Beardsley), and afterwards formed the libretto of an opera by Richard Strauss. The original version was produced in Paris in 1896. The play was produced at the Savoy Theatre, London, on 5 Oct. 1931.

Saluzzo, THE MARQUIS OF, Wautier of Saluces in Chaucer's 'Clerk's Tale', is the husband of Griselda (see *Canterbury Tales*).

Salvation Army, THE, was started as the 'Christian Mission' in Whitechapel in 1865 by William Booth. It was converted into the 'Salvation Army' in 1878, and became a world-wide engine of revivalism.

Salvation Yeo, a character in C. Kingsley's 'Westward Ho!' (q.v.).

Samaritan, GOOD, an allusion to Luke x. 33.

Samian ware, originally pottery made of Samian earth; extended to a fine pottery found on Roman sites.

Samient, in Spenser's 'Faerie Queene', v. viii, the lady sent by Queen Mercilla to Adicia, the wife of the Souldan, received by her with contumely, and rescued by Sir Artegall.

Samos, a large island in the Aegean, the birthplace of Pythagoras. It was a special seat of the worship of Hera (q.v.).

Samoyed, the name of a Mongolian race inhabiting Siberia. Milton, 'Paradise Lost', x. 696, refers to 'Norumbega and the Samoed shore'.

Sampson, DOMINIE, a character in Scott's 'Guy Mannering' (q.v.). His favourite expression of astonishment is 'Prodigious!'

Samson Agonistes, a tragedy by Milton (q.v.) (1671), in the same volume as 'Paradise Regained' (q.v.). In form it is modelled on Greek tragedies. 'Samson Agonistes' (i.e. Samson the Athlete or Wrestler) deals with the last phase of the life of the Samson of the Book of Judges (xvi), when he is a prisoner of the Philistines and blind, a phase which presents a certain pathetic similarity to the circumstances of the poet himself when he wrote the play.

Samson, in the prison at Gaza, is visited by friends of his tribe (the Chorus), who seek to comfort him; then by his old father Manoa, who holds out hope of securing his release; then by his wife Dalila, who seeks pardon and reconciliation, but being repudiated shows herself 'a manifest serpent in the end'; then by Harapha, a strong man of Gath, who taunts Samson. He is finally summoned

to provide amusement by feats of strength for the Philistine lords, who are celebrating a feast to Dagon. He goes, and presently a messenger brings news of their destruction and the death of Samson, by his pulling down of the pillars supporting the roof of the place in which they were.

Samuel, a Hebrew prophet. After the defeat of the Israelites by the Philistines, he rallied the people, and became their ruler. The two books of the O.T. called after him were not written by him, but cover the history of Israel from his birth to the end of the reign of David.

Sancho Panza, the squire of Don Quixote (q.v.), who accompanies him in his adventures and shares their unpleasant consequences. His conversation is full of common sense and pithy proverbs.

Sand, GEORGE, the pseudonym of ARMANDINE LUCILE AURORE DUPIN, *Baronne Dudevant* (1804–76), French novelist. She was married young, and after some years separated from her husband. She subsequently had relations with Alfred de Musset and the composer Chopin, which influenced her work.

Sandburg, CARL (1878–1967), American poet. He challenged contemporary taste by his use of colloquialisms and free verse, and became the principal among the authors writing in Chicago during and after the First World War. He published 'Chicago Poems' (1916), 'Smoke and Steel' (1920), 'The American Songbag', a collection of folksongs (1927), 'Good Morning America' (1928), 'Complete Poems' (1950), and a monumental life of Abraham Lincoln (6 vols., 1926–39).

Sandford and Merton, The History of, a children's tale by T. Day (q.v.), of which vol. i appeared in 1783, vol. ii in 1787, and vol. iii in 1789.

It consists of a succession of episodes in which the rich and objectionable Tommy Merton is contrasted with the virtuous Harry Sandford, a farmer's son, and the moral is drawn by the Revd. Mr. Barlow, their tutor. It is written, without the least sense of humour, to illustrate the author's doctrine that virtue pays.

Sandra Belloni, originally entitled *Emilia in England*, a novel by Meredith (q.v.) (1864). The sequel of the story is in the author's 'Vittoria'.

Sandys, GEORGE (1578-1644), a traveller in Italy, Turkey, Egypt, and Palestine. His chief works were a translation of Ovid's 'Metamorphoses' (1621-6), a verse 'Paraphrase upon the Psalmes' (1636), and 'Christ's Passion, a Tragedy', a verse translation from the Latin of Grotius (1640). He is of some importance in the history of English verse.

Sanger, JOHN (1816-89), the celebrated circus proprietor. In his later years John Sanger was known as Lord John Sanger.

Sanglier, SIR, in Spenser's 'Faerie Queene', V. i, the wicked knight who has cut off his lady's head, and is forced by Sir Artegall to bear the head before him, in token of his shame. He is thought to represent Shane O'Neill, second earl of Tyrone (1530?-67), a leader of the Irish, who invaded the Pale in 1566.

Sangrado, DR., a quack physician in 'Gil Blas' (q.v.), the whole of whose science consisted in bleeding his patients and making them drink hot water.

Sangreal, SANGCREAL, the Holy Grail, see *Grail*.

Sanhedrin, the name applied to the highest court of justice and supreme council at Jerusalem in N.T. times.

Sansfoy, Sansjoy, and **Sansloy,** three brothers in Spenser's 'Faerie Queene', I. ii. 25 et seq. Sansfoy ('faithless') is slain by the Red Cross Knight, who also defeats Sansjoy ('joyless'), but the latter is saved from death by Duessa. Sansloy ('lawless') carries off Una and kills her lion (I. iii). This incident is supposed to refer to the suppression of the Protestant religion in the reign of Queen Mary.

Sanskrit, the ancient and sacred language of India, the oldest known member of the Indo-European family of languages. The extensive Hindu literature from the Vedas downward is composed in it.

Santa Claus, a contraction of St. Nicholas, who is supposed to come, on the night before Christmas Day, to bring presents for children. St. Nicholas was the patron saint of children.

Santayana, GEORGE (1863-1952), a Spaniard brought up in Boston and educated at Harvard, where he became professor of philosophy in 1889. He was an eminent speculative philosopher, of a naturalist tendency and opposed to German idealism, whose views are embodied in his 'Life of Reason' (1905-6). He later modified and supplemented his philosophy in a series of five books, 'The Realms of Being' (1923-40). The most notable among his other writings are 'Soliloquies in England' (1922), essays on the English character, and 'Character and Opinion in the United States' (1920), one of several studies of American life. He also examined the American tradition in his only novel, 'The Last Puritan' (1935).

Sapper, the pen-name of H. C. McNEILE (1888-1937), author of the popular 'Bulldog Drummond' stories about the British ex-army officer who foils the activities of Carl Peterson, the international crook.

Sappho (*fl.* 7th cent. B.C.), a poetess of great genius and passionate energy, a native of Lesbos. Only a few fragments of her work survive, marked by melody and fire. The story of her throwing herself into the sea in despair at her unrequited love for Phaon is probably a later fable. The SAPPHIC STANZA (used by Horace with some modification of its rules) is only one of the many metres that Sappho employed. It consists of $-\cup-\bar{\cup}-\cup\cup-\cup-\bar{\cup}$ thrice repeated, and followed by $-\cup\cup-\bar{\cup}$.

Sapsea, MR., in Dickens's 'Edwin Drood' (q.v.), mayor of Cloisterham.

Saracen, a name whose ultimate etymology is obscure. Among the later Greeks and Romans it was applied to the nomadic tribes of the Syro-Arabian desert. Hence it was used for an Arab, and by extension a Muslim, especially with reference to the Crusades.

Sardanapalus, the last king of Assyria, notorious according to legend for his luxury and effeminacy.

Sardanapalus, a tragedy by Lord Byron (q.v.) (1821).

It was written at Ravenna and the materials were taken from the 'Bibliotheca Historica' of Diodorus Siculus, but freely treated. Sardanapalus is represented as a luxurious but courageous monarch. When Beleses, a Chaldean soothsayer, and Arbaces, governor of Media, lead a revolt against him, he shakes off his sloth, and, stimulated by Myrrha, his favourite Greek slave, fights bravely in the van of his troops. Defeated, he makes provision for the safe withdrawal of his queen, Zarina, and his supporters, prepares a funeral pyre round his throne, and perishes in it with Myrrha.

Sargeson, FRANK (1903–), New Zealand novelist, author of 'A Man and His Wife' (1940), included in a collection of short stories entitled 'That Summer' (1946), and the novel, 'I Saw in my Dream' (1949), the first part of which appeared as 'When the Wind Blows' in 'Penguin New Writing' (see *New Writing*).

Sarmatia, used occasionally by English poets to signify Poland.

Sarpedon, a Lycian prince, son, according to one story, of Zeus and Laodamia, an ally of the Trojans in the Trojan War, who was slain by Patroclus.

Sarra, the city of Tyre in Phoenicia, celebrated for its purple dye, referred to by Milton, 'Paradise Lost', xi. 240.

Sarras, in the legend of the Grail (q.v.), the country to which Joseph of Arimathea fled from Jerusalem.

Sartor Resartus: The Life and Opinions of Herr Teufelsdröckh, by T. Carlyle (q.v.), originally published in 'Fraser's Magazine' in 1833–4; first English edition, 1838.

This work was written under the influence of the German romantic school and particularly of Jean Paul Richter (q.v.). It consists of two parts: a discourse on the philosophy of clothes (*sartor*

resartus means 'the tailor repatched') based on the speculations of an imaginary Professor Teufelsdröckh; and a biography of Teufelsdröckh himself, which is in some measure the author's autobiography.

Sartre, JEAN-PAUL (1905–), French existentialist philosopher and critic (see *Existentialism*). He has also, as novelist and dramatist, conveyed his philosophical ideas to a wide public in France and other countries. His plays include 'Les Mouches' (1942) and 'Huis Clos' (1944).

Sassenach, representing the Gaelic *sasunnach*, the name given by the Gaelic inhabitants of Great Britain and Ireland to their 'Saxon' or English neighbours.

Sassoon, SIEGFRIED (1886–1967), poet, whose vivid and often satirical war poetry expresses his bitterness towards hypocrisy and romanticism. His published works include 'The Old Huntsman' (1917), 'Counterattack' (1918), 'Satirical Poems' (1926), 'The Heart's Journey' (1928), 'Collected Poems' (1947); the semi-autobiographical fiction, 'Memoirs of a Fox-Hunting Man' (1928), 'Memoirs of an Infantry Officer' (1930), and 'Sherston's Progress' (1936); and a biography of George Meredith (1948).

Satan, from a Hebrew word *sātān*, meaning 'adversary', commonly used as the proper name of the supreme evil spirit, the Devil.

Satanic School, THE, Southey's designation (in the Preface to the 'Vision of Judgment', q.v.) for Byron, Shelley, and their imitators.

Satire, from the Latin *satira*, a later form of *satura*, which means 'medley', being elliptical for *lanx satura*, 'a full dish, a hotch-potch'. The word has no connection with *satyr*, as was formerly often supposed. A *satire* is a poem, or in modern use sometimes a prose composition, in which prevailing vices or follies are held up to ridicule.

In English literature, satire may be held to have begun with Chaucer (see particularly the prologue to 'The Canterbury Tales'); he was followed by many 15th-cent. writers including Dunbar. Skelton, the first great English satirist, used the octosyllabic metre, and a rough manner which was to be paralleled in later times by 'Hudibras' Butler and Swift. Gascoigne (q.v.) in his 'The Steele Glas' (1576) was probably the first Elizabethan satirist; his works were perhaps unknown to Joseph Hall (q.v.) who in his 'Virgidemiarum' (1597) made this claim for himself. With Hall are to be grouped Lodge in his 'Fig for Momus' (1595), and Marston. Their works, based largely on Juvenal, are mostly of poor quality. Donne's satires of the same period have greater merit.

Samuel Butler, in 'Hudibras', followed a more English and less classical tradition. The great age of English satire, however, began with Dryden who perfected the epigrammatic and antithetical use of the heroic couplet for this purpose. The cool, good-humoured scorn of his satire is perhaps more effective (e.g. in 'Absalom and Achitophel') than the bitter brilliance of Pope, his greatest follower. Swift was a master of satirical prose (see *Gulliver's Travels* and *A Tale of a Tub*). Gay, Prior, and Young are best known among the many satirists of the Augustan period. The same tradition was followed by C. Churchill (q.v.) and brilliantly revived by Byron in 'English Bards and Scotch Reviewers', and in his 'Vision of Judgment'. The Victorian era produced on the whole no satirists of note. In modern times, Hilaire Belloc, Chesterton, and Roy Campbell (in the 'Georgiad') have contributed to a moderate revival of the tradition, but the more effective modern satire has been in prose, e.g. in the writings of Evelyn Waugh (q.v.).

Satiromastix, or The Untrussing of the Humorous Poet, a comedy by Dekker (q.v.), printed in 1602.

Jonson in his 'Poetaster' had satirized Dekker and Marston, under the names of Crispinus and Demetrius, while he himself figured as Horace. Dekker here retorts, bringing the same Horace, Crispinus, and Demetrius on the stage once more. Capt. Tucca (of the 'Poetaster') turns effectively on Horace the flow of his profanity. Horace's peculiarities of dress and appearance, his vanity and bitterness, are ridiculed; and he is finally untrussed and crowned with nettles.

The satirical part of the play is set in a somewhat inappropriate romantic framework.

Saturn, an ancient Italian god of agriculture, subsequently identified with the Cronos (q.v.) of Greek mythology. He was thought to have been an early king at Rome where he civilized the people and taught them agriculture. His reign was so mild and beneficent that it was regarded as the Golden Age.

Saturnalia, an ancient Roman festival in honour of Saturn and (originally) to celebrate the sowing of the crops. It was a period of general festivity, licence for slaves, giving of presents, lighting of candles, the prototype, if not the origin, of our Christmas festivities.

Saturnian Age, the Golden Age, the *Saturnia regna* of the Roman poets. See *Saturn.*

Saturnian metre, the metre used in early Roman poetry, before the introduction of the Greek metres. The rhythm depended on the arrangement of accented syllables.

Satyr, in Greek mythology, one of a class of woodland spirits, in form partly human, partly bestial, supposed to be the companions of Dionysus (q.v.).

The chorus of the Greek satyric drama (q.v.) was composed of satyrs. The confusion between *satyric* and *satiric* (see *Satire*) occasioned in the 16th-17th cents. the frequent attribution to the satyrs of censoriousness as a characteristic quality.

Satyrane, SIR, in Spenser's 'Faerie Queene' (I. vi), a knight, 'plain, faithful, true, and enemy of shame'. He rescues Una from the satyrs, perhaps symbolizing the liberation of the true religion by Luther.

Satyric drama, the fourth play in the tetralogy of the ancient Greeks, a semi-serious, semi-mocking presentation of a legendary theme. The 'Cyclops' of Euripides (q.v.) is the only complete extant satyric drama.

Satyricon, see *Petronius*.

Saul, (1) the first king of Israel (1 Samuel x); (2) Saul of Tarsus, afterwards St. Paul (Acts vii. 58 and the following chapters).

Saul, an oratorio by Handel (1739), containing the famous Dead March.

Savage, CAPTAIN, in Marryat's 'Peter Simple' (q.v.), the first captain under whom the hero serves.

Savage, RICHARD (*d.* 1743), probably of humble birth, claimed to be the illegitimate son of the fourth Earl Rivers and of the wife of the second earl of Macclesfield. The romantic story of his birth and ill-treatment as given in Samuel Johnson's long and interesting life of him is now generally disbelieved. He wrote several second-rate comedies and poems, including 'The Wanderer' (1729) and 'The Bastard' (1728), a censure on his supposed mother, the first part of which is vigorous and effective, and contains the often-quoted line, 'No tenth transmitter of a foolish face'. He was condemned to death in 1727 for killing a gentleman in a tavern brawl, but pardoned. He died in great poverty.

Savile, GEORGE, *marquess of Halifax* (1633-95), one of the first writers of political pamphlets, is chiefly remembered for his 'Character of a Trimmer' (1688), a brilliant piece of writing, in which he urged Charles II to free himself from the influence of his brother. He also wrote some pleasant essays. He saved the throne in 1679-81 by his resolute opposition to the Exclusion Bill. He is the 'Jotham' of Dryden's 'Absalom and Achitophel' (q.v.).

Savile, SIR HENRY (1549-1622), was secretary of the Latin tongue to Queen Elizabeth, and one of the scholars commissioned to prepare the authorized translation of the Bible. Savile assisted Bodley in founding his library and left a collection of manuscripts, now in the Bodleian Library.

Savonarola, FRA GIROLAMO (1452-98), Dominican monk, an eloquent preacher, leader of the democratic party in Florence after the expulsion of the Medici. His influence was gradually undermined, and he was executed as a heretic. There is a careful study of his character in G. Eliot's 'Romola' (q.v.).

Savoy Operas, see *Gilbert and Sullivan Operas*.

Savoyard, (1) a native or inhabitant of Savoy; (2) a member of the D'Oyly Carte Company which originally performed the Gilbert and Sullivan operas (q.v.) at the Savoy Theatre.

Sawyer, BOB, a character in Dickens's 'The Pickwick Papers' (q.v.).

Saxo Grammaticus, a Danish historian of the 13th cent., author of 'Gesta Danorum', a history of the Danes in Latin, partly mythical. This contains the legend of Hamlet.

Saxon, the name of a Germanic people which in the early centuries of the Christian era dwelt in a region near the mouth of the Elbe, and of which one portion, distinguished as ANGLO-SAXONS, conquered and occupied certain parts of south Britain in the 5th and 6th cents., while the other, the OLD SAXONS, remained in Germany. The name *Anglo-Saxon* (q.v.) has been extended to the entire Old English people and language before the Norman Conquest.

Saxon shore, THE, the eastern and southern coasts of England from the Wash to Shoreham which in the 4th cent. were exposed to the attacks of Saxon raiders and were governed by a military officer known as the *Comes* or Count of the Saxon shore.

Sayers, DOROTHY LEIGH (Mrs. Fleming) (1893-1957), detective story writer, creator of the master-detective Lord Peter Wimsey. Among her best-known novels are: 'Murder Must Advertise' (1933), 'Gaudy Night' (1935), and 'Busman's Honeymoon' (1937). She also wrote plays on religious themes, such as 'The Man Born to be King' (1942), and made

translations of Dante's 'Inferno' (1949)
and 'Purgatorio' (1955).

Scald, see *Skald*.

Scales, GERALD, a character in Bennett's
'The Old Wives' Tale' (q.v.).

Scaliger, JOSEPH JUSTUS (1540-1609), the
son of Julius Caesar Scaliger (q.v.), was
the greatest scholar of the Renaissance;
he has been described as 'the founder of
historical criticism'. He edited Manilius
(1579), reconstructed the lost chronicle of
Eusebius, and issued critical editions of
many classical authors.

Scaliger, JULIUS CAESAR (1484-1558).
Besides polemical works directed against
Erasmus (1531), he wrote a long Latin
treatise on poetics, scientific commentaries
on botanical works, and a philosophical
treatise. These show encyclopaedic knowledge and acute observation, marred by
arrogance and vanity.

Scallop-shell, the badge of the pilgrim.
Pilgrims returning from the shrine of St.
James at Compostella were accustomed to
wear a scallop-shell found on the Galician
shore.

Scamander, a river of Asia Minor, flowing into the sea near Troy.

Scapin, in the 'Fourberies de Scapin' of
Molière (q.v.), the type of rascally
resourceful servant who gets out of difficulties by his audacious lies.

Scaramouch, adaptation of the Italian
scaramuccia meaning 'skirmish', a stock
character in Italian farce, a cowardly and
foolish boaster, who is constantly cud-
gelled by Harlequin.

Scarlet, or SCADLOCK, WILL, one of the
companions of Robin Hood (q.v.).

Scarlet Letter, The, a novel by Hawthorne (q.v.) (1850).

The scene of the story is Boston, in the
Puritan New England of the 17th cent.
To this place an aged and learned Englishman has sent his young wife, intending to
follow her, but is delayed. He arrives to
find her, Hester Prynne, in the pillory,
with a babe in her arms. She has refused
to name her lover, and has been sentenced
to this ordeal. The husband assumes the

name of Roger Chillingworth and obtains
from Hester an oath that she will conceal
his identity. Roger Chillingworth, in the
character of a physician, applies himself
to the discovery of her paramour. Hester's
lover is, in fact, the Revd. Arthur Dimmesdale, a young and highly revered minister
whose lack of courage has prevented him
from sharing Hester's punishment. The
author traces the steps by which Chillingworth discovers him. When Dimmesdale
at the end of seven years is reduced to the
verge of lunacy and death, Hester proposes to him that they shall flee to Europe.
But he puts it from him as a temptation of
the Evil One, makes public confession on
the pillory, and dies in her arms.

Scarlet Pimpernel, The, see *Orczy*.

Scarlet Woman, THE, an abusive term
applied to the Roman Catholic Church in
allusion to Rev. xvii. 1-5.

Scarron, PAUL (1610-60), a French
burlesque dramatist and novelist, married
Françoise d'Aubigné, later the celebrated
Mme de Maintenon.

Scazon, from a Greek word which means
'limping, halting', a modification of the
iambic trimeter in which a spondee or
trochee is substituted for the final iambus.
It is also called *Choliamb*.

Scenario, a sketch or outline of the plot
of a play or film, giving particulars of the
scenes, situations, etc.

Scenes of Clerical Life, a series of three
tales by G. Eliot (q.v.), published in two
volumes in 1858, after having appeared
in 'Blackwood's Magazine' in the previous
year. The three tales are 'The Sad
Fortunes of the Rev. Amos Barton', 'Mr.
Gilfil's Love-Story', and 'Janet's Repentance'.

Sceptic, in philosophy, originally a
follower of the school of Pyrrho; popularly
applied to one who maintains a doubting
attitude with reference to some particular
question or to assertions of apparent fact.

Schamir, in Rabbinical and medieval
myth, the impersonation of a mysterious
force which enabled Solomon to build his
temple without the use of iron.

Scheherazade or SHAHRAZAD, in the 'Arabian Nights' (q.v.), the daughter of the vizir of King Shahriyar, who married the king, and escaped the death that was the usual fate of his wives by telling him the tales which compose that work.

Schelling, FRIEDRICH WILHELM JOSEPH VON (1775-1854), German philosopher. He was a disciple at first of Fichte (q.v.), but soon departed from his doctrine. Schelling makes the universe rather than the *ego* the element of reality. In his later writings his philosophy took a more religious tinge.

Schiller, JOHANN CHRISTOPH FRIEDRICH VON (1759-1805), German dramatist and lyric poet, the chief figure of the 'Sturm und Drang' (q.v.) period of German literature. Schiller first came into prominence and struck the note of revolt in his prose drama, 'Die Räuber' ('The Robbers', 1781). The crudities which marred this play disappear in great measure in Schiller's next dramatic work, the blank-verse 'Don Carlos' (1787); but he reached the summit of his dramatic power in the long historical tragedy 'Wallenstein' (1799) (translated into English verse by S. T. Coleridge in 1800).

Schiller was no less great as a writer of reflective and lyrical poems and of ballads, and his best work of this kind belongs to the period of his intimacy with Goethe. Schiller was also author of philosophical and historical works.

Schism, THE GREAT, the state of divided allegiance in the Western Church due to the election of rival Italian and French popes (Urban VI and Clement VII) in 1378.

Schlegel, AUGUST WILHELM VON (1767-1845), a German Romanticist, chiefly known in England for his translation into the German language, with the assistance of his wife and others, of the plays of Shakespeare.

Schlegel, FRIEDRICH VON (1772-1829), younger brother of August Wilhelm von Schlegel (q.v.), notable for his studies of the history of literature.

Schliemann, HEINRICH (1822-90), the celebrated German archaeologist, who excavated Troy, Tiryns, and Mycenae.

Scholar-Gipsy, The, a poem by M. Arnold (q.v.) (1853).

The poem, pastoral in setting, is based on an old legend, narrated by Glanvill (q.v.) in his 'The Vanity of Dogmatizing', of an 'Oxford scholar poor' who, tired of seeking preferment, joined the gipsies to learn their lore, roamed the world with them, and still haunts the Oxford countryside. With this is woven a wonderful evocation of that landscape, and reflections on the contrast between the concentration and faith of the scholar-gipsy and

'this strange disease of modern life'.

Scholasticism, or the doctrines of the Schoolmen (q.v.), the predominant theological and philosophical teaching of the period 1100-1500, in the main an attempt to reconcile Aristotle with the Scriptures, reason with faith. In the 14th cent., after Ockham, scholasticism, as an intellectual movement, had exhausted itself.

Scholemaster, The, see *Ascham*.

Schoole of Abuse, see *Gosson*.

School for Scandal, The, a comedy by R. B. Sheridan (q.v.), produced in 1777.

In this play, his masterpiece, the author contrasts two brothers, Joseph Surface the hypocrite, and Charles Surface the good-natured reckless spendthrift. Charles is in love with Maria, Sir Peter Teazle's ward, and his affection is returned; and Joseph is courting her for her fortune, while at the same time making love to Lady Teazle. Sir Peter, an old man who has married a young wife six months before, is made miserable by her frivolity. The scandal-mongers, Sir Benjamin Backbite, Lady Sneerwell, and Mrs. Candour, provide the background. Sir Oliver Surface, the rich uncle of Joseph and Charles, returns unexpectedly from India and decides to test the characters of his nephews. He visits Charles in the character of a moneylender, and Charles lightheartedly sells him the family pictures, but refuses to sell at any price the portrait of

Sir Oliver himself, and thus wins the old man's heart. Meanwhile Joseph receives a visit from Lady Teazle in his library and attempts to seduce her. The sudden arrival of Sir Peter obliges Lady Teazle to hide behind a screen. The arrival of Charles sends Sir Peter in turn to cover. Sir Peter takes refuge in a cupboard. The conversation between Joseph and Charles proves to Sir Peter that his suspicion of Charles's attachment to his wife was unfounded, and the throwing down of the screen reveals Lady Teazle. Sir Oliver visits Joseph in the character of a needy but deserving relative applying for assistance, which Joseph refuses. This completes the exposure of Joseph. Charles is united to Maria, and Sir Peter is reconciled to Lady Teazle.

Schoolmen, the succession of writers, from about the 11th to the 15th cent., who treat of logic, metaphysics, and theology, as taught in the 'schools' or universities of Italy, France, Germany, and England, that is to say on the basis of Aristotle and the Christian Fathers, whom the schoolmen endeavoured to harmonize. Among the great Schoolmen were Peter Lombard, Abélard, Aquinas, Duns Scotus, and Ockham (qq.v.).

Schoolmistress, The, see Shenstone.

Schopenhauer, ARTHUR (1788-1860), the author of a pessimistic philosophy embodied in his 'Die Welt als Wille und Vorstellung' (1819, 'The World as Will and Representation'). According to this, Will, of which we have direct intuition, is the 'thing-in-itself', the only reality. Asceticism, and primarily chastity, are the duty of man. God, freewill, and the immortality of the soul, are illusions.

Schreiner, OLIVE EMILIE ALBERTINA (1855-1920), published under the pseudonym 'Ralph Iron' in 1883 the most successful of her works, 'The Story of an African Farm'. Her 'Women and Labour' appeared in 1911, and an uncompleted novel 'From Man to Man' posthumously in 1926. She married in 1894 a South African politician, Samuel Cron Cron-

wright, who wrote an introduction to this last work.

Schubert, FRANZ PETER (1797-1828), the Austrian composer, who in his short life produced several operas, ten symphonies, and much other music. He was one of the greatest of song-writers.

Science Fiction, the current name for a class of prose narrative which assumes a technological or scientific advance, or depends upon an imaginary and spectacular change in human environment. Although examples exist from the time of Lucian (q.v.), it was not until the end of the 19th cent. that the form as described above emerged. The works of Jules Verne (q.v.) have always been popular in England, but the first successful English author was H. G. Wells (q.v.), whose stories include several of the themes later dominant: invasion from outer space ('The War of the Worlds', 1898), biological change or catastrophe ('The Food of the Gods', 1904), time travel ('The Time Machine', 1895), and air warfare ('The War in the Air', 1908).

Since the Second World War scientific developments and their possible consequences have been reflected in fictional form by motifs such as interplanetary travel, robots or mechanical brains, and atomic hand-weapons; and the destruction of the world as a result of its own technological achievements has been a favourite theme. But the scientific element is often ancillary to an inquiry into the nature of man and his behaviour.

Scipio Africanus Major, PUBLIUS CORNELIUS (236/5-*c.* 183 B.C.), the conqueror of Spain, and of Hannibal at the battle of Zama (202 B.C.), and one of the greatest of the Romans.

Scogan, HENRY (1361?-1407), a poet and a correspondent of Chaucer, to whom the latter addressed an 'envoy' or verse epistle. He was tutor to four sons of Henry IV.

Scone stone, a stone supposed to have been brought to Scone in Scotland from Tara in Ireland, and used as the coronation stone of the Scottish kings. Edward I had it removed to Westminister Abbey, where it was placed under the coronation chair, and still remains.

Scorpio, the eighth sign of the zodiac; also a constellation.

Scotist, a follower or disciple of Duns Scotus (q.v.), whose system was in many respects opposed to that of Thomas Aquinas. The followers of the latter were known as 'Thomists'.

Scotland Yard, in Whitehall, near Charing Cross, London, was the headquarters of the Metropolitan Police *c*. 1842-90; these were moved to New Scotland Yard, near Westminster Bridge, in 1890, and to Broadway, Westminster, in 1967.

Scott or SCOT, MICHAEL (1175?-1234?), a scholar of Scottish birth, who studied at Oxford and on the Continent, and was attached to the court of the Emperor Frederick II, probably in the capacity of official astrologer. Legends of his magical power have served as a theme to many great writers from Dante ('Inferno', C. xx, 116) to Sir W. Scott ('The Lay of the Last Minstrel').

Scott, MICHAEL (1789-1835), author of 'Tom Cringle's Log', which was published in 'Blackwood's Magazine' in 1829-33. It gives vivid and amusing pictures of life in Jamaica and the islands of the Caribbean Sea in the early days of the 19th cent.

Scott or SCOT, REGINALD (1538?-1599), author of 'The Discoverie of Witchcraft' (1584). This was written with the aim of preventing the persecution of poor, aged, and simple persons who were popularly believed to be witches, by exposing the impostures on the one hand, and the credulity on the other, that supported the belief in sorcery.

Scott, ROBERT FALCON (1868-1912), captain R.N., Antarctic explorer, was author of 'The Voyage of the Discovery' (1905), a record of the first National Antarctic Expedition (1901-4); and of the notable journal, published as 'Scott's Last Expedition' in 1913, kept during the second Antarctic expedition (1910-12),

the last entry in which was made as the writer was dying, storm-bound by a blizzard on his return from the South Pole.

Scott, SIR WALTER (1771-1832), was called to the bar in 1792. His interest in the old Border tales and ballads had early been awakened, and was stimulated by Percy's 'Reliques', and by the study of the old romantic poetry of France and Italy and of the modern German poets. He devoted much of his leisure to the exploration of the Border country. In 1802-3 appeared the three volumes of Scott's 'Minstrelsy of the Scottish Border' (a collection of ballads, historical, traditional, and romantic, with imitations in a separate section); and in 1805 his first considerable original work, the romantic poem, 'The Lay of the Last Minstrel' (q.v.). He then became a partner in James Ballantyne's printing business, and published 'Marmion' in 1808. This was followed by 'The Lady of the Lake' in 1810, 'Rokeby' and 'The Bridal of Triermain' in 1813, 'The Lord of the Isles' in 1815, and 'Harold the Dauntless', his last long poem, in 1817. Scott promoted the foundation in 1809 of the Tory 'Quarterly Review' (q.v.)—he had previously been a contributor to 'The Edinburgh Review' (q.v.), but seceded from it owing to its Whig attitude. Eclipsed in a measure by Byron as a poet, in spite of the great popularity of his verse romances, he now turned his attention to the novel as a means of giving play to his wide erudition, his humour, and his sympathies. His novels appeared anonymously in the following order: 'Waverley' (q.v.), 1813; 'Guy Mannering' (q.v.), 1815; 'The Antiquary' (q.v.) in 1816; 'The Black Dwarf' and 'Old Mortality' (q.v.) together in 1816 as the first series of 'Tales of My Landlord'; 'Rob Roy' (q.v.) in 1817; 'The Heart of Midlothian' (q.v.), second series of 'Tales of My Landlord', in 1818; 'The Bride of Lammermoor' and 'A Legend of Montrose', the third series of 'Tales of My Landlord', in 1819; 'Ivanhoe' (q.v.), 1819; 'The Monastery', 1820; 'The Abbot',

1820; 'Kenilworth' (q.v.), 1821; 'The Pirate', 1821; 'The Fortunes of Nigel' (q.v.), 1822; 'Peveril of the Peak', 1823; 'Quentin Durward' (q.v.), 1823; 'St. Ronan's Well', 1823; 'Redgauntlet', 1824; 'The Betrothed' and 'The Talisman' (q.v.) together as 'Tales of the Crusaders' in 1825; 'Woodstock', 1826; 'Chronicles of the Canongate' (containing 'The Highland Widow', 'The Two Drovers', and 'The Surgeon's Daughter'), 1827; 'Chronicles of the Canongate' (second series): 'St. Valentine's Day, or The Fair Maid of Perth', 1828; 'Anne of Geierstein', 1829; 'Tales of My Landlord' (fourth series): 'Count Robert of Paris' and 'Castle Dangerous' in 1831. In 1826 James Ballantyne & Co. became involved in the bankruptcy of Constable & Co., and Scott, as a partner of the former, found himself liable for a debt of about £114,000. He shouldered the whole burden himself, and henceforth worked heroically, shortening his own life by his strenuous efforts, to pay off the creditors who received full payment after his death.

Scott's 'Life' by John Gibson Lockhart (q.v.), published in 1837-8, is one of the great biographies of English literature. Scott's 'Journal' was published in 1890 and again in 1939-46, in three volumes, edited by J. G. Tait. An edition of his letters in twelve volumes was published by Sir H. J. C. Grierson (1932-7). 'Sir Walter Scott: the Great Unknown', by Edgar Johnson, was published in 1970.

Scottish Chaucerians, a name given to a group of 15th-16th-cent. Scottish writers, of whom James I, Henryson, Dunbar, and Gavin Douglas (qq.v.) are the chief, who show in a greater or less degree the influence of Chaucer.

Scottish Text Society, THE, founded in 1882 for the purpose of printing and editing texts illustrative of the Scottish language and literature, has issued editions of many works of general literary interest, such as 'The Kingis Quair', Barbour's 'Bruce', and the 'Basilikon Doron', and the poems of Dunbar, Henryson, Drummond of Hawthornden, and Sir D. Lyndsay (qq.v.).

Scotus, JOANNES DUNS, see *Duns Scotus.*

Scotus or **ERIGENA, JOHN** (*fl.* 850), was employed as teacher at the court of King Charles the Bald, afterwards emperor, *c.* 847. The leading principle of his philosophy, as expounded in his great work, 'De Divisione Naturae', is that of the unity of nature, proceeding from God, through the creative ideas to the sensible universe, which ultimately is resolved into its first Cause. He was thus one of the originators of the mystical thought of the Middle Ages.

Scourers or **SCOWRERS,** in the 17th-18th cents., a set of men who made a practice of roistering through the streets at night, frequently referred to in the literature of the period (Wycherley, Gay, 'The Spectator', etc.).

Scourge of God, name given to Attila (q.v.).

Scriblerus Club, an association of which Pope, Swift, Arbuthnot, Gay, Parnell, Congreve, Lord Oxford, and Atterbury were members, formed about 1713. They undertook the production of the 'Memoirs of Martinus Scriblerus' (see *Martinus Scriblerus*), designed to ridicule 'all the false tastes in learning, under the character of a man of capacity enough, that had dipped into every art and science, but injudiciously in each'.

Scrooge, a character in Dickens's 'A Christmas Carol' (q.v.).

Scrutiny, a quarterly review aimed at raising the critical standards for English literature and culture, which ran from 1932 to 1953 with F. R. Leavis (q.v.) as its chief editor. The complete series was reissued in twenty volumes in 1963.

Scudamour, SIR, in Spenser's 'Faerie Queene', Bk. IV, the lover of Amoret, who is reft from him on his wedding-day by the enchanter Busyrane.

Scudéry, MADELEINE DE (1607-1701), one of the most voluminous writers of French heroic romances. Her principal work was 'Artamène, ou le Grand Cyrus' (10 vols., 1649-53). The English translation was very popular, cf. Pepys ('Diary', 12 May 1666).

Scylla, a nymph loved by Poseidon, or according to Ovid by Glaucus, one of the deities of the sea, was changed by Circe (q.v.) into a monster, and threw herself into the sea between Italy and Sicily, opposite the whirlpool of Charybdis (q.v.), and became a danger to mariners. The passage of the straits is the theme of part of the twelfth book of the 'Odyssey'.

Scythrop, in Peacock's 'Nightmare Abbey' (q.v.), a caricature of Shelley.

Seafarer, The, an Old English poem of some 120 lines, included in the 'Exeter Book' (q.v.), discussing the miseries and the attractions of life at sea, and passing to a comparison of earthly pleasures and heavenly rewards. Recent interpretations have attempted to relate it to the practice of penitential pilgrimage, or (with 'The Wanderer', q.v.) to the Christian tradition of man as an exile from Paradise wandering as a pilgrim on the earth.

Sea-green Incorruptible, a name applied to Robespierre (q.v.) by T. Carlyle in his 'French Revolution'.

Seagrim, MOLLY, a character in Fielding's 'Tom Jones' (q.v.).

Seasons, The, a poem in blank verse, in four books, one for each season, and a final 'Hymn', by James Thomson (1700-48, q.v.) (1726-30).

'Winter' was the first of the four 'Seasons' written and published (1726).

Next came 'Summer' (1727), which sets forth the progress of a summer's day, includes two narrative episodes (of the lover Celadon whose Amelia is struck by lightning, and of Damon who beholds Musidora bathing).

'Spring' appeared in 1728. The poet describes the influence of the season on inanimate objects, on vegetables, brute beasts, and lastly man, with a final panegyric on nuptial love.

'Autumn' followed in 1730. This part includes the episode of Palemon who falls in love with Lavinia, a gleaner in his fields (the story of Boaz and Ruth).

The poem is completed by the 'Hymn' to Nature (1730).

Sebastian (1554-78), king of Portugal, killed at the battle of Alcazar. Dryden's play, 'Don Sebastian', refers to this monarch.

Sebastian, (1) in Shakespeare's 'The Tempest' (q.v.), brother to the king of Naples; (2) in his 'Twelfth Night' (q.v.), brother to Viola.

Sebastian, ST., a Roman soldier and Christian martyr who was shot to death with arrows, about A.D. 288. He is commemorated on 20 Jan.

Second Nun's Tale, The, see *Canterbury Tales*.

Sedan, the scene of the defeat of the army of Napoleon III by the Germans on 2 Sept. 1870, and of the French emperor's surrender; the central incident of Zola's 'La Débâcle'.

Sedgemoor, in Somerset, the scene of the battle of 6 July 1685 in which Monmouth was defeated by the Royal troops.

Sedley, MR., MRS., JOSEPH, and AMELIA, characters in Thackeray's 'Vanity Fair' (q.v.).

Sedley, SIR CHARLES (1639?-1701), famous for his wit and urbanity and notorious as a fashionable profligate, was the author of two indifferent tragedies and three comedies. Of these the best are 'Bellamira', produced in 1687, and 'The Mulberry Garden', partly based on Molière's 'L'École des Maris', produced in 1668. Sedley also wrote some pleasant songs: 'Phillis is my only joy', etc. He figures in Dryden's 'Essay of Dramatick Poesie' (q.v.) as Lisideius, who defends the imitation of French comedy in English.

Seeley, SIR JOHN ROBERT (1834-95), professor of Latin at University College, London, and of modern history at Cambridge from 1869 until his death. In 1865 he published anonymously his 'Ecce Homo', a survey of the life of Christ. His historical works, designed to promote a practical object, the training of statesmen, include: 'The Expansion of England in the Eighteenth Century' (1883) and 'The Growth of British Policy' (1895).

Sejanus, his Fall, a Roman tragedy by Jonson (q.v.), first acted in 1603, Shakespeare and Burbage having parts in the cast.

The play deals with the rise of the historical Sejanus, the confidant of the emperor Tiberius, his machinations with a view to securing the imperial throne, his fall and execution.

Selborne, *Natural History and Antiquities of,* see *White* (G.).

Selden, JOHN (1584-1654), an eminent lawyer and bencher of the Inner Temple. He won fame as an orientalist by his treatise 'De Diis Syris' (1617), and subsequently made a valuable collection of oriental manuscripts. His 'Table Talk', containing reports of his utterances from time to time during the last twenty years of his life, composed by his secretary, Richard Milward, appeared in 1689. He wrote, besides important legal treatises, 'Illustrations' to the first eighteen 'songs' of Drayton's 'Polyolbion' (q.v.).

Selden Society, THE, was founded in 1887 by Maitland (q.v.), for the publication of ancient legal records.

Selene, in Greek mythology, the goddess of the moon, the Luna of the Romans. In later myths she is identified with Artemis (Diana).

Seleucids, THE, the dynasty founded by Seleucus Nicator (one of the generals of Alexander the Great), which reigned over Syria from 312 to 65 B.C., and subjected a great part of western Asia.

Self-Help, a work by Smiles (q.v.) (1864), which enjoyed great popularity and was translated into many other languages.

Selim, the hero of Byron's 'Bride of Abydos' (q.v.).

Selima, Horace Walpole's cat, whose death by drowning in a bowl of goldfish was lamented in a poem by Gray.

Seljuk, the name of certain Turkish dynasties that ruled over large parts of Asia from the 11th to the 13th cents.

Selkirk, ALEXANDER (1676-1721), joined the privateering expedition of Capt. William Dampier (q.v.) in 1703. Having quarrelled with his captain, Thomas Stradling, he was, at his own request, put ashore on the uninhabited island of Juan Fernandez in 1704, and remained there until 1709, when he was rescued by Capt. W. Rogers (q.v.). His experiences there formed the basis of Defoe's 'Robinson Crusoe' (q.v.) and are the subject of a poem by Cowper (q.v.).

Semele, a daughter of Cadmus (q.v.) and Harmonia, was beloved by Zeus. The jealous Hera persuaded her to entreat her lover to come to her with the same majesty that he approached Hera. Zeus came accordingly attended by lightning and thunderbolts, by which Semele was instantly consumed. Her child, however, was saved, and was known as Dionysus (q.v.).

Semiramis, a mythical queen of Assyria. She married Ninus, king of Assyria, the reputed founder of Nineveh, and succeeded him on the throne. She built many cities, and some of the great works of the East are by tradition ascribed to her.

Semitic, meaning originally 'of or pertaining to the Semites', the descendants of Shem the son of Noah, is used in a linguistic sense to designate that family of languages of which Hebrew, Aramaic, Arabic, Ethiopic, and ancient Assyrian are the principal members.

Sempronius, (1) in Shakespeare's 'Timon of Athens' (q.v.), one of the false friends of Timon; (2) a character in Addison's 'Cato' (q.v.).

Seneca, LUCIUS ANNAEUS (*d.* A.D. 65), the philosopher, was tutor to the young Nero, and when the latter became emperor was one of his chief advisers, and exerted himself to check his vices. He was accused of participating in the conspiracy of Piso and was ordered to take his own life, which he did with stoic courage. His writings include works on moral philosophy and nine tragedies in a rhetorical style; whence 'Senecan' tragedy.

Senecan tragedy. The plays of Seneca exercised great influence on medieval playwrights who used them as models for literary imitation. They were edited by Nicholas Trivet (1260-1330), and in the 15th and 16th cents. there was a considerable vogue in Italy for Senecan tragedy. The plays of Giraldi (1504-73)—notably his 'Orbecche' (1541)—and of Ludovico Dolce (1508-68) were particularly famous. The same movement in France had its effect on Buchanan's Latin plays and on the plays of Jodelle and Garnier, and both the Italian and the French fashion influenced English drama in the 16th cent.

The characteristics of the Senecan tragedy were: (1) a division into five acts with Choruses—and in the English imitations often a dumb show expressive of the action; (2) a considerable retailing of 'horrors' and violence, usually, though not always, acted off the stage and elaborately recounted; (3) a parallel violence of language and expression.

'Gorboduc' (q.v.) is a good example of a Senecan tragedy in English. The fashion, which developed in learned rather than popular circles, was short-lived, and was displaced by a more vital and native form of tragedy. But its elements persisted in Elizabethan drama and may be traced in such plays as 'Tamburlaine the Great' or 'Titus Andronicus'.

Senior, NASSAU WILLIAM (1790-1864), professor of political economy at Oxford, 1825-30 and 1847-52. Besides important political articles, he wrote 'An Outline of the Science of Political Economy' (1836), etc. He also wrote a notable series of reviews of the Waverley Novels: 'Essays on Fiction' (1864).

Sennacherib, the subject of Byron's poem, 'The Destruction of Sennacherib', was king of Assyria 705-681 B.C.

Sense and Sensibility, a novel by Jane Austen (q.v.), begun in 1797 and published in 1811. A first sketch of the story, read by the author to her family in 1795, was entitled 'Elinor and Marianne'.

Mrs. Henry Dashwood and her daughters, Elinor and Marianne and Margaret, are left in straitened circumstances, for her husband's estate has passed to her stepson, John Dashwood. Henry Dashwood, before his death, has urgently recommended to John the interest of his stepmother and sisters. But John's selfishness defeats his father's wish. Mrs. Henry Dashwood and her daughters accordingly retire to a cottage in Devonshire, but not before Elinor and Edward Ferrars, brother of Mrs. John Dashwood, have become mutually attracted. In Devonshire Marianne is thrown into the company of John Willoughby, an attractive but unprincipled young man, with whom she falls desperately in love. Willoughby suddenly departs for London. Presently Elinor and Marianne also go to London, on the invitation of their friend, Mrs. Jennings. Here Willoughby shows complete indifference to Marianne, and finally, in an insolent letter, informs her of his approaching marriage to a rich heiress. Marianne, whose sensibility is extreme, makes no effort to control the outward symptoms of her grief. Meanwhile Elinor has learnt under pledge of secrecy from Lucy Steele, niece of a former tutor of Edward Ferrars, that she and Edward have been secretly engaged for four years. Elinor, whose sense and self-control are in strong contrast to Marianne's weakness, conceals her distress. Edward's engagement, which was kept secret owing to his dependence on his mother, now becomes known to the latter. In her fury at Edward's refusal to give up Lucy, she dismisses him from her sight, and settles on his younger brother, Robert, the property that would otherwise have gone to Edward. At this conjuncture a small living is offered to Edward, and the way seems open for his early marriage with Lucy. But now Robert, his brother, falls in love with Lucy, who, finding her interest in a marriage with the more wealthy brother, throws over Edward and marries Robert. Edward, delighted to be released from an engagement that he has long regretted, at once proposes to Elinor and is accepted. Marianne is finally won by her old admirer, Colonel Brandon, a quiet serious man of five-and-thirty, whose modest attractions had been completely eclipsed by his brilliant rival.

The cheerful, vulgar Mrs. Jennings, her silly daughter, and Mr. Palmer, her ill-mannered son-in-law, are among the amusing characters in the story.

Sensitive Plant, The, a poem by P. B. Shelley (q.v.) written in 1820.

The poet's spirit is represented as a 'sensitive plant' tended by a lady, the ideal of beauty. The lady dies, and death and corruption settle on the garden. This awakens in the author the question whether, seeing that beauty is permanent, it is not life that is unreal.

Sentimental comedy. Comedies of the type first written by Steele (q.v.) and others, and continued throughout the 18th cent., setting a fashion which Goldsmith and Sheridan (qq.v.) challenged. They were written first in reaction against the immorality of the Restoration drama and attempted to show, as a rule, the just rewarding of virtues and vices.

Sentimental Journey through France and Italy, A, by Mr. Yorick, a narrative by Sterne (q.v.) of his adventures in France in 1765-6 (1768).

The work was to consist of four volumes, of which only two were finished. In it, the humour of 'Tristram Shandy' gives place to sentiment as the predominant element. The author travels to Calais, Amiens, Paris, through the Bourbonnais, and nearly to Modane, where the book abruptly ends. At every turn he meets with a sentimental adventure, and finds pleasure in everything.

Sentry, CAPTAIN, see *Spectator*.

Septuagint, The (commonly designated LXX), the Greek version of the O.T. which derives its name from the story that it was made by seventy-two Palestinian Jews at the request of Ptolemy Philadelphus (q.v.); or it may have been so

called because it was authorized by the seventy members of the Jewish sanhedrin.

Seraph, in biblical use (Isa. vi. 2), one of the creatures with six wings seen in Isaiah's vision as hovering over the throne of God. By Christian interpreters the Seraphim were from an early period supposed to be a class of angels. In the system of the Pseudo-Dionysius, the chief source of later angelology, the Seraphim are the highest, and the Cherubim the second, of the nine orders of angels (q.v.).

Serbonian Bog or LAKE, a great morass near the coast of Lower Egypt, cf. Milton, 'Paradise Lost', ii. 593.

Serendipity, from *Serendip*, a former name for Ceylon, a word coined by Horace Walpole, who says (letter to Mann, 28 Jan. 1754) that he had formed it on the title of the fairy-tale 'The Three Princes of Serendip', to signify the faculty of making happy discoveries by accident, which these princes possessed.

Serious Call to a Devout and Holy Life, see under *Law* (*W.*).

Serpentine verse, a metrical line beginning and ending with the same word, in allusion to the representation of a serpent with its tail in its mouth.

Servetus, MICHAEL (MIGUEL SERVETO) (1511-53), a Spanish physician and theologian, published in 1531 'De trinitatis erroribus' directed against the doctrine of the Trinity, and in 1553 'Christianismi restitutio'. He had to flee to Geneva, but was arrested and burnt by order of Calvin.

Sesame and Lilies, two lectures by Ruskin (q.v.) (1865), to which a third was added in the revised edition.

The first lecture, 'Sesame: of Kings' Treasuries', deals principally with the questions what to read and how to read. The second, 'Lilies: of Queens' Gardens', treats of the sphere, education, and duties of women of the privileged classes. The third lecture, delivered in 1868, is on 'The Mystery of Life and its Arts'.

Session of the Poets, see *Suckling*.

Sestina, a poem of six six-line stanzas (with an envoy) in which the line-endings of the first stanza are repeated, but in different order, in the other five.

Sestos, on the European shore of the Hellespont, at its narrowest part, famous as the residence of Hero (q.v.). Here Xerxes built a bridge of boats when he invaded Europe.

Setebos, a god of the Patagonians, worshipped by Caliban's mother, Sycorax (in Shakespeare's 'The Tempest', q.v.). Pigafetta's description of Patagonia had been translated, and Drake and Cavendish had visited the country, when Shakespeare wrote 'The Tempest'.

Settle, ELKANAH (1648-1724), the author of a series of bombastic dramas which endangered at court Dryden's popularity as a dramatist. Settle's heroic play, 'The Empress of Morocco', in particular, had considerable vogue. Dryden satirized Settle as Doeg in the second part of 'Absalom and Achitophel' (q.v.).

Seven against Thebes, The, a tragedy by Aeschylus (q.v.), for the subject of which see *Eteocles.*

Seven Bishops, THE, Sancroft, archbishop of Canterbury, and six other bishops, who in 1688 signed a petition asking that the clergy should be excused from reading in their churches James II's second 'Declaration of Indulgence'. James regarded this as an act of rebellion; the bishops were tried for seditious libel and found not guilty, to the intense joy of the nation.

Seven Champions of Christendom, The Famous Historie of the, a romance by R. Johnson (q.v.), printed about 1597. The book, the contents of which are inspired by the old romances of chivalry, was widely read, and influenced Spenser.

Seven Cities, THE ISLAND OF THE, or **ANTILIA,** a fabulous island believed in the 14th and 15th cents. to exist in the Atlantic.

Seven Deadly Sins, usually given as Pride, Lechery, Envy, Anger, Covetousness, Gluttony, Sloth; frequently personified in medieval literature. Cf. 'Piers Plowman', Passus V (B), Chaucer's

'Parson's Tale', and Spenser's 'Faerie Queene', I. iv.

Seven Lamps of Architecture, The, a treatise by Ruskin (q.v.) (1849).

This was an incidental work, composed while 'Modern Painters' (q.v.) was being written, and deals with the leading principles of architecture. As a whole, the work is a defence of Gothic, as the noblest style of architecture.

Seven Sages of Greece, THE, the list of these commonly given is: Thales of Miletus, Solon of Athens, Bias of Priene, Chilo of Sparta, Cleobulus of Lindus in Rhodes, Periander of Corinth, and Pittacus of Mitylene. Their teaching was handed down in aphorisms such as 'know thyself'.

Seven Sages of Rome, The, a metrical romance of the early 14th cent. It is interesting as one of the earliest instances in English of the form of short verse-story subsequently adopted by Chaucer in 'The Canterbury Tales'.

Seven Seas, THE, the Arctic, Antarctic, North and South Pacific, North and South Atlantic, and Indian Oceans. 'The Seven Seas' is the title of a collection of poems by Kipling (q.v.) (1896).

Seven Sisters, or **SEVEN STARS, THE,** the Pleiades (q.v.).

Seventh Heaven, THE, see *Heaven.*

Seven Wonders of the World, THE, the seven structures regarded as the most remarkable monuments of antiquity, viz. the Egyptian Pyramids, the Mausoleum at Halicarnassus, the Hanging Gardens of Babylon, the temple of Artemis at Ephesus, the statue of Zeus by Phidias at Olympia, the Colossus at Rhodes, and the Pharos at Alexandria, or, according to another list, the walls of Babylon.

Seven Years War, THE, or **Third Silesian War,** the war waged by France, Austria, and Russia against Frederick the Great (q.v.) of Prussia, who was assisted by Hanoverian troops and subsidies from England, 1756-63.

Severn, JOSEPH (1793-1879), painter, a friend of Keats (q.v.); he accompanied

Keats to Italy in 1820 and attended him at his death.

Severus, WALL OF, a reconstruction by the Emperor Septimius Severus, about the year 208, of the Wall of Hadrian (q.v.).

Seward, ANNA (1747-1809), the 'Swan of Lichfield', bequeathed her poetical works to Sir W. Scott, who published them with a memoir in 1810. Six volumes of her letters appeared in 1811. She frequently met Dr. Johnson and supplied Boswell with particulars concerning him.

Sewell, ANNA (1820-78), remembered particularly as the author of 'Black Beauty', the 'autobiography' of a horse (1877).

S.F., abbreviation of Science Fiction (q.v.).

Shadow, SIMON, in Shakespeare's '2 Henry IV', III. ii, one of Falstaff's recruits.

Shadwell, THOMAS (1642?-1692), dramatist and poet, produced the 'Sullen Lovers', based on Molière's 'Les Fâcheux', at Lincoln's Inn Fields, London, in 1668. His dramatic pieces include an opera, the 'Enchanted Island' (from Shakespeare's 'The Tempest'), 1673, 'Timon of Athens' (1678), 'Epsom Wells' (1673), and 'Bury Fair' (1689). The last two give interesting pictures of contemporary manners. Shadwell was at open feud with Dryden from 1682, the quarrel arising out of some qualified praise bestowed by the latter on Ben Jonson. The two poets repeatedly attacked one another in satires, among which were Dryden's 'The Medal' and 'Mac Flecknoe' (qq.v.), and Shadwell's 'The Medal of John Bayes' (1682) and a translation of the 'Tenth Satire of Juvenal' (1687). Shadwell superseded Dryden as poet laureate at the revolution, but his claims to the position were not high.

Shaftesbury, ANTHONY ASHLEY COOPER, *first Baron Ashley* and *first earl of Shaftesbury* (1621-83), a statesman prominent on the king's side in the Parliamentary War, and after the Restoration as a member of the Cabal and chancellor. After his dismissal he was leader of the opposition, and a supporter of Monmouth. He was satirized as Achitophel in Dryden's 'Absalom and Achitophel' (q.v.).

Shaftesbury, ANTHONY ASHLEY COOPER, *third earl of* (1671-1713), excluded by ill-health from active politics, devoted himself to intellectual pursuits, and in particular to moral philosophy. His principal writings are embodied in his 'Characteristics of Men, Manners, Opinions, Times' (1711). Shaftesbury was influenced by Deism; he was at once a Platonist and a churchman, an opponent of the selfish theory of conduct advocated by Hobbes (q.v.).

Shaftesbury, ANTHONY ASHLEY COOPER, *seventh earl of* (1801-85), philanthropist, active in many movements for the protection of the working classes and the benefit of the poor.

Shahrazad, see *Scheherazade.*

Shakespeare, WILLIAM (1564-1616), was born at Stratford-on-Avon, and baptized on 26 April 1564. Shakespeare's father was a husbandman at Stratford and held various municipal offices. The poet was educated at the free grammar school at Stratford. He married in 1582 Anne, daughter of Richard Hathaway of Shottery. He left Stratford about 1585 having spent, it has been suggested, some time as a schoolmaster, and is next heard of in London, where he became acquainted with Lord Southampton, his principal patron. He was probably engaged in some subordinate capacity at one of the two theatres (The Theatre or The Curtain) then existing in London, and afterwards became a member of the Lord Chamberlain's (after the accession of James I, the King's) company of players, which acted at the Theatre, the Curtain, the Globe (q.v.), and from *c.* 1609 at the Blackfriars Theatre (q.v.). His earliest work as a dramatist, the three parts of 'Henry VI', dates from 1590-1. This, and Shakespeare's other plays and poems, are the subject of separate articles in the present book. 'Henry VI' was followed by 'Richard III' and 'The Comedy of Errors' in the theatrical season of 1592-3, and by

'Titus Andronicus' and 'The Taming of the Shrew' in 1593-4. The attribution of 'Titus Andronicus' to Shakespeare has been much questioned. Shakespeare published the poems 'Venus and Adonis' and 'The Rape of Lucrece' respectively in 1593 and 1594, each with a dedication to Henry Wriothesley, earl of Southampton, with whom, in the latter year, he was, it seems, on terms of intimate friendship. The 'Sonnets' (q.v.) were printed in 1609, but the bulk of them appear to have been written between 1593 and 1596, and the remainder at intervals down to 1600. 'The Two Gentlemen of Verona', 'Love's Labour's Lost', and 'Romeo and Juliet' (Shakespeare's first tragedy) are assigned to 1594-5; 'Richard II' and 'A Midsummer Night's Dream' to 1595-6. Shakespeare purchased 'New Place', the second largest house in Stratford, in 1597, but does not appear to have settled permanently there till 1611. 'King John' and 'The Merchant of Venice' are assigned to 1596-7, the two parts of 'Henry IV' to 1597-8. Shakespeare's most perfect essays in comedy, 'Much Ado about Nothing', 'As You Like It', and 'Twelfth Night', belong to the years 1598-1600, together with 'Henry V' and 'Julius Caesar'. 'Hamlet' and 'The Merry Wives of Windsor' (the latter, according to tradition, written by order of the Queen) are assigned to 1600-1, 'Troilus and Cressida' and 'All's Well that Ends Well' to the next two theatrical seasons. Then came the accession of James I, who (according to Ben Jonson), no less than Elizabeth, held Shakespeare in high esteem. A period of gloom in the author's life appears to have occurred about this time, manifested in the great tragedies, and succeeded, about 1608, by a new outlook in the final romances. The probable order and dates of the plays of the reign of James are given as follows by Sir E. Chambers: 'Measure for Measure' and 'Othello', 1604-5; 'King Lear' and 'Macbeth', 1605-6; 'Antony and Cleopatra', 1606-7; 'Coriolanus' and 'Timon of Athens', 1607-8. 'Pericles',

'Cymbeline', and 'The Winter's Tale' are assigned to the next three seasons; and 'The Tempest', probably the last drama that Shakespeare completed, to 1611-12. 'Two Noble Kinsmen' (q.v.) and 'Henry VIII', in which Fletcher is often thought to have collaborated, were written in 1612-13.

Two sonnets and three poems from 'Love's Labour's Lost' appeared in 'The Passionate Pilgrim, by W. Shakespeare' (1599), the bulk of the volume being by others. Shakespeare's name was also appended to 'a poetical essaie on the Turtle and the Phœnix', which was published in Robert Chester's 'Love's Martyr', a collection of poems by Marston, Chapman, Jonson, and others, 1601. Shakespeare may have had some part in the authorship of the historical play 'Edward III', published in 1596, and 'Sir Thomas More' (q.v.).

Shakespeare now abandoned dramatic composition. He spent the concluding years of his life (1611-16), mainly at Stratford, but paid frequent visits to London till 1614, and continued his relations with actors and poets till the end. He purchased a house in Blackfriars in 1613. He drafted his will in Jan. 1616, and completed it in March. He died 23 April (o.s., i.e. 3 May), and was buried in Stratford Church, where before 1623 a monument, with a bust by a London sculptor, Gerard Johnson, was erected.

Two portraits of Shakespeare may be regarded as authenticated, the bust in Stratford Church, and the frontispiece to the folio of 1623, engraved by Martin Droeshout. But Droeshout is unlikely to have had personal knowledge of the poet. Shakespeare appears to have written his name usually 'Shakspere', sometimes in abbreviated form, but the main signature to the poet's will is 'Shakspere'. The form generally accepted is 'Shakespeare', being that in which the name appears in most of the contemporary editions of his plays and in the dedicatory epistles to the authorized editions of 'Venus and Adonis' and 'The Rape of Lucrece'.

Shakespeare's plays were first collected in 1623, when a folio edition was published containing all the canonical plays excepting 'Pericles'. Further folio editions appeared in 1632, 1663, 1664, and 1685. The first attempt to produce a critical edition of Shakespeare was that of Rowe (q.v.) (1709); he provided lists of dramatis personae and a systematic division into acts and scenes. Pope's edition followed (1725) and the valuable emendations of Theobald (q.v.). Johnson's edition appeared in 1765. Capell, Malone, and Steevens were other important 18th-cent. students of Shakespeare. The Cambridge Shakespeare in 1863-6 (2nd ed. by Aldis Wright in 1891-3) formed the basis of Wright's 1874 Globe edition, which provides the standard line numbering. The edition of separate plays by Quiller-Couch and J. D. Wilson (Cambridge, 1921-62) deals fully with textual problems; and Sir E. K. Chambers's 'William Shakespeare, a Study of Facts and Problems' (1930) is the standard life.

Shakespeare-Bacon Controversy, see *Baconian Theory*.

Shallow, in Shakespeare's '2 Henry IV', a foolish country justice. He appears again in 'The Merry Wives of Windsor'. Shallow perhaps represents Sir Thomas Lucy of Charlecote (he is identified by his coat of arms bearing 'luces', 'Merry Wives', I. i), and the mention of the killing of his deer perhaps has reference to a poaching incident in Shakespeare's early days. But much doubt has been thrown on the story and its application to the Lucys of Charlecote. L. Hotson ('Shakespeare versus Shallow', 1961) suggests that Shakespeare was satirizing William Gardiner the Surrey magistrate with whom he had quarrelled; his arms impaled three luces.

Shalott, THE LADY OF, Elaine, the fair maid of Astolat (see *Launcelot of the Lake*), the subject and title of a poem by Tennyson.

Shamela Andrews, An Apology for the Life of Mrs., a skit on 'Pamela' (q.v.), perhaps by Fielding (q.v.).

Shamrock, THE, adopted as the national emblem of Ireland because (according to a late tradition) it was used by St. Patrick to illustrate the doctrine of the Trinity.

Shandean, having the characteristics of 'Tristram Shandy' (q.v.).

Shandon, CAPTAIN, a character in Thackeray's 'Pendennis' (q.v.).

Shandy, TRISTRAM, WALTER, and MRS., and CAPTAIN TOBIAS, see *Tristram Shandy*.

Shan van Vocht, The, the title of an Irish revolutionary song of 1798, meaning 'the poor old woman', i.e. Ireland.

Sharp, REBECCA ('BECKY'), the principal character in Thackeray's 'Vanity Fair' (q.v.).

Sharp, WILLIAM ('FIONA MACLEOD') (1855-1905), wrote under his own name lives of D. G. Rossetti (1882), Shelley (1887), etc., also volumes of poems, and romances. He began to write mystical prose and verse under the pseudonym 'Fiona Macleod' in 1893.

Shavian, having the characteristic humour of G. B. Shaw (q.v.).

Shaving of Shagpat, The, an Arabian Entertainment, a story by Meredith (q.v.) (1856).

Shaw, GEORGE BERNARD (1856-1950), born in Dublin, came to London in 1876 and became a member of the Fabian Society (q.v.), for which he wrote political and economic tracts. He also applied himself to public speaking, and in 1885 took to journalism. He had meanwhile begun to write for the stage, and at once showed his unorthodox turn of mind and distrust of accepted institutions. 'Widowers' Houses' (begun in collaboration with William Archer) was produced in 1892, and subsequently included in the collection of 'Plays: Pleasant and Unpleasant' (1898). These were followed by 'Three Plays for Puritans' (1901) and 'Man and Superman' (1903). The latter, described as 'A Comedy and a Philosophy', introduces Shaw's conception of the 'Life

Force', a power that seeks to raise mankind, with their co-operation, to a higher and better existence. The same doctrine appears in 'Heartbreak House' (1917) and in 'Back to Methuselah' (1921), in which the causes of the failure of our civilization, as demonstrated by the Great War, are examined. The best known of Shaw's other plays are the following: the powerful and effective historical drama 'Saint Joan' (1924); 'Arms and the Man', 'Candida', 'Mrs. Warren's Profession', and 'You Never can Tell' (in 'Plays: Pleasant and Unpleasant'); 'Caesar and Cleopatra' (in 'Three Plays for Puritans'); 'John Bull's other Island' and 'Major Barbara' (1907); 'Fanny's First Play' (1911); 'Pygmalion' (1912); 'The Apple Cart' (1929); 'Too True to be Good' (1932); 'Village Wooing' (1933); 'The Millionairess' (1936); and 'Good King Charles's Golden Days' (1939). Among his other writings should be mentioned the important Prefaces to the plays, the novel 'Cashel Byron's Profession' (1886), 'The Intelligent Woman's Guide to Socialism and Capitalism' (1928), and 'Adventures of a Black Girl in search of God' (1932).

Shaw, HENRY WHEELER (1818–85), who wrote under the pseudonym 'Josh Billings', an American comic essayist and witty philosopher.

Sheffield, JOHN, *third earl of Mulgrave*, and afterwards *first duke of Buckingham and Normanby* (1648–1721), a patron of Dryden and friend of Pope. He is remembered as the author of the 'Essay on Satire', published anonymously. He also wrote an 'Essay upon Poetry', of no great value, and some fluent verses.

Shelley, MARY WOLLSTONECRAFT (1797–1851), the daughter of W. Godwin (q.v.) and Mary Wollstonecraft (q.v.) and second wife of P. B. Shelley (q.v.). She was author of 'Frankenstein, or the Modern Prometheus' (q.v., 1818), 'The Last Man' (1826, the story of the gradual destruction of the human race, with the exception of one man, by an epidemic), 'Valperga' (1823, a romance of Italy in the Middle Ages), and the autobiographical 'Lodore' (1835).

Shelley, PERCY BYSSHE (1792–1822), was educated at Eton and University College, Oxford, publishing, while at the former, 'Zastrozzi', and in 1810 'St. Irvyne', romances in the style of 'Monk' Lewis. From Oxford he was sent down in 1811 after circulating a pamphlet on 'The Necessity of Atheism'. In the same year he married Harriet Westbrook, who was aged sixteen, and from whom he separated after three years of a wandering life, during which he wrote 'Queen Mab' (q.v., piratically published in 1821). Some portions of this were subsequently remodelled as 'The Daemon of the World'. He left England in 1814 with Mary Godwin (see preceding entry), to whom he was married after the unhappy Harriet had, in 1816, drowned herself in the Serpentine; Claire Clairmont, Mary's step-sister, accompanied them. Shelley's 'Alastor' (q.v.) was written near Windsor and published in 1816. In the same year began his friendship with Byron, with whom Shelley and Mary spent the summer in Switzerland. To this period belong the 'Hymn to Intellectual Beauty' and 'Mont Blanc'. The winter of 1816–17 he spent at Marlow, and wrote, among other poems, 'Laon and Cythna' (q.v.), subsequently renamed 'The Revolt of Islam' (q.v., 1818), and the fragment, 'Prince Athanase'. In 1818 Shelley left England for Italy, translated Plato's 'Symposium', finished 'Rosalind and Helen' at Lucca, and in the summer, at Byron's villa near Este, composed the 'Lines written in the Euganean Hills'. He visited Byron at Venice, where he wrote 'Julian and Maddalo' (q.v.), and at the end of the same year the 'Stanzas written in dejection, near Naples'. Early in 1819 he was at Rome. Here, stirred to indignation by the political events at home, and in particular by the Peterloo affair, he wrote the 'Masque of Anarchy', an indictment of Castlereagh's administration. He also published 'Peter Bell the Third', a satire on Wordsworth. The same year, 1819, saw the publication of 'The Cenci' (q.v.) and the composition of his great lyrical drama, 'Prometheus Unbound' (q.v., 1820). At the end of 1819 the Shelleys moved to Pisa, and it was now that he wrote some of his finest lyrics, including the 'Ode to the West Wind', 'To a Skylark', and 'The Cloud'. His 'Oedipus Tyrannus, or Swellfoot the Tyrant', a dramatic satire on George IV's matrimonial affairs, appeared in 1820. To this period also belong the apologue of 'The Sensitive Plant' (q.v.); the 'Letter to Maria Gisborne' (the outcome of an intellectual friendship); the Odes 'to Naples' and 'to Liberty'; the notable 'Defence of Poetry' (1821), a vindication of the elements of imagination and love in poetry against the strictures of his great friend, T. L. Peacock, in 'The Four Ages of Poetry'; 'Adonais' (q.v., 1821); and 'Epipsychidion' (q.v., 1821).

Shelley removed in April 1821 to Lerici on the shores of the bay of Spezia, and completed his lyrical drama, 'Hellas' (1822), inspired by the struggle of Greece for freedom. He had also been at work on the drama, 'Charles I', which remained unfinished. On 8 July 1822 he was drowned, in his 30th year, while sailing near Spezia. He was at the time engaged on his uncompleted poem, 'The Triumph of Life'. The last period also saw the production of some of his most beautiful lyrics, 'O, world! O, life! O, time', 'When the lamp is shattered', and the love poems inspired by Jane Williams.

Shenstone, WILLIAM (1714-63), a contemporary of S. Johnson (q.v.) at Pembroke College, Oxford. As a poet much of his work is criticized for an artificial prettiness similar to that which he pursued in adorning his estate at the Leasowes, near Halesowen. His best-known work is 'The Schoolmistress' (1742), a poem in Spenserian stanzas describing a village school.

Shepheards Calender, The, was the earliest important work of Spenser (q.v.) (1579). It consists of twelve eclogues, one for each month of the year, written in different metres, and modelled on the eclogues of Theocritus, Virgil, and more modern writers, such as Baptist Mantuan and Marot. They take the form of dialogues among shepherds, except the first and last, which are complaints by 'Colin Clout', the author himself. Four of them deal with love, one is in praise of Elysa (Queen Elizabeth), one a lament for a 'mayden of great bloud', four deal allegorically with matters of religion or conduct, one describes a singing-match, and one laments the contempt in which poetry is held.

Shepherd, LORD CLIFFORD, THE, Henry de Clifford, *fourteenth Baron Clifford* (1455?-1523), celebrated in Wordsworth's 'Brougham Castle' and 'The White Doe of Rylstone'.

Shepherd, THE ETTRICK, see *Hogg*.

Shepherd of Salisbury Plain, The, a famous tract by Hannah More (q.v.).

Shepherd's Calendar, The, a volume of verse by J. Clare (q.v.).

Shepherd's Hunting, The, pastorals written by Wither (q.v.), in the Marshalsea.

Shepherd's Week, The, a series of six pastorals by J. Gay (q.v.) (1714).

They are eclogues in the mock-classical style, presenting shepherds and milkmaids, in their grotesque reality, designed to parody those of Ambrose Philips (q.v.).

Sheppard, JOHN (1702-24), 'Jack Sheppard', a famous thief and highwayman, who after repeated escapes from prison, was hanged at Tyburn. He was the subject of tracts by Defoe, of many plays and ballads, and of a novel by W. H. Ainsworth.

Sheraton, THOMAS (1751-1806), furniture-designer. His books of designs, 'The Cabinet-Maker and Upholsterer's Drawing Book' (1791), 'The Cabinet Dictionary' (1802-3), and 'Cabinet-Maker, Upholsterer and General Artist's Encyclopaedia' (1804), were immensely popular and influential.

Sheridan, MRS. FRANCES (1724-66), the mother of Richard Brinsley Sheridan, was author of the 'Memoirs of Miss Sidney Bidulph' (1761-7, a novel after the manner of 'Pamela'), and of 'The Discovery', a comedy successfully produced by Garrick in 1763.

Sheridan, RICHARD BRINSLEY (1751-1816), the son of Thomas Sheridan (an actor and author). His comedy, 'The Rivals' (q.v., written when the author was only 23), was acted at Covent Garden in 1775. 'St. Patrick's Day' and 'The Duenna' were played in the same year. He acquired Garrick's share in Drury Lane Theatre in 1776, and in 1777 produced there 'A Trip to Scarborough' and 'The School for Scandal' (q.v.). His famous farce, 'The Critic' (q.v.), was given in 1779. He was returned to parliament in 1780 as a supporter of Fox, and thereafter devoted himself to public affairs. He was arrested for debt in 1813, and in his last years suffered from brain disease.

Sheriffs of Bristol, A Letter to the, see *Letter to the Sheriffs of Bristol.*

Sherlock, THOMAS (1678-1761). As master of the Temple (1704-53) he obtained reputation as a preacher, and rose successively to the sees of Bangor, Salisbury, and London (1748-61). He took part in the Bangorian controversy (q.v.), and published, among other works, 'A Tryal of the Witnesses of the Resurrection of Jesus' (1729).

Sherlock Holmes, see *Holmes (Sherlock).*

Sherriff, ROBERT CEDRIC (1896-1975), playwright and novelist. His best-known play 'Journey's End', based on his letters written from the front in the First World War, was produced in 1929. He has written several novels, the first, 'A Fortnight in September' (1931), being the best known; also a number of screenplays which include 'Good-bye Mr. Chips' (1936), and 'The Dam Busters' (1955).

Sherwood, MRS. MARY MARTHA (1775-1851), *née* Butt, was author of numerous popular books for children and young people, the best known of which is 'The History of the Fairchild Family' (3 parts, 1818-47).

She Stoops to Conquer, or The Mistakes of a Night, a comedy by Goldsmith (q.v.), produced in 1773.

The principal characters are Hardcastle, Mrs. Hardcastle, and Miss Hardcastle their daughter; Mrs. Hardcastle's son by a former marriage, Tony Lumpkin, a frequenter of the 'Three Jolly Pigeons', idle, cunning, and mischievous, and doted on by his mother; and young Marlow. His father, Sir Charles Marlow, has proposed a match between young Marlow and Miss Hardcastle, and the young man and his friend, Hastings, accordingly travel down to pay the Hardcastles a visit. Losing their way they arrive at night at the 'Three Jolly Pigeons', where Tony Lumpkin directs them to a neighbouring inn, which is in reality the Hardcastles' house. The fun of the play arises largely from the resulting misunderstanding, Marlow treating Hardcastle as the landlord of the supposed inn, and making violent love to Miss Hardcastle, whom he takes for one of the servants. The arrival of Sir Charles Marlow clears up the misconception and all ends well.

The mistaking of a private residence for an inn is said to have been founded on an actual incident in Goldsmith's boyhood.

She would if she could, the second of the comedies by Etherege (q.v.), produced in 1668.

Shibboleth, the Hebrew word used by Jephthah as a test-word (Judges xii. 4-6), hence a word or formula used as a test for members of a party, etc.

Shimei, in Dryden's 'Absalom and Achitophel' (q.v.), Slingsby Bethel, the sheriff of London and Middlesex. The reference in the name is to 1 Kings ii. 37 et seq.

Shipman's Tale, The, see *Canterbury Tales.*

Ship-money, an ancient tax to provide ships, revived by Charles I (with an extended application to inland counties). The imposition was one of the causes that led to the Civil War.

Ship of Fools, The, an adaptation of

the famous 'Narrenschiff' of Sebastian Brandt. The 'Narrenschiff' was written in the dialect of Swabia and first published in 1494. It became extremely popular and was translated into many languages. Its theme is the shipping off of fools of all kinds from their native land to the Land of Fools.

It was translated into English 'out of Latin, French, and Doche' by Alexander Barclay (q.v.) (1509); the translation is not literal but is an adaptation to English conditions, and gives a picture of contemporary English life. The work is interesting as an early collection of satirical types. Its influence is seen in 'Cocke Lorell's Bote', a popular satire of the 16th cent.

Ships, FAMOUS, see *Argonauts* (for *Argo*), *Ark, Beagle, Bounty, Cutty Sark, Golden Hind, Great Eastern, Mary Celeste, Mayflower, Revenge*.

Shipton, MOTHER, according to tradition, a witch and prophetess who lived in Yorkshire at the end of the 15th cent.

Shipwreck, The, see *Falconer (W.)*.

Shirburne Ballads, The, edited in 1907 by Andrew Clark from a manuscript of 1600-16 (a few pieces are later) at Shirburne Castle, Oxfordshire, belonging to the earl of Macclesfield. The collection contains ballads not found elsewhere, dealing with political events, with legends and fairy tales, or with stories of domestic life. Some of them are homilies.

Shirley, a novel by C. Brontë (q.v.) (1849).

The scene of the story is Yorkshire and the period the latter part of the Napoleonic wars, the time of the Luddite riots. Robert Gérard Moore, a mill-owner of determined character, persists in introducing the latest labour-saving machinery, undeterred by the opposition of the workers. To overcome the financial difficulties that hamper his plans he proposes to Shirley Keeldar, a young lady of wealth, though he loves the gentle and retiring Caroline Helstone. Robert is contemptuously rejected by Shirley, and, when the end of

the war releases him from his embarrassments, marries the faithful Caroline. Meanwhile Shirley and Robert's brother, Louis, successfully overcome the difficulties in the way of their mutual love. In Shirley Keeldar, Charlotte Brontë depicted the character of her sister Emily, as she saw it.

Shirley, JAMES (1596-1666), took Anglican orders, but was presently converted to the Church of Rome and became a schoolmaster. He followed the earl of Newcastle in the Civil War, after which he returned to the profession of schoolmaster.

Shirley wrote some forty dramas, of which the greater number are extant. The tragedies include: 'The Maid's Revenge' (1626), 'The Traitor' (1631), 'Love's Cruelty' (1631), and 'The Cardinall' (1641). He also wrote comedies of manners and romantic comedies, including: 'Changes, or Love in a Maze' (1632, the interchanges of affection between three pairs of lovers), 'Hyde Park' (1632), 'The Gamester' (1633, adapted by Garrick and others), 'The Imposture' (1640). Shirley also wrote 'The Contention of Ajax and Ulysses' (1659), a dramatic entertainment ending with the famous dirge

The glories of our blood and state
Are shadows, not substantial things.

He was disparaged by Dryden ('Mac Flecknoe'), but his reputation was revived by Charles Lamb.

Shirley, JOHN (1366?-1456), said to have been a traveller in various lands. He translated from the French and Latin and transcribed the works of Chaucer, Lydgate, and others; it is on his authority that various poems are attributed to Chaucer.

Shiva, see *Siva*.

Shoemaker's Holiday, The, or A pleasant comedy of the Gentle Craft, a comedy by Dekker (q.v.) (1600).

Rowland Lacy, a kinsman of the earl of Lincoln, loves Rose, the daughter of the lord mayor of London. To prevent the match, the earl sends him to France in command of a company of men. Lacy resigns his place to a friend, and, disguised as a Dutch shoemaker, takes service with Simon Eyre, who supplies the family of the lord mayor with shoes. Here he successfully pursues his suit, is married, and is pardoned by the king. The most entertaining character in the play is that of Simon Eyre, the cheery, eccentric master-shoemaker, who becomes lord mayor of London. See also *Deloney* (*T.*).

Shore, JANE (*d.* 1527?), mistress of Edward IV. She was the daughter of a Cheapside mercer and wife of a Lombard Street goldsmith, and exercised great influence over Edward IV by her beauty and wit. She was accused by Richard III of sorcery, imprisoned, and made to do public penance in 1483, and died in poverty.

She is the subject of a ballad included in Percy's 'Reliques', of a remarkable passage in Sir Thomas More's history of Richard III, and of a descriptive note by Drayton ('England's Heroical Epistles'). Her adversities are the subject of a tragedy by Rowe (q.v.).

Short, CODLIN AND, see *Codlin*.

Shortest Way with the Dissenters, see *Defoe*.

Shorthouse, JOSEPH HENRY (1834-1903), author of 'John Inglesant' (q.v., 1881), and other novels of less importance.

Short Parliament, THE, the first of the two parliaments summoned by Charles I in 1640. It was dissolved after it had sat for three weeks.

Short View of the Immorality and Profaneness of the English Stage, see *Collier*.

Shropshire Lad, A, see *Housman* (*A. E.*).

Shrove-tide, the period immediately preceding Lent, formerly marked by a final indulgence in merry-making, eating, and drinking.

Shylock, the Jewish usurer in Shakespeare's 'The Merchant of Venice' (q.v.), said to have been drawn from Roderigo Lopez, the queen's Jewish physician, hanged in 1594 on a charge of conspiring to murder her.

Sibylline Books, THE, see *Sibyls*.

Sibylline Leaves, a volume of poems by S. T. Coleridge (q.v.).

Sibyls, THE, certain inspired women, who flourished in different parts of the ancient world, at Cumae, Delphi, Erythraea in Ionia, etc. The best known is the Cumaean sibyl, who was beloved by Apollo, and who accompanied Aeneas in his visit to the infernal regions. The three *Sibylline Books* were said to have been sold to Tarquin II by one of the sibyls. These were probably written in Greek, and were kept, under the custody of special officers, in the temple of Jupiter Capitolinus. They were consulted in times of national calamity. When the temple of Jupiter was burnt down in 83 B.C., the books were destroyed. Thereupon a fresh collection of sibylline prophecies was made in Asia Minor and the Greek cities of Italy and Sicily. They continued to be consulted occasionally for several centuries.

Sicilian Vespers, THE, a general massacre of the French in Sicily in 1282, of which the signal was the tolling of the bell for vespers.

Sick Man of Europe, THE, a term frequently applied during the latter part of the 19th cent. to Turkey.

Siddartha, see *Buddha*.

Siddons, MRS. SARAH (1755-1831), the sister of J. Kemble (q.v.), the actor, probably the one great tragedy queen that Britain ever produced. She first attracted attention in the part of Belvidera in Otway's 'Venice Preserv'd', and was subsequently famous in her impersonation of Lady Macbeth and of the heroine in Rowe's 'Jane Shore'.

Sidgwick, HENRY (1838-1900), was from 1883 professor of moral philosophy at Cambridge. A follower in economics and politics of John Stuart Mill, his most important work as a philosophical writer relates to ethics, and his reputation rests on his 'Methods of Ethics' (1874).

Sidney, ALGERNON (1622-83), the grandnephew of Sir Philip Sidney, and younger brother of Waller's 'Sacharissa', took up arms against Charles I and was wounded at Marston Moor. He was employed on government service until the Restoration, but his firm republicanism was the source of hostility to Cromwell. At the Restoration he refused to give pledges to Charles II, and lived abroad in poverty and exile until 1677. He was sent to the Tower of London after the discovery of the Rye House Plot, and was executed on Tower Hill. He wrote 'Discourses concerning Government', first printed in 1698, and a treatise on 'Love', published in 1844. He is the 'later Sidney' to whom Wordsworth refers in his sonnet, 'Great men have been among us'.

Sidney, SIR PHILIP (1554–86), son of Sir Henry Sidney (who was thrice lord-deputy of Ireland) and of Leicester's sister, became intimate with Sir F. Greville (q.v., Lord Brooke) and Camden (q.v.), and was favoured by Sir William Cecil (Lord Burghley). In 1583 he married Frances, daughter of Sir Francis Walsingham. In 1576 he became acquainted with Walter Devereux, first earl of Essex, and his daughter Penelope, to whom he addressed the famous series of sonnets known as 'Astrophel and Stella' (q.v.), written during 1580–4. He saw much of Spenser at Leicester House, and received the dedication of his 'Shepheards Calender'. He became a member of the Areopagus (a club formed chiefly for the purpose of naturalizing the classical metres in English verse, which included Spenser, Fulke Greville, Harvey, Dyer, and others). In 1586 he joined as a volunteer the attack on a Spanish convoy for the relief of Zutphen. Here, on 22 Sept., he received a fatal wound in the thigh. His death evoked elegies by Spenser ('Astrophel'), Matthew Roydon (included after 'Astrophel' in Spenser's works), James VI, Breton, Drayton, and others.

Sidney exercised an extraordinary influence on the poets of his own and the following generations, heightened, perhaps, by the romantic character of his personal history. None of his works appeared in his lifetime; the 'Arcadia' (q.v.)

was first published in 1590; the 3rd edition (1598) included his 'Apologie for Poetrie' (q.v.) and 'Astrophel and Stella' (q.v.), of which an unauthorized edition had appeared in 1591.

Sidney Bidulph, The Memoirs of Miss, see under *Sheridan (Mrs. F.).*

'Sidney's sister, Pembroke's mother', see *Pembroke.*

Sidonia, in Disraeli's 'Coningsby' and 'Tancred' (qq.v.), a wealthy and powerful Jewish banker.

Sidonius Apollinaris (c. A.D. 431–84), the foremost representative of Latin literature of his time, author of letters and of poems.

Sidrophel, the astrologer in Butler's 'Hudibras' (q.v., II. iii). He is supposed to represent Sir Paul Neal, a conceited member of the Royal Society.

Siege of Corinth, The, a poem by Lord Byron (q.v.) (1816), founded on the story of the siege by the Turks, in 1715, of Corinth, then held by the Venetians.

Siege of Rhodes, The, the first attempt at English opera, by D'Avenant, performed in 1656.

Dramatic performances having been suppressed by the Commonwealth government, D'Avenant obtained authority in 1656 to produce at Rutland House an 'Entertainment after the manner of the ancients'; it was accompanied by vocal and instrumental music, composed by Henry Lawes. Immediately after this prologue was given 'The Siege of Rhodes' (at first in one, but in 1662 in two parts), a heroic play, the 'story sung in recitative music'. The play deals with the siege of Rhodes by Solyman the Magnificent, and the devotion by which Ianthe, wife of the Sicilian Duke Alphonso, saves her husband and the defenders of the island.

Siege Perilous, see *Round Table.*

Siegfried, the hero of the first part of the 'Nibelungenlied' (q.v.).

In Wagner's opera, 'Siegfried', the hero, son of Siegmund and Sieglinde, slays Fafner, the giant snake who guards the stolen Rhine-gold, and obtains the magic ring and the 'tarn-helm' which enables him to assume any shape he pleases. He passes through the flames that surround Brynhilde and awakens her, and they plight their troth. The story is concluded in the 'Götterdämmerung' (q.v.).

Sigismonda (Ghismonda), in Boccaccio's 'Decameron' (iv. i), daughter of Tancred, prince of Salerno. Her father, having discovered her love for his squire Guiscardo, slew the latter and sent his heart in a golden cup to Sigismonda, who took poison and died. The father, repenting his cruelty, caused the pair to be buried in the same tomb. The story is the subject of Dryden's 'Sigismunda and Guiscardo'. and of Robert Wilmot's 'Tancred and Gismund'.

James Thomson's tragedy 'Tancred and Sigismunda' (1745) deals with a different story.

Sigurd the Volsung and the Fall of the Niblungs, The Story of, an epic in four books, in anapaestic couplets, by W. Morris (q.v.), founded upon the 'Volsunga Saga', and published in 1876.

The first book of this, Morris's most important work, recounts the grim tale of Sigmund, the father of Sigurd, and the three other books deal with the story of Sigurd himself.

Sikes, BILL, a character in Dickens's 'Oliver Twist' (q.v.).

Silas Marner, a novel by G. Eliot (q.v.) (1861).

Silas Marner, a linen-weaver, has been driven out of the small religious community to which he belongs by a false charge of theft, and has taken refuge in the agricultural village of Raveloe. His only consolation in his loneliness is his growing pile of gold. This is stolen from his cottage by the squire's reprobate son, Dunstan Cass, who disappears. Dunstan's elder brother, Godfrey, is in love with Nancy Lammeter, but is secretly married to a woman of low class in a neighbouring town. This woman carries her child one New Year's Eve to Raveloe, intending to force her way into the Casses' house; but

dies in the snow. Her child, Eppie, finds her way into Silas's cottage, is adopted by him, and restores to him the happiness which he has lost. After many years, the draining of a pond near Silas's door reveals the body of Dunstan with the gold. Moved by this revelation, Godfrey, now married to Nancy, acknowledges himself the father of Eppie and claims her, but she refuses to leave Silas.

Silence, in Shakespeare's '2 Henry IV' (q.v.), a country justice.

Silent Woman, The, see *Epicœne.*

Silenus, a Satyr, the foster-father and attendant of Dionysus (q.v.), generally represented as a fat old man, riding on an ass, intoxicated, and crowned with flowers.

Silures, an ancient British tribe that inhabited the south-east part of Wales.

Silurist,. THE, see *Vaughan.*

Silver-fork, a term used to designate a school of novelists about 1830 (Mrs. Gore (q.v.) and others), distinguished by an affectation of gentility.

Silvia, a character in Shakespeare's 'The Two Gentlemen of Verona' (q.v.).

Simenon, GEORGES (1903-), Belgian-born novelist, a prolific, widely read and widely translated author of crime fiction. His stories create their effect by atmosphere and psychological intuition rather than by intricacies of plot. His detective-superintendent Maigret, who dominates many volumes, has become one of the famous crime-investigators of modern fiction.

Simile (Lat. *simile*, like), an object, scene, or action, introduced by way of comparison for explanatory, illustrative, or merely ornamental purpose. Cf. metaphor.

Simnel, LAMBERT (*fl.* 1475-1525), of humble parentage, was persuaded to give himself out as Edward, earl of Warwick, son of the duke of Clarence. He was crowned at Dublin as Edward VI (1487), and crossed to England, where the force that he brought with him from Ireland was utterly defeated by Henry VII. Simnel was pardoned and employed as a turnspit in the royal kitchen.

Simon Eyre (*d.* 1459), according to Stow, a draper who became mayor of London. He figures in Dekker's 'The Shoemaker's Holiday' (q.v.).

Simonides (*c.* 556–*c.* 468 B.C.), the first great lyric poet of Greece as a whole. His most distinctive work was in his epigrams, notable for their simplicity and power. Some fragments of his poetry survive.

Simon Magus, the sorcerer of Samaria referred to in Acts viii. 9–13. His attempt to purchase miraculous powers by offering the Apostles money is alluded to in the word *Simony*.

Simplicissimus, the name of a well-known German comic paper, founded in 1896.

Sinbad, see *Sindbad of the Sea*.

Sinclair, UPTON (1878–1968), American novelist and journalist. Sinclair was a novelist with a strong sociological bias, and most of his books were written in protest against abuses due to the industrial system. His chief works are: 'The Jungle' (q.v., 1906), 'King Coal' (1917), 'The Brass Check' (1919), 'Oil' (1927), 'Boston' (1928), and 'Dragon's Teeth' (1942).

Sindbad of the Sea, or *Sindbad the Sailor*, one of the tales in the 'Arabian Nights' (q.v.).

Sindbad, a rich young man of Baghdad, having wasted much of his wealth in prodigal living, undertakes a number of sea-voyages as a merchant and meets with various marvellous adventures. The best known are those of the Roc, a huge bird that could lift elephants in its claws, and of the Old Man of the Sea.

Sinfiotli, in W. Morris's 'Sigurd the Volsung', the son of Sigmund and Signy. He appears in 'Beowulf' (q.v.) as Fitela.

Singleton, *Adventures of Captain*, a romance of adventure by Defoe (q.v.) (1790).

Sinn Fein (pron. 'Shin Fane'), 'ourselves', the policy of the Irish Republican party, formulated in 1902; also used for the party itself.

Sinon, see *Horse (The Trojan)*.

Sir Charles Grandison, The History of, a novel by S. Richardson (q.v.) (1754).

As in Richardson's previous novels, the story is told by means of letters. The beautiful and accomplished Harriet Byron comes to London, where she attracts many admirers. Among these, Sir Hargrave Pollexfen, rich, arrogant, and unscrupulous, presses his court. Infuriated by Harriet's refusal, he has her carried off from a masquerade, and forcibly removes her in a coach to the country. The coach is fortunately stopped by that of Sir Charles Grandison, a gentleman of high character, by whom Harriet is rescued. Sir Charles and Harriet fall in love, but the former is precluded from offering marriage. When living in Italy, he has rendered great services to the noble family of the Porrettas, and a quasi-engagement has been formed between him and Clementina Porretta. The difference of their religion has hitherto made it impossible to arrive at an agreement with the parents, and Clementina's mind becomes deranged by her unhappiness. As she gets better, however, she decides that she cannot marry a heretic. Sir Charles is released, and is united to Harriet Byron.

Sirens, THE, fabulous creatures, two (or three) in number, who had the power of luring men to destruction by their song; they lived in an island off the SW. coast of Italy. Odysseus, informed of the power of their voices by Circe, when passing by this point stopped the ears of his companions with wax and caused himself to be tied to the mast of the ship, and so passed them in safety ('Odyssey', xii).

Sir Gawain and the Green Knight, see *Gawain and the Green Knight (Sir)*.

Sirius, see *Dog-star*.

Sir Launcelot Greaves, The Adventures of, a novel by Smollett (q.v.).

Sir Launfal, a poem by Thomas Chestre (*fl.* 1430). Sir Launfal, a Knight of the Round Table (q.v.), leaves the court, offended by the reputed misconduct of Queen Guinevere.

The story occurs in the 'Lays' of Marie de France (q.v.).

Sirmio, a promontory on the southern shore of the Lago di Garda (*Lacus Benacus*), on which Catullus (q.v.) had a villa.

Sir Orfeo, a metrical romance of the Middle English period, in which the classical story of Orpheus (q.v.) and Eurydice is reproduced in Celtic guise.

Sir Patrick Spens, the title of an old Scottish ballad, on the subject of Sir Patrick's dispatch to sea, on a mission for the king, in winter; of his foreboding of disaster; and of his destruction with his ship's company. The ballad is in Percy's 'Reliques'. Scott, in his version, makes the object of Sir Patrick's expedition the bringing to Scotland of the Maid of Norway.

Sirvente, a form of poem or lay, usually satirical, employed by the troubadours. Apparently from Fr. *servir*, to serve, but the connection is not clear.

Sister Anne, see *Blue Beard*.

Sister Helen, a poem by D. G. Rossetti (q.v.) (1870).

The poem presents in semi-dramatic form the story of a woman who destroys her unfaithful lover by melting his waxen image, and thereby loses her own soul.

Sistine Chapel, THE, built by Pope Sixtus IV in 1473 in the Vatican. It was decorated by Perugino, Botticelli, and later by Michelangelo.

Sisyphus, a legendary king of Corinth, famous for his cunning, who outwitted Autolycus (q.v.). After his death, Sisyphus, on account of misdeeds variously related, was condemned in hell to roll to the top of a hill a large stone, which when it reached the summit rolled back to the plain, so that his punishment was eternal.

Sitwell, DAME EDITH (1887-1964), poet and critic, the daughter of Sir George and Lady Ida Sitwell. From 1916 to 1921 she edited 'Wheels', an annual anthology of modern verse. During the 1920s she published a number of volumes of verse in which she exploited the musical qualities of language, sometimes at the expense of any clear meaning. Her recital of some of these poems, under the title 'Façade', to music by William Walton at the Aeolian Hall in 1923 caused something approaching a riot. Volumes of her 'Collected Poems' appeared in 1930, 1954, and 1957. She also published biographical studies, notably 'Alexander Pope' (1930) and 'The English Eccentrics' (1933). Her later verse developed a graver tone, in 'Street Songs' (1943), 'Green Song' (1944), and 'Song of the Cold' (1945).

Sitwell, SIR OSBERT (1892-1969), brother of Edith and Sacheverell Sitwell (qq.v.). He published a number of volumes of verse, mostly light and satirical in character, short stories, including 'Triple Fugue' (1924), and novels, of which 'Before the Bombardment' (1926) is considered the best. His autobiography (5 vols., 1944-50) is especially remarkable for the account of the eccentric and dominating personality of his father.

Sitwell, SACHEVERELL (1897-), brother of Edith and Osbert Sitwell (qq.v.). His 'Selected Poems' were published in 1948. His poetry has affinities with that of his sister, but is technically more traditional. He is chiefly known for his essays and criticism of the arts, including 'A Life of Liszt' (1936), 'La Vie Parisienne' (1937), and 'Sacred and Profane Love' (1940), and for his travel writings.

Siva or SHIVA, the third god of the great Hindu triad, of which Brahma and Vishnu are the other two members. He is the god of destruction, and of the regeneration which follows it, and is generally worshipped under a phallic symbol.

Skald, an ancient Scandinavian poet, a term usually applied to the poets of the Viking period. The Skaldic verse is extraordinarily elaborate in metre and alliteration.

Skeat, WALTER WILLIAM (1835-1912), was appointed in 1878 professor of Anglo-Saxon at Cambridge. He began his great edition of 'Piers Plowman' in 1866. His seven-volume edition of Chaucer appeared in 1894-7. Skeat founded the English Dialect Society in 1873, which prepared the way for the 'English Dialect Dictionary' (edited by Joseph Wright, 1896-1905). Skeat's 'Etymological Dictionary' (1879-82, revised and enlarged, 1910) was begun with the object of collecting and sifting material for the New English Dictionary. He wrote many textbooks for schools and universities, and did much to popularize philology and old authors. He also, in his later years, led the way in the systematic study of place-names.

Skeffington, SIR LUMLEY ST. GEORGE (1771-1850), a fop and playwright, satirized by Byron ('English Bards and Scotch Reviewers', 599) and Moore.

Skeggs, CAROLINA WILHELMINA AMELIA, in Goldsmith's 'The Vicar of Wakefield' (q.v.), one of the fine ladies introduced to the Primroses by Squire Thornhill.

Skelton, JOHN (1460?-1529), was created 'poet-laureate' by the universities of Oxford and Cambridge, an academical distinction. He became tutor to Prince Henry (Henry VIII), and enjoyed court favour, was admitted to holy orders in 1498 and became parson of Diss in Norfolk. His principal works include: 'The Bowge of Court' (a satire on the court of Henry VII); the 'Garlande of Laurell' (a self-laudatory allegorical poem, describing the crowning of the author among the great poets of the world); 'Phylyp Sparowe' (a lamentation put into the mouth of Jane Scroupe, a young lady whose sparrow has been killed by a cat); 'Colyn Cloute' (a complaint by a vagabond of the misdeeds of ecclesiastics), which gave suggestions to Spenser. Not only this last poem, but also his satires 'Speke, Parrot', and 'Why come ye nat to courte', contained attacks on Cardinal Wolsey. As a result Skelton was obliged to take sanctuary at Westminster, where he died. His most vigorous poem was 'The Tunning of Elynour Rumming'. His play of 'Magnyfycence' is an example of the Morality (q.v.). In this allegory, Magnificence, symbolizing a generous prince, is ruined by mistaken liberality and bad counsellors, but restored by Goodhope, Perseverance, and other similar figures.

His favourite metre was a 'headlong voluble breathless doggerel', 'which has taken from its author the title of Skeltonical verse' (Churton Collins). Cf. his own description in 'Colyn Cloute', ii. 53-8.

Sketches by Boz, a collection of sketches of life and manners, by Dickens (q.v.), first published in various periodicals, and in book form in 1836-7 (in one volume, 1839). These are some of Dickens's earliest literary work.

Skewton, THE HON. MRS., in Dickens's 'Dombey and Son' (q.v.), the mother of Edith, Dombey's second wife. See also *Cleopatra*.

Skimpole, HAROLD, a character in Dickens's 'Bleak House' (q.v.).

Skinfaxi ('shining-mane'), in Scandinavian mythology, the horse of the sun.

Skionar, MR., a character in Peacock's 'Crotchet Castle' (q.v.), perhaps a caricature of Coleridge.

Slawkenbergius, HAFEN, in Sterne's 'Tristram Shandy' (q.v.), the German author of a Latin treatise on noses, one of whose Rabelaisian tales is given at the beginning of vol. iv.

Slay-good, in Pt. II of Bunyan's 'The Pilgrim's Progress' (q.v.), a giant whom Mr. Greatheart killed.

Sleary, the circus proprietor in Dickens's 'Hard Times' (q.v.).

Sleeping Beauty, The, a fairy tale, translated from the French of Perrault (q.v.), by Robert Samber (1729?).

Seven fairies are invited to attend the baptism of the daughter of a king. An old fairy has been overlooked and comes unbidden. Six of the first fairies bestow on the child every imaginable perfection. The old fairy spitefully pronounces that she shall wound herself with a spindle and die. The seventh fairy, who has purposely kept in the background, amends this fate, converting the death into a sleep of a hundred years, from which the princess will be awakened by a king's son. So it

S

falls out, and the fairy puts everyone in the castle also to sleep so that the princess may not wake up all alone. In due course the prince comes and wakens the sleepers.

Sleepy Hollow, The Legend of, a humorous tale by W. Irving (q.v.).

Slender, a character in Shakespeare's 'The Merry Wives of Windsor' (q.v.).

Slick, SAM, see *Haliburton.*

Slipslop, MRS., a character in Fielding's 'Joseph Andrews' (q.v.).

Slop, DR., in Sterne's 'Tristram Shandy' (q.v.), a bigoted and clumsy physician.

Slough of Despond, THE, in Bunyan's 'The Pilgrim's Progress' (q.v.), a miry place on the way from the City of Destruction to the wicket-gate.

Slowboy, TILLY, a character in Dickens's 'The Cricket on the Hearth' (q.v.).

Sludge, DICKIE, or 'Flibbertigibbet', a character in Scott's 'Kenilworth' (q.v.).

Sludge, 'the Medium', see *Mr. Sludge.*

Slumkey, THE HONOURABLE SAMUEL, a character in Dickens's 'The Pickwick Papers' (q.v.).

Sly, CHRISTOPHER, see *Taming of the Shrew.*

Small House at Allington, The, a novel by A. Trollope (q.v.) (1864).

This, though not in the Barsetshire series of novels, deals with some of the same characters.

Smart, CHRISTOPHER (1722–71), was author of two volumes of 'Poems' (1752 and 1763); the 'Hilliad' (1753), a satire on John Hill, the quack doctor; a paraphrase of the Psalms; and translations of Phaedrus and Horace. But he is chiefly remembered for his 'Song to David' (1763), a song of praise of King David, as the great poet and author of the Psalms, containing splendid imagery. Smart, who was a friend of Dr. Johnson, declined into insanity and debt.

Smectymnuus, the name under which five Presbyterian divines, Stephen Marshal, Edmund Calamy, Thomas Young, Matthew Newcomen, and William Spurstow, published a pamphlet attacking episcopacy. The name is a combination

of their initials. It was answered by Bishop Hall (see *Hall, J.*), and defended by Milton in his 'Animadversions upon the Remonstrant's Defence against Smectymnuus' (1641), and his 'Apology against a Pamphlet . . . against Smectymnuus' (1642), which contains an interesting account of Milton's early studies.

Smedley, FRANCIS EDWARD (1818–64), a cripple from childhood, was author of some pleasant novels, blending romance with sport and adventure. The most popular of these was 'Frank Fairleigh' (1850).

Smee, a pirate in Barrie's 'Peter Pan' (q.v.).

Smelfungus, see under *Smollett.*

Smike, a character in Dickens's 'Nicholas Nickleby' (q.v.).

Smiles, SAMUEL (1812–1904), devoted the leisure of a varied career to the advocacy of political and social reform on the lines of the Manchester School, and to the biography of industrial leaders and humble self-taught students. He achieved great popular success with 'Self-help' in 1859, 'Character' (1871), etc.

Smith, ADAM (1723–90), was appointed professor of logic at Glasgow in 1751, and in 1752 of moral philosophy. He became the friend of Hume (q.v.). In 1759 he published his 'Theory of the Moral Sentiments', which brought him into prominence. In 1764 he visited France, where he saw Voltaire, and was admitted into the society of the 'physiocrats' (q.v.). After his return he devoted himself to the preparation of his great work, 'An Inquiry into the Nature and Causes of the Wealth of Nations' (q.v.) (1776). This revolutionized the economic theories of the day. Smith edited the autobiography of Hume in 1777, and was a member of the Literary Club (see *Johnson, S.*).

Smith, ALEXANDER (1830–67), published in 1853 'A Life Drama' and other poems, which were received at first with enthusiasm, and were satirized by Aytoun (q.v.) in 'Firmilian'. He published sonnets on the Crimean War in 1855 jointly with

S. T. Dobell (q.v.), and 'City Poems' in 1857, containing 'Glasgow', his finest work in verse, giving a sombre picture of the city.

Smith, GEORGE (1824-1901), joined in 1838 the firm of Smith & Elder, publishers, and in 1846 became sole head of the firm. The chief authors whose works he published in his early career were John Ruskin, Charlotte Brontë, whose 'Jane Eyre' he issued in 1848, and W. M. Thackeray, whose 'Esmond' he brought out in 1851. In 1865 Smith (with Frederick Greenwood) founded 'The Pall Mall Gazette' (q.v.), which remained his property till 1880. In later life his chief authors included Robert Browning, Matthew Arnold, (Sir) Leslie Stephen, and Miss Thackeray (Lady Ritchie), all of whom were intimate personal friends. He was founder (1882) and proprietor of the 'Dictionary of National Biography' (q.v.).

Smith, HARRIET, a character in Jane Austen's 'Emma' (q.v.)

Smith, or GOW, HENRY, the hero of Scott's 'Fair Maid of Perth'.

Smith, HORATIO (HORACE) (1779-1849), brother of James Smith (q.v.), became famous as the joint-author, with him, of 'Rejected Addresses' (1812, q.v.) and of 'Horace in London' (1813). He subsequently wrote novels, of which the best is 'Brambletye House' (1826), an imitation of Sir Walter Scott, the story of a young Cavalier in the days of Cromwell and Charles II.

Smith, JAMES (1775-1839), elder brother of H. Smith (q.v.), solicitor to the Board of Ordnance, produced with his brother the 'Rejected Addresses' (q.v., 1812) and 'Horace in London' (1813).

Smith, CAPTAIN JOHN (1580-1631), set out with the Virginia colonists in 1606 and is said to have been rescued by Pocahontas (q.v.) when taken prisoner by the Indians. He was author of 'The General History of Virginia, New England, and the Summer Isles' (1624), and of a 'Sea Grammar' for young seamen (1626-7).

Smith, MARY, the narrator of the story in Mrs. Gaskell's 'Cranford' (q.v.).

Smith, SYDNEY (1771-1845), resided for a time, as tutor of Michael Hicks Beach, at Edinburgh, where he was intimate with Jeffrey, Brougham, and Horner, and with the first two of these founded 'The Edinburgh Review' in 1802. In 1807 he published the 'Letters of Peter Plymley' in defence of Catholic emancipation. He was noted for his exuberant drollery and wit, which were principally displayed in his conversation, but are also seen in his numerous reviews and letters.

Smith, WAYLAND, see *Wayland the Smith*.

Smith, SIR WILLIAM (1813-93), remembered as the editor and part author of the 'Dictionary of Greek and Roman Antiquities' (1842), and of other educational works. He was editor of 'The Quarterly Review', 1867-93.

Smith, WILLIAM ROBERTSON (1846-94), theologian and Semitic scholar, was dismissed (1881) from his chair at the Free Church College, Aberdeen, for the advanced character of his biblical articles in the 'Encyclopaedia Britannica' (9th ed.), of which work he became co-editor in 1881. He was professor of Arabic at Cambridge from 1883.

Smollett, TOBIAS GEORGE (1721-71), was educated at Glasgow University, but left without means of support. He sailed as surgeon's mate on the 'Chichester' in 1741, was present at the attack on Cartagena, and remained some time in Jamaica, where he married. In 1744 he returned to London, practised as a surgeon, and wrote his novels, which appeared as follows: 'Roderick Random' (q.v.) in 1748, 'Peregrine Pickle' (q.v.) in 1751 (revised edition, 1758), 'Ferdinand Count Fathom' in 1753, 'Sir Launcelot Greaves' (the story of an 18th-cent. Don Quixote) in 1760-2, and 'Humphry Clinker' (q.v.) in 1771. In 1753 he had settled at Chelsea, editing the new 'Critical Review' in 1756, and bringing out a large 'History of England'. Ill health sent him abroad in 1763, and in 1766 he published his entertaining but ill-tempered 'Travels in France and Italy', which procured for him, from Sterne, the nickname of 'Smelfungus'. In 1769 appeared his coarse and vigorous satire on public affairs entitled 'The Adventures of an Atom'. He died at Monte Nero near Leghorn.

Smorltork, COUNT, in Dickens's 'The Pickwick Papers' (q.v.), 'the famous foreigner' at Mrs. Leo Hunter's party.

Snagsby, MR. and MRS., characters in Dickens's 'Bleak House' (q.v.).

Snake, a character in Sheridan's 'The School for Scandal' (q.v.).

Snark, The, see *Hunting of the Snark*.

Sneerwell, LADY, one of the scandalmongers in Sheridan's 'The School for Scandal' (q.v.).

Snevellicci, MR., MRS., and MISS, in Dickens's 'Nicholas Nickleby' (q.v.), actors in Crummles's company.

Snobs of England, The, by one of themselves, a collection of papers by Thackeray (q.v.), republished as 'The Book of Snobs' (1848).

Snodgrass, AUGUSTUS, a character in Dickens's 'The Pickwick Papers' (q.v.).

Snorri Sturlason (1178-1241), an Icelandic historian, author of the 'Heimskringla' (q.v.) or history of the kings of Norway, and of the prose 'Edda' (q.v.).

Snout, TOM, in Shakespeare's 'A Midsummer Night's Dream' (q.v.), a tinker.

Snow, SIR CHARLES PERCY (1905-   ), novelist, was a professional scientist in his early career. His first novel was a detective story, 'Death under Sail' (1932), followed by 'New Lives for Old' (1933) and 'The Search' (1934). Since then he has undertaken a novel sequence entitled 'Strangers and Brothers' (the title of the first volume, 1940). Succeeding novels in the series are 'The Light and the Dark' (1947), 'Time of Hope' (1949), 'The Masters' (1951), 'The New Men' (1954), 'Homecomings' (1956), 'The Conscience of the Rich' (1958), 'The Affair' (1960), 'Corridors of Power' (1964), and 'The Sleep of Reason' (1968), and have a setting largely academic and scientific—

the 'Two Cultures' of his Rede Lecture at Cambridge, 1959.

Snubbin, MR. SERJEANT, in Dickens's 'The Pickwick Papers' (q.v.), counsel for the defendant in Bardell *v*. Pickwick.

Snuffy Davie, or DAVIE WILSON, in Scott's 'The Antiquary' (q.v.), the hero of a favourite story of Monkbarns.

Snug, in Shakespeare's 'A Midsummer Night's Dream' (q.v.), a joiner.

Social Contract, The, the English title of 'Du Contrat Social', by J. J. Rousseau (q.v.).

Socialism, a theory or policy of social organization that aims at the control of the means of production, capital, land, property, etc., by the community as a whole, and their administration or distribution in the interests of all. G. B. Shaw (q.v.) published in 1928 'The Intelligent Woman's Guide to Socialism and Capitalism'.

Society for Pure English, THE, or S.P.E., was founded in 1913, the original committee consisting of H. Bradley, R. Bridges, Sir Walter Raleigh (qq.v.), and Logan Pearsall Smith (1865-1946). The object of the promoters was to guide popular taste and the educational authorities in matters connected with the use and development of the English language.

Socinianism, the doctrine of Lelio Sozzini (Socinus) and his nephew Fausto Sozzini (1539-1604) that Jesus was not God but a divine prophet of God's word.

Socrates (469-399 B.C.), the great Greek philosopher, was a man of uncouth appearance and was married to Xanthippe, who had the reputation of being a scold. Turning aside from the physical speculations of the earlier philosophers, he devoted himself to the investigation of virtue, that which makes a good citizen. He frequented public places, conversing with all and sundry, interrogating those who had a reputation for wisdom, and refuting them. He thus made enemies and was finally accused of impiety by one Meletus, condemned by a narrow majority of the judges, and sentenced to death (by drinking hemlock). Socrates wrote nothing, but the general method and tendency of his teaching are preserved in the Dialogues of Plato (q.v.).

The SOCRATIC METHOD of instruction was by questions aptly proposed so as to arrive at the conclusion he wished to convey.

Sodom and Gomorrah, the cities destroyed, on account of their wickedness, in the days of Lot and Abraham (Gen. xiii, xviii, and xix).

Sofa, The, the name of Bk. I of Cowper's 'The Task' (q.v.). Also the name of a licentious oriental romance by Crébillon the younger (1740).

Sohrab and Rustum, a poem by M. Arnold (q.v.) (1853).

Sohrab was a son of the Persian hero, Rustum (see *Rustem*). Unknown to his father Sohrab has joined the Tartar forces of Afrasiab, and gained great renown for his prowess. The Tartar host is attacking the Persians, and Sohrab challenges the bravest of the Persian lords to meet him in single combat. Rustum, now an old man, but still their greatest warrior, answers the challenge, but he does not know that Sohrab is his son, nor does Sohrab know that he is fighting with his father, until the old man, at a crisis of the struggle, shouts 'Rustum'. His son recoils at the name, and is struck down. Before dying, he reveals to Rustum that he has killed his son.

Soldan or SOULDAN, THE, in Spenser's 'Faerie Queene', v. viii, represents Philip II of Spain.

Solecism, an impropriety or irregularity in speech, diction, or manners; from a Greek word meaning barbarous, stated by ancient writers to refer to the corruption of the Attic dialect among the Athenian colonists of Soloi in Cilicia.

Soliloquy, a speech made without, or regardless of the presence of hearers, especially in plays. In Elizabethan times, and indeed until the comparatively modern vogue for more realistic drama came in, it was an ordinary and convenient way either of imparting informa-

tion to the audience, or of developing the action of the play: cf., for example, Hamlet's famous soliloquies.

Solomon, a great and wealthy king of Israel (10th cent. B.C.), son of David and Bathsheba, famous as the builder of the Temple and for his wisdom, illustrated by his judgement in the dispute about the child (1 Kings iii. 16–28).

Solomon Daisy, in Dickens's 'Barnaby Rudge' (q.v.), the parish clerk and bell-ringer at Chigwell.

Solomons, IKEY, JUNIOR, the pseudonym under which Thackeray (q.v.) wrote 'Catherine'.

Solon (*c.* 638–558 B.C.), the great Athenian legislator, celebrated for his wisdom. He was appointed archon in 594 B.C., and he reformed the constitution, introducing some democratic features. The constitution that he set up was overthrown by Peisistratus.

Solymean, of or belonging to Jerusalem. 'Solymean rout' is used in Dryden's 'Absalom and Achitophel' (q.v.) for the London mob.

Somerset House, London, in which are housed the offices of the Revenue Department, the principal Probate Registry, and the registrar-general of Births, Marriages, and Deaths.

Somerville, EDITH ŒNONE (1858–1949), Irish novelist, who collaborated with her cousin Violet Martin ('Martin Ross') (1862–1915) in a series of admirable tales of Irish life, some humorous, some tragic, including 'The Real Charlotte' (1894), 'Some Experiences of an Irish R. M.' (1890), 'Further Experiences' (1908), etc.

Somerville, WILLIAM (1675–1742), author of 'The Chace' (1735), a poem consisting of four books of Miltonic blank verse, which treats of hounds and kennels, hare-hunting, fox-hunting, and otter-hunting, with literary digressions on oriental methods of the chase.

Somnium Scipionis, from Bk. VI of Cicero's 'de Republica', is a narrative placed in the mouth of the younger Scipio Africanus, largely modelled on the fable of

Er, the son of Arminius, in Plato's 'Republic'. It has been preserved for us in the commentary of Macrobius (Cicero's text is lost). A poetical summary of it occurs in Chaucer's 'Parlement of Foules', and it is referred to by him in other passages.

Sompnour's or *Summoner's Tale, The*, see *Canterbury Tales*.

Song of Solomon, The, otherwise 'The Song of Songs', one of the poetical books of the O.T., at one time attributed to King Solomon, now considered, on linguistic grounds, to be of later date.

The allegorical interpretation of the poem is now generally abandoned, and it is regarded as a love drama.

Song of the Shirt, The, a poem by T. Hood (q.v.), published in the Christmas number of 'Punch' for the year 1843; one of Hood's best-known poems, presenting a picture of the overworked and underpaid sempstress.

Song of the Three Holy Children, The, a portion of the Book of Daniel regarded as apocryphal, purporting to be the prayer and song sung by the three Jews in Nebuchadnezzar's fiery furnace. The latter part figures as the 'Benedicite' in the order for Morning Prayer of the Anglican Church.

Songs before Sunrise, see *Swinburne*.

Songs of Experience, and *Songs of Innocence*, see *Blake*.

Song to David, see *Smart*.

Sonnet, a poem consisting of fourteen lines (of eleven syllables in Italian, twelve in French, and ten in English), with rhymes arranged according to one or other of certain definite schemes, of which the Petrarchan and the Elizabethan are the principal.

The Petrarchan sonnet was introduced into England by Wyatt and Surrey (qq.v.) in the early 16th cent. The rhyme scheme was a b b a a b b a for the *octave* or *octet*, followed by six lines (*sestet*) rhyming usually c d c d c d or c d e c d e. The Italian form had traditionally a definite break in the thought of the poem between the *octet* and *sestet*—a break not always

observed by English imitators. The Petrarchan sonnet never became generally popular, probably because of the difficulty of its rhyme scheme, though Milton, Keats, Wordsworth, and others used it. Milton's 'On his being arrived to the Age of 23' (with the *sestet* rhyming c c e d c e) and Wordsworth's 'Milton! thou shouldst be living at this hour:' (with the *sestet* c d d e c e) or 'Scorn not the sonnet' (with a *sestet* c d c d e e) are good examples.

The Elizabethans adapted the sonnet form in various ways. Spenser, for example, in his 'Amoretti' evolved a rhyming scheme a b a b b c b c c d c d e e, but this ingenious linking of rhymes has found few followers. The arrangement which became the standard English form of the sonnet was that followed by Daniel and Drayton, and made famous by Shakespeare. It is simply three quatrains followed by a couplet, i.e. a b a b c d c d e f e f g g; in its traditional Elizabethan form the last couplet served either to summarize or else in epigrammatic form to serve as an antithesis to the rest of the sonnet.

Sonnets from the Portuguese, a series of sonnets by E. B. Browning (q.v.) (1850), inspired by passionate devotion to her husband. The Portuguese prototypes were probably Camoëns' sonnets to Catarina.

Sonnets of Shakespeare, The, were printed in 1609, but the bulk of them were probably written between 1593 and 1596, the remainder between 1596 and 1600. Most of them trace the course of the writer's affection for a young patron of rank and beauty, and may be addressed to William Lord Herbert, afterwards earl of Pembroke, or Henry Wriothesley, earl of Southampton. The publisher, Thomas Thorpe, issued the 'Sonnets' in 1609 with a dedication to 'Mr. W. H., the onlie begetter of these ensuing sonnets'. Other characters are alluded to, who evidently played a real part in Shakespeare's life, a stolen mistress (40–2), a rival poet (83–6), a dark beauty loved by the author (127 et seq.).

For the form of these poems, see *Sonnet*.

Sophism, a specious but fallacious argument, used either deliberately to mislead or to display ingenuity in reasoning.

Sophist, in ancient Greece, one who undertook to give instruction in intellectual and ethical matters in return for payment; contrasted with 'philosopher', and frequently used as a term of disparagement.

Sophocles (496-406 B.C.), one of the three great Attic tragedians. He won his first victory as a tragic poet in 468 B.C., when he defeated Aeschylus. After this he was regarded as the favourite poet of the Athenians. His tragedies are more human, less heroic, than those of Aeschylus; but he differed from Euripides, to use his own words, in representing men as they ought to be, while Euripides exhibited them as they are. He is the most effective of the three poets as a dramatist, both by his use of tragic contrast in his situations and by his gift of depicting character. His extant plays are: 'Oedipus the King', 'Oedipus at Colonus', 'Antigone', 'Electra', 'Trachiniae' (on the death of Hercules), 'Ajax', and 'Philoctetes'.

Sophonisba, daughter of Hasdrubal, a Carthaginian general. She was betrothed in early life to Masinissa; but her father, in order to gain an alliance, married her to Syphax. Masinissa, fighting in alliance with the Romans, defeated Syphax and captured Sophonisba. Masinissa decided now to marry Sophonisba, but was ordered by Scipio to surrender her. Masinissa, to save her from captivity, sent her a bowl of poison, and this she voluntarily drank, and died.

The story has been made the subject of various plays, notably by Marston (q.v.) in his 'Sophonisba' (printed in 1606), where, however, considerable liberties are taken with the facts; also by Lee (1676) and Thomson (see below), and by Corneille.

The line 'Oh! Sophonisba, Sophonisba, Oh!' is from 'The Tragedy of Sophonisba', 1730 (III. ii), by James Thomson (q.v., 1700-48), and was parodied by Fielding in his 'Tom Thumb'—'O Huncamunca, Huncamunca O!'. Johnson ('Lives of the Poets') quotes the burlesque 'O Jemmy Thomson! Jemmy Thomson, O!'

Sorbonne, The, a theological college in Paris founded by Robert de Sorbon about 1257. The Sorbonne is now the seat of the University of Paris and of the faculties of science, literature, and the *hautes études*.

Sordello, a Provençal poet, born near Mantua about 1180, who became in popular tradition a hero of romance. Dante mentions him repeatedly in his 'Purgatorio'.

Sordello, a poem by R. Browning (q.v.) (1840).

The action takes place at the time of conflicts of the Guelphs and Ghibellines (*c.* 1200). Eccelino, lord of Vicenza, has been exiled from his city, and his wife, Adelaide, has been saved with her infant son by the archer, Elcorte. Retrude, wife of Eccelino's ally, Salinguerra, is also saved, but dies after giving birth to Sordello. Adelaide passes Sordello off as the son of Elcorte and brings him up as her page. He is gifted with an imaginative nature and devotes himself to a poetic, unreal life. At a crisis in the political struggle, his identity as the son of Salinguerra is revealed, and power and eminence come within his grasp. But he cannot bring himself to accept the lower, practical course of action. In the struggle of decision, he dies.

But while the outline of the narrative is simple enough, 'Sordello', the story of the 'development of a soul', is in its details and allusions one of the most difficult of Browning's works to interpret.

Sorrel, Hetty, a character in George Eliot's 'Adam Bede' (q.v.).

Sorrows of Werther, see *Goethe*.

Sortes Virgilianae, the attempt to foretell the future by opening a volume of Virgil at hazard and reading the first passage lit on.

Sotadic, a satire after the manner of Sotades, an ancient Greek poet noted for the coarseness and scurrility of his writings. The word is also used of a line capable of being read in the reverse order, like a palindrome (q.v.).

Sotheby's, in New Bond Street, London, saleroom for books, paintings, *objets d'art*, etc.

Soul's Tragedy, *A*, a drama by R. Browning (q.v.), in two parts (1846), the first part in verse, the second in prose.

The drama treats humorously the 'tragedy' of the degradation of the soul of Chiappino, a citizen of Faenza in the 16th cent.

South, ROBERT (1634-1716), a great court preacher, favoured by Charles II. He was homely, pithy, and often very humorous in the pulpit. His 'Animadversions' (1690) contain a crushing attack on the famous preacher and Dean of St. Paul's, W. Sherlock.

South Sea Company, THE, was formed in 1711 by Harley (later earl of Oxford) to trade with Spanish America under the expected treaty with Spain. A bill was passed in 1720 by which persons to whom the nation owed money were enabled to convert their claims into shares in the Company, and the shares rose in value from £100 to £1,000. The Company shortly afterwards failed. The collapse of the South Sea scheme caused widespread ruin. The whole affair was known as the SOUTH SEA BUBBLE.

The SOUTH-SEA HOUSE, where the Company had its offices, is the subject of one of Lamb's 'Essays of Elia' (q.v.).

Southcott, JOANNA (1750-1814), a religious fanatic. In 1792 she began to write doggerel prophecies and to claim supernatural gifts, and in time attracted a very large number of followers. She died of brain disease, leaving a sealed box with directions that it should be opened at a time of national crisis. It was opened in 1927 and was found to contain nothing of interest.

Southdown, COUNTESS OF, a character in Thackeray's 'Vanity Fair' (q.v.).

Southerne or SOUTHERN, THOMAS (1659-1746), spent his life in London, where he was the friend of Dryden, for several of whose plays he wrote prologues and epilogues. He wrote several comedies, but is remembered for his two tragedies, 'The Fatal Marriage' (1694) and 'Oroonoko' (1695), both founded on novels by Mrs. Behn (q.v.).

Southey, ROBERT (1774-1843), was expelled from Westminster School for a precocious essay against flogging, and proceeded to Balliol College, Oxford. He made the acquaintance of S. T. Coleridge and joined in his scheme for a 'pantisocratic' settlement. He married Edith Fricker (*d.* 1837), whose sister became the wife of Coleridge, in 1795. He published 'Thalaba' in 1801, 'Madoc' in 1805, 'The Curse of Kehama' in 1810, 'Roderick, the Last of the Goths' in 1814, 'A Tale of Paraguay' in 1825, and 'All for Love' in 1829. He worked at translations from the Spanish, and in 1808 became a regular contributor to 'The Quarterly Review'. His 'Life of Nelson' was expanded from an article in 1813. In the same year he accepted the laureateship, which had been offered to Scott. His 'Wat Tyler', a short drama 'written in three days at Oxford' in 1794, was surreptitiously published in 1817, and in consequence of its crude political sentiments, Southey was attacked as 'a renegado'.

Southey wrote an immense amount both of verse and prose. His longer poems are little read now, but were praised by contemporaries so diverse as Scott, Fox, and Macaulay, and admired even by Byron, who hated the author. He is now best known by some of his shorter pieces, such as 'My days among the dead are past', 'The Battle of Blenheim', etc. He was an excellent letter-writer, and three editions of his voluminous correspondence, none of them complete, have been published.

Southwark, the 'south work' or bridgehead at the south end of London Bridge. It is specially famous in literary history on account of its ancient inns and theatres. The Tabard and the White Hart inns were there, also Burbage's 'Globe' theatre, and Henslowe's 'The Hope' and 'The Rose'.

Southwell, ROBERT (1561?-1595), a member of an old Catholic family, was educated at Douai, took Roman orders, and came to England in 1586 with Henry Garnett (who was subsequently executed for complicity in the Gunpowder Plot). He became in 1589 domestic chaplain to the countess of Arundel, was captured when going to celebrate mass in 1592, repeatedly tortured, and executed after three years' imprisonment. His poems were mainly written in prison. His chief work was 'St. Peter's Complaint' (1595), a long narrative of the closing events of the life of Christ. He also wrote a 'Fourefould Meditation of the foure last things' (1606), and many shorter devotional poems of a high order, notably 'The Burning Babe', praised by Ben Jonson.

Sowerberry, an undertaker in Dickens's 'Oliver Twist' (q.v.).

Spanish Bawd, The, see *Celestina*.

Spanish Curate, The, a comedy by J. Fletcher (q.v.) and probably Massinger (q.v.), composed and produced in 1622.

Spanish Fryar, The, a comedy by Dryden (q.v.).

Spanish Gipsy, The, a romantic comedy by T. Middleton (q.v.) and W. Rowley (q.v.), acted in 1623 and printed in 1653. It is based on two novels by Cervantes.

Spanish Gypsy, The, a dramatic poem by G. Eliot (q.v.) (1868).

Spanish Main, THE, the mainland of America adjacent to the Caribbean Sea. In later use, also, the sea contiguous to this.

Spanish Tragedy, The, a tragedy in blank verse by Kyd (q.v.), acted 1592, printed 1594.

The political background of the play is the victory of Spain over Portugal in 1580. Lorenzo and Bel-imperia are son and daughter of Don Cyprian; Hieronimo is marshal of Spain, and Horatio is his son. Balthazar is son of the viceroy of Portugal and has been taken prisoner by Lorenzo and Horatio. He courts Bel-imperia, and

his suit is favoured by Lorenzo. Lorenzo and Balthazar discover that Bel-imperia loves Horatio, and come upon them at night in Hieronimo's arbour, where they kill Horatio and hang him to a tree. Hieronimo discovers who are the murderers and plots with Bel-imperia their destruction. For this purpose he engages them to act with Bel-imperia and him, before the court, a play that suits his revengeful purpose. In the course of this Lorenzo and Balthazar are killed, Bel-imperia stabs herself, and Hieronimo takes his own life.

Interpolations were made in the play as originally written, probably by Ben Jonson, and the play as revised was very popular, though ridiculed by writers of the time. There are certain points of resemblance between the play and 'Hamlet', of which Kyd is thought possibly to have written an early version.

Sparkler, EDMUND, a character in Dickens's 'Little Dorrit' (q.v.).

Sparsit, MRS., a character in Dickens's 'Hard Times' (q.v.).

Spartan, an inhabitant of Sparta. The Spartan characteristics, to which the adjective in modern use refers, were simplicity, fortitude, and brevity of speech.

Spasmodic School, a term applied by Aytoun (q.v.) to a group of poets chiefly represented by P. J. Bailey, Dobell, and Alexander Smith (qq.v.).

S.P.C.K., the Society for Promoting Christian Knowledge, was founded in 1698. One of its primary objects was the setting up of charitable schools for the instruction of poor children. The Society was also a publishing agency for the dissemination of works of a Christian character.

S.P.E., the Society for Pure English (q.v.).

Spectator, The, a periodical conducted by R. Steele (q.v.) and Addison (q.v.) from 1 March 1711 to 6 Dec. 1712. It was revived by Addison in 1714, when eighty numbers were issued. 'The

Spectator' was the successor of 'The Tatler' (q.v.). It appeared daily. Addison and Steele were the principal contributors, in about equal proportions. Other contributors were Pope, Tickell, Eustace Budgell, A. Philips, and Eusden (qq.v.).

It purported to be conducted (see the first two numbers) by a small club, including Sir Roger de Coverley, who represents the country gentry; Sir Andrew Freeport, Capt. Sentry, and Will Honeycomb, representing respectively commerce, the army, and the town. Mr. Spectator himself, who writes the papers, is a man of travel and learning, who frequents London as an observer. The papers are mainly concerned with manners, morals, and literature. Among their pleasantest features are the character sketches, notably in the Coverley papers, and the short stories or episodes.

Spectator, The, a weekly periodical started in 1828 as an organ of 'educated radicalism'.

Speculum Meditantis or *Mirour de l'Omme*, a didactic poem of 30,000 lines in French by Gower (q.v.).

It relates the contest of the seven vices and the seven virtues for the possession of man, and concludes with the Gospel narrative. The description of the estates of man presents a valuable picture of contemporary society.

Speed, JOHN (1552?–1629), historian and cartographer, made various maps of English counties, and was encouraged by Camden, Cotton, and others to write his 'Historie of Great Britaine' (1611). The maps were far more valuable than the history; they began about 1607 and an atlas of them appeared in 1611.

Speed the Plough, a play by T. Morton (q.v.), produced in 1798.

Mrs. Grundy, who has since become the symbol of the British idea of propriety, is constantly referred to in the play, though she never appears in it.

Speke, JOHN HANNING (1827–64), explorer, set out under (Sir) Richard Burton (q.v.) in 1856 to investigate Lake Nyasa, and discovered Lake Tanganyika and Victoria Nyanza. He published in 1863 his 'Journal of the Discovery of the Source of the Nile'.

Spencer, HERBERT (1820–1903), trained as an engineer, gave up this profession early and devoted himself to philosophical study and writing.

Spencer was the founder of evolutionary philosophy, pursuing the unification of all knowledge on the basis of a single all-pervading principle, that of evolution, but recognizing the insolubility of the ultimate riddle of the universe.

His theory of a physical system leads up to an ethical system, to which in his mind all else was subordinated. But here he is less successful in producing a self-consistent whole. For Spencer was essentially an individualist, and his effort is to reconcile utilitarian with evolutionary ethics. He had to confess that for the purpose of deducing ethical principles 'the Doctrine of Evolution has not furnished guidance to the extent I had hoped'.

Spencer has been diversely judged. Carlyle called him 'the most immeasurable ass in Christendom'.

Spender, STEPHEN (1909–), poet and critic; joint editor of the magazine 'Encounter'. During the Spanish Civil War he did propaganda work in Spain for the Republican side. His work includes 'Collected Poems' (1954), a verse play, 'Trial of a Judge' (1938), political and literary studies such as 'Forward from Liberalism' (1937), 'Life and the Poet' (1942), 'The Creative Element' (1953), 'The Struggle of the Modern' (1963), and an autobiography, 'World within World' (1951).

Spenlow, DORA, in Dickens's 'David Copperfield' (q.v.), the hero's 'child-wife'.

Spenlow and Jorkins, in Dickens's 'David Copperfield' (q.v.), a firm to whom Copperfield is articled. Jorkins seldom appears, but Spenlow makes his supposed intractable character the ground for refusing any inconvenient request.

Spens, Sir Patrick, see *Sir Patrick Spens*.

Spenser, EDMUND (1552?-1599), was educated at Merchant Taylors' School and Pembroke Hall, Cambridge. While still at Cambridge, he contributed in 1569 a number of 'Visions' and sonnets (from Petrarch and Du Bellay) to an edifying 'Theatre for Worldlings'. To his 'green youth' also belong the 'Hymnes in honour of Love and Beautie' (not published till 1596). Spenser obtained in 1578, through his college friend G. Harvey (q.v.), a place in Leicester's household, and became acquainted with Sir Philip Sidney (q.v.). With Sidney, Dyer, and others, he formed a literary club styled the 'Areopagus'. In 1579 he began 'The Faerie Queene' (q.v.) and published 'The Shepheards Calender' (q.v.), which was enthusiastically received. In 1580 he was appointed secretary to Lord Grey de Wilton, then going to Ireland as lord deputy, and in 1586 acquired Kilcolman Castle in county Cork. Here he settled and occupied himself with literary work, writing his elegy 'Astrophel' (q.v.) on Sir Philip Sidney, and preparing 'The Faerie Queene' for the press, three books of this work being entrusted to the printer on the poet's visit to London in 1589. He reluctantly returned to Kilcolman, which he regarded as a place of exile, in 1591, and penned 'Colin Clouts come home againe' (q.v., printed 1595). The reputation of 'The Faerie Queene' led the printer, Ponsonby, to issue in 1591 Spenser's minor verse and *juvenilia*, in part rewritten, as 'Complaints, containing sundrie small poems of the worlds vanitie'. In 1594 Spenser married Elizabeth Boyle, whom he had wooed in his 'Amoretti', and possibly celebrated the marriage in his splendid 'Epithalamion' (the two were printed together in 1595). He published the second instalment of three books of 'The Faerie Queene' and 'Foure Hymnes' in 1596, being in London, where he wrote his 'Prothalamion' (q.v.) and also his well-informed, though one-sided, prose 'View of the Present State of Ireland'. His castle of Kilcolman was burnt, Oct. 1598, in a sudden insurrection. He died in distress, if not actual destitution, in London, and was buried near Chaucer in Westminster Abbey.

Spenserian stanza, the stanza invented by Edmund Spenser (q.v.), in which he wrote 'The Faerie Queene'. It consists of eight five-foot iambic lines, followed by an iambic line of six feet, rhyming a b a b b c b c c.

Sphinx, THE, in Greek legend, a monster generally represented with a woman's bust on a lion's body. It frequented the neighbourhood of Thebes, propounded enigmas and devoured the inhabitants if they were unable to explain them. The Thebans were told by an oracle that the Sphinx would destroy herself as soon as one of her riddles was explained. Creon, the regent of Thebes, promised his crown and his sister Jocasta in marriage to whoever should solve the riddle. This was done by Oedipus (q.v.), and the Sphinx, on hearing the correct answer, dashed her head against a rock and expired.

The legend may have come from Egypt. The most famous figure of the Sphinx is near the Great Pyramid at Ghizeh, Egypt.

Spinoza, BENEDICT (BARUCH) DE (1632-77), a Jew of Portuguese origin, born at Amsterdam. He was expelled from the Jewish community on account of his criticism of the Scriptures. The principal source of his philosophy was the doctrine of Descartes, transformed by a mind steeped in the Jewish Scriptures. Spinoza rejected the Cartesian dualism of spirit and matter, and saw only 'one infinite substance, of which finite existences are modes or limitations'. Among his conclusions are determinism, a denial of the transcendent distinction between good and evil, and a denial of personal immortality.

Spinoza's famous 'Ethics', finished about 1665, was not published until 1677, after his death. His morality is founded on the 'intellectual love' of God. Man is moved by his instinct to develop and perfect himself, and to seek this development in the knowledge and love of God.

Spinoza founds his political doctrine on man's natural rights. Man, in order to obtain security, has surrendered part of his rights to the State. But the State exists to give liberty, not to hold in slavery. Spinoza's 'Tractatus Theologico-politicus' was published in 1670; his unfinished 'Tractatus Politicus' in 1677.

Spirit of Patriotism, A Letter on the, a political treatise by Viscount Bolingbroke (q.v.) (1749).

Written in retirement at Chanteloup, it represents Bolingbroke's final attitude in political affairs.

Spiritual Quixote, The, or the Summer's Ramble of Mr. Geoffry Wildgoose, a novel by Richard Graves (q.v.) (1772).

Geoffry Wildgoose, having imbibed the doctrines of the Methodists, sets forth, accompanied by his Sancho Panza, Jerry Tugwell, the village cobbler, to preach those doctrines about the Midlands. The book throws light on the life of the roads and inns in the 18th cent. and there is a pleasant sketch of Shenstone (q.v.) and the Leasowes.

Spleen, The, see *Green (Matthew).*

Splendid Shilling, The, a burlesque poem by J. Philips (q.v.) (1705).

The poet sings in Miltonic verse, with much show of classical learning, the contrast between the possessor of the splendid shilling and the penurious poet.

Spondee, a metrical foot composed of two long syllables.

Sponge, Mr., the hero of 'Mr. Sponge's Sporting Tour' by R. S. Surtees (q.v.) (1853), with pictures by Leech, one of the best of the author's hunting novels.

Spoonerism, see *Metathesis.*

Sporus, the name under which Pope (q.v.) satirizes Lord Hervey (q.v.) in his 'Epistle to Dr. Arbuthnot' (ll. 305 et seq.). The original Sporus was an effeminate favourite of the Emperor Nero.

S.P.Q.R., initial letters of *Senatus Populusque Romanus,* 'the Senate and People of Rome'.

Sprat, Jack, see *Jack Sprat.*

Sprat, Thomas (1635-1713), bishop of Rochester and dean of Westminster, remembered for his history of the Royal Society (q.v.), of which he was one of the first fellows. He is thought to have had a share in Buckingham's 'Rehearsal' (q.v.).

Spy, The, a novel of the American Revolution, by J. F. Cooper (q.v.) (1821).

Square, in Fielding's 'Tom Jones' (q.v.), an inmate of Mr. Allworthy's household.

Squeers, Wackford, in Dickens's 'Nicholas Nickleby' (q.v.), the headmaster of Dotheboys Hall. He has a heartless wife, a spiteful daughter in Miss Fanny, and a spoilt son in Master Wackford Squeers.

Squire, Sir John Collings (1884-1958), poet, critic, and anthologist. He became literary editor of the 'New Statesman' in 1913. He published numerous volumes of verse, critical works, essays, short stories, and an autobiography.

Squire of Dames, a humorous character in Spenser's 'Faerie Queene', III. vii.

Squire of Low Degree, a metrical romance of the early 14th cent.

The squire tells his love to the princess of Hungary, who consents to wed him. But the meeting is seen by an interfering steward, who reports to the king and gets killed by the squire for his pains. The squire is imprisoned by the king and is mourned as dead by the princess for seven years, in spite of the king's offer of a variety of delights. The king is at length forced to relent, the squire is released, goes forth on a knightly quest, and finally marries the princess.

Squire of Low Degree, The, in Spenser's 'Faerie Queene' (q.v.), is Amyas.

Squire's Tale, The, see *Canterbury Tales.*

Staël, Anne Louise Germaine de (1766-1817), the daughter of Jacques Necker, the French minister of finance, and of Suzanne Curchod, the 'first and only love' of Gibbon. She married (1785) but was later separated from the Baron de Staël-Holstein, Swedish ambassador in Paris. A woman of remarkable intellectual gifts and openness of mind, she received in her Paris salon, on the eve of the Revolution, the most progressive elements in French society. She rendered her greatest service to literature in 'De l'Allemagne' (1810–13), in which she introduced to the French the great literary and philosophic movement that had been proceeding in Germany during the previous half-century. Mme de Staël also wrote two novels, 'Delphine' (1802) and 'Corinne' (1807), which reflect the frustrations and conflicts of her own life. She had many passionate friendships, notably with Benjamin Constant.

Stafford blue, 'to clothe in Stafford blue' is to beat black and blue, with a play on 'staff'.

Stagirite or STAGYRITE, THE, Aristotle, born at Stageira in Macedon.

Stalky & Co., tales of schoolboy life, by Kipling (q.v.) (1899).

Standard English, the standard form of the language as distinct from illiterate or dialect speech.

An early attempt to normalize the language was made towards the end of the OE. period when West Saxon clearly became the standard literary form. The Norman Conquest destroyed its prestige and English was written or spoken in all varieties of dialect until, at the close of the 14th cent., the dialect of London attained pre-eminence. This dialect was based on that of the East Midlands with Kentish and Middlesex influences. It became pre-eminent because of the increasing importance of London as the centre of law, government, and trade in England. By Caxton's time its position as the standard form of English was recognized although, till well on in the 18th cent., country people of the upper as well as of the lower classes often continued to speak their regional dialects. In these centuries, nevertheless, Standard English had outgrown its regional basis and had established itself as a class dialect throughout England, the dialect, that is, of the upper and educated classes, or, as Chester-

field called it, 'the use of the best companies'.

In the modern period, Standard English has become not the exclusive prerogative of the upper classes but rather of the educated middle classes, and could be defined as the language of these classes in southern England—for the north still has differences. It seems likely, however, that radio and television, by reason of their wide audience, will gradually widen the basis of Standard English as we know it now.

Standish, MILES, see *Miles Standish.*

Stanhope, LADY HESTER LUCY (1776–1839), was the niece of William Pitt and kept house for him from 1803 till his death in 1806, gaining a reputation as a brilliant political hostess. In 1810 she withdrew from Europe, and in 1814 established herself for the rest of her life in a ruined convent at Djoun in the Lebanon. Here she lived with a semi-oriental retinue which she ruled despotically. In later years her debts accumulated, her eccentricity increased, and she sought to replace her waning political prestige by an undefined spiritual authority. She became a legendary figure in her lifetime and was visited by many distinguished European travellers. Celebrated accounts of their visits to her were written by Lamartine in 'Voyages en Orient' and Kinglake in 'Eōthen'.

Stanley, SIR HENRY MORTON (1841–1904), was sent in 1869 by Gordon Bennett, proprietor of 'The New York Herald', to find David Livingstone (q.v.), who was believed to be lost in Central Africa. Stanley found him at Ujiji, and published his adventures in 'How I found Livingstone' (1872). 'Through the Dark Continent' (1878) relates his experiences while crossing equatorial Africa in 1874–7.

Stanley, SIR HUBERT, *Approbation from, is praise indeed*: from 'A Cure for the Heartache', v. ii, by T. Morton.

Stanza (an Italian word, apparently new in Shakespeare's time—cf. 'As You Like It', II. v), meaning a group of lines into which verse is divided. Stanzas may be of all types in length and metrical form. See, particularly, *Spenserian stanza, rhyme-royal, quatrain.*

Staple of News, The, a comedy by Jonson (q.v.), first acted in 1625, in which on the one hand he satirizes the credulity of the age, and on the other illustrates the use and abuse of riches.

Star-chamber, THE, an apartment in the royal palace of Westminster in which during the 14th and 15th cents. the chancellor, treasurer, justices, and other members of the king's council sat to exercise jurisdiction.

The COURT OF STAR-CHAMBER was developed from the above judicial sittings in the 15th cent. Its procedure in the reigns of James I and Charles I made it a proverbial type of an arbitrary and oppressive tribunal.

Stareleigh, MR. JUSTICE, in Dickens's 'The Pickwick Papers' (q.v.), the judge in the case of Bardell *v.* Pickwick.

Star-spangled Banner, The, the American national anthem since 1931, is said to have its origin partly in the air of 'To Anacreon in Heaven', a convivial song of the Anacreontic Society of London (1771). To this tune Francis Scott Key, an American, set the words of a patriotic hymn on the occasion of the British attack on Fort McHenry in 1814.

Starveling, in Shakespeare's 'A Midsummer Night's Dream' (q.v.), a tailor, who is cast for the part of 'Thisby's mother' in the play of 'Pyramus and Thisbe'. He has nothing to do or say.

Stationers' Company, THE, was incorporated by royal charter in 1557. No one not a member of the Company might print anything for sale in the kingdom unless authorized by special privilege or patent. Moreover, by the rules of the Company, every member was required to enter in the register of the Company the name of any book that he desired to print, so that these registers furnish valuable information regarding printed matter during the latter part of the 16th cent. The Company's

control of the printing trade waned during the 17th cent., to be revived, in a modified form, under the Copyright Act of 1709. (See also under *Copyright.*)

Statius, PUBLIUS PAPINIUS (*c.* A.D. 40-*c.* 96), a Roman poet, author of a 'Thebaid' in twelve books (on the expedition of the 'Seven against Thebes'). Pope and Gray translated portions of the 'Thebaid'.

Statue and the Bust, The, a poem by R. Browning (q.v.) (1855).

Staunton, SIR GEORGE, *alais* GEORGE ROBERTSON, in Scott's 'The Heart of Midlothian' (q.v.), the lover, and subsequently husband, of Effie Deans.

Stead, WILLIAM THOMAS (1849-1912), was assistant editor (John Morley being editor) of 'The Pall Mall Gazette', 1880-3, and editor, 1883-8, in which capacity he initiated many social and political movements. Stead was drowned in the disaster of the 'Titanic'.

Steele, SIR RICHARD (1672-1729), was born at Dublin, in the same year as Addison (q.v.), and was educated with him at the Charterhouse. He was subsequently at Merton College, Oxford, whence he entered the army as a cadet in the Life Guards. As a result of a poem on Queen Mary's funeral dedicated to Lord Cutts, colonel of the Coldstream Guards, he became his secretary and obtained the rank of captain. He published 'The Christian Hero' in 1701, in which he first displayed his missionary and reforming spirit. In the same year he produced his first comedy, 'The Funeral', in which, breaking away from the conventions of the Restoration drama, he tried to present virtue and vice in their true aspects. Neither this nor his two next comedies, 'The Lying Lover' (1703) and 'The Tender Husband' (1705), proved very successful. In 1709 he started 'The Tatler' (q.v.), which he carried on with the help of Addison till January 1711. In conjunction with Addison he carried on 'The Spectator' (q.v.) during 1711-12. This was followed by 'The Guardian', to which Addison, Berkeley, and Pope contributed, and which was attacked by the Tory 'Examiner'. In 1713 he was elected M.P. for Stockbridge. In 1714 he published 'The Crisis', a pamphlet in favour of the Hanoverian succession, which was answered by Swift (q.v.), and led to Steele's expulsion from the House on 18 March 1714; and during the same year conducted 'The Lover', a paper in the manner of 'The Spectator'. The tide turned in his favour with the accession of George I. He was appointed supervisor of Drury Lane Theatre, and to other posts, and was knighted in 1715. His last comedy, 'The Conscious Lovers', based on the 'Andria' of Terence and embodying some of his views on social questions, was produced in 1722. Money difficulties forced him to leave London in 1724, and he died at Carmarthen. His moving letters to his wife, Mary Scurlock, were published in 1787.

Steele Glas, *The*, a satire in verse by Gascoigne (q.v.) (1576).

Steenson, WILLIE, 'Wandering Willie', the blind fiddler in Scott's 'Redgauntlet'.

Steerforth, JAMES, a character in Dickens's 'David Copperfield' (q.v.).

Steevens, GEORGE (1736-1800), a well-known Shakespearean commentator. He assisted Dr. Johnson in his 'Lives of the Poets', and was a member of 'The Club'. He assisted Tyrwhitt (q.v.) in his edition of the 'Rowley Poems', but declared his disbelief in them.

Stein, GERTRUDE (1874-1946), American writer and critic. She left the United States in 1902 and lived in France, writing and encouraging writers. She was deeply interested in style and her experiments influenced many of her contemporaries. She wrote poetry, short stories, novels, criticism, and autobiography, and was one of the leading and most stimulating figures of her time. Among her many books are 'Three Lives' (1908) and 'The Making of Americans' (1925), fiction; 'Tender Buttons' (1914), poetry; 'Composition and Explanation' (1926) and 'Narration' (1935), criticism; and 'Picasso'

(1938). Her autobiography, 'The Autobiography of Alice B. Toklas' (1933), is written as if by her confidante and secretary.

Steinbeck, JOHN ERNST (1902-68), American novelist, born in California. He took his native State as the background for his early short stories and novels, and described the life of those working on the land with realism and understanding. His best-known works are 'Tortilla Flat' (1935); 'Of Mice and Men' (1937), a story of two farm labourers, one of huge strength and weak mind, exploited and protected by the other, and his masterpiece, 'The Grapes of Wrath' (1940), an epic account of the efforts of an emigrant farming family from the dust bowl of the West to reach the 'promised land' of California. Among his later novels, which are often marred by sentimentality, are 'East of Eden' (1952) and 'Winter of Our Discontent' (1961). Steinbeck was awarded a Nobel Prize in 1962.

Stella, the name under which Sir P. Sidney (q.v.) celebrated Penelope Devereux in his sonnets. She was daughter of the first earl of Essex, and when a girl was destined by her father to be Sidney's wife. The project was abandoned and she married Robert, the second Lord Rich, and after being divorced by him, Charles Blount, Lord Mountjoy, afterwards earl of Devonshire.

Stella, Swift's name for Esther Johnson, see *Swift*, and in particular the account there of the 'Journal to Stella'.

Stella, in Waller's (q.v.) poems, is Lady Dorothy Sidney, daughter of Robert Dudley, earl of Leicester.

Stendhal, pseudonym of HENRI BEYLE (1783-1842), one of the greatest of French novelists. His two great novels are 'Le Rouge et le Noir' (1830) and 'La Chartreuse de Parme' (1839), and on the strength of these he has been accorded by modern critics a place in French fiction equal in importance to that of Balzac.

Stentor, the name of a Greek warrior in the Trojan War ('Iliad', v. 785) 'whose voice was as powerful as fifty voices of other men'.

Stephano, a drunken butler in Shakespeare's 'The Tempest' (q.v.).

Stephen, ST., the first Christian martyr, one of the 'seven men of honest report' chosen as deacons at Jerusalem, accused of blasphemy, and stoned to death (Acts vi and vii).

Stephen, SIR JAMES FITZJAMES (1829-94), rose to be legal member of the Governor-General's council in India (1869-72) and a judge of the high court (1879-91). He contributed to magazines, and many of these contributions are collected in 'Essays by a Barrister' (1862) and the three series of 'Horae Sabbaticae' (1862, etc.). In his 'Liberty, Equality, Fraternity' (1873) he severely criticized Mill's utilitarian position in the latter's essay 'On Liberty'.

Stephen, JAMES KENNETH (1859-92), known as 'J.K.S.', was the author of some brilliant light verse, collected in 'Lapsus Calami' and 'Quo Musa Tendis' (1891).

Stephen, SIR LESLIE (1832-1904), brother of Sir J. F. Stephen (q.v.), was educated at Trinity Hall, Cambridge, where he became tutor, having taken orders.

Stephen's reading of Mill and Kant inclined him to scepticism and he relinquished orders after the Act of 1870. In 1864 he came to London for a literary career and contributed critical studies to various periodicals, which were collected in 'Hours in a Library' (1874-6-9). In 1876 appeared his 'History of English Thought in the 18th century', reviewing the position of the chief writers in the great philosophical controversies of that age. He contributed a number of biographies to the two series of 'English Men of Letters', and accepted in 1882 the editorship of the 'Dictionary of National Biography' (q.v.), himself contributing many of the most important notices, especially of the 18th- and 19th-cent. worthies.

Leslie Stephen was the model from which Meredith drew Vernon Whitford, 'a Phoebus Apollo turned fasting friar',

in his 'The Egoist' (q.v.). His first wife was Harriet Marian, Thackeray's younger daughter. Virginia Woolf (q.v.) was his daughter by his second wife, Julia Prinsep.

Stephen of Blois, king of England, 1135-54.

Stephens, JAMES (1882-1950), Irish poet and story-writer, whose best-known work is the prose fantasy, 'The Crock of Gold' (1912).

Sterling, JOHN (1806-44), chiefly remembered as the centre of a literary group known after him as the STERLING CLUB (founded 1838), which included such men as Carlyle, Tennyson, John Stuart Mill, Lord Houghton, and Francis Palgrave. His 'Life' by Carlyle was published in 1851.

Sterne, LAURENCE (1713-68), took orders and became vicar of Sutton-on-the-Forest in 1738, where he remained till 1759, marrying Miss Elizabeth Lumley in 1741. His 'small, quiet attentions' to various ladies disturbed his conjugal life, and his wife became insane in 1758. He began 'Tristram Shandy' (q.v.) in 1759, volumes i and ii being published in 1760. He came to London and was well received in society, and in 1760 published the first volumes of his 'Sermons of Mr. Yorick'. But 'Tristram Shandy', of which four more volumes appeared in 1761, was denounced by Dr. Johnson, Richardson, Horace Walpole, Goldsmith, and others, on moral and literary grounds. Volumes vii and viii of 'Tristram Shandy' appeared in 1765, in which year began his seven months' tour in France and Italy, of which the French part is described in his 'A Sentimental Journey' (q.v., 1768). Volume ix of 'Tristram Shandy' appeared in 1767, also volumes iii and iv of his 'Sermons'. He met in London Mrs. Eliza Draper, for whom he kept the journal addressed to her from April to Aug. 1767. He died of pleurisy in his Old Bond Street lodgings, insolvent. The publication of the 'Letters of Yorick to Eliza' was authorized by Mrs. Draper in 1775. The best early edition of the collected works (with letters and Hogarth's plates) appeared in 1780.

Sternhold and Hopkins, THOMAS STERNHOLD (d. 1549) and JOHN HOPKINS (d. 1570), joint versifiers of the Psalms. A collection of forty-four of these versified psalms appeared in 1549. In 1562 'The Whole Book of Psalms' by Sternhold, Hopkins, Norton, and others, was added to the Prayer Book.

Stevenson, ROBERT LOUIS (originally LEWIS) BALFOUR (1850-94), entered Edinburgh University in 1867 and studied engineering, but soon abandoned this for the law. An affection of the lungs led to his frequent journeys in search of health. His 'Inland Voyage', describing a canoe tour in Belgium and France, was published in 1878, and his 'Travels with a Donkey in the Cevennes', the description of a tour taken in 1878, in the following year. Though very ill with tuberculosis, he contributed to various periodicals and wrote a number of essays, short stories, and fragments of travel and autobiography, collected in 'Virginibus Puerisque' (1881), and 'The New Arabian Nights' (1882). To the same categories belong 'Prince Otto' (1885), 'The Merry Men' (1887), 'Across the Plains' (1892), 'Island Nights' Entertainments' (1893), 'In the South Seas' (1896). Long before this Stevenson had become famous by the publication in 1883 of 'Treasure Island' (q.v.). This was followed by 'The Strange Case of Dr. Jekyll and Mr. Hyde' (1886) and a series of romances: 'Kidnapped' (1886) and 'Catriona', its sequel (1893), 'The Black Arrow' (1888), 'The Master of Ballantrae' (1889), the unfinished masterpiece, 'Weir of Hermiston' (1896), and 'St. Ives' (published in New York, 1897, and in London, 1898), also unfinished, but completed by Sir A. T. Quiller-Couch. In collaboration with Lloyd Osbourne, Stevenson wrote 'The Wrong Box' (1889), 'The Wrecker' (1892), and 'The Ebb-Tide' (1894). In 1888 Stevenson had set out for the South Seas and settled in Samoa, where he bought the 'Vailima'

property and temporarily recovered his health. There he died suddenly from rupture of a blood-vessel in the brain, and there he was buried. Stevenson wrote some remarkable poetry, collected in 'A Child's Garden of Verses' (1885) and 'Underwoods' (1887).

Stewart, DUGALD (1753-1828), professor of moral philosophy at Edinburgh from 1785 to 1810, in which post he exercised a powerful influence on Scottish thought. He was a disciple of Thomas Reid (q.v.). His works, collected by Sir William Hamilton, were published 1854-60 (11 vols.).

Stewart, FRANCIS, *alias* SERGEANT BOTHWELL, a character in Scott's 'Old Mortality' (q.v.).

Stewart of the Glens, JAMES, a character in R. L. Stevenson's 'Kidnapped' (q.v.) and 'Catriona'; a real character too, who was executed for a murder which he did not commit, after trial by a jury of Campbells (the foes of his clan).

Steyne, MARQUIS OF, a character in Thackeray's 'Vanity Fair' (q.v.).

Stichomythia, in the classical Greek drama, dialogue in alternate lines of verse, employed in sharp disputation. The form is sometimes imitated in modern drama, e.g. in the dialogue between Richard III and Elizabeth in Shakespeare's 'Richard III', IV. iv.

Stiggins, MR., a character in Dickens's 'The Pickwick Papers' (q.v.).

Still, JOHN (1543-1608), bishop of Bath and Wells. He was supposed to be the author of 'Gammer Gurton's Needle' (q.v.), but the ascription is doubtful.

Stillingfleet, EDWARD (1635-99), bishop of Worcester from 1689, a popular preacher and author of 'The Irenicum' (1659), suggesting a compromise with the Presbyterians.

Stirling, EARL OF, see *Alexander* (*Sir W.*).

Stockton, FRANK R. (1834-1902), American writer of humorous fiction, remembered as the author of 'Rudder Grange' (1879), 'The Lady or the Tiger' (1882), and many other short stories.

Stoics, a school of Greek philosophers, founded by Zeno (q.v.) of Citium about 310 B.C., which derives its name from the fact that Zeno taught under the 'Stoa Poikile' or 'Painted Portico' of Athens. Though the stoic doctrine embraced a complete philosophical system, its chief importance lies on the moral side. It held that happiness consists in liberation from the bondage of the passions and appetites, and in approximation to God by obeying his will; that virtue is thus the highest good, and suffering a matter of indifference. Among the illustrious Stoics of antiquity were Epictetus, Seneca, and Marcus Aurelius (qq.v.).

Stones of Venice, The, a treatise in three volumes by Ruskin (q.v.) (1851-3).

It was written while the production of 'Modern Painters' was still proceeding. Its purpose is to glorify Gothic and expose 'the pestilent art of the Renaissance' by attacking it in its central stronghold, Venice.

Stonewall Jackson, a nickname of General Thomas Jonathan Jackson (1824-63), a brilliant general on the Confederate side in the American Civil War.

Story of an African Farm, The, a novel by Olive Schreiner (q.v.).

Story of Rimini, The, see Hunt (*J. H. L.*).

Story of Thebes, The, see Lydgate.

Stow, JOHN (1525?-1605), chronicler and antiquary. He occupied himself from 1560 in collecting and transcribing manuscripts, and in producing original historical works, spent all his fortune on his literary pursuits, and existed for some time upon charitable contributions. He was the most accurate and businesslike of the historians of his century. His chief productions are: 'The Woorkes of Geffrey Chaucer', 1561 (his further notes on Chaucer being subsequently printed by Thomas Speght, 1598); Matthew Paris's 'Chronicle', 1571; Thomas Walsingham's 'Chronicle', 1574; 'The Chronicles of England', 1580 (in subsequent editions styled 'The Annales of England'); the second edition of Holinshed's 'Chronicle',

1585-7; and lastly 'A Survey of London', 1598 and 1603.

Stowe, MRS. HARRIET ELIZABETH BEECHER (1811-96), sister of Henry Ward Beecher (1813-87, divine and religious author and journalist), was a school-teacher before her marriage. Her famous anti-slavery novel, 'Uncle Tom's Cabin', appeared in the 'National Era' in 1851-2, and in book form in 1852. 'Uncle Tom's Cabin', by its presentment of the sufferings entailed on the Negroes by the system of slavery, did much to hasten the abolition of slavery in America.

Strabo (*b. c.* 63 B.C.), author of a history, continuing that of Polybius, which is lost, and of an important historical geography of the Roman Empire.

Strachey, (GILES) LYTTON (1880-1932), the author of a work of literary criticism, 'Landmarks in French Literature' (1912), became widely known in 1918 by his 'Eminent Victorians', biographies of Cardinal Manning, Florence Nightingale, Dr. Arnold, and General Gordon. The preface to 'Eminent Victorians' expounded Strachey's method, avoiding 'scrupulous narration' and attacking 'his subject in unexpected places', shooting 'a sudden revealing searchlight into obscure recesses, hitherto undivined'. This book was followed by a life of Queen Victoria in 1921, 'Books and Characters' in 1922, 'Elizabeth and Essex' in 1928, and 'Portraits in Miniature' in 1931.

Stradivarius, the latinized form of the name of Antonio Stradivari (1644?-1737), a famous maker of stringed musical instruments, born at Cremona. The name is also applied to violins of his making. Stradivarius is the subject of a poem by G. Eliot (q.v.).

Strafford, SIR THOMAS WENTWORTH, *first earl of* (1593-1641), became informally Charles I's chief adviser in 1638. He took command in 1640 of Charles I's force in Yorkshire against the invading Scots army. He was impeached by the Commons in 1640, but as it was manifestly impossible to convict him of high treason, a bill of attainder was substituted in 1641, and assented to by Charles in fear of mob violence. He was executed on Tower Hill in May 1641. He was nicknamed 'Black Tom Tyrant'.

Strafford, a tragedy by R. Browning (q.v.), produced in 1837 at Covent Garden, with Macready in the title-role and Helen Faucit as Lady Carlisle. The play was not successful on the stage and ran for only a few nights.

The tragedy deals with the close of Strafford's career.

Strap, HUGH, a character in Smollett's 'Roderick Random' (q.v.).

Straw, JACK, see *Jack Straw*.

Strawberry Hill, near Twickenham, about ten miles W. of the centre of London. Horace Walpole (q.v.) settled there in 1747, making it into 'a little Gothic castle'. 'Strawberry Hill Gothic' is a common term for any example of romantic gothicized architecture of the period.

Stream of consciousness, a method used by certain novelists to describe the inmost thoughts and feelings of their characters. In place of objective description or conventional dialogue the character's thoughts, feelings, impressions, or reminiscences are given, often repetitively and without logical sequence or syntax, as they flow through his consciousness. A pioneer in the use of this technique, which revolutionized the form of the novel, was Dorothy M. Richardson (q.v.); she was followed most notably by Virginia Woolf and James Joyce (qq.v.).

Strephon, the shepherd whose lament forms the opening of Sidney's 'Arcadia' (q.v.), adopted as a conventional name for a rustic lover.

Strickland, AGNES (1796-1874), was author (in collaboration with her elder sister, Elizabeth) of the successful 'Lives of the Queens of England' (1840-8), and 'Lives of the Queens of Scotland and English Princesses' (1850-9). She wrote other historical biographies, and a novel.

Strindberg, AUGUST (1849-1912),

Swedish dramatist and novelist, a misogynist, and a disciple of Nietzsche; author, among other works, of the three plays, 'The Father', 'Miss Julia', and 'The Creditors'.

Strode, RALPH (*fl.* 1350-1400), scholastic philosopher and logician. He entered into controversy with Wycliffe, and Chaucer dedicated to him and to Gower his 'Troylus and Cryseyde'.

Strong, CAPTAIN or CHEVALIER, a character in Thackeray's 'Pendennis' (q.v.).

Strong, DR., in Dickens's 'David Copperfield' (q.v.), an amiable old schoolmaster.

Strophe, from the Greek word meaning 'turn', part of a Greek choral ode sung as the chorus proceeded in one direction, followed by the *antistrophe*, when they turned and proceeded in the opposite direction (see *Alcman*).

Struldbrugs, see *Gulliver's Travels*.

Strutt, JOSEPH (1749-1802), author, artist, engraver, and antiquary, was author of many works valuable for their research and engravings. An unfinished novel by Strutt was completed by Sir W. Scott ('Queenhoo Hall'), and suggested to him the publication of his own 'Waverley'.

Struwwelpeter, see *Hoffmann* (H.).

Stuart, DANIEL (1766-1846), journalist, is remembered as having purchased 'The Morning Post' in 1795 and 'The Courier' in 1796, and raised both papers to importance by his management. There is a pleasant sketch of him in C. Lamb's 'Newspapers Thirty-five Years Ago'.

Stubbes or STUBBS, PHILIP (*fl.* 1583-91), a Puritan pamphleteer, author of 'The Anatomie of Abuses' (1583), a denunciation of evil customs of the time which, in the author's opinion, needed abolition. It contains a section on stage plays and is one of the principal sources of information on the social and economic conditions of the period. It was answered by Nash in the 'Anatomie of Absurditie' (1589).

Stubbs, WILLIAM (1825-1901), became a fellow of Trinity College, Oxford, and was for seventeen years rector of Navestock in Essex. He was much interested in the publication of the Rolls series, and succeeded Goldwin Smith as Regius professor of history at Oxford in 1866. He published a large number of volumes of the Rolls series, but the works by which he is most widely known are his contributions to English constitutional history: the edition of the 'Select Charters and other Illustrations of English Constitutional History' (1870), and 'The Constitutional History of England in its Origin and Development' (1874-8).

Stukeley, a character in George Peele's 'Battle of Alcazar'. The real Thomas Stucley or Stukeley (1525?-1578) was said to be a natural son of Henry VIII. He was an adventurer who had an amazingly varied career and was finally killed at the battle of Alcazar.

Sturla Thordsson (*c.* 1241-84), nephew of Snorri Sturlason (q.v.), Icelandic historian, author of the 'Sturlunga Saga', a vivid picture of old Icelandic life.

Sturm und Drang (storm and stress), the name (taken from the title of an absurd romantic drama of the American War of Independence by the German, Klinger, 1775) given to a period of literary ferment which prevailed in Germany during the latter part of the 18th cent. The principal figures of the movement were Schiller, Goethe, and Herder (qq.v.).

Stutly, WILL, one of the legendary companions of Robin Hood (q.v.).

Stylite or STYLITES, an ascetic who lived on the top of a pillar. The best known of these ascetics was Simeon, a Syrian, who is said to have spent thirty years on a pillar near Antioch before his death in A.D. 459. He is celebrated in Tennyson's poem, 'St Simeon Stylites'.

Styx, connected with the Greek στυγεῖν to hate, στυγνός hateful, gloomy, a river of Hades or the lower world, over which the shades of the departed were ferried by Charon, and by which the gods swore their most solemn oaths. In the 'Odyssey' (x. 515) the Acheron is the principal river of Hades, of which the Pyriphlegethon,

and the Cocytus, a branch of the Styx, are tributaries.

Sublime, On the, see *Longinus.*

Sublime and Beautiful, A Philosophical Enquiry into the Origin of our Ideas of the, a philosophical treatise on aesthetics by E. Burke (q.v.) (1756).

Sublime Porte, THE, see *Porte.*

Subtle, the Alchemist, in Jonson's comedy of that name (q.v.).

Subtle Doctor, THE, *Duns Scotus* (q.v.).

Suckling, SIR JOHN (1609-42), travelled in France and Italy, and was knighted on his return in 1630. He returned to London in 1632 and lived at court in a style of great splendour. He became a leader of the Royalist party in the early troubles; then fled to France and is said by Aubrey to have committed suicide in Paris. His chief works are included in 'Fragmenta Aurea' (1646), and consist of poems, plays, letters, and tracts, among them the famous 'Ballad upon a Wedding'. His 'Session of the Poets', in which the various writers of the day, including Ben Jonson, Carew, and D'Avenant, contend for the laurel, appeared in 1637; it is interesting as an expression of contemporary opinion on these writers. Suckling's play, 'Aglaura' (with two fifth acts, one tragic, the other not), appeared in the same year. It contains the famous lyric, 'Why so pale and wan, fond lover?'. 'The Goblins', his best play, was acted in 1638.

Suddlechop, BENJAMIN and DAME URSULA, characters in Scott's 'The Fortunes of Nigel' (q.v.).

Sullivan, SIR ARTHUR SEYMOUR (1842-1900), composed in 1866 the comic opera, 'Cox and Box', and in 1871 'Thespis', the libretto of which was by W. S. Gilbert (q.v.), the beginning of a collaboration which produced the famous Gilbert and Sullivan operas (q.v.). He composed a setting for Longfellow's 'Golden Legend' (1886); also cantatas, oratorios, and a great deal of sacred music.

Sumer is icumen in, the first line of what is believed to be the earliest extant English lyric. It was probably written in the first half of the 13th cent.; the author is unknown. The music to which it was sung still survives.

Summa Totius Theologiae, see *Aquinas*.

Summers, WILL, Henry VIII's jester.

Summerson, ESTHER, in Dickens's 'Bleak House' (q.v.), one of the narrators of the tale.

Summoner's Tale, The, see *Canterbury Tales*.

Sunium, the ancient name of Cape Colonna, celebrated in the last stanza of Byron's 'The Isles of Greece'.

Surface, JOSEPH and CHARLES, characters in Sheridan's 'The School for Scandal' (q.v.).

Surgeon's Daughter, The, a novel by Sir W. Scott (q.v.), published in 1827 as one of the stories in 'Chronicles of the Canongate'.

Surly, a character in Jonson's 'The Alchemist' (q.v.).

Surrealism, a movement in literature and art which began in Paris *c.* 1924. It was an attempt to express the subconscious without the restraint of reason, e.g. by automatic writing and the juxtaposition of incongruous ideas or objects.

Surrey, HENRY HOWARD, (by courtesy) *earl of* (1517?-1547), the poet, was son of Thomas Howard (afterwards third duke of Norfolk). He was condemned and executed on a frivolous charge when barely 30 years old.

His works consist of sonnets and miscellaneous poems in various metres, notable for their grace and finish. Like Wyatt (q.v.), he studied Italian models, especially Petrarch, and shared with Wyatt the merit of bringing the sonnet from Italy into England. He had the greater merit of introducing, in his translation of the 'Aeneid' (Bks. II and IV), the use of blank verse. The subject of many of his love-poems was 'The fair Geraldine', Elizabeth, daughter of the ninth earl of Kildare. Forty of his poems were printed in Tottel's 'Miscellany', 1557.

Surtees, ROBERT SMITH (1805-64), author of a number of humorous sporting novels.

With Rudolph Ackermann the younger, he started in 1831 'The New Sporting Magazine', to which he contributed the sketches of Mr. Jorrocks, the sporting grocer, subsequently republished as 'Jorrocks's Jaunts and Jollities' (1838). This was followed by 'Handley Cross' (1843), 'Hawbuck Grange' (1847), etc. John Leech's illustrations to most of his books add greatly to their interest.

Survey of London, A, see *Stow*.

Susanna, The History of, one of the apocryphal books of the O.T., detached from the beginning of the book of Daniel. Susanna was the wife of Joakim, a rich man dwelling in Babylon. She was accused of unchastity by two elders, because she had repelled their advances. Daniel exposed the plot by examining the elders separately; their evidence conflicted and they were put to death.

Svengali, see *Trilby*.

Swallow, the mare of Hereward the Wake (q.v.); according to the chronicles the ugliest as well as the swiftest of her time.

Swan, THE MANTUAN, Virgil (q.v.).

Swanhild, according to the 'Volsunga Saga' (q.v.), the daughter of Sigurd.

Swan of Avon, THE, Shakespeare, so called by Jonson.

Swan of Lichfield, see *Seward*.

Swan of Usk, THE, Henry Vaughan (q.v.), from his poem 'Olor Iscanus'.

Swedenborg (SWEDBERG), EMANUEL (1688-1772), Swedish philosopher, scientist, and mystic. He enjoyed visions culminating in 1745 in a revelation, and thereafter devoted his life to the interpretation of the Scriptures. According to his theosophic system, God, as Divine Man, is infinite love and infinite wisdom, from whom emanate the two worlds of nature and spirit, distinct but closely related.

Sweedlepipe, PAUL or POLL, a character in 'Martin Chuzzlewit' (q.v.).

Swidger, PHILIP, WILLIAM, and MILLY, characters in 'The Haunted Man' (q.v.).

Swift, JONATHAN (1667-1745), was born in Dublin and educated at Kilkenny

Grammar School, where Congreve (q.v.) was his schoolfellow. He was a cousin of Dryden (q.v.). He was admitted (1689) to the household of Sir W. Temple (q.v.), where he acted as secretary. He wrote pindarics, one of which provoked, according to Dr. Johnson, Dryden's remark, 'Cousin Swift, you will never be a poet.' He returned to Ireland, was ordained (1694), but came back to Temple in 1696, when he edited Temple's correspondence, and in 1697 wrote 'The Battle of the Books' (q.v.), which was published in 1704, together with 'A Tale of a Tub' (q.v.), his celebrated satire on 'corruptions in religion and learning'. At Moor Park he first met Esther Johnson ('Stella'). On the death of Temple in 1699, Swift went again to Ireland, and was given a prebend in St. Patrick's, Dublin. In the course of numerous visits to London he became acquainted with Addison, Steele, and Halifax. He began in 1708 a series of pamphlets on church questions with his ironical 'Argument against abolishing Christianity'. Amid these serious occupations, he diverted himself with the series of squibs upon the astrologer John Partridge (1708-9, see under *Bickerstaff*), and his poems depicting scenes of London life, which were published in 'The Tatler' (1709). Disgusted at the Whig alliance with dissent, he went over to the Tories in 1710, attacked the Whig ministers in 'The Examiner' (q.v.), which he edited, and in 1711 wrote 'The Conduct of the Allies' and 'Some Remarks on the Barrier Treaty', pamphlets written to dispose the mind of the nation to peace. He became dean of St. Patrick's in 1713. He had already begun his 'Journal to Stella', which is a series of intimate letters (1710-13) to Esther Johnson and her companion Rebecca Dingley, partly written in baby-language, recounting the details of his daily life while in London. Swift's relations with Stella have remained somewhat obscure; she was his worshipper, and he respected her and returned her affection. Whether he ultimately married her

is uncertain. Stella died in 1728. Another woman, Esther Vanhomrigh (pron. 'Vanummery'), entered into his life in 1708; she fell deeply in love with him, received some measure of encouragement, and his final rupture with her about 1723 led to her death. The story of their love-affair is related in Swift's poem, 'Cadenus and Vanessa' (q.v.). In 1714 he joined Pope, Arbuthnot, Gay, and others in the celebrated Scriblerus Club (q.v.). He returned to Ireland in August 1714 and by his famous 'Drapier's Letters' (q.v., 1724) he prevented the introduction of 'Wood's Half-pence' into Ireland. He published 'Gulliver's Travels' (q.v.) in 1726, and paid a last visit to England in 1727. He wrote some of his most famous tracts and characteristic poems during his last years in Ireland, 'The Grand Question Debated' (1729), 'A Complete Collection of Polite and Ingenious Conversation' (1738, q.v. under *Conversation*), and the ironical 'Directions to Servants' (written about 1731). He kept up his correspondence with Bolingbroke, Pope, Gay, and Arbuthnot, attracted to himself a small circle of friends, and was adored by the people. For a time before his death he was insane. He was buried by the side of Stella, in St. Patrick's, Dublin, his own famous epitaph, 'ubi sæva indignatio ulterius cor lacerare nequit', being inscribed on his tomb. His indignation at oppression and unfairness was genuine. His writing was sometimes coarse, but never lewd. His political works are founded on common sense, and he had no party bias. Nearly all his works were published anonymously, and for only one, 'Gulliver's Travels', did he receive any payment (£200).

Swinburne, the quartermaster in Marryat's 'Peter Simple' (q.v.).

Swinburne, ALGERNON CHARLES (1837-1909), was educated at Eton and Balliol College, Oxford, and was early united by ties of friendship with Rossetti and his circle. His first published volume, 'The Queen Mother. Rosamond. Two Plays'

(1861), attracted no attention, but 'Atalanta in Calydon' (1865), a drama in the classical Greek form, with choruses that revealed Swinburne's unsurpassed mastery of melodious verse, brought him celebrity. In 1866 followed the first series of 'Poems and Ballads' (containing 'Laus Veneris', 'Dolores', and 'A Litany', among other notable poems), which, by its outspoken repudiation of conventions and its pagan spirit, incurred censure. 'A Song of Italy' (1867) and 'Songs before Sunrise' (1871), written during the struggle for Italian independence, show his political idealism. The second series of 'Poems and Ballads', more subdued in tone and subject than the first, was published in 1878. 'Songs of the Springtides' and 'Studies in Song' (1880) are marked by the author's passion for the sea. 'Mary Stuart', the third drama of a trilogy, appeared in 1881, and 'Tristram of Lyonesse', a romantic poem in rhymed couplets, considered by many Swinburne's most perfect work, in 1882.

Of Swinburne's prose works of literary criticism, the most notable were his 'Essays and Studies' (1875), and his monographs on Shakespeare (1880), George Chapman (1875), and other Elizabethan dramatists. He also wrote acute and interesting criticisms of many more modern writers, from Blake to the Brontës and Charles Dickens. His letters were edited by Cecil Y. Lang (6 vols., 1959-62). See also *Watts-Dunton*.

Swing, CAPTAIN, an imaginary person to whom about 1830-3 were attributed a number of outrages against farmers who had adopted the use of agricultural machinery.

Swiss Family Robinson, The, the romance of a family wrecked on a desert island, written in German by Johann Rudolf Wyss (1781-1830), a Swiss author, professor of philosophy at Bern. It was published in two parts in Zürich in 1812-13 and the first English translation was a year later.

Swithin or SWITHUN, ST. (*d.* 863), was appointed by King Egbert tutor of his son Ethelwulf. On the latter's accession Swithin was consecrated bishop of Winchester, and was one of the king's chief counsellors. He is commemorated on 15 July. There is a legend that if it rains on this day there will be rain for the next forty days.

Swiveller, DICK, a character in Dickens's 'The Old Curiosity Shop' (q.v.).

Sword-dance, a medieval folk custom, of ritual origin, probably symbolizing the death and resurrection of the year. The stock characters were the fool, dressed in the skin of an animal, and the 'Bessy' a man dressed in woman's clothes. In many of the extant dances one of the characters is surrounded with the swords of the other dancers or slain. The characters were introduced in rhymed speeches. The sword-dance is one of the origins of the Mummers' play (q.v.) and so of English drama. See also *Revesby Play*.

Sybaris, an ancient Greek town in southern Italy, so notorious for its luxury that the name *Sybarite* became proverbial for a voluptuary.

Sybil, or The Two Nations, a historical novel by Disraeli (q.v.) (1845), in which he depicts the conditions prevailing among the working classes in the early years of Queen Victoria's reign, the overcrowding in miserable tenements, the inadequate wages, the 'truck' system, and the selfishness of many of the landlords and employers; and relates the agitation against them that led up to the Chartist riots. The 'Two Nations' of the title are the rich and the poor.

Sycorax, in Shakespeare's 'The Tempest' (q.v.), a witch, the mother of Caliban.

Syllepsis, a figure of speech by which a word, or a particular form or inflexion of a word, is made to refer to two or more other words in the same sentence, while properly applying to or agreeing with only one of them, or applying to them in different senses; e.g. 'Miss Bolo went home in a flood of tears and a sedan chair'. Cf. *Zeugma*.

Sylph, one of a race of beings or spirits supposed to inhabit the air, originally in the system of Paracelsus (q.v.), who similarly imagined gnomes inhabiting the earth, nymphs the water, and salamanders fire.

Sylvanus Urban, the pseudonym of E. Cave (q.v.).

Sylvia, see *Silvia*.

Sylvia's Lovers, a novel by Mrs. Gaskell (q.v.) (1863).

Symbolism, a movement in French poetry which began about 1880, when the poems of Mallarmé and Verlaine (qq.v.) were becoming known, and reached its height about 1890. The poetry aimed to evoke rather than describe, and its matter was impressions, intuitions, sensations.

Symbolism in Russia was the leading literary movement from 1894 to about 1910.

Symkyn, SYMOND, the miller of Trumpington in Chaucer's 'The Reeve's Tale' (see *Canterbury Tales*).

Symonds, JOHN ADDINGTON (1840–93), suffered long from ill-health and spent much of his life in Italy, writing under difficulties. His largest work, a 'History of the Renaissance in Italy' (1875–86), containing much valuable information, is a series of picturesque sketches rather than a continuous treatise. His other works include 'Studies of the Greek Poets' (1873), 'Sketches in Italy and Greece' (1874), a translation of the autobiography of Benvenuto Cellini, short volumes on Ben Jonson, Sidney, and Shelley, and several volumes of verse.

Symons, ARTHUR (1865–1945), poet and critic. He was a prolific writer, and his early verse, published between 1889 and 1899, was typical of the literary fashions of the nineties. His critical work includes 'An Introduction to the Study of Browning' (1886) and 'The Symbolist Movement in Literature' (1899).

Symposium, The, or *The Banquet*, the title of a dialogue by Plato in which Socrates, Aristophanes, Alcibiades, and others, at the house of the poet Agathon, discuss the nature of love. It is also the title of a dialogue by Xenophon, in which Socrates and others are the speakers.

Synaeresis, the sounding of two separate vowels as a diphthong, as when *aerial* is pron. *airial*; the opposite of *diaeresis*.

Synecdoche (pron. 'sinékdoki'), a figure of speech by which a more comprehensive term is used for a less comprehensive or vice versa, as whole for part or part for whole, e.g. 'Oxford won the match', where 'Oxford' stands for 'the Oxford eleven'.

Synge, JOHN MILLINGTON (1871–1909), educated at Trinity College, Dublin, spent his early manhood in Paris. There in 1899 he met W. B. Yeats (q.v.), who persuaded him to apply his talents to the description of Irish peasant life. 'The Aran Islands' is a series of descriptive essays based on his visits to the Islands from 1898 to 1901 and published in 1907. His remarkable dramas followed in quick succession; 'The Shadow of the Glen' was performed in 1903, 'Riders to the Sea' in 1904, 'The Well of the Saints', 1905, 'The Playboy of the Western World', 1907, and 'The Tinker's Wedding', 1907. The unfinished verse drama, 'Deirdre of the Sorrows', was written when Synge was dying, and published in 1910. His 'Collected Works' were published in four vols. (1962–8).

Synonym, strictly a word having the same meaning as another; but more usually one of two or more words having the same general sense, but possessing each of them meanings or shades of meaning or implications not shared by the other or others; e.g. kill, slay, slaughter.

Synoptic Gospels, THE, those of Matthew, Mark, and Luke, so called as giving an account of the events from the same point of view, or under the same general aspect.

Syntax, DR., see *Combe*.

Syphax, see *Sophonisba*. Also a character in Addison's 'Cato' (q.v.).

T

Tabard Inn, THE, in Southwark, the scene of the assembling of the pilgrims in Chaucer's 'The Canterbury Tales' (q.v.). The inn survived until 1875.

Tabaret, PÈRE, the amateur detective in Gaboriau's novels of crime (see also *Lecoq*).

Tacitus, GAIUS(?) CORNELIUS (*c*. A.D. 55-*c*. 117), the Roman historian, of whose works the following survive in whole or in part: (1) 'Dialogus de Oratoribus'; (2) 'Vita Agricolae', especially interesting for its account of the Roman conquest of Britain; (3) 'Germania', a description of the Germanic peoples and their institutions; (4) 'Historiae', A.D. 68-96, of which we have only a portion; and (5) 'Annales', comprising the period from the death of Augustus to the death of Nero in A.D. 68, of which again the extant portion is incomplete. Tacitus was the son-in-law of Agricola and the intimate friend of the younger Pliny (q.v.). 'Tacitean' prose is incisive, polished, and epigrammatic; it contrasts with the ample periods of the Ciceronian style.

Tackleton, a character in Dickens's 'The Cricket on the Hearth' (q.v.).

Tadpole and **Taper,** in Disraeli's 'Coningsby' and 'Sybil', typical party wire-pullers.

Tagore, SIR RABINDRANATH (1861-1941), Indian poet. Of his works, which are marked by deep religious feeling, a strong sense of the beauty of earth and sky in his native land, and by love of childhood (especially in 'The Crescent Moon'), many have been translated into English. Tagore wrote mainly in Bengali, but he also wrote in English and translated into English some of his Indian writings.

Taillefer, a minstrel in the army of William the Conqueror, who, at the battle of Hastings, is said to have encouraged the Normans by singing of the deeds of Roland.

Taine, HIPPOLYTE (1828-93), French philosopher, critic, and historian, whose theories of 'la race, le milieu et le moment' were concerned with the influence of environment and heredity on the development of human character. His works include 'Histoire de la littérature anglaise' (3 vols., 1863) and 'Origines de la France contemporaine' (1875-94).

Tale of a Tub, A, a comedy by Jonson (q.v.), licensed in 1633, the last play that the author put on the stage.

Tale of a Tub, A, a satire in prose by Swift (q.v.), written, according to his own statement, about 1696, published 1704.

The author explains in a preface that it is the practice of seamen when they meet a whale to throw him out an empty tub to divert him from attacking the ship. Hence the title of the satire, which is intended to divert Hobbes's 'Leviathan' and the wits of the age from picking holes in the weak sides of religion and government. The author proceeds to tell the story of a father who leaves as a legacy to his three sons, Peter, Martin, and Jack, a coat apiece, with directions that on no account are the coats to be altered. Peter symbolizes the Roman Church, Martin (from Martin Luther) the Anglican, Jack (from John Calvin) the dissenters. The sons gradually disobey the injunction. Finally Martin and Jack quarrel with the arrogant Peter, and then with each other, and separate. The narrative is freely interspersed with digressions, on critics, on the prevailing dispute as to ancient and modern learning, and on madness—this last an early example of Swift's love of paradox and of his misanthropy. The free comments of the satire prevented Swift from preferment in the Church.

Tale of Chloe, The, a short novel by G. Meredith (q.v.) (1879).

Tale of Two Cities, A, a novel by Dickens (q.v.) (1859).

The 'two cities' are Paris, in the time of the French Revolution, and London. Dr. Manette, a French physician, having been called in to attend a young peasant and his sister in circumstances that made him aware that the girl had been outrageously treated and the boy mortally wounded by the Marquis de St. Évremonde and his brother, has been confined for eighteen years in the Bastille to secure his silence. He has just been released, demented, when the story opens; he is brought to England, where he gradually recovers his sanity. Charles Darnay, who conceals under that name the fact that he is a nephew of the marquis, has left France and renounced his heritage from detestation of the cruel practices of the old French nobility; he falls in love with Lucie, Dr. Manette's daughter, and they are happily married. During the Terror he goes to Paris to try to save a faithful servant, who is accused of having served the emigrant nobility. He is himself arrested, condemned to death, and is saved only at the last moment by Sydney Carton, a reckless wastrel of an English barrister, whose character is redeemed by his generous devotion to Lucie. Carton, who strikingly resembles Darnay in appearance, smuggles the latter out of prison, and takes his place on the scaffold.

The book gives a vivid picture (modelled on Carlyle's 'The French Revolution') of Paris at this period, and the opening scene of the coach-drive to Dover is one of the finest things in Dickens. The novel was dramatized by F. Wills under the title 'The Only Way' (1890).

Tales in Verse, a collection of poems by Crabbe (q.v.) (1812).

Tales of a Grandfather, The, a history of Scotland to the close of the Rebellion of 1745-6, by Sir W. Scott (q.v.) (1827-9). A later series (1831) deals with the history of France.

The 'Tales' were designed in the first instance for the author's grandson, John Hugh Lockhart ('Hugh Littlejohn'). After a prefatory chapter on the period of the Roman occupation, the tales proceed to the period of Macbeth, and thence through Wallace and Bruce right through the history of Scotland down to the '45.

Tales of My Landlord, four series of novels by Sir W. Scott (q.v.): 'The Black Dwarf', 'Old Mortality' (1st Series); 'The Heart of Midlothian' (2nd Series); 'The Bride of Lammermoor', 'A Legend of Montrose' (3rd Series); 'Count Robert of Paris', 'Castle Dangerous' (4th Series). Jedediah Cleishbotham, schoolmaster and parish clerk of Gandercleugh, by a fiction of Scott, sold these tales to a publisher. They were supposed to be compiled by his assistant Peter Pattieson from the stories told by the landlord of the Wallace Inn at Gandercleugh. The title of the series is a misnomer, as Scott himself admitted, for the tales were not told by the landlord; nor did the landlord have any hand in them at all.

Tales of Soldiers and Civilians, a collection of short stories by Ambrose Bierce (q.v.), subsequently entitled 'In the Midst of Life'.

Tales of the Crusaders, two novels by Sir W. Scott (q.v.), 'The Betrothed' and 'The Talisman' (q.v.).

Tales of the Hall, a collection of poems by Crabbe (q.v.) (1819).

Talfourd, SIR THOMAS NOON (1795-1854), judge and author, is principally remembered as the friend of C. Lamb, whose 'Letters' and 'Memorials' he published in 1837 and 1848 respectively.

Talisman, The, a novel by Sir W. Scott (q.v.) (1825), forming part of the 'Tales of the Crusaders'.

The story presents the forces of the Crusaders, led by Richard I of England, encamped in the Holy Land, and torn by the dissensions and jealousies of the leaders. The consequent impotence of the army is accentuated by the illness of Richard. A poor but doughty Scottish crusader, known as Sir Kenneth or the Knight of the Leopard, encounters a Saracen emir, with whom, after an inconclusive combat, he enters into prolonged conversation, and mutual esteem springs up between them. This emir proves subsequently to be Saladin himself, and he presently appears in the Christian camp in the disguise of a physician sent by the Soldan to Richard, whom he quickly cures. Meanwhile the Knight of the Leopard, set to guard during the night the banner of England, is lured from his post by Queen Berengaria, Richard's wife, who sends him an urgent message purporting to come from Edith Plantagenet, between whom and the knight there exists a romantic attachment. During his brief absence, his faithful hound is wounded, and the English flag torn down. Sir Kenneth, thus dishonoured, narrowly escapes execution at Richard's order by the intervention of the Moorish physician, who receives him as his slave. Kindly and honourably treated by Saladin, he is sent, in the disguise of a black mute attendant, to Richard, whom he saves from assassination. Richard pierces through Sir Kenneth's disguise and gives him the opportunity he desires of discovering the hand that wounded the hound and tore down the standard. As the Christian princes and their forces defile past the re-erected standard, the hound springs on Conrade of Montferrat and tears him from his horse. A trial by combat is arranged, in which Sir Kenneth defeats and wounds Montferrat, and is revealed to be Prince David of Scotland. The obstacle which his supposed lowly birth presented to his union with Edith Plantagenet is thus removed.

Talmud, The, in the wide sense, the body of Jewish civil and ceremonial traditionary law.

Talus, in Greek mythology, a man of brass, made by Hephaestus.

Another Talus, a nephew of Daedalus (q.v.), was a mythical person to whom was attributed the invention of the saw and other industrial devices. Daedalus, jealous of his skill, threw him down from the Acropolis of Athens.

Talus, a character in Spenser's 'Faerie Queene' who represents the executive power of government. He attends on Artegall (q.v.), wielding an iron flail, with which he dispatches criminals.

Tamberlane, see *Timur*.

Tamburlaine the Great, a drama in blank verse by Marlowe (q.v.), written not later than 1587 and published in 1590. It showed an immense advance on the blank verse of 'Gorboduc' (q.v.) and was received with much popular approval.

Pt. I of the drama deals with the first rise to power of the Scythian shepherd-robber Tamburlaine. Tamburlaine's unbounded ambition and ruthless cruelty carry all before him. His ferocity is softened only by his love for his captive, Zenocrate.

Pt. II deals with the continuation of his conquests, which extend to Babylon, whither he is dragged in a chariot drawn by the kings of Trebizond and Soria, with the kings of Anatolia and Jerusalem as relay, 'pampered jades of Asia' (a phrase quoted by Pistol in Shakespeare, '2 Henry IV', II. iv); it ends with the death of Zenocrate, and of Tamburlaine himself. See *Timur*.

Tamerlane, a tragedy by Rowe (q.v.), produced in 1702, of some historical interest, because under the name of Tamerlane the author intended to characterize William III, while under that of Bajazet he held up Louis XIV to detestation. The play was, for more than a hundred years, annually revived on 5 Nov., the date of William III's landing. See *Timur*.

Taming of the Shrew, The, a comedy by Shakespeare (q.v.) with perhaps a collaborator, was probably written about 1594, partly adapted from a play, 'The Taming of a Shrew', which had appeared in 1594, and partly based on the 'Supposes' of Gascoigne (q.v.). It was first printed in the folio of 1623.

The play is introduced by an 'induction' in which Christopher Sly, a drunken tinker picked up by a lord and his huntsmen on a heath, is brought to the castle, sumptuously treated, and assured that he is a lord who has been out of his mind, and is set down to hear the following play, performed for his sole benefit by strolling players.

Petruchio, a gentleman of Verona, of shrewd wit and imperturbable temper, determines to marry Katharina, the notorious termagant elder daughter of Baptista, a rich gentleman of Padua. He carries his courtship through with a high hand, undeterred by her rude rebuffs, but affecting to find her courteous and gentle. Then the taming begins. He humiliates Katharina by keeping her waiting on the wedding-day, and at last appearing clad like a scarecrow. He cuffs the priest, refuses to attend the bridal feast, and hurries his wife off, on a sorry horse, to his home. On arrival, he refuses to let her eat or sleep, on the pretext that the food and bed prepared are not good enough for her, and distresses her by other mad pranks. Finally he takes her back to her father's house, which she reaches completely tamed. Meanwhile Bianca, Katharina's younger sister, has been won by Lucentio, who has made love to her while masquerading as a schoolmaster. Hortensio, the disappointed suitor of Bianca, has married a widow. At the feast which follows there is a wager among the bridegrooms which wife shall prove the most docile; Petruchio wins triumphantly.

Tamora, a character in Shakespeare's 'Titus Andronicus' (q.v.).

Tam o' Shanter, a poem by Burns (q.v.).

Tancred, or The New Crusade, a novel by Disraeli (q.v.) (1847), a companion work to his two principal political novels, 'Coningsby' and 'Sybil'. It combines an earnest vindication of the claims and destinies of the Jewish race with a humorous presentment of the aspirations of a visionary young English nobleman to regenerate the world.

Tancred and Gismund, or *Gismond of Salerne,* a play by R. Wilmot (q.v.) and others, published in 1591. (See *Sigismonda.*)

Tancred and Sigismunda, a tragedy by J. Thomson (1700–48, q.v.), published in 1745, produced (with Garrick as Tancred) in 1752.

Tannhäuser (pron. 'Tanhoizer'), a German minnesinger (q.v.) of the 13th cent. the subject of a legend embodied in a 16th cent. ballad. According to this, as he rode by the Hörselberg in Thuringia, he was attracted by the figure of a beautiful woman, in whom he recognized Venus. She beckoned him into a cave, where he spent seven years in revelry. Smitten by his conscience he then left the 'Venusberg' and went to Rome to seek absolution from the pope. His Holiness replied that it was as impossible for Tannhäuser to be forgiven as for his dry staff to burgeon and Tannhäuser departed in despair. But after three days, the staff broke into blossom. The pope sent hurriedly for Tannhäuser, but he was nowhere to be found. He had returned to Venus.

The story is the subject of an opera by Wagner and of Swinburne's 'Laus Veneris'.

Tanqueray, The Second Mrs., a successful play by Pinero (q.v.).

Tantalus, in Greek mythology, the father of Pelops and Niobe (qq.v.). He is represented as punished in hell, for a sin variously related, by being set, thirsty and hungry, in a pool of water which recedes when he attempts to drink it, and under fruit-trees whose fruit he tries in vain to reach.

Tantivy, a nickname given to the post-Restoration high-churchmen and Tories especially in the reigns of Charles II and James II.

Taoism. One of the so-called 'Three Teachings' of China, the other two being Confucianism and Buddhism (qq.v.). Taoism maintained that all moral judgements were relative, and idealized a time of primitive bliss unmarred by intellectual evaluations. The Taoist aim was a return to the state of pure experience and an unthinking conformity with the Tao or 'Way' of Nature; and mystical practices were used to attain its goal. Unlike Confucianism, Taoism suited the private contemplative life; it inspired poets and artists, and strongly influenced Ch'an (Zen) Buddhism.

In later centuries Taoism deteriorated into a polytheistic religion, but its great works continued to be admired. They are the 'Chuang-tzu', a masterpiece of intellectual power, poetic imagination, and literary skill dating from about 300 B.C., and the much-translated 'Tao te ching' ("Classic of the Way and its Power"), a pithy and difficult work written at about the same time, but attributed to a legendary figure called Lao-tzu.

Tapley, MARK, see *Mark Tapley*.

Tappertit, SIMON, in Dickens's 'Barnaby Rudge' (q.v.), Gabriel Varden's apprentice.

Tara, the hill of, in County Meath, Ireland, in early times the residence of Irish kings.

Targum, a word meaning 'interpretation', the name given to several Aramaic translations, interpretations, or paraphrases of the various divisions of the O.T., made after the Babylonian captivity.

Tarlton, RICHARD (*d.* 1588), actor, a man of humble origin and imperfect education, who was introduced to Queen Elizabeth through the earl of Leicester. He became one of the Queen's players in 1583, and attained an immense popularity by his jests, comic acting, and improvisations of doggerel verse. He led a dissipated life and died in poverty. Many fictitious anecdotes connected with him were published, notably 'Tarlton's Jests' (1592?-1611?) in three parts.

Tarquins, THE, Tarquinius Priscus and Tarquinius Superbus (6th cent. B.C.), the fifth and seventh legendary kings of Rome, of Etruscan origin. The former reigned with moderation and popularity. The second, his son, was noted for his tyranny

and arrogance, and the Romans rose in rebellion and expelled the Tarquins from Rome.

Tartar, MR., a character in Dickens's 'Edwin Drood' (q.v.).

Tartarus, one of the regions of Hades where the most impious and guilty among mankind were supposed to be punished. According to Virgil it was surrounded by three impenetrable walls and the burning waters of the river Phlegethon.

Tartuffe, LE, in Molière's comedy of that name, an odious hypocrite.

Task, The, a poem in six books by Cowper (q.v.) (1785).

Cowper's friend, Lady Austen, having suggested to him the sofa in his room as the subject of a poem in blank verse, the poet set about the task. Its six books are entitled, 'The Sofa', 'The Time-piece', 'The Garden', 'The Winter Evening', 'The Winter Morning Walk', and 'The Winter Walk at Noon'. Starting with a mock-Miltonic narrative of the evolution of the sofa, Cowper soon turns to himself and his delight in rural scenes. Similarly the later books give a detailed account of the joys of domestic life in the country. There are interspersed many long didactic passages, condemning the evils of the day, the failings of the clergy, the mischiefs of profusion, the cruelty of certain sports, and the disadvantages of town life in general.

Tasso, TORQUATO (1544-95), son of Bernardo Tasso (author of an epic on Amadis of Gaul). His chief works were the 'Jerusalem Delivered' (q.v.) (1581 and 1593); an epic, 'Rinaldo'; a pastoral, 'Aminta'; and a tragedy, 'Torrismondo'.

Tate, NAHUM (1652-1715), wrote an adaptation of 'King Lear' (in which Cordelia survives and marries Edgar), which held the stage for many years; and with Dryden's assistance the second part of 'Absalom and Achitophel' (q.v.); also the libretto of Purcell's opera 'Dido and Aeneas'. With Nicholas Brady he published in 1696 the well-known metrical version of the Psalms that bears their name. He was appointed poet laureate in 1692. He was pilloried in 'The Dunciad' (q.v.).

Tatler, The, a periodical started by R. Steele (q.v.) in April 1709. It appeared thrice a week until Jan. 1711.

According to No. 1, it was to include 'Accounts of Gallantry, Pleasure, and Entertainment . . . under the article of White's Chocolate House'; poetry under that of Will's Coffee-house; foreign and domestic news from St. James's Coffee-house; and so on. Gradually it adopted a higher mission. The evils of duelling and gambling are denounced in some of the earlier numbers, and presently all questions of good manners are discussed from the standpoint of a humaner civilization, and a new standard of good taste is set up. The ideal of a gentleman is examined and its essence is found to lie in forbearance. The author assumes the character of Bickerstaff (q.v.), the marriage of whose sister, Jenny Distaff, with Tranquillus gives occasion for treating of happy married life. The rake and the coquette are shown in their true light, and virtue is held up to admiration in the person of Lady Elizabeth Hastings—'to love her is a liberal education'. Episodes and short stories illustrate the principles advanced.

From an early stage in the history of 'The Tatler', Steele had the collaboration of Addison (q.v.), who besides notes and suggestions contributed a number of complete papers.

Tattycoram, in Dickens's 'Little Dorrit' (q.v.), a foundling brought up in the Meagles household.

Tauchnitz, CHRISTIAN BERNHARD VON (1816-95), the founder of a publishing house at Leipzig which in 1841 began the issue of a 'Collection of British and American Authors' for sale on the Continent, followed by a collection of English translations of German authors.

Taurus, the Bull, the second of the zodiacal constellations, containing the groups of the Pleiades and the Hyades, and the great star Aldebaran. The sun enters the zodiacal sign Taurus on 2 May.

Tawdry, see *Audrey*.

Taylor, EDWARD (1645?-1729), American poet and divine, born in England, emigrating to Boston in 1668. His devotional poems remained in manuscript and were not published until 1937, when their importance to the history of early American letters was at once recognized. He belongs to the metaphysical tradition of George Herbert and Francis Quarles (qq.v.).

Taylor, SIR HENRY (1800-86), held an appointment in the Colonial Office from 1824 to 1872, during which time he published a number of plays in verse. 'Philip van Artevelde' (1834), his masterpiece, is remarkable as a study of character, and also displays his lyrical faculty. There is an interesting critical introduction to the play.

Taylor, JANE (1783-1824) and ANN (1782-1866), authors of books for the young, published 'Original Poems for Infant Minds' in 1804, which attained immense popularity, and 'Rhymes for the Nursery' (1806), which included 'Twinkle twinkle, little star'.

Taylor, JEREMY (1613-67), was chaplain to Laud and Charles I, and was appointed rector of Uppingham in 1638. He was taken prisoner in the Royalist defeat before Cardigan Castle in 1645, and retired to Golden Grove, Carmarthenshire, where he wrote most of his greater works. After the Restoration he was made bishop of Down and Connor, and subsequently of Dromore. He died at Lisburn and was buried in his cathedral of Dromore. His fame rests on the combined simplicity and splendour of his style, of which his 'Holy Living' and 'Holy Dying' (1650-1) are perhaps the best examples. Among his other works, the 'Liberty of Prophesying', an argument for toleration, appeared in 1646; his 'Eniautos' or series of sermons for the Christian Year, in 1653; 'The Golden Grove', a manual of daily prayers, in 1655.

Taylor, JOHN (1580-1653), the 'water-poet', was apprenticed to a waterman, became a Thames waterman, and collector of the Lieutenant of the Tower's perquisite of wine. He increased his earnings by rhyming, and showed a marked talent for expressing himself in rollicking verse and prose. He obtained the patronage of Jonson and other men of genius, and diverted both court and city. He published in 1630 a collective edition of his works, 'All the Workes of John Taylor, the Water Poet'.

Taylor, PHILIP MEADOWS (1808-76), an Indian officer and 'Times' correspondent in India from 1840 to 1853, was author of 'The Confessions of a Thug' (1839), a very successful book.

Tchaikovsky, PETER ILITCH (1840-93), an eminent Russian composer, whose works are marked by the national spirit and the power of portraying every variety of emotion. They include several operas, six symphonies (of which the last three are the best known), pianoforte concertos, etc.

Tchehov, ANTON PAVLOVICH, see *Chekhov*.

Tearsheet, DOLL, a character in Shakespeare's '2 Henry IV' (q.v.).

Tears of the Muses, The, a poem by Spenser (q.v.), included in the 'Complaints' (1590). In this the poet deplores, through the mouth of the several Muses, the decay of literature and learning.

Teazle, SIR PETER and LADY, characters in Sheridan's 'The School for Scandal' (q.v.).

Te Deum, an ancient Latin psalm of praise, so called from its opening words. The authorship is traditionally ascribed to St. Ambrose (*c.* 340-97, bishop of Milan); but modern scholars incline to attribute it to Niceta of Remesiana.

Teian Muse, THE, Anacreon (q.v.).

Teiresias, see *Tiresias*.

Telemachus, a son of Odysseus and Penelope (qq.v.), who was still a child when his father went to the Trojan War. At the end of the war, when his father did not return, Telemachus went to seek him, accompanied by Athene in the guise of Mentor, and visited Menelaus and Nestor to obtain information. On his return to Ithaca, where the suitors of his mother had conspired to slay him, his father, who had just returned, was revealed to him by Athene. Together they brought about the destruction of the suitors.

Telford, THOMAS (1757-1834), a great civil engineer and road and bridge builder. He was an intimate friend of Campbell and Southey, and made an interesting journey through Scotland with the latter and wrote an account of it.

Tell, WILLIAM, a legendary hero of the liberation of Switzerland from Austrian oppression. The stories concerning him differ in details, but in its generally accepted form the legend represents him as a skilled Swiss marksman who refused to do honour to the hat of Gessler, the Austrian bailiff of Uri, placed on a pole, and was in consequence arrested and required to hit with an arrow an apple placed on the head of his little son. This he successfully did, and with a second arrow shot Gessler, subsequently stirring up a rebellion against the oppressors. These events are placed in the 14th cent. But Swiss historians have shown that there is no evidence for the existence of a real William Tell. He is the subject of a play by Schiller (q.v.).

Tellus, the name under which the Earth was worshipped at Rome, corresponding to the Greek Ge.

Tempe, a valley in Thessaly, celebrated for its beauty, cool shades, and warbling birds.

Tempest, The, a romantic drama by Shakespeare (q.v.), was probably written in 1611 and the latest of his completed works. It was not printed till the folio of 1623. The story of the exiled magician and his daughter had figured in a recent German play, and other literary sources have been suggested. Shakespeare has worked into the play details of the shipwreck on Bermuda of Sir G. Somer's ship the 'Sea-Venture' in 1609. He may have got the name of the god Setebos from Richard Eden's 'History of Travaile' (1577).

Prospero, duke of Milan, ousted from his throne by his brother Antonio, and turned adrift on the sea with his child Miranda, has been cast upon a lonely island. This had been the place of banishment of the witch Sycorax. Prospero, by his knowledge of magic has released various spirits (including Ariel) formerly imprisoned by the witch, and these now obey his orders. He also keeps in service the witch's son Caliban, a misshapen monster, the sole inhabitant of the island. After Prospero and Miranda have lived thus for twelve years, a ship carrying the usurper, his confederate, the king of Naples, and the latter's son Ferdinand, is by the art of Prospero wrecked on the island. The passengers are saved, but Ferdinand is thought by the rest to be drowned, and Ferdinand thinks the rest are drowned. Ferdinand and Miranda are thrown together, fall in love, and plight their troth. Ariel, by Prospero's orders, subjects Antonio and the king of Naples to various terrors. Antonio is cowed; the king repents his cruelty, is reconciled with Prospero, and his son Ferdinand is restored to him. All ends happily, for the ship is magically restored and Prospero and the others prepare to leave the island, after Prospero has renounced his magical faculties. Caliban, whose intercourse with Stephano, a drunken butler, and Trinculo the jester, has provided some excellent fooling, is left, as before, the island's sole inhabitant.

Templars, KNIGHTS, an order founded about 1118, whose profession was to safeguard pilgrims to Jerusalem. From a state of poverty and humility they became so wealthy and insolent that the order was suppressed by the kings of Europe in their various dominions with circumstances, especially in France, of great cruelty.

Temple, MISS, in Charlotte Brontë's 'Jane Eyre' (q.v.), the kindly manager of the Lowood Asylum.

Temple, THE, a district of London lying between Fleet Street and the Thames, took its name from the Knights Templars (q.v.), who owned it from about 1160 until their suppression.

The TEMPLE GARDEN is the scene, in Shakespeare's '1 Henry VI' (II. iv), of the plucking of the white and red roses of York and Lancaster; and in '1 Henry IV', III. iii, the prince makes an appointment with Falstaff in the Temple Hall (an anachronism, Loftie points out).

Temple, SIR WILLIAM (1628–99), was envoy at Brussels in 1666, and visited The Hague, where he effected the triple alliance between England, Holland, and Sweden (1668). He married in 1655 Dorothy Osborne, whose letters to him were published in 1888, and again in a better edition in 1928. He settled first at Sheen and later at Moor Park, near Farnham, where he was much occupied with gardening, and where Swift (q.v.) was an inmate of his household. His principal works are an 'Essay upon the Present State of Ireland' (1668), and three volumes of 'Miscellanea' (1680, 1692, and 1701). The second of these contains his best-known essay, 'Of Ancient and Modern Learning', which, by its uncritical praise of the spurious epistles of Phalaris (q.v.), exposed the author to the censure of Bentley (q.v.) and led to a vigorous controversy.

Tenant of Wildfell Hall, The, see *Wildfell Hall.*

Ten Days that Shook the World was written by John Reed, a correspondent of the American Socialist press, and first published in England by the British Communist Party in 1926, with an introduction by Lenin. Reed records the rise of the Bolsheviki, and his story, as he explains in his preface, dated 1 Jan. 1919, is 'what happened in Petrograd in November, 1917, the spirit which animated the people, and how the leaders looked, talked, and acted'. The material comes from Reed's own notes, and from Russian, English, and French newspapers and the *Bulletin de la Presse* issued daily by the French Information Bureau.

Teniers, DAVID, the Younger (1610–90), Flemish painter, chiefly of genre scenes of peasants and topers. His father, David Teniers the Elder (1582–1649), painted chiefly religious subjects, and his son, David (1638–85), was also a painter.

Tennant, WILLIAM (1784–1848), a parish schoolmaster learned in oriental languages, remembered in a literary connection for his poem in six cantos, 'Anster Fair' (1812), a mock-heroic description of the humours of the fair.

Tenniel, SIR JOHN (1820–1914), illustrator. He worked for 'Punch' from 1850, and from 1864 succeeded Leech as its chief cartoonist. 'Dropping the Pilot' (1890), referring to Bismarck's resignation, is one of his best-known cartoons. His illustrations for 'Alice in Wonderland' (1865) and 'Through the Looking-Glass' (1871) are perfect examples of the integration of illustration with text.

Tennyson, ALFRED, *first Baron Tennyson* (1809–92), educated at Trinity College, Cambridge, where he became acquainted with A. H. Hallam (q.v.). He won the chancellor's medal for English verse in 1829 with a poem, 'Timbuctoo'. 'Poems, by Two Brothers' (1827) contains some of his earlier and unimportant verse. In 1830 he published 'Poems, chiefly Lyrical' (including 'Claribel' and 'Mariana'), which were unfavourably reviewed by Lockhart and Wilson, and in 1832 travelled with Hallam on the Continent. Hallam died in 1833, and in that year Tennyson began his 'In Memoriam' (q.v.) expressive of his grief for his lost friend. He became engaged to Emily Sellwood, to whom, however, he was not married until 1850. In 1833 he published a further volume of 'Poems', containing 'The Two Voices', 'Œnone', 'The Lotos-Eaters', 'A Dream of Fair Women' ('Tithonus', published in 1860, belongs also to this period); and in 1842 an edition of his poems in two volumes, which

included some of his finest work: the 'Morte d'Arthur' (the germ of the 'Idylls'), 'Locksley Hall', 'Ulysses', 'St. Simeon Stylites', etc. In 1847 he published 'The Princess' and in 1850 'In Memoriam', and was appointed poet laureate in succession to Wordsworth in the latter year. He published 'Maud' in 1855, and in 1859 four 'Idylls of the King' (q.v., Enid, Vivien, Elaine, Guinevere), which finally established his fame and popularity. 'Enoch Arden' appeared in 1864 (the volume included his popular dialect poem, 'The Northern Farmer: Old Style'); 'The Holy Grail' in 1869; 'The Last Tournament', privately printed in 1871, and 'Gareth and Lynette' in 1872. In 1880 appeared 'Ballads and other poems', which includes, besides 'The Voyage of Maeldune' and 'Rizpah', the fine war ballads 'The Revenge' and 'The Defence of Lucknow'. Tennyson published 'Tiresias, and other poems' in 1885, 'Locksley Hall, sixty years after' in 1886, and 'Demeter, and other poems' (including 'Merlin and the Gleam', the lines 'To Virgil', and 'Crossing the Bar') in 1889. Tennyson was buried in Westminster Abbey. A life of him by his son was published in 1897.

Tennyson, FREDERICK (1807–98), elder brother of A. Tennyson (q.v.), contributed to the 'Poems, by Two Brothers' (1827), and published 'Days and Hours' (1854), etc.

Tennyson Turner, CHARLES (1808–79), elder brother of A. Tennyson (q.v.), contributed to 'Poems, by Two Brothers' (1827), and published from time to time volumes of sonnets.

Terence (PUBLIUS TERENTIUS AFER) (*c.* 190–159 B.C.), the Roman comic poet, a native of Africa, author of six comedies, four of which are adapted from Menander: 'Andria', 'Hecyra' ('The Mother-in-Law'), 'Heautontimoroumenos' ('The Self-punisher'), 'Eunuchus', 'Phormio', 'Adelphoe'.

Teresa, ST. (1515–82), a Spanish saint and author, who entered the Carmelite sisterhood and became famous for her mystic visions. Her works include 'El Camino de la Perfección' and 'El Castillo interior'. Her 'Book of the Foundations' narrates her ceaseless journeys and the continually growing labour of organizing the Carmelite order. She is commemorated on 15 Oct.

Tereus, see *Philomelia*.

Termagant, the name of an imaginary deity held in medieval Christendom to be worshipped by the Muslims: in the mystery plays represented as a violent overbearing personage; hence 'a bully', and later 'a virago'.

Terpander, the father of Greek music, a native of Lesbos, who probably flourished in the 7th cent. B.C.

Terpsichore, one of the Muses (q.v.), who presided over dancing.

Terror, THE, see *Reign of Terror*.

Tertium quid, 'some third thing', something indefinite, related in some way to two definite or known things, but distinct from both.

Terza rima, the measure adopted by Dante in the 'Divina Commedia', consisting of lines of five iambic feet with an extra syllable, in sets of three lines, the middle line of each rhyming with the first and third lines of the next set (a b a, b c b, c d c, etc.).

Tessa, a character in George Eliot's 'Romola' (q.v.).

Tess of the D'Urbervilles, *A Pure Woman*, a novel by Hardy (q.v.) (1891).

Tess Durbeyfield is the daughter of a poor, foolish villager of Blackmoor Vale, whose head is turned by learning that he is a descendant of the ancient family of the D'Urbervilles. Tess is seduced by Alec, a young man of means whose parents bear the surname D'Urberville with doubtful right to it. Tess gives birth to a child, which dies in infancy. Some time later, while working as a dairymaid on a large farm, Tess becomes engaged to Angel Clare, a clergyman's son. On their wedding-night she confesses to him the affair of Alec; and Angel abandons her.

Misfortune and hardship come upon her and her family, and accident throws her once more in the path of Alec D'Urberville. After some pathetic appeals to her husband, she is driven to accept the protection of Alec. Clare, returning from Brazil repentant of his harshness, finds her in this situation. Maddened by this second wrong that has been done her by Alec, she murders him to liberate herself. After a brief period of concealment with Clare in the New Forest, Tess is arrested, tried, and hanged. '"Justice" was done, and the President of the Immortals (in Aeschylean phrase) had ended his sport with Tess.'

Testament of Beauty, The, see *Bridges*.

Testament of Cresseid, The, see *Cresseid*.

Testament of Love, The, see *Usk*.

Tester, apparently a corruption or perversion of *teston*, a name for the *teston* or *testoon* (shilling) of Henry VIII, especially as debased and depreciated; subsequently a colloquial or slang term for sixpence.

Tethys, in Greek mythology, one of the deities of the sea, daughter of Uranus and Ge, and wife of Oceanus; her daughters were known as the Oceanides.

Tetrachordon, the third of Milton's pamphlets on divorce, dealing (whence its name) with four sets of passages from Genesis, Deuteronomy, the Gospel of St. Matthew, and the First Epistle to the Corinthians. Milton also wrote two sonnets on the subject of this pamphlet.

Tetterbys, THE, characters in Dickens's 'The Haunted Man' (q.v.).

Teubner, BENEDICT GOTTHELF (1784–1856), the founder of a publishing and book-selling business in Leipzig, famous for its editions of the ancient classics.

Teucer, a son of Telamon and half-brother of Ajax (q.v.), and the best archer in the Greek army before Troy.

Teufelsdröckh, HERR, see *Sartor Resartus*.

Thackeray, ANNE ISABELLA, see *Ritchie*.

Thackeray, WILLIAM MAKEPEACE (1811–63), educated at Charterhouse, and at Trinity College, Cambridge. Here he studied little, and left in June 1830 without a degree, after making friends with Edward FitzGerald, Tennyson, and others. In 1831 he entered the Middle Temple, but soon gave up the legal profession. In 1833 he became proprietor of 'The National Standard', for which he wrote and drew. It had a short existence, and Thackeray settled in Paris to study drawing. He returned to England in 1837 and contributed to 'Fraser's Magazine' 'The Yellowplush Correspondence' (in which Mr. Yellowplush, an illiterate footman, relates his social experiences) and wrote reviews for 'The Times' and other papers. 'Some Passages in the Life of Major Gahagan' appeared in 'The New Monthly Magazine' in 1838-9, and 'Catherine', narrated by 'Ikey Solomons, junior', in 'Fraser's Magazine' in 1839-40, the latter being an attempt to ridicule the exaltation of crime in fiction. 'A Shabby Genteel Story' appeared in 'Fraser' in 1840, 'The Paris Sketch-Book, by Mr. Titmarsh' in the same year, and 'The Great Hoggarty Diamond' in 1841. In these last two works Thackeray assumed the pseudonym of Michael Angelo Titmarsh. In the character of George Savage Fitz-Boodle he contributed to 'Fraser' in 1842-3 the 'Fitz-Boodle Papers', the confessions of an elderly clubman of the flames inspired in his susceptible heart. Fitz-Boodle reappears in 'Men's Wives', a series printed in 'Fraser' in 1843. 'Bluebeard's Ghost' and 'The Irish Sketchbook' by M. A. Titmarsh were published in the same year; and in 1844 Thackeray, in the character again of Fitz-Boodle as editor, contributed to 'Fraser' 'The Luck of Barry Lyndon'. Thackeray began his contributions to 'Punch' in 1842; of these the best known are 'The Diary of Jeames de la Pluche' (1845-6) and 'The Snobs of England' (1847, afterwards published as 'The Book of Snobs'), a denunciation of social pretentiousness. Even before the 'Snobs' were completed, the serial numbers of 'Vanity Fair' (q.v.) had begun to appear, followed by those of 'Pendennis'

(q.v.) in Nov. 1848, 'Esmond' (q.v.) in 1852, and 'The Newcomes' (q.v.) in 1853-5. Meanwhile Thackeray had begun to publish the tales ('Mrs. Perkins's Ball', 'Our Street', 'The Rose and the Ring', etc.) reprinted in 'Christmas Books' (1857). In these, and in the burlesque 'Legend of the Rhine' (1845), 'The Kickleburys on the Rhine', and 'Rebecca and Rowena' (q.v.) (1850), Michael Angelo Titmarsh reappears as author. Thackeray lectured on 'The English Humourists of the Eighteenth Century' in 1851 (published in 1853) and on 'The Four Georges' in 1855-6 (published in 1860). In 1852 he went on a lecturing tour to America, and the result was the sequel to 'Esmond', 'The Virginians' (q.v.), published in serial numbers in 1857-9. Mention should be made of Thackeray's ballads and other rhymes, written at various periods of his life, and in various moods.

There is a biography of Thackeray by A. Trollope in the English Men of Letters series (1879), and Lewis Melville published another, in two volumes, in 1910.

Thaïs, (1) an Athenian courtesan who, according to legend, accompanied Alexander on his Asiatic conquests and caused him to burn the royal palace of Persepolis. The incident is treated in Dryden's ode, 'Alexander's Feast'; (2) an Egyptian courtesan, the subject of a novel by Anatole France (q.v.).

Thaisa, in Shakespeare's 'Pericles' (q.v.), the wife of Pericles.

Thalaba the Destroyer, a poem by Southey (q.v.) (1801).

Thaler, see *Dollar.*

Thales (*c.* 624-546 B.C.), one of the seven wise men of Greece, the first to calculate with accuracy a solar eclipse. He may be considered the founder of the first Greek School of philosophy.

Thalia, the Muse (q.v.) of comedy and pastoral poetry.

Thamuz or THAMMUZ, a Syrian god, referred to by Milton in 'Paradise Lost', i. 446-52.

Thamyris, a Thracian musician mentioned by Homer ('Iliad', ii. 594). (Cf. Milton, 'Paradise Lost', iii. 35.)

Theatre. The English theatre grew out of two traditions, one that was based on the church, using altar and chancel for liturgical performances, the other on early strolling players, using merely a trestle with perhaps some sort of back-cloth. The medieval theatre, set up on benches, on a cart, or on an open village green, had regularly a *platea* or flat, where the main business of the play was done. The whole stage was, however, often divided up into 'mansions' or separate parts representing 'Heaven', 'Hell', etc., the *platea* in front being used for any general unlocalized action. In medieval miracle plays (q.v.), these 'mansions' were often on separate carts, so that different parts of the play were being performed simultaneously while the procession moved through the town. They had sometimes a two-floored stage, where the lower room was used for dressing with a ladder to the upper stage. Medieval audiences demanded a variety of stage properties; mechanical contrivances like a 'Hell's mouth' whose jaws opened and shut, seem to have been popular.

These different traditions were carried into Elizabethan times. Then when a company of actors, instead of having to wander the country, came to stay in one place and played regularly, an inn-yard was the most suitable place for performances. Trestles made the stage: patrons watched from seats on the stage itself, from the yard, or from windows round the yard which made a kind of gallery. Windows near the stage were often used in the action of the play itself. Famous inns where plays were given in the 16th cent. were the 'Cross Keys', the 'Bel Savage', the 'Bell', the 'Bull', the 'Boar's Head' at Whitechapel, and the 'Saracen's Head' at Islington.

These features were embodied in the first regular theatres built, in 'The Theatre', 1576 (which was rebuilt as the 'Globe' in 1599), and in 'The Curtain' at Shoreditch, 1577. Other theatres, such as the 'Rose' at Southwark, 1592, were built in the same period. They had normally a stage which projected into the audience (so that the audience were on three sides of the actors), an upper stage or balcony which could represent anything from a castle wall (cf. 'King John') to the Capulet's balcony (cf. 'Romeo and Juliet'); beneath it was an inner stage often covered with a curtain (Prospero, for example, would be 'discovered' here, in his cell, in the first act of 'The Tempest'); and behind this the dressing-room. Actors used few properties and relied on their words to convey illusions of time and place, but a great deal of money was spent on rich and elaborate costumes.

There were also in Elizabethan times 'private' theatres which differed by being smaller and being roofed in, such as 'The Blackfriars', 1596. Children's companies regularly performed in 'private' houses.

During the 17th cent., no great development took place, but generally the period saw a change to something nearer the modern stage. D'Avenant (q.v.) and John Webb, who had been Inigo Jones's assistant, when they built their theatre after the Restoration, introduced the 'apron stage' which ran in behind a proscenium. Actors still came forward to deliver their lines but the probability of a flat stage, cut off from the audience, was nearer. Indeed, during the 18th cent., the modern theatre practically came into being, and developments since have been mainly technical, such as the introduction of stage-lighting (formerly when the play was not given in the day-time, as it was regularly in Shakespeare's time, lights were burnt throughout the hall) from the Continent by Garrick.

Thebes, the chief town of Boeotia in Greece, supposed to have been founded by Cadmus, and the scene of the misfortunes of Oedipus (q.v.). It was the birthplace of Pindar. For the war of THE SEVEN AGAINST THEBES, see under *Eteocles*.

This war was the subject of a long epic poem, 'The Thebaid', by the Roman poet Statius (q.v.).

Thebes, The Story of, see *Lydgate*.

Theism, which in its general sense means belief in a deity, or deities, as opposed to *atheism*, or in one deity as opposed to *polytheism* or *pantheism*, is especially used in the sense of belief in one God as Creator and Ruler of the universe, without denial of revelation. In this use it is distinguished from *deism*, which is belief in the existence of a Supreme Being as the source of finite existence, with rejection of revelation and the supernatural doctrines of Christianity.

Themis, the daughter of Uranus and Ge, mother of Prometheus, and by Zeus, mother of the Fates. She was the goddess of law and equity.

Thenot, (1) a shepherd in Spenser's 'The Shepheards Calender' (q.v.); (2) a character in Fletcher's 'The Faithful Shepherdess' (q.v.).

Theobald, LEWIS (1688-1744), author of poems, essays, and dramatic works, published in 1726 his 'Shakespeare Restored', exposing the incapacity as a critic shown by Pope in his edition of Shakespeare. Pope, infuriated, made Theobald the hero of his 'Dunciad' (q.v.). But we owe to Theobald's edition of Shakespeare (1734) many valuable restorations and emendations, among others the admirable touch in the death of Falstaff, 'a' babbled of green fields' ('Henry V', II. iii).

Theocritus, the great Greek pastoral poet, lived in the 3rd cent. B.C. His 'Idylls', in which he depicts the everyday life of the people of the country, were the first examples of pastoral poetry in the literature of Greece, and were imitated by Virgil and others in Roman literature.

Theodore (602?-690), was consecrated archbishop of Canterbury by Pope Vitalius in 668. He imposed the Roman order and was the first archbishop to whom (according to Bede) the whole English church agreed in submitting.

Theodore and Honoria, one of the 'Fables' (q.v.) of Dryden. The story is from Boccaccio's 'Decameron' (v. viii).

Theodoric, see *Dietrich of Bern.*

Theophrastus (*d. c.* 287 B.C.), a Greek philosopher, native of Lesbos, and pupil of Aristotle. His interest in connection with English literature lies in his 'Characters', brief but graphic descriptions of various types of human failings, illustrated by typical actions. They served as a model to J. Hall (q.v.), to Overbury (q.v.), to Earle in his 'Microcosmographie' (q.v.), and others, and contributed in some degree towards the evolution of the English essay.

Theory of Moral Sentiments, a philosophical work by Adam Smith (q.v.) (1759).

Theosophy, from a Greek word meaning wisdom concerning God or things divine, a term applied in the 17th cent. to a kind of speculation, such as is found in the Jewish Cabbala, which sought to derive from the knowledge of God contained in secret books, or traditions mystically interpreted, a profounder knowledge and control of nature than could be obtained by the current philosophical methods. It was often applied specifically to the system of Jacob Boehme (q.v.).

In more recent times it has been adopted by the THEOSOPHICAL SOCIETY, an association founded at New York in 1875 by Col. H. S. Olcott, Madame Blavatsky, and W. Q. Judge, its professed objects being: (1) to form the nucleus of a universal brotherhood; (2) to promote the study of Aryan and other Eastern literature, religions, and sciences; (3) to investigate the unfamiliar laws of nature and the faculties latent in man.

Theresa, ST., see *Teresa.*

Thersites, the most querulous and illiberal of the Greek host in the Trojan War. He was killed by Achilles (q.v.) for laughing at the latter's grief over the death of Penthesilea. He figures in Shakespeare's 'Troilus and Cressida' (q.v.).

Thesaurus of English Words and Phrases, see *Roget's Thesaurus.*

Theseus, a son of Poseidon, or, according to a later legend, of Aegeus, king of Athens, and of Aethra, daughter of the king of Troezen, where he was brought up. In due course he was recognized by Aegeus as his son, and achieved many great feats, among others the destruction of the Minotaur (q.v.) with the help of Ariadne, daughter of Minos, whom he carried off and subsequently deserted in Naxos. His return to Athens occasioned the death of Aegeus, who threw himself into the sea when he saw his son's ship approaching, with black sails, hoisted in error, the signal of ill success. Thesus then ascended the throne of Athens. He overcame the Amazons and carried off their queen, Hippolyta. He descended to the infernal regions to carry away Proserpine, but Pluto defeated the attempt. Theseus suffered imprisonment in hell, until released by Hercules. He was also husband of Phaedra (q.v.) and father of Hippolytus (q.v.).

Theseus, the duke of Athens in Shakespeare's 'A Midsummer Night's Dream' (q.v.).

Thespis, a Greek poet of Attica, who lived in the 6th cent. B.C. He is important in the history of tragedy, for he is said to have introduced an actor in performances which had hitherto been given by a chorus alone.

Thetis, one of the sea deities, daughter of Nereus and Doris, who became the wife of Peleus (q.v.). It was foretold that her child would be greater than his father, a prophecy that was fulfilled by the birth of her son Achilles (q.v.).

Thibault, J. A., see France (A.).

Thierry and Theodoret, a tragedy by J. Fletcher (q.v.), with perhaps the collaboration of Beaumont and Massinger, printed in 1621.

Thirty-nine Articles, THE, see Articles of Religion.

Thirty Tyrants, THE, an Athenian oligarchy of thirty magistrates imposed by Sparta upon the Athenians at the close of the Peloponnesian War (403 B.C.).

Thisbe, see Pyramus.

Thomas, DOUBTING, an allusion to John xx. 25, 'Except I shall see in his hands the print of the nails . . . I will not believe.'

Thomas, DYLAN (1914-53), poet, born in Swansea. His poetry, which is full of vitality and, especially in his earlier work, powerful but often obscure imagery, has had a tremendous influence on the younger poets of his generation, and has also roused profound controversy among the critics. He died during a lecture tour of the United States, by which time he was already something of a legend for his poetry readings, his talk, and his Bohemianism. His volumes of poetry include 'Eighteen Poems' (1934), 'Twenty-five Poems' (1936), 'The Map of Love' (1939), 'Deaths and Entrances' (1946), and 'Collected Poems' (1952). His prose includes 'Portrait of the Artist as a Young Dog' (1940) and 'Adventures in the Skin Trade' (1955), both semi-autobiographical. 'Under Milk Wood', a play for voices, had its first public hearing in May 1953, at Cambridge, Mass., when he read it himself in a still unfinished version. He completed it later and it was published in 1954.

Thomas, EDWARD (1878-1917), wrote biographical and topographical works and, when he was over 30, began to compose verse at the suggestion of Robert Frost (q.v.). He was killed in Flanders during the First World War. His verse shows a loving and accurate observation of the English pastoral scene. His 'Collected Poems' appeared in 1920.

Thomas à Becket, ST. (1118?-70). Henry II appointed him chancellor, and made him his intimate friend and companion. In 1162 Thomas reluctantly became archbishop of Canterbury, and thereafter opposed the king's measures against the excessive privileges of the Church. The king in a passion made use of hasty words which led four knights to slay the prelate, who met his death with splendid courage, in his own cathedral on 29 Dec. 1170. His shrine became the most famous in Christendom and Henry II did penance at his tomb. Thomas à Becket was canonized in 1173 and his festival is observed on 29 Dec. He is the subject of dramas by G. Darley, Tennyson, and T. S. Eliot (qq.v.).

Thomas à Kempis (THOMAS HÄM-MERLEIN or HÄMMERKEN) (1380-1471), born at Kempen, near Cologne, became an Augustinian monk and wrote Christian mystical works, among which is probably to be included the famous 'De Imitatione Christi', which has been translated from the Latin into many languages (into English in the middle of the 15th cent.). It obtained wide popularity by its simplicity and sincerity and the universal quality of its religious teaching.

Thomas the Rhymer, see *Erceldoune*.

Thomist (pron. 'Tōmist'), a follower of the scholastic philosopher, Aquinas (q.v.). Cf. *Scotist*.

Thompson, FRANCIS (1859-1907), lived a life of ill-health and, for a time, of extreme poverty, from which he was rescued by Alice Meynell (q.v.) and her husband. His first volume of 'Poems' (1893) included his famous 'Hound of Heaven' (describing the poet's flight from God, the pursuit, and the overtaking), which shows the influence of Crashaw (q.v.). This was followed by 'Sister Songs' in 1895, and 'New Poems' in 1897. His prose work includes 'Health and Holiness' (1905) and an 'Essay on Shelley' (1909).

Thomson, JAMES (1700-48), began early to write verse that showed his fondness for rustic scenes. He came to London in 1725 and under stress of poverty wrote 'Winter', the first of his 'Seasons' (q.v.), which appeared successively in 1726-30. He made the acquaintance of Arbuthnot, Gay, and Pope, found patrons, and eventually, through the influence of Lord Lyttelton, received a sinecure. In 1734-6 he published his long poem 'Liberty'. He produced a series of tragedies, 'Sophonisba' (1730), 'Agamemnon' (1738), 'Edward and Eleanora' (1739); 'Tancred

and Sigismunda' (1745) and 'Coriolanus' (1749) were produced after his death. In 1740 was performed the masque of 'Alfred' by Thomson and David Mallet (q.v.) containing 'Rule, Britannia', which was probably written by the former. Thomson published in 1748 'The Castle of Indolence', which contains a portrait of himself as an inmate of the castle, contributed by Lord Lyttleton. His 'Seasons' first challenged the artificiality of English poetry, and inaugurated a new era by their sentiment for nature.

Thomson, JAMES (1834-82), the child of poor parents, made friends with Charles Bradlaugh (q.v.), wrote for the 'National Reformer', and took an active part in the propaganda of free thought. He lived a sad and isolated life in London, aggravated by insomnia and addiction to drink. His chief poem, 'The City of Dreadful Night', a powerful and sincere expression of an atheistic and despairing creed, was contributed to the 'National Reformer' in 1874. It was republished with other poems in 1880. He wrote under the initials B.V. (for Bysshe [Shelley] Vanolis [Novalis]).

Thone, in Milton's 'Comus', 675:

Not that nepenthes which the wife of Thone

In Egypt gave to Jove-born Helena, a reference to Homer's 'Odyssey', iv. 228, where Helen, to divert Menelaus and Telemachus from their gloomy thoughts, casts a drug into their wine, which Polydamna, wife of Thon, a woman of Egypt, had given her.

Thopas, The Tale of Sir, see *Canterbury Tales*.

Thor, in northern mythology, the god of thunder, son of Odin (q.v.), and one of the three great gods (Odin, Thor, and Frigga) of the Scandinavians.

Thoreau, HENRY DAVID (1817-62), was a friend of Emerson (q.v.) and, in his own words, 'a mystic, a transcendentalist, and a natural philosopher to boot'. He rebelled against the Puritanism of New England and against the materialistic values of modern society, and in search of the simple life built himself a cabin by Walden Pond, where he lived on an expenditure of a few dollars for two and a half years. He was an ardent lover and observer of nature, and his 'Walden or Life in the Woods' (1854), his best-known work, is admirable chiefly for his descriptions of natural phenomena. His interesting and important 'Journal' was printed in fourteen volumes in 1906 (reprinted 1963).

Thorndyke, Dr., in the detective stories of Richard Austin Freeman (1862-1943), 'a barrister and doctor of medicine', 'probably the greatest criminal lawyer of our time' and 'the leading authority on poisons and crimes connected with them' ('As a Thief in the Night'). His companion and foil is Dr. Jervis; his laboratory assistant, Polton.

Thornhill, Sir William and **Squire**, characters in Goldsmith's 'The Vicar of Wakefield' (q.v.).

Thorpe, John and **Isabella**, characters in Jane Austen's 'Northanger Abbey' (q.v.).

Thoth, an ancient Egyptian god, identified by the Greeks with their Hermes.

Thousand and One Nights, The, the 'Arabian Nights' Entertainments' (q.v.).

Thrale, Hester Lynch, Mrs. (1741-1821), the friend of Dr. Johnson, was married against her inclinations to Henry Thrale, the son of a wealthy brewer. Her intimacy with Dr. Johnson became famous, Johnson at one time being almost domesticated at Thrale's house at Streatham Park. After Thrale's death she married Gabriel Piozzi, an Italian musician. In 1786 she published her 'Anecdotes of the late Samuel Johnson', which gave a lively picture of the Doctor, and in 1788 her correspondence with him.

Thraso, a braggart soldier in Terence's 'Eunuchus'.

Three Clerks, The, a novel by A. Trollope (q.v.) (1858), which gives some glimpses of the author's youth.

Three Men in a Boat, see *Jerome* (*Jerome K.*).

Three Musketeers, The, ('Les Trois Mousquetaires'), one of the most popular of the romances of Dumas (q.v.) the elder (1844).

With its sequels 'Twenty Years After' and 'The Vicomte de Bragelonne' it deals with the life of a poor Gascon gentleman, d'Artagnan, who comes to Paris in the reign of Louis XIII to join the king's musketeers, gets involved with three members of that force, Athos, Porthos, and Aramis, and thereafter becomes their friend and shares their many heroic adventures.

Thrie Estaitis, Ane Pleasant Satyre of the, see *Lindsay* (*Sir D.*).

Through the Looking-Glass, a book for children by Lewis Carroll (see *Dodgson*) (1872).

Alice (see *Alice's Adventures in Wonderland*) walks in a dream through the looking-glass into Looking-Glass House, where she finds that the chessmen, particularly the red and white queens, are alive; meets with Tweedledum and Tweedledee and Humpty-Dumpty; and so forth. The story ends with Alice, who has the red queen in her arms, 'shaking her into a kitten' (for she had gone to sleep playing with the black and white kittens). The well-known verses about the Jabberwock, and the Walrus and the Carpenter, occur in the course of the story.

Thucydides, the great Athenian historian, was born about 460 B.C. and died in the early years of the 4th cent. His history, which deals with the great war between Athens and Sparta down to the year 411 B.C., is concise sometimes to the point of obscurity, but is marked by scrupulous accuracy and also by a gift for expressing the sadness of a tragic story. It is noteworthy, moreover, as the first work of the kind in which events are traced to their cause and their political lessons brought out.

Thule, an island in the northern seas, first mentioned by Pytheas, a Greek navigator of the 4th cent. B.C. It may have been Iceland, or Norway, or the Shetlands. Ultima Thule, 'farthest Thule', is used figuratively for the uttermost point attainable.

Thumb, TOM, see *Tom Thumb*.

Thurber, JAMES (1894-1961), American short-story writer, humorist, and illustrator. He was a staff writer on, and later a frequent contributor to, 'The New Yorker' (q.v.). He had a delightful vein of fantasy and comedy, which appeared in both his prose and drawings. Among his many books are 'The Owl in the Attic and Other Perplexities' (1931), 'The Seal in the Bedroom and Other Predicaments' (1932), 'My World—and Welcome to It' (1942), 'Men, Women, and Dogs' (1943), 'The Thurber Carnival' (1945), and 'Thurber Country' (1953).

Thurio, a character in Shakespeare's 'The Two Gentlemen of Verona' (q.v.).

Thwackum, in Fielding's 'Tom Jones' (q.v.), the tutor of Tom and Blifil.

Thyestes, see *Atreus*.

Thyrsis, A Monody, to commemorate the author's friend, Arthur Hugh Clough, who died at Florence 1861, by M. Arnold (q.v.) (1867).

The poem, pastoral in form, and containing frequent reference to 'The Scholar-Gipsy' (q.v.), combines a lament for the dead friend with an exquisite description of the Oxford country, similar to that found in the earlier poem.

Tibbs, BEAU, see *Beau Tibbs*.

Tibert, see *Tybert*.

Tibullus, ALBIUS (*c.* 60-19 B.C.), a Roman elegiac poet, a contemporary of Virgil and Horace.

Tickell, THOMAS (1686-1740), contributed verse to the 'Guardian', 'Spectator', and other publications, and was author of a poem 'On the Prospect of Peace' (1712). He enjoyed the patronage of Addison and is chiefly remembered as having occasioned the quarrel between Pope and Addison by publishing a translation of the first book of the 'Iliad' at the same time as Pope, at Addison's instigation as Pope supposed.

Tigg, MONTAGUE, a character in Dickens's 'Martin Chuzzlewit' (q.v.).

Till Eulenspiegel, see *Eulenspiegel*.

Tillotson, JOHN (1630-94), a 'latitudinarian' who became archbishop of Canterbury. His sermons, marked by lucidity of style, were very popular, and earned the approval of Dryden.

Tilney, GENERAL, and his sons and daughter, characters in Jane Austen's 'Northanger Abbey' (q.v.).

Timber, or Discoveries made upon Men and Matter, by Jonson (q.v.), printed in the folio of 1640, a collection of notes, extracts, and reflections on miscellaneous subjects, made in the course of the author's wide reading, varying in length from a single sentence to short essays. They are, for the greater part, adapted from Latin writers.

Time and Tide, by Weare and Tyne, twenty-five letters by Ruskin (q.v.) on the laws of work, addressed to a working man of Sunderland (1867). They are in effect essays on social reconstruction, expressions of Ruskin's aspirations for a happier world and the disappearance of luxury and poverty, greed and suffering.

Times, The, was founded under the name of 'The Daily Universal Register' on 1 Jan. 1785 by John Walter, the name being changed to 'The Times' in 1788. The founder and his son, also named John Walter, introduced great improvements both in the mechanism of newspaper printing, and in the collection of intelligence. Among the famous editors of 'The Times' have been Thomas Barnes (1817-41) and John Thaddeus Delane (1841-77). The latter was followed by Thomas Chenery, and in 1884 by G. E. Buckle. 'The Times' was one of the first papers to employ special foreign correspondents (Henry Crabb Robinson, q.v., was sent out to North Germany in this capacity in 1807) and war correspondents (W. H. Russell, in the Crimea). Among notable men of letters who contributed to 'The Times' in early days were George Borrow (from Spain), Leigh Hunt, and Disraeli ('Runnymede Letters').

Times Literary Supplement, The, was first published on 17 Jan. 1902 under the editorship of Mr. (later Sir) Bruce Richmond, and has since then appeared weekly. It contains articles and reviews, correspondence on bibliographical and other subjects, and a record of current literary publications.

Timias, in Spenser's 'Faerie Queene', Prince Arthur's squire, represents Sir Walter Ralegh.

Timon, a misanthropical citizen of Athens who lived about the time of the Peloponnesian War, the subject (1) of one of Lucian's finest Dialogues; (2) of Shakespeare's 'Timon of Athens' (q.v.).

Pope's Timon, in 'Moral Epistles', iv. 98 et seq., an example of ostentatious wealth, was perhaps drawn from the duke of Chandos.

Timon of Athens, a drama by Shakespeare (q.v.) written probably about 1607, perhaps left unfinished or written in collaboration with another dramatist; not printed until the first folio.

The material of the play is in Plutarch's 'Antony', Lucian's 'Misanthropos', and an anonymous play 'Timon' in the Dyce MS. Timon, a rich and noble Athenian of good and gracious nature, having ruined himself by his prodigal liberality to friends, flatterers, and parasites, turns to the richest of his friends for assistance in his difficulties, and is denied it, and deserted by all who had previously frequented him. Cursing the city, he betakes himself to a cave, where he lives solitary and misanthropical. While digging for roots he finds a hoard of gold, which has now no value for him. His embittered spirit is manifested in his talk with the exiled Alcibiades, the churlish philosopher Apemantus, the thieves and flatterers attracted by the gold, and his faithful steward Flavius. When the senators of Athens, hard pressed by the attack of Alcibiades, come to entreat him to return to the city and help them, he offers them his fig-tree, on which to hang themselves as a refuge from affliction. Soon his tomb

is found by the sea-shore, with an epitaph expressing his hatred of mankind.

Timur or *Timur-Leng* ('Timur the Lame'), corrupted to *Tamerlane* or *Tamberlane* (*d.* 1405), a descendant in the female line from Genghis Khan (q.v.), established himself in Samarkand and extended his rule by terror and desolation over parts of Turkestan, Siberia, Persia, and India, assuming the title of the Great Khan. He captured Delhi and founded the Mogul dynasty in India. (See also *Tamburlaine the Great*.)

Tindal, WILLIAM (*d.* 1536), see *Tyndale*.

Tintagel, a castle on the N. coast of Cornwall, of which ruins remain. It figures in Malory's 'Morte Darthur'.

Tiresias or TEIRESIAS, a Theban soothsayer, who was struck with blindness in his youth. As some compensation, he was given the power of prophecy, and a staff which guided his footsteps. He advised the Thebans in the wars of the Seven against Thebes and the Epigoni. He lived to a great age. His daughter Manto was also a prophetess.

The legend of Tiresias is the subject of a dramatic monologue by Tennyson and of a poem by Swinburne.

'Tis Pity she's a Whore, a tragedy by J. Ford (q.v.) (1633).

The play deals with the guilty passion of Giovanni and his sister Annabella for each other. Being with child, Annabella marries one of her suitors, Soranzo, who discovers her condition. Soranzo invites Annabella's father and the magnificoes of the city, with Giovanni, to a sumptuous feast, intending to execute his vengeance. Although warned of Soranzo's intentions, Giovanni boldly comes. He has a last meeting with Annabella just before the feast, and to forestall Soranzo's vengeance, stabs her himself. He then enters the banqueting-room, defiantly tells what he has done, fights with and kills Soranzo, and is himself killed.

Titania, in Shakespeare's 'A Midsummer Night's Dream' (q.v.), the queen of the fairies, and wife of Oberon.

Titans, THE, sons and daughters of Uranus and Ge (qq.v.). They included Cronos (Saturn), Rhea, Oceanus, Tethys, and Hyperion. The legend says that Uranus had thrown his elder sons into Tartarus, and that Ge incited the Titans to rise against him. This they did, deposed Uranus, and raised Cronos to the throne. Subsequently Zeus (q.v.) revolted in turn against Cronos and the other Titans, and with the help of thunder and lightning hurled them from heaven. (This contest is sometimes confused by the poets with the rising of the Giants (q.v.) against Zeus and the later gods.)

Tithonus, a son of Laomedon, king of Troy. He was so beautiful that Aurora (q.v.) became enamoured of him. Zeus granted him immortality at the goddess's request; but she omitted to ask at the same time for perpetual youth, and he soon became old and decrepit.

Tennyson presents him, in a dramatic monologue, lamenting his unhappy fate.

Titian (*c.* 1487/90-1576), TIZIANO VECELLI, Venetian painter. He excelled as a painter of portraits, and of sacred and mythological subjects.

Titivil or TUTIVILLUS, a medieval word of unknown origin, the name of a devil said to collect fragments of words dropped, skipped, or mumbled in the recitation of divine service, and to carry them to hell to be registered against the offender. Hence it became a name for a devil in the mystery plays, and hence again it passed into popular speech as a term of reprobation, a scoundrel, villain. Titivil was evidently in origin a creation of monastic wit.

Titmarsh, MICHAEL ANGELO, see *Michael Angelo Titmarsh*.

Tito Melema, a character in G. Eliot's 'Romola' (q.v.).

Titus Andronicus, a tragedy attributed to Shakespeare (q.v.), acted and printed in 1594. The extent of Shakespeare's share in the authorship is uncertain.

It deals with the revenge exacted by Titus Andronicus, a Roman general under the Empire, for the revolting atrocities committed against Lavinia his daughter, his sons, and himself, and for the murder of his daughter's lover, by Tamora the captive queen of the Goths, her sons, and her paramour, Aaron the Moor. ('Andronicus' in the play is accentuated on the second syllable; in Latin it is 'Andronícus'.)

Tiu, TIW, TYR, an ancient Teutonic deity, a war-god identified with the Roman Mars, commemorated in our 'Tuesday'.

Tobit, The Book of, a romance of the Jewish captivity, forming part of the Apocrypha.

Todgers, MRS., a character in Dickens's 'Martin Chuzzlewit' (q.v.).

Tolkien, JOHN RONALD REUEL (1892-1973), Merton professor of English language and literature at Oxford, 1945-59. He published a number of philological and critical studies as well as novels based on a mythology of his own: 'The Hobbit' (1937); and 'The Lord of the Rings', a sequence in three volumes: 'The Fellowship of the Ring' (1954), 'The Two Towers' (1954), and 'The Return of the King' (1955).

Toller, ERNST (1893-1939), German revolutionary poet and dramatist, author of 'The Machine Wreckers' (1923), 'Masses and Man' (1923), 'The Swallow Book' (1924), and an autobiography of post-war Germany, 'I was a German'.

Tolosa, GOLD OF, gold plundered by the Roman consul, Quintus Servilius Caepio, in 106 B.C. from a temple at Tolosa. The phrase is used to signify ill-gotten gains.

Tolstoy, COUNT LEO NIKOLAEVICH (1828-1910), Russian writer. He was of noble birth and heir to large estates, but his intense sincerity of thought gradually led him to abandon his normal career. He arrived eventually at intellectual conclusions which involved non-resistance to evil, the abolition of governments and nationality, of churches and dogmas, but involved also belief in God and love of men. His chief importance rose from his amazing power, which entered into his books, whether they were discussions, novels, plays, or exhortations. This power spread his influence far beyond Russia, and made him something like a prophet to many minds in the West. His chief novels are: 'War and Peace' (1865-72, an epic tale of the Napoleonic invasion), 'Anna Karenina' (1875-6), 'The Death of Ivan Ilyitch' (1884), 'The Kreutzer Sonata' (1890), 'Resurrection' (1899).

Of his other books, 'What is Art?' (1898) is a profound analysis of the nature of art; 'Confession' (1882) is an auto-biographical description of the great spiritual crisis of his life; 'What then must we do?' (1886) is a study of economic conditions. Besides these, there are essays and short stories, all full of the same power and intensity, and the plays, of which 'The Power of Darkness' (1886) is the greatest.

The union of a great moral conviction and realistic details, and an immense imaginative vision, combine to make him one of the great European writers.

Tom Brown's Schooldays, see *Hughes*.

Tom Cringle's Log, see *Scott* (*M.*, 1739-1835).

Tom Folio, see *Rawlinson* (*T.*).

Tom Jones, a Foundling, a novel by H. Fielding (q.v.) (1749), consisting of eighteen 'books', each preceded by an introductory chapter in the nature of an essay on some theme more or less connected with the story, in the manner subsequently adopted by Thackeray and George Eliot. These essays contain some of Fielding's best prose.

The plot of this, which is generally regarded as Fielding's greatest work, is briefly as follows. Tom Jones is a foundling, discovered one night in the bed of the wealthy and benevolent Mr. Allworthy, who gives him a home and educates him, but presently repudiates him. The causes which lead to Tom's dismissal are several. In the first place Tom, a generous, but too human, youth, has incurred his benefactor's displeasure by his amour with Molly Seagrim, the keeper's daughter.

Then he has fallen in love with the beautiful Sophia (daughter of the bluff irascible foxhunter, Squire Western). He has incurred the enmity of his tutor, the pedantic divine, Thwackum, and, in a less degree, of his colleague, the hypocritical philosopher, Square. And lastly he is the victim of the cunning misrepresentations of young Blifil, who expects to marry Sophia himself, and hates Tom. Tom sets out on his travels, accompanied by the schoolmaster, Partridge, a simple lovable creature, and meets with many adventures, some of them of an amorous description. Meanwhile Sophia, who is in love with Tom and determined to escape from the marriage with Blifil to which her despotic father has condemned her, runs away from home, with Mrs. Honour, her maid, to a relative in London. Finally Tom is discovered to be the son of Allworthy's sister, the machinations of Blifil are exposed, Sophia forgives Tom his infidelities, and all ends happily.

Tommy Atkins, a familiar name for the typical private soldier in the British Army; arising out of the casual use of this name in the specimen forms given in the official Army regulations from 1815 onwards.

Tom o' Bedlam, a wandering beggar. After the dissolution of the religious houses, the poor wandered over the country, many assuming disguises calculated to obtain them charity. Among other disguises some affected madness, and were called Bedlam Beggars. Edgar, in 'King Lear', II. iii, adopts this disguise.

Tom Sawyer, a novel by Mark Twain (see *Clemens*).

Tom Thumb, an old nursery tale, of which there are several Northern versions.

According to the English tale, Tom was the son of a ploughman in the days of King Arthur, and he was as tall as the ploughman's thumb. His diminutive size was the occasion of many absurd adventures, as when he was swallowed by a cow, was carried off by a raven, and was swallowed by Giant Grumbo.

Tom Thumb, a Tragedy, a burlesque of

contemporary playwrights by H. Fielding (q.v.), first acted in 1730; reissued, enlarged, in 1731 as 'The Tragedy of Tragedies; or the Life and Death of Tom Thumb the Great'.

Tono-Bungay, see *Wells* (*H. G.*).

Tonson, JACOB (1656–1736), publisher. He purchased the copyright of 'Paradise Lost', and published many works by Dryden and Addison, besides Rowe's 'Shakespeare' and an edition of Beaumont and Fletcher. He was secretary to the Kit-Cat Club (q.v.). His publishing business was continued by his nephew and great-nephew, who bore the same name as he. Pope (adapting Dryden) mentions Tonson in 'The Dunciad' as 'left-legged Jacob', but his other references to him are more kindly.

Toodle, POLLY and ROBIN ('Rob the Grinder'), her son, characters in Dickens's 'Dombey and Son' (q.v.). Polly was Paul Dombey's foster-mother.

Tooke, JOHN HORNE (1736–1812), vigorously supported Wilkes (q.v.) in connection with the Middlesex election. He published ' *Ἔπεα πτερόεντα*, or the Diversions of Purley', a work which established his reputation as a philologist. He was more than once in conflict with the authorities, was fined and imprisoned for sedition, and was tried for high treason and acquitted.

Toots, MR., a character in Dickens's 'Dombey and Son' (q.v.).

Topsy, in Mrs. Beecher Stowe's 'Uncle Tom's Cabin' (see under *Stowe, Mrs. H. B.*), a little slave girl who asserted that she had neither father nor mother, and being asked who made her, replied 'I spect I grow'd'.

Torquemáda, TOMÁS DE (1420–98), a Spanish Dominican monk, appointed in 1483 the first inquisitor-general by Ferdinand and Isabella. Hence his name became a synonym for a cruel persecutor.

Tory, from an Irish word meaning 'pursuer', was a name applied in the 17th cent. to the dispossessed Irish, who became out-laws. In 1679–80 it was applied as a nickname by the Exclusionists to those who opposed the exclusion of the Roman Catholic James, duke of York, from the succession to the Crown. Hence, from 1689, it became the name of one of the two great political parties in England, that which sprang from the 17th-cent. Royalists or Cavaliers. For some years after 1689 the Tories leant more or less decidedly towards the dethroned House of Stuart. But from the accession of George III they abandoned this attitude, retaining the principle of strenuously upholding the constituted authority and order in Church and State. The opposition to the growing demands of Liberalism, a consistent antagonism to measures for widening the basis of parliamentary representation, etc., became their most marked characteristic. As a formal name 'Tory' was superseded by 'Conservative' about 1830.

Tottel, RICHARD (*d.* 1594), a publisher, chiefly known as the compiler (with Grimald, q.v.) of 'Songs and Sonnets', known as 'Tottel's Miscellany' (1557), comprising the chief works of Wyatt and Surrey (qq.v.).

Touchstone, a clown in Shakespeare's 'As You Like It' (q.v.).

Tourneur, TURNOUR, or TURNER, CYRIL (1575?–1626), dramatist. Practically nothing is known of his life. Of his two plays (assuming that they are both his, which is contested), 'The Revenger's Tragedy', was published in 1607. It deals with the revenge of Vendice for the murder of his betrothed lady by the licentious duke, and for the attempt of the duke's son, Lussorioso, to seduce Vendice's sister, the chaste Castiza. It is a gloomy work, relieved by the poetic beauty of several passages and the tragic intensity of the plot. 'The Atheist's Tragedy' appeared in 1611. (The dates and order of the two plays, however, are disputed.)

Toussaint L'Ouverture (1743–1803), to whom Wordsworth addressed a sonnet, was a Negro revolutionist who made himself master of the French colony of San

Domingo (Haiti) when the decree of 1791 freeing the Negroes was revoked. For some years he administered the island with great success, but he was overcome by the forces of Buonaparte and transported to France, where he died.

Towneley Mysteries, see *Mysteries.*

Town Mouse and Country Mouse, a fable told by Horace (Sat. II. vi) and by La Fontaine (though the latter substitutes rats for mice). The city mouse, contemptuous of the country mouse's cave and humble fare, invites it to a sumptuous supper in its palace. But the feast is disturbed by an alarm, and the mice scurry away. The country mouse concludes that it prefers its wood and cave free from surprises, and its homely fare.

M. Prior (q.v.) was at least part-author of the 'Hind and Panther transvers'd to the tale of the Town Mouse and the Country Mouse'.

Tow-wouse, Mr. and Mrs., characters in H. Fielding's 'Joseph Andrews' (q.v.).

Toxophilus, see *Ascham.*

Tractarian Movement, see *Oxford Movement* and next entry.

Tracts for the Times, a series of tracts on religious subjects, of which the principal authors were Newman, Keble, R. H. Froude, and Pusey (qq.v.) (1833–41).

The first tract was by Newman, 'Thoughts on the Ministerial Commission, respectfully addressed to the Clergy', and the most famous, 'Tract XC', was also by him. See *Oxford Movement.*

Traddles, a character in Dickens's 'David Copperfield' (q.v.).

Trafalgar (formerly pron., as in Spanish, Trafalgar'), BATTLE OF, fought on 21 Oct. 1805.

Tragedy, a word derived from the Greek τραγῳδία, apparently meaning 'goat-song'. As to the reason of the name many theories have been advanced, some even disputing the connection with goat. It is applied to a play or other literary work of a serious or sorrowful character with a fatal or disastrous conclusion; also to that branch of dramatic art which treats of

sorrowful or terrible events in a serious and dignified style.

English tragedy, as it developed in the 16th cent., was less clearly related than comedy (q.v.) to the earlier native forms inherent in miracle and morality plays, though it derived its dramatic conventions from the same source. The main impulse was foreign, Italian through French, and introduced to England by the middle of the 16th cent. a number of Senecan tragedies (q.v.) modelled on strictly classical forms. 'Gorboduc' (q.v.), 1561, is one of the most famous examples of an early tragedy of this type: it derived its merits from certain elements of a native tradition rather than from its adherence to the Senecan model. The form was nevertheless learned rather than popular. At the same time troops of wandering players were evolving the more popular form of historical chronicle play which had the blood-thirstiness of Senecan tragedy, was itself often tragic in denouement, and though rougher in style, possessed greater realism. The two forms coalesced at the end of the century in the plays of Marlowe, Kyd, and others to produce a tragic drama which, while based on popular appeal, had all the elements of great art.

Marlowe's 'Tamburlaine the Great' (q.v.) has the formlessness of a chronicle play relieved by magniloquent language: his 'Doctor Faustus' (q.v.) explored the psychological tragedy which was to characterize Shakespeare's tragic period. It is possible that Kyd (q.v.) wrote an early form of 'Hamlet' before 1590; his Spanish Tragedy' (q.v.), 1592, was one of the most popular of all Elizabethan plays, reverting as it does to an earlier and cruder type. About this time there appeared also an example of 'domestic tragedy' in 'Arden of Feversham' (q.v.), a type of drama that was to reappear in Heywood's 'A Woman Kilde with Kindnesse' (q.v., 1603), and a hundred years later again in the plays of Lillo (q.v.). Historical tragedy was developing contemporaneously: all the elements of pure tragedy can be found in

Shakespeare's 'Richard II' or 'Julius Caesar' or again in Ben Jonson's 'Sejanus' and 'Catiline' where he attempted to regain strict classical forms.

After the period of Shakespeare's great tragedies—'Hamlet', 'Othello', 'King Lear', 'Macbeth'—a period roughly 1600-8, there was a brief fashion, exemplified in the works of Webster and Tourneur (qq.v.), for a poetic and very Italianized 'tragedy of blood'. Chapman's 'Biron' and 'Bussy d'Ambois' plays have, besides their writer's very individual touch, an affinity to Marlowe. The succeeding years, with their emphasis on romantic comedy and the development of the masque (q.v.), produced few great tragedies. Ford, the last of the Elizabethans, recaptured some of their glories in 'The Broken Heart' and ''Tis Pity she's a Whore' (qq.v.), but generally there was little real merit or attempt at genuinely tragic forms.

The heroic drama of the Restoration, imitating in heroic couplets Marlowe's grandiloquence, had the merits of opera rather than tragic drama. Sometimes, e.g. in Dryden's 'All for Love' (q.v.)—written incidentally in blank verse—there is real feeling, and Otway (q.v.) was a genuine tragic poet. The early years of the 18th cent. saw some attempts, e.g. by Rowe, Dennis, Addison, and others, to write classical drama, but their works were flat and sterile. Lillo's plays, already mentioned, had considerable merit, but the fashionable poetic tragedy of the period —cf. the plays of James Thomson (q.v.) or Johnson's 'Irene'—had little except eloquence to commend them; and there was no revival similar to that produced by Sheridan and Goldsmith in comedy, of earlier tragic glories.

The decline into melodrama continued throughout the 19th cent. The modern period has seen the influence from abroad of Strindberg, Ibsen, and Maeterlinck (qq.v.), and certain German authors, e.g. Ernst Toller, and occasional successes in realistic modern tragedy.

Tragedy of Tragedies, see *Tom Thumb, a Tragedy*.

Tragic Comedians, The, a novel by G. Meredith (q.v.) (1880).

Traherne, THOMAS (1636?-1674), a writer of religious works, both in prose and verse, 'Christian Ethics' (1675), 'Poems' (1903), and 'Centuries of Meditation' (1908), marked by originality of thought and by a remarkably musical quality. The poems were discovered in manuscript by Bertram Dobell and edited by him; they show striking anticipation of Wordsworth and Blake.

Traitor, The, a tragedy by James Shirley (q.v.), produced in 1631 and printed in 1635.

Trajan (MARCUS ULPIUS TRAIANUS), Roman emperor, A.D. 98-117. His victories are commemorated on TRAJAN'S COLUMN in Rome.

Transcendental, a word that signifies, in the philosophy of Kant (q.v.), not derived from experience but concerned with the presuppositions of experience; pertaining to the general theory of the nature of experience or knowledge.

Transcendental Club, founded in America in 1836 by Emerson (q.v.) and others, the embodiment of a movement of thought, philosophical, religious, social, and economic, produced in New England between 1830 and 1850 by the spirit of revolutionary Europe, German philosophy, and Wordsworth, Coleridge, and Carlyle (qq.v.).

Trapbois, and his daughter MARTHA, characters in Scott's 'The Fortunes of Nigel' (q.v.).

Traveller, The, a poem by Goldsmith (q.v.) (1764), his earliest production under his own name. It is dedicated and addressed to his brother, a country clergyman. The author, in the character of a traveller, places himself on the summit of the Alps, and compares social and political conditions in the countries that he sees, noting the inconveniences of each, and endeavouring to show that there may be equal happiness in other states though differently governed from our own. Johnson contributed nine lines to the poem, ll. 420, 429-34, 437-8.

Travels in France, a record of travel in that country during the years 1787-90, by A. Young (q.v.) (1792). Visiting France shortly before and during the Revolution, Young draws attention to the defective social and economic conditions of the *ancien régime*.

Travels with a Donkey, see *Stevenson (R. L.)*.

Treasure Island, a romance by R. L. Stevenson (q.v.), published in book form in 1883.

The narrator is the lad, Jim Hawkins, whose mother keeps the 'Admiral Benbow' somewhere on the coast in the west of England, in the 18th cent. An old buccaneer takes up his quarters at the inn. He has in his chest information, in the shape of a manuscript map, as to the whereabouts of Capt. Flint's treasure. Of this his former confederates are determined to obtain possession. But Jim Hawkins outwits them, secures the map, and delivers it to Squire Trelawney. The squire and his friend Dr. Livesey set off for Treasure Island in the 'Hispaniola' schooner, taking Jim with them. Some of the crew are the squire's faithful dependants, but the majority are old buccaneers recruited by the plausible one-legged villain, Long John Silver. Their design to seize the ship and kill the squire's party is discovered by Jim, and after a series of thrilling fights and adventures, is completely thwarted; and the squire, with the help of the marooned pirate, Ben Gunn, secures the treasure.

Treatise of Human Nature, A, a philosophical work by Hume (q.v.) (1739-40).

It is convenient to consider this work, composed before the author was five-and-twenty, together with the 'Enquiry concerning Human Understanding' (1748) and the 'Enquiry concerning the Principles of Morals' (1751), which are recastings of the earlier treatise in the light of a maturer judgement. Hume's purpose in these is to correct and complete the philosophy of Locke and Berkeley as set forth in the 'Essay concerning Human Understanding' (q.v.), and in the earlier works of Berkeley (q.v.). Whereas his predecessors had maintained a distinction between reason on the one hand and the effects of sensation and experience on the other, Hume endeavours to show that our 'rational' judgements are simply impressions associated by custom, expectations resulting from experience. The problem of knowledge, in his treatment, becomes the problem of causation, instead of the problem of substance.

The second and third books of the 'Treatise' are occupied with an examination of the passions, and with morals. As regards the latter, he rejects the view that the distinction between right and wrong is one of reason. It derives from a sentiment of approval or disapproval of an action which arises in one's breast. At the same time Hume comes finally to the conclusion that the happiness of others and the happiness of oneself are not discordant but harmonious aims.

Trelawny, of the ballad, see *Hawker*.

Trelawny, EDWARD JOHN (1792-1881) the friend of Shelley, who was present at Leghorn when Shelley was drowned, was author of the remarkable 'Adventures of a Younger Son' (1831), and of 'Records of Shelley, Byron, and the Author' (1858).

Trench, RICHARD CHENEVIX (1807-86), dean of Westminster and archbishop of Dublin. He was the author of works dealing with history and literature, poetry, divinity, and philology. As a philologist, and notably by his 'The Study of Words' (1851), he popularized the scientific study of language. His sonnets, lyrics, and hymns show much poetic ability.

Trent, the detective in E. C. Bentley's (q.v.) 'Trent's Last Case'.

Trent, FRED, a character in Dickens's 'The Old Curiosity Shop' (q.v.). His sister is 'Little Nell'.

Trent, COUNCIL OF, see *Council of Trent*.

Trevelyan, GEORGE MACAULAY (1876-

1962), son of Sir G. O. Trevelyan (q.v.), appointed Regius professor of modern history at Cambridge in 1927 and Master of Trinity in 1940. He was author of three remarkable works on Garibaldi, 'Garibaldi's Defence of the Roman Republic' (1907), 'Garibaldi and the Thousand' (1909), and 'Garibaldi and the Making of Italy' (1911); also of a 'History of England' (1926), 'English Social History' (1944), etc.

Trevelyan, SIR GEORGE OTTO (1838–1928), nephew of Lord Macaulay (q.v.), entered parliament in 1865 and held at various times important offices. The first of his great works, 'The Life and Letters of Lord Macaulay', appeared in 1876; the second, 'The Early History of Charles James Fox', in 1880, which gives a striking picture of social and political England in the later part of the 18th cent.

Trevisa, JOHN DE (c. 1340–1401), translated Higden's 'Polychronicon' (see *Higden*) in 1387, adding an introduction and short continuation, one of the early examples of English prose, written in a vigorous and colloquial style.

Triads, in ancient Welsh literature, verses celebrating famous subjects of tradition; a form of composition characterized by an arrangement of subjects or statements in groups of three. There are satirical allusions to these 'triads' in Peacock's 'The Misfortunes of Elphin'.

Triamond, in Spenser's 'Faerie Queene', IV. iii and iv, the Knight of Friendship.

Tribrach, a foot consisting of three short syllables.

Tribulation Wholesome, a character in Jonson's 'The Alchemist' (q.v.).

Trilby, a novel by Du Maurier (q.v.) (1894).

It is the tragic story of Trilby O'Ferrall, an amiable artist's model in Paris, with whom various young English art-students fall in love. She becomes a famous singer under the mesmeric influence of Svengali, a German-Polish musician, but loses her voice when the latter dies, and herself languishes and dies soon after.

Trilogy, in Greek antiquities, a series of three tragedies (originally connected in subject) performed at Athens at the festival of Dionysus. Hence any series of three related dramatic or other literary works.

Trim, CORPORAL, one of the principal characters in Sterne's 'Tristram Shandy' (q.v.).

Trimalchio, a type of ostentatious extravagance and gluttony. He figures in an incident in the 'Satyricon' of Petronius (q.v.).

Trimeter, see *Metre* and *Iambic*.

Trimmer, originally applied to one who trims between opposing parties in politics; hence, one who inclines as his interest dictates. But Lord Halifax in his 'Character of a Trimmer' (1682) accepted the nickname in the sense of 'one who keeps even the ship of state'.

Trinculo, a jester in Shakespeare's 'The Tempest' (q.v.).

Triolet, a poem of eight lines, with two rhymes, in which the first line is repeated as the fourth and seventh, and the second as the eighth.

Triplet, three successive lines of verse rhyming together, occasionally introduced among heroic couplets, e.g. by Dryden.

Trip to Scarborough, A, a comedy by R. B. Sheridan (q.v.) produced in 1777.

The plot is that of Vanbrugh's 'The Relapse' with some modifications.

Trismegistus, see *Hermes Trismegistus*.

Tristan l'Hermite, a character in Scott's 'Quentin Durward' (q.v.).

Tristan und Isolde, a music-drama by R. Wagner (q.v.).

Tristram. The story of Tristram and his love for Iseult is much older than the parallel tale of Launcelot and Guinevere, and in its earlier form was not connected with the Arthurian cycle.

In Malory's 'Morte Darthur', Tristram is son of Meliodas, king of Lyonesse. Tristram is sent to Ireland to be cured of a wound. Owing to his skill with the harp he is received with favour by the king and is placed in the care of his daughter, La

Beale Isoud. Tristram and she fall in love. The queen discovers that their guest is the knight who slew her brother, and Tristram leaves the court after exchanging vows of fidelity with Isoud, and returns to Cornwall. After a time King Mark, being jealous of Tristram and desirous to destroy him, sends him to Ireland to ask the hand of La Beale Isoud, whose praises he has heard from Tristram. Tristram, having rendered an important service to the king of Ireland, asks as reward the hand of Isoud for King Mark. Isoud and Bragwaine, her attendant, set off with Tristram. Mark and Isoud are married, but the relations between Tristram and Isoud continue, till the lovers are betrayed to Mark. Tristram leaves the court of Mark and, fighting for King Howel of Brittany, falls in love with Isoud la Blanche Mains and marries her, 'almost forsaking' Isoud of Ireland. However, on the invitation of the latter he returns privily to Cornwall. He is banished thence and is welcomed at Arthur's court, where he shows his prowess in many contests. Finally it is stated that Mark slew Tristram as he sat harping before La Beale Isoud.

But a more romantic ending is given in one of the manuscripts and has been adopted and developed by later poets. Tristram, in Brittany, is wounded by a poisoned arrow. Feeling that he is dying, he sends a messenger for Isoud of Ireland. If she comes, the ship that brings her is to set a white sail, if not, a black. Isoud of Brittany overhears, and when the ship returns tells Tristram the sail is black. Tristram in despair turns his face to the wall and dies (cf. the story of Theseus, q.v., and Aegeus). Isoud of Ireland finds her lover dead, lies down beside him, and dies.

Tristram and Iseult, a poem by M. Arnold (q.v.) (1852).

The subject is the death of Tristram (q.v.) in Brittany.

Tristram of Lyonesse, a romance in couplets by Swinburne (q.v.) (1882), which tells the tale of Tristram (q.v.).

Tristram Shandy, The Life and Opinions of, a novel by Sterne (q.v.), of which vols. i and ii appeared in 1760, vols. iii to vi in 1761-2, vols. vii and viii in 1765, and vol. ix in 1767.

In spite of the title, the book gives us very little of the life, and nothing of the opinions, of the nominal hero, who gets born only in vol. iv, and breeched in vol. vi, and then disappears from the story. Instead we have a group of humorous figures: Walter Shandy of Shandy Hall, Tristram's father; 'my Uncle Toby', his brother, wounded in the groin at the siege of Namur, whose hobby is the science of attacking fortified towns; Corporal Trim, his servant, wounded in the knee at Landen, devoted to his master. Behind these three major figures, the minor characters, Yorick the parson, Dr. Slop, Mrs. Shandy, and the widow Wadman, play more elusive parts.

The book is chiefly occupied with exposing the author's own personality and whimsical imaginations.

Triton, a sea deity, son of Poseidon (Neptune) and Amphitrite.

Triumph of Life, The, an uncompleted poem by P. B. Shelley (q.v.), in *terza rima*, published after his death, an allegory of which the sense is obscure. The poet sees a vision of the human multitude, and in the midst of it the Triumph passes, the chariot of Life the Conqueror, trampling on youth, and dragging others in chains. The vision passes to the allegory of a single life, which after a youth of aspirations, succumbs to the same mystery.

Triumph of Mammon, see *God and Mammon*.

Trivia, or The Art of Walking the Streets of London, a poem by J. Gay (q.v.), in three books (1716).

In this entertaining work, on the model of Swift's 'City Shower', the author takes the reader through the streets of London, first by day and then by night. The poem is a mine of information on 18th-cent. manners.

Trivium, in the Middle Ages, the lower

division of the seven liberal arts, comprising grammar, logic, and rhetoric. Cf. *Quadrivium*.

Trochee, a metrical foot consisting of a long followed by a short syllable; in accentual verse, of an accented followed by an unaccented syllable.

Troglodyte, a cave-dweller. The ancients (Pliny, Strabo, etc.) mention races of Troglodytes in Ethiopia and elsewhere.

Troilus and Cressida. This story has no basis in classical antiquity but was developed from an episode in the 'Roman de Troie' of Benoît de Sainte-Maure, by Guido da Colonna in the 'Historia Trojana', by Boccaccio in 'Filostrato', by Chaucer, by Lydgate in his 'Troy-Book', by Henryson, by Shakespeare, and by Dryden.

The first of these makes *Briseida* (Homer's Briseis) the daughter of Calchas (see *Briseis* and *Chryseis*), and Troilus and Diomede her successive lovers. *Briseida* was changed to *Griseida* by Boccaccio, and to *Cryseyde* by Chaucer. The story is that of the love of Troilus, a son of Priam, for Cressida, daughter of Calchas the priest, who, foreknowing the fall of Troy, has fled to the Greeks but left his daughter in Troy. Cressida returns the love of Troilus, and Pandarus acts as go-between. But an exchange of prisoners is arranged and Cressida is sent to the Greek camp, where Diomede urges his suit and is finally preferred to Troilus. Troilus and Diomede meet in the field but neither kills the other. Troilus is at last killed by Achilles.

Chaucer's poem, 'Troylus and Cryseyde', probably written between 1372 and 1386, contains some 8,200 lines of rhyme-royal; in it the poet enriched the story as he got it from Boccaccio by the vivid and humorous figure of Pandarus and by the development of the character of Cressida.

Shakespeare's Cressida, on the other hand, is 'a giddy girl, an unpractised jilt, who falls in love with Troilus, as she afterwards deserts him, from mere levity and thoughtlessness of temper' (Hazlitt).

Shakespeare's play, produced probably in 1602, and printed in 1609, presents, as background to the story, the principal characters of the 'Iliad': Agamemnon, Ajax, Ulysses, Nestor, Achilles sulking in his tent, the railer Thersites; and on the Trojan side, Priam, Aeneas, Hector and Andromache, Paris, and Helen. The death of Hector at the hands of Achilles is summarily dealt with.

Trojan Horse, THE, see *Horse* (*The Trojan*).

Trojan War, see *Troy*.

Troll, in Scandinavian mythology, one of a race of supernatural beings formerly conceived as giants, now in Denmark and Sweden, as dwarfs or imps.

Trollope, ANTHONY (1815–82), entered the General Post Office as a clerk in 1834 and proved himself an active and valuable public servant. His first novels were: 'The Macdermots of Ballycloran' (1847) and 'The Kellys and the O'Kellys' (1848). 'The Warden' (1855), the first of the Barsetshire series, was a moderate success. But from this point his popularity as a novelist steadily increased. His output was considerable, having regard to the fact that his official work was arduous; it was achieved by a mechanical regularity in his writing which he has himself described. His chief remaining novels were: 'Barchester Towers' (1857), 'Framley Parsonage' (1861), 'Orley Farm' (1862), 'The Last Chronicle of Barset' (1867), 'Phineas Finn' (1869), 'Phineas Redux' (1874). Trollope also published various books of travel and a monograph on Thackeray (1879). His interesting 'Autobiography' appeared in 1883.

Trollope, FRANCES (1780–1863), *née* Milton, the mother of A. Trollope (q.v.). When her family were reduced to poverty she supported them by writing novels, of which the best known is 'The Widow Barnaby' (1838).

Trompart, in Spenser's 'Faerie Queene', II. iii, attends Braggadochio (q.v.) as his squire, and with him is finally exposed and beaten out of court.

Trophee, an unknown writer mentioned by Chaucer in 'The Monk's Tale' (l. 127). A marginal note in the Ellesmere and Hengwrt MSS. says, 'Ille vates Chaldeorum Tropheus'.

Trotcosey, in Scott's 'The Antiquary' (q.v.), a favourite subject of reference by Jonathan Oldbuck; the house of Monkbarns stood on the lands of the ancient abbey of Trotcosey.

Trotter, JOB, in Dickens's 'The Pickwick Papers' (q.v.), Jingle's servant.

Trotwood, BETSEY, a character in Dickens's 'David Copperfield' (q.v.).

Troubadours, poets composing and singing in Old Provençal during the 12th and 13th cents. They were famous for their mastery of verse forms in the lyric, and for the conception of courtly love (q.v.) which is first found in their poetry. William count of Poitiers and duke of Aquitaine is the first known troubadour; Jaufre Rudel invented the theme of the 'distant love'; Bernart de Ventadour was acknowledged as the most truly lyric in inspiration, while Arnaut Daniel was praised by Dante as the finest craftsman among the troubadours. (See also *Provençal*.)

Trouvères, poets composing narrative, dramatic, satiric, lyric, and comic verse in the north of France during the Old French period. They might be professional entertainers, *clercs* or, when courtly society developed, feudal lords composing the fashionable courtly lyrics. Chrétien de Troyes (q.v.) was a *clerc*; Conon de Béthune was a courtly poet, a noble of Picardy who took a prominent part in the Fourth Crusade.

Troy or ILIUM, a city that stood near the Hellespont and the river Scamander in the NW. of Asia Minor. According to legend, as related by Homer in his 'Iliad', Troy was the capital of King Priam, and was for ten years besieged by the Greeks. See *Agamemnon, Menelaus, Helen, Paris, Achilles, Horse (The Trojan)*, etc.

Troy, SERGEANT, a character in Hardy's 'Far from the Madding Crowd' (q.v.).

Troy-book, a poem in five books, in tensyllable couplets, written by Lydgate (q.v.) (1412–20). It tells the 'noble storye' of Troy, following the Latin history of Guido da Colonna (which had drawn largely on the apocryphal tales of Dictys Cretensis and Dares Phrygius, qq.v.), and serves in some sort as an introduction to the story of the Trojan settlement of England by Brutus, great grandson of Aeneas, told by Geoffrey of Monmouth and Wace. In the third book, in connection with the story of Troilus and Cressida, he introduces a tribute to his 'maister Chaucer'.

True Law of Free Monarchies, The, a political treatise attributed to James I (1603), written to combat the Calvinistic theory of government advocated by George Buchanan. It sets forth the doctrine of the divine right of kings, and of the king's responsibility to God alone.

Trulliber, PARSON, a character in Fielding's 'Joseph Andrews' (q.v.).

Trumpet-Major, The, a novel by Hardy (q.v.) (1880), one of Hardy's simplest and pleasantest tales, with hardly a trace of irony or bitterness. It is set in the time of the Napoleonic wars.

Trumpington, THE MILLER OF, the miller in 'The Reeve's Tale' in Chaucer's 'The Canterbury Tales' (q.v.).

Tuck, FRIAR, see *Friar Tuck*.

Tulkinghorn, MR., a character in Dickens's 'Bleak House' (q.v.).

Tulliver, MR. and MRS., and TOM and MAGGIE, the principal characters in G. Eliot's 'The Mill on the Floss' (q.v.).

Tully, see *Cicero*.

Tunning of Elynour Rumming, The, a poem by Skelton (q.v.), a vigorous Hogarthian description of contemporary low life.

Tupman, TRACY, a character in Dickens's 'The Pickwick Papers' (q.v.).

Tupper, MARTIN FARQUHAR (1810–89), published in 1838–42 his 'Proverbial Philosophy', commonplace maxims and reflections couched in a rhythmical form, which achieved extraordinary popularity.

Turberville or **TURBERVILE**, **GEORGE** (1540?-1610?), published 'Epitaphs, Epigrams, Songs, and Sonets' (1567), 'Poems describing ... Russia' (1568), 'The Booke of Faulconrie' (1575), and various translations from Ovid and modern Italians. He familiarized the employment of Italian models, and shows the influence of Surrey and Wyatt (qq.v.).

Turgenev, **IVAN SERGEYEVICH** (1818-83), Russian novelist. His novels examine, in personal terms, social and political problems of 19th-cent. Russia. He lived much abroad, was more 'Western' in spirit than most major Russian writers and received a correspondingly more immediate recognition outside Russia. His most important novels are 'A Nest of Gentlefolk' (1859), 'Fathers and Sons' (1862), 'Smoke' (1867), and 'Virgin Soil' (1877).

Turgot, **ANNE ROBERT JACQUES** (1727-81), an able financier and one of the *Physiocrats* (q.v.).

Turk Gregory, in Shakespeare's '1 Henry IV', v. iii, where Falstaff compares his deeds in arms with those of 'Turk Gregory', is a facetious combination of the characters of 'terrible Turk' and militant pope (Gregory VII).

Turn of the Screw, The, a masterpiece of supernatural fiction by Henry James (q.v.), published in 1898.

Turner, **CHARLES TENNYSON**, see *Tennyson Turner*.

Turner, **JOSEPH MALLORD WILLIAM** (1775-1851), landscape painter. He exhibited at the Royal Academy from 1791, becoming an Academician in 1802. After studying the Dutch landscape painters and Claude, he developed an interest in romantic subjects, such as storms at sea and mountains. The first volume of Ruskin's 'Modern Painters' (q.v.) was written to defend Turner against criticism, and it assured his reputation.

Turnus, a king of the Rutuli, and a brave warrior, who fought against Aeneas. He

was killed by Aeneas in single combat (Bk. XII of the 'Aeneid').

Turpin, **RICHARD** (?1706-39), the famous highwayman, was arrested for horsestealing and hanged at York. He figures in Ainsworth's 'Rookwood'.

Turveydrop, father and son, characters in Dickens's 'Bleak House' (q.v.).

Tusher, **THE REVD. THOMAS**, chaplain to the Castlewood family in Thackeray's 'Esmond' (q.v.), subsequently a bishop and the first husband of Beatrix Esmond (see *Virginians*).

Tusitála, a Samoan name, meaning 'teller of tales', for R. L. Stevenson (q.v.).

Tusser, **THOMAS** (1524?-1580), agricultural writer and poet, published his 'Hundreth good pointes of husbandrie' in 1557 (amplified in later editions) in verse of quaint and pointed expression. It is a collection of instructions on farming, gardening, and housekeeping, together with humorous and wise maxims on conduct in general.

Tutivillus, see *Titivil*.

Twain, **MARK**, see *Clemens (S. L.)*.

Tweedledum and Tweedledee, the expression arose from an 18th-cent. epigram (by Byrom?) on Handel and Buononcini. Tweedledum and Tweedledee figure in L. Carroll's 'Through the Looking-Glass', where they engage in a notable battle.

Twelfth Day, 6 Jan., the twelfth day from the Nativity, also called the feast of the Epiphany, was formerly celebrated as the closing day of the Christmas festivities, with special reference, some think, to the Magi (q.v.) or Wise Men of the East.

Twelfth Night, Or what you will, a comedy by Shakespeare, produced probably in 1600-1, and first printed in the folio of 1623. The story was probably taken from an English rendering of a tale in Cinthio's 'Hecatommithi', or from Bandello or Belleforest.

Sebastian and Viola, twin brother and sister, and closely resembling one another, are separated in a shipwreck off the coast of Illyria. Viola, brought to shore in a boat, and disguised as a youth Cesario, takes service as page with Duke Orsino, who is in love with the lady Olivia. The latter rejects the duke's suit and will not admit him to her presence. Orsino makes a confidant of Cesario and sends her to press his suit on Olivia, much to the distress of Cesario, who has fallen in love with Orsino. Olivia in turn falls in love with Cesario. Sebastian and Antonio, captain of the ship that had rescued Sebastian, now arrive in Illyria. Cesario, challenged to a duel by Sir Andrew Ague-cheek, a rejected suitor of Olivia, is rescued from her predicament by Antonio, who takes her for Sebastian. Antonio, being arrested at that moment for an old offence, claims from Cesario a purse that he had entrusted to Sebastian, is denied it, and haled off to prison. Olivia coming upon the true Sebastian, takes him for Cesario, invites him to her house, presses her suit on him, finds him not unwilling, and marries him out of hand. Orsino comes to visit Olivia. Antonio is brought before him, claims Cesario as the youth he has rescued from the sea; while Olivia claims Cesario as her husband. The duke, deeply wounded, is bidding farewell to Olivia and the 'young dissembler' Cesario, when the arrival of the true Sebastian clears up the confusion. The duke, disappointed of Olivia, and becoming conscious of the love that Viola (as Cesario) has betrayed, turns his affection to her, and they are married.

The humour, which abounds in the play, is chiefly provided by the sub-ordinate characters, who have no essential connection with the plot, Sir Toby Belch, uncle to Olivia; Sir Andrew Aguecheek, his friend; Malvolio, the pompous conceited steward to Olivia; Maria, her attendant; and the clown, Feste. The play contains one of the most beautiful of Shakespeare's songs, 'Come away, come away, death'.

Twitcher, JEMMY, in Gay's 'The Beggar's Opera' (q.v.), one of Captain Macheath's associates, who betrays him.

Two Drovers, The, a short story by Sir W. Scott (q.v.), one of the 'Chronicles of the Canongate' (1827).

Two Foscari, The, a historical tragedy by Lord Byron (q.v.) (1821).

Two Gentlemen of Verona, The, a comedy by Shakespeare (q.v.), one of his early works, probably of 1594-5, first printed in the folio of 1623. The story is taken from Montemayor's pastoral romance 'Diana'.

The two gentlemen of Verona are the friends Valentine and Proteus. Proteus is in love with Julia, who returns his affection. Valentine leaves Verona for Milan 'to see the wonders of the world abroad', and there falls in love with Silvia, the duke of Milan's daughter. Presently, Proteus is sent also on his travels, and exchanges vows of constancy with Julia before starting. But arriving at Milan, Proteus is at once captivated by Silvia, and, betraying both his friend and his former love, reveals to the duke the intention of Valentine to carry off Silvia. Valentine is banished and becomes a captain of robbers, and Proteus continues his court of Silvia. Meanwhile Julia, pining for Proteus, comes to Milan dressed as a boy and takes service as Proteus' page, unrecognized by him. Silvia, to escape marriage with Thurio, her father's choice, leaves Milan to rejoin Valentine, is captured by robbers and rescued from them by Proteus. Proteus is violently pressing his suit on Silvia when Valentine comes on the scene. Proteus is struck with remorse, and his contrition is such that Valentine is im-pelled to surrender Silvia to him, to the dismay of Proteus' page, the disguised Julia. She swoons, and is then recognized by Proteus, and the discovery of her con-stancy wins back his love. The duke and Thurio arrive. Thurio shows cowardice in face of Valentine's determined attitude, and the duke, approving Valentine's spirit, accords him Silvia. Launce, the clownish servant of Proteus, and his dog Crab 'the sourest natured dog that lives', provide some drollery.

Two Noble Kinsmen, The, a play by J. Fletcher (q.v.), probably with the collaboration of Shakespeare, printed in 1634.

The play, which deals with the story of Palamon and Arcite, follows fairly closely the story as told by Chaucer in 'The Knight's Tale' (see *Canterbury Tales*).

Two on a Tower, a novel by Hardy (q.v.) (1882).

Two Years Ago, a novel by C. Kingsley (q.v.) (1857), dealing with some of the moral problems and material evils of contemporary English life, notably the need for sanitary reform.

Tybalt, a character in Shakespeare's 'Romeo and Juliet' (q.v.). For the allusion in the play to cats in connection with his name, see *Tybert*.

Tybert or TIBERT, the cat in 'Reynard the Fox' (q.v.). The name is the same as Tybalt (see the dialogue between Mercutio and Tybalt in Shakespeare, 'Romeo and Juliet', III. i).

Tyburn, the name of an ancient manor, north-west of the old city of London, celebrated as the place of execution of malefactors until 1783.

Tyler, WAT (*d.* 1381), the leader of the peasants' revolt of 1381; the subject of a drama by Southey.

Tyndale, WILLIAM (*d.* 1536), the translator of the Bible, formed the project of translating the Scriptures into the vernacular, but finding difficulties in England, went to Hamburg for the purpose. He visited Luther at Wittenberg, and commenced printing his translation of the

N.T. at Cologne in 1525. He completed the work at Worms and introduced copies into England, which were denounced by the bishops and destroyed. He himself was arrested for heresy, imprisoned at Vilvorde in 1535, and strangled and burnt at the stake there, in spite of Cromwell's intercession. Tyndale was one of the most remarkable of the Reformation leaders; his original writings show sound scholarship, but his translation of the Bible, the accuracy of which has been endorsed by the translators of the Authorized Version, is his surest title to fame.

Typee, see *Melville* (*H.*).

Typhon or TYPHOEUS, in Greek mythology, a terrible monster, son of Tartarus and Ge, and father of various other monsters.

Tyr, see *Tiu*.

Tyrannic Love, or *The Royal Martyr*, a heroic play in rhymed couplets by Dryden (q.v.) (1669).

The play, which contains some beautiful passages, is marred by absurdities, which provided material for ridicule in 'The Rehearsal' (q.v.).

Tyrtaeus, a poet who lived at Sparta about the middle of the 7th cent. B.C., and by his war-songs and elegiac lays encouraged the Spartans in their war with the Messenians (685-668 B.C.).

Tyrwhitt, THOMAS (1730-86), remembered for his edition and exposure of the 'Rowley Poems' (see *Chatterton*), in the authenticity of which he originally believed; for his 'Observations . . . upon . . . Shakespeare' (1766); and still more for his studies of Chaucer, whose 'Canterbury Tales' he edited in 1775-8.

U

Udall or **UVEDALE, NICHOLAS** (1505–56), dramatist and scholar, successively headmaster of Eton and Westminster. He was author of 'Ralph Roister Doister' (q.v.), the earliest known English comedy. He translated selections from Terence and other works, and wrote Latin plays on sacred subjects.

Udolpho, Mysteries of, see *Mysteries of Udolpho*.

Ulfilas or **WULFILA** (A.D. 311–81), a Christian of Cappadocian origin, was consecrated bishop of the Arian Visigoths in 341. He translated the Bible into Gothic from the Greek. Fragments of this translation survive, and are of great value to the philological study of the Germanic languages.

Ulrica, in Scott's 'Ivanhoe' (q.v.), the old sibyl who sets fire to the castle of Torquilstone and perishes in the flames.

Ultima Thule, see *Thule*.

Ultramontane, lit. 'beyond the mountain', applied to those who hold extreme views on the Pope's authority.

Ulysses, see *Odysseus*.

Ulysses, a novel by James Joyce (q.v.), first published in Paris in 1922. Copies of the first English edition were burned by the New York post office authorities, and the Folkestone Customs Authorities seized the second edition in 1923. Various later editions appeared abroad and, after the United States District Court found the book not obscene in 1933, an unlimited edition appeared in America and in England in 1937.

The novel deals with the events of one day in Dublin in June 1904. The principal characters are Stephen Dedalus (the hero of Joyce's earlier 'Portrait of the Artist as a Young Man'); Leopold Bloom, a Jewish advertisement canvasser; and his wife Molly. The plot follows the wanderings of Stephen and Bloom through Dublin, and their eventual meeting. The last chapter is a monologue by Molly Bloom. The various chapters roughly correspond to the episodes of Homer's 'Odyssey': Stephen representing Telemachus, Bloom Odysseus, and Molly Penelope. In the course of the story a public bath, a funeral, a newspaper office, a library, public houses, a maternity hospital, and a brothel are visited. The style is highly allusive and employs a variety of techniques, especially those of the stream of consciousness and of parody, and ranges from extreme realism to fantasy.

Umbriel, 'a dusky melancholy sprite' in Pope's 'The Rape of the Lock' (q.v.).

Una, in Bk. 1 of Spenser's 'Faerie Queene', typifies the true religion. She is separated from the Red Cross Knight (q.v.) of Holiness (the Anglican Church) by the wiles of Archimago (q.v.), but meets and is protected by a lion (England), until the latter is killed by Sansloy (see under Sansfoy), who carries Una off to a forest. She is rescued by fauns and satyrs, and is finally united to the Red Cross Knight.

Uncial, in connection with writing, is applied to letters having the large rounded forms (not joined to each other) characteristic of the chief Greek and Roman book script of the 4th to the 8th cents. The term is commonly explained as meaning originally 'letters of an inch long'.

Uncle Remus, see *Harris (J. C.)*.

Uncle Silas, a novel by Sheridan Le Fanu (q.v.), published in 1864.

Uncle Toby, MY, Capt. Shandy, uncle of the nominal hero of Sterne's 'Tristram Shandy' (q.v.).

Uncle Tom's Cabin, a novel by Harriet Beecher Stowe (q.v.), published in book form in 1852.

Uncommercial Traveller, The, a collection of tales and sketches of places and manners, and of institutions needing reform, by Charles Dickens (q.v.), issued in 1861 and 1866. It contains some of Dickens's best literary work.

Understanding, LORD, in Bunyan's 'Holy War' (q.v.), the lord mayor of Mansoul.

Under the Greenwood Tree, a novel by Hardy (q.v.) (1872), an idyll, set in the rustic scene of Mellstock village, of two young lovers, Dick Dewy and Fancy Day, the schoolmistress.

Underwoods, a collection of 'lesser poems' by Jonson (q.v.) (1640). It includes the famous poem to Shakespeare.

Unfortunate Traveller, The, or the Life of Jacke Wilton, a prose tale of adventure by T. Nash (q.v.) (1594), the earliest picaresque romance in English, and the most remarkable work of the kind before Defoe. The whole story is told with much spirit and wit.

Uniformity, ACT OF, passed in 1559, forbade the use of any form of public prayer other than the second prayer-book of Edward VI (with some modifications).

Unitarian, a member of a religious body that affirms the single personality of the Godhead, as opposed to believers in the Trinity.

Unities, THE, three principles of dramatic composition, viz. that a play should consist of one main action, occurring at one time (not longer than the play takes to perform), and in one place; expanded from Aristotle's 'Poetics' by 16th-cent. Italian critics, and by French classical dramatists of the 17th cent. The Unities were often modified; e.g. the time limit was extended to twenty-four hours, and the place to one house or town, rather than one room or street.

University Wits, name given to a group of Elizabethan playwrights of whom Nash, Greene, Lyly, and Lodge were the chief.

Unto This Last, four essays on economics by Ruskin (q.v.) (1860-2).

This was the earliest of Ruskin's economic treatises. He first deals with wages and employment, and discusses the nature of true wealth, to be distinguished from the riches obtained at the cost of making others poor. His final plea is for 'Not greater wealth, but simpler pleasure'.

Ruskin's views were derided at the time, but many of the reforms that he advocated have since been adopted.

Urania, the Muse (q.v.) of astronomy.

Uranian Aphrodite or URANIAN VENUS, the 'Heavenly Aphrodite', distinguished from APHRODITE PANDEMOS, the Aphrodite of the World, was the goddess of pure and ennobling love.

Uranus, the personification of the sky, the most ancient of the Greek gods and the first ruler of the universe. He married Ge, the earth, and was father of the Titans, including Cronos, who ousted him from his throne.

Urban, SYLVANUS, the pseudonym of E. Cave (q.v.), and, by succession, of the later editors of 'The Gentleman's Magazine'.

Uriah the Hittite, an officer in David's army, the husband of Bathsheba, whom David caused to be killed in battle (2 Sam. xi).

Uriel, one of the seven archangels enumerated in the 'Book of Enoch' (see under *Angel*). Milton ('Paradise Lost', iii. 690) makes him 'Regent of the Sun', beguiled by Satan in spite of his sharp sight.

Urizen, in the mystical poems of Blake (q.v.), a grim old giant, the symbol of restrictive morality, identified with Jehovah. Also a symbol of the bondage of man to the senses.

Urn Burial or *Hydriotaphia,* a treatise by Sir T. Browne (q.v.) (1658).

The point of departure is the discovery of some ancient sepulchral urns in Norfolk, which leads the author to consider the various modes of disposal of the dead recorded in history and practised in Britain, urns and their contents, funeral ceremonies, and immortality or annihilation. The tone is meditative and mystical, and the style reaches the highest level of rhetorical prose.

Ur of the Chaldees, the city where, according to the book of Genesis, Abraham settled, and whence he migrated northwards to Haran. Excavations by Sir Leonard Woolley have resulted in discoveries of great interest.

Urquhart or URCHARD, SIR THOMAS (1611–60), author and translator. He published a book of 'Epigrams' in 1641. He followed Prince Charles (later Charles II) to Worcester, where many of his manuscripts were destroyed by the Parliamentarians. He was imprisoned during 1651–2, and died abroad. His best-known work is a translation of the first three books of Rabelais (q.v.) (1653–93). He wrote a number of curious treatises on mathematics, linguistics, etc.

Ursula, ST., a British saint and martyr, daughter of a 'Christian British King'.

There is no mention of St. Ursula before the 10th cent., several hundred years after her supposed martyrdom. Details of the story appear in the 12th cent., and it is told by Geoffrey of Monmouth.

Usk, THOMAS (*d.* 1388), the author of 'The Testament of Love', formerly ascribed to Chaucer, was under-sheriff of London by Richard II's mandate in 1387, and was proceeded against by the 'Merciless' parliament in 1388 and executed. 'The Testament of Love' is an allegorical prose work written by Usk in prison to enlist sympathy.

Ussher, JAMES (1581–1656), archbishop of Armagh. He wrote much on theological subjects, and was learned in patristic literature and ancient Irish history. But his chief work is the 'Annales Veteris et Novi Testamenti', a chronological summary in Latin of the history of the world to Vespasian, of extraordinary critical quality.

Uther Pendragon, in the Arthurian legend, king of the Britons and father of Arthur (q.v.).

Utilitarianism, an essay by J. S. Mill (q.v.) (1861).

In this work, Mill, while accepting the Benthamite principle (see *Bentham*) that Utility, or the greatest happiness of the greatest number, is the foundation of morals, departs from it by maintaining that pleasures differ in kind or quality as well as in quantity, 'that some *kinds* of pleasure are more desirable and more valuable than others'; also by recognizing in 'the conscientious feelings of mankind' an 'internal sanction' to be added to Bentham's 'external sanctions'.

Utopia, the principal literary work of Sir T. More (q.v.), is a speculative political essay, written in Latin (1516). The subject is the search for the best possible form of government. More meets at Antwerp a traveller, one Raphael Hythloday, who has discovered 'Utopia', 'Nowhere land'. Communism is there the general law, a national system of education is extended to men and women alike, and the freest toleration of religion is recognized. The work at once became popular, and was translated into English in 1551, and into French (in 1530), German, Italian, and Spanish.

Utrecht, PEACE OF, the peace concluded in 1713, which terminated the War of the Spanish Succession.

Uzziel, one of the angels. In Milton's 'Paradise Lost', iv. 781–2, he is 'next in power' to Gabriel.

V

Vae Victis!, Latin, 'Woe to the vanquished!', the exclamation attributed to Brennus, the Gaulish conqueror of Rome (390 B.C.) (Livy, v. 48).

Valdarno (*Val d'Arno*), the valley of the Arno, in which Florence is situated, referred to by Milton in 'Paradise Lost', i. 290.

Valentine, one of the 'Two Gentlemen of Verona' in Shakespeare's play (q.v.).

Valentine and Orson, an early French romance, which has been attached to the Carolingian cycle.

The story appeared in English about 1550. A ballad in Percy's 'Reliques' deals with it.

Valentine's Day, ST., 14 Feb., on which day two martyrs of the name were executed, one a Roman priest, the other a bishop of Terni. There was an ancient practice among young people in England of choosing, by lot or otherwise, on St. Valentine's day, a sweetheart or a special friend for the ensuing year, and of sending a present to the person so chosen. Its origin is obscure. A rural tradition that birds choose their mates on the day in question is referred to by Chaucer ('The Parlement of Foules', 309), by Shakespeare ('A Midsummer Night's Dream', IV. i), and by Herrick in 'Hesperides'.

Valentinian, a tragedy by J. Fletcher (q.v.), produced between 1610 and 1614.

Valerian, the husband of St. Cecilia, whose story is told in Chaucer's 'The Second Nun's Tale' (see *Canterbury Tales*).

Valhalla, in Scandinavian mythology, a hall in Gladsheim (the residence of Odin), destined for the reception of dead heroes.

Vali, in Scandinavian mythology, the youngest son of Odin, who avenges Balder by slaying Hödur (qq.v.), the two deaths

perhaps symbolizing the changes of the seasons. He is one of the survivors of Ragnarök (q.v.).

Valkyries, THE, in Scandinavian mythology, the messenger maidens of Odin. Their special function was to kill the heroes selected for death in battle, and to conduct them when dead to Valhalla.

Valley of Humiliation, THE, in Bunyan's 'The Pilgrim's Progress' (q.v.), the place where Christian encounters Apollyon.

Valley of the Shadow of Death, THE, see Ps. xxiii. 4. Christian in 'The Pilgrim's Progress' (q.v.) passes through it.

Vallombrosa, a valley some twenty miles east of Florence, referred to by Milton in 'Paradise Lost', i. 303.

Vallon, ANNETTE (see under *Wordsworth, W.*).

Vamp, MR., in Peacock's 'Melincourt' (q.v.), a caricature of Gifford (q.v.).

Vanbrugh, SIR JOHN (1664–1726), dramatist and architect. In 1696 he produced 'The Relapse, or Virtue in Danger' with immense success, and 'The Provok'd Wife' in the following year. His other principal comedies are 'The Confederacy' (1705) and 'The Provok'd Husband', which he left unfinished and Cibber (q.v.) completed and brought out in 1728. As a playwright he offers a strong contrast to his contemporary, Congreve, in that he paid no attention to style. He wrote as he talked. He, together with Congreve, was specially attacked by Collier (q.v.) in his 'Short View'.

Vanbrugh's first building was Castle Howard, 1699–1726. This already shows the grandeur and dramatic quality of his style, which reaches its climax in Blenheim Palace (q.v.). Hawksmoor (q.v.) assisted him in many of his projects.

Vance, PHILO, the detective in a series of stories of crime by the American author,

Van Dine (Willard Huntington Wright, 1888-1939).

Vancouver, GEORGE (1758-98), explorer, accompanied James Cook on his second voyage, and was subsequently sent on a voyage of discovery to Australia and the North Pacific (1791-5). His 'Voyage of Discovery to the N. Pacific' was published posthumously in 1798.

Vandals, a Germanic tribe which in the 4th and 5th cents. A.D. invaded western Europe, and established settlements in various parts of it, finally in 428-9 migrating to northern Africa. In the year 455 their king, Genseric, led a marauding expedition against Rome, which he took and sacked. The Vandals were overthrown by Belisarius in 533; this was a great misfortune for Christendom, for it let in the Muslims in the 7th cent.; and these, not the Vandals, completed the ruin of Roman Africa and Mauretania.

Van Dyck, see *Dyck* (*Sir A. v.*).

Vanessa, Swift's name for Esther Vanhomrigh. See *Swift*.

Van Eyck, JAN, see *Eyck* (*J. v.*).

Van Gogh, VINCENT, see *Gogh* (*V. v.*).

Vanhomrigh, ESTHER (1690-1723), see *Swift*.

Vanity Fair, in Bunyan's 'The Pilgrim's Progress' (q.v.), a fair set up by Beelzebub, Apollyon, and Legion, in the town Vanity, through which pilgrims passed on their way to the Eternal City.

Vanity Fair, a novel by Thackeray (q.v.), published in monthly numbers in 1847-8.

The novel is principally concerned with the parallel careers of two strongly contrasted characters: Rebecca (Becky) Sharp, clever, unscrupulous, and courageous, and Amelia Sedley, a pretty, gentle, unintelligent creature, whose father is a rich man of business. The pair are brought together as girls at Miss Pinkerton's Academy. We follow Becky through her attempt to capture the fat Jos Sedley, Amelia's brother, to the home of the dirty, cynical, old Sir Pitt Crawley, where she is engaged as governess and captivates Sir Pitt himself and his rich sister Miss Craw-

ley. The baronet on the death of his wife proposes to her, and brings to light the fact that Becky has overreached herself by getting secretly married to Rawdon, Sir Pitt's second son and the favourite of Miss Crawley; a revelation that infuriates Sir Pitt and Miss Crawley, and loses Rawdon his aunt's inheritance.

Meanwhile Amelia's father is ruined by speculations, and her intended marriage with a young officer, George Osborne, is forbidden by Osborne's purse-proud father. Amelia is heartbroken at the desertion of George, a worthless fellow whom she blindly adores. Captain Dobbin, George's fellow-officer, her honest and unselfish worshipper, brings George to a sense of the shabbiness of his conduct, and the marriage takes place in defiance of old Osborne, who utterly repudiates his son. Then follows the campaign of Waterloo, and the chief actors are brought together at Brussels, where George, before being killed in the battle, engages in an intrigue with Becky, now Mrs. Rawdon Crawley.

Much of the remainder of the story is occupied with the skilful generalship by which the undaunted Becky wins her way into the highest society, first in Paris, then in London, in spite of poverty and disadvantages of birth.

Amelia, plunged in grief by the loss of the husband she still worships, lives a life of poverty and humiliation which the devoted Dobbin has secretly done his best to alleviate. After ten years Dobbin comes home from India, but though Amelia is grateful to him, the memory of her husband still stands between her and him. It is only after Becky has revealed to her George's infidelity that room is made in her heart for Dobbin, whom she finally marries.

Vanity of Human Wishes, The, a poem by S. Johnson (q.v.) (1749). It is an imitation of the Tenth Satire of Juvenal.

The poet considers the various objects of human ambition and indicates their vanity.

Varangians, THE, the Scandinavian rovers who in the 9th and 10th cents. overran Russia and reached Constantinople. They figure in Scott's 'Count Robert of Paris'.

Varden, GABRIEL, a character in Dickens's 'Barnaby Rudge' (q.v.), father of Dolly Varden.

Variorum or VARIORUM EDITION, an edition, especially of the complete works of a classical author, containing the notes of various editors or commentators.

Varney, RICHARD, a character in Scott's 'Kenilworth' (q.v.).

Vasco da Gama, see *Gama*.

Vathek, An Arabian Tale, written in French by W. Beckford (q.v.), (translated into English, 1786), said to have been written in three days and two nights. It is founded on Eastern tales.

Vatican, THE, the palace of the pope on the Vatican Hill in Rome. It contains the Sistine Chapel (q.v.), the Vatican Library, and galleries of pictures, sculptures, and *objets d'art*.

Vaudeville (from *vau de vire,* in full *chanson du Vau de Vire,* a song of the Valley of the Vire in Normandy), a light popular song or a stage performance of a light and amusing character interspersed with songs. Now used for a revue or variety entertainment, not necessarily musical.

Vaughan, HENRY (1622–95), is noteworthy for his 'Silex Scintillans', a collection of religious poems (including the magnificent 'They are all gone into the world of light'), of which the first part was published in 1650, and the second in 1655. Of his profane works, 'Poems' appeared in 1646, 'Olor Iscanus' (the Swan of Usk) in 1651, and 'Thalia Rediviva' (including a section of 'Pious Thoughts and Ejaculations') in 1678. He was known as the 'Silurist' because of his love for his native county of Brecknockshire, anciently inhabited by the Silures.

Vaux, ROLAND DE, the baron of Triermain, see *Roland de Vaux*.

Vaux, THOMAS, *second Baron Vaux of Harrowden* (1510–56), a contributor to 'Tottel's Miscellany' (q.v.), principally remembered as the author of 'The aged Lover renounceth Love', the source of the song mumbled by the grave-digger in 'Hamlet'.

Veal, MRS., see *Defoe*.

Veck, TOBY ('Trotty'), a character in Dickens's 'The Chimes' (q.v.).

Veda, one or other of the four ancient sacred books of the Hindus. The date of the Vedas is unknown, but they are among the most ancient literary works of the world.

Vega, LOPE DE (1562–1635), the founder of the Spanish drama, and the author of a great number of plays, poems, and romances, which have been a source of inspiration to European literature in general, particularly to that of France.

Velasquez, DIEGO RODRIGUEZ DA SILVA (1599–1660), Spanish painter. He was appointed court painter to Philip IV in 1623. The realism of his work influenced the French Impressionist painters of the 19th cent.

Vendice or VINDICE, the chief character in 'The Revenger's Tragedy', ascribed to Cyril Tourneur (q.v.).

Veneering, MR. and MRS., in Dickens's 'Our Mutual Friend' (q.v.), types of flashy social parvenus.

Venetia, a novel by Disraeli (q.v.) (1837).

The story is partly based on the life of Byron with some admixture of that of Shelley, but is placed in the latter part of the 18th cent.

Veni, vidi, vici, Latin, 'I came, I saw, I conquered', words which Suetonius in 'Lives of the Caesars' (*Julius,* 37) says were displayed before Julius Caesar in his Pontic triumph (after his victory over the rebel Pharnaces II, 47 B.C.).

Venice Preserv'd, or a Plot Discovered, a tragedy in blank verse by Otway (q.v.), produced in 1682, a work of considerable dramatic power and poetic merit.

The play with Betterton as Jaffier and Mrs. Barry as Belvidera was very well received, and was frequently revived.

Venn, DIGGORY, the reddleman in Hardy's 'The Return of the Native' (q.v.).

Ventidius, (1) in Shakespeare's 'Timon of Athens' (q.v.), one of the faithless friends of Timon; (2) in Shakespeare's 'Antony and Cleopatra' (q.v.) and in Dryden's 'All for Love' (q.v.), Antony's general.

Venus, identified with the Aphrodite of the Greeks and the Astarte of the Syrians, was the Roman name for the goddess of beauty and love. Zeus gave her in marriage to Hephaestus (Vulcan). She was unfaithful to him, was found in the arms of Ares (Mars), and was exposed to the ridicule of the gods. By various gods she became mother of Eros (Cupid), Harmonia, Hermaphroditus, and Priapus. She became enamoured also of Adonis, and of Anchises (by whom she was mother of Aeneas). In the contest with Hera and Athene for the golden apple, the prize was awarded to her by Paris. The most celebrated of her statues was that in her temple at Cnidos, by Praxiteles.

Venus, MR., a character in Dickens's 'Our Mutual Friend' (q.v.).

Venus and Adonis, a poem in six-lined stanzas by Shakespeare (q.v.) (1593), dedicated to Henry Wriothesley, earl of Southampton. It was probably Shakespeare's first published work. Venus, in love with the youth Adonis, detains him from the chase, and woos him, but cannot win his love. She begs him to meet her on the morrow, but he is then to hunt the boar. She tries in vain to dissuade him. When the morning comes she hears his hounds at bay, and, filled with terror, goes to look for him, and finds him killed by the boar.

Vercelli Book, a codex of OE. manuscripts in the possession of the chapter of Vercelli in N. Italy. It is unknown how it came into their keeping. It contains prose sermons and religious poetry, particularly the 'Andreas', Cynewulf's (q.v.) 'Elene', and 'The Dream of the Rood'.

Vercingetorix, the chief of the Arverni, who roused his countrymen to resist Julius Caesar and carried on the struggle against him with great ability, as described in Caesar's 'Commentaries' (Bk. VII).

Verdant Green, The Adventures of Mr., see *Bradley (E.)*.

Verdi, GIUSEPPE (1813-1901), the great Italian composer of operas. His most important works were: 'Rigoletto' (1851), 'Il Trovatore' (1853), 'La Traviata' (1853), 'Aïda' (1871), 'Otello' (1887), and 'Falstaff' (1893).

Vere, AUBREY DE, see *De Vere (Aubrey)*.

Verges, a character in Shakespeare's 'Much Ado about Nothing' (q.v.).

Vergil, see *Virgil*.

Vergil, POLYDORE (1470?-1555?), a native of Urbino, who came to England in 1502. He published his 'Anglicae Historiae Libri XXVI' in 1534-55, a chronicle of special value for the reign of Henry VII.

Verisopht, LORD FREDERICK, a character in Dickens's 'Nicholas Nickleby' (q.v.).

Verlaine, PAUL (1844-96), French poet who died in poverty after a life in which bouts of alcoholism alternated with periods of repentance and religion. His verse is evocative, rhythmic, and musical ('De la musique avant toute chose' was his advice to poets).

Vermeer, JAN (1632-75), of Delft, Dutch painter. Only about forty paintings by him are known, mostly interiors.

Verne, JULES (1828-1905), French novelist, who achieved great and enduring popularity by the combination of adventure with popular science in such books as the 'Voyage au centre de la Terre' (1864), 'Vingt mille lieues sous les mers' (1869), and 'Le Tour du monde en quatre-vingts jours' (1873).

Verner, KARL ADOLPH (1846-96), a philologist of Copenhagen. 'Verner's Law', which completes 'Grimm's Law' (see *Grimm, J. L. C.*) of consonantal variations in the Aryan languages, was a notable advance in the science of comparative philology.

Vernon, DIANA, the heroine of Scott's 'Rob Roy' (q.v.).

Veronica, ST., in Christian legend, the

woman of Jerusalem whose cloth or ker-chief was used to wipe the face of Christ on the way to Calvary, and retained miracu-lously impressed upon it his features.

Vers libres, or free verse, verses in which various metres, or various rhythms, are combined, or the ordinary rules of prosody disregarded.

Vertumnus, an Italian deity, worshipped as the god of the changing year, and the giver of fruits.

Vesta, akin to the Greek goddess Hestia, was worshipped by the Romans as goddess of the hearth. Her circular temple stood in the forum. In it the sacred fire was tended by the VESTAL VIRGINS. These were originally drawn from patrician families and were required to remain celibate for thirty years. In cases of violation of their vow, they were buried alive.

Vholes, a lawyer in Dickens's 'Bleak House' (q.v.).

Vicar of Bray, The, the title of a well-known song of unknown authorship, dating from the 18th cent. The subject is a time-serving parson, who boasts that he has accommodated himself to the reli-gious views of the reigns of Charles, James, William, Anne, and George, and that whatsoever king may reign he will remain Vicar of Bray.

Vicar of Christ, a title first assumed by Pope Innocent III (1198–1216).

Vicar of Wakefield, The, a novel by Goldsmith (q.v.), written in 1761-2 but not published until 1766. Goldsmith received £60 for the manuscript.

The story is told by the Revd. Dr. Primrose, the Vicar, kindly, charitable, and devoid of worldly wisdom. His wife, Deborah, is proud of her house-keeping and her six children, two girls, Olivia and Sophia, and four boys (see *Primrose*). The Vicar loses his independent fortune through the bankruptcy of a merchant. They move to a new living under the patronage of a certain Squire Thornhill. Thornhill, who is an unprincipled ruffian, seduces Olivia after a mock ceremony of

marriage, and deserts her. She is dis-covered by her father and brought home, but his humble vicarage is destroyed by fire. He himself is thrown into prison for debt at the suit of Thornhill; and George Primrose, who challenges the latter to a duel to avenge his sister, is overpowered by ruffians and likewise sent to prison. The Vicar's second daughter, Sophia, is forcibly carried off in a postchaise by an unknown villain, and Olivia, who has been pining away since her desertion, is reported to the Vicar to be dead. All these misfortunes he bears with fortitude and resignation.

On their removal to their new vicarage the Primrose family had made the acquain-tance of a certain Mr. Burchell, who appears to be a broken-down gentleman, kind-hearted but somewhat eccentric. By good fortune he is now the means of rescuing Sophia. It thereupon appears that he is in reality the benevolent Sir William Thornhill, the squire's uncle. The squire's villainy is now exposed, and at last all ends happily. Sir William mar-ries Sophia. Olivia is found not to be dead, and her marriage to the squire is shown to have been, contrary to his intentions, legal. The Vicar's fortune is restored to him, and George marries the young lady of his heart.

Vice, THE, a fool or buffoon introduced into some of the interludes (q.v.) and later moralities (q.v.). The character was prob-ably evolved from the merry and mis-chievous devil 'Tutivillus' (see *Titivil*), one of the stock figures of mysteries and moralities.

Vice Versa, a novel by F. Anstey (q.v.) (1882), the story of the misadventures of Mr. Bultitude, a father who, by the action of an Indian charm, is transformed into the physical appearance of his schoolboy son, while the son takes the outward form of his father; each retaining their original mental characteristics. Mr. Bultitude has to go to school while Dick remains at home and behaves as a schoolboy might be expected to behave.

'Vicisti, Galilaee', the last words, according to legend, of Julian the Apostate (q.v.).

Victor and Cazire, the pseudonyms under which P. B. Shelley (q.v.) and Elizabeth Shelley published 'Original Poetry' in 1810.

Victoria (1819–1901), queen of England, 1837–1901. The 'Letters of Queen Victoria' have been issued in three series, in 1907, 1926–8, and 1930–2. Her 'Leaves from a Journal of Our Life in the Highlands, 1848–61' appeared privately in 1867, and publicly in 1868. A second part, 'More Leaves', followed in 1883, covering the years 1862–3.

Victorian, an epithet applied to anything (spiritual or material) or to a person (author, artist, politician, etc.) considered typical of the reign of Queen Victoria. Among the characteristics of the age in allusion to which the term is sometimes used are its improved standard of decency and morality; a self-satisfaction engendered by the great increase of wealth, the prosperity of the nation as a whole, and the immense industrial and scientific development; conscious rectitude and deficient sense of humour; an unquestioning acceptance of authority and orthodoxy.

Vignette, an ornamental design on a blank space in a book, especially at the beginning or end of a chapter, of small size, and unenclosed in a border. The word is a diminutive of the Fr. *vigne*, a vine; originally meaning an ornament of leaves and tendrils.

Vigny, ALFRED VICTOR, *Comte de* (1797–1863), French poet, dramatist, and novelist, an early leader of the Romantic movement in French literature.

Vikings, the Scandinavian adventurers who from the 8th to the 11th cent. practised piracy at sea and committed depredations on land as far as the Mediterranean.

Village, The, a poem by Crabbe (q.v.) (1783), in which the poet presents the life of the rustic poor unidealized, in sombre colours.

Village Blacksmith, The, a poem by Longfellow (q.v.) (1841).

Villanelle, a poem, usually of a pastoral or lyrical nature, consisting normally of five three-lined stanzas and a final quatrain, with only two rhymes throughout. The first and third lines of the first stanza are repeated alternately in the succeeding stanzas as a refrain, and form a final couplet in the quatrain.

Villette, a novel by C. Brontë (q.v.) (1853).

The story, which is a rehandling of material already dealt with in 'The Professor' (then unpublished), reflecting the personal experiences of the authoress, is that of the life of an English girl without beauty, money, or friends, who obtains, in order to support herself, a post as teacher in a girls' school at Brussels. The drabness of the story is redeemed by its biographical aspect and by the drawing of the characters, particularly of Monsieur Paul, Madame Beck, and the heroine herself.

Villon, FRANÇOIS (*b.* 1431), French poet, a poor scholar of the university of Paris, who spent a riotous life between the tavern and the prison, and narrowly escaped the gallows for theft. Gay, witty, ironic, melancholy, he struck a new note in his lyrics, in which he sang the experiences of his own life. His chief works are the 'Petit Testament', the 'Grand Testament', and a number of *ballades* and *rondeaux*, of which the best known, the 'Ballade des Dames du temps jadis', was translated by D. G. Rossetti (q.v.).

Vincent de Beauvais, a 13th-cent Dominican, author of the 'Speculum Majus', an enormous compilation of all the knowledge of the time, mentioned by Chaucer in the prologue to 'The Legend of Good Women'.

Vincentio, (1) the duke in Shakespeare's 'Measure for Measure' (q.v.); (2) a character in his 'The Taming of the Shrew' (q.v.).

Vincy, ROSAMUND, a character in G Eliot's 'Middlemarch' (q.v.).

Vindication of Natural Society, *A*, a treatise by E. Burke (q.v.), published in 1756.

This is one of the first of Burke's published writings. It is an ironical answer to Bolingbroke's indictment of revealed religion, in imitation of his style and in the form of a *reductio ad absurdum*.

Vindication of the Rights of Woman, see *Godwin* (*Mrs. Mary Wollstonecraft*).

Vindice, see *Vendice*.

Vinegar Bible, THE, an edition of the Bible printed by Baskett (q.v.) at Oxford in 1716-17, so called from the misprint of the word 'vinegar' for 'vineyard' in the heading of Luke xx.

Vinland, the region of North America where, according to the Norse sagas, a settlement was made by Norsemen in the early years of the 11th cent. It appears to have been in the neighbourhood of Cape Cod. The name is derived from the grapes said to have been found there by the discoverers.

Viola, the heroine of Shakespeare's 'Twelfth Night' (q.v.).

Violenta, one of the dramatis personae of Shakespeare's 'All's Well that Ends Well' (q.v.) who appears only once (III. v) in the play and does not speak; sometimes referred to as typical of a nonentity.

Virelay, a song or short lyric piece, of a type originating in France in the 14th cent., usually consisting of short lines arranged in stanzas with only two rhymes, the end-rhyme of one stanza being the chief one of the next.

Virgidemiarum, Sex Libri, by J. Hall (q.v.), a collection of satires on the abuses of the day, in the spirit of Juvenal. The first volume was published in 1597 and the second in 1598.

Virgil (PUBLIUS VERGILIUS MARO) (70-19 B.C.), the Roman poet. His chief works were the 'Aeneid', the epic poem of the Roman people, recounting the adventures of Aeneas; the 'Georgics', a didactic poem on the cultivation of the soil, and the rearing of cattle and bees; and the 'Eclogues' or 'Bucolics', imitations of the pastorals of Theocritus. See also *Sortes Virgilianae*, and below, *Virgil's Fourth Eclogue*.

Virgil, POLYDORE, see *Vergil* (*P.*).

Virgilia, in Shakespeare's 'Coriolanus' (q.v.), the wife of Coriolanus.

Virgil's Fourth Eclogue, written in 40 B.C. and hailing the birth of a child who should bring back the golden age, was interpreted by the early Church and in the Middle Ages as a prophecy of Christ. The identity of the child to whom Virgil was really referring has not been fully established.

Virgil's Gnat, a poem by Spenser (q.v.), adapted from the 'Culex' attributed to Virgil.

Virginia, a daughter of the centurion, Lucius Virginius. Appius Claudius, the decemvir, became enamoured of her and sought to get possession of her. For this purpose she was claimed by one of his favourites as daughter of a slave, and Appius in the capacity of a judge gave sentence in his favour. Virginius arrived from the camp and plunged a dagger into his daughter's breast to save her from the tyrant. He then rushed to the camp with the bloody knife in his hand. The soldiers, incensed against Appius Claudius, marched to Rome and seized him. But he destroyed himself in prison. The story (which is in Livy, iii. 44 et seq.) is the basis of Macaulay's (q.v.) lay 'Virginia'.

Virginians, The, a novel by Thackeray (q.v.), published in twenty-four serial numbers, Nov. 1857 to Sept. 1859.

The author relates the fortunes of the descendants of Colonel Henry Esmond (see *Esmond*), in particular of the twin sons, George and Henry, of his daughter Rachel. Rachel has married a Warrington (ancestor of the friend of Pendennis) and survived him as owner of an estate in Virginia. George Warrington, the elder twin, disappears in General Braddock's disastrous expedition against Fort Duquesne, and is believed to have perished. His younger brother, now regarded as the heir of a great property, visits England, and is received with questionable cordiality by his cousins of the Castlewood family. With them is the dominating character of the book, Baroness Bernstein, the Beatrix Esmond of the earlier novel, who has buried her first husband, Tom Tusher, the bishop, and the second, the baron, and is now a stout sardonic old lady with a very dark pair of eyes, who conceives a strong affection for Harry. Harry, who is a frank, open-handed, but stupid fellow, plunges into a course of dissipation which lands him in a sponging-house, whence he is rescued by his brother George, who has survived his wounds and spent eighteen months as a prisoner in French hands. Harry enters the army, serves with distinction under Wolfe, returns to Virginia, and marries the daughter of his mother's housekeeper, Mrs. Mountain. George settles in London and leads a struggling life; for his tyrannical mother, whose love is centred on Harry, cuts off supplies when he marries Theo, the daughter of the gallant but impecunious old General Lambert. In time, however, he inherits the Warrington property, and his troubles come to an end.

The book contains a vivid account of the rakish and unprincipled society of the day, and introduces Wolfe and Washington. The latter part deals with the American War of Independence.

Virgin-Martyr, The, a tragedy by Massinger and Dekker (qq.v.), printed in 1622.

Virgin Queen, a name for Queen Elizabeth I of England.

Virgo, a zodiacal constellation and the sixth sign of the zodiac, which the sun enters about 20 Aug.

Virtues, see *Angel.*

Virtues, in scholastic philosophy, comprised the three THEOLOGICAL VIRTUES, faith, hope, and charity, and four CARDINAL VIRTUES, justice, prudence, temperance, and fortitude.

Vishnu, in Hindu mythology, the second god in the triad (Brahma, Vishnu, and Siva), regarded as the preserver. Vishnu

shares with Siva the principal worship of modern Hindus, Brahma having fallen into the background.

Vision concerning Piers the Plowman, The, see *Piers Plowman.*

Vision of Judgment, A, a poem in hexameters by Southey on the death of George III (1821).

The preface, in defence of this metrical innovation, contains, in a digression, a violent attack on the works of Byron.

The poem was amusingly parodied by Byron in 'The Vision of Judgment' (q.v.).

Vision of Judgment, The, a satirical poem by Lord Byron (q.v.), published in 'The Liberal' in 1822.

In 1821 had appeared Southey's 'A Vision of Judgment' (q.v.), containing in the preface a violent attack on Byron's works. Byron replied in the appendix to 'The Two Foscari' and in the present satire, a travesty of Southey's poem, in which, besides holding up the poet laureate to derision, he treats the subject of the late King George III's appearance before the tribunal of heaven very disrespectfully if very humorously.

Vision of Mirza, The, an allegory by Addison (q.v.), published in 'The Spectator' (No. 159). Mirza has a vision of human life in the form of a bridge, over which the multitudes are passing, some dropping through concealed trap-doors into the flood beneath.

Visions of the Daughters of Albion, a poem by Blake (q.v.).

Vita Nuova, see *Dante.*

Vitruvius, POLLIO (*fl.* 40 B.C.), Roman architect and author of 'De architectura', the only surviving classical treatise on architecture.

Vittoria, a novel by G. Meredith (q.v.) (1867).

The scene is laid in northern Italy in the period of the first rising of 1848, at the inspiration of Mazzini, against the Austrian domination. Against this background we have a continuation of the romance of 'Sandra Belloni'.

Vittoria Corombona, see *White Divel.*

Vitus, St., the son of a Sicilian nobleman, who is said to have suffered martyrdom under Diocletian. The saint is especially invoked in cases of *chorea*, the disease otherwise known as St. Vitus's Dance.

Vivian Grey, a novel by Disraeli (q.v.) (1826–7). This was the first of Disraeli's novels, written when he was only 21.

Vivien, see *Lady of the Lake*, *Merlin*, *Merlin and Vivien*.

Volpone, or *The Fox*, a comedy by Jonson (q.v.), first acted in 1606 and printed in 1607.

Volpone, a rich Venetian without children, feigns that he is dying, in order to draw gifts from his would-be heirs. Mosca, his parasite and confederate, persuades each of these in turn that he is to be the heir, and thus extracts costly presents from them; Corvino even sacrifices his wife. Finally Volpone, to enjoy the discomfiture of the vultures who are awaiting his death, makes over his property by will to Mosca and pretends to be dead. Mosca takes advantage of the position to blackmail Volpone; and Voltore, a lawyer, who has aided Volpone in the infamous conspiracy against Corvino's wife, reveals the whole matter to the senate; whereupon Volpone, Mosca, and Corvino receive the punishment they merit.

Volsung, in Icelandic legend, a descendant of Odin, and the father of Sigmund and grandfather of Sigurd.

Volsunga Saga, a prose version of a lost cycle of heroic songs of which fragments survive in the poetic Edda (q.v.), dealing with the families of the Volsungs and the Nibelungs. It has been translated by W. Morris and E. Magnusson (1888). See *Sigurd the Volsung*.

Voltaire (1694–1778), the name assumed by François Marie Arouet and by which he is generally known. He was born in Paris, and spent the years 1726–9 in exile in England, owing to a quarrel with a French noble. Here he wrote the 'Lettres philosophiques' (1734), one of his masterpieces. In 1750 Frederic II of Prussia tempted him to Potsdam, but king and philosopher presently disagreed, and in 1753 Voltaire settled at Ferney on the shores of the Lake of Geneva. He returned to Paris when 84 years old and enjoyed there a brief period of glory before his death.

A sceptic in philosophy, rejecting all systems, he was a believer in God, though he condemned particular religions. His anti-clericalism, his wit, and his style have made him one of the most famous of French writers, and one of the leaders of free thought everywhere. His influence on the French Revolution, which in 1778 he declared had 'already come and even gone too far', was wholly on the practical side (e.g. on statesmen like Danton). Dreamers (e.g. Robespierre) were more influenced by Rousseau.

The best known of his works, of which he left seventy volumes, are, besides the 'Lettres philosophiques': his history of the 'Siècle de Louis XIV' (1751), his amusing satirical tales 'Zadig' (1748) and 'Candide' (1759), and his correspondence with D'Alembert. Voltaire wrote a number of tragedies on classical subjects, and a few comedies. In his 'Lettres sur les Anglais', he condemned Shakespeare for lack of taste and ignorance of the classical rules of the drama (see *Montagu, Mrs. E.*).

Voltore, a character in Jonson's 'Volpone' (q.v.).

Volumnia, in Shakespeare's 'Coriolanus' (q.v.), the mother of Coriolanus.

Voragine, Jacobus de, see *Golden Legend*.

Vortigern, a legendary king of Britain in the 5th cent. who, it is said, usurped the crown. About 449 he invited the Jutes to England to aid him against the Picts, after which the Jutes declined to go away again. The story is in Layamon's 'Brut', ll. 14255–396.

Vortigern and Rowena, a pseudo-Shakespearian play forged by W. H. Ireland (q.v.), on the story of Vortigern (q.v.).

Vox Clamantis, a poem of 10,000 lines in Latin elegiacs by Gower (q.v.), recounting the Peasants' Rising of 1381 and exposing the corruption of contemporary society, especially in its political aspect.

Vulcan or MULCIBER, the Roman equivalent of the Greek god HEPHAESTUS. He was the god of fire and the patron of workers in metal.

Vulgar Errors, the usual name for *Pseudodoxia Epidemica, or, Enquiries into very many received Tenents and commonly presumed Truths*, a treatise by Sir T. Browne (q.v.) (1646).

This was the author's longest work. He first analyses the causes of mistaken popular beliefs, then ranges over a vast number of legends and beliefs, discussing them with a pleasant irony and quaint fancy.

Vulgate, THE, a term applied particularly to St. Jerome's Latin version of the Bible completed *c.* 404. The CLEMENTINE text of this, a recension made by order of Clement VIII (1592-1605), is the authorized text of the Roman Catholic Church. See *Bible*.

W

Wace of Jersey (*d.* after 1171), wrote *c.* 1154 a 'Geste des Bretons', dedicated to Eleanor, queen of Henry II, embodying the Arthurian legends, based on Geoffrey of Monmouth (q.v.). This was one of the sources of Layamon's 'Brut' (see *Layamon*).

Wackles, MRS. and the MISSES MELISSA, SOPHY, and JANE, in Dickens's 'The Old Curiosity Shop' (q.v.), kept a 'Ladies' Seminary' at Chelsea.

Wade, MISS, a character in Dickens's 'Little Dorrit' (q.v.).

Wade's boat, in Chaucer's 'The Merchant's Tale' (see *Canterbury Tales*), l. 179, a disputed reference. According to Skeat's note Wade was a famous hero of antiquity who is mentioned in various poems and in Malory's 'Morte Darthur', VII. ix. He was the son of Wayland the Smith (q.v.) and the king's daughter, and had a magic boat called Wingelock (French *Guingelot*, see *Gringolet*). A 12th-13th-cent. English reference to Wade is recorded in 'The Academy' (1896), i. 137, 157.

Wadman, WIDOW, in Sterne's 'Tristram Shandy' (q.v.), occupies the house next to that of 'my Uncle Toby' and tries to secure him for a husband.

Wagg, MR., in Thackeray's 'Vanity Fair' (q.v.), a satellite of Lord Steyne. His name has allusion to Theodore Hook (q.v.).

Wagner, the attendant of Faust in Marlowe's 'Doctor Faustus' (q.v.) and in Goethe's 'Faust'.

Wagner, (WILHELM) RICHARD (1813-83), German musician and poet, who by the combination of these twin arts in his great music-dramas ('Der Ring des Nibelungen' (q.v., 1853-70), 'Tristan und Isolde' (1865), the 'Meistersinger' (1868), 'Parsifal' (1882), etc.), and also by his critical work, 'Oper und Drama' (1851), exerted a powerful influence on German music and literature.

Wainewright, THOMAS GRIFFITHS (1794-1852), wrote art-critiques for 'The London Magazine' during 1820-3 and exhibited at the Royal Academy. He was a forger and a suspected poisoner, and died a convict in Tasmania. He was the original of Varney in Bulwer Lytton's 'Lucretia' and suggested to Dickens his sketch, 'Hunted Down'. He was a friend of Charles Lamb and the subject of an essay by Oscar Wilde (qq.v.).

Wakefield Plays, see *Miracle Plays*.

Wakem, MR. and PHILIP, characters in G. Eliot's 'The Mill on the Floss' (q.v.).

Waldeck, MARTIN, the subject of a legend from the German interposed in

Scott's 'The Antiquary' (q.v.), a charcoal-burner enriched by gold obtained from the demon of the Harz Mountains, whose wealth brings him to an evil end.

Walden, or Life in the Woods, a narrative by H. D. Thoreau (q.v.), published in 1854.

Waldenses or WALDENSIANS, the adherents of a religious sect which originated in the south of France about 1170 through the preaching of Peter Waldo, a rich merchant of Lyons. They rejected the authority of the pope and various rites, and were excommunicated in 1184 and subjected to persecution. Their persecution by the duchess-regent of Savoy in 1655 led to Milton's noble sonnet, 'Avenge, O Lord, thy slaughtered saints'.

Waldhere, the name given to two short fragments (11th cent.) of an OE. epic poem preserved in the Royal Library at Copenhagen.

We know from other sources that Waldhere was the son of a king of Aquitaine, who was given up to Attila, king of the Huns, and became one of his generals, but escaped with Hiltgund (daughter of a king of Burgundy), to whom he had been betrothed when young. In the course of their flight they were waylaid, and Waldhere, after slaying his assailants in a first encounter, was surprised and wounded on the following day, but was able to continue his journey and was finally married to Hiltgund. The fragments give speeches that pass just before the second fight.

Waley, ARTHUR DAVID (1889–1966), poet and authority on Chinese and Japanese literature. He is probably best known for his translations of Chinese poetry which he first published in 1918, and for his translation (6 vols., 1925–33) of the 11th-cent. Japanese novel 'The Tale of Genji'. His other works include 'The Nō Plays of Japan' (1921), 'The Analects of Confucius' (1938), 'Monkey' (1942, tr. of a 16th-cent. Chinese novel), 'The Poetry and Career of Li Po, A.D. 701–762' (1951), and a miscellany, 'The Secret History of the Mongols and other Pieces' (1964).

Wallace, ALFRED RUSSEL (1823–1913), joined Henry Walter Bates, the naturalist, in 1848 in a trip to the Amazon for the collection of specimens. The expedition is described in Wallace's 'Travels on the Amazon and Rio Negro' (1853). A further voyage to the Malay Archipelago (1854–62) is described in his 'Malay Archipelago' (1869). It was in 1858 that the idea of natural selection as the solution of the problem of evolution flashed upon him, and he at once communicated it to Darwin. The outcome, a testimony to the generosity of both the great biologists, was the famous joint communication to the Linnean Society on the theory of evolution.

Wallace, EDGAR (1875–1932), a very prolific author, one of the masters of the pure 'thriller', among whose numerous works it is almost impossible to select the most notable. A few landmarks are: 'The Four Just Men' (1905) and its followers, 'Sanders of the River', 'The Angel of Terror' (novels); 'The Terror' (1927), 'The Squeaker' (1927), 'On the Spot' (plays).

Wallace, SIR WILLIAM (1272?–1305), the Scottish patriot of the time of Edward I, who devoted his life to resistance to the English, is the subject of a long poem by Henry the Minstrel (q.v.), 'Blind Harry'.

Wallenstein, ALBRECHT EUSEBIUS VON (1583–1634), an Austrian general celebrated for his campaigns in the Thirty Years War. His career is the subject of a great historical trilogy by Schiller (q.v.), of which the two last parts were translated by S. T. Coleridge (q.v.).

Waller, EDMUND (1606–87), entered parliament early and was at first an active member of the opposition. Later he became a Royalist, and in 1643 was leader in a plot ('Waller's plot') to seize London for Charles I. For this he was imprisoned, fined, and banished, but, on betraying his associates, spared execution. He made his peace with Cromwell in 1651 and returned to England. He was restored to royal favour on the Restoration. After the death of his first wife (in 1634) he had paid unsuccessful court to Lady Dorothy Sidney, whom he celebrated in poems as 'Sacharissa'. Waller was a precocious poet. His verse is of a polished simplicity, and was highly commended by Dryden. Some of his best work belongs to his later period: the 'Panegyric to My Lord Protector', the 'Instructions to a Painter' on the battle of Sole Bay, and 'Of the Last Verses in the Book'. His earlier pieces, 'On a Girdle' and 'Go, lovely Rose!', are also well known.

Walpole, HORACE, *fourth earl of Orford* (1717-97), fourth son of Sir Robert Walpole, travelled in France and Italy with Gray (q.v.) in 1739-41. In 1747 he settled at Strawberry Hill, Twickenham, which he made into 'a little Gothic castle', and where he collected articles of virtu, and established a printing-press. Here he printed Gray's two Pindaric odes and his own 'Anecdotes of Painting in England' (which still retain importance). In 1764 he published his 'Gothic story', 'The Castle of Otranto' (q.v.). It is on his letters that Walpole's literary reputation rests. They are remarkable both for their charm and their autobiographical, social, and political interest.

Walpole, SIR HUGH SEYMOUR (1884-1941), novelist, among whose chief works are: 'Mr. Perrin and Mr. Traill' (1911), 'Fortitude' (1913), 'The Cathedral' (1922); and a historical sequence comprising 'Rogue Herries' (1930), 'Judith Paris' (1931), and 'The Fortress' (1933).

Walpole, SIR ROBERT, *first earl of Orford* (1676-1745), was prime minister and chancellor of the exchequer, 1715-17, and again 1721-42; he laid the foundations of free trade and modern colonial policy. He was the father of Horace Walpole (q.v.).

Walpurgis Night, so called by association with St. Walburga (an English nun who in the 8th cent. helped to convert the Germans to Christianity and who is commemorated on 1 May), the night before 1 May, when, according to popular superstition in Germany, the witches and the Devil hold a festival.

Walton, IZAAK (1593-1683), was the friend of Donne, of Sir Henry Wotton, and of Bishops Morley, Sanderson, and King. He published 'Lives' of the following: John Donne (q.v.) in 1640, Sir Henry Wotton (q.v.) in 1651, Richard Hooker (q.v.) in 1665, George Herbert (q.v.) in 1670, and Bishop Sanderson in 1678. The 'Compleat Angler' (q.v.), by which he is chiefly known, first appeared in 1653, largely rewritten in the second edition (1655). See also *Cotton* (*C.*).

Walton, SIR WILLIAM TURNER (1902-   ), composer. He became closely associated with the Sitwells (qq.v.) and his early composition 'Façade' (1923) consisted of poems of Edith Sitwell read to the accompaniment of flute, clarinet, trumpet, saxophone, 'cello, and percussion. His other works include the overture 'Portsmouth Point' (1926), 'Belshazzar's Feast' (1931), an oratorio with text by Osbert Sitwell based on the Book of Daniel, 'Symphony' (1935), 'Crown Imperial' (1937), and a Chaucerian opera 'Troilus and Cressida' (1954). He has also written music for the screen versions of 'Henry V', 'Hamlet', and 'Richard III'.

Walwain, see *Gawain*.

Wamba, in Scott's 'Ivanhoe' (q.v.), the devoted jester of Cedric the Saxon.

Wanderer, The, an OE. poem of 115 lines, included in the 'Exeter Book' (q.v.), telling of the wanderings of a man who has lost his lord. He dreams of his former happiness, and reflects on the vicissitudes of human life. See also *The Seafarer*.

Wandering Jew, THE, a Jew condemned to wander about the world until Christ's second coming, because, according to the legend, as Christ bore the cross to Calvary, the Jew chid him, and urged him to go faster.

A pamphlet was published at Leyden in 1602 relating that Paulus von Eizen, bishop of Schleswig, had in 1542 met a Jew named Ahasuerus, who admitted that he was the Jew in question. The story became popular, and many instances of the appearance of the Wandering Jew are recorded from the 16th to the 19th cents.

The legend of the Wandering Jew has been made the subject of many German works, and Goethe designed a poem on the subject.

Wanderings of Cain, The, a prose-poem by S. T. Coleridge, written in 1798. The work was undertaken in conjunction with Wordsworth, who was to have written the first canto. Coleridge wrote the second canto; but the work was then abandoned, and 'The Ancient Mariner' was written instead.

Wandering Willie, Willie Steenson, the blind fiddler in Scott's 'Redgauntlet' (q.v.), 'Wandering Willie's Tale' is an episode in the novel.

'Wandering Willie' is also the name of a song by Burns.

Wanley, HUMFREY (1672-1726), began life as a draper's assistant at Coventry, but read widely and went to Oxford in 1695, and was an assistant in the Bodleian Library in 1696. He displayed remarkable skill in palaeography. He produced in 1705 a catalogue of Anglo-Saxon manuscripts, which is still the standard work.

Wantley, The Dragon of, see *Dragon of Wantley.*

War and Peace, a novel by Tolstoy (q.v.), published 1865-72.

Warbeck, PERKIN (1474-99), the impostor who gave himself out for Richard, duke of York, son of Edward IV. For Ford's play see *Perkin Warbeck.*

Warburton, JOHN (1682-1759), herald and antiquary, an indefatigable collector who owned many rare manuscripts.

Most of the rare Elizabethan and Jacobean plays in his possession were through his own 'carelessness and the ignorance' of Betsy Baker, his servant, 'unluckily burned or put under pye bottoms'. Some of the burnt manuscripts were unique.

Warburton, WILLIAM (1698-1779), rose to be bishop of Gloucester in 1759. He was much engaged in theological controversy, writing with vigour and arrogance. He brought out in 1747 an edition of Shakespeare which was sharply criticized, and in 1751 an edition of Pope's works (he had been left Pope's literary executor). He was a bad scholar, a literary bully, and a man of untrustworthy character.

Ward, ARTEMUS, see *Browne (C. F.).*

Ward, EDWARD ('Ned') (1667-1731), tavern-keeper and writer of Hudibrastic doggerel verse and coarse humorous prose, is remarkable for his sketches of London life and characters. Some of the best of these are contained in 'The London Spy' (1698-1709).

Ward, MARY AUGUSTA, better known as MRS. HUMPHRY WARD (1851-1920), was granddaughter of Thomas Arnold of Rugby. She wrote her first novel, 'Miss Bretherton', in 1884. She embodied in her most famous novel, 'Robert Elsmere' (1888), her view that Christianity could be revitalized by emphasizing its social mission and discarding its miraculous element. Mrs. Humphry Ward was an active opponent of the extension of the franchise to women.

Warden, HENRY, in Scott's 'The Monastery' and 'The Abbot', an earnest Protestant divine.

Warden, The, a novel by A. Trollope (q.v.) (1855), the first of the Barsetshire series, and the first of Trollope's novels that met with success. The story is continued in 'Barchester Towers' (q.v.).

Wardle, MR., a character in Dickens's 'The Pickwick Papers' (q.v.).

Wardour, SIR ARTHUR, and his son and daughter CAPTAIN REGINALD and ISABELLA, characters in Scott's 'The Antiquary' (q.v.).

Wardour Street, the name of a street in London, which was formerly occupied mainly by dealers in antique, and imitation-antique, furniture. Hence 'Wardour-Street English' is applied to the pseudo-archaic diction affected by some modern writers, especially of historical novels.

Ware, THE BED OF, see *Bed of Ware.*

Waring, one of the 'Dramatic Romances' of R. Browning (q.v.) (1842).

The poem is the reminiscence of a friend, Domett (q.v.), who has left England.

Warner, WILLIAM (1558?-1609). His chief work is 'Albion's England', a metrical British history, with mythical and fictitious episodes. Meres, in his 'Palladis Tamia' (1598), associated him with Spenser as one of the two chief English heroic poets. Drayton also eulogized him.

Warrington, GEORGE, a character in Thackeray's 'Pendennis' (q.v.), who figures also in 'The Newcomes'. He is a descendant of the Warringtons of 'The Virginians' (q.v.).

Wars of the Roses, THE, the prolonged struggle between the houses of York and Lancaster, whose badges were respectively a white and a red rose. The wars began in 1455 in Henry VI's reign and ended with the defeat and death of Richard III at Bosworth in 1485, and the accession of Henry VII, who, by marrying Elizabeth of York, united the two lines.

Wart, THOMAS, in Shakespeare's '2 Henry IV', one of the recruits for Falstaff's force.

Warton, JOSEPH (1722-1800), brother of T. Warton (q.v.), held various livings and was a conspicuously unsuccessful headmaster of Winchester (1766-93). He was a literary critic of wide knowledge and independent judgement, and is principally known for his 'Essay' on Pope (1756 and 1782), in which he criticized the 'correct' school of poetry.

Warton, THOMAS (1728-90), brother of J. Warton (q.v.), was professor of poetry at Oxford (1757-67) and subsequently Camden professor of history, and poet laureate in 1785, an appointment that was celebrated in the 'Probationary Odes'. He was the author of a 'History of English Poetry' (1774-81), a valuable pioneer work; and 'Observations on the Faerie Queene of Spenser' (1754). He edited the early poems of Milton and the famous miscellany of university verse entitled 'The Oxford Sausage' (1764). Warton was a real predecessor of the Romantic school, and a much bigger man than has been (until recently) recognized.

Warwick, MRS., the heroine of Meredith's 'Diana of the Crossways' (q.v.).

Warwick the King-maker, Richard Neville, *earl of Warwick* (1428-71), instrumental in placing Edward IV on the throne in 1461, and in restoring Henry VI in 1470; killed at Barnet, 1471.

'The Last of the Barons' (q.v.), by Bulwer Lytton (q.v.), deals with the life of Warwick.

Washington, BOOKER TALIAFERRO (1856-1915), born a Negro slave, devoted himself to raising the moral and intellectual status of his fellow Negroes. He was an eloquent speaker and voluminous writer. His works include an interesting autobiography, consisting of two parts, 'Up from Slavery' (1901) and 'Working with Hands' (1904).

Washington, GEORGE (1732-99), was appointed commander-in-chief of the Continental Forces in the War of American Independence. He was president of the American convention of 1787, and first president of the United States (1789).

George Washington figures in Thackeray's 'The Virginians' (q.v.).

Watchman, The, a political and literary journal issued by S. T. Coleridge (q.v.) from 1 March to 13 May 1796.

Water Babies, The, A Fairy Tale for a Land-Baby, by C. Kingsley (q.v.), published in 1863.

The story tells, with much pleasant humour, how little Tom, the chimney-sweep, employed by the bully, Mr. Grimes, runs away, falls into a river, and is turned into a water-baby. In the river and sea he makes intimate acquaintance with all sorts of aquatic creatures.

Waterloo, a village to the S. of Brussels, where, on 18 June 1815, was fought the battle in which Napoleon was finally and decisively defeated. The word 'Waterloo' is used allusively for a decisive contest.

Water-Poet, THE, see *Taylor (John)*.

Watling Street, one of the great Roman roads of Britain, which ran from Dover, through Canterbury, past the ancient city of London, through St. Albans, and across England to Chester.

In Chaucer's 'The Hous of Fame', ii. 431, the eagle draws the poet's attention to the Milky Way and says:

And some, parfay,
Callen it Watling Street.

Watson, DR., in the cycle of stories by Sir A. Conan Doyle (q.v.) relating to Sherlock Holmes, the detective, is a stolid medical man, Holmes's companion and assistant in his adventures, and his chronicler.

Watson, THOMAS (1557?-1592), published in 1582, 'Ἑκατομπαθία, or Passionate Centurie of Loue', eighteen-line English poems (called 'sonnets'), reflecting classical and French and Italian poems, and being in some cases translations; this is his most important work. A few previously unpublished poems by him appeared in 'The Phoenix Nest' (1593) and 'England's Helicon' (1600). His sonnets appear to have been studied by Shakespeare and other contemporaries. He was the 'Amyntas' of Spenser's 'Colin Clouts come home againe' (q.v.).

Watson, SIR WILLIAM (1858-1935), poet, whose chief works were: 'Lachrymae Musarum' and 'Lyric Love' (1892), 'The Year of Shame' (1896), 'The Heralds of the Dawn' (1912), 'Collected Poems' (1906).

Watsons, The, an unfinished fragment of a novel by Jane Austen (q.v.), written about 1805 and appended by J. E. Austen Leigh to the second edition of his 'Memoir of Jane Austen' (1871); reprinted, Oxford, 1927. The authoress completed little more than the *mise en scène* of the story.

Watteau, JEAN ANTOINE (1684-1721), French genre-painter, famous for his pictures of *fêtes champêtres*, and of shepherds and shepherdesses in the fashionable costumes of the early 18th cent.

Watts, ISAAC (1674-1748), the son of a Nonconformist schoolmaster, is remembered as the author of 'Divine Songs for Children', 1715, containing such well-known lines as:

Let dogs delight to bark and bite,
For God hath made them so;

and the lines about the little busy bee. He also wrote a number of hymns, some of which have obtained a wide popularity, including, 'O God, our help in ages past' and 'When I survey the wondrous Cross'.

Watts-Dunton, WALTER THEODORE (1832-1914), gave up his profession of solicitor to devote himself to literary criticism, on which subject he contributed many valuable articles to 'The Athenaeum'. His novel 'Aylwin' (1898) met with great success. Watts-Dunton had met Borrow (q.v.) in 1872, and his recollections of him may be read in his editions of 'Lavengro' (1893) and 'The Romany Rye' (1900).

Watts-Dunton befriended Swinburne in his declining health, took him to his house at Putney, and exercised a devoted and tactful control over him.

Waugh, EVELYN ARTHUR ST. JOHN (1903-66), novelist. His work is mainly satire, sophisticated and witty, and includes the following novels: 'Decline and Fall' (1928), 'Vile Bodies' (1930), 'Black Mischief' (1932), 'A Handful of Dust' (1934), 'Scoop' (1938), 'Put Out More Flags' (1942), 'Brideshead Revisited' (1945), 'The Loved One' (1948), the trilogy: 'Men at Arms' (1952), 'Officers and Gentlemen' (1955), and 'Unconditional Surrender' (1961), 'The Ordeal of Gilbert Pinfold' (1957). He also wrote a life of Edmund Campion (1935).

Waverley, the first of the novels of Sir W. Scott (q.v.) (1814).

Edward Waverley, a young man of romantic disposition, has been brought up in part by his father, a Hanoverian in politics, in part by his uncle Sir Everard Waverley, a rich landowner of Jacobite leanings. Obtaining a commission in the army in the year 1745, he joins his regiment in Scotland, and there, while on leave, visits his uncle's friend, the baron of Bradwardine, a kind-hearted old Jacobite, and attracts the favourable notice of the gentle Rose Bradwardine, his daughter. Impelled by curiosity, he visits Donald Bean Lean, a Highland freebooter, and Fergus Mac-Ivor Vich Ian Vohr of Glennaquoich, a young Highland chieftain. While at Glennaquoich, he falls in love with Fergus's sister Flora. These visits, injudicious in an officer of the British army at a time of acute political tension, compromise Edward with his colonel, and he finds himself accused of fomenting mutiny in his regiment, and is finally cashiered and arrested. From imprisonment he is rescued by the action of the devoted Rose, and, under the influence of a sense of unjust treatment, of Flora's enthusiasm, and of a gratifying reception by Prince Charles Edward, he joins the Jacobite forces. At the battle of Prestonpans he has the good fortune to save from death Colonel Talbot, a distinguished English officer, and the influence of the latter, after the final defeat and dispersal of the Pretender's army, is the means of securing Edward's pardon. Meanwhile Edward has been decisively rejected by the spirited Flora, and has turned his affections to the milder and more congenial Rose, to whom in due course he is married.

Wayland or WELAND THE SMITH, the Vulcan of Scandinavian mythology.

He is the *Wieland* of German epics, who fashioned the famous sword Mimung. There are traces of his legend in England. He was supposed to have his forge in a dolmen near the White Horse on the Berkshire Downs (see Scott's 'Kenilworth').

Way of All Flesh, The, a novel by S. Butler (1835-1902, q.v.) (1903).

In the form of a novel, brilliant with wit and irony, Butler here presents a study of one of his favourite themes, the relations of parents to children, a study embittered by some of his own recollections.

Way of the World, The, a comedy by Congreve (q.v.), produced in 1700. This is the most finished of Congreve's comedies, but it was not very well received and the author in disgust renounced any further writing for the stage.

Besides the finished portrait of Millamant, the heroine, finely-tempered in sense and intellect, Congreve's most brilliant creation, there are several amusing characters.

Weak ending, the occurrence of an unstressed syllable (such as a preposition, conjunction, or auxiliary verb) in the normally stressed place at the end of an iambic line.

Wealth of Nations, Inquiry into the Nature and Causes of the, a treatise on political economy by Adam Smith (q.v.) (1776).

Adam Smith's work is the first comprehensive treatment of the whole subject of political economy, and is remarkable for its breadth of view. The 'Wealth of Nations' sets out with the doctrine that the labour of the nation is the source of its means of life. In a more advanced state of society three elements enter into price —wages, profit, and rent—and these elements are discussed separately.

The author's political economy is essentially individualistic; self-interest is the proper criterion of economic action. But the universal pursuit of one's own advantage contributes, in his view, to the public interest.

Webb, MARY (1881-1927), author of novels descriptive of the Shropshire country, including 'Gone to Earth' (1917), 'Precious Bane' (1924).

Webster, JOHN (1580?-1625?), collaborated with Dekker and other dramatists in a number of comedies, 'Westward Hoe' and 'Northward Hoe' in 1603-4 (printed in 1607), and with Rowley in 'A Cure for a Cuckold' (printed 1661). He completed for the stage Marston's 'Malcontent' (1604). His tragedies, founded on Italian *novelle*, show that he approached in tragic power nearest to his contemporaries to Shakespeare; they are 'The White Divel' (q.v.), produced *c.* 1608;

'Appius and Virginia' (perhaps partly by Heywood), *c.* 1609; 'The Duchess of Malfi' (q.v.), *c.* 1614.

Webster, NOAH (1758-1843), American lexicographer, remembered for his great 'American Dictionary of the English Language' (1828), of which there have been several subsequent editions.

Wedgwood, JOSIAH (1730-95), the founder of the celebrated pottery works at 'Etruria' (a village which he built for his workmen near Stoke-on-Trent).

THOMAS WEDGWOOD (1771-1805), son of Josiah, was the first to produce (unfixed) photographs, and was a generous patron of S. T. Coleridge.

Wegg, SILAS, in Dickens's 'Our Mutual Friend' (q.v.), a one-legged impudent old rascal.

Weir, MAJOR, in Scott's 'Redgauntlet', Sir Robert Redgauntlet's monkey in 'Wandering Willie's Tale', named after a famous wizard.

Weir of Hermiston, an unfinished novel by R. L. Stevenson (q.v.) (1896). The fragment does little more than set the scene and present the chief characters, but it includes some of Stevenson's finest work.

Weland the Smith, see *Wayland the Smith*.

Well-Beloved, The, a novel by Hardy (q.v.), published serially in 1892, reissued in revised form in 1897.

The scene is the 'Isle of Slingers', that is, Portland, and the tale deals with the peculiar temperament of its inhabitants.

Weller, SAMUEL, in Dickens's 'The Pickwick Papers' (q.v.), Mr. Pickwick's devoted servant.

Weller, TONY, in Dickens's 'The Pickwick Papers' (q.v.), a coach-driver, the father of Sam Weller.

Wells, CHARLES JEREMIAH (1800-79), author, under the pseudonym of H. L. HOWARD, of 'Joseph and his Brethren: a Dramatic Poem' (1824). In 1876 (and in the World's Classics in 1908) this was republished with an essay by Swinburne. It was greatly admired by Rossetti.

Wells, HERBERT GEORGE (1866-1946), the son of a small tradesman, was apprenticed to a draper in early life, a period of which reflections may be seen in some of his best novels ('The History of Mr. Polly', 'Kipps', 'The Wheels of Chance'). He followed the teaching profession until 1893, when he definitely adopted that of letters.

Wells's novels divide themselves broadly into three groups: (1) fantastic and imaginative romances, in which, after the manner of Swift in 'Gulliver's Travels', the author projects himself to a distant standpoint—the moon, the future, the air—and views our life from outside, e.g. as an angel sees it ('The Wonderful Visit'); (2) novels of character and humour, of which 'The History of Mr. Polly' (1910) is the type; (3) discussion novels—discussion, that is, in the main, of human ideals and progress.

Wells's publications include: 'The Time Machine' and 'The Wonderful Visit' (1895), 'The War of the Worlds' (1898), 'Love and Mr. Lewisham' (1900), 'The First Men in the Moon' (1901), 'Anticipations' (sociological essays, 1902), 'The Food of the Gods' (1904), 'A Modern Utopia' and 'Kipps' (1905), 'The War in the Air' (1908), 'Tono-Bungay' (1909, one of Wells's most remarkable works, a picture of English society in dissolution in the later 19th cent., and of the advent of a new class of rich), 'The Country of the Blind' (1911), 'Mr. Britling sees it through' (1916), 'Short History of the World' (1922), 'The Shape of Things to Come' (1933).

Wemmick, in Dickens's 'Great Expectations' (q.v.), clerk to Mr. Jaggers the lawyer.

Wentworth, SIR THOMAS, see *Strafford*.

Werewolf or WERWOLF, a person who (according to medieval superstition) was transformed or was capable of transforming himself at times into a wolf. The belief in werewolves was widespread in England, Wales, Ireland, and the greater part of the Continent, down to the 17th cent., and is hardly extinct everywhere even today.

Werner, a tragedy by Lord Byron (q.v.) (1822).

Werther, The Sorrows of Young, see *Goethe*.

Wesley, CHARLES (1707–88), a brother of J. Wesley (q.v.), founded, while a student at Christ Church, a 'methodist' society of pious young men. To this society belonged John Wesley and George Whitefield, and these, with Charles himself, were the principal leaders of the Methodist movement. From a literary standpoint, Charles Wesley is remembered as the composer of a very large number of hymns, including 'Jesu, lover of my soul'.

Wesley, JOHN (1703–91), brother of Charles Wesley (q.v.), was a man of real and deep learning, and of autocratic temper. He published twenty-three collections of hymns (1737–86) and his collected prose 'Works' (1771–4). His 'Journal' is remarkable for its pathos, humour, and observation of mankind. Southey's 'Life of John Wesley', perhaps one of the best biographies in the language, was published in 1820. See also *Methodism*.

Wessex, the kingdom of the West Saxons, who established themselves in Hampshire early in the 6th cent., and extended their dominion north and west. It included Hants, Dorset, Wilts, Berks., and part of Somerset. Ultimately, under Egbert, Alfred, and their successors, the kingdom of Wessex developed into that of England.

'Wessex' is used by Hardy (q.v.) to designate the SW. counties, principally Dorset, which are the scene of his novels.

West, DAME REBECCA (1892–   ), novelist, critic, and political writer. Her novels include 'The Return of the Soldier' (1918), 'The Judge' (1922), 'Harriet Hume' (1929), 'The Thinking Reed' (1936), and 'The Fountain Overflows' (1957). Her other work includes 'The Strange Necessity' (essays and reviews, 1938), 'Black Lamb and Grey Falcon' (a book about Yugoslavia, 1942), 'The

Meaning of Treason' (a study of traitors, 1949), and 'The Court and the Castle' (a study of political and religious ideas in imaginative literature, 1958).

Western, SQUIRE and SOPHIA, characters in Fielding's 'Tom Jones' (q.v.).

Westlock, JOHN, a character in Dickens's 'Martin Chuzzlewit' (q.v.), at one time pupil of Mr. Pecksniff.

Westminster Abbey: Edward the Confessor passed much of his reign at Westminster and built a great church for the monks there. It was rebuilt by Henry III and added to and partly reconstructed in subsequent reigns. 'Poets' Corner' in the S. transept contains the monuments or other memorials of Chaucer, Spenser, Shakespeare, Ben Jonson, Milton, and other British authors.

Westminster Review, The, was founded in 1824 by Bentham (q.v.), with the assistance of James Mill (q.v.), as the organ of the philosophical radicals.

Westward Ho!, a novel by C. Kingsley (q.v.) (1855).

This was the most successful of the author's novels, and is a patriotic tale of adventure, Jesuit intrigue, and naval enterprise of the time of Queen Elizabeth. The hero, Amyas Leigh, takes part in the military measures against the Spaniards who landed at Smerwick in 1580, in the course of which he takes prisoner a Spanish captain, Don Guzman. The latter, while on parole in Devonshire, falls in love with the beautiful Rose Salterne, and induces her to leave her home, marries her, and carries her off to the Spanish main. Amyas and his brother Frank, and other disappointed suitors of Rose, with Salvation Yeo, sail in pursuit, but with tragic results. Rose, brought under suspicion by their action, falls a victim of the Inquisition, together with Frank Leigh. Amyas and his ship's crew wander for three years in South America, capture a Spanish galleon and return to England. The last chapter of the book are devoted to Amyas's pursuit of his vengeance on Don Guzman, for which the arrival of the Armada provides an opportunity. But Providence takes the vengeance out of his hands. After a long pursuit the Spaniard is wrecked and drowned, and Amyas is struck blind by lightning.

Westward Hoe, a comedy by J. Webster and T. Dekker (qq.v.), printed in 1607, but entered at the Stationers' Hall in 1605.

Weyman, STANLEY JOHN (1855-1928), author of several good historical romances in the vein of Dumas and R. L. Stevenson, including 'A Gentleman of France' (1893), and 'Under the Red Robe' (1896). In his finest book, 'Ovington's Bank' (1922), he dealt with England in the period after the Napoleonic wars.

Wharton, EDITH (1862-1937), American novelist. She was a friend of Henry James (q.v.) and deeply influenced by him, but her work is original and of distinct character. She excelled in both the short story and the novel. Her chief books were 'The House of Mirth' (1905), 'Ethan Frome' (1911), 'The Age of Innocence' (1920), 'Glimpses of the Moon' (1922), 'Hudson River Bracketed' (1929), 'The World Over' (1936).

Whately, RICHARD (1787-1863), principal of St. Alban Hall, Oxford, 1825-31, and professor of political economy, 1829-31. He was appointed archbishop of Dublin in the latter year. His fame rests chiefly on his 'Logic' and 'Rhetoric' (1826 and 1828). In theology he showed himself a critic of dogma, and was a supporter of the Broad Church views.

What you Will, (1) sub-title of Shakespeare's 'Twelfth Night' (q.v.); (2) a comedy by John Marston (q.v.), printed in 1607, containing, it is said, some satire of Ben Jonson.

Wheel, in prosody, see *Bob and Wheel*.

Whetstone, GEORGE (1544?-1587?), author of miscellaneous verse and prose tales, is principally remembered for his 'Promos and Cassandra' (1578), a play in rhymed verse (based on a tale in Cinthio's 'Hecatommithi'), which provided the plot for Shakespeare's 'Measure for Measure'

(q.v.), and is an early example of English romantic comedy.

Whig, a word probably shortened from *Whiggamore*, originally applied to the Covenanters in the west of Scotland in 1648. About 1679 it was applied to the Exclusionists, who opposed the succession of James II to the Crown. Hence from 1689 it came to be used for an adherent of one of the two great political parties in England. Since the middle of the 19th cent. the term has been mostly superseded by *Liberal*.

Whig Examiner, The, a literary and political periodical published by Addison (q.v.). Five numbers appeared in Sept. to Oct. 1710.

Whiskerandos, DON FEROLO, in Sheridan's 'The Critic' (q.v.), the lover of Tilburina.

Whistler, JAMES ABBOT MCNEILL (1834-1903), painter and etcher, born at Lowell, Massachusetts. He settled in England in 1866, living in Chelsea. In reaction against Victorian subject pictures, he called his paintings by such names as 'symphony' or 'nocturne' to emphasize their aesthetic qualities. In 1878 he brought a libel action against Ruskin for condemning his 'Nocturne in Black and Gold' and was awarded a farthing's damages. He published 'The Gentle Art of Making Enemies' (q.v.) in 1890. Whistler was a friend of Oscar Wilde (q.v.).

Whitaker's Almanack, founded in 1868 by Joseph Whitaker (1820-95), a publisher, and at one time (1856-9) editor of 'The Gentleman's Magazine'. It is a compendium of general information.

White, GILBERT (1720-93), spent most of his life as curate of Selborne, refusing various livings in order to remain in his beloved birthplace. He began in 1751 to keep a 'Garden Kalendar' and later a 'Naturalist's Journal'. He made the acquaintance of two distinguished naturalists, Thomas Pennant and the Hon. Daines Barrington, with whom from 1767 he carried on a correspondence which formed the basis of his 'Natural History and Antiquities of Selborne' (1789).

White, HENRY KIRKE (1785-1806). By a volume of verses (1803) he attracted the favourable notice of Southey, who thereafter protected him, and wrote a memoir of him in 1807 after his death. He was praised by Byron, but little survives of his work except one or two hymns ('Oft in danger, oft in woe').

White, JOSEPH BLANCO (1775-1841), was a friend of Whately (q.v.), and, when the latter was appointed archbishop of Dublin, accompanied him there as tutor to his son. He wrote the sonnet on 'Night and Death' (1828), which Coleridge declared the finest and most grandly conceived sonnet in our language.

White, PATRICK (1912-), Australian novelist, author of 'Happy Valley' (1939), 'The Living and the Dead' (1941), 'The Aunt's Story' (1948), 'The Tree of Man' (1956), 'Voss' (1957), 'Riders in the Chariot' (1961), and 'The Burnt Ones' (1964).

White, TERENCE HANBURY (1906-64), is best known for his novels on the Arthurian legend, published under the title 'The Once and Future King' (1958). He also wrote 'Farewell Victoria' (1933), a novel, and 'The Goshawk' (1951), an account of how he trained a hawk. 'The Book of Beasts' (1954) is a translation from a 12th-cent. Latin bestiary.

White, WILLIAM HALE (1831-1913), known as a writer under the pseudonym MARK RUTHERFORD. His literary work began with the publication in 1881 of 'The Autobiography of Mark Rutherford', followed in 1885 by its sequel 'Mark Rutherford's Deliverance', works of intimate spiritual self-revelation, marked by sincerity and depth of feeling and ironic humour. His other imaginative works included: 'The Revolution in Tanner's Lane' (1887) and 'Pages from a Journal' (1900).

White Company, THE, a body of English mercenaries led by the condottiere Hawkwood (q.v.) about 1360 into Italy. Sir A. Conan Doyle (q.v.) wrote a spirited story with this title about a similar company.

White Cross Knights, the *Hospitallers of St. John of Jerusalem* (q.v.).

White Divel, The, or *Vittoria Corombona*, a tragedy by J. Webster (q.v.), produced *c*. 1608, published in 1612. The play is founded on events that took place in Italy in 1581-5.

The duke of Brachiano, husband of Isabella, is weary of her and in love with Vittoria, wife of Camillo. Flamineo, brother of Vittoria, helps Brachiano to seduce her, and contrives the death of Camillo, while Brachiano causes Isabella to be poisoned. Flamineo quarrels with his young brother, the virtuous Marcello, and kills him. The duke of Florence avenges his sister Isabella by poisoning Brachiano, and two of his dependants kill Vittoria and Flamineo. The play contains many splendid passages, including the famous dirge by Cornelia, the mother of Marcello, over her dead son, 'Call for the robin-red-breast, and the wren' (Act v. iv).

Whitefield, GEORGE (1714-70), joined Charles Wesley's 'Methodist Society', and undertook a missionary journey to Georgia in 1738. He subsequently engaged in evangelical preaching in other parts of America, adopting Calvinistic views, so that his followers and those of Wesley separated and formed rival parties. He compiled a hymn-book (1753) and published sermons and autobiographical writings.

White Friars, THE, the Carmelites (q.v.).

White Hart Inn, THE, in Southwark, is referred to by Shakespeare in '2 Henry VI', iv. viii, as the headquarters of Jack Cade. There, at a later period, Mr. Pickwick first met Sam Weller. It survived until 1889.

Whitehead, ALFRED NORTH (1861-1947), professor of philosophy at Harvard University, the author of many important philosophical and mathematical works, including 'Principia Mathematica' (with Bertrand Russell, 1910), 'Symbolism' (1927), 'Adventures of Ideas' (1933).

Whitehead, WILLIAM (1715–85), produced at Drury Lane in 1750 a tragedy 'The Roman Father' (a version of Corneille's 'Horace') which was highly successful. He was appointed poet laureate in 1757. His productions in this capacity met with much unfriendly comment, but his earlier productions are not without merit.

White Jacket, by Herman Melville (q.v.) (1850), a fictional narrative based on the author's life as a common seaman aboard a frigate in the U.S. Navy.

White's, a chocolate-house in St. James's Street, London, started in 1697 by Francis White. The first number of 'The Tatler' announced that accounts of gallantry, pleasure, and entertainment would emanate from White's Chocolate House.

White Ship, The, a poem by D. G. Rossetti (q.v.), included in 'Ballads and Sonnets' (1881).

The butcher of Rouen, Berold, tells the story of the sinking of the 'White Ship' in which Prince William, son of Henry I, was returning with his half-sister from France.

White Surrey, Richard III's horse (see Shakespeare, 'Richard III', v. iii).

Whitman, WALT (1819–92), became an office boy at 11 years of age, and subsequently a printer, wandering schoolteacher, and contributor to, and editor of, various magazines and newspapers. Deeply affected by the teachings of Emerson (q.v.), he published his first edition of 'Leaves of Grass' in 1855, twelve poems. In this volume and its numerous subsequent enlarged editions, Whitman made himself a champion of American intellectual independence. During the Civil War he acted as a volunteer hospital visitor, an experience which affected him deeply, as can be seen in his prose 'Memoranda during the War' (1875) and in the poems he published under the title 'Drum-Taps' in 1865. In the 'Sequel' to these poems (1866) appeared the great elegy on Abraham Lincoln. In spite of his achievement, Whitman was disregarded by the public at large. He offended some by his outspokenness on sexual matters, but he also won admirers, some of the warmest being Englishmen, such as Swinburne and W. M. Rossetti (qq.v.).

Whit-Sunday, the seventh Sunday after Easter, observed as a festival of the Christian Church in commemoration of the descent of the Holy Spirit on the day of Pentecost.

Whittier, JOHN GREENLEAF (1807–92), American poet who began life as a farmer's boy. His poetical instincts were aroused by reading Burns's poetry, and he was from early years an industrious writer. He edited various periodicals and became an ardent abolitionist, and secretary of the American Anti-Slavery Society. He has always been a popular poet in America, owing in part to the transparent sincerity and nobility of his character, in part to the appeal to the young made by his ballads. He published many volumes of poems, of which a final collected edition appeared in 1888–9.

Whittington, RICHARD (*d.* 1423), rose to be lord mayor of London, 1397–8, 1406–7 (a year of plague), and 1419–20. He was a liberal benefactor of the city. The popular legend of Whittington and his cat, the germ of which is probably of very remote origin, is not known to have been narrated before 1605.

Whole Duty of Man, The, a devotional work (1658) in which man's duties in respect of God and his fellow men are analysed and discussed in detail. The book, by internal evidence, is the work of a practised divine, perhaps Richard Allestree (1619–81), chaplain in ordinary to the king. It had enormous popularity, lasting for over a century; it is comparable in this respect only to the 'De Imitatione Christi' and to Law's 'Serious Call'.

Who's Who, an annual biographical dictionary of contemporary men and women. It was first issued in 1849.

Whymper, EDWARD (1840-1911), a pioneer of Alpine climbing. He related his experiences in 'Scrambles in the Alps' (1871).

Whyte-Melville, GEORGE JOHN (1821-78), a captain in the Coldstream Guards, he served in the Crimea. He was killed in the hunting-field. His novels, in many of which hunting figures largely, include 'Digby Grand' (1853), 'Holmby House' (1860), 'The Gladiators' (1863), 'Roy's Wife' (1878), and 'Black but Comely' (1879).

Whythorne, THOMAS (1528-96), educated at Magdalen College, Oxford. After three years as 'servant and scholar' in the household of John Heywood (q.v.) he became a teacher of music and composer of madrigals. His autobiography, 'A Book of Songs and Sonetts', discovered in manuscript in 1955, was edited by J. M. Osborn and published in 1961. It is not only an interesting document of Tudor life and poetry and music, but also, because Whythorne wrote in his own phonetic system, a key to the pronunciation of his day.

Wickfield, MR. and AGNES, characters in Dickens's 'David Copperfield' (q.v.).

Widdicombe Fair, the title of a popular song which has become the accepted Devonshire song. The date of words and tune is probably the end of the 18th cent.

Widsith, a poem of 143 lines in Old English, so named after its opening word. It is included in the 'Exeter Book' (q.v.).

Widsith, a wandering minstrel, belonging to the Myrging tribe, speaks of his travels and the kings he has heard of. The kernel of the poem may belong to the 7th cent. or an even earlier date. It was elaborately edited by R. W. Chambers, 1912.

Wieland, see *Wayland.*

Wieland, CHRISTOPH MARTIN (1733-1813), German poet and writer of romances, whose best-known works are light ironic verse-tales, drawn from medieval or oriental sources, of which

'Oberon' (on the story of Huon of Bordeaux, 1780) is a good example.

Wife of Bath, see *Canterbury Tales.*

Wilberforce, WILLIAM (1759-1833), M.P. for Yorkshire, devoted himself to the cause of the abolition, first of the slave-trade, then of slavery, and to other philanthropic projects. He published in 1797 'A Practical View of the Prevailing Religious System of Professed Christians', a work that had an immense influence.

Wilcox, MRS. ELLA WHEELER (*née* Wheeler) (1850-1919), American poet and journalist, described as 'the most popular poet of either sex and of any age, read by thousands who never open Shakespeare'. She began to publish poems in 1872, and her last volume, 'Poems of Affection', was published posthumously in 1920. Her 'Collected Poems' were published in 1921.

Wild Boar of the Ardennes, see *Ardennes.*

Wild, JONATHAN (1682?-1725), worked as a buckle-maker in London. He became head of a large corporation of thieves, gained notoriety as a thief-taker, and was ultimately hanged at Tyburn. His 'Life and Actions' were related by Defoe (1725). For Fielding's satire see *Jonathan Wild the Great.*

Wilde, OSCAR FINGAL O'FLAHERTIE WILLS (1854-1900), poet and dramatist, educated at Trinity College, Dublin, and Magdalen College, Oxford, gained at the latter the reputation of founder of an aesthetic cult, which was caricatured in Gilbert and Sullivan's comic opera, 'Patience'. He published his first volume of 'Poems' in 1881, followed by several works of fiction, including 'The Picture of Dorian Gray' (1891), and several sparkling comedies, of which the best known are 'Lady Windermere's Fan', produced in 1892; 'A Woman of No Importance', in 1893; and 'The Importance of being Earnest', in 1895. His play 'Salomé' (in French, see *Salome*) was published in 1893. In 1895 he was sentenced to two years' imprisonment with hard labour for homosexual practices. After his release he lived abroad and finally settled in Paris, where he died. The most remarkable of his works were the 'Ballad of Reading Gaol' (1898) and 'De Profundis' (1905), written about his imprisonment.

Wilder, THORNTON NIVEN (1897-1975), American novelist and dramatist. His best-known novels are 'The Bridge of San Luis Rey' (1927) and 'Ides of March' (1948). He scored considerable success in the theatre with 'Our Town' (1938) and 'The Skin of Our Teeth' (1942).

Wildeve, DAMON, a character in Hardy's 'The Return of the Native' (q.v.).

Wildfell Hall, The Tenant of, a novel by A. Brontë (q.v.) (1848).

The tenant of Wildfell Hall is Helen Graham, said to be a widow. Her youth and beauty, her secluded mode of life, and her silence as to her antecedents, set the tongues of local gossips wagging. Gilbert Markham, the narrator of the tale, a young gentleman farmer and her neighbour, who has fallen in love with her, is loyal in his conviction of her innocence until he overhears her in affectionate conversation with Lawrence, her landlord.

The threatened rupture of relations between Gilbert and Helen forces the latter to confide her secret to her lover, in the form of her diary, which occupies a great part of the book. In this she recounts her youthful marriage with Arthur Huntingdon, a drunken profligate, her efforts to reclaim him, until his shameless conduct forces her to seek the asylum of Wildfell Hall, provided for her by Lawrence, who is her brother. Soon after the revelation of her secret to Gilbert, Helen returns to her husband to nurse him in an illness which proves fatal. The discovery that Helen is now wealthy is an obstacle to the renewal of Gilbert's suit, but this is finally overcome.

Wildfire, MADGE, see *Murdockson*.

Wild-Goose Chase, The, a comedy by J. Fletcher (q.v.), acted with great success in 1621, and printed in 1652.

Wilfer Family, THE, characters in Dickens's 'Our Mutual Friend' (q.v.).

Wilfrid or WILFRITH, ST. (634-709), bishop of York, of which see he was twice deprived. He was instrumental in winning the adherence of King Oswy of Northumbria to the Roman, as opposed to the Columban, Church (synod of Whitby), and was involved in other ecclesiastical disputes. He is commemorated on 12 Oct. 'The Conversion of St. Wilfrid' is a beautiful tale in Rudyard Kipling's 'Rewards and Fairies'.

Wilkes, JOHN (1727-97), after marrying an heiress much older than himself, led a life of dissipation and became a member of the Medmenham Abbey (q.v.) fraternity. He founded in 1762 'The North Briton' (q.v.) in which he skilfully attacked the government of Lord Bute. His prosecution for libel in connection with No. 45 of this paper led to his expulsion from the House of Commons, and outlawry. He retired to Paris, whence he returned in 1768 and was elected M.P. for Middlesex, and his outlawry was reversed. He was again expelled from the House in 1769 for a libel in the 'St. James's Chronicle', and three times re-elected for Middlesex, his elections being each time annulled. He finally took his seat in 1774.

A man of much wit, ability, and determination, though of low moral standard, and an idol of the London mob, he was the means of asserting and securing several of our most valuable political rights.

Willbewill, THE LORD, a character in Bunyan's 'The Holy War' (q.v.).

Willet, JOHN and JOE his son, characters in Dickens's 'Barnaby Rudge' (q.v.).

William I, of Normandy, 'The Conqueror', king of England, 1066-87.

William II, or RUFUS, king of England, 1087-1100.

William III and Mary, king and queen of England from 1689. Mary died in 1694, William in 1702.

William IV, king of England, 1830-7.

William de la Marck, see *Ardennes*.

William of Cloudesley, see *Adam Bell*.

William of Malmesbury (*d.* 1143?), historian, was born between 1090 and 1096. He was educated at Malmesbury Abbey, and became librarian. His works include 'Gesta Regum Anglorum', covering the period from A.D. 449 to 1127; its sequel 'Historia Novella', dealing with English history to 1142; 'Gesta Pontificum Anglorum', finished 1125; and 'De Antiquitate Glastoniensis Ecclesiae', written between 1129 and 1139. William of Malmesbury is not only a historian of high authority, but a picturesque and vivacious writer. The 'Gesta Regum' has two passages about Arthur, whom William regards as a great warrior, while discrediting many of the stories about him.

William of Newburgh (1136-1198?), author of a 'Historia Rerum Anglicarum' in Latin, covering the period from 1066 to 1198, but mainly devoted to the reigns of Stephen and Henry II. It is the best historical work extant by an Englishman of this period.

William of Palerne, one of the earliest of the 14th-cent. alliterative English romances, of some 5,500 lines and probably from a Latin source.

Williams, CALEB, see *Caleb Williams*.

Williams, JOHN (1761-1818), satirist and miscellaneous writer, best known by his pseudonym ANTHONY PASQUIN. He was associated with various journals in Dublin and London, and wrote formidable theatrical criticisms. In 1797 he took out a libel action in respect of the poem, 'The Baviad', by William Gifford (q.v.), but failed when it was shown that he had himself libelled every respectable character in the kingdom from the sovereign down. He emigrated to America and died in poverty.

Williams, MICHAEL, in Shakespeare's 'Henry V' (q.v.), one of the English soldiers.

Williams, TENNESSEE (1914-), American dramatist. He made his reputation with 'The Glass Menagerie' (1945) and was even more successful with 'A Streetcar Named Desire' (1947), a violent and effective study of sexual aberration, set in the South. Among other plays on related sensational themes are 'Rose Tattoo' (1951) and 'Cat on a Hot Tin Roof' (1955). His novel, 'The Roman Spring of Mrs. Stone', was published in 1950.

Williams, WILLIAM CARLOS (1883-1963), American poet. He published many volumes of verse, of which the most ambitious is 'Paterson' (in five books, 1946-58).

Will-o'-the-Wisp, see *Ignis Fatuus*.

Willoughby, SIR CLEMENT, a character in Fanny Burney's 'Evelina' (q.v.).

Willoughby, JOHN, a character in Jane Austen's 'Sense and Sensibility' (q.v.).

Will's Coffee-house, was at No. 1 Bow Street, at the corner of Russell Street. It was frequented in the 17th and 18th cents. by authors (notably by Dryden, Wycherley, Addison, Pope, and Congreve), wits, and gamblers. The first number of 'The Tatler' (q.v.) announced that all poetry appearing in it would be under the article of Will's Coffee-house.

Wilmot, ROBERT (*fl.* 1568-1608), dramatist, published in 1591 'The Tragedie of Tancred and Gismund, or Gismond of Salerne'. Act II is by Henry Noel, Act IV by Hatton (q.v.). The play is founded on a tale by Boccaccio (see *Sigismonda*).

Wilson, ALISON, a character in Scott's 'Old Mortality' (q.v.).

Wilson, JOHN (1627?-1696), became a barrister of Lincoln's Inn and recorder of Londonderry. His principal plays are two comedies on the Jonsonian model, 'The Cheats' (1664) and 'The Projectors' (1665), and a tragedy, 'Andronicus Comnenius' (1664).

Wilson, JOHN (1785-1854), was elected professor of moral philosophy at Edinburgh University on the strength of his Tory principles in 1820. He joined the editorial staff of 'Blackwood's Magazine' (q.v.) in 1817, and contributed to it the greater number of the 'Noctes Ambrosianae' (q.v.), in which he figures as 'Christopher North'. He joined with Lockhart and Hogg in the production of the famous 'Translation from an Ancient Chaldee Manuscript', in which Edinburgh notabilities were satirized in scriptural language ('Blackwood', Oct. 1817). Wilson was one of the first critics to do justice to the poetry of Wordsworth.

Wilson, THOMAS (1525?-1581), privy councillor and secretary of state in 1578, published the 'Rule of Reason' in 1551, and the 'Art of Rhetorique' in 1553. The latter is noteworthy in the history of English literature; in it the author urges the importance of writing of English matters in the English tongue, avoiding affectations and latinisms.

Wilton, JACKE, see *Unfortunate Traveller*.

Wimble, WILL, in Addison's 'The Spectator' (q.v.), a friend of Sir Roger de Coverley.

Wimsey, LORD PETER, the detective hero of many stories by Dorothy L. Sayers (q.v.).

Winchilsea, ANNE FINCH, *countess of* (1661-1720), a writer of pleasant occasional verse (praised by Sir E. Gosse) and a friend of Pope and Rowe (qq.v.). Wordsworth found affinities in some of her work.

Winckelmann, JOHANN JOACHIM (1717-68), the founder of the modern study of Greek sculptures and antiquities. By his understanding of the ideal of Greek art, its spiritual quality, and its sense of proportion, he exerted an immense influence on subsequent thought and literature (e.g. on Goethe).

Windsor Forest, a pastoral poem by A. Pope (q.v.) (1713), combining descriptions of the English countryside and field sports, with historical, literary, and political passages.

Winkle, NATHANIEL, a character in Dickens's 'The Pickwick Papers' (q.v.).

Winkle, RIP VAN, see *Rip van Winkle*.

Winner and Waster, Good Short Debate between, an alliterative poem composed in the middle of the 14th cent., discussing the economic problems of the day. It perhaps contributed to inspire the 'Vision concerning Piers the Plowman' (q.v.).

Winter's Tale, The, a play by Shakespeare (q.v.), probably produced in 1609-10, and based on Robert Greene's 'Pandosto' (q.v.). It was not printed until the folio of 1623.

Leontes, king of Sicily, and Hermione, his virtuous wife, are visited by Leontes' friend, Polixenes, king of Bohemia. Leontes, presently filled with a baseless suspicion of the relations of Hermione and Polixenes, attempts to procure the death of the latter by poison, and on his escape imprisons Hermione, who in prison gives birth to a daughter. Paulina, wife of Antigonus, a Sicilian lord, tries to move the king's compassion by bringing the baby to him, but in vain. He orders Antigonus to leave the child on a desert shore to perish. He disregards a Delphian oracle declaring Hermione innocent. He soon learns that his son, Mamillus, has died of sorrow for Hermione's treatment, and shortly after that Hermione herself is dead, and is thereupon filled with remorse. Meanwhile Antigonus leaves the baby girl, Perdita, on the shore of Bohemia, and is himself killed by a bear. Perdita is found and brought up by a shepherd. When she grows up, Florizel, son of King Polixenes, falls in love with her, and his love is returned. This is discovered by Polixenes, to avoid whose anger Florizel, Perdita, and the old shepherd fly from Bohemia to the court of King Leontes, where the identity of Perdita is discovered, to Leontes' great joy, and the revival of his grief for the loss of Hermione. Paulina offers to show him a statue that perfectly resembles Hermione, and when the king's grief is intensified by the sight of this, the statue reveals itself as the living Hermione, whose death Paulina had falsely reported in order to save her life. Polixenes is reconciled to the marriage of his son with Perdita, on finding that the shepherd-girl is really the daughter of his former friend Leontes. The rogueries of Autolycus, the pedlar and 'snapper-up of unconsidered trifles', add gaiety to the later scenes of the play; and his songs, 'When daffodils begin to peer' and

'Jog on, jog on, the foot-path way', are famous.

Wireker, NIGEL (*fl.* 1190), author of 'Speculum Stultorum', a satire on monks, an elegiac poem recounting the adventures of Burnell the Ass (q.v.). It is referred to in Chaucer's 'The Nun's Priest's Tale'.

Wisdom of Solomon, one of the books of the Apocrypha (q.v.), attributed by tradition to Solomon's authorship, but probably from a Greek original of a period little anterior to Christianity.

Wise Men of Gotham, see *Gotham*.

Wise Men of Greece, see *Seven Sages of Greece*.

Wishfort, LADY, a character in Congreve's 'The Way of the World' (q.v.).

Witch, The, a play by T. Middleton (q.v.), written before 1627, not printed until 1778.

Part of the interest of the play lies in the comparison between Middleton's Hecate and the witches in Shakespeare's 'Macbeth'. Charles Lamb in his 'Specimens' has indicated the difference between them.

Witchcraft, The Discoverie of, see *Scott (R.)*.

Witches' Sabbath, see *Sabbath (Witches')*.

Witch of Atlas, The, a poem in *ottava rima* by P. B. Shelley (q.v.), written in 1820.

The poet invents the myth of a beautiful and beneficent witch, the daughter of Apollo, who can see the souls of men under their mortal forms, blesses those whom she sees most beautiful, but 'writes strange dreams upon the brain' of those who are less beautiful, and mischievously crosses their purposes.

Witch of Edmonton, The, a tragic-comedy by Dekker, J. Ford, W. Rowley (q.v.), 'etc.' (as the title states), first performed probably in 1623, but not published until 1658.

The old woman of Edmonton, who is persecuted by her neighbours until she sells her soul to the devil in order to be revenged on them, and becomes the witch

that they have called her, provides the title for the play, but has little connection with the main plot. This part is notable for the characteristic sympathy shown by Dekker for the poor outcast.

Witch of Endor, THE, see *Endor*.

Wither, GEORGE (1588–1667). His satires, 'Abuses stript and whipt' (1613), in spite of the innocuous character of their denunciations, earned him imprisonment in the Marshalsea. There he wrote five pastorals under the title of 'The Shepherd's Hunting', containing some of his best verse, a continuation of the 'Shepherd's Pipe' which he had written in conjunction with William Browne (q.v.), the 'Willie' of these eclogues. His 'Fidelia', a poetical epistle from a faithful nymph to her inconstant lover, appeared in 1617 and again, with the famous song, 'Shall I, wasting in despair', in 1619. In 1622 appeared his 'Mistress of Phil'Arete', a long panegyric of his mistress Arete; also the collection of pieces called 'Juvenilia', containing most of his best work. After this he became a convinced Puritan and published principally religious exercises. His 'Collection of Emblemes' was published in 1634–5 (see *Emblem-book*).

Witterly, MR. and MRS., in Dickens's 'Nicholas Nickleby' (q.v.), typical snobs.

Wits, The, a comedy by D'Avenant (q.v.), published in 1636.

Witwoud, and his half-brother SIR WILFULL WITWOUD, characters in Congreve's 'The Way of the World' (q.v.).

Wives and Daughters, the last and unfinished novel of Mrs. Gaskell (q.v.) (1864–6).

Wizard of the North, THE, Sir W. Scott (q.v.).

Wodehouse, SIR PELHAM GRENVILLE (1881–1975), humorous novelist, among whose chief works are: 'Uneasy Money' (1917), 'Piccadilly Jim' (1918), 'The Indiscretions of Archie' (1921), 'The Clicking of Cuthbert' (1922); and the series of Jeeves stories (from about 1917 onwards), which have been collected in 'My Man Jeeves', 'The Inimitable Jeeves', 'Carry on, Jeeves', 'Very Good, Jeeves', and 'The Jeeves Omnibus'.

Woden, the OE. name of the god called in Norse Odin (q.v.), from whom our 'Wednesday' or 'Woden's day' is derived.

Woeful Countenance, THE KNIGHT OF THE, Don Quixote (q.v.).

Woffington, MARGARET (1714?-1760), 'Peg Woffington', the celebrated actress. Her amours were numerous and for some time she lived with Garrick. For Charles Reade's novel concerning her, see *Peg Woffington*.

Wolcot, JOHN (1738-1819), 'PETER PINDAR', published his satirical 'Lyric Odes to the Royal Academicians' in 1782-5, followed by a mock-heroic poem, 'The Lousiad' in 1785, and various satires on George III. He was attacked by Gifford in 'The Anti-Jacobin'. His 'Bozzy and Piozzi', in which Boswell and Mrs. Thrale set forth their respective reminiscences of Dr. Johnson in amoebaean verse, appeared in 1786. He had a gift for the comical and mischievous exposure of foibles, but his work suffers from vulgarity of thought and inelegance of style.

Wolfe, CHARLES (1791-1823), was the author of the splendid lines on 'The Burial of Sir John Moore' (apparently based on Southey's narrative in the 'Annual Register', and first published in the 'Newry Telegraph' in 1817).

Wollstonecraft, MARY, see *Godwin* (*Mrs. M. W.*).

Wolsey, THOMAS (1475?-1530), cardinal; his fall from power is depicted in Shakespeare's 'Henry VIII' (q.v.).

Woman in the Moone, The, a prose play by Lyly (q.v.) (1597).

Woman in White, The, a novel by Wilkie Collins (q.v.) (1860), one of the first detective stories, notable for the characterization of the villain Count Fosco.

Woman Kilde with Kindnesse, A, a domestic tragedy by T. Heywood (q.v.), acted about 1603, printed in 1607.

Frankford, a country gentleman, is the husband of Anne, a 'perfect' wife. But his happiness is ruined by the treachery of

Wendoll, a guest to whom Frankford has shown every kindness and hospitality. Frankford sends Anne to live in comfort in a lonely manor-house, only prohibiting her from seeing him or her children again. She dies from remorse, after having sent for Frankford to ask forgiveness on her death-bed.

This play, in which pathos and manliness are blended, is considered Heywood's masterpiece. It opens with a pleasant hawking scene.

Women beware Women, a tragedy by T. Middleton (q.v.), published in 1657, thirty years after his death.

Wonders of the World, THE SEVEN, see *Seven Wonders of the World*.

Wood, ANTHONY, or, as he latterly called himself, ANTHONY À WOOD (1632-95), antiquary and historian. He prepared a treatise on the history of the University of Oxford, which was translated into Latin and edited (with alterations) by Dr. John Fell (q.v.), dean of Christ Church, and published as 'Historia et Antiquitates Univ. Oxon.' (1674). Wood published 'Athenae Oxonienses' (1691-2), a biographical dictionary of Oxford writers and bishops, containing severe judgements on some of these, and was expelled from the University in 1693 as a consequence.

Wood, ELLEN, better known as MRS. HENRY WOOD (1814-87), novelist, among whose best-known works are 'East Lynne' (1861) and 'The Channings' (1862).

Woodcourt, ALLAN, a character in Dickens's 'Bleak House' (q.v.).

Wooden Horse of Troy, THE, see *Horse* (*The Trojan*).

Woodforde, THE REVD. JAMES (1740-1803), author of the 'Diary of a Country Parson' (5 vols., 1924-31), which gives a vivid picture of the life of the period in college and country parish, with special reference, incidentally, to what was eaten and drunk.

Woodhouse, MR., in Jane Austen's 'Emma' (q.v.), the father of Emma.

Woodlanders, The, a novel by Hardy (q.v.) (1887).

Wood's half-pence, see *Drapier's Letters*.

Woodstock; or, The Cavalier. *A tale of the year 1651*, a novel by Sir W. Scott (q.v.) (1826). The work was written when misfortunes were heaping themselves upon the author: his financial ruin, the death of his wife, and the illness of his beloved grandson.

The period is that of the Civil War, and the story centres in the escape of Charles II from England after the battle of Worcester. The portrait of Cromwell has been criticized; the author makes, it is said, the mistake of representing Oliver as being in supreme power before he became lord protector in 1653. But the work gives a vivid picture of a reckless cavalier, Roger Wildrake; of the Revd. Nehemiah Holdenough, Presbyterian minister of the town of Woodstock; of Puritan soldiers and preachers (including Joseph Tomkins, the steward of the parliamentary commissioners, a mixture of hypocrisy and enthusiasm); and of plotters and spies on both sides.

Woolf, VIRGINIA (1882–1941), daughter of Sir Leslie Stephen (q.v.), author of fiction: 'The Voyage Out' (1915), 'Night and Day' (1919), 'Jacob's Room' (1922), 'Mrs. Dalloway' (1925), 'To the Lighthouse' (1927), 'Orlando: A Biography' (1928), 'The Waves' (1931), 'The Years' (1937), 'Between the Acts' (1941); essays and other works: 'The Common Reader: First Series' (1925), 'Second Series' (1932), 'A Room of One's Own' (1929), 'Flush: A Biography' (1933), 'The Death of a Moth' (1942), 'A Haunted House' (1943), 'The Moment' (1947), 'The Captain's Death Bed' (1950), 'Granite and Rainbow' (1958). 'A Writer's Diary' (1953) was selected and edited by her husband, Leonard Woolf.

Virginia Woolf contributed to the development of the art of fiction. From 'Jacob's Room' to 'Between the Acts' she continued to experiment with the form of the novel, minimizing the importance of facts, events, and character analysis in order to concentrate on the moment by moment experience of living. She eliminated the author as narrator or commentator. She was also a distinguished critic. In 'A Writer's Diary' her reflections upon each of her works from its conception to its accomplishment convey a vivid impression of the joys and agonies of creative effort.

Woolsack, THE, the usual seat, without back or arms, of the lord chancellor in the House of Lords. The term is often used allusively to signify the lord-chancellorship.

Wooster, BERTRAM (familiarly known as 'Bertie'), an amiable, vacuous young man-about-town in the stories of P. G. Wodehouse (q.v.); the employer of Jeeves (q.v.).

Wopsle, MR., a character in Dickens's 'Great Expectations' (q.v.).

Worde, WYNKYN DE (active 1477–1535), printer, born at Worth in Alsace. His real name was Jan van Wynkyn. He came to London *c.* 1477 and became Caxton's (q.v.) assistant, inheriting his press on Caxton's death in 1491. He printed nearly 800 books, including new editions and broadsides. Among the most notable were 'The Golden Legend' (1493), the 'Vitae Sanctorum Patrum' of St. Jerome, translated by Caxton (1495), 'Le Morte Darthur' (1498), and 'The Canterbury Tales' (1498).

Wordsworth, DOROTHY (1771–1855), sister and constant companion of W. Wordsworth. Her 'Journals' were edited by W. Knight, 1896 and 1904. A life and study of her by E. de Selincourt appeared in 1933.

Wordsworth, WILLIAM (1770–1850), was educated at the grammar school of Hawkshead and St. John's College, Cambridge, leaving the University without distinction. In 1790 he went on a walking tour in France, the Alps, and Italy. He returned to France late in 1791, and spent a year there. The revolutionary movement was then at its height and exercised a strong influence on his mind. While in France he fell in love with the daughter of a surgeon at Blois, Annette Vallon, who bore him a daughter (see Émile Legouis, 'William Wordsworth and Annette Vallon', 1922). The episode is in part reflected in 'Vaudracour and Julia', written in 1805. In 1793 he published 'An Evening Walk' and 'Descriptive Sketches' (of the Alps), his first serious poetical efforts. When the French Revolution was followed by the English declaration of war and the Terror, Wordsworth's republican enthusiasm gave place to a period of pessimism, which manifested itself in his tragedy, 'The Borderers', written in 1795-6. He received in 1795 a legacy of £900, left to him by his friend Raisley Calvert, a mark of Calvert's confidence in Wordsworth's genius. In the same year Wordsworth made the acquaintance of S. T. Coleridge (q.v.). A close and long-enduring friendship developed between the poets, and Wordsworth, with his sister Dorothy and Mr. and Mrs. Coleridge, lived for a year in close intercourse at Alfoxden and Nether Stowey in Somerset. Together the poets published in 1798 'Lyrical Ballads' (q.v.), which marked a revival in English poetry, but was unfavourably received. Together also, at the end of the same year, the poets went to Germany, Wordsworth and his sister wintering at Goslar. Here Wordsworth began 'The Prelude' (q.v.) and wrote 'Ruth', 'Lucy Gray', 'Nutting', the lines on 'Lucy' (q.v.), and other poems. In 1799 he settled with his sister at Grasmere, where he spent the remainder of his life (at first at Dove Cottage). In 1800 appeared an enlarged edition of the 'Lyrical Ballads', with a critical essay named 'Observations', expounding Wordsworth's principles of poetry, to which was added in 1802 an appendix on 'Poetic Diction'. This edition of the 'Lyrical Ballads', and particularly the 'Observations', were received with extreme hostility by the critics, which left Wordsworth unmoved. To the year 1800 belongs 'Michael', one of the most harmonious of Wordsworth's poems. He married in 1802 Mary

Hutchinson of Penrith. Events abroad now changed his political attitude to one of patriotic enthusiasm, while the death of his brother John in 1805 and the physical decline of his friend, S. T. Coleridge, deeply affected him. In 1805 he completed 'The Prelude', which, however, was not published until after his death. In 1807 he published poems, including the odes to 'Duty' (written in 1805) and on 'Intimations of Immortality', 'Miscellaneous Sonnets', and 'Sonnets dedicated to Liberty'. He now moved to Rydal Mount, Grasmere, which he occupied till his death. He toured in Scotland in 1814, and in that year published 'The Excursion' (q.v.). 'Peter Bell' (q.v., written in 1798) and 'The Waggoner' (written in 1805) appeared in 1819. The 'Ecclesiastical Sonnets' appeared in 1822. He travelled on the Continent in 1820, 1823, and 1828, publishing in 1822 a volume of poems entitled 'Memorials of a Tour on the Continent'. In 1843 he succeeded Southey as poet laureate. His biography was written by M. Moorman (2 vols., 1968).

Worldly Wiseman, MR., in Bunyan's 'The Pilgrim's Progress' (q.v.), an inhabitant of the town of Carnal Policy, who tries to dissuade Christian from going on his pilgrimage.

Worthies of England, The, by Fuller (q.v.), published in 1662, after his death.

The work is a kind of gazetteer of England, in which the author takes the counties one by one. After these come short biographies, not devoid of humour, of the local saints, martyrs (i.e. persons who suffered for the Protestant faith), prelates, statesmen, etc.

Worthies of the World, THE NINE, were 'three Paynims, three Jews, and three Christian men', viz. Hector of Troy, Alexander the Great, and Julius Caesar; Joshua, David, and Judas Maccabaeus; Arthur, Charlemagne, and Godfrey of Bouillon (Caxton, Preface to the 'Morte Darthur'). The list of worthies in

Shakespeare's 'Love's Labour's Lost', v. ii, is not quite the same, for it includes Pompey and Hercules.

Wotton, SIR HENRY (1568-1639), became agent and secretary to the earl of Essex, 1595, and was employed by him in collecting foreign intelligence. He was employed on various diplomatic missions from 1604 to 1624. A collection of his poetical and other writings appeared under the title 'Reliquiae Wottonianae' (containing his famous 'Character of a Happy Life' and 'On his Mistress, the Queen of Bohemia'—'You meaner beauties of the night') in 1651. His 'Life' was written by Izaak Walton (1670).

Would-be, SIR POLITICK and LADY, characters in Jonson's 'Volpone' (q.v.).

Wrayburn, EUGENE, a character in Dickens's 'Our Mutual Friend' (q.v.).

Wreck of the Hesperus, The, a poem by Longfellow (q.v.) (1841).

Wren, SIR CHRISTOPHER (1631-1723), a prominent member of the group of scholars who later were founder members of the Royal Society (q.v.). He was appointed professor of anatomy at Gresham College, London, in 1657, and Savilian professor of astronomy at Oxford in 1661. His first architectural works were the chapel of Pembroke College, Cambridge (1663-5), and the Sheldonian Theatre, Oxford (1664-9). A few days after the Fire of London in 1666 he presented a plan for rebuilding the City, but it was not adopted. He was, however, made surveyor in charge of the City churches, and designed fifty-two of them. He had prepared a scheme for repairing St. Paul's before the Fire, and when, in 1668, it became clear that it must be rebuilt, he prepared designs. Work began on the new building in 1675 and it was finished in 1710. Wren became surveyor-general of the king's works in 1688/9; he designed part of Whitehall Palace (destroyed by fire, 1698), Kensington Palace, extensions to Hampton Court, Chelsea Hospital, and part of Greenwich Hospital. His university buildings include the library of

Trinity College, Cambridge, and Tom Tower, Christ Church, Oxford.

Wren, JENNY, the business name of the doll's dressmaker in Dickens's 'Our Mutual Friend' (q.v.). Her real name was Fanny Cleaver.

Wulfila, see *Ulfilas*.

Wulfstan (*d.* 1023), archbishop of York, author of homilies in the vernacular, including a famous address to the English ('Sermo Lupi ad Anglos'), in which he describes the desolation of the country owing to the Danish raids, and castigates the vices and demoralization of the people.

Wuthering Heights, a novel by E. Brontë (q.v.) (1847).

The central figure of this sombre and highly imaginative story is Heathcliff, a gipsy waif of unknown parentage, picked up by Mr. Earnshaw in the streets of Liverpool and brought home and reared by him as one of his own children. Bullied and humiliated after the elder Earnshaw's death by Earnshaw's son Hindley, Heathcliff's passionate and ferocious nature finds its complement in Earnshaw's daughter, Catherine, and he falls passionately in love with her. Overhearing her say that it would degrade her to marry him, he leaves the house. Returning three years later he finds Catherine married to the insignificant Edgar Linton. Being possessed of money, he is welcomed by Hindley, a coarse-natured gambler, who is now married. Heathcliff's vindictive nature henceforth has full play. His violent love for Catherine brings her to her grave at the birth of her daughter Cathy. He marries Edgar's sister Isabella, not loving her, and cruelly maltreats her. He gets Hindley and his son Hareton completely in his power, brutalizing the latter in revenge for Hindley's treatment of himself when a child. His attempt to destroy the houses of Earnshaw and Linton fails in the end from lack of resolution, and at his death Hareton and Cathy are left to be happy together.

Wyatt, SIR THOMAS (1503?-1542), held various posts at home and abroad, including that of ambassador to Charles V (1537-9), in the service of Henry VIII. He was a close student of foreign literature, and (with Surrey, q.v.) introduced the sonnet (q.v.) from Italy into England. His first published works appeared as 'Certayne Psalmes . . . drawen into Englyshe meter' (1549), and many of his poems, which include rondeaux, lyrics, and satires in heroic couplets, were issued by Tottel (q.v.) in his 'Miscellany' (1557). He was a lyric poet of the purest note.

Wycherley, WILLIAM (1640-1716). His first play, 'Love in a Wood, or St. James's Park', a comedy of intrigue of which St. James's Park furnishes the scene, was acted in 1671 and published in 1672. His second play, 'The Gentleman Dancing-Master', was acted in 1671 or 1672; 'The Country Wife' in 1672 or 1673; his last play, 'The Plain Dealer', probably in 1674. His 'Miscellany Poems' (published in 1704) led to a friendship with Pope, who revised many of his writings. Lamb classes him with Congreve as one of the best masters of 'Artificial Comedy'. Wycherley was labelled by Macaulay as licentious and indecent. The present view of him is that he was a satirist more savage than Congreve, but a poet less sensitive. Contemporaries named him 'manly Wycherley'.

Wycliffe, JOHN (c. 1320-84). A realist in philosophy and a religious reformer, he advocated the poverty of the clergy and attacked church endowments. His 'De Dominio Divino' (1376) expounds the doctrine that all authority is founded on grace; which leads to the idea that wicked kings, popes, and priests should have no power. The Lollards adopted and exaggerated his views. From a literary standpoint he is chiefly notable as having instituted the first translation into English of the whole Bible, himself translating the Gospels, probably the New Testament, and possibly part of the Old Testament. See also *Bible* (*The English*).

Wynkyn de Worde, see *Worde*.

Wyntoun, ANDREW OF (1350?-1420?), a canon regular of St. Andrews and author of 'The Orygynale Cronykil', a metrical history of Scotland from the beginning of the world to the accession of James I. He becomes a valuable authority in the later part of the work.

X

Xanadu, in Coleridge's 'Kubla Khan' (q.v.), the place where the Khan decreed 'a stately pleasure-dome'. The name is taken from the passage in 'Purchas his Pilgrimes' which inspired the poem. J. L. Lowes in his 'The Road to Xanadu' (1927) reconstructs, with the aid of one of Coleridge's notebooks (of the years probably 1795-8), the process by which the images in the poem were drawn from various sources.

Xanthippe, the wife of Socrates (q.v.), said to have been a scold.

Xenocrates (396-314 B.C.), a native of Chalcedon and a Platonic philosopher.

Xenophanes (c. 576-480 B.C.), a Greek poet, formerly thought to have been the founder of the Eleatic School of philosophy. He taught that God was the eternal and immutable unity pervading the universe.

Xenophon, an Athenian, probably born about 430 B.C., was, when young, a pupil of Socrates. He joined the Greek contingent raised by the younger Cyrus in 401 for his war with Artaxerxes. After the battle of Cunaxa, Xenophon was elected one of the generals of the Greek force, which was left in a dangerous situation between the Tigris and Euphrates, and took a leading part in the memorable retreat thence to the Black Sea.

Xenophon's principal writings include: the 'Anabasis', or history of the expedition of the younger Cyrus and the retreat of the Greeks; the 'Cyropaedia', a political romance based on the history of Cyrus, the founder of the Persian monarchy; and the 'Memorabilia' of Socrates and the 'Symposium', in which he expounds and defends the doctrines and character of the great philosopher.

Xerxes (519–465 B.C.), king of Persia, the son of Darius I. He invaded Greece, overcame the resistance of Leonidas at Thermopylae, but was defeated at Salamis (480 B.C.). He is the King Ahasuerus of the Book of Esther.

Y

Yahoo, see *Gulliver's Travels*.

Yale University, originally founded as a school at Saybrook, Connecticut, in 1701, was transferred to New Haven, Connecticut, in 1716 and called Yale College in consequence of benefactions received from Elihu Yale (1648–1721), a native of Boston, Massachusetts, who entered the service of the East India Company, and became governor of Madras. It received a new charter in 1745 and assumed the name of Yale University in 1887.

Yarrow, THE, a river in Selkirkshire that joins the Ettrick near Selkirk. It has inspired many poets, from the author of the ballad 'The Dowie Houms of Yarrow' onwards, including Hamilton of Bangour, the Revd. John Logan (1748–88), James Hogg, Scott, and Wordsworth.

Year, THE, in England from the 13th cent. began on 25 March (the Annunciation), having previously begun on Christmas Day. To harmonize the legal year with that of Roman Catholic countries (since 1583) and of Scotland (since 1600), also with common usage in the kingdom, an Act of 1751 prescribed that from 1752 the year should begin on 1 Jan.

Year Books, reports of English common law cases for the period 1292–1534, of great interest from a historical as well as a legal standpoint. They were succeeded by the law 'Reports'. F. W. Maitland (q.v.) began editing them, and the work is still going on.

Yeast, a novel by C. Kingsley (q.v.), published in 'Fraser's Magazine' in 1848.

This was the first of Kingsley's novels and is crude as a literary work. It deals with some of the social and religious problems of the day (the miserable conditions of the rustic labourer, the game laws, and the Tractarian movement), largely by means of dialogues between the hero and various other characters.

Yeats, WILLIAM BUTLER (1865–1939), was born in Dublin. For three years he studied at the School of Art in Dublin, where with a fellow student, George Russell ('AE') (q.v.), he developed an interest in mystic religion and the supernatural. At 21 he abandoned art as a profession in favour of literature, writing 'John Sherman and Dhoya' (1891) and editing 'The Poems of William Blake' (1893), 'The Works of William Blake' (with E. J. Ellis, 3 vols., 1893), and 'Poems of Spenser' (1906). A nationalist, he applied himself to the creation of an Irish national theatre, an achievement which, with the help of Lady Gregory (q.v.) and others, was partly realized in 1899 when his play, 'The Countess Cathleen', was acted in Dublin. The English actors engaged by the Irish Literary Theatre gave place in 1902 to an Irish amateur company, which produced Yeats's 'Cathleen ni Houlihan' in that year. The Irish National Theatre Company was thereafter created, and acquired the Abbey Theatre (q.v.) in Dublin. Yeats's early study of Irish lore and legends resulted in 'Fairy and Folk Tales of the Irish Peasantry' (1888), 'The Celtic Twilight' (1893), and 'The Secret Rose' (1897). Irish traditional and nationalist themes and the poet's unrequited love for Maud Gonne, a beautiful revolutionary, provided much of the subject-matter for 'The Wanderings of Oisin and other Poems' (1889), 'The Land of Heart's Desire' (1894), 'The Wind among the Reeds' (1899), 'The Shadowy Waters' (1900), and such of his later plays as 'On Baile's Strand' (1904) and 'Deirdre' (1907).

With each succeeding collection of poems Yeats moved further from the elaborate, Pre-Raphaelite style of the 1890s. 'In the Seven Woods' (1903) was followed by 'The Green Helmet and Other Poems' (1910), 'Poems Written in Discouragement' (1913), 'Responsibilities: Poems and a Play' (1914), and 'The Wild Swans at Coole' (1917). In 1917 he married Georgie Hyde-Lees, who on their honeymoon attempted automatic writing, an event that exercised a profound effect on his life and work. His wife's 'communicators' ultimately provided him with the system of symbolism described in 'A Vision' (1925) and underlying many of the poems in 'Michael Robartes and the Dancer' (1921), 'Seven Poems and a Fragment' (1922), 'The Cat and the Moon and Certain Poems' (1924), 'October Blast' (1927), 'The Winding Stair' (1929), 'Words for Music Perhaps and Other Poems' (1932), 'Wheels and Butterflies' (1934), 'The King of the Great Clock Tower' (1934), 'A Full Moon in March' (1935), 'New Poems' (1938), and 'Last Poems and Two Plays' (1939). In the poems and plays written after his marriage he achieved a spare, colloquial lyricism wholly unlike his earlier manner.

Yeats served as a senator of the Irish

Free State from 1922 to 1928. He was awarded the Nobel Prize for Literature in 1923.

Yeats also published collections of essays and edited many books, the most important being 'The Oxford Book of Modern Verse' (1936). He wrote good letters, and five major collections have been made.

Yellow-backs, cheap editions of novels, so called from being bound in yellow boards. They were the ordinary 'railway novels' of the seventies and eighties of the last century.

Yellow Book, The, an illustrated quarterly which appeared from 1894 to 1897. Many distinguished writers and artists contributed to it, notably Aubrey Beardsley and Max Beerbohm, Henry James, Edmund Gosse, Walter Sickert, etc.

Yellow Journalism, a name given to the sensational journalism of America which developed about 1880. The YELLOW PRESS is a term applied in England to sensational periodicals and newspapers.

Yellowplush, MR. CHARLES JAMES, a footman, a character assumed by Thackeray (q.v.), as observer of manners, and also as literary critic, in several of his earlier works.

Yeo, SALVATION, a character in C. Kingsley's 'Westward Ho!' (q.v.).

Yeobright, CLYM, THOMASIN, and MRS., characters in Hardy's 'The Return of the Native' (q.v.).

Yeoman's Tale, The, see *Canterbury Tales.*

Ygerne, see *Igraine.*

Yggdrasil, in northern mythology, the world tree, an ash, representing all living nature, which connects heaven, earth, and hell. Under its branches sit the Norns (q.v.). The dragon Nidhöggr gnaws at its root in Niflheim, an eagle sits at its summit, and the squirrel Ratatösk runs up and down to sow strife between the two. Our maypoles and Christmas trees are said to be derived from this conception. See also *Jack and the Beanstalk.*

Yonge, CHARLOTTE MARY (1823-1901),

came under the influence of John Keble (q.v.), who urged her to expound his religious views in fiction. 'The Heir of Redclyffe' (1853) first brought her popular success. She issued in all 160 books, including a life of Bishop Patteson (1874), a 'History of France' (1879), and a 'Life of Hannah More' (1888).

Yorick, (1) in Shakespeare's 'Hamlet' (q.v., v. i), the king's jester. He is perhaps to be identified with Tarlton (q.v.); (2) 'the lively, witty, sensible and heedless parson' in Sterne's 'Tristram Shandy' (q.v.). Sterne adopted 'Yorick' as a pseudonym in his 'Sentimental Journey' (q.v.).

Yorkshire Tragedy, A, a play published in 1608 and stated in the title to be written by Shakespeare, but internal evidence and the late date make it extremely improbable that he had any part in its authorship.

The play is based on certain murders actually committed in 1605.

Young, ARTHUR (1741–1820), the son of a Suffolk clergyman, became well known as an agricultural theorist, though unsuccessful as a practical farmer. He wrote a large number of works on agricultural subjects. His power of political and social observation is shown by his 'Political Arithmetic' (1774) and his 'Tour in Ireland' (1780), but his fame rests chiefly on his 'Travels in France' (q.v., 1792).

Young, EDWARD (1683–1765), took orders and became rector of Welwyn in 1730, where he spent the remainder of his long life, never receiving the ecclesiastical promotion to which many of his contemporaries thought him entitled. His literary work includes two plays, 'Busiris', a tragedy of violence and ungoverned passion, successfully produced at Drury Lane in 1719, and 'The Revenge', another tragedy, produced at the same theatre in 1721. In 1725–8 he published a series of satires under the title 'The Universal Passion' (the Love of Fame), which were witty and brilliant, and were much admired. In 1742–5 appeared the work by which he is principally remembered, 'The Complaint, or Night Thoughts on Life, Death, and Immortality' (see *Night Thoughts*), which immediately became very popular. He published 'The Brothers', a tragedy written long before, in 1753, and 'Resignation', his last considerable poem, in 1762.

Younger Son, The Adventures of a, see *Adventures of a Younger Son.*

Ysolde or YSOUDE, see *Iseult.*

Yule, from the OE. *geol*, Christmas Day or Christmastide, corresponding to the Old Norse *jól*, a heathen feast lasting twelve days, and (later) Christmas.

Yule, SIR HENRY (1820–89), was, with Arthur Coke Burnell, originator of 'Hobson-Jobson' (q.v.).

Yvetot, see *Roi d' Yvetot.*

Ywain and Gawain, a verse-romance of the 14th cent., translated from the French of Chrétien de Troyes.

Z

Zadig, a satirical romance by Voltaire (q.v.).

Zany, from the Italian *zani*, the name of servants who act as clowns in the 'Commedia dell' Arte', a comic performer attending on a clown. Hence an attendant, follower (almost always in a contemptuous sense); or a buffoon; or a fool, simpleton.

Zanzis, a supposed poet referred to by Chaucer in 'Troylus and Cryseyde', iv. 414. The name perhaps arises from a misreading of Boccaccio's text.

Zapolya, a 'dramatic poem . . . in humble

imitation of the *Winter's Tale* of Shakspeare', by S. T. Coleridge (q.v.) (1817).

Zarathustra, see *Zoroaster*.

Zarathustra, *Thus spake*, the chief work of Nietzsche (q.v.).

Zastrozzi, see *Shelley (P. B.)*.

Zeal-of-the-land Busy, a character in Jonson's 'Bartholomew Fayre' (q.v.), a typical religious humbug.

Zeitgeist, German, the spirit or genius which marks the thought or feeling of a period.

Zenelophon, see *Cophetua*.

Zeno, the founder of the Stoic school of philosophy (close of the 4th cent. B.C.). For his ethical teaching see under *Stoics*. Another Zeno, of Elea (*c.* 450 B.C.), was a disciple of Parmenides (q.v.) and expounded his philosophy.

Zenocrate, the wife of Tamburlaine, in Marlowe's 'Tamburlaine the Great'.

Zephon, in Milton's 'Paradise Lost', iv. 788, a 'strong and subtle Spirit'.

Zephyrus, in Greek mythology, the personification of the west wind. He was the father of Xanthus and Balius, the horses of Achilles.

Zeugma, a figure of speech by which a single word is made to refer to two or more words in a sentence, especially when properly applying in sense to only one of them; e.g. 'See Pan with flocks, with fruits Pomona crowned'. Cf. *Syllepsis*.

Zeus, the greatest of the Greek gods, in whom the myths of many different nations centred. The Roman god Jupiter was identified with him, and the Greek myths transferred to him. His worship was widespread and of great solemnity. He was regarded as the king and father of gods and men, with power over all other deities save the Fates.

Zimri, (1) in 1 Kings xvi, the servant of Asa, king of Judah; (2) in Dryden's 'Absalom and Achitophel' (q.v.), in allusion to the above, represents the duke of Buckingham.

Zodiac, from the Greek ζῴδιον, a sculptured figure (of an animal), a sign of the zodiac; a belt of the celestial sphere extending 8 or 9 degrees on each side of the ecliptic within which the apparent motions of the sun, moon, and planets take place. It is divided in twelve equal parts called *signs*. These are named after the twelve constellations (Aries, Taurus, Gemini, Cancer, Leo, Virgo, Libra, Scorpio, Sagittarius, Capricornus, Aquarius, Pisces) with which at a former epoch they severally coincided approximately. They no longer do so owing to the precession of the Equinoxes.

Zoilus, a grammarian of Amphipolis, of the period of Philip of Macedon. His name became proverbial as that of a carping critic, on account of his strictures on Homer, Plato, and Isocrates.

Zola, ÉMILE (1840–1902), the principal figure in the French school of naturalistic fiction, of which 'Thérèse Raquin' (1867) is his first example. After 1870 he set about his principal work, 'Les Rougon-Macquart', a series of twenty novels in which he departs from the limited themes of the novel of his day to display the whole panorama of 19th-cent. French life. In the Dreyfus case Zola intervened on the side of truth with memorable vigour (notably in his letter to 'L'Aurore', 'J'accuse!').

Zophiel, in Milton's 'Paradise Lost', vi. 535, one of the 'victor Angels'.

Zoroaster, the Greek form of *Zarathustra*, the founder of the Magian system of religion, probably a historical personage who has become the subject of legends; a Persian who is believed to have lived in the 6th cent. B.C.

The essential feature of Zoroastrianism is the existence of two predominant spirits: Ahura-Mazda (Ormazd) the wise one, the spirit of light and good; and Ahriman, the spirit of evil and darkness.

Zuleika, (1) according to Muslim tradition, the name of Potiphar's wife; (2) the heroine of Byron's 'The Bride of Abydos'.

Zuleika Dobson, see *Beerbohm*.

Zweig, ARNOLD (1887–1968), German novelist, known in England as the author of 'Der Streit um den Sergeanten Grischa' (1928, 'The Case of Sergeant Grischa').

Zwingli, ULRICH (1484-1531), a famous Swiss leader of the Reformation. He first found his inspiration in Erasmus and Luther, but soon drew away from the latter, and by 1525 had rejected the mass altogether; and this split Switzerland into Catholic and Protestant cantons. It ended in civil war, in which Zwingli was killed in battle.